A COLLECTION
OF THE
INSCRIPTIONS ON COPPER-PLATES AND STONES
IN THE
NELLORE DISTRICT

A COLLECTION

OF THE

INSCRIPTIONS ON COPPER-PLATES AND STONES

IN THE

NELLORE DISTRICT

MADE BY

ALAN BUTTERWORTH,

OF THE INDIAN CIVIL SERVICE (MADRAS)

AND

V. VENUGOPAUL CHETTY,

OF THE INDIAN CIVIL SERVICE (MADRAS)

IN THREE PARTS

PART I

GYAN

Published by

Gyan Publishing House
5, Ansari Road
Daryaganj, New Delhi-110002
Phone: 011-47034999, 9811692060
E-mail: books@gyanbooks.com

Distribution Network
gyanbooks.com
India, USA, Canada, UK, Australia, France

ISBN : 978-81-212-3814-4 (Set)
ISBN : 978-81-212-9725-7 (HB)
First Published, 1905

2nd Impression 2020

Printed at: Gyan Press, Delhi.

A Collection of the Inscriptions on Copper-Plates and Stones in the Nellore District, Part I
Author: Alan Butterworth, V. Venugopaul Chetty

A COLLECTION

OF THE

INSCRIPTIONS ON COPPER-PLATES AND STONES

IN THE

NELLORE DISTRICT.

MADE BY

ALAN BUTTERWORTH,

OF THE INDIAN CIVIL SERVICE (MADRAS)

AND

V. VENUGOPAUL CHETTY,

OF THE INDIAN CIVIL SERVICE (MADRAS).

IN THREE PARTS.

PART I.

MADRAS:

PRINTED BY THE SUPERINTENDENT, GOVERNMENT PRESS.

1905.

NELLORE DISTRICT MAP
SHOWING
DISTRIBUTION OF INSCRIPTIONS
Places where Tamil inscriptions are found are noted in Antique figures.
A few places are omitted as not being found on the Survey Maps.
SCALE OF MILES
KANIGIRI
UDAYAGIRI
KAVALI
ATMAKUR
RAPUR
VENKATAGIRI
PODILI
NORTH ARCOT
CHINGLEPUT
KURNOOL
CUDDAPAH
KISTNA
BAY OF BENGAL
From Cumbum
From Badvel
From Vontimitta
From Pullampet
To Yerpedu
To Renigunta
To Madras
Photo-Print, Survey Office, Madras
1908

GENERAL CONTENTS.

PART I.

PART II.

PART III.

APPENDICES.

PREFACE.

THE publication of this collection of the Stone and Copper-plate inscriptions of the Nellore district as it existed in 1903 has been rendered possible by the generosity of the Government of Madras under whose orders it was printed at the Government Press.

The work was undertaken in the belief that the records of a district situated as Nellore is would contain a lot of new matter of historical importance. This hope has not been realized. The great bulk of the inscriptions consists of grants to tanks and temples which are of no interest whatever and perhaps only one inscription (No. 26 of Kandukúr) can be pointed to as having a real historical motive. The collection supplies a few new historical names, mostly of only local importance, and fixes a few doubtful dates but of the condition of the country and the people in past ages it tells us nothing. In short the principal fruit of our labours is that we have saved epigraphists from wasting time on the exploration of a barren area.

2. The information supplied by the inscriptions being so scanty, the history of the district as revealed by them can be compressed into a few lines.

To begin with, it will be noted that records anterior to the twelfth century are rare. The wonder is, indeed, that so many have survived, having in view the indifference of the people to ancient remains. Nor are officials free from blame in this matter as is testified to by the old buildings of the Collector's cutcherry at Nellore in the construction of which inscribed stones have been freely employed.

The centuries subsequent to the eleventh are fairly prolific in remains, the thirteenth century being especially well represented.

The epigraphical history of the district begins with Copper-plate No. 24. This is a grant by the Western Chalukyan King Vikramáditya I in the seventh century. It records the gift of a village which has not been identified. Assuming that the grant relates to the Nellore district, we find in it an indication of the dispossession of the Pallavas from this part of the East Coast by the Western Chalukyan dynasty.

It is probable that the next glimpse of the past is obtained through No. 54 of Gúdúr which gives a Pallava king reigning over part of the district in subordination, apparently, to the Western Chalukyans. This inscription may be assigned with probability to the eighth century.

After this we seem to hear no more of the Western Chalukyans or of the main line of the Pallavas and for a long period we lose sight altogether of the southern part of the district. In the north, however, we have clear indications in the ninth and tenth centuries to show that it then formed a part of the Eastern Chalukyan dominions and towards the close of the latter century the Bána dynasty appears on the scene as is proved by a single inscription from Podili.

Another gap occurs at this stage and the records are silent until the close of the eleventh century when we come upon traces of the Chóḷas and their main line is not lost sight of until the second half of the thirteenth century. It seems to have governed through the agency of viceroys or petty chiefs, mainly of Pallava and Chóḷa descent, and most of the inscriptions relating thereto come from the southern part of the district. From the north the Eastern

Chalukyan-Chóḷas were ousted by the Kákatíyas who, by the middle of the thirteenth century or earlier, had acquired Ongole, Podili and Darsi. Later on the borders of the Kákatíya kingdom were pushed farther downwards and only the extreme south is free from Kákatíya inscriptions. Early in the fourteenth century we lose sight of the Kákatíya dynasty whose authority was acknowledged by various petty chiefs of Yádava, Chóḷa and other lineages. After this, the northern part of the district fell into the hands of the Reḍḍi dynasty which ruled there from the middle of the fourteenth century to about the middle of the fifteenth. In this district its head-quarters seem to have been Chunḍi.

Meanwhile, in the south, authority appears to have been exercised by chiefs of Chóḷa descent, some of whom assume the imperial title and carry on the Chóḷa dominion into the fourteenth century. There are not wanting, also, slight traces of Pánḍyan sovereignty, one Pánḍyan inscription being so late as the close of the fourteenth century.

All these dynasties, in the north and the south, were absorbed by the Vijayanagar Empire, the first traces of which are found early in the fourteenth century and when Krishnadévaráya had expelled the Gajapatis of Orissa who, for a brief period, held a part of the district, the whole of Nellore seems to have acknowledged his authority. That was early in the sixteenth century and the district remained a part of the shattered Vijayanagar Empire until the middle of the following century, for it is not until 1640–41 that we find references to Abdullah Kutb Sháh of Golkonḍa and the latest Vijayanagar inscription is dated 1662–63.

The later history of the district need not be alluded to.

3. It will be seen that we have collected about 903 inscriptions. With one exception no inscriptions subsequent to the eighteenth century have been included; otherwise we may fairly claim that the collection is practically complete. The distribution of the inscriptions has been indicated in the accompanying map which distinguishes the places where Tamil inscriptions have been found. Mr. V. Venkayya contends on page 7 of the Epigraphical Report for 1903-04 that the prevalence of Tamil inscriptions in the south indicates that in modern times the Telugu language has extended southwards. The facts derived from the present collection are these :—In Súlúrpet out of 20 inscriptions, 4 are Telugu and all these seem to be comparatively modern; a similar remark applies to Venkatagiri where there are 5 Telugu out of a total of 27; Gúdúr has 118 inscriptions, of which 22 are Telugu and of these one is dated in the thirteenth century; Rápúr shows 67 Telugu inscriptions out of a total of 79 and some of the former are dated in the thirteenth and fourteenth centuries; a similar remark applies to Nellore which possesses 64 Telugu inscriptions in a total of 124. Old Telugu inscriptions are thus not unknown in the southern part of the district, just as old Tamil inscriptions occur in such unquestionably Telugu taluks as Átmakúr, but, on the whole, Mr. Venkayya's conclusions seem to be correct, for it may be said as a general thing that Chóḍa or Chóḷa inscriptions are in Telugu in the north of the district and in Tamil in the south. The line of division between the two languages may, in the thirteenth century, have lain in the Nellore taluk but Rápúr seems to have always been Telugu. Now-a-days the dividing line roughly coincides with the southern boundary of the district. It may be mentioned that a few Tamil inscriptions were found at

Pákála in Kandukúr taluk, but they are merely private grants.

4. It will be observed as one of the defects in this collection that the system of transliteration into English characters is not invariable. For example, the palatal 'S' is sometimes represented as 'Ṣ' and sometimes as 'Ś'. Such variations are a consequence of collaboration by several workers.

5. In Appendix I we have brought together to the best of our very limited ability the information available in respect of the several dynasties who have left traces of their presence. Other appendices and a glossary have been inserted for convenience of reference.

6. It remains to acknowledge assistance. In the first place we tender hearty thanks to Mr. V. Venkayya, the acting Government Epigraphist of Madras, for help rendered to struggling amateurs. This gentleman most kindly transliterated for us nearly all the Chalukyan inscriptions and some of the others.

The transcription and translation of the Tamil inscriptions were done by M.R.Ry. T. P. Krishnaswámi Sástri of the Revenue Secretariat, and our thanks are due to him for the trouble he took.

In the working out of the Sanskrit inscriptions Mr. Venugópál Chetti was much assisted by the late Inguva Pattábhi Ráma Sástrulu of Ongole.

The exceedingly laborious task of transcribing the Telugu inscriptions fell mainly to the lot of M.R.Ry. Pólúr Venkatáchalam of the Nellore Local Fund Department, who also helped in the translation of some of them and did such Canarese work as there was. We take the opportunity to thank him.

We are also under obligation to Saiyid Mustafa Khán Sáhib, the Huzur Sheristadar of Nellore, for his kindness in dealing with the Persian inscriptions.

We must not forget to mention those also to whose lot fell the toilsome and uncommonly hot work of taking the impressions. They are the late Mailapur Krishnaswámi Mudaliar, Múchi of the Collector's office, Vemula Ádanna, Múchi of the Sub-Collector's office, and Fasi-uddín, Collector's dáláyat.

For assistance rendered by several of the Divisional officers, Tahsildars, Deputy Tahsildars and other gentlemen, we must express our obligation in general terms. We have acknowledged their assistance in, we hope, all cases in the body of the collection.

Finally we have to thank Mr. R. Hill and his successor Mr. T. Fisher and their subordinates of the Government Press for the care and skill shown in printing from manuscripts which were often well-nigh illegible.

7. A few photographs have been inserted in the collection. These were taken by Mr. Venugópál Chetti and M.R.Ry. V. Subba Rao, Minor Irrigation Overseer, and have been reproduced at the Survey Office.

8. Undoubtedly, in dealing with this mass of inscriptions, we have made many errors and we are fully conscious of our inability to do justice to the task we have undertaken. With this confession we hope to disarm the criticism of epigraphists.

A. B.
C. V.

October 1904.

POSTSCRIPT TO THE PREFACE.

Just as this book was about to issue, M.R.Ry. P. Venkatáchalam forwarded copies of three additional copper-plate grants. There being no time to incorporate and discuss them in the body of the work, the translations of two of them and an abstract of the third (all supplied, with his usual kindness, by Mr. V. Venkayya) have been relegated to a postscript at the end of the book (see pages 1421 *a—e*).

Of these the first inscription was found among the effects of a Sanyási and was secured by the Deputy Tahsildar of Addanki, from whose office it was sent to the Government Museum, Madras. It is, apparently, about to appear in *Epigraphia Indica* where it will doubtless be fully discussed.

The second and third inscriptions are in the possession of M.R.Ry. Nágarája Suryanáráyana Ráo Pantulu Gáru of Nellore, who kindly allowed *facsimile* impressions to be taken. Both these inscriptions relate to the village of Chandalúru in the Addanki division.

Our remarks about the Pallava and Eastern Chalukyan dynasties in the preface and elsewhere need modification with reference to these newly-discovered and ancient grants.

September 1905.

ABBREVIATIONS USED IN THIS WORK.

Prefixed to a Number	A.	stands for	Átmakúr Taluk.
,,	,,	C.	,,	Copper-Plate.
,,	,,	D.	,,	Darsi Division.
,,	,,	G.	,,	Gúdúr Taluk.
,,	,,	KG.	,,	Kanigiri ,,
,,	,,	KR.	,,	Kundukúr ,,
,,	,,	KV.	,,	Kávali ,,
,,	,,	N.	,,	Nellore ,,
,,	,,	O.	,,	Ongole ,,
,,	,,	P.	,,	Podili Division.
,,	,,	R.	,,	Rápúr Taluk.
,,	,,	S.	,,	Súlúrpet (or Pólúr) Division.
,,	,,	U.	,,	Udayagiri Taluk.
,,	,,	V.	,,	Venkatagiri Division.

B.	stands for	Brown's Telugu Dictionary.
Epig. Carn.	,,	Epigraphia Carnataca.
E.I.	,,	Epigraphia Indica.
I.A.	,,	Indian Antiquary.
M.P.C.	,,	Madhurántaka Pottapi Chóḷa.
M.K.	,,	Mukkanṭi Káduveṭṭu.
M.M.	,,	Mahá Mandaléṣvara.
M.	,,	Srímanmahámandaléṣvara.
	,,	Wilson's Glossary of Revenue terms.

A COLLECTION

OF THE

COPPER-PLATE AND STONE INSCRIPTIONS

IN THE

NELLORE DISTRICT.

COPPER-PLATE INSCRIPTIONS.

COPPER-PLATE No. 1. (A.D. 1390–91.)

[Parachúr grant of king Dévaráya. (S.S. 1312.)]

Note.

The subjoined inscription is edited from the original preserved in the Collector's office, Nellore. It consists of two plates, 9 inches long and 3½ inches wide, which are engraved breadthwise.

The characters are Telugu while the language is Sanskrit. No distinction is observed between short i and long i, nor between d and dh.

Mr. Sewell gives a summary of this grant in Vol. II of his Antiquities (*No. 94, p. 15*). Some of the verses have apparently been misplaced. Mr. Sewell does not seem to have noticed this and hence his inability to understand the grant.

The inscription begins with an invocation to Vishnu in his Boar incarnation (V. 1). Next V. (2) contains an invocation to Gaṇésa. Without any preface the name of Harihara is introduced in V. 3 and in V. (4) his liberality to Brahmans is praised; V. (5) says that Dévarája was the son of Harihara; V. (6) praises his valour. V. (7) states that he undertook a military expedition under the orders of his father and returned victoriously. In V. 8 it is stated that a minister gave a village to Chennu Bhaṭṭa, a Brahman, under the orders of Dévarája. Evidently no copper grant was issued by Dévarája, for the donee went to his son Rámachandra who was the lord of Udayádri (Udayagiri) and asked for a record of the boundaries of the village granted to him (Vs. 9 and 10).

Rámachandra made an enquiry and confirmed the grant (V. 10). The grant having been made by his father, the inscription is in the name of Dévarája; V. 12 and 13 record this fact. After obtaining his desire, the donee offered benedictions to the donor Dévarája and his son Rámachandra (Vs. 14 and 15); V. 16 states that the *ṣlókas* of this grant were composed by Ṣrí Devarája Miṣra the court poet of Rámachandra. The inscription closes with one of the customary imprecatory verses.

The object of the grant is a village measuring 15 *manḍyas* in extent, lying on either side of the river *Audala*, near *Parachúr* village in the kingdom of Addanki. It is understood that there is a river Audala between Guntur and Addanki. 'Manḍya' is some measure of land.

The donee was Chennu Bhaṭṭa, of the *gótra* of Bháradvája and of the Rig Véda. He is said to have been master of the Purános.

The date of the grant is given as 'Ṣaka Rúpálayé.' Mr. Sewell says that this is unintelligible, but the system of denoting numerals by letters is explained on p. 79 of Burnell's Palæography where it is shown that *r* represents 2, *p* 1, *l* 3, *y* 1. Thus Rúpálayé = 1312, the digits being transposed.

The Harihara referred to in this grant must be Harihara II, and the Dévaráya referred to was his son Dévaráya I. The grant furnishes the information that Dévaráya I had a son named Rámachandra, who was appointed Yuvarája and lord of Udayagiri.

As regards the transposition of some of the verses: V. 6, 7 instead of following V. 5 are inserted at the top of the second plate, first side, and the first line of V. 14 is written at the end of the first plate, second side, instead of at the top of the second plate, second side.

Translation.

First plate, first side.

V. 1. May the glorious primeval Boar—who bore (on his tusk) the charming (moist) earth like a beautiful damsel wet with perspiration engendered by embrace with her beloved—protect you!

V. 2. I salute (Ganésa) the power that transcends matter, the dispeller of the array of obstacles, the destroyer of the mountains of sins, the first cause of the worlds.

V. 3. There was a king Harihara, of unlimited glory, whose fame was brilliant as sheets of snow, and whose mind was illumined by the desire of liberality.

V. 4. By him Indra and other gods are made suppliants for sacrifice in the house of Brahmans, which is delightful with the windows of the balconies of beautiful mansions exceedingly fragrant with the appearance of smoke proceeding from the fire kindled with many oblations of ghee and which is filled with the shouts of rivalry of the gods who have arrived there having been invoked by their respective hymns.

V. 5. To him was born Dévarája, by the blow of whose long sword numerous hostile kings were slain, and whose arms moved like the Mantha mountain to churn the ocean which was the multitude of valiant hostile kings.

V. [1] 6. The regions of the earth being pervaded by the flames issuing from the fire of his valour, darkness obtained entry only in the caves which were the hearts of hostile kings.

V. 7. Having for a long time carried out a fierce military expedition by order of his father king Harihara, accompanied by the six components of the army, he, the king, reached quickly the city.

First plate, second side.

Vs. 8. Once, a minister, having pleased the king Ṣrí Dévarája, gave at his command that village consisting of a measured extent of land as a gift at the festival of Purári (Ṣiva).

Vs. 9 and 10. This Chennu Bhaṭṭa went to the excellent son of king Ṣrí Dévarája who was seated on the throne of the Karnáṭa kingdom and who was an Indra on earth, and applied to that Yuvarája (crown prince) for a document showing the boundaries of that village of his. He, the Udayádri Rája, having made an enquiry into the former grant of his father, accordingly granted (the request).

V. 11. Since then its name was called Dévaráyapuram. He, Rámachandra, subjugated (hostile) kings, was the lord of Udayádri city (and) by his skill vanquished the Mussalman king.

Second plate, first side.

Vs. 12 and 13. In the Ṣaka year denoted by (the chronogram) *rúpálayé* (1312), in the year Pramóda, in the month Jyéshṭha, on the full moon day, on Friday, Dévaráya, the

[1] First two lines of second plate, first side.

ornament of kings, being in the holy place where pleasant winds blow from the excellent Tungá river (Tungabhadrá), gave an excellent land to Chennubhaṭṭa of the *gótra* of Bháradvája, of the Ṛig Véda, and master of the path of the Puránas, the land lying on the two banks of the river named Audalá near Parachúr (village) in Addanki ráshṭra (kingdom)—measuring 15 *maṇḍyas*. Boundary stones marked with figures of the sun and the moon are planted here all round.

V. [1]14. May the king named Ṣrí Dévarája, who excels in valour, ruling the Vijayanagar kingdom as long as the moon lasts, enjoy happiness!

Second plate, second side.

May his son, the illustrious Rámachandra, conqueror of hostile kings in battles, who bears the title of Yuvarája, be victorious on earth for 1,000 years!

V. 15. Accordingly the famous Ṣrí Dévárája Miṣra, the court scholar of the best of kings Rámachandra, wrote (this) charitable edict.

V. 16. This general maxim of kings should always be observed by you; thus Rámachandra again and again entreats all these future kings.

Ṣrí Rámachandra.

First plate, first side.

1. श्रीःअव्याद्वः प्रथमः पोत्रीसरसामुद्वहन् रसां । प्रियांगसं-
2. गसंजातस्पांद्रस्वेदोदयामिव ॥ (*v.* 1) [2] पदनपारणं वन्दे प्र-
3. त्यूहव्यूहवारणं दारणं दुरिताद्रिणां जगतामादि-

[1] Last line of first plate, second side, and first three lines of second plate, second side.

[2] Read प्रचार.

4. कारण ॥ (2) आसीदसीममहिमा हिमानि [1] विलसद्यशाः । राजाहरिहरः त्याग-

5. रागरंजितमानसः ॥ (3) आज्यप्राज्यहविस्समिद्धहुतभग्धूमो [2]

6. द्रमाविर्भवद्भूयस्सौरभसाधुसौधवलभीवातायनो-

7. द्रासिनि । तत्तन्मंत्रनिमंत्रितागतसुराहंपूर्विकापूरिते थेना-

8. कारिषत।र्तिनो [3] द्विजगृहे सत्राय शक्रादयः॥ (4) तस्मादजायत निजा

9. यतखड्गधारासंपातपाटितपरश्शतवैराजः [4] । उद्दामवामनर-

10. पालकुलाब्धि [5] मंदिमंथाचल प्रलद्दोरिह [6] देवराजः ॥ (5)

First plate, second side.

1. भौमः कदाचित्परितोष्यभूपं श्रीदेवराजं तदनुज्ञ-

2. यैव । ग्रामं व्यदात्तं मितभूमिभागं सत्रेपुरारेःखलु

3. संप्रदानं ॥ (8) कर्णाटराज्यासिंहासनमध्यासेदुषो वरं तन-

4. यं । श्रीदेवरायनृपतेःस्स चेन्नुभट्टो धरामरेन्द्रमगात् ॥ (9)

5. व्य [7]जिजपत्तं युवराजमेतत्स्वग्रामदेशांक [8] लेख-

6. नाय । पितुः पुरा दानमसौ विमृश्य तथान्वजानादु-

7. दयाद्रिराजः ॥ (10) देवरायपुरीमत्युदिनं [9] तन्नाम तत्प्रभृति

8. सू [10]कृतभूपः । रामचंद्र उदयाद्रिपुरींद्रः प्रौढिनिर्जित-

9. तुरुष्कनरेन्द्रः ॥ (*v.*11) [11] आचंद्रंविजयाभिधाननगरी राज्यं

Second plate, first side.

1. यस्यप्रतापानलजृंभमाणज्वालावलिद्धे [12] भुवनांतराले ।

2. तमः परंप्रापदा [13]नुप्रवेशं प्रत्यर्थिपृथ्वीपतिहृद्दरीषु ॥ (6) हरि-

---

[1] Read मानीत्रि. [2] Read भुग्धूम. [3] Read र्थिनो.

[4] Read वैरिराजः [5] Read मंथि. [6] Read प्रचल.

[7] Read जिज्ञपत्तं. [8] Read त्रिलेखनाय, उशाकलेख in original.

[9] Read त्युदितंतन्ना. [10] Read सोकृत. [11] आनं in original.

[12] Read र्लीढे. [13] Read प्रापदनु.

3. हरनृपतः पितुर्न्नियोगाच्चिरमुररीकृतचंडदंडयात्रः ।

4. ससरभसमलं [1] पुरिमुपागात्सहकृतषड्विधसैनिको नृपालः ॥ (7) तस्मि-

5. न्नुत्तुंगतुंगाजलमहितमरुत्सेविते [2] पुण्यदेशे शाके रूपा-

6. लयेब्दे नरपतितिलको देवरायः प्रमोदे । ज्येष्टाराकाख्यप-

7. र्वण्युशनासि दिवसे [3] चेन्नुभट्टाय भारद्वाजायर्ग्वेदिने दात्परिक-

8. लितपुराणाधूने क्षेत्रमग्र्यं ॥ (12) अद्दंकिराष्ट्रपरुचूरुगकादला- [4]

9. ख्य स्रोतस्तटाद्वितयगामिनि भूमिभागे । मण्डियपंचदश-

10. परिमितेत्रसीमाचंद्रार्कचान्हित [5] शिलाः परितोनिरवाताः ॥ (13)

Second plate, second side.

1. प्रशाशत्सुख [6] भूयाद्भूमिपतिः प्रतापमहितः श्री-

2. देवरायाह्वयः । तत्सूनुर्युवराजपट्टच [7] भुवि

3. श्रीरामचंद्राभिधः श्रीमानाजिषु वैरिराजविजयी जी-

4. यात्सहस्रंसमाः ॥ (14) रामचंद्रनृपास्थानी विद्वा-

5. नद्वा यशोधनः । श्री देवराजमिश्रोयं व्यलि-

6. खद्धर्मशासनं । (15) सामान्योयं धर्मसेतुर्नृपा-

7. णां काले काले पालनीयो भवाद्भिः ॥ इत्थंसर्वा(नेता)न् मा- विनः पार्थि-

8. वेंद्रान् भूयोभूयो याचते रामचंद्रः ॥ (16) श्रीराम चंद्र.

---

[1] Read पुरी. [2] मस्त्पाविते in original [3] दिनेहे in original.

[4] Read गतौदला. [5] Read चिन्हित. [6] Read सत्सुखी.

[7] Read पट्टण.

Copper-plate No. 2. (A.D. 1435-36 ?)

[Tiruvíḍu grant.]

Note.

[This is a Telugu copper-plate grant and is edited from the original preserved in the Collector's office, Nellore. Mr. Sewell refers to it (No. 66, page 9, Vol. II).

The engraving is excellent and the orthography calls for no remarks.

The cyclic and S.S. dates do not agree.]

Translation.

Hail! On Monday, the 15th of the bright fortnight of Kártika (month) of the year Párthiva, corresponding to 1357 of the illustrious, victorious and prosperous Ṣáliváhana Ṣaka era — Dévaráya Voḍaya Gáru of the *gótra* of Káṣyapa, after making prostrations to the illustrious lotus feet of the illustrious Ahóbaḷa déva, the deity of Tiruvíḍu, who is the Lord of Vaikunṭa Déṣa of Kali Yuga, who is the ruler of the crores of worlds of the whole universe, and who is called Náráyaṇa, whose vehicle is the bird Garuḍa, who is the establisher of the path of the Védas and who is the illustrious inaugurator of the philosophy of the illustrious Ṣrí Rámánuja,[1] gave the (following) charitable deed so that religious merit might accrue to his father Parvataráya, his mother Párvatí Déví, his grandfather Rámachandra Ráya, and his grandmother Lakshmí Déví. We have given the village named Tiruvíḍu which is in the bed of the tank named Karakili and which lies on the northern bank of the *Pináki* (Pennéru),

[1] Rámánuja, the Vaishnavite reformer, flourished in the twelfth century of our era.

in the Pánkanánḍu district in Udayagiri kingdom belonging to us, to the deity Ahóbaḷéṣvara of Tiruvíḍu, after pouring water into the hands of Purushóttamayya, ṣon of Padmanábhayya, who is of the *gótra* of Paráṣara, and follower of the Yajuṣ Sákhá and who is the temple servant of Ahóbaḷadéva, for providing all kinds of enjoyments (to the deity), so that the deity may enjoy the eight powers and the eight enjoyments. Having accepted this, may the deity deign to protect us!

The protection of another's gift is twice as meritorious as one's own gift. By resuming another's gift, one's own gift becomes inefficacious.

Verily the country to the extent of three 'Yójanas' surrounding the temple of Ahóbaḷa Nṛisimha is a hundred times more sacred than Gayá, Prayág and Káṣi.

Obeisance to Ṣrí Narasimha!

Obeisance to Ṣríman Rámánuja!

Ṣrí Ráma.

First side.

1. స్వస్తిశ్రీ విజయాభ్యు
2. దయ శాలివాహ
3. న శకవరుషంబు
4. లు ౧౩౫౭ అగున
5. ట్టి పార్థివ సంవత్స
6. ర కార్తీక శు ౧౫
7. శో-స్వస్తిశ్రీ కలియు
8. గ వైకుంఠ దేశ అఖి
9. లాండకోటి బ్రంహ్మాం
10. డనాయక అభంగ
11. గరుడనారాయ
12. ణ వేదమార్గప్రతి

Second side.

13. ష్టాచారియ్య శ్రీరామా
14. నుజ దరుశన స్థాపనా
15. చారియ్యు లాన తిర్వ్వశ్రీ అవు
16. ళ్ళదేవర శ్రీపాదప
17. ద్మంబులకు కాశిపగో
18. తృలైన దేవరాయవొ
19. డయలు గారు తమ
20. తండ్రి పర్వతరాయ
21. లకున్ను తల్లిపార్వ్వతి
22. దేవికిన్ని తమ తాత రా
23. మచందురాయ రా
24. యలకున్ లక్ష్మిదేవి
25. కిన్ని దర్మ్మం అగునట్లు

Third side.

26. గాను సాష్టాంగ్గ దణ
27. ం వెట్టియిచ్చిన దర్మశ
28. శాసనము మాకు
29. ంజెల్లివుదయగిరి
30. రాజానపాంకనా
31. ండ్లిలోను పినా
32. కినది వుత్తరభాగా
33. న కరకిలి చెరువులో
34. ను తిరిపీడు అగ్రా
35. మము తిరిపిటి అవు
36. భ ళైశ్వరుక్ని అం
37. గరంగవైభవాల

Fourth side.

38. కున్ను ఆరగింపులకు
39. న్ అష్టైశ్వర్యాలు గల్గు
40. నట్టుగాన్ను అష్టభోగా
41. లుకల్గునట్టుగాను పా
42. దాశలయజాస్యఖా
43. ధ్యాయులైన అవుబళ
44. దేవరస్థానికులు. పద్మ
45. నాభయ్యగారి పుత్రు
46. ండగుపురుషోత్తమ
47. య్యంగారి హస్తంలోను
48. దారవోశి అవుబళే
49. శ్వరునికి సమర్పింగ్స్తిమి అ
50. వధరించి మన్నును ర
51. క్షింపు నవధరించ్చిడిన్

Fifth side.

52. స్వదత్తా ద్విగుణం పుణ్యం పరదత్తానుపాలనం పరదత్తాపహారే

53. ణ స్వదత్తంనిష్ఫలంభవేత్తు ॥ అహోబళనృసిహాశ్చసమంతా

54. ద్యోజనత్రయం।గయా ప్రయాగ కాశీభ్య సత్యం శతగుణాధి

55. కం శ్రీ నరసింహ్వాపనమః శ్రీమతే రామానుజాపనమ॥ శ్రీరామ.

Copper-plate No. 3. (A.D. 1429-30.)

[Lingampáḍu. Grant of Dévaráyá II (Vijayanagar). S.S. 1351.]

Note.

This grant consists of three copper plates strung on a ring bearing the usual emblem of the Vijayanagar dynasty. The plates excluding the circular portion at the top are $5\frac{1}{2} \times 7\frac{1}{2}$ inches. The first and third plates are inscribed on the inside only, while the second is inscribed on both sides. The writing is in the Nandinágari alphabet and in excellent preservation and the language is Sanskrit verse.

The inscription records that king Dévaráya II of Vijayanagar gave the village of Lingampád which was thenceforward surnamed Pratápadévaráyapuram, along with Tanḍa (Taḍa) to Annamárádhya, otherwise known as Kompalli, the son of Mallikárjuna. The village Lingampáḍu was situated in *Paḍanáḍu*, in the Chandragiri *Rájya*, in the Porúr *ṣíma*, and to the south of the river Svarnamukhi. The date of the grant was the 12th of the bright half of Kártika of 1351 S.S. and cyclic year Saumya.

The donee is said to have been the governor of the northern gate of Srísaila, and a worshipper of Ṣiva. His religious sanctity is curiously described; it was so great that when the Panchákshara and a Rudráksha bead having one face were placed on one scale and he sat on the other, the latter went up. The exact meaning of this is not quite clear as the inscription in this portion is apparently corrupt. He was an Árádhya (a Ṣaiva sect) and was named *Annam*, but his popular name was Kompalli.

The inscription resembles that of the Satyamangalam grant of the same king (E.I., Vol. III, p. 35) and the verses relating to the genealogy of the donor are identical with a few variations.

The date of the Satyamangalam grant is 1346 S.S.

The Moon }
| } Mythical.
Yadu }
|
Sangama I, had several sons.
|
Bukka I, married Gaurámbiká
|
Harihara II.
|
Pratápa Dévaráya I = Hémámbiká.
|
Víra Vijaya = Náráyanámbiká.
|
Dévaráya II.

The engraver was Muddana, son of Vírana and he is described as Ṣásanácháryavarya, the best of edict-engravers.

Translation.

First plate, second side.

Adoration be to Ṣrí Gaṇádhipati (Gaṇéṣa)!

V. 1. Salutation be to Ṣiva, who is beauteous with the moon, as with a *chámara*, kissing his lofty head, and who is the main pillar of the creation of the city of the three worlds!

V. 2. May the wonderful elephant[1] whose pleasure-park sages call the Vedas, bring you great happiness!

V. 3. May Hari, to whom lifting up the earth (when) in the form of a boar, the ocean became a pleasure-pond, bring you prosperity!.[2]

---

[1] Ganéṣa who has the face of an elephant.

[2] This is an invocation to Vishnu in his boar incarnation.

V. 4. From the milky ocean arose the flower of the waters (the moon) which is fresh and never withered and which Íṣvara (Ṣiva) wears on the head.

V. 5. The descendant of him (the moon), who is the storehouse of eternal fragrance, named Yadu, was the wonderfully sweet fruit of penance performed by the earth.

V. 6. In his lineage which was characterized by valour, there was a king named *Sangama.* The celestial river (Ganges) shone, having its bed formed by his fame, as it were.

V. 7. Amongst the sons of him (Sangama) who was the treasure of all gems, king *Bukka* became universal sovereign as the 'kaustubha' among gems.

V. 8. The son of him (*Bukka*) whose wife was Gaurámbiká, was king *Harihara,* who was excellent in modesty, who wore great glory as a necklace.

V. 9. Who verily traversed the fourteen worlds with the fame of the sixteen mahádánas (great gifts) (performed by him) reaching all the quarters (of the world).

V. 10. His son was named *Pratápa Dévaráya* whose prowess was like that of Indra, who on account of his virtues was as it were the delight of his subjects incarnate.

V. 11. Having consumed (as a sacrifice) the fuel which is his enemies in the fire which is his valour on the (marriage) [1] altar which is the battle field, the goddess of victory was taken in marriage by this hero.

V. 12. The son of him (Pratápa Dévaráya), whose wife was Hémámbiká, was the heroic king *Vijaya,* eminent in

---

[1] This is all very fanciful. The destruction of enemies is compared to a marriage ceremony.

modesty, the treasury of knowledge and skilled in solving difficult matters.

V. 13. The queen of him (Vijaya) who was the store-house of compassion was Náráyanámbiká as Mahá-Lakshmi was of Ṣaura (Krishna) and Párvati was of Ṣankara (Ṣiva).

Second plate, first side.

V. 14. Resplendent on earth is king *Dévaráya*, the giver (of gifts), the excellent fruit of their austerities in previous births in the form of a son.

V. 15. Which king they style another Vikramáditya in valour, another Bhója in enjoyment, and a Kubéra in liberality.

V. 16. Whom kings served with *chámaras* and other emblems of royalty, belonging to Abhanga,[1] Vanga, Kalinga, Vanga and other kingdoms, held by themselves.

V. 17. Who is Rájádhirája, valiant, who is Rájaparaméṣvara, who is great with the *biruda* "Bháshalanghitabhúpálabhujanga" (the paramour of kings who break their word).

V. 18. Who has the surname Múrurâyaragaṇḍa (the conqueror of the three kings, viz., Chera, Chola and Pándya), who is Pararáyabhayankara (the terror of other kings), and who is eulogized by panegyrists as Hindu-ráyasuratrána (a Sultan among Hindu kings).

V. 19. He, the foremost of the glorious, king Prauḍha (Déva)ráya, in the town named Vijaya which has for its moat the glorious Tungabhadra,

---

[1] It is not known what kingdom is referred to by Abhanga and it is curious that Vanga is mentioned twice, probably we should read Anga for Vanga in one case.

V. 20. In the Ṣaka year reckoned in order by the moon (1), the arrows (5), Ráma (3), and the moon (1) *i.e.*, 1351, in the year Saumya in the month of Kártika, on an auspicious day,

V. 21. On the 12th of the bright half, on a very holy occasion, being on the bank of the Tungabhadra river, in the presence of Virúpáksha (gave the following gift),

V. 22. To the descendant of the Kaunḍinya *gótra*, the follower of the excellent Ápastamba *sútra*, who is glorious, the student of the Yajuṣ ṣákha, who is brilliant in virtue,

V. 23. Who is the son of the Brahman Mallikárjuna, who is of unlimited spiritual power, who is intent on the performance of the good deeds prescribed by the *Srautas* and the *Smártas*, who is intelligent,

V. 24. Who is a fit person for receiving gift of land, who is the foremost of Brahmans, who is modest, distinguished, famous and high-souled,

V. 25. He has studied four Vedas and understood them by the Ṣaiva scriptures; he is the lord of the northern gate at Ṣríṣaila, and is renowned on earth,

V. 26. He placed the mantra consisting of five letters (Námas Ṣiváya) and a Rudráksha having one face on one scale (and he himself sat on the other). Oh wonder, he went up.

V. 27. He is known as *Kompalli*, and is a worshipper of Ṣiva at the six times. To the learned man named *Annamárádhya*, who is versed in the Védas and the Védángas,

Vs. 28 to 32. (Dévaráya) gave joyfully after making libation of water and gift of gold the village named Lingampáḍu, surnamed Pratápadévaráyapuram, along with the village Tanḍa (Taḍa ?), situated in the Chandragiri *rájya*, in the country named Paḍanáḍu, in the famous *síma* Porúr, excellent, situated to the south of the Svarnamukhi river, as a *Sarvamánya*, with its four boundaries everywhere, together with its treasures and hidden deposits, with its water and stone, with its *akshini* and *ágámi*, with its actuals and outstandings; (he gave) this as *ékabhóga sarvamányam* to last as long as sun and stars last.

Third plate, first side.

V. 33. This copper edict has been inscribed by Muddanácharya, son of Vírana, the best of edict-engravers.

[Imprecatory verses.] Ṣrí Virúpáksha.

First plate, second side.

1. श्रीगणाधिपतयेनमः । नमस्तुंगशिरश्चुम्बि चन्द्रचाम-
2. रचारवे । त्रैलोक्यनगरारंभमूलस्तंभाय शंभवे । (॥ 1)भू
3. यस्यय[1] भवतां भूत्यै भूयादाश्चर्यकुंजरः । आहुर्विहारं-[2]
4. कांतारं आगमांन्यस्य[3] योगिनः (॥ 2) क्षेमं वःप्रचुरीकु-
5. र्याद् क्षोणिमम्युद्धरं[4] हरिः । क्रोडाकृतेरभूतस्य[5] क्रीडा-
6. पल्वलमंबुधिः । (॥ 3) अस्ति क्षीरार्णवोद्भूतमपां पुष्पाम-[6]
7. नुत्तमं । [7]अम्लानमविनिर्माल्यमाधत्तोशिरसी-
8. श्वरः । (॥ 4) सदामोदानिधेस्तस्य संताने[8] यदुसंज्ञिते।[9]
9. अभूदाश्चर्यमाधुर्यं वसुधायास्तपः फलं । (॥ 5) सं-
10. गमो नाम राजा भूसारभूते[10] तदन्वये । रेजे यस्य

---

[1] Read भूयस्यै.
[2] Read हारकां.
[3] Read आगमान् यस्य.
[4] Read धरन् हरिः.
[5] Read यस्य.
[6] Read पुष्पम
[7] Or read अम्लानमविनिर्माल्यं.
[8] Or read सन्तानो.
[9] Or read सञ्ज्ञया.
[10] Read राजासीत् सारभूते or राजाभूत्सारभूते.

11. यश(:)सिद्धसरणीव सुरापगा। (॥ 6) सर्वरत्ननिधे-

12. स्तस्य संराडासीत्तनूभुवां। मथो[1] बुक्कमहीपालो

13. मणिनामिव[2] कौस्तुभ(:)। (॥ 7) तस्य गौरांबिकाजाने-

14. स्तनयो(विनयो)न्नत(:)। हारगौरयशःपूरदारी[3] हरि-

15. हरश्वरेः। (॥ 8) यः षोडशमहादान(य) शसा दिग्वि-

16. हारिणा। भूयसोप्यगमनूनं[4] भुवनानि

17. चतुर्दश। (॥ 9) प्रतापदेवरायस्य[5] पुत्र(:)सुत्राम-

18. विक्र(मः)। प्रमोद इव मूर्त्तोयं प्रजानां स्वगुणै-

19. रभूत्। (॥ 10) प्रत्यर्थिसमिधो हुत्वा प्रतापाग्नि[6]-

20. रणं(।)गणे। विहितो येन[7] विजयश्री-

21. करग्रह(:)। (॥ 11) तस्य हेमांबिकाजानेस्तनयो विन-

22. येन्नतः। विद्यानिधिर्विशेषज्ञो वीरो विज-

23. यभूपतिः। (॥ 12) दयानिधेरभूत्तस्य दवा नाराय-

24. णांबिका। शौरेरिव महालक्ष्मीः शंकरस्येव

Second plate, first side.

25. पावता। (॥ 13) पुत्ररूपं तयोः श्लाघ्यं पूर्वजन्म-

26. तपःफलं। देवरायमहीपालो दाता दि[8]-

27. व्यति भूतले। (॥ 14) विक्रमो[9] विक्रमादित्यं भो-

28. गैर्भोजमिवापरं। राजा राज्ञां वितरण रा-

29. जानं य[10] प्रचक्षते। (॥ 15) अभंगवंगकालिंगवंगा-

30. द्यैश्चामरादिभिः। राजानोयं निषेवंते राज-

---

[1] Read ध्ये.
[2] Read णीनामिव.
[3] Read धारी.
[4] Read भूयसाध्यगमन्नूनं.
[5] Read रायाख्यः.
[6] Read प्रतापाग्नौ.
[7] Add वीरेण.
[8] Read दीव्यति.
[9] Read विक्रमैः or विक्रमे.
[10] Read राजराजं वितरणे राजानंयं.

31. चिह्नैःस्वयंधृतैः । (॥ 16) राजाधिराजस्तेजस्वी यो राज-
32. परमेश्वरः । भाषालंधितभूपालभूजंग-
33. विरुदोन्नतः । (॥ 17) मूरुरायरगंडांकः परा-
34. यमयंकर । हिंदुरायसुरत्राण[1] वंदिवर्गे-
35. ण वाणतुं[2] (॥ 18) श्रीतुंगभद्रापरिधे नगरे विज-
36. याह्वये । पुण्यश्लोकाग्रगण्यो सौप्रौढरायम-
37. हीपति(:) (॥ 19) शसिसायकरामेंदुशकवर्षक-
38. मादिषु । सौम्यसंवत्सरे मासि कार्तिक्यां
39. तु शुभे दिने । (॥ 20) शुक्लपक्षे च द्वादश्यां पुण्य-
40. काले विशेषतं(तः) । तुंगभद्रानदीतीरे वि-
41. रूपाक्षस्य संनिधौ । (॥ 21) (कौ)ण्डिन्यगोत्रसंभूतव-
42. रापस्तंबसूत्रिणे । यशास्विने यजु(:)शाखा-
43. ध्याइ(यि)ने गुणशालिने । (॥ 22) मल्लिकार्जुनवर्याय[3] पु-
44. त्रायामिततेजसे । श्रौतस्मार्तसदाचारनि-
45. रताय मनीषिणे । (॥ 23) भूदानपात्रभूताय भूमि-

Second plate, second side.

46. देवाग्रयाइ(यि)ने । विनीताय विशिष्टाय विख्या-
47. ताय महात्मने । (॥ 24) शैवशास्त्रपरिज्ञातचतुर्वेद-
48. परायणे (णः) । श्रीशैले उत्तरद्वारनायको घुवि[4]
49. विशतुः[5] । (॥ 25) तुलामारोहयामास सहपंचारी-
50. णय[6] । रुद्राक्षेणैकवक्तण[7] चित्रं तत्र समारुह[8]-
51. त् (॥ 26) कोंपल्लिनाम विख्यात(:)षक्कार[9]शिवपूजकः ।

---

[1] Read त्राणो. [2] Read वर्ण्यते. [3] Read वर्यस्य.
[4] Read भुवि. [5] Read विश्रुतः. [6] Read सहपंचाक्षरेण यः.
[7] Read कस्वक्षेण. [8] Read समारुहत. [9] Read पट्टकाल.

52. अंनमाराध्याविदु(षे)वेदवेदांगवेदिने । (॥ 27) चंद्र-
53. गिर्याह्वये राज्ये पडनाडुमहीतले । पोरूरु-
54. सीमविख्यातपितिष्टित[1]मनुत्तमं[:] । (॥ 28) सुवर्ण-
55. मुखिनद्याया[2] दक्षिणं दिशमाश्रितं । तंडं च
56. ग्रामसंयुक्तं लिंगंपाड्डितिनामकं (॥ 29) प्रतिना-
57. म प्रतापाख्यदेवरायपुरं तथा । सर्वमान्यं त्र-

Second plate, second side.

58. तुः सीमा संयुतं च समंततः । (॥ 30) निधिनिक्षेपसं-
59. युक्तं जलपाषाणसंयुतं । अक्षिण्यागामिसहि-
60. तं सिद्धसाध्यसमन्वितं । (॥ 31) ये(ए)कभोगामिदंसर्व
61. मान्य [मा] चंद्रतारकं । सहिरण्यपयोधारापूर्वकं
62. दत्तवानमुदा (॥ 32).

Third plate, first side.

63. शासनाचार्यवर्येण वीरणस्य सुतेन च । मुद्दद
64. ण[3]चार्यनाम्ना वै लिखितं तांब्रशासनं ॥ (॥ 33)
65. दानपालन &c.

Usual imprecatory verses.

75. रामचंद्रः ॥

श्रीविरूपाक्ष.

---

[1] Read प्रतिष्ठित.

[2] Read मुखरीनद्यादीक्षण दिश.

[3] Read ना.

Copper-plate No. 4. (A.D. 1746-47.)

[From Rámayyapaṭnam, Kandukúr Taluk.]

Note.

[1. Records the agreement of certain Lambáḍi salt traders to pay Re. 1 per *puṭṭi* of salt bought by them to Báva Mohandás Rághavadás and his heirs for maintaining the (Bairági) *maṭham* at Rámayapaṭnam, Kundukúr taluk.

2. Date—S.S. 1668—A.D. 1746.

3. Language—Telugu. The front side records the above said agreement and on the reverse are inscribed a few of the customary imprecatory verses in Sanskrit.]

[Obeisance to Ṣrí Ráma.]

This is the deed of gift executed by the Lambáḍis named (here comes a list of names) to Báva Mohandás Rághavàdás on the 7th of the bright half of Mágha of the year Akshaya, corresponding to the illustrious, victorious, and prosperous S.S. year 1668. In fasli 1156 we settled to give one rupee per *puṭṭi* of salt purchased by Brinjáris (salt traders) to maintain the charity in your *maṭham* at Bandar Rámayapaṭnam. Therefore we, the salt traders who trade at Pákala, Binginapalli and Tummalapenṭa of Sarkár Udayagiri, Zuvvaladinne, Krishṇapaṭnam and Gangapaṭnam of Sarkár Sarvepalli, and Gógulapalli, Isikipalli and Allúru of Sarkár Kambham, and other ports on the coast and we, the Lambáḍis or whoever we be; bind ourselves to continue in the above said manner the charity in your *maṭham* to your sons and grandsons in succession as long as the sun and moon endure. This deed of gift has been executed in these terms with our consent.

[Two imprecatory verses.]

శ్రీరామా.

స్వస్తిశ్రీ విజయాభ్యుదయ శాలివాహన శకవరుషంబులు ౧౬౬౮ అగునేటి అక్షయనామ సంవత్సర మాఘ శు ౭ లు బావా మోహన దాసు రాఘవదాసుగారికి దోమాపతు ఖిమాసవాయి బాణాసామాష కిరాశంద్దాము టలయ్యా ఖమాఝూజనరపతు కాదలాతు గిరిద్దర ఖిలాపతు రామదాసు మిరుజార్ఘు నోతుతింమ్మ శ్యైజెమపతు జివాహెము తాళ్ళాబగ్గి ఖిమతాళ్ళాపతు చంద్ద్రాలికరు పాపాతరతాకురు వగైరాముాడు బూక్యాదిపాగంగ్గు షేతాపతుహాటి చాకాపతు లో వగైరా సత్తాలినుపాదాబుక్యా తెరపడముదు వగైరా లంబాడిబ్రాయించియిచ్చిన దానపత్రం. స్న ౧౧౫౬ ఫసలి బందరు రామయపట్నంలోను మీమఠం ధర్మంనడిచేటందుకు మఠాలాకు బంజారీలు పట్టెవుప్పుకు ఖ ౧కి రూపాయనిపరురష చేసినాముగనుక పాకల బింగినపల్లె తుమ్మలపెంట సరకారు వుదరగిరి జువ్వలదిన్నె క్రిష్ణాపట్నం గంగపట్నం సరకారు సర్వేపల్లి యిశికిపల్లి గోకులపల్లి అల్లూరు సరకారు కంభంవగైరా కరవాక[1] బందర్లలో పట్టెలంబాడీలు యెకులావారు పటినా యీ సదరపా వ్రాశినప్రకారం మీమఠానకు ధర్మ్మం మీ పుత్రపవుత్ర పారంపరియంత్తగం ఆచంద్రార్కస్థాయిగాను నడిపించగలవారము యిటని మారాజిని వ్రాయించ్చి యిచ్చిన దానపత్రముసరి॥

దానపాలనయోర్మధ్యే దానాచ్ఛ్రేయోనుపాలనం దానాత్స్వర్గమవాప్నోతి పాలనాదచ్యుతంపదం॥

స్వదత్తా ద్విగుణంపుణ్యం పరదత్తాను పాలనం పరదత్తాపహారేణ స్వదత్తం నిష్ఫలంభవేత్ ॥

---

[1] కరవాక. = On the coast.

Copper-plate No. 5. (A.D. 1406–07.)

[The Málakonda temple grant of Kandukúr Taluk. Telugu.]

Translation.

Prosperity! Hail! On the 15th of the bright fortnight of Vaiṣákha of the year Vyaya, corresponding to the illustrious Saka year 1328, Mahárája Srí Mallaya Reḍḍi, the son of Srígiri Reḍḍi, grandson of Pina Kómati Reḍḍi, and great grandson of Vémaya Reḍḍi, who (Vémaya) had the *birudas* Jagannobbaganḍa (the sole hero of the world), Jita Gópála[1] (the conqueror of Gopála), Pallava Trinétra, Vairivíra (the hero to enemies), Basava Sankara, who (Vémaya) was the builder of (the flight of) steps at Srísaila (Parvata), and the giver of unlimited land and the gifts prescribed by Hémádri, issued this charitable edict to Málekonḍa Késava Díkshit, the priest of Vishnu of Mályádri (Málakonḍa), the son of Rangá Chárya and grandson of Peddayya, of the Parásara *gótra*, of the Ápastamba *sútra*, and of the Yajussákhá. We have granted on this holy occasion with libation of water the hereditary right of worshipping Vishnu at the villages Cherukúru, Kámayapalli, Ádúru, and Penṭaréla, and their hamlets, which are attached to Chunḍi in Kandukúru. Therefore you and your sons and grandsons should enjoy this for ever as long as the sun and moon last.

Verses. The protection of another's gift is twice as meritorious as one's own gift.

---

[1] Perhaps we should read Jagatgópála as in K.R. 18.

By resuming the gift of another one's own gift becomes inefficacious.

[This is] the signature of Mallaya Reḍḍi.

1. శ్రీ స్వస్తిశ్రీ శకవర్షంబ్బులు ౧౩౭౮ అగునేటి వ్యయ సంవత్స
2. ర వైశాఖ శు ౧౫ యజుశ్శాఖాధ్యాయ నాపస్తంబసూత్ర పరా
3. శర గోత్ర పెదయ్యపౌత్ర రంగాచార్య పుత్రమాల్యాద్రి హారిపూజా
4 పరులైన మాలెకొండ కేశవ దీక్షితులవారికి జగనొబ్బగం
5. డ జితగోపాల పల్లవత్రినేత్ర వైరివీర బసవశంకరాది బిరుదులుంగ
6. ల పర్వతానసోపానాలు నిస్సిమభూదానహేమా
7. ద్రి. దానాలున్ను చేశిన వేమాయ రెడ్డింగారి నప్తృలు
8. న్ను పినకోమటి రెడ్డింగారి పౌత్రులున్ను శ్రీగి
9. రి రెడ్డిగారి పుత్రులున్ను ఆయిన మహారాజశ్రీ
10. మల్లాయరెడింగారు వ్రాయించియిచ్చిన ధ
11. ర్మశాసనం కందుకూరికి చెల్లె చుండి సంమ చెరు
12. కూరు కామయపల్లి ఆదూరు పెంటరేల యీ క
13. సుపాలు పీటిపలెలుకూడా విష్ణుదేవాలయా
14. ల అర్చకమిరాశి యీ పుణ్యకాలమందు ధారా
15. గ్రహితం చేస్తిమిగనుక ఆచంద్రార్కస్థాయి
16. గా పుత్రపౌత్ర పారంపర్యంతరం మీరు అను
17. భవించుకునేది ॥ శ్లోకం ॥ స్వదత్తా ద్విగుణంపుణ్య
18. ం పరదత్తానుపాలనం । పరదత్తాప హారేణ స్వ
19. దత్తం నిష్ఫలం భవేత్ ॥ శ్రీ శ్రీ శ్రీ శ్రీ శ్రీ మల్లయ
20. రెడ్డివ్రాలు

COPPER-PLATE No. 6. (A.D. 1602–03.)

[Mangalampád grant of Venkaṭa I.]

Note.

The original of this grant was secured from its owner by Rao Sahib T. Raghaviah, Deputy Collector of Gudur Division. It consists of five plates measuring 8⅓ inches long and 7 inches wide, the first and last of which are inscribed on their inner sides only. The plates are held together by a ring passing through their upper part which is rounded at the top. They are in a state of excellent preservation.

The grant throughout is in the Nandinágari alphabet and the language is Sanskrit. It is entirely in verse of various metres. The letters are very clearly engraved and it is noteworthy that very few mistakes are found in this grant. The orthography calls for no special remarks.

The grantor is Venkata I, who also issued the Vilapaka grant (Ṣaka 1523).

The date of the grant is Ṣaka 1524 or A.D. 1602–03, cyclic year Ṣubhakṛit, on the 12th day of the month of Ashádha.

The donee was Ṣrí Rangarája, son of Jagannáthárya, grandson of Ṣrí Rangarájárya, of the *gótra* of Atri, of the Ápastamba *sútra*, and foremost of the students of the Yajuṣ Ṣákhá. His genealogy is traced up to one Védántódayana, who was the cook of Ṣrí Rámánujárya (the Vaishnava philosopher) and who was famed for his shastraic lore.

From this inscription we learn that Kavitárkíkasimha, *i.e.*, Védántáchárya or Déṣika, the Vaishnava philosopher, was a disciple of Várihamsámbuváha, and descendant of the above said Védántódayana.

The object of the grant is the village of Mangalampáḍ *alias* Pórúr, surnamed Jagannáthapuram, situated in the kingdom (Rájya) of Chandragiri, in the division of Paḍanáḍu, north of Santavélúr, east of Ugumudípera *agrahára*, south of Uchúr and west of Ilúr. It is stated that the gift was made before the deity Venkaṭéṣa.

The Vamṣávali (genealogy) of the grantor is identical with that of the Vilapaka grant (Vol. IV, E.I., p. 272) and the verses of the two grants are identical throughout except in a few places. No new historical information is accordingly furnished.

The stanzas of this grant were composed by Chidambara Kavi, sister's son of Ṣiva Súrya, the king of poets.

The engraver is said to have been Kámayárya, the son of Gaṇapárya, the brother of Vírana (probably the same individual who engraved the Vilapaka grant.)

Like the Vilapaka grant, this grant bears at the end the colophon Ṣrí Venkaṭéṣa (Vishnu) in Telugu characters.

Translation.

First plate, second side.

Salutation to Ṣrí Venkaṭéṣa!

V. 1. I seek refuge in that pair of substances,[1] by virtue of whose touch a stone became the gem of women, and which is deserving of worship by the gods (or the wise).

V. 2. I seek refuge in Vishvakséna, whose courtiers, over a hundred in number, the elephant-headed (Ganéṣa) and others, destroy the obstacles of (his) devotees.

---

[1] The pair of substances are the two feet of Ráma. When he once trod on a stone, it immediately became a woman. She was Ahalyá, the wife of Gautama, who had been condemned by her husband for unfaithfulness to become a stone.

V. 3. Victorious is the luminary (the Moon), which is the left eye of Hari, which arose from the ocean of milk, which is the support of the chakóras,[1] and which is productive of longevity to the gods.

V. 4. His grandson was Purúravas, the son of Budha. His son was Áyus. From him was born Nahusha. After him was Yayáti. Then from him was born Puru.

In his race arose King Bharata. In his lineage was Santanu.

The fourth after him was Vijaya (Arjuna). From him was born Abhimanyu. Then came Parikshi(t).

V. 5. The eighth in descent from him was Nanda.[2] Ninth from him was born king Rája Chalikka;[3] the seventh from him was Rája Naréndra, who was devoted to Śrípati (Vishnu); the tenth after him here (*i.e.*, on earth) was Vijjaléndra.[4] The third after him was born Víra Hémáliráya,[5] lord of Máyápuri, devotee of Murári (Vishnu).

V. 6. Fourth after him was born king Táta Pinnama, at whose sight the assemblage of enemies got frightened. Then was born king Somadéva, who in one day captured seven forts from the enemy. To him was born an heroic son, named king Rághavadéva. Then was the glorious King Pinnama.

V. 7. King Bukka was the son of him (Pinnama) who was the lord of the city of Áravíḍu,[6] (Bukka) whose

---

[1] The *chakóras* are fabulous birds supposed to feed on moonbeams.

[2] Nanda—the composer seeks to connect the family of the donor with previous dynasties, *e.g.*, Nanda, Chálukya and Kálachúri. The Nanda dynasty was subverted by the Mauryas.

[3] Chalikka and Rája Naréndra are Chálukyas.

[4] Vijjaléndra was of the Kálachuri dynasty.

[5] Víra Hémáliráya, lord of Máyápuri was probably the Kálachuri king Permádi; (S.S. 1050) E.I., Vol. III, p. 238.

[6] Araviḍu; perhaps Áravéḍu near Ráyachóṭi in Cuddapah district.

splendour was increasing, and by whom even the kingdom of Sáluva Nrisimha[1] was firmly established.

Second plate, first side.

V. 8. Bukka, the ornament of kings, who was a very tree of paradise to learned men, married the lovely Ballámbiká, who in the beauty of her body surpassed the nymphs of heaven, and who was of estimable character, just as Vishnu (married) Lakshmí.

V. 9. As the daughter of Kalaṣámbudhi (Lakshmí) obtained (a son) the flower-arrowed (Káma) from Mádhava, as the daughter of the chief of mountains (Párvatí) obtained Kumára from Ṣankara, as Ṣachí obtained Jayanta from the lord of the gods (Indra), so did Ballamá obtain from king Bukka, a son Rámarája, who was renowned in the world.

V. 10. Having vanquished by the great valour of his arm in battle the army of Sapáda,[2] though consisting of 70,000 horse, he seized from him the fort of Avanigiri,[3] and suddenly put to flight even Kásappudaya who excelled Indra in valour.

V. 11. He, whose prosperity was increasing, captured the fort of Kandanavólu[4] by the excessive strength of his arm. Having partaken of the poison administered by his relations, he converted it into ambrosia, (*i.e.*, did not die) owing to his devotion to the feet of Hari who was present there.

V. 12. Resplendent was Lakkámbiká, the queen of the glorious king Rámarája, who was a philosopher's

---

[1] From this it appears that he was the minister of Sáluva Narasimha (S.S. 1404) the third king of the second Vijayanagar dynasty.

[2] Sapáda—A certain chieftain; not, apparently, identified.

[3] Avanigiri not known.

[4] Kandanavólu—Kurnool.

stone to the assemblage of scholars, as Lakshmí, the wife of the lotus-eyed Vishnu.

V. 13. Owing to his many austerities he had a son, the illustrious king Rangarája, the light of the lunar race. When his power was resplendent, O wonder! even the eyes of the beautiful-eyed (ladies) of (his) enemies became bright.[1]

V. 14. Having obtained as consort the virtuous Tirumalámbika, who captivated the heart by her virtues, who eclipsed even the renown of Arundhati[2] by the beauty of her character and who surpassed the fame of Vasumatí[3] in patience, just as the moon (obtained) Róhiní, he, the foremost of heroes, rejoiced.

V. 15. This very valiant king begot these sons in succession on queen Tirumalá: the heroic Rámarája, versed in politics, the excellent Tirumalaráya and king Venkaṭádri.

V. 16. This hero Rámarája, having slain in battle his enemies who were the scourges of the whole earth, whose fame was as celebrated as that of Bharata, Manu, Bhagíratha and other kings, ruled the circle of the earth.

V. 17. Hearing the succession of his gifts sung by Vidyádhari women in accompaniment to the sound of their lutes resonant on account of their being struck with their nails, the tree of the city of the gods appears to plunge entirely into the ocean under the semblance of its reflection.

---

[1] *I.e.* he killed his enemies. Their widows could not use collyrium to their eyes which therefore appeared white though filled with tears. Not only were the eyes of his own ladies bright owing to his success, but also those of his enemies' widows. Hence the wonder.

[2] Arundhatí—wife of Vasishṭha—type of chastity.

[3] Vasumatí—the earth—type of patience.

V. 18. Ṣrí Vara (Víra?) Venkaṭádri Rája shone on earth, resembling Lakshmana in beauty, surpassing the roar of thunder-clouds by the twang of his bowstring and causing great delight to the minds of his friends.[1]

V. 19. Amongst the three sons of king Ṣrí Ranga, king Tirumala Mahárája, of great prowess, wise, having subdued hostile kings in battle, and having been anointed to peerless sovereignty, ruled the whole earth, as Hari among the trinity.

V. 20. When the installation of this, the foremost of the famous and the moon of kings, took place, this earth being sprinkled with the water (poured out) on the occasion of numerous gifts attained as it were the position of queen.[2]

V. 21. Then shone his son, Ṣrí Rangaráya, famous, the bestower of wealth on dependants, the collection of the long accumulated merit of Ṣrí Vengalámba, and whose hand eclipsed the celestial tree (in liberality).

Third plate, first side.

V. 22. When his installation ceremony was performed according to the prescribed rules by the best of

---

[1] The epithets in this verse apply both to king Venkatádri and Lakshmana, brother of Ráma.

Lakshmana cháru murti:

(1) in the case of Venkatádri, resembling Lakshmana in beauty.

(2) in the case of Lakshmana—having a form possessing auspicious marks.

Méghanádha—

(1) roar of thunder clouds, in the case of Venkatádri.

(2) Indrajit, son of Rávana, who was defeated by Lakshmana—in the case of Lakshmana.

Sumitrásaya—

(1) The desire of friends—in the case of Venkatádri.

(2) The desire of Sumitra, who was the mother of Lakshmana—in the case of Lakshmana.

[2] One of the ceremonies at the coronation of a king was to bathe him and his queen with sacred water.

Brahmans, when the cloud of his hand rained everywhere gold, waves of fame rose everywhere in the ten directions, and the fierce forest-fire which was the poverty of the good was quenched.

V. 23. Then his younger brother Venkaṭapati Ṣrí Dévaráya, the son of Tirumala Ṣrí Dévaráya, the fruition of the great religious merit of previous births of Ṣrí Vengalámba, devoted to the protection of the learned, and seated on the throne of universal sovereignty, like the tree of paradise (standing) on Mount Méru, ruled the whole earth with righteousness.

V. 24. Having been anointed according to the prescribed rules by the spiritual preceptor of his *gótra*, the famous Tátayárya, who was the ornament of the wise, just as the descendant of the Raghu family himself (Ráma) by the husband of Arundhatí (Vasishṭha), (and) having quickly destroyed the demons who were the Yavanas [1] (as Ramá), ruling the earth, he was triumphant.

V. 25. His queens, Ṣrí Venkaṭámbá, Pedayovayámba, Ṣrí Krishnámba, Kódamámba, and Ṣrí Rághavámba resembled his three *Ṣaktis*,[2] *Níti*,[3] and *Dayá*.[4]

V. 26. Having been forcibly deprived of quantities of horses, elephants, weapons, umbrellas, etc., in a battle by the excellent soldiers of the army of him (Venkatapati) whose bravery was renowned, Mahamanda Sáhu,[5]

---

[1] The Yavanas referred to here were the Muhammadans आशर:= demon. Ráma destroyed the demons. This king destroyed tne Yavanas.

[2] The three *Ṣaktis* are the three elements of regal power—(1) Prabháva = majesty, (2) Utsáha = energy and (3) *Mantra* = counsel.

[3] Níti = Polity or politics.

[4] Dayá = Mercy.

[5] Mahamanda Sáhu is the Sanskritized form of Muhammad Shah who was king of Golkonḍa from A.D. 1581 to 1611.

son of Malikibharáma,[1] returned home in despair, shorn of splendour, and thus day by day made his name significant.

V. 27. Behaving like a grandfather to friends and foes, intent on giving refuge to enemies who bowed to him; his splendour was thus eulogized by all men "he is the crusher of the pride of Avahaluráya."

V. 28. Whose prosperity is radiant, having the title *manyaraganḍa* (hero to mountain chiefs), having titles, possessed of heroes who were able to vanquish the king of Utkala (Orissa) whose might was great, the punisher of the assemblage of enemies with the fierce strength of his arm, having the great title *ganḍaraguli-mányapuli* (a wild tiger to wicked kings).

V. 29. The central gem (the lord) of the necklace which is the city of Áravíḍu,[2] dallying with the powerful goddess of valour, broad-armed like the lord of serpents (Ṣésha), acquiring the title *manḍalíkadharaníraráha* (the boar on earth among provincial chiefs).

V. 30. *Venga-Tirubhuvanamalla,* an Arjuna in the science of the battle-field, *Urugula-suratrána*[3] (the Sultan of Orangal), the devotee of Hari (Vishnu),

V. 31. The best of kings, known as "Rámabhadra in battle," whose *biruda* is described as *Nánávarṇa Srí Mandalíkaganda* (the hero of provincial chiefs of all castes),

---

[1] Malikibharama is the Sanskritized form of Málik Ibrahim. He was the father of Muhammad Shah and Sultán of Golkonda. There is here a play upon the name of Mahamanda Sáhu.

[2] Áravíḍu is, perhaps, a village 16 miles from Ráyachoṭi in Cuddapah district.

[3] Suratrána is the Sanskritized form of Sultán.

V. 32. The foremost of kings descended from the *gótra* of Atri, of great renown, possessing an army of excellent horse,[1] and endowed with great intelligence, he had as his vassals, the Araṭṭas and Magadhas (lit. his rank was honoured by the Araṭṭas and Magadhas),

V. 33. Resplendent with righteousness like Yudhishṭhira,[2] the lord of the city of Kalyána,[3] accomplished in arts, *Chálikka chakravarti* (the emperor of the Chálukyas), and shining with the great crown of gems,

V. 34. Having the glory of the title *ébirudaráyaráhutavésyaikabhujanga* (the sole paramour of the prostitutes who are the troops of kings having all titles), having beautiful fame due to the proclamation of the *biruda Oddiyaráyadisápaṭṭa*[4] (the vanquisher of the king of Orissa),

V. 35. Whose cheeks resembled the moon, who eclipsed the god of love[5] in beauty, the hero who punished kings who break their word, the protector of the nine continents of the earth,

V. 36. Having the title Rájádhirája, whose gifts are like those of Kubéra,[6] surnamed *múruráyaragaṇḍa* (the vanquisher of the three kings), possessing fame surpassing Méru,

V. 37. Indifferent to other men's wives, the terror of other kings, devoted to the protection of the good, the

---

[1] Dhaṭṭá = Daṭṭu (Canarese) = a crowd, an army.

[2] Ṣalyári, a rare word = Yudhishṭhira whose uncle was Salya, king of Madra

[3] The birudas Venga Tribhuvana Malla and Kalyánapurádhipa are meant to show connection with the eastern and western Chálukyas.

[4] Oddiya is Orissa.

Disápatta (Canarese) = causing (enemies) to be scattered in all directions.

[5] Asamakánda — Asamabána = the number of whose arrows is odd (five *i.e.*, the god of love).

[6] Amhati — an unusual Sanskrit word = gift.

destroyer of the tiger-like wicked,[1] having the title *aríbhagandabhérunda* (the eagle to the elephants which are his enemies), the store of ambrosia which is faith in Vishnu,

V. 38. He was eulogized daily by the crowd of bards, singing with folded hands "be victorious, live long," with these and other titles.

V. 39. His glory was sung by the Kámbhója, Bhója, Kalinga, Karaháta, and other kings who became his doorkeepers.

V. 40. He, Venkaṭapati, the foremost of kings, who surpasses the assemblage of ancient kings in policy, who is a tree of paradise to the crowd of scholars, having won the throne of Karnáṭa by the might of his arm, having subdued his enemies from the bridge (Rámésvaram) as far as the Himálayas, and joyfully ruling the whole earth, is resplendent.

Vs. 41 and 42. In the Ṣaka year, reckoned by the Védas (4), the eyes (2), the arrows (5), and the moon (1), *i.e.*, 1524, in the year Ṣubhakrit, in the month of Áshádha, in the bright fortnight, on the auspicious twelfth *tithi*, under a sacred asterism in the presence of the lotus feet of Ṣrí Venkaṭéṣa, who is the store-house of bliss,

V. 43. To the excellent Ṣrí Rangarája of the illustrious *gótra* of Atri, who is famed as the ornament of the earth, the follower of the excellent Ápastamba *sútra*, the foremost of the students of the Yajuṣ Ṣákhá.

V. 44. There was a great man named Vedántódayana, who was the cook of the illustrious Rámánujárya and who was famed for his learning in all the scriptures.

---

[1] Dushtaṣárdúlamardana — the tiger was the emblem of the Chola king. The biruda may refer to this; it would then mean the vanquisher of the wicked Chóla king.

V. 45. In his lineage arose a great man named Várdihamsámbuváha, whose disciples Kavitárkikasimha (Védántáchárya, known as Déṣikáchárya) and others were renowned on earth.

Vs. 46 to 51. In his family arose Ṣrí Rangarájárya of great intelligence. To his grandson who commented on the two schools of the Vedánta (*i.e.*, the Sánskrit and the Drávida or Tamil Schools), the son of the excellent Bráhman Jagannátha, who was a proud lion to the mad elephants who are his opponents in controversy, who was intelligent, and who was renowned for having everywhere promulgated the Vedic conduct; to the excellent Srí Rangarájá, who was (as it were) the accumulation of virtues, the self-chosen lord of the goddess of universal sovereignty of the Vaishnava creed, who reached the summit of altruistic acts, who is skilled in selecting learned men who observe good conduct, whose lotus-mind delighted in the contents of the eighteen Puránas, the best in righteous acts, of pure disposition of mind, who by daily giving food pleased the crowd of all Brahmans, and who was possessed of knowledge and modesty,

Vs. 52-to 57. The village named Mangalampáḍu situated in the kingdom (*Rájya*) of Chandragiri, connected with Paḍanáḍu, having (also) the name Pórúr, lying to the west of the village Ilupúr, lying to the north of the village called Santavélúru, lying to the east of the *agrahára* Ugumuḍipera, and lying to the south of the village named Uchchúru, well known by its other name Jagannáthapuram, free from all taxes, with the four boundaries everywhere, together with its treasures, hidden deposits, stones, water, and every thing which it does or may contain, with its *akshini* and *ágámi*, with its trees, having wells, cisterns, tanks, embankments and gardens, to be enjoyed as a single share, to be enjoyed in succession by sons, grandsons, and others (of the grantee) as long as the moon and sun endure, subject to right of gift, mortgage, sale or transfer,

V. 58. Surrounded by many assiduous and amiable learned men, who followed the path of the Ṣrautas, who excelled in speech, and who were headed by his domestic chaplain, the glorious king Víra Venkaṭapati Mahárâya, after making gift of gold and libation of water, joyfully gave.

V. 59. This is the charter of Ṣrí Venkaṭapatiráya, the best of kings, the great king, the famed, who is a very moon to the lotuses which are scholars.

V. 60. At the bidding of Ṣrí Venkaṭapatiráya, Chidambara Kavi, who acquired an exalted position on account of being the sister's son of Ṣiva Súrya, the king of poets, composed the verses of this copper-plate grant.

V. 61. Under the orders of king Ṣrí Venkaṭapatiráya, Kámayárya, son of Ganapárya, the brother of Vírana, engraved this copper-plate grant.

V. 62. Of giving and protecting (another's gift) protecting is superior to giving; by giving, one attains heaven, but by protecting one gets imperishable bliss.

V. 63. The protection of another's gift is twice as meritorious as gift by one self; by resuming another's gift one's own gift becomes inefficacious.

V. 64. Whoever resumes land given by himself or another is reborn a worm in ordure for 60,000 years.

V. 65. There is only one sister of all kings in this world, to wit, land bestowed on Bráhmans, who is not to be enjoyed nor married.

V. 66. "This general duty of kings should always be observed by you," (thus) does Rámachandra again and again exhort all future kings.

Ṣrí Venkatésa.

First plate, second side.

1. श्री वेङ्कटेशा(य)नमः ॥ यस्य संपर्कपुण्येन नारीरत्न-
2. मभूच्छिला । यदुपास्यं सुमनसां तद्वस्तुद्वन्द्वमाश्र-
3. य ॥ (*v.* 1) यस्य द्विरदवक्त्राद्याः पारिषद्याः परःशतं । वि-
4. घ्नं निघ्नन्ति भजतां विष्वक्सेनं तमाश्रये ॥ (2) जय-
5. ति क्षीरजलधेर्जातं सव्येक्षणं हरेः । आलम्बनं
6. चकोराणाममरायुष्करं महः ॥ (3) पौत्रस्तस्य पुरूरवा बुध-
7. सुतस्तस्यायुरस्यात्मजः संजज्ञे नहुषो ययातिर-
8. भवत्तस्माच्च पूरुस्ततः तद्वंशे भरतो बभूव नृपति-
9. स्तत्संततौ शंतनुः तत्तुर्यो विजयो भिमन्युरुदभूत्तस्मा-
10. त्परीक्षि(त्) ततः ॥ (4) नन्दस्तस्याष्टमोभूत्समजनि नवमस्त-
11. स्य राज्ञश्चलिक्कक्ष्मापस्तत्सप्तम(:) श्रीपतिरुचिरभ-
12. वद्राजपूर्वो नरेन्द्रः । तस्यासीद्विज्जलेन्द्रो दशमयि-[1]
13. वनृपा[2]वीरहेमाड्डिरायस्तार्तीयोको मुरारी कृतन-
14. तिरुदभूरतस्य[3] मायापुरीशः ॥ (5) तत्तुर्योजानि ताताापि-
15. न्नममहीपालो निजालोकनत्रस्तामित्रगणस्तता-
16. जानि हरन् दुर्गाणि सप्ताहितात् । अह्नैकेन स सो-
17. मदेवनृपति स्तस्यैव जज्ञे सुतो वीरो राघवदेवरा-
18. डिति ततः श्रीपिन्नमोभून्नृपः ॥ (6) आरवीटिनगरी-
19. विभोरभूदस्य बुक्कधरणीपातिस्सुतः । येन सालु-

[1] Read इ.

[2] Read हनृपो.

[3] Read दभूत्तस्य.

Second plate, first side.

20. वनृसिंहराज्यमभ्येधमानमहसा स्थिरीकृतं ॥ (7) स्वः का-
21. मिनी (:) स्वतनुकान्तिभिराक्षिपन्तीं बुक्कावनीपतिलको बुध-
22. कल्पशाखी। कल्याणिनीं कमलनाभ इवाब्धिकन्यां बल्लांबि-
23. कामुदवहद्बहुमान्यशीलां ॥ (8) सुतेव कलशाम्बुधेस्सुरभि-
24. लाशुगं माधवात्कुमारमिव शंकरात्कुलमहीभृतः क-
25. न्यका । जयन्तममरप्रभोरपि शचीव बुक्काधिपाच्छ्रतं ज-
26. गात बल्लमालभत रामराजं सुतं ॥ (9) सहस्रैस्ससत्त्या सहित-
27. मपि यस्मिन्धुजनुषां सपादस्यानीकं समिति भुजशौर्ये-
28. ण महता । विजित्यादत्ते स्मादवनिगिरिदुर्गं विभुतया वि-
29. धूतेन्द्रंकास(:)प्पुडयमपि विद्राव्य सहसा ॥(10) कन्दनवोलिदु-
30. र्गमुरुकंदलदभ्युदयो वाहुवलेन यो बहुतरेण विजित्य ह-
31. रेः। सन्निहितस्य तत्र चरणाबुषु भक्ततया ज्ञातिभिरार्पि-
32. तं सुधयतिस्म निषेव्य विषं ॥ (11) श्रीरामराजाक्षितिपस्य
33. तस्य चिन्तामणेरर्थिकदंबकानां । लक्ष्मीरिवांभोरुहलो-
34. चनस्य लक्काम्बिकामुष्य महिष्यलासीत ॥ (12) तस्याधिकै-
35. स्समभवत्तनयस्तपोभिश्च श्रीरंगराजनृपतिश्शशिवं-
36. शदीपः। आसंन् समुल्लसति[1] धामानि यस्य चित्रं नेत्राणि
37. वैरिसुदृशां च निरञ्जनानि ॥ (13) सतीं तिरुमलांबिकां चरि-
38. तलीलया रुन्धतीप्रथामपि तितिक्षया वसुमतीयशो-
39. रुन्धतीं । हिमांशुरिव रोहिणीं हृदयहारिणीं सद्गु णै-

Second plate, second side.

40. रमोदत सधर्मिणमियमवाप्य वीराग्रणीः ॥ (14) राचितनयवि-
41. चारं रामराजं च धीरं वरतिरुमलरायं वेङ्कटाद्रिक्षितीशं ।

---

1 There is a dot in the text after आसन् which is superfluous.

42. अजनयत स ये[1] तानानुपूर्व्या कुमारानिह तिरुमलदेव्यामेव रा-
43. जा महौजाः ॥ (15) सकलभुवनकण्टकानरातीन् समिति-
निहत्य स-
44. रामराजवीरः । भरतमनुभगीरथादिराजप्रथितयशाः
45. प्रशशास चक्रमुर्व्याः ॥ (16) वितरणपरिपाटीं यस्य विद्याधरी-
46. णां ननखरमुखरबीणानादगीता (म्) निशम्य । आनुकलमय[2]-
47. मावालांवुबिंबापदेशादमरनगरशाखी लज्जया मज्ज-
48. तीव ॥ (17) व्यराजत श्रीवरवेंकटाद्रिरा न[3]क्षितौ लक्ष्मण
चारु-
49. मूर्तिः । ज्याघोषदूरीकृतमेघनादः कुर्वन् सुमित्राशय-
50. हर्षपोषं ॥ (18) त्रिषु श्रीरंगक्ष्मापरिबृढकुमारेष्वाधिरणं
51. विजित्यारिक्ष्मापान् स्तिरुमलमहारायनृपतिः । महौ-
52. जा स्साम्राज्ये सुमतिरभिषिक्तो निरुपमे प्रशास्त्युर्वीम् स-
53. र्वामपि तिसृषु मूर्तिष्विवहरिः ॥ (19) यशस्विनामग्रसरस्य
54. यस्य पट्टाभिषेके सति पार्थिवेन्दोः । दानाम्बुपूरैरभि-
55. षिच्यमाणा[4] देवीपदं भूमिरियं दधाति ॥ (20) अनन्तरं त-
56. (त्) तनयः प्रतीत(ः) चकास्ति हस्तापजिताद्विशाखी[5] ।
श्रीवेंगलां-
57. बाचिरपुण्यरासि(शिः) श्रीरंगराय(ः) श्रितभागधेयः ।(॥ 21) य-
58. था विधि महीसुरोत्तमकृताभिषेकोत्सवे यदीय-
59. करवारिदे कनकवृष्टिदे सर्वतः । यशोमयतर-

Third plate, first side.

60. ङ्गिणी दशादिगन्तर जृंभते सतां प्रशमितोभवत् कृप-
61. णतोरुदावानलः ॥ (22) विद्वत्राण[6] परस्ततस्तदनुजः श्रीवेंगलां-

---

[1] Read एता.
[2] Read अनुकलमय.
[3] Read द्रिराजः.
[4] Read ना.
[5] Read युशाखी.
[6] Read विद्वत्त्राण.

62. बापुरा पुण्योत्कर्षफलोदयास्तिरुमलश्रीदेवरायात्मभूः
63. संतानद्रारिव स्थितस्सुरगिरौ साम्राज्यसिंहासने स-
64. र्वां शास्ति नयेन वेंकटपतिश्रीदवरायो समाम ।[1] (॥ 23) यथा
रघु-
65. कुलोद्वह(:) स्वयमरुंधतीजानिना स्वगोत्रगुरुणा सुधीति-
66. लकतातयार्य्येण यः । यथाविधि यशस्विना विरचिताभिषे-
67. कः क्षणाद्विभिद्य यवनाशरान्विजयते प्रशासन्मही (॥ 24)
श्री-
68. वेंकटांबा पेदयोबमांबा श्रीकृष्णमांबापि च कोंडमांबा
69. श्रीराघवांबेति च भान्ति देव्यः शक्तित्रयीनीतिदयायि (याइ)
70. वास्मिन् । (॥ 25) यस्यातिप्रथितैाजशो[2] रणमुखे सेनाभटैरुद्ध-
71. टै स्साटोपाहतसैन्धवद्विपघटाशस्त्रातपत्रादिभिः[3] । निर्वि-
72. ण or ण्णो मलिकीभरामतनुभूः संप्राप्य गेहं महैर्मन्दरस्तन्
73. महमंदशाहुरयते सार्थाविधा[4]मन्वहं । (॥ 26) उभयदलपि-
74 तामहो नतानामभयपदार्पणतत्परो रिपूणां । अयमव-
75. हलुरायमानमर्द्दी त्यखिलजनैरभिधीयमानधामा (॥ 27)
76. तांडवितोदयो बिरुदमंन्यरगंड तयो[5]र्दूदण्डबलोत्कले-
77. न्द्रजयपंडितवीरयतः । चंण्डिमशालिबाहुवलदंडि-
78. तवैरिगणो गंडरगूलिमंन्यपुलि मान्यमहाबिरुदः (॥ 28)
79. सारवीररमया समुल्लसन्नारवीटिपुरहारनाय-

Third plate, second side.

80. कः । कुण्डलीश्वरमहाभुज(:) श्रयन् मण्डलीकधरणीवरा-
81. हतां । (॥ 29) वेंगात्रिभुवनमल्ल(:) संख्यक्षितिकलार्जुनः । उरि-
82. गोलसुरत्राणो हरिगोचरमानसः । (॥ 30) राज्ञां वरो रणमुख-

---

[1] Read रायः क्षमां.
[2] Read सो.
[3] Read मः
[4] Read - भिधा-
[5] Read यतो.

83. रामभद्र इति श्रुतः । वर्नित[1] विरुदो नाना वर्न [2] श्रीमण्डली-
84. कगंड इति । (॥ 31) आत्रेयगोत्रजानामग्रसरो भूभुजामुदा-
85. रयशाः । अतिबिरुदतुरगघट्टो मतिगुरुरारट्टमगधमा-
86. न्यपदः । (॥ 32) शळ्यालि(रि)नीतिशाली कल्याणपुराधिपः कलाचतुरः ।
87. चालिक्कचक्रवर्ती माणिक्यमहाकिरीटमहनीयः । (॥ 33)ए बिरु-
88. दरायराहुतवेश्यैकभुजंगबिरुदभरितश्री(:) । रम्यतरकी-
89. र्तिरोडिडयरायादिशापट्टबिरुदघोषेण । (॥ 34) ओषधिपत्युप-
90. माइ(यि) तगंडस्तोषणरूपजितासमकांडः । भाषगेतप्पुव
91. रायरगंड(:)पोषणनिर्भरभूनवखंडः । (॥ 35) राजाधिराजबि-
92. रुदो राजराजसमांहातिः । मूरुरायरगंण्डाङ्को मेरुल-
93. ङ्घियशोभरः (॥ 36) परदारेषु विमुखः पररायभयंकरः । शि-
94. ष्टसंरक्षणपरो दुष्टशार्दूलमर्द्दनः । अरीभगंण्डभेरुं:
95. डो हरिभक्तिसुधानिधिः । (॥ 37) इत्यादिविरुदैर्वन्दितत्या
96. नित्यमभिष्टुतः । जयजीवेति वादिन्यांजलितांजालि-
97. बंद्धया [3] (॥ 38) कांभोजभोजकालिंगकरहाटादिपार्थिवैः ।
98. प्रतीहारपदं प्राप्तैः प्रस्तुतस्तुतिघोषणः । (॥ 39) सोयं नीति-

Fourth plate, first side.

99. जितादिभूपतितति(:) सुत्रामशाखी सुधीसार्थानां
100. भुजतेजसा स्ववशयन् कर्णाटसिंहासनं । आसेतोर-
101. पि चाहिमाद्रि विमतान् संहृत्य शासन् मुदा[:] । सर्वो-
102. र्वीं प्रचकास्ति वेंकटपति(:) श्रीदेवरायाग्रणीः (॥ 40) वेदने-
103. त्रकलंबेन्दुगणिते शकवत्सरे । संवत्सरे शुभकृति

---

[1] Read वर्णित. [2] Read वर्ण.

[3] Read वादिन्या जनितांजलिबंधया.

104. मासे चाषाढसंज्ञिके । (॥ 41) पक्षे वलक्षे पुण्यर्क्षे पुण्यायां
105. द्वादशीतिथौ । श्रीवेंकटेशपादाब्जसन्निधौ श्रेयसां नि-
106. धौ । (॥ 42) श्रीमदात्रेयगोत्राय धराभरणकीर्तये । वरा-
107. पस्तम्बसूत्राय यजुश्शाख्यग्रयाइ(यि)ने । (॥ 43) श्रीमद्भा
मानु-
108. जार्यस्य यो माहनासिको महान् । प्रख्यातः सर्वशा-
109. स्त्रेषु वेदान्तोदयनाह्वयो । (॥44)वारि(द?)हंसांबुवाहाख्यस्त-
110. द्वंशे भून्महाहियः ।[1] कवितार्किकसिंहाद्याः यच्छिष्या
111. भुवि विश्रुताः । (॥ 45) अभू(त) श्रीरंगराजार्यस्तद्वंशे यो म-
112. हामतिः । तस्य पौत्राय वेदान्तद्वयव्याख्यानशा-
113. लिने । (॥ 46) प्रतिवादीन्द्रमत्तेभद्वसिंहस्य धीमतः ।
114. ख्यातस्य वैदिकाचारस्थापकत्वेन सर्वतः । (॥ 47) ज-
115. गन्नाथार्यवर्य्यस्य पुत्राय गुणराशये । शिष्टवै-
116. ष्णवसाम्राज्यश्रीस्वयंवरकामिने(॥ 48) परोपका-
117. रकृत्येषु परां प्रौढिमुपेयुषे । शिष्टाचारप-

Fourth plate, second side.

118. रित्राणविद्वज्जनविचक्षणे[2] । (॥ 49) अष्टादशपुराणा-
119. र्थहृष्टाशयसरोरुहे । नीतिकार्यधुरीणाय निर्म-
120. लस्वान्तवृत्तय ।(॥ 50) नित्यान्नदानसंतुष्टानिखिलाद्विजसं-
121. सदे । श्रीरंगराजवर्य्याय विद्याविनयशालिने । (॥ 51)
122. श्रीचंद्रगिरिराज्यस्थं पडनाडुसमन्वितं । पोरू-
123. रुनामसंयुक्तं मङ्गलंपाडुनामकं । (॥ 52) ईलुपूर्नामकग्रा-
124. मात् प्रतीच्यांदिशि संस्थितं । संत्तवेलूर्नामकस्य ग्राम-
125. स्स्योत्तरतः स्थितं । (॥ 53) ऊगूमूडिपेरग्रहारात्पूर्वस्यां दि-

---

[1] Read महान्हिः

[2] Read विचक्षणे.

126. शि संस्थितं। उच्चूरिनामकग्रामाद् दक्षिणस्यां दिशि स्थि-
127. तं। (॥ 54) प्रतिनाम्ना जगंन्नाथपुरामित्यतिविश्रुतं। (॥ 54½) सर्वमान्यं
128. चतुः सीमासंयुतं च समन्ततः। निधिनिक्षेपपाषाणासि-
129. द्धसाध्यजलान्वितं। (॥ 55) अक्षिण्यागामिसंयुक्त मेकभोग्यं
130. सभूरुहं। वापीकूपतटाकैश्च कच्छारामैश्च संयुतं। (॥ 56)
131. पुत्रपौत्रादिभिर्भोग्यं क्रमादाचन्द्रतारकं। दानाध-
132. मनविक्रीतियोग्यं विनिमयोचितं। (॥ 57) परीतः प्रय-
133. तैः स्निग्धैः पुरोहितपुरोगमैः। विविधै र्विबुधैः श्रौत-
134. पथिकैरधिकैर्गिरा। श्रीवीरवेङ्कटपतिमहारायम-
135. हीपतिः सहिरंण्य[1]पयोधारापूर्वकं दत्तवान्मुदा।(॥ 58) श्री-

Fifth plate, first side.

136. वेङ्कटपतिरायक्षितिपतिवर्य्यस्य कीर्तिधुर्य्यस्य
137. शासनमिदं सुधीजनकुवलयचंद्रस्य भूमहेन्द्रस्य। (॥ 59) श्रीवें-
138. कटपतिरायगिरा शिवसूर्य्यकवीन्द्रभागिनेयतया। क-
139. लितोन्नति श्चिदंबरकविरवदत् ताम्रशासनश्लोकान्। (॥ 60) श्री-
140. वेंकटपतिरायक्ष्मापतिदेशेन कामयाचार्य्यः। गणपार्य्य-
141. तनय (सुतः)शासनमलिखदिदं वीरणानुजस्ताम्रं। (॥ 61) दानपालन-
142. यो र्मध्ये दानाच्छ्रेयो नुपालनं। दाना (त्) स्वर्गमवाप्नोति पालनाद-

[1] The anusvára is superfluous.

143. च्युतं पदं । (॥ 62) स्वदत्ताद्विगुणं पुंण्यं परदत्तानुपालनं पर-
दत्ता-

144. पहारेण स्वदत्तं निष्फलं भवेत् । (॥ 63) स्वदत्तां परदत्तां
वा योहरेत

145. वसुन्धरां । [1] सष्ठिवर्षसहस्राणि विष्टायां जायते कृमिः
(॥ 64) [2] ये-

146. कैवभगिनी लोके सर्वेषामेव भूभुजाम् । न भोज्या न
करग्राह्या

147. विप्रदत्ता वसुंधरा (॥ 65) सामान्योयं धर्मसेतुः नृपाणां कोल
कोलं

148. पालनीयो भवद्भिः । सर्वानेतान् भाविनः पार्थिवेन्द्रान् भू-

149. यो भूयो याचते रामचन्द्रः (॥ 66)

श्री वेंकटेश.

COPPER-PLATE No. 7. (A.D. 1647–48.)

[Utsúr grant of Ranga VI of Karnáṭa, S.S. 1569.]

Note.

This grant is transcribed from the original copper-plates. Like the Mangalampád grant it consists of five plates, the first and last of which are inscribed on the inner sides only.

The grant was issued by King Ranga VI of Karnáṭa in Ṣaka 1569 (A.D. 1647) in the year Sarvajit, in the month of Chaitra on *Ṣrí Rámanavami* of the bright fortnight. It records the gift of Utsúr village surnamed Vilásapuram, situated in the *rájya* of Chandragiri and the

---

[1] Read ष.

[2] Read ए.

síma of Pórúr to the Brahman named Anantácháirya, son of Anantasáyanárya and grandson of Kedámbi Anantárya, who belonged to the Átréya *gótra*, followed the Ápastamba *sútra* and studied the Yajuṣ Ṣákhá. The gift was made in the temple of Ṣrírangam, situated "between the two Káveris."

The composition of the verses is said to have been by Rámakavi, son of Kámakóti, and grandson of Sabhápati. This Rámakavi also composed the Kallakurchi grant of Ranga VI (I.A., Vol. XIII, page 153). The engraver of that grant, viz., Sómanáthárya, son of Kámaya and grandson of Ganapayárya, engraved this grant also.

The language throughout is Sanskrit and the character is Nandinágari. The whole is in verse of various metres.

The *Vamṣávali* given in this grant is identical with that furnished by the *Kaḻḻakurchi grant* (I.A., p. 153), the verses in both being identical almost throughout. The numbers of the corresponding verses in the Kaḻḻakurchi grant are printed within brackets.

The orthography calls for no special remarks, all peculiarities having been noticed by previous editors of the Karnáṭa grants (Kaniyur, Vilapaka, Kondayata and Kaḻḻakurchi). There are numerous mistakes in the text. They have been corrected in the text as otherwise the foot-notes would be unduly numerous.

Translation.

The first twenty verses are the same as in the Mangalampáḍ plates.

V. 21. As the four Védas, Sáma and the others, were produced from the mouth of the Creator; as the four methods of diplomacy, conciliation (Sáma) and the others, were produced from the warlike Satyavák; as the four sons, Ráma and the others, were born to Dasaratha; so four sons of immeasurable glory were born to him (Tirumala), the diadem of kings. [V. 18.]

V. 22. To him there were (born) king Raghunátha, Ṣrí Rangaráya, who was a *párijáta*[1] to dependants, Ṣrí Rámarája, the moon of the earth, and the celebrated Venkaṭadévaráya. [V. 19.]

V. 23. Amongst those brothers, Ṣrí Rangaráya, who reached the farther shore of the milk-ocean of politics, and who was renowned in the eight quarters, was installed sovereign of the kingdom of Penugonḍa. [V. 20.]

V. 24. Then Ṣrí Venkaṭapatidévaráya, brilliant in polity, ruled the earth, beautifying the ten regions with his fame. [V. 21.]

V. 25. To his elder brother the Lord Rámarája, whose deeds put the celestial tree to shame, were born Tirumalarája and the famous Ṣrí Rangaráya. [V. 22.]

V. 26. To Ṣrí Rangaráya, of these two, were born sons, excelling in modesty, endowed with compassion, learned and glorious. [V. 23.]

V. 27. Amongst those sons of king Ṣrí Rangaráya, king Ṣrí Rámaráya shone for a long time, being beyond the reach of the poetry of the best of poets, as the Kaustubha amongst the gems sprung from the ocean. [V. 24.]

V. 28. Formerly by the celebrated Rámaraja[2] who resembled Ṣrí Ráma in beauty, were begotten five sons,

---

[1] Párijáta a mythical tree of paradise.

[2] Rámarája referred to in v. 28 is not the same Rámarája who is mentioned in v. 27, but is Tirumala's elder brother Rámarája. The word *purvam* in v. 28 and v. 35 shows this clearly. This has been pointed out by Dr. Hultzsch (Vol. XIII, p. 153, *Ind. Ant.*).

possessed of increasing fortune, clever in protecting the world, followers of the path of polity, and anxious to grant the desires of the crowd of learned men as the (five) trees of the residence of the gods (heaven) from the milk-ocean. [V. 25.]

V. 29. Amongst those kings of famous deeds, Ṣrí Rangarája, the moon of the earth, became renowned in the three worlds like the *párijáta* among celestial trees. [V. 26.]

V. 30. The horses which have been abandoned by hostile kings who were eager to flee through great fear at the very sound of his drum in battle are rolling on the ground from fatigue. Do they sweep away the foot-prints of (their) owners which are marked with waterpots, umbrellas, flags, &c., but which have become (mere) ornaments of the forest, fearing that he would pursue them (their owners) (in case their foot-prints were visible)? [V. 27 *cf.* Kaniyur grant Vol. III, E.G., p. 243.]

V. 31. By the great grace of the lord of Séshagiri (Vishnu) who was pleased with his excellent austerities Ṣrí Rangárája had two sons, of lovable beauty, and resembling Indra in happiness. [V. 27.]

V. 32. (They) two named Peda Venkaṭéndra and the lord Pinavenkaṭa, who were anxious to protect (their) subjects, and able to destroy the cruel (Khara) and the wicked (Dúshana) [1], caused delight (to the world) like Ráma and Lakshmana. [V. 28.]

V. 33. Of these two, the illustrious king Peda Venkaṭéndra was the superior in age, valour, liberality,

[1] Khara and Dúshana were two demons destroyed by Ráma and Lakshmana.

magnanimity, fortitude, learning and all other virtues. Thinking that the sea may become land, being filled with the dust raised by his army, when he proceeds on expeditions for learning the art of destroying his enemies, Hari took up his abode in his heart.[1] [V. 29.]

V. 34. When this son of Şrí Rangarája, Venkaṭadévarája, the best of kings, was anointed to the kingdom of Penugonḍa, wise men also were anointed with (gifts of) gold. [V. 30.]

V. 35. The glorious king Venkaṭádri, who was renowned as he was the younger brother of his (Peda Venkaṭa's, or Venkaṭa II's) grandfather (Ráma referred to in V. 28), became the object of grace of the self-chosen consort of Lakshmí (Vishnu), was a very lion who took the vow to destroy the mad elephants which were his proud enemies, and resembled a new Bhója[2] skilled in protecting the assemblage of poets. [V. 31.]

V. 36. His son was the glorious king Ranga, who was the ocean of virtues, and on account of the excellence of whose liberality the tree of paradise dwells (*i.e.*, hides itself) somewhere in the garden of heaven. [V. 32.]

V. 37. On account of his good deeds accumulated in previous births, to this king of marvellous virtue was (born) a son Gópála, foremost of kings, whose majesty resembled that of Indra, and who having himself granted the desired boons of all learned men on earth, made (men) forget Bhója and other kings who were accomplished in gifts. [V. 33.]

---

[1] The sea is the proper abode of Hari; fearing it may become land he moves to Venkaténdra's heart.

[2] Bhója was a great patron of learning.

V. 38. He, the blessed, associated with his wife, worshipped with prayers the lord of Venkaṭaṣaila (Tirupati). Then that god, the granter of boons, being pleased, said to him out of mercy. [V. 34.]

V. 39. "I have now been incarnated on earth as a renowned son named Ṣrí Rangaráya in consequence of the power of the severe austerities of China (Pina) Venkaṭádri just as formerly the son of Vásudéva named Krishna became incarnate on account of the severe austerities of Bala's enemy (Indra). As Nanda formerly considered him (Krishna) as his son, consider Ṣrí Rangaráya as your son."[1] [V. 35.]

V. 40. King Gópála rejoiced, having obtained, for the protection of the earth (and) for the perpetuation of his family, a son, the glorious king Rangaráya, whose beauty resembled that of the consort of Ṣrí (Vishnu).

V. 41. To protect good men, and to destroy the pride of the wicked, resembling in beauty the destroyer of the great pride of Kamsáṣura (*i.e.*, Krishna), this Rangarája is seated on the peerless throne of universal sovereignty, to which he was installed as king, and which is daily eulogized with devotion by the kings of various countries.

V. 42. Ṣrí Ranga, the foremost of kings, whose kingship was bestowed by (the deity) Ṣrí Rangéṣvara, who received presents from the kings of the Bhójas and Magadhas who prostrated themselves at his lotus-feet, and whose lotus-feet were placed on the heads of (*i.e.*, who was honoured by) all the kings of earth, ruled with great

---

[1] V. 39. This verse shows that Ranga was only the adopted son of Gópála and that he was the son of China (Pina) Venkatádri.

righteousness the earth whose girdle is the seven oceans. [V. 36.]

V. 43. He who resembles the sea in great depth, the sole excellent capturer of the fort of Cháurási,[1] who causes great terror to the minds of hostile kings of the eight quarters; devotee of the bearer of the bow *Ṣárgna* (Vishnu). [V. 37.]

V. 44. The vanquisher of enemies, who is a very celestial tree to mendicants, *hosabirudaragaṇḍa*, *ráya-ráhuttaminda*, blessed in famous deeds, the possessor of the dignity of the famous titles *mannyán sámula*[2] and others, the vanquisher of the assemblage of enemies.

[V. 40. Of Kondayata grant p. 131; I.A., Vol. XIII.]

V. 44½. Possessing prosperity which is radiant, having the *biruda biruda manneragaṇḍa* (the hero or vanquisher of mountain chieftains having titles), associated with heroes who were able to vanquish the mighty king of Utkala (Orissa).

V. 45. Dallying with the powerful goddess of valour, he is the central gem (lord) of the necklace which is the city of Áravíḍu, strong-armed like the lord of serpents (Sésha), who acquires the title *Mandalíkadharanívaráha* (the boar on earth among provincial chiefs). [V. 38.]

V. 46. The foremost of kings descended from the *gôtra* of Atri, of great renown, whose cheeks resembled the moon, who eclipsed the god of love in beauty.

V. 47. The hero who punished kings who break their word, the protector of the nine continents of the Earth, having the title Rájádhirája, whose gifts resemble those of Kubéra.

---

[1] Cháurási — Hindustani = *84*.

[2] Sámula—Arabic (?) = confederate. Mannyán = mountain chiefs.

V. 47½. Having the *biruda Múrurâyaraganda* (the vanquisher of the three kings), possessing fame surpassing Méru.

V. 48. He, the glorious Rangaráya, who surpasses the multitude of ancient kings in policy, who is a very tree of paradise to the crowd of scholars, having won the throne of Karnáṭa by the might of his arm, having subdued his enemies from Ramésvaram as far as the Himálaya and joyfully ruling the whole sea-girt earth, is resplendent.

Vs. 49 and 50. In the Ṣaka year, reckoned by the planets (9), the seasons (6), the arrows (5), and the moon (1), (*i.e.*, 1569), in the year named Sarvajit, in the month named Chaitra, in the bright fortnight, on the sacred day called *Ṣrí Rámanavami*,[1] being in the presence of Ṣrí Rangéṣvara who resides between the two Káverís (the two branches of the Káveri at Ṣrírangam). [Vs. 41 and 42.]

V. 51. To him who is the descendant of the *gótra* of Atri, follower of the Ápastamba *sútra*, the foremost of students of Yajuṣ Ṣákhá, the granter of boons,

V. 52. Who is of immeasurable glory, and of spotless fame, who is the grandson of Kéḍámbi Anantárya, and the son of Ananta Ṣáyanayárya,

V. 53. To the excellent (Brahman) Anantácharya, the ornament (of men), the great-souled, who pleased Brahmans following excellent customs with gifts of delicacies,

V. 54. The gem of the court of kings, the protector of all relations, who single-handed was eloquent in expounding the established Vaishnava scriptures,

---

[1] The ninth day in the fortnight sacred to Ráma.

V. 55. Who is clever in expounding the doctrines of the two famous schools of the Védánta (*i.e.*, the Sanskrit and the Drávida or Tamil Schools), whose mind is a very bee at the lotus-feet of Ṣrí Ráma.

Vs. 56 to 59. The excellent village named Útsúr, situated in the illustrious *rájya* of Chandragiri, and in the *síma* of Pórúru, well known as Niḍuganṭakóṭa, celebrated as Piḍanáḍu, lying to the east of Mangavéru, to the south of Tatrayali village, to the west of Moduga-lapályа, and to the north of Mangalampáḍu, (?), (the village) otherwise named Vilásapuram, rich in all crops.

Vs. 60 to 62. [Same as Vs. 55, 56 and 57 in Manga-lampáḍu grant.]

V. 63. Surrounded by many assiduous and amiable learned men, who follow the Vedic path, who excel in speech, and who are headed by the family priest, king Ṣrí Rangaráya who is worthy of being revered by intelligent men, joyfully gave with libation of water and gift of gold.

V. 64. This is the charter of the great king Víra Ṣrí Rangaráya, the famous, the moon to the lotuses which are scholars.

V. 65. At the bidding of Víra Ṣrí Rangaráya, Ráma-kavi, son of Kámakóṭi, and grandson of Sabhápati, composed the text of this inscription.

V. 66. Under the orders of king Víra Rangaráya, Sómanátháryа, the son of Kámaya and the excellent grandson of Ṣrí Ganapayárya, engraved this inscription.

Imprecatory verses (as in Mangalampád grant).

Ṣrí Ráma.

NOTE.—The mythical ancestors according to the Utsúr, Mangalampád and other grants are –

The Moon
|
Budha
|
Purúravas
|
Áyu
|
Nahusha
|
Yayáti
|
Púru
|
Among his descendants Bharata
|
Do. do. Santanu.
|
The fourth after him Vijaya (*i.e.*, Arjuna)
|
Abhimanyu
|
Parikshit

The eighth after him Nanda (5)
„ ninth „ Chalikya
„ seventh „ Rájanarêndra
„ tenth „ Bijjala
„ third „ Hemali. lord of the Town of Máya (?)
„ fourth „ Pinnama I (6)—Historical.

The historical genealogy of the third Vijayanagar dynasty follows as below from
Pinnama I
|
Sómadeva
|
Rágavadêva
|
Pinnama II
|
Bukka
Psotector of Sáluva Nrisimha (of Vijayanagara)
married Ballamá
|
Rama (I)
married Lakká
|
Ranga (I)
married Tirumalá

Children of Ranga (I):

- Rama (II) married a sister of Sadásiva of Vijayanagara, killed 1565 A.D.
  - Ranga (IV) one of five brothers
    - Pedavenkata or Venkata II (Grant S. 1568).
    - Pinavenkatá or China Venkata III
      - Ranga (VI) (donor of Utsúr grant) date S,S. 1599 adopted by Gópála.
- Tirumala (I) married Vengalá.
  - Raghunátha.
  - Ranga (II).
  - Ráma (III).
    - Tirumala (II).
    - Ranga (III).
      - Rama (IV).
  - Venkata I (donor of Mangalampád grant.) S.S. 1524.
- Venkatádri
  - Ranga (V)
    - Gopála
      - Ranga (VI), adopted son.

(See E.I., Vol. III, p. 238).

Venkata I, donor of Mangalampád grant (S.S. 1524).

Ranga VI, donor of Utsúr grant (S.S. 1569).

The first twenty verses (57 lines) are the same as those in Mangalampád plates.

Second plate, second side.

58. सामादयो विधिमुखादिव सत्यवाचा (चः) सामाद्युपा-
59. यनिवहायिव [1] सांयुगीनात्। रामादयो दशरथादिव
60. राजमौलेस्तस्मादमेययशसस्तनया बभू(भू)वुः। (॥ 21) राजा
61. तता भूद्रघुनाथनामा श्रीरङ्गराजः श्रितपारिजा-
62. तः। श्रीरामराय(ः) शिशिरांशुरुर्व्यां विख्यातिमान्वेंक-
63. टदेवरायः। (॥ 22) श्रीरङ्गराय(ः)सहजेषु तेषु पारंगतो
नीति-
64. पयःपयोधेः। अष्टासु दिक्षु प्रथितः स [2] लेमे[ः] पट्टाभि-
षेकं पे-
65. नगोण्डराज्ये (॥ 23) अथ श्रीवेंकटपतिदेवरायो नयोज्ज्वलः
अ-
66. वनीमतिष [3] त्कीर्त्या दिशो दश विशोभयन्। (॥ 24)
तज्ज्यायसः सुर-
67. द्रुमलज्जावहचारितरामराजविभोः। जातस्तिरुमलरा-
68. जःख्यातश्रीरङ्गरायोपि। (॥ 25) तयोः श्रीरङ्गरायस्य
तनया वि-

Third plate, first side.

69. नयाधिकाः। अजायन्त दयावन्त(ः)श्रुतवन्तो यश-
70. स्विनः। (॥ 26) श्रीरङ्गरायनृपतेस्तनयेषु तेषु पारं गिरा-
71. माधि(ति)गतः कविपुङ्गवानां। रत्नेषु कौस्तुभयि [4] वाम्बुधि-

---

[1] Read इव.

[2] Omit visarga after लेभे.

[3] Read अशिषत्.

[4] Read इवा for यिवा.

72. संभवेषु श्रीरामरायनृपति(:) सुचिरं विलासीत्[1] । (॥ 27) पूर्व

73. विशृत[2] रामराजनृपते(:) श्रीरामभद्राकृतेः कल्याणोद-

74. यशालिनरतनुभवं[3] पञ्च प्रपञ्चावने । दक्षा नीतिपथा-

75. नुगाः समभवन् क्षीरापगाकामिनो गीर्वाणालयभूरु-

76. हा इव बुधश्रणीष्टदानोत्सुकाः । (॥ 28) विख्यातचर्येषु नृपेषु ते-

77. षु श्रीरङ्गराज(:) शिशिरांशुरुर्व्याः । विश्वत्रये विश्रुत-कीर्त्ति-

78. रासीत्सौरेषु सालेष्विव पारिजातः । (॥ 29) दङ्केरीघन-भांकृ-

79. तिश्रंवणतो भीत्या महत्या रिणे[4] प्रत्यर्थिक्षितिपैः फला[5]- यन-

80. परै र्मुक्ता लुटन्त(:) श्रमात् । कान्ताराभरणीभवन्ति कल शच्छत्र-

81. ध्वजाङ्काश्चितान्युन्मार्जंत्यधिभूपदानि तदनुव्रज्जाभिया[6] किं

82. हयाः । (॥ 30) श्रीरङ्गराजस्य तपोविशेषैः संतोषणः[7] शेषागिरीश्वर-

83. स्य । कारुण्यभूम्ना कमनीयशोभौ पुत्रावभूतां पुरुहूतभोगौ (॥ 31)

84. पेदवेंकटेन्द्रपिनवेंकटाधिराडि(पावि)ति नामकौ प्रकृतिपालनो-

85. त्सुकौ । खरदूषणप्रहतिदक्षिणावुभौ ददतः प्रमोदमिव ।

86. रामलक्ष्मणौ । (॥ 32) श्रीशाली पेदवेंकटेन्द्रनृपतिर्जे (ज्ये)-ष्ठो वयो-

---

[1] Read व्यलासीत्. [2] Read विश्रु. [3] Read नुभवाः.

[4] Read रणे. [5] Read पला. [6] Read व्रज्या,

[7] Read संतोषिणः.

87. भिस्तयोः शौर्यौदार्यगभीरताधृतिकलापूर्वैश्च स-
88. र्वै र्गुणैः। यस्यारातिनृपालभेदनकलायात्रासु
89. सेनारजःपूरै र्भूर्जलधिर्भवेदिति हरिश्चित्ते
90. श्रधत्ते [1] स्थितिं। (॥ 33) श्रीरङ्गराजेन्द्रकुमारकेस्मिन् वी-
रो-
91. त्तमे वेंकटदेवराये। पट्टाभिषिक्ते पेनुगोण्डराज्ये
92. तदाभिषिक्ताः सुधियोऽपि हेम्ना। (॥ 34) ख्यातस्तस्य पिता-
महा

Third plate, second side.

93. नुजतया श्रीवेंकटाद्रिक्ष्मापालः श्रीललनास्वयंव-
94. तपतेर्जातानुकम्पास्पदं। आसीदुद्धतशत्रुगंधकर-
95. टिप्रध्वंसबद्धव्रतो हर्यक्षः कविलोकरक्षणकलाप्रत्य-
96. ग्रभोजाकृतिः। (॥ 35) तस्य श्रीरङ्गपति(ः) क्षोणीपति।
रात्मभूर्गुणा-
97. ब्धिरभूत्। यस्यौदार्यमहिम्ना कल्पतरुः क्वापि नन्दने
वसति। (॥ 36)
98. राज्ञस्तस्य गुणाद्भुतस्य सुकृतैः प्राचीनजन्मार्जितैः
99. पुत्रोभून्पुरुहूतकल्पमहिमा गोपालराजाग्रणीः। सर्वेषां
100. विदुषां समीहितफलं दत्वा जगत्यां स्वयं यो विस्मारय-
101. ति स्म दानचतुरान्भोजादिकान पार्थिवान्। (॥ 37)
सोयं प्रियासह-
102. चरः (प्रियाभिः) सुकृती तपोभिराराधयद्वेङ्कटशैलनाथं।
प्रीतस्तदा-
103. नीमगदीदभीष्टदायी स देवः कृपया तमेनं। (॥ 38) पुत्रः
सन्ध-

---

[1] Read चित्तेस्य

104. रणीमवाप्यमधुना श्रीरङ्गरायाभिधो विख्यातश्चिनवें-[1]

105. कटेन्द्रनृपते रुग्रैस्तपोवैभवैः । पूर्वं श्रीवसुदेवभू वैलरिपोः

106. कृष्णभिधोयं यथा नन्दः प्रागिव तं सुतं कलयतां-[2]
श्रारग-

107. रायाभिधं । (॥ 39) श्रीरंगरायाक्षितिनायकं तं श्रीकान्त-
रूपं

108. क्षितिरक्षणाय । अवाप्य पुत्रं कुलवृद्धिहेतोः गोपाल
राज(:)

109. समभून् प्रहृष्टः । (॥ 40) सोयं श्रीरंगरायक्षितिपतिरवितुं
सज्ज-

110. नान् दुर्जनानां गर्वध्वंसायु[3] कंसासुरमदगरिमध्वंसि-

111. नो रूपधारी । प्राज्यंसाम्राज्यसिंहासनमधिवसति प्र-

112. त्यहं भक्तिपूर्वं नानादेशावनीशैर्विनुतमनुपमं प्राप्तरा-

113. ज्याभिषेकं(कः) (॥ 41) श्रीरंगेश्वरदत्तराज्यमहिमा श्रीरंग-
रायाग्र-

114. णीः पादांभोजविनम्रभोजमगधक्ष्मापार्पितप्राभृतः ।

115. सर्वेषां पृथिवीभुजामधिशिरो विन्यस्तपादांबुजः पृथ्वीं

116. पालयते नयेन महता सप्तार्णवीमेखलां । (॥ 42) वारासि
गांभीर्य-

117. विशेषधुर्यश्चौराशिदुर्गैकविभालवर्यः । पराष्ट-

Fourth plate, first side.

118. दिश्रायमनःप्रकामभयंकरः शार्ङ्गधरान्तरङ्गः । (॥ 43)[4]

119. हतारिपुरनिमषीनांकहो याचकानां होसाविरु-

---

[1] Read पिन.

[2] Read कलयतं.

[3] Read यु.

[4] Read शि.

120. दरगण्डो रायराहुत्तमिण्डः । महितचारितधन्यो मन्त्रि-

121. यान्शामुलादिप्रकटितविरुदश्रीः पाटितारातिलो-

122. कः । (॥ 44) तांडवितोदयो विरुदमनेरगंडतयो [1] दंड-बलो-[2]

123. त्कलेन्द्रजयपंडितवीरयुतः । (॥ 44½) सारवीररमया समु-

124. ल्लसन् आरवीटिपुरहारनायकः । कुण्डलीश्वरमहा-

125. भज(:) श्रदन्मण्डलीकधरणीवराहतां । (॥ 45) आत्रेयगोत्र-

126. जानामग्रसरो भूभुजामुदारयशाः (। 45½) ओषधिपत्युपमा-

127. यु(यि)तगडंः स्तोषणरूपजितासमरखंडः [3] । भाषेगे तप्पुवरा

128. यरगंडः पोषणनिर्भरभूनवरवंडः (॥ 46½) राजाधिराजविरु-

129. दो राजराजसमाहतिः[4] । मूरुरायरगंडाङ्को मेरुलंघि-

130. यशोभरः । (॥ 47½) सोयं नीतिजितादिभूपतितति(:) सुत्रामशाखी सुधी-

131. सार्थानां भुजतेजसा स्ववशदन्कर्णाटसिंहासनं । आ सेतोर-

132. पि चाहिमाद्रि विमतान्संहृत्य शासन्मुदा सर्वोर्वी प्रचकास्ति

133. सिंधुपरिगां [5] श्रीरंगरायाग्रणीः । (॥ 48) अहर्तुबाणचं-

134. द्राख्यगणिते शकवत्सरे । सर्वजिन् नामकेवर्षे मासि चै-

135. त्राभिधानके । (॥ 49) शुक्लपक्षे च पुण्यायां श्रीरामनौम्यां ति-

136. थौ । वुभयकावेरिमध्यस्तं [6] श्रीरंगेश्वरसन्निधौ । (॥ 50) आत्रेय-

137. गोत्रजाताय आपस्तंबाख्यसूत्रिणे । यजुश्शाखूयवताम-[7]

---

[1] Read युतो. [2] Read दण्डबलो. [3] Read कांडः

[4] Read समाहृतिः [5] Read —खां—

[6] Read उभयकावेरीमध्यस्थ. [7] Read खावतां

138. ग्रयायिने भीष्टदायिने । (॥ 51) केडांभिअनन्तार्यस्य पौ-
त्रायामि-

139. ततेजसे । अनन्तशायनयार्यस्य(शयनार्यस्य) पुत्रायानघकी
र्तये । (॥ 52)

140. अनन्ताचार्यवर्याय शेखराय महात्मने । मिष्टान्नदान-

141. संतुष्टशिष्टाचाराद्विजन्मने। (॥ 53) राजन्यास्थानरत्नाय र-

Fourth plate, second side.

142. क्षितासे(शे) षबन्धवे । वैष्णवागमसिद्धान्तवावदू-

143. कैकशालिने । (॥ 54) विख्यातोभयवेदान्तव्याख्यावैभ-
वशा-

144. लिने । श्रीरामचरणांभोजभ्रमरायितचेतसे । (॥ 55) श्री-

145. चंद्रगिरिराज्यस्थं पोरूरिसीमकेस्ति (स्थि)तं । पिडनाडिति

146. विख्यातं निडुगंटकोटेति विश्रुतं (॥ 56) बलिवलपतु[1]संयुक्तं

147. सर्वसस्यसमन्वितं । मंगनेरुपूर्वभागे तत्रयालिग्रा-

148. मदक्षिणे । (॥ 57) मोदुगलपाल्यपश्चिमायां । मंगलंपाडु

149. वुत्तर । (॥ 57½) वूचूरुग्रामरत्नस्य[2] सर्वसस्यसमन्वितं । श्री-

150. विलासपुरमिति[3] प्रतिनामसमान्वितं । (॥ 59) सर्वमान्यं

151. चतुःसीमासहितं समंततो । निधिनिक्षेपपाषाण-

152. सिद्धसाध्यजलान्वितं । (॥ 60) अक्षिण्यागामिसंयुक्तं ए-
कभो-

153. ग्यं समूरुहं । वापीकूपतटाकैश्च कच्छारामैश्च संयु-

154 तं । (॥ 61) पुत्रपौत्रादिभिः भोग्यं क्रमादाचंद्रतारकं । दाना-

155. घमनविक्रीतियोग्यविनिमयोचितं । (॥ 62) परीतः प्रदत्तैः

---

[1] बलि tax, वलपतु village servants (?). [2] Read रत्नंतद्.

[3] Here the plate is a little worn.

156. स्निग्धैः पुरोहितपुरोगमैः विविधैर्विबुधैः श्रौतप-

157. थिकैराधिकैर्गिरा । श्रीरगरायभूपालो माननी-

158. यो मनस्विनां सहिरण्यपयोधारापू(व)क दत्तवा-

159. न्मुदा ॥ (63)

Fifth plate, first side.

160. वीरश्रीरंगरायक्षितिपतिवर्यस्य कीर्तिधु-

161. र्यस्य । शासनमिदं सुधीजनकुवलयचन्द्रस्य भू-

162. महेन्द्रस्य । (॥ 64) वीरश्रीरंगरायोक्त्या प्राह पौत्रः सभा-

163. पतेः । कामकोटीसुतो रामकविः शास(न)वाङ्मयं । (॥ 65) वीर-

164. (श्री)रगरायक्ष्मापीतेदशेन सोमनाथार्यः । शासनमलिखत कामयत

165. नयः श्रीगणपयार्थपौत्रमणिः । (॥ 66) दानपालनयो-

166. र्मध्ये दानाच् श्रेयोनुपालनं । दानात् स्वर्गमवप्नोति पाल-

167. नादच्युतं पदं । (॥ 67) स्वदत्ताद्द्विगुणं पुण्यं परदत्तानुपालनं ।

168. प रदत्तापहारेण स्वदत्तं निष्फलं भवेत् । (॥ 68) स्वदत्तां प

169. रदत्तां वा यो हरेत वसुंधरां षष्टिवर्षसहस्राणि वि-

170. ष्टायां जायते क्रिमिः । (॥ 69) ये(ए) कैव भगिनी लोकेसर्वेशामे-

171. व भूभुजां। न भोज्या न करग्राह्या विप्रदत्ता वसुंधरा (॥ 70)

172. सामान्योयं धर्मसेतुर्नृपाणां काले काले पालनी-

173. यो भवद्भिः । सर्वानेतान्भाविनः पार्थिवेन्द्रान्भूयो

174. भूयो याचते रामचन्द्रः । (॥ 71) श्री

श्रीराम.

Copper-plate No. 8. (A.D. 1652–53 ?)

[Telugu. Grant of Singáreḍḍipalli.]

Translation.

Hail! On the 15th day of the bright fortnight of Chaitra of the year Nandana, corresponding to the year 1573 of the illustrious, victorious and prosperous Ṣálivá-hana Ṣaka era,[1] Mahárája Rája Ṣrí Váḍa Peda Venkaṭádri Náyanimgáru executed and granted an edict of gift of land as follows to Kandáḷḷa Doḍḍayá Cháryulu Ayyavárlugáru, who is the establisher of the path of the Vedas and promulgator of the two schools of Vedánta philosophy (*i.e.*, Drāviḍa and Sanskrit).

We re-name Singáreḍḍipalle Máchireḍḍipalle, situated in Ṣítárámpuram taluk (Sammatu) which was graciously given by the Rája as a Jaghir, as Ayyaváripalli. Áḍúri Góvindácharlu, Ṣésham Rághavá Cháryulu, Garimeḷḷa Vóbuḷácháryulu, Náranapáṭi Bhávaná Cháryulu, Vinnapála Venkaṭá Cháryulu, Rámáyanam Tirumalá Cháryulu, Sálagrámam Narasimhá Cháryulu and Mahankáḷi Varadá Cháryulu, &c., said that the boundaries in the eight directions of the *agrahāram* should be within the limits of my jurisdiction and that the boundaries on the eight sides should be settled and that a deed of gift should be granted. Therefore the details of the edict granted are :—

[Here follows a long list of the boundary points.]

Having fixed inscribed stones in this manner we have given the entire *agrahāram* in the name of Sítáráma to the abovesaid Brahmans together with its treasures,

[1] A.B.—The years do not agree.

hidden deposits and stone. Thus having established 12 shares for the Brahmans, having apportioned two shares to the village Karanam, Nellúru Gópáḷayyagáru, and having appointed the respective *Méradars* and given suitable lands to these, we have made over the *agrahá-ram* to you. Therefore you, your sons and grandsons, should enjoy the various kinds of grain yielded by this and live happily as long as the sun and the moon last. This document showing boundaries has been engraved by Boggavarapu Nágabattuḍu according to a draft written by Sádhu Lingaráju.

(Signed) VENKÁTADRI NÁYUDU.

Ṣrí Síta Ráma.

NOTE.—See note to next grant.

స్వస్తి శ్రీ విజయాభ్యుదయ శాలివాహాన
శకవరుషంబులు ౧౫౭౩ అగు నేటి నంద్దన
నామసంవత్సర చైత్రశుద్ధ ౧౫ లు శ్రీమద్వే ద
మార్గ ప్రతిష్ఠాపనాచార్యోభయ వేదాం
త్తప్రవర్తకులయిన కందాళ్ల దొడ్డయా
చార్యుల అయ్యవార్ల గారికి రాజేరా
జశ్రీ వాడపెద వెంకటాద్రి నాయనింగారు
వ్రాయించియిచ్చిన భూదాన ధర్మశాసన
పత్రికె క్రమమెట్లన్నను రాయుఃవారు
మన్నించిన మాజాగీరు శీతారామాపురం
సమతులో శింగారెడ్డిపల్లె మాచిరెడిపల్లె
కు ప్రతినామము అయ్యవారిపల్లె అని ని
ర్ణయించి ఆదూరి గోవిందాచార్యులు శేషం
రాఘవాచార్యులు గిరిమెళ్ల వోబుళాచార్యు
లు నారణపాటి భావనాచార్యులు విన్నపాల
వెంకటాచార్యులు రామాయణం తిరుమ

లాచార్య్యులు-సాలగ్రామం నరశింహ్మాచా
ర్య్యులు మహంకాళ్ళి వరదాచార్య్యులు మొద
అయినవారు అష్టదిక్కులనదులు మాపొలి
మేరకు లోకటుగా కావలెను అష్టదిక్కులకు
పొలిమేర యెర్పరచి శాసనములు వేయించి
యిప్పించ్చుమంటిరి గనుక శాశనములు వేయిం
చినవివరము తూర్పునకు సోంపల్లె వాగు
పడమటివొడ్డున మఱ్ఱిమాను దగ్గరను హ
నుమంతశాశనము రాయి ౧ ఆశాశనా
నకు కోనంపల్లె పిచ్చిగుంట్లపల్లె తూర్పు కూ
డలినశాశనము రాయి ౧ ఆశాశనానకు
దక్షిణం సూరయపల్లె సోంపల్లెకోనంప
ల్లెకూడలిన శాశనము రాయి ౧ ఆశాశనా
నకుదక్షిణం గుండాలమఱ్ఱివాగు దక్షిణ
పువొడ్డున పుట్టుబండను శాశనము రా
యి ౧ ఆశాశనానకు దక్షిణంవూరు
గాయలబోడు తూర్పుభాగాన శాశ
నమురాయి ౧ ఆశాశనానకు వూరు
గాయలబోట చెరిసఘానకలు జువ్విమా
నుకిందను శాశనము రాయి ౧ ఆశా
శనానకు పడమర పరికెలగొందిదిన్నె
నుశాశనము రాయి ౧ ఆశాశనా
నకు పశ్చిమర వల్లభరాయుని కుంట
దక్షిణపుకొమ్ము కటువను
శాసనము రాయి ౧ ఆశాశనానకు
వాయువ్యాన వేపల వాగుదక్షిణం నూ
నెశిడయపల్లె పాటికూడలిన శాశన
మురాయి ౧ ఆశాశనానకు వుత్తరపు
భాగాన బోటిమీదను శాశనము రా

యి ౧ ఆశాశనానికి వుత్తరంబోటికెంద పిల్లగో
వుల తిప్ప దక్షు(ణ)పు భాగాన శాశనము రా
యి ౧ అశాశనానికి వుత్తరం పిల్లగో
వులతిప్ప చెరిసభానకలు జువ్విమాని
కిందను శాశనము రాయి ౧. అశాశ
నానకు శింగారెడ్డిపల్లెకు పడమర గు
రునాధునిమగ్రికి దక్షిణం మడిమాకుల
సందువాగువొడ్డున శాశనం రాయి ౧
ఆశాశనానకు వుత్తరం మల్లపలెతూ
ర్పునవాగువొడ్డు చింతమానుకిందను
శాశనము రాయి ౧ ఆశాశనానకు
వుత్తరం వుప్పరపల్లె మల్లపల్లె కూడ
లి తకెర్కన్న దిన్నె చేను పశ్మటి గట్టున
శాశనం రాయి ౧ ఆశాశనానకు వు
త్తరం వుప్పరపల్లె దక్షిణంవాగు వుత్తరా
నశాశనము రాయి ౧ అశాశనానకు
వుత్తరదిశకు కొమ్మలమగ్రి వుత్తరాన
వాగు వుత్తరపువొడ్డున శాశనము రా
యి ౧ ఆశాశనానకు నెమలి దిన్నె
చినవుప్పరపల్లె కూడలిన మగ్రిమాను
పడమట పాలబరిగె మానుదగ్గర శాశనం
రాయి ౧ ఆశాశనానికి తూర్పు నెమ
లిదిన్నెకోట దక్షణాన శాశనం రాయి ౧
ఆశాశనానికి దక్షణం పెద్దవాగు తూ
ర్పుశాశనం రాయి ౧ యీప్రకారము
గా శాశనము వేయ్యించి నిధినిక్షేప పాషా
ణములతోకూడా సర్వ అగ్రహారము
అయ్యవార్లగారికి శ్రీ శీతారామార్ప
ణముగా సమర్పిస్తిమి గనుక అయ్యవా

ళ్లగారు ౧౭ స్వాస్థ్యములు నిర్ణయించి
గ్రామకరణాలు నై రు గోపాళయ
గారికి కరిణీకంతోకూడా ౨ స్వాస్థ్య
ములు నిర్ణయించి ఆయామేరగాండ్ల
ను నిర్ణయించి వాండ్లకు తగుమాత్రం
పాలంయిచ్చి అగ్రహారము మీస్వాధీ
నచేశి-గనుక యిందులవుండిన నానాధా
న్యములు మీ పుత్రపౌత్రపారంపర్యం
తం ఆచంద్రార్కస్థాయిగా అనుభ
వించి సుఖాన వుండుకునేది ॥ సాధులిం
గరాజుగారి లిఖిత ప్రకారము బొగ్గవర
పు నాగాబత్తుడు చెక్కిన హద్దు పత్రి॥
వెంకటాద్రినాయుడి చేవ్రాలు॥
శ్రీ శీతారామా॥

Copper-plate No. 9. (A.D. 1687–88?)

[Telugu. Grant of Singáreḍḍipalli.]

Translation.

Hail! On the 5th day of the bright fortnight of Ṣrávaṇa of the year Prabhava, corresponding to the year 1608 of the illustrious, victorious and prosperous Ṣáli-váhana Ṣaka era [1] the conditions of the charitable deed executed and granted by Mahá Rája Rája Ṣrí Váḍa Peda Venkaṭádri Náyanimgáru to—Ádúri Govindáchá-ryulu, Adúri Rangacháryulu, Ṣésham Rágbavácháryulu, Ṣésham Venkaṭácháryulu, Garimeḷḷa Vóbuḷácháryulu, Garimeḷḷa Venkaṭácháryulu, Náranapuram Bhávaná-cháryulu, Náraṇapuram Kóḍanda Rámácháryulu, Vínna-pála Venkáṭacháryulu, Rámáyaṇam Tirumalácháryulu,

---

[1] *N.B.*—The years do not agree.

Sálagrámam Narasimháchháryulu, and Mahankáḷi Varadácháryulu, etc., who are the establishers of the illustrious path of the Vedas and promulgators of the two schools of Védánta philosophy, are as follows :—

In the taluk (*Sammatu*) of Ṣíta Rámápuram given to us as a Jághir by the Rája, we have renamed Singáreḍḍipalle-Máchireḍḍipalle as Ayyavár ipalle, fixed its boundaries and granted it by this deed. In respect of wet fields under the tank now constructed by us the eastern boundaries of Singáreḍḍipalle-Máchireḍḍipalle are—the stone under the Mámilla banyan tree lying by the side of the *Vágu* which is to the south of the stone at the junction of Nemalidinne and Chinnavapparapalle; to the south of that stone is the stone under the tamarind tree belonging to Gára Pápayagáru; to the south of that stone is the stone under the mushti (*nux vomica*) tree standing on the southern side of the supply channel of the Tadinálakunṭa; to the south of that stone is the trunk of the Pacháre (*Dalbergia paniculata*) tree standing in the Erra fields; to the south of that tree are round and rough stones under a Boḍu (hillock); according to the limits detailed in this manner by Sádhu Achchanna and Páṇem Venkaṭa we have taken Singáreḍḍipalle.

We give water to the fields of Kancharipéṭa and Gajjalapalle which were declared in writing to be clubbed with the fields of Nemalidinna.

We confirm the 14 *vrittis* including that of the karanams formerly settled, fix for each share as much land as can be sown with 5 *túms* of seed. We give to Agastyarája Channamarája as much wet land as can be sown with 5 *túms* and 5 *gorrus* of dry land.

Further we give sufficient land to the *Méradárs.*

We give the remainder of the village as an *agrahâram* in the name of Ṣítáráma. Therefore you, your sons, and grandsons should enjoy the various kinds of grain raised on these fields as long as the sun and moon exist and live happily.

[Two imprecatory verses.]

(Signed) VENKAṬÁDRI NÁYUḌU.

Ṣri Síta Ráma.

NOTE.—This inscription was copied by M.R.Ry. M. Ṣítárámayya Gáru, Tahsildar of Udayagiri, from a copper-plate in the possession of the Garimeḷḷa family of Singáreḍḍipalli. The donor is said to have been a petty Rája of Sítarámpuram, a village of Udayagiri taluk.

స్వస్తి శ్రీ విజయాభ్యుదయశా
లివాహన శకవర్షంబులు ౧౬౦౮ అగు
నేటి ప్రభవనామ సంవత్సర శ్రావణ శుద్ధ
౫ లు శ్రీమద్వేదమార్గ ప్రతిష్ఠాపనా
చార్యోభయులు వేదాంద ప్రవర్తకులయిన
ఆదూరి గోవిందాచార్యులు రంగాచార్య
లు శేషం రాఘవాచార్యులు వెంకటాచా
ర్యులు గరిమెళ్లి వోబుళాచార్యులు వెం
కటాచార్యులు నారణపురం భావనాచా
ర్యులు కోదండ్రామాచార్యులు విన్నపా
ల వెంకటాచార్యులు రామాయణం తిరు
మలాచార్యులు సాలగ్రామం నరుశింహా
చార్యులు మహంకాళి వరదాచార్యులు మొ
దలయినవారికి మహారాజ రాజశ్రీ వా
డపెద వెంకటాద్రినాయునింగారు వ్రా
యించ్చియిచ్చిన ధర్మశాసన పత్రిక క్రమమే
ట్లన్నను, రాయలవారు మర్నించిన మాజా
గీరు శీతారామాపురము సముతులో శిం

గారెడ్డి పల్లె మాచిరెడ్డిపల్లెకు ప్రతినా
మం అయ్యవారిపల్లె అనినిర్ణయించి
హద్దులు నిర్ణయించి వ్రాయించియిచ్చినం
దుకు యిప్పుడు మేము కట్టించిన చెర్వు
క్రిందను మాగాణినిమిత్తము శింగారెడ్డి
పల్లె మాచిరెడ్డిపల్లెకు పూర్వం హద్దులు
నెమలిదిన్నెచిన వుప్పరపల్లెకూడలిరా
తికి దక్షిణం వాగువొడ్డున మామిళ్ల మ
ర్రిక్రిందనురాయి, ఆరాతికి దక్షిణం
గార పాపయగారి చింతమానుక్రింద
నురాయి, ఆరాతికి దక్షిణం తదినాల
కుంటలోకివచ్చేవొందురు దక్షిణపు వొ
డ్డున ముష్టిమానుక్రిందను రాయి ఆరా
తికి దక్షిణం యర్రచేలల్లో మొద్దుపచ్చా
రిమాను ఆమానుకు దక్షిణంబోటిక్రిం
ద పలుగురాతిగుండ్లు యీ ప్రకారం అని
పాధు అచ్చన్నపాణెం వెంకటచెప్పిన హ
ద్దుప్రకారం శింగారెడ్డిపల్లె మెము తీసు
కొని నెమలిదిన్నె పొలములో కట్టుగా
వ్రాశియిచ్చిన కంచరిపేట గజ్జలపల్లె పొ
లానకు నీళ్లుయిచ్చి మునుపు నిర్ణయిం
చిన వృత్తులు కరణాలతోకూడా ౧౪ కి
స్వాస్తియం వఖంటికి ఖ ౦౹౦ యేడు
ముమడి యిప్పుడు నిర్ణయించినది అగ
స్త్యరాజు చన్నమహారాజుగారికి ఖ ౦౧౦ యె
డుముమడి ౫ గొర్లవెలిగడ ఆయా
మేనగాండ్లకు తగుమాత్రము యిచ్చి మి
గిలిన అ౹ హరము శ్రీ శీతారామా
ర్పణంగా యిస్తిమి గనుక యిందుల వ

డిన నానా ధాన్యములు మీ పుత్రపౌ
త్ర పౌరంపర్యంతం ఆ చంద్రార్క స్తా
యిగా అనుభవించుకొని సుఖాన వుం
డుకునేది ॥ స్వదత్తా పుత్రికాధా
త్రీ పితృదత్తా చ సోదరీ । అన్యదత్తా
భ వేన్మాతా విప్రదత్తా వసుంధరా॥
మద్వంశజాః పరమహీపతి వంశ
జావా యే భూమిపాస్సతతముజ్వ
లధర్మచిత్తాః । మద్ధర్మమేవ సతతం
పరిపాలయంతే తత్పాదుకాద్వ
యమహం శిరసావహామి ॥ వేంక
టాద్రినాయుడి చేవ్రాలు । శ్రీశీ
తారామా॥

Copper-plate No. 10. (A.D. 1536-37.)

[Pólépalli grant of Achyutaráya. Ṣaka 1458.]

Note.

This grant is referred to by Mr. Sewell under the village of Pólépalli in Darsi division. It is in the possession of the shrótriemdar who kindly lent it.

The plates are three in number, each being about 8 inches broad and 11 inches long. The ring with the seal connecting them is said to have been lost. Plates 1 and 2 are engraved on both sides while plate 3 is engraved only on one side at the bottom. The engraving is excellent throughout, but the text contains numerous mistakes.

The characters are Nandinágari, excepting the words *Srí Virúpáksha* at the end which are in large Canarese characters. The language is Sanskrit, and excepting the initial invocation Ṣrí Ganádhipatayénamah, the whole is in verse of various metres.

Lines 1–79 are almost identical with lines 1–91 of the Unamanjéri plate of Achutaráya (Vol. III, E.G., p. 151). Lines 1–62 are also found in the Hampi inscription of Krishṇaráya (E.G., Vol. II, p. 363.)

The grant is one of Achyuténdra. From line 1–79 is given an account of Achyuta and his predecessors. Lines 79–97 give the grant proper. Lines 99–102 give the name of the poet and the engraver. Lines 102–109 are the usual imprecatory verses.

No fresh historical information is furnished by the present grant. The genealogy given is—

Timma=Dévakí
|
Íṣvara=Bukkamá
|
Tippáji=Narasa=Nágalá
| |
Víra Nrisimha. Krishnaráya.

Verse 14 of the Unamanjéri plate which gives the relationship between Achyuta and Krishnaráya is omitted in the present grant. That verse says that Narasa had by a third wife Obámbiká a son named Achyuténdra.

The grant proper (lines 79 to 97) states that Achyuténdra, being on the bank of the river Tungabhadra, on the 12th lunar day of the bright half of Kártika—the day when Vishnu rises from his sleep—of S.S. 1458, corresponding to the cyclic year Durmukhi, in the presence of the deity Viṭṭhaléṣvara, granted the village of Pólépalli, situated in the *Mahárájya* of Koṇḍavíḍu in the district (*ṣíma*) of Kocherlakóṭa *alias* Yeruvanáḍu.

Apparently on account of this the village came to be called Achyuténdrapuram. The boundaries are—

North—Chandavaram.
South—Rudrasamudram.
East—Chákicherla.
West—Lakshmípuram.

Pólépalli is still a shrotriem in Darsi Division.

The donee was Annama, the son of Chintupalli Singanárya, descendant of the *gótra* of Viṣvámitra, follower of the Áṣvaláyana *Sútra*, and student of Rikṣákhá.

The composer of this grant was Sabhápati, probably the same poet who composed the Unamanjéri and other Vijayanagar grants. The engraver is Víranáchárya, the son of Mallana, the engraver of the Unamanjéri and other grants.

TRANSLATION.

Adoration be to the Lord of hosts (Ganéṣa)!

V. 1. Salutation be to Sambhu (Siva) who is beautiful as with a chámara[1] with the moon which kisses his lofty head,[2] and who is the main pillar of the creation of the city of the three worlds.

V. 2. May the staff—like tusk of Hari (Vishnu) who assumed in sport the form of a boar [3]—resting on which the earth with Mount Meru as its apex resembled an umbrella—protect you.

V. 3. May that lustre, which dispels the darkness of obstacles, which though an elephant was born of the

---

[1] Chámara—the Yak's tail, used as a flywhisk—also as an ornament on the heads of horses and elephants.

[2] The moon is supposed to rest on the head of Ṣiva.

[3] This refers to the boar incarnation of Vishnu.

daughter of the mountain and which is worshipped even by Hari (Vishnu), cause prosperity.[1]

V. 4. From the milky ocean which was churned by the gods arose like fresh butter the luminary (moon) by which darkness is dispelled.[2]

V. 5. He had a son Budha whose name was true to its meaning owing to his unequalled austerities. He had a son Purúravas in consequence of his austerities. Áyus was the son of him (Purúravas) who destroyed the lives (Áyus) of his enemies with the valour of his arm. His son was Nahusha. His son was Yayáti, a hero in battle and renowned on earth. The son of him who was the husband of Ṣrí Dévayáni was Durvasu who was like Vasu.[3]

V. 6. In his lineage shone king Timma, the husband of Dévakí, famed among the kings of the Tuḷuvas[4] like Krishna in the race of Yadu.

V. 7. From him was born king Íṣvara, the husband of Bukkamá, and the fearless and righteous crest-jewel of kings.[5]

---

[1] The invocation is to Ganésa. There is a pun on the words Gaja and Hari. Gaja = elephant and Agaja means (1) not an elephant, also daughter of Aga, *i.e.*, Parvatí—Ganéṣa though Gaja (elephant) was the son of Agaja, *i.e.*, of Parvatí, wife of Ṣiva. Hari = (1) lion, (2) Vishnu. Generally Hari (the lion) is a foe of Gaja (elephant). Here Hari (Vishnu) worshipped Gaja (Ganéṣa).

[2] The allusion is to the churning of the ocean of milk by the gods. The moon is supposed to have then sprung from it.

[3] There is a play on the word Vasu and the latter part of Durvasu. The Vasus were originally a class of gods. Vasu subsequently came to be identified with Vishnu.

[4] Timma is said to be of the race of the Tuluvas. This suggests that the second Vijayanagar kings originally came from the Tulu country in S. Canara. It appears further that there was no direct family relationship between the first and second Vijayanagar dynasties. See the remarks of Dr. Hultzsch on the similar Hampi grant at page 361 of Volume I, E.I.

[5] Agunabhramsam = (1) not deviating from virtue ; (2) not getting loose. There is a pun on *guna* which means (1) quality ; (2) string passing through the jewel.

V. 8. By him, the handsome son of Dévakí, was begotten king Narasa, as Káma by the son of Dévakí,[1] (Krishna).

V. 9. Rendered famous for various good deeds, with a delighted mind, surrounded by wise men, he again and again made the sixty kinds of gift according to prescribed rules, at Rámésvaram and every other holy place, thus increasing (lit. rendering superfluous) his great renown which was sung by the denizens of the three worlds.

V. 10. Having quickly dammed the Kávéri which was swiftly flowing with copious water, and having crossed it, he captured the enemy alive in battle, subdued his kingdom and Srírangapatnam and planted a triumphal pillar. He thus shone, his deeds being eulogized in the three worlds.

V. 11. He conquered the Chéra, the Chóla, the Pándya who was the lord of Madura and whose ornament was honour, the Mussalman, fierce in valour, the Gajapati king and others. Becoming very famous from the banks of the Ganges to Lanka, and from the eastern to the western mountains, he extended his rule on the heads of kings like a garland.[2]

Vs. 12 and 13. Two sons—the princes Víra Nrisimhéndra and Krishnaráya—a brave but modest—were born to Nrisimha by his queens Tippáji and Nágalá Dévi as Ráma and Lakshmana (were born) to Dasaratha by Kausalyá and Srí Sumitrá.

V. 14. The glorious Víra Nrisimha, seated on the jewelled throne in Vijáyanagar, excelling in fame and

---

[1] This is simply a play on the word Dévakí.

[2] This is a common simile in Sanskrit poetry, meaning that he made them his vassals.

righteousness even Nṛiga, Nala, Nahusha and other kings on earth, being praised by Brahmans, and having himself won the hearts of all, ruled the kingdom from the Bridge (Ráma's) [1] to Mount Suméru, and from the eastern to the western mountain.

V. 15. He made various gifts at (Chidambaram) the hall of gold, [2] at the temple of Ṣrí Virúpáksha,[3] at the town of the illustrious Lord (deity) of Kálahasti,[4] at Venkaṭádri (Tirupati),[5] at Kánchi, at Ṣríṣaila,[6] at Sóna Ṣaila,[7] at the great Harihar,[8] at Ahobala,[9] at Sangama,[10] at Sríranga,[11] at Kumbhaghóna,[12] at the holy place Mahánandi [13] where sin is destroyed and at Nivritti.[14]

V. 16. By the streams of water poured out on the occasion of the numerous and various great gifts performed by him at Gókarna,[15] Rámasétu,[16] and all other holy places in the world, the ardent desire of (Indra) the bearer of the thunderbolt, who was intent on clipping the wings of the mountain which was sunk in the ocean[17]

---

[1] Sétu is Rama's bridge—said to have been built for him to cross the sea and get to Lanka (Ceylon).

[2] Hall of gold—Chidambaram in South Arcot district.

[3] This is the temple at Hampi.

[4] Kálahasti—in North Arcot district.

[5] Tirupati—in North Arcot district.

[6] Ṣrí Ṣaila—in Kurnool district on the bank of the Tungabhadra.

[7] Ṣóṇaṣaila—Tiruvannámalai in South Arcot district.

[8] Harihar—in Mysore.

[9] Ahóbala—in Kurnool district.

[10] Sangam—in Nellore.

[11] Sríraugam—in Trichinopoly.

[12] Kumbhaghona—this is the modern Kumbhakónam.

[13] Mahánandi—in Kurnool district.

[14] Nivritti—? not known.

[15] Gókarna— in Dharwar District.

[16] Rámasétu—Ráma's bridge.

[17] This refers to the story of the mountain Ménaka hiding itself in the ocean from fear of Indra.

which was dried up by the dust raised by the assemblage of his prancing horses, was frustrated.

V. 17. He performed (the following gifts):—

The mundane egg, the circle of the universe, a pot containing the five elements, a jewelled cow, the seven oceans, a tree and creeper of paradise, a golden cow of plenty, a globe of gold, a horse chariot of gold, gold of the weight of a man, a thousand cows, a golden vessel, an elephant chariot of gold and five ploughs.[1]

Vs. 18 and 19. Now that this Indra of the earth, renowned for his virtues, having ruled the extensive kingdom without hindrance, has gone to heaven as if to rule the sky also, the glorious king Krishnaráya, of invincible valour, bears the earth on his arms like a jewelled bracelet.[2]

V. 20. Probably suspecting that by the spreading of his glory the universe would everywhere become one mass of light, formerly Ṣiva (to distinguish himself from the rest) became possessed of an eye in the forehead, even the lotus-eyed (Vishnu) became one with four arms, the lotus-born Brahma became one with four faces, Káli bore the sword, Ramá (Lakshmí) took up a lotus, and Vání (Sarasvatí) bore a Vína (lute) in her hand.[3]

V. 21. Was it in anger that he dried up the seven oceans with the heaps of dust of the earth torn up by the horses of his vast forces lest perchance they give refuge to his enemies, and created of his own accord as their substitutes rows of oceans with the unlimited waters

---

[1] These are given in the Dána Kánda (gift chapter) of Hindu law books.

[2] Mahabhujáh means one who has broad shoulders. The reading Mahimbhuji—is better.

[3] The idea is that everything became white with the lustre of Krishnaráya's fame, these gods and goddesses included. To distinguish themselves from other objects they assumed the several marks referred to in the verse.

which were poured out on the occasion of the great gifts, viz., the mundane egg (Brahmáṇda), a Méru of gold (Svarṇaméru), &c.

V. 22. Desiring that the assemblage of suppliants should long enjoy the wealth given by him, probably to obstruct the progress of the chariot of the sun, this lord of the earth planted everywhere in the earth firmly-fixed pillars of glory, resembling (Méru) the residence of the Gods, towering up to the sky and marked with the (history of) his expeditions for the conquest of all the quarters and with his titles.

V. 23. Again and again for securing great happiness he made the various gifts prescribed in the sacred books, the weight of a man in gold, etc., along with all minor gifts, according to the prescribed rules at Kánchi, Ṣrí Ṣaila, Ṣónáchala, Kanaka Sabhá (Chidambaram), Venkaṭádri (Tirupati) and other temples and at holy places of pilgrimage.

V. 24. He had the following and other *birudas* :—

The angry punisher of hostile kings, he whose shoulders are broad as those of Ṣésha (the world-serpent), he who is able to protect the earth, the punisher of untruthful kings, the satisfier of beggars, he who is fierce in battle ;

V. 25. Rájádhirája, Rájaparaméṣvara, the conqueror of the three kings (Chéra, Chóla and Pándya), the terror of other kings ;

V. 26. The Sultan [1] among Hindu kings, the destroyer of the wicked who are like tigers, [2] Vírapratápa (he who is famed for valour).

---

[1] Suratrána—is the Ṣanskritized form of Sultan.

[2] The tiger was the emblem of the Chólas—this biruda may simply mean *the conqueror of the Chóla king.*

V. 27. He is served by the Anga, Vanga, Kalinga and other kings who address him:—"Deign to look on me, O Mahárája, live, be victorious!"

V. 28. Seated on the jewelled throne at Vijayanagar, king Krishṇaráya, whose liberality is worthy of being praised by learned men, who eclipses in righteousness Nṛiga and other kings, increasing the prosperity of the assemblage of mendicants, shines with glory from the eastern hill to the slopes of the western hill, from the end of the Himálayas to the Sétu (Bridge).

V. 29. After Krishnaráya went to the world of the gods (*i.e.*, died), his younger brother Achyuténdra, whose deeds are virtuous, the vanquisher of his enemies, the meditator on Hari, the granter of boons to learned men, having become master of the whole earth, is resplendent.

V. 30. The moon of his fame moves over the earth and waxes on all lunar days. It increases the delight of the world, waxes by day and by night along with the lotuses. (This is a contrast between the moon and the moon of his fame.)

V. 31. (The text is doubtful, Professor Keilhorn gives a conjectural rendering of this verse):—

"Seeing how the multitude of his horses, humbling the conceit of the winds, has created darkness by the immense clouds of dust which it raises with its hoofs, one feels inclined to ask whether, eager to destroy the opponent forces, Achyuténdra angrily is drying up the ocean, because it impedes the progress of his chargers.' (Foot-note 12, Vol. III, E.I., p. 153.)

V. 32. His *chámaras* are waved by the hands of the rows of wives of his hostile kings to whom the prison house has become a residence; he has many *birudas*, viz., Rájádhirája,[1] Pararájabhayankara,[2] Eka Víra,[3] &c.

V. 33. By whom frequently the sixteen kinds of gifts were performed at Gókarna, Sangama, Nivritti, Suvarna Sabhá,[4] Sónádri,[5] Parvata,[6] Vrinchipuram and Kánchi, and at Ṣrí Kálahasti town, and at Kumbhaghóna.

V. 34. This ocean, whose water is being drunk by the clouds, which was drunk and thrown out by Agastya, which was heated by the crest of the fire of the arrows of Rághava (Ráma), which is ever being heated by the internal flames of fire proceeding from the mouth of Vaḍava—which thus gets dry, appears indeed full with the copious water of his gifts.

V. 35. He is always eulogized by the Anga, Vanga, Kalinga and other kings "be victorious, live long, O Mahárája!"

V. 36. Triumphant is king Achyuta, seated on the jewelled throne, residing at Vijayanagar, resplendent with fame, surpassing in polity the whole collection of kings, Nṛiga, Nala, Nahusha, &c., possessed of unequalled valour of arm and liberality.

Vs. 37 to 48. In the Ṣaka year 1458, in the year Durmukhi, on the holy 12th lunar day of the bright fortnight of the month Kártika—the day when Vishnu rises from his sleep—Achyuténdra who is revered among intelligent men, being on the bank of the Tungabhadra, in the temple of Viṭṭhalóṣvara, having purified himself by bathing, with an attentive mind, wearing two washed

---

[1] Rájádhirája—paramount lord. [2] The terror of other kings.

[3] The sole hero.

[4] Suvarna Sabha = hall of gold—Chidambaram.

[5] Ṣónádri—same as Sóna Ṣaila—Tiruvannámalai in South Arcot district. This verse is slightly different in Unamanjéri plate.

[6] Parvata—Ṣrí Parvata, *i.e.*, Ṣrí Ṣaila.

garments and wearing suitable ornaments, surrounded by assiduous and amiable learned men who are followers of the Ṣrautas and excel in eloquence, and who are headed by the family priest joyfully gave with gold and a libation of water to Annama the son of Chintapalli Singanárya who is of the *gótra* of Viṣvámitra, who is a follower of the Áṣvaláyana *sútra*, who is a student of the Riksákhá, who is versed in the Vedas, Vedánta and Ágamas, who is wise, who is acquainted with the Dharma prescribed in all the *Ágamas* (scriptures), who is devoted to the six sacraments, the village known on earth as Pólépalli, situated in the great kingdom of Kondavídu, in the district of Kochérlakóṭa *alias* Yeruva náḍu, lying to the east of the village named Lakshmípuram, to the south of the large village Chandavaram, to the west of the village Chákicherla, and north of Rudrasamudram—adorned with the surname Achyuténdrapuram—free from all taxes, up to its four boundaries everywhere, together with the eight enjoyments, to wit, treasures, hidden deposits, stones and other things, abounding in all kinds of produce, to be enjoyed as a single share, together with its trees, possessing wells, cisterns, ponds and tanks—to be enjoyed in succession by sons, grandsons, and other descendants as long as the sun and the moon last—subject to gift, mortgage and sale.

V. 49. This is the edict of Achyutaráya whose kingship was bestowed by Achyuta (Vishnu), who grants the desires of the learned, and who curbs the conceit of his enemies.

V. 50. At the command of Achyuténdra Mahárája, Ṣabhápati composed this copper-plate edict in sweet verse.

V. 51. The artizan Ṣrí Víranácharya, son of Mallana, engraved (this) copperplate edict of Achyuténdra Maháraya.

Vs. 52 to 56 and 102 to 109. [Imprecatory verses.]

"Ṣrí Virúpáksha."

First plate, second side.

1. श्रीगणाधिपतये नमः । (॥) नमस्तुङ्गशिरश्चुम्बिचन्द्र-
चामरचारवे । त्रैलो-

2. क्यनगरारंभमूलस्तंभाय शंभवे । (॥ 1) हरेर्लीलावराहस्य
दंष्ट्रादण्डः

3. स पातु वः । हेमाद्रिकलशा यत्र धात्री छत्रश्रियं दधौ । (॥ 2)
कल्याणाया-

4. स्तु तद्धाम प्रत्यूहतिमिरापहं । यद्गजोप्यगजोद्भूतं हरिणापि च

5. पूज्यते । (॥ 3) अस्ति क्षीरमयाद्देवैर्मथ्यमानान्महांबुधेः ।
नवनीतमि-

6. वोद्भूतमपनीततमोमहः । (॥ 4)[1] तस्यासीत्तनयस्तपोभिरतुलैरन्वर्थ-

7. नामा बुधः । पुण्यैरस्य पुरूरवा भुजबलै रायुर्द्विषां नि
घ्नतः । त-

8. स्यायु र्नहुषो स्य तस्य पुरुषो युद्ध ययातिः क्षितौ । रव्या
तस्तस्य तु दुर्व-

9. सुर्वसुनिभः श्रीदेवयानीपतेः । (॥ 5)[2] तद्वंशे देवकीजानिर्दि
दीपे तिमभूप-

10. तिः । यशस्वी तुलुवेन्द्रेषु यदोः कृष्णायि(इ)वान्वये । (॥ 6)
ततो मुद्धुक्कमाजानिरी-

11. श्वर[ः] क्षितिपालकः । अत्रासमगुणभ्रंशं मौलिरत्नं मही-
भुजां (॥ 7) सर-

---

[1] Verses 1 to 4—Metre Anushtubh. [2] V. 5—Metre Śárdúlavikrídita.

12. सादभूत्तरमान्नरसावनिपालकः । देवकीनंदन(ना)त्कामो देवकी

13. नन्दनादिव । (॥ 8)[1] ।विविधसुकृतो[2]द्दाम(ो)रामेश्वरप्रमुखे मुहुर्मु दितहृद-

14. य(:) स्थाने स्थाने व्यधत्त यथाविधि[:] । बुधपरिवृतो नाना दानानि

15. यो भुवि षोडश त्रिभुवनोद्गीत[3] ख्यातयशः[4] पुनरुक्तयन् । (॥ 9) कावेरी-

16. माशु बध्वा[5] बहुलजलरयां तां विलङ्घ्यैव शत्रुं जीवग्राहं ग-र्वं

17. हीत्वा श (स)मिति भुजबलात्त च राज्यं तदीयं (।) कृत्वा श्री-रङ्गपूर्वंतदपि

18. निजवसे(शे) पट्टणं यो बभासे[।] कीर्त्तिस्तंभं निरवाय त्रिभुवन भवनस्तू-

19. यमानापदानः । (॥ 10)[6] चेरं चोलं च पाण्ड्यं तमपि च मधुरावल्लभं मान-

20. भूषं । वीर्योदग्रं तुरुष्कं गजपतिनृपतिं चापि जित्वा तदन्यान् ।

21. आगंगातीरिलंकाप्रथमचरमभूभृत्तटान्तं नितान्तं । ख्यात(:)क्षो-

22. णीपतीनां स्रजमिव शिरसां शासनं यो व्यतानीत (॥ 11) तिप्पाजी-

23. नागलादेव्योः कौशल्याश्रीसुमित्रयोः । देव्योरिव नृसिंहा (हेन्द्र) त्त-

24. स्मात्पांक्तिरथादिव । (॥ 12) वीरौ विनयिनौ रामलक्ष्मणाविव नन्दनौ(।)जा-

---

[1] Verses 6 to 8—Metre, Anushtubh.

[2] V. 9—Metre Harini.

[3] Read त्रिभुवनजनोद्गीतं in Unamanjéri plate.

[4] Read स्फीतं यशः in Unamanjéri plate.

[5] Read बद्ध्वा.

[6] Vs. 10 and 11—Metre Sragdharâ.

25. तौ वीरनृसिंहेन्द्रकृष्णरायमहीपती । (॥ 13)[1] वीरश्रीनारसिंह-रस विज-

26. यनगरे रत्नसिंहासनस्थः कीर्त्या नीत्या निरस्यन्नृगनलनहुषा-

27. नप्यवन्यामथान्यान् । आसेतोरासुमेरो रवनिश्वर[2] नुतः स्वै-रमा-

28. चोदयाद्रेरापाश्चात्याचलात्ता[3]दखिलहृदयमावर्ज्य राज्यं शशा-

29. स । (॥ 14) नानादानान्यकार्षीत्कनकसदसि यः श्रीवि-रूपाक्षदेवस्थाने

30. श्रीकालहास्तीशितुरपि नगरे वेंकटाद्रौ च कांच्यां । श्री-शैले

Second plate, first side.

31. शोणशैले महति हरिहरे होबले संगमे च श्रीरंगे कुंभघो-

32. णे हततमसि महानन्दितीर्थे निवृत्तौ । (॥ 15) गोकर्णे रामसेतौ जग-

33. ति तदितरेष्वप्यशेषेषु पुण्यस्थानेष्वारब्धनानाविधबहुलमहादा-

34. नवारिप्रवाहैः । यस्योदंचत्तुरंगप्रकरखुररजःशुष्यदंभोधिमग्न-

35. क्ष्माभृत्पक्षच्छिदोद्यत्तरकुलिशधरोत्कुण्ठता[4] कुंठिताभूत् ।(॥ 16) ब्रह्माण्डं वि-

36. श्वचक्रं घटमुदितमहाभूतकं रत्नधेनुं । सप्तांभोधिं च कल्पक्षिति-महाति-

37. लतके[5] कांचनीं कामधेनुं । स्वर्णक्ष्मां यो हिरण्याश्वरथमपि तुला-पूरु-

---

[1] Vs. 12 and 13—Metre Anushtubh.

[2] Read अवनिसुर

[3] Read आचालान्तादखिल.

[4] Read धरोत्कण्ठता.

[5] Read कल्परुहलतके in Unamanjéri plate. कल्पक्षितिरुहलतिके, in Sadâsivarâya's plates.

38. षं गोसहस्त्रं[1] हेमगर्भं कुंभंकनककरिरथं पंचला(ङ्) गल्यतानान् (नीत्) (॥ 17)[2] प्राज्यं प्रशा-

39. स्य निर्विघ्नं राज्यं द्यामिव शासितुं । तस्मिन् गुणेन विख्याते क्षितेरिन्द्रे दि-

40. वंगत । (॥ 18) ततोप्यवार्यवीय(:) श्रीकृष्णरायमहीपतिः - बिभर्त्ति मणिकेयू-

41. रनिर्विशेषं महाभुजाः[3] (॥ 19) [4]कीर्त्त्या यस्य समंततः प्रसृतया विश्वं रुचैकयं व-

42. जेदित्याशङ्क्य पुरा पुरारि(र)भवः[5] भालेक्षणः प्रायशः । पद्मा-क्षोपि चतुर्भुजो-

43. जनि चतुर्वक्त्रश्च भवद्भूत (क्रो भव[6]त्पद्मभूः) काली खड्ग मधाद्रमा च कमलं वीणां च वाणी

44. करे । (॥ 20) [7] शत्रूणां वासमेते ददत [8]यिति रुषा किंनु सप्तां-बुराशीन् नानासेनातु-

45. रंगत्रुटितवसुमतीधूलिकापालिकाभिः (।) संशोप्य स्वैरमेतत्प्रति-

46. निधिजलधिश्रेणिका यो विधत्ते ब्रह्माण्डस्वर्णमेरुप्रमुखनिजम-

47. हादानतोयैरमेयैः । (॥ 21) महत्तामर्थिसार्था(:) श्रियं(मिह) सुचिरं भुंजता-

48 मित्यत्रेत्य। प्रायः मत्पूहहेतोरतपनरथगतेरालयं[9] देवतानां। त-

49. त्तद्दिग्जैत्रयात्रयापि च विरुदपदैराङ्कितांस्तत्र तत्र स्तंभान् जातप्र-

---

[1] हेमाश्वं is inserted in Unamanjéri plate.

[2] Vs. 14 to 17 Sragdharâ.

[3] Read महीं भुजे.

[4] Vs. 18 and 19 Anushtubh.

[5] Read अभवद् for अभवः

[6] Read वक्त्रोभवत्.

[7] v. 20 Ṣárdúlavikrídita.

[8] Read ददत इति.

[9] Professor Kielhorn prefers आलयान्; v. 23 is not found in Unamanjéri plate. Vs. 21 to 23 Sragdharâ.

50. तिष्ठान् व्यतनुत भुवि यो भूभृदभ्रंकषाग्रान् । (॥ 22) कांची-श्रीशैलशोणाच-

51. लकनकसभावेंकटाद्रिप्रमुख्येष्वावर्त्यावर्त्य सर्वेष्वतनुत विधि-

52. वद्भूयसे श्रयसे यः । देवस्थानेषु तीर्थे'वापि कनकतुलापूरुषा-दीनि ना-

53. नादानान्येवोपदानैरपि सममखिलैरागमोक्तानि तानि । (॥ 23) रोषकृतप्र-

54. तिपार्थिवदंडः शेषभुजः क्षितिरक्षणशौण्डः। भाषगेतप्युवरायर-गंडः पो-

55. षकृदर्थिषु यो रणचण्डः । (॥ 24) राजाधिराजयि(इ)युक्तो यो राजपरमेश्वरः । मू-

56. रुरायरगंडश्च परराजभयंकरः । (॥ 25) हिंदुरायसुरत्राणोदुष्ट-शार्दूल-[1]

57. मर्दनः । वीरप्रतापयि(इ)यादि विरुदैरुचितैर्युतः । (॥ 26) आ-लोक्य महारा-

58. ज जयजीवेति वाधि(दि)भिः । अंगवंगकलिंगीयैराजाभिः से-व्यते च यः । (॥ 27)

59. सत्यौदार्यः[2] सुधीभिः स विजयनगरे रत्नसिंहासनस्थः क्ष्मापा-लान् कृ-

60. ष्णरायक्षितिपतिरधरीकृत्य नीत्या नृगादीन् । आ पूर्वाद्रेरथा-स्तक्षिति-

61. रधकटकादा च हेमाचलांतादासेतोरर्थिसार्थश्रियमिह बहली -

62. कृत्य कीर्त्या समथः (समिंधे)[3] । (॥ 28[4]) कृतवाति सुरलोक कृष्णराये निजांशं तदनु

---

[1] Read दुष्टशार्दूलमर्दनः vs. 24 to 27 not found in Unamanjéri plate.

[2] Read स्तुत्यौदार्यः

[3] बभासे for सामिन्धे in Unamanjéri plate.

[4] Metre of verse 28 Sragdhará ; metre of verse 29 Máliní.

63. तद्नुजन्मा पुण्यकर्माच्युतेन्द्रः । [1] प्रकटमवनिलोकं स्वांशमे-

64. त्यारिजेता विलसति हरिजेता [2] विद्वदिष्टप्रदाता । (॥ 29) यत्कीर्तिर्नं-

Second plate, second side.

65. द्रश्चरति क्षमायां तिथिष्वशेषासु विवर्धते च । तनोति च-

66. क्रस्य मुदं समिंद्धे दिवा च सायं कुमुदैर्विरुंद्धे (॥ 30) मदं मनसि मा-

67. रुतं शिथिलयत्य[3]मेयैरयैर्यदश्वनला[4]खुरैः क्षितिरजोभिरुत्थापितैः ।

68. अजीजनादिति कुथा किं[5] विशोषयत्यंबुधिं बलप्रमथनस्यनारे-

69. ये विरोधिनं वाजिनं । (॥ 31) कारागृहाकलितवासविरोधि[:] भूपदारावली-

70. करविचालितचामरस्य । राजाधिराजपरराजभंयकरैकवीरादि-

71. कानि बिरुदानि बहूनि यस्य । (॥ 32) गोकर्णसंगमनिवृत्ति सुवर्णसभाशोणाद्रि (सुवर्णसंसच्छोणाद्रि)

72. पर्वतविरिंचिपुरेषु कांच्यां । श्रीकालहस्तिनगरेपि च कुंभघोणदानानि षो-

73. डशबहूनि कृतानि येन । (॥ 33) अंभोदेन निपीयमानसाले] लोगस्त्येन पी-

---

[1] आखिलमवनिलोकं in Unamanjéri plate.

[2] हारिचेता in Unamanjéri plate. After verse 29 another verse is inserted in Unamanjéri plate.

[3] Read शितिलयन्त्यमेयै. Verse 30 Upajáti.

[4] Read यदश्वपटली, verse 31 Prithvi. Professor Kielhorn suggests मे यस्तमो and बलप्रमथनोद्यतो.

[5] Read क्रुधा किमु : verses 32 and 33 Vasantatilaká, verse 33 is slightly different in Unamanjéri plate. After verse 33 a verse is inserted in Unamanjéri plate.

74. तोछितस्तत्तो [1] राघवसायकाधि स्तिखया [2] संतप्यमानान् सदा [3]। अन्तस्थै-

75. र्वडवानलशिखाज्वालैर्विशुष्को [4] ध्रुवं यद्दानांबुघनांबुधिरसौ [5]

76. पूर्गः समुद्योतते । (॥ 34) अंगेनापि कलिंगेन वंगेन च परै- र्नृपैः । जयजीव

77. महाराजेत्यनिशं गीयते च यः। (॥ 35) स जयति नरपालो रत्न- सिंहासन-

78. स्थो विजयनगरवासी कीर्त्तिपूर्त्या विलासी । नृगनलनहुषादी- निच-

79. यान् राजनीत्या निरुपमभुजवीर्यो दार्यभूरच्युताख्यः । (॥ 36) शालिवाह-

80. ननिर्णीते शकाब्दे स चतुःशतैः । अष्टपंचाशदधिकैः संख्याते दश-

81. भिःशतैः॥ दुर्मुख्यां वत्सरे मासि कार्तिके शुक्लपक्षके । उत्थान- द्वादशी (श्यां)

82. चैव पुण्यायां च महातिथौ । (॥ 37) तुंगभद्रानदीतीरे विट्ठले- श्वरसंनिधौ ।

83. स विश्वामित्रगोत्राय आश्वलयायनसूत्रिणे । ऋक्शाखाध्या- इने [6] वेदवे-

84. दांतागमवेदिने । (॥ 38) चिन्तपल्लीसिंगणार्यनन्दनो अंनम- सुधी [7] सकला-

---

[1] Read पीतोज्झितस्तत्तो.

[2] Read सायकाग्नि शिखया.

[3] Read संतप्यमानः सदा

[4] वडवमुखानल शिखाजालै र्विशुष्को in Unamanjéri plate.

[5] अयं for असै in Unamanjéri plate. Read यद्दानांबुघ्नुनीभिरंबुधिरसौ.

[6] Read ध्यायिने.

[7] The nominative is suddenly used here instead of the dative case.

85. गमधर्मज्ञ षट्कर्मनिरताय च। (॥ 39) कोण्ड वीडीमेहाराज्ये[1] मंडल(मंडले) परि-

86. शोभिते । येरुवनाडुविख्यातकोचेर्लकोटसीमानि । (॥ 40) लक्ष्मीपुराभि-

87. धग्रामात्पूर्वस्यां पूर्वांदिशमाश्रितं। चंदवरमहाग्रामनाम्नो दाक्षि-

88. णत(:)स्थितं। (॥ 41) चाकिचेर्रे(र्ले)ति विख्यातग्रामात् पश्चिमत(:)स्थितं। ग्रामाद्र(द्) रु-

89. द्रसमुद्रा[यां] दुत्तरं(रां) दिशमाश्रितं। (॥ 42) पोलेपल्लामिधग्रामं नामा(ग्रामनाम्ना)-

99. नं च भुवि विश्रुतं। अच्युतेन्द्रधुरं[2] चेति प्रतिनामोपशोभितं। (॥ 43) स-

90. र्वमान्यं चतुःसीमासंयुतं च समन्ततः। निधिनिक्षेपपाषा-

91. णाद्यष्टभोगैश्च संयुतं। (॥ 44) विविधैः फलैर्युक्तमेकभोग्यं सभू-

92. रुहं। वापीकूपतटाकैश्च कच्छेनापि च संयु । (॥ 45) पुत्रपौत्रादिभि-

93. र्भोग्यं क्रमादाचन्द्रतारकं। दानस्याधमनस्याा विक्रय-

94. स्यापि चोचितं। (॥ 46) यथाविधि कृतरन नशुचिर्भूत्म [3]समाहित।

95. :वसानो वाससी धौते यथोचितं[4] विभूषणैः ॥ (47) परीत(:) प्रयतैस्स्निग्धैः

96. पुरोहितपुरोगमैः। अच्युतेन्द्रमहारायो माननीयो मनास्विनां। साहि-

97. रण्यपयोधारापूर्वकं दत्तवान् मुदा ॥ (॥ 48)

---

[1] Ral महाराज्ये.

[2] धरं is probably a mistake for पुरं.

[3] Read कृतस्नानाः शुचिर्भूत्वासमाहितः.

[4] यथोचितविभूषणाः.

98. पूरयतो बुधवांच्छं[1] पारयतो वैरिभूभुजां गर्वं[2] । अच्युतविहित-

99. विभूते रच्युतरायस्य शासनं तदिदं । (॥ 49) अच्युतेन्द्रमहा-रायशासने-

100. न सभापतिः। अभाणीन् मृदुसंदर्भं तदिदं ताम्रशासनं। (॥ 50) अच्युते-

101. न्द्रमहारायशासनं मल्लणात्मजस्त्वष्टा श्रीवीरणाचार्यो अ(व्य)-लिखत ता-

102. म्रशासनं। (॥ 51) दानपालनयो र्मध्ये दानात् श्रेयोऽनुपा-लनं । दानात्स्वर्गम-

103. वाप्नोति पालनादच्युतं पदं। (॥ 52) स्वदत्ताद्द्विगुणं पुण्यं परदत्तानु-

104. पालनं। परदत्तापहारेण स्वदत्तं निष्फलं भवेत् । (॥ 53) स्वदत्तां परदत्तां

105. वा यो हरेत वसुंधरां षष्टिंवर्षसहस्राणि विष्टायां जायते क्रि-मः[3] । (॥ 54)

106. येकैव[4] भगिनी लोके सर्वेषामेव भूभुजां । न भोग्या न करग्रा-ह्या वि-

107. प्रदत्ता वसुंधरा। (॥ 55) सामान्योयं धर्मसेतुनृपाणां काले का(ले) पालनी-

108. यो भवद्भिः । सर्वानेतान् भाविनः पार्थिवेन्द्रान् भूयो भूयो या-चते राम-

109. चन्द्रः ॥ (॥ 56)

श्री विरूपाक्ष ।

---

[1] वांच्छा in Unamanjéri plate. Read वांच्छां.

[2] वैरिभूपांचत्तमदं in Unamanjéri plate. The metre is Gíti.

[3] Read कृमिः

[4] Read एकैव.

COPPER-PLATE No. 11.

[Grant of Penubarti.]

Note.

This was received through M.R.Ry. Rám Mohun Singh, Taluk Sheristadar, from the Village Munsif of Penubarti, Rápur taluk. There were three plates which were dug up long ago, and only one plate is now to be found. It is engraved on only one side and contains 34 lines or so in Nandinágari, identical with the first 34 lines of the Pólépalli grant.

COPPER-PLATE No. 12. (A.D. 1438-39 ?)

[Telugu. Grant from Varadarájasvámi temple at Kocherlakóṭa, Darsi Division. The years do not agree.]

TRANSLATION.

May there be prosperity ! Hail ! On the 15th of the bright half of Mágha of the year Vijaya, corresponding to the year 1360 of the illustrious, victorious and prosperous Ṣálivábana Ṣaka era, Rája Ṣrí Velugóṭi Kastúri Rangapati Náyaningáru presented fields as a *mányam* (to wit) eight *Kuchchalas* of dry land and wet land sowable with 18 *túms* of paddy, to Varadarájasvámi of Kocherlakóṭa, who is the lord of all the crores of worlds, for offerings and worship with a lamp, and two maunds a month for lighting the perpetual lamp. He has presented this on the holy occasion of a lunar eclipse. Therefore, any one failing to maintain the charity will incur the sin of killing his parents, cows and Brahmans at Benáres.

[One imprecatory verse.]

First side.

శుభమస్తు। స్వస్తిశ్రీ జయాభ్యుదయ శా
లివాహన శకవర్షంబులుం ౧౩౬౦
అగునేటి విజయనామ సంవత్సర మా
ఘ శుద్ధ ౧౫ లు శ్రీమదఖిలాండకో
టి బ్రహ్మాండనాయకులైన కొంచెర్లకో
ట వరదరాజస్వామికి నైవేద్య దీపారాధ
నకుగాను రాజశ్రీ వెలుగోటి కస్తూరి రంగ్గపాతి
నాయనిగారు సమర్పించ్చిన మాన్య
క్షేత్రము వెలిపాలం యెనిమిది కుచ్చళ్లు
వరిమడి పద్యెనమందుం నిత్య అ
ఖండనకు మాసనకు రెండ్డు మణా
వుఘ సోమోపరాగ పుణ్యకా
లమండ్ను సమర్పించ్చినారు గనుకను
యీధర్మానకు యెవరుతప్పినా త
మ తల్లితండ్రిని గోబ్రాంహ్మల వార
ణాసిలో వధించ్చిన పాపానపో

Second side.

వువారు॥ స్వదతా ద్విగుణం
పుణ్యం పరదత్తానుపాలనం ప
రదత్తాపహారేణ స్వదత్తం
నిష్ఫలం భవేత్॥

COPPER-PLATE No. 13. (A.D. 1541–42.)

[Yadavalli grant of Achyuta. S.S. 1463.]

Note.

The subjoined inscription is edited from the original copperplates preserved in the Collector's office at Nellore. They are three in number. The engraving is on both sides of the second plate, but only on one side of plates 1 and 3. In the last plate there is blank space in the middle. The plates are 11 inches long and 8 inches wide..

The characters are Nandinágari excepting the words "Ṣrí Virúpáksha" at the end which are in large Canarese characters. The language is Sanskrit except in the portion giving the boundaries of the village granted which is in Telugu. The Sanskrit portion except the initial invocation to Gaṇéṣa is in verse. The text is full of mistakes and obscure in places.

This inscription is identical with the Pólépalli grant down to line 72; in it however occur two additional verses, viz., 8 and 9 which are found in the Hampi inscription of Krishnaráya. (E.I., Vol. I., p. 361.)

The grant proper begins in the middle of the third plate and records that Achyuténdra being on the bank of the Tungabhadra, in the presence of the deity Virúpáksha, on the 12th lunar day of the bright half of Kártika—the day when Vishnu rises from sleep—in S.S. 1463, in the cyclic year Plava, gave the village named Yadavalli, situated in the *síma* of Pánganáḍu attached to Udayagiri (province), in Chirumana *sthala,* to a learned Brahman Tirumala Bhaṭṭa, son of Bhairava Bhaṭṭa, of the Kaundinya *gótra,* of the Ápastamba *sútra* and the Yajuṣ Śákhá.

The village was consequently surnamed Achyuténdrapuram. A village named Dhárávali was given for its support.

The donee is said to have blessed Achyuta after receiving the gift.

The poet and engraver of this as of Pólépalli grant were Sabhápati and Víranácharya respectively.

TRANSLATION.

Vs. 1 to 7. Same as in Pólépalli grant.

V. 8. Oh Wonder! Though he was the son of the glorious Dévakí (like Krishna), though he had lotus eyes (like Vishnu), though he obtained tribute (Bali) by valiant deeds which were able to conquer the three worlds (as Vishnu who conquered Bali by three strides extending over the three worlds), though he bore in his hand the conch and the discus (like Vishnu), he became still more celebrated by the name of 'Íṣvara,[1] as he acquired prosperity (bhúti),[1] universal respect, and the daughter of a king!

V. 9. Like another sun, fond of dwelling only on earth, rising day and night, surrounded by poets and learned men, fond of war, exceedingly renowned from the eastern to the western ocean, from the bridge to Mount Méru, he killed the enemies the Mandéhas,[2] and was resplendent, eclipsing the celestial trees by his gifts.

---

[1] Íṣvara (Ṣiva) had ashes (bhúti), universal worship and Párvatí (daughter of a mountain).

Bhúbrit = (1) a king, (2) a mountain.

[2] The Mandehas are Rákshasas who endeavoured to destroy the sun.

[Then follow verses identical with verses 8 to 36 of the Pólépalli grant with slight variations.]

V. 37. In the Ṣáliváhana Ṣaka year, reckoned in order by 1,000, 400, and 63, (*i.e.*, 1463), in the year Plava, in the excellent month Kártika, on the 12th *tithi*, the day when Vishnu rises from sleep, at a holy time and on an auspicious day.

V. 38. Being on the bank of Tungabhadrá, in the presence of Vírúpáksha, in the hall of gifts which is the abode of the great tree of paradise and other (celestial) trees,

V. 38½. King Achyuténdra, serene, and magnanimous, (gave the following village),

V. 39. to the descendant of the Kaundinya *gótra*, student of the excellent Ápastamba *sútra*, who is glorious, student of Yajus *Sákhá*, who is brilliant in virtues,

V. 40. to Tirumala Bhaṭṭa, son of Bhairava Bhaṭṭa, who is well versed in the Tantras, Logic, and Mahábháshya (grammar),

V. 41. who has studied, taught, and retains in his memory history and the ṣástras, whose intellect is able to distinguish Dharma from Adharma,

V. 42. who is fit to receive gift of land, who is the foremost of Brahmans, who is modest and eminent, to the intelligent man named Tirumala Bhaṭṭa,

Vs. 43 to 47. The village named Yadavalli, situated in the *ṣíma* named Pánganáḍu attached to Udayáchala (Udayagiri), in the *sthala* of the village named Chirumana, to the north of that village, possessing all estimable qualities, bearing the surname Achyuténdrapuram, beautiful and marked by all excellences, and the village named Dhárávali for the maintenance of that village, together with its treasures, hidden deposits, minerals, everything that is and that may be discovered, and water, with the *akshiní* and the *ágámi*, together with the eight enjoyments, with its wells, cisterns, ponds and banks, to be enjoyed by sons and grandsons, and other descendants in succession as long as the moon and sun last.

V. 48. Achyuténdra Mahárája, who is worthy of honour by intelligent men, being surrounded by many assiduous and amiable scholars, who follow the path of the Śrautas, who excel in eloquence, and who are headed by the domestic chaplain, joyfully gave with libation of water and gift of gold.

V. 49. Then Tirumala Bhaṭṭa with a pleased mind blessed him saying "Achyuténdra Mahárája, may you have long life."

V. 50. The boundaries of the *agrahára* in the direction east, &c., are described in the colloquial language (Telugu) in order by their respective marks.

Lines 92 to 96. (Here come the boundaries in Telugu written in Sanskrit characters.)

V. 51. This is the edict of Achyutaráya who satisfies the desires of learned men, and curbs the pride of mind of foes, and whose prosperity (kingship) was bestowed by Achyuta (Vishnu).

V. 52. Under the orders of Achyuténdra Maháráya, Sabhápati composed this copper-plate inscription in sweet verse.

V. 53. At the bidding of Achyuténdra Maháráya, the artizan Śrí Víranácharya, the son of Mallana engraved this copper-plate edict.

[The grant closes with five of the usual benedictory and imprecatory verses.]

Śrí Virúpáksha.

(Verses 1 to 7 as in the Pólépalli grant.)

पद्माक्षोपि[1] बलिजिन्निजैस्त्रि

11. भुवनाक्रान्ति[2]क्षमैर्विक्रमैः शंखं चक्रमपि श्रयन्निजकरे श्री-
देवकीनन्दनः । भू

12. त्वाप्यद्भुतमीश्वरोऽयमिति यो भूयस्तरां पेप्रथे भूतिं चाखिलपूज्य-
तामतिभृ

13. शं भूभृत्सुतामाश्रितः । (॥ 8) भूवासकपराऽपरो रविरिव
प्राप्तोदयोऽहर्निशं । योम-

14. न्देहरिपूनहन्कविबुधोपेतोऽनपेतो रणात् । आपूर्वापरवारिराशि
नितरा

15. मासेतु हेमाचलं विख्यातो विहसंश्च यो वितरणैर्व्यद्योततद्यो-
तरून् । (॥ 9) स-

(For the first part see Pólépalli and Hampi grants.)

Second plate, second side.

72. ॥ (36) शकाब्(दे) साळिवाहस्य सहस्रेण चतुःशतैः । त्रयः
षष्टि समायुक्ते प्रा-

73. कृते गणिते क्रमात् । भवसंवत्सरे श्लाघ्ये कार्तिके मासि सं-
स्थिते । उत्थानद्वाद-

74. शीतिथ्यां । पुण्यकाले सुभे दिने[3] ।(॥ 37) तुंगभद्रानदीतीरे
विरूपाक्षस्य संनिधौ । महा-

75. कल्पलताशने यस्थानंदानमंटपे[4](॥ 38) सुप्रसन्नो महोदारा ।
अच्युते न्द्रमहीपा

76. तिः । (॥ 38½) कौंडिन्यान्वयसंभूतवरापस्तंभ(ब)सूत्रिणे । यश-
स्विने यजुशाखाध्यायिने

---

[1] पि is superfluous for the metre.

[2] Read भुवनाक्रान्ति.

[3] Read शुभेदिने.

[4] Read कल्पलतादीनामास्थाने.

77. गुणशालिमे। (॥ 39) भैरवभट्टपुत्राय तिरुमलभट्टाख्यशालिने। तन्त्रतर्कमहा-

78. भाष्यप्रतिभाप्रभविष्णवे। (॥ 40) अधीताध्यापितज्ञाताधृतचारित्रशास्त्रिणे। धर्मा-

79. धर्मपयो व्यक्तेमरालायुतं[1] बुद्धये। (॥ 41) भूदानपात्रभूताय भूमिदेवाग्रयायिने।

80. विनीताय विशिष्टाय तिरुमलभट्टाख्यधीमते। (॥ 42) उदयाचलसंबंधे पांग-

81. नाडाख्य सीमनि। चिरुमनग्रामनामाख्यस्थले सस्योपशोभितः[2] (॥ 43) तद्ग्रामउत्त-

82. रे भागेयद्वल्लीतिविश्रुतं। सर्वलक्षणसंपन्न(न्नं)प्रतिनाम प्रकल्पितं।(॥ 44) अच्युते-

83. न्द्रपुरं रम्यं सर्वलक्षणलक्षितं। (॥ 44½) ग्रामग्रासार्थमस्यैवथारावलीतिना-

84. मतः। निधिनिक्षेपपाषाणसिद्धसाध्यजलान्वितः[3]। (॥ 45) अक्षिण्यागामिसहितं

85. अष्टभोगसमन्वितं। वापीकूपतटाकैश्च कच्छेनापि समन्वितं। (॥ 46) पुत्र-

86. पौत्रादिभिर्भोग्यं क्रमादाचन्द्रतारकं। दानस्याधमनस्यापि विक्रयस्यापि

87. चोचितं। (॥ 47) परीतः प्रयतः[4] स्निग्धैः पुरोहितः[5] पुरोगमैः विविधैः विबुधैः श्रौतः[6]

---

[1] Read व्यक्तिमरलायितबुद्धये

[2] Read शोभितं.

[3] Read न्वितं.

[4] Read प्रयतैः

[5] Omit the visarga after पुरोहित.

[6] Read श्रौत.

88. अधिकैरधिकं[1] गिरा। अच्युतेन्द्रमहारायो माननीयो मनस्विनां। स।हिरण्य-

89. पयोधारापूर्वकं दत्तवान् मुदा। (॥ 48) तिरुमलभट्टः संतुष्टमनसा चकाराशि-

90. षः। अच्युतेन्द्र महाराय(श्र्) चिरंजीवी भवत्विति। (॥ 49) तैस्तैः समन्ततः चिह्नैः इदं[2]

91. प्राच्यादिषु क्रमात् सीमान[3] साग्रहारस्य[4] लिख्यंते देशभाषया। (॥ 50) तूर्पुकु

Third plate, first side.

92. नागत।निकुंट अङ्गेया।नक थलग्गुलमोडु वंदुरु। दक्षनान-

93. कु कंदादुलगुंट दक्षणपु कांमु यरवंदुरु। नैरुतिकि चिरुम-

94. नचेरुवुकट्टमीदि नछराइ(यि)। पडुमाटिकि मोंडि कट्टमीदि गंगादेविगुडि।

95. वायव्यानकु तेलचौठ वेसिनराइ(यि)। उत्तरानकु तिप्पपडुमाटि रालगुंट

96. ईशान्यानकु नछगुंड्लवांगु ॥ पूरइतो[5]वुदवांचतं[6]वाइतो[7] वैरिचित्त-

97. मदं। अच्युताविहितभूत[8]अच्युतरायस्य शासनं तदिदं ॥ (॥ 51)

Blank space.

98. अच्युतेन्द्रमहारायशासनेन सभापति(:) अभाणी (त्) मृदुसंदर्भं तदिं[9] ताम्र-

---

[1] Read पथिकैरधिकैर्गिरा.

[2] इदं is probably a mistake for दिक्षु.

[3] Read सीमान:

[4] Read अस्याग्रहारस्य.

[5] Read पूरयतो.

[6] Read बुधवांच्छा.

[7] Read पारयतो.

[8] Read विभूतेः

[9] Read तदिदं.

99. शासनं। (॥ 52) अच्युतेन्द्रमहारायशासनान् मल्लणात्मजः त्वष्टा श्रीवीरणाचार्यो

100. लिखितं[1] ताम्रशासनं। (॥ 53) दानपालनयोर्मध्ये दानाच्छ्रेयोनुपालनं। दानात्स्वर्गम-

101. वाप्नोति पालनादच्युतं पदं।(॥ 54) स्वदत्ताद्द्विगुणं पुण्यं परदत्तानुपालनं परद-

102. त्तापहारेण स्वदत्तं निष्फलं भवेत्। (॥ 55) स्वदत्तां परदत्तां वा यो हरेत वसुंधरा(म्)ष-

103. ष्टिर्वरुष[2] सहस्राणि विष्ठायां जायते कृमिः। (॥ 56) एकैव भगिनी लोके सर्वेषां भूमु-

104. जां न भोज्यं[3] न करग्राह्यं[4] विप्रदत्तावसुंधरा। (॥ 57) सामान्योयं धर्मसेतुः नृपाणां काले

105. काले पालनियो[5] भवाद्भिः सर्वानेतान् भाविनः पार्थिवेन्द्रान् भूयोभूयो याचते रामचन्द्रः। (॥ 58)

Copper-plate No. 14.

[Mámidipúṇḍi grant of Sadáṣivaráya. S.S. 1471. A.D. 1549–50.]

Note.

The grant consists of three plates, the first and last of which are engraved on the inner side only, while the middle is engraved on both sides. They have raised rims to protect the writing and are connected by a ring on which there is a seal representing a boar, the sun and the moon.

The writing of the inscription is Nandinágari. throughout except in the case of the final words Ṣrí

---

[1] Read ऽलिखत्तत्.

[2] Read षष्टिवर्ष.

[3] Read भोग्या.

[4] Read ग्राह्या.

[5] Read पालनीयो.

Virúpáksha. The writing is crowded with the exception of the usual opening words 'Ṣrí Gaṇádhipatayénámah.' The whole is in Sanskrit verse. The boundaries however of the village granted are given in Telugu.

The inscription is one of Sadáṣivaráya and bears a general resemblance to the British Museum plates of the same king (E.I., Vol. IV., pages 12–22), and the first forty-two verses in both are identical.

Vs. 1 to 42 give the genealogy of Sadáṣivaráya. Vs. 43 and 44 give the date of the grant. Vs. 45–49 describe the donee Ácharayya, a learned Brahman, son of Anantayárya.

Vs. 49 to 56 state that the village of Mámiḍipúnḍi, situated in Udayagiri *rájya*, in Pákanáḍu and in Sarvapalli *síma*, and surnamed Ṣrí Rangarájapuram, was granted with the usual rights.

Vs. 57 to 67 give the genealogy of Timmarája, at whose request Sadáṣiva made the gift, and contain a eulogistic account of his virtues.

Bukka of Áravíḍu married Ballámbiká.

|

Rámarája (Rama I of Carnatic) married Lakkámbiká.

|

Rangarája (Ranga I) married Tirumalámbiká.

|

Rámarája (Rama II) who married a sister of Sadáṣiva. — **Timmarája (Tirumala I).**

Thus Timmarája was the younger brother of Ráma II. Tirumala is the general form of the name.

The British Museum grant was made at the request of Ráma II, ruler of the Carnatic.

After V. 70 the boundaries of Mámidipúṇḍi the village granted are given in Telugu written in Sanskrit characters.

V. 71 says that Sadáṣivaráya made the gift.

Vs. 72 and 73 give the name of the composer and the engraver, viz., Sabhápati Svayambhú and Ṣrí Víraṇácharya, respectively.

The inscription closes with five imprecatory verses.

Translation.

[The first forty-two verses are not translated as being identical with those of the British Museum plates of the same king—see E.I., Vol. IV, pp. 12–22.]

Vs. 43 and 44. In the Ṣaka year, reckoned by the moon (1), the horses (7), the oceans (4), and the moon (1), *i.e.*, (1471), in the year Saumya, in the month of Ṣrávana, on Monday the holy 12th *tithi* of the bright fortnight, being on the banks of the Tungabhadra in the presence of Viṭṭhaléṣvara, (Sadáṣivaráya gave).

Vs. 45 to 49. To the scholar named Ácharayya, who is a very tree of paradise born from the milk-ocean of the Gautama *gótra*, who is a lion to the elephants which are his controversialists, who is of the excellent Ápastamba *sútra*, who is glorious, who is a student of Yajuṣ *ṣákhá*, whose mind is always devoted to the performance of the six sacraments, whose armour is the Véda, whose dictum settles disputes regarding the six Ṣástras, who has studied the established doctrine of the Vaishnava scriptures, who is a Brahmavádi (Vedántist), who is the expounder of the meaning of the Ṣrí Bháshya to classes of distinguished disciples, whose mind is resplendent through taking refuge at the lotus feet of Srí Venkatésa, who is the excellent son of the illustrious Anantayárya, who is upright, and whose speech is true and pleasant.

Vs. 49 to 56. The village named Mámidipúndi, otherwise named the famous Srírangarájapuram, situated in Udayáchala (Udayagiri) *rájya*, in Pákanádu, in the *síma* named Saryapalli, possessed of great fame, lying to the east of the excellent village Tállapúdi, to the south of the well-defined boundary of the two villages Piditapólu and Musidikádu, to the west of the proper boundary of the two villages Nellatúr and Krishnaráyapattanam, and to the north of the village named Mutkúr, rich in all kinds of corn, up to its four boundaries everywhere, with its treasures, hidden deposits, minerals (stones), actuals, outstandings and water, with its *akshiní* and *ágámi*, abounding in trees, having cisterns, wells, ponds, embankments, and gardens, as a *sarvamánya* to be enjoyed as a single share, to be enjoyed by sons, grandsons and other descendants of the grantee in succession as long as the moon and sun endure, subject to gift, mortgage and sale and subject to transfer.

V. 57. There was a king of great prowess, who was a very tree of paradise on earth, Bukka of the famous Áravídu (city). His wife was Ballámbiká as the daughter of Pulóma was of Purandara (Indra).

V. 58. From him was born Rámarája as Káma from the lotus-eyed Lord of all the worlds (Vishnu). His queen was Lakkámbiká, blessed, the gem of the world of kings in virtues, as Rati (wife of Káma).

V. 59. From him was born the excellent king Srí Rangarája, the gem of the lunar race, who by his splendour obtained the position of the central gem (lordship) in the middle of the necklace consisting of provincial chiefs (*i.e.*, he became the lord of provincial chiefs).

V. 60. The queen of this (king), who was accomplished in gifts, was Tirumalámbiká, as Dévasénâ was of Sénâní (Kumára), and as Damayanti was of Nala.

V. 61. In consequence of his many austerities, he had a son, king Şri Rámarája, the light of the lunar race. To the extent that his splendour shone in the world, even the eyes of the ladies of his enemies became white (devoid of collyrium).

V. 62. Resplendent is his younger brother Timmarája, the outer yard of whose house is wet with the water poured out on the occasion of gifts, and by the shower of whose arrows the fire which is the valour of all kings is quenched.

V. 63.[1] Whose enemies in battle, being made to move round by the array of his troops, became cowards, like wives showing signs of love, having tremor, perspiration and horripilation.

Vs. 64 to 68. Complying with the request of this hero Timmarája, who is accomplished in gifts and virtuous, who is the treasury of mercy, who is *anṭembaraganḍa* (the disgracer of those of whom the *birudas* are proclaimed), who is of the lunar race, who is the ornamental gem of the Átréya *gótra*, who is the supporter of the Dharma (promulgated by) Manu, who is a sun to the collection of lotuses which are scholars, who has vanquished the valour of his enemies, who resembles Nahusha, who is *Nánávarṇaşrímanḍálikaganḍa* (conqueror of chieftains of various castes), who has the *biruda ébirudaráyaráhuta-*

---

[1] Verse 62 is obscure. The meaning given is that suggested by Dr. Prof. Kielhorn in B.M. plate grant. Makaránkita = (1) full of love, or (2) made to move round by the *makara* (array) of his troops.

veṣyaikabhujanga (the unique paramour of the prostitutes who are the troopers of kings possessing all kinds of *birudas*), whose pleasure is to destroy chiefs having *birudas*, who is victorious, who has the *biruda Dharaní-varáha*, (the boar that supports the earth) as he is famed for supporting the earth, and who is the dwelling house of modesty, liberality, magnanimity and faith.

V. 69. Sadáṣivaráya, who deserves to be honoured intelligent men, surrounded by many assiduous and amiable scholars, who are followers of the Ṣrauta, who excel in speech, and who are headed by the domestic chaplain, joyfully gave with libation of water and gift of gold.

V. 70. The boundaries of the village in the directions east, etc., with their respective marks are written in order in the provincial language (Telugu).

(*Telugu.*)

The eastern boundary of Mámiḍipúnḍi (is) the bund between Nérarladoruvu and Alluladoruvu in Nuyyala-guṭṭa at the junction of Krishnaráyapaṭṭanam and Nelaṭúr.

South-east: the anthill at the junction of Krishna-ráyapaṭṭanam, Mutukúru and Mámiḍipúnḍi.

South: the white stone in the bed of Pinacheruvu at the junction of Mámiḍipúnḍi and Mólúru.

On the south-west: Yallaguṇṭa at the junction of Mámiḍipúnḍi and Móluru.

On the west: the rough stone at the junction of Mámiḍipúnḍi and Tállapúḍi.

On the north-west: the rough stone to the north of the Daipyálavániguṇṭa, at the junction of Mámiḍipúnḍi and Piḍitipólu.

On the north: Chauṭaguṇṭa at the junction of Mámidipúṇḍi and Musidikáḍu.

On the north-east: the *balusu* (*Canthium parviflorum* according to Brown) tree beyond the Kallaṭivágu at the junction of Mámiḍipúṇḍi and Nelaṭúr.

(*Sanskrit.*)

V. 70. This is the charter of Sadáṣivaráya, who is charming, the best of kings, the foremost of the famous, who is like Ráma in wielding the bow, and who is devoted to unlimited gifts.

V. 71. At the bidding of the glorious Sadáṣivaráya, the court poet Sabhápati Svayambhú thus composed the text of the copper plate edict written in a simple and charming style.

V. 72. Under the orders of Sadáṣivaráya, the engraver Ṣrí Viraṇácharya son of Víraṇa engraved the copper-plate edict.

[Five imprecatory verses.]

Up to the 11th line of second plate, second side, the text consists of the first 40 verses of B.M. Plates.

Second plate, second side.

Line 12. चन्द्राश्वार्णवशीतांशुसंख्या-

13. ते शकवत्सरे । सौम्यसंवत्सरे मासि श्रावणे शशिवासरे (॥ *v.* 43) पक्षे वलक्षे पुण्यायां द्वा-

14. दश्यां च महातिथौ । तुंगभद्रानदी तीरे विट्ठलेश्वरसंनिधौ (॥ 44) गौतमान्वय दु-

15. ग्धाब्धि कल्पवृक्षायितात्मने । वादिवारणसिंहाय वरापस्तंब-सूत्रिणे । (॥ 45) यशस्वि-

16. ने यजुश्शाखाध्यायिने बुद्धिशालिने । षट्कर्मसंततोपात्रनर्मणे[1]वेदवर्मणे । (॥ 46)

---

[1] Perhaps the text is संततापात्मनर्मणे.

17. षण्णामपि च शास्त्राणां निर्णायकनिजोक्तये। वैष्णवागम-सिद्धान्तवेदिने ब्रह्म-

18. वादिने। (॥ 47) विशिष्यशिष्यवर्गाणां श्रीभाष्यार्थोपदेशिने। श्रीवेंकटेशपादांबुजादाब्जा-

19. श्रयणोल्लासिचेतसे । (॥ 48) श्रीमतोनंतयार्यस्य सुपुत्राय सुवृत्तये। आचारय्याभिधाना-

20. य सूरय सूनृतोक्तये। (॥ 49) उदयाचलराज्यस्थं पाकनाडौ कृतांस्थितिं सर्थपल्याख्यसी-

21. मायां संप्राप्तं ख्यातिमुत्तमां। (॥ 50) ताल्लपूडिवरग्रामात्प्रा-चीमाशामुपाश्रितं। पिडिता-

22. पोलु मुशिडिकाडु ग्रामद्वयस्य च। (॥ 51) प्रख्याताद्युक्त सीमांताद् दाक्षिणस्यां दिशिस्थितं। ने

23. ल्टूरोः कृष्णरायपट्टणस्य द्वयोरपि। ग्रामयोः युक्तसीमान्तात् पश्चिमां दिशमाश्रितं। (॥ 52) मु-

24. त्कूरुनामकाद्ग्रामात् संप्राप्तं दिशमुत्तरां। विख्यातश्रीरंगरा-जपुरमित्यपराभिधं। ग्रा-

25 मं मामिडिपूंडच्याख्यं सर्वरुस्योपशोभितं। (॥ 53) सर्वमान्यं चतुस्सीमासंयुतं (च) समंततः।

26. निधिनिक्षेपपाषाणसिद्धसाध्यजलान्वितं। (॥ 54) अक्षिण्या गामिसंयुक्तमेकभोग्यं सभूरु-

27. हं। वापीकूपतटाकैश्च कच्छारामैश्च संयुतं। (॥ 55) पुत्र पौत्रादिभिर्भोग्यं क्रमादाचंद्रता-

28. रकं। दानाधमनविक्रीतियोग्यं विनिमयोचितं। (॥ 56) भूकल्प-शाखी प्रथितारवीटिबुक्क्ष

29. मापोरितं पुरुप्रतापी । बह्लांबिका तस्य बभूव पत्नी पुरंदरस्येव पुलोमकन्या [:] (॥ 57) अरमा

30. दशोषभुवनावनवारिजाक्षात शृंगारराजवत् (द) जायत राम-राजः । धन्या गुणेन धर-

31. णीवरलोकरत्नं लक्कांबिका रतिरिवाभवदस्य देवी । (॥ 58) तस्मादभूदैन्दववंशरत्नं श्रीरं-

32. गराजक्षितिपालवर्यः । [अभजत] यो मंण्डलधीश्वरहारवल्यां मध्येऽभवन्नायकतां[1] महिम्न । (॥ 59) यस्य

33. दानधुरीणस्य देवी तिरुमलांबिका । देवसेनेव सेनान्यो दमयन्ती नलस्यवा । (॥ 60) तस्या-

34. धिकै(:) समभवत्तनय[:]स्तपोभिः श्रीरामराजनृपतिः शशिवंश दीपः । यस्योज्वलददूजग-

35. ति[2] धाम यथा तथा[3] संनेत्राणि वैरिसुदृशां च निरंजनानि (॥ 61) दानांबुना व्यारवीलमेदिनी-

36. क[:][4]स्तस्यानुजो राजति तिमराजः । शौर्यानलः सर्वमहीपतीन शान्तो यदीयैः शरवृ-

37. ष्टिपातैः (॥ 62) सकंपस्वेदरोमांचास्समरे मकरांकिताः । यस्याधि[5] सुरता स्तत्यः शत्रवो

Third plate, first side.

1. भीरवोभवन् । (॥ 63) तस्य दानधुरीणस्य धार्मिकस्य द-
2. यानिधेः । अत्रेंबरगंडस्य[6] हरिणांकान्ववायिनः[7] । (॥ 64)

---

[1] Read मध्येऽभजन्नायकतां.

[2] Read यस्याज्वलद् जगति.

[3] Read तथासन्नेत्राणि.

[4] The text conveys no meaning. The reading may be दानांबुनार्द्रांकितमेदिनीकः or दानांबुनाद्राङ्कणमेदिनीकः or is it क्षालितमेदिनीकः

[5] Read -यस्यावि-

[6] Prof. Kielhorn suggests बिरुदांतेंबरगंडस्य for the sake of metre.

[7] In the B.M. Plate we have हरिभक्ताग्रयायिनः

3. आत्रेयगोत्रालंकारमणे र्मनुनयस्थितेः। सूर्य्यब्जवनसूर्य्यस्य सूदि-

4. तारातितेजसः (॥ 65) नहुषोपमस्य नानावर्णश्रीमंण्डलीक-गंडस्य। ये बिरुदराय-

5. राहुत्त(त)वेश्यैकभुजंगबिरुदभरितस्य(॥ 66)विख्यातबिरुदमांन्नि-यविमालललीलस्य

6. बिजयशीलस्य। विश्वंभराभृतिस्फू(सु)तविश्रुतधरणीवराहबिरु-दस्य। (॥ 67) विनयौ-

7. दार्ढ्यगांभीर्यविश्वासवासवेश्मनः[1]। वीरस्य तिमराजस्य विज्ञप्ति-मनुपालयन्। (॥ 68) परीतः

8. प्रयतैः स्निग्धैः पुरोहितपुरोगमैः। विविधैर्विबुधैः श्रौतपथिकै-रधिकैर्गिरा। सदाशिवम-

9. हारायो माननीयो म(न)स्विनां। संहिरण्यपयोधारापूर्वकं दत्तवान् मुदा (॥ 69) ग्रामस्यास्यैव सीमा-

10. नो दिक्षु प्राच्यादिषु क्रमात्। तत्तच्छिह्नसमायुक्ता लिख्यंते देशभाषया। (॥ 70) ई ग्रामानकुपोलिमे-

11. र। मामिडिपूडिकि तूर्प्पुमेर। कृष्णरायपट्णनेलटूरिसंधु मु-ख्यलगुट्ट नेरेलेदोरुवु अ-

12. ह्युल दोरुवु नडिविगट्ट अग्नेयं कृष्णरायपट्ण मुत्तुकूरुमामिडि-पूडिसंधुपकुकेल-

13. पुट्ट दक्षिणं(:) मामिडिपूडि मोलुरिसंधु। पिनचेरुवु तोट्टन तेह्लरायि। निरृऋतिभागं मामि-

14. डिपूडिमोलूरिसंधुयह्लगुंट पडमर मामिडिपूडि ताह्लपूडि संधु चडिपिरायि वा-

15. यव्यः मामिडिपूडिपिडितापोलिसंधु दैप्यालवानिगुंटकु उत्तर-चिडापिरायि। उत्तरं

---

[1] In the B.M. Plate we have विक्रमवासवेश्मनः

16. मामिडपूडि मुशिडिकाडुसंघु चौटगुंट । ईशान्यं । मामिडि-पुंडि नेलटूरिसं-

17. घु कछेटिवागुकु आवलिबलसुलमिद्दा । श्री

18. सरससदाशिवरायक्षितिपतिवर्यस्य कीर्तिधुर्यस्य । शासनमिदं सरासन[1] दाशर-

19. थेरमितहेमदानरतेः । (॥ 71) मृदुपदमिति ताम्रशासनार्थं महित । सदाशिवरायसास[2]-

20. नेन । अभणदनुगुणं वचोमहिम्ना सरसतरेण सभापतिस्स्वयंभूः (॥ 72) सदाशिवमहा-

21. रायशासनाद्वीरणात्मजः । त्वष्टा श्रीवीरणाचार्यो व्यलिखत्तां प्रशासनं । (॥ 73) दानपाल-

22. नयोर्मध्ये दानाच्छ्रेयोनुपालनं । दानात्स्वर्गमवाप्नोति पाल-नादच्युतंपदं । (॥ 74) स्वद-

23. त्ताद्द्विगुणं पुण्यं परद्त्तानुपालनं । परदत्तापहारेण स्वदत्तं निष्फलंभ-

24. वेत् । (॥ 75) स्वदतां परदत्तां वा यो हरेत वसुंधरां । षष्टिं वर्षसहस्राणि विष्टायां

25. जायते क्रिमिः । (॥ 76) एकवै भगिनी लाके सर्वेषामेव भूभुजां । न भोग्या न करग्रा-

26. ह्या विप्रदत्ता वसुंधरा । (॥ 77) सामान्योयं धर्मसेतुर्नृपाणां काले काले पालनी-

27. यो भवाद्भिः । सर्वानेतान्भाविनः पार्थिवेंद्रान्भूयो भूयो याचते रामचंद्रः (॥ 78) श्री

श्रीविरूपाक्ष.

---

[1] Read शरासन.

[2] Read रायशासनेन.

(To face page 109.)

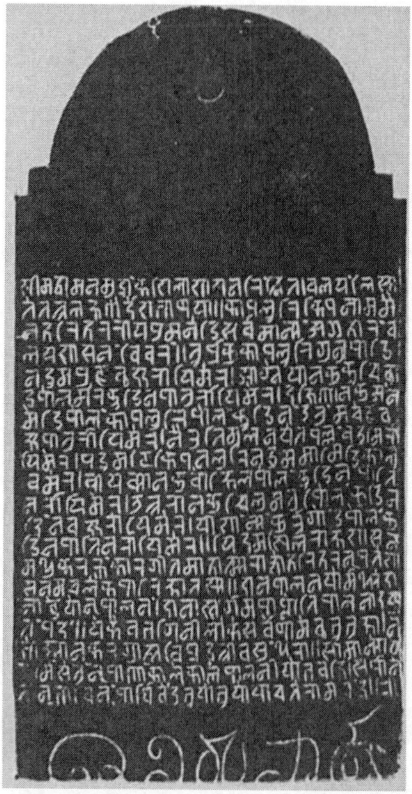

COPPER-PLATE NO. 15.

(4)

(To face page 106.)

COPPER-PLATE NO. 15.

(3)

(To face page 109.)

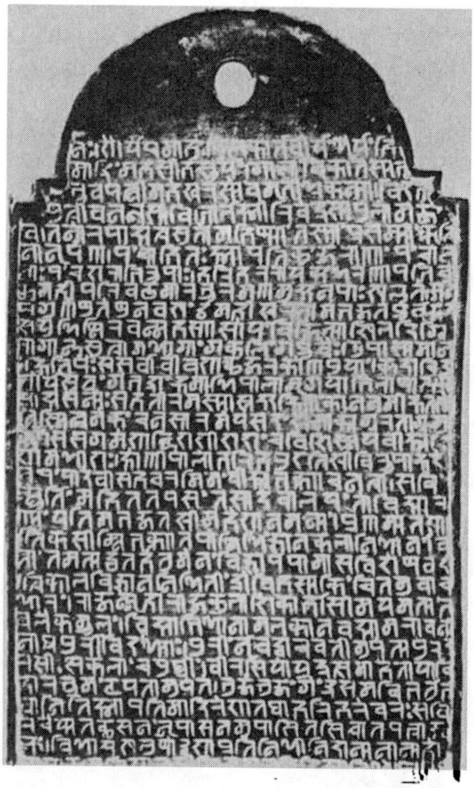

COPPER-PLATE NO. 15.

(2)

(To face page 109.)

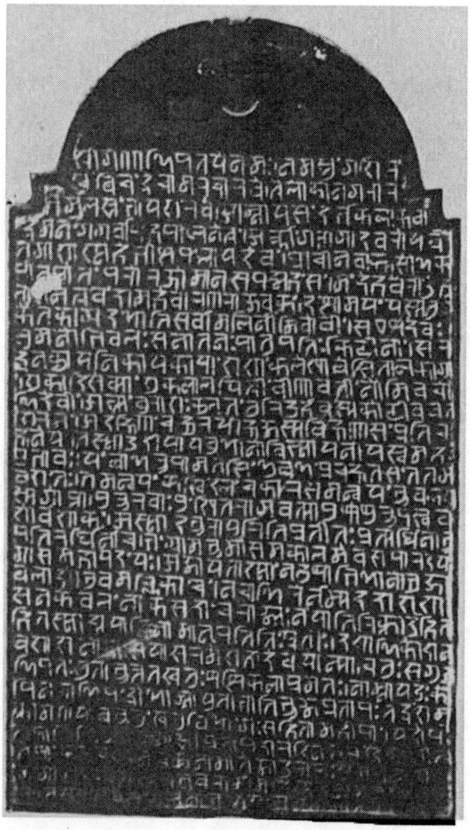

COPPER-PLATE NO. 15.

(1)

Copper-plate No. 15.

[Kapalur grant S.S. 1258. (A.D. 1336-37.)]

[From the Collector's office, Nellore.]

Note.

The following grant is published from the original copper-plates which are kept in the Collector's office, Nellore. The plates are three in number of which the first and the third are engraved on only one side.

The engraving is clear but in places some letters appear to have been erased. The character is Nandinágari but the formation of the letters is quite modern and in certain letters it is very similar to Dévanágari. This fact shows that the document is a fabrication.

There are numerous mistakes in the inscription. These are pointed out in the foot-notes.

The grant consists of fifty Sanskrit verses, and a portion in Telugu giving the boundaries of the village granted.

The first five verses are invocations to deities. Vs. 6 to 13 give the mythical genealogy of the first Vijayanagar dynasty tracing it to the moon. The first king was Bukka, whose wife was Mégámbiká. Next came his son Sangama whose wife was Gálámbiká; he had five sons Harihara, Bukka, Kampa, Mára and Muddana. (Vs. 14 to 18). The next king was the eldest of these, viz., Harihara. V. 19 states that he ruled the whole earth having conquered all the quarters of the earth and that his capital was Kunjarakóna (the elephant valley).

Vs. 20 to 27 relate the circumstances under which Harihara came to found the city of Vidyánagar. Once when out hunting in the forest to the south of the Tungabhadra, he saw a hare attack a dog and wondered. Thinking it to be a wonderful event and perceiving that the hare was Virúpáksha, he went to and sought counsel of the sage Vidyáranya, who was practising austerities in the temple of Virúpáksha. The hermit said that the place was fit to be the residence of a royal dynasty, asked him to build a city called Vidyánagar and prophesied the future glory of his race.

Next we come to the grant proper which states that Harihara gave an Agrahára named Hariharapuram to a Brahman named Ananta Súraya, son of Sankukéśava, of the Viṣvámitra *gótra* and the Áṣvaláyana *sútra*. Vs. 39 to 41 say that he divided the village into 60 shares, kept 30 for himself and gave the other 30 to Brahmans. Only 5, however, of these sharers holding 11 shares are given in the inscription (Vs. 41 to 45).

V. 46 says that boundaries were fixed with stones stamped with the seal bearing the figure of the Vámana incarnation (dwarf).

Then there is a Telugu passage giving the boundaries and the inscription closes with three of the usual imprecatory verses.

The date of the inscription is S.S. 1258. V. 29 says that the grant was made after the coronation of the king.

Translation.

Adoration be to Ganádhipatí (Ganéṣa)!

V. 1. Salutation be to Ṣiva, who is charming with the moon, as with a *chámara*, which kisses his lofty head, and who is the main pillar of the creation of the city of the three worlds.

V. 2. We salute for the fruition of our desire the god who is the author of the art of the composition of the Véda, whose eye in the forehead destroyed the pride of Káma, who has his consort (in) the (left) half of his body.[1]

V. 3. We adore the elephant-faced (Ganéṣa), who is a young pigeon in the mansion which is the Véda (*i.e.*, who is to be known by the Véda), who is the swan on the lotus which is the mind of those who are free from passion[2] (and) who has the eyes: the enemy of the mandéhas (*i.e.*, the sun), the moon and fire.

V. 4. May this god, the eternal, the Lord of Boars (the Boar incarnation of Vishnu), whose Kétaki flower in the form of a tusk bears the whole earth like a female[3] bee (or swarm of bees) and who is praised by the gods, protect (you).

V. 5. I praise the goddess of speech (Sárasvatí), whose body resembles (in splendour) the sky with its autumnal clouds,[4] whose hair is decked with the digit of the moon, who is worshipped by Ṣuka and other sages, who caresses a parrot and who has a lute.

V. 6. The son[5] of this ocean (milk-ocean) was the moon, the crest-jewel of Ṣiva, whom now the learned call the left eye of Vishnu.[6]

---

[1] *Avaródha* generally means *harem*, here it means *wife*.

[2] The expression means also the swan of the lotuses found in the Mánasa lake which is free from dirt.

[3] The earth which is black resting on the Boar's tusk which is white resembles a female bee (which is black), resting on the Kétaki flower (which is white).

[4] Sarasvatí is supposed to be white.

[5] *Kulatantu* the thread or perpetuator of the family. The moon is supposed to have been produced from the ocean at the time of churning.

[6] The moon is said to be the left eye and the sun the right eye as Vishnu.

V. 7. From him (the moon) arose (one) whose name was Budha, the greatness of whose intellect was wonderful, whom the wise always call the ocean of the nectar of knowledge.

V. 8. In course of succession a certain ruler of the circle of the earth adorned that race (viz.) Purúravas, who resembled the flower-arrowed (Káma) in beauty, who brought under his control Urvasi (a celestial nymph) on account of the existence of intense love.

V. 9. From him there was a king famed as Áyu, who caused *Mahápadam* simultaneously to (his) enemies and suppliants in *Sangrámabhúmi*.

[NOTE.—There are puns on the words *Sangrámabhúmi* and *Mahápadam*. In the case of enemies he caused a great calamity in *Sangrámabhúmi*, *i.e.*, the battle field: in the case of suppliants he caused to be produced an exalted position in *Sangrámabhúmi*, *i.e.*, a country abounding in excellent villages]

V. 10. From him sprang Nahusha (lit. whose name was Nahusha), who by the strength of his arm not only ruled the sea-girt earth in such a manner that his feet were adorned by kings but also the kingdom of the dwellers of heaven (the gods).

(The allusion is that Nahusha once obtained the position of Indra).

V. 11. Born to him who surpassed in mercy, the king named Yayáti, famous (and) excelling in compassion, sported with Dévayáni, as the vanquisher of the demons (Vishṇu) with Lakshmî.

V. 12. From him (Yayáti), who was the lord of the four seas, sprang a son versed in the sixty-four arts; resplendent is the king named Yadu, possessed of splendour, and strong-armed.

V. 13. Kings arose who were pearls of his race and who were possessed of the four members of the army (chariots, elephants, horses and infantry); the moonlight which was the smile of the wives of his enemies was dispelled by the sun which was the prowess of Yadu.

[NOTE.—The meaning is that Yadu destroyed his enemies and their wives were thus deprived of their cheerfulness.]

V. 14. In their race was a certain king named Bukka whose valour was difficult to rival. Mégámbiká was that king's wife as the daughter of the ocean (Lakshmí) was of Vishnu.

V. 15. From him was born Sangama, the might of whose arm was sung everywhere, whom they here call indeed Kártavírya in valour, the Himálayas in courage, and the sun in splendour.

V. 16. Gálámbiká was his wife as the daughter of the mountain (Párvatí) was of Mahéṣvara (Śiva), as the Vidarbha princess (Damayantí) was of Nala, as Lakshmí was of Vishnu, and as the daughter of Pulóma was of Indra.

V. 17. Five excellent sons, who were lions to the elephants which were wicked kings, and who resembled the five-arrowed (Káma) in beauty, were begotten by that blessed king on that queen.

V. 18. They were indeed King Harihara, King Kampa, King Bukka, King Mára and King Muddana. But the eldest (*i.e.*, Harihara) amongst them who were of spotless virtues, resembling Yudishṭhira in splendour, attained the sovereignty of the earth consisting of the nine continents (lit. pieces).

V. 19. Having conquered all the quarters of the world beginning with (the territories of) the Angas and Kalingas, possessed of Indra's splendour, and being honoured by kings, he ruled the whole earth at the city of Kunjarakóṇa. (This is probably a Sanskrit rendering of Ánegonḍa and means the elephant-valley.)

V. 20. Once through desire of hunting, having crossed the (river) Tungabhadrá with his army, having reached its bank, the king saw a forest to the south of it.

V. 21. Having beheld in that forest a certain hare engaged in copulation, which was fierce and was biting a dog and (its companion)[1] the female hare, the lord of men (the king) wondered.

V. 22. Having perceived this (hare) to be Ṣrí Virúpákshadéva associated with Pampádévi, and humble with devotion, king Harihara, went to the hermit Vidyáraṇya the incarnation of spiritual knowledge, whose austerity was honoured and who was like another glorious Mahéṣána (Śiva), (who resided) near his (Virúpáksha's) temple.

V. 23. Having saluted in his vicinity with reverence (Vidyáranya) who was the store-house of austerity, and the receptacle of knowledge and arts, and who was very praiseworthy, he related this incident whose explanation was very wonderful.

V. 24. Having smiled a little, (Vidyáraṇya) the storehouse of knowledge of the three times (past, present and future), the best of ascetics, said (as follows) to that hero: "Oh king, this country deserves to be the residence of a family of great kings and the sole source of great power.

Vs. 25 and 26. Oh Lord, found a city named Vidyá, as beautiful as Alaka (Kubéra's city), which shall be a

---

[1] The passage here is obscure. The reading is conjectural. The fact of the male hare attacking a dog caused surprise in the mind of the king who thereupon thought it must be a holy place where such a thing could happen and went to Vidyáraṇya to seek advice.

forest of learning (Irá = Sárasvatí, learning); and having reached the city having nine gates, and endowed with the glory of Indra, you bear (will bear) the whole earth on your arm which resembles the lord of serpents (Sésha) and which has attained the state of (has become) the pleasure-grove of the Ṣrí (goddess) of war who has been captured (by you) in battles." He thus instructed the king.

V. 27. Having accordingly obeyed his command, occupying the seat of kings (throne), conspicuous with an excellent white umbrella, having indeed performed gifts which were even greater than the sixteen gifts (prescribed in the Law Books) he, king Harihara, shone in the extensive town named Vidyá.

V. 28. In the year of (the Ṣaka) king (Nripa) having the number 8, 5, 2, 1, (*i.e.*, 1258), in the bright fortnight of Mádhava (Vaiśákha) of (the year) Dhátṛí, under the auspicious Pushya star and Hari *lagna* and on the 7th (*tithi*).

V. 29. After the festival of coronation, being in the auspicious presence of Pampá Virúpáksha Mahéṣvara, the great king who was truthful and valiant founded an *Agrahára.*

V. 38. King Harihara, who is worthy of honour among wise men, joyfully gave with gift of gold and libation of water.

Vs. 33, 34 and 35. the great village Kápalur, fit to be the residence of wise men, situated in the *rájya* (kingdom) named Chendragiri in Paḍanáḍu *síma* (district), in the holy and beautiful *sthala* (place) of the river Svarnamukhyá (Mukhi is the usual form), to the east of Panalúru, to the south of Chilalúru, to the west of

Gunupáḍu, and to the north of Ánaméḍu, well known by the surname Hariharapuram, as a *sarvamánya*, up to its four boundaries everywhere.

V. 36. Along with its hidden treasures, deposits, stone, actuals, outstandings and water, with the *akshini*, and *ágámi*, as an *éka bhógyam*, together with its trees.

V. 37. Together with its ponds, wells, tanks and embankments, to be enjoyed in succession by sons, grandsons and others as long as the moon and stars endure.

Vs. 30, 31 and 32. To Ananta Súraya, son of Ṣanku Késava Bhaṭṭa, of the *kula* (*gótra*) of Viṣvámitra, of the Áśvaláyana *sútra*, student of Rikśákhá, versed in the Véda, the Védánta, and the Ágamas, devoted to the good conduct laid down in the Śrauta and Smárta (*sútras*) intelligent, who was a fit recipient of gift of land, the foremost of Brahmans, modest, distinguished, famous and great-souled.

Vs. 39 and 40. The owner of the village having received the *agrahára*, having divided 60 *vriṭṭis* into two halves, and having retained one half of those (for himself), joyfully presented 30 *vriṭṭis* to Brahmans. The *vritti* holders with their *gótra* and *sútra* are—

Vs. 41 to 45—

Name of Sharer.	Father's Name.	Gótra.	Sútra.	Shares.
1. Singábhaṭṭa ...	Anantaya	Bháradvája.	Rik ...	3
2. Mallubhaṭṭa ...	Timmana	Śrívatsa. ...	Yajus ...	2
3. Pochana	Náganárya ...	Káśyapa ...	Do. ...	2
4. Mallubhaṭṭa ...	Mádhava	Śánḍilya ...	Do. ...	2
5. Náribhaṭṭa ...	Chellapilla	Harita ...	Do. ...	2
			Total ...	11

V. 46. The boundaries demarcated with stones stamped with the illustrious Vámana (dwarf) seal are described in the provincial language (Telugu) by their respective marks.

[Here follows a Telugu passage giving the boundaries.]

V. 47. This is the edict of King Harihara, the sole Párijáta of the earth, whose greatness is sung by the humming of the bees which are the conquests of all kings.

Vs. 48 to 50 are three of the usual imprecatory verses.

Ṣrí Virúpáksha.

First plate, second side.

1. श्रीगणाधिपतये नमः । नमस्तुंगशिर-
2. श्चुम्बिचंद्रचामरचारवे । त्रैलोक्यनगरारं-
3. भमूलस्तंभाय शंभवे ॥ (1) आम्नायसंदर्भकलाकवी-
4. न्द्रमनंगगर्वापहफालनेत्रं । अर्धांगभागादवरोधवं-
5. तमाशास्महे भीष्टफलायदेवं ॥ (2) प्राचीनवाक्सौध-
6. कपोतपोतं परोरजो मानसपद्महंसं । मंदेहवैरीन्दुहु-
7. ताशनेत्रं वंदामहे वारणराजवक्त्रं ॥ (3) दंष्ट्रामयं यस्यतु
8. कैतकाग्रं दधाति सर्वा मलिनीमिवोर्वी । सएष देवः
9. सुमनोभिवन्द्यः सनातनः पातु पतिः किटीनां ॥ (4) स-
10. शारदाभ्राभ्र निकाशकायां शशांकलेखोल्लसितालकाग्रां-
11. शुकादिसेव्यां शुकलालयित्रीं वीणावतीं नौमि वचो-
12. धिदेवीं ॥ (5) अस्यांबुराशेः कुलतंतुरिंदुः देवस्य को-
टीरवतं-
13. सरत्नं । अदक्षिणं चक्षुरधोक्षजस्य[1] वि(च)क्षणा[2] संप्रतिच-

---

[1] हेवस्य in text.

[2] च is omitted in text in the word विचक्षणाः.

14\. क्षते यं ॥ (6) तस्मादुदीयाय न्नुधा[भि]धानो [1] विस्मापनीय-

15\. प्रतिभा प्रभावः। यं वोधरूपामृतसिंधुबंधुं प्रचक्षते संततमेव

16\. संतः ॥ (7) तमन्वयं कश्चिदलंचकार समन्वयं भूतल-

17\. यस्य गोप्ता । पुरूरवाः पुंखितरागवत्याः [2] पुष्पेषुरूपस्रव

18\. शोर्वशीकः ॥ (8) अस्मादभूदा [3] युरिति प्रतीतः प्रत्यःर्थिनांभू-

19\. पतिराथनां च । संग्रामभूमौ समकालमेव संपादया- [4]

20\. मास महापदं यः ॥ (9) अजायतास्मान्नहुषाभिधानो-भुजा-

21\. बलाद्योभुवमह्लिकांच [5] । नराधिपै [6] र्नम्यदशं [7] शशा-

22\. स न केवलं नाकसदां च राज्यं ॥ (10) न यातिरिक्तात [8]-

23\. हितस्माद् ययाति नामा नृपति(ः)तिः [9] प्रतीः (प्रतीतः)[10]। दयाधिकोदान-

24\. वशासनोवासिया [11] स रेमे सह देवयान्या ॥ (11) चतुः समु-

---

[1] भि is omitted in the text. Read तस्मादुदेतिस्मवुधाः भिधानौ.

[2] रागवत्याः does not suit the sense. Read रागवृत्या or रागवत्वात्.

[3] दभूरायु in text.

[4] संपारदया in text.

[5] Read बलाद्यो भुवब्धिकांचीं.

[6] नाचाधिपै in text.

[7] Read नम्यपदं.

[8] Read रक्तादुदितो.

[9] One ति is superfluous.

[10] तः of प्रतीतः omitted in text.

[11] सिया in text. Read श्रिया.

25. द्राधिपतेः सुतो भूत्ततश्चतुः षष्टिकलाप्रतीतः [1] । नाम्ना यदुःको-

26. पि नराधिपेन्द्रो धाम्ना युता भाति भुजप्रतापः ॥ (12) तद्वंशमु-

27. क्तामणयो बभूवुः श्चतुर्विधांगैः सहिता महीपाः । यदोःप्र-

28. तापारिहिम [2] भानुनारताप्रतपदरा [3] स्मितचंद्रिकासीत् ॥ (13)-

29. तेषां कुले कश्चन बुक्कनामा तेजोदुरापः समभून महीपः-

30. मेंगाबिका तस्य बभूव राज्ञी [4] मोदिन्युदन्वत्तनयाधिवि-

31. वा ॥ [5] ॥ (14) तस्यां भवसंगम [6] नामधेयेः सरस्वतीगीतभजोपमा-

32. नः [7] । शौर्ये यमाहुः किल कार्तवीर्यं धैर्ये हिमा-

33. द्रिं महसीह सूर्यं ॥ (15) गालांबिका तस्य ब-

34. भूव पत्नी महेश्वरस्येव महीध्रकन्या । विदर्भ-

35. पुत्रीव नलस्य विष्णो र्लक्ष्मीरिवेन्द्रस्य पुलोमजे-

36. व ॥ (16) । तनोरपाद्यत्रसुतो [8] सुता मांहिष्यां तस्यां-प्रसम्यां [9] कृति-

37. नानृपेण । पंचाहितक्ष्मापतिकुंजराणां पंचान-

---

[1] प्रमेतः in the text is a mistake for प्रतीतः.

[2] प्रतापाहिमभानुना is the correct reading.

[3] Read प्रतीपदारस्मित.

[4] राज्ञी is probably a mistake for राज्ञः.

[5] The letters in the 31st line which is at the bottom of the plate are crowded and hence not clear. मेदिनी is probably a mistake for गेहिनी; the reading is probably गेहिन्युदन्वत्तनये व विष्णोः.

[6] Read तस्याभवत्संगम.

[7] Read ससत्वतोगीतभुजाप्रतापः.

[8] Read तेनोदपाद्यन्त.

[9] Read प्रशस्याः.

(1) (2)

38. नाः पंचशराभिरूपाः ॥ (V. 17) हरिहरराय कम्पधरणी-

पति बु-

(3) (4) (5)

39. क्कमहीपरिवृढमारभूरमणमुद्धनृपाः खलु ते । अन-

40. घगुणेषु तेपु नवखण्डमहीश्वरतामभजत पूर्वजः

41. सतुयुधिष्टिर वन्महसा ॥ (18) सोयं निर्जित्याखिलदिग्वि-

42. भागान् सुत्रामधामांगकलिंग पूर्वैः[1] 1 उपास्यमानः

43. क्षितिपै श्च सर्वामुर्वीमशात् कुञ्जरकोण पुर्यां ॥ (19)-

कदाचिदु-

44. त्तीर्य स तुंगभद्रां क्षमाधिपालो मृगयाशिलाषदा[2] आ-

45. साद्य सैन्यैः सह तीरमस्यास्तद्दक्षिणं काननमीक्षतेस्य ॥

(20)

46. तस्मिन्वने कंचनसारमेय सदंशनाकाग्ररताग्र[3] मु-

47. ग्रं । स संगमेशाक्षि शशी शशं[4] च विसिस्मये वी-

क्ष्यदि-

48. शामधीशः[5] ॥ (21) क्षोणीपालो हरिहरइति श्रीवि-

रूपाक्षदे-

49. वं पंपादेवीसहचरमिमं वीक्ष्य भक्त्या च नम्रः[6] । सं

विन्-

---

[1] Better पूर्वान्.

[2] Read भिलाषात्.

[3] The text is not clear here. संदंशनैकाग्ररताग्रमुग्रं is proposed.

[4] I propose संगमासक्तशशं शंशी च.

[5] दिशामधीशः which means regent of the quarters does not suit the context. Read विशामधीश· lord of men. विशंपतिः.

[6] भता च नत्वा in text. The form of the letter त्वा ; is quite modern.

50. मूर्तिं[1] महिततपसं तस्य देवालयांते[2] (।) विद्यार-
51. ण्यं यतिमभजत श्रीमहेशानमन्यं ॥ (22) प्रणाम्य तस्यां
52. तिकसीम्नि भक्त्या तपोनिधिं ज्ञानकलानिधानं । वृ-
53. त्तांतमत्यद्भुतहेतुमेनं विज्ञापयामास विशेषवंद्य ॥ (23)-
54. त्रिकालविज्ञाननिधि(र्य)तीन्द्रो विहस्य किंचित्तमुवाच-
55. वीरं ।[3] राजन्महाराजकुलासिकाहासीभियमत्यंत-
56. बलैकमूलं ॥ (24) विद्याभिधानामलकानवद्यामिरावनं-
57. नाथ पुरीं विदध्याः । पुरीं नवद्वारवतीमुपेत्य पुरंद-
58. रश्रीःसकलांच पृथ्वीं ॥ (25) वीरश्रियो युद्धसमाहृतायाः वि-
59. हारभूमंटपतामुपेते । भुजेभुजंगेन्द्रसमे बिभर्ति[5] भ-
60. वानिति क्ष्मापतिमादिदेश ॥ (26) तथा हरिहरेश्व[6] सवि-
61. रचय्य[7] तच्छासनंनृपासनमुपासितसितातपत्रोज्व-
62. ऌः[8] विधाय खलु भोढशाप्रतिनिधोनि दानान्यहो[9]-
63. व्यराजत[10] विशालसीम्नि नगरे[11]. हि विद्याभिधे[12] ॥
(27)

---

[1] सवि at the end of line 49 in the text and न्मूर्तिं at the beginning of 50th line is written as नूर्तिं.

[2] देवालयेतो in text.

[3] Vidyáranya here asks Harihara to found the city of Vidyánagar.

[4] युद्रसामाहताया in text.

[5] बभर्तु in text.

[6] हरिहरेश्वर in text.

[7] रचैय्यं in text.

[8] Read मपास्थितो च्छ्रितसितातपत्रोज्वलः-

[9] दान्यनान्यहा in text.

[10] व्यराजम in text.

[11] नगर in text.

[12] The two letters (अष्ट) seem to have been engraved and then erased at the end of line 63. They are again written at the begin[n]ing of line 64.

Second plate, second side.

64. अष्टपंचयुगलैकसंख्यया संयुते नृप-

65. शकस्य वत्सरात् (रे) । धातृमाधववलक्षे(क्ष)सप्त-

66. मीं पुष्यतारहरिलग्नके भुजे ॥ (28) पट्टाभिषेको-

67. त्सवतः परस्ता(त्) पंपाविरूपाक्षमहेश्वरस्य । सत्स-

68. न्निधौ सत्यपराक्रमस्तु चक्रे महान्भूपतिरग्रहारं ॥ (29) वि-

69. श्वामित्रकुलीनाय आश्वलायनसूत्रिणो । रुकृशरवाध्या ।-

70. यिने वेदवेदान्तागमवेदिने ॥ (30) शंकु(?)केश[1] वभट्ट-स्यसून-

71. वेनंतसूरये । श्रौतस्मार्तसदाचार निरताय मनीषि-

72. णे ॥ (31) भूदानपात्रभूताय भूमिदेवाग्रयायिने विनी-

73. ताय विशिष्टाय विख्याताय महात्मने । (॥ 32) चंद्र गिर्या-

74. ख्यराज्ये तु पडनाडोस्तु सीमनि । नद्याः सुवर्णमुख्या-

75. याः[2] स्थले पुण्ये मनोहरे ॥ (33) प्राग्भागे पनलूरो स्तुचिल-

76. लूरोस्तु दक्षिणे । प्रतीच्यां गुनुपाडोस्तु उत्तरे चा-

77. नमेडुतः । कापलूरं महाग्रमं वासयोग्यं मनी-

78. षिणां ॥ (34) प्रातिनाम्ना हरिहरपुरमित्येव विश्रुतं[3] ।

79. सर्वमान्यं चतुः सीमासंयुतं च समंततः ॥ (35) निधि-

80. निक्षेपपाषाणसिद्धसाध्यजलान्वितं । अक्षिण्यागाभि-

81. संयुक्तमेकभोग्यं सभूरुहं ॥ (36) वापीकूपतटाकादिक च्छेना-[4]

---

[1] शकुकेशव in the text.

[2] यास्तु in the text.

[3] विरप्तं for विश्रुतं in the text.

[4] कधे for कच्छे in text.

82. पि च संयुतं । पुत्रपौत्रादिभिर्भोग्यंक्रमादाचन्द्रतार-

83. कं ॥ (37) हरिहरमहारायो माननीयो मनस्विनां । सहिर-

84 ण्यपयोधारपूर्वकं दत्तवान्मुदा ॥ (38) ग्रामस्य यजमान-

85. स्तु प्रतिगृह्याग्रहारकं । परिकल्प्य स वृत्तीस्तु षष्टि

86. चार्धं तदर्धकं ॥ (39) संस्थाप्य वृत्तीः त्रिंशत्ताः द्विजेभ्यो दत्त-

87. वान् मुदा । वृत्तिमंतो विलिख्यन्ते गोत्रसूत्रपुरस्सरं ॥ (40)

88. भारद्वाजकुलोद्भूतो बह्वृचो नंतयात्मजः । सिंगाभट्टः

89. सदाचारः वृत्तित्रयमिहाश्नुते ॥ (41) श्रीवत्सगोत्रसंभू-

90. तो याजुष स्तिम्मनात्मजः । मल्लभट्टस्तु दांतोयंवृत्ति-

91. [1]द्वयमिहाश्नुते ॥ (42) काश्यपस्तु यजर्वेदी नागणार्यस्य

92. नन्दनः । पोचनाख्यः सुशीलोयं वृत्तिद्वयमिहाश्नते ॥ (43)

93. शाण्डिल्यगोत्रसंभूतमाधवस्य तनूभवः । याजुषो मल्लभट्टा-

94. ख्यो वृत्तिद्वयमिहाश्नुते ॥ (44) हरितस्तु यजुर्वेदीचेल्लपि-

95. ल्लात्मजः सुधीः । विद्वां स्तु नारिभट्टोयं वृत्तिद्वयमिहाश्नुते ॥ (45)

Third plate, first side.

96 श्रीमद्वामन मुद्रांकशिलाशासनचिह्नित । अवधयोलिख्यं-

---

[1] द्व the shape of the letter is quite modern.

(*Telugu.*)

97. ते त्र लक्षणैर्देशभाषया ॥ (46) कापलूरिकिपरनाममै-

98. नहरिहररायपुरमनेडिसर्वमान्यं अग्रहारं व-

99. ध य शासनं विवरं ॥ तू र्पुकुकापलूरिगुनुपाडि-

100. नडुमपुट्टछुद्ददरायिमेर । आग्नेयानकु कुचिका-

101. डुपोल्मेरकूडिन पातुरायिमेर । दक्षिणानकु अंन

102. मेडिपोलं कापलूरिपोलं कूडिनद्दुतुंमचेट्टव

103. ट्टपातुरोयिमेर । नैरुतिमूल नर्यतपल्लं नहुमिरा

104. यमेर । पडमटिकिपनुलुरिनडुममामिडिकालु

105. व मेर । वायव्यानकुवोजिलपोल कूडिनपाति

106. न रोयि मेर । उत्त्ररानकु चिलुमतुपोलं कूडिन-

107. दि नवब्रदरोयिमेर । यीशान्यं कुर्रुगोड पोलंकू-

108. डि नपातिन रायिमेर ॥ यि[1] दमरिवलराजशासन-

(*Sanskrit.*)

109. मधुकरकं का [2]रगीतमाहात्म्य [3]राज्ञो हरिहरनृपतेःशा-

110. सनमचलैकपारि जातस्य ॥ (47) दानपालनयोर्मध्येदा-

111. नाच्छ्रयोनुपालनं । दानत्स्वगमवाप्नोतिपालनादच्यु-

112. तं पदं ॥ (48) एकैवभगिनी लोके सर्वेषामेव भूभु-
जां । नभो-

113. ग्या न करग्राह्या विप्रदत्ता वसुधरा ॥ (49) सामान्योय-

114. धर्मसेतु र्नृपाणां कालेकाले पाललनीयो भवद्भिः । सर्वानि-

115. तान् भाविनः पार्थिवेन्द्रान् भूयोभूयो याचते रामचन्द्रः ॥
(50) ॥ श्री विरूपाक्ष

---

[1] Read इद.

[2] Read झेंकार.

[3] Read माहात्म्यं । In other inscriptions it is महात्मनः.

COPPER-PLATE No. 16. (A.D. 1515–16.)

Nágulavaram grant of Krishnaráya, S.S. 1437.

[From the Collector's office, Nellore.]

Note.

The following transcript was made from the original copper-plates which are preserved in the Collector's office, Nellore. They are five in number measuring 9 inches × 7¼ inches. Their tops are a little raised and have holes for a ring which is not now in existence. The inscription is in Nandinágari and with the exception of the portion giving the boundaries is in Sanskrit verse. The letters are very badly shaped and the text is full of mistakes.

The grant is one of Krishṇadévaráya. The first 46 lines which give an account of his predecessors are the same as in other similar grants (*vide* Pólépalli grant) and have not been transcribed. The next portion says that Krishṇadévaráya defeated Vírabhadra Gajapati, son of Rudra of Koṇḍavíḍu, captured him, and made him his servant. We know that this was in S.S. 1437. The date of the grant was 1437; evidently it immediately followed the capture of Koṇḍavíḍu.

The gift was of Nágulavaram to a Brahman astronomer named Súra Bhaṭṭa, son of Rámabhaṭṭa and of a field named Timmayapáḷem and measuring 2,250 *kuṇṭas* for the maintenance of that village. It was made at the request of Gaṅga Reḍḍi or Gangádhara, son of Viṭṭa, who had the *birudas* Karpúravasantaráya, Kancharkaládri, Basava Śankara, Ghaṇṭánáda, Suhémádridánachintámani, Rája-véśyá Bhujanga, Chanchumallúra Chúrakára, Jagannab-baragaṇḍa and Rúpanáráyaṇa. He was evidently a Reḍḍi chief who accepted Krishnaráya's lordship at the very commencement of his exploits on the east coast.

His name does not, it seems, appear in any other recorded inscription.

Some of the *birudas* are those of the Reḍḍi chiefs:—
Karpúra Vasantaráya, the king of spring; the king evidently participated in the spring festival in which camphor used to be scattered about.

Kanchárkaládri--is not intelligible.

Basava Śankara—a form of Śiva.

Ghantánáda—who has the right to be heralded by a bell.

Hémádridána Chintámani—a philosopher's stone in giving the gifts prescribed by Hémádri, *i.e.*, one who gave all these gifts.

Rájavéśyá bhujanga—the paramour to the prostitutes who are other kings.

Chanchumallúra Chúrákára--the destroyer of Chanchumallúra (?)

Jagannabbaraganḍa—the sole hero in the world.

Rúpanáráyaṇa--a Náráyaṇa in beauty.

Translation.

The first 46 lines are not translated.

Vs. 1 and 2. In the Śáliváhana Śaka year 1437, in the year Yuva, in the month of Śrávaṇa, in the bright fortnight, on the holy full moon day, (*i.e.*, on the day of a lunar eclipse (lit. when the moon was swallowed by Ráhu).

V. 3. Being in the presence of Mallikárjuna at the shrine of Bháskara in Ṣríśaila (Krishnadévaráya made the following grant).

Vs. 3 to 5. Having captured alive in battle Vírabhadra Maháráya, son of king Rudra, in the city of Konḍavíḍu and having made him who had come under his control by the strength of his arm his servant, Krishnadéva Mahárâya, king of the Carnatic, (became) renowned.

Vs. 5 to 10. King Gangá Reḍḍi, who was the moon of the ocean of the glorious Panṭa race, the son of king Viṭṭa (Chinta ?), the best of rulers of the earth, who never even in a dream even uttered the words "There is nothing" (*i.e.*, I cannot give you anything) to suppliants; he has the *biruda* "Santatakarpúra Vasantaráya" on earth; his seal (bears) the titles "Kanchárkaládriráya" and "Basava Śankara," the lord who is heralded by a bell, who is a glorious "Hémádridána Chintámani," who is adorned with "Ráyavéśyábhujanga" and other *birudas*, who is "Chanchumalluchúrakára," and who has the *biruda* "Rúpa Náráyana;"

V. 10. Who is resplendent with the *biruda* "Jagannabbaragaṇḍa."

Vs. *10* and *10½*. He, Gangádhára, being devoid of fear, pleased Krishnaráya, the lord of the Carnatic, with the valiant deeds achieved by his arm; beholding him he said:—

Vs. 11 to 13. "O King Krishnaráya, whose lotus feet are made resplendent by the rubies of the diadems of kings, who hast the *biruda* 'Múruráyaraganda,' "O my Lord, many forts will come to us this year"; thus often, O my Lord, the Brahman (named) Súraya formerly said; whose grandfather is Ráyaja. He is versed in phonetics, and in the science of omens, he is skilled in predicting the future, he is a master of the *mantras* and knows the meaning of the Védas.

V. 14. Seeing his proficiency in (the science of) the movements of the planets, being delighted in mind, I shall give this Brahman the village Nágulavaram.

V. 15. May the village bringing fame to you, O my Lord, and an illustrious copper-plate charter for it be granted by my Lord to the astronomer Súraya."

Vs. 16 and 17. Having heard this, having at once presented a quantity of cloths and ornaments to the wise Súryárya, and having pleased (him), Krishnaráya said "I will give the village Nágulavaram mentioned by you to him" and granted (it).

Vs. 17 to 21. Krishnadéva Maháráya, who is worthy of honour among wise men, being surrounded by many assiduous and amiable learned men who are followers of the path of Dharma, who excel in eloquence and who are headed by the family priest, joyfully gave with libation of water and gift of gold, the village as a *sarvamánya*, up to its four boundaries everywhere, with its hidden treasures, deposits, stones, actuals, outstandings and water, with its *akshini* and *ágámi*, with its ponds, wells, tanks and embankments, as an 'ékabhógyam,' with its trees, to be enjoyed in succession by sons, grandsons, etc., (of the grantee) as long as the moon and the sun endure.

Vs. 22 and 23. Having granted the village, the king gave a copper-plate edict appertaining to it. The description of that village Nágulavaram is now given.

Vs. 23 to 26. It is situated in the *rájya* of Udayáchala (Udayagiri), and in the *síma* named Jaladanki; it is well known and is included in Pákanáḍu.[1] It lies to the east of the village Jakképalli, Gumudvúru, to the south of the hamlets named Ámódúlu and Tállúru, to the

---

[1] On p. 56 of Epig. Ind., Vol. V, it is stated that Pákanáḍu extended from Konḍaviḍu to Kandukúr. The present inscription shows that the southern boundary must be shifted below Kandukúr. Verse 37 indicates that this copper plate was not prepared at the time of the grant. Verses 3 to 5 hardly seem relevant to the grant.

south-west of the *agrahára* Biṭraguṇṭa, to the west of the town Chágavólu, to the north-west of the town Dámavaram, and to the north-east of the village Vítupódu.

Vs. 27 and 28. The owner of the village is next written. Súrabhaṭṭa of the Rébha Káṣyapa *gótra*, son of Ṣrí Rámabhaṭṭa, intelligent, follower of the Rig Véda, versed in the (science of), the movements of the stars, passed master in *yantras* (astronomical and other instruments), an astronomer versed in the science of Yámala [Rudrayámala a certain treatise on *mantra*] and of good character.

V. 29. The Mahárâya and Gangá Reḍḍi having given the village,—May Súrayárya, the owner of the village, prosperously flourish for a long time on earth.

V. 30. This is the edict of the heroic Krishṇaráya, who is a very tree of paradise to suppliants on earth, and whose hand resembles in (making) gifts the tree of Balaṣásana (Indra) (*i.e.*, the tree of paradise).

V. 31. By the order of Krishnadéva Mahárâya, Sabhápati (the Court poet) composed this sweet composition of the copper-plate edict.

V. 32. Next are described in the provincial language (Telugu) the boundaries—the banks, trees and stone pillars of that village beginning from the east.

[Here comes a long list in Telugu of the boundary marks of the village which it is unnecessary to translate.]

Stanzas 20, 21 and 22 of Pólépalli grant.

V. 33. In the Ṣaka year, reckoned by the sages (7), the Rámas (3), and the worlds (14), in 1437 (in Telugu figures), in the holy Yuva year, in the auspicious month named Ṣrávana, on the full moon *tithi*, when the moon had gone into the mouth of Ráhu (*i.e.*, on the day of lunar eclipse), the victorious and glorious king Ṣrí

Krishnaráya gave the village Nágulavaram to the astronomer Súra.

Vs. 34 to 36. For the subsistence of that village Nágulavaram the king gave a field named Timmayapálem measured up to the margin of the tank, situated in wet fields, having water, rich in paddy, marked by a stone idol of the *múlasthána* Siva and measured with a pole of 32 feet in length. He granted 2,000 + ¼ (*i.e.*, of 2,000) or 2,500 *kuntas*.

V. 36½. "Let the high-souled (Súraya) enjoy this (village) as long as the moon and stars endure."

V. 37. Having said this, the heroic Krishnaráya, king of kings, prosperously ruled the kingdom for a long time with fame, righteousness and valour.

Vs. 38 and 39 are two common imprecatory verses.

V. 40. They do not call poison, poison. The property of a Brahman is called poison. Poison kills one alone, but the property of a Brahman kills sons and grandsons.

Vs. 41 and 42 are two other common imprecatory verses.

Srí Virúpáksha.

Second plate, second side.

The first forty-six lines are identical with the verses at the beginning of Pólépalli grant.

47. शालिवाहनि [1] निर्णीते शकाब्दे सचनुः शतेः । सप्तत्रिश-

48. त्समायुक्तैः संख्याते दशाभिः शतैः । [॥ 1] युवसंवत्सरे शुक्लपक्षे श्रा-

[1] Read शालिवाहननिर्णीत.

49. वणमासिच । पौर्णमास्यां पुण्यायां[1] राहुग्रस्तेनिशाकरे ॥
[2] श्री-

50. शैले भास्करक्षेत्रे मल्लिकार्जुनसंनिधौ । [2]वीरभद्रमहारायं
तनयंरु-

51. द्रभूपतेः ॥ [3] जीवग्राहं गृहीत्वाजौ[3] कृत्वाकिंकरमा[5]
त्मनः । कोंडवी-

52. डिपुरं[4] वाहा[5] बलेनतामवशं गते[6] ॥ [4] क्रिष्णदेवमहारयः[7]
ख्यातः कर्णाट-

53. केश्वरः । क्रिष्णरायं महीपालमौलिलालितशासनं ॥ [5]
तं दृष्वा नरना-

54. थःश्री[8] पंटवंशाब्धि-चंद्रमाः ।

55. वित्त[9] क्ष्मापसुतो गंगारेड्डिर्भूनाय- ।

56. कोत्तमः ॥ [6] नास्तीति शब्दमात्रं स्वमेपि च याचके-
षुनोक्तो[10]यः । सोपि

57. धरण्यां संततकर्पूरवसंतराय बिरुदांकः ॥ [7] कंचार्क-
लाद्रि-

Third plate, first side.

58. रायबक(स)व[शंक]रांकितशासनः। घांटानाद[11] सुहमाद्रिदा

59. नवचिन्तामणि विभुः ॥ [8] रायवेश्याभुजंगादिबिरुदांकित-
शोभनः च-

---

[1] Read सपुण्यायां on account of metre.

[2] There seems to be a break here.

[3] त्वाजा in the text.

[4] Read पुरे.

[5] बांहा in the text.

[6] गतः in the text.

[7] Is after श्री in text.

[8] Here क्रि is written for कृ in कृष्णराय throughout.

[9] The letters वित्त are not clear. The name may be chinta.

[10] Read नोच्चे.

[11] Read घंटानाद

60. चुमछ्चूरकारो रूपनारायणांकितः ॥ [9] जगन्नब्बरगं-
डांकबिरु-

61. देन विराजितः । गंगाधरोपि श्री क्रिष्णरायंकर्नाटकेश्वरं ॥
[10] सं-

62. तोषर्द्धि हतत्रासः[1] स्वभुजार्जितविक्रमैः । [$10\frac{1}{2}$] भूपा-
लमौलिमाणिक्य-

63. रंजितांध्रिद्वयांबुज । मूरुरायर गंडांक क्रिष्णरायमहीपते ॥
[11] स्वामि-

64. न्नो बहवो दुर्गाः संभवंतीह वत्सरे । इत्युक्तोयंतु[2] दैवज्ञः
पूर्वस्मिन्

65. बहुधाप्रभो ॥ [12] स्वरज्ञः शकुनज्ञश्च दैवज्ञो मंत्रपारगः
वेदार्थ-

66. वित्सूरयार्यो रायजोस्य पितामहः ॥ [13] अस्य ग्रहगति-
ज्ञत्वं वीक्ष्याहं

67. हर्षमानसः । दास्यामिनागुलवरग्राममस्मै द्विजायच ॥ [14]
भवत्की-

68. र्तिकरं ग्रामं तस्य श्रीताम्रशासनं । स्वामिनादि(दी)यतां
देवसूरज्यौति-

69. षिकायच ॥ [15] । इति श्रुत्वा क्रिष्णरायो वस्त्राभरणसं-
चयं । दत्वासंतोष्य[3]

70. सूरयार्याय धीमते ॥ [16] त्वयोक्तंनागुलवरमस्मै दस्यामि
सहसामिस्वया-[4]

---

[1] The verses 4 to $10\frac{1}{2}$ have no predicate.

[2] The lines in the text are not clear here. इत्युक्तोयंतु is perhaps a mistake for इत्युक्तवांस्तु.

[3] Three syllables are wanting here.

[4] Read दास्यामहत्यदात्.

71. त् । सर्वमान्यं चतुःसीमासंयुतंचसमंततः ॥ [17] निधि निक्षेपपाषाण-

72. सिद्धसाध्यजलान्वितं । अक्षिण्यगामिसंयुक्तमेकभोग्यंसमू-रुहं ॥ [18]

73. वापीकूपतटाकैश्चकच्छेनापिसमन्वितं । पुत्रपौत्रादिभि र्भोग्यं-

74. क्रमादाचंद्रतारकं ॥ [19] परीतः प्रयतैः स्निग्धैः पुरोहित[1] पुरो-

75. गमैः । विविधै र्विबुधै र्धर्मपथिकैरधिकै र्गिरा ॥ [20]

76. ष्णदेवमहारायो॰ माननीयो मनस्विनां । साहिरण्य-

77. पयोधारापूर्वकं दत्तवान्मुदा ॥ [21] ग्रामं दत्वा महारायोददौ-

78. तत्ताम्रशासनं ॥ [22] तन्नागुल्वरग्रामलक्षणं वक्ष्यतेधुना । उदया-

Third plate, second side.

79. चलराज्यस्थं जलदंक्याख्यसीमानि ॥ [23] विख्यातंपां-कनाड्वंतर्भा-

80. वंचापिसमाश्रितं । जक्केपल्लिगुमुद्रूरुग्रामतः प्राग्दिशिस्थितं ॥ [24] चा-

81. मोदुलुताल्लूरु[नाम]पल्लीभ्यां दक्षिणे स्थि[त]तं । बिटगुंटाग्रहा-रस्य नैरृत्यां दि-

82. शि संस्थितं ॥ [25] चोगवालुपुरात्पश्चात् स्थितं दामवं-रात् पुरात् । वायव्यां-

83. दिशि वेतुपोडुग्रामस्ये शान्यतः स्थितं [॥ 26] लिख्यते-ग्राममनाथस्तु वेदवेदां-

84. गपारगः । रेभकाश्यपगोत्रश्रीरामभट्टात्मजः सुधीः ॥ [27] बहु-

---

[1] पु is repeated in the text.

85. चः सूरभट्टार्यो ज्योतिषांगतिकोविदः । यंत्रज्ञो भूभगोलज्ञो[1]

86. यामलज्ञः सुशीलवान् ॥ [28] दत्वाग्रामं महारयो गंगारे-
-ड्डिश्च भूतले ।

87. ग्रमाधिपः सूरयार्यो वर्त्तते सुचिरं श्रिया ॥ [29] तदिद-
-15मवनीवनीपक-

88. चि विबुधरायस्य[2] क्रिष्णरायस्य । शासनमिति बल-

89. शासनतरुकरदा-

90. नस्यसापदानस्य [॥ 30] क्रिष्णदेवमहारायशासनेनसभा-
-पतिः । अभाणी- ।

91. त्मृदुसंदर्भंतदिदं ताम्रशासनं ॥ [31] तस्य ग्रामस्य
सामान[3]

92. जलाशयमहातरून् । प्रागादितः शिलास्तंभान् लिख्यते
देशभाष-

93. या ॥ [32] ॥ बूरितूर्पुयाचेर्वुकट्ट[अ]ाआग्नेयं बूडिद-

94. पाडुपडमरपारिनर्चीकिरेनुलकट्टवमीदि वेलगचेट्टु । करकट्ट ।
तेरुपुडटिगडि उय्यालपल्लि-

95. यरेशानिकुंट । आपडमटिकरकट्टमीदि विदुलप-

96. डियकालुव धारमारचेट्टु । वागुदांटिवीकिरेनुल-

97. करकट्ट । आकरकट्टदक्षिणं नल्लगुल्लवा-

98. गु, नल्लगुंल्लवागु नैरुति पेद्दद तिपूप ॥

---

[1] भूगोल and भगोल (astronomy).

[2] रायसो in text. The reading should be मवनीवनीपकविबुधराजस्य.

[3] The construction of the sentence is wrong. It may be corrected to तस्य ग्रामस्य सामीनः जलाशयमहीरुहाः । प्रागादितः शिलास्तंभाः लिख्यन्ते देशभाषया ।

Fourth plate, first side.

99. आवलिवादरगट्ट । आवलिनछुगुंछुउ-
100. न्न पेदनचेलुमलकुंठ । आ पडमर पेद्दु चवुलु ।
101. आ नैऋति औदूदलरेवटि दीक्षणं वेलंगलकुंठ । आप-
102. डमर वालुंगुलमुय्यचु निलुवुरायि । आउत्तरं मछ्लपगुं-
103. टलोनि पानुरायि । आकुंटकुनूर्पुगा बारिन करकट्ट मदिसू
104. र्यचंद्रलुवोट्टिन पेद्ददनछुगुंडु । पलुगुराछुकट्ट
105. व आ उत्तरंगानु पारिन करकरकट्ट । जुव्वुल-
106. गुंटतोट्टुकालुवलकट्टमीदि निलुवुरायि । आजु-
107. व्वुल्वगुंटतूर्पु चेलिक्यलोनि जुव्विमानु । ऊरिकिवाय-
108. व्यं चितमानि उत्तरं मोरवंपु निलुवुरायि उत्तरं
109. चवलका तूर्पु मुंच्चुमरि । आ तूर्पु बट्टगुणा-
110. लगुटं । अंटुकु ईशान्यभाननुरेंटगुटकु-
111. पच्चालदिन्न । व्रालुव्रासिन निलुवुरायि मछ्लगुंट ।
112. आ तूर्पुमूय्यलगुंट अनो निलुवुरायि । आदक्षि-
113. णं करवहि कलेवलकुंटआग्नेयंकडु-
114. वदंड निलुवुरायि । यर्रचेरुवु दक्षिणपु को-
115. मु निलुवु रायि ॥ * *

Lines 115 to 119. Verse 20 in Pólépalli grant.

Fourth plate, second side.

Lines 119 to 123. Verse 21 in Pólépalli grant.

123. * * ॥ शाकाब्दे.
124 मुनिरामलोकसद्दशे [1] । १४३७ शुद्धे । युवे वत्सरे मा-
125. सि श्रावणसंज्ञिते शुभतरे सत्पूर्णिमायां तिथौ ।
126. राहोराननगे विधौ सविजयश्री क्रिष्णरायो ददौ

---

[1] सद्दशे is a mistake for सहिते.

127. सूरज्यौतिषिकायनागुलवरं ग्रामं महीवल्लभः ॥ [33]
128. तन्नागुलवरग्रामग्रातार्थं प्रददौ प्रभुः । नाम्ना
129. तमभयपाल्यं च तटाकप्रांतसंमितं[1] ॥ [34] केदारसं-
130. स्थितं क्षेत्रं सजलं व्रीहिपूरितं । मूलसयन वहेसा-
131. शसाद्वाबिंध[2] शिलांकितं ॥ [35] द्वात्रिंश[3] त्पादमि-
तिना

Fifth plate, first side.

132. शलोकेन विनिर्मितं । द्विसहस्त्रमितान् कुंटान् सपा-
133. दसहितान्[4] ददौ ॥ [36] आचंद्रतारकं चैतिअनुभ-
विति (चानुभवत्विति) मही
134. पमि[ः । ॥36½] इत्युक्त्वा राजराजेंद्रः क्रिष्णरायः प्रता-
प(व)ा-
135. न् । क्रीत्यी र्त्या[5] प्रतापेन राज्यं[6] चक्रे चिरं श्रिया ॥
[37][7] एकै-
136. व भगिनी लोके सर्वेषामेव भूभुजां । न भोग्यानकरग्राह्या
विप्रदत्ता
137. वसुंधरा ॥ [38] स्वदत्ताद्द्विगुणं पुण्यं परदत्तानुपालनं ।
परदत्तापहारे-
138. ण स्वदत्तं निष्फलं भवेत् ॥ [39] न विषं विषमित्याहु
र्ब्रह्मस्वं विष मुच्यते । वि-
139. षमेकाकिनं हन्ति ब्रह्मस्वं पुत्रपौत्रकं ॥ [40] स्वदत्तां
परदत्तांवा यो हरे-

---

[1] समिरं in text.

[2] The reading may be मूलस्थानमहेशानबिंब्रशिलिशिलाङ्कितं.

[3] द्वत्रंश in text.

[4] सपादुसाहितान् in text.

[5] कीर्त्या नीत्या.

[6] रा is written as ग ।

[7] त stands for ए.

140. त दसुंधरां । षष्टिं वर्षसहस्राणि विष्टायां जायते कृमिः ॥ [41] ॥

141. सामान्योयं धर्मसेतु र्नृपाणां कालेकाले पालनीयो भवद्भिः ।

142. सर्वानेतान् भाविनः पार्थिवेंद्रान् भूयो भूयो याचते रामचंद्रः ॥ [॥ 42] श्री विरूपाक्ष

Copper-plate No. 17. (A.D. 1254–55.)

[Śárngapuram grant of Śárngadhara.] (S.S. 1176.)

Note.

This grant is engraved on five copper-plates 10 inches × $5\frac{1}{4}$ inches connected by a ring whose exterior diameter is 4 inches. The ring bears a seal the figure on which is not clear owing to corrosion. The plates are all engraved on both sides and the edges have not been raised as in most grants. On the left of the first side of the first plate are figures of the *chakra*, *śanku*, and boar one below the other, and between the figure of the *śanku* and the boar is the letter *Śrí* engraved in big type.

The character is Telugu and the language is Sanskrit verse with the exception of the part relating to the boundaries of the village which was granted. The writing is in a fair state of preservation. The letters on the first plate are small while those on the other plates are big. The writing is breadthwise. The first verse is an invocation to the Boar incarnation of Vishnu. Verse 2 says that there was a Kákati king by name Prólaya. Verses 3 to 7 relate to his grandson Gaṇapati. Verse 8 says that Gaṇapati's vassal was Mádhava, son of Sauri

Suvara. From verse 9 it appears that he was the ruler of Addanki in Ongole taluk, Nellore district. Verse 9 says that Mádhava's son was Ṣárngadhara, of the Ṣálankáyana *gótra*. He is the donor of this grant—he was also known as Chakra Náráyaṇa[1].

The inscription next says that for the merit of his master (Gaṇapati) Śárngadhara granted the village of Ṣárngpuram to Brahmans with a gift of cash after making due obeisance to them. The date of the grant was Monday; the 10th *tithi* of the bright fortnight of Phálguna of the year Ánanda, corresponding to S.S. 1176. The year is given both in Telugu figures and by the usual method of reckoning by names denoting digits.

Forty-seven shareholders are enumerated with their *gótra*. Of these the first forty-two have equal shares; the last three are said to be *nischala bháginas* the meaning of which term is not clear; it probably means 'invariable shareholders' and the 43rd and 44th shareholders get 2 shares. Each share consists of one *gócharma*. Verse 28 says that 1 *gócharma* = 10 *nivartanas* and 1 *nivartana* = 30 rods (*daṇḍam*, measured with a rod of 10 cubits (*hasta*).

Next comes a description of the boundaries in Telugu.

Vs. 29 to 34 are 5 of the usual imprecatory verses.

At the end of line 87 is engraved the figure of a *chakra*.

The inscription then invokes the blessing of the Boar. At the beginning of line 88 is the figure of the boar.

The grant closes with a verse stating that king Ṣrí Chakra Náráyana (Ṣárngadhara) granted the village

---

[1] Chakra Náráyaṇa is simply a title of Ṣárngadhara.

Śárngapuram to learned Bráhmans. The plate was got from the *archaka* of the temple at Mannepalli of Darsi Division. We are told that a hamlet called Sárnapuram exists in the Ongole taluk.

TRANSLATION.

V. 1. Om! Hail. May the Boar, the glorious supporter of the earth (Vishnu), the beloved consort of his wife, viz., the earth, give (happiness) to all up to the mountain which encircles the earth who formerly, joyfully desiring to take her away (from the ocean), made his broad, delicate and white tusk which dispels misfortunes a present to her like a very beautiful kétaki flower.

V. 2. King Prólaya, who is the ornament of the glorious Kákati race, who is very renowned in the world, he alone is sung by poets as king Bali in (of) the Kali age.

V. 3. By the power of austerities performed (by him) formerly (*i.e.*, in previous births), and by the austerities of the whole world there was born to that king a son who was a ruler of the world as if Mahádéva (Ṣiva) himself.

V. 4. This king was surely Mahádéva the lord of the Universe; if not, how indeed can Gaṇapatidéva himself have been his son?

V. 5. When king Gaṇapati, the store-house of knowledge and the embodiment of pleasure was born, the whole Universe opened (with joy) just as the lotus (opens) when the moon rises.

V. 6. His belly is not hanging (*i.e.*, large like that of Gaṇapati, Gaṇésa), nor was there association with the double-tongued (*i.e.*, snakes); nor is his face crooked. Oh wonder that he is called Gaṇapati by people!

V. 7. By fulfilling the desires of suppliants, by seizing the wealth of enemies and by protecting the host of kings he is surely Gaṇapati himself.

V. 8. There is a king Mádhava, who is a very bee delighting in the pollen which is the service of the lotuses which are his feet (of Ganapati), son of Sauṛi Suravara, brave by reason of being compassionate.

V. 9. There was born to the ruler of the city of Addanki a good son, a ruler of men, of the Ṣálankáyana *gótra*, destroyer of enemies, of excellent fame, named Śárngadhara (bearer of the discus).

V. 10. Honoured for his might resembling that of all the regents of the earth he always delighted all (his) subjects; he is praised as the moon by them.

V. 11. In Sáka whose year was Ánanda, reckoned by the tastes (6), the sages (7), the Ṣivas (11), in 1176 (in Telugu figures), on the 10th (*tithi*) of the bright fortnight of Tapasya (Phálguna), on Monday,

V. 12. Having respectfully summoned Brahmans who were thoroughly versed in the Vedas and vedangas, and who were endowed with virtues, and having honored (them) according to the prescribed rules,

V. 13. That king, having wished "May there be religious merit to my Lord," gave to them the village called Ṣárngapuram with a gift (of money).

V. 14. Having given the village up to the boundaries, along with the eight enjoyments, and with power and ownership, to these (Brahmans), he, possessed of modesty, said (as follows).

V. 15. "My folded hands are raised to the head (*i.e.*, I give salutation) to those (rulers) who protect my charity whether (those) rulers are of my lineage, or of the lineage of my enemies or others."

V. 16. The recipients there (of the charity) are—

Names of Brahmans.	Name of Gótra.
1. Ṣrídhara	Śrívatsa.
2. Koppana	
3. Kosanéyárya	
4. Muppana	Háriti.
5. Kéśava	
6. Ananta	
7. Perumádi	
8. Komana	
9. Viṭṭala	
10. Pekana	
11. Ranganátha	
12. Kéśava	
13. Máraya	
14. Prólidéva	
15. Nágadéva	
16. Márayárya	
17. Ellayárya	Śáṇḍilya.
18. Kommanárya	
19. Muttanárya	
20. Dévana	
21. Áditya	Kauṇḍinya.
22. Svámidéva	
23. Kámana	
24 Máraya	
25. Vennaya	
26. Bólaya	
27. Prólaya	Kauśika.
28. Dévana	
29. Prólidéva	
30. Kéśava	
31. Dónayárya	Bhárgava.
32. Kommanárya	Káśyapa.
33. Kéśavárya	
34. Śúranárya	

Names of Brahmans.		Name of Gótra.
35. Rebbana	... ...	Bháradvája.
36. Remana	... ...	
37. Nágadéva	... ...	
38. Kommanárya	... ...	Âtréya.
39. Tammenárya	... ...	
40. Bolayárya	... ...	
41. Erram Potárya	...	
42. Vishnuvriddha	...	Gautama.
43. Kámadéva	... ...	Śáṇḍilya.
44. Oppanárya	... ...	
45. Márayárya	... ...	Háriti.
46. Nárayana	... ...	Kauṇḍinya.
47. Súrana ...	... ...	

V. 26. All the (first) forty-two recipients are equal sharers. But the last three are invariable sharers (?)

V. 27. The middle two, Oppana (and the other) have here $\frac{1}{4}$ of 8, *i.e.*, 2 shares (?)

For each of these a land measuring only one *gocharma* is apportioned.

V. 28. A *nivartana* consists of 30 rods measured with a rod of 10 cubits in length. Ten of those (*nivartanas*) is a *gocharma*. By gift of that (*i.e.*, a góchARMA), imperishable bliss accrues.

Then the marks of the boundaries (are given) in the provincial language (Telugu).

(Here follows a long passage giving the boundaries which it is unnecessary to translate).

[Imprecatory verses.]

V. 29. The earth has been given by many kings commencing with Sagara. Of whomsoever the land is, of him is the merit.

V. 30. A charity made even by an enemy should be protected with care. An enemy indeed is an enemy. Charity may not be the enemy of any one.

V. 31. Of giving (oneself) and of maintaining (another's grant), the maintenance (of another's grant) is superior to giving (oneself). By giving (oneself) one obtains heaven; (but) by protecting (another's gift) one gets imperishable bliss.

V. 32. He who resumes land given by himself or by another is reborn a worm in ordure for 60,000 years.

V. 33. Whoever misappropriates one cow, or one gem, or one inch of land even, goes to hell up to the dissolution of the elements.

V. 34. This general bridge of morality of kings should be followed constantly by you. Thus Ráma-chandra entreats again and again all these future kings.

May the illustrious Boar protect!

May there be great prosperity!

[Here is a figure of a discus]—the discus ||

[Here is a figure of a boar]—the Boar ||

Ṣrí Ṣrí Ṣrí!

V. 35. The illustrious Chakra Náráyana, the accomplished, the ruler of earth, having worshipped Brahmans who were descended from a pure race, who were spotless, purified by good acts (Karma—sacrament or rite), devoted to study and teaching (of the vedas), perfect, devoted to dharma, proper, versed in Kalpa (rules of ritual), commentaries, logic and ethics, gave them (the village) Ṣárngapuram.

First plate, first side.

1\. ओं। स्वस्ति श्री धरणी[1]वरो वितरतादाचक्रवाळं किरिर्वि-श्व स्मै

2\. वसुधावधूप्रियवरः स स्तांजगांसुमुधा[2] । तस्यै स्वीय.

3\. विशालकोमलासितां दंष्ट्रामरिष्टापहां कतक्याः कुसुमं

4\. यथातिसुभगं कुर्वन् पुरोपायनम् (1) श्रीकाकतिकुलतिल-

5\. कप्रोलयभूपोति विश्रुतो लोके। कलिकाले बलिराजः केवल-

6\. मेवैषगीयते कविभिः । (2) तस्यपुराकृततपसां प्रभाव-तः सवलो-

7\. कतपसाच । समजायत भुवनपतिः स्वयमिव नृपतेः सुतो

8\. महादेवः । (3) नूनं स्वयमेवासौ भुवनपति र्भूपातिर्महा-

9\. देवः । नो चेद्गणपतिदेवः कथमिव तस्य स्वदंसुतो भूया-त् ॥ (4) उ-

10\. दिते गणपति नृपतौ कळानिधावमृतमूर्तौ च । उदमील-दखिलभु-

11\. वनं कैरव मिवकुमुदबांधवे भ्युदुते ॥ (5) नोलंबमानमुदरं

12\. नैवास्य जनो[3] द्विजिह्वजनभावः । नचवक्रमस्य तुण्डं गण-पतिरि-

13\. त्युच्यते जनैश्चित्रं । (6) अ र्थिजनार्थ विधानात्प्रत्य-र्थार्थापदायना(र्थिजन्मर्थहरण्पत)

First plate, second side.

14\. च्चा(श्च)पि । नरपतिगणपालनतो नूनमसौ गणपतिः स्वयंदे-वः । (7) तच्चरणकम-

---

[1] Read धरणीधरो. [2] Read यस्तांश्रिहर्षुर्मुदा । [3] Read नैवाप्यज्ञानि.

15. लसेवापरागपरितुष्टमानसभ्रमरः । शौरिसुवरवरतनुजः क-
रुणा-

16. धीनो स्तिमाधवो नृपतिः ॥ (8) अहंकिपुरेशादतस्तनूजो-
जनि[1] प्रजे-

17. शानः। शालंगायनगोत्रश्शार्ङ्गधरः शत्रुशासनः सुयशाः ॥
(9) अपिसर्व्व-

18. लोकपालप्रभावसंभावितः प्रजाः सर्व्वाः । आनंदयन्ननस्तं
द्विजराजः

19. कीर्त्यते सदा ताभिः ॥ (10) शाकेरसमुनीशान ११७६
गणितानंदवत्सरे(।) तप-

20. स्ये शुक्लपक्षस्य दशम्यां सोमवासरे । (11) अहूय ब्राह्म-
णान्भक्त्या

21. वेदवेदाङ्गपारगान् । श्रुतशील गुणोपेतान् संपूज्य च यथा-
विधि । (12)

22. भूयात्स्वस्वामिने पुण्यमित्याशास्य स भूपतिः । तेभ्यः सद-
क्षिणं ग्रा-

23. मं प्रादाच्छार्ङ्गपुराभिधं । (13) अष्टभागयुतं तेजःस्वा-
म्याम्यां चसमायु-

24. तं । आसीमा[2]ग्रामभेतेभ्यो दत्वाह विनयान्वितः ॥ (14)
स्ववंश्याः शत्रुः-

25. वंश्या वा परेवास्युं न्नराधिपाः । येपालयन्तिमेधर्मं तेभ्योमू-

Second plate, first side.

26. र्ध्नि कृतो ञ्जलिः । (15) तत्रप्रतिग्रहीतार आर्य्यौ श्रीध-
रकोम्मनो । कोसने-

---

[1] Read पुरेशात् सततनूजोजनि.

[2] Read आसीमग्राम.

27. यार्य इत्ये ते त्रय(:)श्रीवत्सगोत्रिण: । (16). मुप्पन:
केशवोऽनंत: मेरुमा-

28. दिश्च कोमन: । विठ्ठल: पेकनोरंगनाथ: केशवमारयौ ॥
(17) प्रोलिदे-

29. वो नागदेवो मारयार्य इतीरिता: । त्रयोदशद्विजवरा आ-

30. र्या हारीतगोत्रिण: ॥ (18) एछयार्य: कोम्मनार्यो मुत्तना-

31. र्येश्च देवन: । शाण्डिल्यगोत्रिणश्चैतेचत्वारो द्विजपुंग-

32. वा: । (19) आदित्य: स्वामिदेवश्च कामनो मारयस्तथा ।
वेन्न-

33. यो बेलयश्चेति कौंडिन्या: षड्वि[1]जोत्त मा: (20) प्रोल-
योदे-

34. वन: प्रोलिदेव: केशव इत्यमी । चत्वार: कौशिकाविप्रा-
दोन-

35. यार्यश्च भार्गव: (॥ 21) कोम्मनार्य्य: केशवार्य्य: सू-

36. रनार्य्यश्च काश्यपा: । रेब्बनो रेमनो नागदेवश्चेति द्वि-
जो-

Second plate, second side.

37. त्तमा: । (22) भारद्वाजास्त्रयो प्येते आत्रेय: कोम्मना-

38. र्य्यक: । तम्मेनार्य्यो बोलयार्य एछपोतार्य्य

39. इत्यमी । (23) गौतमो विष्णुवृद्धश्च कामदेवो द्विजो-
त्तम: । शा-

40. ण्डिल्यगोत्रसंभूतो ओप्पनार्य्यो द्विजोत्तम: । (24)
हरितान्व-

41. यसंभूतो मारयार्य्यो महाद्विज: । नाराय-

42. ण: सूरनश्च द्वावार्य्यौ कुण्डिनान्वयौ ॥ (25) इति प्रति-

---

[1] Read षड् द्विजो.

43. ग्रहीतारः सर्वोंपि समभागिनः । द्विचत्वारंशदंत्यास्तु
44. त्रयो निश्चलभागिनः । (26) मध्यस्थो ओप्पनार्य्यस्तु द्वये
45. ष्टर्धार्धभागिह ॥ प्रत्येकमेषां गोचर्ममात्रं

Third plate, first side.

46. क्षेत्रं प्रकल्पितं ॥ (27) दशहस्तेन दण्डेन त्रिंशद्दण्डा निवर्त-
47. मं । तान्येव दश गोचर्म तद्दानाद च्युतंपदं ॥ (28) अ-
48. थ सीमालक्षण्यान्यंध्र[1] भाषया ॥ *Telugu.* तूर्पुनगुंड-
49. कंम । अनंतरमालंजपाटि दक्षिणान वांगु । अ-
50. टुवच्चि देवतगुंडि तूर्प्पुन ननुमनंगूरिडोंक उति-
51. पुट्ट । अटुवच्चियसवलकुंट । अटुमड्डुपुगावच्चिनंन्नूरीशा-
52. न्यान कुशदर्भपडिय । अटुवच्चि नंनूरिवायव्यान नेल-
53. पडिय। अटुवच्चि(न)नूरिनैरृतिगोिल्लकुंट । अटुवाच्चि
54. नेत्रपाट । आग्नेयान पुद्द । अटुवाच्चि चिलुकलोटितूर्पुन

Third plate, second side.

55. नेत्रकुंट । चिलुकलोटि पडमट नेरु वांगु कूटमि । अ-
56. टुवच्चि कलवुलकुंट । अटुवच्चिलोंतुवांगु येंटं
57. गलाशिनकूटमि । अटुत्पटिदक्षिणान मड्डुपुगां दूर्पु
58. वाच्चिकोटिकालगट्ट पडुमटिप्रांतमु । अनंतरमा-
59. बोंमरमुगट्ट अटुमड्डुपुगांबीयि तू-
60. र्पुन वेमुलकालुव । अटुवाच्चियाग्नेयमु-
61. मूल दूबलगुंट । अटुवाच्चिमोगलिगुंडालपं-
62. चकुलगट्टु । अटुवच्चि नैऋतिमूलनेलगुंट । अ-
63. टुमड्डुपुगावाच्चि पडुमाटिसीमलुनेलपड्ड

[1] Read न्यांध्र.

Fourth plate, first side.

64. मुतोडिदूब । पूटि दक्षिणानंबोदटिताडिदूब ।
65. एटियुत्तरानंबक्कलपोदरु । अटुवच्चिव्राप्पिकुं-
66. ट । अटुमडुपुंगां दूर्पुवच्चि गुट्टतोटिपुट्ट । अटु अटु-
67. अटुवच्चिरेंटकुंटलु । अटुवच्चिचिलुकलेटिदक्षिणा-
68. नं चट्टतोडिगुड्ड । एटियुत्तरानं बक्कलतोडि-
69. पुट्ट । अटुवच्चि वायव्यमुदिक्कुवांगु । अटुवच्चिमं-
70. रूयनकुंट । अटुवच्चि ईशान्यमुदिक्कुन मांडूके-
71. श्वरमु पडुयटगुंडकंम । दीनिकिस्थलमु लंजेपा
72. डुंनु पिनक्कुंकुपाडुन्नु क्षेत्रमुपाडुन्नु । चाला-

Fourth plate, second side.

73. निकोंरकु मंगिलिगुंडालपोलमंदु पेट्टिंनारु ।

(Sanskrit.)

74. बहुभिर्वसुधादत्ता राजभिः सगरादिभिः ।
75. यस्ययस्ययथाभूमिस्तस्य तस्य तथाफ-
76. लं ॥ (29) शत्रुणापिकृतो धर्म्मो रक्षितव्यः प्रयत्न-
77. त शत्रु रेवाहिशत्रुः स्याद्धर्मः शत्रुर्नकस्यचित (30) ॥
78. दानपालनयोर्मध्ये दानाच्छ्रेयोऽनुपालनं । दानात्स्वर्ग-
79. मवाप्नोतिपालनादच्युतंपदं ॥ (31) स्वदत्तां परदत्तां
80. वायोहरेद्धि वसुंधराम् । षाष्टिं वर्षसहस्राणि
81. विष्ठायां जायते कृमिः ॥ (32) गामेकां रत्निका-

Fifth plate, first side.

82. मेकांभूमेरप्येकमङ्गलं । हरन्नरकमा- ।
83. मोति यावदाभूतसंप्लवं ॥ (33) सामान्योयं

(To face page 149.)

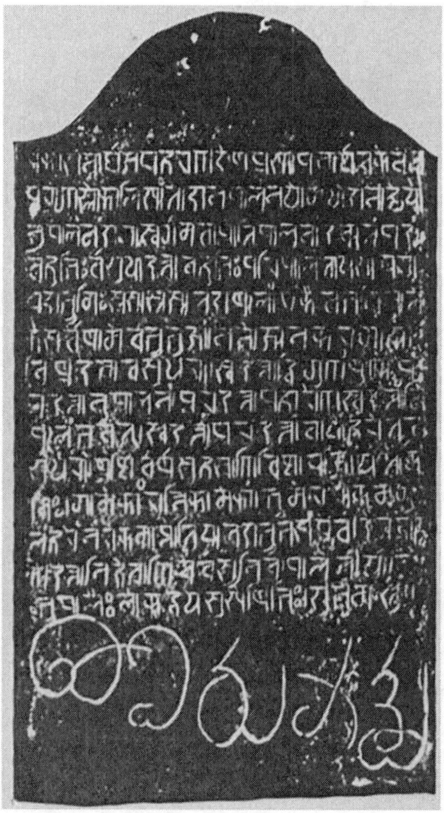

COPPER-PLATE NO. 18.

(8)

(To face page 140.)

COPPER-PLATE NO. 18.

(5)

(To face page 149.)

COPPER-PLATE NO. 18.

(To face page 149.)

COPPER-PLATE NO. 18.

(3)

(To face page 149.)

COPPER-PLATE NO. 18.

(2)

(To face page 140.)

COPPER-PLATE NO. 18.

(1)

84. धर्मसेतु नृपाणां कालेकाले पालनीयो
85. भवाद्भिः । सर्वानेतान् भाविनः पार्थिवें-
86. द्रान्भूयोभूयोयाचते रामचंद्रः ॥ (34) श्रीं-
87. धरणीधरोरक्षतु । मंगळमहाश्री चक्रं ॥
88. वराहः ॥ श्री श्री श्री ॥ विप्रांच्छुद्धाकु-
89. लोद्भवानविकलान्सत्कर्मभिः संस्कृतान् स्वाध्या-

Fifth plate, second side.

90. याध्येयने रतानविक्रुतान्धर्मैरतान्संग-
91. तान् । कल्पव्याकृतितर्कनीतिनिपुणानभ्य-
92. र्च्य तेभ्यः कृती प्रादाच्छार्ङ्गपुरंधराप-
93. रिवृढः श्रीचक्रनारायणः ॥ 35 ॥

COPPER-PLATE No. 18.

[Chéjerla grant of Dévaráya II, S.S. 1351.]
(A.D. 1428-29.)

From the Collector's office, Nellore.

Note.

The grant is engraved on five copper-plates $7\frac{3}{4}$ inches × $5\frac{3}{4}$ inches with curved tops. The ring connecting them now is an ordinary one and is apparently not the original one as it bears no seal. The first and the last plates are engraved on one side only while the others are engraved on both sides. The plates are numbered at the top in Telugu figures and raised at the rims to preserve the writing.

The characters are Nandinágari and the language is Sanskrit verse except in the case of the portion giving boundaries which is in Telugu. The whole writing is in an excellent state of preservation. On the second side of plate III two lines seem to have been engraved and then erased and there is consequently a blank space. There is a large number of mistakes in the text.

The grant is one of Pratápa Dévaráya (Dévaráya II) and after tracing the dynasty to the moon, who was the mind-born son of Vishnu, gives the following genealogy—

Harihara.
|
Dévaráya.
|
Vijaya Bukka.
|
Pratápa Dévaráya.

It was made at the request of Paṇṭa Mailára, who was the great grandson of Súra, the grandson of Póta, and the son of Mumbámbá and Mummaḍíndra. He was evidently a vassal chief of the Reḍḍi caste and the inscription says that he served Dévaráya in battle and gave him valuable presents. The king who was pleased with him offered him a boon, but the latter asked for the grant of a village to holy and learned Brahmans. Mailára had the *birudas* Dharanívaráha, Ghaṇṭánáda, and Chauhattamalla.

The date of the grant was the Śaivatami (Śivarátri) day of the month of Mágha in the year Kílaka in S.S. 1351. The grant was made in the temple of Virúpáksha, who resides in Hémakúta in Bháskarakshétra on the Tungabhadra.

The object of the grant was the village formerly named Pólavaram but designated Chéjerla at the time of the grant, and situated in Púnginádu on the banks of the Kundi (Gundlakamma). It is the village Chéjerla in

Ongole taluk. The Brahman sharers whose fathers, *gotras* and *sákhás* are given, were 54 and the shares were 80. Three shares were given to the deities, Ráméśvara, Sóméśvara, Kéśava, Vighnéśvara and the goddess Puttalamma of Chéjerla.

The boundaries are given in Telugu and Sanskrit.

The grant concludes with some imprecatory verses and the colophon Ṣrí Virúpáksha.

TRANSLATION.

Adoration to Gaṇádhipati (Gaṇéśa.)

V. 1. May the illustrious primeval Boar, being carried upwards by whom (being married by whom) the earth became impregnated with gems, be auspicious to you!

V. 2. May the elephant (Gaṇéṣa), whose trunk is always moist with flowings from his temples, having worshipped whom Śiva and others obtain the fruition desired (by them), bring you happiness!

NOTE.—These are puns on the words दान: and कर: *Nityadánárdra-karah* means also one whose hand is wet with constantly making gifts.

V. 3. May the moon, the store-house of ambrosia of the gods, wearing whose digit the lord of the Universe (Śiva) became Rájaśékhara (moon-crested), be a source of delight to you!

V. 4. From the moon who was born from the mind of the primeval man (Vishnu) arose the race of the Yadus in which, as the fruit of Vásudeva's merit, appeared Hari himself (in the form of Krishna) associated with the hosts of gods.

V. 5. In that pure race was born a king named *Harihara*, of pure character, just as the moon (was born) from the milk-ocean.

V. 6. The two (functions), the protection of the good and the punishment of the wicked, are indeed divided in (between) Hari (Vishnu) and Hara (Śiva) ; but the lord (Harihara) made these two functions one (*i.e.*, combined them in himself).

V. 7. His son was the glorious *Dévaráya*, of great fortune, who attained glory, who was a very king of the gods (Indra) on earth, and who by constantly (making) gifts expunged the word "give" in the case of enemies (when addressed to them) and suppliants (when addressed by them).

V. 8. From him who was the store-house of virtue was born, as Jayanta from Indra, king Vijaya Bukka, who was eminent, by whom enemies were vanquished, and who resembled Vijaya (Arjuna).

V. 9. His son was *Pratápa-Dévaráya*, of unlimited glory, (and) accomplished in courting beauties, viz., fortune, fame, earth and Sarasvatí.

V. 10. Being enthroned at Vijayanagar which had come to him by the succession of his family, he conquered (both) internal and external enemies by his intellect and valour (respectively).

V. 11. Being designated by the term Rája on account of his pleasing men because he protects the system of castes. He protected the earth which has the four oceans for its girdle under one rule (umbrella) (*i.e.*, as universal sovereign).

V. 12. Him the learned constantly call—*Múruráya-raganḍa*, (the champion or vanquisher of the three kings), *Ariráyavibhálaka* (the destroyer of hostile kings), and *Hinduráya suratrána* (a Sultan among Hindu kings).

V. 13. Formerly Ráma, son of Daṣaratha, had (the attributes) magnanimity, fortitude, valour, courage, mercy, liberality, truthfulness and reverence; (but) now it is king Dévaráya (who possesses these virtues).

V. 14. King Mailára was assiduous in serving his (Dévaráya's) feet, with (his) wisdom, devotion, and valour, just as Hanumán was in respect of those of Ráma.

V. 15. Who was the great grandson of king *Súra*, who was the grandson of king Póta, who was the son of Mumbámba and Mummadíndra, and was of pure conduct.

V. 16. Who had the *biruda Dharanívaráha*, (the boar on earth), and was famed as Chauhattamalla (a hero whose strength is that of four elephants, or a hero resembling the four-armed, *i.e.*, Vishnu). Panṭa Mailára caused fear to hostile provincial chiefs by the ringing of his bell.

V. 17. In this manner doing by various means what was pleasing and good to the king, destroying wicked kings by his wisdom and valour, always paying homage (to the king) with different kinds of gems and excellent articles, with his mind intent on (the king's) service, he caused delight to the mind (of the king).

V. 18. Then Pratápa Dévaráya, being pleased with his service and valour, and having honoured Mailára, joyfully granted him a boon.

V. 19. He, the victorious, asked a boon—not horses nor elephants, nor ornaments, nor wealth—but the good of his lord and of himself.

V. 20. "Oh king, honour with the grant of an excellent village those gods on earth (Brahmans), in whom Mahéṣvara and other gods reside, in whom the Védas with their Angas dwell, and who are devoted to religion."

V. 21. Then being thus requested by him king Mailára, king Dévaráya surnamed Pratápa, with a delighted mind.

V. 22. Being on the bank of the Tungabhadrá river in the holy shrine of Bháskara, in the presence of Virúpáksha who dwells on the Hémakúṭa,

V. 23. In the Śaka year, reckoned by the moon (1), the arrows (5), the fires (3), and the moon (1), (*i.e.*, 1351), in the (cyclic) year Śrí Kílaka, in (the month of) Mágha, on the holy occasion relating to Śiva, the glorious lord Dévaráya joyfully gave to Brahmans the auspicious village, well known as Pólavaram, (situated) on the bank of the Kunḍi river (Gundlakamma), in the *vishaya* of Púnginádu, having surnamed it Chéjerla.

V. 24. The apportionment of the shares of the Brahmans, with their *Śákhá*, (school of the Véda), name and *gótra*, in this *agrahára* whose eight kinds of ownership and enjoyment were given to them is (hereunder) written. (List omitted.)

The marks of the boundaries of this village in the eight directions, commencing from the east and proceeding to the right, are written, as stated, in Sanskrit interspersed with the provincial language (Telugu), thus—

V. 54. On the east the boundary is the river Mudigunḍi which has large waves, extending from the north-eastern corner up to the south-eastern limit.

V. 55. Then on the resplendent southern side of that, from the south-east corner up to the limit of the path to Alúr, the boundary is the same river Mudigundi which flows on bright with rows of fish springing in it.

V. 56. The ancients call the unequalled channel which carries pure water from the path to Alúr up to the south-western corner the Pámulakálva and fix it as the boundary.

V. 57. Having made obeisance to the glorious Dévaráya, king Mailára, whose mercy is great, caused the district from here up to the river Mudigundi to be given to the best of Bráhmans.

Hence from to-day the boundary of Alúr village commencing from Pámulakálva up to the south-western corner as far as the (river) Mudigundi is also the boundary of the *agrahára* Chéjerla.

V. 58. I proceed next to describe in detail in order the well-known marks of the boundary in the western direction beginning from the south-western corner as far as the north-western corner.

V. 59. First there is the Bhútala gunta, then there is the limit of the Bóyachintala; and then there is the large well-known white "*uppi*" bush growing on a '*Nélaputta,*' (a low ant-hill).

V. 60. Then the black '*uppi*' bush growing on a *Nélaputta.* Next as you go on in the north-western corner is the mark Godungigattu.

V. 61. I next write down the well-known marks of the boundary in the northern direction, beginning from the north-western up to the north-eastern corner.

V. 62. In the north-west there is indeed the famous bush of black '*uppi*' trees standing on a *Nélaputta.* Beyond that there is Godungigattu, next Golamillagunta.

V. 63. Then there is a black '*tumma*' tree on a *Nélaputta;* beyond that shines Pótugattu. Next in the north-east corner with that at its apex is the Peyyalavágu with the mark "Toranaputta" (?)

V. 64. Then king Panta Malla (*i.e.,* Mailára) having established the Bráhmans, who were the best of those that knew Brahma, having obtained the fruition of his birth, and being pleased with himself.

V. 65. With folded hands entreats future kings. "This charity of mine should be maintained by you."

It has thus been said by Rámachandra.

[First imprecatory verse.]

For the exaltation of the virtue of protection (of a grant) and for the condemnation of the sin of resumption a few old verses are here written :—

[Imprecatory verses.]

V. 72. He who seizes one cow, one ornament, or even one inch of land goes to hell (and stays there) until the final dissolution of the elements.

V. 73. Lands and wealth given to the gods and Brahmans should be protected by kings who desire happiness in both the worlds.

May there be prosperity!

Ṣrí Virúpáksha!

First plate, second side.

1. श्रीगणाधिपतयेनमः ॥ श्रीमानादिमभूदारः श्रेयसेभूय-
2. सेस्तुवः । येनोद्धाहमवाप्यासीद्रत्नगर्भा वसुंधरा ॥ (V. 1) हेरं-
3. बो नित्यदानार्द्रकरः शर्म तनोतु वः । यमाराध्य महेशा-
4. द्या लभते वांछितं फलं ॥ (V. 2) सुधागारं सुमनसां चंद्रः प्र-
5. ह्लादनोस्तुवः । आसीद्यस्य कलां[1] बिभ्रद् भूतेशो राजशे-खरः ॥ (V. 3) पुं-
6. सः पुराणस्य मनःप्रसूते रिंदोर्य्य[2] दूनां प्रबभूववंशः । यत्रा-
7. विरासी द्वसुदेवभाग्यं हरिस्स्वयं देवगणै रुपेतः ॥ (V. 4) त-
8. स्मिन्विशुद्धजनने जातो हरिहराह्वयः । विशुद्धचरि-

---

[1] कलां is omitted in the line and inserted at the top of the plate.

[2] र्य्य is written at the top of the line.

9. तो राजा दुग्धाब्धाविव चंद्रमाः ॥ (v. 5) शिष्टावनं दुष्ट-
निवा-

10. रणं च द्वयं विभक्तं हि हरौ हरेच । चकार तत्कार्य-

11. मभिन्नरूपं बिभ्र त्तदीयं[1] महिमानमा[2]ख्यां [॥] (V. 6) तदा-
त्मजो

12. भूतलदेवराज[3] श्रीदेवरायोभवदूर्जितश्रीः । दाने-

13. नदेहीतिपदं ममार्ज प्रत्यर्थिनांयो मुहरर्थिनांच ॥ (V. 7)

14. अथ जयंत इवामरनायका द्गुणनिधे रुपलब्ध-

15. जनिस्ततः । विजयबुक्कमहीपतिरुन्नतो विजित-

16. शत्रुरभू द्दि[4]जयोपमः ॥ (V. 8) प्रतापदेवरायोभूत् तत्सूनु-

17. रमितोत्सवः । श्रीकीर्ति धरणी[5] वाणीकांतालालन-

18. दक्षिणः ॥ (V. 9) सिंहासनरथो[6] विजयनगरे स्वकुलाग

19. रिपूनाभ्यंतरान्बाह्यान जयद्बुद्धि[7] विक्रमैः ॥ वर्णाश्रम-

20. नुपालनरंजितजनवर्ध्मानराजपदः । चतुरुद-

Second plate, first side.

21. धिमेखलांकामेकच्छत्रामपालयद्वसुधां ॥(V. 11)मूरुरायरगडां-

22. कमारिरायविभालकं । हिंदुरायसुरत्राणं यमाहुरनि-

23. शंबुधाः ॥ (V. 12) गांभीर्यधैर्यतेजोवीर्यकृपौदार्यसत्यमर्यादा

24. धत्ते दशरथतनयो रामः प्रागद्या[8] दवराजेंद्रः॥ (V. 13)
दक्षस्तत्पा-

25. दसेवायामासीन्मैलारभूवरः । हनुमानिव रामस्य प्रज्ञा-

---

[1] Read विभुः तदीयं.

[2] Read महिमानमाप्यास्यां.

[3] Read राज:.

[4] रुद्धि in the text.

[5] य for ध in text.

[6] स्था for य in text.

[7] द्ध in text.

[8] Read प्रागद्यदे.

26. भक्तिपराक्रमैः॥ (V. 14) नप्तायः सूरनपतेः पौत्रिः[1] पातेमही-
भुजः ।

27. पुत्रः पवित्रचारित्रो मुंमांबामुंमडीन्द्रयोः ॥ (V. 15) धरणीवरा-

28. हबिरुदोयो वाचौहत्तमल्लविख्यातः । अरिमण्डलीक-

29. भीषण घंटानादः[2] सपंटमैलारः॥ (V. 16) विविधकरणैरेवं

30. राज्ञः प्रियं हितमाचरन्नहितधरणीपालान् भिंदन स्व

31. बुद्धि[3] पराक्रमैः। विविधमणिभि(:)श्लाघ्यै द्रव्यैः पदे परिपू-

32. जयन्नकृतमनसः प्रीतिं सेवानिरूढमना(:)स्वयं[4] (V. 17)
प्रताप-

33. देवरायोस्य सेवापौरुषतोषितः । मानयित्वाथमैलारं

34. तस्मै वरमदान्मुदा ॥(V. 18) नहयान्न चमातंगान्न भूषान[5] चसं-

35. पदः । स्वामिनः स्वस्य च हितमयाचत कृती वरं[6] प्र-
तिष्ठि-

36. तायत्रमहेश्वराद्याः सांगाश्ववेदानिवसंति येषु । ता-

37. न् धर्मनिष्ठान् धरणीसुरेन्द्रान्(।)संभावयग्रामवरे-

38. ण राजन् ॥ (V. 20) इति विज्ञापितस्तेन राजा
मैलारभूभुजा ।

39. देवरायः प्रतापांकस्तदा[7] संतुष्टमानसः ॥ (V. 21) पवित्रेभा-

40. स्करक्षेत्रे तुंगभद्रानदीतटे । हेमकूटनिवासस्य वि-

41. रूपाक्षस्य सन्निधौ ॥ (V. 22) शाके भूमिशराग्निचंद्रगुणिते
श्री-

42. कीलके वत्सरे माघे शैवतमोविशेषसमये श्रीदेवराय-

43. प्रभुः । कुंडारोधसि पूंगिनाटिविषये चेजेर्लनामांकितं कृ

---

[1] Read पौत्रः.

[2] There is an unnecessary stroke after घंटा in the text.

[3] In the text we have बुद्धि.

[4] स्वयां in text.

[5] In the text भूषानू च.

[6] वरां in the text.

[7] तहा in the text.

Second plate, second side.

44. त्वापोलवरप्रासीद्धिमादिशत् ग्रामंद्विजेभ्यः शुभ ॥ (V. 23) दत्ता-
45. ष्टैश्वर्यभोगे स्सिन्नग्रहारे द्विजन्मनां । सशाखाह्वयगो-
46. त्राणां भागक्लृप्तिर्विलिख्यते ॥ (V. 24) अर्हत्यापस्तंबः का-
47. श्यपगोत्रो हि कामनतनूज । पेद्दिरिह सप्त-
48. भागान् भागंचार्धं च नल्लनप्यायः (नार्योयः) ॥ (V. 25) कौण्डिन्याया-
49. जुषः पोतिभट्टपुत्रोन्नमो र्हति ॥ (V. 26) भागंचार्धंच
50. नूंकस्यस्तनयोप्पतथार्हति आपस्तंबः काश्य-
51. पगोत्रो गूडपाटितिप्पनो भागं । भागं च बकम-
52. ल्लोभागांस्त्रीन्[1] गायपं,डितोर्हतिच ॥ (V. 27) आपस्तंबो गौत-
53. मगोत्रोर्हति रालपाल्लिपेर्द्दिद्दौ । भागौ[1] स नरह-
54. रिरपि[2] (चाप)द्यौ हरितकुलसुधी[3] स्तु पेद्दि स्त्रीन् ॥ (V. 28) अ-
55. र्हति मत्तयालिंगः शौनकगोत्रोत्र याजषो भा-
56. गं । तच्छाखीकौण्डिन्यो नरहरिरपि पोतिभट्टसुत ए-
57. कं ॥ (V. 29) कौण्डिन्यौ याजुषौ वेलंगूरितल्लयनंदनौ । शि
58. मनश्चौभलश्चैव द्वौ द्वौ भागाविहार्हतः ॥ (V. 30) कौण्डि-न्यातु
59. याजुषा वेलंगूरिनागयनंदनाः । सार्धं भागमिहा-
60. र्हंति मारुलक्कयतल्लनाः ॥ (V. 31) कौण्डिन्यो याजुषो
61. प्यत्र भागमेकं त्रिविक्रमः । तादृशः पेद्दिरप्ये-
62. कमारेमंचिसुतोर्हति ॥ (V. 32) गौतम आपस्तंबो भा-
63. गं मोट्टुपाल्लिशिंगनोर्हति सः । तच्छाखः कौण्डिन्यो-
64. भागं गुद्दूरिशिंगनश्चैकं ॥ (V. 33) याजुषोर्हति कौण्डि-

---

[1] भागैस्त्रि in text. [2] पिचापिद्यो in text.

[3] कुलसुहृद्दुपेद्धि in text.

Third plate, first side.

65. डि[1] न्यो भागार्धं मिरुवन्नमः । भागं तद्वद आत्रेयो भट्टभा-

66. णस्तथार्हति ॥ (V. 34) कौण्डिन्योयाजुषो रामाभट्टो भागमि-

67. हार्हति । त्रीन् पादान् तत्सुतः शिंगनाख्यः पादं त-

68. थान्नमः ॥ (V. 35) आपस्तंबो भारद्वाजः कोवूरि अन्नमो भागं ।

69. अर्धं तु चेन्नमल्लोर्हत्यर्धं ताडिपर्तिपोलश्च ॥ (V. 36) तच्छा-

70. खागोत्रोर्हति भागमसौ बिट्टगुंटशिंगाख्यः । नागमभ-

71, ट्टश्चैकमथात्रेयः सोध अ(?)शिंगनश्चैकं ॥ (V. 37) श्रीवत्सो या-

72. जुषो लक्कमात्मजो भागमध्यमः । ओरुगंटी हरिहरः

73. कौण्डिन्यश्चैकमर्हति॥(V. 38) हारीतो याजु षे भागं जन्नवाड-

74. सदाशिवः । पाराशरो मद्दिपाटिकामनो द्वाविहा-

75. र्हति ॥(V. 39) भागं शुक्लयजुर्वेदः काश्यपश्चिट्टयार्हति। दौहि।

76. त्रः अच्चमांबायाः भागमेकस्तथाविधः ॥ (V. 40) आत्रेयो या-

77. जुषो भागद्वयं पिल्लयनागणौ । भार्गवौ त्वादित्यतिक्कौ

78. भागमेकैकमर्हतः ॥ (V. 41) याजुषः कोम्मनो भागं मैत्राव-

79. रुणगोत्रजः । सार्धभागं कौशिकोर्हत्यादित्यो नागणा-

80. र्यजः ॥ (V. 42) त्रिविक्रमस्तल्ल भट्टः सुपाणिरपि लक्कणः एकै-

81. कमर्हतो भागं काश्यपा[2] आश्वलायनाः॥ (V. 43) पेद्धयतिप्पणना

82. मा भारद्वाजोत्र भागमृग्वेदः । शिंगयनरहरिरप्यर्ह-

83. ति विश्वामित्रगोत्रजो भागं ॥ (V. 44) कृष्णाख्यो भागमृग्वेदी मौल-

---

[1] डि is repeated in text. [2] वाश्व लायनौ in text.

84. भार्गवगोत्रजः । वासिष्ठो वासुदवोपि भागमेकमिहार्हं ॥
85. ति ॥ (V. 45) ऋग्वेदो माचिभट्टो भारद्वाज स्तु भागमर्धयुतं। तद्रू-
86. वेदोवासिष्ठ स्तोयरणाख्यश्च भागमर्हति यः ॥ (V. 46) नर-सिंहभ-
87. ट्टनामा भारद्वाजोत्र मंचिभट्टसुतः । ऋग्वेदोर्हति भागं

Third plate, second side.

88. चंनमल्लो वत्सगोत्रजश्चैकं॥(V. 47) ऋग्वोदिनौ कानकामौवि-
89. श्वामित्रकुलोद्भवौ [1]। द्वौ द्वौ भागौ पंगुलूरीशिंगणो-मल्लण-
90. स्तथा ॥ (V. 48) कौशिकौ याजुषौ च त्रीन् भागान् माचण-तिप्पणौ
91. माध्यंदिनः काशिनाथो भागस्यार्द्धं तथार्हति ॥ (V. 49)
92. मामिल्लपल्लिमारप्रियपुत्रो नरहरिर्यं-
93. जुश्शाखः। एकं भागमिहार्हति भारद्वा-
94. जान्वये जातः ॥ (V. 50) श्रीमत्काश्यपगोत्रोर्हत्ये-
95. कं भागमग्रहारेस्मिन् । रेंटालशबूद-
96. पूर्वी गणमुलगंगाधरो यजुर्वेदः ॥ (V. 51) ना-
97. यिनार्यस्य रेस्तु in text) दौहित्रो भागमेकंतु याजुषः।
98. शाण्डिल्यगोत्रसंभूतो दे व राम (रंम in text) इहा-र्हति ॥ (V. 52)

Two lines seem to have been engraved and then erased. hence there is blank space here.

99. रामेश्वरसोमेश्वरदेवावेकं
100. च केशवश्चैकं। विघ्नेश्वरोर्धमर्हत्यर्धं

[1] कलौं इ ॥ द्विभाहै in text.

101. चेंजेर्लपुट्टलांबा च ॥ (V. 53) अस्य ग्रामस्याष्टदि-
102. क्सीमाचिह्नानि देशभाषोपेतया गीर्वा-
103. णवाण्या प्रादक्षिण्येन प्राचीमारभ्य यथाक्र
104. मं लिख्यंते । यथा ॥ आरभ्य गौरीरमण-

Fourth plate, first side.

105. स्य कोण मावह्निकोणावधि दीप्यमाना । प्रा-
106. च्यां दिशि प्रौढ तरंगमाला सीमा स्रवंती मुदि-
107. गुंडि नामा ॥ (V. 54) ततः स्फुरन्त्यां दिशि दक्षिणस्या मा
108. रभ्यतं हव्यवहस्यकोणं । आलोलमानोन्मद
109. मीनपंक्ति रालूरिमार्गावधिसैव सभि ॥ (V. 55) आर
110. लूरिमार्गाद्रजनीचरेन्द्रकोणावधि स्वच्छजलं
111. वहंतीं । कुल्यामतुल्यां प्रवदंतिसीमां प्राज्ञो ज-
112. नाः पामुलकालुवेति ॥ (V. 56) अत्र विशेषो लिख्यते।
113. श्रीदेवरायस्य कृतप्रणामो मैलारभूपो म-
114. हितानुकंपः । अदापयत् भूसुरपुंगवेभ्यः
115. सीमामितो प्या मुदिगुण्डिनद्याः ॥ (V. 57) तस्मादद्यप्रभृ-
116. ति पामुलकालुवामारभ्य मुदिगुंडिपर्यंता नि रृ
117. ति कोणावधिः(।) आलूरिनाम्नो ग्रामस्य सीमापि चेंजे-
118. र्लग्रहारस्य सीमैव ॥ ततः प्रचेतो दिशि विश्रुता-
119. नि चिह्नानि सीम्नो विद्गणोमिसम्यक् । आर-
120. म्य कोणं रजनीचरस्य यावन्मरुत्को-
121. णमिहक्रमेण ॥ (V. 58) प्रथमं भूतुल गुंटस्ततः प-
122. रं भवति बोयचिंतलावधिः । तदनंतरं च

Fourth plate, second side.

123. सु महान् विख्यातो नेलपुट्टनेल्लुप्पि पोदः ॥ (V. 59)
124. नेलपुट्टोपरि ततो नल्लुप्पिपोद एव च । क्र
125. मात् गोडुंगिगट्टुश्च चिह्नं कोणे नभस्वतः ॥ (V. 60) त-
126. तः परं यक्षपते र्दिशायामारभ्य तद्गंध-
127. वहस्य कोणं । आशंभुकोणावधिविश्रुतानि (चिह्नानि)
128. सीम्नःपरितो लिखामि ॥ (V. 61) वायव्यकोणे खलुनेलपु-
129. ट्टोपरिस्थ नल्लुप्पि पोदः प्रतीतः । गो-
130. डुंगिगट्टुस्तु ततः परस्तात्ततः परस्तात्
131. गोलमिल्लगुंट्टः ॥ (V. 62) स्यान्नेलपुट्टोपरिनल्ल-
132. दुम्मस्ततः परं राजति पोतुगट्टः । त-
133. न्मस्तकं तोरणपुट्टचिह्न मैशानके
134. पेय्यलवागु रेव ॥ (V. 63) इतिस्वयं प्रति-
135. ष्ठाप्य ब्राह्मणान् ब्रह्मवित्तमान् ।
136. अवाप्यजन्मसाफल्यंमात्मना हर्षमुद्वहन् ॥ (V. 64)
137. भवद्भिः पालनीयो मे धर्मोयमिति भाविनः । कृतां-
138. जलिः पार्थयतेपंट मल्ल(ो)महीपतीन् ॥ (V. 65) रामचन्द्रेणा-
139. प्येव मेवोक्तं ॥ सा(मा)न्योयं धर्मसेतुर्नृपाणां कालेका-
140. ले पालमीयो भवाद्भिः [।] सर्वानितान्[1] भाविनः पा्र्थि
141. वेन्द्रान् भूयो भूयो याचते रामचन्द्रः ॥ (V. 66) पालनपुण्य-

Fifth plate, first side.

142. प्रशंशनार्थं अपहरण दोषप्रख्यापनार्थं च केचित्
143. पुराणश्लोका लिख्यन्ते ॥ दानपालनयोर्मध्ये दानाच्छ्रयो
144. नुपालनं । दानात्स्वर्गमवाप्नोति पालनादच्युतं पदं ॥ (V. 67)

---

[1] सर्वानेतेन्.

145. बहुभिर्वसुधादत्ता बहुभिः परिपालिता । यस्य यस्य
146. यदाभूमि स्तस्य तस्य तदाफलं ॥ (V. 68) एकैव भगिनी लो-
147. के सर्वेषामेवभूभुजां । नभोज्या नकरग्राह्या
148. विप्रदत्तावसुंधरा ॥ (V. 69) स्वदत्ताद् द्विगुणं पुण्यं प-
149. रदत्तानुपालनं । परदत्तापहारेण स्वदत्तं नि-
150. ष्फलंभवेत् ॥ (V. 70) स्वदत्तां परदत्तांवा यो हरेतव-
151. सुंधरां । षष्ठिंवर्षसहास्राणि विष्टायां जायते कृ-
152. मिः ॥ (V. 71) गामेकांरत्निकामेकां भूमेरप्येकमंगु
153. लं । हरन् नरकमाप्नोति यावदाभूतसंप्लवं ॥ (V. 72) देवब्राह्म-
154. णदत्तानि क्षेत्राणि च वसूनिच । पालनीयानि
155. भूपालैः लोकद्वयसुखैषिभिः ॥ (V. 73) शुभमस्तु ॥

श्री विरूपाक्ष.

Copper-plate No. 19.

[Malliyapúnḍi grant of Amma Rája II, East Chálukyan king (about 867 Śaka—945–46 A.D.]

Note.

The original of the subjoined inscription was discovered by Mr. Venugopal Chetti in the Rámalingéṣvara svámi temple of Madanúr, a village about 10 miles from Ongole, Nellore district. It records a grant of the village named Malliyapúnḍi, over twenty miles off. As to when it came into the possession of the temple authorities, no information is available. Through the kindness of the Rája of Venkatagiri Mr. Venugopal Chetti was enabled to get a loan of the copper-plate and prepare the transcript and translation.

The document is engraved on five copper-plates with raised rims, each measuring 9 inches long. There is writing only on the inner sides of the first and fifth plates while the other plates bear writing on both sides. The plates are joined by nearly a circular ring whose thickness is 2 inches and diameter 4½ inches. To the ring is attached a beautiful circular seal which measures 2½ inches in diameter and bears the usual Chálukyan symbols—a recumbent boar, the moon, and an elephant-goad; across the centre is written the legend "श्रीत्रिभुवनांकुश" (Śrí Tribhuvanánkuṣa) and at the bottom is represented a lotus flower. The seal stands on an expanded lotus flower.

The plates and the seal are on the whole in excellent preservation. The characters are neatly engraved and there are no peculiarities in the orthography which is of the east Chálukyan style. The errors found in the inscription are noted in the foot-notes to the translation. One however is worth mentioning here; in line 47; after काधिपतिः, वृंत्त (vrintta) is written by mistake for वृत्तं (vrittam), the *anusvára* being placed before त्त instead of after it.

The inscription opens with an invocation to the Jain religion, because the gift therein made is to a Jain temple. The grant of Amma II published in Volume VII, E.I., page 185, was also to a Jain temple.

Then there is the usual genealogy beginning with Kubja Vishnuvardhana, but very little new information of historical value is supplied. In the foot-notes any special points are referred to. In line 14 Vijayáditya III is called Parachakraráma, a surname not to be found in other inscriptions. As in some other Chálukyan inscriptions, here also the reign of Yuddhamalla, the son of Tála, is not mentioned, possibly because, as

Dr. Hultzsch suggests, he was considered a usurper. His name is however mentioned amongst the rival claimants who fought for the Veṅgi kingdom after the death of Vikramáditya. The other claimants are given as Rája Mártáṇḍa and Kaṇṭhiká Vijayáditya—names not traceable in other inscriptions. The fortunes of these are given in detail—Rája Mártáṇḍa was slain, and the other two were banished by Chálukya Bhíma II. Regarding Chálukya Bhíma II our grant gives a poetical account of his valour and greatness.

The donor was Amma Rája II and the inscription states that he was crowned in his twelfth year, in the Śaka year 867, *i.e.*, 945–46 A.D. This date is given in another inscription of the same king, I.A., Volume VII, page 16. It is noteworthy that these two inscriptions contain a few almost identical sentences and verses.

The grant proper begins with the statement that Ammarája sends an order to the residents of the 'Vishaya' or district of *Kommanáṇḍu.* It then proceeds to mention the donee—a Jain temple called Kaṭakábharaṇa or ornament of Kaṭaka, constructed by Duggarája, to the south of the village of Dharmapuram which O. 39 and O. 40 seem to identify with Dharmavaram in Ongole taluk. Duggarája was Kaṭakarája (superintendent of the royal camp). His genealogy is briefly given as—

Krishnarája.
|
Katakádhipati (name not given).
|
Vijayáditya.
|
Duggarája, founder of the Jain temple in question.

It is said that this temple was presided over by a Jain saint named Diradéva, disciple of Divákara, a saint who was the first disciple of Jinanandi who was of the Śrí Yápuníya Sangha and of the Nandigachcha.

The grant consisted of the gift of Malliyapúṇḍi village. Its western boundary is Kalvakúri, and its northern is Dharmapuram. So its exact situation is identifiable though there is now no village named Malliyapúṇḍi.

The inscription states that the gift was made on the occasion of Uttaráyaṇa or the winter solstice. Its date is not given, but it must be after 867 Śaka, the year of the grantor's coronation.

The purpose of the grant was for the repairs of the abovesaid Jain temple and for the performance of worship, etc., therein.

The 'vijñapti' or executor of the grant is mentioned as Kaṭakarája, the superintendent of the royal camp or fort (probably Kocherlakóṭa, *vide* O. 46). That the term Kaṭaka denotes a fixed local area seems clear from the fact that the temple is called "the ornament of the Kaṭaka" and from O. 46 where a village is described as attached to Kocherlakóṭa Kaṭaka. "Fort" seems to be a better rendering than "royal camp" which suggests a mere temporary encampment.

TRANSLATION.

Lines 1 to 3. May there be always prosperity to the religion of the illustrious lord Jinéndra, which has vigorously spread (in the world), which is praised in the three worlds and which is the support of the magnificent Dharma, by whose power vices caused by the wicked Kali age and those springing from delusion and evil propensities on earth do not spread and (by whose power) there is always peace of (in) the earth.

Lines 3 to 8. Hail! Kubja Vishnuvardhana, the brother of Satyásráya Vallabhéndra, who adorned the race of the illustrious Chálukyas, who are of the *gótra* of the Mánavyas, who are praised throughout the whole universe, who are the descendants of Háriti, who have obtained sovereignty by the excellent grace of Kauṣiki,[1] who are protected by the assemblage of the divine mothers, who contemplate the feet of the lord Mahásénа,[2] who have subjugated the territories of their enemies in an instant at the mere sight of the excellent sign of the Boar which they had acquired through the grace of the Lord Náráyaṇa, (and) whose bodies have been purified by baths performed after celebrating horse sacrifices, reigned over the territory of Vengi for eighteen years.

Lines 8 and 9. His son Jayasimha (reigned) for thirty-three (years).

Line 9. Vishnuvardhana, the son of his younger brother Indrarája, (ruled) for nine (years).

Lines 9 and 10. His son Mangi Yuvarája (prince regent) (ruled) for twenty-five (years).

Line 10. His son Jayasimha (ruled) for thirteen (years). His younger brother Kokkili (ruled) for six months.

Lines 10 and 11. His elder brother Vishnuvardhana, having expelled him, (reigned) for thirty-seven years. His son Vijayáditya Bhaṭṭáraka (reigned) for eighteen (years).

Lines 11 and 12. His son Vishnuvardhana (ruled) for thirty-six (years).

Lines 12 and 13. (His son) the wise king Vijayáditya, who was as valiant as a lion and was surnamed Naréndra-

---

[1] Kauṣikí—Párvatí, wife of Śiva. [2] Mahásénа—Skanda, son of Śiva.

mṛigarája (a lion among kings) reigned for forty-eight years.

Line 13. His son Káli Vishnuvardhana (ruled) for a year and half.

Lines 14 to 16. His son Vijayáditya, whose other name was Parachakrarárma,[1] having in a great battle heavily defeated Mangi, the king of the Nodamba[2] Ráshtra (kingdom) who had taken refuge in the hills of Gangakúta,[3] and having fought with Sankila,[4] the king of Saṭṭala,[4] who was joined by the fierce Vallabha,[5] protected the earth for forty-four years.

---

[1] Vijayáditya III according to other inscriptions was called Gunaga, Gunagánka or Gunakenalla. According to the present inscription his surname was Farachakra Ráma, *i.e.*, one who was like Ráma (Parasuráma) to other kings, *i.e.*, the terror of other kings.

[2] Nodamba or Nolamba. The Nolambavádi which included Bellary and part of Mysore was ruled at one time by a branch the Pallava dynasty.

[3] Gangakúṭa is perhaps the Chakrakúṭa of other inscriptions.

[4] Saṭṭalas—probably a mistake for *Raṭṭ-ila, i.e.*, the Ráshṭrakúṭas.

In the original we have योयाययित्वा which makes no sense. It may be a mistake for योधयित्वा = having fought.

In other inscriptions these deeds are referred to, *e.g.* :—

Vol. VII, E.I., p. 189, Gunaga (Vijayáditya III) is described as 'one to whose arms great honour was paid by the Vallabha king' (Vallabhanripa samabhyarchitabhujah).

Vol. IV, p. 239, we have "the great lord Gunaga Vijayáditya . . . the hero who played the game of ball on the battle field with the head of Mangirája, who burnt Chakrakúṭa, who frightened Sankila, residing in Kíranapura (and) joined by Krishna, who restored his dignity to Vallabhéndra . . . ".

Ind. Antiquary XII, p. 221, Vijayáditya III "prompted by the lord of the Raṭṭas, having conquered the unequalled Gangas, cut off the head of Mangi in battle, and, having frightened Krishna and Sankila, he completely burnt their city."

In *South Ind. Ins.*, Vol. I, pp. 38, 39 and 42, Vijayáditya "was renowned through killing Mangi and burning Kíranapura."

Our inscription states that Mangi was a Nodamba king and that Sankila was a Raṭṭa king.

[5] The Vallabha here referred to must be the Krishna who is elsewhere said to have been in alliance with Sankila. It seems clear then that the identification of this Krishna with a Ráshtrakúṭa king is correct. But see E.I., Vol. IV, p. 227.

Lines 16 to 18. Then Chálukya Bhíma, the son of his younger brother Vikramáditya who was appointed Yuvarája,[1] (ruled) for thirty years. His elder brother (son) Vijayáditya[2] (ruled) for six months. His eldest son Ammarája (ruled) for seven years.

Lines 18 and 19. Then king Tála, the son of Yuddhamalla the paternal uncle of Chálukya Bhíma, having overcome his (Ammarája's) infant son[3] (ruled) for a month.

Lines 19 to 22. Then the illustrious Vikramáditya, the son of king Chálukya Bhíma, of very great prowess, having an army of fierce elephants, having slain in a fierce battle that king Tála along with the assemblage of the various feudatories who had large forces, wisely ruled the sea-girt earth for a year.

Lines 22 to 24. Then after the death of Vikramáditya, like Rákshasas (after the setting of the sun), the claimant princes, emulating one another, intent on harassing the subjects, desirous of getting sovereignty, Yuddhamalla, Rája Mártánḍa, Kanṭhiká Vijayáditya and others engaged in war.[4]

---

[1] Yuvarâja = Heir apparent.

[2] Vijayáditya IV is here said to be the elder brother of Chálukya Bhíma. This is a mistake, as in other inscriptions, he is given as his son; even in this inscription in line 23 he is correctly given as his son.

[3] Bála or infant son—whose name was Vijayáditya. He is said to have reigned half a month.

[4] According to other inscriptions Bhíma, another son of Ammarája, succeeded Vikramáditya and ruled for eight months; he was succeeded by Yuddhamalla, son of Tála. As in some other inscriptions, the reign of Yuddhamalla is not noted in our inscription apparently because he was considered a usurper. His name is however given as one of the claimants who fought for the kingdom; the others being Rája Mártánḍa and Kanṭhiká Vijayáditya. The last named seems to be Kanṭhiká Béṭa, the youthful son of Amma I, who was dethroned by Tála and founded a fresh line, for which see p. 4 of the E.R. for 1893–94. Our inscription tells us that Rája Mártánḍa was slain, while the other two were banished from the country by Chálukya Bhíma II.

On page 46, *S.I. Inscriptions*, Vol. I, Dr. Hultzsch says in a note that Rája Mártánḍa was a surname of Chálukya Bhíma II. In the present inscription, Rája Mártánḍa was one of the rival *dáyádis* slain by Chálukya Bhíma II.

Lines 24 and 25. Thus five years passed in mere war. Then he succeeded,

Lines 25 and 26. Who slew Rája Mártánḍa amongst them in a battle; and by whom Kanṭhiká Vijayáditya and Yuddhamalla were banished from the country.

Lines 26 to 28. By the edge of the scimitar wielded by his club-like arms, many other honourable kings also, who were spoiled by evil course of conduct, who were causes of trouble to the country, and who were famous, were brought to destruction.

Lines 28 and 29. The command of him who was waging fierce battle was worn on the head (honoured) like a garland by kings who were devoted to him.

Line 29. The fire of his anger does not turn back without having entirely consumed the assemblage of enemies.

Line 30. His pure fame does not keep quiet without pervading[1] the whole world.

Line 31. The store of his wealth which was like a beap of clouds verily rains on the good crop, viz.,[2] men who are being daily scorched by the excessive heat of poverty.

Line 32. He, Rájabhíma, the son of Vijayáditya, the grandson of Chálukya Bhíma, wisely ruled the earth for 12 years.

---

[1] नभ्रमत् means 'not wandering.' The idea is that his fame was always in motion over the earth, *i.e.*, ever increasing.

Both in this and in the following sentences न—न, two negatives are used to express an affirmative.

[2] जनसस्ये—makes no sense. It is probably a mistake for जनसस्य. A poor man is compared to crops withered by heat and the king's wealth is compared to clouds which rain on them.

Lines 32 and 34. To him whose form was like that of Mahésvara, from Lókamahádévi whose beauty was like that of Umá, was born Ammarája who was like Kumára.

Lines 34 and 35. The soles of his feet were marked with the signs:—lotus flower, umbrella, chowri, the water-pot and the elephant-goad; he had shining arms as massive as bars of iron and hanging as far as the knee.

Lines 35 to 38. His shoulders were like the summits of the Himálayas; he was learned in the science of kings, and skilled in the use of various weapons. He vanquished the assemblage of his enemies. He was versed in the treatises on elephants and horses. He was a very bee at the lotus feet of Hara (Siva). He was illustrious, a very tree of paradise to poets and singers, a very cow of plenty to Bráhmans, hermits, the poor, the blind and relations, a very philosopher's stone to the assemblage of beggars, the gem of kings of the earth. He was like the sun by reason of his excessive brilliance.

Lines 38 to 41. In the Śaka year reckoned by the mountains (seven), the flavours (six) and the Vasus (eight), *i.e.*, (S.S. 867) in this month of Márgaṣírsha on the thirteenth day of the dark fortnight, on Friday, under the constellation Maitra, under the zodiacal sign of Dhanus (bow), when the sun was in 'ghaṭa' (water-jar), and in the 12th year of his age, he assumed the crown to the delight of the world, like the mountain of dawn bearing the sun.[1]

Lines 41 and 42. He, Ṣrí Vijayáditya Ammarája, the asylum of the whole universe, the great king, the supreme lord of kings, very righteous, thus commands all the

[1] In the inscription in S.A., Vol. VII, p. , Dr. Fleet reads रविवारव= like the sun on the mountain of dawn; the simile is not quite intelligible there.

householders of the district of Kammanáṇḍu headed by the headmen.

Lines 43 and 44. Nobles[1] (Áryáh).

He, the hero of Páṇḍaranga, consumed Kíranapuram, the residence of Kṛishṇarája, as Śiva burned Tripuram; therefore the enumeration of the valiant exploits of him whose fame is pure, is impossible even to one with a thousand mouths.[2]

Line 45. His son had his forehead adorned with the pure and white insignia of royalty of Kaṭaka.

Lines 45 and 46. His son Vijayâditya was the ruler of Kaṭaka.[3]

Verses 46 to 48.[4] His son Duggarája was the receptacle of virtuous qualities, pious, truthful, charitable, enjoyer of luxuries, great-souled, conqueror in battles, the abode of the goddess of victory.

Even his sword was ever for the protection of the fortune of the Chálukyas; and his family[5] was famous for the support of the excellent and great kingdom of Vengi.

---

[1] The visarga is omitted after आर्या.

[2] The reading and translation of lines 43 and 44 are conjectural as the original here is apparently full of mistakes. कृष्णराजास्ततय: makes no sense. It is proposed to read कृष्णराजास्थितं य : he who burned Kíranapuram where Krishnarája dwelt, for Sankila dwelt at Kíranapuram and Krishna his ally may have dwelt there too. मुखसहस्र — the allusion is probably to Śésha who is fabled to have 1,000 mouths.

[3] Dr. Fleet in Vol. VII, E.I., pp. 183 to 185, discusses the meaning of the word Kaṭakarája and concludes that it denotes an official post, that of the Governor or superintendent of the royal camp (*Kaṭaka*).

[4] Ajñapti or Vijñapti = a command. In inscriptions it denotes the *dùtaka* or messenger whose duty it was to communicate the grant to the local authorities (Vol. VII, E.I., p. 183).

वृंत्त in the original is evidently a mistake for वृत्तं = verse, the *anusvára* being placed before त्त by mistake instead of after it. It denotes that what follows is verse.

[5] वंश: = (1) a bamboo, (2) family. There is here a pun on the word and therefore अवलंबाय (= for support) is used, a bamboo being used for that purpose.

Lines 48 and 49. An excellent temple of Jina, which was very charming, was constructed by him, to the south of Dharmapuri, and there is a holy temple auspiciously named the "ornament of Kaṭaka."[1]

Lines 50 and 51. There was the lord of saints Jinanandi, who was the chief of the holy Kótimaduva *gaṇa* of the Ṣrí Yápuniya Sangha, belonging to the holy and venerable Nandi *gachcha*, and who was equal to a Ganadhara[2].

Lines 51 and 52. His first disciple was Divákara, famous in the earth, the best of sages, who was the repository of supreme knowledge, great-souled, who was himself like the Jinas in the aggregate of virtues.

Lines 52 and 53. His disciple was the illustrious sage Díradéva, the store-house of austerities, wise, whom the world esteems as endowed with the greatness of power to command.[3]

Lines 53 to 56. The executant of this charity is Kaṭakarája. On the occasion of a winter solstice, after

---

[1] Kaṭakábharana, "the ornament of Kaṭaka," is the name of the temple.

[2] The text of lines 51 and 52 is obscure and the reading is only provisional. The *Yâpaniya Sangha* was a sect of the Jains whose members "had the appearance of Digambaras, but the observances of Śvétambarás (Vol. IV, E.I., p. 339).

Nandigachcha' was one of the four *gachchas* or schools of Digambara Jain ascetics. The four *gachchas* were—

(1) Nandigachcha, (2) Sarasvati gachcha, (3) Bhárati gachcha and (4) Syéna gachcha; Jinanandi was of the Nandigachcha.

Sangha = Fraternity—the clergy of the Buddhists as well as of the Jains.

A *gaṇa dhara* was the teacher of a *gaṇa* or sect.

[3] Pratihárya Śakti—probably a technical expression of Jainism. It is interpreted as Prabhu sakti—the power of lordship or power to rule men.

Lines 54 and 55. The portion of the inscription giving the purposes for which the gift was made is apparently wrongly engraved. Satra means 'charity'.

There is a village named Kalvakur even now in Addanki division of Ongole taluk.

Dharmapuram also is a village in the same neighbourhood.

making a libation of water, the hamlet named Malliya-púndi is given exempt from all taxes to the temple of Jina named Kaṭakábharaṇa which is presided over by him, for the restoration of whatever may have been broken or torn, and for the performance of offering, worship and *satra* (giving food).

Lines 56 and 57. Its village boundaries are—

On the east—Manjunúru ;
On the south—Yinimili ;
On the west—Kalvakúru ; and
On the north—Dharmapuram.

Lines 57 to 60. The field boundaries of this village are—

On the east—Gollavi gunṭa ;
On the south-east—Ráviaperíacheruvu ;
On the south—the demarcation stone ;
On the south-west—the demarcation stone ;
On the west—Malkaparṛakoṛabóyu-taṭáka ;
On the north-west—the demarcation stone ;
On the north—Dúva cheruvu ;
On the north-east—the boundary is the same as the boundary of the field named Ervókachénu of Kalvakúru.

First plate, second side.

1. भद्रं स्यातात्रिजन्नुतायसततं श्रीमज्जिनेन्द्रप्रभो रुद्दमातततंशा-सना-

2. य विलसद्धर्म्मावलंबायच । सामत्थ्यी त्त्रवलु यस्य दुष्कालि-कृता दोषाश्चमिश्चांद्भवा (:) दु

3. वृद्धत्तानि च भूतले न विनता शान्तिश्च नित्यंक्षिति (:)[1] ॥ स्वस्ति श्रीमतां सकलभुवनसं-

4. स्तूयमानमानव्यसगोत्राणां हारितिपुत्राणां कौशिकि(को)वरप्र-सादलब्धरा

5. ज्यानाम्मातृग(ण)[2] परिपालितानां स्वामिमहासेनपादानुध्या यिनां भगव-

6. न्नारायणप्रसादसमासादितवरवराहलांच्छनेक्षणक्षणवशी कृता-रातिमण्डला-

7. नामश्वमेधावभृथस्नानपवित्रीकृतवपुषां चालुक्यानांकुलमलं-करिष्णोस्सत्याश्र-

8. यवल्लभेन्द्रस्यभ्राता कुब्जविष्णुवर्द्धनोष्टादश वर्षाणिवेंगि-मण्डलमपालयत् । तदात्म-

Second plate, first side.

9. जोजयसिंहस्त्रयस्त्रिंशतं । तदनुजेन्द्रराजनन्दनो विष्णुवर्द्ध-नोनव । तत्सूनुर्म्मङ्गियुवराज-

10. ष्पः पंचविंशतिस्तत्पुत्रो जयसिंहस्त्रयोदश । तदवरज(:)[3] कोकिलिष्षण्मासान् । तस्य ज्येष्ठभ्राता

11. विष्णुवर्धनस्तमुच्चाट्य सप्तत्रिंशतानि(शंत) वर्षाणि । तत्पुत्रो-विजयादित्यभट्टारकोष्टादश । तत्सुतो

12. विष्णुवर्द्धनष्षट्त्रिंशतं(तत्सुतो)[4] ॥ नरेन्द्रमृगराजाख्य(ो)-मृगराजपराक्रमः । विजयादित्य-

13. भूपालः चत्वारिंशत्समाष्टधीः[5] ॥ तत्पुत्रः कलिविष्णुवर्द्धनो ध्यर्द्धवर्षं । त-

---

[1] Read क्षिते: or the reading should be शान्ताश्च नित्यं नित्यं.

[2] ण after मातृग is omitted in the original.

[3] Visarga is omitted in the original.

[4] तत्सुतो omitted in the plate.

[5] ष्टधा: stands here for : सुधी:

(To face page 164.)

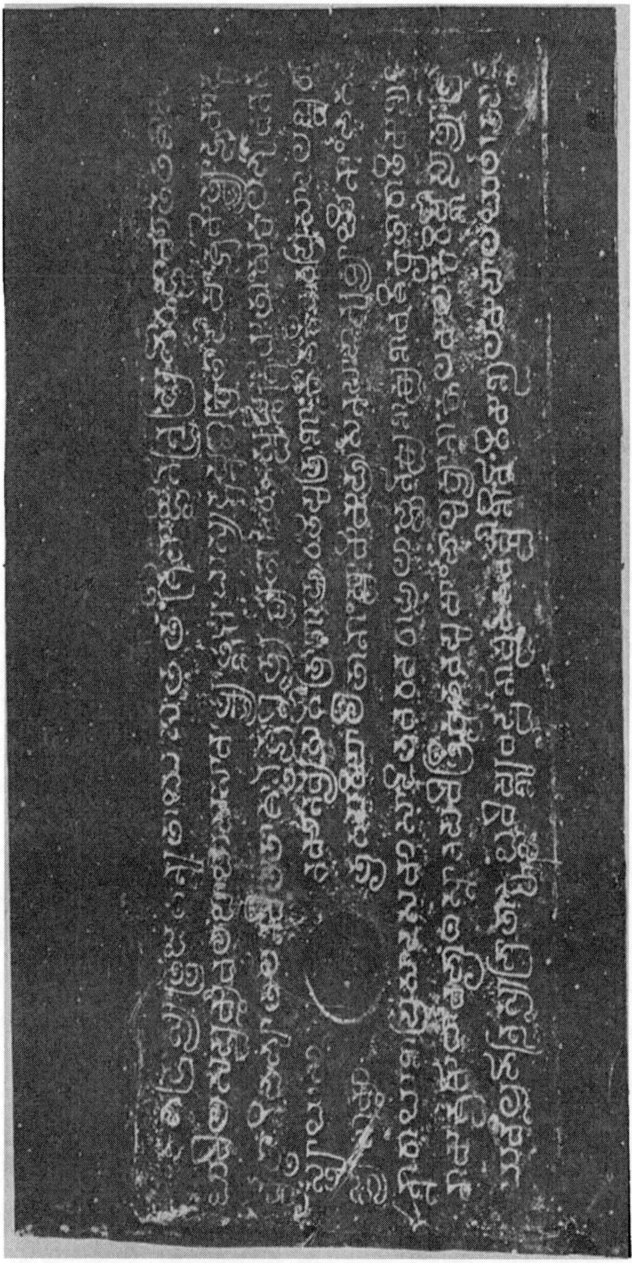

COPPER-PLATE NO. 19.

(1)

(To face page 164.)

COPPER-PLATE NO. 19.

(2)

(To face page 164.)

COPPER-PLATE NO. 19.

(3)

(To face page 164.)

COPPER-PLATE NO. 19.

(4)

(To face page 164.)

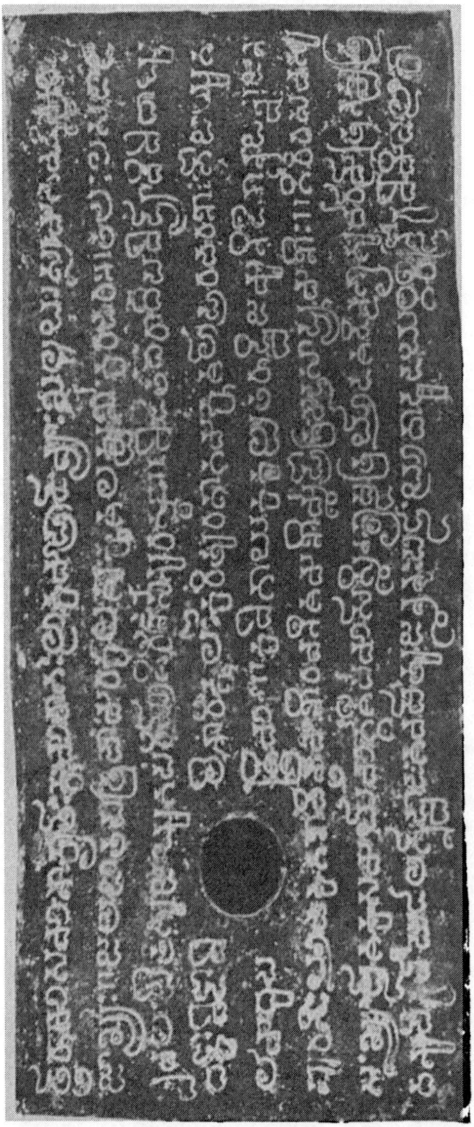

COPPER-PLATE NO. 19.

(5)

(To face page 164.)

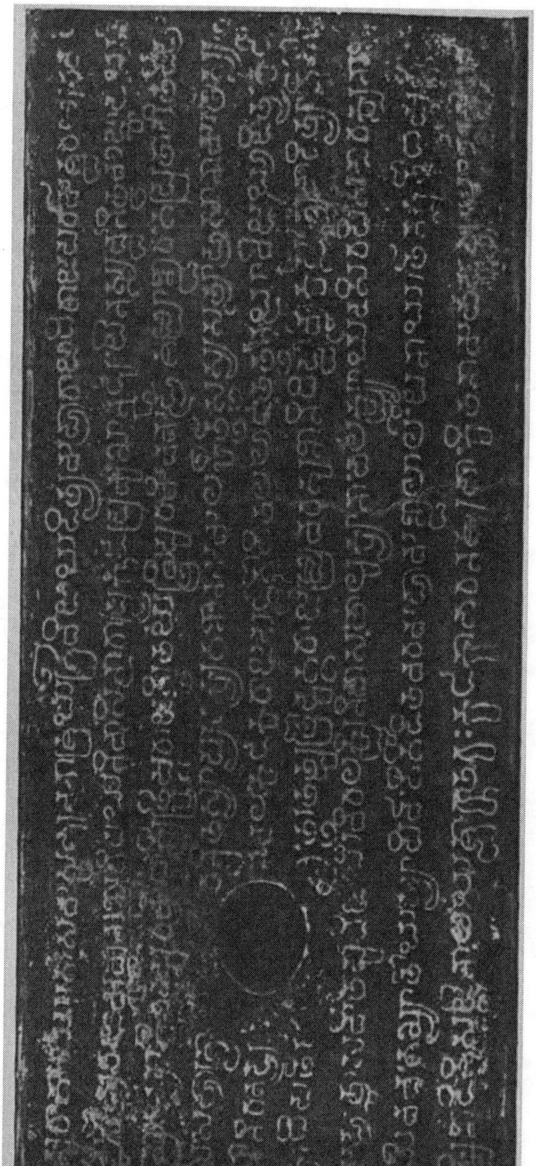

COPPER-PLATE NO. 19.

(6)

(To face page 161.)

COPPER-PLATE NO. 19.

(7)

14. त्पुत्रः परचक्ररामापरनामधेयः(॥) हत्वा भूरिनोदम्रा(म्ब)ष्टनृपार्ते मंमिम्महासंग-

15. रे गङ्गानाश्रित गङ्गकुट[1] शिखरान्त्रिजित्य(तं) सद्दल(।)धि(र्धा) शं संकिलमुग्रवल्लभयुतं यो चा

16. यथित्वा[2] चतुश्चत्वारिंशतमब्दकांश्चविजयादित्योररक्षाक्षितिं ॥ तद्दनुजस्यलब्ध

Second side.

17. यौवराज्यस्य विक्रमादित्यस्य सुतश्चालुक्यभीमस्त्रिंशतं। तस्या-ग्रनो[3] विजयादित्यः

18. षण्मासान्। तदग्रसूनुरम्मराजस्सप्तवर्षाणि। तत्सूनुमाक्रम्य बालं चालुक्यभीमपि-

19. तृव्ययुद्धमल्लस्य नन्दनस्तालनृतो मासमेकं ॥ नानासामन्त-वग्गैराधिकवलयुतैर्भ

20. त्तमातंग सेनो हत्वातं तालराजं विषमरणमुखे सार्द्धमत्यु-ग्रते-

21. जाः। एकाब्दं सम्यगम्भोनिधि वलयद्युतामन्वरक्षद्धरित्रा श्रीमान चालुक्य-

22. भीमक्षितिपतितनयो विक्रमादित्यभूपः ॥ पश्चादहमहामिकदप विक्रमादित्यारत-

23. मने राक्षसा इव प्रजाबाधनपरा दायादराजपुत्रा राज्या-भिलाषिणो युद्धमल्लरा-

---

[1] Ought to be गांगकूट गंगाकूट ; if the latter is inserted the metre would be faulty.

[2] Read योधयित्वा.

[3] This is a mistake for अनुज्ञो as will be seen from other inscriptions. Ought to be सुतः.

24. जमार्त्तण्ड [ल][1] कण्टिकाविजयादित्यप्रभृतयो विग्रहीभूत आसन्। विग्र-

Third plate, first side.

25. हेणैव पंचवर्षाणिगतानि (।) ततः (।) यो वधद्रिाजमार्त्तण्डा-न्तेषां येन रणे कृतो[2] क-

26. ण्टिकाविजयादित्ययुद्धमल्लो ?[3] विदेशगो[4] ॥ ? अन्येमान्य मही भृतोपिबहवो दु-

27. ष्टप्रवृत्ताद्धताः देशोपद्रवकारिणः प्रकटिताः कालालयप्रा-पिताः। दोर्द्दण्डेरि-

28. तमण्डलाग्रलतया युस्योग्रसंग्रामका वाज्ञा[5] तत्परभृ[6] नृ-पैश्च

29. शिरसा मालेव सन्धायिते ॥ नादग्धा? विनिवर्त्तते रिपु-कुलं कोपाग्निरामूल-

30. तः शुभ्रं यस्य यशो न लोकमाखिलं सन्तिष्टते न भ्रमत् [।] द्रव्यांभोधरराशि(जि)रप्यनुदिन-

31. मू सन्तप्यमाने मृशं दारिद्र्योग्रतरातपेनजनसेससस्ये[7] न नो वर्षति ॥ स चालुक्यभीमनत्ता वि-

32. जयादित्यनन्दन(:)। द्वादशाव्यात्समास्सम्यक राजभीमो धरा-तलं ॥ तस्य महेश्वरमू

Third plate, second side.

33. र्त्ती रुमासमानाकृतेः कुमाराभः। लोकमहादेव्याः खलुयस्स-[8] मांभवदम्मरा-

---

[1] ल seems to be superfluous.

[2] Read कृतौ.

[3] Read मल्लौ.

[4] Read गौ.

[5] Read संग्रामकस्याज्ञा.

[6] Read भूनृ.

[7] Read जनसत्सस्ये.

[8] Read समभवत् for समाभवत.

34. जाख्यः ॥ जलजातपत्रचामर कलशांकुशलक्षणां क [र] चरणतलः । लसदाजा-

35. न्ववलंबितभुजयुगपरिघो गिरीन्द्रसान्वं [1] सः ॥ विदितधराधिप-विद्योविविधायु-

36. धकोविदो विलीनारिकुलः करितुरगागमकुशलो हरचरणा-म्भोजयुग-

37. लमधुप श्रीमान् ॥ कविगायककल्पतरु द्विजमुनिदीनान्ध-बन्धुजन-

38. सुरभि । याचकगणचिन्तामणि रवनीशमणिर्म्महोग्रमहसाद्यु-मणिः ॥ गिरिरसकमु-

39. सख्याऽदे शकसमये मार्ग्गशर्षिमासेस्मिन् । कृष्णत्रयोदश-दिने भृगुवारे मैत्रनक्षत्रे ॥

40. धनुषिरवौ घटलग्ने द्वादशवर्षे तु जन्मनः पट्टं । यो धादु-दयगिरीन्द्रो [2] रविमिवलोका-

Fourth plate, first side.

41. नुरागाय ॥ स समस्तभुवनाश्रय श्रीविजयादित्य महाराजाधि-राजपरमेश्वरपरमधा

42. र्म्मिकोम्मराजः कम्मनाण्डुविषयनिवासिनो राष्ट्रकूटप्रमुखान् कुटुंबिनस्सर्व्वानित्त(त्थ)माज्ञापयति ।

43. आर्या(:)। किरणपुरमधार्क्षन्क्रि (त्क्र) ष्णराजस्तितय (तदीय or तृतीय ?) स्त्रिपुरमिव महेशःपाण्डरंग प्रतापी। तादि-हमु-

44. खसहस्रै (स्रै) रन्वितस्याप्यशक्य(मू) गणनम(।)मलकीर्त्ते-स्तस्य सत्साहसानाम् ॥ तस्यात्म-

---

[1] नु in the original. [2] रीन्द्रेरविरिव in Inscription Vol. VII. S.A.

45. जो निरवद्यधवलकटकराजपट्टशोभितललाटः तत्तनयो विज-यादित्य (:) कट-

46. काधिपति(:)। वृंत्त (वृत्तं)। तत्पुत्रो दुग्गराजःप्रवरगुण-निधि र्द्धार्मिकस्सत्यवादीत्यागी भोगी

47. महात्मा समितिषु विजयी वीरलक्ष्मीनिवासः। चालु क्यानचां लक्ष्म्या यदसिरपि सदा रक्षणाय

48. यि(इ)व [1] वंश (:) ख्यातो यस्यापि वेंगि(वेंगी)गदितवरमहा-मण्ड लांलंबनाय। (॥) तेन कृतो धंम्मपुरी द-

49. क्षिणदिशि साज्जिनालयश्चारुतरः। कटकाभरणशुभांकितनाम च पुण्यालंयो वसति (।)

Fourth plate, second side.

50. श्रीयापुनीय शंह (संघ) प्रपुज्य (प्रपूज्य) कोठिमदुव गणेशमुख्यो यः। पुण्यारुह (हे) नन्दिगच्छो जिननान्दिमुनाश्वरो-थग-

51. णधरसदृशः। तस्यात्रशिष्यः प्रथितो धा (ध) रायां दिव (वा) कराख्योमुनिपुगवो भूत। यम् (:) केवलज्ञाननिधि-

52. र्म्महात्मास्वयं जिनानां शद्रशो (सदृशो) गुणैघे। श्रीमानिरदव (श्रीमान्दिरदेव) मुनिस्सुतपोनिधि रभवदस्य शिष्यः (।) धीमां(न्) य

53. स्प्रातिहार्य्यमहिमा [2] संप्पन्नमिवाभिमन्यते लोकः। तदधिष्ठित कटकाभरणजिनालया-

54. य कटकराजविज्ञप्ते (प्ति): खण्डस्फुटनवकृत्यैपिलि (बालि-प्रपूज(जा)दिसत्रसिद्धयर्थम्। यु (उ)

55. त्तरायननिमित्ते मल्लियपूण्डिनामग्राम(ा)टिका सर्व्वकरपरि-हारमुदक

---

[1] Read येव.

[2] महिम संपन्न is the proper form.

56. पूर्व्व(मू)कृत्वा दत्ता। अस्य ग्रामावधयः पूर्व्वतः मंजुनूरु दक्षिणतः यिनिमिलि। पश्चिम-

57. त कल्त्रकूरु॥ यु(उ)त्तरतः धर्म्मपुरमु॥ ये(ए)तद्ग्रामस्य क्षेत्रावधयः पूर्व्वतः गोल्लवि

58. गुण्ट। आग्नेयतः रावियपेरियचेऌरुवु। दक्षिणतः स्थापित शिरा। नैरित्यस्थ(स्था)पितशिलैव

Fifth plate, first side.

59. पाश्चिमतः मल्कपल्लुकोल्लुवायुतटाकश्च॥ वायव्यतः स्य(स्य-)पताशेलत्रै। उत्तरतः दुवचरुवु

60. ईशान्यां कल्त्रकरि एवौंकचेनि सीमैव सीमा॥

COPPER-PLATE No. 20.

[Biṭraguṇṭa grant of Sangama II (S.S. 1278). (A.D. 1356–57?).]

Abstract.

This grant has been already published in the 3rd volume of E.I., pp. 21 to 35.

The plates are five, measuring 10 inches × 5¼ inches. The ring connecting them is lost. The writing is in Telugu and the language is Sanskrit verse.

The inscription opens with an invocation to the Boar incarnation of Vishnu and then introduces the first Vijayanagar king Sangama. Verses 3 and 4 say that he had five sons—Harihara, Kampa, Bukka, Márapa and Muddapa. The first two ruled one after the other. The donor was Kampa's son Sangama II, whose name is not given in any other inscription.

The date of the grant was the new moon day of the third month of Durmukhi in S.S. 1278.

The object of the grant was the village of Biṭraguṇṭa. It was given to 28 Brahmans at the request of the king's preceptor Ṣríkanṭhanátha. The village was hence surnamed Ṣríkanṭhapuram. The occasion is said to be the anniversary of the king's father's death. From this it is to be gathered that Sangama II ascended the throne in S.S. 1277 (*see* E.I. III, p. 23).

The inscription also records the grant of another village Sunkésari.

It is recorded that the writer was Bhóganátha, the Court jester of Sangama II.

Copper-plate No. 21.

[Copper-plate grant of Sómavarapáḍu, Ongole taluk.]

Translation.

The following are the terms of the *paṭṭa* (deed of gift) granted to Kákolli Náráyaṇa Pandit of Konḍavíḍu on Thursday, the 15th of the bright fortnight of Kumbha in the 23rd year of the reign of Ṣrí Vírabhadraráya Maháráya who is Mahánubháva, Paramabhaṭṭáraka, a great devotee of Śiva and Vishnu, who resembles Náráyana in beauty of form, who is well versed in all branches of knowledge, who is a new incarnation of the god of love, who is a great warrior, fearless in battle, the lord of the Drávila maṇḍala (country), the lord of Kalubarga the capital of the Carnatic yielding a revenue of nine crores.

We have granted to you with libation of water the village of Sómavaram in the *ṣíma* of Addanki as an

(Between pages 182 and 183.)

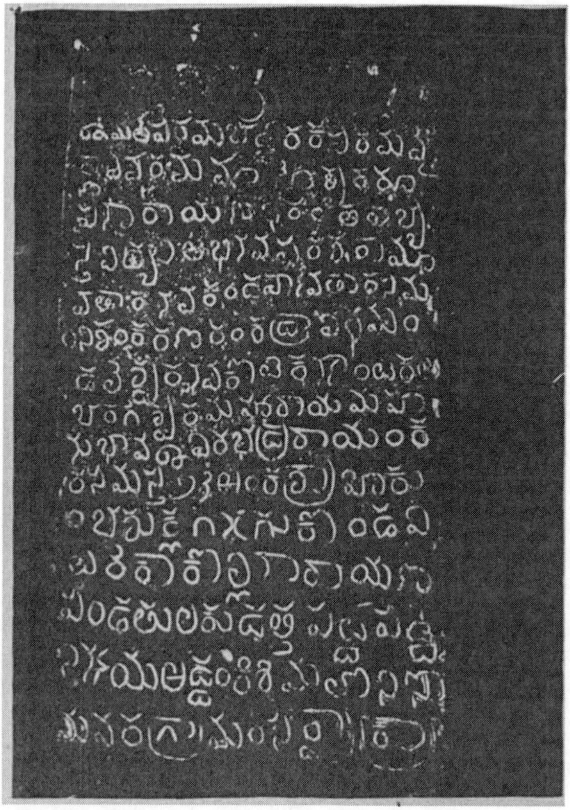

PART OF COPPER-PLATE NO. 21.

(Between pages 182 and 183.)

TERMINATIONS OF COPPER-PLATES NOS. 21 & 22.

absolute gift and as a *sarvamánya*. You should enjoy it as long as the moon and sun endure.

[One imprecatory verse.]

Seal.

NOTE.—This is a single copper-plate engraved on both sides. At the end there are some peculiar symbols which seem to be the seal of the donor. We have not been able to identify the king, but from C.P. 22 it appears that he and Venkataráya Pratápa Rudradéva were Kàkatíyas.

First side.

1. శ్రీమత్ పరమభట్టారక పరమవై
2. ష్ణవ పరమమాహేశ్వర రూ
3. ప నారాయణ నిరంతరాభ్య
4. స్త విద్యా అభినవ పరశరామా
5. వతార నరకండవాణవతారనమ
6. ర నిశంకరణరంకద్రావిళమం
7. డలేశ్వర నవకోటిః నాణంటకలు
8. బరగేశ్వర మహారాయ మహా
9. నుభావశ్రీ వీరభద్రరాయం క
10. ర సమస్త ౧౩ అఃక శ్రాహి కు
11. ంబ శుక్ల ౧౫ గు కొండవి
12. ట కేశాకొల్లినారాయణ
13. పండితులకు దత్తపట్టా పట్ట
14. నినణయ అర్ధంకి శీమలోని సో
15. మవర గ్రామం సర్వా గ్రా

Second side.

16. ంతంగాను సర్వమాన్యంగా
17. నుధార ఓసియిస్తిమి ఆచం
18. ద్రాకణం అనుభవించిది। దానపా

19. లనయోర్మధ్యే దానాచ్ఛ్రేయోను
20. పాలనం । దానాత్స్వర్గ మవా
21. ప్నోతి పాలనాదచ్యు
22. తం పదం ॥.

COPPER-PLATE No. 22.

[Copper-plate grant of Vankayapáḍu and Gunḍimalla villages by Rudradéva Mahárája.]

TRANSLATION.

The charitable edict issued by Víra Ṣrí Gajapati Káketa Rudra Venkaṭaráya Ṣrí Pratápa Rudradéva Mahárájulungáru, lord of Gauḍa, ruler of Kalubarga, capital of the Carnáṭic yielding a revenue of nine-crores, on Monday, the 30th of the dark fortnight of Makara, in the 19th year of his victorious reign, on the holy occasion of Ardhódaya in the *Kaṭaka* of Velupu-konḍa to Kákolli Timma Pandit is as follows. After pouring water in the hand we have granted the two villages Vankáyapáḍu in the Danḍampáḍu (sub-division) of Addanki and Gunḍimalla in the Danḍampáḍu (sub-division) of Ammanabrólu, free of all taxes to you for your sole enjoyment. You, and your sons and grandsons in succession, should enjoy the produce of these two villages in perpetuity as long as the sun and moon exist.

[One imprecatory verse.]

Seal.

NOTE.—This is a single copper-plate. Both sides are engraved. The inscription closes with some letters which seem to form the seal. The plate was got from the karnam of Guḍimélapáḍu in Ongole taluk.

First side.

1. వీరశ్రీ గజపతి గౌడేశ్వర నవకోటికనా౯
2. ంట కలు బురిగేశ్వర కాకేత రుద్రవెంక౯
3. ట రాయశ్రీ ప్రతాపరుద్రదేవుమహా
4. రాజాంకరు విజయరాజ్యే కాకొల్లి తిమ్మా
5. పండితులకు దిల్లాధమ్మా౯శాసన వ
6. ట్ట సమస్త ౧౯ సాంక౯ శ్రాహిమఃకరక్ష్మ
7. ష్ణ ౩౦ సోవేలుపు కొండకటకాయిాని
8. అధో౯దయ పుణ్యకాలాన శ్రీ హస్తా
9. నను ధారాపూవ్వ౯కంగాను పాణిచ్చ
10. డాధిల్లా అద్దంకి౯ దండ్డపాటలోనివం
11. కాయపాడున్ను అమ్మనంబోలిదండ
12. పాటలోని గుండిమడాను యిాగ్రా
13. మాలు రెండున్ను మీరు యేకభోగంగాను
14. చత్రి ఆవేదనలున్ను మానియిస్తిమి అందు
15. లఫలం మీపుత్రపౌత్ర పారంపర్యం
16. గాను అచంద్రాక౯ స్దాయిగాను అనుభ
17. వించ్చి బ్రతికెడి ఏకైవ భగినీలోకే స

Second side:

18. ర్వేషామేవ భూబు(భు)జాం । నభోజ్యా(గ్యా) నక
19. రగ్రాం(గా)హ్యా లి(ఖి)ప్రదత్తా వసుంధరా ।
20. ఖ . . . . . .
21. . . . .

.

Copper-plate No. 23.

[Kuchipúḍi grant of Achyutadéva. Telugu (S.S. 1270). (A.D. 1347–48.)]

Translation.

Hail! On the 15th of the bright-half of Kártika of the year Sarvajit, corresponding to 1270 of the illustrious, victorious and prosperous Śáliváhana Śaka era, (Achyutadéva Mahárája), who belongs to a *ṣákhá*, a *sútra*, and a *gótra*, who is a swan taking refuge in the lotus feet of God himself, who is the grandson of Anantadéva Maháráya, who is the son of Nrisimhadéva Maháráya, who has the *birudas*—Ṣrímad Rájádhirája, Rájaparaméṣvara, Múruráyaraganḍa, Ashtadigráyamanóbhayankara, Bhasadappupararáyaraganḍa, Púrvapaśchimádéśa, Karnáṭa Lakshmí Manóhara—the sovereign who is enthroned at Vijayanagar (gave this edict)—"Ándrapaṭnam was established by Brahma, Parvatam by Vishnu, the *bilam* (cave) by Śiva, Ganga by Ánjanéya. There is no rebirth to one who has been to the temple of Rámalinga which was consecrated by Ráma."

These are the terms of the charitable edict relating to the gift of land executed and granted by Achyutadéva Maháráya, after making obeisance with prostrations to Ṣrí Ándra Rámalinga Svámi, who is the supreme lord of the whole world and who resides in Podili *ṣíma*. A field of 10 *kuchchalas* in the village named Kuchipúḍi, a wet field which can be sown with 10 *túms* (of seed) under the Marripúḍi tank, half a *kuchchala* of land in every village situated in this *ṣíma*, *méras* of 2 measures on every *puṭṭi* of produce, and a fee of Rs. 2 on every Rs. 100 (of revenue). We have settled these terms and granted the above to you on the holy occasion of Parva. Therefore the income derived from these should be utilized for offerings and worship with lights, for the great festivals during Navarátri, the month of Kártika, the month of Dhanus, and Ṣivarátri, for the worshippers and for the offering of 1,000 Bilva leaves on Mondays. On Sunday eight Brahman travellers going on the old road should be fed with food and water. In this manner may you be pleased to maintain the charity always and protect us. May Ándralingéṣvarasvámi deign to accept the eighe species of ownership of this charity.

V. I bear on my head the two feet of Rudra which Hari in the form of a boar, having dug the earth, did not see (*i.e.*, though he dug as far as the nether regions he could not find Rudra's feet).

The signature of Achyutadéva Mahárája.

NOTE.—There are good reasons to doubt the genuineness of this grant which was obtained through M.R.Ry. C. Ráma Rao, Deputy Tahsildar of Podili division, from the Archaka of the Rámalingéśvara temple at Kúchipúḍi. The writer was evidently ignorant of the *śákha*, *sútra* and *gótra* to which Achyutadéva belonged; his grandfather's name differs from that commonly accepted and the value of the grant is suspiciously large. The date is, of course, wrong and, as the Śaka and cycle years correspond, the error, which amounts to about 200 years, is not likely to be due to a mere slip.

First side.

శ్రీరామా

1. స్వస్తి శ్రీ విజయాభ్యుదయ శాలివాహన శక
2. వర్షంబ్బులు ౧౨౭౦ అగు నేటి సర్వజిత్తునా
3. మ సంవ్వత్సర కార్త్తిక శుద్ధ ౧౫ లు శాఖా
4. సూత్రగోత్రాది సాక్షాద్భగవద్విగ్రహ పాదా
5. రవింద్వాశ్రితహంశః అనంత్త దేవమహారాయు
6. లుగారి పౌత్రులుఁన్ను నృశిఁహ్వ దేవమహారా

7. యులుగారి పుత్రులుంన్ను శ్రీమద్రాజాధిరాజరాజ.
8. పరమేశ్వర మూరురాయరగండ్ల అష్టధిగ్రామ (హె)
9. భయంకరఃరభాస తప్పుపరరాయరగండ్ల పూర్వప
10. శ్చమ దిశాకర్ణాటరాజ్యలక్ష్మీ మనోహారవిజ
11. యనగర శింహాసనాధీశ్వరులు, బ్రంహ్మనిర్మా
12. ణంద్రపట్నం విష్ణునిర్మాణ పర్వతం శంబోబిల
13. ంచ్చ రిర్మాణాం సార్వకాలేషు శాశ్వితంగంగ్గాని
14. ర్మాణాంజ్ఞనేయం రామచంద్ర పతిష్ఠితం రా
15. మలింగ్గాలయం దృష్ట్వా పునర్జన్మంనవిద్యతే ।
16. శ్రీమత్సమస్తలోకాధీశ్వరులవై పాదిల సీమ
17. లోవుంన్న అంద్రరామలింగస్వామివారికి సాష్టా
18. ంగ్గ దండ్డప్రణామంబ్బులు చేశి అచ్చుతదేవమహారాయు
19. లు వ్రాయించ్చియిచ్చిన భూధానధర్మశాసన క్రమ
20. ము యల్లన్నను, కూచిపూడి అనెగ్రామములో
21. ౧ం పదికుచ్చళ్ల పొలము మర్రిపూడి చెరువుకింద్ద
22. పంద్దుము విత్తులవరిమిడి, శిమామూలము గ్రా
23. మాదులకు వూరికి అరకుచ్చలపొలము, పండినఫ
24. లాదులుకు పుట్టికి ముంతెడుమేర యీశీమయెత్తి
25. న రూకలుకు నూటికిమాడ లెఖరుసుము, యీలా
26. గునవిర్ణయము చెశి యధావర్వ పుంణ్యకాలమ
27. ంద్దు నత్మకుసమర్పింస్తిమిగనుకు యింద్దులఫలం
28. నివెదన దిపారాధనలుకు నవరాత్రిళ్లు కార్తీక
29. మాసము ధనుర్మాసము శివరాత్రి మహో
30. త్సవాదులుకు పరిచారకులుకు యింద్దువాసర
31. మునసహస్ర బిల్వదళసమర్పణవెళను ఆది

Second side.

32. మార్గానడిచెవరదెశి బ్రాహ్మణులకుయెనిమి
33. దిమంద్దికి అంన్నోదకములు యిప్పింంచ్చి యీలా

(To face page 189.)

COPPER-PLATE NO. 24.

(2)

(To face page 189.)

COPPER-PLATE NO. 24.

(I)

34. గున అనుగ్రహించ్చి సార్వకాలము మంమ్మున

35. రక్షించ్చునెలెను యీధర్మము అష్టభోగస్వాధమ్యే

36. ము అంద్రరామలింగ్గస్వామి అవుధరించ్చుగా

37. క । [1]హరిఃవరాహరూపెణ । భిత్వాచలమవ్ర

38. ష్టభే । యోరుద్రపాదౌ తౌ భక్త్యా శిరసా ధారయామ్య

39. హం । అచ్యుత దేవమహారాయులు వ్రాలు

COPPER-PLATE No. 24. (A.D. 663-64?)

[Talamanchi grant of the Western Chálukyan king Vikramáditya I.]

Note.

These plates are three in number and were found by a resident of Tallamanchi and given to the Collector of Nellore. They measure $7\frac{1}{2}$ inches × $3\frac{1}{4}$ inches and are connected by a ring, the seal on which is much erased and bears the figure of a boar. The first and third plates are engraved only on one side. The grant was by the Western Chálukyan king Vikramáditya I. The characters are of the usual western Chálukyan style. The only noteworthy point is the use of the symbol ∝ for final *m*. Except in one portion the writing is well preserved. A photograph is annexed.

---

[1] The text is possibly as follows :—

37. हारे: वाराहरूपेण । भित्त्वा तलमद्द

38. ष्टवान् । यौ रुद्रपादौ(तौ) भक्तया । शिरसा धारयाम्य

39. हं ॥

Compare with this inscription those in Volume VI, *I. Antiquary*, p. 75; Volume VII, *I. Antiquary*, p. 219. The name of the dynasty Chálukya is given with the vowel of the first syllable short.

The object of the grant is the village of Edusanti situated to the north of Kororukonṭa. The donee is the king's spiritual preceptor Mégháchárya of the Vasisbṭa *gótra*. The date is the sixth year of the reign of the king. Dr. Fleet places Vikramáditya I about 580 S.S. (Vol. VII, I.A., 218.)

The inscription was engraved by Ṣrí Vajravarma of the Vaidya family. It closes with a benediction on Brahmans and cows.

TRANSLATION.

Verse. Victorious is the Boar form, which was manifested of Vishnu, which made the ocean tempestuous (and) which had the earth resting on the tip of its lofty right tusk.

The great grandson of Śrí Pólikési (Pulikéṣi) Vallabha Mahárája, who adorned the race of the Chálukyas who are illustrious, who are of the lineage of Mánavya which is praised throughout the whole universe, who are the descendants of Háriti, who have been fostered by the seven mothers who are the seven mothers of the world, who have uninterruptedly obtained prosperity through the protection of Kártikèya, and who have subjugated all kings in an instant at the sight of the sign of the Boar which they had acquired through the grace of the Lord Náráyaṇa and whose body was purified by baths taken after performing horse-sacrifices,

The grandson of Ṣrí Kírtivarma Prithivi Vallabha Mahárája, whose pure fame was established in the territories of the hostile kings of Vanavási and other countries which had been invaded byhis valour;

the beloved son of Satyáśráya Śrí Prithiví Vallabha Mahárájádhirája Rájaparaméśvara, who acquired the title of Paraméṣvara (supreme lord) by defeating Śrí Harsha-varddhana [1] the warlike supreme lord of the whole region of the north;

the unrepulsed Vikramáditya, Vikramáditya Satyáṣráya Śrí Prithivi Vallabha Mahárájádhirájaparaméśvara, whose enemies were vanquished by (the valour of) his own arm which resembles (in vastness) the body of the serpent by which the burden of the earth is borne (*i.e.*, Ádiṣésha), who has many wounds concealed by his armour, having regained the fortune of his father which was eclipsed by the triad of kings,[2] with the sole help of the excellent horse named Chitrakantha and of the pure, sharp and brilliant sword which exults in tasting the blood of hostile kings in many famous battles, bearing singly the burden of the whole kingdom which was firmly established, and having reinstated in that triad of kingdoms by word of mouth (verbal command) the property of gods and grants to Brahmans which had lapsed, for the increase of religious merit and fame, having vanquished in battle hostile kings in all quarters, and having obtained the fortune of his own family and (having attained) the status of Paraméśvara (supreme lordship), commands all.

"Be it known to you! In the 6th year of our prosperous and victorious reign, in the month of Śrávaṇa,

---

[1] King of Canouj. [2] The triad of kings, *viz.*, Pándya, Chóla and Chéra.

at solar eclipse, the village Edusanti, situated to the northern side of the village named Korurokonṭa, has been given by us with libation of water, free from all taxes, to our *guru* Srí Méghácbárya, who is learned in the Védas with their Angas and Upángas, who is of the *gótra* of Vasishṭa, for the acquisition of religious merit and fame by our parents and ourselves, to last as long as the sun, moon, earth and ocean exist. It should be protected by those who wish to acquire fame just like their own gift.

V. It is very easy to give one's own property; but the protection of the grant of another is difficult.

V. (If it is asked which is more meritorious) giving (oneself) or preserving (another's grant), preservation is better than giving.

And it has been said by the blessed Vyása, who compiled the Védas.

V. Land has been enjoyed by many kings beginning with Sagara; he, who for the time being possesses land enjoys the benefit of it.

V. Whoever appropriates land given by himself or another is reborn a worm in ordure for 60,000 years.

This edict of the family of Ṣrí Méghácbrya has been written by Śrí Vajra Varma of the Vaidya family (caste).

May there be prosperity to cows and Brahmans!

Ṣrí!

NOTE.—This inscription was discovered about 12 years ago by a servant of Adapalli Venkaṭa Reḍḍi of Párlapalli while ploughing some land known as Talamanchipádu in Talamanchi of Nellore taluk where a flourishing village is said to have once stood. The plates were got for us by the Deputy Tahsildar M.R.Ry. A. Ananta Náráyana Śástri and have been sent to the Madras Museum at the request of the owner.

First plate, second side.

1. जयत्याविष्कृतं विष्णोर्व्वाराहं क्षोभितार्स्म(र्ण)वं। दक्षिणोन्नतदं-ष्ट्राग्रविश्रान्तभु-

2. वनंवपुः ॥ श्रीमतां सकलभुवनसंस्तूयमानमानव्यसगोत्राणां हा-रितिपुत्रा-

3. णां सप्तलोकमातृ(तृ)भिस्सप्तमातृभि रभिवर्धितानां कार्तिकेयप-रिरक्षणप्राप्तक-

4. ल्याणपरंपराणां भगवन्नारायणप्रसादसमासादितवराहलान्छ-नेक्ष-

5. णक्षणवशीकृताशेषमहींभृतां चलिक्यानां कुलमलंकरिष्णो-रश्वमे-

6. धावभृथस्नानपवित्रीकृतगात्रास्य श्रीपालिकेशिवल्लभमहारा-ज-

7. स्य प्र पौत्रः पराक्रमाक्रान्तवनवास्यादिपरनृपतिमण्डलप्रणि-बद्धविशुद्ध-

8. [विशुद्ध] कीर्त्ति[1] [श्री कीर्त्ति] श्रीकीर्त्तिवर्म्मपृथिवीवल्ल-भमहाराजस्य पौत्रः समर-

9. संसक्त सकलोत्तरापथे श्वरश्रीहर्षवर्द्धनपराजयोपलब्धपर-मेश्वरा-

Second plate, first side.

10. परनामधेयस्य सत्याश्रय श्रीपृथिवीवल्लभमहाराजाधिराजप-रमेश्वर-

11. स्य प्रियतनयः चित्रकण्ठाख्य प्रव(र)तुरं गमेनैकेनैवप्रतीताने-कस-

---

[1] Read कीर्तेः.

12. मरमुखेषु रिपुनृपतिरुधिरजलास्वादनरणयज्वऊ [1] दमलनिशि-
तनिंस्त्रि श-

13. धारयाच धृतधरणीभर भुजंग भोगसद्दशनिजभुजाविजित-
विजिर्ग(गी)षुः-

14. आत्मकवचावमग्रानेकप्रहारस्वगुरो(ः)श्रियमवनिपतित्रितया-

15. न्तरितां(।) या(मा)त्म सात्कृत्यकृत्यै [2] काधिष्टिताशेषराज्य-
भरस्तस्मित्राज्य-

16. त्रयेच नष्टानि देवरवब्रह्मदेयानि धर्मयशोभिवृद्धये रवमुखे-
नस्था-

17. पि त [3] च[4]रणाशिरासि रिपुनरेन्द्रान्दिशि दिशि जित्वा रववं
शजां लक्ष्मीं प्राप्यच-

18. परमेश्वरतामनिवाधि(रि)तविक्रमादित्यः विक्रमादित्यसत्याश्र-
यश्रीप्ट-

19. थिवीवल्लभमहाराजाधिराजपरमेश्वरस्सर्वानाज्ञापयति विधि-
त [5]-

Second plate, second side.

20. यस्तु भो स्माभिः प्रवर्द्धमाननिजयराज्यषट्संवत्सरतमे श्राव-

21. णमास(से)सूर्यग्रहणे उदक[।]पूर्व्वं सांगोपाङ्गवेदविदुषेवासिष्ट-

22. सगोत्राय श्री मेघाचार्य्याय स्वकीयगुरवे कोळ्नूकोन्ठ ?
ग्राम-

23. स्योत्तरपार्श्वे एदुसात्ति न्नाम ग्रामः माता पित्रो रात्मनः-

24. प्पु(पु) ण्ययशोवाप्तये सर्व बाधा [6] परिहारंदत्तं [7]। आच-
न्द्रार्क-

---

[1] Read रणदुज्वल or र (स) नायमान.

[2] Read कृतेका.

[3] Read स्थापमित्वा.

[4] There is a dot after च

[5] Read विदित.

[6] वों in original.

[7] Read दत्त:.

25. धरात्मिवस्थिति(?)समकालं यश श्चिर्चीषुभि(:)स्वदत्ति [1] निर्व्वि
शेषंपरि-

26. पालनीयं॥ स्वन्दातुं सुम(द्द)च्छक्यं दुःखमन्यस्य पालनं। दानं-
27. वा पालनं वेति दानाच्छ्रेयोनुपालनं ॥ वि

Third plate, first side.

28. उक्तंच भगवतावेदव्यासेन व्यासे । वहुभिववसुधा[2]भुक्ति
29. राजभिस्सगरादिभिः । यस्ययस्य यदाभूमिस्तस्यतस्य
30. तथाफलं॥ स्वदत्तां दतां वा योहरेतवसुन्धरांषष्टिंव
31. र्षसहस्राणि विष्टायांजायते क्रिमिरिति । श्रीमेघाचा
32. र्यस्यान्वयस्यशासनं वैद्यान्वयं(य)श्रीवज्र वर्मना(ण)लिखितं।
33. स्वस्त्यस्तु गोब्राह्मणेभ्यः ॥ श्री ॥

---

[1] Read स्वदत्त. [2] Read वसुन्धरां.

STONE INSCRIPTIONS.

Atmakur (1). (A.D. 1616–17.)

[Amánicheruvella. Telugu. To north near tank bund.]

Translation.

May there be prosperity! Hail! On the 12th of the bright fortnight of Kártika of the year Nala, corresponding to the illustrious, victorious and prosperous Sálivábana Saka year 1538, Srímad Rájádhirája Rája-paramésvara Srí Víra Pratápa Srí Víra Venkatapati-ráyadéva Mahaáráyalayyaváru . . . . . to Kampi Náyadu. This charitable edict was granted by Mára Kampi Náyániugáru to Kandagada Guruvayya. For worshipping Kóna Vallabharáya of the southern Sara-vólu, situated in Udayagiri *Síma* which was granted to us by the Rája, we have granted that village to you. Therefore, having come with your family to Udayagiri and taken up your residence there, worship Sarvésvara and, listening to my advice and that of my son Appánáyundu, enjoy that village, you, your sons and grandsons, in perpetuity as long as the sun and moon endure.

* * * *

1. శుభమస్తు స్వస్తిశ్రీ
2. జయాభ్యుదయ శాలివాహన శకవర్షంబులు
3. ౧౫౩౮ అగునేటి నళసంవత్సర కార్తిక శు ౧౨ లు
4. శ్రీ మద్రాజాధిరాజ రాజపరమేశ్వర శ్రీ వీరప్రతా

5. వ శ్రీ వీర వేంకట పతిరాయదేవ మహారాయ
6. లయ్యవారు . . . . . . కంపినాయనికి
7. మారకంపినాయనింగారు (కంద) కడ గురువయ్య
8. కు ఇచ్చిన ధర్మశాసనం మాకు రాయలువారు పా
9. లించిన ఉదయగిరిశీమలోను దక్షిణపు శరవాళు కొ
10. న వల్ల భరాయని శేవ సేసుకొని వుండేనిమిత్తం ఆగ్రామం
11. మీకు ఇస్తిమిగనుక విటకుకుటుంబసమేతంగాను
12. వచ్చి వుదయగిరిలో కాపురాలువుండి సర్వేశ్వరు
13. ని సేవచేసుకొని మేముచెప్పిన బుద్ధిమంతులున్ను
14. మాకొమార అప్పానాయండుచెప్పిన బుద్ధి
15. మంతులును పుత్రపౌత్రపా
16. రంపర్యంతమున్ను ఆచంద్రార్కస్థాయిగా
17. ను అనుభవించి బ్రతుకువారు . . ఎను

Note.—This Mára Kampi Náyuḍu was perhaps a member of the family referred to in U. 23.

Atmakur (2).

[Amánicheruvella. Telugu. South of village.]

Translation.

Salutation be to the illustrious Rámánuja. May there be prosperity! . . . .

1. శ్రీమతే రామానుజాయ
2. నమః । శుభమస్తు
3. ణమై శ్రీ పంచకి
4. . తా . ధాతంభు తె
5. వన్యవ . తెలవు
6. . వ పరమతవర్జణ
7. . వ హార్యమంత్యభు

8. . . . . వ . గాను వమమి
9. గ్రపు . ణ దివ్యాప్రవీణ
10. సభలో . వడుపూర్వ్వ
11. వ . . డెనం . న పర్వ
12. . . . . డింగాను
13. . . . . త్రవిక్వత
14. . . చా . ఖండుశెసి
15. శావునుడు . రి ఇయ్య
16. . నం ఇను . డు . చలక్రినా
17. చిన్నమయవవాడు
18. . వనమమ . . . . . .
19. . . రన . . . . ప్రతిహా
20. . . . .

ATMAKUR (3). (A.D. 1628–29.)

[Anantaságaram. Telugu and Sanskrit in Telugu character. On a stone near sluice of tank between Manchálapalli and Mustafapuram. The Sanskrit portion is a summary of the Telugu.]

TRANSLATION.

Hail! On Wednesday, the 3rd *tithi* of the bright fortnight of the month of Vaiṣákha, the day which is called Akshakaratritíya[1] and which is the birthday of Balabhadra of the year Vibhava, corresponding to the year 1550 of the illustrious and prosperous Ṣáliváhana era, while Ṣrímad Rájádhirája, Rájaparaméṣvara, Ṣrí Víra Pratápa, Ṣrí Víra Rámadéva Mahárája, seated on (his) diamond

---

[1] Akshayatritíya is the 3rd of the bright fortnight of Vaiṣákha.

throne, was ruling the kingdom of the earth, while Venkaṭapati Náyaningáru, who is the moon of the ocean of the race of Padmanáyaka, who is an Arjuna in war, who is the paramour of the prostitutes who are princes possessing all titles, who bears the *biruda* Kánchikavátaṭachúrakáruḍu (?),[1] who is of the Récherla *gótra*, who is the son of Kumára Timmanáyaningáru and the grandson of Veligóṭi Peda Tonḍamanáyaningáru, was ruling the *Símas* of Rápúru, Nellúru, Pórúru, Káḷahasti, Konḍamapáḍu, Venkaṭagiri, Korṭúru and other places which were granted as an *amaram* (to him) by Ráma-dévaráyaluváru, the channel of the Muddala tank of Anantaságaram *agrahára* having fallen into disrepair, Raghupati Ammagáru who is as holy as Ṣrí Mahá Lakshmi, Śarasvati and Párvati, who is the daughter of Muchintala Rangappa Náyaniváru, and the wedded wife of Veligóṭi Komára Timmanáyaningáru, and who is the mother-of-pearl of the pearl, to wit, Venkaṭapati Náyaka, caused to be erected in the village of Mustafapuram 33 pillars on the weir (of the tank) with walls and steps on both sides in stone, and also caused the tank bund to be strengthened by earth-work so that it may last as long as the sun and moon endure, the former weir having . . . . Ṣrí, Ṣrí.

Sanskrit portion.

King Venkaṭanáṭhachandra . . . . son . . . of the Ṣrí Récherla *gótra* of the Veligóṭi family

* * * *

Raghupatyambá, mother of . . . .

---

[1] The destroyer of the door of Kánchi (?)

* * * *

addicted to making gifts . . . .
constructed the weir and bund of the tank of Anantaságaram.

Raghupatyambá, the wife of Kumára Timmapati the ornament of kings, the daughter of Ṣrí Bangéṣvara.

Rácha Raghupatyambe . . . the frontal gem of Ṣrímat Veligóṭi Venkaṭapatinátha. This is the edict of the tank of Anantaságaram. The weir of Anantaságaram tank . . . . fixed with stone pillars. Ṣrí, Ṣrí

1. స్వస్తి
2. శ్రీ జయాభ్యుదయ శాలివాహ
3. న శకవరుషంబులు ౧౪౪౦ యగు
4. నేటి విభవసంవత్సర వైశాఖశుద్ధ ౩
5. బలభద్రజయంతి త్రికాద్యష్టకర
6. త్రితీయప్రియుక్త బుధవారంనాడు
7. . . . . శ్రీమద్రాజాధిరాజ
8. రాజపరమేశ్వర శ్రీవీరప్రతాప శ్రీ
9. వీర రామదేవ మహారాయలు వ
10. జ్రఖచిత భద్రశింహాసనారూఢుం_
11. పృథివీ సాంమ్రాజ్యం చేయుచుండంగా
12. పద్మనాయక పాథోధి (?) చంద్రుండును సం
13. గ్రామ పార్థుండున్ను సర్వబిరుద కొమా
14. ర వేశ్యాభుజంగుండున్ను కాంచ్చికవా(త)
15. ట చూరకారుడున్ను రేచర్లగోత్ర
16. పవిత్రుండున్ను వెలిగోటి పెదకొం
17. డమ నాయనింగారి పౌత్రులున్ను
18. కొమార తిమ్మనాయనింగారి పుత్రు
19. లైన వెంకటపతినాయనింగారు తమ
20. కు రామదేవరాయలు అమరానకు

21. పాలించిన రాపూరు నెల్లూరు పోరూ
22. రు కాళహస్తి తొండమపాడు వెం
23. కటగిరి కోట్టూరారు మొదలయిన శీమ
24. లు పాలింపుచుండంగాను ॥ శ్రీమహా
25. లక్ష్మీ సరస్వతి పార్వతీ సమాన పవిత్రచ
26. రిత్రురాలయిన ముచ్చింతల రంగప్ప నా
27. యనింవారికి బుత్రిఅయిన వెలిగోటి
28. కొమార తింమానాయనింగారికి ధ
29. ర్మ దేవి అయిన వెంకటపతి నాయక ము
30. క్తాఫల శుక్తియైన రఘువతంమ్మగారు
31. అనంతసాగర మహాగ్రహార మండ్లలచె
32. రువు కాల్వ శిథిలమై వుండ్డగానున్న
33. ముస్తా పురమునందున
34. మునుపు అలుగుపని . కుం . . . . .
35. ంచి చెరువుకట్ట మట్టిపని వేయించేటట్టు
36. గానున్న అలుగుకు ముప్పదిమూండు శిలా
37. స్తంభాలు నిలిపి యిరుగడల సంతనిసారువ
38. లు సొపానాలు కలుగుకట్టుగాను ఆచంద్రా
39. కర్కాస్తాయిగాను కట్టించెను శ్రీనిభా

Sanskrit.

40. లకు మాంబిక . . . . .
41. శృతః ॥ శ్రీరెచర్ల పౌత్ర పవిత్రవెలిగోటి
42. టి వంశమణోభి జా. . . భూమో
43. పుత్రవేంకట నాథచంద్రేశ్వరం
44. ఆ . ధార . . యిగాభి మాతృరఘుపత్యంబ
45. సంకాశ . . ద్రద (. . శ్రీదేవిమానసరిఘా
46. బోలలిదళ పారమా విలాసనల శ్రీ
47. . తృబలా రథదాసారతోక రుచి

48. . . పరివాహించ అను త్తసా

49. గర (కపుణం) తోటక సేతుంపరి వాహా

50. . . దోధిదాతుజా రఘుపత్యంబా

51. . రిమణి భూపోత్తంసకుమారతింమ్మ

52. పతిభార్యచ ముచ్చియ శ్రీరంగేశ్వరవు

53. త్రి రాచరఘు పత్యంబ జనను శ్రీమతు

54. వెలుగోటి వెంకటపతి నాంధ చింతామణి సే

55. య యహంత మనంత్తసాగర తటకస్య శ్రాస

56. నం) (శ్రీమల్లిలగినిగి) శ్రీభవ్యవిభవేచ శూద్దతృతి

57. య్యాయ సితిభానుజ పంచకయాపింశ

58. లాస్తంబా యువవాస్రాబవైశాఖ

59. వి వ్రాటంపువలం జాశాయలి . . . నం

60. రచాంచదనంత సాగరతుటకస్యపరివా

61. హం (గిద) శ్రీ శ్రీ.

ATMAKUR (4).

[Anantaságaram. - Telugu. In tank bed to the north.]

TRANSLATION.

The boundary stone planted by Ráyasam Koṇḍa Marusayya.

1. రా యస
2. ము కొండ్డ
3. మరుసయ్య
4. వారి సం
5. ధి రాయి

ATMAKUR (5). (A.D. 1520–21.)

[Anantaságaram. Telugu. In tank bed.]

TRANSLATION.

On Thursday, the 15th of the bright fortnight of Jyéshṭa of the year Vikrama, Ráyasam Koṇḍa Marusayya (planted) the boundary stone. Ṣrí, Ṣrí, Ṣrí!

1. విక్రమ సంవత్స
2. ర జేష్ట శు ౧౫ గు
3. రాయసం కొం
4. డ మరుసయసం
5. ధ్వ రాయి శ్రీ శ్రీ
6. శ్రీ

ATMAKUR (6). (A.D. 1520–21.)

[Anantaságaram. Telugu. On tank bund above Gollabháma temple.]

TRANSLATION.

May there be prosperity! Hail!

On Thursday, the 15th day of the bright fortnight of Jyéshṭa of the year Vikrama, corresponding to the year 1444 of the illustrious, victorious and prosperous Ṣaka era, while Ṣríman Mahárájádhirájá, Rájaparaméṣvara Ṣrí Víra Pratápa Ṣrí Víra Krishṇadéva Mahárája, seated on the diamond throne at Vijayanagar, was ruling the whole kingdom of the earth, Mahá Rája Ṣrí Ráyasam Koṇḍa Marusayyagáru the agent (Káryakarta) of the throne of the Ráya (king of Vijayanagar) caused to be constructed a tank at Anantaságaram for the religious merit of his mother Sankáyamma and his father Timmarusayyagáru Ṣrí, Ṣrí, Ṣrí! In the name of Sankáyamma and Timmarusu he caused to be constructed a temple. . . . and (gave) *vrittis* (shares) to Brahmans. Those who obstruct (this) will incur the sin of killing near the Ganges. Having founded the endowment as charity (for the merit of) Timmaya and Ṣrí Krishnaráya . . . . . (he) set up images of Íṣvara Tripurántaka.

[One imprecatory verse.]

Note.—The cyclic year differs by one year from the S.S. year.

1. శుభం ము। తినా (?) ॥
2. స్వస్తి శ్రీ జయాభ్యుదయ
3. శాలివాహన శకవర్ష
4. ంబులు ౧౪౪౪ అగు
5. నేంటి విక్రమ సంవత్సర
6. జేష్ట శు ౧౫ గు। శ్రీమన్మ
7. హా రాజాధిరాజ రాజ
8. పరమేశ్వర శ్రీ వీరప్రతాప
9. శ్రీ వీర క్రిష్ణదేవరాయ
10. మహారాయులు విజయ
11. నగరంమందు వజ్రసింహా
12. సనారూఢులై సకలసా
13. ంబ్రాజ్యము చేయుచుండ్గ
14. ంగాను రాయసింహ్వో
15. సనానకు కార్యకర్తలై
16. నట్టి మహారాజ శ్రీ

Second side.

17. రాయసం
18. కొండమరు

19. సయ్యంగా
20. రు తమ తల్లి
21. సంకాృయమ్మ
22. ంగారికిన్ని
23. తమ తండ్రి
24. తిమ్మరుసయ్య
25. ంగారికిన్ని పు
26. ణ్యము గాను
27. అనంత సా
28. గరము చెరువ్వ
29. కట్టించెను
30. శ్రీ శ్రీ శ్రీ
31. శ్రీ సంకుృ యంమ
32. భైర తిమ్మరుసయ్య
33. పేరను గుడికట్టించి
34. . . . కట్టించె
35. ను బ్రాంహాణ్రవి
36. త్తులు . . .
37. . . . యువ్వారైన
38. విఫలంచేసిన గంగ్గ క
39. ర్ణం వధియించిన
40. పాపానం బోవువారు
41. ధర్మ ప్రీతి స్వాస్త్య
42. నుంచేసి తిమ్మయ
43. శ్రీ క్రిష్ణరాయలకు
44. . . . . .
45. . . చేసిరి . ఈ
46. శ్వరునికి త్రిపురాం
47. తకేశ్వరుని . . .

48. . . . .
49. . . ప్రతిష్ట చేయిం
50. చె। స్వదత్తా ద్విగుణం పు
51. ణ్యం పరదత్తానుపాలనం
52. పరదత్తాపహారేణ
53. స్వదత్తం నిష్ఫలం భవేత్

ATMAKUR (7). (A.D. 1246–47.)

[Annamasamudram. Telugu. From a stone in the tank bed. In one or two places the text is obscure.]

TRANSLATION.

Hail! On Friday, the 11th day of the bright fortnight of Bhádrapada of the year Parábhava, corresponding to the year 1168 of the illustrious Ṣaka era, Hail! Ṣríman Mahámaṇḍaléṣvara Allu Tirukáḷatidéva Mahárája, who is endowed with the honour consisting of all names and titles, while ruling at the city of Kánchi, holding pleasant communication (with his feudatories), consecrated Dánava Murári Perumándi Déva at Ṣrí Átukúru (Átmakur) for the religious merit of his father-in-law Tirukáḷadéva Mahárája and for the increase of his own life, health and wealth and caused to be built a temple and manḍapas to that deity. He made a gift for (providing) enjoyments in perpetuity to last as long as the sun and moon exist. May there be great prosperity!

He made a gift of (lease of) 4 *paṭṭus* of paddy field out of Prabhu mányam [1] (Government land) measured by

---

[1] This phrase perhaps means land granted by the State for the private use of a subordinate ruler.

the 20-span (pole) of this village; 20 *paṭṭus* of dry Government land measured by the (pole of) 26 of the same spans of this village . . . . (the rate is) a *máḍa* for 2 *paṭṭus* of kóru land; on dry land it is a *máḍa* per *paṭṭu*; a *máḍa* per 4 *paṭṭus* in excess (?) of *kóru* dry land. This is the rate for *kóru* land for all expenses for them.

Rámireḍḍi should pay in the month of Vaiṣákha of every year 130 *máḍas* on the gross income towards all the expenses of the deity irrespective of the vicissitudes of the season, acts of the king, acts of God, excess of rain and drought. This lease should continue as long as the moon and the sun endure.

First side.

1. స్వస్తి శ్రీశక వరు
2. షంబులు ౧౧౬౮
3. అగు నేంటి
4. పరాభవ సంవ
5. త్సరమున భాద్రప
6. ద శుద్ధ ౧౧ శుక్రవార
7. మున స్వస్తి సమస్తంబు
8. నామాంక మాదిశా ప్ర
9. శస్తి సహితం శ్రీమను
10. మహా మండ్డలేశ్వర అ
11. ల్లు తిరుకాళతి దేవ
12. మహారాజు కాంచీ
13. పట్టణంబున సు
14. ఖ సంకథా వినోదంబు

15. ల రాజ్యంబు సేయుచుండి

16. తమ మామ తిరుకాళ

17. దేవ మహారాజునకు

Second side.

18. పుణ్యముగాను

19. తనకు ఆయు

20. రారోగ్యైశ్వరియా

21. భివృద్ధ్యర్థము

22. గాను శ్రీ ఆతూర

23. రిలోన దానవ

24. మురారి పెరుమా

25. ండిదేవర ప్రతిష్ట

26. సేసి ఆ దేవరకు

27. గుడి మండపా

28. లు గట్టిస్తిమి మీరు

29. ఆచంద్రార్కస్థాయి

30. గాను రాగభోగ

31. ములకిచ్చె మ

32. హాళ మహా

33. శ్రీ శ్రీ శ్రీ

Third side.

34. ఇయూరని జేనను

35. ఎం జేనకొలను ప్ర

36. భు మాన్యము వరి

37. చేను నాలుగు పట్ల

38. ఇజేనన అడ జేన

39. ల కొలయ ప్రభు

40. మాన్యము వెలిసేను

41. ఇరువది వట్లు ఊ

42. రను వెలిచేను మడి

43. ము పాలి కోరు నేల రె

44. ం డి పట్టికి మాడవె

45. లిసేను పటిమాడా ? వె

46. లి కోరు నేలపఇంటి

47. నాలుగు వట్లమాడా

48. ను ఇమేర కోరునకు

49. ఆరికి సెలవుగాను

50. సర్వా—యమునకు

51. రామిరడి దేవరకు

52. వైశాఖ మాసమున

Fourth side.

53. ను పంటాను నూ

54. ట ముప్పది

55. మాడలు పెట్టి

56. ం గలవారు రా

57. జికము వైవి

58. కము అతివ్రిష్టి
59. అనావ్రిష్టి అర
60. సి కొణువారు ఇ
61. గుప్త అచంద్రా
62. కర్ణస్థాయికంము
63. చెల్లెడి। స్వదత్తం
64. పరదత్తం వా
65. యో హరేతి వసు
66. ంధరా షష్టివర్ష
67. సహస్రాణి విష్ఠా
68. యాం జాయతే క్రి
69. మి। శ్రీ లక్ష్మీలు

Atmakur (8).

[Annamasamudrampéṭa. Persian. From the mosque.]

Translation.

This mosque is just like the famous mosque of the Prophet of Medina. May the praise of God be on him and on his descendants.

هذالمسجد سمي مسجدالنبي المدني صلي الله عليه وآله وسلم •

(To face page 211.)

ATMAKUR NO. 9.

ATMAKUR (9). (A.D. 1762–63.)

[Annamasamudrampéṭa. Persian. From the mosque.]

TRANSLATION.

Muhammad.	(c) In Thy honour is said "Thy hand is over the hand of all."	(b) I begin in the name of God who is the most compassionate and most merciful.	(a) Towards Thee all devout persons turn just as they do towards the kibla in prayers.	Alláh.
[Alluding to the meaning of Rahmat-ul-lah, *i.e.*, the compassion of God.]	(e) (Since) Thy name bears the impress of the sentence "no one can despair of the mercy of God."	......	(d) Thou art the hope of compassion for every one.	
*' Umr.	(h) Just like Abraham, thou hast built the temple of God.	(g) There is no God but one God, and Muhammad is the Messenger of God.	(f) Thy grace sends forth blessings every moment just like the great pilgrimage at Mecca.	* Abu Bakr.
	(j) "*Rahmat-ul-lah built the temple at Jerusalem.*"	......	(i) The announcing angel (Hátif) said as to the date of the mosque.	
*Ali (for Haidar).	(m) Chancel and pulpit—	(l) Era of construction of mosque Hijra 1176. One thousand one hundred seventy-six Hijra.	(k) —Lamp and mosque.	* Usmán.

---

* These words refer to the names of the four Khálifs, Ali's name being represented as Haidar.

(j) When worked out gives the date of the Hijra 1176 or 1762–63 A.D.

$n = 50$				
$m = 40$				
$u = 6$	$m = 40$	$a = 1$	$r = 200$	$a = 1$
$d = 4$	$s = 60$	$k = 100$	$h = 8$	$l = 30$
$n = 50$	$j = 3$	$s\ (s) = 90$	$m = 40$	$l = 30$
$d = 4$	$d = 4$	$y = 10$	$t = 400$	$h = 5$
154	107	201	648	66

	(c)	(b)	(a)	
محمد *	بشانت فوق ایدهم یداللہ*	بسم اللہ الرحمن الرحیم	توئی اهل یقین را عین قبلہ *	اللہ *
	(e)		(d)	
	زطغراسکہ زد من رحمت اللہ *	......	بهر کس را توئی امید رحمت *	
	(h)	(g)	(f)	
عمر*	خلیل آسا نمودی کعبۃ اللہ *	لاالہ الااللہ محمد رسول اللہ *	بہر دم فیض تو چون حج اکبر*	وابوبکر*
	(j)		(i)	
	نمودند مسجد افضل رحمت اللہ *	......	کہ هاتف گفت در تاریخ مسجد *	
	(m)	(l)	(k)	
علی*	محراب و منبر*	تاریخ بنائی مسجد سنہ ۱۱۷٦ یکهزار و یکصد و هفتاد و شش هجری *	چراغ و مسجد *	عثمان *

Atmakur (10). (A.D. 1781–82.)

[Annamasamudrampéṭa. Arabic. On a stone near the mosque.]

Translation.

(1) Continued severe illness which wears out a patient.

(2) Death as compared with such illness is contemptible.

(3) Indeed, O Ayesha,[1] such illness embitters life.

---

[1] Presumably the name of some lady of the family.

(4) Death is near to prove this fact (*i.e.*, whether death or such illness is easier to bear).

Hijra 1196.

(۱) دنف يذوب بدا يه

(۲) والموت دون بلايه

(۳) ان عايشه عاش منغص

(۴) والموت دون بلايه

NOTE.—For the translation we are endebted to Ghulám Mahmúd Sáhib, Manager of the Surgeon-General's Office, Madras.

ATMAKUR (11). (A.D. 1279-80?)

[Átmakúr. Telugu. From Alaganáthasvámi temple.

TRANSLATION.

Hail! On Friday, the 13th of the dark fortnight of Kártika, corresponding to the illustrious and prosperous (Ṣaka) year 1201, Dhí Bahava (?) Mahárája and the Kápús and (Karnams) of Jilleri [constructed] a temple to Aḷaha-purapatidéva of Átukúr and gave with libation of water . . . . gave to last (as long as the sun and moon endure).

1. స్వస్తి శ్రీ శుభజాతకవరుషంబు
2. లు ౧౨౦౧ వగు నేంటి కార్తిక బహు
3. ళ ౧౩ శుక్రవారాన ధీ బహావ
4. మహారాజులుం జిల్లెటి కాంపు
5. [లు కరణాలు] ఆతుకూరి అళహాపురప
6. తి దేవరగుడి . . . . పుల కానిదేవ

7. రకు ధారాపూ [ర్వకముసేసి] సమర్ప

8. ముసేసిరి [ఆచంద్రార్క ముం] . . . . గానిచ్చె

NOTE.—Átukúr is Atmakúr. The letters within brackets are uncertain. There is probably some mistake in the name of the rája who cannot be identified. A king Bhava appears in O. 13.

ATMAKUR (12).

[Átmakúr. Telugu. From the same temple.]

TRANSLATION.

The Karnam of Átmakúr village, son of Tirumalayya, has made prostrations to Alaganátha Svámi on the 2nd day of the bright fortnight of Áshádha of the year Bhava, corresponding to . . . of the victorious and prosperous Ṣálivábana Ṣaka era. May it cause great prosperity.

1. స్వస్తి విజయాభ్యుదయ శాలివాహ
2. న శకవర్షంబులగు - బవ సంవత్సర ఆషా
3. ఢ శుద్ధ ౨ లు అలగనాధునికి ఆత్మకూ
4. రి గ్రామకరణం తిరుమలయ్య కు
5. మారుడు దండాలు సమర్పించి
6. నాడు శ్రీ శ్రీ శ్రీం జయన్య

ATMAKUR (13). (A.D. 1277-78.)

[Átmakúr. Telugu. From same temple.]

TRANSLATION.

Hari! Óm! Hail! On Sunday, the 13th day of the bright half of Phálguṇa of the year Íṣvara, corresponding to the year 1199 of the victorious and prosperous

Ṣaka era, Átukúri Vámana Prichudévaḍu (gave) to Nambi Upureḍi Súraya, the temple servant of Átukúri Aḷahápatidéva, for the religious merit of his father . . . . dramuváru, and of Immaḍi Tiruvengaḍappadási to last as long as the moon and sun exist . . . .

1. హరి ఓం స్వస్తి శ్రీ శుభజాతక వ
2. రుషంబులు ౧౧౯౮ అగునే
3. ంట్టి ఈశ్వర సంవత్సర పాల్గుణ
4. శుద్ధ త్రయోదశీని ఆదివారము
5. నాండు ఆతుకూరి వామన ప్రి
6. చుదేవడు ఆతుకూరి అళహాపతి
7. దేవరవారికి స్థానపతినంబి ఉపురెడి సూరయ దమ తండ్రి
8. . . . ద్రమువారికిని పుణ్యముంగా నిమ్మడివీర తిరువే
9. ంకడప్పదాసికిని ఆచంద్రార్కము వారికిని ధమ్మంగాం బంపురితిని

Átmakur (14). (A.D. 1274–75 ?)

[Átmakúr. Tamil. Alaganáthaswámi temple.]

Translation.

Harih! Hail! Prosperity! In the Śaka year one thousand one hundred and ninety-eight which corresponds to the cyclic year Bháva, Káraikiḻánbhaṭṭan gave free of tax as gift to the god Aḻagaperumáḷ of Áttakkúr

[1] ஹரி: ஸ்வஸ்தி ஸ்ரீ ஸகவருஷம் ஆ-
[2] யிரத்து ஒருநூற்றுத்தொ-
[3] ண்ணூற்றெட்டாவது
[4] பாவஸம்வத்ஸரத்து காரை-
[5] கிழான்பட்டன் தேவதா-

[6] ணங்கள் நாயநார்க்கு நில [மா]-
[7] க ஆத்தக்கூர் அழகப்பெரு-
[8] மாளுக்கு திருவிடையாட்ட-

NOTE.—The S.S. and cyclic years do not agree.

ATMAKUR (15).

[Atmakur. Telugu. From the tank bund.]

TRANSLATION.

Velidanḍḍa Konéru Timmarasu Mánapati (king), the worshipper of Ṣrí Venkaṭéṣvarasvámi's feet.

1. శ్రీ వెంకటేశ్వరస్వామి పాద
2. శేవకుడు వెలిదండ్ల కోనేరు
3. తిమ్మరసు
4. మానపతి.

NOTE.—The word మానపతి stands detached.

ATMAKUR (16). (A.D. 1549–50 or 1556–57 ?)

[Atmakur. Telugu. From same place.]

TRANSLATION.

This tank (was) constructed by Kónéṭi Timma Rájayya on Thursday, the 13th day of the bright fortnight of Pushyam of the year Naḷa (?) corresponding to the year 1471 of the victorious and prosperous Ṣáliváhana Ṣaka era. Ṣrí Rámáchandra's feet are (my) sole refuge. May it cause great prosperity. The charity should be continued.

1. విజయాభ్యుదయ శాలివాహన శకవరు
2 షంబ్బులు ౧౪౭౧ అగు నేటి నర[1] సంవ్వర[2] పుష్య
3. [3]ఖు ౧౩ గు నాండు కోనేటి తిమ్మరాజయ్య
4. గట్టించ్చిన చెరువు శ్రీరామచెంద్రా నీపాద
5. మెగటి శ్రీ శ్రీ శ్రీం జయునూ ధర్మ్మాం న
డపవలెనూ

NOTE.—The S.S. year 1471 does not correspond with the year Nala of the southern cycle.

ATMAKUR (17). (A.D. 1548–49.)

[Battepáḍu. Telugu. On a well to south of village.]

TRANSLATION.

Hail! On Wednesday, the 5th of the bright fortnight of Bhádrapada of the year Kílaka, corresponding to the year 1471 of the illustrious, victorious, and prosperous Ṣáliváhana Ṣaka era, while Ṣrímat Rájádhirája Rája-paraméṣvara Ṣrí Víra Pratápa Ṣrí Sadáṣivadévaráya, seated on the diamond throne at Vijayanagar, was ruling the whole earth, Ṣríman Mahámaṇḍaléṣvara Rámaráju Timmayadéva Mahárája under the orders of Sadáṣivaráya honoured Mangaḷa Konḍóji and issued a charitable edict on stone granting an *inám*. The barbers[4] of Baṭṭepáḍu a village in Udayagiri *rájya* have (represented matters) to the State. Therefore this is the charitable edict exempting them from the fines levied for breaking rules of caste (Kulasiddháyálu?), marriage fees, presents, and *veṭṭi*

---

[1] నర for నల [2] For సంవత్సర [3] For శు

[4] Mangaḷavánḍlu = barbers. Several other inscriptions to the same effect occur. See KG. 20 where we have Timmóju Konḍóju and P. 35 where we have Timmóju Konḍóju Bhadróju. The dates do not support the view that the several inscriptions relate to father, son and grandson.

taxes as a *sarvamánya* as long as the sun and moon endure. Whoever fail to observe the conditions of this charitable edict will incur the sin of killing cows and Brahmans near the Ganges. Srí.

1. స్వస్తి శ్రీ జయాభ్యుదయ
2. శాలివాహన శకవరుషంబులు
3. ౧౪౭౧ అగు నేంటి కీలక సంవత్సర
4. భాద్రపద శు ౫ బు శ్రీమద్రాజా
5. ధిరాజ రాజ పరమేశ్వర శ్రీ వీరప్రతాప
6. ఉ శ్రీ సదాశివదేవ మహారాయలుంగారు విజ
7. యనగరమందు వజ్ర సింహాసనారూఢులై సకల సా
మ్రాజ్య
8. మున్ను చేయుచుండఁగాను శ్రీమన్మహా మండలేశ్వర
రామరాజు తిం
9. మ్మయ్య దేవ మహారాజులుంగారు సదాశివరాయలయ్యా
వారి
10. ఆనతిని రామరాజుంగారు మంగళకొండ్డోజును మనిం
చ్చియి
11. చ్చిన రాతిమాన్యం ధంమ్మశాసనము వుదయగిరిరాజ్యం
లోని బట్టె
12. పాటి మంగ్గళవాండ్లు నగరికిం బెట్టియిచ్చిరి కుళసిద్ధా
యాలు
13. గవ్యం కాని కేలుసః సర్వమైన వెట్టివేములు మాన్యాలు
గాను సర్వమాన్యంగా
14. ను ఆచంద్రార్కస్థాయిగాను మాని యిచ్చిన ధర్మశాస
నము యీ
15. ధర్మశాసనం ప్రకారము యెవ్వరు తప్పినాను గంగ్గక
ర్త్తను గోవు
16. బ్రాహ్మణను చంపినపాపాన పోవువారు శ్రీ.

ÁTMAKUR (18).

[Battepáḍu. Tamil. From four sides of a stone opposite the Śiva temple. Only a portion of one side can be deciphered.]

TRANSLATION.

Hail! Prosperity! In the thirty-fifth year of the reign of the emperor of the three worlds, the glorious KULÔTTUNGACHÔḶADÊVA, I, the glorious Madurântaka-pottapichôḷa *alias* Nallaśittiyaraiśan of Nellúr . . to the god the glorious Râmêśvara on behalf of king . . . gaparangêśvara Udayân of Melaivâśal (a village) of Nellûrnâḍu (a sub-division) of Jayankoṇḍachôḷa maṇḍalam. . . . .

[1] ஸ்வஸ்தி ஸ்ரீ
[2] திரிபுவநச்ச-
[3] க்கரவத்திகள்
[4] [ஸ்ரீகு]லொத்துங்-
[5] கசொழதெவற்-
[6] குயாண்டு முப்ப-
[7] த்தஞ்சாவது
[8] [நல்லூர்] ஸ்ரீம■-
[9] ராந்தகப்பொ-
[10] த்தப்பிச்சொ-
[11] ழநென் நல்-
[12] ல சித்தியரை-
[13] சநென் ஜெய-
[14] ங்கொண்டெ-
[15] சாழமண்டல-
[16] த்து நெல்லூர்-
[17] நாட்டு மெலை-
[18] வாசல் கொங்-
[19] . கபரங்கிசுர-

[20] முடையா-
[21] ன் பக்கல் ஸ்ரீ
[22] ராமெழுராமுடை-
[23] யா . . .

NOTE.—The Uḍaiyán referred to was apparently some petty chief.

ATMAKUR (19).

[Bhímavaram. Telugu. To the north.]

TRANSLATION.

Hail! On . . . year . . . Ṣrí Ṣaka year . . . Ṣrímat . . ṛája . . . . granted this charitable edict . . . . . father Gontappa Náyuḍu . . his mother Góva . . . . granted fields . . . . raised a temple to the deity.

1. స్వస్తిశ్రీ సకవరుషంబులు . . .
2. . . . .
3. . . . . . సంవత్సర
4. . . . .
5. . . . శ్రీమతు . . .
6. . . రాజ . నాది . క . .
7. . . జు విడిక . . . . .
8. . రు డారాజు . . . . .
9. ః దమ్మ్రసాసనము . గంగా
10. మనముకుంమువ . జా . .
11. న . వము . . . తల్లి
12. తండ్రి . గొండప్పనాయ . . . .
13. తమతల్లిగోవ . . .
14. . . గాను . . .

15. హావన . . . తల్లి
16. కొజు నమతండి
17. రపవతాగ . . . పతి
18. ప్ప ాెయించేనుదామవడిత
19. ప్రాసాదమెత్తించెదేవరకు

ATMAKUR (20).

[Bommavaram. Telugu. To west of village.]

TRANSLATION.

First side.

Hail! On . . . . . Ṣrí Ṣaka year . . . . .

Second side.

As the tank of Bommavaram, situated in Udayagiri *Síma* which was granted to us as an *amaram* by Ṣrí Ra [nga] rájayyavàru, is in ruins

* * * *

First side.

1. స్వస్తిశ్రీ శకవషఁం
2. బులు ౧ . . . . అను
3. . . . . . .
4. . . . . . .
5. . . . . . .
6. . . . . . .
7. . . . . . .
8. . . . . . .
9. . . . . . .

10. . . . . . .
11. . . . . . .
12. . . . . . .
13. . . . . . .
14. . . . . . .
15. . . . . . .
16. . . . . . .
17. . . . . . .
18. . . . . . .
19. . . . . . .
20. . . . . . .
21. . . . . . .
22. . . . . . .
23. . . . . . .
24. . . . . . .
25. . . . . . .

Second side.

1. . . . .
2. శ్రీక . . రాజయ్యవా
3. రు మాకు అమరము
4. లకు పాలించినవుద
5. యగిరి శీమలోను
6. బొమ్మవరంగ్రామం చె
7. రువు తెగి ఖిలమై వుం
8. డంగాను మేము .
9. . . . . . రి
10. . . . లు . . . లు
11. . ము . లు గుణించి . .
12. . . . . . .

13. . . . .
14. . లార . మా . .
15. . . cప:డ . .
16. మామడిమీ . లుపుట్టి
17. ౧ టం గుంచాలు వుద
18. యం గెలు . వ . . .
19. డి పాడిగు . . పా
20. దరమ . . . .
21. రిగు ౧౦ కి . . . .
22. యామంద . . .
23. . . . .
24. . . . .
25. . . ఇ . . .
26. . తి . . . .

ATMAKUR (21).

[Bommavaram. Telugu. On road to west of village. Three sides of a stone.]

TRANSLATION.

(Salutation be to) Ṣrí Ráma.

The village of Bommavaram in Udayagiri *Ṣíma* granted to us as an *amaram* by Ṣrí Rangarájulaváru. . . . . 3 *puṭṭis* . . . . as charity . . . . we have exempted . . .

* * * *

First side.

1. శ్రీరామ
2. శ్రీ రంగరాజులవా

3. రు మాంకు అమరమునకు
4. పాలింపుంచినట్టి వుద
5. యగిరి సీమలోని
6. బొమ్మవరంగ్రామం . .
7. రు మతికి ఖ 3 పుట్లు .
8. . ర్యంగాను ఖను . .
9. . . . . రంగ
10. రాజుగారి గరి . ము
11. . . . . . .
12. వరాఇమానితిమి
13. . గంగాంద . . .
14. మా . డిమా . పపు .
15. . . . గుంటలు పుబా
16. పురాలు . . . .
17. ది పాడిగ . . . . రు .
18. డి . . . . నమడి .
19. . . ౧౦ కి . . . .
20. యీమర్యాదను . . .
21. . . . . . .
22. . . ంలోనిపి . . .
23. . . . .
24. . . . .
25. . . . .

Second side.

* * * *

Third side.

1. యీ చెరు

* * * *

14. . . . చిన

* * * *

16. . . నజ

* * * *

19. . . తాం

* * * *

20. . జ . . బాం

* * * *

NOTE.—This Ṣrí Rangarázulaváru is perhaps the Ṣrí Rangaráyulu Ayyaváru of U. 24.

ATMAKUR (22).

[Cheruvupalli. Telugu. On two stones opposite Rámalingam temple.]

TRANSLATION.

First portion.

. . . Ṣrí. . . .

be granted . . in perpetuity as long as the sun and moon endure.

[Two imprecatory verses.]

Second portion.

. . . . . Saka.

* * * *

They will incur the sin of killing their parents .

* * * *

Third portion.

. . . . they . . . . . to last in perpetuity as long as the sun and moon endure . . .

[Three imprecatory verses.]

May it cause great prosperity!

First portion.

1. . . . .
2.
3.
4.
5.
6. . . పాపానం
7. . . . . .
8. . . . . .
9. . . . . .
10. . . . చెయ్యడము
11. . . చంద్రము .
12. . . పరచి . .
13. . . . ఆచంద్రార్కస్థా
14. ఇగా నిచ్చెను ॥ స్వదత్తం
15. పరదత్తంవాయో
16. హారేతి వసుంధరా షష్టి
17. వర్షసహస్రాణి వి
18. ష్టాయాం జాయతేక్రిమి (1) బహు
19. భిర్వ సుధాదత్త బహుభిన్నానుపాలి
20. తా యస్య యస్యయదాభూమి
21. తస్య తస్య తదాఫలం (2)

Second portion.

1. . . శకవ
2. . . . . య
3. . . . . .
4. . . . . .
5. . . . సహా
6. . . . . ంగ
7. . . . . పం
8. . . . . మా
9. . . . . ణు
10. . . . . నేసి
11. ఆ . . . తల్లితం
12. డ్రుల . . . సిని
13. . . మనంబో .
14. . . లోని మహా
15. . . . ల నాయ్యా
16. . . . . .
17. . . . . .

Third portion.

1. వావిర సారింగ
2. లో దయరు ఆ
3. చంద్రార్కా స్థాయి
4. గానున్న . . .
5. . . వారు ప్రితి . .
6. చ్చి . . . . . .
7. స్వదత్తం పరదత్తంవా
8. యోహారేతి వసుం
9. ధరా షష్టిర్వర్ష

10. సహస్రాణి
11. విష్టాయాం జాయ
12. తెక్రిమిః (1) స్వదత్తా
13. ద్విగుణంపుణ్యం
14. పరదత్తాను పా
15. లనం పరదత్తాప
16. హారేణ స్వదత్తం
17. నిష్ఫలంభవేత్ (2)
18. దానపాల నయో
19. ర్మధ్యే దానచ్ఛ్రేయో
20. నుపాలనం దానా
21. త్స్వర్గ మవాప్నో
22. తి పాలనాదచ్యు
23. తంపదం (3) ॥ మం
24. గళమహా
25. శ్రీ శ్రీ

ATMAKUR (23). (A.D. 1697–98?)

[Chézerla. Telugu. In Chennakéṣavasvámi temple.]

TRANSLATION.

Hail ! On Friday, the 30th of the dark fortnight of Jyéṣṭha of the year Íṣvara, corresponding to the year 1609 of the illustrious and prosperous Ṣáliváhana Ṣaka era, on the holy occasion of a solar eclipse the following charitable edict was given with libation of water by Ṣrímat (Dávu Suratrána ?) Máradattamgáru, who is all-powerful, to Chennakéṣavadéva (deity) of Chéjarla and to Náganátham Timmávójhulu, who is of the *yajus sákhá* and of the Kaundinya *gótra*. They should enjoy the village . . . . which is attached to Udayagiri *rájya* and subject to us with its eight species of enjoyment and eight species of ownership. Half of the village is set apart for the deity for performing *tírtha mahótsava* to the deity. If any fail in this charity he will incur the sin of killing cows and Brahmans on the banks of the Ganges.

[Two imprecatory verses.]

The temple servant (*sthánapati*) of this deity is . . . . Chennakéṣava . . . .

NOTE.—The cyclic and S.S. year do not correspond. Members of the Kauṇḍinya gótra appear as makers or recipients of grants in C.P. 3, C.P. 13, O. 102 and O. 111 as well as here. The donor is not identifiable.

1. స్వస్తి శ్రీ శుభ శాలివాహన శకవర్షంబులు ౧౬౦౯
2. అఋనేంటి యీశ్వరసంవత్సర జేష్ట బ౩ం భృగువారము।
సూర్య
3. గ్రహణ పుణ్యకాలమందును శ్రీమతు దావు సురత్రాణు
4. లు సర్వబలైవ మార దత్తంగారు కేజల్ల చెన్నకేశవ
5. దేవరికిన్ని యజుశ్శాఖా కౌండిన్యగోత్రం నాగా
6. నాధుం తిమా వోఝుఃకున్ను దారవోశి యిచ్చిన
7. ధర్మశాసనం వుదయగిరి రాజ్యంలోను మాకుం
8. (. . జెల్లె . . . గ్రామము)
9. శ్రీ అష్టభోగ తేజస్వామ్యాలున్ను అనుభ
10. వించువాండు దేవునికి సగమున్ను దేవుని
11. కిని తీర్థమహొత్సవం సాగించేది యీ ధ
12. ర్మానకు యెవ్వరు గనక తప్పినాను గ
13. ంగ కెతర గోబ్రాంహ్మనిన్ని చంపిన
14. పాపానం బోవువారు ॥ స్వదత్తా ద్విగు
15. ణం పుణ్యం పరదత్తానుపాలనం పర
16. దత్తాపహారేణ స్వదత్తం నిష్ఫలం భవేత్ (1)

17. యేకైవ భగినీ లోకే సర్వేషామేవ భూభుజాం
18. న భోగ్యా న కరగ్రాహ్యా విప్రదత్తా వ
19. సుంధరా (2) యీ దేవునికి స్తాన
20. వతి . . . ణమ పెత్తోవ్వదింశశి
21. స్వామి చెన్నకేశవ

ATMAKUR (24). (A.D. 1187–88?)

[Chiramana. Sanskrit in Telugu character and Telugu. Near a well to north of village.]

TRANSLATION.

(Sanskrit verse.) The sun and moon, wind and fire, the sky, the earth, water, heart and Yama, day and night, the two twilights and dharma know the disposition of man. (Telugu.) In the Ṣaka year 1109 Dámanenḍu consecrated Kéṣavadéva of Chirumana and Doḍḍaka Dámanáyaka, Baiyapa Náyaka, Dámi Náyaka and Nallamgáṭi Náyaka of Gollapúnḍi presented with libation of water a jonna field under the Mandu tank, and Maḍamareḍḍi's field for the religious merit of their parents. Whoever thinks of injuring this (charity) will be considered to have killed a tawny cow near the Ganges and to have drunk (its) blood from the skull of his parents. The *vritti* of the temple of Ṣrí Çhirumana Kéṣavadéva should be cultivated with second crop also . . . ?

1. आदित्यचंद्रावतिलोन
2. लश्चद्यौर्भूमिरापोहृदयं
3. यमश्चवहश्चरात्रिश्च उभेच

---

[1] मनश्च—Manas (mind) is the more usual reading.

4. संध्येषर्मश्चजानातिनरस्यवृत्तं ॥
5. శకవరుషంబులు ౧౧౦౭ దామనెం
6. డు చిఱుమన కేశవ దేవర ప్రతిష్ట సే
7. సి గొల్ల పూండి దొడ్డ కదామనాయకు
8. ండును బైయపనాయకుండును దా
9. మినాయకుండును నల్లంగాటినాయ
10. కుండును తమ తల్లితండ్రులకు ధర్మ
11. వుగా ధారవోసినాండ్రు చెఱువు
12. ను జొన్నచేను మెడమరడ్డి చేంను
13. నిచ్చిరి దీనిం నెవ్వడేని చెఱు సదలంచి
14. న వాని గంగ్గకఱుత కవిలం వధించి రక్తం
15. తమ తల్లి తండ్రుల కపాలమున బె
16. ట్టి త్రాగినవారు శ్రీ చిఱుమన కేశవ
17. దేవరగుడికి ప్రతిష్టకాంఱుతోప్పండే
18. ది వీరప్రతిష్టఇడి వాండు

ATMAKUR (25). (A.D. 1284–85 ?)

[Chiramana. Telugu. On west wall of Chandra-maulésvara temple.]

TRANSLATION.

On Thursday, the 13th day of the bright fortnight of Bhádrapada, corresponding to the Ṣaka year 1207, in the kingdom of Hail! Ṣríman Mahámaṇḍalésvara Vijaya-gaṇḍa Gópáḷa Mahárája, who is possessed of divine glorious titles, who is of the race of Parna (read Parama ?), who is holy by reason of being of the *gótra* of Bháradvája, whose banner is a club, whose ensign is the bull, who is the supreme lord of the city of Kánchi the best of cities, who possesses an excellent boon from the goddess Kámakóṭí and is Jagatgópála.[1] Hail! Ṣrí Káma Náyaka, and Devináyaka, the sons of Ṣrímat Golapúndi Késima Náyaka, who is possessed of divers glorious titles, who wears a bracelet and necklace adorned with the rays of excellent gems, who is the lord of Orriyúru, the best of cities, Gaṇḍaragaṇḍa,[2] Prajamecchugaṇḍa,[3] Panditapuṇḍaríkashandamártánda,[4] Burágaṇḍanitalagóluganḍa,[5] and Badhyamahárájasthápanácharya[6]—gave four *paṭṭus* of paddy field to dancing girls for performing dancing in the temple of Chirumana Mallikárjuna which is maintained on charity; also (the field called) kalavulachénu in rear of Kani cheruvu, high level fields in wet lands, 1,000 *kuntas* in the block of land called Kanchenángá, and dry land consisting of four *paṭṭis* in the field called Penumani in Graddaguṇṭa Révaṭa measuring 4,000 *kuntas*; for dancing girls who perform worship a paddy field of 750 *kuntas* in the field called Ánagiḍa chénu—for dancing girls who perform worship dry land of 4,000 *kuntas* in Graddakunṭa Révata. If the dancing girls themselves lease out the lands given to them the *kápus* who rule the village will treat them as "sarvamánya." For worshipping Ṣrí Balidéva should be spent . . . . . .

---

[1] Protector of the world.

[2] Gaṇḍaragaṇḍa = hero of heroes.

[3] Prajamecchugaṇḍa = a hero who is praised by the people.

[4] Panditapuṇḍaríkashaṇḍamártánda = a sun to the collections of lotuses which are learned men.

[5] Burágaṇḍanitalagóluganḍa = the hero who cut off the head of Burágaṇḍa.

[6] Badhyamahárájasthápanácharya = one who reinstates kings who have been taken prisoners. Badhyamahárája is perhaps the same as Badhyamadrarája in Ins. No. 55.

	Na. (tám))
For the cows and oxen of the temple	$7\frac{1}{2}$
Fire-wood for cooking	$\frac{1}{2}$
Conch blower	$1\frac{1}{2}$
Gardener	1
Grass-cutter	$\frac{1}{2}$
Potter	$\frac{1}{2}$

Paddy field for the conch blower $\frac{3}{4}$ *kunta.*

The *Kápus* should cultivate the paddy fields given to the temple for its share, and give each year 155 *puṭṭis* of paddy, and a half share in the second-crop paddy, they should raise gingelly, flax, kāru jonna, and green gram on dry lands, and pay at the rate of $\frac{3}{4}$ *máḍa* on female cloths. The *Kápus* should conduct the charity perpetually. They should not allow the lands of the deity to lie waste. They should not sell the calves of the deity. This is a *sarvamánya* for the worshippers. Those who obstruct this charity will incur the sin of killing a tawny cow near the Ganges and of drinking its blood.

[Two imprecatory verses.] Ṣrí! Ṣrí! Ṣrí!

NOTE.—This Gollapuṇḍi family is mentioned in A. 26 and A. 38 also. In the latter Gollapayinḍi Biyyappa Náyaka is called the Protector of the kingdom of Erra Siddha.

1. శకవరుషంబులు
2. ౧౨౦౭ గు నేంటి భాద్రప
3. ద శుద్ధ త్రయోదశి గురువార
4. మునాండు స్వస్తి పర్ణవంశోద్భ
5. వ భారద్వాజగోత్ర పవిత్ర ఖట్వాంగధ్వ
6. జ త్రిపభలాంచన కాంచీపుర వరాధీశ్వ
7. ర కామకోట్యంబికా లబ్ధ వరప్రసాద జ
8. గదగోపాళ నామాది ప్రశస్తి సహితం
9. శ్రీ మన్మహా మండలేశ్వర విజయగం

10. డ గోపాళమహారాజు రాజ్యమున స్వస్తి
11. గుణమణి కిరణాలంక్రిత కేయూరహార ఒఱ్రి
12. యూరి పురవరాధీశ్వర గండరగండ ప్ర
13. జమెచ్చుగండ పండిత పుండరీకషం
14. డ మార్తాండ ఋరాగండనితల గోలుగం
15. డ బద్దమహారాజ స్థాపనాచార్యునా
16. మాది ప్రశస్తి సహితం శ్రీమతు గొలపూ
17. ండి కేశిమనాయకుని కొడుకులు శ్రీ కామనా
18. యకుండును దేవినాయకుండును ధర్మ
19. వృత్తియైన చిఱుమన మల్లికార్జున దే
20. వరగుడి రంగభోగార్థముగాను భో
21. గమువారికిచ్చిన వరిచేను పట్టునాల్గు
22. కనిచెఱువువె
23. నకకలవులచే
24. ను మడిచేనమె
25. ట్టదొంపుటానున్న కం
26. చెనాంగా వట్టి నేలిగు
27. ౧౦౦౦ వెలిసేను గ్రద
28. గుంటరేవట పెనుమ్రు
29. నిచెలనాల్గు వట్లుగు
30. ౪౦౦౦ అర్చనభోగ
31. మువారికి అనగిడచే
32. న వరిచేను గు ౬౫౦ ఆ
33. ర్చన భోగమువారికి
34. వెలిసేను గ్రద్దగుంటరే
35. వటగు ౪౦౦౦ భోగము
36. వారికిచ్చిన చేలువారే
37. డునం గోరికిచ్చిన ఉనతె
38. లికంగాంపులూ సర్వ

39. మాన్యముగం జెల్లింప
40. ంగలవారు మగుచు శ్రీ
41. బలిదేవర ఆరగింపు
42. నకూ మోచికూటకవల
43. సితెవకూం జెల్లంగలది
44. పడ్లు ఎడ్లు
45. దేవర ఆలము
46. వున ౭౪ వంట చెఱి
47. కులకున ౪ సంకువాని
48. కిన ౧౪ తొంటవానికి
49. న ౧ కసవ్రువానికిన ౪
50. గిడపవారికిన ౪ సంకు
51. వారికి వరిచేనుగు ౮౪
52. భోగము వరిచేలు
53. పాలికిదున్ని పంటాను
54. నూటపపదేనుపుట్లు
55. వడ్లు కారువరిసగం
56. బావికింని నువ్వు (గో
57. ధుమ) కారుజొన్న పె
58. సరువెలిసేను. కోకనుం
59. కమ్మకోర అర్ధిపట్టి
60. ముకరాలు మాడాన్న
61. లెకరాడుని కాంపులెల్ల కా
62. లము బెట్టంగలంవారు
63. దేవరచేలుతో వెట్టంగల
64. వారుగారు దేవుగోతియలు
65. అమ్మింగలివారుగారు పూ
66. జారులకు సర్వమాన్యము
67. ఇ దమ్మువు ఎవ్వరు విఘల

68. ము చేసినా గంగకఱ్త కపిలం బొడిచి
69. నెత్తురు దావిన పాపానఁ బోవువారు
70. సామాన్యోయంధర్మసేతుర్నృపాణాం
71. కాలే కాలే పాలనీయో భవద్భిః। సర్వా
72. నేతాన్భావినః పార్థివేంద్రాన్భూయో
73. భూయో యాచతే రామచంద్రః॥ స్వద
74. త్తం పరదత్తం వా యో హరేత వసుం
75. ధర షష్టివర్షసహస్రాణి వి
76. ష్ఠాయాం జాయతే క్రిమిః॥ శ్రీ శ్రీ
77. శ్రీ

Atmakur (26).

[Chiramana. Tamil. South wall of Chandramaulés̩vara temple.]

Translation.

Hail! Prosperity! In the eighteenth year of the reign of the emperor of the three worlds, the glorious Kulôttungachô̱ladêva, Gollappûṇḍi Nâyakkar left free of taxes, to last as long as the moon and sun endure, to Kêśavaperumâḻ of Se̱ruḍinai (situated) in Angaḍipâttanâḍu (a sub-division) of Jayankoṇḍachô̱lamaṇḍala, Erâḍi tank, the wet lands under it and temple lands, (after having) provided a supply channel (for the tank).

He who obstructs this (charity) will incur the sin of killing a tawny cow on the banks of the Ganges.

(This is the signature of) of the man who possesses rights in the temple, Koppaiyâ̱lvân the son of A̱rivariyapirân.

[1] ஸ்வஸ்தி ஸ்ரீ த்ரிபுவ[னசக்ரவத்திக]-
[2] ள் ஸ்ரீ குலொத்துங்கசொழதெவர்க்கு
[3] யாண்டு பதினெட்டாவது ஜயங்-
[4] கொண்டசொழமண்டலத்து
[5] அங்கடிபாத்தநாட்டு செறுடிணையி-
[6] ல் கெசவப்பெருமாளுக்கு கொல்ல-
[7] ப்பூண்டி நாயக்(கர)கரொம் விட்டதி-
[8] ருவிடையாட்டம் எராடியெரியும் இ-
[9] திக்கிழ் நிர்நிலமும் கொயிலுநிலம்
[10] 'ஓடவெட்டியும் விட்டொம் சந்-
[11] த்ர ஆதித்தவரை செல்லக்கடவதாக இ-
[12] து விலக்கினார் கெங்கையிடைக்கு-
[13] மரியிடைக்குராற்பசுக்கொ-
[14] ன்றான் பாவத்தைப்படுவா[ந்]
[15] இக்கொயில் காணியுடையா-
[16] ன் அழிவரியபிரான் மகன் [ெ]-
[17] [சா]ப்பையாழ்வான் ||

Atmakur (27).

[Jammavaram. Telugu. East of the tank.]

Translation.

On Sunday the 5th of the bright fortnight of Mágha of the year Viḷambi, Maparusayya, son of Ṣrímat Sáluva Narusappayya, granted *méras* at 1 *kuncha* for the tanks constructed (by him) at the village of Jammalamaḍuvu. We have granted 100 *kunṭas* of wet land in Jalatiramalatala as a *sarvamánya* for the religious merit of the illustrious (Rája).

1. విళంబిసంవత్సర మాఖ శు ౫ ఆ శ్రీమ
2. తుసాలువ నరుసప్పయ్యా కుమారుఁడు మపరుసయ్యా

3. జంమలమడుపు గ్రామాన వేయించ్చిన చెరువు
4. లుగ్ యిచ్చిన చెరువుకుంచాలు తిప్ప శ్రీ శ్రీ
5. వారికి-పుణ్యంగాను
6. జంతిరామలటలవరి
7. మడి గుంటలు ౧౦౦ సర్వమా
8. న్యంగాను ఇస్తిమి

ATMAKUR (28). (A.D. 1519-20.)

[Kaluváyi. Telugu. On bank of tank to west of village.]

TRANSLATION.

Hail ! On Thursday, the 15th day of the bright fortnight of Vaiṣákha of the year Pramádi, corresponding to the year 1441 of the illustrious and auspicious Ṣaka era, while Ṣríman Mahárájádhirája Rája Paraméṣvara Ṣrí Víra Pratápa Ṣrí Víra Krishṇadéva Maháráya was ruling the whole earth, Ráyasam Koṇḍamarusumgáru, for the religicus merit of his father Timmarusumgáru and his mother Sankáyammagáru, caused to be constructed the Kaluváyi tank, got images of Malalamma and Bírapa Déva made, set them up, and caused to be built temples (for them). Ṣrí, Ṣrí.

1. స్వస్తి శ్రీ శుభశకవర్షంబులు
2. ౧౪౪౧ అగు నేటి ప్రమాదిసం
3. వత్సర వైశాఖ శు ౧౫ గు శ్రీమ
4. న్మహా రాజాధిరాజ రాజపరమే
5. శ్వర శ్రీవీరప్రతాప శ్రీ వీరక్రిష్ణ
6. దేవమహారాయలు సకలసా
7. ంబ్రాజ్యము సేయుచుండ్డంగా

8. ను రాయసము కొండమ
9. రుసుంగారు తమ తల్లిసంకా౯
10. యమ్మంగారికిన్ని తమతండ్రి
11. తింమరుసుంగారికిన్ని పు
12. ణ్యముగాను కలువాయిచెరు
13. వుగట్టించ్చి మల లమ్మాను బీ
14. రపదేవరాను చేయించి
15. ప్రతిష్ట చేసిరి గుళ్లునుగట్టిం
16. చిరి శ్రీ శ్రీ

Atmakur (29). (A.D. 1275–76.)

[Kámireḍḍipáḍu. Telugu. Near Durgamma temple.]

Translation.

Hail! While Ṣríman Mahámaṇḍaléṣvara (Náne) déva Mahárája was ruling as universal sovereign at Nellore, holding with delight pleasant communication (with his feudatories), Hadapamunu Lunkkarája, the servant of the king, gave . . twenty . . for providing offerings to Durgáparaméṣvari on the festival day of Mahá Lakshmi on Sunday, the 10th day of the bright fortnight of Ásvayuja of the year Yiva (Yuva), corresponding to the illustrious, victorious and prosperous Ṣaka year 1197, for his own religious merit. Itama Reḍḍi and Maratóya, rulers of Anuyúru, gave this formerly to Durga with libation of water. They shall maintain this charity as long as the sun and moon exist. Those who think of obstructing this charity will incur the sin of killing a tawny cow near the Ganges.

1. స్వస్తి శ్రీమన్మహామండలేశ్వర
2. (నానే) దేవమహారాజులు నెల్లూరను
3. సకలసాంమ్రాజ్యం జేస్తుండి సుఖసంకథా
4. వినోదంబుల రాజ్యంబు చేయుచుండంగాను
5. రాజానకు నిజభ్రిత్యుండైన హదవము
6. సలుంకిర్రాజా సుఖానుంను శ్రీ జ
7. య్యాభ్యుదయ శకవర్షంబులు
8. ౧౧౯౭ నేంటి యువ సంవత్సర
9. మున ఆశ్వయుజ శుద్ధ ౧౦ లు ఆ
10. దివారమున మహాలక్ష్మీదేవి
11. పండువనందనకుం పుణ్యముగా
12. దుర్గా పరమేశ్వరికి నవేద్యమునకు తం
13. . నికిరుపవి . . . .
14. . . . . తము
15. . . . . వాలు . . . . .
16. పూర్వకమున స్వామికిం అను
17. యూరిప్రభువులు దుర్గామంను
18. దీనియితమ రెడిమారతోయ
19. ధారాపూర్వకము సేసిరి ఇ దర్మ
20. వు ఆచంద్రార్కస్థాయిగాం జెల్లి
21. ంచ్చువారు॥ యి ధర్మవునకు ఎ
22. వ్వర విఘ్నము దలంచినాను గంగకలు
23. తం గవిల వధియించిన పాప్పానం బోవువారు

ATMAKUR (30).

[Kólagoṭla. Telugu. In a field west of village.]

TRANSLATION.

On . . . . . of Kártika of the year Vikṛiti, Kámana, the son of . . . Basavarusayyapati, and Annam Gáru of the Kárumanchi family, issued this charitable edict for Basavayya déva of Kólagoṭla. To the north of the village well, he granted . . . . a field as a *mányam*. Therefore whoever fails (in preserving this) will incur the sin of killing a cow and a Brahman. If it is given to *jangams* they should enjoy it. May it cause prosperity !

1. వికృతిసంవత్సర కార్తిక . .
2. . . రలు బసవరసయ్యపతి కొడుకు
3. (కామన) కారు మంచ్చింగారల అ
4. న్నంగారు కోలగోట్ల బస్వయ్యదేవర
5. కు యిచ్చిన ధర్మశాసనంబమూ
6. రిబావివుత్తరం బాతని (న. గింతంట)
7. చేనుమాన్యం యిచ్చెను గనుక యె
8. వ్వరు తప్పినాను గోవు బ్రాంహ్మణి
9. ం చంప్పినపాపాన
10. బోదురు జంగాలకి
11. చ్చిన శేశుక బ్రితు
12. కువారు శ్రీ శ్రీ శ్రీం జే
13. యును

Atmakur (31).

[Kólagoṭla. Telugu. From stone in front of Nága-varuppu temple.]

Translation.

On Monday, the 30th day of the dark fortnight of Nija Áshádha of the year Chitrabhánu, Viḍayanchami Jangamayya, the *Mahápátra* (minister) of Ṣríman Mahá manḍaléṣvara Ṣrí Víra Pratápa Ṣrí Virúpáksha Ráya Maháráya executed this charitable edict to certain persons :—(Here follows a list of them.)

He presented in charity the village Kámpu Kímasi to Jagadíṣa (lord of the world) of Sangam situated in Pákanáḍu *sthala* in Udayagiri *Rájya*. Jangamayyagáru performed this gift for the religious merit of Ṣríman Mahá Virúpákshadévaráya Maháráya . . . . Maintain that charity and acquire merit. They should enjoy this village as a *sarvamánya* in perpetuity as long as the sun and moon exist.

[One imprecatory verse.]

Note.—The date may be 1462–63 and the reference to Vírupáksha the son of Dévaráya II.

1. చిత్రభానుసంవత్సరనిజ ఆషా
2. ఢ బ ౩౦ సో । శ్రీమన్మహామండలే
3. శ్వర శ్రీవీరప్రతాప శ్రీవిరూ
4. పాక్షరాయ మహారాయల వా
5. రికిం మహాపాత్రులు వార
6. ణాసి బసువయ్యంగారికిన్ని రా
7. జ రామదేవదాగసిద్ధయ్యం
8. గారికిన్ని వేదాంతయ్యంగా
9. రికింన్ని సివరాత్రి బసవయ్యం

10. గారికిన్ని సూరయ నాగయ్య

11. గారికిన్ని వారణాశి లిం

12. గయ్యంగారికిన్ని కొండ

13. ని వీరయ్యంగారికిన్ని చిట్టి

14. య్యంగారికిన్ని టిళ దేవమ

15. ంగయ్యంగారికిన్ని అయ్య

16. యారయ్యంగారికిన్ని విడ

17. యంచమిస జంగమయ్య

18. ంగారిలు దామిచ్చెన ధర్మ

19. శాసనాపత్రం వుదయ

20. గిరిరాజ్యానను

21. పాంకనాంటిస్థల

22. ములోను సంగా

23. ము శ్రీ జగధీసునకు

24. కాంపుకీమసిగ్రామము

25. జంగమయ్యగారు శ్రీమన్మహా

26. విరూపాక్ష దేవరాయమ

27. హారాయలకు పుణ్యం

28. గాను యీ దానం సేసి

29. నవారముంన్ను ఆదిపాలిం

30. చి పుణ్యంలానను సే

31. యండి . . . .

32. ఆ గ్రామము సర్వమాన్యముగా

33. ను ఆచంద్రార్క స్థాయిగాను

34. అనుభవించువారు । స్వ

35. దత్తాద్విగుణం పు ణ్యం పరదత్తాను

36. పాలనం పరదత్తాపహారేణ స్వ

37. దత్తం నిష్ఫలం భవేత్ ?

ATMAKUR (32).

[Kólagoṭla. Telugu. In a field to the north of the village. Illegible.]

ATMAKUR (33).

[Kórimerla. Telugu. Opposite Nágavarappamma temple.]

TRANSLATION.

Hail ! . . . . Ṣrí Ṣaka year . . . . . on the occasion of Makara Sankránti . . . deity . . . .

* * * *

whoever injures . . . . .

1. స్వస్తిశ్రీ శక
2. వర్షంబులు
3. లు . . .
4. మకర సంక్రాం
5. త్తిని . . .
6. . దేవర . .
7. . వ . . రక
8. . . దమ . .
9. . రో . . .
10. ము . మ . రంక
11. లకం . వవెరు
12. . . .
13. వడు . .
14. చెరిచినవాండు
15. ండు . . నుం

ATMAKUR (34).

[Kóṭítírtham. Telugu in old characters. From Koṭéṣvarasvámi temple. Incomplete.]

TRANSLATION.

Hail! Prosperity!

Niḍugaṇḍi (?) having abandoned enjoyment and desire, went in quest of Vidháta (Brahma).. Vidháṇḍu (Brahma) said "thou art not fit for this now; thou hadst better live in Niḍukóṇḍi Dévádi Kóṭíṣvaram which is to the south of the Peṇṇa and do penance (as) a deer (*i.e.*, live upon leaves, &c.)." He came and performed the penance and God revealed himself to him.

1. స్వస్తిశ్రీ నిడుగణ్డి . . . భోగకామా
2. తీకుర్త్తై విధాత్రుం గానం బోయిన విధా
3. ణ్డు . నీవిప్రుడిన్దుల కోర్వ్యణ్డవు గావుం పెణ్ణ
4. దక్షిణభాగంబున నిడుకోణ్డి దేవాదికోటీశ్వరం
5. బుననుండి హారణిమృగంబ . య్తపంబు సేయుంబోమ
6. నిన వచ్చి తపంబు సేసినం దేవరు ప్రత్యక్షంబయి

NOTE.—Mr. V. Venkayya supplied the transliteration.

ATMAKUR (35). (A.D. 1612-13).

[Kullúru. Sanskrit in Telugu character and Telugu. Near Ṣiva temple.]

TRANSLATION.

(*Sanskrit verses.*)

On Monday, the auspicious *tithi*, the 12th of the dark fortnight of Kártika in Parídhávi, in the illustrious Ṣáliváhana Ṣaka year reckoned by the oceans (4), three, the arrows (5), earth (1), *i.e.*, (1534), the weir of the tank bund built with stone pillars was constructed to-day by the lord Rudra, the moon of the illustrious (family of) Chintapaṭla, in the town of Kullúru. This verse is composed by Náganárya, the moon of the family of the illustrious Jallipalli to the perpetual delight of all learned men.

(*Telugu prose.*)

Prosperity! Hail! On Monday, the 12th of the dark fortnight of Kártíka of the year Páridhávi, corresponding to the year 1534 of the illustrious, victorious and prosperous Ṣáliváhana Ṣaka era, while Ṣrímad Rájádhirája Rájaparaméṣvara Ṣrí Víra Pratápa Ṣrí Víra Venkaṭapatiráya was ruling the kingdom of the earth, Venkaṭapati Náyaningáru, who is the moon of the ocean of the race of Padmanáyaka, who is the conqueror of the territory called Panchapáṇḍya, who is an Arjuna in war, who is the paramour of the prostitutes who are the princes bearing all *birudas*, who is pure by reason of descent from the *gótra* of Récherla, who is the grandson of Velugóṭi Peda Konḍama Náyuḍu and who is the son of Komára Timmanáyuḍu, sent for Rudrappa, who is the ruler of the *ṣíma* of Kullúru, who is skilled in ruling that kingdom, who is holy by reason of his descent from the *gótra* of Paisála, and who is the grandson of Chintapaṭla Singama Náyuḍu and the son of Chenchama Náyuḍu, at Kullúr which was granted to him (Venkaṭapati Náyaningáru) for ruling as an *amaram* by Venkaṭapatiráya and addressed him thus "You have restored the sluice of Anantaṣágaram tank which was in disrepair; you have constructed the eastern weir of Kaluváyi tank and are keeping the tank in good order. Deeds of charity like topes, topes in tanks, wells, etc., are meritorious services. So construct the eastern weir of Kullúr tank for the religious merit of my father Komára Timmanáyuḍu." Thus the assembly commanded him. Therefore Rudrappa Náyuḍu fixed 33 stone posts on the tank weir, built side walls on the two sides and constructed a flight of steps in stone so as to last in perpetuity as long as the sun and moon endure, Ṣrí!

(*Telugu verse.*)

Chenchaya Rudra Sauri, who is the resident of Chintapaṭla, who is the abode of Ṣrí, and who is delightful by reason of his charming qualities, planted 33 stone pillars on the weir of the Nallacheruvu of Kullúr, pillars which resemble the beautiful jewelled chariots of Indra who has come to bathe here, which are, as it were, high peaks to those who come with the desire of seeing the bund of the tank, which are, as it were, emblems of the good fame acquired by the lord of the earth, who is famous in polity—which, kissing the sky, resemble the pinnacles of Varuṇarája, and which are set with pearls.

NOTE.—From R. 60 we learn that Kanchamma was the mother of this ruler of Kullúru *ṣíma* and that he built a sluice for Tegacherla tank.

1. वर्षे श्रीमति शालिवाहनशके वार्धित्रिबाणोर्विरासंख्याके परिधाविनींदुसाहि

2. तोर्जद्वादशिसत्तिथौ कृष्णेकारि तटाकसेतुपरिवाहः कुल्लुरीपट्टणे शैलस्तंभधृढोद्य

3. रुद्रविभुना श्रीचिंतपट्लेंदुना (स)श्लोकोयं रचितः श्रीमज्जाछिप- छ्वि कुलेंदुना । ना

4. गनार्येन सर्वेषां विदुषां संमुदेन्वहन् ॥

5. శ్రీ స్వస్తి శ్రీ జయాభ్యుదయ శాలివాహన శకవర్షంబు లు ౧౫౩౪ అగు

6. నేంటి పరిధావి సంవత్సర కార్తీక బ ౧౨ సో। శ్రీమ ద్రాజాధిరాజ రాజపరమేశ్వ

7. ర శ్రీవీరప్రతాప శ్రీ వీరవేంకటపతిరాయలు పృథ్వీ సాం మ్రాజ్యం శేయుచు

8. వుండంగాను పద్మనాయక వంశాభోది చంద్రుండున్ను పంచ పాండియ ధరావిభాళుండు

9. ను సంగ్రామ పార్థుండున్ను సర్వబిరుదకొమార వే శ్యా భుజంగుండున్ను రేచెర్లగోత్రపవిత్ర

10. డున్ను వేలుగోటి పెదకొండమనాయని పౌత్రుండున్ను కొమారతింమానాయనిన

11. ందంను అయిన వేంకటపతినాయనింగారు తమకు వెంకట పతిరాయలు అమరానకు పాలిం

12. చుటకు యిచ్చిన కుల్లూరిని కుల్లూరి శీమప్రభులున్నూ। త ద్రాజ్యభారధురంధరుండు

13. ను పశాలగోత్రపవిత్రుండును చింతపట్ల శింగమనాయని పౌత్రుండును చంచమనాయని

14. పుత్రుండునైన రుద్రప్పనురావించ్చి అనంతసాగరపు చె రువు తూము ఖిలపడి వుండంగాను పునరు

15. ద్ధారికముచేసినావు కలువాయచెరువు తూర్పువలుగుక ట్టించ్చి చెవ్పు నీవుప్రతిముఖంచేయించిన తోంపులు చెవ్పులతో

16. ంపులు బావులుమొదలయిన పుణ్యాలు వుార్జితమై వుంన్న కార్యానంగనుక తమతండ్రికొమారతింమానాయనికి పు

17. ణ్యంగాను కులూరిచెరువు తూర్పుపలుగుకట్టించుమని సభవారునూనంనా ఆనతిచ్చెగనక చెరువుకు

18. అలుగుముప్పదిమూడు శిలాస్తంభాలు నిలిపి యిరుగడల సంతని సారువులు సొపానాలు కలుగు

19. కట్టంగాను ఆచంద్రార్కస్థాయిగా రుద్రప్పనాయిండు కట్టించినది శ్రీ

20. అకగాహనేహ సమాయాత విభుధరా టకమనీయ్య మణి శతాంగములనంగ తాటాక సేతు

21. సందర్శనేచ్ఛాగతస్థిత సమున్నత మహాశిఖరులనగ। నీలినుజ్వలధరానేతృసంపాదితమూ

22. తీర్భసతీర్తీర్మూర్తులనగ। ముక్తామణీయుక్తమో హనాంబరచుంబ్బివరుణరాజన్యగో

23. పురములనగ। నిలిపెంగులూరినలచెర్వులుగునంస్థు। ముప్ప దియు మూడురాకం

24. భములుంజెలంగ। చింతపట్ల పురస్థాయి శ్రీనిధాయి। రుచిర గుణహరిచెంచయ

25. రుద్రశౌరి॥

ATMAKUR (36).

[Kullúru. Telugu. From the Calingulah of the tank.]

TRANSLATION.

The weir work done by Marára Duggaraju Vírappa. Imminilu has written (this).

1. . . . . . .
2. . . . . . .
3. , శ్రీశినం హని
4. మరార దుగ్గ
5. రాజువీరప్ప
6. శేయించిన
7. అల్లుపని
8. యి మింని
9. లు వ్రాసినా
10. ండు

ATMAKUR (37).

[Mahimalúru. Telugu. On a fallen stone by a small tank to north of village.]

TRANSLATION.

On Thursday, the 15th of the bright fortnight of Márgaṣira of the illustrious year Vyaya, Madhura Perumáḷḷa Rája, son of Kulaṣékhara Maṇḍana Perumáḷḷa Ráju, the emperor of the three worlds, and Káḷati Ráju, son of Kulaṣékhara Kávéri, issued this charitable edict as a gift to the gods Múlasthána Íṣayadéva and Nágéṣvaradéva of Mahimalúru. We have given with libation of water on the holy occasion of a lunar eclipse on Thursday, the 15th of the bright fortnight of Márgaṣira of that year 100 *kunṭas* of land under the Rámamaḍi Pina Cheruvu in Mahimalúru which is situated in Giribhávivelibóyaviḷa which is attached to our chiefdom. This should be utilized for offerings to the deities in perpetuity to last as long as the moon endure. Whoever cause obstruction to this charity will incur the sin of killing a tawny cow near the Ganges.

Hrim Ṣri!

NOTE.—We have not been able to identify this emperor. The name and the reference to Madura suggest a Páṇḍyan. Mr. Sewell on pages 70 and 72 of Vol. 2 of "Antiquities" mentions two inscriptions of Kulaṣékhara Perumál from Tinnevelly. They are of the 16th century and can hardly have any connection with the emperor of this inscription.

1. శ్రీ వ్యయసంవత్సర మార్గ్గసిర సు ౧౫ గు త్రిభువనచ
2. క్రవర్తి కులశేఖరమండన పెరుమాళ్ళరాజు కుమా
3. రుండు మధురపెరుమాళ్ళరాజున్ను - కులశేఖరకా
4. వేరి కుమారుండు కాళతిరాజున్ను మహిమలూరి

5. మూలస్తాన యీాశయదేవరకున్ను నాగేశ్వరదేవరకు
6. ంన్ను దేవదానముగాను యిచ్చిన ధంమ్మశాసనం
7. ము మానాయంకరానకుం జెల్లివుండే గిరిభావివెలి
8. బోయవిళలోని మహిమలూరను తత్సంవత్సర మా
9. ర్గసిర సు ౧౩ ను సోమగ్రహణ పుణ్యకాలానను ధార
10. పోసియిచ్చినవి రామంమడిపిన చెరవుక్రిందను
11. నూరుగుంటలుంన్నా ఆచంద్రస్తాయిగాను దేవ
12. ళ్లకు నవద్యాలకు[1] చెల్లంగగలది ఇ ధర్మానకు
13. యవ్వరు విఘ్నమాచరించినా వా
14. రు గంగకర్త కవిల చం
15. పిన పాపానం బోవువారు
16. శ్రీం శిరి.

ATMAKUR (38). (A.D. 1217–18?)

[Mahimalúru. Telugu. From the Vishnu temple.]

TRANSLATION.

Hail! On Wednesday the 8th of the bright fortnight of Jyéshṭa . . . . corresponding to the Ṣri Ṣaka year 1139, Bammináyakuḍu, younger brother of Gollapayinḍi Biyyapa Náyakuḍu, the protector (*pratipálaka*) of the kingdom of Hail! Erra Siddanadéva Chóḍa Mahárája, on whose (Erra Siddana's) lotus feet are set the eyes of Trilóchana[2] and all other kings, who (Erra Siddana) is the jewelled lamp of the race of Karikála by whom (Karikála) the dam[3] of the Kávéri was built, who (Erra Siddana) is the elephant-goad to wicked princes,

---

[1] Read నైవేద్యాలకు. [2] The allusion is to the Pallava dynasty.

[3] See note on page 1250.

Ṣríman Mahámaṇḍaléṣvara, the supreme excellent lord of Orayúru, the best of cities, who is the vanquisher of rival chiefs, who is a glorious Náráyaṇa, Ayyana Singa,[1] who is eminent in valour, who has levied tribute from Kánchi, and who is Bhujabaḷa Víra (a strong-armed hero), who (Biyyapa Náyaka) wears on his arms an armlet adorned with the rays of numerous excellent gems, who has a broad chest marked by the embraces of the orbs of the bosom of Lakshmí, who is Ṣésha (the serpent bearing the earth) of Prattikoṇḍa[2] hill—the illustrious (?)—the ornament of the race of Manma, who is the hero of heroes, who is the hero praised by his subjects, who is the sun to the host of lotuses which are learned men, who has set up the kingdom of the Chóḍa Mahárája, who has acquired great wealth, Ṣríman *Mahápradhání* (prime minister), and who is the commander-in-chief of all the forces . . . . having propitiated Chenna Kéṣavadéva of Mahimalúru which is the capital of Tónkakúḍúrunáḍu in Tiruvaḍi Kavalillu(?) in Pánkanáḍu, gave villages (names doubtful) . . . . having constructed . . . . for them every year a field . . . . for his parents . . . . Vávillapalli . . . founded this endowment. Whoever does not maintain the gift but obstructs it will incur the sin of killing 1,500 tawny cows on the Ganges.

[One imprecatory verse.]

Note.—This Bammi Náyaka may be the Bhíma Náyaka of R. 37. He may have succeeded his brother in the post of Commander-in-chief (Sáhiṇi).

---

[1] Ayyana Singa—the lion of his father. Regarding this title, see *Ind. Ant.*, Vol. XV., p. 276.

[2] We have not been able to discover any Prattikonda in Nellore district.

1. స్వస్తిశ్రీ శకవర్షంబులు ౧౧౩౯
2. అగు నేంటి జేష్ట శుద్ధాష్టమియు
3. బుధవారమునాండు స్వస్తి
4. చరణ సరోరుహవిహితవిలో
5. చన త్రిలోచన ప్రముఖాఖిలపృథి
6. వీశ్వరకారిత కావేరితీరకరికా
7. లకులరత్న ప్రధీపాహితకుమా
8. రాంకుశశ్రీ మన్మహామణ్డలేశ్వ
9. రఉఱయూరిపుర వరాధీశ్వర
10. దాయాది మణ్డలీక దిశాపట్ట
11. * వైరి పురటికీర్తినారాయణ
12. ఆయ్యనసింగసాహసోత్తుం
13. గ్గ కాంచింగప్పమురిన్న భుజ
14. బళవీర ఎఱ్ఱసిద్ధనదేవచోడ
15. మహారాజుల రాజ్యప్రతిష్ఠా
16. లకుండును స్వస్తిసమస్తగు
17. ణమణి కిరణాలంకృత కే
18. యూరహార దారణదో
19. ర్వ్యజిత విస్తార లక్షణ ల
20. క్ష్మీ కుచకలశ . . . .
21. . లక్షిత విశాల వక్షస్థ
22. ల (ప్రత్తికొండరద్రిశేషము)
23. (ని మానమహాస్వవమన్మ)
24. కులతిలకగండరగండ జ
25. గమెచ్చు గండపండిత పు
26. ండరీకషండ మార్తాండ
27. చోడమహారాజరాజ్య
28. ప్రతిష్టత విభవానేకస
29. ంచ్చితశ్రీ మన్మహాప్రధాని

30. సమస్తసేనాధి పతియు
31. నునైన గొల్లపఙండిబియ్య
32. పనాయకుని తమ్ముండు
33. బమ్మినాయకుండు పాం
34. కవాంటి తిరువడికవలి
35. ంటిలోని తోంక కూడూరునాంటి
36. కిరాజధానియైన మహి
37. మలూరజన్న కేశవదే
38. వరకుబ్రీతిగా సేసిమహి
39. మలూరిని రతిడిడామా
40. రమునం గరిదమూతం
41. బాదారము (వరముగల)
42. ఇచ్చి డీనికి . . . . ల . .
43. (యేకత కండమున ప)
44. (మముంగట్టి) . . . . . .
45. (యిచ్చివీల్ల కుపంటనుం)
46. (డిమవేమవ . . . . .)
47. (గలచే నుకుం . . . తర)
48. (పలికకొమ . . . తట)
49. (ప్పు విచిభైరవనేండుమర)
50. (గా పావనభట్లును . తమత)
51. (ండికిం తల్లికిం . . . . పక)
52. (. కొమకు . . . . . మ)
53. (మందిద్రి . . . . . రు)
54. (నమెరగావాంవిలిపల్లి పలిక)
55. (ం . వీరు . వాండుమర)
56. (లితుం . . . . . ంలు .)
57. (. . . . . . .)
58. . . . . . . (మంది)

59. (తొడిదిం . షెం . నాను .)
60. (గట్టినవాండు . . . .)
61. వృథము బెట్టిదానమును సె
62. ళ్లించకను లేక విపులము సే
63. సేవాండుగంగకర్తృవేయుం
64. నేనూరు కవిలలం బొడ్చి
65. నపాపానంబోయినవారు
66. స్వదత్తం పరదత్తంవాయో
67. హారేతి
68. వసుం
69. ధరాష
70. ష్టివర్ష
71. షసహా
72. స్రాణి వి
73. ష్టాయాం
74. జాయ
75. తే క్రి
76. మి

ATMAKUR (39). (A.D. 1409–10.)

[Mangampalli (hamlet Guḍiguṇṭa). Telugu. South of Chennakéṣavasvámi temple.]

TRANSLATION.

Prosperity! Hail! On Thursday, the 10th of the bright fortnight of Ṣrávaṇa of the year Viródhi, corresponding to the year 1331 of the prosperous Ṣaka era, while Ṣríman Mahá Rájádhi Rája Rájaparaméṣvara Ṣrí Víra Pratápa Dévaráya Oḍayalu, son of Ṣrí Harihararáya, was ruling with pleasure the kingdom at Vijayanagar as the lord of the four seas, Appalayya, of the Yajus Ṣákha, of the Bháradvája *gótra,* and son of Mádhava Jósyulu who is the son of Yéputtila Appaya Jósyulu, constructed this on an auspicious day which is regarded with esteem by the whole world and which is appropriate for making gifts, charity, &c., at Bahadurpuram, otherwise called Guḍakunṭṭu, situated to the west of Anantaságaram on the banks of the river Penna in the country (déṣa) of Bóyavihára, in the kingdom of Udayagiri, to Chennakéṣvaradéva and to Ṣrí Rangamanátha who is honoured as the consort of Ṣrí, to last as long as the sun and moon exist, for the religious merit of his parents Mádhavajósyulu and Jábálika. May his fame in the shape of that dancing-hall (Rangamanḍapam) last eternally as long as the moon and stars exist. May the grace of that Chennakéṣava be eternally propitious to Appalu, son of Mádhava Jósyulu, and grant him eternal prosperity. May that Appana Jósyulu live long! May there be great prosperity!

1. శ్రీ స్వస్తి శ్రీ శకవర్షం బుడయంబు
2. లు ౧౩౩౧ అగునేటి విరోధిసంవత్సర శ్రావణ
3. శు ౧౦ గురువారమందు శ్రీమన్మహారా
4. జాధిరాజ రాజపరమేశ్వర శ్రీహరిహ
5. రరాయని కుమారుండు శ్రీవీరప్రతాపదేవ
6. రాయఒడయలు విజయనగరమందు సు
7. ఖానను చతుస్సముద్రాధీశ్వరుడై రాజ్యం
8. చేయుచుండంగాను యజుః శాఖా భార
9. ద్వాజగోత్రం యేపుట్టిల అప్పయజోస్యు
10. ల కొడుకు మాధవజోస్యులకొడుకు అప్పలయ్య
11. ఉదయగిరి రాజ్యమందుల బోయవిహార
12. దేశంలోపలను పెన్నకటక తీరమందున

13. అనంతసాగరానకు పడుమటను గుడకుంట్లు
14. లనెటి బహాదురిపురమందు సకలజగధారా
15. ధ్యమై సకల దానధర్మాది చెంతిలమనోరథ
16. మైన శుభదినమందు చెన్నకేశ్వర దేవరకు
17. నిలశ్రీశా మహాత్ములైన శ్రీరంగమనాథునకు
18. మును ఆచంద్రార్కముగా యిచ్చినట్టిగాను దీని
19. తల్లిదండ్రులు మాధవజోస్యులుకును జా
20. బాలికకుచు సుకృతంగాను కట్టించిరి యీ
21. న ఆ రంగమంటప రూపమైన కీర్తి ఆచంద్ర
22. క తారకము ఔనట్లుగాన స్థిరమై ఉండుంగా
23. క ఆ శ్రీ చెంనకేశ్వరకృప మాధవజోస్యుల కొ
24. డుకు అప్పలుకు నిత్యమై స్థిరలక్ష్మీవౌనట్టుగా
25. ను నిత్యసంపదలునూ ఇచ్చుగాక ఆ యప్పన
26. జోస్యు.. ఆయుక్మంతుడు అయెడుమ మంగ.
27. ళమహా శ్రీ శ్రీ శ్రీ

Atmákur (40). (A.D. 1610–11.)

[Minagallu (hamlet Venkatreḍḍipalli). Telugu. Near Lingarázu Gunṭa.]

Translation.

Hail! On the 30th of Márgasira of the year Sádháraṇa, corresponding to the illustrious, victorious and prosperous Ṣáliváhana Ṣaka year 1532, Veligóṭi Timmanáyaningáru issued this charitable edict to Lingaráju, karnam of Minnakallu . . . . . We have given you 100 *kunṭas* of wet land within the four boundaries in Minakallu as a *sarvamánya*. Therefore you should enjoy it as long as the sun and moon endure

1. స్వస్తిశ్రీ జయాభ్యు
2. దయ శాలివాహ
3. న శకవరుషంబులు
4. ౧౫౩౨ అగు నేంటి సాధార
5. రణసంవత్సర మార్గశిర ౩౦ లు
6. వెలిగోటి తింమానాయనింగా
7. రు మిన్నకంట్టి కరణంలింగ్గ
8. రాజుకు ఇచ్చిన ధర్మశా
9. (సనం) మింనకంటను (వనుయల్లచను
10. స్సిమాన) నూరుకుంటలమ
11. డికారుకాదాసు సర్వమాన్యంగాని
12. స్త్రిమి గనక అచంద్రార్కంగాను అ
13. ను భవించివారు . . .
14. . . . .
15. . . . .

ATMAKUR (41).

[Minagallu (hamlet Lakkirázupalli). Telugu. In Muppu Seṭṭi's tope to the north.]

TRANSLATION.

On . . . . the 12th of the dark fortnight of Márgaṣira . . . . Náráyaṇa Ráju . . . .

1. లా . . . .
2. మార్గశిర బ ౧౨
3. . . వారంనం నారా
4. యణరాజు పాలె
5. ంబ . నేంటిసం

6. . . మేరలోకట

7. . ణం గా షేటు

8. . . . . .

9. మ . . నారు

Atmakur (42).

[Minagallu. Telugu. On the boundary of Nallarázupáḷem.]

Translation.

Ranganátharájungáru . . . . gave . . . Ranganátha of Mahimalúru which was granted as an *amaram* . . . .

1. . . . .

2. తిరుమలకువని . .

3. . . సంభవల్ల . . .

4. కు అమరాలకుమ . . .

5. పాలించిన మహిమలూరి

6. ని రంగనాంథుండు . రంగ

7. నాంథ రాజుంగారు . .

8. . లిచ్చినకా(ందటు) మేర

9. . కరాజుంగారి నీతరు .

10. . . . . .

Atmakur (43).

[Návúru. Tamil. To east of Nágéṣvara temple.]

Translation.

Hail! Prosperity! In the thirty-ninth year of the reign of the emperor of the three worlds, the glorious

Kulôttungachôḻadêva, (in the temple) of Tirunâgíśvara who is the presiding deity (Múlasthána) at Nâvalûr.

[1] ஸ்வஸ்தி ஸ்ரீ தி
[2] ஹுவனச்சக்ரவத்-
[3] திகள் ஸ்ரீகுலொத்-
[4] துங்க சொழதெவர்-
[5] க்கு யாண்டு நடு-
[6] சூ ஆவது நாவூரி-
[7] ல் மூலஸ்தாநமாந-
[8] திருநாகீஸ்வரமுடை-
[9] டயார்கொ

Atmakur (44).

[Návúru. Telugu. Defaced stone to south of Polé-ramma temple.]

Translation.

. . . . . Two *paṭṭus* of paddy field to him . Whoever obstruct this charity will be considered to have killed a tawny cow near the Ganges.

1. . . . . వ షం
2. . . . .
3. . . . లు .
4. . . నవ . .
5. . . నికిని వారి
6. కివరిచేను పట్లు ౨ ఇది
7. ట్టి దమ్మాకు యెవ్వరు వి
8. ఘ్నము సేసిన గంగకటత
9. కవిలం పొడిచినవారు

Atmakur (45).

[Návúru. Telugu. To the east of Panchaliṅgála temple.]

Translation.

Prosperity! Hail! Ṣríman Mahámaṇḍaléṣvara Rájádhirája Paramakusálava (?) Próshi Errasidi Rája, Hari Bairapa Náyaka, Ammanáyaka and Pahinḍináyaka, all of Gandavárаṇamupáḍu, having consecrated Siddhanáthadéva in the name of their fathers, gave *vrittis* as follows for enjoyments and decorations to that deity: a *paṭṭi* of *kóru* land, a dry field of one *paṭṭi* to the north, 100 *ṛaṭṭis* of wet field in rear of Maṭṭiváḍicheruvu which is of medium soil among wet fields (?) May there be great prosperity! . . . .

. . . . It appears he has done that work.

NOTE.—This Errasiddhi may be Erra Siddhanadéva Choḍa.

1. శ్రీ స్వస్తి
2. శ్రీమన్మహా
3. మండలేశ్వర
4. రాజాధి
5. రాజ పర
6. మకుసాల
7. వప్రోషి
8. ఎఱసిది
9. రాజుగం
10. డ వారణ
11. ముపాటి
12. హరిబై
13. ప వనా

14. యకుండు
15. ంను అంమ
16. నాయకు
17. ండూన్న ప
18. హిండినా
19. యకుండు
20. న్న తమ త
21. ండ్రి పెరసి
22. ద్ధనాధదే
23. వరప్రతి
24. ష్టశేసి ఆ
25. దేవర అం
26. గబోగ
27. మునకూ
28. రంగబో
29. గమునకు
30. ద్రిత్తికోరు
31. పట్టిచేలు
32. న్న నుత్త
33. రమున
34. నుండేటి
35. పొలము
36. వేలి చేణి
37. ప ౧ మ
38. ట్టివాడిచె
39. ఊవువె
40. నకమాగలి
41. నడితర
42. ం వరిచే

43. ను పట్టి
44. ని నూటు
45. మంగళ
46. మహా శ్రీ
47. డల ఆపని
48. కట్టినట

ATMAKUR (46).

[Pedda Annalúru. Near tank sluice. Under water and so not taken.]

ATMAKUR (47). (A.D. 1486–87.)

[Pelléru. Telugu. Opposite Chennakéṣavasvámi temple. Partially defaced.]

TRANSLATION.

(Obeisance to) Ṣrí Ráma! Hail! On the 15th of the bright half of Vaiṣákha of the year Parábhava, corresponding to the year 1409 of the illustrious, victorious, and prosperous Ṣaliváhana Ṣaka era, Ṣrímat Ko . . . náyanimgáru . . . . having constructed at Prátapáḍu . . . .

1. శ్రీరామ స్వస్తి శ్రీ జయాభ్యుద
2. య శాలివాహాన శకవర్షంబు
3. లు ౧౪౦౯ అగునేంటి పరాభవసంవ
4. ర వైశాఖ శుక్ల ౧౫ లు శ్రీమతు కొ
5. (. . .) నాయనింగారు చుంచు
6. . . . . ప్రాతపాట్న చి నచె

7. . . . . కంగానుకట్టించి
8. . . టన్న . . కుం
9. . . . తనిసలు.
10. గనా భని. .
11. ఙ

ATMAKUR (48). (A.D. 1621–22.)

[Pelléru. Telugu. In front of Síta temple.]

TRANSLATION.

Hail! On Monday, the 15th day of the bright half of Srávaṇa of the year Durmati, corresponding to the illustrious, victorious and prosperous year 1544 of the Ṣálivàhana Ṣaka era, in the kingdom granted by Ṣrímat Rájádhirája Rája Paraméṣvara Ṣrí Víra Pratápa Ṣrí Víra Venkaṭapatidéva Maháráya, who, seated on the diamond throne, was ruling the kingdom of the earth, to Veligóṭi Komára Timmánáyaningáru, in Nellúru *síma*, Venkaṭapatináyaningáru gave the village Pellerlu as an *amaram* to Chintagumpalli Basappa Náyaningáru. Therefore the terms for providing channels for the people this year are: the produce raised on dry fields should be divided into four shares, of which three should go to the ryot and one to the estate every year. The grain raised under the tanks should be divided into three shares, of which two should go to the ryot and one to the estate every year. In this manner whoever is the ruler should cause to be done.

1. స్వస్తి శ్రీ విజయాభ్యుదయ
2. శాలివాహన శకవరుషంబు

3. లు ౧౫౪౪ అగు నేటి దుర్మతిన
4. ంవత్సర శ్రావణ శు ౧౫ సో। శ్రీమద్రాజాధిరాజ
5. రాజపరమేశ్వర శ్రీవీరప్రతాప శ్రీవీరవేంకటపతి
6. దేవ మహారాయలయ్యవారు వజ్రసింహాసనారూ
7. ఢులై పృథివి సాంమ్రాజ్యం శేయుచుణ్డ వెలిగోటి కొ
8. మార తింమ్మానాయనింగారికి యిచ్చిన రాజ్యం
9. లో నెల్లూరి శీమలోని పెళ్లెగ్లు అను గ్రామం వెంకట
10. పతినాయనింగారు చింతగుంపల్లి బసవ్వనా
11. యనింగారికి అమరానకు యిచ్చిరిగనక . . . .
12. . . . . . చెవుణనిమిత్తం యీసంవ్వత్సరా
13. న ప్రజలకు కాపులకు యిచ్చిన వివరం వెలిబోలాను పం
14. డినట్టి ధాన్యం శ్రాహి ౪ లెఖను కాంపుకు పాళ్లు ౩
15. మూడునగరికి పాలి లెఖను చెరువులకింద్ద పండినట్టి దా
16. న్యం శ్రాహి ౩ లెఖను కాంపుకు పాళ్లు ౨ ను నగరికి
17. పాలి లెఖను యీప్రకారంగాను యవ్వరు యేలినా జరు

పువారు.

Atmakur (49).

[Peramana. Telugu. Near Tummalamma temple.]

Translation.

The temple caused to be erected for (the goddess) Tummalamma by Báchámu Akkayya and Inagureḍḍi Krishnamma on the 2nd day of the bright fortnight of Mágha of the year named Ṣubhakṛit.

1. సుభకృతు
2. నామసంవత్సర
3. మాఖసుద్ద

4. విదియలు బా
5. చాము అక్క
6. యయినగు
7. రెడ్డి క్రిష్ణమ్మ
8. కట్టించిన తుమ్మ
9. లంమ్మ దేవాలయం॥

ATMAKUR (50). (A.D. 1771–72.)

[Peramana. Telugu. Near Tummalamma temple.]

TRANSLATION.

Hail! On the 30th day of the dark fortnight of Áṣvija of the year Khara, corresponding to the year 1693 of the illustrious Ṣáliváhana Ṣaka era, the Dommaras, viz., Kútumgópála, the daughter of Bussáreḍḍi the proprietor of the dramatic company, Changálu, the daughter of Mallároḍḍi and others gave a charitable edict to the great ṣakti (goddess) Tummalamma of Permana who is otherwise called Mahákáḷi and Mahádurgí. (Signatures of) the Dommaras who roam over the earth carrying a drum named *Gangaḍólu* (?)

1. స్వస్తి శ్రీశాలివాహన
2. శకవర్షంబులు
3. ౧౬౯౩ అగునేటి
4. ఖర సం॥ ఆశ్వీజ బ
5. ౩౦ లు మహాకాళి మహా
6. దుర్గి అగునటి పెర్మనతుం
7. మ్మలంమ్మ మహాశక్తింకి కూ
8. తుంగోపాళ నాటకరాయ

9. బుస్సారెడ్డి కూతురు మల్లారెడ్డి
10. కూతురు చంగ్గలు వగైరా దొమ్మలున్
11. శేఖంచ్చి ఇచ్చి ధర్మశాసనం మీ
12. గంగడ డోలు
13. పట్టైభూమి
14. ని తిరిగ దో
15. మ్మల్లున్ ॥

ATMAKUR (51). (A.D. 1274–75?)

[Peramana. Telugu. Near Áñjanéya temple.]

TRANSLATION.

Hail! On Thursday, the 5th day of the dark fortnight of Chaitra, corresponding to the year 1196 of the illustrious Ṣaka era, when the Mahárája was ruling, his (the Mahárája's) subordinate (శంకలుడు) Ḍámirapu Ráminávaḍu and Malli Náyaḍu presented as a gift the village of Yoḍalrupáḍu, to last as long as the sun and moon exist, for the religious merit of Nágadéva Mahárája. May it cause great prosperity! Whoever cause obstruction to this will incur the sin of killing a tawny cow on the banks of the Ganges and the sin of cooking and (eating) . . . . in the skulls of their parents.

1. స్వస్తి శ్రీ సకవరుషంబు
2. లు ౧౧౯౬ అగునేంటి
3. చైత్ర బహుళ పంచమి గురు
4. వారమునాండు మహారా
5. జురాజ్యమున నాగదేవమ
6. హా రాజునకు ధర్మువు

7. గా నాతని శంకలుడామి
8. అపురామి నాయిండు
•9. మల్లినాయిండును
10. మనదవదానముగా
11. రెూండ్లుపాటి
12. విడిచితిమి
13. ఆచంద్రాకర్కము
14. గా మంగళమా
15̣. హాః శ్రీ శ్రీ శ్రీ ఊ
16. వంద్ర సైసినవారు
17. గంగ కలుత గవి
18. లం బొాడిచినవారు వం
19. డికోని తమ తల్లిదం
20. డ్రుల కపాలములో
21. (కుడిచిన పాపాన పోదురు)

ATMAKUR (52).

[Pongúru. Telugu. On western boundary.]

TRANSLATION.

Hail! On the 15th of the bright fortnight of . . . . of the year . . . . . . corresponding to the illustrious, victorious and prosperous Ṣáliváhana Ṣaka year . . . . on the holy occasion of a lunar eclipse, while . . . . Oḍayalu was ruling the earth, ... the son of Polináyaku, son of Malallimpáḍu . . . . granted . . . . with libation of water. Whoever obstructs the donee will be regarded as having eaten from the skull of his eldest son and will incur the sin of killing a tawny cow on the Ganges.

[One imprecatory verse.]

1. (స్వస్తిశ్రీ జయాభ్యుదయ శాలివాహనశకవర్షంబులు .
2. ...) అగునేంటి . త్ర . సంవత్సర .... శు
౧౧ సోమ
3. గ్రహణపుణ్యకాలమందు . . . . .
4. ఒడయలు ప్రిదివిరాజ్యము చేయుచుండగాను
5. మలల్లంవాడుకో (డుకు) పొలినా(యకుని)కు
6. మారుండుతాను . దమ . . .
7. ను తిరుమలయ్య . . . . . . లవ
8. త . . . .
9. (. . . పుడండ . బను) ధారాపూర్వకముగాను
10. యిస్తిమి యాశ్రితులకు యవ్వరు విఘలముచేసినాను
11. తనపెద్దకొడుకు కపాళనకుడిచినారు గంగ్గకఅత
12. ను కపిలచంపిన పాపానంబోదురు స్వదత్తాద్విగు
13. ణంపుణ్యం పరదత్తానుపాలనం పరదత్తా
14. పహారేణ స్వదత్తం నిష్ఫలంభవేతు.

ATMAKUR (53). (A.D. 1602–03.)

[Prabhagiripaṭṇam. Telugu. From stone in front of Perumáḷasvámi temple.]

TRANSLATION.

Hail! On the 11th day of the bright fortnight of Kártika of the year Ṣubhakṛit, corresponding to the year (1524) of the illustrious, victorious and prosperous Ṣálivábana Ṣaka era, while Ṣrímad Rájádhi Rája Rája Paraméṣvara Ṣrí Víra Pratápa Ṣrí Venkaṭaráya Maháráyulu, seated on the diamond throne at Vijayanagar, was ruling the kingdom of the earth, Ṣríman Mahámaṇḍaléṣvara Muddayadéva Mahárája, son of (Koṇḍa . . .) déva Mahárája issued this charitable edict to Ṣrí Chennakéṣavaráya of Paṭnam (Prabhákara Paṭnam). We have given on the holy occasion of the 11th day of the bright fortnight of Kártika the village Nandiráyuni, (Nandiráyi?) situated in the *ṣíma* of Prabhákarapaṭnam attached to the kingdom of Udayagiri, which was bestowed on us for our chiefdom by Ṣríman Mahámaṇḍaléṣvara Satti Rája Ṣrí Muddayya Déva Mahárája, for providing incense, light, and offerings, and all enjoyments (to the deity). Therefore this is the charitable edict given to Ṣrí Chenna Kéṣavadéva bestowing all the produce, &c., grain and income derived from that village.

[One imprecatory verse.]

Whoever injures this charity will incur the sin of killing cows and Brahmans near the Ganges.

1. స్వస్తి శ్రీజయాభ్యుదయ శాలివాహన శక వరుషంబులు (౧౫౨౪)

2. అగు నేంటి శుభకృతు సంవత్సర కార్తిక శు ౧౧ శ్రీమ

3. ద్రాజాధిరాజ రాజపరమేశ్వర శ్రీవీర ప్రతాప శ్రీవేంక టరాయమహా

4. రాయలు విజయనగరమందు వజ్ర సింహాసనారూఢులై పృథ్వి సాం

5. బ్రాజ్యం చేయుచుండ్డంగాను శ్రీమన్మహామండ్డలేశ్వర (కొండం . . . . మ)

6. . దేవమహారాజులంగారి కొమారుండు ముదయ్యదేవ మహారాజుల

7. ంగారు పట్నం శ్రీచన్న కేశవరాయనికి యిచ్చిన ధర్మ శాశనపత్రము శ్రీమన్మ

8. హా ఖండ లేశ్వర సత్తిరాజు శ్రీముద్దయ్య దేవమహారా జులంగారు మాకు

9. నాయంకరానకుం పాలించ్చనవధరించ్చె వుదయగిరి రా జ్యాన్ను చెల్లె ప్రభాకరపట్న

10. ం శీమలోని నందిరాయుని ధూవ దీవ నైవేద్యాలకున్ను అ

11. ంగ్గరంగ్గవైభవాలకున్ను (కార్తీక శు) యేకాదశి పుణ్య కాలమున నారవ (?) (ఇస్తి)

12. మిగనుర ఆగ్రామానంగలిగిన సకల ఫలాదులున్ను సక ల ధాన్య

13. దాయమున్ను ప్రకారం శ్రీచన్న కేశవ దేవునికి యిచ్చిన ధర్మశాసనము

14. స్వదత్తాద్విగుణం పుణ్యం పరదత్తానుపాలనం పర దత్తా పహారేణ

15. స్వదత్తం నిష్ఫలం భవేతు యీపుణ్యం యవ్వరు చెర్పి నా గంగకర్త గో

16. బ్రాహ్మల వధియించ్చిన పాపాన పోఇనవారు

ATMAKUR (54). (A.D. 1581–82.)

[Punugóḍu. Telugu. Near Nallúruvári well to west of village.]

TRANSLATION.

(Adoration be to) Ṣrí Nílakanṭhéṣvara! On Monday, the 30th day of the dark fortnight of the month of Vaiṣákha of the year Vishu, corresponding to the year 1503 of the illustrious, victorious and prosperous Ṣáli-váhana era, Chintanúri Kéṣanáyuḍu, while ruling the village of Ponungóḍu, this day consecrated the image of Nílakanṭhéṣvara, and for providing incense, lamps, and the 16 services (to the deity) founded an endowment in the village consisting of one *puṭṭi* . . . . of paddy fields in Vutla ana . . . . dry field of 2 *gorrus* in Savulagaṭṭu. We have presented all this land as a *sarva-mányam*, with libation of water to Ṣrí Nílakanṭhéṣvára to last as long as the sun and moon exist. Therefore whoever fails in this charity will incur the sin of killing a cow and a Brahman near the Ganges.

[One imprecatory verse.] Ṣrí!

NOTE.—Chintanuri Kéṣanáyuḍu is not mentioned elsewhere and was evidently a person of no importance; perhaps merely a village headman.

1. శ్రీ నీలకంఠేశ్వర శ్రీ జయాం
2. భ్యుదయ శాలివాహనశక
3. వరుషంబులు ౧౫౦౩ అ
4. గు నేటి విషు సం
5. వత్సర వైశాఖ (మాస)
6. వు బావుల 30 సో మార
7. లోన పానుంగోటి
8. గ్రామం చింత నూరి (కే)
9. శనాయండు యేలుచు
10. యీాదివసమందు నీల
11. కంఠేశ్వరున్ని ప్రతిష్ఠ సే
12. యించ్చి ధూపదీప
13. షోడచోప
14. పచారాల
15. కున్ను గ్రామా
16. నె సాగించ్చి
17. న స్వాద్యం
18. మేరఖ ౧

19\. . . . . . . న్నవు
20\. . . . . పు
21\. . . . . ద్దు
22\. . . . .
23\. వరిమడిం పూట్ల అన . ,
21\. ండుకటును వెలిచేను సా
25\. పులగట్టి స్థలాన్ను రెండుగోర్లు
26\. ను ఇంతవట్టున్ను నీలకంఠే
27\. శ్వరునికి ధారవోసి . సర్వ
28\. మాన్యంగాను ఇచి ఆ
29\. చంద్రార్క స్థాయిగాను ఇ
30\. స్థిమి గనుక యీ పుణ్యా
31\. నకు యవ్వరు తప్పి
32\. నాను గంగ్గకత్త గో
33\. బ్రాంహాన్ని వధించిన
34 పాపానం బోవా
34\. రు । స్వదత్తాద్విగు
36\. ణం పుణ్యం పరదత్తా
37\. నుపాలనం పరదత్తాపహారేణ స్వ
38\. దత్తం నిష్పలం భవేత్ శ్రీ

ATMAKUR (55). (A.D. 1290–91.)

[Rájavólu. Telugu. Near the calingulah of the tank.]

TRANSLATION.

Hail! On Monday the 10th of the bright fortnight of Áshádha of the year Vikṛiti, corresponding to the Ṣrí Saka year 1212, in the kingdom of Ṣríman Maṇḍaléṣvara Malidéva Mahárája, son of (Hail) Ṣríman

Mahámaṇḍaléṣvara Vijayádityadévamaháràja who is endowed with all the glory of titles. Hail! Pinnama Náyakuḍu, son of (Hail) Manḍi Súnki Náyakuni Kéṣava-náyaka, who is *Bayya* (?), possessed of various other titles and who is the son of Hail! Badhyamadra Ráju, who wears an armlet adorned with the rays of numerous excellent gems, the supreme lord of Orayúru the best of cities, the hero of heroes, the hero praised by his subjects, a sun to the host of lotuses which are learned men, gave with libation of water (the village of) Bayinḍipáḍu as an *ékabhógam* (to be enjoyed as a single share) to the deity Anḍama of Koḍumana which belongs to him and is situated in Angaḍamantanáḍu, to last as long as the moon and the sun endure.

[Three imprecatory verses.]

NOTE.—The inscription gives us—

Badhya Madra Ráju
|
Mandi Súnki Náyakuni Késava Náyaka
|
Pinnama Náyaka.

and the first is said to have ruled at Orayúru. These chiefs do not appear to be mentioned elsewhere. In the note on p. 72 of Vol. III of E.I. Uraiyúr is identified with the suburb of Trichinopoly of that name and is described as being formerly a capital of the Chola kings.

First side.

1. స్వస్తిశ్రీశక
2. వరుషంబులు
3. ౧౨౧౨ విక్రమ
4. సంవత్సర ఆ
5. షాఢశుద్ధద
6. శమిసోమవా
7. రానస్వస్తిసమ
8. స్తప్రశస్తిసహి

9. తంశ్రీమన్మహా
10. మండలేశ్వర
11. విజయాదిత్య
12. దేవమహారా
13. రాజులకొడుకుశ్రీ

Second side.

14. మనుమండలేశ్వర
15. మలిదేవమహారా
16. జులరాజ్యమున
17. స్వస్తియనేకగుణ
18. మణికిరణాలంక్రిత
19. ఒరయారిపురవా
20. రాధీశ్వరగండ్డర
21. గండ్డప్రజమెచు
22. గండ్డపండ్డితపు
23. ండ్డరీకషండ్డమా
24. ర్తాండబద్యమ
25. ద్రరాజుకొడుకు
26. బయ్యనామాది
27. ప్రశస్తిసహిత

Third side.

28. శ్రీమతు
29. లు మండిస్నూ
30. ంకి నాయకుని
31. కేశవనాయ
32. కుని కొడుకు పి
33. న్న మనాయకు

34. ండ్డు అంగ్గడ
35. మంతనాంట్టి
36. లోందమ్రవిత్తి
37. న్నైనకొండు
38. మన అణ్డమ
39. ందేవరకు
40. బయిండిపా
41. డు యేకబో
42. గమా చంద్రార్క-
43. ముగా ధారపోసి

Fourth side.

(Imprecatory verses.)

ATMAKUR (56).

[Ṣríkolanu. Sanskrit in Telugu characters and Telugu. Near a well to east of village.]

TRANSLATION.

Hail! Prosperity! Adoration be to Mallikárjuna, the lord of Ṣrí Parvata.

May Mallinátha protect you, he, by whom the enemies of the gods have been vanquished, who alone is able to protect all, by whom the host of miseries has been destroyed, by whom the path to heaven is established, whose ornament is the moon, who in all ways pleases his devotees, and whose consort is the daughter of the mountain.

* * * *

Victorious is Ṣrí Muppaḍéndra, who is adorned with the aggregate of all forms of wealth, on whom Kákati Rudra Déva having placed the burden of his kingdom . . . . .

NOTE.—Muppaḍi Náyaḍu was the Prime Minister of Pratápa Rudradéva (*vide* other inscriptions).

Telugu.

* * * *

On an auspicious occasion on Monday the 14th of the dark fortnight of Mághá of the year . . . . corresponding to Ṣaka year 12 . . .

* * * *

having set up the deity . . . . with gift of gold

* * * *

should continue . . .

* * * *

should belong to them

* * * *

will incur the sin of killing his mother . . . .

1. स्वस्तिश्रीश्रीपर्वत
2. याशमाह्लिखाजुर्न देवाय
3. नमः । जितविबुधावि
4. पक्षसर्वयैवादक्ष
5. :क्षपितदुरितवर्गः
6. स्थंभितस्वर्गमार्गः
7. शिशिरकरविभूषस्सोवि
8. ताश्रेषतोषिगिरिदु
9. हितुस्सनाधपातुवोम
10. ह्विनार्थः ॥ सतिरारि

11. स . . रमवरमेह
12. . तरा . कूलाशिशरवश
13. . . रमां . . यमवे
14. . . . . . कमा . कम
15. णविंस . . . हमित
16. चुवालि जरकाकतीकु
17. लदावश्रीमद्रमा .
18. . शाज्ञातिपरिवृढप्रौढ
19. आहवह . . नबल
20. . नपशाडम जबला . न
21. . . त्रपालंत्रत्य . क
22. प्र . नृरि प्रगुणमाणि
23. . . प्रभावाप्रम
24. . ग . भोशुक्तिमु
25. क्ति . . रमरतरुस्त्व
26. रूपाणांनिजाप्तक्षोणि
27. श्रीमुप्पडेंद्रोजय
28. तिविभवसभारंमडी
29. कृतप्राज्ञांत
30. निजराज्यभारंनिरंत्तरा
31. काकतिरुद्रदेवः (व)
32. . ఐ . వేమర
33. . గణాను . నామ
34. . భ కాంయ . .

Second side.

1. ధిర . . . . .
2. గగనం . . . . .
3. గ నంతం . . . . .
4. . బ . మా . . . బ
5. . . . . లి సెవా . .
6. . . వా స్తిర్ల . . ఙ్వ
7. . . ద్వనతుతి . . . .
8. . పంజం . . . .
9. . తిమిది రెఫజ నబి
10. . . . . సర వరుష
11. & 12. ంబులు ౧౨ . . అగునే
13. ంటి . . . త్తి సంకత్స
14. ర మాఘ బ ౧ర లుసో వారా
15. న పుణ్యకాలమున . . స్వ
16. . . న శ్రీపర్వ్య
17. . . పు . . చ . . శ్రీ
18. మ . . . దివ్య . . .
19. . న శ్రీ . . . . . .
20. . . రు . డు . . నుం
21. . . ధవ . . . ప
22. . . త . . వారులగను. త్రు
23. . . రు . . . . . . యి
24. రాం . . . . పాంకనా
25. ంటిలోన . . .
26. . . . . .
27. అయిపెరి . . . . . తముదేవర
28. ప్రతిష్టచేసి . . . సహిర
29. . వ . . . . .

30. ద . . రవలుఃబ్బ మును
31. . వభు . . .
32. . ములుసఃర్గ . .
33. నతాంచెల్లంగెది . . .
34. . . యమి . వము . .
35. వలోన
36. . . మయము
37. . . పుత్రిక . .
38. విరికి చెల్లగలదియన్న
39. గలవారిబెఃహంకడాంక
40. యీాన మిల్లలకు యల్లలవాం
41. . . . మల్పి కాండవ
42. . . కలమ లంకవిసంతా
43. . . తమతల్లిని వఖించ్చిపాం
44. పానంబోయినవారు.

ATMAKUR (57). (A.D. 1286–87.)

[Vasili. Telugu. From outside of Varadarájasvámi temple.]

TRANSLATION.

May there be prosperity. Dharma! Hail! On the day of Makara Sankránti, Wednesday, the 10th of the bright fortnight of Pushya of the year Vyaya, corresponding to the year 1208 of the illustrious Ṣaka era, Hail! [Ṣríman Mahámaṇḍaléṣvara ma . . . . Déva Mahárája gave for the religious merit of his father and his mother . .

1. శుభమస్తు ధర్మ్మం
2. స్వస్తి శ్రీశకవర్షంబులు ౧౨౦౮

3. అగునేంటి వయ సంవత్సర పౌష్య శుద్ధ దశమి బు
4. ధవారము మకర సంక్రాంతినాండు
5. స్వస్తి శ్రీమన్మహా మహామండలేశ్వర మ
6. . . . . దేవమహారాజు
7. లు తమ తండ్రికిన్ని తమ తల్లికిన్ని
8. ధర్మార్థముగాను ఇచ్చిన .

ATMAKUR (58).

[Vasili. Telugu. From inside Varadarájásvámi temple.]

TRANSLATION.

We the Dommaras who play on drums and perform on poles have presented this to the deity for the religious merit of (. . . .) in perpetuity to last as long as the sun and moon exist. If any one obstructs this charity he will incur the sin of killing cows at Benares. In these terms this charitable edict has been executed with the consent of all our caste people.

(The) signature of China Viréṣam with the consent of all these people. Ṣrí! Ṣrí! Ṣrí!

ర్థ ధర్మంగాను ఆచంద్రార్కస్థాయిగాను
స్వామి వారికి సమర్పించినాము డోలుగ
డవేసి ఆడె దొమ్మలుర యిందుకు యెవ
రు యీ ధర్మానకు అడ్డిచేసినవారికి కాశిలో గో
హత్య చేసిన పాపాన పోదురు యిటని మాకులం వా
రి అంద్దరి సమ్మతిని వ్రాయించ్చి యిచ్చిన ధర్మసా
సనపు పత్రిక వీరందరి సమ్మతిని చినవిరే
శం వ్రాలు శ్రీ శ్రీ శ్రీ

DARSI (1). (A.D. 1272–73.)

[Aluvalapáḍu. Telugu. North of Ánjanéya temple.]

TRANSLATION.

Hail! Ṣríman Mahámanḍaléṣvara Tripurári Déva Mahárája, who is the director of 72 offices, who is the worshipper of the lotus feet of Rudradéva Mahárája the ornament of the Kákatiya family, who (Rudradéva) is the ruler of many countries, who is the supporter of the four castes, who is the disperser of the army of the western king Dámódara, who is the only hero, who is the incarnation of valour, who is a perfect Révanta amongst those who are mounted on very unruly horses, who is Náráyaṇa and who is the beloved consort of the goddess of victory, who is terrible in battle, before whom the courage of all kings is paralyzed, with the collection of whose fame the foreheads of the maidens of the cardinal points are marked, who surpasses in liberality Káma Dhénu (cow of plenty) and Kalpa Druma (tree of plenty), the collection of rays from the nails of whose feet is kissed by the edges of the jewelled crowns of all kings who bowed to him, who (Tripurári) has acquired the lordship of the whole kingdom, who is of great prowess, who has the titles Chalamattugaṇḍa, Múruráya-jagadaḷa, Maṇḍalíka Bramha Rákshasa, Gaṇḍa Penḍáru, Hail! on the holy occasion of a lunar eclipse, on Wednesday, the 15th of the bright fortnight of Śrávaṇa of the year Ángirasa, corresponding to the year 1194 of the Ṣrí Śaka era, he gave for providing enjoyments to Ṣrí Tripurántakadéva, the village of Aluvalapáḍu in Póliganḍa *Sthala* with its four boundaries and with its income, after pouring water into the hand of Ṣrímat Triyambaka Śivácharya, the worshipper of the illustrious lotus feet of Ṣrí Tripurántaka Déva, for the increase of his life, health and wealth, in perpetuity to last as long as the sun and moon endure.

[Three imprecatory verses.]

Whoever thinks otherwise of this charity will incur the sin of killing ten thousand black cows on the banks of the Ganges.

(May it cause) great prosperity!

NOTE.—

Révanta—son of the sun.

Diṣápatta—Canarese = scatterer to all the points of the compass. Dámódara was apparently a Kaḍamba king, *vide* p. 93, Vol. XXI, I.A.

"Chalamattigaṇḍa" or Chalamartigaṇḍa was a biruda of the Kákatiyas.

Mururáya Jagadala, probably means the conqueror of the three kings.

Maṇḍalīka Brahma Rákshasa a very Brahma Rákshasa to provincial chiefs.

Gaṇḍa Penḍáru—Canarese; the meaning is not clear.

1. స్వస్తిశ్రీ మన్మ హామండ
2. లేశ్వర బాహాత్తరనియో
3. గాధిపతి అనేక దేశాధి
4. పతి చాతుర్వర్ణ్ణసము
5. ద్ధరణ పశ్చిమరా య
6. దామోదర సైన్యదిశా
7. పట్ట ఏకాంగవీర వీ
8. రావతార అతివిషమ
9. హాయారూఢ ప్రౌవు
10. ఢరేఖారేవంత విజయ
11. లక్ష్మీకాంతనాయకనా
12. రాయణ కదనప్రచ

13. ండ స్తంభః స్తంభిత స

14. కలక్షితిపాలశౌర్య్యా

15. యశస్తోమతిలకిత

16. ది గంగనాముఖ వి

17. తరణ గుణవినిర్జ్జిత కా

18. మధేను కల్పద్రుమ

19. ప్రణత సకలనరప

20. తి మణిమకుట కోటి

21. మకరికా చుంబ్యమా

22. న చరణ నఖకిరణ

23. కందళ కాకతికుల

24. తిలక రుద్రదేవ

25. మహారాజచరణ

26. నళిన యుగళ సమా

27. రాధన సమధిగత

28. సకల రాజ్యాధిపత్య

29. మహా విభవ చల

30. మత్తుగండ మూ

31. రురాయ జగదళ

32. మండలీక బ్రంహ

33. రాక్షస గండ పెండా

34. రు త్రిపురారి దేవ

35. మహారాజులు త

Second side.

36. మకు అయు

37. రారోగ్యైశ్వర్యా

38. భి వ్రిద్ధిగాను స్వ

39. స్తి శ్రీ శకవరు

40. పంబులు ౧౧౯౪
41. అగునేంటి ఆం
42. గిర సంవత్సర
43. శ్రావణ శు ౧౫ బు
44. నాండు సోమ
45. గ్రహణ పుణ్య
46. కాలమందు
47. శ్రీ త్రిపురాం
48. త్తక దేవర అం
49. గరంగభోగా
50. లకు శ్రీత్రిపు
51. రాంతక దేవ
52. రు దివ్యశ్రీపా
53. దపద్మారాధ
54. కులైన శ్రీమ
55. తు త్రియంబ
56. క శివాచా
57. ర్యుల హా స్త
58. మందు పోలి
59. గండ స్థాలము
60. లోని ఆలువు
61. లపాడు అనెం
62. డి యూరు చ
63. తుస్సీమంబూ
64. ను సకలాయ
65. సహితమూ
66. గాను దారా
67. పూర్వకము
68. సేసి ఆచంద్రా

69. ర్క స్థాయిగా
70. నిచ్చిరి .
71. స్వదత్తాం పరదత్త

Third side.

72. ం వాయోహరేత
73. వసుంధరాం। ష
74. ష్టివర్ష సహస్రా
75. ణి విష్టాయాంజా
76. యతే క్రిమిః॥ స్వద
77. త్తా ద్విగుణంపుణ్య
78. ం పరదత్తానుపా
79. లనం పరదత్తాప
80. హారేణ స్వదత్తం ని
81. ష్ఫలంభవేత్॥ సా
82. మాన్యోయంధర్మ
83. సేతుంనృపాణాం కా
84. లే కాలే పాలనీయో
85. భవద్భిః। సర్వానేతా
86. న్భావినః పార్థివే
87. ంద్రాన్ భూయో భూయో యా
88. చతేరామచంద్రా॥
89. ఈ ధర్మ్మ వునకు
90. ఎవ్వరైన అన్యధా త
91. లంచిన వారు గంగా
92. తీరమందలి పదివే
93. లు కపిలగోవుల వ
94. ధియించిన పాపా
95. నం బోవువారు।మ
96. ంగళ మహా శ్రీ శ్రీ.

Darsi (2).

[Annavaram Agraháram. Telugu in Chálukyan character at the 26th mile on the road.]

Translation.

In the kingdom of (Hail!) . . . Ṣrí Vikramáditya Mahárája, descendant of the Ṣrí Chálukya dynasty. . . . one . . . . as an ancient *vritti* . . . . (rest unintelligible).

1. స్వస్తిశ్రీ చాళుక్య వంశోద్భవ శ్రీ విక్రమాదిత్యమహా
2. రాజుల రాజ్యమ్మునన్దున పూర్వ్వవృత్తికి వకబు వెజ్జ్వన
3. కొడువట్టి దత్తియాచ . . . వలుజేసి నిల్పె విద్ధవుమవి
4. ప్రకచఃభూన్ను

Darsi (3). (A.D. 1709–10 or 1726–27.)

[Baḍuguléru. Telugu. Stone near a well. The two lines printed last may form part of another inscription. They appear in a corner of the stone.]

Translation.

Obeisance to Ṣrí Ráma! Hail! On the 10th of the bright fortnight of Áṣvija of the year Viródhi, corresponding to the year 1649 of the illustrious, victorious and prosperous Śáliváhana Śaka era, Máchavarapu Múrti Ráju, the karnam of the village of Baduguléru, Ganṭa Yarrá Reḍḍi, descendant of the Kúnapaiḍipáḷḷa *gótra*, ditto Timmá Reḍḍi, Mullangi . . . gáru of the

Innúḷḷa *gótra,* — Mullangi (Gaṭṭá) Reḍḍi, Pálu Erra Reḍḍi, Vinnapála Timmá Reḍḍi, Nádipálu Vagapálu . . .

NOTE.—The cyclic and S.S. years do not correspond.

1. శ్రీరామాస్వస్తిశ్రీ విజయాభ్యు
2. దయ శాలివాహన శకవర్షంబు
3. లు ౧౬౭౪ అగునేంటి విరోధినా
4. మ సంవత్సర అశ్వీజ శు ౧౦ లు
5. బద్ధులెటిలో గ్రామకరణం
6. మాచవరపు మూర్తిరాజు, కూన
7. పైడిపాళ్లగోత్రోద్భవులయిన గం
8. ట్టాయర్రా రెడ్డి ఆతింవమ్మారెడ్డి యిం
9. న్నూళ్లగోత్రులయ్యి ముల్లంగి .
10. యగారు వనిల . . .

(1) మాదముల్లంగి గట్టారెడ్డిక్కి పాలు యల్లుగ్గె
(2) ర్రారెడ్డి విన్నపాల తిమ్మారెడ్డి నా
ది పాలువగపాలు

DARSI (4).

[Bhaṭlapalli. Telugu. In a field to the north.]

TRANSLATION.

Bhíma Mallaparáju, son of Nandipáṭi Akkiráju.

1. నంద్దిపాటి
2. అకిర్రా
3. జు కొ
4. మారుండు
5. భీమ మల్ల
6. ప రాజు

DARSI (5).

[Bhaṭlapalli. Telugu. In a garden to west.]

TRANSLATION.

Adoration to Ṣrí Ráma, Bhavánı́, Ṣankara, and Bhramarámba Amba.

On the 5th of the bright fortnight of Mágha of the year Vikriti, this well is the charity of Karan Ráju Bhaṭu Rámaráju, resident of Bhaṭlapalle *agrahára*. I have caused to be constructed a temple of Śiva to Mallésvara for dedication to Sámbaṣivá.

1. శ్రీరామ భవానీశం
2. కరారా బ్రమరాంబ అంబ
3. వికృతినామ సంవత్స
4. ర మాఘశుద్ధ ౫ లు భట్ల ప
5. ల్లె అగ్రహారికుడు కరంరాజు
6. భటురామరాజు భావి అయ
7. నధర్మం సాంబశివా పుణ్యం
8. గ్గాను మల్లేశ్వరునికి శివాల
9. యంకట్టిస్తిని.

DARSI (6). (A.D. 1291-92?)

[Bhímavaram. Telugu. Opposite Bhímésvara temple.]

TRANSLATION.

Hail! On . . . . day, the 5th of the bright fortnight of Márgaṣira of the year Khara, corresponding to the year 1212 of the illustrious and prosperous Śaka era, ... Chóḍamalidéva Mahárája consecrated the image of Gópálanátha in Bhímavaram and presented to the deity a field where 4 *puṭṭis* and 10 *túms* can be sown for providing *Amritapaḍi* (food for the God) worship, &c., . . . and a wet field for maintaining a light for the religious merit of Pratápa Rudradéva Mahárája.

Second side.

As a *mányam* free from taxes . . . . Ridhadha Baliráju presented . . . . . . rája presented for the religious merit of Mópu Venkamgáru. The agent for this is Késava Peddingáru, son of Valaráṇakanambigáru, who should maintain this in perpetuity as long as the sun and moon endure.

Whoever thinks of causing trouble to this *vritti* will go to hell.

NOTE.—The cyclic and S.S. years do not correspond. Khara is S.S. 1214 current.

1. స్వస్తిశ్రీ శుభశకవర్షంబులు
2. ౧౨౧౨ అగునేంటి ఖరసం
3. వత్సర మార్గశిర శు ౫ . . వారంమున
4. . రా . చోడమలిదేవ మహారాజులంగా
5. రు భీమావరంలో గోపాలనాథనిం ప్ర
6. తిష్టసేసి ప్రతాపరుద్రదేవ మహారా
7. జునకుం బుణ్యముగాను దేవ
8. రకును అమ్రుతపడి అర్చ్చ
9. నాదులకుంబెట్టిన క్షేత్రం
10. ఖ ౪ న ౧౦ నీరునేలదిపాదిక
11. . . నుగూను ఇంత్తకు
12. . . . . . .

Second side.

13. . ం బంగ మాన్యముగా
14. . . . రిధధ బలిరాజు పెట్టెం.

(To face page 291.)

DARSI NO. 7.

15. . రాజు మోపు వెంకంగారికిం బు
16. ణ్యముగాను వెటించె॥ ఇంతవ
17. ట్టుకు అదిష్టా॥ వలరాణకనంబి
18. . . గారి కొడుకు కేశవపెద్దింగారు
19. ఆచంద్రార్కర్క స్థాయిగాం॥ ఇవ్రిత్తి
20. కి ఊపద్రం ఎవ్వండే ఘటించినా వినాయి
21. . కనర్రకొనంబడుదురు.

Darsi (7).

[Bódanampáḍu. Telugu. On tank bund north of village. This is on two sides of a stone. A photograph of one side is annexed. The character is Chálukyan, but we have not been able to make out the sense. The transcription seems to be as under.]

1. హాకా
2. . .
3. వి రూపతి
4. సి (వెచ్చి .
5. . . .
6. . వ్విసమ
7. తిరా . క్ష
8. తివిరి . .

Second side.

(9) . సాతి .
(10) క్ష . ల .
(11) . జ హాన
(12) ద్ధు రావిమ

(13) . బ్య అడ
(14) రేవపు వ
(15) కి దత్తినార
(16) స్వస్తి శ్రీసతి

DARSI (8).

[Boddikúrapáḍu. Telugu. Opposite Vishnu temple.]

TRANSLATION.

Hail ! May there be prosperity ! . . . . gáru karnam . . . . . should maintain the charity.

1. స్వస్తి శుభమస్తు
2. . . . . సు
3. రవనికి . న . . . య
4. . . నిలాశుకవ . .
5. . . . . . నవా . .
6. . ఇ . చిన . . .
7. నికిపు . . . నచి .
8. . . . .
9. . . . . . కిచెప . వ . .
10. గారు కర్ణంమా . . .
11. ధర్మాని జేయంగలవారు.
12. . . మార్తాండ . .
13. . . . . . శన్యలాబి . . ధ
14. . . దావ . . . . .
15. రపసు . వదను . దృకా
16. . . డితువిరమ . . .
17. తాని . మత్తానని . కాతు

18. . . . భగావరశ

19. . . . . . .

20. (మడాల నమకరమా)

Darsi (9). (A.D. 1494–95.)

[Chandalúru. Telugu. On a stone in the bed of the tank.]

Translation.

Hail! On Thursday, the 15th of the bright fortnight of Kártika of the year Ánanda, corresponding to the year 1416 of the illustrious Śaka era, Kasvánénigáru, son of Bállimalli Abbanéni, caused to be dug two channels, one at the southern end of the tank bund and the other at the northern end of the tank bund and strengthened the tank for the religious merit of his son Dhadhipati Ráo who was ruling Chandalúru. May it cause great prosperity!

Note.—Dhadhipati Ráo was apparently an official or petty chief. His name does not occur elsewhere in this collection.

1. స్వస్తిశ్రీ శకవరుషంబులు ౧౪౧౬ అగునేంటి ఆనంద సంవత్సరనం

2. కార్తిక శు ౧౫ గు బాల్లిమల్లి అబ్బానేని కుమారుడు కస్వా

3. నేనిగారు చందలూరు యేలుచును తమకొమారు

4. డు ధధిపతిరావుకుం పుణ్యంగాను చెర్వుదక్షిణ

5. పు కొంమ్మకాలువాను చెర్వువుత్తరపుకొంమ్మకా

6. లువాను యీ రెండు కాల్వలు తవ్వి చెర్వువూజీ

7. తము తాన చేయించెను మంగళమహా

8. శ్రీ శ్రీ శ్రీ శ్రీ శ్రీ.

DARSI (10). (A.D. ?)

[Darsi. Telugu. On stone in front of Śiva temple.]

TRANSLATION.

Hail! While Ṣríman Mahámaṇḍaléṣvara Kákatiya Pratápa Rudradéva Mahárája was ruling the earth, holding pleasant converse (with his feudatories), on the holy occasion of Vishu Sankránti, in the year Rudhiródgári, Tattinúri Nándévarájulu gave for providing enjoyment to Svayambhudéva of Darisi — a field of 5 *puṭṭis* at Pondukamúr, 2 *puṭṭis* in the north of Sámantapúḍi, 3 at Chaṭralakunṭa, *i.e.*, 10 *puṭṭis* in all, as a *sarvamánya* for the religious merit of the Mahárája and of his own father Jayadévaningáru.

NOTE.—The cyclic and S.S. years do not correspond. Is this Jagadeva the general of Ganapati?

1. స్వస్తి శ్రీమన్మహా
2. మండలేశ్వర కాకతి
3. య్య ప్రతాపరుద్ర
4. దేవమహారాజు
5. లు సుఖసంకథావినో
6. దమ్ము నంబ్రిదివి రాజ్యం
7. బు చేయుచుండం తాము
8. రుధిరోద్గారి సంవత్సర
9. విషుసంక్రాంత్తి పుణ్య
10. కాలమున్ను తత్తినూరి
11. నాందేవరాజులుమ
12. హారాజులకును తమ
13. తండ్రి జయదేవనిం
14. గారికిని పుణ్యము

15. గాను దరిసి స్వయంభు
16. దేవరకు బోగవ్రిత్తి షాం
17. దుకమూరి చేలు ఖ ౫
18. సామంతపూండిని ఉత్తర
19. ఖ ౨ చట్రలకుంట
20. కడ ఖ ౩ వెర
21. సి ఖ ౧౦ ను స
22. ర్వమాన్యము
23. గా నిస్తిమి.

Darsi (11).

[Darsi. Telugu. From Śiva temple.]

Translation.

On the 5th of the dark fortnight of Mágha of the year Ṣrímukha, Chennam Seṭṭi of the *Kummara* (potter) caste caused to be built a temple to Chenamalaya (Śiva) at Pólavaram for the religious merit of his mother Dáḍema and his father Gópī Ṣeṭṭi.

1. శ్రీ ముఖసంవత్సర మా ఖ బ ౫ లు
2. కుమ్మఱ చన్నం సెట్టి తమ తల్లి దా డెమ
3. కును తమతండ్రి గోపి శెట్టికిన్ని పుణ్యం
4. గాను పోలవరపు చెనమలయగుడికట్టి
5. ంచెను.

DARSI (12). (A.D. 1313–14.)

[Darsi. Telugu. In front of stone bearing a Hanuman.]

TRANSLATION.

Hail! On the 15th day of the bright fortnight of Kártika in the year Pramádícha, corresponding to the illustrious Ṣaka year 1235, under the orders of Pótaya Sáhiṇamgáru the servant of Ṣríman Manḍalêṣvara Káka-tiya Pratápa Rudradéva Mahárája, Mallinandévaṇam-gáru planted a garden for Ṣríman Tripurántaka Mahádéva in Tripurántaka (village) to secure long life, health, and increase of wealth for his liege lord Pratápa Rudradéva Mahárája and gave for the site of that garden land of 3 *puṭṭis* and 16 *túms* in the fields of Darisi to the south of the village and land of one *puṭṭi* and 4 *túms* in Podukamúru to the north of the street—in all 5 *puṭṭis*. He granted (this land) as a *vritti* to last as long as the sun and moon last. It is a *sarvamánya*, free from all taxes.

(Verse.) The protection of land given by another is twice as meritorious as giving (land) one self. By resuming what has been given by another one's own gift becomes inefficacious.

1. స్వస్తి శ్రీశకవరుషంబులు ౧౨౩౫ అగు నేంటి
2. ప్రమాదీచ సంవత్సర కార్త్తిక శు ౧౫ స్వస్తి శ్రీమన్మ
3. ండలేశ్వర కాకతియ్య ప్రతాపరుద్ర దేవమహారాజుల

భృత్యుడు

4. పోతయ సాహిణంగారి ఆనతిని మల్లినందేవణంగారు
5. తన్నేలినస్వామి ప్రతాపరుద్రదేవమహారాజులకాయురా
6. రోగ్యైశ్వర్యాభివృద్ధిగాను త్రిపురాంతకములోను
7. త్రిపురాంతక శ్రీమన్మహాదేవరకుం బువ్వుందో
8. ట పెట్టించ్చి ఆ తోటవట్టునకై దరిసిపొలాలనను ఊ
9. రిదక్షిణానను మోట్టితెగటను ఖ 3 న ౧౬ పొడుకమూరి

10. తెరువు ఉత్తరానను ఖ ౧ నర అటువెరశి ఖ ౫ ఇ
11. చ్చెను వ్రిత్తిగాను ఆచంద్రార్కస్థా ఇగాను ఇచ్చి
12. రి పంగ్గ ములేదు సర్వమాన్యము ॥
13. స్వదత్తాద్ద్విగుణం పుణ్యం పరదత్తాను పాలనం
14. పరదత్తాపహారేణ స్వదత్తం నిష్ఫలంభవేతు.

Darsi (13). (A.D. 1384–85?)

[Darsi. Telugu. On a stone near the Achanna-cheruvu.]

Translation.

Prosperity! Hail! On Thursday the 15th of the bright fortnight of Mágha of the year Rákshasa, corresponding to the illustrious Śaka year 1317, Śríman Maṇḍaléṣvara Ásnadéva Mahárája, while ruling the kingdom of the earth and holding pleasant converse (with his feudatories), caused to be constructed a tank to last as long as the sun and moon endure in the name of his mother Áryamadévi.

Hail! Gonkaráju was the lord of the earth, surrounded by enemies having many hosts of elephants; he had a high and broad chest which was embraced by the goddess Lakshmí, his consort was Sandhyádéví; he was the emperor of the kingdom of Káma; he was a graceful king in the world; he was the beloved of the world, he was the supreme lord of great kings; *Parama Bhaṭṭáraka*;[1] he was the hero of many battles; the goddess of victory was pleased to look at him with a thousand rays (flames); he was the descendant of the race of Panéndra

---

[1] Parama Bhaṭṭáraka = very religious.

(lord of snakes); his emblems are the elephant, crocodile, serpent and boar; he wears the discus like Narasimha and Ráma; his territory is girt by the girdle of the four oceans, his throne is invulnerable, he wears a jewelled diadem and a *laládapaṭṭa* (ornament for the forehead), his excellent body has been rendered holy by bathing in the Ganges which is 1,000 *yójanas* away; he is a born *Karṇa* (*i.e.*, liberal); he has a triad of umbrellas with white handles; his emblem is the moon adorned with the serpent, he is of the Vishnu family, he is the ornament of the lunar race, he is of the Hárita *gótra*, he is the protector of unborn children; he is a tree of paradise to dependants, a protector of refugees; he has planted pillars of victory in the mountains to the east and west of the Mahánadi river; he is the ornament of the Vishnu family; the lord of the three worlds, he is Góvinda, he is a moon, he is the punisher of his enemies, he is a Bhíma who punishes the elephants who are his enemies, he is the hero among the men of the three worlds . . . ? he is the spoiler of the kingdoms of his foes . . ? he is *Óm Náráyaṇa*; he is a descendant of the race of *Nága* (serpent); he is the vanquisher of the three crowns (kings), he is *Britti Manivvara Gaṇḍa*,[1] he is the ocean of truth, an Arjuna in war, he is an emperor. . . . ? Gonkaráju had all these titles. His son was Manabali Dévaráju, his son was Nágaráju, his son was Pótaráju, his son was Vémula Mali Dévaráju, his son was Núnkaráju, his son was Ásna Dévaráju, his son was Núnkaráju, his son was Óbalāyya. The *agrahára*s granted by Ásna Dévaráju of Darasi for the religious merit of the aforesaid :—We have granted Pina Pántaḍa

[1] Britti Manivvara Gaṇḍa—Canarese = Yama.

to Gurudévara. We have granted Peda Pántaḍa to the *maháјanas* (elders), in the presence of Cherumanagoṇḍa Payyarája, Nárapararáju and Mantriráju, for the merit of our grandfather. We have granted an *agrahára* to the *mahájanas* in the presence of Siddhavarupu Kalapa Maláya Singaráju, and Jakkapeddi Gangu Mantriráju, at the junction of Darsi and Chandalúru for the religious merit of our excellent son Núnkaráju and in his name we have built in the *régaḍa* (black cotton soil) fields of Darsi the tank called Pápirávigunṭa and have granted 100 *kunṭas* as *agrahára* to Guru Dévara for his religious merit. We have granted to the *mahájanas* of Chirumana Goṇḍa, a fertile field yielding *sáma* crop at the junction of Tangéḍa Vancha and Chirumanagoṇḍa for the maintenance of the village. We have given Pandaráju *agrahára* and a dry field in Edara village between Edara and Púrimiṭṭa in the name of Maluḍu Vémula Mali Dévaráju, grandson of Manva Malidévaráju; also Goranṭla field which is 4 *gorrus* in extent under the Edara tank at the junction with Púrimiṭṭa.

Third side.

Having sold the land which is our *vritti*, we have given the front portion of the garden to Chilukúri Anamaráju Mantaráju and Dáyá Vírayya.

We have given an *agrahára* to Beli Núntu Alikharáju, and Mantriráju at the junction of Darsi and Dévarapu, in the name of Ásnadévaráju for our own religious merit.

We have caused to be constructed a temple to Pratápa Gópinátha of Darsi for the religious merit of our parents; we have caused to be constructed a tank in the name of our mother Lakshyama Dévi and have caused to be erected a pillar. We have given 20 *puṭṭis* of land in Úrachénu to the north of Darsi to Bójuri Váju, the Vójulu (artizan) who constructed this temple.

[One imprecatory verse.]

Those who injure this charity will incur the sin of committing the five cardinal sins.

Those who maintain the charity according to the orders of Pratápa Gópinátha will acquire great merit (?).

Note.—This inscription is difficult to decipher and render. The translation is conjectural in parts. The S.S. and cyclic years differ widely. The mother of Ásnadéva is given in one place as Aryamadévi and in another as Lakshyamadévi; one or other is doubtless a mistake in transcription.

1. శ్రీ స్వస్తి శకవరుషంబులు ౧౩౧౭ యెగునేంటి
2. రాక్షస సంవత్సర మాఘ శు ౧౫ గు । నాండు
3. స్వస్తిశ్రీమ్న మండలేస్వర ఆస్నదేవమహా
4. రాజులు శుఖసంఖతా వినోదంబునం బ్రి
5. దివిరాజ్యంబు సేయుచుండి తమతల్లి ఆర్య
6. మ దేవులపేరను ఆచంద్రార్కముగాను చె
7. ఱువు గట్టించ్చి । స్వస్తి అనేక కరి మకర నికరప
8. రిబంతపరిత భూతలాధిప లక్ష్మిసమాలి
9. ంగితోత్తుంగ విశాలవక్షస్తల సంధ్యాదేవిల
10. సాధన కామసామ్రాజ్య భూరి భారజగతి లలి
11. త భూక్షర భార జగతివల్లభ మహానృపతివు పరమస్వర
12. పరమ భట్టారక అనేకసమర సంఖట్టన వీరవిజయల
13. క్ష్మి లక్షిత సహస్రకిరణనికర పణేంద్రకుఒస
14. ంభవ కరిమగహోరగవరాహలాంచెన నారసింహ్మరా
15. మ చక్రాయుధ చతురుదధి వేలావలయవలక్షిత
16. అయోధ్య సింహాసన మణిమగుట లలాట ప
17. ట్టవర్ణన, ఒక్కింశతశతయోజన గంగాసలిలాత్యా
18. స విశదపవిత్రి కృతమణిఘాత్రక జాతక

19. నర్గ దండ ధవళచ్ఛత్ర త్రయ యురగపూషణ
20. యుత చంద్రలాంచన విష్ణు వంశోద్భవనుంగా
21. చెంద్రాన్వయకులతిలక హారితగోత్ర అజాతగ
22. ర్బ రక్షణం ఆశ్రితజన కల్పవృక్ష శరణా
23. గత రక్షక మహానది తటనిర్ఘాత పూ
24. ర్వ పశ్చిమశైలాతలస్తంభన విష్ణుకు

Second side.

1. ఽమండన త్రిభువన కర్తాతురాయ సిధుగోవింద శిత
2. కర దండితారికరభీమ బోగావతిఖిలంబాన్వగర్ మత్య
3. ద్భుతాంత త్రిబువనకులధీర (బాతర్గంబులాకు ఆతా
4. రకీర మండలికాం చోంబులార) బరమంకల చూఱకా
5. ర వుభయదళపూజ లింగనం ఓంనారాయణ నాగవంశో
6. ద్భవ మూన్మూశిలగండ భృత్రిమునివ్వరగండ సత్యరత్నా
రక ఆహ
7. వార్జున చెక్రవర్తి (ఆపోదతిసహస్రనోదశ కీలద్వ్యం
తుర్గ లా
8. జినాం) అనంతము పాదశంఖాతం యత్నతెమాధమయా
9. య్యన సంతానం గోంకరాజు, అతనికొడుర్గ మనబలిదేవ
రాజుఅ
10. తనికొడుర్గ నాగరాజు అతనికొడుర్గ పోతరాజు అతనికొ
డుకు
11. వెములమలి దేవరాజు ఆయనకొడుర్గ నూంకరాజు ఆ
12. యన కొడుర్గ అన్న దేవరాజు ఆయనకొడుకునూంకరాజు
ఆత
13. నికొడుకు ఓబళయ్య విరిర్గపుణ్యంగాను దరశి అన్నదేవ
రాజు
14. యిచ్చిన అగ్రహారాలు పినపాంతడ గురు దేవరకు

15. యిస్తిమి పెదపాంతడ తమతాతలకు పుణ్యముగాను బి
ఱుమ

16. నంగొండ బయ్యరాజు నారవరాజు । మంత్రిరాజు వీరు
17. సహితమందున మహాజనాలకుని స్తిమి । దరశిచెంద
18. లూరి సందుకట్టున తనకొడుకు నూంకరాజు పరనుతి
19. యనకు పుణ్యముగాను శిద్ధవరపు కలపమలాయశి
20. ంగ రాజు జకరు పెద్దిగంగు మంత్రిరాజు వీరుసహిత
మున

21. మహాజనులకు అగ్రహారము యిస్తిమి । రాకట దరిశి
22. పొలములోను కొంతచెను వాపిరావికుంట చెఱువు ఊ
23. కట్టించ్చి నూరుకుంటలు వారికి పుణ్యముగాను గురుదేవ
24. రకు అగ్రహారము యిస్తిమి । తంగెడవంచ చిఱుమన
25. ంగొండ సందుకడుసామున్పైఱు ఊ ఉలి పొలము గ్రా
26. మగాసము చిఱుమనగొండ మహాజనాలకు ని
27. స్తిమి పూరి మిట్టయుదర సందుకట్టున యుడఱిపొ
28. లము గొంతమెట్ట మన్వమలిదేవరాజు మన్నుండు
29. మలడు వేముల మలిదేవరాజు పేరనుపంద
30. రాజు అగ్రహారము యిస్తిమి, యీదరచెరువుక్రింద
31. గోరంటలచెను పూరిమిట సందుకటున నాల్గుగోఱులు

Third side.

1. తనభూమి యిచ్చి
2. న ప్రవిత్తిచెను యిపుడు
3. స్థలము అమ్మి
4. ముందటి తోట
5. మఱలు చిలుకూరి అ
6. న్నమరాజు మంత రా
7. జునుం దాయా వీర
8. యకును యిస్తిమి

9. దరసి దేవరవు స
10. ందు కట్టిన అన్న దేవ
11. రాజుల పేరను తనకు
12. ం బుణ్యంబు గాను
13. బెలినూంతు అలిఖ
14. రాజు, మంత్రిరాజు
15. అగ్రహారము యిస్తి
16. మి తమమాతాపితా
17. లకుం బుణ్యంబుగాను
18. దరశి ప్రతాపగోపినా
19. తనిగుడిగట్టించి తమత
20. ల్లి లక్ష్మదేవుల పేర
21. ను చెరువు గట్టించి స్త
22. ంభము వేయిస్తిమి, యీ
23. గుడిగట్టిన వోజులబో
24. జురి వాజుకుంబెట్టిన
25. ట్టిది దరసి ఉత్తరానను
26. ఖ ౨ం రు ఉరచేను యిస్తిమి
27. స్వదత్తా ద్విగుణ
28. ం పుణ్యం పరదత్తాను
29. పాలనం పరదత్తాప
30. హారేణ స్వదత్తం నిష్ఫల
31. ం భవేత్ ॥ యిదత్తడి
32. బాపినవారు వ
33. ంచ మహాపాతకం
34. ప్రతాప గోపినాతని ఆ
35. జ్ఞవర పరధరుముపు నాఖ ౧
36. ఆశ్రితులు.

DARSI (14).

[Dékanakonda. Telugu. To the west. On a stone standing on a rock.]

TRANSLATION.

Sidhiráju Timmaráju who caused to be constructed a *bóghma aṇḍapa* (pleasure hall) to Ṣrí Chennaráya caused this pillar to be erected.

1. శ్రీ చెన్నరాయఁకు
2. బోగ మండపం కట్టిం
3. చిన సిధిరాజు తింమ
4. రాజు వ్రూడిగంవెట్టి యె
5. త్తించిన కంబము.

DARSI (15). (A.D. 1541–42.)

[Dévavaram. Telugu. Near the well. On four sides of a stone.]

TRANSLATION.

(Adoration be to) Śrí Ráma! Prosperity!

Hail! On Thursday the 1st of the dark fortnight of Jyéshṭha of the year Plava, corresponding to the illustrious, victorious and prosperous Śáliváhana Śaka year 1464, Venkaṭapati, of the Parakūṭla *gótra*, grandson of Ṣésam Rangappagáru, and son of Chennappagáru, performed an act of charity in constructing this well. The act of charity was performed for the religious merit of Gádi Lakshmínarasimha.

[One imprecatory verse].

(Adoration be to) Śrí Ráma! Ṣésam Venkaṭapati constructed a well in the village of Divvaram (Dévavaram) which belongs to Râja Śrí Gummaḍappa Rágha-vappa Náyaningáru and (thus) performed an act of charity. Therefore the details of the gifts made by the *kápus* are :—

we have granted garden land containing 2 *gorrus* at a rent of 6 (?)

Signature of Venkaṭádri Náyaningáru.

Signature of Gópála Venkaṭanarasu the karnam of the village.

Signatures of Chippiri Venkaṭapati and Ambatti Buchi Reḍḍi, the Peddakápu.

NOTE.—Gummadappa Rágbavappa Náyaningáru does not appear elsewhere in this collection. He was probably an ordinary land owner.

1. శ్రీరామ శ్రీ
2. స్వస్తి శ్రీ విజ
3. యాభ్యుద
4. య శాలివాహ
5. న శకవరుషం
6. బ్బులు ౧౭౬౭
7. అగునేటి ప్లవ
8. నామ సంవ
9. త్సర జ్యేష్ట బ
10. హుళ్యమి గు
11. రువారం వః
12. కూట్ల గోత్రో
13. ద్భవులైన శేస
14. ం రంగప్పగారి
15. పౌత్రులుంన్ను
16. చంన్నప్పగారి
17. పుత్రుడుంన్ను

Second side.

18. అయినా వెం
19. కటపతి
20. తవ్వించి
21. న బావి ధ
22. ర్మం గాది ల
23. క్ష్మీ నరస్సు
24. మ్మ పు
25. ణ్యంగా చే
26. శిన ధర్మం
27. దానపాల
28. నయోర్మ
29. ధ్యే దానా శ్రే
30. యోనపా
31. లనం దానా
32. స్వర్గ మవా
33. ప్నోతి పాల
34. నాదచ్చ్యుత
35. తంపదం.

Third side.

36. శ్రీరామా
37. రాజ శీ
38. గుంమడ
39. ప్ప రాఘు
40. వప్ప నాయు
41. నింగా రికి
42. మిశానా
43. కునడిచె

44. మాంజెవి_
45. వ్వరంలో
46. శిసం వెం
47. కటపతి
48. భావి తవి
49. ంచి ధర్మ్మాం
50. చేసే గనుక
51. కాపులు యి
52. చ్చిన వివర
53. ం తోటగా ఎ
54. కి. సర్వ్వం మా
55. త్రాగ ౬ ఆరు

Fourth side.

56. యిచ్చినా
57. ము వెంకటా
58. ద్రినాయ
59. నింగారి వ్రా
60. లు గ్రామఃకరు
61. ణం గోపాలు
62. ని వెంకటను
63. రు.సువ్రాలు
64. పెద్దకాపులు
65. చిప్పిరి వెం
66. కటపతి ఆ
67. ంబత్తి బు
68. చ్చిరెడ్డి వ్రా
69. లు

DARSI (16).

[Donakoṇḍa. Telugu. In the temple of Gangamma.]

స్వస్తి శ్రీ . . సంవత్సరా
. . . . ది నన్ని
. . ప్రతిప్ప శిదినె
. . ముది చరిపనిసీ
. . . . చి యుదీ
. . రెక వురి . .
. . . .

DARSI (17).

[Donakoṇḍa. Telugu. On a stone in the temple of Madiyaladévata.]

TRANSLATION.

On the 15th of the bright half of Nija Áṣvija of the year Nala, the perpetual devotion of Pótaya Jayaliḍu, son of Vengaḷa, the *pújári* (priest) of Ṣrí Donakoṇḍa Gangádévi.

1. నలసంవత్సర
2. నిజ ఆశ్వీజశు
3. ౧౫ లు శ్రీ దోన
4. కొండ్డ గంగదె
5. వరి పూజరి
6. వెంగ్గళ కోమా
7. రుండు పోత
8. య జయాలిడు
9. సదాసివ శ్రీ.

Darsi (18).

[Donakonḍa. Telugu. Stone in Gangamma temple.]

Translation.

In the Śaka year . . . . when Víra Pratápa Ṣrí Kṛi(shna)ráya was ruling at Vidyánagar . . . presented to Gangá Paraméśvarí of Donakonḍa . . . to last as long as the moon . . . .

[One imprecatory verse.]

1. ం శకవరు . . . . . రుష
2. య . . .
3. ఆ . . .
4. . . . . .
5. ష్ఠ పూర్వ కమాద . ద . .
6. దాలిప్పగె . . .
7. యాగ్గనిదివ్య . . .
8. వీరప్రతాపంకు . .
9. రాయులు విద్యానగరమందు.

Second side.

10. . . ౯దివిత్తే .
11. . యని వఠంగా లజ్య అశ్వ
12. . . . . ం మిరం నింసవ
13. ని దొనకొండ గంగాపరశ్వమేరికి ఆచం
14. . . . . తస్వదత్తం .
15. . . . .
16. . . . .
17. . కు . సా. . . .
18. కిమి . స్వద . . .

DARSI (19). (A.D. 1406-07).

[Donakonḍa. Telugu. On a stone in the temple of Gangamma.]

TRANSLATION.

Hail! On the 5th day of the dark fortnight of Kártika of the year Vyaya, corresponding to the year 1328 of the illustrious Śaka era, while the 56 countries were prosperous with good crops, while the village of Donakonḍa was flourishing, while the son of Dévaráya Maháráyulu was ruling the kingdom, while Kapratidéva *alias* Cháma Voḍayalu was ruling the village, for the religious merit of Doṇakonḍa Tirumandulapu Tinuṭijika's sons and for himself, he constructed *maṇḍapas*, constructed a stone temple to Mánkalamma (goddess), constructed a temple to the *virlu* (heroes) and caused to be raised a fortified enclosure. He did this to last as long as the sun and moon exist.

May it cause great prosperity!

NOTE.—The allusion is, no doubt, to Rámachandra son of Dévaráya I and governor of Udayagiri. His rule extended over Addanki Ráshtra (see C.P. 1) and Donakonḍa probably fell within the boundaries of that *ráshtra*.

The other persons named in this inscription are not referred to elsewhere in this collection and were doubtless of no importance.

First side.

1. స్వస్తి శ్రీశ
2. కవరుషంబులు
3. ౧౩౨౮ అగునేం
4. టివ్యయసంవ
5. త్సరకార్తిక బ ౫

6. ఆమై యారు
7. దే శాఖ నువ్వీర
8. లు సుభిక్షముగా
9. నున్న దొనకొండ
10. గ్రామము వూ
11. జీతముగానున్న
12. దెవరాయ మ
13. హారాయలు
14. కొమారుం

Second side.

15. డు గ్రా
16. జ్యమెలు
17. చుం
18. డగాను
19. క ప్రతిదే
20. వయుని
21. చామ
22. వొడ
23. యలు
24. గ్రామ
25. మేలు
26. చుం
27. డంగాను

Third side.

28. దొణకొండతి
29. రు మంద్దులపు
30. తినుటిజికకొ
31. మాళ్లకు పుణ్యం

32. ముగాను త
33. . . . .
34. న ఱంగల పున్న్యము
35. గా మంటపాలు
36. వెట్టించి మాం
37. కలన్మాకు కల్లురు
38. డి గట్టించి వీరలు
39. గుడి గట్టించి ప్రాకా
40. రము కోటవెట్టిం
41. చెను. ఆచంద్రార్కస్థా
42. యిగాను చెసెను మ
43. ంగళమహా శ్రీ శ్రీ శ్రీ.

Darsi (20). (A.D. 1432–33.)

[Donakoṇḍa. Telugu. On a stone in the temple of Gangamma.]

Translation.

May there be prosperity . . . .
(Mám ?) Kalá Paraméṣvari
Venkaṭápúri Rámayyagáru at Donakoṇḍa, the following inscription was inscribed on stone by Pinnamma Naiḍu, the younger brother of Vemá Náyanimgáru.

Hail! On the 11th of the bright fortnight of Kártika of the year Paridhávi, corresponding to the year 1354 of the illustrious Śaka era, for the religious merit of Ṣríman Mahárájádhirája, Rájaparaméṣvara, Ṣrí Víra Pratápa Dévaráya Maháráyulu . . . . Dévamahárájú, son of Gummaḍúri Konḍurájú Chinni Rájú gave this charitable edict to Gangá Paraméṣvarí, goddess of all the sciences. We have presented to the *dévata* (goddess), being in the presence of Vírúpáksha (who resides) on the banks of the Tungabhadra, the village . . . . which is attached to our chiefdom with libation of water and gift of gold for the performance of *játara* (festival) and for providing all enjoyments to the Ammangáru (Gangamma), to last as long as the sun and moon exist.

[Imprecatory verse.]

NOTE.—The Gummaḍúri family is alluded to as chiefs of an area which included Donakonḍa village in D. 23 under date 1427–28. The Kámayadéva of KV. 40 is probably different from the Kámayadéva of D. 23 and no other references to these chiefs seem to have been found:

1. శుభమస్తు . . .
2. మాం కలా పరమేశ్వరి । వెంకటా
3. పూరి రామయ్యగారు దొన
4. కొండని ప్రమాణానం ప్రవిదా
5. కి) వేమానాఇనింగారి తమ్ము ం
6. డు పింన మ్మనా ఇండు శిలాలిఖిం
7. తము శె ఇంచిన వివరము
8. స్వస్తి శ్రీ శకవర్షంబులు ౧౩౪౯
9. నగునేంటి పరిధావి సంవత్సర కా
10. ర్తిక శు ౧౨ శు శ్రీ మన్మహారాజా
11. ధి రాజ రాజపరమేశ్వర శ్రీ
12. వీరప్రతాప దేవరాయ మహా
13. రాయులకు పుణ్యముగా
14. ను గంగాపరమేశ్వరమ్మ
15. కు . . . గుమ్మడూరి కొ
16. ండంరాజు చిన్నిరాజుల కుమా
17. రుం . . . దేవమహారాజు
18. సకలకలా పరమేశ్వరికి ఇచ్చిన

19. దర్మ శాసనం మాకునాయం
20. కరాన కు నడచివచ్చినయి ఆంవలో
21. . . . యేటి తెరువు
22. . . . ను మలవుపు
23. . . ఫలము దినాలప్రటిన
24. * * * *

Second side.

25. ఖడిన్ని జాతర
26. రలు దీనపుట్లు
27. పడిన జాతర
28. గాను అంక్యం
29. గారికి అంగరం
30. గ బోగాల కుం
31. ను తుంగ భ
32. ద్రా తీరమం
33. దు విరూ పాక్ష
34. దె వర సంనిధి
35. ని స హిరణ్యో
36. దక దారా ద
37. త్తము సేసి దేవ
38. తకు ఆచంద్రార్క
39. స్తా ఇగాను ఇ
40. స్తిమి ॥ స్వదత్తా ద్వి
41. గుణం పుణ్యం
42. పరదత్తాను పాల
43. నం పరదత్తా ప
44. హారేణ స్వదత్తం
45. నిష్ఫలం భవేత్తు.

DARSI (21).

[Donakonḍa. Telugu. On stone in front of Gangamma temple.]

TRANSLATION.

. . . . In the month of Vaiśákha of the year Nala . . . .

నల సంవత్సర వైశాఖమాస . . .

. సగ డొన కొండ నంక . . .

. డు యి చా . . .

. పెరా . . .

DARSI (22). (A.D. 1525-26.)

[Donakoṇḍa. Telugu. In front of Gangamma temple. The inscription is difficult and the translation conjectural in parts.]

TRANSLATION.

May there be prosperity ! Hail !

On Monday, the 15th of the bright fortnight of Pushya of the year Párthiva, corresponding to the year 1447 of the illustrious, victorious and prosperous Śáliváhana Śaka era, on the holy occasion of a lunar eclipse after worshipping the very glorious Virúpáksha and Viṭhaléṣvara (we gave to) Ṣri Gangá Paraméṣvari Parabrahma of Donakoṇḍa . . . . While Ṣríman Mahárájádhirája, Rájaparaméṣvara, Múruráyaragaṇḍa, Ariráyavibhála,

---

Múruráyaragaṇḍa = the vanquisher of the three kings (Chéra, Chóḷa and Páṇḍya). Ariráya vibhála = the destroyer of hostile kings. Púrva dakshina paschima samudrádhíśvara the lord of the eastern, southern and western seas. Yavanarájyasthápanáchárya, establisher of the kingdom of the Yavanas (Muhammadans). Ashtadigráyamanóbhayankara, the terror of the minds of kings of the eight cardinal points. Básaduppuvaráyaragaṇḍa, he who punishes kings who break their word;

Ashtadigráyamanóbhayankara, Básadappuvaráyaraganda, Púrva dakshina paschima samudrádhíṣvara, Yavanarájyasthápanácharya, the conqueror of Aṣvapati and Gajapati, Ṣrí Víraprátápa Ṣrí Krishnaráya Maháráyulu, seated on the diamond throne at Vidyánagar, was ruling the earth. . . . .

Yeddu Mummayya Bagádingáru having seen (addressed ?) the following leaders of the cowherd (Gópa) caste, chiefs of the Yedu (Yadu) caste and lions among Gollas which castes (?) are the door-keepers to Ṣrí Krishṇaráya Déva Maháráya, to wit :—Timapanáyunḍu, Ádipanáyunḍu, Nasapanáyunḍu, Bhanḍármu Peddapanáyunḍu, Bórisú Bairinenḍu, ditto Nágatáta, Avasaram Basivinenḍu, Kírtilayyangáru, and people of various *gótras* in the royal abodes of the above and others, (thereupon) the people of the Yádava *gótra* rejoicingly besought Krishṇaráya Maháráya to bestow upon Gangá Paraméṣvari the village of Dévara Donakonḍa which is the principal seat of the Nandagópa caste and the Badugula caste (?). (Accordingly) he caused a charitable edict to be issued granting the village of Donakonḍa in perpetuity as long as the sun and moon endure, with its four boundaries, together with ponds, wells, tanks, hidden treasures, deposits, etc., ... for providing means of enjoyment and sacred food to Gangá Paraméṣvari.

[V. 1. An ordinary inprecatory verse.]

V. 2. Even a charity founded by an enemy should be assiduously protected; the enemy indeed is an enemy, but (the) charity (performed by him) is not anyone's enemy.

* * * *

May it cause great prosperity to Yeddu Mummayya Bagádingáru!

NOTE.—We find the Baḍugula people mentioned again in K.R. 26 where it is said under their chief Káṭam Rázu they were defeated by Nallasiddhi of Nellore. The date of that battle is given as A.D. 863 which is no doubt, erroneous; probably it occurred in the 13th century. The family apparently rose to a position of some power in the northern part of Nellore district. They do not seem to be mentioned in any of the heretofore-published inscriptions. See note under K.R. 26.

Yeddu Mummaya Bagádingáru is not mentioned elsewhere.

1. శుభమస్తు
2. స్వస్తిశ్రీ జయాభ్యుదయ శాలివాహన
3. శక వర్షంబులు ౧౪౪౭ అగునెంటి పా
4. ర్థివ సంవత్సర పుష్య శు ౧౫ సో। సోమగ్రహణ
5. పుణ్యకాలమందు అతిమహింపు విరూపా
6. క్ష వీరలేశ్వర దేవర్లకు అర్పించి శ్రీదానకొం
7. డ గంగాపరమేశ్వరి పరిబ్రహము। శ్రీమ
8. న్మహారాజాధి రాజ రాజపరమేశ్వరమూ
9. రురాయరగండ అరిరాయవి భాళ అష్టది
10. గ్రాయమనోభయంకర బాస దప్పు వరా
11. యర గండ పూర్వ దక్షిణ పశ్చిమ సముద్రా
12. ధీశ్వర యవనరాజ్య స్థాపనాచార్య అశ్వ
13. పతి గజపతి విభాళ శ్రీ వీరప్రతాపశ్రీ క్రి
14. ష్ణరాయ మహారాయలు విద్యానగరమందు
15. వజ్ర సింహాసనంబున పృధ్వీరాజ్యం సేం
16. యుచుండంగాను శ్రీకృష్ణరాయ దేవమహా
17. రాయులద్వార పాలకులైన గోపకుల వర్ధను
18. లున్ను యెదుకుల శ్రేష్టులున్ను యలగోల
19. సింహ్యాలున్నైన తింమపనాయుండు ఆ
20. దిపనాయుండు నరసప నాయుండు భండార

21. ము పెద్దవనాయుండు బోవి సూబైరినెండ్లు అ
22. నాగశాత అవసరం ఒసివినెండు కీతి౯లయ్యం
23. గారు వీళ్లు మొదలైన రాయసింహాసనందు ని
24. ంగలగోత్రవారిని యెద్దుముమ్మ, య
25. బగా దింగారు పొడగనినంద గోపాలక ప్రజంస్వ
26. బ్రిశివింబ్యడుగుల వారికి మూలస్థానమైన దే
27. వర దొనకొండ గంగా పరమేశ్వరి౯గానీ మింస
28. యాదవగోత్రంవారు సంతోషించ్చి క్రిష్ణరాయమ
29. హారాయుఃకు విన్నపము సేసి గంగాపర
30. మేశ్వరి అంగరంగవైభవాల
31. కున్ను అమ్రుత పంళ్లకున్ను చెల్లి
32. ంచె టట్టుగాను దొనకొండగ్రా
33. మము వాపికూప తటాక నిధి
34. నిక్షేపాది సహాగాను చెతు
35. శ్సీ మాను ఆచం ద్రాక౯స్థా ఇ.గా
36. స మపి౯ంచిన దమ౯ శాసనము.
37. स्वदत्तां परदत्तां वायोहरे
38. ति वसुंधरां षष्टिर्वर्षसह
39. स्राणि विष्टायां जायतेक्रमिः (॥ 1)
40. शत्रुणापिकृतोधर्मः पालनी
41. यः प्रयत्नतः। शत्रुरेवह
42 तशात्रुः स्याद्धर्मःशत्रुर्नकस्याचेत। (॥ 2)
43. చప్పన్న దేశాల కొలంగోమ
44. రికోసుకుం పాటి శావదెండు
45. యెద్దుముం వయ బగాది గా
46. రు మంగళ వహ శ్రీ శ్రీ శ్రీ
47. ంజేయును.

DARSI (23). (A.D. 1427-28.)

[Donakonḍa. Telugu. From Gangamma temple.]

TRANSLATION.

May there be prosperity! Hail!

On Thursday, the 15th of the bright fortnight of Mágha of the year Plavanga, corresponding to the year 1349 of the illustrious Saka era, this charitable edict was granted by Rámayadéva Mahárája, son of Ṣríman Mahámaṇḍaléṣvara Anṭyambaragauḍa[1] Gummuḍúri Kámayadéva Mahárája to Kalá Paraméṣvari (goddess) of Donakonḍa which is attached his chiefdom and is situated in Pinayerruvu for the religious merit of Ṣríman Mahámaṇḍaléṣvara Rájádhirája, Rájaparaméṣvara, Ṣrí Víra Pratápa Dévaráya Maháráya. Five *túms* per *puṭṭi* according to the lease of the tank were formerly given to the rulers from the income of the goddess (?) . . . . This is to be relinquished by the rulers commencing from the 1st of the bright half of Kártika of the year Plavanga.

* * * *

This is the charitable edict issued to Gangáparaméṣvari of Donakonḍa as an act of charity to last as long as sun and moon exist.

[Two imprecatory verses.]

Will incur the sin of . . . .

Will incur the sin of . . . .

NOTE.—See note under D. 20.

1. శ్రీ శుభమస్తు ॥ స్వస్తిశ్రీ
2. శకవర్షం బులు ౧౩౪౯
3. అగునెంటి ప్లవంగ సంవత్స

[1] Anṭyambaragaṇḍa = the vanquisher of chiefs whose titles are proclaimed.

4. ర మాఘ శు ౧౫ గు శ్రీమం
5. న్మహా మండలేశ్వర రాజాధి
6. రాజ రాజపరమేశ్వర శ్రీవీర
7. ప్రతాప దేవరాయ మహారాయల
8. కుు పుణ్యముగాను శ్రీ మన్మహామ
9. ండలేశ్వర అంత్యంబరగండ గుం
10. ముడూరి కామయదేవ మహారా
11. జుల కుమారుండు రామయ దేవ
12. మహారాజులు పినయెఱువలో
13. ను తమనాయం కరానకుం జెల్లె దో
14. నకొండనుంకలాపరమేశ్వరికి ఇ
15. చ్చినధర్మశాసనం పూర్వాన అంమ్మ
16. ంగారి నియపురాజ్యంవారికి యెందుం
17. ౧ కిం చెర్వు గుత్తట . . . ప్లవంగ సంవత
18. ర కార్తిక శుద్ద ౧ ఆరభ్యంగాను వండెటికిన్ని
19. గుత్త ధాన్యము రాజ్యమువారుమాని పూ
20. . . .
21. . . . వం
22. డిన ధాన్యము వీరికి . . . .
23. . రకం
24. అట్లుగా . . . . .
25. య్యం గాను తమ తల్లిదం
26. డ్రుల దర్మముగాను . . . ఆచం
27. ద్రార్కస్థాయిగాను దొనకొండగంగా
28. పరమేశ్వరికియిచ్చి వ్రాయిం
29. చిన ధర్మము శాసనము స్వదత్తం
30. పరదత్తం వాయో హరేతి
31. వసుంధరా షష్టివర్ష సహ
32. స్రాణి విష్టాయాం జాయతేక్రిమి॥

33. స్వదత్తా ద్విగుణాంపుణ్యాం పరదత్తా
34. ను పాలనం పరదత్తాప హారేణ స్వ
35. దత్తం నిష్ఫలం భవేత్ ॥ ఎ . . . త
. . . ఇంచు . . . . శా అంబ
. . . . దోషా
పాపంబునం బోవు వారు.

DARSI (24). (A.D. 1267–68.)

[Edururállapáḍu. Telugu.]

TRANSLATION.

Hail! On Thursday, the 15th of the bright fortnight of Kártika of the year Prabhava, corresponding to the year 1189 of the illustrious Śaka era—Hail! As charity on behalf of Ṣríman Mahámanḍaléṣvara Singayadéva Gaḍidéva, who is the sovereign of the earth, on whose lotus feet the eyes of Trilóchana (Pallava) and all other kings are set, who is the jewelled lamp of the race of Karikála by whom the dam[1] of the Kávéri was built, of unlimited valour, who is a constant worshipper of the consort of Lakshmi, the brave, the lord of Orriyúr the best of cities, the Tripura Trinétra (Śiva the destroyer of three cities) of Kánchipura, who is of the Káśyapa *gótra*, who is possessed of all praiseworthy attributes consisting of these and other titles, and for the religious merit of Rudramahárája the ruler of Konḍavíḍu in the kingdom, and for the religious merit of his parents and of himself, Ṣrímat Komminṇáyunḍu, the governor (Rakshádhíṣvara) of Táḍlúru, gave the following charity

---

[1] Alluding, probably, to the Grand Anikat of the Káveri, *see page 1250*.

as dharma to his lord Mallináthadéva of Pratishṭapura for providing worship and all enjoyments. I have given Koddipáṭi Eṟṟanṭi cheruvu (tank) to the south of Edurulapáḍu in Peddakolam Khandrika (sub-division of a village) and a mango tope in rear of it to Nágésvaradéva. The temple servant Prólamaráju should maintain this and enjoy happiness.

[Two imprecatory verses.]

Those, who deny the existence of this (charity), will incur the sin of killing cows near the Ganges and will be considered to have eaten food from the skull of their eldest son.

1. స్వస్తిశ్రీ శకవర్షంబ్లు ౧౧౮౯ అగు
2. నేంటి ప్రభవ సంవత్సర కార్తిక శుద్ధ ౧౫ గు
3. స్వస్తి చరణాంభోరోరుహాలిహిత విలోచన
4. త్రిలోచన ప్రముఖాఖిల ప్రిథివీశ్వరకారి
5. త కావేరితీర కరికాలకులరత్న ప్రదిప అపరి
6. మిత ప్రతాప సతతహిత దివ్యార్చిత లక్ష్మీశ్వర ఒఱ
7. యూరి పురవరాధీశ్వర కాంచిపుర త్రిపుర త్రి ణేత్ర
8. కాస్యపగోత్ర నామాది సమస్త ప్రశస్తి సహితం
9. శ్రీ మన్మహామండలేశ్వర శింగయదేవగడిదేవఱ
10. దర్మంగా రాజ్యంబున కొన్డవీటి నేలిన రుద్ర మ
11. హారాజులకును బుణ్యముగాను శ్రీమతు
12. తాన్లూరి పురవరాధీశ్వరుండైన కొమ్మినాయుండుత
13. న్ను నేలినప్రతిష్టపుర మహాదేవమల్లి నాథదేవరకు ద
ర్మంగా
14. పూజలకును అంగ్గరంగ్గ భోగానంకూను తమతల్లి
15. తండ్రులకు పుణ్యముగాను తనుకుం బుణ్యముగాను
16. ఇచ్చిన ధర్మము యదురాళ్లను ఊరిదక్షిణానను పె
17. ద్దకొలను ఖండ్రికనూను నాగేశ్వర దేవరకు కొద్దిపా

18. టి ఎఱ్ఱింటిచెఱువ్వను ఆచెర్వ్వ వెనకమావిడి
19. తోంటనూ ఇస్తానపతి ప్రోలుమరాజు దీనినడపి
20. సుఖం బనుభవించెడివారు । స్వదత్తా ద్విగుణం
21. పుణ్య పరదత్తాను పాలనం పరదత్తా పహారేణ స్వద
22. త్తం నిష్ఫలం భవేత్ ॥ స్వదత్తం పరదత్తం వాయోహ
23. రేతివ సుంధరా షష్టివర్ష సహస్రాణి విష్టాయా
24. ంజాయతే క్రిమి । దీన్ని లేదన్నవారు గంగకఱుతర
25. రికపిలింబొడిచిన పాపానంబో ఇ పెద్దకొడుకును
26. కపాళానం గుడించినవారు.

DARSI (25). (A.D. 1254–55.)

[Gangavaram. Telugu. In tank bed.]

TRANSLATION.

Hail! He who is intent on worshipping the lotus feet of Gaṇapatidéva Mahárája who (Ganapati) is Ṣríman Mahámandaléṣvara, who is the director of 72 offices, who is the ruler of many countries, who is the supporter of the four castes, who is the scatterer to all points of the compass of the army of the western king Damodara, who is the one and only hero, who is the incarnation of valour, who is a perfect Révánta (son of the sun) amongst those who are mounted on most unruly horses, who is a Náráyaṇa, the beloved of the goddess of victory, who is terrible in battle, before whose columnar arms the courage of every king is paralysed, who with his wide-spread fame marks the foreheads of the maidens of the cardinal points, who is a Karna in liberality, who excels (in liberality) Kámadhénu (cow of plenty) and Kalpadruma (tree of plenty), the collection of the rays from the nails of whose feet kissed by the row of the edges of the jewelled crowns of prostrate rulers, who is the ornament of the Kákati race, who (the donor) is a very Bramha Rákshasa Gaṇḍa to provincial chiefs, who is Penḍáru Ganḍa, who is Bráhmana Véda,[1] (Hail !) gave on Thursday the 13th of the bright fortnight of Mághá of the year Ánanda, corresponding to the year 1176 of the era of Ṣálivâhana, with libation of water, to Ṣrímat Śánta Śivaguru déva, who is the worshipper of the divine and illustrious lotus feet of Tripurántakadévara, and whose head is adorned with the excellent lotus feet of Śrímat Rájá Gurudéva, the village named Chalamati Gandapuram, situated in the *Kampana* of Amavakalamári with its four boundaries to last as long as the sun and moon endure, for setting up (the image of) Ṣrí Rangéṣvara in the holy place of Tṛipurántaka.

NOTE.—The donor of this grant was apparently the same as that of No. 28. For Ṣrímat Rája Gurudéva we should perhaps read Ṣrímat Ṣiva Gurudéva as in No. 28. He was perhaps the religious instructor of the donee. *See* also No. 74.

1. శ్రీ స్వస్తిశ్రీ మన్మహామండలేశ్వర బాహ
2. త్తర నియోగాధిపతి అనేక దేశాధిపతి
3. చాతుర్వర్ణ్య సముద్ధరణ పశ్చిమరాయ
4. దామోదరా సైన్యదిశాపట్ట పకాంగవీర వీ
5. రావతార అతివిషమ హయారూఢ
6. ప్రౌఢ రేఖారేవంత విజయలక్ష్మీకాం
7. తనాయక నారాయణ కదనప్రచండ
8. దోస్తంభ కుంభిత సకలక్షితి పాలశౌర్య

[1] Bráhmana Véda probably means one who is a Védântist.

9. యశస్తో మతిలకిత దిగంగనాముఖ విత
10. రణకర్ణా వినిర్జిత కామదేను కల్ప
11. ద్రుమ ప్రణతసకల నరపతిమణి
12. మకుటకోటి మకరికా చుంబ్యమాన
13. చరణ నఖకిరణ కందళి కాకతికులతి
14. లక గణపతి దేవమహారాజు చరణనళి
15. నయుగళ సమారాధన తత్పర మండ
16. లీక బ్రంహరాక్షస గండ పిండారుగండ
17. ఱౌ బ్రాంహ్మణవేద స్వస్తిశ్రీ శుభశకవర్షం
18. బులు ౧౧౭౬ గు నేంటి ఆనంద సంవ
19. త్సర మాఘ శుద్ధ ౧౩ గురువారము నా
20. ండు స్వస్తిశ్రీమతు రాజగురు దేవరు
21. ల వరపాద సరోజ భూషితమస్తకులు
22. శ్రీ త్రిపురాంతకదేవర దివ్యశ్రీ పాద
23. పద్మారాధకులైన శ్రీమతు శాంతశివ
24. గురు దేవరుంకు అమవకల మారిక
25. ంపనములోన పలికించిన చలమతి
26. గండాపురము[1] అనెడి యూరు చతుసీమ
27. మూను శ్రీత్రిపురాంతక తీర్త్థము శ్రీ
28. రంగేశ్వరదేవర ప్రతిష్టచాయను దక్షిణ
29. గాను ధారాపూర్వకము సేసి ఆచంద్రార్క స్తాఇ
30. గానిచ్చిరి.

NOTE.—*Nishka* is a coin of variable value.

[1] Gangavaram was apparently formerly called Chalamati Gaṇḍapuram, the town of Chalamatti Gaṇḍa (a biruda of the Kákati kings).

Darsi (26).

[Gangavaram. Telugu. Ánjanéya temple.]

Translation.

While Pratápa Rudradéva Mahárája was ruling the earth, Hail! Ṣrímat Dévádaṭi Vuddangáru . . . .

1. ప్రతాప రుద్రదేవమ
2. హా రాజులు ప్రిథి విరా
3. జ్యము చేయుచుండ
4. గాను స్వస్తి శ్రీమతుదే
5. వాదటి వుద్దంగా(రు)

* * * *

Darsi (27).

[Gangavaram. Telugu. From tank bed.]

Translation.

Hail! Ṣríman Mahámaṇḍaléṣvara Kákatiya Ganapatidéva Mahárája presented Chalamatti Gaṇḍápuram with all its income to Ṣrí Tipurántaká Mahádévéṣvara and other gods for . . . . festivals . . .

1. స్వస్తిశ్రీ మన్మహామ
2. ండలేశ్వర కాకతియ గ
3. ణపతిదేవమహారాజులు
4. శ్రీ తిపురాంతక మహా దే
5. వేశ్వరులు మొదలయిన దేవర్లకు
6. . . . . రాది దేవరా
7. అని నిచ్ఛలమత్తి గండా
8. పురము సకలాయస
9. హితంబుగా నిచ్చిరి.

DARSI (28). (A.D. 1254–55.)

[Gangavaram. Telugu. In tank bed.]

TRANSLATION.

On Thursday the 13th of the bright fortnight of Mágha of the year Ánanda, corresponding to 1176 of the Ṣrí Śaka era,

Prosperity! Hail! Ṣríman Mahámaṇḍaléṣvara Ḥaridéva Chóḍa Mahárájulu, on whose lotus feet the eyes of Trilóchana and all other kings of the earth are set, who is the jewelled lamp of the race of Karikála by whom the dam of the Kávéri was built, who is the elephant-goad of wicked princes, gave with libation of water the village named Chalamati Ganḍapuram, situated in the *Kampana* of Amavakala Méri, with its four boundaries, for setting up the image of Ṣrí Paru (Parama?) Mahéṣvaradéva at the holy place of Ṣrí Tṛipurántaka to last as long as the sun and moon endure to Ṣrímat Śánta Śiva Gurudéva, who is the worshipper of the divine and illustrious lotus feet of Ṣrí Tṛipurántakadéva and whose head is adorned with the lotus which is the foot of (Hail) Ṣrímat Śívagurudéva.

[One imprecatory verse.]

1. శ్రీ స్వస్తి చరణసరోరుహ. [వి]
2. విహితవిలోచన త్రిలోచనప్ర
3. ముఖాఖిల పృథ్వీశ్వర కారి
4. త కావేరితీర కరికాలకుల ర
5. త్నప్రదీపాహిత కుమారాంకుశ శ్రీమ
6. న్మహా మండలేశ్వర హాఱిదేవచోడ
7. మహారాజులు శ్రీశకవరుషంబు
8. లు ౧౧౭౬ అగునె టి ఆనందసం

9. వ్వత్సర మాఘశుద్ధ ౧౩ గురువా
10. రమునాండు స్వస్తిశ్రీ మ
11. తు శివగురు దేవరులచరణ
12. సరసీరుహాభూషిత మస్తకుండు
13. శ్రీత్రిపురాంతక దేవరు దివ్యశ్రీ
14. పాదపద్మారాధకులైన శ్రీమతు శాం
15. తశివగురుదేవరులకు ఆమ
16. వంకలమారీ కంపనములోన ప
17. రికించిన కలమతి గండాపురము
18. ంమనెడి యూరు చతుస్సీమము
19. ను శ్రీత్రిపురాంతక తీర్త్థవని శ్రీ
20. పరమహేశ్వర దేవర ప్రతిష్టచా
21. యుటకుగాను ధారాపూర్వ్వ
22. కము శేశి ఆచంద్రార్క్కముగాను
23. ఇచ్చిరి॥ స్వదత్తాంపరదత్తాం వాయో హ
24. రేతివసుంధరాం షష్టివర్షవర్ష సహ
25. స్రాణి విష్టాయాం జాయతే క్రిమి॥

DARSI (29).

[Guḍipáḍu. Telugu. Opposite Vénugópálasvámi temple.]

TRANSLATION.

This is the Bṛindávanam (basil garden) planted by . . . . Kumára Mallana for the religious merit of . . . .

1. . . . కు పుణ్యంగా
2. . . కుమారమల్లనవెట్టించిన బృందావనం
3. . . . తోంట

DARSI (31). (A.D. 1672–73.)

[Kallúru. Telugu and Sanskrit in Telugu character. On tank bund near Gangádhara temple.]

TRANSLATION.

May there be prosperity! Hail! On the 1st of the bright half of Bhádrapada of the year Paridhávi, corresponding to the year 1594 of the illustrious, victorious and prosperous Ṣáliváhana Ṣaka era, this is the Pedda Samudram tank caused to be constructed by Médarameṭla Peddammangáru of the *gótra* of Tammanúru, the great granddaughter of Ráyavináyani Gópála Náyaniváru of the *gótra* of Mádáli, the granddaughter of Rangappa Náyaniváru, and the daughter of Veṅkaṭádri Náyaniváru.

I bear on (my) head the sandals of those kings, either descendants of my line or descendants of other royal lines, who, always resplendent with charitable thoughts, protect my charity.

1. శుభమస్తు
2. స్వస్తిశ్రీ జయాభ్యుదయ శాలివాహ
3. నశకవర్షంబ్బులు ౧౫౯౪ అగునేంటి పరిధా
4. వి సంవత్సర భాద్రపద శు ౧ లు మాదాలగోత్రోద్భవులై
5. న రాయవినాయని గోపాళనాయనివారి ప్రపౌ
6. త్రినున్ను రంగప్పనాయనివారి పౌత్రికానున్ను వెం
7. కటాద్రినాయనివారి పుత్రికాను అయినట్టువం
8. ట్టి తంమనూరిగోత్రులైన మేదరమెట్ల పెద్దమ్మ
9. ంగారుకట్టించిన పెద్దసముద్రం చెర్వు
10. मद्वंशजाः परमहीपतिवंशजा वा ये भूमि

11. पास्सतत मुज्वलधर्मचित्ता: । मद्धर्ममेव सततं प
12. रिपालयंतु [1] तत्पादुका द्वयमहं
13. शिरसा वहामि ॥

DARSI (32). (A.D. 1370–71?.)

[Kallúru. Telugu. On tank bund near Gangádhara temple.]

TRANSLATION.

Hail! On the 1st of the dark half of Pushya of the year Sádháraṇa, corresponding to 1 (2) 92 of the Ṣrí Ṣaka era, we gave the wet field formerly belonging to Gangéṣvaradéva, ¼ of the field in front of the western sluice and also a dry field ¾ *puṭṭi* in extent and named Nángaṭichálu Ŕépáḍa, by the street of Sómepalli. These three fields were given so that they might be enjoyed as before. Those who cause obstruction . . . . . (Those who protect it) . . will acquire merit.

1. స్వస్తి శ్రీ శక
2. వర్షంబులు ౧ (౨)
3. ౯౨ అగునేంటి
4. సాధారణ సం
5. వత్సర పుష్య బ ౧
6. గంగేశ్వర దేవునికిపూ

Second side.

7.ర్వమునందు చెల్లేనీరునేల
8. పడమటి తూము మొగద

---

[1] Read ति.

9. లన పాలికి చేసున్న సోమెపల్లి తెరు
10. వునాంగటిచాలు తెపాడను వెళ ౻

Third side.

11. చేనుమూండుమ పూర్వ్వక్రమాన
12. (చెన్నేట్లుగా) ను ఇచ్చితి విఘ్న
13. . . . . . ద్య . . . . .
14. . . . . . ం
15. . . . . . లం
16. పుణ్యాం నం బోదురు.

DARSI (33). (A.D. 1370–71.)

[Kallúru. Telugu. From four pieces of a stone on tank bund near Gangádhara temple.]

TRANSLATION.

Hail! On Saturday, the 10th of the dark fortnight of Pushya of the year Sádhárana, corresponding to 1292 of the illustrious Ṣaka era, Anapóti Náyundu presented an oil mill to Gangésvaradéva for providing an oil bath (for the god) for the religious merit of his uncle Bári Náyudu, and his aunt Núnkasáni.

Whoever causes obstruction by not maintaining this oil mill will incur the sin of killing children near the great Ganges. Those who protect (it) will acquire merit.

1. స్వస్తిశ్రీ శకవర్షంబు
2. లు ౧౨౯౨ అగునేం
3. టి సాధారణసంవత్స
4. ర పుష్యబ ౧౦ వ[1] । గంగేశ్వ

---

[1] (వ stands for వడివారము = Saturday.)

5. రదేవుకి·ఉవ్యధార
6. కు ౧ గానుగు అనపో
7. తినా ఇండు తమ
8. పెదతండ్రి ఖారినా

Second side.

9. ఇనక్ని తమపెదతల్లి
10. నూంకసానికిన్ని పుణ్యా
11. ముగాను ఇచ్చెను

Third side.

12. ఇగానుగు చెల్లనీకవి
13. ఘ్నముచేశినవారు పె
14. దగంగ కటితశిశు వ
15. ధ చెశినవారువో
16. ఇనందోషాన బోవువారు
17. పాలించిన పుణ్యాన
18. ంబో ఇనవారు.

DARSI (34). (A.D. 1612–13.)

[Kambhampáḍu. Telugu. To south of Ánjanéya temple.]

TRANSLATION.

Hail! On Wednesday, the 5th of the bright fortnight of Śrávaṇa of the year Parídhávi, corresponding to the year 1534 of the illustrious, victorious and prosperous Śáliváhana Śaka era, this temple was caused to be erected for dedication to the god by Bháva Siripurapu Yatni Maṇiráju to Ṣrí Sómésvara for the religious merit of his *guru* Ṣrí Parvatáráḏhya, his grandfather Víramaráju, his grandmother Vírama, his father Lakna, his mother Vírama and his elder brother Jaggaráju (?). The signature of Kunchanapalligiri Bhaktu.

1. స్వస్తిశ్రీ జయాభ్యుదయ శాలివాహాన శఖ వరుషంబ్బులు ౧౨౩౪ అగునేటి

2. పరీధావిసంవత్సర శ్రావణశ్శు ౫ బు శ్రీసోమేశ్వరునికి తమ గురుశ్వశివుడు శ్రీపర్వతా

3. రాధ్యలుహన్ను తమతాతవీరమరాజు ముత్వవీరమ తండ్రి లక్న తల్లివీరమఅం (న జ)గరా

4. జుకున్నుసుకృతంగా భావశిరిపురపు యత్నిమణిరాజు (గట్టించ్ని దేవస్థా)నం సివా

5. ప్పణం । కుంచనపల్లిగిరి భక్తుని వ్రాలు॥

Darsi (35). (A.D. 1310–11.)

[Kocherlakóṭa. Sanskrit in Telugu character and Telugu. Near Vírannabávi.]

Translation.

V. 1. May the staff-like tusk of Hari, the sportive Boar, protect you—resting on which (the tusk), the earth with mount Méru as its apex appeared like an umbrella.

May well-being be conferred on you by the heap of wet rice placed by Brahma on the head of Śambhu (Ṣiva) at the time of (his) marriage with Gaurí (Párvatí) which grain, resembling a collection of pearls issuing from a pearl oyster, seems as though it had developed into the Moon and his wives.

Hail! On Monday, the 10th of the bright fortnight of Jyéshṭha of the year Sádháraṇa, corresponding to the Ṣrí

Śaka year 1232, while (Hail!) Pratápa Rudradéva Mahárája, who is the ornament of the Kákati race which is renowned in the whole world, was ruling the earth, Śrímat Dévari Náyaningáru whose columnar arms are of peerless might, who is *Chalamarti gaṇḍa*, who has caused to fade the plantain flower which is the fame of hostile kings with the heat of his excessive valour, who is a master of polity, the hero of the world, who has cut down hostile kings with his sharp sword in the fury of the battle field, who is eulogized as Trinétra, who is honoured by intelligent men, who is the ocean of gems, to wit, noble qualities, who is the Vírabhadra of the Kaliyuga, who is a host of suns to the darkness of hostile armies, who is the champion over treacherous people (Dróhara gaṇḍa ?) by whom the consort of Párvatí (*i.e.* Śiva) is constantly worshipped, who is the excellent son of Śríman Máchaya Náyaka and who is a sun to the lotuses which are poets, set up (the images of) Gauríśvara, Sóméśvara and Mahádéva in the shape of three peaks (by constructing temples with three pinnacles) at Kottacheṛla and Mácheṛla.

Having appointed Dálamu Varadanna and Tammaḷḷa Peddini as priests, he granted the following *vritti* fields with libation of water as *sarvamányas* free from all burdens and taxes for (providing) decorations to the deities (here follows a list of the *vrittis*),

also a *pullari mányam* (a grant of pasture land free of tax?) for the cattle belonging to the deity, the *sunkam* as a *sarvamánya* (evidently a grant of the proceeds of some tax) the tax raised from Kómiṭis (Bachchulu) on shops daily at dra (?) $\frac{1}{4}$ of $\frac{3}{4}$ or $\frac{3}{16}$ as a *sarvamánya*. The rulers have given all these. *Méras* should be collected from every village in the country at 1 *túm* on every heap of grain, and in towns, such as

Krottacherla, &c., where taxes are levied on merchandize at nu (?) ¼ + 1 on every headload of all kinds of grain. They should on the whole (average) be collected at 1 ta (?), and at du (?) ¼ + 1. One ka (?) of land is given under the tank (?); grain at 1 *puṭṭi* should be collected at Rájépalli for the religious merit of Dévaṛi Náyuningáru. All this should be maintained as long as the sun and moon endure.

May there be prosperity!

[Three imprecatory verses.]

Adoration be to the Lord of Śríśaila!

Adoration be to Tripurántaka Déva!

At Aḍaviguḍipáḍu ... ... 1 Ré (?) of wet land,

At Chandalúru ... ... ½ Ré (?) of wet land

are given by Dévaráyudu, Rámayya and Ti . . . . for (providing) sacred food to the deity.

Those who violate this will be considered to have killed a Brahman.

NOTE.—The latter portion is obscure.

Krottachera or Krottacherla is Kocherlakóṭa.

NOTE.—There is a rather interesting *Sthalapuráṇa* in the temple at Kocherlakóṭa which name, it appears, is a contraction for Kottacheru-vulakóṭa. It begins with the remark that Mallikharjuna Gaṇapati ruled over the *síma* of Singarikonḍa (Singaráyakonḍa?) with Manginapúḍi (Mangyanapúḍi?) as his capital. He was succeeded by his son Gajapati, who, in the year Manmatha, corresponding to the Śaka year 918, built the fort Kottacheruvulakóṭa, laying it out so as to correspond with the area over which his dogs had been chased by a hare. He then amalgamated the *símas* of Dévarakonḍa and Santa Singarikonḍa which formed (part of?) the country known as Yeruvanáḍu and styled the new territory Kochcherlakóṭa *Síma*. He dwelt in his new fort for a short while and then went to Telingána. Gajapati's son was Mukkanṭi who ruled over Kaḷinga and appointed Mallaparáju, the karnam of Kochcherlakóṭa, to be his representative there, with Pólireḍḍi as commandant of the fort. Sometime afterwards Pratápa Rudra invaded Kochcherlakóṭa *Síma* with nine lakhs of archers and besieged the fort for thirteen years. In the course of the siege the gallant karnam, the commandant, and one Bhaṭṭu sallied out and in a severe battle killed eleven chiefs but were themselves slain. Then follows a song sung by the body-guard (భటులు) in honour of the karnam.

The story goes on that Pratápa Rudra then obtained possession of Kochcherlakóṭa and granted the position of *Sthala Karnam* of the *síma* to Káḷamráju, son-in-law of Pavani Yugandharuḍu who was minister to Pratápa Rudra's son. Afterwards one Turumeḷḷa Abburáju was associated with Káḷamráju by an edict issued by Pratápa Rudra on Sunday the 15th of the bright fortnight of Márgaṣira of the year Vikriti, corresponding with the Ṣaka year 1033. Pratápa is here described as the son of Kákaṭarudra and grandson of Ṣiva Dévaka Oḍiyalu, and as ruling at Orugallu. It appears that he presented on this occasion to the joint *sthala karnams* a town which he had founded under the name of Prátáparudrasamudram and Manginapúḍi "which has existed from ancient days." He also gave them the four villages of Gajjalakonḍa, Kámepalli, Dévarakonḍa and Peddavaram subject to payment of 300 *máḍas* (a year ?).

Pratápa Rudra is said to have reigned for 24 years and to have been succeeded by his son Haripálaka who reigned for 8 years.

Subsequently "in the year Dundubhi, corresponding to 1065 of the Ṣaliváhana Ṣaka era, the Gajapati family again wanted to rule over these lands" and in the year Raktákshi, corresponding to the Ṣaka year 1067, their minister, Gópáráju Rámanna, made certain grants and confirmed Rudra's edict in favour of the two *sthala karnams*. He is said to have "reigned" for 38 years and it would follow that the descendants of Pratápa Rudra must have been ousted in Ṣaka 1065 from this territory by the descendants of the old rulers.

The *puráṇa* goes on that in Vikári or 1102 Ṣaka, Polaya Vémareḍḍi of the Góna family, came to the throne and that he built the temples in Ṣríṣaila and reigned for 12 years. He was followed by his son Anapóta Bhúpatireḍḍi who reigned for 30 years and by his grandson Ana Vémareḍḍi who reigned for 15 years. The last-named's son Komára Vémareḍḍi followed with a reign of 25 years and *his* son Korivémareḍḍi with a reign of 4 years. The last-named was followed by his son Komaragirireḍḍi who reigned 14 years. "These Reḍḍis ruled for a period of 100 years" and, all this time, the sthala karnamship was being held by generation after generation of the Káḷamráju and Turimaḷḷa families. We now come to Pramádi, corresponding to the Ṣaka year 1222, when the "Ráyulavárn" are said to have been reigning. Achyutadévaráyulu is said to have reigned "for sometime" as did his son Pravududévaráyulu and his grandson Narasimhadévaráyulu. The last-named's son Achchitadévaráyulu, "setting Krishṇadévaráyulu in front," [1] conquered extensively and ruled for some years. While he was on his way to Vijayanagaram with some idols, he chanced to visit Kochcherlakóṭa and was so pleased with it and the ancient temple built by Gajapatiráju that he also built a temple there and set up an image therein. He then went on to Vijayanagaram.

The *puráṇa* proceeds that Achyutadévaráyulu came to the throne at the end of the reign of Nṛisimhadévaráyulu and he sent for the edicts of Pratápa Rudra, had copper-plate grants issued in confirmation thereof, set up some stone edicts and confirmed certain gifts made by Polaḍu [2] "who once carried the State umbrella."

Afterwards one Singaráju filed a suit for the office of karnam against the Kálamráju and Turimaḷḷa families and the case was settled at Vijayanagaram before the "Ráyulu" in favour of the old families.

"Later on" Rámappayya, son-in-law of (Achyuta) Ráyulu, came to the throne and he reigned "for some time" and it is stated that the Ráyulu family ruled for 200 years.

We now come to Alamgir Pádisháh who came to the throne in Vikári, corresponding to the Ṣaka year 1402, and it seems that that monarch appointed one Ravilla Timma Náyuḍu to rule over this part of the country. The latter established his capital at Panchagullapáḍu in Kóṭa *Síma*, ruled there and was succeeded by his son Venkaṭáḍri Náyuḍu who granted Kochcherlakóṭa as a jághir to six of his

---

[1] The Telugu is పురస్కరించుకుని. It apparently means "assisted by." Several Telugu Brahmans have stated that this is the meaning of the passage but possibly it merely means that Krishnaráya preceded him on the throne.

[2] This Póladu is said by tradition to have been granted for a time by a member of the Kákatiya family the right to use the royal seal and make grants. Probably he was the Polaya Vémareḍḍi who became independent of the Kákatiya dynasty in A.D. 1328 and founded the Reḍḍi dynasty (*see* p. 22, E. R. for 1899-1900).

relatives whose acts in founding suburbs, temples, etc., in and about Kochcherlakóṭa are described and the "Náyapanéni" family is said to have held sway there for many years, that family being apparently the family composed of the six related jághírdars.

The *puráṇa* then reverts to Venkaṭádri Náyuḍu who was succeeded by his son Malla Náyuḍu and his grandson Uddanda Malla Náyuḍu and at this time litigation for the sthala karnamship was renewed, this time by a faithless proxy, one Konḍappa, who had "stolen the *danḍa kavila*" (family chronicle), but the traitor was routed during the rule of Vengamanáyanivárn and the vigorous old families retained their cherished office.

"Then," goes on the *puráṇa*, "the Sarkar granted Arikaṭla *Síma* for the maintenance of the Rávilla family and annexed and kept the remainder of the kingdom" (whatever that may mean).

We now come to Vikriti corresponding to S.S. 1513 when "Sherlashá Dágir Kodávaddi (Khuda-u-din) Sultán Khájalálukhál," Jaghirdar of Murtijánagar (?) and Cuddapah, acquired, (on behalf of "Kadakusháh" of Golkonḍa), Vinukonḍa, Bellamkonḍa, and Murtijánagar from "Kodávaddi" and also the 18 Parganas of Khamman Sarkar of Cuddapah Subha, viz., Khamman (Kambham), Dupáḍu, Yeruva, Márella, Pálnáḍu, Kárempúḍi, Tumurugóḍu, Tangéḍu Mácherla, Gurzala, Panchamahal, Podili, Kóṭa, Darsi, Pelluru, Chímakurti, Addanki, Ammanabrólu and Kandukúru. These were divided among various great Kháns who failed to pay the vanji (tribute ?) and rebelled, but were suppressed by an army from Golkonḍa and "Málisham Muhammad Shásu" was placed in control of the country. He was afterwards removed in favour of "Singini Nilandánu," appointed on behalf of Muhammad Darkhini (Dakhani) Pádisháh. He was followed by Shaikh Muhammad Khán who demolished the temples in Podili. Then came Makkili, then Abhiryárámarázu, then Muhammad Khásim Khán Góri, then Miṭṭakonḍaráju, then Sambaráyunivárn, then Chinna Kopparáju, then Mangaráju, then Purushottamaráju, then Sámbaráju then Rámaráju, then Velagaráyanivárn. This brings us to Durmukhi or S.S. 1604 when, during the reign of Táneshá, Akkanna, Mádanna and Suryaprakáṣa Rao, one Jillalla Mangaparáju held the local governorship (?). He was followed by Barige Undanda Ráo and he by Pidila Lingappa Pantulu and he by Kónéṭi Ráo. During all this time the two families of Káḷamrázu and Turimalla held the sthala karnamship. The next governor was

Chalichelamala Jayaváru Reḍḍi who built a fort in Kochcherlakóṭa and refused to pay tribute and was consequently turned out in favour of Damera Biṭṭha Náyuḍu and Vengama Náyuḍu and was beheaded by the Sarkar in Krodhana corresponding to the S.S. year 1608.

Here the *puráṇa* ends after professing to trace the local history for nearly 700 years. It will be observed that, according to the *puráṇa*, for nearly 600 years the office of sthala karnam never passed out of the hands of the two families on whom it was originally bestowed.

See note in App. I about this *purána*.

1. स्विस्ति ॥ हरेर्लीलावराहस्य दंष्ट्रादंडः स पातु वः । हमाद्र-
2. कलशा यत्र धात्रीच्छत्राश्रियं दैधा ॥ (v. 1) गौरापाणग्र-
3. हणसमये मूर्ध्नि शंभोर्विधात्रा विन्यस्त-
4. स्ते दिशतु कुशलं राशिरार्द्राक्षतानां ।
5. मुक्तास्फोटप्रसृमरमणिस्तोमसा-
6. म्येन येन प्रालेयांशुः परिणत इव
7. प्रेयसीभिर्विभाति ॥ (v. 2) స్వస్తిశ్రీ శకవర్షంబులు

౧౨౩౨

8. అగునేంటి సాధారణ సంవత్సర జేష్ట శు ౧౦ సో స్వ
9. స్తి సమస్త భువన ప్రశస్త కాకతి కులతిలక ప్రతాపరుద్రదే
10. వ మహారాజు పృధివి రాజ్యము సేయుచుండంగా
11. ను అతులబలబాహుదండ చలమర్తిగండ ప్రబల
12. ప్రతాపోష్మ ప్లాపిత ప్రతి నృపతి యశః కందళక నయనా
13. యక జగద్ధళ సమర సీమసరభససముత్థాత ఖడ్గధా
14. రావిదారిత వినుతశ్రుత్రజ వర్ణితత్రినేత్ర మనీషిజన
15. మాననియ్య మహాగుణరత్న సముద్ర కలియుగవీర
16. భద్ర ప్రతి బల తిమిరమార్తాండస్థోమ ద్రోహరగండ స
17. ంత్తత సమారాధ్యమాన పార్వతీ నాయక, శ్రీమన్నాచ
18. యనాయకు సుపుత్రుండ్డనుం గవికమల మిత్రుండు
19. నైన శ్రీమద్దేవరి నాయకుంగారు క్రొత్త చెల్లిను మాచెల్లిను

20. గౌరీశ్వర సోమేశ్వర మహాదేవరలనుం త్రికూట ప్రతి
ష్ఠజే

21. సిటి దాలము పరదన్న తంమళ్ల పెద్దిని పూజాన్యయుక్తి
నింగా

22. నియమించ్చిరి దేవరల అంగ్గ భోగాలకు వంగ్గతప్పం సేసిప

23. న్ను సర్వ మాన్యముగా ధారాపూర్వకము సేసియి
చ్చిన వ్రిత్తి

24. క్షేత్రాలు క్రొత్త చెఱ్ఱను ఖ ౧ నిర్న్వెలరే ౧ గురాల
చెఱువు

25. ను తోంటలు ౨ మాన్యపు గానుగులు ౨ మారక

26. గ్రాన నిర్న్వెలరే ౩ తనూర్పాట ఖ ౧ బొడిచెల్లి ఖ
౧ వెలికాలచె

27. ఱ్ఱ నిర్న్వెలరే ౨ వెలిసేను ఖ ౧ లోకాంకల్ల ఖ ౧ తువటి
మింనిని

28. ర్న్వెలరే ౨ గొబ్బూర వెలిసేను ఖ ౧ దోరణాల వెలిసె
ను ఖ ౧

29. నిర్న్వెలరే ౨ అయనముకుర్తల వెలిసెను (ఖ) ౧ కర్లోడ
ఖ ౧

30. నాయుని పల్లిని ఖ ౧ వెరసి వెలి సేనులు ఖ ౧౦ నిర్న్వె
లరే ౧౦.

31. తోంటలు ౨ దేవర పసులకు పుల్లరి మాన్యమున్ను సు

32. ంకం సర్వమాన్యంగానున్ను అంగటిముద్ర సుంకం వ
ల్ను నిత్యద్రమ్మన్ను

33. బచ్చులు డీయం సర్వ మాన్యంగానుంన్ను

Second side.

34. (ఋ) వ భూమి ప్రభువులూనిట్టున్నిచ్చెను మేరలు దేశా

35. నందు ఊరూరను రాసి తూములున్ను క్రొ

36. చ్ఛల్లి పేంటె మొదలైన సుంకె పేంటల తలపాంకలంచు
37. నను ।౧ పోంకలుండి బయలుంగన్న నానాధాన్యా
38. లూను ।౧ ను ఉభయము ప ౧ న్న చేమూట పెర। ౧ ధు
39. నున్నలాకుం చుఱ్వ క ౧ న్న దేవరినాయునింగా

౭౬౦ బు

40. ణ్యాముగాను పశ్చిమిగ్యుం రాజేపల్లి ఖ ౧ న్న ఇంత్త వ
41. ట్టుఅచెంద్రస్థాఇగాం చెల్లంగలది మంగళమహా
42. శ్రీ శ్రీ శ్రీ సామాన్యోయం ధర్మసేతున్నృ
43. పాణాం కాలేకాలేపాల నియోజ్యాభవద్భిః । సర్వానే
44. తాన్భావినః బార్థివేంద్రా న్భూయో భూయో యాచ
45. తే రామచెంద్రః ॥ స్వదత్తాద్విగుణంపుణ్యం పరదత్తా
46. నుపాలనం । పరదత్తాపహారేణ స్వదత్తం నిష్ఫలం భ
47. వెత్ ॥ స్వదత్తాం పరదత్తాంవ్వాయో హరేతవసుంధ
48. రా షష్టిర్వర్ష సహస్రాణి విష్టాయాం జాయతే
49. క్రిమిః॥ శ్రీశైలనాధాయనమః । శ్రీతిపురా
50. ంతక దేవాయనమః ॥ అడవిగుడిపాటను నీరు నేల రే

౧ ప

51. (.) చెందలూర నీరు నేలరె॥ దేవరాయడు రామయ తి
52. (. ౦) గొన్నారు (తలముడిపుంబె) అమృతపల్లి యిచ్చెను
53. యిందుకు తప్పినవారు గోబ్రాహ్మణ్ని వధించినవారు

Darsi (36).

[Kócherlakóta. Telugu. At gate of temple of Ṣrí Varadarája Svámi. Unintelligible.]

1. ఋవెట
2. ఉన్న చెలు
3. మ్మడులిడ
4. అంకిచ

DARSI (37). (A.D. 1533–34.)

[Kocherlakóṭa. Telugu. On a stone in the temple of Varadarájasvámi.]

TRANSLATION.

May there be prosperity! Hail! On the 11th of the bright fortnight of Márgaśira of the year Vijaya, correpronding to the year 1455 of the illustrious, victorious and prousperous Śáliváhana Śaka era, Chintaguṇṭa Chennamaráju, having constructed a temple to Janárdanadéva of Kocherlakóṭa for the religious merit of Mannárappa Náyaniṁgáru, set up the image of Janárdanadéva and gave a paddy field in rear of the Nágulacheruvu and two dry fields in Muddapáḍu village for the performance of the marriage festival and for providing food (*amṛitapaḍi*) for the deity to last as long as the sun and moon exist.

We have given with libation of water . . . . dry field, a (half?) paddy field under the tank of (Netya . . . . nunala?); one-half of a *maḍi* (wet field) under the tank Asna Gangala, in all 2 wet *maḍis*.

May the deity enjoy these fields for his *amṛitapaḍi* (food) as long as the sun and moon exist, with the eight powers and enjoyments, to wit, treasures, hidden deposits, trees, minerals, *akshini* and *ágámi*, actuals and outstandings.

Whoever be the ruler of Kocherlakóṭa, if he does not maintain *amritapaḍi* for the deity, he will incur the sin of killing cows and Brahmans near the Ganges.

1. శుభమస్తు ॥ స్వస్తి శ్రీ జయాభ్యు
2. దయ శాలివాహాన శకవష౯
3. ంబులు ౧౪౫౫ అగునేంటి విజ

4. యసంవత్సర మార్గశిర శు ౧౧
5. మన్నారప్పనాయనిం గారికిం బు
6. ణ్యముగాను చింతకుంట్ల చెన్నమ
7. రాజు కొచ్చెర్ల కోటజనార్దన దే
8. వ్వరుకు నగరు గట్టించి జనార్దనుడి
9. ని ప్రతిష్ఠ చెసి చంద్రార్కం గా
10. ను వివాహం సాగంగాను దేవుని
11. అమృతపళ్లకు నాగుల చెరువు వెన
12. . క ఒకవరి మడిన్ని ముద్దపాటి
13. పొలానను వెలిపొలం రెండున్న
14. వెలి చేనున్న
15. పుట్టి నెయ్య
16. ప్మాల చెరువులు
17. వరిమడి అ
18. స్న గంగల చెరువు
19. క్రింద అద్దమడిన్ని
20. వుభయం వరిమడు
21. లుగ దారపొస్తి
22. మిగాన అపొలా
23. న నిధినిక్షేపతరు
24. పాషాణ అక్షీణ్యా
25. ఆగామి సిద్ధి సాధ్య
26. ంబులని యెనిమిది
27. బోగ తెజస్వామ్య
28. లున్ను యుందాను ఆచ
29. ంద్రార్కముగా
30. స్వామి అమృత పడు
31. లకు అనుభవిం
32. చురవధరించెడి

33. కోచర్ల కోటనయెవ్వ
34. డుఏలినాను వా
35. డు దేవర అమృతవ
36. ల్లకు సాగించక త
37. ప్పితిరా గంగకతీ
38. ను గోబ్రాహ్మల వధి
39. ంచిన పాపానం బోవువారు

DARSI (38). (A.D. 1167–68 ?)

[Kocherlakóta. Telugu. In the temple of Varadarájasvámi.]

TRANSLATION.

Hail! On Sunday, the 1st of the dark fortnight of Mágha, corresponding to the year 1089 of the illustrious Śaka era, Malli Peddidévulu gave a *paṭṭu* of land in perpetuity as long as the sun and moon exist for providing worship and daily offering to Ṣrí Varadaṛájasvámi for the religious merit of Ṣríman Mahámaṇḍaléṣvara Panṭṭadéva Chóḷa Mahárájulu. Hail!

1. స్వస్తి శ్రీ శకవర్షంబులు
2. ౧౦౮౯ గు నేంటి మాఘ బ
3. హుళ ౧ నాదివారమున శ్రీమ
4. న్మహా మండలేశ్వర పంట్టదేవ
5. చోళమహారాజులకు బుణ్యం
6. బుగ మల్లి పెద్దిదేవులు శ్రీమ
7. న్మహా శ్రీ వరదరాజస్వామిపూ
8. జకు నివేద్యమునకు . . .
9. . . . పట్టు పొలము
10. . . నా చంద్రార్కము

DARSI (39). (A.D. 1141–42?)

[Kocherlakóṭa. Telugu. From Varadarájasvámi temple.]

TRANSLATION.

Hail! On Wednesday, the 14th of the dark fortnight of (not legible) of Durmukhi (Durmati?), corresponding to the year 1064 of the illustrious Ṣaka era, 15 *túms* of wet land in rear of Jamasamudram of Krottacheruvu was . . . . to Ṣrí Mallaṇadéva . . . . as long as the sky exists (?)

Those who fail to keep it up are murderers of pious Bráhmans.

1. స్వస్తి శ్రీమతు శకవర్షంబు
2. లు ౧౦౬౪ అగు దుర్ముఖి
3. సంవత్సర బహుల ౧౪ యు బుధ
4. వారమునం క్రొత్త చెఱువున జమ
5. సముద్రం వెనుకన ౧౫ నీటి
6. నెలన్ని శ్రీమల్లణ దేవరకు [నాకమా
7. లంచి ది(వ)ం కలయుంతకు] నిచ్చిరి
8. . . . ఇది నడపనివారు దే
9. వబ్రాంహాల జంపినవారు

DARSI (40). (A.D. 1144–45?)

[Kocherlakóṭa. Telugu. From Varadarájasvámi temple.]

TRANSLATION.

Hail! On Thursday, the 11th of the dark fortnight of Vaiṣákha, corresponding to the year 1066 of the illustrious Śaka era, they gave 1 *puṭṭi* and 10 *túms* of wet land under *Vémácheruvu* of Krottacheruvu [1] to Srídéva, and 1 *putti* and 10 *túms* to Késava for providing daily offerings and food. Those who fail to keep it up are murderers of Déva (pious) Brahmans.

1. స్వస్తి శ్రీమతు శకవర్షంబు
2. ములు ౧౦౬౬ అగు నేటి వైశా
3. ఖ బ ౧౧ గురువారమును క్రొత్త
4. చెఱువుల వేమా చెఱ్వ వెనక వరి
5. పొలము శ్రీ దేవరకు ఖ ౧ న ౧౦
6. కేశవరకు ఖ ౧ న ౧౦ దండూయము
7. తో తనుస్థానిత్యలుకు అమృతపడ్డ
8. కు నిచ్చిరి ఈ ధర్మాన్ని నడప
9. నివారు దేవబ్రాహ్మలు జం
10. పినవారు.

Darsi (41). (A.D. 1134–35.)

[Kocherlakóṭa. Telugu. On a pillar in the temple of Varadarájasvámi.]

Translation.

Hail! On Monday, the 15th of the dark fortnight of Márgaṣira of the year Ánanda, corresponding to the year 1057 of the illustrious, victorious and prosperous Sáliváhana Śaka era, Tullilla Pemmaráju caused to be constructed a mukhamandapa (entrance-porch) in the temple of Srí Varadarájasvámi. The Mirásidar of this is Kócherladésa Pándyagiri. He has half a share here, he has half a share in Bandiveligandla (?) His sons Kabunáthulu, Tarchalappa Mádirájavarudu (?)

---

[1] Krottacheruvu or Krottacheruvulakóṭa is the old name of Kocherlakóṭa.

1. స్వస్తి శ్రీ విజయాభ్యుదయ
2. శాలివాహన శకవర్షం
3. బులు ౧౧౫ అగు ఆన
4. ౦ద సంవత్సర మార్గశిర బ ౧౫
5. యిందువారం శ్రీ వరదరాజ
6. స్వామివారి సన్నిధానమందు
7. తుల్లిళ్ల పెఁమ్మరాజుకట్టించిన
8. ముఖమంటపము యీయన
9. కు మిరాశి కోచర్ల దేశపాం
10. డ్యాగిరి సఖముంన్న బండి
11. వెలిగండ్లలో [సఖం విర్ల]
12. పుత్రులు [కబునాథు
13. లు తగ్గులప్ప మాదిరా
14. జపరుడు.]

DARSI (42).

[Korlamadugu. Telugu. In a street. Illegible.]

1. . . . వుకిశ
2. . . . వచ్చ
3. . . . .

DARSI (43). (A.D. 1150-51 ?)

[Kottapalli. Telugu. Stone in front of Sómésvara temple.]

TRANSLATION.

Hail! In the year Pramódúta corresponding to 1079 of the Śaka era.

Śríman Mahámandalésvara Vijayádityadéva Mahárája, who is descended from the family of Mukkanti Káduvettu, gave to Srí Sómésvaradéva of Kórradlamadugu a field of ten *túms* of paddy on the northern side of the village and to the east of Irumáṭi. This *vritti* is given with libation of water to Muppana Paṇḍita. He should enjoy this happily as long as the sun, moon and stars exist.

[One imprecatory verse.]

(He who obstructs the charity) will be considered to have killed 1,000 tawny cows near the Ganges and to have taken food from the skull of his eldest son. This is a charity given to a deity.

NOTE.—We should perhaps read S.S. 1073 which corresponds with Pramoda.

స్వస్తి సకవర్షంబులు ౧౦౭౯ నెంటి ప్రమోదోత సంవత్సరమున

1. శ్రీ ముక్కంటి కాడు వెట్టి వంశావతారులై
2. న శ్రీమన్మహా మండలేశ్వర విజయా
3. దిత్య దేవ మహారాజులు కోఊడ్ల మగ్గు
4. ను శ్రీ సోమేశ్వర దేవరకు యిచ్చిన
5. చెనుయూరి యుత్తరభాగమున ఇరుమాటి తూ
6. ర్పున [పంబండుము పుర్వయముప్పజారి]
7. అయ్యిముప్పన పండితులుకు ధారాపూర్వకం
8. చేసిన వృత్తి ఇది యాచంద్రార్కతారకా శుఖన్బ
9. యన్భవింపగలవారు ॥ స్వదత్తాం పరదత్తాంవా
10. యోహరేతి వసుంధరాం షష్టివర్షసహస్రాణి వి
11. ష్టాయాం జాయతే క్రిమీ ॥ గంగకత్తాను వేయి కపిలలును
12. వధ సేసినవారు పెద్దకొడుకు కపాలానమా
13. ఢు వట్టినవారు ఇ దేవదత్తివి

NOTE.—The following old forms of letters appear :—

Darsi (44).

[Kurichéḍu. Telugu. In the temple.]

Translation.

Ṣrí Ṣrí Ṣrí! Tammaḷa Vírajiyyalu and his wife Dáda Sáni daily make one thousand salutations together to Ṣrí Káḷahasti Íṣvara of Kurichéḍu.

1. శ్రీకురిచెటి కాళ స్తి యీశ్వరు
2. ని శ్రీ శ్రి శ్రి తంమ్మళ వీరజియ్యాలు ఆ
3. యిన పెండ్లము దాదసానిన్ని
4. దేవుని నిత్యసహస్ర దండాలు.

Darsi (45). (A.D. 1170–71 ?)

[Kurichéḍu. Telugu. From Śiva temple.]

Translation.

(Adoration be to) Ṣrí Ráma! Hail! On Monday, the 11th of the dark fortnight of Śrávaṇa, corresponding to 1092 of the Ṣrí Śaka era, Palukúri . . . . gave a paṭṭu of wet field as a charity for providing a perpetual lamp to Divyakírti Vara Mahádéva of Kurichéḍu . . . . for the religious merit of Ṣrímat Kulóttunga Rájéndra Chóḍa Maháraja. He presented this charity to last as long as the sun, moon and stars endure.

* * * *

1. శ్రి రామ
2. స్వస్తి శ్రీ శకవ
3. రుషంబులు ౧౦౯౨ అగునే
4. టి శ్రావణ బహుళ యేకాదశి సో

5. ·మవారమః నాండు కురుచేటి
6. దివ్యకీర్తి వరమహాదేవునకు
7. పలుకూరి · · · కో
8. · · · · అ శ్రీమతు
9. కులోత్తుంగ రాజేంద్ర చోడ
10. మహారాజులకు పుణ్యంగా హరి
11. . సాక్షి ధర్మ్మము అఖండదీపముకు వరి
12. పొలము పట్టు · · · కిచ్చినట్టి
13. యీ ధర్మం ఆ చంద్ర తారార్కము .
14. గ సత్రాజు సమర్పించిరి · · ·
15. నుంగ . య .. కయీ . లువతి .

DARSI (46). (A.D. 1415–16.)

[Mangyanapúḍi. Telugu. Near a well.]

TRANSLATION.

Hail ! On Thursday, the 5th of the bright half of Vaisákha of the year Manmatha, corresponding to 1337 of the Śrí Ṣaka era, while Dévaráya Maháráyulu was ruling the earth, at that time, Jannappa Murárinéni Chennammanéndu, son of Jédévaráṇa Jannapanéni Bamminâyuḍu, gave this endowment . . . . He gave fields of 4 *puṭṭis* in all to Vallaki Peddi Avubaḷa Reḍḍi, Vendiganja Reḍḍi, Vinapeddi Avubaḷa Reḍḍi, and Piná Siganti Reḍḍi, to the north of the village (he constructed) Kanyacheruvu . . . and gave this charter . . . . .

They should maintain this charity . . . .

* * * *

we shall . . . . we shall utilize these for the deity.

* * * *

NOTE.—We find the donor and his father mentioned again in KG 34; big landholders no doubt.

1. స్వస్తి శ్రీ శకవర్షంబులు ౧౩౩౭ అగు
2. నేంటి మంన్మథసంవత్సర వైశాఖ శు ౫ గు। దేవ
3. రాయ మహారాయలు పృథివిరాజ్య
4. ం శేయుంగాను ఆ కాలమందును జే దేవరా
5. ఌజంనప నేని బంమినాయని కొడు
6. కు జంనప్పాను మురారి నేని చెంనను నే
7. ండును యిచ్చిన మరియ్యాదెమ్మంగేన
8. పూండ్లివల్లకి పెద్ది అహబలి రెడ్డి వెంకిగం
9. జ రెడ్డి విన పెద్ది అవుబళ రెడ్డి పినాసి
10. ంగంటి ప్పి రెడ్డికిన్ని వెర్సిఖ ర నే
11. లను ఇచ్చిన చెఱ్వుగట్టి పవసాపి
12. శాసనం పూరివుత్తరపు కాలు
13. వ కంన్యచెర్వు (ద) గిడి సఁమఁదానకు
14. సవండ్లముప కురె
15. . సమతుతుఁఌ కా
16. ఇ పున్యం చెలింఁచియేని బడివారు
17. ను కోరుగొనువారము . . . . మ
18. . . . దేవరవాడికి చెల్లించ్చినవారము
19. మెవ్వగ అను మోదము
20. . . . ండు మహ . ం చ్చివాండు.

DARSI (47). (A.D. 1429–30.)

[Mangyanapúḍi. Telugu. On tank bund to the east.]

TRANSLATION.

May there be prosperity! Hail!

On Wednesday, the 5th of bright half of Ṣrávaṇa of the Saumya year, corresponding to the illustrious, auspicious and prosperous Ṣaka year 1351, while Dévaráya Mahárayulu, the son of Ṣríman Mahámandaléṣvara Ṣrí Pratápa Vijaya Bukkaráya Maháráyulu, was ruling the kingdom of earth, Manginapúnḍi which was attached to Pratáparáyulu's dominion was made over (at the request of) Chilalasalu Vissanu Oḍayamgáru . . . . to be ruled by Káḍiruchiráju Lingaráju. A charitable edict was issued by Manchirájungáru, Dáché Singamalireḍḍi, Ádipareḍḍi; Vallabhareḍḍi, Nárapareḍḍi, Bámpireḍḍi, Ménkala Náinḍu, Venkareḍḍi, Busireḍḍi, Kommireḍḍi, and Malareḍḍi, to Víreḍḍi for the tank. In the days of Ratnáyammagáru, as the tank in front of the village of Manginapúnḍi was in ruins, it was ordered to be maintained at the instance of the local officer (adigáru) Bommaráju Singaráju out of 10 *marutu* of land given for the tank by Nágaráju the chief officer of your village, two *marutu* of land as *mányam* . . . . and one *puṭṭi* of dry land were given for the maintenance of the tank.

This should be taken by . . . . for the religious merit of . . . . We have given fields in the same manner as before. They should keep the fields in proper order and enjoy them by cultivating them. These *mányams* should be shared as before. One share should go to Malireḍḍi, one share to Tippareḍḍi, one share to Nárapareḍḍi, one share to Bámpireḍḍi and one share to

Ménkala Náyunḍu, etc. If any one speak ill of . . . . (they will incur the sin . . . . .) on the bank of the Ganges.

* * * *

1. శుభమస్తు స్వస్తిశ్రీ శుభజాత కాబ్యుదయ
2. శకవరుషంబులు ౧౩౫౧ అగునేంటి సౌమ్య సంవత్స
3. ర శ్రావణ శు ౫ బు శ్రీమన్మహా మండలేశ్వర శ్రీ
4. ప్రతాప విజయ బుక్కరాయ మహారాయల కు
5. మారుండు దేవరాయ మహారాయలు పృథివీ
6. రాజ్యం చెయంగాను మంగినపూండి ప్రతాపరా
7. యల ఒళబండారానకుం చిలలసలు పిస్సను ఒ
8. డయంగారి . రంకనువిం . . కాది రు
9. చి రాజులింగ రాజుంగారి దులపు కావచేసెను
10. మంచిరాజుంగారు డాచె సింగమలిరెడ్డి ఆదివరె
11. డ్డి వల్లభరెడ్డి నారపరెడ్డి బాంపిరెడ్డి మేంకల
12. నాయఁడు వెంకారెడ్డి బుసిరెడ్డి కొంమిరెడ్డి పులరె
13. డ్డి దరమాంమగాను వి రెడ్డింగారికి యిచ్చినచెరు
14. వు ధర్మశాసనము మంగినపూండి వూరిముంగ
15. లిచెరువు ఖిలమై ఉండంగాను రత్నాయమ్మంగా
16. రి కాలమందు మీరు ఆచెరువుకుగాఫ .
17. . . . . . మనివారి అధికారి బొమ్మరాజు శింగ్గరా
18. జుంగారి పంపున మీవూరి అధికారంచేసి నాగరాజుం.
19. . . రాజుంగారిచేత మీరు యిప్పించుకుని . .
20. . . రంగ్గచెరుమీదను అచ్చుకట్టుగట్టను
21. యిచ్చిన పదిమరుతులలోన రెండుమరుతులు
22. . చెరువునకు మాన్యముగాను వెలిచేను
23. . . . . . దెనిమణుంగు పుట్టెండుచేనును నిచ్చిరి
24. . . . . లపాతి పుణ్యంబుగాను కొనెవారు అంక
25. రానను చెరువు . . . . . . నుకన తిరిగానన

26. మున్ను మాకు వారిచ్చిన క్రమానన చెలి స్తిమి
27. గాన అచ్చుకట్టిగట్టి వ్యవసాయంచేసి సుఖంగాను
28. ఖాలుఅనుభవించ్చిది స్తానమా న్యాలుపూ
29. వఁర్మయ్యార్వమలి రెడ్డివోక బాలుతిప్పారెడ్డి
30. వోకబాలునారపరెడ్డి వోకబాలు బాంపిరెడ్డి
31. వోకపాలు మెంకలనాయుండు మోదలైనవా
32. రును వోకపాలున్ను చేరునువాడు యె . . .
33. . . యవ్వరు ఆడినాను గంగకర్తఁ
34. . . . రహితం రాలర

DARSI (48). (A.D. 1145–46.)

[Mannepalli. Sanskrit in Telugu character and Telugu. From two fragments of a stone opposite Chennakéṣava temple.]

TRANSLATION.

(Sanskrit verse.) The son of the illustrious Pottapi Nanni Chóḍa was the illustrious king Venka. His (Venka's) son was king Káma who is a thunderbolt in destroying the mountains which are the abode of his enemies. (His) son was the illustrious king Balli, who is the moon to the ocean which is the solar race, who has acquired merit by the worship of the lotus feet of Gaurínátha (Śiva) and who is the ocean of kindness.

(Telugu.) Hail! Sríman Mahámanḍaléśvara Ballichóḍa Mahárája on whose lotus feet the eyes of all kings Trilóchana and others are set, who is the jewelled lamp of the race of Karikála by whom the dam[1] of the Kávérí was built, and who is an elephant-goad to wicked

---

[1] See note on p. 1250.

princes, on the occasion of Uttaráyaṇa Sankránti, corresponding to 1067 of the Ṣrí Śaka era, gave in perpetuity, to last as long as the sun, moon and stars endure, Dévarampalli in the wet fields south of Manyapalli in Gunḍikarrti to Ṣrímat Mallésvara Mahádévaru of Manyapalli which is part of our property for sacrifices, worship, offerings, lighting and decoration to his person (the priest of the temple should take possession of it) he, his sons, and his grandsons should enjoy it and maintain the charity. On these conditions we have granted. Those who cause obstruction to this charity will be regarded as having killed a tawny cow on the banks of the Ganges and as having committed murder at Benares.

[One imprecatory verse.]

1. श्रीमत्पोत्तपिनन्निचोडतन-
2. यः श्रीवेंकभूपालकः तत्पु-
3. त्रोरिपदावलापहपविः कामाक्षिती[1]-
4. नायकः सूनुः सूर्यकुलान्वयाम्बुधिशशी-
5. श्रीबाह्लिभूपालकः गौरीनाथपदाब्ज-
6. वन्दितगुणः सौजन्यरत्नाकरः ॥ स्व-

The metre is 'Ṣárdúlavikríḍitam.'

7. స్తి చరణసరోరుహ విహిత విలోచ
8. న త్రిలోచన ప్రముఖాఖిల పృథివీశ్వ
9. ర కారిత కావేరితీర కరికాలకులర
10. త్న ప్రదీపాహిత కుమారాంకుశ శ్రీమ
11. న్మహా మండలేశ్వర బల్లిచోడ మహారా
12. జులు శ్రీసకవర్షంబులు ౧౦౬౭ గు

---

1 (क्षिति) *kshiti* is the correct form but the metre requires (क्षिती) *kshití*.

13. నేంట్టి ఉత్తరాయణ సంక్రాంత్తిని
14. మిత్తమున మాజీవితవర్గ్గమైన
15. గుండ్డికత్తిలోని మన్యపల్లి శ్రీ శ్రీ
16. మద్ మల్లీశ్వర మహాదేవ
17. రకు బల్యర్చ్చన నివేద్య దీపాంగ్గ భోగరా
18. గం బులకు మన్యపల్లి దక్షిణము
19. బల్లములోని దేవరము పల్లియా
20. చంద్రార్కతారకముగాని గుటి స్వా
21. . నాది . . . . . . లుగను
22. . . . . . .
23. పుత్రాను పౌత్రికము సేకొని నడపం
24. గ్గలవాండుగా నిచ్చితిమి యి ధర్మ్మము
25. నకు విఘ్నము సేసినవారు గంగ్గక
26. త్తిం గవిలలంబొడ్చినవారు వారణా
27. సి వచ్చినవారు ॥ స్వదత్తం పరదత్తం వా
28. యో హరేతి వసుంధరా షష్టిర్వర్షస
29. హస్రాణి విష్టాయాం జాయతే క్రిమిః॥

Darsi (49). (A.D. 1166–67.)

[Mannepalli. Sanskrit in Telugu character and Telugu. On road to Viṭhalapuram.]

Translation.

(Sanskrit verse.) The son of the illustrious Pottapi Nanni Chóḍa was the illustrious king Venka. His son was king Káma who is a thunderbolt in destroying the mountains which are the abode of his enemies. His son was the illustrious king Balli, who is the moon to the ocean which is the solar race, who has acquired merit by the worship of the lotus feet of Gaurínátha (Śiva) and who is the ocean of kindness.

(Telugu.) On the occasion of Uttaráyaṇa Sankránti, corresponding to the year 1088 (S.S.), Śríman Mahámaṇḍaléśvara Balli Chóḍa Mahárájulu on whose lotus feet the eyes of all kings, Trilóchana and others, are set, who is the jewelled lamp of the race of Karikála by whom the dam of the Kávérí was built, and who is the elephant-goad to wicked princes.[1] . . . . granted 3 *puṭṭis* for providing oblation, sacrifice, food and daily offering to Ṣrí Chóḍeśvara Mahádévaru of [2] Manyapalli in [3] Guṇḍakaḍu which is our property, *viz.*, 2 *puṭṭis* to the *pújári* (priest) of this temple, Báma Jíyya, and 1 *puṭṭi* for (keeping up) the perpetual lamp. Báma Jíyya should receive these, and he, his sons and grandsons enjoy happiness. This was given so that it may be maintained on these terms.

NOTE.—The donor in this inscription is the same as that in Darsi (48), and the first portions in both are identical.

1. श्रीमत्पोत्तपिनान्नि
2. चोडतनयः
3. श्रीवेंक्कभूपा
4. लकः तत्पुत्रोारि
5. पदाचलापह
6 पाव: कामाक्षितीना
7. यकः सूनुस्सूर्य
8. कुलान्वयांन्नु
9 धिशाशी श्रीबल्लिभूपालकः गौरीना

---

[1] This verse is the same as in Darsi (48). [2] Manyapalli in Darsi.
[3] Gundikarri in Darsi.

10. थपदाब्जवीदं

11. तगुणस्सौजन्यरत्नाक

12. रः ॥ స్వస్తి చరణ సరో

13. రుహ విహితవిలో

14. చన త్రిలోచన ప్ర

15. ముఖాఖిల ప్రిథివీ

Second side.

16. శ్వర కారిత కా

17. వేరితీర కరికా

18. ల కులరత్న ప్ర

19. దీపాహిత కు

20. మారాంకుశ శ్రీ

21. మన్మహా మ

22. ండ్డ లేశ్వర బల్లి

23. చోడ మహారా

24. జులు ౧౦౮౮ ఉ

25. నట్టి యుత్తరా

26. యణ సంక్రాంతి

27. నిమిత్తమున మా

28. జీవితవర్గమైన గుం

29. డ్ల కడీలోని మన్య

30. వల్లి శ్రీచోడేశ్వ

31. ర మహాదేవర

32 కు హావిబలి

Third side.

33. నమో పడిపని

34. వేద్యంబులకు

35. ం బెట్టిన ఖ ౩ ఐగు

36. డిబోజారి బా-
37. మజీ య్యకు ఖ ౨
38. దేవర అఖం
39. డ్డ దీపమున
40. కుగాన ఖ ౧ దీ
41. కిం జేకొని బా-
42. మజీయ్యపు
43. త్రాను పౌత్రికము
44. సుఖమనుభవించ
45. ం గలవాండు జల్లె
46. టి . . .
47. చ్చినదా . . .

Darsi (50). (A.D. 1537–38.)

[Márella. Telugu. Opposite Vénugópálasvámi temple.]

Translation.

Prosperity! Hail! On Saturday the 7th of the bright fortnight of Śrávaṇa of the year Hévilambi, corresponding to the year 1459 of the illustrious, victorious and prosperous Śáliváhana Śaka era, Koṇḍamaráju of the Kaṇva *Śákhá*, of the Bháradvája *gótra*, grandson of Márella Nágaráju and son of Abbalaráju, caused to be constructed a temple and caused to be set up the image of Madanagópinátha.

Ṣrí Hari!

1. శ్రీ స్వస్తి శ్రీజయాభ్యు
2. దయ శాలివాహన శకవష౯

3. ంబులు ౧౪౫౯ అగు నేటి హేవి
4. ళంబి సంవ్వత్సర శ్రావణ శుద్ధ
5. ౭ వ । కాంణ్వ శాఖాన్వయుడై
6. న భారద్వాజ గోత్రుండైన మా
7. రేళ్ల నాగరాజు పౌత్రుండైన అబ్బల
8. రాజు పుత్రుడైన కొండమ రా
9. జు దేవస్థానంగట్టించ్చి మదనగోపి
10. నాథని ప్రతిష్ట సేయించ్చెను॥
11. శ్రీ హరి।

Darsi (51).

[Mullamúru. Telugu. On Ánjanéya stone near Vénugópálasvámi temple.]

Translation.

(Adoration be to) Ṣrí Ráma.

On the 10th day of the bright fortnight of Mágha of the year Ánanda, Rampa Anantabhaṭlu caused this edict to be inscribed.

The *méras* to Ṣrí Hanumán (are) at 2 a[1] (*aḍḍa* ?) for every *puṭṭi*.

1. శ్రీరామం
2. ఆనంద సం
3. వత్సర మాఘ
4. శు ౧౦ లు
5. రంపఅన
6. ంతభట్లు శాసనం

---

[1] May stand for aḍḍa = 2 mánikas.

7. వే ఇంచెను
8. శ్రీ హాను
9. మంతుడు
10. మేర ఖ ౧ కి
11. అ॥ లేఖ..

DARSI (52). (A.D. 1586–87?)

[Náyuḍupáḷem. Telugu. On Bollikonḍa in front of Temple.]

TRANSLATION.

(Adoration be to) Ṣrí Ráma! Hail! On Thursday the 10th of the bright fortnight of Kártika of the year Vyaya, corresponding to 1519 of the Ṣrí Śáliváhana Śaka era, Singaráju, karnam of Machchapuram, Gangaráju's son Konḍamaráju, Venggaráju son of Konḍamaráju, and Vóbuḷuráju son of Venggaráju, who caused to be set up the image of Anumanta (Hunumán) Perumáḷ of Machchapuram Bollikonḍa after making ceaseless prostrations, presented for *amritapaḍi* (sacred food) to Hanumanta $\frac{1}{16}$ field to the east of the Banri sluice for the religious merit of their ancestors. We have also presented at ($\frac{1}{8}$) *túm* on every *puṭṭi* (measured) at the threshing floor of all kinds of grain raised in our karnam *mányam* land.

[One imprecatory verse.]

NOTE.—The cyclic and S.S. years do not correspond.

1. శ్రీరామా స్వస్తిశ్రీ శాలి
2. వాహాన శకవర్షంబ్బులు ౧౫౧౯
3. అగు నేటి వ్యయసంవత్సర కార్తీక

4. శు ౧౦ గు। మచ్చపురం బొల్లికొండ్డ
5. అనుమంత్త పెరుమాళ్ల ప్రతిష్ట
6. శేయించ్చిన మచ్చపురపు కరణం
7. శింగ్గరాజు గంగరాజు కొమారుండు
8. కొండ్డమరాజు కొండ్మరాజు కొమారు
9. డు వెంగ్గరాజు వెంగరాజు కొమారు
10. డు వోబుళ్రాజు తమ పెద్దలకు పు
11. ణ్యంగాను అనంతములైన శేవ .
12. హానుమంతుని అమృతపళ్లకు గా
13. బంటితూము తూర్పున పరకచేనున్ను స
14. మపీఁం స్తిమి మాకరిణీకపుమాన్యం
15. లోను పండిన నానాధాన్యాలు పాలిన
16. పుట్ల కల్లాను ఖ ౧ కి = [1]ఖై సాగిం స్తి
17. మి ॥ స్వదత్తా ద్విగుణంపుణ్యం
18. పర దత్తాను పాలనం. పరదత్తాప
19. హారేణ స్వదత్తం నిష్ఫలం భవే
20. త్ ॥

DARSI (53). (A.D. 1529–30.)

[Pólavaram. Telugu. In the garden of K. Kóṭi Reḍḍi.]

TRANSLATION.

Hail! On the holy occasion of Krishṇáshṭami (birth of Kṛishṇa) the eighth of the dark fortnight of Śrávaṇa of the year Viródhi, corresponding to the year 1451 of the illustrious, victorious and prosperous Śáliváhana era, Ráyasam Ayyappa, with mind solely intent on making

---

[1] = this symbol stands for ⅛ túm.

gifts, after making many prostrations to the lotus feet of Ṣrí Tiruvenkaṭádri, the lord of the four worlds, and after pouring water, issued a charitable edict of gift of land the particulars of which are . . . .

Second side.

While Ṣrímad Rájádhirája, Rájaparaméṣvara, Ashṭadigrájamanóbhayankara,[1] Ṣrí Víra Pratápa Ṣrí Kṛishṇadéva Maháráyalu was ruling the earth . . . . . .

Ayyaparusayya, ... the son of Vémarusayya and the subordinate of Ráyasam Timmarusayya, who is of the Áṣvaláyana *sútra*, of the Bháradvája *gótra*, and student of the Rik *Śákhá*, has reverently given with libation of water, with all rights to land and water, (?) for providing *amṛitapaḍi* (sacred food) to Ṣrí Tiruvenkaṭádri Nátha the lord of the four worlds, the village of Pólavaram situated in Addanki *síma* in Konḍavíḍu *rájya* which (*ṣíma*?) he has been pleased to give us for our chiefdom.

Third side.

We have given this for the religious merit of Kṛishṇadéva Mahárája. The progeny of those who fail to uphold this charity will go to hell. Whosoever transfers (to?) Konḍamayya, (or?) the sons of his family . . . . shall be liable to . . . .

[One imprecatory verse.]

1. స్వస్తిశ్రీ విజయాభ్యు
2. దయ శాలివాహన శక
3. వర్షంబులు ౧౪౫౧ అ
4. గు నేంటి విరోధి సంవత్స

[1] He who causes terror to the minds of kings of the eight quarters.

5. ర శ్రావణ బ కృష్ణాష్టమీ
6. పుణ్యకాలాన శ్రీచతుర్భు
7. వనా ధీశులైన శ్రీ తిరువెం
8. కటాద్రినాధని శ్రీపాదపద్మ
9. ంబులకు రాయసం అయ్యవ
10. దా నేకాగ్ర సాష్టాంగ్గ ద
11. ండప్రణామంబులు సమర్పి
12. ంచ్చి ధారబోశిన భూదా
13. న ధర్మ శాసన క్రమమెట్లన్నను
14. . . . . .
15. . . . . .

Second side.

16. శ్రీమద్రాజాధి రాజరాజపర
17. మేశ్వర అష్టదిగ్రాజరాజమనోభ
18. యంకర శ్రీ వీరప్రతాప శ్రీకృ
19. ష్ణ దేవమహారాయలు
20. పృద్వీసామ్రాజ్యాన . . .
21. మిమానా అంకధానకుంబా
22. లించంగా వధరించిన
23. కొండవీటిరాజ్య అద్దంకిశీమ
24. లోని పోలవరగ్రామము శ్రీ
25. చతుర్భువనాధీశ్వరులైన
26. శ్రీ తిరువెంకటాద్రి నాధుని
27. కి ఆశ్వలాయన సూత్రులు భా
28. రద్వాజసగోత్రులు రుకుశాఖా
29. ధ్యాయులైన రాయసం తిమ్మర్సయ్యఃవి
30. త్యులు వేమరుసయ్యవారి
31. పుత్రులయిన అభిమానంబుగ
32. భూ వారి పూర్నసుధారగాను

33. అయ్యప్పరుసయ్య శ్రీ తిరు
34. వెంకటాద్రినాధని అమృ
35. తపల్లకు ధారబోసిఇస్తిమి

Third side

36. కృష్ణదేవ మహారా
37. యలకుంబున్య
38. ముగాను ఇస్తిమి
39. ఇద్ధర్మానకు ఎవ్వరు
40. తప్పినాను వారికులకో
41. న్న నరకానపోదురు ఎవ
42. రైనుకొండమయ్య చెల్లించి
43. నాను వారికులకోమరు
44. లును . కు . . . గల్లునిచ్చి
45. డివారుగా జనపదస్తు ప
46. డుమరు॥స్వదత్తా ద్విగుణ
47. ం పుణ్యం పరదత్తానుపాల
48. నం పరదత్తాపహారేణ స్వ
49. దత్తం నిష్ఫలం భవేతు॥

Darsi (54).

[Pólavaram. Telugu. From Śiva temple.]

Translation.

On Sunday the 5th of dark half of Mágha of the year Ṣrímukha, Kummaṛa Channam Ṣeṭṭi caused to be constructed a temple to Channamalaya of Pôlavaram for the religious merit of his mother Dádema and his father Gópi Ṣeṭṭi.

1. శ్రీముఖ సంవత్సర మాఘ బ ౫ ఆ
2. కుమ్మఱి చన్నంశెట్టి తమతల్లిదాదెమ
3. కున్న తమతండ్రి గోపిశెట్టికిన్ని పుణ్యం
4. గాను పోలవరపు చన్నమలయ గుడిగట్టి
5. ంచ్చెను॥

Darsi (55).

[Potakamúru. Telugu. Below Dhvajasthambam of Vénugópálasvámi temple. Unintelligible.]

1. కాగోస . వ . న విభుండు
2. వుదకంబుగొనఁ ఖధా
3. త్రిం గులవ్రతమని శిలా
4. ఉ రంబులోనం ఇతి
5. టి . . . దేవిమి
6. తా ఆ . . సాక్షిగా
7. . . . . .

Darsi (56). (A.D. 1448–49.)

[Pótavaram. Telugu. To west of Rámalingasvámi temple.]

Translation.

May there be prosperity! Hail! On Monday the 12th of the bright fortnight of Vaiśákha of the year Vibhava, corresponding to the illustrious Ṣaka year 1370, Panṭa Burrela Chinama Reḍḍingáru set up the images of Achchaḍa Pótavara, Ráma Déva, and Ṣrí Kéśava Perumáḷ and founded an endowment with libation of water for providing daily offerings to those deities consisting of 10 *túms* of dry land in Reḍḍipáḍu and a wet field of 10 *kunṭas* in Reḍḍipáḍu.

1. శుభమస్తు - స్వస్తిశ్రీశక
2. వరుషంబు ౧౩౪౦ అ
3. గుణెంటి విభవ సంవత్సర వై
4. శాఖ శు ౧౨ సో । వంట్టబు తెల
5. చినమరెడ్డింగారు అచ్చడపోతవరా
6. నను రామాదేవరాను శ్రీకేశవపెరుమా
7. ళ్లాను ప్రదిష్టసేసి అదేవుళ్లకు
8. నివేద్యాలకు దార
9. వోశి పెట్ని మీదేవరకు వెలి
10. చెను రెడ్డిపాటిని వందు
11. మున్నూ వంగమడిరె
12. డిపాటిని పదికుం (టలు)

Darsi (57). (A.D. 1219-20?)

[Potlapáḍu. Telugu. Opposite the Vírabhadra temple.]

Translation.

Hail! Tripurántaka Mahárája, who is the servant of the feet of Rudradéva Mahárája, who (Rudradéva) is Ṣríman Mahámanḍaléśvara, who is the lord of many countries, who is the supporter of the four castes, who is the destroyer of the army of the western king Dámódara, who is the incarnation of fame, who is a perfect Révanta amongst those who are mounted on very unruly horses, who is the beloved consort of the goddess of victory, who is a Náráyaṇa, who is fierce in war, by whose columnar arms is made motionless the valour of all kings, with the might of whose fame the faces of the women of the cardinal points are marked, who is a Karna in making gifts, who has eclipsed Kámadhénu and Kalpadruma (in liberality), the collection of the rays of the nails of whose feet is kissed by the array of the edges of the jewelled diadems of all kings whose praises are sung, who is the ornament of the illustrious Kákati dynasty, who (Tripurántaka) is brave, who has acquired the lordship of the whole kingdom, whose power is equal to that of a god, who is *Chalamattigaṇḍa,* who is the vanquisher of the three kings, who is a Brahmarákshasa to provincial chiefs, who is Gaṇḍa Penḍáru.

Hail ! On Thursday, the 15th of the bright fortnight of Áśvíja of the year Pramádi, corresponding to the auspicious Śaka year 1151, on the holy occasion of a lunar eclipse made this gift for providing decorations, daily worship, sandal, musk, camphor, saffron, milk, &c., to Śrí Tripurántaka Śríman Mahádéva . . . . . and to the dancing girls of the temple . . . . . to last in perpetuity as long as the sun and (moon) endure, to secure increase of life, health, wealth and success . . . .

Tripurántakadéva . . . former *vritti* . . . . Tripurántaka.

[One imprecatory verse.]

whoever causes obstacles to this charity, will incur the sin of killing a tawny cow on the banks of the Ganges, and will be regarded as having eaten from skull of his eldest son.

May it cause great prosperity !

NOTE.—The cyclic and S.S. years do not agree. The Śaka date is almost certainly wrong.

1. స్వస్తి శ్రీమన్మహామండలేశ్వ
2. ర అనేక దేశాధిపతి చాతువ
3. ర్ణ సముద్ధరణ పశ్చమరాయ దా
4. మోదర సైన్యదిశావట్ట లలాట
5. కీర్త్తిఅవతార అతివిషమహా
6. యారూఢప్రౌఢరేఖా రేవంత
7. విజయలక్ష్మీకాంతనాయ
8. క నారాయణ కథనప్రచండ
9. దోస్తంభ స్తంభిత సకలక్షితిపా
10. లశౌర్య్య యశస్తోమతిలకిత
11. దిగంగనాముఖ వితరణక
12. ర్ణావినిర్జిత కామధేనుకల్పద్రు
13. మా వర్ణిత సకలనరపతిమ
14. ణిమకుటకోటీర మకరికా
15. చుంబ్యమానచరణ నఖకిరణ కంద్ద
16. ళ శ్రీకాకతికులతిలక రుద్రదేవ
17. మహారాజచరణ విదేయ
18. . . . . ధీరసమధి
19. గతసకలరాజ్యాధిపతి
20. (దైవత) విభవ చలమర్త్తిగ
21. ండ్ల మూరురాయ జగద
22. మండలీక బ్రహ్మరాక్షస
23. గండపెండారు త్రిపురాంతక
24. మహారాజులు తమకు ఆ

Second side.

25. యురారోగ్యైశ్వర్యాభివృద్ధిగ
26. విజయార్థముగాను స్వస్తి
27. శుభ శకవరుషంబులు ౧౧౫౧

28. అగునేంటి ప్రమాదిసంవత్సర ఆ
29. శ్వీజ శు । ౧౫ మ నాంటి సోమగ్రహ
30. ణపుణ్య సమయమందు శ్రీ
31. త్రిపురాంతక శ్రీమన్మహాదేవ
32. రకు శ్రీఅంగభోగము నిత్యా
33. చఁన గంధకస్తూరి కర్పూర కుంకు
34. మ క్షీర . నిలజ . లకు గుడినాను
35. లకూను . . తస . . . . . .
36. ద్యకము . . . .
37. క్ర . . . . .
38. ల . . . . .
39. . .
40. . నుస
41. . . .
42. స్థా . . . , .
43. . . . .
44. . . . .
45. . . . .
46. . . . .
47. . . . .
48. . . . . . .
49. . . . .
50. . . త్రిపురాంత్త
51. కదేవ . . . పూర్వఁత్రవిత్తి
52. . . త్రిపురాంతక . . శాకతలం
53. . . . . కృతిమత .
54. . . కజు
55. . యమ . వ . హయకు . దయ
56. . చిత . . . నివితేయతి . క్షిణర

57. . . . . సముల . . . .

58. . . . . నాయంత

Third side.

గామేక

రత్రికామేకా భూమే

రప్యేక మంగుళం

యావన్నరకమాప్నోతి

తావదాభూత సం

ప్లవం । ఇధమఃము

కు యవ్వారైన విలంఘు

ము తలంచినవా

రు గంగాతీరమందు క

పిలగోవును వధించ్చి

వారు పెద్దకొడుకు

కపాలమునం కూడు

కుడిచినవారు

. . . .

. . . .

. . . . కా .

. . . . . మాం

గళమహా శ్రీ శ్రీ

DARSI (58).

[Potlapáḍu. Sanskrit in Telugu character and Telugu. In front of Vírabhadrasvámi temple.]

TRANSLATION.

(End of one imprecatory verse.) Whoever seizes even one cow, or one jewel, or one inch of land obtains (remains in) hell until the final destruction of the elements.

2. Whoever among the maintainers of this charity thinks of causing obstacles to this charity will incur the sin of killing a black cow on the banks of the Ganges, and (eating) from the skull of his eldest son.

* * * *

May it cause great prosperity!

1. वत् ॥ गामेकां
2. रात्निकामेकां भूमे-
3. रप्येकमङ्गुलं । ह
4. रन्नरकमाप्नोति
5. यावदाभूतसं-
6. प्लवं ॥ ఈధర్మ్మపా
7. లకులెవ్వరైన విఘంఘ్య
8. ము తలంచినవారు
9. గంగాతీరమున గ
10. పిల గోవు వధించి
11. దమ పెద్దకొడుకు
12. కపాలమునందు
13. . . . హ్లాముదిరా

14\. . . . . ం చి

15\. జగం . . డల

16\. . . . . ం మో.

17\. . . . . మం

18\. గళ మహా శ్రీ శ్రీ

19\. శ్రీం జేయును.

Darsi (59).

[Potlapáḍu. Telugu. In front of Vírabhadrasvámi temple.]

Translation.

Hail! Ṣrí Tripuráridéva Mahárája, who is the worshipper of the lotus feet of Rudradéva Mahárája, Ṣríman Mahámanḍaléśvara, who (Rudradéva) is the ruler of many countries, who is the supporter of the four castes, who is the destroyer of the army of the western king Dámódara, who is the one and only hero, who is the incarnation of valour, who is a perfect Révanta (son of the sun) amongst those who are mounted on very unruly horses, who is a Náráyaṇa, the beloved of the goddess of victory, who is terrible in battle, before whose columnar arms the courage of all kings is paralyzed, who with the might of his fame marks the foreheads of the maidens of the cardinal points, who is a Karṇa in liberality, who is a Káma to beautiful women, who is a Kalpadruma (tree of plenty) to relatives, the collection of the rays from the nails of whose feet are kissed by the array of the edges of the jewelled crowns of prostrate rulers, who is the ornament of the Kákati family, who (Tripuráridéva) has acquired the lordship of the whole kingdom, whose majesty is great, Chalamartiganḍa,[1] Múruráya Jagada[2] Manḍalíka Bramharákshasas,[3] Ganḍa Penḍáru,[4] (gives) for his

* * * *

1. స్వస్తిశ్రీ మన్మహా మండలేశ్వ
2. ర అనేక దేశాధిపతి చాతుర్వర్ణ
3. సముద్ధరణ పశ్చమరాయదా
4. మోదరా సైన్యదిశాపట్ట పకాంగవీ
5. ర వీరావతార అతివిషమహ
6. యారూఢ పౌఢరేఖా రేవంత
7. విజయలక్ష్మీకాంత నాయ
8. క నారాయణ కదనప్రచండ,
9. దోస్తంభగుంభిత సకలక్షితిపా
10. ల శౌర్య్య యశస్తోమతిలకిత
11. దిగంగనాముఖ వితరణకర్ణ
12. కామిని జనకామ బంధుకల్పద
13. మ ప్రణతసకలనరపతి మ
14. ణి మకుట కోటి మకరికాచుం
15. బ్యమాన చరణ నఖకిరణకంద
16. ళ కాకతికుల తిలక రుద్రదేవ
17. మహారాజచరణ నళిన యు
18. గళ సమారాధక సమధి

---

[1] Chalamartiganḍa is a variant of Chalamattiganḍa.

[2] Múruráya Jagada is the same as Múruráya Jagadala, the vanquisher of the three kings, Chéra, Chóḷa and Páṇḍya.

[3] Manḍalíka Brahmarákshasa = who was a very fierce demon to provincial chiefs.

[4] Ganḍa Penḍáru = a Canarese title, the meaning of which is not known to us.

19. గత సకల రాజ్యాధి
20. భవధర్మవిభుధ చలమర్తిగ
21. ండమూరురాయజగద
22. మండలీక బ్రంహ్మరాక్షస గ
23. ండ పెండారు త్రిపురారిదేవ
24. మహారాజులు తమకుల

DARSI (60). (A.D. 1219–20?)

[Potlapáḍu. Telugu. Opposite Vírabhadrasvámi temple.]

TRANSLATION.

For the benefit of the temple of Umésvarasvámi of the village.

* * * *

Hail! On Tuesday, the 15th of the bright half of Áṣvija of the year Pramádi, corresponding to 1157 of the illustrious and auspicious Śaka era, on the holy occasion of a lunar eclipse . . . . to Ṣríman Mahádéva of Ṣrí Tripurántaka for providing decorations for the person, daily decorations, musk . . . . (of the rest only a few words legible here and there).

NOTE.—The cyclic and S.S. years do not correspond.

* * * *

1. యూరి యుమేశ్వర స్వామివారి
2. ఆల్లయానర్తముగాను స్వస్తి
3. శ్రీ శుభ శకవరుషంబులు ౧౧౫౭
4. అగునేటి ప్రమాది సంవత్సర ఆ
5. శ్వీజ శుద్ధ ౧౫ మనాంటి సోమగ్రహ

6. ణ పుణ్యసమయమందు శ్రీ
7. రపురాంతక శ్రీమన్మహాదేవ
8. త్రికు శ్రీ అంగభోగార్థము నిత్య
9. శ్రీరంగకస్తూరికయ పూలకుం
10. . నలాని . జన
11. . ము . . వస . . .
12. ద్రా . ముసెవ
13. . గా
14. .
15. .
16. .
17. .
18. .
19. * * * * *
20. చిత త్రిపురా . . . . శానతలది
21. . . కృతిమెత
22. . . . . ణకంటము
23. . యమునిషి . రతీయక
24. . వక్ష్యంభవంతు . . వతేనీయని తేషుస్వైర్ష
25. . వీదా . నా . . త . . దె
26. చగు

Darsi (61). (A.D. 1718–19?)

[Rájampalli. Telugu. In front of Gópálasvámi temple.]

Translation.

Hail! On the 11th of the bright half of Kártika of the year Viḷambi, corresponding to 1651 of the illustrious, victorious, and prosperous Śálivâhana Śaka era, Gópanangáru, descendant of the Damarti *gótra*, grandson of Dhúḷipáḷḷa Akkanangáru and son of Gurvanangáru, had the consecration of the temple performed in the temple of Gópálasvámi of Rájyampalli. Kárumanchi Mallavaráju is the worshipper of Gópálasvámi. To the three artizans who carved this temple, Kákumáni Vírayya, Nalla Sítarayya and Varadáyuḍu of Ammanabrólu, Gópanna granted a charity. He gave a field named maṭa (?) and the field named (pallimuntham ?) in Rájámpalli village.

* * * *

Note.—The S.S. and cyclic years do not correspond. Probably the S.S. date should be 1641.

1. స్వస్తి శ్రీ విజయా
2. భ్యుదయశాలివా
3. హానశకవరుషంబ్బు
4. లు ౧౬౫౧ అగు నేట్టి విళంబినా
5. మ సంవత్సర కార్తీక శు ౧౧ లు రాజ్యం
6. పల్లి గోపాలస్వామి దేవాలయం
7. లో దమర్తి గోత్రోద్భవులైన ధూళిపాళ్ల
8. అక్కనంగారి పౌత్రులున్ను గుర్వనంగారిపుత్రు
9. లైనగోపనంగారు చేసిన దేవాలయ
10. ప్రతిష్ట। గోపాలస్వామికి కారుమంచ్చి
11. మల్లవరాజు శేవకుండు। యీ దేవాలంచెక్కినదిబ
12. త్తులు అమ్నం బ్రోలయన్నయకాకుమాని వీరయనల్లసీత

రయ

13. వరదాయుడు ముగ్గిరికిన్ని గోపన్నయిచ్చిన దర్మంరాజంపల్లి
14. గ్రామమందున మటను చేలను ఇచ్చెను పల్లెముంతుమంచెను

* * * *

Darsi (62). (A.D. 1675–76.)

[Rájampalli. Telugu. Opposite Janárdanasvámi temple.]

Translation.

Hail! On the 10th of Śrávaṇa of the year Rákshasa corresponding to 1597 of the illustrious, victorious and prosperous Śáliváhana Śaka era, the fields presented to Gópála of Rájampalli for food (*amritapaḍi*); fields at Kesimpáḍu . . . .
These fields were presented to Gópála of Rájampalli. If any one fails, he will displease Hari (?)

Those who obstruct this charity will incur the sin of killing cows and Bráhmans near the Ganges. Śri! Śri!

1. స్వ స్తి శ్రీజయాభ్యుదయశాలి
2. వాహనశకవరుషంబులు
3. ౧౫౯౭ అగునేంటి రాక్షసనం
4. వత్సర శ్రావణ శుద్ధ ౧౦ లు రాజంపల్లి
5. గోపాలానికి అమ్రుతపళ్లకును
6. ఇచ్చినక్షేత్రాలు . . కేసింపాటి
7. . . . క్షేత్రము (వియలక్షేత్రవుం.
8. వారును విధమటి ౯ క్షేత్రాలు) ఇ . రాజం).
9. పల్లినిం గోపాళునికి సమప్పిం౯ం
10. చిన యీక్షేత్రము దప్పిన హరిపాదా
11. లు యీధర్మావునందును .యెవ్వరు
12. తప్పినాను గంగకటుతగోవు బ్రాహ్మ నివధిం
13. చిన పాపానం బోవుట శ్రీ శ్రీ

DARSI (63). (A.D. 1402-0.)

[Rájampalli. Telugu. Opposite Janárdanasvámi temple.]

TRANSLATION.

(a)

Hail! On Thursday, the 10th of the bright fortnight of Kártika of the year Chitrabhánu, corresponding to 1324 of the illustrious Ṣaka era, Tátireḍḍi and Sándrámalapalli Singama Ṣeṭṭi caused to be consecrated Ṣrí Gópináthadéva of Rájyapalli.

At the time of consecration Rájannamgáru dedicated fields in Rájyampalli to Perumál namely, dry fields 2½ *puṭṭis* wet field 2½ *marutus*.

Hamahvári Vallabharáyuḍu presented 10 *túms* in Paiṭipáḍu. Dharu Mantri Ráju 5 *túms*. Irugaráju gave 6 *puṭṭis* . . . ayilunḍu gave 10 *puṭṭis* . . . . Ṣrí Dadhiráju 10 *túms*.

(b)

On the 10th of the bright fortnight of Ṣrávaṇa of the year Sádháraṇa, Dinaka Reḍḍi presented in Pámúr 1 *puṭṭi*, Rupinakari Dompi Sénu Sanapa (?) presented to the deity 2 (?) *túms* (?) of land in front of Ayyarájukunṭa in Dhúlipálla.

* * * *

Bochchula Bhíminénḍu presented in Krottapalli 10*na*. The field given by Bannamanénḍu at Annavaram is 10*na*.

(c)

On the 9th of the dark fortnight of Pushya of the year Viródhikrit Kancherla Konḍama Náyunḍu presented to the aforesaid Gópinátha of Rájampalli a field of 2 *kunṭas* in Rájampalli to the south of the village near the Kóṭi-vulungu and a wet field to the west of Gópinátha (temple)-0-1$\frac{1}{8}$.

Therefore whoever obstructs this charity will incur the sin of killing cows and Bráhmans near the Ganges.

May it cause prosperity.

Note.—These inscriptions are on two sides of one stone. The date of the first only is ascertainable.

1. స్వస్తి శ్రీ శఖవ్వరుషం
2. బులు ౧౩౭౮ అగునే
3. టి చిత్రభానుసక్వత్సర
4. కార్తీక సు ౧౦ గు రా
5. జ్యంపల్లిశ్రీ గోపీనాతన
6. దేవరను తాతిరెడ్డెనింగా (రు)
7. సాంద్రాంమల పల్లిసింగ
8. మ సెట్టింన్నిప్రదిష్టసే ఇ
9. ంచ్చిరి ప్రదిష్టకాలమం
10. దు రాగన్నంగారు పెరుమా
11. ళ్లకు రాజ్యంపల్లినిసమ
12. ం ర్పించిన క్షేత్రము ఖ ౨ ॥
13. నీరునేలమర్తులు ౨ ॥
14. పైటిపాటను హామహ్వా
15. రి వల్లభరాయండు స
16. మర్పించిన క్షేత్రంన ౧౦
17. ధరంమంత్రిరాజుగారు
18. ంను సమర్పించ్చిన్న క్షేత్రంన౫
19. ఇరుగరాజు ఇచ్చిన క్షే
20. త్రము ఖ ౬. . .
21. అఖిలుండఖం ౧౦ శ్రీ
22. దధిరాజు ఇచ్చినచేనున ౧౦

Second side.

23. దినకతెడ్డింగారు
24. పామూరంబెట్టి
25. న క్షేత్రం ఖ ౧
26. సాధారణసంవత్సర శ్రావణ
27. శు ౧ంధూలిపాళ్లనురుపిన
28. కరిదాంపి సేనుసోనప యిచ్చిన
29. క్షేత్రం అయ్యరాజు కుంట ము
30. ందిరను ం౨ [1] క్షేత్రం
31. స్వామికి సమర్పించ్చె
32. ను శ్రీ
33. క్రొత్తపల్లినిబొచ్చు
34. ల బిమినేండువెట్టిన
35. క్షేత్రంన ౧౦
36. అంనవరానబం
37. నమనెండు వెట్టినక్షే
38. త్రం న ౧౦
39. విరోధకృత్ సవ్వత్సర
40. పుష్యబ౯ ఆరాజంప్ప
41. ల్లి గోపినాధనికి కంచ్చె
42. ర్లం కొం ష్ణనాయిండు
43. రాజంపల్లిని ఇచ్చినక్షే
44. త్రం వూరికిదక్షిణా
45. న కోటివెలుంగు వ
46. ద్దిచేను కు ౨ న్న గో
47. పి నాధనిపమ
48. టి వరిమడి ౧ ॥ ను
49. ఇస్త్రిమి ఇంకుకు యు

[1] The symbols used are ౯ ౧.

50. వ్వరుదప్పినాను-గంగక
51. త్తీర గోవు(బ్రాంహ్మాని చ
52. ంప్పి పాపానంబోవురు
53. శ్రీ శ్రీ శ్రీం జేయును

Darsi (64).

[Rudrasamudram. Telugu. On tank bund.]

Translation.

The *mányam* granted to the Upparas (diggers) on the 15th of Nija Bhádrapada of the year Viródhi for their having constructed the tank is . . . . *puṭṭi* and one *kuncham*. For this, one *puṭṭi* of Váviḷḷapalli paddy as measured at Váviḷḷapalli lying near Yerra-cheruvu is granted as Tank *méra* (?). They have founded this for the religious merit of their parents. Whosoever obstruct this will incur the sin of killing cows and Brahmans on the banks of the Ganges. They will incur the sin of killing their parents at Benares.

1. విరోధిసంవత్సర ని జ భాద్రపద శు ౧౫ లు
2. చెరువు కట్టించినందుకు వేసిన నిమిత్తౌవుప్ప
4. రవారికి ఇచ్చిన మాన్యం . . . ఖ ౧
3. కుంచాలు ఇంమ్కుగా చేరు ఉమేర (య
5. ర చె అగుట్టునవున్న వావిళ్లిపల్లి గ్రామమే
6. ర ఖ ౧ కు పునవావిళ్లపల్లిదాన్యానకు
7. (. . . . .) తమత
8. ల్లితండ్రాదులకు ధర్మవుగాను
9. ప్రతిష్టించిరి ఎవరుతప్పినాను గంగ

10. కత౯గోవు బ్రాంహ్మాణిచంప్పించిన పా

11. పాన.బోవువారు తమతల్లితంండ్రుల

12. వారణాసిలోవధి ఇంచ్చినపాపానంబోవు

13. వారు ॥

DARSI (65). (A.D. 1538–39.)

[Sámantapúḍi. Telugu. On wall of Ánjanéya temple.]

TRANSLATION.

Hail! On Sunday, the 15th of the bright fortnight of Jyéshṭha of the year Viḷambi, corresponding to the year 1460 of the illustrious, victorious and prosperous Ṣáliváhana Śaka era, Bháskarayyangáru, who is of the Arṭári *gótra*, who is the grandson of Sáminéni and son of Mummaṇi caused to be constructed a temple in the village of Sámantapúnḍi and set up the image of Ṣrí Hanumanta for the religious merit of his son Yellaya and of his daughter-in-law Yellama. Ṣrí, Ṣrí, Ṣrí, Srí, Srí!

1. స్వస్తి శ్రీ జయాభ్యుదయశాలివాహాన శకవరుషంబులు

2. ౧౪౬౦ అగునేటి విళంబి సంవత్సరా జేష్ట శు ౧౫ ఆ

అటా౯రి

3. గోత్రులైనశామినేని పౌత్రులైనముమ్మణిని పుత్రుండైన

4. బాసకరయ్యంగారు తమకొమారుండు యల్లయకును తను

5. కోడలుయల్లమకును పుణ్యముగాను సామంతపూండిగ్రా

6. మానను దేవస్థానంగట్టించె శ్రీహనుమంతుని ప్రదిష్ట శ్రీశ్రీశ్రీ

శ్రీశ్రీ।

DARSI (66). (A.D. 1535–36.)

[Sámantapúḍi. Telugu. Opposite Chennakéśava temple.]

TRANSLATION.

Hail! On Thursday, the 15th of the bright fortnight of Chaitra of the year Manmatha, corresponding to the year 1458 of the illustrious, victorious and prosperous Ṣáliváhana Ṣaka era, for the religious merit of Appalayya, who is the son of Pallela Basuvánáyaningáru and who is of the illustrious *gótra* of Veruṭla, his mother Mádammangáru caused to be made a temple, a tope and a tank to Kéśavanátha of Sámantapúnḍi. Ṣrí, Ṣrí, Ṣrí, Ṣrí, Ṣrí!

1. స్వస్తిశ్రీ జయాభ్యుద
2. య శాలివాహన శక
3. వరుషంబులు ౧౪౫౮
4. అగు నేంటి మన్మథసంవత్స
5. ర చైత్ర శు ౧౫ గు శ్రీమతు
6. వెరుట్ల గోత్రులైన పల్లెలబ
7. సువానాయునింవారి కొమా
8. రుండు అప్పలయ్యకుం బుణ్య
9. ముగాను వారి తల్లిమాదంమ్మం
10. గారు సామంతపూండి కేశవనా
11. ధని గుడినివనము చెరువు
12. శేయుంచెను శ్రీ శ్రీ శ్రీ శ్రీ శ్రీ.

Darsi (67). (A.D. 1328–29 ?)

[Ṣivarámpuram. Telugu. To the west in a tamarind tope.]

Translation.

Hail ! On Friday, the 5th of the bright fortnight of Kártika of the year Jayavibha (Vibhava ?) corresponding to 1250 of the illustrious, victorious and prosperous Ṣaka era, we have presented a wet field of 4 *kuṇṭas* under the tank of Pollaboyaniyúru to Agastalinga for the religious merit of Bayyaparáju and Márasániamma.

Whoever obstructs (this) will incur the sin of killing cows and Brahmans near the Ganges.

1. స్వస్తిశ్రీ జయాం అభ్యు
2. దయ సక వరుషంబు
3. లు ౧౨౫౦ అగు నేంటి జ
4. య విభ సంవ్వచ్ఛర కా
5. ర్తిక శు ౫ శు బయ్య ప
6. రాజునికిన్ని మారసా
7. ని అమ్మకును పుణ్య
8. ముగాను పొల్లబో
9. యని యూరు యీం
10. చెర్వు క్రింద్దను అగ
11. స్త లింగ్గానకు వరిచే
12. ను నాల్గు గుంటలు
13. యిస్తిమి పవ్వరాణ
14. విఘాతము చేసిన
15. గంగ కత్తర బ్రాంహ్మడి.

Second side.

16. సు గో°వుం జం

17. పిన దో°షాన బా°

18. వువాంరు

DARSI (68). (A.D. 1147–48 ?)

[Ṣivarámpuram. Telugu. To north of Agasthéṣvara temple.]

TRANSLATION.

First side.

Hail! Ṣríman Mahámaṇḍaléṣvara Balayachóḍadéva Mahárája on whose lotus feet the eyes of Trilóchana and all other kings of the earth are set, who is the jewelled lamp of the race of Karikála by whom the dam[1] of the Kávéri was built, who is the goad of wicked princes,

Second side.

in the year Prabhava, corresponding to 1 (069) of the Ṣaka era, gave a *paṭṭi* field under Díchinachúḍni tank to the deity Agastir a of Sthánamápáliṭidána (?) for a perpetual lamp.

* * * *

Third side.

(Those who obstruct this charity) will be regarded as having killed cows near the Ganges and as having eaten from the skull of their eldest son.

* * * *

---

[1] See foot-note on p. 1250.

Fourth side.

Whoever does not maintain . . . . . Five *puṭṭis* of land were given to the *pújári* (priest) and a *puṭṭi* of land to Sasaradaku Báyaku at Brammapuram (?)

NOTE.—The figures showing the S.S. year are not quite clear.

First side.

1. స్వస్తి చరణ సర
2. సిరుహ విహితవిలో
3. చన త్రిలోచన ప్ర
4. ముఖాఖిల పృథివీ
5. శ్వర కారిత కావేరితీర
6. కరికాలకుల రత్నప్ర
7. దీపాహిత కుమారాం
8. కుశ శ్రీ మన్మహా మం
9. డలేశ్వర బలయచో
10. డదేవ మహారాజులు

Second side.

11. శక వరుషం
12. బులు ౧(౦౬౯)
13. అగు ప్రభావా
14. య సంవత్స
15. ర స్తానమాపౌలి
16. టి డాన అగస్తి
17. ర దేవరకు దీ
18. చిన మాడ్ని
19. చెఱువ క్రింద
20. పట్టినెల యివి
21. అఖణ్డ వత్తి కి

22. ముంగురుగంస

23. . . . . రివి వ

Third side.

24. ల . వ వగంగకతలమొ

25. దవుల పొడిచినవారు

26. తన పెద్దకొడుకు కపాలా

27. నీ కుడిచినట్టు మ

28. ల్ల న్యావస . . కొమ్ము

29. న కలుపాయ గత్తవిన

30. . . . . వణ్య

Fourth side.

31. నడవకా

32. ఎవరు పూజారి

33. కినేల ఎనుపు

34. ట్లును సనరదకు

35. బాయకు పుట్టి

36. ని బమ్మపురం

37. వని . డనం

DARSI (69). (A.D. 1218–19 ?)

[Sómavárapádu. Telugu. On a big rock near Gangamma temple.]

TRANSLATION.

Hail! Ṣríman Mahámaṇḍaléṣvara Paraméṣvara Abhidéva Malidéva Mahárája, who is a descendant of an excellent race, who is the ornament of the Pallava dynasty, who is of the Bháradvája *gótra*, who holds as ensign (?)

the lovely half moon, whose flag bears the emblem of a club (weapon of Ṣiva), who is Révanta in riding troublesome horses, who is the lord of Kánchi the best of cities, who is the (abode of) the grace of Kámakótyámbiká and Varadarája, whose crest is the bull, who is . . . Venkaṭanátha, who is an Arjuna in valour, who honours his servants, who delights his relations, who is the protector of the world, who is a Bhairava marked by firmness of character, who is a Náráyaṇa on earth, who is a young Káma, whose lotus-like feet are chafed by the jewelled diadems of many hostile kings, who is the upholder of the duties relating to the four castes, who has granted seven cows and an *agrahára* in the eastern quarter of Ṣrí Parvata (Ṣríṣaila), who sports with the axe in water (?), who is the ocean of perpetual gifts, who is descended from the race of Mukkanṭi Káḍveṭṭu, on the occasion of Vishu Sankránti corresponding to (the Śaka year) 1140, set up the image of Mallikhárjunadéva in (Viddárakántarapuram ?) and caused a temple to be built (for it).

* * * *

[Unintelligible; relating to lands constituting the gift.]

1. స్వస్తి శ్రీమన్మహామండలేశ్వర
2. పరమేశ్వర పరమవంశోద్భవ పల్లవ
3. కులతిలక భారద్వాజగోత్ర లలితార్ద్ధచంద్ర
4. ధర ఖట్వాంగధ్వజ కడుహయారూఢ రేఖా
5. రేవంత కాంచీపురవరాధీశ్వర కామకోట్యంబి
6. కావరదరాజప్రసాద వ్రిషభలాంచన వెంగడనాధనో
7. డువడి సాహసార్జున నిజసేవకాభావ బంధుజనానంద్ధ జ
8. గదగోపాల జలదంకిర్భైరవ భువనినారాయణ కుమార

కంద

9. ర్ప అనేకరిపునృపతిమణిమకుటఘటితచరణారవింద

10. చాతుర్వర్ణాన్వర్ణధర్మార్ధధర్మప్రతిపాలిత శ్రీపర్వతపూ
ర్వదిగుభా

11. గాగోసప్తసతాగ్రహారప్రతిష్ఠిత గదాజలక్రీడ నిత్యదాన

12. సముద్ర ముకరంటికాద్వెట్టివంశావతారుండైన అభిదేవ
మలి దేవమ

13. హారాజులు ౧౧౮౦ నేటివిషుమసంక్రాంతినిమిత్తమున
(ఖిద్దారకాంతరవరమున)

[The following lines have an arched form.]

1. మల్లికార్జున దేవరలను
ప్రతిష్టించి గుడిగట్టిరి (దాలు) గ్రామం . . .
.

2. దీనికిం లాంమేరగు . . డనూతు పెట్టిన మేరయును
పెద్ద
గంగకరత . . . .

3. . . . . . నాలువ . . . .
నమెట్టమాస పూర్వానుండి నడుపుకాండున్న
రక . . . పెలికొలము మంది
మడి . . . . వము త్తరానమసు
త్తిమ

(1) యె
(2) కిలనుతయు
(3) సిభరిగి వెనమగుంట
(4) కండుగుడింతొడ్డూడిమహిమనపరమాగలిగుండు . .
మ . .

(5) . . తభ అతవినింమపుట్లూ తొడ్లూరి పొలమున
(6) . . . వలమురంపానిలవరు . . తాతమునారు . . .
(7) . వేహారాలుంకగరతు . . . . అడ్డికెపి

DARSI (70). (A.D. 1305–06.)

[Táḷḷúru. Telugu. Near Vénugópálasvámi temple.]

TRANSLATION.

Hail! On Monday, the 2nd of the bright fortnight of Vaiṣákha of the year Viśvávasu, corresponding to the year 1227 of the illustrious and auspicious Śaka era, when Chennakéśava Perumáḷ of Táḷḷúru was consecrated, Koṇḍapi Váyapóti Náyuḍu caused to be constructed the temple and *manḍapa*, bought and gave 10 (*túms*) of paddy field in Chintaguṇṭa swamp as a *mányam* for the religious merit of his parents. In the same locality Mummaḍi, the son of Pádumákshuḍu and Ṣríranganáthuḍu, son of Kanchikuḍu, bought and gave *mányam* of land for the religious merit of their parents and this field is ten *túms*. . . . . .? Hail! For the religious merit of Ṣríman Mahámanḍaléśvara Pratápa Rudradéva Mahárája beside what Dóchayadéva gave himself . . .

1. స్వస్తిశ్రీ శుభ శక వరుషంబులు
2. ౧౨౨౭ అగునేంటి విశ్వావసు సంవత్సర వై
3. శాఖ శుద్ధ ౨ సో । తాళ్లూరి చన్నకేశవ పెరు
4. మాళ్లు ప్రతిష్టకాలమైనప్పుడు కొండపివా
5. యపోతి నాయుడు తమతల్లి దండ్రు
6. లకుఁ బుణ్యముగాను గుడి మంటపం
7. కట్టించియిచ్చిరి మూల్యమిచ్చికొన్న
8. ది యిచ్చింది చింతగుంటపఱ్ఱను ఖండుం
9. వరిచేను న ౧౦ పాదుమాక్షుడి కొడుకు ము
10. మడి తమతల్లిదండ్రులకు బుణ్యము
11. గాను కంచికుడికొడుకు శ్రీంరగనాథు

12. డు కొంతమూల్యమిచ్చికొని యిచ్చింది
13. యీపొలానను ఖండుముచేసున ౧౦ (రు
14. పిచయు నానాదేసి నిచింది చండు
15. ండేసిరి వీసాములు)॥ స్వస్తిశ్రీ
16. మన్మహా మండలేశ్వర ప్రతాప రుద్రదేవ
17. మహారాజులకు (బుణ్యముగాను)
18. దోచయందేవ స్వయ
19. ముగా నిచ్చిందిగాన

* * * *

Darsi (71).

[Táḷḷúru. Telugu. Near Ánjanéya's temple.]

Translation.

You, your sons and grandsons should enjoy in comfort, as long as the sun and moon last, this charity which has been granted to you after making libation of water and gift of gold with the sun and moon as witnesses. In these terms the edict has been caused to be engraved on stone for (the deity) Gópinátha. Those who fail to keep up this charity will be regarded as having incurred the sin of killing cows and Brahmans near the Ganges. Those who violate this charity will be considered to have taken their birth in the womb of a donkey and will go to hell in the next world. Whoever maintains this charity, I shall bear his feet on my head.

[Note.—The first two lines are illegible.]

1. . . .
2. . . (మందమారితి కనక)
3. సూర్యచంద్రులు సాక్షిగాను, సహిరం
4. ణ్యక దాన దారా దారా పూర్వకముగాను ధారవో
5. సి యిచ్చిన ధర్మమును మీపుత్రపౌత్ర పారంప
6. ర్యంతము ఆచంద్రార్కముగాను అనుభవించ్చి
7. బ్రతుకువారు యీ ప్రకారం గోపినాథుని
8. కిగాను శిలాశాసనముగాను వ్రాయించెను
9. యీ పుణ్యమునకు యెవ్వరు. దప్పినాను గంగకతెర్లను
10. గోవు బ్రాహ్మల జంపించిన పాపానబోయి
11. నట్టివారు యీ పుణ్యంయెవ్వరు దాటి నడచినా
12. గాడిదె కడుపునందు బుట్టినట్టివారు పరమందు
13. నరకం అనుభవించెవారు యీ దర్మ్మ సెఇంచిన
14. దర్మము ఎవ్వరు జరపినాను వారిపాదాలు
15. శిరస్సున ధరించు వాండు ॥

DARSI (72). (A.D. 1272–73.)

[Tammalúru. Telugu. West of village.]

TRANSLATION.

Hail! On Thursday, the 5th of the bright fortnight of Phálguṇa of the year Angírasa, corresponding to 1194 of the illustrious and auspicious Śaka era, while, Hail! Kákatíya Rudráyyadéva Mahárája, ruler of the three worlds, was ruling the earth. Mallanadévilammangáru, daughter of Ṣrí Gópāḷadéva who is the paternal uncle of

Hail! Ṣríman Mahámaṇḍaléṣvara Chakra Náráyaṇa Ṣrí Mádhavadévarája (?) the governor of Addenki *sthala*, had the image of Gópíśvaradéva set up in the name of her father at Tammalúr, caused the pinnacles of the temple to be erected and gave a dry field, a *paṭṭi* field (?) two paddy fields and in Mattulúr a flower garden—all to last as long as the sun, moon and stars exist to the deity for providing daily worship and all enjoyments, and to the dancing girls of the temple.

[Imprecatory verses.]

(1) స్వస్తి శ్రీశుభశకవరు
(2) షంబులు ౧౧౯౮ అగు
(3) నేంటి అంగీరస సంవత్సర
(4) ఫాల్గుణశుద్ధ పంచమియు
(5) గురువారము నాండుస్వ
(6) స్తి త్రిభువనాధిపతి కా
(7) కతీరుద్రాయ్యదేవ మహా
(8) రాజులు ప్రిథివిరాజ్య
(9) ముసెయంగాను అద్దె
(10) ంకి స్థలసాధ్యకుండు
(11) ను స్వస్తి శ్రీమన్మహా
(12) మండలేశ్వర చక్రనా
(13) రాయణ శ్రీమాధ
(14) వ దేవరాజుల
(15) పిన్న తండ్రి శ్రీ గో
(16) పాళదేవని కూంతు
(17) ఉ మల్లణ దేవిఅమ్మ
(18) ంగారు తంమలూరన
(19) తమతండ్రి పేరింట్టి గో
(20) పీశ్వరదేవర ప్రతిష్ఠ

(21) చేసి గుడి గలాశింపం
(22) గట్టించి దేవరకు ' నిత్య
(23) నివేద్య అంగరంగబో
(24) గానకును గు
(25) డి ప్రానివారికి
(26) నివెలి పొలమూ
(27) ను పట్టి సేనున్నా వ
(28) రిపొలము రె
(29) ండు మత్తులూ
(30) రుపుర్వ్యందోంట
(31) ను అంతపట్టును
(32) ఆచంద్రార్కతార
(33) కముగా చెల్లని
(34) స్త్రిమి । స్వదత్తం
(35) పరదత్తంవా యోహ
(36) రేతివసుంధరా షష్ఠి
(37) వర్షసహస్రాణి వి
(38) ష్టాయాం జాయతెక్రిమి.

Darsi (73). (A.D. 1586–87.)

[Tsalivendra. Telugu. Below hill near figure of Gangamma.]

Translation.

Hail! On the 15th of the bright fortnight of Pushya of the year Vyaya, corresponding to 1509 of the illustrious Ṣaka era, Timmánáyaningáru, of the *gótra* of Inigela, son of Dámera Késamanáyaḍu of the lineage of

Padmanáyaka, caused Tellamgaḍḍa tank to be built, caused (an image of) Gangádévi to be made, caused it to be set up, and issued a charitable deed with libation of water giving a *kuchchala*[1] field to the east to that deity. If any persons obstruct this charity by levying a grazing fee on this field or a tax for the use of the tank water they will incur the sin of killing cows and Brahmans near the Ganges.

1. స్వస్తి శ్రీ శకవర్షం
2. బులు ౧౫౦౯ అగు
3. నేంటివ్యయ సంవత్సరపు
4. వ్య శు ౧౫ లు పద్మనాయక వంశస్తు
5. లున్న ఇనిగెల గోత్రులున్న
6. అఇన దామెర కేసమనా ఇనిం
7. కుమారుండు తింమ్మానాఇనిం
8. గారు తెల్లంగడ్డ చెరువు గట్టిం
9. చ్చి గంగ్గాదేవిని శేఇంచ్చి ప్రతి
10. ష్ట శేఇంచి ఆదేవరకు తూ
11. ర్పుతట్టున కుచ్చలచేనుధారవోశి ఇచ్చినధర్మశాసనం యీచేనికి
12. గాని చెరువుకు నీళ్ల పుల్లరిగొనికాని యెవ్వరు ధర్మాంద ప్పినాను
13. గంగ్గకరుత గోబ్రాంహ్మణవధ శేసిన పాపానంబోవువారు.

---

[1] This means a field measuring 8 gorrus or about 25 acres.

DARSI (74).

[Tummerlapáḍu. Telugu.]

TRANSLATION.

Hail! Along with a house which was built for Ṣrímat Ṣánta Ṣivagurudévaru, who is the worshipper of the divine and illustrious lotus feet of Ṣrí Tripurántakadéva and whose head is adorned with the unequalled lotus feet of Ṣrímat . . . . (for Ṣivaguru *vide* Gangavaram inscriptions (Nos. 25 and 28)).

The village named Pótalapáḍu with its four boundaries was presented with gift of gold to Ṣrí Gangéśvaradévaru of the holy place of Ṣrí Tripurántaka for providing the eight enjoyments (for the deity) to last as long as the moon and stars endure. . . . .

1. స్వస్తి శ్రీమతుం . . .
2. నతుల చరణ సరసీరుహా
3. పూజితమ స్తకులు శ్రీత్రిపు
4. రాంతక దేవర దివ్యశ్రీపాద
5. పద్మారాధకులైన శ్రీమతుశాంత
6. శివగురు దేవరులకు చెఱువ.క
7. ట్టించిన కట్టడముతోన పోత
8. ల పాడు అనెడు యూరు చతు
9. స్సీమమూను శ్రీ త్రిపురాంత్త
10. క తీర్థము శ్రీ గంగేశ్వర దేవర
11. కు అష్టబాగంస దక్షిణరతి
12. . . . . ఆచంద్ర
13. (తారకముగాను) దేవరకు

14. . . . . (నడు) పింప

15. . . . .

16. . . . .

17. . . . .

Darsi (75).

[Vémparála. Telugu. On road to Kambhampáḍu.]

Translation.

I intended to divide

* * * *

The yard of a donkey will be put into the mouth of any one who says that this is not the boundary (?)

1. కడపోప
2. లిడిబం
3. పింపతలచితి
4. మేరకాదన్నవారి
5. నోరిది గాడద
6. మోడ్డ

[1] Gudur (1).

[Akkampéṭa. Telugu. On the Nandi miṭṭa.]

Translation.

Hail ! On the occasion of Vishama Sankránti, corresponding to the illustrious and auspicious Ṣaka year 1505, for the religious merit of Ṣríman Mahá maṇḍa . . . . Bhujabala . . . . Nalla Siddana Déva Chóḍa Mahárájulu, the receiver of tribute from . . . . for performing daily offerings to Ṣrí Yajnéṣvara of Kháḍipúnḍi . . . . granted . . . . field . . . . charity . . . . of killing a tawny cow.

---

[1] Note.—The Manager of the Kalahasti Estate has sent us a translation of an inscription of Ṣrí Ranga Rája dated in the 'Thathu' year (?) corresponding to S.S. 1489. (Probably the year Dhátá and S.S. 1499 should be read.) Ranga Rája was then reigning at Chandragiri and the boundaries of his kingdom are described as follows :— "The village Padunathi and remarkable dry rivers on the east; the village Pillusrí with its sacred fig tree and the other important village Audalimala with the river Lavana kuri close by on the north; on the south-west the river Chekkangaguni and the western sea and Durgaráyapatnam with its 'caldera' (screw pine ?) grove and also the village Nithimakulu; and on the north-eastern and western sides of this Samasthánam there are, on the west, a small tank and the village Tirumúr near the village of Samativatari and, on the north-east, the villages of Mamuluki and Vengalapuram." So the translation given us runs but the cardinal points are evidently wrongly rendered; *for* east we should apparently *read* west, *for* north, south and so on. Durgaráyapatnam is plainly Duggarázupaṭnam, a village on the coast in Gudur taluk and Vengalapuram and Tirumúr are in the Tiruvallúr taluk of Chingleput. The other boundaries of the kingdom we do not trace.

1. స్వస్తి శ్రీ శుభ శకవర్షంబులు
2. ౧ . ౦౫ గు నేంటి విషువసంక్రాంతి
3. నిమిత్యమున శ్రీ మన్మహామండ
4. . . . ౦.భం గప్పముకొన్న భుజబల . :
5. . గల్ల సిద్దనదేవచోడ మహారాజులకు దన్మ
6. పుగాను . . . ఖాడిపూండి శ్రీ యజ్ఞేశ్వరుని
7. కి నిత్యనివేద్యమునకుం భాస్వతీలా . .
8. దేవరులు దుక్కిండి . . డి పొలము . . . .
9. దేపరల య . తము . . . . . .
10. . . . . నిచ్చిరి ధర్మ
11. . . . . . కీడించిన గవిలలంబొడిచినవారు
12. . . . . . . న . . . . .

GUDUR (2).

[Akkampéṭa. Telugu. In Paddapáṭi field.]

TRANSLATION.

The inscription planted by Rámachendra Súrapa on Monday the 30th of the dark fortnight of Chaitra in the year Raudri. Whoever covets the *méra* grain of the tank and does not give it will be considered to have been born to a donkey.

1. రౌద్రి సంవ్వత్సర
2. చైత్ర బ ౩౦ సో రామ
3. చెంద్ర సూరపవే
4. ఇంచిన శాసనం
5. చెరువు మేరధా
6. న్యం ఇయ్యక ఎ

7. వ్వరు ఆసించిన
8. గాడిదకు పుట్టి
9. నవాండు . .

Gudur (3).

[Brahmadévam. Telugu. In a street to the south.]

A fragment relating to work done to a tank and a tope.

Gudur (4).

[Chennúru. Tamil. From wall of Chennakéṣvara temple.]

Translation.

Hail! Prosperity! In the 13th year of the reign of the emperor of the three worlds, the glorious Vírarájéndrachóḻadéva, in the month of Ani, we three—Médabhaṭṭan, Śámibhaṭṭan and Śankarabhaṭṭan, (having assembled) at the temple of Nílakaṇṭha at Cheṛuvanûr sold our shares at Kumbakkappúṇḍi to Puḍólabhaṭṭa, the son of Anniṭṭa (Agnishṭa), so that he may enjoy the share just as we enjoyed (*i.e.* with all our rights) it before, in order to marry Perumáḷ, the son of Méḍabhaṭṭan.

This is the signature of these including Tiruvégambamuḍaiyár. This is the signature of Perumáḷ (the son of) Méḍabhaṭṭa. This is the signature of these including Sámibhaṭṭan. This is the signature of Sámibhaṭṭan. This is the signature of Perumáḷ (the son of) Sámibhaṭṭan.

We, Tiruppaṇi Vayirágiyáṇḍár, Váśi Reḍḍi, Jelatangipuḍi Reḍḍi, Tikkama Reḍḍi (and) Paḍukama Reḍḍi—the sons of Chakkami Reḍḍi, bear witness to this.

[1] திரிபுவனச்சக்கரவத்திகள் ஸ்ரீ விராராஜெந்த்ரசொழ-தெவர்க்கு யாண்டு ௰௩ ஆவது ஆனி [ம]ாஸத்தில் செறுவனூரில்

[2] மெ[ட]பட்டனும் சாமிபட்டனும் சங்காபட்டனும் இம்மூவொம் நிலகண்டதெவர்கொயில் இம்மூவ[ரு]-ங்கும்-

[3] ம்பக்கப்பூண்டியில் மூவர்பங்கும் நாங்கள் மூன்னுள் அநுபவித்த[ப]டியெ அன்னிட்டமகன் புடொல ப-ட்டனுக்-

[4] கு [இக்கா]ணிவிற்று மெடபட்டன் மகன் பெருமா-ளுக்கு விவ[ா*]கம் பண்ணுகைக்கு புடொலபட்ட - னுக்கு விலையற விற்று-

[5] ப்பெ [ரிய]றைகொண்டொம் இவை திருவெகம்ப-முடையார் உள்ளிட்டார் எழுத்து இவைமெடபட்-டன் பெருமாள் எழுத்து

[6] இவை சாமிபட்டன உள்ளிட்டார் எழுத்து இவை சொமபட்டன் எழுத்து இவை சாமிபட்டன் பெரு-[மா*]ள் எழுத்து இப்படி அறி-

[7] வொம் திருப்பணி வயிராகியாண்டாரொன் சக்கமிரட்-டி கு[ம]ாரரொன் வாசிரொட்டியென் செலதங்கிபு-டொட்டியென் திக்கமரட்டியென்

[8] [படு]கமரட்டியென்.

Gudur (5 to 8).

Chennúru.

The Chennakéṣava temple at Chennúru supplies the following Tamil inscriptions which are not worth printing *in extenso* :—

(5) 18th of Rájarájadéva, gift of a lamp by Náma-ṣivayya.

(6) 19th Rájarájadéva (?) gift of a lamp by Náma-ṣivayya.

(7) A list of persons who presented a lamp.

(8) S.S. 11(4 (A.D. 1242-43?) being the 27th of Rájarájadéva. Gift of a lamp by Pimináyakkan.

Gudur (9 to 18).

Chennúru.

The Sómésvara temple at Chennúru supplies the following Tamil inscriptions which are not worth printing:—

(9) S.S. 1191 (A.D. 1209-70?). Records apparently the gift of a pillar.

(10) 30th of Rájarájadéva gift of 1½ *máḍai* for a lamp by Eraman.

(11) S.S. 1190 (A.D 1268-69?). Gift of a pillar and a drum (?)

(12) 28th of Rájarájadéva. Gift of 1½ *máḍai* for a lamp by Isan Kosan.

(13) 26th of Rájarájadéva. Gift of 1½ *máḍai* for a lamp by Bhayiri Chetti.

(14) 15th of Rájarájadéva. Gift of 1 *máḍai* for a lamp.

(15) Gift of a lamp in the reign of Kulóttungachóḷa.

(16) An unintelligble fragment.

(17) S.S. 1171 (A.D 1249-50 ?. Records the names of a number of people who presented lamps.

(18) Records the names of persons who have given lamps.

GUDUR (19). (A.D. 1698-99 ?.)

[Chitéḍu. Sanskrit in Telugu character and Telugu. East of village.]

TRANSLATION.

The lunar year should be adopted for transacting secular business in this country. On the 2nd of the dark fortnight of Nija Jyéshṭha of the year Bahudhánya, corresponding to the year 1619 of the Śaliváhana Śaka era, Lakshamma Gáru, the elder sister of Krishnappa Gáru, the son of Chiṭṭeṭi Janganna Gáru, built a temple, tank, and *maṇḍapa,* and granted this charitable edict as charity to last as long as the sun and moon endure. All kinds of good will accrue to those who protect my charity and great sin will accrue to those who neglect it.

1. अस्मिन् देशे लोकव्यवहारा-
2. र्थं चांद्रमानाब्दो ग्रा
3. ह्यः । శాలివాహాన శకవర్ష
4. ంబులు ౧౬౧౯ యగు బహు
5. ధాన్య సంవత్సర నిజజేష్ట బ
6. ౨ లు చిట్టెటి జంగ్గనగారి కొ
7. మారుడు క్రిష్ణప్పగారి జేష్ట
8. భాతృలక్ష్మంమ్మగారు ఆలు
9. కము కోనేరు మంటపము
10. కట్టించి ఆచంద్రార్కముగా
11. ధర్మస్తితి చేశిన ధర్మశా
12. సనముం నాధర్మము
13. సంరక్షణ చేశినవారికి స
14. కల శ్రేయములు కలు

15. గును అశ్రద్ధఁజేసి
16. నంగారు బహుదోషః
17. ము సంభవించు
18. ను

Gudur (20 to 33).

Gúdúru.

The Aḷaganáṭha temple at Gúdúr supplies the following Tamil inscriptions which are not worth printing *in extenso.* The place is described as Kumulúr in Mélaipaṭṭayanáḍu, a sub-division of Jayankoṇḍachóḷa-maṇḍalam:—

(20) 29th of . . . . Chóḷadéva. Gift of a *máḍai* for lamp by Áchchamallináyakkan.

(21) A fragment relating to a lamp.

(22) 25th of Rájarájadéva. Records a gift by Tiru . . . nár Kániyáḷan *alias* Vikramachóḷa Múvéndai.

(23) Records a gift by Jakkama Reḍḍi, son of Káviri Muppi Reḍḍi of Vilakkaṇḍai.

(24) 25th of Rájarájadéva. Records the gift of a lamp by Káppén.

(25) 26th of Rájarájadéva. Gift of 1¼ *máḍai* for a lamp by Chóḍi Saṭṭi.

(26) 36th of Rájarájadéva. Gift of 1½ *máḍai* for a lamp by Nágen.

(27) S.S. 1169 (A.D. 1247–48 ?). Gift of 1½ *máḍai* for a lamp by Mádanimári Seṭṭi.

(28) 18th of Rájarájadéva. Gift of 1¼ *máḍai* by Kámayan.

(29) S.S. 1[1]98 (A.D. 1276–77?). Gift of 1½ *máḍai* for a lamp by Irásáni, wife of Pálama Reḍḍi.

(30) 25th of Rájarájadéva. Gift of 51 *máḍai* for a lamp by Káppen *alias* Lakshmaṇadásan.

(31) 19th of Rájarájadéva. Gift of 1¼ *máḍai* for a lamp by Erama Reḍḍi.

(32) Gift of 2 *máḍai* for a lamp by Páchchaperumáḷ Cheṭṭi.

(33) 35th of Kulóttungachóḷa. Gift of lands.

GUDUR (34).

[Gunupáḍu. Tamil. From pillar of manḍapa of Puttanáthasvámi temple.]

TRANSLATION.

Hail! Prosperity! In the 27th year of the reign of the emperor of the three worlds, the glorious Kulóttuṅgachóḷadéva, I Madurántakapottapichóḷa *alias* Nallasidharasa gave with libation of water to the God at Tiruvengaḍam free of tax from the month of Chitra (of this year) the village of Vélúr in Melaippaṭṭayanáḍu including all kinds of taxes small and big (*chilvari* and *peruvari*) to last as long as the moon and sun.

I, Nallasiddarasa, (gave) to the god at Tiruvengaḍam. He who causes injury to this (charity) will incur the sin of killing a tawny cow and a Brahman on the banks of the Ganges.

[1] ஸ்வஸ்திஸ்ரீ திரிபு-
[2] வனச்சக்கிரவத்தி-
[3] கள் ஸ்ரீகுலோத்-
[4] துங்க சோழதே-

(To face page 406.)

PART OF GUDUR NO. 34.

[5] வற்கு யாண்டு
[6] உயிள வது சித்தி-
[7] ணைமாஸமுதல் ம-
[8] துராந்தகப்பொத்-
[9] தப்பிச்சொழநாக ந-
[10] ல்லசித்தரசனென்
[11] திருவெங்கடமுடை-
[12] டயானுக்குதிருவிடை-
[13] யாட்டமாக மெலை-
[14] ப்பட்டயநாட்டில்
[15] வெலூர் எப்பெற்-
[16] பட்ட சில்வரி பெருவ-
[17] ரி உட்படச்சந்திர-
[18] ாதித்தவரை செல்-
[19] லக்கடவதாக நி-
[20] ர் வாற்துக்குடுத்-
[21] தென் நல்லசித்த-
[22] ரசனென் திருவெ-
[23] ங்கடமுடை-
[24] யானுக்கு இது-
[25] க்கு அழிவுசெய்த-
[26] ாந் கெங்கைக்-
[27] கரையிற்குராற்ப-
[28] சுவும் பிராமண-
[29] னையும் கொந்-
[30] றான் பாபங்கொ-
[31] ள்வான்.

GUDUR (35).

[Gunupáḍu. Sanskrit in Grantha character. From ceiling of Puttanáthasvámi temple.]

TRANSLATION.

This states that one Bhímarája constructed a palace as pleasing as the Kailása to Mahádéva. The first few words evidently refer to some date.

[1] ஸ்ராஶ்விபஜ-
[2] ஹவஶ்ரா० ஶ்ரீ
[3] ஷீமராஜ நா-
[4] த்நா கேஸராஸ-
[5] கைலஸஶிவ-
[6] மமோநாஹம-
[7] ஹாதேவ-
[8] ப்ராஸாதஸ்தி-
[9] மகோரஸ
[10] ம०ஃ

GUDUR (36).

[Ípúru. Tamil. From north gate of Chenna-késava temple.]

TRANSLATION.

In the year Śobhakrit, Uśaka Muhamad, the son of Á. Silaimán erected (this) tomb and palli (mosque).

[1] ஸொர்[ப]க[ஞு]த்திவருஷம் ஆ-
[2] சிலேமான் மக-
[3] ன் உசகமுகமட்
[4] கல்லறையும் (ப்)-
[5] பள்ளியவாயும் வைத்தான்.

Gudur (37).

[Ípúru. Tamil. On lintel of south gate of Chenna-késava temple.]

This records that two rooms were built in the mosque and that wages were given by one Mulla Mohidin Shah and it refers to some land as belonging to the mosque. It ends with saying that he who obstructs this charity will not prosper for seven births.

[1] பள்ளிக்கு இரண்டு அறை கல்லாலெ ச-
[2] மைத்தொம் இது கூலிக்குடுத்து மொல்-
[3] லா மொகதின்சா . . ஒருவரும் தாதவில்-
[4] .. . த ஒண்ணுது பள்ளி நிலம் யாதொருத்த-
[5] ன் அகிதம் பண்ணின் எழுசன்ம நாசம் அகுவன்.

Gudur (38).

[Jatlakondúru (hamlet Bandepalli). Telugu. In field No. 138.]

Translation.

On the 13th of the dark fortnight of Kártika of the year Viródhi, corresponding to the Sálivâhana Saka year . . . . Rájasrí . . . . Ayyaváru granted this *mányam* to Hussain Muhammad. Those who protect it . . . . whoever obstructs and covets that *mányam* will go to perdition. In these terms is this edict issued.

Srí Ráma.

1. శాలివాహన శక
2. వరుషంబులు అగు నేటి

3. విరోధినామ సంవ్వత్సర (కా
4. ర్తిక) బహుల ౧౩ రాజశ్రీ . . .
5. య్యవారు హుసేనుమహాదు . .
6. నైకె ఇచ్చినమాన్యాం ఇదిపాలించెడువారు . . .
7. చెందనక ఆమాన్యంయవరు అ . . .
8. చ్చినాను అధోగతి బడువాండు ఇ-
9. ట్లనిబద్ధ । శ్రీరామ. ॥

GUDUR (39). (A.D. 1256–57.)

[Kistnapatam. Tamil. North wall of Siddhéṣvara-swámi temple.]

TRANSLATION.

Hail! Prosperity! In the expired Śaka year 1178 corresponding to the 13th year of the reign of the emperor of the three worlds, the glorious Víraréjéndra-chóḻadéva, on the date corresponding to Saturday with the *nakshatra* Róhini, the thirteenth day of the bright half of the month of Mahara, all the men of the town of Kollatturai *alias* Gaṇḍagópálapaṭṭana and the foreigners of the eighteen countries, having assembled together at the sacred flower garden of Désnáyakan attached to the temple of Chandirattiraipiḷḷaiyár, gave to the god Manu-masiddhéśvara of this town money (amount not clear owing to the portion being mutilated) (to be spent as follows):— . . . .

¼ *chinnam* for upper and lower female cloths.

1 *mádai* for a *vessel.*

1 *mádai* for *sacred ashes.*
¼ *mádai* for cloth.
¼ *mádai* for *vidava*.(not understood).
½ *mádai* for *kalava* (not understood).
⅛ *chinnam* for *kámarasavalli* (not understood).

We all—the townsmen (of Kollatturai) and the foreigners of the eighteen countries, gave the above, agreeing to continue (them) as long as the moon and sun last.

This (charity) is (placed under) the protection of all the Máhésvaras.

In the thirteenth year (of the reign of the above mentioned king), Urúdaiyán Madapalisvámi gave for sacred food to Tirupallirainácchiyár, (the goddess of the sacred bed-room), 300 *kulis* of arable land free of tax, to last as long as the moon, at Iruvulavánigi in Munaiyúr, (after) demarcating (the same) with stones.

In the 15th year (of the reign of the above mentioned king) under the order (according to the letter) of Manumasiddharasar, Ânda . . . kilán (*alias*) Tiruvarangamudaiyár gave, free of tax, to the above mentioned goddess . . . of arable land.

In the 16th year (of the reign of the above mentioned king) Danmapálan gave to the above mentioned goddess . . *kulis* of arable land to be spent on the great night (Sivarátri).

. NOTE.—The regnal year was first read as the 21st, but on check *in situ* seems to be the 13th. But the S.S. year also is not very clear.

[1] ஸ்வஸ்தி ஸ்ரீ சகரையாண்டு [௲ளஎ௰அ] செல்லாநின்ற தி-
ரிபுவனச்சக்கரவத்திகள் ஸ்ரீ வீரராஜெந்த்ர-

[2] சொழதெவ[ற்கு யாண்டு ௨௰]க வது மகரநாயற்று
பூர்வபக்ஷத்து த்ரயொதஸியும் சனி[க்கிழ]மையும்

[3] பெற்ற ரொஹணி நாள் கொல்லத்துறையான கண்ட-
கொபால பட்டினத்து ஊ[ர் வரும்] பதினெண்ஸமு-

[4] தி ஸமூஹ [வா] தெசிகளும் இவ்வனைவொம் சந்தாத்-
திளைப்பிள்ளையார் கொயிலில் தெசிநாயகன் திரு-நந்[தா]-

[5] வனத்து நிறைந்து இரு [ந்து] இவ்வூரில் உடையார்
மனுமஸித்திஸ்வரமுடையநாயனார்க்கு திருப்படி-

[6] [க்கு] . . . வை[த்து]க்குடுத்து [இவ்] வூர் தெ-
வற்கு மலைமண்டலத்தாண . . . இவ்வெரிக்கிழ் துறை
யனா-

[7] . . . . . த்து [மாடை] ஒன்றுக்[கு] கொள்ளு-
மவன் ஒருகாசுமவற்கு[ம] வன் ஒருகாசும் செ . . . .
க்காசு [ச]ய

[8] . . ற்கும் வ . . . க் கொன்றுக்குக்காசு சாசய
கொள்ளுமவன் கால்சின்னமும் புடவைக்கும் கிழாடைக்கு-

[9] [மாகதந்த] கால்சின்னமுமாக கலம் ஒன்றுக்கு மாடை
ஒன்றும் தொனூ[ருக்கு] மாடை ஒன்றும் வெட்டிக்கு

[10] மாடை கால் [விட]வுக்கு மாடை கால் கலவத்துக்கு
மாடை அரை காமரசவல்லிக்கு சின்னம் அரை தூ-

[11] [ளி]க்கு சின்னம் அரை ஆக இப்படி வைத்துக்குடுத்-
தமிது ஸஞ்ராதித்தவரை செல்லக்கடவதாக சம்மதி-

[12] த்தொம் ஊர்வரும் ஸமூஹபரதெசிகளும் இவ்வனை-
வொம் இது ஸ்ரீமாஹெஸ்வரரக்ஷை

[13] யரூவது . திருப்பள்ளியறைநாச்சியாருக்கு அமுது-
படிக்கு ஊருடையான் மடபளிசுவாமிகள் முனையூரில் இரு
வள-

[14] வாங்கியில் கல்லடித்து ஸஞ்ராதித்தவரை ஸர்வமானி
ய-மாகயிடுவித்த [துர்] ஒன்றினால் விளைநிலங்குழிமுன்னூறு.

[15] யரு-வது . மெற்படி[யாற்]கு நாயினார் மனுமசித்த-
னாசர் திருமுகப்படி ஸர்வமானியமாக ஆண்ட . . க்கிழான்
திருவர[ங்கமு]டையார்-

[16] [வை]த்த விளை நிலங்குழி . . . . . மேசா-வது மெற் படிய[ாற்கு] மஹாராராவுக்கு நன்றாக தன்மபால[கிடு] வித்த வி [ளைநிலங்]குழி . . . . .

Gudur (40).

[Kistnapatam. Telugu and Tamil. From a stone in a street bearing also a Tamil inscription.]

This is a grant given by certain *kápus* but the inscription is fragmentary and unintelligible.

వెలుసపా
శ్రా ?
టిలురాయ వి-భు
వేడిశను కాంపులు
నజ్యాచేను పెరికిం
పవత్తే్చరులకుంన్ను
తానాపంత్తులవారి
చెఱ్క ఇచ్చిన శాసనం
యీా పడిన ఆచం
క-స్త్రాయిగా
ను శాశనంము
ం మిపచ్చు ఇష్టవ
త్ర-నము నిండాను
కారిపు ఎక్కడినది
శ్రీ విరూపా
క్ష దేవరాను
మంగళముహా
శ్రీ శ్రీ శ్రీ

Gudur (41).

[Kistnapatam. Tamil. To the east in the dhoby's inam. Illegible.]

Gudur (42). (A.D. 1408-09.)

[Kistnapatam. Tamil. In a house in Ayyavárappa Khandriga.]

Translation.

Hail! Prosperity![1] In the expired Śaka year 1330 corresponding to the cyclic year Sarvadhári, during the reign of the glorious provincial chief (Mahámaṇḍaléśvara), Ráyavibhála, the chastiser of three kings (Múváráyaragaṇḍa), Víradévaráya, the son of Harihararáya, on Monday bearing the (nakshatra) *punarpúśa* the tenth day of the bright half of the month of Paṅguni, one . . . . the charity of Manusiddharaśa in Ponmanáśariyar street at Rájavibháṭapaṭṭinam in Nellúrnáḍu.

[1] ஸ்வஸ்திஸ்ரீமக் மஹாமண்டலெஸ்வரரு ராய விஹாடூ-ெ[வ] ராய

[2] ரமஹ்ணு[ர்] அரிஅரராயன் குமாரன் ஸ்ரீவிரதெவராயனுக்கு

[3] யாண்டு சகாப்தயாண்டு ௲௩௱௩௰ யிதன் மெல் செல்-

[4] லாநின்ற சவ்வதாரி வருஷம் பங்குனிமாதத்து பூ-[ர்வ]பக்ஷத்து தசமியும்-

[5] புனர்பூசமும் திங்கள்கிழமையும் பெ[ப*]ற்ற நாள் [நெல்லூ]ர் நாட்டில் இராயவிபாட-

[6] ன்பட்டினத்தில் பொன்மஞசரியர் தெருவில் மனுமசித்தரயர் தன்ம ஒரு

[7] . . . .

---

[1] These two words are in Telugu charactor.

GUDUR (43).

[Kistnapatam. Tamil. From a stone bearing also a Telugu inscription. It consists of two fragments which are unintelligible.]

[1] செலுத்-
[2] த கடவெ-
[3] ன் இந்தப்ப-
[4] . . க்குத்த-
[5] ங்ககட்டு.
[6] ணல்லாதவ-
[7] லபா
[8] நாரணெ

[1] ரதன் காளுசெ-
[2] ப்பாதெ . கள-
[3] ற்லும் . லெ
[4] நாற்பால் எல்லை-
[5] யில் இதற்கு கு-
[6] டிகளும் . லு
[7] மெல் வடக்கெ-
[8] லும் குடிகளுக்கு-
[9] ம் குடுத்த சிலை
[10] சாதனம் இப்பட்-
[11] டணத்துக் குச்-
[12] சந்தானம் இல்-
[13] லாதவொருலு-

GUDUR (44).

[Kistnapatam. Tamil. From steps of shrine of Siddhêṣvara temple.]

Abstract.

This inscription which is dated in the 26th year of the reign of some king (name not clear) records the erection of a *gópuram* and a *maṇḍapam* for some Vaishnava god (*perumáḷ*), and the gift of 300 *pon* the sale-proceeds of certain lands for oblations of rice and a lamp to the same god.

[1] . . . . . . யாண்டு உ௰௬ ஆவது ரக்க . . . . . ஸ்ரீ-

[2] மாக . . . . ள . . . ணத்தில் மலைமண்-டலத்து . லகூத்தா-

[3] டை . . . . ப் பெருமாள் சந்திராத்திரை-மண்டபத்திற்கும்

[4] லை . . . . . . கொபுரமு மண்டபமும் கட்டுவித்து

[5] . . . . டகித்த . . குடி வெரி . . . . கூவிக்கும் இடையநா . . . வித்து-

[6] [கொயில் பிரா]மணர் வசம் அமுதுக்கு ஸாவ . . . நெய் . . .

[7] . . . . . . ய் திருவிளக்குக்கு ஸால இருநா . . . . . அமுதுக்கு நில-

[8] . . . . . . செயளந்து விற்று வருஷ௪ ஒன்றுக்கு அமுதுக்கு மு-

[9] ந்நூறு பணம் பிராமணர் கையில் குடுத்து நின்றது திரு . . .

[10] . . . . . . த்துவராகவும் இந்த தன்மத்துக்கு நன்மை செய்தவன் தலை

[11] . . . . ப் பிள்ளையாரும் இளைய நயினை

Gudur (45). (A.D. 1279–80.)

[Kistnapatam. Tamil. From south wall of Siddhéṣvara temple.]

Translation.

Hail! Prosperity! In the expired Śaka year 1201 which corresponded to the 2nd year of the reign of the emperors of the three worlds, the glorious Irumaḍi Tirukkáḷattidéva, the merchants of the *náḍus*, towns, hills and the five *manḍalams* and all the five hundred foreigners (coming from) the other illustrious eighteen countries (residing in) Kóḻḻitturai *alias* Gaṇḍagópálapaṭṭanam assembled at Tirukkávaṇam on the date (corresponding to) Saturday, the 10th day of the bright half of the month of Mína which bore the *nakshatra* Róhini. (According to their proposals) we gave for expenses connected with building, sacred food and ornaments for the god Manumasiddhísvara of this village, one-fourth per cent. on the appraised cost of all the bags exported and imported at this port.

We, all the merchants from the *náḍus*, towns, hills and five *manḍalams* and all the foreigners from all the eighteen countries, gave this one-fourth per cent. to be paid to this deity as long as the moon and sun last.

This (charity) is (placed under) the protection of all the *Máhéṣvaras*.

[1] ஸ்வஸ்தி ஸ்ரீ சகரையாண்டு ௲௨௱௧ செல்லாநின்ற திரி-புவனச்சக்க-

[2] ரவத்திகள் ஸ்ரீ இருமடிதிருக்காளத்திதெவர்க்கு யாண்-டு ௨-வது செ-

[3] கால்லித்துறையான கண்டகொபாலபட்டினத்து நாடு-நக-

[4] ரமலைமண்டலம் ஐஞ்சு உள்ளுவணி கம்பிபதினெண்-
பூமி ஸுதேஸபாதே-

[5] சிகளும்இவ்வனைவொம் ஐந்நூற்றுவன் திருக்காவண-
த்து நிறைந்து

[6] இருந்து செய்தபடி மினகாயற்றுவ—முல்லு—வெவக்ஷத்து-
உஹஸியும் ச[னி]க்-

[7] கிழமையுமான ரொஹணி நா[ள்*] இவ்வூரில் உடை-
யார் மனுமலிஸி-

[8] ஸ்ரீ உடைய நாயனார்க்கு திருப்பணி அமுதுபடி சாத்-
துப்-

[9] படி உள்ளிட்டனவைய்யிற்றுக்கு உடலாக வைத்துக்-
கொடுத்த இவ்-

[10] வூர்த்துறையில் எறு சாக்கு இறங்கு சாக்குகள் மதிக்கு
மிடத்து

[11] நூற்றுக்குக்கால் வைத்துக்குடுத்தொம் இந்நூற்றுக்-
குக்கா-

[12] லும் இந்நாயனார்க்கு சந்திராதித்யவரை செல்லக்கடவ
தாக

[13] வைத்துக்குடுத்தொம் நாடு நகரம் மலைமண்டலம்

[14] ஐஞ்சு வண்ணவணி குரம்பி நாநாதெசிய பதினெண்-
ஷ—மிஸு-

[15] தேஸ்வாரதெசிகள் இவ்வனைவொம் இது ஸ்ரீ ராஜ-

[16] ஸ்ரீ ரக்ஷை

GUDUR (46). (A.D. 1548–49.)

[Kistnapatam. Telugu. To south near Salt Cottars.]

TRANSLATION.

May it be well! On Wednesday the 4th of the bright fortnight of Bhádrapada of the year Kílaka, corresponding to the year 1470 of the illustrious, victorious and prosperous Ṣáliváhana Ṣaka era, Venkana, son of

Achchinéni Rámanáyaḍu, the agent of Ṣríman Mahámaṇḍaléṣvararámaráju Timmayadéva Mahárajulu Gáru issued this charitable edict . . . . the charitable edict granting as a *sarvamánya* . . . . Ṣrí Ráma

1. శుభమస్తు
2. స్వస్తి శ్రీ జయాభ్యు
3. దయ శాలివాహ
4. న శకవర్షంబులు
5. ౧౪౭౦ అగునే
6. ంటి కీలక సంవ
7. త్సర భాద్రపద శు ౪
8. బు । శ్రీ మన్మహామ
9. ండలేశ్వర రామరా
10. జు తింమయదేవ
11. మహారాజులుం
12. గారి కార్యకర్త
13. లైన అచ్చినేని రా
14. మినాయని కొడుకు
15. వెంకన చేయించ్ని ధర్మ

Second side.

1. . . . .
2. . . . .
3. . . . . . .
4. . . . . . .
5. . . . . . . చేయంగ
6. . . . . . . చ్చిన
7. నాము . . . ను.

8. . న . . . . .
9. సర్వ మాన్యంగా
10. ను. ఇచ్చినధర్మశాసనం.
11. . వ్య . భః రు .
12. శికి . . ణ్యం
13. . . . . .

Third side.

1. . . . .
2. ం తినువాడు.
3. శ్రీరామ
4. . . .
5. . . .
6. యొకంబు .
7. యు త . .
8. . . . .
9. . . . .
10. . . . .

GUDUR (47).

[Kistnapatam. Telugu. In field to west. Mostly illegible.]

GUDUR (48).

[Kóṭa. Telugu. Opposite Sóméṣvara temple.]

TRANSLATION.

On the second of the bright fortnight of Mágha of the year Kálayukti, Ṣríman Mahámaṇḍaléṣvara Aliya

(Rávulaya) Dévamahárájulum Gáru, the agent (kár-yakartá) of Ṣrímad Rájádhi Rája, Rája Paraméṣvara, Ṣrí Sadáṣiva Déva Mahárájulayyavaru, issued this charitable edict . . . to barber Konḍóji . . . as a *sarva-mánya* . . . to last as long as the sun and moon exist. Those who cause obstacles to it will incur the sin of killing a cow and a Brahman.

Note—This Konḍoji receives a grant in P. 35 and K.G. 20 also. *For* Rávulaya *read* Rámaya?

1. కాళయుక్తి సంవ
2. త్సరమా ఘ శు ౨ లు
3. శ్రీ మద్రాజాధిరా
4. జరాజ పరమేశ్వర
5. శ్రీ సదాసివ దేవమ
6. హారాజు లయ్య .
7. వారి కార్యకర్తలైన
8. శ్రీమత్ మహామహా
9. మండలేశ్వర అలి
10. య (రావులయ) దే
11. వ మహారాజుల
12. ం గారు మంగళ
13. కొండోజికి

Second side.

14\. . మంగ . .

15\. . మాకు చ .

16\. . . చలద్వల

17\. . . రిబతివారి

18\. . . . . .

19\. . . . . .

20\. . . . . . .న్యం
21\. చెయించిన ధర్మశాసనం
22\. ముల . .
23\. . . . .
24\. . వినహాగాను సర్వఁమా
25\. గాను . . . . సూర్య చంద్రు
26\. లుగలంత కాలము . .
27\. . . విఘలింబు చే
28\. సిన గో బ్రాంహ్మలం
29\. వధించిన పాపానం
30\. బోయిన వారు.

GUDUR (49).

[Kurucherlapáḍu. Telugu. East of village on tank bund.]

TRANSLATION.

The edict issued by Surabhiváru on . . . . of the bright fortnight of Áshádha of the year Raudri for the religious merit of Venkaṭapati Ráyuḍu. Whoever appropriates the *méra* grain of the tank and does not give it will be regarded as having been born to a donkey.

On one *puṭṭi* 1 kuncham and 2 measures.

1\. రౌద్రి సంవత్స
2\. ర ఆషాఢ శుద్ధ . . .
3\. వెంకటపతిరా .
4\. ఇవికి పుణ్యంగా
5\. సురభివారు వే
6\. ఇంచిన శాసనం

7. చెఱ్వు మేరధాన్య
8. ం ఇయ్యక ఏవ
9. రు పుచ్చుకుం
10. న్నా గాడిదెకు
11. పుట్టిన వాడు
12. ఖ ౧ కి ౦౦ ౹౨

GUDUR (50). (A.D. 1192–93 or 1193–94.)

[Kurucherlapáḍu. Tamil. To west of village in a yard.]

TRANSLATION.

Hail! Prosperity! In the expired Ṣaka year 1114 corresponding to the cyclic year Pramádi, which was the 16th year of the reign of the emperor of the three worlds, the glorious Kulóttuṅgachóḻadéva, on Saturday, with the (*Nakshatra*) Anusha of the bright half of the month of Makara, Madurántakapóttapichóḻan (*alias*) Rájagaṇḍa-gópálan *alias* the glorious Ranganáthan (gave) to (the god) Gópálaperumáḷ at Nellúr *alias* Vikramasingapuram (situated) in Paḍaináḍu in Chedikulamáṇikkavaḷanáḍu (a sub-division) of Jayankoṇḍachóḻamaṇḍalam land in Nellúr tank in Siṅgapaináḍu as exclusive property as a *sarvamánya* free of tax to last as long as the sun and moon endure.

NOTE.—The cyclic and S.S. years differ by a year. *For* Singapai we should probably *read* Singaṭṭai. The Ṣaka date was first transcribed as 1131 but on check *in situ* appears as 1114.

[1] ஸ்வஸ்தி ஸ்ரீ சகரையாண்டு
[2] ஆ[ா]ண்டிக செல்லா நி[ன்]-
[3] ற [ப்ரமாதி] ஸம்வத்ஸ-

[4] ரத்து திரிபுவனச்சக்க-
[5] ரவத்திகள் [ஸ்ரீ குலோத்து]-
[6] [ங்க சோழதேவர்]க்கு யா-
[7] ண்டு ய[சா]ஆவது மகரநாய-
[8] ற்று [வ—லு—பக்ஷ]த்து [சனிக்கிழ]-
[9] மையில் அனுழமும் பெற்றநாள்
[10] ஜயங்கொண்டசோழமண்-
[11] டலத்துச் செதிக்குலமாணிக்-
[12] கவனநாட்டுப்படைநாட்-
[13] டு நெல்லூரான விக்கிரமசிங்-
[14] கபுரத்து
[15] கோபாலபெருமாளு-
[16] க்கு மதுராந்தகப்பொத்-
[17] தப்பிச்சோழன் இராஜ-
[18] கண்டகோபாலன் ஆன
[19] ஸ்ரீரங்கநாதன் சிங்க-
[20] பைநாட்டு [நல்]லூர் செ-
[21] லவிலவர் திருவிடை-
[22] யாட்டமாகச் சந்திரா
[23] தித்தவரை ஸலு—மாணியம-
[24] ாக செல்வதாக வித்து

. . . .

Gudur (51).

[Maḍamannúru. Tamil. From tank bed. Incomplete.]

Translation.

Hail! Prosperity! In the thirty-second year of the reign of the emperor of the three worlds, the glorious Tribhuvanavíradéva, Iráyán Koḷaraivachchiyán Akkan of Murinóttamangalam (situated) in Valluvanádu (a sub-division of Malaimandalam dug a tank in (the village of) Maduvanúr (situated) in Singattainádu (a sub-division) of Jayankondachólamandalam. For the protection of this tank and this village he gave at the place where the ceremonies for the protection of the village were performed two *pattitarai* (pattis of land?) one *pattitarai* to Śríkári Máśidáśar for a sacred flower garden and one *pattitarai* to Tirumanojñadáśardáśar for the sacred kitchen, for the god at Tiruvéngadam.

. . . .

NOTE.—Tribhuvana Víradéva is a name of Kulottunga III. *See* p. 220, Vol. IV, p. 199, Vol. V, and pp. 135 and 136 of Vol. VII, E.I.

[1] ஸ்வஸ்தி ஸ்ரீ த்ரிபுவநச்சக்ரவத்திகள் ஸ்ரீ த்ரி-
[2] புவனவீரதெவர்க்கு யாண்டு முப்பத்திர-
[3] ண்டாவது ஜயங்கொண்டசொழமண்டல-
[4] த்துச்சிங்கட்டைநாட்டு மடுவனூரில் மலை-
[5] மண்டலத்து வள்ளுவநாட்டு முரிநொத்தமங்-
[6] கலத்து இராயான் கொளரைவச்சியான் அக்-
[7] கன் ஏரி கல்லி இவ்வூர்க்கு ரக்ஷை பண்ணி-
[8] ன இடத்து இவ்வேரிக்கும் ஊர்க்கும் ரக்ஷை-
[9] யாகத்திருவெங்கடஉடையானுக்குத்திரு-
[10] நந்தவனத்துக்கு ஸ்ரீகாரி மாசிதாஸர் வசம் ஒ-
[11] ருப்பட்டிதறையுமடப்புறத்துக்கு திருமனொ-
[12] [ஜ்ஞ]தாஸர்தாஸர் வசம் ஒரு பட்டிதரையுமின்னல் இ-
[13] ரண்டு பட்டிதறையும் படிக்கு கிழக்குப்பொக

* * * *

Gudur (52). (A.D. 1712–13.)

[Maḍamannúru, Telugu. In a street.]

Translation.

Hail! On the 10th of the bright fortnight of Kártika of the year Nandana, corresponding to the illustrious, victorious and prosperous Ṣáliváhana Ṣaka year 1634, Gurappallita Bhásandáru, the secretary (mudrakarta) of Rávéla Muddukrishṇappa Náyani Váru issued this charitable edict for the tanks of Madamanúru. They should give 1 *túm* in each *puṭṭi* of all grain and produce raised in this village. Whoever, not maintaining this, covets or causes obstacles will incur the sin of killing a cow and a Brahman on the Ganges, and will be regarded as having been born in the womb of a donkey. If any one injures this his wife will be ravished by a Mádiga.

1. స్వస్తి శ్రీ జయాభ్యుదయ
2. శాలివాహన శకవర్షంబులు ౧
3. ౬౩౪ అగునేటి నందన సంవత్సర
4. కార్తిక శు ౧౦ లు రావేలముద్దుక్రి
5. ష్ణప్పనాయనివారి ముద్రకర్త గురప్ప
6. ల్లి (త) భాసంగారు మడమ నూరు చెరు
7. వులకు వేయించిన ధర్మశాసనం
8. యీగ్రామాన పండ్డిన నానాధాన్యము
9. సకలాయుఖ ౧కి ౦౧ యివ్వగలవారు
10. యివ్వరునడిపించకున్న యివ్వరు అపేక్షి
11. ంచ్చినా యివ్వరు విఘాతం చేశినా వా
12. ండు గంగకర్త గోబ్రాంణిం జంపినవాండు
13. ను వారు గాడిదకడుపునబుట్టేను
14. యిందుకు యవరు తప్పేట్టు

15. చెశినా పాడాలిని మాదిగవాం
16. డు దెంగ్గేది

GUDUR (53).

[Mallam. Tamil. East wall of Subrahmanyéṣvara temple.]

TRANSLATION.

Hail! Prosperity! In the 26th year of the reign of the emperor of the three worlds, the glorious Kulottuṅga Choḷadéva, who was pleased to take Madurai and the crowned head of the Páṇḍyan, I, Peddaraśar the son of Rájarájapaṭṭaivattiyarasar, the lord of the best of cities Ahischatra, the lord of the Phaṇámaṇḍala, Ṣivapádasékhara, who belonged to the pure Atríya gótra, gave to the god Subrahmanyapiḻḻaiyar at Tiruvánbúr (situated) in Kíḻa paṭṭaiyanáḍu in Paiyúriḻaṅgóṭṭam (a sub-division) of Jayankoṇḍachóḻamaṇḍalam, as temple lands, in the lands belonging to (the village of) Iṇaiyúr.

This land is bounded on the west by the big road of Rájarájan, on the north by the tank bund, on the east by the boundary of Árúr and on the south by the boundary of Kongil. I, Peddarasan, the son of Rájarájapaṭṭavattiyarasar gave all the lands enclosed within the above-mentioned four boundaries, wherever the monitor lizard runs and the tortoise creeps, demarcated with stones as temple land, with all the taxes taken off, to last as long as the moon and the sun, the same being engraved in stone.

Those who cause hindrance to this charity shall incur the sin of killing a tawny cow on the banks of the Ganges.

The feet of those who protect this charity are on my head.

This (charity is placed under) the protection of all the Máhéśvaras.

NOTE.—Among the mean and miserable religious edifices of Nellore, the Subramanya temple at Mallam or, rather, the Maṇḍapam thereof may pass as ornate. The Telugu people seem never to have possessed the architectural skill of the Tamils. The original type of temple in Nellore seems to be a plain oblong building with a roof slightly barrelled externally and containing a cell faced by a few squat pillars. Sometimes the outer wall is broken up into pillars; oftener the wall is solid. We take the opportunity to suggest that the well-known *Amalaka* ornamentation which is common here as elsewhere is a representation of the common pumpkin known here as gummaḍi káya (*Cucurbita maxima*).

[1] ஸ்வஸ்திஸ்ரீ திரிபுவனசக்கரவத்திகள் மதுரையும் பாண்டி-யன் முடித்த-

[2] லையுங்கொண்டருளிய ஸ்ரீ குலோத்துங்கசோழதேவற்-கு யாண்டு

[3] உ௰சுவது ஜெயங்கொண்டசோழமண்டலத்துப்பை-யூரிளங்கோட்டத்து-

[4] க்கிழைப்பட்டையகாட்டுத் திருவான்யூர் ஸுப்ர-ஹ்மண்யபிள்ளையாற்கு ஸ-

[5] ஹிஷ்த்ரவாரவாராயஸ்ல ப்ரஹ்மதேஸாயிவதி [ஷ]ணா-ஜ்ஞய-

[6] ராயிஸர ஸிவபாதஸேகர ஞுதேரயமோதரவகிர இராஜ-

[7] [ர]ாஜப்பட்[டைவ]த்தியரசர் மகன் பெத்தரசனென் இன்றையனுற்[கு]

[8] தெவதானமாக இவையூர் நிலத்தில் இராரான்[1] பெரு-வ[ழி]க்கு மெற்-

[1] Read இராஜராஜன்.

(To face page 429.)

GUDUR NO. 54.

[9] கும் ஓட்டை ஏரிக்கரைக்கு வடக்கும் ஆறூர் எல்லைக்கு கிழக்கு-

[10] ம் கொங்கில் எல்லைக்குத் தெற்கும் இன்னான்கு எல்லை-க்கு

[11] உட்பட்ட நிலம் உடும்பொடி ஆமை நடந்த நிலம் எ-

[12] ல்லாம் எப்பெற்பட்ட இறைகளுந்தவுர்த்து இறையிலி-

[13] தெவதானமாக சந்த்ராதித்தவரை செல்வதாக நாற்பால் எல்லையுங்-

[14] கல்லு நட்டு ஶிலாலெகை பண்ணிக்குடுத்தென் இரா-ஜராஜ-

[15] பட்டை[வ]த்திஆரசர் மகன் பெத்தாசனென் இத் தன்மத்துக்கு

[16] இலங்கணம் பண்ணுவார் கங்கைக்கரையிற்குரால் பசு--

[17] க் கொன்றான் பாபத்தைப்படுவான் இத்தர்மத்தை ரக்ஷி-ப்-

[18] பான் வாதங்கள் என்தலை மெலெ இதுவஜாலெஹ-

[19] ஹூராரலெக்ஷ

Gudur (54).

[Mallam. Tamil in character of the Pallava type. From the floor of the Subrahmanyéśvara temple.]

Translation.

Hail! Prosperity! In the 15th year of the reign of Nandipóttaraśar, we, the men of the district (náḍu), the villagers and the heads of assemblies, gave at the order of Chaḷukkiaraśar on the petition of Áḷuvaarasar to (the god) Subrahmanya at Tiruvánbúr (situated) in Paiyyúriḷaṅgóṭṭam, 35 kaḷañji of gold given in that year and also the kaḷañju of gold given by Maduvár for (maintaining) lamps (?)

May this charity be not interfered with.

[1] ஸ்வஸ்தி ஸ்ரீ நந்திப்பொத்தரசர்க்கு[ப்ப]-
[2] திணைந்தாவது பெய்யூரிள[ங்கொ]-
[3] ட்ட[த்*]து திருவான்பூர் ஸபாஸர்வஜனமு[ம் அ]-
[4] [வ்]வ,[ற்]றைப்பொக் அபிம்[பத்தைங்க]-
[5] மூஞ்சி [கொ]ள்ளும் மதுவாரட்டு[வித்த]
[6] கழஞ்சு பொன்னும் விளக்க . . .
[7] [ப்] புறமாக ஆ[ளுவ]அரசர் வி[ண்ண]-
[8] ப்பத்தினுக் சளுக்கிஅரசராண-
[9] த்தியாக ப்பணித்தொம் நாட்டா-
[10] ரும் ஊராரும் ஆள்வாரும். அரமறவற்க

GUDUR (55 TO 80).

Mallam.

The Subramanya temple at Mallam is covered with Tamil inscriptions, all of which have been translated. Some have been given above. The rest relate merely to grants of land, money, lamps and so on and it would be a waste of labour to print them *in extenso*. A summary is given below. The village is described as Tiruvánbúr, situated in Okkáṭṭunáḍu in Kíḻaippaṭṭaiyanáḍu in Paiyúrilaṅgoṭṭam, a sub-division of Jayankoṇḍachoḻa-maṇḍalam.

(55) 26th of Kulóttunga Chóḻa. Donor Uḍaiyappa-náyakkan.

(56) 27th of Rájarájadéva. Donor Chémiyánḍán son of Sámi Ruttan *alias* Nánádési Malaimaṇḍala Náḍáḻván.

(57) 24th of Vijayagaṇḍagópáladéva. Donor Sataya Vaḻittunai Apparaśa.

(58) 11th of Rájarájadéva. Donor Siddaraśa, brother-in-law of Madurántaka Pottapi Chóḻa *alias* Erasiddaraśa.

(To face page 430.)

GUDUR NO. 66.

(To face page 430.)

GUDUR NO. 75.

(59) 19th of Rájarájadéva. Donor Maduràntaka Pottapichóḷa *alias* Erasiddaraśa.

(60) 13th of Rájarájadéva. Donor Maduràntaka Pottapichóḷa *alias* Tirukkálattidéva *alias* Gaṇḍagópála.

(61) 9th of Rájarájadéva. Donor Aṭṭamasiddi Bhuvané Kaní Kadhéran *alias* Páṇḍya Gaja Késari *alias* Rája Brahma Chóḷa Vaitumbana *alias* Vaṇan Mahárájan *alias* Madanudévan *alias* Dasaiyaraśan.

(62) 4th of Rájarájadéva. Donor Chíramáṇḍai.

(63) 20th of Vikrama Varmadéva.

(64) A.D. 1314–15.

(65) 5th of Rájarájadéva. Donor Vikramachóḷa Múvendavéḷán *alias* Eriyamireḍḍi Muppi Reḍḍi.

(66) A.D. 1289–90. Donors Sáminàyakkar, Sandamanáyakkar and another.

(67) 9th of Víragaṇḍa Gópáladéva. Donor Tyágasamudrapaṭṭai Mallidévaraśan.

(68) Donor Návan Póyáṇḍán.

(69) 21st of Vijayagaṇḍa Gópáladéva. Donors the Cheṭṭis of Vikramasingapuram *alias* Nellúr.

(70) 36th of Kulóttungachóḷa.

(71) 12th of Rájarájadéva. Donor Chenavaṇi *alias* Iḍaikkamináṭṭuvéḷán *alias* Pichchan *alias* Tiruvékambamuḍaiyán *alias* Rájánáráyaṇavéḷán.

(72) 17th of Kulóttungachóḷa. Donor Sivapútan *alias* Vánavanáyakan *alias* Baladévan.

(73) 22nd of Rájárájadéva. Donor Maruduḷán, the commander-in-chief (senápati) of Ulagáḷuḍaiyan (the ruler of the world).

(74) 21st of Vijayagaṇḍagópáladéva. Donors Álikkonraikiḷán *alias* Irájamallan *alias* Karumbáṇḍai and his brother Peṛṛu Piḷḷai.

(75) 11th of Vijayagaṇḍa Gópáladéva. Donor Chakkama Reḍḍi, son of Viḷakkandai Káviriyár *alias* Vikramachóḻa Múvveḷár *alias* Muppi Reḍḍiyár.

(76) 27th of Kulóttungachóḻa. Donor Mayilamadévi Pattaraśa, son of Madurántaka Pottapichóḻa *alias* Nallasiddaraśa.

(77) 3rd of Alluntirukkáḷattidéva *alias* Gaṇḍagópála Mahárája. Donor Tiruchchiṟṟambalamuḍaiyán *alias* Váḻavaṇḍán.

(78) 18th of Rájárájadéva (who took Madura and the crowned head of the Páṇḍyan). Donor Śiddaraśa, son of Kulóttungachóḻa paṭṭai Śékharadéva, the lord of the best of towns Ahischatrapura, the lord of the middle country, the lord of the Paṇamaṇḍala, having the *biruda* Śivapádaśékhara and belonging to the Átriya *gótra*.

(79) 21st of Rájarájadéva. Donor Tirukkáḷattivéḷán, son of Vilakkandai Káviri *alias* Vikramachóḻa Múvéndavéḷán *alias* Muppi Reḍḍi.

(80) 27th of Vijayagaṇḍagópáladéva. Donor Déśavéḷán *alias* Tennaviḻupparaiyan *alias* Varantarumperumál.

Gudur (81).

[Muṭṭumbáka. Tamil. To the west in No. 136. Illegible.]

Gudur (82). (A.D. 1533–34.)

[Muttukúr. Telugu. South of village.]

Translation.

Prosperity! May it be well! On the 30th of the dark fortnight of Vaiṣákha of the year Vijaya, corresponding to the illustrious, victorious and prosperous Sáliváhana

Ṣaka year 1456, Tiṃmanáyaningáru, the agent of the affairs (káryakartá) of Ṣríman Mahámanḍaléṣvara Salaká (Ráju ?) Tirumala Déva Maháráyalu, after making obeisance, issued this charitable edict to Nágéṣvara Déva of Muttukúru. The village of Muttukúru in Sariyapalli *Síma* is granted with gift of gold and libation of water to you . . . . for providing worship with incense and lamps, daily offerings, and all enjoyments and marriage festivities for the religious merit of Tirumalaráya . . . . after making salutations . . . . therefore this charitable edict has been issued so that the deity may enjoy the charity as long as the sun and moon endure.

[One imprecatory verse.]

Charitable edict on stone.

[Another imprecatory verse.]

May it cause great prosperity !

Whoever injures this edict . . . .

First side.

1. శ్రీశుభమస్తు
2. స్వస్తిశ్రీవిజ
3. యాభ్యుద
4. యశాలివా
5. హానశకవ
6. రుషంబులు
7. ౧౪౫౬ అగు
8. విజయ సంవ
9. త్సరవయి
10. శాఖబ ౩౦
11. ముత్తుకూరి

12. నాగేశ్వరదేవు
13. నికి శ్రీమన్మ
15. హామండలేశ్వర
16. సలకా . . .
17. తిరుమలదే
18. వ మహారాయుల
19. వారి కార్యకర్త
20. లయినట్టి తిం
21. మ్మనాయనింగా
22. రు దండముసమర్పి
23. ంచ్చియిచ్చిన ధర్మ
21. శాసనం. సరియపల్లి
25. శీమలోను ముత్తుకూ
26. రిగ్రామం మీ (.)

Second side.

27. . . . .
28. ధూపదీప నైవేద్యా
29. లకును అంగ్గరంగ్గవైబ
30. భవాలకును తిరుమ
31. ల రాయవారికి పు
32. ణ్యంగాను సహిర
33. ణ్యోదక దానధారా
34. పూర్వకముగాను దే
25. వునికి కల్యాణం అ
36. వధరించడముకు .
37. . . . డండము.
28. సమర్పించ్చి సర్వ.
33. . . . . గనుక

40. ఇ అ . . .
41. ఆచంద్రార్కము
42. గాను అవధరి
43. ంపునని దండం
44. సమర్పించియిచ్చి
45. నధర్మశాసనము । స్వద
46. త్తాంద్విగుణంపుణ్యం
47. పరదత్తానుపాలనం ప
48. రదత్తాపహారేణ స్వ
49. దత్తం నిష్ఫలం భవేత్
50. శిలాధర్మశాసనము.

Third side.

51. దానపాల
52. నయోర్మధ్యే
53. దానాచ్ఛ్రే
54. యోనుపాల
55. నం దానా
56. స్వర్గమవా
57. ప్నోతి పాలన
58. త అచ్చుదం।
59. పదం ॥
60. శ్రీ శ్రీ శ్రీ
61. ం జేయును
62. యీధర్మశాస
63. నం చెప్పిన
64. అహారిం
65. చిన విర
66. (చారుండు)

67. . . .

68. . . .

69. . . .

70. . . .

71. . . .

GUDUR (83). (Subsequent to A.D. 1791–92.)

[Mutyálapáḍu (hamlet Writersaṭram). Telugu. Near the Chattiram.]

TRANSLATION.

Hail! Prosperity! On the 15th of the bright fortnight of Jyéshṭha of the year Viródhikṛit in the Ṣáliváhana year 1713, Kaligiri Venkaṭáchalam Gáru caused a reservoir to be dug in the fields of Mutyálpáḍu on the road leading to Káṣi and Rámésvaram, constructed a rest house in the village and continued the charity. Afterwards his second brother, Kaligiri Rámayya Gáru continued the charity in the same manner. Then his third brother Kaligiri Ṣéshayya continued the charity in his days and after him the above said Venkaṭáchalayya Gáru's grandson, Kaligiri Sundarayya maintained the charity for a few days and on the 5th of the bright fortnight of Mágha of the year Durmukhi constructed a charitable rest house and a tiled house and entered the house on Thursday, the 2nd of the dark fortnight of Áshádha of the year Ṣárvari (?)

1. స్వస్తి శ్రీ । శా । వా । ౧౭౧౩ । విరోధికృతునామ సంవ్స

2. త్సర జేష్టశుద్ధ ౧౫ లు కలిగిరివెంకటాచలంగారు ము

3. త్యాలపాటి పొలంలో కాశీరామేశ్వరపు ఘాటలో
4. కోనేరు తొవ్వించ్చి వూరితో సత్రంకట్టించి ధర్మం
5. నడిపిస్తువచ్చినారు తదనంతరం వారి రెండో స
6. హోదరుడయిన కలిగిరి రామయ్యగారు అ
7. దేప్రకారం ధర్మంజరిగిస్తువచ్చిన తర్వాత మూడో స
8. హోదరుడయ్ను కలిగిరి శేషయ్యగారున్ను ఆ ధ
9. ర్మంపరిపాలనచేస్తూవచ్చి ఆయనదినములలోను
10. న్ను వారికి పింమ్మటనున్ను సదరహి వెంకటాచలయ్యగా
11. రి మనముడైన కలిగిరి సుందగయ్య కొన్నిదినములు సదరు
12. ప్రకారం ధర్మమునడిపిస్తువచ్చి దుర్ముఖి సంవత్సర మాఖశ్శు
౫ లు
13. ధర్మసత్రం పెంకుటియిల్లు కటించి శార్వరిసం॥ ఆషా
14. ఢ శు ౨ గురువారం॥ శ్రీం॥ మం॥ గృహప్రవేశం అయ్ను
॥ ౭ ॥

GUDUR (84). (A.D. 1688–89.)

[Nárikéḷḷapalli. Telugu. In a street.]

TRANSLATION.

Hail! On . . . . of the bright fortnight of Pushya of the year Vibhava, corresponding to the year 1610 of the illustrious Ṣáliváhana Ṣaka era, under the orders of Rávela Muddu Krishnappa Náyaniváru, Yiravarapu Timmanna Gáru granted this charitable edict . . . . it is ordered that *kunchams* should be collected for the tank in the village of Nárikéḷḷapuri which was granted to us as an *amaram* in Sariyapalli *síma* . . . . they should do work to the tank with the grain. The méradar or amaradar or the sandháta, whoever rules the village, should do work to the tank and not covet the tank *méras.* Whoever covets the tank *kunchams* will incur the sin of killing a cow and a Brahman on the Ganges. The wife of the man who covets that grain will be given to the Veṭṭi. In these terms has the charitable edict been issued.

Ṣrí Ráma.

Ṣrí.

1. (స్వస్తి శ్రీ శాలివా)హన శ
2. క వర్షంబులు (౧౬.౧౦) అగు
3. విభ సంవత్సర పుష్యశు
4. . లు రావేలముద్దు క్రి
5. ష్ణప నాయనివారి ఆన
6. మితిని యిరవగపు తి
7. ంమ్మనంగారు వేయి
8. ంచ్చిన ధర్మశాసనం స
9. రియపల్లి శీమలోను
10. మాకు అమరానకుపా
11. లించిన నారికేళ్లపు
12. రిగ్రామాన చెరువు
13. . . . . . చ్చాలు
14. . చుం . . . ధాన్య
15. ము చెరువుపనిముఖం

Second side.

16. శేయించగలవారు
17. మేర అమరం . .
18. సంధాతన . .
19. ం థోరయవరు రమేలి
20. నాను చెరువుమేరధా
21. న్యం ఆశించక చెర్వు

22. పనిముఖం చెయిం
23. చం గలవారు చెర్వుకు
24. ంచాలధాన్యం యివ్వ
25. రు ఆశించినాను గ
26. ంగ్గక స్త్రీ గో బ్రాంహ్మ
27. ణ వధించ్చిన పాపాన
28. ం బోదురు ఆధాన్యం
29. ఆశించినవాని ఆలిని
30. వెట్టివానికి యిచ్చేది.
31. యిట్లని వేయించిన
32. ధర్మశాసనం శ్రీరా
33. మా శ్రీ శ్రీ శ్రీ శ్రీ

Gudur (85). (A.D. 1263–64.)

[Punjulúrupáḍu. Tamil. To north of village. Illegible in the middle.]

Translation.

Hail! Prosperity! In the expired Śaka year 1185 corresponding to the 20th year of the reign of the emperor of the three worlds, the glorious Víra Rájéndrachóḻadéva, on Friday which bore the *nakshatra* Magha and which corresponded to the 11th day of the bright fortnight of the month of Tulá (the grant appears to be of some land, but the portion dealing with this is not decipherable) . . . . . to the lord Sántíśvara at Vikramaśiṅgapuram *alias* Nellúr (a town) in Miḍai (Paḍai?) náḍu (situated) in Chédikulamáṇikkavaḷanáḍu (a sub-division) of Jayaṅkoṇḍachóḻamaṇḍalam . . . . .

I, Perumáḷ Cheṭṭi, gave this, as temple land (dévadánam) to this god with libation of water to last as long as the moon and sun endure.

[1] ஸ்வஸ்தி ஸ்ரீ ஸகல-
[2] ருஷம் தூாஅம [ரு]
[3] [சென்ற] திரிபுவன-
[4] சக்கிரவத்திக-
[5] ள் ஸ்ரீ [வீரராஜெ]-
[6] [ந்ரு]சொழெ[த]வற்கு
[7] யாண்டு உம ஆவது
[8] துலாநாயற்று பூ-
[9] ர்வபக்ஷத்து ஏகா-
[10] [த]சியும் மகமும் ெ-
[11] பற்ற வெள்ளிக்கி[ழ]-
[12] மை நாள் ஜயங்ெ-
[13] காண்டசொழம-
[14] ண்டலத்துச்செதி-
[15] குலமாணிக்கவள-
[16] நாட்டில் மிடை[நா]-
[17] ட்டு விக்கிரமசிங்க-
[18] புரமான நெல்லூ[ரி]-
[19] ல் உடையார் ஸா[க்ஷி]-
[20] ஸ்வரமுடையநாய-
[21] . . . . கு வி . . .
[22] . . . .
[23] . . . . ளிகு . .
[24] . டி . . மா . .
[25] செல்லக்கட[வதா]-
[26] க இவ்வூர் . . .
[27] கெல்லை பொற்பொ-
[28] . . . . . .
[29] ளக . . . ண்ட-

[30] டிவெ . . டை-
[31] . உட்பொக . . .
[32] உளர . . த . மு-
[33] . . . . . .
[34] வதாகவும் . . .
[35] . யாட்ட . . .
[36] . . ருகுதி ரி . . .
[37] . ந பாமாத்தப்ப .
[38] . . . . ன்ம
[39] . . . . . ஹெ-
[40] . . . . விலைகுத்து
[41] [இ]ன்றுயனுற்கு தெ-
[42] வதானமாக தாரா-
[43] பூஜைம் பண்ணிவித்-
[44] து சந்திராதித்தவ-
[45] ரை செல்லக்கடவ-
[46] தாகக்குடுத்தென்
[47] பெருமாள்செட்டி

GUDUR (86).

[Reḍḍipāḷem (hamlet Panṭrangam). Tamil. From Panḍaranga temple.]

TRANSLATION.

Hail! Prosperity! In the 36th year of the reign of the emperor of the three worlds, Tribhuvanavíradéva, I, Sittaraśan, the son of the provincial chief of the middle country (mattimadésam) Rájarájapaṭṭaipeṭṭaraśan, presented one sacred lamp in the temple of the lord Panḍaraṅga (situated in) Pérúrnáḍu in Payvattirikóṭṭam (a subdivision) of Rájéndrachóḷamanḍalam, as charity on behalf of my elder sister Páchchaldéví the consort of Madurántakappottapichóḻa (*alias*) Manumasittarasan.

*   *   *   *

(For this lamp) I, Rájarájapaṭṭaisittarasa, gave the tax on vémugar (?) the tax on house front (doors), the tax on looms, the tax on goldsmiths, and the temple dues on the garden lands.

We three, the Śiva *Brahmans* of the temple, Paṇḍaraṇgabhaṭṭa, Náṟpatteṇṇáyirabhaṭṭa and Paṇmáhéśvarabhaṭṭa, having bound ourselves to pay the interest on this gold and maintain a sacred perpetual lamp as long as the moon and sun last, have received (the money).

Those who obstruct this charity will incur the sin of stabbing a tawny cow on the banks of the Ganges.

(This charity is placed under) the protection of all the Máhéśvaras.

[1] ஸ்வஸ்தி ஸ்ரீ திரிபுவநச்சக்கரவத்திகள் திரிபுவநவிர-
தெவற்கு யாண்டு ௩௰௪ வது இராஜெந்திர சொழமண்டலத்-
து பவ்வத்திரிக்கொட்டத்துப் பெறூர்நாட்டில் உடையார்-
பண்ட-

[2] ரங்கருடைய நாயனூற்கு மத்திமதெசத்தில் மகாமண்-
டிவிகந் இராஜராஜப்பட்டைபெத்தரைசர் மகந் சித்தரை-
சநென் எங்கள் தமக்கையார் மதுராந்தகப் பொத்தப்-

[3] பிச்சொழமநுமசித்தரைசர் தெவியார் பாச்சல்தெ-
வியாற்குத்தந்மமாக நாந் வை(ய்)த்த திருநந்தாவிளக்கு ஒந்-
றுக்கு வெ[முகற்] காணிக்கையும் வாசற் சிந்நமும் தறி இறை-
தட்-

[4] டாரப்பாட்டமும் தொட்டக்காட்டில் தெவதானத்திற்-
காணிக்கையும் விட்டெந் இராஜராஜ ப்பட்டைசித்தரைசநெந்
இப்பொந் [பொலி][யூ*]ட்டுக்கொயிற் சிவபிராம்மணந் பண்-
டரங்கபட்டநு-

[5] ம் நாற்பத்தெண்ணாயிரபட்டரும் பந்மாஹேஶ்வரப-ட்டரும் திருநுந்தாவிளக்கு சந்திராதித்தவரை செலுத்தக்கட-வோமாக கை(ய்)க்கொண்டோம் இம்மூவோரும் இத்தந்ம-

[6] மிரக்ஷுவார் கெங்கைக்கரையில் குராற்பசுக்குத்திநார் பாபத்தெ படுவார் பந்மாஹேஶ்வர ரக்ஷை.

Gudur (87).

[Reḍḍipáḷem (hamlet Pantrangam). Tamil. From Panḍaranga temple.]

Translation.

In the 32nd year of the reign of Kulóttuṅgachóḻa-déva who abolished tolls we gave for as long as the moon and sun last to the gods Pavanavináyakadéva and Paṇḍa-raṅgésvara who were pleased to reside at the great city of Kákandi in Kaḍalkoṇḍa Pavvaṭṭirikóṭṭam (a sub-division of) Rájendrachóḻamaṇḍalam (called after) the emperor of the three worlds, the unequalled among kings, as tax-free temple lands . . . . *kudir* (?) including the *Neḍuṅgudir* (?) situated in Kaṇḍári Kaḍakambákkam in Kíḻaipaṭṭaiyanáḍu.

The boundaries of the land on the four sides are on the west the backwaters of Paṇḍitturai and Pammal, on the north . . . . on the east the backwaters of Táḻaiyappáḍu and the south by the drainage channel of the boundary.

We gave to these gods the forests, fields, wells sunk in the land and trees growing upon the land included within these four boundaries, the income from the internal revenue, the income in gold, and the miscella-neous dues as tax-free *dévadánam*. Whoever obstructs this (charity) will incur the sin of killing a tawny cow on the banks of the Ganges.

This (charity is placed under) the protection of all the Máhésvaras.

[1] திரிபுவந சக்ரவத்தி கொநெரிமென்கொண்டா-
[ெ*]ஜ[ந்*]திர சொழமண்டலத்துக்கடல்கொண்ட்டபல்வத்திரி-
கொட்டத்தில் காகந்திமாநகரில் பூசைகொண்டருளும் பவ-
ணவிநாயகதெ-

[2] வரும் பண்டரங்கிசுரமுடையநாயனாற்(க்)கு சுங்கந்தவி-
ர்த்த குலொத்துங்கசொழ தெவற்(க்)கு யாண்டு ௩௰௨ ஆவ-
து நாளில் ஊந்த நாயநாற்(க்)குக்கிழைப்பட்டைய நாட்டில்-
கண்டாரி கட-

[3] கம்பாக்கம் கிர்ப்பம நெடுங்குதிர் உட்ப்பட்டகுதிற்களு-
ம் இந்நாயநாற்(க்)கு இறையிலிதெவதாநமாக நாற்பாலெல்லை-
க்கு மெல்பாற்கெல்லை பண்டித்துறைகழிக்கும் பம்மல்கழி-
க்கு . . . . த்தெற்கும் கிழ்பார்க்கெல்லை தாழை-
யபாட்டிற்கழிக்கு மெற்(க்)கும் தென்பாற்(க்)கெல்லை எல்லைக்-
கால்கழிக்கு[வ]டக்கும் இந்நாற்(ப்)பாக்கு நடு உட்பட்ட காடு-
ங்கழியும் கிழநொக்கிந கிணறும் மெல்நொக்-

[4] கிந மரமும் இந்நாயநாற்(க்)கு சந்திராதித்தவரை ஆய
மந்தராயப்பாட்டம் பொந்நாயம் சில்லறைகளகப்பட் இறை-
யிலிதெவதாநமாக விட்டொம் இதுக்கு இலங்கனம் பண்ணி-
நாந் கெங்கைக்கரையிற்குராற் பசுகொந்ந பிரம்மகத்தியில் படு-
வாந் இது [ஸ்ரீ]மாஹெஸ்வரர் ரக்ஷெ.

Abbreviation.

Gudur (88 to 105).

Reḍḍipálem.

Besides the inscriptions printed above, the Paṇḍaranga temple at Panṭrangam, hamlet of Reḍḍipálem, contains the following Tamil inscriptions which it is not thought worth while to print. The locality is described as Paṇḍarangam in Péṛúrnáḍu in Pavaṭṭirikóṭṭam, a sub-division of Jayaṅkoṇḍachóḻamaṇḍalam or Rájéndrachóḻamaṇḍalam. The village is also apparently sometimes described as "the great city of Kákanḍi in Kaḍalkoṇḍa Pavattirikóṭṭam":—

(88) 8th of Rájarájadéva, gift of a lamp by Mummuḍivaitumba Mahárájan *alias* Vishnudévan, *alias* Durai Araśan.

(89) 29th of Kolóttungachóḻa. Gift of 13 *máḍai* for a lamp by Táttán Tanapalapanmamuḍaiyan a merchant of Conjeevaram.

(90) S.S. 1185 (expired) (A.D. 1263-64) and 20th of Víraréjéndrachóḻadéva. Gift of 1 *máḍai* for a lamp by Tikkánai Áṇḍán.

(91) 7th of Vijayagaṇḍagópála. Gift of an image of the goddess of Tirukkámakóṭṭam.

(92) 36th of Tribhuvana Víradéva. Gift of 98 "full grown, undying and unaging" sheep for a lamp by Irumaḍiśṛiyádéví wife of Rájarájapaṭṭai Siddaraśa and daughter of Uraiyúr Chóḻan *alias* Śúraḻvár Kaṭṭidévar.

(93) 3rd of Rájarájadéva. Gift of 5 lamps by Váṇiyan Nalluḻán *alias* Chéramán Toḻan *alias* Páváṇḍán.

(94) 8th of Vikramachóḻadéva. Gift of land in several villages.

(95) Two fragments.

(96) 6th of Kulóttuṅgachóḷa *alias* Chokkanáyanár. Records a grant of land.

(97) Fragment relating to a grant of land.

(98) 5th of Vijayadéva. Grant of a lamp.

(99) 14th of Rájarájadéva. Grant of a lamp.

(100) Records a grant of land.

(101) 32nd of Kulóttuṅgachóḷa. Grant of cattle for the maintenance of a lamp.

(102) Illegible inscription.

(103) Ditto.

(104) Ditto.

(105) Ditto.

Gudur (106).

[Raṭṭamala. Tamil. To east of Prasanna Kálahasti Íṣvara.]

Translation.

Hail! Prosperity! On the 14th of the month of Tai in the year . . . I, Pottappichembar, gave with libation of water to Ádirájáttidéva Tribhuvananáyaka, all my rights in the lands, tank, backwater and wells after having caused this (temple) to be built.

He who obstructs this charity will incur the sin of giving pain to tawny cows, divine Brahmans and *Ṛishis*. Salutation to Buddha.

Note.—Note the reference to Buddha. The last four lines are part of a separate inscription.

[1] ஸ்வஸ்தி ஸ்ரீமது . . . . .
[2] ௪ தை மீ யசஉ ஆதிரா[சாத்தி]தெ-
[3] வர் திருபுவநநாயகற்கு பொத்தப்பிசெம்பர ன-
[4] ங் காணி எ[றி]க்கழித்தாவு-

(To face page 446.)

GUDUR NO. 106.

[5] முதலுண்டாக சுவந்திரமெல்-
[6] லாம் விட்டுயிதை கட்டிவித்து
[7] தாரை வாத்து குடுத்தெந் யி-
[8] ந்த் தநமத்துக்கு அகிதம் பண்-
[9] ணிநபெர் கெங்கைக்-
[10] ரையில் கார[ப்]-
[10] பசுவை-
[11] யும் தெவப்பிரா-
[12] மணரையும்
[13] யிருஷிகளையும்
[14] [யி]ங்சைபண்ணி
[15] ந தொசத்திலெ
[16] பொகக்கட
[17] வர்
[18] ஙஜோ
[19] வைஷி- .
[20] ஸ
[1] நாநா
[2] தெச இ
[3] ருமக-
[4] ள் ஙி

Gudur (107).

[Sarvepalli. Telugu. On gate of Śiva temple. Illegible.]

Gudur (108). (A.D. 1530–31.)

[Vákáḍu. Telugu. In enclosure of Vishnu temple.]

Translation.

May it be auspicious! Hail! On Thursday the 10th of the bright fortnight of Pushya of the year Vikṛiti, corresponding to the year 1452 of the illustrious, victorious, and prosperous Ṣáliváhana Ṣaka era, while Ṣríman Mahárájádhirája Rájáparaméṣvara, Ṣri Víra Pratápa Achyutaráya Maháráyulu was ruling the earth, Ṣrímán Mahámaṇḍaléṣvara Basava Ṣankara Onḍánemanḍalíkaraganḍa,[1] Guttihannibbaraganḍa,[2] Salaka Ráju Tirumalayya Déva Mahárájulu granted a charitable edict as follows: Being on the banks of the Svarnamukhi on the holy occasion of Makara Sankramaṇa we have given, with gift of gold and libation of water, Nélaṭúru, otherwise known as Achyutaráyapuram and Chirumanambúnḍi in Eastern Paḍanáḍu *síma* in the *Rájya* of Chandragiri, which (*ṣíma*) is attached to our chiefdom for performing the 16 ceremonies to Onkáḍa Aḷaganátha Déva for the religious merit of Achyutaráyulu.

1. శుభమస్తు స్వస్తి శ్రీ జయాభ్యు
2. దయ శాలివాహన శకవర్షంబులు లైన
3. ౧౪౫౨ అగు నేంటి వికృతిసంవత్సర
4. పుష్య శు ౧౦ గురువారాన శ్రీమ
5. న్మహారాజాధిరాజరాజపరమేశ్వర
6. శ్రీ వీరప్రతాప అచ్యుతరాయ మహా
7. రాయలు పృథ్వీరాజ్యం సేయుచు
8. ం డంగాను శ్రీమన్మహామండలేశ్వ
9. ర బసవశంకర ఒండానెమండలీ
10. కర గండగుత్తిహన్నిబ్బరగండసల
11. కరాజు చిన తిరుమలయ్యదేవమ

---

[1] The vanquisher of feudatories possessing titles?

[2] The Gutti conqueror of twelve men?

12. హారాజులు సమర్పించ్చిన ధర్మశాస
13. న క్రమమెట్లన్నను చంద్రగిరిరాజ్యము
14. లోనుమాకునాయంకరానకుం
15. జెల్లెతూర్పుపడనాండి సీమలోని
16. అచ్యుతరాయపురప్రతినామమై
17. ననెల్లటూరును చిరుమనంబూ
18. ండినిబింకాడ అళగనాధదేవుని
19. కి షోడశోపచారాలున్ను నడిచి
20. యట్టుగాను మకరసంక్రమణ
21. పుణ్యకాలమందు సువర్ణముఖీ
22. తీరమందు అచ్యుతరాయల
23. కు పుణ్యముగాను సహిరణ్యోద
24. క దానధారా పూర్వకముగాను స
25. మర్పిస్తిమి।

GUDUR (109). (A.D. 1579–80.)

[Vallúru. Telugu. In street to the west.]

TRANSLATION.

Hail! On the 1st of the dark fortnight of Kártika of the year Pramádi, corresponding to the illustrious victorious and prosperous Sáliváhana Saka year 1502, Srímat . . . Venkaṭádri . . . issued this charitable edict for the *kunchams* for the tank . . . in the village of Vallúru. They must pay as before *méras* at 1 *kuncha* per *puṭṭi* on all kinds of grain raised in the dry fields within the four boundaries of the village of Vallúru, situated in Sarepalli *Ṣíma*, which was granted to him as an *amaram*. Whoever, not maintaining the tank always, misappropriates that grain will incur the sin of killing a cow and a Brahman on the Ganges. He will be considered to have given his (wife's) honour to the *Veṭṭis*, *Málas*, and *Mádigas* of Vallúr, and his wife will be regarded as having been given . . .

1. స్వస్తి శ్రీ విజయాభ్యు.
2. దయ శాలివాహాన
3. శకవర్షంబులు ౧౫౦౭
4. అగు నేంటి ప్రమాది సం
5. వత్సర కార్త్తీక బ ౧ లు శ్రీమ
6. తు . . వెంకటాద్రి . . . .
7. అ . . . . . వల్లూరు గ్రామ
8. త్ర . . . నిగారు చెరువుకుంచా
9. లకు వెళ్ళించిన ధర్మ్మశాస
10. నము తమకు అమరంకు
11. పాలించిన సరె పల్లిశిమాలో
12. వల్లూరిగ్రామంచెరు శీమాముదెవి
13. తరిలోనుగాఖండిన నానాధా
14. న్యంమేరకున్ను పూర్వంనడుస్తావుం
15. డే మర్యాదపుట్టి కుంచాలు
16. యిచ్చి చెర్వ వేళించ్చంగలవారు
17. ఇందుకు యల్లప్పటికి అచ్చెరువు యవ్వరు వే
18. యక ఆధాన్య పుచ్చుకున్నాను వారు
19. గంగకత్తీరాం గోబ్రాహ్మణిజంపిన పా

20. పొనః బోవును వానిమానం వల్లూరి
21. వెట్టి మాలమాదిగెవాండ్లకు ఇ
22. చ్చినవాండె అట్టమీంది ఆలిని
23. యి . . చినవానికి ఇచ్చినవాండు.

GUDUR (110). (A.D. 1614–15?)

[Vanjaváka. Telugu. In enclosure of Chennakéṣava temple.]

TRANSLATION.

Hail! On the 10th of the bright fortnight of Pushya of the year Kródhi, corresponding to the year 1536 of the illustrious, victorious and prosperous Ṣáliváhana Ṣaka era, Venkaṭapati Rájum Gáru, Son of Ṣrí Veligóṭi Rájayyapátúru, issued this charitable edict to the dancers, drummers, pipers and dancing girls after worshipping Chanráya of Vanjivánka. We have given 60 *kunṭas* in Vendavánka and 20 *kunṭas* under the Sarmágunṭa, total 80 *kunṭas*, as a *sarvamánya*. Besides this we have given the lease fees and the pound fees in the town for providing worship with lamps to the deity. Therefore it should be maintained as long as the sun and moon exist.

Whoever fails to continue it will incur the sin of killing a cow near the Ganges . . .

Third side.

The charitable edict granted . . . it should be maintained as long as the sun and moon endure. . .

NOTE.—The S.S. and cyclic year do not agree.

1. స్వస్తి శ్రీ జయాభ్యుదయ
2. శాలివాహన శకవర్షంబు
3. లు ౧౭౩౬ అగు నేంటి క్రోధి
4. సంవత్సర పుష్య శుద్ధ ౧౦ లు
5. శ్రి (వెలి) గోడిరాజయ్య పాతూరి
6. (కు)మారుండు వెంకటపతిరా
7. జుంగారు వంజివాంక చ
8. న్రాయనికి శావసేసినప్పి
9. ంచి నట్టు వాండ్లు డోంఙ్లునా
10. గసరపువారికిన్ని బోగము
11. వారికిన్ని యెవర్రచిన ధర్మ
12. శాసనక్రమము వందవాం
13. కలోనుగు ౬౦ ను సమా
14. గుంటక్రిందుగు ౨౦ న్నుకూ
15. డాగు ౮౦ చేనున్ను సర్వమా
16. న్యముగాను యిస్తిమి యి
17. దిగాక వూళ్లోను కవుల్లా
18. యెమున్ను ౧౦ దెల్ను దేవు
19. నికి దీపారాధనకు యిస్తిమి.
20. గనక ఆచంద్రార్కము
21. నడపంగలవారుయి
22. ది యవ్వరు నడపకున్నాను
23. గంగకర్త గోవుంజంప్పిన
24. పాపానంబోదురు

Second side.

1. కొరి అంగజాల
2. . . . . హంరి

Third side.

1. ఢ్బిర . . . . వనము

చ్చినయిధర్మశాసనం బచ్చులీకూర

2. . . . .

ఆచంద్రార్కము నడపంగలవారు

3. . . . .

. . . .

GUDUR (111). (A.D. 1534–35.)

[Vindúru. Telugu. In a field.]

TRANSLATION.

Adoration be to Piḍúri Nílakanṭhéṣvára. Lingákumára (?) . . .

While Ṣrí Rájádhirája Rájaparaméṣvara Ṣrí Achyutaráya Maháráyalu was ruling the kingdom, on the 3rd of the bright fortnight of Vaiśákha of the year Jaya, corresponding to the Śaka year 1456, on the holy occasion of Akshatadiya,[1] this inscribed eulogy of Vindúru was put up.

Bóḍi Reḍḍi, son of Dinadévi Reḍḍi planted a tope and presented lands for the religious merit of Achyutaráya, and of his own parents . . . .

1. పిడూరినీల
2. ఠేశ్వరా
3. -గాకుమార

---

[1] Akshayatadiya or Akshayatritíya is the 3rd of the bright fortnight of Vaiṣákha—so called because it is supposed to secure permanency to actions performed on that day.

4. మిదె ౧
5. శ్రీ రాజాధిరాజరాజ ప.
6. రమేశ్వర శ్రీ అచ్యుతరాయ
7. మహారాయలు రాజ్యపరి
8. పాలనం సెయుచున్నప్పటి
9. శకవర్షంబులు ౧౪౫౬ చ
10. నునప్పటి జయసంవత్సర వై
11. శాఖశు ౩ బలరామరమనుతెశి
12. అక్షతదియ మన్వాదిపుణ్యకా
13. లమందును విందూరి శాసనస్తు
14. లిదిన దేవిరెడ్డింగారి కుమారుండు
15. బోడిరెడ్డింగారు వనంవెట్టి అచ్యుతరా
16. యలకు పుణ్యంగానున్న తమతల్లి
17. తండ్రింగారికి పుణ్యంగానున్న
18. (మధ్యతనూశివారావోజలుసటి ౧).

GUDUR (112). A.D. (1617-18 ?)

[Víranna Kanupur. Telugu. Near Śiva temple.]

TRANSLATION.

Hail! On the 30th of the dark fortnight of Ṣrávaṇa of the year Pingaḷa, corresponding to the illustrious, victorious and prosperous Ṣálivahana Ṣaka year 1538, while Ṣrímad Rájádhi Rája, Rájaparaméṣvara, Ṣrí Víra Pratápa, Ṣrí Víra Venkaṭapatiráyaluváru, seated on the diamond throne, was ruling the earth, Rávula Vengaḷappa descendant of the *Gótra* of Ḷókapála, grandson of Ṣrí Vengáḷappa, and son of Rávula Venkaṭappa, issued this charitable edict to Visvéṣvarasvámi of Vírannakanupur.

Rávula Venkaṭapati Náyaningáru presented the tax raised in the village of Víranna Kanupur which was granted to him as an *amaram* by Venkaṭapatiráyaluváru as a *sarvamánya* for the religious merit of Venkaṭappa Náyaningáru. This should be maintained as long as the sun and moon endure.

Whoever misappropriates the tax or objects to it will be regarded as having given his (wife's) honour to a gulápuváḍu.[1] Thus has the charitable edict been issued.

NOTE.—Assuming Pingala to be the correct year, it represents the expired S.S. year 1539 and the year 1617–18 of our calendar.

1. స్వస్తి శ్రీ జయాభ్యు
2. దయ శాలివాహన
3. శకవరుషంబ్బులు ౧౫౩౯
4. అగునేటి పింగళ సంవ్వత్సర
5. శ్రావణ బ ౩౦లు శ్రీమద్రా
6. జాధిరాజరాజపరమే
7. శ్వర శ్రీ వీరప్రతాప శ్రీవీర వేంకట
8. టపతి రాయలవారు ప్రజశింహా
9. సనాసీనుండై పృధ్విసాంమ్రాంజ్యం
10. చేస్తుంనుండగాను లోకపాల
11. గోత్రోధ్భవులున్ను శ్రీవెంగళప్పం
12. పౌవుత్రులైన రావుల వెంకటప్ప (పుత్రు
13. లు రావులువెంగళప్ప) వీరన్నకను
14. పూటి విశ్వేశ్వర స్వామికిన్ని యిచ్చిన ద
15. మ శాసనం॥ రావెల వెంకటపతినా

[1] Probably means 'a slave,' from Hind. *ghulám*.

16. ఇనింగారు తనకు వెంకటపతిరాయులువారు
17. అమరానకు పాలించ్చిన విరన్నకనుపూ
18. రిగ్రామానం జెల్లిన సుంఖమ
19. సర్వమాన్యముగాను రావుల వెంక
20. డప్పనాఇనింగారికి బుణ్యంగాను
21. ఇప్పించ్చినం సమ ఆచంద్రార్కం
22. గాను నడపం గలది సుంకము
23. . యు . యెవ్వరు కాంచి ఆక్షేపిం
24., చినాను యీగ్రామం యేలేవారు ఆక్షే
25. పించ్చినాను గుళాపువారి మా
26. నం ఇచ్చినవాండె ఇస్తని
27. ఇచ్చిన ధర్మశాసనం.

GUDUR (113). (A.D. 1559-60?)

[Víranna Kanupur. Telugu. Near Vírabhadra temple.]

TRANSLATION.

Hail! On Wednesday, the 14th of the dark fortnight of Mágha of the year Siddháddri, corresponding to the illustrious, victorious and prosperous Sálivahana Saka year 1475 (?), Allúri Anná Reḍḍi, the agent for the affairs (Káryakartá) of Sríman Mahámanḍalésvara Ráma Ráju Tirumalarájayyaváru issued this charitable edict for the *mukhamanḍapa* of the deity of the hamlet of Kanupur.

We have presented . . . Porávaran . . . . for securing prosperity (portions unintelligible) for the religious merit of Tirumala Rájayyaváru. Whoever violates this will incur the sin of killing a cow and a Brahman near the Ganges.

Ṣrí.

Note.—The date should apparently be S.S. 1481.

1. స్వస్తి శ్రీ జయాభ్యుద
2. య శాలివాహాన శక
3. వరుషంబ్బులు ౧౪౭౫ అ
4. గు నేంటి సిద్ధాద్రి సంవత్సర
5. మాఘ బ ౧౪ బు । శ్రీమన్మ
6. హామండలేశ్వర రా
7. మరాజు తిరుమల
8. రాజయ్యవారి కా
9. ర్య కర్త్తలైన అల్లూ
10. రి అన్నారెడ్డింగారు
11. కనుపూరి పల్లెకు దేవు
12. ముఖ్యమండపాన
13. కు రెడియిచ్చిన ధర్మ
14. శాసనము. మా
15. న్యంబెడికి యకం
16. దిరుమల రాజయ్య
17. వారికి పుణ్యంగాను
18. భద్రకరమ్ముగ పారా
19. వసం యిస్తిమి. యందు
20. కు యవ్వరు తప్పినాను
21. గంగ్గకర్తగో బ్రాహ్మ

22. ని వధించిన పాపానం

23. బోవువారు శ్రీ

GUDUR (114). (A.D. 1555–56.)

[Víranna Kanupur. Telugu. Near Vírabhadra temple.]

TRANSLATION.

Hail! On Monday, the 3rd (or 7th) of the dark fortnight of Mágha of the year Rákshasa corresponding to the illustrious, victorious, and prosperous Ṣáliváhana Ṣaka year 1476, Koṇḍapalli Yallaparáju, the agent for the affairs (Káryakarta) of Ṣríman Mahámaṇḍaléṣvara Ráma Ráju Tirumala Rájayyaváru issued this charitable edict to Íṣvara. He presented . . . in the village of Yaḍimalu in the *síma* of Saryápalli with its four boundaries with libation of water for the religious merit of Tirumala Rájayya . . . . edict . . . will incur the sin of killing a cow and a Brahman on the Ganges.

Ṣrí.

NOTE.—The cyclic and S.S. dates differ by one year.

1. స్వస్తి శ్రీ జయాభ్యుద
2. య శాలివాహన శకవ
3. రుషంబులు ౧౪౭౬
4. అను నేటి రాక్షస స
5. ంవత్సర మాఘబ 3
6. సో॥ శ్రీమన్మహా మండ
7. లేశ్వర రామరాజు తి

8. రుమల రాజయ్యవారి
9. కార్యకర్తలైన కొండపల్లి
10. యల్లప్పరాజు ఇశ్వరునికి
11. ం వేయించిన ధర్మ
12. శాసనం సర్వాపల్లి శీమ
13. లోనియ డిమలుగ్రా
14. మంలో రామలింగ
15. పా . . . యిను చెతుశీ
16. మాను (ధానాధారాపూ)
17. (వక్షకం) . . . .
18. కు తిరుమలరాజు
19. య్యకు పుణ్యముగాను
20. . . . . శాసనం
21. . . . .
22. . . . . . (నూ
24. . .
25. . .
26. . .
27. . .
28. . . తన . .
29. ం కో
30. చమతలిత
31. శు . రు కో .
32. గంగకరుత గోబ్రాంహ్మ

33. ని చంపించ్చిన పాంపాం

34. నం బోదురు.

GUDUR (115). (A.D. 1299–1300.)

[Víranna Kanupur. Tamil. From a stone removed from above the gate of the Vírabhadra temple.]

TRANSLATION.

Hail! Prosperity! In the Śaka year 1222 corresponding to) the cyclic year Vikári, which was the 9th year of the reign of the emperor of the three worlds, the glorious Rájagaṇḍagopáladéva, on the third day of the bright half of the month of Tai which bore the *nakshatra* Aviṭṭa, I, Madurántakapottapichóḷan (*alias*) Rájagaṇḍagópáladévan gave, with libation of water, to last as long as the moon and sun to the god Piḷḷaiyuḍaiya Náráyaṇaperumáḷ for worship on behalf of Tirukkachchanambi residing in the merchant street at Nellúr *alias* Vikramasiṅgapura in Maḍai (Paḍai?) náḍu in Jayakulamáṇikkavaḷanáḍu (a sub-division) of Jayaṅgoṇḍachóḷamaṇḍalam.

If there is any body who obstructs this charity, he will be regarded as having committed the sin of killing cows and Brahmans on the banks of the Ganges.

[1] ஸ்வஸ்தி ஸ்ரீ ஸகவரு-

[2] ஷம் க௲௨௱௨௰௨ வது

[3] விகாரிஸம்வத்ஸரத்-

[4] து திருபுவனச்சகக-

[5] ரவத்திகள் ஸ்ரீ இ-

[6] [ரா]ச கண்டகொ-

[7] பாலதேவற்கு யா-
[8] ண்டு ௨ ஆவது தை-
[9] ய் மாஸத்து பூர்வப-
[10] க்ஷத்து அவுட்டநக்ஷ-
[11] த்திரமும் திரிதியை-
[12] யும் பெற்ற நாள் செ-
[13] யங்கொண்டசோ-
[14] ழமண்டலத்தில் செ-
[15] யக்குலமாணிக்க-
[16] வளநாட்டு மடைந-
[17] ாட்டில் நெல்லூரா-
[18] ன விக்ரமசிங்கபுரத்தி-
[19] ல் வாணிகத்தெருவி-
[20] ல் இருக்கச்சநம்பி திரு-
[21] வாராதநமான பிள்ளை-
[22] யுடைய நாராயணப்-
[23] பெருமாளுக்கு சந்த்ரா-
[24] (ர)தித்தவரை
[25] செல்வதாக
[26] தாரபூர்வ-
[27] [illegible] பண்ணிக்-
[28] குடுத்தே-
[29] ன் மதுராந்-
[30] தகப்பொ-
[31] த்தப்பிச்செ-
[32] சாழன் இராசக-
[33] ண்டகோ-
[34] பாலதே-
[35] வனென் இந்-

[36] ந்த தங்மத்-

[37] தை வில-

[38] க்கிஞருண்-

[39] டாநால் ெ-

[40] ஶங்கை-

[41] க்கறைபில்

[42] மாவேராஹு-

[43] ணவதை

[44] பண்ணிஞன்

Gudur (116).

[Yérigaṭipalli. Tamil. In a street to the east.]

Translation.

This inscription is mutilated at the end so that the object of the grant is not ascertainable. It begins with a short Sanskrit introduction which says that it is the grant of Chitraméḷa (perhaps a surname of Ṣrí Vijayagaṇḍágópáladéva) for the good of all the world. The inscription is dated in the 19th year of the reign of the king Vijayagaṇḍagópáladéva and the date is the 13th day of the bright half of the month of Kaṭaka *nakshatra* Púśa.

[1] ஶ்ரீ . . . . தெ . த்ரயஸ்த்ரைக லொ-

[2] கைக-ஹிதொத்ஸவ வல்லபொ-

[3] கஜிதாஸ்த்ராய சித்ரமேள-

[4] ஸ்ய ஶாஸநம் || ஸ்வஸ்தி தி-

[5] ருவாய்க்கெழ்விமு[ந]னுடைத்தா[ய்]

[6] த்ரிஹுவன சக்ரவர்த்திகள்

[7] ஸ்ரீ விஜயகண்டகோபா-

[8] ல்தேவற்கு யாண்டு ய[க] ஆ-

[9] வது க்கடக நாயற்று பூர்வ-

[10] பக்ஷத்து த்ரயோதஸி பெ-

[11] ற்ற பூ[ஸநக்ஷத்ரத்து] நாள் ஜய-

[12] [ங்]கொ[ண்டசோ]ழ[ம]ண்[ட]-

[13] [ல]த்து . . . .

[14] . டத்து . . டைய பட்-

[15] டயநாட்டு கெகாபடு-

[16] நாட்டுரறன் காட்டன்பட்டு

. . . . . .

Gudur (117).

[Yérúru. Telugu. Near ruined Vírabhadra temple.]

Translation.

. . . . We have ordered that the grain should be utilized on doing work to the tank. Therefore, if the ruler of the village or the agent or any one else take that property or do not repair the bund, he will incur the sin of killing a cow and a Brahman at Benares.

Venkaṭapatiráya.

1\. . . . . . .

2\. . . . . . ర బాద్రప.

3\. . . . . . ంఢ్ల పనాయ

4\. . . . . . రవుకు వే

5\. . . . . పో

6\. . . . . నానా

7\. . . . .

Second side.

8\. ధాన్యాదులు చెరువు వేయించ్చ

9\. క కట్టడ శేసినారముగనక ఆ స్వామ్మి

10\. గ్రామం యేలిదొరగాని కాయ్యాకర్తలు

11\. గాని యవ్వరుగనక పట్టినాంగాని కట్టవేయిం

12\. చ్చక యవ్వరు యియ్యకపోయినా (కాశిలో)

13\. హత్య గోవుబ్రామ్మాణిని వధిఇచ్చినవాండు

14\. వేంకటపతిరాయులు.

Gudur (118).

[Yérúru. Tamil. Over door of Channakéșava temple.]

Translation.

This is the *paḷḷi* (mosque?) founded by Málikáduru (Málik Ḳádr), the son of Silaiyamánár (Sulaimán?) on the first of Ávaṇi of the year Héviḷambi.

[1] எயவிளம்பிவருஷம் ஆவணி

[2] [க]தி . சிலையமாணார்மகன் மாளி-

[3] கதாருவையத்த பள்ளி

KANDUKUR (1). (A.D. 1315–16.)

[Bhímavaram. Telugu. On a stone at the gate of the temple of Chennakéṣava.]

TRANSLATION.

Hail! On the holy occasion of Makara Sankránti of the year Rákshasa, corresponding to the year 1237 of the Ṣaka era—hail! Ṣríman Muppaḍi Náyanka Puraharu, the prime minister (Mahápradháni), who is the servant of Ṣríman Mahámandaléṣvara Kákatíya Pratápa Rudra Déva Mahárája, who is possessed of all praise-worthy attributes, and who is the worshipper of the divine lotus feet of Ṣrí Sómanátha Déva, after pouring water in the hand of Boḷḷeḍla Próli Seṭṭi, caused to be given the field (?) named Nagamandaḍi Prolebóyinini Kuḍiningali (?) as a *sarvamánya* (free grant) to the deity Prasanna Chennakéśavadéva of Bhímavaram *agrahára*, which is situated in Púnginádu, for the religious merit of his master (Pratápa Rudradéva) and of himself. This charity should be kept up as long as the sun and moon endure.

[Imprecatory verse.]

1. స్వస్తి సమస్త ప్రశస్తిసహిత
2. శ్రీమన్మహా మండలేశ్వర కాక
3. తియ్యప్రతాప రుద్రదేవ మహా
4. రాజులకు నిజభృత్యులును
5. శ్రీసోమనాధదేవ దివ్య
6. శ్రీపాధపద్మా రాధకులూ
7. లైనస్వస్తి శ్రీమన్మహాప్రధా
8. ని ముప్పడినాయంకపుర
9. హారు దమకుం బుణ్యముగా

10. న శకవరుషములు ౧౫౩౭
11. అగు రాక్షస సంవత్సర ము
12. కర సంక్రాంతిపుణ్య కా
13. లమునప్పుడు పూంగి
14. నాంటిలోని అగ్రహారం
15. భీమావరము ప్రసన్న
16. చెన్నకేశవదేవర దీపాంగకు
17. నాగమండడి ప్రోలేబోయి
18. నిని కుడిలింగలి సర్వమాన్య
19. ముగాను బొల్లెడ్లప్రోలిసెట్టి
20. చేతను భారవోసి ఇప్పించ్చిరి
21. ఈ ధర్మము ఆ చంద్రార్కమూ
22. గాం చెల్లంగలది । సామాన్యోయ
23. ం ధర్మసేతు నృపాణాం కాలే
24. కాలే పాలనీయో భవద్భిః
25. సర్వానేతాన్ భావినః పార్థి
26. వేంద్రాన్భూయో భూయో
27. యాచతే రామచంద్రః ।

KANDUKUR (2).

[Bhímavaram. Telugu. On a small stone in front of the temple of Ráma.]

TRANSLATION.

The village of Bhímavaram has been bestowed by Ayyapparusayya on Parṇaṣála Narasimha (Narasimha of Singaráyakoṇḍa).

1. పర్నశాలనరశింహానికి అ
2. య్యప్పరుసయ్య సమర్పించి
3. న గ్రామం భీమవరం

KANDUKUR (3). (A.D. 1551–52 ?)

[Bhímavaram. Telugu. Opposite the Rắmasvámi temple.]

TRANSLATION.

Hail! On Thursday the 7th of the dark fortnight of Vaiṣákha of the year Viródhikṛit, corresponding to the year 1475 of the illustrious, victorious and prosperous Ṣáliváhana Ṣaka era, Ṣríman Mahámandaléṣvara . . . a stone pillar. Bhímavarapu . . . we have given a wet field of . . *gorlu* . . . . dry field . . . . . ¼ *puṭṭi* Iruvapalli. We have given with libation of water a field of . . *gorlu* and fifty *kunṭas* of paddy field, to conduct . . . . to . . gáru . in the street of Irópalli. We have given wet field . . . and dry field. Therefore we have given . . . . to Vánduya and 1,000 *kunṭas* of dry land as a sarvamánya to Jámu Gáru. All the crops raised in the village . . . . under the tank . . . continue the choultry shall acquire in perpetuity as long as the moon and sun endure all blessings. Ṣrí, Ṣrí, Ṣrí (One imprecatory verse).

For this he will enjoy all blessings; but whoever violates the charity shall fall into eternal perdition to all generations.

May it cause great prosperity!

NOTE.—The cyclic and Ṣaka years do not quite correspond.

1. స్వస్తిశ్రీ జయాభ్యుదయ శాలివాహన
2. శకవర్షంబులు ౧౪౭౫ అగునేంటి విరో
3. ధికృతు సంవత్సర వైశాఖ బ ౭ గురువారమున శ్రీ
4. మన్మహా మండలేశ్వర అప్రతిక . . . . . చెరు . వి
5. . . . రెడు యిడెమూాడ . . . లు . వడు ఇయ్య

6. . . . సన శిలా స్తంభం । భీమవరపు . . . . . . ము
. . .

7. . . రి . వ . పూర్వాలి . . . దా . . . . . .
తిర .

8. . . . . చెందుగొల్లు . . పాలానంవెలి . .

9. . . . . గుడులును . . . . లతో

10. గంపలో ఇరువల్లి . . . లుపునఖ । చేని స్థిమి

11. . . గ . కాత . . . . .

12. గారికి వుదకంపోశిచ్చిరి దత్తిచెల్లింప . . .

13. గొల్లుచేనున్ను వరిమడి యాబై గుంటలున్ను

14. నడుపం ఇస్తిమి ఇరెవల్లి తెరువునంబెట్టినది

15. మం బరపండు . . . . కి . . .

16. . . వరిమడి . . . . . . చెలున్న . . .

17. . . . ఇస్తిమిగనక . . . . . . తాంము . . . . వాందు
యు

18. కున్ను చలివెందలి . . గంగనున్ను . . . చ . .
ండివా

19. సరికిన్ని కూడాసు జాముగారికిన్ని వెలిపోలము

20. కు ౧౦౦౦ లున్న సర్వమాన్యంగానున్న ఇస్థిమి గ్రా
మాన పండిన

21. నానాధాన్యాలున్న . . నసా . . . చెర్వుక్రింద . .

22. . . లారు యీ . అసాగించేవారు ప్రత్రమ

23. . . . . సాగించేది వారుసత్రము . . నడవంగల

24. వారున్ను ఆచంద్రార్కస్థాయిగాను పొందుతారు శ్రీ శ్రీ శ్రీ

25. స్వదత్తాద్విగుణంపుణ్యం పరదత్తానుపాలనం పరదత్తాపహా

26. రేణ స్వదత్తంనిష్ఫలంభవేతు ఇందుకు సకలఫలము అనుభ
వించు

27. వాండు దప్పినవాండు పుత్రులు పౌత్రులు నరకమున బ

28. వారు శ్రీ శ్రీ శ్రీ జేయును

KANDUKUR (4). (A.D. 1644–45.)

[Boganampáḍu. Telugu. On tank bund.]

TRANSLATION.

Hail! On the 15th of Ṣrávaṇa of the year Táraṇa, corresponding to the year 1566 of the illustrious, victorious and prosperous Ṣáliváhana Ṣaka era, Parachúru Yangana Gáru, the grandson of Timmana Gáru and the son of Vóbhanésuḍu . . . Gáru and descendant of the Chivikápakala *Gótra* gave the villages . . . to . . who is of the fourth caste, the son of Guravayya and the grandson of Ayyappa. In these villages . . . . set up the deities.

1. స్వస్తిశ్రీ జయాభ్యుదయ
2. శాలివాహన శకవర్షంబు
3. లు ౧౫౬౬ అగునేటితా
4. రణ సంవత్సర శ్రావణ
5. శు ౧౫ లు చివికాపక
6. ల గోత్రోద్భవులున్ను
7. తిమ్మనగారి పౌత్రు
8. లున్ను వోభనేశుండ
9. . గారిపుత్రులున్ను అ
10. ఇనపరచూరియంగన
11. ంగారు చతుర్థవంశోద్భ
12. వులున్ను అయ్యపపౌత్రులు
13. లున్ను గురువయ్యంగా
14. రి పుత్రులు అయిన చె . .
15. ఉ . . తి . గో. . . .
16. తనికొ . నేనివ . . . అ
17. సీమలున్ను . జారి

18. అని యిచ్చినాంగాన
19. ఈ గ్రామమాను న . . .
20. . . . అడిగి ప్రతిష్టించెను .
21. . . మి . . .

Second side.

1. . . . . రింత
2. . . తుమ . . జం .
3. జాల . . ౧ జం . .
4. దనహ . . . దిముగతి
5. . . . .
6. . . . .
7. . . . .
8. . . . .
9. . . . .
10. . జెల్లించ . . .
11. క . . ము . . .
12. వుంగామ . . . వి .
13. . . . .
14. . . . చ్చ . . కుం .
15. . క . . . టి . . కు .
16. . . . మి . . . .
17. . . . .
18. . . . .
19. . . . .
20. . . . . . .
21. ధరా . . . . . .
22. కిదిని . . . . .
23. . . . . . .
24. . . . . . .

KANDUKUR (5).

[Chalamachala. Telugu. In a street.]

TRANSLATION.

Adoration be to Ṣrí Rámá, may it be auspicious! Hail! On the 10th . . . . of the year Viródhi, corresponding to the year . . . . of the illustrious, victorious, and prosperous Ṣáliváhana Ṣaka era . . . descendant of the *gótra* of Ganga, grandson of . . . . . son of Balabhadrayya endowed a *mányam* for *méras* to the tank in the village of Chalamachala in Kandukur *síma* which is in his enjoyment and gave a wet field under the tank . . . . 2½ *túms* (?) of wet and dry land under the . . . . To the *Upparas* (diggers) he gave a *mányam* free of tax at one-fourth of a *túm* per *puṭṭi* on all kinds of grain raised on wet and dry lands. Therefore the rulers, whoever take the lease of it, should maintain it in perpetuity as long as the sun and moon endure. Whosoever appropriates it without continuing the charity will incur the sin of killing a cow and a Brahman on the bank of the Ganges and of disobeying his spiritual preceptor. Those who continue this will get all kinds of prosperity, will have increase of progeny and will live happily. May it cause great prosperity!

(Signature.) DÁDANA.

1. శ్రీరామా॥ శుభమస్తు । స్వస్తిశ్రీ జయాభ్యుద
2. య శాలివాహన శకవర్షంబులు . . .
3. అగు నేటి విరోధినామసంవత్సర . . .
4. ౧౦ లు (వలిజరాతి) . . . . .
5. నుధుగం గోత్రోద్భవులయిన డు . . .

6. ంగనంగారి పవుత్రులు బలభద్రయ్యపుత్రులు
7. (ఈధుడని) కందుకూరి శీమలో మాకుం చెల్లె చల
8. మచాల గ్రామాన్ను చెరువు మెరలు మాన్యం ఛేసి
9. (డు వరిక్ర్మమ॰) చెర్వుకింద వరిమడి గాజులు
10. (లి . . . . స్త్రగి) వారిచెలోజనువరిమడివెలిం ౨॥
11. పుష్పరవారికి మాన్యము వరిమడివెలి పాలానపం
12. డిననానాదాన్యాన్ను వండ్లదింప్పులేక ఖం ౦౹ ఖైవె
13. ట్టి యిస్తిమిగనక యిందు అమరము గుత్తచేసిన
14. దొగలు ఆచంద్రాకర్కస్థాయిగా నడుపించగలవా
15. రు యివరు ఆశించ్చి నపహకున్నాను గంగలో గో
16. బ్రాంహ్మలవధించిన పాపానంబోదురు తమ గు
17. రువుల దప్పినట్టె యీధర్మము నడిపించేవారికి సక
18. ల శ్రేయస్సులుంగలిగి పుత్రపౌత్ర బ్రిద్ధిగా బ్రతుకు
19. దురు శ్రీ శ్రీ శ్రీం జెయునూ ॥ దాదనవ్రాలు

KANDUKUR (6).

[Chémeḍadapáḍu. Telugu. On image to south.]

TRANSLATION.

Hail! On Tuesday, the auspicious day, the 13th of the bright fortnight of Mágha of the year Khara, Mallu Bhíma Tammi, son of Dammi púvula Singaya . . . . for his father . . . . for his mother . . . .

1. ఖరసంవత్సర
2. మాఘ శు ౧౩ మ
3. ం దవారు పుణ్యదినసమయం
4. దమ్మిపూవుల సింగయకొమారు
5. డు మల్లు భీమతమ్మి తండ్రి (అ)
6. పనదాన పెద్ది . .
7. తల్లి . . . .

KANDUKUR (7).

[Chémeḍadapáḍu. Telugu. On two sides of a stone to the east.]

TRANSLATION.

Hail! On . . . . Ṣríman Mahámanḍaléṣvara Gópála Mahá Rájulu who is endowed with all eulogistic titles, who is the vanquisher of the three kings . . . for his mother and his gods . (founded this charity).

. . .

NOTE.—Possibly this is Gópála the son of Ranga V.

1. స్వస్తిశ్రీ . . . . .
2. సంవత్సర . . . . .
3. . త్యంబున . త్ర . . .
4. . (శుష) . . . పనాధని . కట్టి
5. (కా . కి . . . . .)

Second side.

1. యశనువమువారినా . .
2. సమస్త ప్రశస్తి సహితం శ్రీమ
3. న్మహామండలేశ్వర మూరురాయరగం
4. డ గోపాలరమహారాజులు తమ
5. తల్లిధమ్మ దేవులకున్ను . . . ముగా
6. . కి . . . .
7. . . . .
8. . . . .

KANDUKUR (S). (A.D. 1387–88.)

[Chennipáḍu. Sanskrit in Telugu character and Telugu. On a stone standing in temple of Sangaméṣvara.]

TRANSLATION.

Sanskrit.

In the Ṣrí Ṣaka year reckoned by the moon (1), Rámas (3), sky (0), and nine (*i.e.*, 1309) in the year Prabhava, on the *tithi* of Dharma (11th) of the bright fortnight of Ásvayuja, he constructed a temple of Ṣiva.

2. He repaired the ruined temple of Sangaméṣvaradéva up to the dome, which is situated on the holy bank of the junction of the rivers Kshíra (Pálêru) and Mákéru, and which is at a place about 15 *yójanas* [1] to the north-east of the peak of Ṣríṣaila.

Telugu.

The regents of the cardinal points Indra, &c., the nine planets, the sun, &c., earth, water, fire, air and ether; day and night, the years, months and seasons, the spirits, the elephants of the eight points of the horizon, ... the animal and vegetable worlds . . . .

NOTE.—The first ten lines are in Sanskrit. The form *kuryât* (may do) is used for *akarôt* (did). The inscription is not complete. The Ṣaka year is denoted as usual by words—but they represent digits from left to right which is not usual.

1. श्रीशकवर्षे शशिरामगगन नव
2. संख्यप्रभवाब्दे । आश्वयुज शु
3. क्लपक्षधर्मतिथौ शिवालयं

---

[1] *Yójana* = 4 kros or probably about 8 miles.

4. कुर्यात । श्रीशैलशिखर आग्ने
5. यभागे पंचादशयो
6. जनविस्तारायामभू
7. मिसमीपक्षीरवाहिनी
8. माकेटिसंगमपुण्यनीर
9. संगमेश्वरदेवखिलमंदिरं
10. शिखरपर्यन्तं कुर्यात । దేవేం
11. ద్రుండమోదలైన దిక్పాలకు
12. లున్ను ఆదిత్యాదినవగ్ర
13. హాలున్ను పృథివ్యప్సుతే
14. జవాయురాకాశములు
15. న్ను అహోరాత్రములుంన్ను
16. సంవత్సరమాసఋతు
17. వులున్ను అశరీరులు
18. అష్టదిగ్గజాలు
19. కులపర్వతంబులున్ను
20. స్థావరలజంగమంబులున్ను
21. యెఱిం

KANDUKUR (9).

[Chennipáḍu. Telugu. On a stone in the temple of Sangaméṣvara. The stone is broken right through on the left side. The inscription as it stands is unintelligible.]

1. . రజో .
2. . మహాసం .
3. . కర్ణాటకదువేం .
4. . ల సత్రహార ప్ర

5. . దిగ్విజయార్చ్జిత గంక
6. . లోక చచువ్వర్న్న శ్రవ
7. . . సురమకుట ఘటిచరణ
8. . . నారాయణ కుమార కందర్పస్వ
9. . . చండ్డ జలదంకరి బుర పభు
10. . . ణా బంధు జనాశ్రయప్రసన్న ప్ర
11. . . డి సర్వప్రాజ్ఞ నిజసేవక భర
12. . . బిడలర్భ, వరప్రసాదకోడువ
13. . . పురవరదీశ్వర కామకోటూం
14. . . లాంచ్ఛన వెంగళ నాథకంచ్చి
15. . . వాము పటి ఘోషణ వృషబె
16. . . ంద్రశ్ఖర ఖట్వాంగధ్వజకడు
17. . . బారద్వాజగోత్ర లలితాదాచవే
18. . . మపల్లవకులతిలక
19. . . రమేశ్వర పరమవంశిడ్భ
20. . . లరాజధిరాజ రాజ ప
21. . . స్వస్తి అనేకమటిమఃడ

Kandukur (10).

[Chennipáḍu. Telugu. On a stone in the temple of Saṅgaméṣvara.]

Translation.

We have granted the two villages Oḍḍumganṭṭu and Chennunipáḍu, with a libation of water, situated at the sacred confluence of the *Kshíra Nadi* (Páléru) and the Mákéru for (providing) *amritapaḍi* (sacred food), all enjoyments and the sixteen kinds of service to Ṣrí Kúḍali[1] Sangaméṣvara, who resides at the confluence of the two

---

[1] Kúḍali = confluence of two rivers.

rivers, as a gift in perpetuity to last as long as the sun and moon exist. We have made the gift with the righteous rulers of the eight worlds (points of the horizon) as witnesses. We shall bear on our head the lotus feet of those righteous persons who know this and, not scorning it, protect the charity.

[One imprecatory verse.]

May it cause great prosperity!

1. శ్రీ కూడలిసంగమే
2. శ్వర మహాదేవుని అమృ
3. తపల్లికును అంగగంగవై
4. భపభోగరాగ షోడశోప
5. చారాలకున్ను ఒడ్డుంగంట్లు
6. చెన్నునిపాడ గ్రామద్వయం
7. ఆ చంద్రార్కస్థాయిగాను క్షీ
8. రనదిమూకేటి కూడలి
9. పుణ్య సంగమంలోను
10. ధారాదత్తంచేసి సమర్పి
11. ంస్తిమి అష్టలోకధర్మ
12. పాలకులుసాక్షిగాను ఇస్తి
13. మి యీధర్మము ఎరింగి
14. న్ని తిరస్కరించక పాలిం
15. చ్చిన పుణ్యులపాదపద్మ
16. ములు తమశిరసున ను
17. ంచుదును। స్వదత్తాద్ద్విగుణ
18. ంపుణ్యం। పరదత్తాను
19. పాలనం। పరదత్తాపహారే
20. ణ స్వదత్తం నిష్ఫలం భ
21. వేత్ ‖ మంగళమహా
22. శ్రీ శ్రీం జేయును.

KANDUKUR (11).

[Chennipáḍu. Telugu. On a stone by the field of Managaváru to the north of the pond of Bade Sahib.]

TRANSLATION.

The charitable edict granted by Jóvipallikha Narasingamanáyaningáru to Jangam Pápaya, the priest of Sangaméṣvara, on Thursday, the 11th of the bright fortnight of Chaitra of the year Vyaya. We have given land—1,000 *kuntas* of dry waste land, as measured with a pole three feet in length, in the field named Puliváguchépu chĕnu in the southern fields of Chenupalli in Chunḍi *Ṣíma* which Konḍamarusayya was pleased to grant to us as an *amaram*, with libation of water, for providing *amritapaḍi* (sacred food) to Sangaméṣvara (whose temple is) on the sacred river at the confluence of the rivers Kshíra (Páléru) and Mákĕru.

They (the donees) should utilize the eight species of enjoyment and ownership with respect to this land for the deity three times a day and enjoy them as long as the sun and moon last. Those who fail to keep up this charity will be regarded as having broken their word (?) and trangressed the regulations of their caste and (the precepts of) their spiritual preceptors; they will incur the guilt of committing sins such as cow-slaughter and Brahmanicide on the banks of the Ganges. The righteous people who protect this charity will have increase of life, health, wealth and progeny, and live for many Brahmakalpas (cycles of Brahma).

[Two of the usual imprecatory verses.]

May it cause great prosperity!

NOTE.—Chenupalli is doubtless the earlier name of Chenupáḍu. Konḍamarusayya is Ráyasam K. the governor of Udayagiri. The grant of Chundi *S.ma* to a stranger indicates the complete suppression of the Reḍḍi line which ruled at Chunḍi.

1. వ్యయసంవత్సర చైత్ర శు ౧౧ గు । జోవిపల్లి ఖ

2. ఃగశింగమనాయనింగారు సంగమేశ్వరుని సమారాధ

3. నకుడు జంగం పాపయకు ఇచ్చిన ధర్మశాసనం । కొండ మురు స

4. య్యవారు మాకు అమరానకు పాలించ నవధరించిన చుండిశీమ

5. లోని చెంనుపల్లె దక్షిణపు పొలంలోను పులివాంగుచేప చేనుబీ

6. డువెలిచెను త్రిపాదపడగులగడను ౧౦౦౦ కుంటల క్షే త్రం క్షీర

7. నది మాకేటికూడలి పుణ్యనదిలోను సంగమేశ్వరుని అ మృతపల్లకు

8. ధారాపూర్వకంగాను సమర్పించ్తిమి ఇ క్షేత్రంవల్లం గల అష్ట

9. భోగ తేజస్వామ్యములు దేవునికి త్రికాలవేళాను అవధ రింపం జే

10. శి అచంద్రార్కం అనుభవించి బ్రతికిడి ॥ ఇ పుణ్యానకు తప్పిన-

11. వారువాచార కులాచారలకు వెలి తమగురువులకుతప్పిన వారు గంగకరు

12. తగోహత్య బ్రంహ్మత్యాది పాతకాలుచేసిన దోషానంబో వువారు ఇ పుణ్యం పాలి

13. ంచిన పుణ్యులు ఆయురారోగ్య అఇశ్వర్యములు పుత్రపౌ త్రాభివ్రిద్ధిం గలిగి అ

14. నేక బ్రంహ్మకల్పాలు బ్రతుకుదురు। స్వదత్తా ద్విగుణం పుణ్యం పరదత్తా

15. ను పాలినం । పరదత్తాపహారేణ । స్వదత్తం నిష్ఫలం భవేత్ ॥

16. స్వదత్తాం పరదత్తాం వా యో హరేతి వసుంధరః । షష్టి వర్ష

17. సహస్రాణి విష్టాయాంజాయతే క్రిమి ॥ మంగమహా శ్రీ శ్రీం జేయః

KANDUKUR (12). (A.D. 1643–44.)

[Chévúru. Telugu. To east of village in field No. 230-A; from four sides of a stone.]

TRANSLATION.

First and second sides.

Ṣrí Ráma! Hail! On Sunday the 15th of the bright fortnight of Mágha of the year Svabhánu, corresponding to 1566 of the illustrious, victorious, and prosperous Ṣáliváhana Ṣaka era . . . . descendant of the Srívatsa *gótra*, follower of the Ápastamba *Sútra* and master of the Yajuṣṣákha, grandson of [Káṭa]mráju, son of Ayyaparáju . . . . Venkaṭa Peda . . . . ráju . . . . Ṣrí Véma . . . . son of . . . . na ráchiráju . . . . land . . . .

Third side.

To continue the *méras* in the village of Chévúr which has been in the enjoyment of Ṣrí Chennakéṣava, (they) granted grain on a field of 10 *puṭṭis*. At that rate the illustrious Reḍḍis . . . . a field in the south-east corner of that village to the Uppara . . . . to last as long as . . . . sun endure as a (sarva)mánya. Kápu Damma Péranṭálu . . . .

Fourth side.

Unintelligible.

NOTE.—This inscription was deciphered by Mr. V. Venkayya. Perhaps for Káṭamrázu we should read Kasuvarázu and compare K.R. 80 and K.V. 1.

First side.

1. శ్రీరామా
2. స్వస్తి శ్రీజ-
3. యాభ్యుద-
4. య శాలివా-
5. హనశకవరుషం
6. బులు .౧౫౬ [౬] అ-
7. గు నేంటి స్వభాను
8. నామసంవత్స-
9. ర మాఘశుద్ధ
10. ౧౫ అ ౧ శ్రీవ-
11. త్స గోత్రోద్భవులు-
12. ంను ఆపస్తంబ-
13. సూత్రులుంను
14. యజుశాఖాధి-
15. నాయకు లుం
16. ను [కాట] మ రా-
17. జుగారి పౌ-
18. త్రులుంను
19. అయ్యపరాజు

Second side.

20. గారి పు-
21. త్రులుం
22. . . .
23. . . .
24. వెంకట
25. పెద . . .
26. . రాజు

27. . . నరా
28. చిరాజు
29. కొమార
30. శ్రీవేమ
31. . . .
32. . . .
33. . . .
34. . . .
35. క్షేత్రము
36. . . .
37. కంమకు
38. . . .
39. . నారు

Third side.

40. శ్రీ చెన్నకేశవా
41. . . . స చె[ల్లి]-
42. వచ్చె శేవూరు
43. గ్రామాన పేరుంన
44. మేర నడపింప
45. ఖ ౧౦ సేనను ధా.
46. న్యాన పె[టి]రి
47. ఆ లెఖన ప్రీతి
48. శ్రీ రెడ్లుగన ఆ
49. వూర . . చేను
50. ఆగ్నేయ మూలవు
51. పరవాని . .
52. పలిమటకెలు .
53. . . దిత్తకాల
54. . . మాన్యం

55. . కాపు దంష్ము

56. పేరంటాలు

57. . లోన . . .

Eight more damaged lines.

Fourth side.

1. దీనికి అ
2. హింతఖిచ్చ [పి]
3. ఖీచ్చన వాణ్డు
4. భారణాసి (ఐ)
5. వెయు గుళ్ళవు
6. వెయు చెఱువు
7. ళు వెయు గవి
8. లాళు వేపురు
9. పాఱను వేవు
10. కన్యళనుము
11. టిచ్చిన (వి)
12. (శ్య) అయ్యో (దు) (॥*)

KANDUKUR (13).

[Chouṭapāḷem. Telugu. Opposite Gógulamma temple.]

TRANSLATION.

On the 12th day of the dark fortnight of Asháḍha of the year Íṣvara . . Chavuṭáripálem . . . .

1. యీశ్వర సం
2. వత్సర ఆషా
3. డబహుళ ౧౨ చవు
4. టారిప్యాలెం

* * * *

Kandukur (14). (A.D. 1613–14.)

[Chuṇḍi (hamlet Linganapáḷem). Telugu. To the west. On four sides of a stone.]

Translation.

Hail! On Sunday the 10th day of the dark fortnight of Chaitra of the year Pramádicha, corresponding to the year 1535 of the illustrious, victorious and prosperous era of Ṣáliváhana Ṣaka, the acts of piety performed by Ayyapiyanḍu Bálinenḍu Virappangári Rapamádharunḍu . . . . . Náyaningáru grandsons of Káminéní Dádi Nāyaningáru, and sons of Vīrararághava Nayaningáru and Konḍamámba, while he was ruling the town of Chunḍi granted to him as an *amaram* by Mahimandu Khulikuḍupullamgáru are as follows . . He gave *méras* and *mányams* in the villages under his jurisdiction to Brahmaréṣvara of Árumúru for daily offerings and worship with a lamp . . (unintelligible).

Second side.

. . . in the villages named . . he founded a village and caused a tank to be constructed in the name of his father Vīralaya. In the name of his mother Konḍamma he founded the village named Konḍa Samudram and gave it as an *Agrahára* to Bodénapalli Gópináthayya's son (Ṣrí Chippalaka Tiruhấram) (?) He caused a well to be sunk in her name in the Nallam Reḍḍi . . . . . varu's yard. To the north of Chunḍi he got a tank constructed in the name of his brother Ayyana and gave *mányams* under it to deities and Brahmans. He got a tank constructed in the name of his younger brother Venkaṭappa to the south of Chunḍi.

He got a tank constructed in the name of his sister Kirtivandé (vi ?) Tirumalamma. He had a tope planted in the name of Dáduva. (?) He dedicated the tanks and villages to those persons in whose name they were respectively constructed.

Third side.

Whoever fail to continue these charities as long as the sun and moon remain will be born in the womb of a donkey. He caused a . . . . constructed for his younger brother Polinéni Khinuláma? Those that continue this in this manner . . . . will incur the sin of .

Fourth side.

He provided for daily offerings and worship with a lamp and arranged the performance of annual festivals. (The temple of) Chuṇḍi Janárdana Svámi being in ruins since the days of the Reḍḍis (Reḍḍi dynasty) he had the temple plastered with chunam set up the deity in the temple and founded an endowment for daily offering and worship with lamps. He founded festivals.

Note.—In K.R. 20 we have Káminéni Muttarázu who was apparently the son of the Polinéni mentioned here. The granter of the amaram must be Muhammad Kuli Kutb Sháh of Golkoṇḍa. The inscription shows that by the beginning of the 17th century the Mussalmans had obtained the sovereignty over the northern part of the district. The use of the name Káminéni seems to show connection with the family of the present Zamíndárs of Chuṇḍi. That estate dates its existence as a jághír or amaram from 1487 (*vide* p. 724 of the District Manual). It may perhaps be regarded as the last surviving fragment in Nellore district of the old Reḍḍi kingdom.

1. స్వస్తి శ్రీజయాభ్యుదయ
2. శాలివాహన శకవరుషం

3. బుబు ౧౪౩౫ అగునేటి ప్రమా
4. దీచసంవత్సర చైత్ర బ
5. ౧౦ ఆశ్రీమన్మహా నాయ
6. కాభాప్పిలైన ఇనుమహానిధి
7. అభవులైయిన కామినేవిదా
8. దినాయనింగారి పవుత్రులు
9. ంన్న వీరరాఘవనాయు
10. నింగారికిన్ని కొండమాంబకు
11. ంన్నపుత్రులయిన అయ్యపి
12. యండు బాలినెండు వీర
13. ప్పంగారి రవమాధరుండు
14. . . . నాయనింగారు
15. మహిమందు ఖులికుడు ఫుల్లం
16. గారు అమరంపాలించ్చని పు
17. . . చుండ్డి పట్టణమేలు
18. చున్నండాజేసిన పుణ్యాలు । ఆరు
19. మూరి . . భ్రమరేశ్వరునికి వ .
20. (రమ్మురా . యం . . తనతో)
21. లు చెడిగ్రామాలను మే
22. రమాన్యాలు సాగించ్చి
23. నిచ్చి నయివేద్య దిపా
24. రాధనలుకు నిచ్చిరి
25. (ను ను) ల గోవులబ్రాంహ)
26. (దివలంసుర నంగియియి)

Second side.

1. అనే గ్రామం యిచ్చిను
2. తమతండ్రి వీరలయ
3. పూరిపేర గ్రామం గట్టిం

4. చ్చి చెరువు గట్టించెను
5. తమతల్లి కొండంగా
6. రిపేర కొండసముద్రము
7. అనేగ్రామము గట్టించి బోదెనప
8. ల్లి గోపినాధయ్యవారి కొమా
9. ళ్లు (శ్రీచిప్లలట లిరుహారల)
10. (శేశెను నల్లందడ్డి వారి పే)
11. దను ఆమెపేరనే భావి గట్టి
12. ంచెను చుండికి పుత్రరాన్నను
13. తమ అన్న అయ్యనపేరను
14. చెరువు గట్టించి ఆ చెరు
15. వు కిందను దేవబ్రియాల
16. కు మాన్యాలు యిచ్చిరిచుండి చ
17. తుణాశంతన తంముండు వె
18. ంకటప్ప పేరను చెరువు గట్టి
19. ంచెను కిర్తివందె దమ చెల్లె
20. లు తిర్మలంమ పేరను చె
21. రువు గట్టించెను దాదువు
22. పేరను (తొంపు) వేయించెను
23. గ్రామాలు చెరువులు యెవ్వ
24. రెవ్వరి పేరను గట్టించెనారు
25. వారి వారిక్ పేరను అచిణం
26. చిరి.

Third side.

1. . అచం
2. ద్రాకణంగా
3. ను నడిపిం
4. చ్చునివారు
5. గాడిద క

6. డుపున బు
7. ట్టిదురు
8. తన తంమ్ము
9. ఁడు పాలినే
10. ని ఖినులామ
11. ంగటించిరి
12. యీ ప్రకారం
13. గాను యవరు న
14. డపిఇంచినేని
15. వారు . . .
16. . . . . ప్ర
17. చ్చువారు . . .
18. నశించిన
19. పాపాన
20. ం బోదు
21. రు.

Fourth side.

1. నిత్య నైవేద్య
2. దిపారాధ
3. నలు కటడ
4. చేసి యాం
5. టను తీర్థ
6. ం సాగించె
7. ను చుండి
8. జనార్థన
9. దేవుండు రె
10. డ్డి వారి నా
11. టి నుండిం

12. స్న ఖిలపడి
13. పుండ్డం
14. గాను దేవ
15. శగ సుంన్న
16. ం శేఖుంచి
17. దేవుని ప్ర
18. తిష్టచేశి ని
19. త్య నైవేద్య
20. దిపారా
21. ధనలు క
22. ట్టడి చేశిరి
23. మహాహాత్స
24. వానుచిన
25. మెరవాడు

KANDUKUR (15).

[Old Chundi. Sanskrit in Telugu character. From a stone outside Rámalingasvámi temple.]

TRANSLATION.

1. May the Boar protect the earth—the god, the lord who sportively supported the earth with his tusk . . .[1]

2. (Some letters are illegible and the meaning is not clear; the words seem to be an invocation to Śiva who has the moon on his crest.)[2]

3. Just as the Brahmans, Kshatriyas and others were born from the body—the mouth, arms, thigh and feet—of Vishnu, the Panṭa race arose from his foot.

---

[1] Portion of this verse is illegible.

[2] Only a few words are legible.

4. From the milky ocean of the Panṭa race arose Alla (*read* Anna?) Bhúpati, whose enemies were crushed by his columnar arms and who honours his kindred.

5. By his son Véma, excellent king, victorious, the vanquisher of foes, who ruled the earth, Kali (Yuga) was made Kritayuga (the first or golden age),

6. Who was Jayanta (son of Indra) by his beauty, Vasanta (spring) in causing delight to men, Yama in battle, Révanta (son of the sun) in horsemanship.

7. The sky seemed as if it were adorned with the rays of the autumnal moon which was his fame; he gave beauty to the moon which has a spot on it (?) [1]

8. He had eleven sons, very intelligent, best of men, resembling Rudra in valour, accomplished in (making) gifts; the most excellent in all qualities. Amongst them one was known as Malla Bhúpa who resembled Káma in beauty, and who was firm in truth; who was like the lord of the rivers (ocean) in depth (magnanimity), and the earth in patience; always devoted to the worship of Śiva, who was as it were another Vishnu in valour.

9. The treasurer and servant of that king was Srí Kóna Singaya Sṛéshti (Kómaṭi), the best of merchants, always devoted to the worship of Śiva,

10. Devoted to the worship of Hara (Śiva), fond of stories of Sadáṣiva (or, always fond of stories of Śiva), truthful in speech, upright in character, renowned for having founded a settlement of his castemen (in that locality),

11. By him this two-roomed mansion of Uméṣvara (?) was caused to be constructed by the residents of the

---

[1] This verse is rather obscure; the reading is uncertain.

town of Chuṇḍi for the delight (merit) of his father who was in heaven.[1]

12. In the year Raktákshi, in the month of Chaitra, on the great *tithi*, viz., the 2nd, (he) gave for securing enjoyment (in heaven), renunciation, &c., to last as long as the sun and moon endure.

13. This village has been given to Bhímésaliṅga to last as long as the earth consisting of seven continents lasts, and as long as the seven mountains endure.

The protection of this charity should be maintained by all kings; this charity must be protected by those like you.

14, 15, 16. [Imprecatory verses.]

17. Next the description of the fields (granted) is written in the Telugu language.[2]

Ṣri! Ṣri!

NOTE.—The inscription is in Sanskrit verses. The writing is not legible in some places.

1. विश्वंभरां व
2. राहोव्याह्रचे
3. यो दंष्ट्रया
4. महीम् । . . . . . .
5. लीला . . . . .
6. संयोग
7. वताद्देवोयं क्री
8. डया विभुः ।(1) तुंडा
9. सप्तर्षित्वामुं . . .
10. । चंद्रमास्सोऽवता . .

[1] Some of the letters of this verse are illegible.
[2] The portion giving the boundaries is missing.

11. जटाजूटकृतास्थितिः । नेपथ्य
12. रतस्य मणि द . . . .
13. तः । (2) मुखबाहूरुपादाब्ज
14. ब्राह्मणक्षात्रियादयः ।
15. विष्णोजार्ता यतस्तन्वोः पादात
16. पटान्वयाभवत् । (3) पंटान्वय
17. क्षीरनिधावुदभूदल्लभू
18. पतिः । दोर्दंडखंडितारा
19. तिः स्वजनप्रतिपूजकः ॥ (4) तस्य
20. पुत्रेण जयिना वेमभूपव
21. रेण गाम् । प्रशासतामित्रजि
22. ता कलिः कृतयुगीकृतः ॥ (5) जगं
23. तो निजरूपेण वसंतो ज
24. नरंजने । कृतांतो योभ
25. वद्युद्धे रेवंतोश्वाधिरोह
26. णे ॥ (6) यस्य कीर्तिशरच्चंद्रचं
27. द्रिकाभूषितं नभः । अं
28. तर्गतकलंकस्य विद्या धत्ते[1]
29. सु[2] रूपतां ॥ (7) तस्य पुत्रा म
30. हाप्राज्ञा एकादश नरोत्तमा
31. ः । तेजसा रुद्रसदृशा अभ
32. वन् दानशौंडिनः । तेषु स
33. र्वगुणश्रेष्ठो मल्लभूप
34. इति श्रुतः । रूपेण मन्म
35. थाकारस्सत्ये च परिनिष्ठितः ।
36. गांभीर्ये सिं

---

[1] Read धत्ते.

[2] Read स.

37. धुराज्ञेन
38. क्षांत्या विश्वं
39. भरासम : ।शि
40. वपूजारतो नि
41. त्यं शौर्ये विष्णु
42. रिवापरः ॥ (8) तस्य
43. राज्ञो धनाध्यक्षः
44. सेवको वणिजां व
45. रः । श्रोकोनशिंग
46. यश्रेष्ठी शिवपूजा
47. रतोन्वहम् ॥ (9) ह
48. रस्य पूजानिरत
49. स्सदा शिवकथाप्रि
50. यः । सत्यवाग्धर्म
51. शीलश्च कुलस्थापन
52. विश्रुतः ॥ (10) तेन द्विभ
53. वनं सौधं चुं
54. डीनगरवासिभि
55. : । उमेश्वर
56. स्वर्गस्थस्य
57. पितुर्मुदे ॥ (11) रं
58. काक्षिवत्सरे
59. चैत्रे द्वितीया
60. यां महाति
61. थौ । आचंद्र
62. तारकं प्रा
63. दाद्भोगत्या

64. गादिसिद्धये ॥ (12)
65. सप्तद्वीपा धरा
66. यावद्यावत्स
67. प्त धराधराः
68. तावद्भी(वे)मेशलिंगाय ग्रामोयं
69. प्रतिपादितः । धर्मानुवर्त्ति
70. नं कार्यं सर्वेम्मेनुजवल्लभहिः[1]
71. सोयं धर्म्मः प्रय
72. त्नेन पालनीयो भव
73. द्भिः ॥ (13) सामान्योयं
74. धर्म्मसेतुर्नृपाणां
75. कालेकाले पालनीय्यो
76. भवाद्भिः । सर्वानेतान्भा
77. विनः पार्थिवेंद्रान्भू
78. योभूयो याचते
79. रामचंद्रः ॥ (14) स्वदत्तां
80. परदत्तां वा यो
81. हरेति वसुंधरां
82. षष्टिवर्षसहस्राणि
83. विष्टायां जायते क्रिमिः ॥ (15)
84. स्वदत्ताद्द्विगुणं पुण्यं
85. परदत्तानुपालनं
86. परदत्तापहारेण स्वद
87. त्तंमपि निष्फलं भवेत् ॥ (16) ततःपरः
88. आंध्रभाषया क्षेत्रानि
89. र्णयो लिख्यते ॥(17) श्री श्री

---

1 Read वल्लभैः.

KANDUKUR (16). (A.D. 1430–31.)

[Old Chuṇḍi. Telugu. From three sides of a stone in front of Kámákshamma temple.]

TRANSLATION.

First side.

Hail! On Thursday, the 11th of the bright fortnight of Phálguna of the year Sádháraṇa, under the Vṛishabha (Ṛishabha) *lagna*, corresponding to the illustrious Ṣaka year 1352, Kommana Sómayájulu, who is the prime minister (Pradháni) of Kómaṭi Reḍḍi, the son of Ṣrígiri Reḍḍi; who (*Kommana*) is of the Maitrávaruṇa *Gótra*, and of the Ápastambha *Sútra*, who is the grandson of Dúbaguṇṭa Máramarájn, who is the son of Rámarája and Brammasáni, and the younger brother of Bairavanna, Mádhavanna, Déchana, and Narahari, and who is the disciple of Amala Bhárata, with the help of his sons Rámachandra and Náráyaṇadévara, who were born to him of his wedded wife Lakkamámba, brought a *Svayambhu Linga* (a natural *linga*) from the Pátálaganga at Ṣríṣaila to the sacred place where he had performed the two sacrifices "Agnishṭoma" and "Atirátri," between the Tumiléru and the Tompéru (two streams) in the town of Chuṇḍi, to the north of Chuṇḍi fort, and set it up as Yajnéṣvaradéva. This Kommana Sómayájulu caused to be built a stone temple and a *manḍapa* for this deity. He set up all around this deity (images of) Vighnéṣvara, Durgá, Gópáladéva and Bhairavadéva, and caused to be erected stone temples for these deities. He planted in that place (two) sacrificial stone pillars for marking the two sacrifices performed by him. He planted a grove all round the *prákára* of that deity (Yajnéṣvara), caused to be built a sacrificial fire-place on the north-west of it, and founded an endowment for providing all enjoyments to that deity.

The sons of the aforesaid Kómaṭi Reḍḍi, viz., Tippaya Reḍḍi, ditto (*i.e.*, Tippaya) Ṣrígiranna, Rámayya, Dévaráyunḍu, Náráyanadéva—granted the following lands, with libation of water, in the presence of Virúpákshadéva, who is on the banks of the Tungabhadra: 3 *puṭṭis* of dry land in Chunḍi; 30 *túms* of dry land in Lingamgunṭa; 2 *marutus* of wet land in Chunḍi in rear of the Prólasamudram tank; and 1 *túm* on every harvested heap of all kinds of grain in Chunḍi and its hamlets, in Lingamgunṭa and in Mompáḍu;

to the aforesaid Gópáladéva: a dry field of 30 *túms* and a *marutu* of wet field in Chunḍi;

to the aforesaid Vighnéṣvara, Durgá, and Bhairava—3 *puṭṭis* of dry land in Chunḍi at 1 *puṭṭi* each; so that the deities may enjoy the eight powers of ownership in them as long as the sun and moon exist.

Second side.

Therefore may every one maintain this charity and not let it go to ruin. Those who obstruct this charity will incur the sin of killing excellent cows and Brahmans on the Ganges.

[One imprecatory verse.]

The good services rendered by Kommana Sómayájulu are: a fresh water well with stone revetment in Kandukúr to the north behind the tank; the tank constructed between Kandukúr and Kóvúr, a well with stone revetment and a grove; a reservoir constructed at the northern end of the bund; a tank constructed to the east of Chunḍi; a well and fig trees planted there; the setting up of Viṣvéṣvaralinga and his temple at the northern end of Chunḍi Prólasamudram tank bund,

Third side.

the fresh water well sunk by Kommana Sómayájulu in the path to the north of Chunḍi fort for the religious merit of his son Hariharanátha (probably deceased). The works caused to be done by Rámachandra, son of the aforesaid Sómayájulu are: the dome of the temple of Núkanamma of Chunḍi; the tank constructed in that village to the north of the hill, and the fig trees planted there. The works caused to be done by his (Rámachandra's) younger brother Nárapurája are: the Chunḍi fort; a tank constructed to the west of the fort connecting Pálanaravakonḍa and Manyamkonḍa (two hills near Chunḍi) a well and a grove there.

NOTE.—The genealogies are as follows:—

Dúbaguntạ Máramarája.
|
Rámarája = Brammasáni.
|
Baira-vanna. | Mádha-vanna. | Déchana. | Narahari. | Kommana Sómayájulu = Lakkamâmba. (Donor)—Prime Minister of Kómati Reḍḍi.

Kommana Sómayájulu's sons:
Hariharanátha (deceased). | Rámachandra. | Náráyanadévara (Nárapurája.)

Srí Giri Reḍḍi.
|
Kómaṭi Reḍḍi—reigning chief.
|
Tippaya Reḍḍi. | Tippaya Reḍḍi Srígiranna. | Rámayya. | Dévaráyunḍu. | Náráyanadévara.

First side.

1. స్వస్తి శ్రీ శకవర్షంబులు ౧౩౫౨ అగునేంటి సాధా
2. ర సంవత్సర పాల్గునశుద్ధ ౧౧ గు నాండు వృషభల
3. లగ్నమునను । చుండి పట్నమందును । శ్రీగిరె డ్డింగా
4. రి కుమారుండు కోమట్రెడ్డింగారి ప్రధాని మైత్రా

5. వగుణగోత్రులు । ఆపస్తంబసూత్రులు దూబగు
6. ంట మారమరాజుంగారి మనుమలు రామరా
7. జుంగారికిన్ని బ్రహ్మసానింగారికిన్ని పుత్రులు బైర
8. వన్న । మాధవన్న । దేచన। నరహరింగారి తమ్ములు అమ
9. లబారతుల శిష్యులు కొమ్మన సోమయాజులు త
10. మ ధర్మపత్ని లక్కమాంబయందుం బడసిన పుత్రులు
11. రామచంద్రుండున్ను । నారాయణదేవరాను చేశిం
12. పంగానుచుండికోట ఉత్తరానను తూము లేటితోం
13. పేటి మధ్యమందును । అగ్నిష్టోమ । అతిరాత్రియజ్ఞాలు
14. రెండున్ను చేసిన పుణ్యస్థలమందును శ్రీ శైలానను పాతాళ
15. గంగలోని స్వయంభులింగముం దెచ్చి ప్రతిష్ట సేశించి
16. న యజ్ఞేశ్వరదేవుండు । యీ దేవునికిని ఆ కొమ్మన సోమ
17. యాజులు కలుగుడిన్ని మండపమున్ను కట్టించి అ దే
18. వునిం దిరిగి రాను విఘ్నేశ్వరునిన్ని । దుర్గని । గోపాళ
19. దేవునిన్ని । బైరవదేవునిన్ని । ప్రతిష్టల్లు సేశించి ఆ దేవళ్ల
20. కును కలుగుళ్లు గట్టించి ఆ ప్రదేశానను తారుచేసిన
21. రెండు క్రతువులకున్ను సిలా యూపస్తంబాలు నిలి
22. పి ఆ దేవుని ప్రాకారము తిరిగిరాను వనము వెట్టి
23. ంచ్చి ఆవాయవ్య భాగమందును గుండాము
24. గట్టించె । ఆ దేవుని అంగరంగ భోగాలకును చేసి
25. న నివార్ణహాము । ఆ కోమ్రరెడ్డింగారి కుమాళ్లు । తి
26. ప్పాయరెడ్డింగారు । అశ్రీగిరన్న । రామయ్య । దేవ
27. రాయుండు । నారాయణదేవరంగారు తు
28. ంగభద్రలోను విరూపాక్షదేవుని సన్నిధిని దారవో
29. సి పెట్టినవిచుండిని వెలిసేను మూండు పుట్లున్ను । లి
30. ంగముగుంటను ముప్పందుమున్ను చుండిం
31. ప్రోలసముద్రము చెఱువు వెనకను వరిచేను రె
32. ండు మఱుతులున్ను చుండిన్ని । చుండిలోని
33. పాలేలాను లింగముగుంటను । బ్రోంపాటను
34. నానాధాన్యాలందున్ను తలరాశితూములున్ను

35. ఆ గోపాలదేవునికి చుండినివెలిసేను ముప్పందు
36. మున్న వరిమఱుతువకటిన్ని, ఆ విఘ్నేశ్వరునికిన్ని
37. దుర్గ్గకిన్ని। భైరదేవునికిన్ని। పేరనుపుట్టెంటి లెఖను
38. చుండినివెలిశేను మూండుపుట్లున్ను ఇంతవట్టు
39. అష్టభోగ స్వామ్యముగాను ఆచంద్రార్క్క స్థా
40. ఇగాను ఇచ్చిరిగాన యీ ధర్మ్మము చెడకు

Second side.

41. ండాను పాలిం
42. చువారు ఇందు
43. కును యవ్వరు త
44. ప్పినాను గంగకఱత
45. ను గంగిగావున్ను
46. బ్రాహ్మనిన్ని చంప్పి
47. న పాపానం బో
48. వువారు॥ స్వదత్తా
49. ం పరదత్తాం వా
50. యో హరేతు వ
51. సుంధరాం ష
52. ష్టివర్ష సహస్రాణి
53. విష్టాయాం జా
54. యతే క్రిమిః॥
55. కొంమన సోమ
56. యాజులు చే
57. సిన దమ్మాలు క
58. ందుకూరను ఉ
59. త్తరానను చెఱువు
60. వెనకను జాకట్నము
61. మంచినీళ్ల నుయ్యి
62. ఆ కందుకూరి కో
63. వూరి నడుమును

64. కట్టించిన చెఱు
65. వున్ను ఱాకట్నము
66. ను ఇన్నీ వనమున్ను
67. ఆ ఉత్తరపుంగొ
68. మ్మునం గట్టించిన
69. కొలను । చుండి
70. తూర్పునను కట్టించి
71. న చెఱువున్నును
72. ఇన్ని అకరూడంబెట్టి
73. న అశ్వద్ధాలున్ను
74. చుండి ప్రోలస
75. ముద్రము చె

Third side.

76. ఱువు ఉత్తరపుంగొమ్మునను విశ్వేశ్వర లింగప్రతి
77. ష్ఠాను ఆ గుడిన్ని । కొమ్మన సోమయాజులు తమ
78. పుత్రుండు హరిహరనాథనికిం బుణ్యముగాను
79. చుండికోట ఉత్తరపువంక దారలోను త్రవ్వించి
80. న మంచినీళ్లబావి । ఆ సోమయాజుల పుత్రు
81. ండు రామచంద్రుండు చేఇంచినవి చుండినినూ
82. కనమ్మ గుడిశిఖరము । ఆ ఊరంగొండ ఉతరా
83. నను కట్టించిన చెఱువున్ను ఆ అశ్వతాలున్ను । ఆ
84. యన తమ్ముండు నారపరాజుంగారు వెట్టించి
85. న (వి) చుండికోట । ఆ కోటపడుమటను పాలనఱి
86. కొండాను మన్యముకొండాను కట్టించిన చె
87. ఱువున్ను అనుఇన్ని అవనమున్ను॥

NOTE.—నూఇ or నూయి. See lines 61, 66, 72, and 87.

A COLLECTION
OF THE
INSCRIPTIONS ON COPPER-PLATES AND STONES
IN THE
NELLORE DISTRICT

A COLLECTION
OF THE
INSCRIPTIONS ON COPPER-PLATES AND STONES
IN THE
NELLORE DISTRICT

MADE BY
ALAN BUTTERWORTH,
OF THE INDIAN CIVIL SERVICE (MADRAS)
AND

V. VENUGOPAUL CHETTY,
OF THE INDIAN CIVIL SERVICE (MADRAS)

IN THREE PARTS
PART II

GYAN

Published by

GYAN

Gyan Publishing House
5, Ansari Road
Daryaganj, New Delhi-110002
Phone: 011-47034999, 9811692060
E-mail: books@gyanbooks.com

Distribution Network
gyanbooks.com
India, USA, Canada, UK, Australia, France

ISBN : 978-81-212-3814-4 (Set)
ISBN : 978-81-212-9724-0 (HB)
First Published, 1905

2nd Impression 2020

Printed at: Gyan Press, Delhi.

A Collection of the Inscriptions on Copper-Plates and Stones in the Nellore District, Part-II
Author: Alan Butterworth, V. Venugopaul Chetty

A COLLECTION

OF THE

INSCRIPTIONS ON COPPER-PLATES AND STONES

IN THE

NELLORE DISTRICT.

MADE BY

ALAN BUTTERWORTH,

OF THE INDIAN CIVIL SERVICE (MADRAS)

AND

V. VENUGOPAUL CHETTY,

OF THE INDIAN CIVIL SERVICE (MADRAS).

IN THREE PARTS.

PART II.

MADRAS:

PRINTED BY THE SUPERINTENDENT, GOVERNMENT PRESS.

1905.

CONTENTS.

PART II.

ABBREVIATIONS USED IN THIS WORK.

Prefixed to a Number	A.	stands for	Átmakúr Taluk.
„	„	C.	„	Copper-Plate.
„	„	D.	„	Darsi Division.
„	„	G.	„	Gúdúr Taluk.
„	„	KG.	„	Kanigiri „
„	„	KR.	„	Kundukúr „
„	„	KV.	„	Kávali „
„	„	N.	„	Nellore „
„	„	O.	„	Ongole „
„	„	P.	„	Podili Division.
„	„	R.	„	Rápúr Taluk.
„	„	S.	„	Súlúrpet (or Pólúr) Division.
„	„	U.	„	Udayagiri Taluk.
„	„	V.	„	Venkatagiri Division.

B.	stands for	Brown's Telugu Dictionary.
Epig. Carn.	„	Epigraphia Carnataca.
E.I.	„	Epigraphia Indica.
I.A.	„	Indian Antiquary.
M.P.C.	„	Madhurántaka Pottapi Chóḷa.
M.K.	„	Mukkanṭi Káduveṭṭu.
M.M.	„	Mahá Mandaléṣvara.
S.M.	„	Srímanmahámandaléṣvara.
W.	„	Wilson's Glossary of Revenue terms.

A COLLECTION

OF THE

COPPER-PLATE AND STONE INSCRIPTIONS

IN THE

NELLORE DISTRICT.

PART II.

KANDUKUR (17). (A.D. 1430-31.)

[Old Chundi. Sanskṛit verses in Telugu character. From the fourth side of the same stone.]

TRANSLATION.

1. May the consort of Ṣrí (Vishnu) protect your eternal happiness—who, in the form of a sportive Boar, lifting up the earth even along with the mountains, is to be praised.

2 and 3. In the Ṣâka year denoted by (the chronogram) *Ṣríṣa Ṣlághyé*, *i.e.*, 1352, on the 8th *tithi* (of Ṣiva) of the bright fortnight in the month of Phálguna, on Wednesday, in the year Sádháraṇa, at the time of the rising of Ṛishabha (lagna), Kommanárya, the son of the minister Ráma, who was initiated (for sacrifice), having performed here the sacrifices Agnishṭóma and Atirátri according to scripture, permanently set up (the image of) Yajnéṣvara.

NOTE.—Kommanárya of this inscription is evidently the same person as Kommana Sómayájulu in No. 16.

1. श्रीशः क्रीडावरा
2. हात्मा पाया
3. द्वो नित्यकौतुकम् ।
4. सगोत्रामपि
5. गोत्रां यः
6. श्लाघनीयस्त
7. मुद्वहन ॥ (1)
8. आशाश्वोब्धि शका
9. ब्दे विमलशिवाति
10. थौ फाल्गुने मा
11. सि वारे । बौधे सा
12. धारणाब्देभ्यु
13. दयति वृष
14. भे रामया
15. मात्यसूनुः ॥ (2)
16. अग्निष्टोमातिरा
17. त्रौ विधिवदिह
18. विधायाध्वरौ
19. तत्प्रदेशे । यज्ञे
20. शस्य प्रतिष्ठाम
21. चलमरचय
22. द्दीक्षितः कोम्मना
23. र्यः ॥ (3)

KANDUKUR (18). (A.D. 1408–09.)

[Old Chundi. Telugu. From one side of a stone near Janárdanasvámi's temple.]

TRANSLATION.

Hail! On Saturday the thirteenth of the bright fortnight of Ṣrávana of the year Sarvadhári, corresponding to the illustrious Ṣaka year 1330, Maláya Reḍḍi, the younger brother of Kómaṭi Reḍḍi, who is the son of Ṣrígiri Reḍḍi, who is the excellent son of Pina Kómaṭi Reḍḍi, who is the son of Malláya Reḍḍi, the younger brother of Vémáya Reḍḍi, who (Vémaya) bore the birudas—Jagannobbagaṇḍa,[1] Jagatgópála,[2] Pallavádítya,[3] Pallavatrinétra,[4] Vairi Víra,[5] Basava Ṣankara, &c., who (Vémaya) built a flight of steps at Ṣríparvata,[6] and who made unlimited gifts of land, and the gifts described by Hémádri, for the purpose of securing the four kinds of human objects, caused to be set up an image of Ṣrí Janárdanadéva in the town of Chunḍi, caused to be constructed a temple and a *maṇḍapa*, bestowed, with libation of water, on that deity 4 *puṭṭis* and 10 *túms* of dry land in the fields of Chunḍi and 2 *marutus* of wet land in rear of Prólasamudram and 5 *túms* of wet land in Chunḍi, presented, with libation of water, the tax of 2 pies on each of his soldiers to provide for the great festivals of that deity, and made an endowment for food, enjoyments and pay (of servants) for the fortnightly and monthly festivals in his capital. Thus he founded a great charity to last in perpetuity as long as the sun and moon endure. May it cause great prosperity!

NOTE.—The genealogy is—

Véma. — Malla.
Malla → Pina Kómati Reḍḍi.
Pina Kómati Reḍḍi → Ṣrígiri Reḍḍi.
Ṣrígiri Reḍḍi → Kómati Reḍḍi. — Malla—Donor, S.S. 1330.

(See No. 17 for continuation of this table.)

[1] The sole hero of the world.
[2] The protector of the world.
[3] The Pallava sun.
[4] Trinétra (Ṣiva) of the Pallavas.
[5] Hero to enemies.
[6] Ṣríṣailam.

1. స్వస్తి శ్రీ శకవర్షంబులు ౧౩౩౦
2. అగునేంటి సర్వధారిసంవత్సర శ్రా
3. వణ శు ౧౩ శ జగనొబ్బగండ్డ జగత
4. గోపాలపల్లవాదిత్య పల్లవ త్రినేత్ర
5. వైరివీరబసవ శంకరాది బిరుదు
6. లంగల వాండైన శ్రీ పర్వ్వతాన·సో
7. పానాలు నిర్మ్మించి నిస్సీమ భూదాన
8. ముసు హేమాద్రిదానాలున్ను చేశి
9. న వేమాయరెడ్డింగారి తమ్ముండై
10. న మల్లాయరెడ్డింగారి కుమారు
11. ండ్లు పినకోమటి రెడ్డింగారి సుపు
12. త్రుండైన శ్రీగిరిరెడ్డింగారి కుమా
13. రుండు కోమటిరెడ్డింగారి తంము
14. ండైన మలాయరెడ్డింగారు చతు
15. ర్వ్వర్ధపురుషార్థసిద్ధికొఱకై చుండి
16. పట్టణమందున శ్రీ జనార్దన దేవ
17. రను ప్రతిష్ట శేయించి గుడిన్ని మ
18. ంటపమున్ను కట్టించి ఆ దేవర
19. కును చుండిపాలానను నాలుగు
20. పుట్లున్ను పండుమువెలి శేనున్ను
21. ప్రోలసముద్రము వెనుకను నీరు
22. నేలరెండు మఱుతులున్ను చు
23. ండిని దేవదాములున్ను దారా పూ
24. ర్వకంగాను సమర్పించి దేవర
25. మహోత్సవాలకు పరివారము
26. చేతను బంటుబడి దుగాండ్లున్ను
27. ధారవోయించి తమ నగరను మా

28. స పక్ష మహోత్సవాలకు పష్లున్ను
29. భోగజీతాలున్ను పెట్టించి ఆచం
30. ద్రార్కస్థాయైన మహాదర్మం చేశిరి
31. మంగళ మహా శ్రీ శ్రీ శ్రీం జే
32. యున్

KANDUKUR (19). (A.D. 1407–08 or 1408–09 ?)

[Old Chundi. Sanskrit verse in Telugu character. From three sides of the same stone.]

TRANSLATION.

V. 1. May Hari protect you, Hari who has assumed the stately form of a boar making a sound as deep as that of a thunder-cloud, who is resplendent with his principal limbs[1] which form the seat (origin) of the four castes and with his minor limbs which cause admiration and on the tip of whose tusks the earth, appearing like a cloud resting at the end of a fresh and lovely crescent of the moon, experiences the pleasure of (being in) a stream of delicious nectar.

2. I worship the elephant-faced god (Ganéśa) who destroys all obstacles. I salute Sarasvatí, who is as

---

[1] Angas—principal limbs—face, arms, thighs and feet from which the four castes arose.

Upangas—minor limbs—eyes, ears, &c., from which the quarters of the world, sun, &c., arose. *Angas* may also mean the six angas or sciences and *upangas* the minor or auxiliary sciences of the vedas. The Supreme Being is said to be the personification of the Vedas. In this case, चातुर्वर्ण्यपदे: = which are the receptacle of the duties of the four castes.

white as the jasmine and the moon and who is the giver of strength.

3. From Vishnu arose a certain caste, eminent in virtue, whose sister was the river (Ganga) on the crest of the braid of hair of Ṣiva.[1]

4. In that caste there was king Vêma, illustrious, the lord of the eastern country, who indeed caused to be forgotten (by his own excellence) the wealth of virtue of Ráma and others.

5. He rendered Ṣrí Parvata[2] accessible to men by (building) a flight of steps; he, the peerless, joyfully presented unlimited land to priests; hostile kings accompanied by *ṣama* ((i) peace, (ii) chants of the Sáma Veda), worship his two feet day and night with the *stóma* ((1) mass, (2) hymn of praise) of the rays of new gems set in their crowns.

6. His younger brother was *Malla*, emperor of the Earth, liberal, a full moon to his dependants, having mighty arms which were as it were mountains of churning to the ocean, to wit, the army of hostile kings.

7. His son was *king Kómaṭi*, a mine of valour, possessed of fame as white as the autumnal moon, a Karna in gift, a Dilípa in mercy, a Dharma in truth, the Earth in patience.

8. His son was *king Ṣrígiri*, who destroyed the pride of his foes, the treasury of wealth, honoured by his younger brothers—king Mácha and the others—who

---

[1] The fourth caste and Ganga (Ganges), were both sprung from the feet of Vishnu and so Ganga is called the sister of the fourth caste.

[2] Ṣríṣaila.

obeyed his commands and who were of very virtuous conduct.

9. Adorned with fame as white as the mountain of snow (Himálaya) and the moon, exclusively devoted to the gifts described by Hémádri, accomplished, the abode of affability, magnanimity and mercy, and the mine of valour.

10. Four sons were born to king Ṣrígiri like the (four) oceans, clever, glorious, heroes, as Ráma and the others to Dasaratha, (to wit) the illustrious *Kómaṭi*, the ornament of kings; the great king *Malla*; the long-lived (áyushman) *Ana Véma* king; and king *Náráyaṇa*.

11. Amongst them *king Malla* was like Bhíshma, being the son of Gangámbika [1], like Arjuna having acquired good fortune [2], like Ṣiva being *Rájamauḷi* (or the crest jewel of kings.) [3]

12. In Káma was fresh beauty, in the ocean immeasurable depth, in Ráma ability to protect, in the sun the production of heat, in the moon the conferring of lustre; so in Mahéndra (Indra or Mount Mahéndra) great power; (but) all these attributes found a fixed abode for long in king Ṣrígiri.

13. In the Ṣaka year reckoned by the sky (0), Rámas (3), fire (3), moon (1), (*i.e.*, 1330)—in the bright fortnight of Ṣrávaṇa, on the day of Káma (13th)—Malla, the diadem of kings, the son of king Ṣrígiri, a tree of paradise to the host of kings of poets, eminent in the aggregate of virtues, victorious, caused to be performed by venerable Brahmans the consecration of Vishnu, of

---

[1] Bhíshma, son of Ganga. Malla's mother was Gangámbika.

[2] Arjita Subhadra = by whom *Subhadra* was won in the case of Arjuna.

[3] Rájamauḷi = the moon-crested—Ṣiva.

glorious splendour and excellent, in the town of Chunḍi.

14. He constructed this temple along with its *maṇḍapa,* which is beautiful, with the *gópura* to the *prákára* (and) also gave to this Janárdana a collection of jewels.

15. (He) the wise presented to him a dry field yielding 4½ *puṭṭis,* and a wet field measuring 2 *nivartanas* [1] in Chunḍi town.

16. He, whose mind is free from envy, celebrates here every year all the holy and glorious *mahótsavas* (great festivals) of this Vishnu.

17. May this God, Janárdana, who has been set up by king Ṣrígiri Malla, and who is the illustrious ornament of the town of Chunḍi and who is of great majesty last up to a *Kalpa* (cosmic period).

18. [One imprecatory verse.]

NOTE.—Genealogy is as follows :—

Véma, *brother of* Malla.
|
Kómati.
|
Ṣrígiri = Gangámbika. — Mácha, etc.
|
Kómaṭi. — Malla Donor, S.S. 1330. — Ana Véma. — Náráyana.

(Compare that in No. 18.)

1. वाराहं वपुरु
2. द्धतं घनघनध्वा
3. नं दधानो हरि
4. श्चातुर्वर्ण्यपदै
5. श्चमत्कृतिकरैं

---

[1] Nivartana = an unknown square measure.

6. गैरुपांगैः
7. स्फुरन् । अव्याख्वा
8. मतिभव्यनव्याहि
9. मरुग्रेखाग्रमे
10. घाकृति र्यद्दं
11. ष्ट्राशिखरे सुखा
12. मृतसरित्संवेदि
13. नी मेदिनी ॥ (1) विघ्नं
14. निघ्नंतमखिलं
15. भजे देवं ग
16. जाननं । वंदे
17. कुंदेंदुधवलां
18. शारदांसार
19. दायिनीं ॥ (2) आ
20. दिनारायणात्क
21. श्रिदासीद्वर्णो गु
22. णोन्नतः । यस्य शं
23. भजटाजूट त
24. टिनी सहजा निजा ॥ (3)
25. तत्राभूद्धेमभू
26. पालः श्रीमान् प्रा
27. गर्णवीश्वरः । रामा
28. दिगुणभूमानं
29. व्यस्मारयदरं स्म
30. यः ॥ (4) यः श्रीपर्वतमा
31. ततान सुगमं सो

32. शानपङ्क्त्या नृणां
33. । निस्सीमां भु
34. वमादरादनुप
35. मो यः श्रोत्रिये
36. भ्यो ददौ । यत्या
37. दद्वयमर्च
38. यंत्यहरहः
39. प्रत्यर्थिपृथ्वीभु
40. जो । मौलिस्थापित
41. नूत्नरत्नकिरणस्तो
42. मेन सामान्विताः ॥ (5)
43. तस्यानुजो मल्लमहीपतींद्रः । श्रीमानु
44. दारः श्रितपूर्णचंद्रः । विरोधिरा
45. जन्यकसैन्यसिंधु । मंथाचलव्यग्र
46. दुदग्रबाहुः ॥ (6) तदात्मजः कोमटिभू
47. मिपालः । शौर्याकरः शारदचंद्रकीर्तिः ।
48. दानने कर्णो दयया दिलीपः । सत्येन धर्मः
49. सहनेन धात्री ॥ (7) तदात्मजः स्तंभितवैरिदंभ
50. : । श्रीसेवधिः श्रीगिरिभूमिपालः । मान्योनु
51. जैर्माचमहीवराद्यै । राज्ञाकरैरद्भुतस
52. च्चरित्रैः ॥ (8) हिमाद्रिशीतांशुयशोव
53. तंसो । हेमाद्रिदानैकरतः कलावान् ।
54. दाक्षिण्यगांभीर्यदयानिवासः शौ
55. याकरः श्रीगिरिभूमिपालः ॥ (9) चत्वार
56. श्चतुरा यथा दशरथाद्रामादयो
57. विश्रुताः । शूराः श्रीगिरिभूमिपादु

58. दभवन् पुत्राः समुद्रा इव । श्रीमान् को
59. मटिभूमिपालतिलको मल्लक्षितीशो म
60. हानायुष्माननवेमभूमिरमणो ना
61. रायणक्षोणिपः ॥ (10) गंगांबिकातनूजो भा
62. ष्म इवार्जुनवदार्जितसुभद्रः । शंभुरि
63. व राजमौलिर्मध्ये मल्लक्ष्मापति
64. रतेषां ॥ (11) कंदर्पे नवसुंदरत्वममि
65. तं गांभीर्यमंभोनिधौ । रामे र
66. क्षणदक्षिणत्वमभवद्भानौ प्रता
67. पोदयः । चंद्रे कांतिकथा तथा विभ
68 विता स्फीता महेंद्रे चिरं । सर्वे श्रीगिरि
69. मल्लभूमिरमणे प्राप्ताः प्रतिष्ठां गु
70. णाः ॥ (12) शाकाब्दे व्योमरामज्वलनशशिगु
71. णे श्रावणे शुक्लपक्षे । कंदर्पाहे कवींद्र
72. प्रकरसुरतरुः श्रीगिरिक्ष्मापसूनुः । म
73. ल्लक्षोणीशमौलिर्महितगुणगणो जिष्णु
74. राधत्त विष्णो । र्विप्रैरार्यैः प्रतिष्ठां प्रकटित
75. विभवां चुंडिपुर्यां प्रवर्याम् ॥ (13) सद
76. नमिदं सहमंटप । मकरोत्प्राकारगो
77. पुरमनोज्ञम् । स जनार्दनदेवाय प्रा
78. दादाभरणजालमपि तस्मै ॥ (14)
79. चुंडिपुरे पां
80. डुभुवं चतु
81. ष्पुटिमर्थवर्धितां
82. तस्मै । द्विनिवर्तन
83. मितिमेष प्रादा

84. त्केदारमेदिनीं प्रा
85. ज्ञः ॥ (15) मल्गरविहि
86. नचेतो महोत्स
87. वान् महितसं
88. स्तुतानखिलान् । प्र
89. तिवत्सरमिह त
90. नुते तस्य श्रीव
91. त्सलांछनस्यासौ ॥ (16)
92. श्रीगिरिमल्ल
93. तपुणिष्टा
94. तोयं जनार्द
95. नो देवः । चुंडि
96. रमंडनश्री
97. राकल्पमनल्प
98. वैभवस्स्थेयात् ॥ (17) न
99. सामान्योयं
100. धर्मसर्तुनृ
101. पाणाम् काले का
102. ले पालनीयो भ
103. वद्भिः । सर्वानेता
104. न्भाविनः पार्थिवें
105. द्रान् भूयो भू
106. यो याचते रामचं
107. द्रः ॥ (18)

KANDUKUR (20). (A.D. 1640–41.)

[Old Chundi. Telugu. From a *mandapa* opposite Janárdanasvámi's temple.]

TRANSLATION.

(Obeisance to) Śrí Ráma! Hail! On the 2nd day of the bright fortnight of Phálguna of the year Vikrama, corresponding to 1563 of the illustrious, victorious and prosperous Śáliváhana Śaka era, Káminéni Muttaráju who is a descendant of the race of Válmíki, who is of the *gōtra* of Ammasáni, who is the grandson of Víra Rághava Náyaningáru and the son of Polinéningáru, (gave) to Víra Battu, the grandson of Inugandi Virá Battu and the son of Ayyappa Battu and . . . the son of Appá Battu and the grandson of Jayavarapu Basava Battu . . . . the field called Núlantachénu in the *Śīma* of Kandukur, in the village of Chundi, to the west of the village, to the east of Baridinatippa, to the north of the field of the Uriminddeváru, to the south of the field of the Alattúriváru and one *kuchchala* in the field called (Nu) lantu to the south of Chundi, to the west of the path to Vitrala, and to the south of the field "Cheruvupalli pálla marri."

This is the charitable deed of gift of land issued to the abovesaid Inagádiya Nimmaya.

In the . . . . granted to us as an *amaram* by Rája Śrí Sultan Abdul Pádúshah. In order that we may keep in good repair the temples in our *Śīma* . .

NOTE.—The name of the donee varies, but the writing is not very clear. The granter of the amaram is Abdulláh Kutb Sháh of Golkonda.

1. శ్రీరామం। స్వస్తి శ్రీ జయాభ్యుద
2. య భలివాన శతవారుషం
3. బులు ౧౫౬౩ అగు నేటి వి
4. క్రమ సంవత్సర బాలు
5. గుణ శు ౧ లు వాల్మీక
6. వంశోద్భవులు అన్మ
7. సానిగోత్ర సంభవులు
8. ంన్న వీరరాఘవ నాయి
9. నింగారి పౌత్రులుంన్న పోలి
10. నేనింగారి పుత్రులైన కామి
11. నేని ముత్తరాజుంగారు ఇను
12. గంది వీరాభత్తుని పౌత్రుడు
13. న్న అయ్యపబత్తుని పుత్రుడు
14. న్న అఇన పీరాబత్తునికింన్ని జ
15. యవరపు బసవాబత్తుని పౌపు
16. త్రుడున్న అప్పాబత్తునిపుత్రుడు

* * * *

17. కంద్దుకూరి శీమలో చు
18. ంఢ్లిగ్రామనను వూరికి పోడ్మట
19. ఖాగన బరిదినతిప్పతూర్పూన పూ
20. రిమింద్దివారిచేనికి వుత్తరం అ
21. లత్తాగివారిచేనికి దక్షానను
22. నూలంతంచేనిన్ని లంతు పేరను
23. కుచ్చల। చుండికి దక్షినానూ వి
24. ట్రలదోవాకుపాడుమను చెరువు
25. పలిపాల్ల మర్త్తి చేనికి దాఉనాన
26. ను అఇనగాదియ నిమ్మయగారికి
27. న్ని ఇచ్చిన భూదాన ధర్మశాస
28. నం మంన్మున మా శీమలో

29. ను దేవళ్లు దేశాలకు పాటు
30. వడురా నెట్టుగాను జేశినాం
31. దులకు రాజశ్రీ సులుతా
32. ను అబ్దులా పామషాంగారు
33. మాకు అమరం పాలించిన

* * * *

KANDUKUR (21). (A.D. 1408–09.)

[Old Chundi. Telugu. From the same maṇḍapa.]

TRANSLATION.

Hail! Mallaya Reḍḍi, the excellent son of Ṣrígiri Reḍḍi,—who (Ṣrígiri) is the grandson of Sríman Vémáya Reddi, who (Vémáya) was addicted to making unlimited gifts of land and who built the flight of steps at Ṣríparvata (Ṣríṣaila)—and of Gangámbá. Hail! On Saturday, the 13th of Ṣrávaṇa in the year Sarvadhári, corresponding to 1330 of the illustrious Ṣaka era, he caused to be set up (an image of) Ṣrí Janárdanadéva in the town of Chundi and caused to be constructed a temple, a *manḍapa*, a *gópura* and an enclosure wall, for the purpose of securing the four kinds of human desires.

1. స్వస్తి శ్రీమన్నిస్సీమ భూదా
2. న నిరతుండై శ్రీ పర్వతా
3. న సోపానాలు నిర్మించిన వే
4 మాయరెడ్డింగారి మను
5. మండైన శ్రీ
6. గిరిరెడ్డింగా
7. రికిన్ని గంగా
8. ంబకున్ను

9. సుపుత్రుండై
10. న మల్లాయ
11. రెడ్డింగారు
12. స్వస్తి శ్రీ శకవర్షంబులు ౧౩౩౦
13. అగునేంటి సర్వధారి సంవత్సర
14. శ్రావణ శు ౧౩ వ। చతుర్ధ
15. పురుషార్థ సిద్ధికొఱకై చు
16. ండిపట్టణమందు శ్రీ జ
17. నార్దనదేవరను ప్రతిష్టసే
18. యించ్చి గుడిన్ని మంట్టపము
19. న్ను ప్రాకార గోపురాలున్ను
20. కట్టించ్చిరి

KANDUKUR (22). (A.D. 1237–38 ?).

[Gudlúr. Telugu. From fallen stone in Nílakanṭhéṣvarasvámi temple.]

TRANSLATION.

Hail ! On the day of Vishama Sankránti in the illustrious Ṣaka year 1159, Chóḍadéva Chóḍa Mahárája, Mallidévarája, and Chikkirája constructed a front hall, a kitchen and a garden well, and having done work to the garden for the merit of their parents, gave one *paṭṭu* of ḍry land for them and four *paṭṭus* of dry land to Padi Mokati Sim Baṭṭi Sánu (?). The Monkatisánulu (?) should lease out the low land in the lands attached to the treasury of Nílakanṭhadéva for a half share of the produce to their friends.

* * * *

[One imprecatory verse.] Ṣrí !

NOTE.—The latter portion of the inscription is obscure.

1. స్వస్తి శ్రీ సఖవర్షంబులు ౧౧౫౯ద
2. వునేండు విషువ సంక్రాంతినాండు
3. చోడదేవ చోడమహారాజును మ
4. లి దేవరాజును చిక్కిరాజునుందమ
5. తల్లిద డ్రులకు దమ్మ్ఁవుగా మో
6. గసాలి గట్టించ్చి మడపాల్లి గటిం
7. చ్చి తోంట్ల నూతి గట్టించ్చి తోంట్లపనిసేసి వాటి
8. కి వెలిసేనుపట్టిపడి మోతికికిశింబట్టి సాను
9. కుంనాలుగువట్టు వెలిసేనునీలకంట్ల (దే)
10. వరభండారువు వరిచేని లోన తగ్గు
11. నేల తమవలచినవారికిసగం బాలికిచ్చి కొ
12. నువారు మోంకతిసానులు। స్వదత్తా పర
13. దత్తం వా హరేతి వసుందరా షష్టివర్షసహ
14. స్రాణి విష్టాం జాయతే క్రిమి శ్రీ

Kandukur (23).

[Guḍlúr. Telugu. On a fallen stone near the temple of Nílakanṭhasvámi.]

Translation.

On Tuesday, the 14th of the bright fortnight of Ṣrávaṇa of the year . . . the illustrious Muppuri (Muppaḍi) Náyakaḍu, who is the (Mahápradháni) prime minister (of Rudradéva) and who is the worshipper of the divine and illustrious lotus feet of (Só)manáthadéva (gave) . . for providing all enjoyments to Ṣrí Nílakanṭhadéva of Guḍlúr which is situated in Púnginádu, for the religious merit of his lord, Hail! Ṣríman Mahámaṇḍaléṣvara Kákatiyya Pratápa Rudradéva Mahárája, and that of his own mother Gaugasánamma and of his father Nágináyaningáru. . . . . .

1. Not found in the inscription.
2. వత్సర శ్రావణ శు ౧౮ మ వారము (సో)
3. మనాథదేవ దివ్య శ్రీపాద పద్మారాధకు
4. లైన శ్రీమన్మహాప్రధాని ముప్పటినాయ
5. ంకడువారు తమ్మునేలిన స్వస్తి శ్రీమన్మహా
6. మండలేశ్వర కాకతియ్య ప్రతాప రు
7. ద్ర దేవ మహారాజులకూను తమ తల్లి
8. దండ్రులు గంగసానమంగారికి నా
9. గినాయనింగారికినిం బుణ్యము గాను
10. పూంగినాంటిలోని గుడ్లూరి శ్రీనీ
11. లకంఠ దేవరకి అంగరంగ బోగా
12. లు . . . . .

Kandukur (24).

[Guḍlúr. Telugu. From a fallen stone in same locality.]

Translation.

On Sunday, the 15th of . . . in the year Íṣvara, Pedda Sináyakunḍu (gave) to Ṣrí Nīlakanṭhadēva of Guḍlúr . . . . to last as long as the sun and moon endure.

[One imprecatory verse.]

The temple of Nílakanṭhadéva should be maintained (Pralamrāju . . . ?)

1. శ్రీ ఈశ్వర సంవత్సరం [గ పృ మ ౫ భు.]
2. . . . . రాజులకు . . .
3. పడిపెద్దసినాయకుండు శకునం

4. ౫ ఆ పంచాదశియు నాదివారమునం
5. గుడ్లూరం శ్రీనీలకంఠ దేవరకుం . .
6. . . . . . . ఆచంద్రార్కతారకం
7. స్వదత్తాం పరదత్తాం వా యో హరేత
8. సార్ణి విష్టాయాం జాయతే క్రిమి
9. (నీల) కంఠదేవర స్థానము నడచె
10. డిన తత్తు . (బ్రలమురాజు
11. కముల ఇత్తూరు ?)

KANDUKUR (25). (A.D. 1544–45.)

[Guḍlúr. Telugu. From pillar in front of Chenna-késavasvámi temple.]

TRANSLATION.

Hail! On Thursday, the 12th of the bright fortnight of Ṣrávaṇa of the year Kródhi, corresponding to the illustrious, victorious and prosperous Ṣálivábana Ṣaka year 1466, Tallayya, the son of Kilári Konḍamanáyaḍu, after making salutations, granted this charitable edict to Chennakéṣvaradéva of Guḍlúr. We have given a field of 4 *gorrus* situated in Râvulaguṇṭa in rear of the *guṇṭa* (pond), a field of 5 *gorrus* to the south of Pakkela guṇṭa, a wet field on which 5 *túms* of seed can be sown, and grain at 1 *túm* on the total produce (of the village?) for providing food (*amritapaḍi*) to the deity. Whoever obstructs this charity will incur the sin of killing cows and Brahmans on the Ganges.

1. స్వస్తిశ్రీ జయాభ్యుదయ శాలివాహన శకవర్షంబులు ౧౪౬౬

2. అగు నేటి క్రోది సంవత్సర శ్రావణ శు ౧౨ గు గుడ్లూరి చెన్నకేశ్వర దేవునికి

3. కిలారి కొండమనాయని కొమారుండు తల్లయ్య దండ్డం
సమర్పించ్చి యి

4. నుల్ఛ్చిన ధర్మశాసనం రావులగుంట్టను సనా

5. గొలుర్ చేనున్న పక్కెరలగుంట దక్షిణం అఖదుగొలుర్
చేనున్న యేందుముపిత్తు

6. ల పట్టు వరిమషిన్ని రాశికి తూమెండేశి కొల్చున్న
దేవునికి అమృతపల్లి

7. కు యిస్తిమి యీ ధర్మానకు యెవ్వరు తప్పిరి గంగ
కత్తర గొబ్రాంహానిం

8. జంప్పిన పాపాన పోదురు

KANDUKUR (26). (A.D. 1258–59 ?)

[Guṇḍlapáḷem. Telugu. From fallen stone in Brahmarêśvara temple.]

TRANSLATION.

Vaiṣampáyana said to Parískhit thus :—

Yama, Ṣaníṣvara, Jamuná (Jumna), Tapati (Tapti), and Vaivasvata Manu, were born to Súrya, the son of Aditi and Kaṣyapa. Many Manavas (men), viz., the Brahmans, the Kshatriyas, the Vaisyas and the Sudras, were produced by Vaivasvata Manu. To them were born eight kings Véna and others. The emperor Purûrava was born to Ilá, daughter of this Manu and Budha, son of Sôma (the moon). Áyu was born to Purúrava and Úrvasi. Nahusha was born to Áyu and Svarbhánu and reigned over the kingdom. Yayáti was born to Nahusha and Priyamana (Priyamvadá) and performed many sacrifices. Yadu was born to this Yayáti and Dévayána, the daughter of Ṣukra. Súra (Sêna) descendant of the noble Yadu race, and of the Átréya *gótra*, made Mathurá his capital and reigned over the country called Mathurá and Súraséna. Formerly, during the time of Vasudéva, the son of Súra, many thousands of chiefs of the Asuras (demons), O King, listen, encroached upon this earth assuming the royal insignia; and this goddess Earth being unable to bear the burden went to Brahmá in the form of a cow and cried before him shedding tears copiously. Brahmá took compassion upon her and went to Vishnu, accompanied by the gods and the goddess Earth. Having chanted the Purushasúkta (a hymn of the Ṛig Veda) he fell into a marvellous trance in which he heard a divine voice. He then explained what he had heard, to the gods and the goddess Earth thus:—"Oh ye gods, go and incarnate yourselves on earth in the Yádava dynasty with your divine power; Vishnu, the consort of the goddess Ṣrí, will be born to Vasudêva and will relieve the earth of her burden. O ye celestial nymphs, incarnate yourselves on earth as beautiful damsels for worshipping Hari. Sésha will also incarnate himself as the elder brother of Hari in order to relieve the earth of her burden." O Lord of the earth! Listen. Dróna was the chief of the Vasus; and Dhará was his wife. This Dróna, who was the chief of the gods, was born as the present Nanda Gópa, and Dhará was born to Yaṣóda and Nanda as *Yógamáyá*. All the cows were produced by the power of the Ṛishis. All the gods were born as cowherds. Dévaki was formerly during the Svayambhava-Manvantara (period) a faithful wife called Priṣni and Vasudéva a Prajápati called Sutapunya. In their second birth they were born as Aditi and Kaṣyapa; and in their third birth they were born as Vasudéva and Dévakí and to them Ráma and Kṛishna were born. The Apsaras (celestial nymphs) were born as daughters of the cowherds. All the Yádavas including Ráma and Kṛishna, together with the cows and cowherds, flourished up to the end of the Dváparayuga. Having destroyed Duryôdhana and others and installed the Pándavas on the throne, they joyfully returned to *Dváraka*. Ṣṛí Kṛishna and all other Yádavas reigned for 36 years. Owing to the curses of the great sage Kanva and Gándhári, one day they observed some bad omens and under the orders of the king left Dváravati to perform pilgrimage. Ṣṛí Kṛishna and other Yádavas including the heroes of the Vrusti (?) (Vṛishni) (?) the Bhója and Andhaka clans fought with one another on the sea-shore, being much intoxicated by drinking, armed with the three-cornered rushes which sprang out of the Musala (pestle), as foretold by the Ṛishi, and perished.

Dváraka then informed the Pándavas of all this. Arjuna went to Dváravati and paid a visit to Vasudéva. "Ṣṛí Kṛishna is dead. The Yádavas have all joined the host of gods (*i.e.* died), and Dváravati will be submerged by the sea." So thinking, Arjuna immediately took with him all the young and the old, the Apsara maids and the milk-maids, to Indraprastha. He installed Vajradhara (grandson of Pradyumna, son of Kṛishna) descendant of the Yádavas on the throne. Having appointed Amṛitagóvinda a grandson of Yádava Gópa as the protector of the cows, he installed him at Ghanavírapur, directing him to look after the cows. Having posted the Yádavas here and there, Arjuna returned to Hastinápura and informed Dharmaja (Yudhishṭira) of this. Some 400 years after the departure of the Yádavas and the Pándavas to enjoy heavenly bliss (*i.e.* their death) Kaliyuga [1] commenced. Vajradéva's son was called Dadhinanga; the descendants of the grandsons of the cowherds flourished at Brindávanam, which is known as Nandavrajam on this earth. The cowherds being delighted with the pasture for cattle settled themselves on the Révata mountain where Amritabhágésvara flourishes as the god of the Yádavas. This god was formerly established there by Vasudéva and Nanda in the presence of Srí Krishna. The son of Upananda and grandson of Góvinda was indeed named Amritabhója after that god. When the merry Janaméjaya invited all the kings and performed a sacrifice he admired his son Vijayámbhója and appointed him governor of the town of Varanápur and they ruled there for sometime.

Era of Kaliyuga.

Vijayámbhója's era during the time of Súdraka Rája	530
Era of Kanakámbhója	490
Era of Gajayámbhója during Vikramárka's time.	430
Era of Ráyambhója	420
Era of Ratnámbhója	402
Era of Viravijaya Rája	390
Era of Padmana Rája during Sáliváhana's time.	354
Era of Sri Kúrma Rája	340
Era of Simhédri Rája during the time of Bhója.	300
Era of Vallu Rája during Chóda's time	195
Era of Pólu Rája	82

[1] Kaliyuga began on the day of Krishna's death.

During the time of Oruganṭi Pratápa, Káṭamrájn, after a reign of 32 years, fought a battle with Nala Siddhi Rája at the junction of Lingálakonḍa and Yaragaḍapáḍu in which the Baḍugulaváru died. 3,965 years had then already passed in the Kaliyuga. The chronicle of the great deeds of these is in accordance with what is stated in the Ádiparva describing the origin of all creation, Anuṣásanaparva, the 10th book of Bhágavata and the Mausalaparva. Just as the Trimúrtis lived with the Ṛishis on Góṣṛinga mountain, the cows which were produced by the power of the descendants of Yámbhója Ṛishi and others lived with Ṣrí Kṛishna; the gods were also born then at the end of Dvápara; Budha (son of the moon), the emperor Purúrava, Yayáti, Súraséna, Vasudéva and Ṣrí Kṛishna were born in the Yádava dynasty. The 72 Niyogams that applied to the above also applied to the Baḍugulaváru (*i.e.*, they possessed similar power?). Owing to a curse that was laid on the descendants of Yayáti, they became cowherds to tend cows and they flourished in thousands. May it cause prosperity!

The cities and countries that were ruled over by the desçendants of Atri: the son that was born from the eye of Atri (*i.e.*, the moon) ruled over the whole world. Purúrava, the grandson of the moon, ruled all over the earth. Yayáti, the grandson of the son of Purúrava became king and ruled over the earth consisting of the nine continents. Yadu, son of Yayáti ruled over heaven (?) Súraséna, of the lineage of Yadu, ruled at Mathurá over the countries called Máthura and Súraséna. His son Vasudéva ruled at the town of Mathurá. Nanda-gopa, his relation, ruled over Répalli. Ṣrí Kṛishna, the son of Vasudéva ruled over Dváravati. The descendants (sons) of Ṣrí Kṛishna by the Gópikas, namely, Vajradhara, Amṛita Góvinda and the six Ambhójas ruled over the kingdom of Indraprasṭha and Ghanavírapur. Padmanábha ruled over a portion of that kingdom. Víravijaya ruled over another portion. Ṣrí Kúrma ruled over Aruntulakóna, Amarávati, Simhádri and Yellamanchi. Vallu Rája ruled for some time over Álavallapur (Alavalapáḍu of Kanigiri?) and Aḍidevịṭi (?). During the time of Pratápa, when the Ála Pola Rája, descendant of Yadu, was ruling over Pina Yerpa and Peda Yerpa, having herds of cattle at Dhanamukonḍa, the king and Padmanáyuḍu, observing that there was no pasture for the cows owing to the drought prevailing in the said Yérpas, migrated with their cows and agreeing to take Pákináḍu on payment of *pullari* (grazing fee) to Siddhi Rája, they entered on the land and grazed (their cattle) there. With the cows that were grazing, he proceeded towards Dhanukoti in the south and paid a visit to its ruler. Thence bringing the cows over rivers and hills, they encamped on the bank of the Penna (Pennér). Nalla Siddhi Rája attacked their cattle. They wandered in forests resting under the shade of trees, left Nellore with their cows and halted at Yarragaḍḍapáḍu. An ambassador of Nalla Siddhi Rája came to demand *pullari* tax. They stoutly refused to pay *pullari* and told him to go away. On such refusal Nalla Siddhi Rája of Nellore led an expedition to Yarragaḍḍapáḍu.

Hail! On Thursday, the 5th day of the bright fortnight of the month of Kârtika of the year Kâḷayukti, corresponding to the year 1170[1] of the Ṣrí Ṣáliváhana

---

[1] The dates do not correspond. The reading is uncertain and probably it should be 1180.

Ṣaka era, when Nalasiddhi Rája of Nellore advanced with an army, Vallu Rája, who was of the Átreya Gótra and who was a Yádava Kshatriya, who was descended from the divine feet of Ṣrí Vishnuyógamáya, the lord of Mathurápura, the renowned destroyer of foes, who was descended from Gópikávallabha of Dváraka and who was of the lineage of the famous Puru, and his sons Pólu Rája and Peddi Rája and their sons and other Yádavas met Siddhi Rája in battle at the junction of Lingalakonḍa and Yaragaḍḍapáḍu in the presence of Soméṣvara and perished. In order to remove the fear of the Yâdavas, the Trimúrtis said to the goddess Yógamáya thus:—"Oh Bhadra! You had better go to the herds of cattle of the Gópikás and Gópálas. Becoming the daughter of Vasudéva and Nanda, you will be the receptacle of much prosperity, and will be worshipped by men. They will give you presents and sacrifices and praise you in eighteen names." The names of the various shrines are given. She is called Hémkriti at Piṭṭápur; she appeared at Dhanamukonḍa; she is known as Bhágirathi on the bank of the Páléru; she appeared to her devotee and conferred heroism to the delight of the Trimúrtis (?).[1] (This is) the holy place of Bhágirathi Durga. This edict has been engraved by Rámayya, son of Konḍayya.

NOTE.—The first part of this inscription consists of extracts from the Telugu Bhárata and Bhágavata. The second part says that a battle took place between Kâṭam Rája and Nalla Siddhi Rája in the time of Pratápa of Orangal (Kákatíya). Káṭam Rázu was apparently a petty chief claiming descent from Kṛishna; his family was called the Baḍugulaváru. The third part says that a battle took place between Vallu Rája of Alavallapur (Alavalapád of Kanigiri ?) and Nalla Siddhi

[1] The passage is obscure and the translation is doubtful.

Rája of Nellore on account of the former refusing to pay grazing tax to the latter. The date of the battle is given as S.S. 1170. It is not clear how Káṭam Rája and Vallu Rája are connected. They both claimed to be of the Yádava dynasty and the inscription in the first part traces their connection with Kṛishna. In this connection see p. 135 of Mr. Sewell's *Lists of Antiquities*, Vol. I, where he quotes Mr. Boswell. " About this period (12th century) the northern parts of the district " were under various petty princes of obscure origin of the Yádava or " shepherd caste. The principal members of the family, whose " exploits from the subject of legendary tale, are the following :—

Annala Valla Ráj.

Simhádri Raj.	Peddi Raj.	Yerramuka Raj.	Nallamuka Raj.	Pala Raj.
Sreerala Raj.	Kantam Raj.			

It is clear that Valla Rázu of the present inscription and his sons Pólu and Peddi Rázu are identical with those named above. Káṭam Rázu can hardly be Kantam Raj because he is said to have been ruling 32 years and it is not likely that he would have had grandfather alive after so long a reign. Who the Ála Pola Rája was is not clear; probably one of the same family.

The language is in many places obscure and the translation conjectural.

The scene of the battle is given as Yarragaḍḍapád. There is a Yerraguḍipád in Ongole taluk, but Mr. Venugopal Chetti thinks that the place referred to is probably the place where the temple of Poleramma now stands, just beyond Alavalapád in Kanigiri taluk.

It will be observed that, then as now, the grazing question was an acute one in the Nellore district.

1. యాదవజల్మం[1] వైశంపా
2. యిందు పరీక్షిత్తుకుఋ
3. ట్లనిఎ అధితికి కశ్యపునకు పుట్టి
4. న వైవస్వతుండను మనువునకు
5. యెముండును శనైశ్వరుం
6. డ్డను యెమునయుందపతియుం

[1] Read జన్మం.

7. బుట్టి గండు వైవస్వతుండను మను
8. పువలన బ్రహ్మ క్షత్రియ వైశ్యసూ
9. ద్రులైన మానవులు అనేకులు పు
10. ట్టిరి. వారికి [1] శేనప్రముఖులైన రాజులు
11. యనమండ్ర పుట్టిరి। ఆ మునిపుత్రి ఐ
12. న యిలగన్య సోమపుత్రుండైన బుధు
13. నకు పురురవ చక్రవర్తి పుట్టె పురూరవు
14. నకు వూర్వశికి నాయువుండు పుట్టె నా
15. యువునకున్ స్వర్భానుయకున్ నభిషుండు పు
16. ట్టె రాజ్యంబు సేసె నభిషునకున్ ప్రియమోను [2]
17. నకున్ యయాది పుట్టి యనాకయాగంబులు సేసె
18. ను యయాదికిని శుక్రుని పుత్రియైన దేవయాన
19. కున్ యదువు జన్మించెను। శీలముగల యదుకులాత్మ
20. జుండు యాత్రియగోత్రజుండ్డు ఆ సూరూను
21. ండను వాండు మధురాపురంబ్బుం దనకు రాజధాని
22. గా మాధురంబులు సూరసేనంబులనియెడి దేశంలేలె పూ
23. ర్వకాలమున అసూరు సునికి పుత్రుం వసుదేవుండు అచట
24. రాజేంద్రవినులొల్గి రాజలాంచ్ఛనంతో వేల
25. సంఖ్యలు దైత్యవిభులుందన్ను। ఆక్రమించ్చిన భూమిభా
26. రమానంజాలక గోరూపునై బ్రహ్మంజేరంబోయి క
27. న్నీరు మున్నీరు రోధనం శాయ కరుణతో భావించి। కమ
28. లభవుండు ధరణి నూరడం బలికి ధాత్రియును వెల్పులు క
29. దిలిరా విష్ణునింగాననెంగి పురుష సూక్తంబు చదవి య
30. ద్భుద సమాధినుండి యొక మాంటవిని వారిజోద్భవు
31. ండ్డు వినుండు వేల్పులు ధరయును నేవిన్న యెట్టి పలుకు
విచారించెద

[1] Read వేన.

[2] Read మను.

32. నని ప్రేరింబలికెందెలియ యాదవకులమున నమరులుమె
దిని

33. సైగ బుట్టం జనుండు మాయంశమునన్ । శ్రీదైత్యుండు
వసుదేవు

34. నకాదరమునం బుట్టి భారమంత్తయుంభాపును హరిపూజా
తాం

35. పుట్టుండు సురకన్యలు భూమియంద్దు సుందరతనులైహరి
కగ్రజు

36. ండై శేషుండు హరికళతోంబుట్టి భారమంతయుం బా
పును। అవనీ

37. శ వినుద్రోణుండనువాండు వసువులయందు ముఖ్యుండు
ధర అ

38. తని భార్య ఆవెల్పుల పెద్ద అ ద్రోణుండు యీ నంద్ద
గోపకుండై జన్మి

39. ంచె ధరయియ్యా హరి యోగమాయ యశోదనందుర
డు గాదై జె

40. ల్మించె[1] యల్లధేనవలెల్ల రుషుల అంశమున జన్మించె సుర
లెల్లగోరక్ష

41. పాలకులై జల్మించ్చె దేవకీసోను తొల్లి స్వాయంభుమను
సంతగంబు

42. న పుస్త్రీయనుప్రతివ్రత నసుదేవుండ్డను [2]సుతుపుణ్యుండను
ప్రజాప

43. తి రెండవజన్మమున అధితియుగస్యపుండును మూండువ
జన్మమున

44 వసుదేవ దేవకి రామక్రిష్ణులు పుష్పలించిరి అత్తరాంగన
లు గోపకన్యలై పు

45. దయించిరి రామక్రిష్ణులు పెద్దలైన సర్వయాదగోపుల
గోపాలురు ద్వాపార అ

---

[1] Read జన్మించె.

[2] Read సు.

46. ంత్యమున కూడవర్తించ్చి అచటంగొనాళ్ళు । దుర్యోధ నాదులం ద్రుంచ్చి పాండ్డ

47. వుల పరగ బట్టంబుగట్టి సంతోషమ్ము న వచ్చే ద్వారకాపు రికికణ్వ మహాము

48. నుల గాంధారిశౌవంవంకను మునుకొని యున్నంగ ము ప్పదియారు వర్షములు

49. శ్రీక్రింష్ణుమొదలైన సర్వయాదవలు రాజ్యంబు సేసిరి । శయ్యం గనొకర్నాండు

50. వుత్పాతములు వొడిమె వుర్వీశుపంపున । జాతరలు శ య్యాను ద్వారవతి

51. కదిలిరి శ్రీక్రిష్ణుయాదవులు సముద్రుడి కడకు జలధితీర మున సవపా

52. సమత్తులై విష్ణు భోజాంత్మక వీరులెల్ల మునివర నిర్ధిష్ట ముస నిర్ధిష్టముస

53. లాం త్మకృములైన[1] మూయ్యంచ్చుతుంగ్గల మొందులాడి మృ

54. తులైరి అంత [2]తారకుండు చని పాండవుల కెరింగి

55. ంచె ।।।

Second side.

1. అర్జునుండ్డు ద్వారావతికి వచ్చి
2. వసుదేవునింగని శ్రీక్రిష్ణుపరమమూ
3. ర్తింగలసె [3]ఆధవులు దేవగణానంగ
4. లసిరి ద్వారావతి వనధి ముంచ్చునని ఆ
5. తుణమె బాలవ్రిద్ధులాను [4]అక్రురాం
6. గ్గనలాను గోపాంగ్గన లాను గొంచ్చు
7. అర్జునుండు యింద్రప్రస్థకుం దె
8. చ్చెను । ఆదవకులకరుండైన వజ్రధరుని

---

[1] Read ముసలాత్తములైన.

[2] Read దారకుండు.

[3] Read యాదవులు.

[4] Read అక్రూరా.

9. ం బట్టంబు గట్టెను । యాదవ గోపికాపౌత్రు
10. ని నేమించ్చి గోవులకు గోరక్షపాలకుడుం జే
11. సి గోవులం గాపాడుమని ఘనవిరవురంబ్బు
12 న అమృతగోవింద్దుని అభిషిక్తు జేసెను యా
13. దవుల అంద్దరిని అకౄడ అకౄడ నిలిపి అర్జును
14. ండు [1]అస్తనాపురికి బోయి దర్మజుకు యెరింగి
15. ంచ్చెను యాదవులు పాండువర్లు స్వర్గాది
16. బోగానకు బోయిన వెనక నన్నూరుయేండ్లకు
17. కలియుగం చొచ్చెను। వజ్రదేవుని పుత్రుండు దధి
18. సంగ్గుండనంగ గోపికల పౌత్రకులవంశకరులు
19. బృంద్దావనమునం ప్రిథివింబెంపొంద్ది నంద్దవ్రజ
20. ంబ్బుకు నలినొప్పుచుండ్డు । ఆవుల మేపుతనలరి
21. గోపకులు రైవతాచలమున రంజిలుచున యా
22. దవులకు దైవమెంతయు నొప్పు అమృత బా
23. గేశ్వరుండంద్దు, వెలిసున్న వసుదేవనందనులు తొ
24. ల్లి శ్రీక్రిష్ణుముందరంగోకుర్లు మీరప్రతిష్టలు శేశి
25. రి ప్రభమీరి వెలయ గోవిందు మనమందు వుపనంగ్దు
26. పుత్రుండ్డు అమృతాంబోజుండని ఆ దేవుపేర వెలయ
27 ంగబెట్టెను విచిదంబుగాను అతని పుత్రుండు విరయాం
28. ంభోజుండు । సంతోషమునసుండ్డ జనమేజయు
29. ండు యజ్ఞంబుసేయ నెల్లరాజులను రప్పించి య
30. జ్ఞముండగంజేసె విజయాంబోజుని మెచ్చి వారణా
31. పురంబ్బున పట్నస్వామిగా జేసి కొంత్తగాలం రాజ్య
32. ంబ్బుసెసిరి । కలియుగాబ్దాః సూద్రికి రాజకాల
33. మున విజయాంబోజాబ్దాః । ౫౩౦ । కనకాంబోజాబ్దాః
34. ।౪౯౦। విక్రమారుడుని కాలమున గజయాంబోజాబ్దా
35. ।౪౩౦। రాయాంబోజాబ్దాః ।౪౨౦। రత్నాంభోజాబా

[1] Read హస్తినాపురి.

36. ః ।౪౦౭। వీరవిజయః రాజాబ్దాః ।౩౯౦। శాలివాహను
విశా

37. లమున పద్మనరాజాబ్దాః ।౩౫౪। శ్రీ కూర్మిరాజాబ్దాః
।౩౪౦।

38. భోజరాజు కాలమున సిమ్హాద్రిరాజాబ్దాః ।౩౦౦।

39. చోడాని కాలమున వల్లురాజాబ్దాః ।౧౯౫। పోలురా

40. జాబ్దాః ।౮౭। వోరుగంట ప్రతాపుని కాలమునకా

41. టమరాజు ।౩౭। రాజ్యం సెసిలింగాలకొండ యరగడ
పాట

42. నునల సిద్ధిరాజుంగూడి యుద్ధంబుసేశి బడుగులవారు

43. చనిపొయ్యెనాంటికి కలియుగంచొచ్చి ।౩౯౭౫। యెంగ్లా

44. యను । విరులమహాత్వం అవివర్ణ సకలభూత సంభవ
అను

45. శాసనీక భాగవత దశమస్కంధమవుసలాన వెళ్లిన
శాస్త్రిధర్మ

46. మిది త్రిమూర్తులు కారణమున గోస్రృంగపర్వతాన తొల్లి

47. యాంబోజరుటి మెదలైన రుమల సంతతిని దేనువులు
క్రిష్టావ

48. తారంన గూడి దేవతులు కూడ వర్తించ్చిరి ద్వాపార అం
త్యము

49. న జన్మించిరి ఆధవు కులమున చంద్రనందను పురూరవ
చక్రవర్తి

50. యయాధి యెదుకులోమ్మజ సూరశేను వసుదేవు పు
త్రుం శ్రీ

51. క్రిష్ణుమగణ క్రిష్ణుమగణ వీరికి నడిచి డెబ్బైరెండు నియో
గాలు బడుగుల

52. వారికి చెల్లును వీరు యయాదివంశం శాపకారణమున

53. గోవుల రక్షింప గోరక్షపాలకులం జేసిర వెలసిరి గోప

54. కులు వేయివేల సంఖ్య ॥ శ్రీ శ్రీగ జేయును ॥

Third side.

అత్రియెముని సంతతిరాజులు యె
లినపట్టణ భూములు అత్రియ నేత్రపుత్రుడు
భూలోకమెల్లాడిపించెను ఆచంద్రసంద
నుపుత్ర పురూరవుండ్డు భూచక్రమెల యే
లెను ఆ పురూరవ పుత్రపౌత్రుండు యయా
దిరాజులై నవఖండ పృధివియేలె యయా
దిపుత్రుండు యధువుయేనాకభూములు
యెలెను యెధుకులోంత్మజు సూరశేను మధు
ర మాధురంబులు సూరసేనంబులనియెడి దేశ
ంబులు యేలెను ఆతని ఆంత్మజుండు వసుదేవు
మధురాపురంబు యేలె అతని భాందువు
నందగోపకుండు రేవుపల్లె యేలె వసు
దేవు పుత్ర శ్రీక్రిష్ణుద్వారవతి యేలేనా
క్రిష్ణగోపికావపుత్రులు వజ్రధరు అ
మృత గోవిందు అంభోజు లాగ్గురు
యింద్రప్రస్థ ఘనపీరపురిరాజ్యంబు
సేశిరి పద్మనాభుండు యెలె యండ్డలి
రాజ్యంబు కొంతయెలె । వీరవిజయు
ండు యేలెను న । శ్రీరామ్మణుండేలెను అ
రుంటుల కోన అమరవతి । సింహ్యాద్రియె
ల మంచ్చి యేలెను వల్లురాజులె ఆంవల్ల
పురము అచట కొన్నాళ్లు అడిదెవి టేనె
ను ఆలపోలురాజు ప్రతాపుని కాలము
న యెదుకులాత్మజులు దనుముకొండ్డ
మండలుడ, పినయెర్ప పెదయెర్ప యేలం
గ యెర్పలకు అనాప్రిష్టిదాంకి ధేనువు
లకు మేంతలేదని రాజుల పద్మనాయుం

28. డుగ్గా వివరించ్చుకొని ధేనువులుగా దారు
29. కదిలిరి పాంకనాడు సిద్ధిరాజుకు పు
30. ల్లరి వొడంబడి భూమినొచ్చి మేపిరి । మె
31. పుతనల నన్న ధేనువులుందాను దత్తణాదనువు
32. కోటికి కదిలి పోఇదనువు కో వల్లభుని దనువుకోవల్లభుని

దశే

33. ంచ్చి నలనన్న దెనువులుందాను మరిలి దిన గిధుల
34. మీందం గదిలివచ్చి పెన్నవెంట విడిశిరి నలసి
35. ద్దివారు యెద్దుల యెసిరిఆదవులవందను ఆండం
36. తరుచాయ అడవుల వంకర రంతుపడె
37. నెల్లూరి ధేనువులుందారు కదిలియ
38. అగడ్డ పాటనిలిచెను నలసిద్ధిరాయ
39. భారిపుల్లరికివచ్చెను దట్టించ్చిరాయ
40. భారిని పుల్లరిలేదు పొమ్మనిరి లేదు పొ
41. మ్మంటేను నెల్లూరి నలసిద్దిరాజు యఅ
42. గడ్డ పాటికి యెత్తివచ్చెను॥

Fourth side.

1. స్వస్తి శ్రీ శాలివాహన శకవ
2. షంబ్బులు ౧౧౭౦ [1] అగునేం
3. టి కాళయుక్తి సంవత్సర కార్తీక
4. శు ౫ గు నెల్లూరి నలసిద్ధిరాజు సవ
5. సెన్నాహం మెరసి । లింగాలకొండ యఅగ
6. డ్డపాటి కూడలి సోమేశ్వరుని సందలిన
7. నాన ఆత్రియగోత్ర యాదవక్షత్రి
8. య మధురాపురమం డీశ్వర శ్రీ
9. విష్ణుయోగమాయ దివ్యశ్రీ పా
10. దక బ్రకట శాత్రవభంజననచ్చెరవుంది

---

[1] Date uncertain; probably 1180.

11. పౌత్రలాయత్తవం గౌరవ పౌరవు
12. ండు ద్వారకాపురి గోపికావల్లభు
13. ని పౌత్రుండు వల్లురాజుంతని సు
14. తులు పోలురాజు పెద్దురాజు వా
15. రిపుత్రులు మొదలైన యాదవులు
16. నలసిద్ధింగూడి యుద్ధము
17. సేసి మృతులైరి । యదువంశ
18. మునకు భయంబ్బుదొలుగునని త్రిమూ
19. ర్తులు యోగమాయాదేవిని యిల్ల
20. నిరి గోపికాజనములు గోపాలకు
21. లున్న పసలమంద్దకు వేంగు భద్ర
22. నీవు వసుదేవనందనులకు గర్భపు
23. త్రికవై నానావిధ సంపదలకు స్తా
24. నకమై మానవులు భక్తింగొలుతు
25. రు కానుకలును బలులు నిచ్చి పద్దె
26. నిమిది నామంబ్బుల గొనియాడు
27. దురు ఇయ్యావ్యస్థానంబులు రా
28. రింగించ్చ వుమిపితాపురి హేంకృతిద
29. నువు కొండ్డుంబ్రత్యక్షమై । పాలేటి
30. తీరంమున భాగిరత్థై నిలిచి భక్తునికి
31. ప్రత్యక్షమై త్రిమూర్తుల మెప్పించి వీ
32. ర మహత్తు ఇప్పించెను భాగీరథి ధుగ్గ
33. స్త్రానం కొండయ్యకొడుకు రా
34. మయ్య వుద్ధరించిన శాసనం॥

KANDUKUR (27). (A.D. 1514–15.)

[Gundlapálem. Partly Sanskrit in Telugu character, partly Telugu. From stone by Bramharéṣvara's temple.]

From line 25, the stone is worn.

TRANSLATION.

Sanskrit verse.

May this deity named Brahmaréṣvara (who resides) specially in the holy place which is to the south-east of Ṣríṣaila always protect the worlds. Ṣrí! Ṣrí!

Telugu.

Hail! On Thursday, the 13th of the bright fortnight of Bhádrapada of the year Bháva, corresponding to the illustrious Ṣaka year 1436, Ráyasam Koṇḍamarusayya—who holds authority to carry out the orders of Krishnaráya in Udayagiri (*i.e.*, viceroy) which is the chief *durgam* in the kingdom of Ṣrí Víra Krishnaráya Maháráya, who (Krishnaráya) is Ṣríman Mahámaṇḍaléṣvara, Rájádhirája, Rájaparaméṣvara, Múruráyaragaṇḍa,[1] Ashṭadikkuráyamanóbhayankara,[2] Báshatappuvaráyaragaṇḍa,[3] Púrvadakshinapaschamasamudrádhísvara,[4] Yavanarájyasthápanácharya[5], and Ṣrí Víra Pratápa—presented the village Árumúruguḍlu[6] which is in Púnginádu and which formerly belonged to Brahmaréṣvara Ṣríman Mahádéva for restoration of the temple (*punaruddhárana*) and for

---

[1] The disgracer of three kings.
[2] The terror of the kings of the eight cardinal points.
[3] The disgracer of kings who break their word.
[4] The lord of the eastern, southern and western seas.
[5] The establisher of the Yávana (Mussalmán) kingdom.
[6] An old name of Gundlapálem apparently.

providing all enjoyments to the deity, to last in perpetuity as long as the sun and moon endure.

(Sanskrit.) [One imprecatory verse.]

(Telugu.) He has given a *paṭṭu* field under Mácha-varam tank . . . under Mópáḍu tank for *punaruddhâraka* to the deity Brahmaréṣvara. Ṣrí, Ṣrí, Ṣrí !

1. श्रीशैल आ (ला) ज्ञे(ग्रे)य दिग्भागे पुण्यक्षेत्रे वि
2. शेषतः । भ्रमरेश्वरोभिधानोयं
3. लोकान् रक्षतु शाश्वतं ॥ श्री श्री
4. స్వస్తి శ్రీ శకవర్షంబులు ౧౪౩౮ అగునేం
5. టి భావ సంవత్సర భాద్రపద శు ౧౩
6. గురువారాన స్వస్తి శ్రీ మన్మహా మండ్డలే
7. శ్వర రాజాధిరాజ రాజపరమేశ్వర మూ
8. రు రాయరగండ్డ అష్ట దికురా
9. య మనోభయంకర బాసదప్పువ
10. రాయరగండ్డ పూర్వ దక్షిణపశ్చ
11. మ సముద్రాధీశ్వర యువన[1] రాజ్య స్థా
12. పనాచార్య్య శ్రీ వీరప్రతాప శ్రీ వీ
13. ర క్రిష్ణరాయ మహారాయలోని గల
14. రాజ్యాలకున్ను మొదలిదుర్గము
15. వుదయగిరికి క్రిష్ణరాయల ఆజ్ఞా
16. ప్ర మాణ్యానను ప్రతిపాలనం శెయ్యను
17. అధికారంగల రాయసం కొండ్డ మరు
18. సయ్యంగారు భ్రమరేశ్వరం శ్రీ మన్
19. మహా దేవునికి పూర్వానఁ గల ఆరు
20. మూరుగుళ్లు పూంగినాంటిలోని ఆ
21. గ్రామము పునరోద్ధారకముగాను దే

---

[1] Read యవన.

22. పుని అంగ్గరంగ్గ వైభవాలకున్ను ఆచ
23. ంద్రార్క స్థాయిగాను సమర్పించెను॥
24. స్వదత్తాం పరదత్తాం వా యో హ
* 25. రేతి వసుంధరాః । షష్టిర్వర్షసహ
26. స్రాణి విష్టాయాం జాయతే
27. క్రిమిః (మాచ) వరం చెరువుకింద్ద
28. (భ్రమరేశ్వ) ర దేవుని పట్టించెను
29. . . . మో పాటిచెరు
30. (వు క్రింద . . .) ష్ఠు
31. . . . యి భ్రమరె
32. (శ్వర దేవునకు) పునరోద్ధా
33. రకముగాను యిచ్చెను
34. శ్రీ శ్రీ శ్రీ

Kandukur (28). (A.D. 1329–30.)

[Gunḍlapāḷem. Sanskrit in Telugu character and Telugu. From stone in same temple.]

Translation.

Adoration to Ánjanéya!

[Sanskrit verse—only a fragment—seems to be an invocation to Brahmarésvaradéva.]

Sanskrit.

In the Śaka year reckoned by 'yama rúpa,' (*i.e.* 1251) in the year Śukla, in the bright fortnight of Mágha on Thursday—on full moon day—on *parva* of the moon (lunar eclipse) the village of Árumúru . . . was presented to Bráhmans to last as long as (the sun and) moon exist.

Telugu.

Ṣrí Víra Pratápa Rudradévapatirája Maháráya (who has the *birudas*) Srí Víra Narapati . . . . lord of the Carnatic country, . . . ari pratápa, &c., presented to Brahmarámésvara Linga of Árumúrugudlu[1] situated in Púnginádu *sthala* which is attached to Udayagiri which is included in his kingdom, that village for the restoration of the temple (*punaruddháraka*) and for providing all enjoyments (to the deity). He presented to this deity dry land, wet land, and *méras* in the villages of Kandukúr *ṣíma*.

(Sanskrit.) [Imprecatory verse.]

1. आंज भान्वर्कं । . . . । श्री आरुमूरु . .
2. वायाशं श्री भ्रमरलिंग . . .
3. वो लिंगं । कटकाधिपतिताम . .
4. . . . रो . . . धि आचंद्रतारकं । . .
5. धर्मो वर्धते वर्धते । श्री शाके यम
6. रूपगणिते अब्दे च शुक्लाह्वये
7. माघे सितपक्षये सुरगुरौ . . .
8. पौर्णमी । तत्काले शशिपर्वणिषु . . .
9. . . . श्री आरमूरिग्रामं । ब्रा[ह्मणे]
10. षु सणर्पमं (गजेष ?) याचंद्र
11. శ్రీ విరనరపతి . . .
12. ప్రౌఢ కనాౕంటక బవదీ శ్వ అరి ప్ర
13. తాప శ్రీ వీరప్రతాప రుద్ర [దేవ]
14. పతిరాయ మహారాయలు నిజ

---

[1] Árumúrugudlu seems to be a former name of Gundlapálem.

15. రాజ్యానకుం జెల్లి యుండెటి
16. ఉదయగిరికి జెల్లియుండె
17. ంటి పూంగినాంటి స్థళంలోని
18. ఆడు మూరుగుళ్ల (భమ రామే
19. శ్వర లింగ్గానకు పునరోద్ధార
20. కంముగాను ఆ గ్రామం అంగ్గ
21. రంగ్గ విభవాలకును సమర్ప
22. ణచేసెను ॥ కందుకూరి శీమ
23. గలం గ్రామాలాను వెలిపా
24. లం పరిమడి మేరలుసహా
25. గార్ను దేవునికి సమర్పణ చే
26. సెను ॥ స్వదత్తాం ద్విగుణం
27. పుణ్యం పరదత్తానుపాలనం
28. పరదత్తాపహారేణ స్వద
29. త్తం నిష్ఫలం భవేత్ ॥

Kandukur (29). (A.D. 1209-10.)

[Gundlapáḷem. Telugu. From stone in same temple.]

Translation.

Hail! On Vaddavâram (Saturday), the 7th of the bright fortnight of Bhádrapada of the year Ṣukla, corresponding to the illustrious Ṡaka year 1132, on the occasion of Kanya Sankránti, Sénángulam, who is the son of Ṣríman Déva of Nellúrikóṭa, and who is the head servant of Ṣríman Mahámanḍaléṣvara Tirukáltidéva Chóḍa Mahárája, granted wet fields in Áramúru which is attached to his chiefdom, and is situated in Púnginádu, as a gift to Bráhmans.

			Pa.[1]
Venka Súryadéva Bhaṭlu	...	...	2½
Anyébhaṭlu	...	...	1½
Víridévara Peddi	...	...	1½
Yerrébhaṭlu	...	...	2
Virikochurépeddi	...	...	2
Potébhaṭlu	...	...	2
Nágadévabhaṭlu	...	...	1½
Appanabhaṭlu	...	...	1½
Dévanabhaṭlu	...	...	1½
Náráyaṇabhaṭlu	...	...	1½

He has given (the lands) to these to last as long as the sun and moon exist.

[One imprecatory verse.]

1. స్వస్తి శ్రీ శకవరుషంబులు ౧౧౩౨
2. నేంటి శుక్ల సంవత్సర భాద్రపద శుద్ధ స
3. ప్తమియు షడ్డవారమున కన్యసంక్రాంత్తి
4. నిమిత్త్యమున శ్రీ మన్మహా మండలేశ్వర తి
5. రు కాత్తిదేవ చోడమహారాజుల మూలబ్రిత్యు
6. లైన నెల్లూరికోట పడవారిలోన శ్రీమదేవని కొడుకు
7. సేనాంగులము పూంగినాంటిలోనం దమ జీవిత
8. వర్గమైన ఆరమూర బ్రహ్మదత్తము గావించి
9. న పరిపాలము వెంకట సూర్య్య దేవభట్లకు ప ౨॥
10. అన్యెభట్లకు ప ౧॥ వీరి దేవనపెద్దికి ప ౧॥
11. ఎఱ్ఱెభట్లకు ప ౨ విరికొచురె పెద్దికి ప ౨ పో
12. తె భట్లకు ప ౨ నాగదేవభట్లకు ప ౧॥ అప్పన
13. భట్లకు ప ౧॥ దేవనభట్లకు ప ౧॥ నారాయ
14. ణభట్లకు ప ౧॥ కిట్లరలు వీరలకాచంద్రా

[1] 'Pa' stands for paṭṭu.

15. కల్పస్థాయి । స్వదత్తం పరదత్తం వా యో హరే
16. తి వసుంధరా షష్టివర్షసహస్రాణివిష్టాయాం జా
17. యతే క్రిమి॥

KANDUKUR (30). (A.D. 1520–21.)

[Jillélamúḍi. Telugu. On shrine of Ánjanéya temple.]

TRANSLATION.

Hail! On Wednesday, the 15th day of the bright fortnight of Vaiṣákha of the year Vikrama corresponding to the year 1442 of the illustrious, victorious and prosperous Ṣáliváhana Ṣaka era while Ráyasamkonḍa Marusayyaváru of the Bháradvája *gōtra* and of the Áṣvaláyana Sútra was the ruler of Udayagiri which is the chief fortress under the royal throne, skilled in bearing the burden of the administration of the domain of Ṣríman Mahámandaléṣvara Rájádhirája Rájáparamésvara, Múruráyaragaṇḍa,[1] Ashtadigráyamanóbhayankara,[2] Básadappuvararáyaragaṇḍa,[3] the lord of the eastern, southern, and western seas, the beloved of the goddess of the Carnatic Kingdom, the lord of the throne of Vijayanagar, Srí Víra Pratápa Ṣrí Krishṇa Dévaráya Maháráya, he addressed the deity Janárdana who manifested himself at Skandasthána (Kandukúr) in the north-eastern quarter of Ṣríṣaila to the great sage Agastya "O Lord of the Universe, the bearer of the conch, the discus, and the club, Janárdana of the town of Kandukúru, adoration be to thee" and issued this charitable stone edict for the

---

[1] Disgracer of three kings.

[2] The terror of kings of the eight cardinal points.

[3] The disgracer of kings who break their word.

village after making prostrations to devotees possessed of truthfulness, modesty and awe. On this day the holy occasion of a lunar eclipse the village of Dávi on the Pāḷéru in Kandukúru *ṣíma* attached to the *rájya* of Udayagiri (is given) as a *sarvamánya*.

1. స్వస్తిశ్రీ జయాభ్యుదయ శాలివాహన శకవర్షం
2. బులు ౧౪౪౭ అగు నేటి విక్రమ సంవత్సర వైశాఖ శు
3. ౧౫ శు శ్రీమన్మహా మండలేశ్వర రాజాధిరాజ రా
4. జ పరమేశ్వర మూరు రాయర గండయష్టదిగ్రాయ
5. మనోభయంకర బాసదప్పువరరాయరగండ్డ పూర్వ ద
6. క్షిణ పశ్చిమ సముద్రాధీశ్వర కర్నాటక రాజ్యలక్ష్మీ మ
7. నోహార విజయనగర సింహాసనాధీశ్వర శ్రీవీరప్ర
8. తాప శ్రీక్రిష్ణదేవరాయ మహారాయల రాజ్యభార
9. ధురంధరులున్ను భారద్వాజ గోత్రోద్భవులున్ను అశ్వలా
10. యనసూత్ర పవిత్రులున్ను ఆ ఇనరాయసంకొండ మ
11. రుసయ్యవారు రాయసింహాసనానకు మొదలి దు
12. ర్గమైన ఉదయగిరి దుర్గాధిపతిత్వము సేసున్ను
13. శ్రీశైలానకు ఆగ్నేయ దిగ్భాగమైన సారండస్థానమం
14. దును అగస్త్యమహామునికిం క్షేత్రమైన జనార్దన
15. దేవునికి శ్రీమత్సకలలోకేశ, శంఖచక్రగదాధర
16. కండుకూరి పురానైక జనార్దన నమోస్తుతే। ఆది
17. సత్య నయభయభక్తులను సాష్టాంగదండ్డ ప్రణామ
18. ంబు సేసి సమర్పించ్చిన గ్రామానకు ధర్మశిలాశా
19. సనము ఉదయగిరి రాజ్యానకుం జెల్లి కందుకూరి శీమ
20. లోని పాలేటిధరిని దావిఅని గ్రామము సర్వమాన్యము
21. గాను నేంటి సోమగ్రహణ పుణ్యకాలమందు

KANDUKUR (31) & (32).

[This inscription was found on a stone built into the Ramasvámi Méḍa in Kandukur town. Mr. Venugopal Chetti had the slab removed to the taluk office.

The inscription is on three sides of the stone.

The inscription is in the Eastern Chalukya character. On the second side the style of writing resembles that of the fifth century. The inscriptions on the other two sides are of another style and of later date.

The characters are beautifully engraved. It has not been found possible to translate the inscription as it is incomplete. The first side contains epithets relative to a king of an Ayodhya dynasty and therefore the inscription evidently refers to some Chalukya king. The language is Telugu. Mr. V. Venkayya assisted in the transliteration which is doubtful in parts. On the opposite page will be found a photograph of the inscription.]

First side.

1. శ్రీనిరవద్యుణ్డు . .
2. సిత్త . . పముణ్డు శివ
3. పదవర . పవిత్రుణ్డ
4. ఖిలుణ్డా నృత రిపు బ
5. లుణ్డామహావరాద్యుణ్డ (రాముణ్డ)
6. యోధ్యా సింహాసనుణ్డ
7. గణిత దాన మాన్యుణ్డు గజ

Second side.

1. లయుణ్డ . . త్వసణ్డ
2. నపణ్డర గుంవ్వ . ఛ్ఛణీయుగాని

(To face page 541.)

KANDUKUR NOS. 31 & 32.

(1)

(To face page 544.)

KANDUKUR NOS. 31 & 32.

(2)

(To face page 544.)

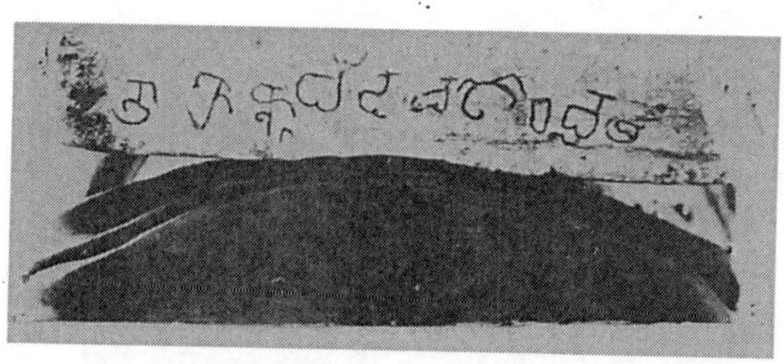

KANDUKUR NOS. 31 & 32.

(3)

3. కోలడితేని కోట్టబుం లోవ్వడి [చి]
4. గోణకేన ల్లాతని పశుపాంతి
5. సలలిత . . . పదగ
6. . . . . న

Third side.

ఆ కాన్న విదభ గోకవ .

Kandukur (33).

[Kandukúr. Sanskrit verses in Telugu character. On a demarcation stone to the west of fort.]

Translation.

1. What merit there is in all holy places, what efficacy there is in all sacrifices—all this merit one acquires by protection of the village (granted as a gift).

2. The merit of one who protects a former gift is greater than that of (the giver of) the former gift; but if a former gift is not protected, it destroys all merit previously acquired (?)

3. Never have I the desire for the enjoyment of celestial maidens; I seek not the glory of acquiring the illustrious place of Brahma and the other (gods); nor does this (my) mind ever think of the eight sorts of wealth (or spiritual powers). But I pray, O Hara, for very deep faith in the lotus of thy feet.

* * * *

First side.

1. सर्वतीर्थेषु यत्पुण्यं
2. सर्वयज्ञेषु यत्फलं
3. । तत्फलं लभते सर्वं
4. ग्रामस्यैवानुपालना

5. त् ।। पूर्वदत्तस्य यत्पु
6. ण्यं पालकस्य ततो
7. धिकं । अपालितं तु (य
8. द्दत्तं पूर्वपुण्याविनाश
कन्)

सातेशखलु

Second side.

सदाकांक्षा नास्ति त्रिदश
वनिताभोगजनिता न या
चे ब्रह्मादिप्रकटपदसं
प्राप्तिविभवम् । न मे चाष्टै
श्वर्यै विशाति सततं
मानसमिदं पदा(ब्जे या)
चेहं निविड(तमभक्ति)
हर तव ॥ . . . . .
तश्रमस्वत . . . . .

KANDUKUR (34).

[Kandukúr. Sanskrit in Telugu character. On the front side north pillar in the mosque in the fort.]

TRANSLATION.

1. May the god (Vishnu) protect the world—the sportive Boar, who resembles a large sapphire in brilliance, who has beautiful tusks, and who is like a black cloud appearing between the portions of the moon which are cut off (by it)[1]—who, while rescuing the earth from the ocean as (he rescues) his devotees from the weight of perils, seemed as if only slightly wet with sweat, though the ocean had merged in him.[1]

---

[1] The two tusks being white and the face of the boar being black.

2. There was a king named *Prólaya*, renowned as Rájaṣirómani[1] (the crest jewel of kings)—omniscient, associated with all auspicious emblems, and adorned with the army consisting of elephants, &c.

3. Rightly is he styled Rájachúḍámani (the crest gem of kings) for, holding arrows springing forth with great energy, he vanquished the enemy, possessed of formidable weapons.[2]

4. His son was *Véma*, resplendent with glory sung by many mouths; the goddess of fame flew up like a row of swans from the mountain which was the enemy who was crushed by his might.[3]

5. He built a flight of steps at Ṣríṣaila (to lead) to the rough Pátálagangapatha; he joyfully presented as much land as was desired to Brahmans. Even to enemies he did only good by establishing them in heaven.[4] What king can bear comparison with this ruler of earth?

6. The younger brother of him (Véma) who was victorious, who caused delight to the host of learned men, and who crushed the crowd of hostile kings, was king

---

[1] Rajaṣirómani = the crest jewel of kings—when applied to Prólaya; also the moon crested (*i.e.,*) Ṣiva.

The epithets apply both to the king and Ṣiva. In the case of Ṣiva, Karimukha = the elephant-faced, or Ganéṣa.

[2] Here also the king is compared to Ṣiva who consumed Káma (Vishamáyudha) possessing an uneven number of weapons (*i.e.*, 5) with his (third) eye (ambaka) starting forth with great wrath.

[3] Véma is here compared to Indra who crushed his enemies, viz., the mountains.

The meaning is —The fame of the enemy on being vanquished flew away like a row of swans fleeing away from a mountain destroyed by Indra.

[4] A comforting way of describing their destruction presumably. Pátálagangápatha is the stream flowing by Ṣrísailam.

Malla, who has the glory of Vishnu, the conqueror of foes.[1]

NOTE.—A few letters are visible at the end of these six verses showing that there was a continuation of this inscription.

This was covered with plaster. For the succeeding genealogy see Nos. 16 and 18. This gives us another name, Prólayya, the father of the Véma and Malla who head the table in No. 18.

1. देवः पातु महेंद्रनीलनिबिडज्योतिस्सुदं
2. ष्ट्रांकुरः प्रांतोद्भिन्नसुधांशुखंडविलसत्का
3. लांबुवाहोपमः अंभोधेर्विपदांभरा
4. द्रसूमतीं भक्तानिवोभ्युद्धरन् किंचित्खिन्न इवा
5. त्मलीनजलधिः क्रीडावाराहो जगत् ॥ (1)
6. आसीत्प्रोलयनामा सॅवज्ञः सर्वमंगलोपेतः
7. करिमुखवलापेशाभो राजशि रोमणिरितिख्यातः (2)
8. राजचूडामणिस्सोयं वैरिणं विषमायुधं
9. अनंगीकृतवान्युक्तमुद्यत्तीव्रानलांचकः ॥ 3 ॥
10. नानामुखोदीर्णवचोविलासो वेमाह्वय
11. स्तस्य कुमार आसीत् यदीयशक्त्या दलितोरगात्राद्धं
12. सावलीवोत्पतिता यशश्रीः । (4) श्रीशैले घटयांचकार वि
13. षमे पाताळगंगापथे सोपानानि यथारुचि क्षितिमदा
14. द्भूदेवताभ्यो मुदा । शत्रूणामपि सौख्यमेव विदधे स्वर्गे
15. प्रतिष्ठापनादस्य क्षोणिभुजस्तुलां कलयते को नाम
16. भूनायकः । (5) बुधव्रजानंदकृतोस्य जिष्णोर्विरोधिभूभृत्कु
17. लभेदनस्य मल्लक्षितीशः प्रातिमल्लजेता रमाधिपश्रीरनुजो ब

---

[1] Véma is compared to Indra and Malla to Vishnu, who is Indra's younger brother.

Jishnu—(1) Indra, (2) Victorious in the case of Véma.

Budha = God in the case of Indra, (2) learned man in the case of Véma.

Bhûbhrit = Mountain in the case of Indra, (2) king in the case of Véma.

Pratimallajêta = Malla was an asura or demon vanquished by Krishna (Vishnu).

Ramadhipa Sri (1) Vishnu, (2) having the glory of Vishnu.

The comparison is entirely based on verbal puns.

18. मूव । (6) ऐराव

19. य

20. ना

KANDUKUR (35). (A.D. 1398–99 ?)

[Kandukúr. Sanskrit in Telugu character. On the south front pillar of the mosque in the fort.]

TRANSLATION.

1. Victorious is Ṣrípati (Vishnu), whose quality of goodness is well known, the Boar, whose might is beyond change and worthy of praise, who, having gently and in sport lifted up the earth endowed with all excellent qualities and submerged in the waters of the ocean, made it happy.[1]

2. There arose a king named Véma in the fourth caste among those castes, viz., the Brahmans, Kshatriyas, Vaisyas and Sudras—who were born from the body[2]—the mouth, arms, thigh and feet (respectively)—of the venerated lord of the world, who is skilled in the art of creating the universe.

3. He gave as much land as was desired to Brahmans and constructed a flight of steps at the Pátálagangápatha.[3] He then caused to be related in Ándhra (Telugu) by Srí Ṣambhudása,[4] the Rámáyana,[5] describing good deeds, and the Harivamsa, and performed the ordinances of gifts and great gifts enumerated by Hémádri.

4. His great prowess shone like a lamp illuminating the whole universe; having dispelled the darkness

---

[1] The earth is compared to a damsel rescued by her lover.
[2] The word "déhát," in the text seems unnecessary.
[3] This is the river at Ṣríṣaila.
[4] Srí Ṣambhudása—another name of the Telugu poet Erra Pregada. He composed the Rámáyana and Harivamsa in Telugu. He was the court poet of Véma.
[5] The reading Rámáyana is conjectural; the word may be Dharmáyana.

of the pride of hostile mischievous kings who were already vanquished by its lustre, it (his prowess) hastens to play with the balls of the heads, shining with diadems of valiant and excellent kings, but is suddenly obstructed by peace sued for by them.[1]

5. His elder brother was *Mácha Sauri*[2]; his younger brother was king *Annaya;* the younger brother of him Annaya was king *Malla.*

6. In his hand was firmly fixed liberality, in his mind ardent fondness for virtue, in his character mercy, in his speech truth, in his side-glance beauty, on his shoulders the earth, (and) in his sword victory.

7. The son of him, king Malla, was king *Kômaṭi* who was skilled in ruling the earth, and who was adorned with virtues.

8. His eldest son by *Gaurámbiká* was king *Ṣrísa Ṣrigiri,* who was possessed of eternal fame, who was glorious and who alone was skilled in ruling the earth; he was devoted to the service of the lotus feet of (his) guru *Ṣrímad Voḍiyaráya Ṣrigiri,* he was eminent in valour and liberality and knew the beauties of song and poesy.[3]

9. He caused to be constructed many thousand huge tanks, which were useful to the public, as deep as the ocean, and famous for producing plenty of crops; and (he) performed the gifts described by Hémádri.[4]

---

[1] This verse is obscure. The text is partially illegible and some letters are missing. The reading is conjectural.

Are Kútabhanjana and Víra Vara names or surnames of two kings vanquished by Véma?

[2] Ṣauri—Krishna.

[3] The metre seems irregular here.

[4] The text is illegible here and the reading is conjectural.

10. The mountain of the gods (Méru) bears resemblance to this king in height (magnanimity when applied to the king), in always being the abode of the gods (the king being the asylum of learned men), and in having gold (urbanity when applied to the king). Having in his hand a bow fit for the gods, skilled (literally, initiated) in protecting the earth and being approved by the gods—Oh, wonder—he purifies us all!

11. Then shines the younger brother of him, Śrígiri, the conqueror of the earth—*Śrí Rácha Véma*, glorious with fame, great in valour, revered by his younger brothers, viz., *Mácha*, lord of earth, *Anna Déva*, king of earth, *Peddi*, ruler of earth—as she, Doḍḍámbiká (shines revered) by her princely son.[1]

12. His enemies who have been exalted by permanent regal fortune (*i.e.*, who are firmly established on thrones) are humbled (by him); those who are smitten down constantly by his sword in battle are easily cast up on the breasts of celestial maidens.[2]

13. By those very blows by which he quenches the valour of his enemies—he, the wise, indeed increases the lustre of his own valour.[3]

14. The sun of his sword annihilates the snow which is the fame of his enemies. This is indeed proper,

---

[1] Doddámbika's son was Kátaya Véma, the minister of Kumáragiri (S.S. 1307—1338). It is assumed that the reference is to Véma's daughter Doḍḍámbiká but it is not very clear why her name is brought in here.

[2] The poet plays on words here—the enemies are thrown *down* by blows in battle but thrown *up* on the breasts of celestial maidens, *i.e.*, they are killed and welcomed by celestial maidens in heaven.

[3] The reading लेदुग्धरसा in the original has no meaning सद्गुद्धिरसौ has been substituted.

for the very thought of him envelops the minds of his enemies in darkness.

15. Hail! Ṣrí Dhananjaya (Arjuna) conquers in war his enemies who have sworn never to flee—who is eminent by reason of the help of the army of Hari (Krishna) (or by the help of Hari and Bala), and by whom the enemy Mahéṣa (Ṣiva) has been vanquished.[1]

16. He, Rácha Véma, the moon of kings, the great glory of whose valour is sung by wise men, caused to be made a tank, useful to the world, in the north-eastern quarter of Baddipunḍi.

17. In the Ṣaka year reckoned by the sky (0), the eyes (2), Rámas (3), the Earth (1), (*i.e.*, 1320), in (the month of) Kártika, on (the day of) solar eclipse, the younger brother of Ṣrígiri, the lord of earth, the lord Rácha Véma, the treasury of wealth, presented that incomparable tank made in Baddepúnḍi[2] to Janárdana, the consort of Lakshmi, (who is) in Skandapura (Kandukúr), for the religious merit of his elder brother.

18. May the regal splendour of king Ṣrí Rácha Véma continue for ever on earth, by the great grace (literally, gracious look) of Janárdana, who resides in Skandapura, and who is pleased with the gift of the tank!

NOTE.—1. This inscription is found engraved on the south front pillar in the mosque in the old fort at Kandukúr. This mosque was evidently a manḍapa in former days.

2. The writing was quite covered with chunam when first seen by Mr. Venugópál Chetti. Even after the removal of the chunam, some of the letters were hardly legible. It has been noted in the footnotes where readings are conjectural.

---

[1] Rácha Véma is here compared to Arjuna. In the case of Rácha Véma Haribalasaháya = with the help of men brave as lions; and Mahéṣa = a great king.

[1] Baddipúnḍi is a village in Kandukúr taluk.

3. The language is Sanskrit and the characters are Telugu. The whole is in verse and consists of 18 verses which are numbered in Telugu numerals.

4. The inscription records (v. 16–17) the dedication of a large tank newly constructed at Baddipúṇḍi, a village in Kandukúr taluk, by Rácha Véma of the Reḍḍi dynasty to Janárdanadéva (the deity) of Kandukúr (Skandapura). The date of the grant was the day of solar eclipse in Kártika in the S.S. year 1320. The dedication was for the merit of his elder brother Ṣrísa Ṣrígiri.

5. After the usual invocation to the Boar incarnation (v. 1) the inscription says that Véma was born in the Súdra caste; v. 3 says that he built a flight of steps to the Pátálagangápatha, which flows near Ṣríṣaila in Kurnool district; it also says that he had the Rámáyana and the Harivamsa related in Telugu by Ṣrí Sambhudása, who we know from Telugu literature was no other than his court poet Erra Prégaḍa. In v. 7, the Guru of Ṣrígiri is given as Ṣrímad Voḍiyaráya Ṣrígiri.

6. The following table exhibits the genealogy as traced out in this and preceding inscriptions:—

Prólayya.
Mácha. Véma. Anna. Malla.
Pina Kómati = Gaurámbiká (son of Malla).
Ṣrísa Ṣrígiri married Gangámbiká. Rácha Véma. (S.S. 1320.) Mácha. Annadéva. Peddi.
Kómati (S.S. 1352). Malla (S.S. 1330). Ana Véma. Náráyana. (sons of Ṣrísa Ṣrígiri and Gangámbiká)
Tippayya Reḍḍi. Tippayya Reḍḍi Ṣrígiranna. Rámayya. Déváráyuṇḍu. Náráyanadévaru. (sons of Kómati)

Verses 12, 13 and 14 are poetical descriptions of the prowess of Rácha Véma. In verse 15 he is compared to Arjuna, every epithet used referring to him and Arjuna. The inscription closes with a benediction on him (v. 18).

1. जयति विदितसत्वः श्रीपतिः स्तब्धरोमा जलधिज
2. लनिमग्नां सादरं लीलया यः । सकलगुणस
3. मेतां गामुदुह्यात्तसौख्यामकृत विकृतिदू
4. रश्लाघनीयानुभावः 1 ॥ लोकेशस्य समस्तलोकजनन
5. व्या(वअ) पारपारंगतस्यासन् वक्त्रभुजोरुपादजनितास्सेव्य
6. स्य देहात्त था विप्रक्ष त्रियवैश्य नामकलिता श्शूद्राह्व
7. यश्चेति ये वर्णा स्तेषु चतुर्थवर्ण उ दभूद्द्मा
8. भिधानो नृपः ॥ 2 ॥ वि प्रेभ्यः प्र ददौ यथे ष्टवसुधां
9. पातालगंगापथे सोपानप्रततिं व्यरी रचदतो रा
10. मायण म सत्कार्ति । आ चांध्रं[1] हरिवंशं मप्यकथ यत् श्रीशंभुदासेन यो हे
11. माद्रेर्गणितांश्चकार च महा दानातिदानव्रतान् ॥ 3 ॥ य स्यादीप्यत सर्वलोकविकस
12. द्दिपः प्रतापो महान् । शोभानिर्जितकूटभंडनरिपु क्ष्मापालगर्वाधतां हत्वा
13. वीरवराधिराजमकुटस्फू र्जच्छिरःकंदुकक्रीडाकिलरया युतोर्थ सहसा तत्सा

[1] Read यश्चान्ध्रं.

14. [1]मयग्रेभवाति[2] ॥ 4 ॥ तस्याग्रजो माचशौरिरनुजन्मान्न
15. याधिपः । तस्यान्नयरयावरज ˘ः प्राभवन्मल्लभूपतिः ॥ 5 ॥ दानं
16. करे चेतासि धर्मलौल्यं । दयाचीरित्रे वचनेषु सत्यं । प्रतिष्ठितं
17. यस्य रमा कटाक्षे । भुजे धरित्रीविजयश्च खड्गे ॥ 6 ॥ तस्य मल्ल
18. महींशस्य पुत्रः कोमटिभूपति   ः । धरापालनधौरेयो बभूव
19. गुणभूषणः ॥ 7 ॥ श्रीशश्रीगिरि भूपतिः स्थिरयशस्तस्याग्रसू
20. नुरसुधीः ख्यातः क्ष्मातलपालनैकनिपुणो गौरांबिका
21. यामभूत् । श्रीमद्वोडियरायश्रीगिरिगुरोः । पादाब्जसेवापरश्शौर्यौदा
22. र्यसमुन्नतश्च गुणवित्संगीतसा हित्ययोः ॥ 8 ॥ जगद्धिता नेकसहस्रा ब्धिसमा
23. नगांभीर्य महातटाकान् । अकारयत्तस्यभरप्रशस्यान् । हेमाद्रिदानानि च यो विधत्ते ॥ 9 ॥
24. औन्नत्येन सदा बुधाश्रय तया कल्याणभावेन च क्षोणीपस्य दिवौकसां वितनुते यस्यो
25. पमां भूभृतः[3] । कृत्वा पाणितलेसुरक्ष मध नुः भूपालने दीक्षितो देवेनानुमतो
26. खिलान्किल पु ˘नात्यस्मानसा धारणं ॥ 10 ॥ त स्यश्रीगिरिभू मिजेतुरनुजश्रीराच वेमाधिपश्री

---

[1] Read—ति.   [2] Read—सामरुद्भोभव.   [3] Read भूधरः.

27. कीर्तिप्रथित प्रतापमाहि तः स्वस्यानुजैः पुजितः माचक्ष्मापातनान्नदेवधरणीपा
28. लेन पेद्दिक्षमापालेनापि विभाति सैव विभुना दोड्डांबिकासू नुना ॥ 11 ॥ भवंति य
29. स्य प्रणतास्सपत्नास्समुन्नताशाश्वतराजलक्ष्म्या । विदारणै [1] खड्गनिपानिता ये स्वस्त्रीकुचाग्रे
30. षु सुखोन्नतास्ते ॥ 12 ॥ कोरोति[2] यो खड्ग पयोदधारानिपातनैश्शांतिं[3] मरिप्रतापं ।
31. तैरेव लेदुग्धरसा[4] स्वकीयप्रतापलक्ष्म्याः प्रतनोति वृद्धिम् ॥ 13 ॥ यशस्तुषारं द्विषताम् यदीयः कृपाण
32. भानुः कुरुते निरस्तं । युक्तं हि ताच्चित्तमहो तदीयं भयांधकारावृतमातनोति ॥ 14 ॥ संशप्तकान् स
33. पत्नान् समरे हरिबलसहायमहनीयः । योजितशत्रुमहेशः । स्वस्ति श्रीमद्धनंजयो जयति ॥ 15 ॥ स राचवेमक्षि
34. तिपालचंद्रो व्यरीरचद्विश्व हितं तटाकं । आग्रेयदिक्सीमनि बद्दिपूंडेरार्यस्तुतस्पीतयशःप्रतापः ॥ 16 ॥
35. शकाब्दे गगनाक्षिरामवसुधा संख्ये ग्रहे कार्तिके भानोश्री गिरिभूमिभर्तुरनुजः श्री
36. राचवेमप्रभुः । पुण्यायाग्रभुवस्तटाकमतुलं तं बद्दिपूंडौ कृतं लक्ष्मीशाय ज
37. नार्दनाय वसते[5] स्कांदे पुरे श्रीनिधिः ॥ 17 ॥ तटाकदानेन जनार्दनस्य संतुष्यतः स्कंदपुरि
38. स्थितस्य कृपार्द्रदृष्ट्या भुवि राज्यलक्ष्मीश्रीराचवेमस्य विभो स्थिरस्तु ॥ 18 ॥

---

[1] Read. सदारणे. [2] Read करोति. [3] Read शान्ति ।

[4] This is unintelligible ; सद्बुद्धियरसौ is proposed ।

[5] वसत seems unnecessary ; read विदधे instead.

KANDUKUR (36).

[Kandukúr. Telugu. From western pillars of mosque in fort].

TRANSLATION.

(*On north pillar.*)

The polished pillar caused to be erected by Lingisetti and Mádhavasetti, sons of Bhandáru Mádha Vóttamasetti of Rávúr. Srí!

(*On south pillar.*)

The polished pillar caused to be erected by Mávuka Ayyapasetti, son of Vinikada Chennisetti.

(*On north pillar.*)

1. రావూరి భండార
2. మాధవోత్తమ సె
3. ట్టి కొడుక్లులింగిశె
4. ట్టి మాధవుశెట్టి సే
5. యించిన వరుంబ
6. ని కంభము శ్రీ||

(*On south pillar.*)

1. వినికడచెన్ని శె
2. ట్టి కొడుకు మావు
3. క అయపశెట్టి సే
4. యించివరుంబని
5. కంభ శ్రీ.

KANDUKUR (37).

[Kandukúr. Telugu. From eastern pillars of mosque in fort.]

TRANSLATION.

(On the north pillar.)

The polished pillar caused to be erected by Bápiráju, son of Guḷḷapalli Gonkaráju for the religious merit of his parents. Ṣrí !

(On the south pillar.)

The pillar caused to be erected by Chennu Ráju, son of Guḷḷapalli Gonkaráju. Ṣrí !

(On the north pillar.)

1. గుళ్లపల్లి గొాంకరాజు
2. కుమారుండు బా
3. పి రాజుగారు త
4. మ తల్లి తండ్రికి
5. పుణ్యముగాను చే
6. యించిన వరువు
7. ంబని కంభము శ్రీ.

(On the south pillar.)

1. గుళ్లపల్లి గొాంకరా
2. జు కుమారుండు
3. చెన్ను రాజు చేఇ
4. ంచిన కంభము శ్రీ

KANDUKUR (38).

[Kandukúr. Telugu. On middle pillars of mosque in fort.]

TRANSLATION.

(On the north pillar.)

The polished pillar caused to be erected by Narasingu, son of Balasáya Singama. Ṣrí!

(On the south pillar.)

The polished pillar caused to be erected by Bandári-seṭṭi, son of Bhanḍári Kámi Seṭṭi and Gópu, son of Bhanḍári Kúnáya. Ṣrí!

(On the north pillar.)

1. బలసాయ శింగము
2. కొడుకు నరసింగు సేఇ
3. ంచిన వరువుంబని
4. కంభము శ్రీ

(On the south pillar.)

1. బండారి కామి శె
2. ట్టి కొడుకు భండా
3. రి శెట్టిన్ని బండారి కూ
4. నాయ కొడుకు గోపు
5. న్ను చేయించిన వరువు
6. ంబని కంభము శ్రీ

Kandukur (39).

[Kandukúr. Telugu. On a stone built into the northern wall of the mosque.]

Translation.

Hail! (this is the charitable edict) given to Kalikéṣvaradêva (deity) of Kandukúr on the holy occasion of *Makara Sankránti* by Ráyasam Koṇḍamarusayyangáru, who is skilled in ruling the kingdom of Ṣríman Mahámaṇḍaléṣvara, Rájádhirája, Rájaparaméṣvara, Múruráyaragaṇḍa,[1] Ashtadigráyamanóbhayankaṛa[2] . . . . Ṣrí Krishna Dévaráya the paramount lord of Vijayanagar, who is a descendant of the *gótra* of Gautama, and who is a pure follower of the Áṣvaláyana *Sútra*, when he was ruling Udayagiri *durgam* . . . .

Note.—Part of the stone is broken, so that the object of the gift and other particulars are not known.

1. స్వస్తి శ్రీ మన్మహా
2. మండలేశ్వర రాజాధి
3. రాజరాజపరమేశ్వర మూరు
4. రాయరగండ అష్టదిగ్రాయ
5. మనోభయంకర విజయనగ
6. రాధీశ్వర శ్రీ విజయ
7. . నారసిహ్వ . .
8. . శ్రీ క్రిష్టదేవ
9. మహా రాయల రా
10. జ్యభార ధురంధరులున్న
11. గౌతమ గోత్రోద్భవులు

---

1 The hero to the three kings—the conqueror of three kings (Chéra, Chóla and Pándya).

2 Who causes terror to the kings of the eight points of the horizon.

12. న్న ఆశ్వలాయన సూ
13. త్ర పవిత్రుల్న అఇన రా
14. యసంకొండ మరుస
15. య్యవారు వుదయగిరి
16. దుర్గాధిపతితత్వము చేయించు
17. కందుకూరి కలికేశ్వర
18. దేవరకు . మకర సంక్రా
19. తి పుణ్యకాలమందు
20. . . . సెసి ఇచ్చిన
21. . . . . .

KANDUKUR (40). (A.D. 1322–23 ?)

[Kandukúr. Telugu. On a stone built into the steps of the Pírla Bhávi.]

TRANSLATION.

Hail! On Monday, the 5th of the bright fortnight of Chaitra in the year . . . corresponding to 1244 of the Srí Ṣaka era, while Ṣríman [Mahámaṇḍaléṣvara] Kákatíya Pratápa Rudradéva Mahá [rája] was ruling . . . Rudradévaningáru (at the request ?) of Kámaya Boppaningáru gave on the auspicious occasion of Ṣivarátri dry fields in the bed of the tank Uḍumulani kunṭa in the fields of Bátupadlakúka of Guḍipáḍu, 1,000 *kunṭas* of dry land in Guḍipáḍu and 1,000 *kunṭas* of wet land for the performance of daily worship to Kalikéṣvaradéva of Kandukúr for the religious merit of that Rája (Rudradéva). We have given dry land as *archana vritti* (share for the worshippers). We have given the Urimi fields, under the same tank as *sarvamánya* (free grant) . . . . we have given . . . .

This is the endowment made by Kámayya Boppaningâru when he was ruling Kandukúru. Whoever causes this charity to be kept up will get religious merit.

NOTE.—The stone was found built into the steps of the well. Mr. Venugópál Chetti had it removed to the Taluk office. As it is broken at the end, some portion of the inscription is missing and the translation given above is more or less conjectural. This Kámayya Boppaningáru is perhaps the official referred to in O. 49.

SUN. MOON. LINGAM.

1. స్వస్తి శ్రీ శక వరుషంబులు ౧౨౪౪ [అగునేంటి దుం దుభి?]
2. సంవత్సర ౣత్ర శు ౫ సో స్వస్తి శ్రీమన్మ [హా మండ లేశ్వర]
3. కాకతియ్య ప్రతాపరుద్రదేవ మహా [రాజులు రా]
4. జ్యము చేయుచుండంగాను ఆరాజులకు దమ్మ
5. ముగాను కామయ బొప్పనింగారిల [. . .]
6. కు రుద్రదేవనింగారు । శివరాత్రి పు[ణ్యకాలమ]
7. పుడు కందుకూరి కలికేశ్వర దేవర[అర్చన బాగా]
8. నకు ఆఘుడుపాటి బాతుపల్ల కూక . . .
9. ని పొలములోని ఉడుములానిగు[ంటకా]
10. డ కొని ఆచెర్వులోపలాను వెలుప[లాను]
11. పొలము ఘడపాటిని వెయికుంట[లున్న]
12. ౧౦౦౦ వల్న నీరునేలగాతునంత వర[కు కొ]
13. ంతవటు వెలిపొలమును గాను అ[ర్చన]
14. వ్రిత్తిగా నిస్తిమి ఆచెట్టున ఢుంనకు . . .
15. ము ఉరిమి చెలఆకొని కదరిశన . . . .
16. లరి సర్వమాన్యముగా నిస్తిమి . . . .
17. యినపుడెది [సా]గిపడుమడిమాన్య . . .
18. . . పులొంటను ఇస్తిమి । కామయ బొప్పని
19. ●గారు కందుకూరు ఏలి యిపుడు చేసిన ధ

20. న్స్వాకు యిధర్మాకు యెవరయినా చెల్లించి
21. పుణ్యము సేసిడి.

KANDUKUR (41). (A.D. 1683–84.)

[Kandukúr. Telugu. On stone near temple of Ítamukkalamma near Taluk Cutcherry.]

TRANSLATION.

Hail! On Tuesday, the 30th day of the dark fortnight in the month of Mágha of the year Rudhiródgári, corresponding to 1606 of the victorious and prosperous Ṣáliváhana Ṣaka era, in the town of Ṣrí Skandapuri (Kandukúr) situated in the kingdom of Udayagiri, when Bálu Panaha Khán, Allisán, Sándatanisánu, Bhódáyya, Nandakhán, Ajyam-Akaram, Sultán Khán, and Dánḍíla-tuhúmgáru were present, when Khán Ajyam Ajyambar Muhammad Khán Sáhib was seated, and when the Desáhis, the Sthalakaranams, the Kasbá Kápus, the Karanams, the Manḍali Kápus, the Désasthas, the Náyaks, the Pámakus (?,) and many others who had come from different directions were seated in the presence of the rulers, the two acrobatic companies of Mannekmári Annáreḍḍi and Mannekmári Pápayya performed various feats on poles and ropes. Then Aṇṇeárḍḍi fell down from the rope and died in the midst of the assembly. The members of this assembly therefore requested the (Muhammadan) ruler to make some provision for the future for the children of the deceased by giving them a village by the tank of this village and to grant them an hereditary inám with full ownership. Therefore they have caused to be executed and given a charitable deed granting one *gorru* of cultivable dry land in the eastern fields of the *kasba* village and as much cultivable wet land as can be sown with 4 *túms* of paddy under the Nallangaṭṭa tank. With the consent of the Kápus and Karnams of the *kasba* village they secured for them hereditary rights of ownership, ordered that the other 24 classes of Dommaras should have no right to it, and caused (this) stone inscription to be planted. Therefore according to this stone inscription the sons and grandsons of these persons Pâpayya and Annâreḍḍi should enjoy these (lands) in peace as long as the sun and moon exist. Ṣrí ! " Of giving and protecting a gift, protecting is more meritorious. By giving oneself, one attains heaven; but by ratifying another's gift, one secures imperishable bliss." Ṣrí.

If any persons, with the sun and moon as witnesses, obstruct the charity and violate the conditions of this stone inscription, granted by this assembly, with the object of making profit in this village, or if they obstruct the other 24 classes of Dommaras in any way, they will understand that they are excommunicated. Ṣrí.

NOTE.--The names of the persons present are in several cases doubtful.

1. శ్రీ స్వస్తి శ్రీ జయాభ్యుదయ శాలి
2. వాహాన శక వర్షంబులు ౧
3. ౬౦౬ అగునేటి రుధిరోద్గారినామసంవ్వ
4. త్సర మాఖ బ ౩౦ అంగారకవార్శ్యం
5. దు। వుదయగిరి రాజ్యమంద్దు చెల్లె శ్రీ
6. సరంధపురి పట్టణమందువ జారం
7. తమకు బాలువనవాఖాను అ
8. ల్లిశాను శాద తనిశాను భోదా య్యావ

9. రిద్దఖానై అజ్యం అకరం సుల్తాను
10. ఖానుదాండీల తుహజాంగారి
11. సదురునను ఖానై అజ్యంబరు మహో
12. మ్మదుఖాను సాహెబులుంగారు కూర్చు
13. ండి దేశాహిస్తల కరణాలు కసు
14. బా కాంపులు కరణాలు మండె[డ]లికాం
15. పులు దేశస్తులు నాయకులు పామ
16. కులు చాలుమూల సమయ సమస్త
17. పెకండ్రులున్ను యేల్నివారి సముఖ
18. మంద్ద కూర్చు

Second side.

19. ండి వుండగాను మన్నెక్మారి అన్నారెడ్డి
20. ఆపాపయ యీ రెండుతెగలవారు
21. న్ను ఖడలువెసుకొని మోకులమీద
22. ను నానా అపుమేళాలు ఆడుచూ వుండ్డం
23. గాను అన్నారెడ్డి మోకుమీదనుండి స
24. భామధ్యమమంద్దు పడి మృతిబొం
25. ంద్దె గనక యీసభవారు అంత్తా ప్రభు
26. వుతో విన్నపంచేసి వీండ్లకు యీ గ్రామం
27. చెరువుకోట్లు గ్రామం ఆయసు విరి
28. ండ్లకు ముంద్దరగతి గల్పించవలెను వీండ్లకు
29. మాన్యా స్వామ్యాలున్ను కాణయాచి
30. స్వాస్త్యం యిప్పించ్చవలెను అని విన్నపం చే
31. శిరి గాన అందుక కసుబాలోనుం తూర్పు
32. పొలానంను కైలిగొత్తందు వెలిపాలము
33. న్ను నల్లంగట్ట క్రిందకైలిలునా తుమువరి
34. విత్తనాల మడిన్ని దానపత్రిక వ్రాయిం
35. చ్చి యిప్పించి కసుబాం కాంపులు కరణాల

36. అడుకొండని కాణయాదిస్వాస్త్యం పిండ్లకు
37. యిప్పించి కడ్మ యిరువైనా ల్గు కులా
38. ల దొమ్మర్లకున్ను పని లేకుండా ని
39. ర్ణయం చేశి శిలాశాసనం వే
40. యించ్చిరి గనక యీ శిలాశాసన ప్ర
41. కారాన యీ పాపయ అన్నారెడ్డిగా
42. రి పుత్ర పౌత్ర పారంపర్యంతమున్ను ఆ
43. చంద్రార్కస్తాయిగాను అనుభవించుకు
44. ఖులై వుండువారు । శ్లో । దానపాలన
45. యోర్మధ్యే । దానాచ్ఛ్రేయోను పాలనం
46. థానా త్స్వర్గమావాప్నోతి । పాలనాద
47. చ్యుతం పదం । శ్లో
48. యీసభ వేయించ్చిన శిలాశాసన
49. ంతప్పి యీ గ్రామాన కట్నం వచ్చునని
50. యవరు అడ్డపడివచ్చినా సూర్యాచ
51. ంద్రమనులు సాక్షిగా యిరవైనా
52. లుగు కులాల దొమ్మర్లకు అడ్డంవచ్చినా
53. వాండ్లు వెలిగాన తెలిశేది. శ్రీ.

KANDUKUR (42). (A.D. 1802-03.)

[Karéḍu. Telugu. On the tank bund.]

TRANSLATION.

Hail! On Wednesday the 13th of the bright fortnight of Ṣrávaṇa of the year Dundubhi, corresponding to the year 1725 of the illustrious, victorious and prosperous era of Ṣáliváhana Ṣaka on August 11 of the year 1802 Pákala Rámanna, the Brahman Karnam of Banginipalle having trodden the boundary between Karéḍu and Bangiuapalle won a victory under the orders of M.R.Ry. John Pinnvarat (Benward) Travers, Collector of Ongole anḍ Nelloré. Therefore this stone inscription was set up under the orders of that lord.

NOTE.—This is inserted though subsequent to A.D. 1799 on account of its curious character. The meaning is probably merely that the Karnam settled the boundary between the two villages. Ongole and Nellore were separate districts before the time of Mr. Travers. The exact meaning of "Mahallát táluká" is not clear; apparently the words mean "appertaining to the jurisdiction of".

1. స్వస్తి శ్రీ విజయాభ్యు
2. దయ శాలివాహన శక
3. వరుషంబులు ౧౭౨౫ అ
4. గు నేటి దుందుభి నామసం
5. వ్వత్సర శ్రావణశు 13 భృగు
6. వారం ౧౮౦౨ సంవ్వత్సర ఆ
7. గోష్టు నెల ౧౧ తేది కరేడు బి
8. ంగినిపల్లె సంద్దు పొలిమేర
9. మహారాజరాజశ్రీ జాన్ పి
10. ను వారతు త్రయివర్సు మహా
11. ల్లాతు తాలూకా నెల్లూరు వం
12. గ్గవోలు కలకటరు ధొరవారి
13. హుకుం ప్రకారం బింగినిపల్లె
14. బ్రాంహాణ కరణం పాకల
15. రామన్న పొలిమేర తొక్కి జ
16. యించినాడు గనుక ప్రభువు
17. వారి హుకుంప్రకారం వేయిం
18. చ్చి శిలాశాసనాలు.

KANDUKUR (43). (A.D. 1400–01?).

[Koṇḍamuḍusupáḷem. Telugu. On stone over Mopáḍ tank sluice.]

TRANSLATION.

Hail! On Monday, the 15th of the bright fortnight of Áshádha of the year Vikrama, corresponding to the illustrious Ṣaka year 1222, while Ṣrígiríṣvara Reḍḍi, the excellent son of Kómaṭireḍḍi, who (Srígiri?) bears the *birudas*—Jagannobhagaṇḍa,[1] Víranáráyaṇa,[2] Bhujabala,[3] Chóla Páṇḍyagajakésari,[4] Vairivíra,[5] Basuva Ṣankara[6] &c.—was ruling, Kómaṭi Rája ordered that the soldiers stationed in the town of Kandukúr, which is ruled by him, should contribute 1 *duggáni* (about 6 pies?) on each house from their pay, and presented this as an endowment to last as long as the sun and moon for providing all enjoyments to Kanda Soméṣvara Déva (the deity) who resides at Kandukúr which is to the south-east of Ṣrí Parvatam (Ṣrí Ṣailam). The king and his subordinates (soldiers) who maintain this charity will acquire merit (?)

Whoever removes this stone (bearing the terms of) this charity will incur the guilt attached to the five cardinal sins.

NOTE.—1222 S.S. expired corresponds to Vikári and not Vikrama which is 1202 expired. Probably we should read S.S. 1322.

1. శ్రీ స్వస్తి శ్రీ శకవర్షంబులు ౧౨౨౨ అగు నే
2. ంటి విక్రమసంవత్సర ఆషాడ శు ౧౫ సో । నాండు

జగనో

---

[1] = the sole hero of the world.

[2] = valiant Náráyaṇa (Vishnu).

[3] = having strength in one's arm; strong-armed.

[4] = the lion to the elephants which are the Chola and Páṇdya kings.

[5] = hero to enemies.

[6] are proper names (?).

3. బ్బగండ్డ వీరనారాయణ భుజబల చోల పాండ్యరాయగజ
4. కేసరి వైరి వీరబసువశంకరాదిబిరుద నిర్వాహకుండైన
కో

5. మల్లెండ్డింగారి సుపుత్రుండు శ్రీగిరీశ్వర రెడ్డి రాజ్యము
6. సేయుచుండం గోమటిరాజు యేలెడిపట్నము
7. కందుకూరి విరపరివారము శ్రీపర్వత ఆగ్నేయ
8. ద్వార నివాసియైన కంద సోమేశ్వరదేవరకును అంగ
9. రంగాభోగార్థము ఆచంద్రార్కముగాను త
10. మ తమ జీతాలవలనం విరను యింటను ఒ
11. కొకర్ల దుగ్గాని తెఖను సమర్పించ్చెను యీ ధర్మ
ము మి
12. గ పరివారము ఏలిక ధర్మంను సాగించిన
13. ఆ యీ యింయీ సుకృతమును బొందెడివి యీ
14. ధర్మమునకును ఎవ్వరు ఉంరాలిని తిసినాను
15. వారు పంచమహాపాతకములుం జ్యేగినారు.

KANDUKUR (44). (A.D. 1650–51.)

[Kondamudusapálem. Telugu. On sluice of tank.]

TRANSLATION.

Hail! On Friday, the 2nd of the dark fortnight of Márgaṣira of the year Vikriti, corresponding to the year 1573 of the illustrious, victorious, and prosperous Ṣáliváhana Ṣaka era, Antóji, the agent of Ṣrí Rámóji Mámbáji Nároji Raghoji Pantulu after making salutations has given, with libation of water, a *kóru* wet land for maintaining the tank *amaram*. It is settled that one *kunchaḍu* of grain for every *puṭṭi* of paddy and of all (other) produce raised under the tanks belonging to us in Kandukúr, which has been given to us by Háji Koti Sultán Abdullá Pádusháh as a *mokhása*, should be collected as tank *kunchas* (méras). We have ordered that the grain thus realized should be given to Upparas (diggers) so that they may keep the tanks in good condition. It should be maintained in this manner for the merit of Háji Kóti Pádusháh. Whoever misappropriate the *kuncha* grain set apart for the maintenance of this tank, not carrying out the provisions of this edict, if they are Muhammadans, will incur the sin of killing a pig at Mecca, if they are Brahmans or Sudras, will incur the sin of killing cows and Brahmans on the Ganges. Hence

* * * *

According to these conditions immediately . . .

This charitable edict . . . . .

Note.—The granter of the mokhása is Abdulláh Kutb Sháh of Golkoṇḍa. Anṭóji is called Havildár in Nos. 47 and 48 and governor of Kandukúr Pargana. In No. 48 Rámóji Mámbáji is described as Phamujudár.

First side.

1. స్వస్తి శ్రీ జయాభ్యుద
2. య శాలివాహన శక
3. వర్షంబులు ౧౫౭౩
4. అగునేంటి వికృతినామ
5. సంవత్సర మార్గశిర బ
6. ౨ శు నాడు శ్రీరామోజి
7. మాంబాజి నారోజి ర
8. ఘోజి పంతులంగారి
9. కార్యకర్తలయిన అ
10. ంతోజీ దండం పెట్టి
11. ధారా పూర్వకంగా
12. కోరుమాంగిలి సెర్వు

13. అమరం పాలించ స
14. మప్పీంవగ చెసితి

Second side.

15. మి. మీాకున్న మాకు
16. హాజికొాతి సులతాను
17. అబ్దుల్లా పాదుశాహిం
18. గారు మాఖా సాయించిన
19. కందుకూరిలో మా్రవిత్తి
20. చెరువులక్రింద్ద వండించ్చి
21. న వడ్లకు సకలాయం పు
22. ట్టి ౧ కి కుంచ్చండ్లి లెఖను చెర్వు
23. కుంచాలు కట్టడాచేసి వచ్చిన ధా
24. న్యం వుప్పలణవశాన యిచ్చి చెర్వు
25. లమీంద పని ముఖంసెయిం
26. చెటట్టుగా కట్టడచెస్తిమి గాన
27. క యీప్రకారం హాజికోతిపా
28. దుశాహింగారికి ధర్మణంగ్గాను
29. నడ్పించెది యీచెరువు కుంచ్చా
30. ల ధాన్యం యీశాసనప్రకా
31. రాన నడిపించక యవ్వరు పు
32. చ్చుకున్నను తురకలయినా

Third side.

33. ను మఖాలో వం
34. ద్ది చంపిన పాపమున
35. బోందురు బ్రాంహ్మలు
36. అయితేను శూద్రులయితేను
37. గంగకర్ణను గో బ్రా
38. హ్మాలం చంప్పిన పాపా

39. నం పోదుగు ఖుద్దున
40. యీ కట్టండ్లప్రకారం యీ .
41. . . . .
42. . . . .
43. యీ ధర్మశాసనం

KANDUKUR (45).

[Kóvúru. Telugu. In a backyard.]

TRANSLATION.

With love . . . . constructed a *mandapa* to Kóvúru Viṣvanátha and founded an endowment of land . . . . whosoever fails to uphold this charity will incur the sin of cow-slaughter and Brahmanicide on the banks of the Ganges.

1. కోవూరు విశ్వనాధనికి ప్రీతించే
2. మండపం . . . చేసిన వృత్తి
3. . . . . . డు ఇధర్మమునకు
4. ఎవరు తప్పినాను గంగ క
5. తర్ను గోవును బ్రాంహాల చం
6. పినవారు.

KANDUKUR (46). (A.D. 1682–83.)

[Máchavaram. Telugu. On a fallen stone by the road side.]

TRANSLATION.

Hail! On Thursday, the 15th of Mágha of the year Dundubhi, corresponding to the illustrious, victorious and prosperous Ṣálivahána Ṣaka year 1604 . . . .

(Illegible.)

The sons of the *Dharmakartás* (trustees of the charity) and . . . . The terms of the charitable edict are—

[This is] the edict founding charities in the villages Máchavaram and Mópád. The existing wells . . . .

The tamarind tope to the east of Guḍlúr; the mango tope to the south of Guḍlúr; the tamarind tope; the plantain garden . . . (to the north of the tamarind) . . . . .

NOTE.—There is also an inscription on an adjacent hill, but it is altogether illegible.

1. స్వస్తి శ్రీ జయా
2. భ్యుదయ శాలివా
3. హన శకవర్షంబు
4. లు ౧౬౦౮ అవు నేంటి
5. దుందుభియను సంవ
6. త్సర మాఘ శు ౧౫ భృగు
7. వాసరంనాడు
8. . . . [అవ్రైయించి
9. నవారునూ   వరదప్ప
10. గారియ దేవహాను
11. మంతుడి చ్చనవుం
12. డ్డి బండిలుండు తము
13. లుశాసనం]   చ్చి
14. రిధర్మకర్తల కొమా
15. ళ్లుంన్ను
16. . . . .
17. . . . .
18. . . . .
19. . . . .

20. . . . .
21. . . . .
22 ధర్మశా
23. సనక్రమ
24. మెఝ్ఘుంన్న
25 ను । మాచ
26. వరం । మో
27. పాడు । యీ
28. గ్రామాదుల ద
29. ర్మము ప్రతి
30. ష్టించిన ధర్మం । సా
31. లు భావులు
32. [ళ్లాల ఖవతం ?] గ్రా
33. మాలంలు గు
34. ఙ్లూరి తూర్పు
35. చింతతోపును
36. గుఙ్లూరి
37. కోను మాపిడి
38. తోపు చింతతోపు
39. లరెటి తోపు [చింత
40. తూర్పు ఉత్తరం]
41. . . . .

Kandukur (47). (A.D. 1650–51.)

[Máchavaram. Telugu. From stone near temple of Perantálu below tank bund.]

Translation.

Hail! On Friday, the 3rd of the bright fortnight of Márgaṣíra of the year Vikriti, corresponding to the illustrious, victorious and prosperous Ṣáliváhana Ṣaka year 1573, Antóji Pantulu Havildár the agent of Ṣrí Rámoji Mambáji[1] Náróji Ṣrí Raghoji Pantulu . . . .

We have granted (*méras*) fixing them at 1 *kunchaḍu* on every *puṭṭi* of paddy and all (other) produce raised under the tanks in the *Ṣíma* of Kandukúr which has been bestowed on us as a *mokhása* by Hazarat Sultán Abdulla Pádusháhi of Hyderabad Sarkár (government). According to the terms fixing a *kunchaḍu* under the tank, the grain should be collected from (the produce under) the tanks, and given to Upparas (diggers) in order that they may keep the tanks in good condition . . . .

Whoever misappropriate the grain, not carrying out the provisions of this edict, if Muhammadans, will incur the sin of killing a pig at Mecca, if Brahmans or Sudras, will incur the sin of killing cows and Brahmans on the Ganges.

If any one does this (*i.e.*, obstructs the charity), of whatever caste he be, his wife will be considered to have been given to a *veṭṭi*. May it cause great prosperity!

First side.

1. స్వస్తి శ్రీ జయాభ్యుద
2. య శాలివాహన
3. శకవర్షంబులు ౧
4. ౫౭౩ అగునేటి వికృ
5. తినామ సంవత్సర మా
6. ర్గశిర శు ౩ శు రోజు
7. శ్రీరామోజి మంబాజి
8. నారోజి శ్రీ రఘోజిపం
9. తులంవారి కార్య

---

[1] Numbáji in 48.

10. క త్తృలైన అంతో
11. జీవ :తులు హా
12. వలదారువారు
13. . . . .

Second side.

1. సరాకారు హైదరా
2. బాదు హాజిరతు సు
3. ల్తాను అబ్దుల్లా పాదుశాహిం
4. గారు మొకరారుచేసి ఇచిన
5. కందుకూరు శిమాలోం చెఱువు
6. క్రిందపండివచ్చినవడ్లకుసకలాయం
7. పుట్టి ౧ కి కుంచడు లెఖను కట్టడచేసి
8. యిస్తిమి . . . చె
9. ర్వు కుంచాల కట్టుప్రకారం వచ్చిన ధా
10. న్యం వుప్పంణ వశాన ఇచ్చి చెర్వు
11. మీంద పనిముఖం చెయించేది
12. . . . . వాడిచ్చావున్నా
13. . . . . ప్రకారాన
14. . . . . .
15. న్యం చెరువు

Third side.

* * * *

1. నం యీ శాసన
2. ప్రకారం నడిపింపక
3. యన్వరు పుచ్చుకున్నా రు
4. అకలయితేను మఖాలో వం
5. ద్ది చంప్పిన పాపానం బోదు
6. రు బ్రాంహ్మలు అయిన నూ

7. ద్రష్ట అయినను గంగకతణం గో
8. బ్రాంహ్మలం జంపినం బోదురు
9. యిందుకు యే కులంవారు అయి
10. నాను వాని ఆలిని వెట్టివా
11. నిట యిచ్చినట్టె శ్రీ శ్రీం
12. జేయును

KANDUKUR (48). (A.D. 1650–51.)

[Máchavaram. Telugu. From a stone near the same temple.]

TRANSLATION.

May the illustrious Ánjanéya help us! Hail! On Friday, the 3rd of the bright half of Márgaṣira of the year Vikriti, corresponding to the year 1573 of the illustrious, victorious, and prosperous Ṣáliváhana Ṣaka era, this edict was executed and granted by us, Challá Timmireḍḍi, and Mummaḍi Timmireḍḍi and others whose names are engraved on the inscribed stone containing our family pedigree near (the temple of) Hanumán, which is close to the temple built on Nélatippa situated in these rocky fields, and by the *Dharmakartás* (trustees) who constructed the tanks. Its terms are: on all kinds of produce raised from the wet fields irrigated by the tanks of these four villages, *i.e.*, Kandukúr, Konḍamuḍusupáḷem, Mópáḍu, and Máchavaram, which were given to us as a *mokhása* (?) by the orders of Hajarat Sultán Abdulla Pádusháhim of Hyderabad Sarkár and which are situated in Kandukúru Pharagana which is in the jurisdiction of Antóji Pantulu, Havaldár and agent of Rája Ṣrí

Raghóji [1] Numbâji Nárójí Rághóji the Phamujudár (commander-in-chief), grain at one *kuncha* on every *puṭṭi* should be given to the Voddars Taníru Góvindu, Taníru Nárâyuḍu, Taníru Venkaṭaya, Taníru Narasaya, Taníru Pápaya, and Taníru Venkaṭarámuḍu, who originally put up the bunds of these tanks, and have been maintaining them, who are residents of Mópáḍu and Máchavaram, and who are Peddabóyas (?). These six persons should get the tank *kunchas* as written above, and in addition land on which six *túms* of seed can be sown, in the Chintaléṭi Báḍava field situated in the wet fields of Mópáḍu, and land on which six *túms* of seed can be sown, in the *váka* field (field where there is percolation of water) situated to the south-east of Nélatippa in the fields of Máchavaram; in all land on which twelve *túms* of seed can be sown as an entire *inám*. They have also the privilege of grazing their cattle and sheep without paying *pullari* (grazing fees). Moreover the other Voḍḍars of these four villages who do *amji* work (customary labour) to the tanks along with these are exempted from *pullari*. Further only these persons should perform the duties of *nírukaṭṭu* (distributor of water) for all the wet fields under these tanks. For this service they are given land on which four *túms* of seed can be sown in the Báḍava (moist land) situated to the west of Nágula well in the fields of Mápáḍu and land on which four *túms* of seed can be sown in the *váka* under the bund to the south of the sluice in the fields of Máchavaram; in all, land on which eight *túms* of seed can be sown as *nírukaṭṭu mànyam* (grant for looking after the distribution of water). Under the orders

---

[1] Rámoji in No. 47.

of the Mahárája Ṣrí it is settled that the *méra*, *mánya*, and *pullari*, should be given as a *surva inám*. For this purpose to obviate the necessity of issuing *sannads* or *dumbalas* not only has this stone edict been engraved, but we have also executed and granted them a copper-plate deed of gift. Therefore in order that they, their sons, grandsons and progeny, may enjoy in this manner as long as the sun and moon exist, we, the aforesaid rulers of the present day, and their officers have jointly given this agreement. Therefore future rulers and their officers, the villagers, and all other people should cherish and maintain this charity. In the rainy season after the *amji-workers* dig the caliugulas and sluices, these (Voḍḍars) should do earth-work and also *amji* work along with the *amji-workers*. When the tank is full, these (Voḍḍars) should carefully observe the places which are unsafe and do the needful repairs. They should look after the tanks along with the villagers, *mudáms*, *veṭṭis*, *Mádigaś* and others. According to the customary supply of water of the villages water should be distributed by them without waste to the wet lands. We have issued orders in these terms. Therefore in this manner it should be carried out for the religious merit of Házarat Sultán Abdul Pádusháhigáru. Whoever obstruct this charity or misappropriate the proceeds, whether they be the rulers, or their officers or other people, or the villagers, or any one else, if the obstructors are Muhammadans they will incur the sin of killing a pig at Mecca; if they are Brahmans or Sudras they will incur the sin of killing cows and Brahmans on the banks of the Ganges. Those who obstruct this (charity), to whatever caste they may belong, will have many births in the hell called *kumbhipáka* and finally will be born in the sixth caste (as animals). This stone inscription has been engraved in the presence of the five elements and the thirty-three crores of gods.

First side.

1. శ్రీ ఆంజనేయా సహాయం। స్వస్తి
2. శ్రీ జయాభ్యుదయ శాలివాహన శక వ
3. ర్షంబులు ౧౫౭౩ అగునేటి వికృతినామ
4. సంవత్సరమార్గశిరశుద్ధ 3 శుక్రవారం గోజుం ఋా
5. దిప్పిపాల్యా యిక్కడ నేలదిప్పగుడిదాపున హనుమంతు

ని సమీపాన వుం

6. డ్డె మా వంశావళీ శాసనపు బండ్లమీద చెక్కించ్చిన పేర్ల
7. గల చల్లా తిమ్మిరెడ్డి ముమ్మడి తిమ్మిరెడ్డి వగైరాలము

. న్ను చెర్వులు వేయించినధర్మకర్తలమున్ను అయిబ్ర

మేము

9. వ్రాయించ్చిన ధర్మశాసన క్రమమెట్లంటన్నను రానరిశీ

రఘో

10. జి నుంబాజీ నారోజా రాఘోజా ఫముజుదారు పంతు
11. లంగారి కార్యకర్తలైన అంత్రోజి పంతుల హ
12. వాలదారుగారు ఫరగణాకందుకూరు
13. సర్కారు హయిదరాబాదు హజిర్యతు సు
14. ల్తాన్అబ్దుల్లా పాదుషాహింగారు మొక
15. ర్రరుచేసి మాకు పరుమానా దయచేయించివున్న
16. కంద్దుకూరు కొండ్లముద్సుపాలెం మోపాదు మా
17. చవరం యీనాల్లు గ్రామాదుల చెర్వులక్రింద పారు
18. దలమాంగిలి పాలంలో పండించినపంట సకలాయం
19. ఖ ౧ కి ౦౦। తీర్ను యీ చెర్వులకు గడ్లలు యెత్తించిన

వాండ్లుం

20. న్ను పనిముఖించేయించ్చినవాండ్లున్ను మోపా

డు మాచవరం కాపరస్తులున్నా పెద్దబోయ లుగా యేర్పడివుంన్న వొడెలు। తన్నీరు గోవిం దు। అ నారాయుడు। అ వెంకటయ। అ సర్సయ। అ పావయ। అ వెంకటామడు అన యీ ఆగుర రింన్ని వయ్ని వ్రాసినప్రకారం చెర్వుకుంచాలున్న యి దిగాక మోపాటి మాగాణి పొలంలో చింతలేటి బాడ్వాపట్టుతుర్రం ఖం। ౧ విత్తనాల పట్టున్నా మాచ వరం మాగాణి పొలంలో నేలతిప్ప దక్షిణం తూర్పున నుండ్డెవాక లోంతట్టు ఖం। ౧ విత్తనాలపట్టున్నా జ్మలా తీసి ఖం ౪ ౨ విత్తనాల పట్టు పొలం మాన్యంగా నున్నా వీండ్లకు వుండె పశ్వులు సన్నజీవాలు న్నాపుల్లరి లేకుండానున్నా యిదేగాక వీండ్లతోపాటు చెర్వుల అంజీపనిచేశే యీ నాల్గుగ్రామాదలలో వుండ్డె వొడ్డెలు పుల్లరిమాత్రం లేకుండ్డానున్నా మరి న్నా యీ చెర్వులకింది మాగాణిపొలం యావత్తు కుంన్నా వీండ్లే నీరుకట్టుపనిన్ని చూచేలాగ్నునున్నా యి ంద్దుకుగా మోపాటిపొలంలో నాగుల భావిపడ్మటి బాడవపట్టుమ్నుం ౦౮ విత్తనాలపట్టున్నా మాచవరం పొలంలో పెద్దతూము దక్షణాం కట్టకింది వాక పట్టు ౦౮ విత్తనాలపట్టున్న జ్మలా ఖం। ౩ విత్త నాలపట్టు నీరుపట్టు మాన్యంగానున్నా నిరుర్వ చేషియిచ్చేలాగ్నునున్నా మహారాజే శ్రీగారికట్టడ ప్రకారం మేరామాన్యములు పుల్లరింన్ని సర్వం యింనాముగా స్నదు దుంబాలాలు కూడా పనిలేకుం డ్డా యిచ్చేలాగున నిర్నయించ్చి యీ శిలాశాసనం చెక్కించడం మాత్రమేకాకుండ్డా వీండ్లకు మేము తాంబ్రంశాసనం దానపత్రంగ్గా వ్రాసియిస్తి మి గనుక యీప్రకారం వీండ్ల పుత్రపౌత్రపా రంపర్యా ఆ చంద్రార్కస్థాయిగా అనుభ

50. ఖించేలాగున్ను మేమున్ను యిప్పుడు వుండ్డే సదరు
51. ప్రభువులున్ను వారి వ్యాపారస్తులున్ను సహా
52. యిస్తిమి గనుక యిఖమీద వొచ్చే ప్రభువులు
53. న్ను వారితరపు వ్యాపారస్తులున్ను గ్రామ

Second side.

54. సులున్ను యింకాను యిత
55. రమయిన లోకులు సమేతు
56. న్ను యీ ధర్మంయెంకు అభి
57. మానం వుంచి నడిపించవలెను।
58. యీ చెర్వుల అల్లులకిన్ను తూము
59. లకున్ను వర్షాకాలంలో అంజీలు అ
60. కు కోసిన తర్వాత మంన్ను పోశేలా
61. గూను అంజీలతో పాటు అంజీవని చే
62. శేలాగూను నిండ్లు చెర్వులప్పుడు అపా
63. యం వొచ్చే స్తలాలుకిం కనిపెట్టి పనిము
64. ఖంచేయిస్తూన్ను గ్రామస్తులు ముదాం
65. వెట్టి మాదిగలు వగైరాలతోకూడా చే
66. ర్వులు కాపాడేలాగున్ను గ్రామాసుల
67. మామూలు వకబడిప్రకారం దరోబ
63. స్తు మాగాణికి విస్తరించి వజ్జు పోనివ్వ
69. కుండా కిల్లు కట్టించేలాగుననున్ను క
70. ట్టెళ్లు చేస్తిమి గనుక యీ ప్రకారం మాజ
71. రతు సుల్తాను అబ్దుల్లా పాదుంపాహిం
72. గారికి పుణ్యముగా నడిపించవలెను । యీ
73. ధర్మాని యెవ్వరు విఘాతంచేసినా యీ
74. ద్రవ్యం యెవరు అపహరించ్చినా వారు ప్ర
75. భువులుగాని వారి యిలాకా వ్యాపారస్తు
76. లుగాని యింకా యితరులయిన్ను లోకులు

77. గాని గ్రామస్తులుగాని యెవ్వరైనా ఆటంకర్యం
78. చేస్తూన్నారో వారు తురకలైతే మక్కా
79. లో పందినిచంపిన పాపాన్ని పొందుదురు బ్రాహ్మ
80. ణులున్నూ శూద్రులున్నూ అయితే గంగాతీరాన్న
81. గోబ్రాంహ్మణుల జంప్పిన పాపానం బోదురు
82. దీనిరి యేకులంవారు విఘ్నము చేస్తారో వారు అ
83. నేక జంన్మాలు కుంభీపాకమనెడు నరకాన్న పొంద్ది ష
84. ష్టమ కులమందు జన్మింతురు యిటు పంచ్చ
85. మహాభూతాలు సాక్షిగాను ముప్పయిమూ
86. డుకోట్ల దేవతుల సాక్షిగాను వ్రాయిం
87. చ్చిన శిలాశాసనము.

KANDUKUR (19).

[Málakonḍa Hill. Telugu. From pillar of Narasimha-svámi temple.]

TRANSLATION.

On the 12th of the bright fortnight of Kártika in the year Plava, they have constructed a *manḍapa* to Narasimha of Ṣrí Málakonḍa. The perpetual devotion of Jayavarapu Nimmaya.

NOTE.—Mr. Boswell in the District Manual talks of a grant appertaining to the Málakonḍa temple. It is identical with No. (79) of Singaráyakonḍa and Mr. Boswell probably incorrectly ascribed it to the Málakonḍa temple.

1. ప్లవ సంవత్సర కా
2. ర్తిక శుద్ధ ౧౨
3. శ్రీయుమాల కొం
4. డ్డ నరశింహ్మలకు
5. మండపము శేశిరి
6. జయవరపు నిమ్మ
7. య నిత్యశావా.

KANDUKUR (50). (A.D. 1268–69.)

[Pákála. Telugu. On a stone in front of the Ṣiva temple.]

TRANSLATION.

Hail! On the day of Vishumat Sankránti, on the 10th day of the bright half of Chaitra of the year Vibhava, corresponding to the illustrious Ṣaka year 1190, (Ru) dra Pregaḍa, the prime minister (Maháپradháni) of the illustrious (Rudradéva?) gave 600 *kunṭas* of wet land under the pond of Birrala Rémaḍuvu, to wit, wet land near Sévákaṭṭam, paddy fields irrigated by the water of Biṭraguṇṭa tank, and 12,500 *kunṭas* of land on the north and east of Brammireḍḍipalli, as an endowment to Rámalingadéva for providing all enjoyments, for the religious merit of Rudradéva and his own parents, to last as long as the sun and moon last.

[One imprecatory verse.]

Sun. Moon.

1. స్వస్తి శ్రీ శ
2. క వరుషంబు
3. లు ౧౧౯౦ అగు నే
4. ంటి విభవ సంవ
5. త్సర చైత్ర శు ౧౦
6. విషుమత్ సంక్రా
7. ంతినాండు శ్రీ [రుద్ర
8. దేవ-] మహా॰ ప్రధాని
9. [రు]ద్ర ప్రెగడ రు
10. రుద్రదేవరకు దమ
11. దల్లి తండ్రులకు
12. పుణ్యముగాను

13. శ్రీరామలింగ
14. దేవరకు అంగ
15. రంగ భోగానకు ధమ్మ్రా
16. ంగ్గాను ఇచ్చిన వరి
17. సేను సేవాకట్టం
18. చెల్లె పొలము బి
19. జ్రాల తెమడువు
20. నా నీరుపాము
21. ను ౬౦౦ బిట్ర
22. గుంట చెఱువ్నీ
23. ఱిం బండె వరిచె
24. ను బ్రహ్మిరెడ్డి ప
25. ల్లి ఉత్తరానాం దూ
26. ప్పూణానాను గుం
27. ౧౨౫౦౦ ఆచం
28. ద్రార్కము
29. స్వదత్తం పర
30. దత్తాం వా యా
31. హారేతి వసు
32. ంధరా షష్టి
33. వ్వరుషసహస్రా
34. ణి విష్టాయాం జా
35. యతే క్రిమి.

KANDUKUR (51).

[Pákála. Telugu. On the bell in Ṣiva temple.]

TRANSLATION.

On the 7th of the bright fortnight of Pushya in the year named Khara, Battula Śarabhá Reḍḍi and Chinna Lingá Reḍḍi caused this bell to be made for Rámalinga svámi of Pákala for the merit of Himaḍaka Péranṭála.

ఖరనామసంవ్వాత్సర పుష్యశుద్ధ ౭ లు
పాక్ల రామలింగస్వామికి హిమడక పె
రంటాలకి వి శేషంగాను బత్తుల శ
రభారెడ్డి చిన్నలింగ్గారెడ్డి చేయించిన
ఘంట.

KANDUKUR (52). (A.D. 1302–03.)

[Pákála. Telugu. On a stone pillar in the Śiva temple.]

TRANSLATION.

Hail! On Thursday, the 1st of the bright fortnight of Márgaṣira in the year named Ṣubhakrit, corresponding to 1224 of the illustrious Ṣaka era, we have given for the performance of occasional festivals (?) to Ṣríman Mahá Rámanáthadéva of Pákála *vrittis* (shares of land) for Brahmans near Vailumulaguṇṭa, 960 *kunṭas* of dry land at Biṭraguṇṭa which were purchased and given, and wet land under the Amudamaḍuvu to last as long as the sun and moon endure.

1. స్వస్తిశ్రీ శకవరుషంబులు
2. ౧౨౨౪ వగునెంటి శుభకృ

3. ఖనామసంవత్సర మార్గశిర
4. శు ౧ గు పాకల శ్రీమ
5. న్మహా రామనాథదేవర
6. కును అవసరధ్యాయము
7. దునకు వైలుములగుం
8. ట్ట మరు
9. ట్టి బ్రాహ్మ
10. ణ వ్రిత్తు
11. లు బిట్ర
12. గుంటను
13. టికి ఇచ్చి
14. న వెలిచేను గు
15. ర్టెం అంముద మడు
16. వుక్రింద నీరునెలం నిం
17. ని ఆచంద్రార్కముగాను
18. నిస్తిమి.

KANDUKUR (53). (A.D. 1273–74.)

[Pákála. Telugu. On a stone pillar in the Ṣiva temple.]

TRANSLATION.

Hail! On . . . day of Uttaráyana Sankránti in the year Ṣrímukha, corresponding to 1195 of the illustrious Ṣaka era, (Sítaya) the younger brother of Periya Reḍḍi Náyani, the karnam of this village, presented . . . . for the perpetual lamp to Ṣrí Rámálingasvámi of Pákala, for the *archakas* rice at the rate of . . . for the religious merit of his parents and of himself and of

Pedda Seṭṭi Náyaḍu . . . the share Tamminenḍu (?) should keep up the perpetual lamp as long as the sun and moon endure.

1. స్వస్తి శ్రీ శకవరుషంబులు
2. ౧౧౯౪ అగు నేంటి శ్రీము
3. ఖ సంవత్సరమునందు
4. . . ఉత్తరాయణస
5. ంక్రాంతినాండు యీాయూ .
6. రి కరణము పెరియరె
7. ట్టి నాయని తమ్ముండు
8. (శీతయ) తమతల్లి దండ్రు
9. లకు తమకున్న పెద్ద
10. సెట్టి నా్న యనికిపుణ్య
11. ంగాను పాకల శ్రీరామలి
12. ంగదేవరకు అఖండదీ
13. పానకిచ్చిరి అర్చకులకు
14. పడిబియ్యంము లెఖ
15. . . . . .
16. * * * *
17. * * * *
18. * * * *
19. ప్రిత్తి తంమి నెండు
20. ను అఖండ దీప
21. ము ఆచంద్రకము నడు
22. పంగలవారు.

Kandukur (54). (A.D. 1320-21.)

[Pákála. Telugu. On a stone pillar in the Śiva temple.]

Translation.

Hail! On Sunday, the 6th of the bright fortnight of Chaitra of the year Raudri, corresponding to the year 1242 of the illustrious Ṣaka era, while Ṣríman Mahámaṇḍaléṣvara Kákatíya Pratápa Rudradéva Mahárája was ruling the kingdom of the earth in agreeable interchange of communications (with his feudatories ?), Hail! The Kómaṭis (Nagaramlónivâru) of Nellore who were ruling the illustrious village of Pákala gave a field on which 5 *túms* of seed can be sown . . . . The perpetual lamp should be kept up as long as the sun and moon endure. The temple servants should see that this (charity) is maintained.

1. స్వస్తి శ్రీమన్మహా మ
2. ండలేశ్వర కాకతియ్య
3. ప్రతాపరుద్ర దేవ మ
4. హారాజులు శుఖ
5. సంగతా వినోదం
6. బునం పృథి
7. వీ రాజ్య
8. ంబు చే
9. యు
10. చుం
11. డంగా
12. శఖవరుష
13. ంబులు ౧౨౪౨

14. గువె ంటిరౌద్రి సం
15. వత్సర చైత్ర శు
16. ద్ధ ౬ ఆ। స్వస్తి శ్రీ
17. పాకల [గ్రామం యేలుచు
18. ఉండిన్ని ?] నెల్లూరి
19. నగరములోని వా
20. రియుందు
21. పదుము
22. విత్తుల
23. సెను.
24. . .
25. . అఖం
26. డ దీపంబు సూర్యచ
27. ంద్రులు గలిగిన కాలము
28. చెల్లునది ఇందుకు స్తానా
29. పతులు చెల్లించగలవారు.

KANDUKUR (55). (A.D. 1320–21.)

[Pákála. Telugu. On a stone pillar in the Ṣiva temple.]

TRANSLATION.

Hail! On Sunday, the 6th of the bright fortnight of Chaiṭra of the year Raudri, corresponding to the illustrious Ṣaka year 1242, while Ṣríman Mahámaṇḍaléṣvara Kákatîya Pratápa Rudradéva Mahárája was ruling the kingdom of the earth, holding pleasant communications (with his feudatories ?)—Hail! A wet field on which five *túms* of seed can be sown (is given) to Ṣrí Rámayadéva of Pákala by the Kómaṭis (?) of Nellore. The perpetual lamp given by Nitya Dipila (?) the son of Pérla

Seṭṭi, should be kept up as long as the sun and moon endure. The temple servants of this temple should see that this lamp is kept up.

1. స్వస్తి శ్రీమన్మహా
2. మండలేశ్వర కాక
3. తియ్య ప్రతాప
4. రుద్రదేవ మహా
5. రాజులు సుఖసంక
6. థా వినో
7. దంబు .
8. నం ప్రి
9. థివి రా
10. జ్యంబు
11. చేయు
12. చుండంగా శకవరుష
13. ంబులు ౧౨౮౨ గు నెం
14. టి రౌద్రిసంవత్సర చైత్ర
15. శు ౭ ఆ। స్వస్తి శ్రీపాక
16. ల రామయ్యదేవునికి . .
17. నెల్లూరి నగరము వా [రివా ?]
18. రి యందు పదు [ము విత్తుల మ ?]
19. డియ పెర్ల సెట్టికొడుకు నిత్యది
20. పిళ పెట్టిన అఖండదీపంబు
21. సూర్యచంద్రులు గలంత
22. కాలమున్ను చెల్లంగలది
23. ఇ దీపము ఇకుడిస్తానా
24. ప్రతులు
25. చెల్లింప
26. గలవారు.

KANDUKUR (56).

[Pákála. Tamil. From Rámalingaswámi temple.]

TRANSLATION.

We four persons of this place, *viz.*, Púśári, Kóyiméṇáke, Rámaṇ and Vallen, received one Gaṇḍagópálamáḍai [1] for one evening lamp presented to the god Ilaṇgaśenukuḷiya. We bind ourselves to maintain (this charity) as long as the moon and sun last.

If any one obstructs this charity he will incur the sin of killing a tawny cow on the banks of the Ganges.

[1] . . . . -த்-
[2] துக்கு கொண்டு
[3] விட்ட இலங்கசெனுகு-
[4] [சழிய] நாயனார்க்கு வை-
[5] த்த சந்திவிளக்கு ஒன்று-
[6] க்குக்குடுத்த கண்-
[7] [ட]கொபாலந் மாடை-
[8] ட ஒன்றும் கைக்கொண்-
[9] டொம் இத்நாகத்தில்
[10] பூசாரி கொயிமெநா-
[11] கெ இராமநும் வல்லெ-
[12] னு இந்நால்வரும் ச-
[13] ந்திராதித்தவரை செ-
[14] லுத்தக்கடவோ
[15] ம்
[16] இத்
[17] தந்ம
[18] ம் இல-
[19] ங்கக-

[1] Some sort of coin evidently; the máḍai of king Gaṇḍagópála.

[20] ம் பண்-
[21] ணினி-
[22] வன்த்-
[23] ஈருண்-
[24] டாகில்
[25] கங்கை-
[26] ககரை-
[27] யில் கு-
[28] ராற்பசு
[29] வை கெ-
[30] ரன்றுநப-

KANDUKUR (57). (A.D. 1272–73 ?)

[Pákála. Tamil. From Rámalingaswámi temple.]

TRANSLATION.

In the Ṣaka year 1194, in the month of Ávaṇi, on the day of Urosaṇi aṭṭaputagi (?) . . . . Paṭṭaṇangiḻán, (*alias*) Kuḻamban (*alias*) Aṛamana of Uttaramélúr, presented a sacred flower garden to . . . . deity in the town of . . . . Chalamattigaṇḍa . . . . For its maintenance he presented 500 *kuḻi* of land to the deity . . . .

[1] சகரையாண்டு ஆா-
[2] கூடுசவது ஆவணிமாச[த்தி]-
[3] ல் உரொசணியு அட்டபுதகி நாள்
[4] . . . : . ரநசலமத்திகண்ட
[5] . . . டணத்தில் நாயகா-
[6] . . . நா . தெவர்கு உத்-
[7] [த]ரமெரூரில் பட்டணங்-
[8] கிழாக்குழம்பன் அறமகெ-

[9] ந் இந்நாயனாற்கு கொண்டு-
[10] விட்ட திருநந்தாவநமு-
[11] [ம்] இதுக்கு காணியாக கொ-
[12] ண்டுவிட்ட உடையாற்கு
[13] . ண்டாட்டில் புக்குபுலி
[14] . . . குழி நய நாயநார்
[15] . . . திருப்புரத்த

KANDUKUR (58). (A.D. 1277–78.)

[Pákála. Tamil. From the image of Vignéṣvara.]

TRANSLATION.

In the expired Ṣaka year one thousand one hundred and ninety-nine, on the date corresponding to Monday, the fifth day of the first (bright) half of the month of Kaṛkaṭaka (kárttika) . . . . which I Korran Paṇḍári received for the god[1] at Pákkal.

[1] [சகர]யாண்டு [ஆ]-
[2] [யிர]த்தொருநூ[ற்]-
[3] [று]த்தொண்ணூ-
[4] ற்று ஒன்பது [செ]
[5] ல்லாநின்ற [கற்]-
[6] கடகநாயற்று-
[7] ப்பூர்வபக்ஷத்து
[8] பஞ்சமியும் திங்-
[9] கட்கி ழமையும்
[10] பெற்ற நாள் பா-
[11] க்கவில் இ[ந]ா[ய]
[12] [னு]தேவற்[க்]கு ந-
[13] ாங் கொற்றன் [ப]-
[14] [ண்டாரி] கொண்ட

---

[1] Name not clear.

KANDUKUR (59).

[Peddakanḍlaguṇṭa. Telugu. To east of village.]

TRANSLATION.

On the 15th day of the bright fortnight of Kártika of the year (Promódúta). . . . for the religious merit of his father and mother with the goddess Earth and the god of rain as witnesses . . . . will maintain. .

1. ధరణీ దేవిని వా
2. నదేవరసాక్షిగాను
3. (ప్రమాదూత)
4. సంవత్సర కార్తిక
5. శుద్ధ ౧౫ . . . . .
6. . . . ంగారు . .
7. . . గళా . తల్లికిన్ని .
8. తండ్రికిన్ని పు
9. ణ్యము . . . .
10. . . . అ . య . . . .
11. . . నడపినవారు . .
12. . . . .

KANDUKUR (60). (A.D. 1258-59 ?)

[Penṭrála. Telugu. From one side of a fallen stone near the river.]

TRANSLATION.

On Thursday the 15th of the bright fortnight of Áshádha of the year Kálayukti, corresponding to the year 1179 of the illustrious and auspicious Ṣaka era Ṣríman Mahámaṇḍaléṣvara Bhujabala Víra Manma Siddaya

Déva Mahárájulu gave an Agrahára for enjoyment to the Puróhit (priest) of the deity Márgamu Pahindimukkala Márga Náráyaṇa Perumál, through the agency of the son of Márgamu Pahinḍimukkala Víra Tiruvengaḷa the illustrious establisher of the path of the Védas, to last as long as the sun and moon endure . . . . The Nambi Tiruvengaḍaya and Padmanábha . . . . for enjoyment . . . . 1,000 *kunṭas*, 1,000 *kunṭas* for the marriage festival of the deity . . . .

NOTE.—The cyclic and Ṣaka dates differ by a year. This guru Márganur Pahinḍimukkala Víra Tiruvengala does not seem to be mentioned outside this group of Kandukúr inscriptions.

1. శ్రీ శుభ శకవరుషంబులు
2. ౧౧౭౯ అగునేటికాళ
3. యుక్తి సంవత్సర ఆషాఢ
4. శుద్ధ ౧౫ గురువారాన శ్రీ
5. మన్మహా మండలేశ్వర భు
6. జబళ వీరమన్మ సిద్ధయదే
7. వ మహారాజులు శ్రీమతువే
8. ద మార్గ ప్రతిష్టాచార్యు
9. లైన మార్గము పహిండిము
10. క్కల వీరతిరువెంగళ కొమా
11. రుని పురుషాకారన . . క
12. ఖండు . . . . .
13. లునారా . . మార్గము పహిం
14. డి ముక్కల మార్గనారాయ
15. ణప్పెరుమాళ్ల పురోహితు
16. లకు అగ్రహారము ఆ చంద్రా
17. ర్కముగ నిస్తిమి . . . .
18. . తిరువెంకడయ నంబిపద

19. మసాభ . . . .
20. భోగము . . . .
21. . .
22. . . వ
23. మ .
24. తిరు
25. . .
26. తి
27. కు ౧౦౦౦
28. పికి . . . ౧౦౦౦
29. . పి
30. . . ౪౧౦ . . . . రికితిరు
31. కళ్యాముకు . . . . .
32. లనుకు
33. నిప . . . . వతిమ
34. రాయ . . . . . .
35. కలకాండ . . . .
36. త్రకునుకు . . .
37. . కు . . . . .
38. . కూనుకు
39. . కొరకు
40. కొవసి
41. రివసి
42. కటర . తి . హా . కికు .
43. కు . . . . రికి . . బ్రవి
44. కువిరి
45. రికి
46. . .
47. . .

Kandukur (61). (A.D. 1259–60 ?)

[Penṭrála. Telugu. From another side of the same stone.]

Translation.

On Thursday, the 10th of the bright fortnight of Vaiṣákha of the year Siddhárthi, corresponding to the year 1180 of the illustrious and auspicious Ṣaka era, Ṣríman Mahámaṇḍaléṣvara Alláḍu Suddha Déva Mahá Ráju, grandson of Podakanúrisiddi Ráju, who is a descendant of the race of Mukkanṭikáḍuveṭṭu, gave to last as long as the sun and moon endure for providing sacred food and all kinds of enjoyment to the illustrious Pahinḍi Mukkala Márga Nárayaṇa Perumál through the agency of the son of the illustrious Márgamu Pahinḍimukkala Víra Tiruvengaḷa, the establisher of the path of the Védas, for the prosperity of the kingdom of Ṣríman Mahámaṇḍaléṣvara Bhujabala Víra Manma Siddaya Déva Chóḍa Mahárájulu.

Note.—The cyclic year corresponds with S.S. 1182 current.

1. శ్రీ శుభ శకవరుషంబులు
2. ౧౧౮౦ అగు నేంటి సి
3. ద్ధార్థి సంవత్సర వైశా
4. ఖ శుద్ధ ౧౦ గురువారాన శ్రీ
5. మన్మహా మండలేశ్వర
6. ముక్కంటికాడు వెట్టువంశావ
7. తారుడైన పొ (ద) కనూరి సిద్ధిరాం
8. జమనుమండు అల్లాడు శుథదే
9. వ మహారాజు శ్రీమన్మహా మండ్డ
10. లేశ్వర భుజబళ వీరమన్మసిద్ధ
11. యదేవచోడ మహారాజులకు
12. రాజ్యాభివ్రిద్ధిగాను శ్రీమతు వేదమా

13. ర్గ ప్రతిష్టాచార్య్యులైన మార్గము
14. పహిండి ముక్కుల వీర తిరువెం
15. గళ కొమారుని పురుష కారానకుక్కే
16. ంధామతుల్లైన పహిండిముక్కుల
17. మార్గనారాయణ పెరుమాళ్ల
18. అమృదపడి చాతదర్మకున్ను
19. అంగరంగ బోగాలకును ఆచ
20. ంద్రార్క ముగాని స్తిమి

Kandukur (62). (A.D. 1260–61 ?)

[Penṭrála. Telugu. From the same side of the same stone.]

Translation.

On Thursday, the 5th of the bright fortnight of Chaitra of the year Raudri, corresponding to the year 1181 of the illustrious and auspicious Ṣaka era, Madusúdhana Déva Mahárája, the grandson of the Ṣríman Mahámanḍaléṣvara Andulúri Vijayaditta Déchini who is descended from the race of Mukkanṭi Káḍuveṭṭu, granted Veligandla Márga Náráyaṇapuram as *Agrahára* to the puróhit (priest) of Márga Náráyaṇa Perumál through the agency of the son of Márgamu Pahinḍimukkala Víra Tiruvengaḷa the illustrious establisher of the path of the Védas, for the prosperity of the kingdom of Ṣríman Mahámanḍaléṣvara Immaḍi Ganḍa Gópáḷa Vijayáditta Déva Mahárájulu.

Note.—Raudra is S.S. 1183 current.

1. శ్రీ శుభ వరుషంబులు
2. ౧౧౮౧ అగు నేంటి రవు

3. ద్రి. సంవత్సర చైత్ర శుద్ధ ౫
4. గురువారాన శ్రీ మన్మహా మండ్లే
5. శ్వరముక్కంటి కాడువెట్టివంశావతా
6. రులైన అందులూరి విజయదిత్త దే
7. చిని మనుమండు మదనసూదనదే
8. వమహారాజు శ్రీ మన్మమహామ
9. ండలేశ్వర ఇమ్మడి గండకోపా
10. ళ విజయాదిత్త దేవమహారా
11. జులకు రాజ్యాభివ్రిద్ధిగాను
12. శ్రీమతు వేదమార్గ ప్రతిష్టా
13. చార్యులైన మార్గము వహి
14. ండిముక్కల వీరతిరువెంకళ కు
15. మారుని పురుషాకారాన మా
16. ర్గనారాయణ పెరుమాండ్ల
17. పురోహితులకు వెలిగండ్ల
18. యిన మార్గనారాయణ పుర
19. ము అగ్రహారము ఆ చంద్రార్కము
20. గా నిస్తిమి

KANDUKUR (63). (A.D. 2161–62.)

[Penṭrála. Telugu. From another side of the same stone.]

TRANSLATION.

On Thursday, the . . . . of the bright fortnight of Phálguṇa of the year Durmukhi, corresponding to the year 1183 of the illustrious and auspicious Ṣaka era, Siddama Dévulu Vijaya Dévaṇḍu, son of Ṣríman Mahámaṇḍa-léṣvara Ka . . ráya Bhíma Déva Mahárájn, who is a descendant of the race of Mukkanṭi Káḍuveṭṭu, granted the villages Marripalli and Álápálapalli for celebrating new moon festivals, for sacred food and sandalwood at Vishuvena Sankramáṇa to Ṣrí Márga Náráyana Perumáḷ through the agency of the son of Ṣrímad Márgama Pahiṇḍi Mukkala Víra Tiruvengaḷa, the illustrious establisher of the path of the Védas, for the prosperity of the kingdom of Ṣríman Mahámaṇḍaléṣvara Bhujabaḷa Víra Manma Siddaya Déva Chóḍa Mahárájulu, to last as long as the sun and moon endure. The boundaries of these lands are, on the east a cart track, on the south-east Indum Channel and Indula Channel Maḍuka (Maḍugu ?), on the south the Mannéru, on the south-west Marrula Ganga, on the west Tiruvaḷikáḍu, on the north-west Rri (?) Donakoṇḍa, on the north Kanyamérru and, on the north-east Déva Dona Gaṭṭu. The fields within these boundaries belong to the deities and Brahmans. The length of the pole with which these fields are measured is 13 *báras*. Those who violate this will be considered to have killed a tawny cow on the Ganges. They will incur the penalty attached to the five cardinal sins.

[One imprecatory verse.]

1. శ్రీశుభ శకవరుషంబులు
2. ౧౧౮౩ అగు నేటి దుర్మ్ముఖ
3. సంవత్సర ఫాల్గుణ శుద్ధ
4. గురువారాన శ్రీ మన్మహా
5. మండలేశ్వర ముకర్ంటి(కాడువె)
6. ట్టు వంశావతారులైన శ
7. రాయభీమదేవ మహారా
8. జా కొడుకు సిద్ధమదేవుల విజ
9. దేవండు శ్రీ మన్మహామ:డలే
10. శ్వర భుజబళవీరమన్మసి

11. దయదేవ చోడమహారా
12. రాజులకు రాజ్యాభివ్రిద్ధిగాను
13. శ్రీమతు వేదమార్గ ప్రతిష్టా
14. చాయ్యులైన మార్గముస
15. హిండిముకుల వీరతిరు
16. వేంగళకొమారుని పురు
17. షాకారాన శ్రీమార్గనా
18. రాయణ పెరుమాడ్ల అమా
19. వాశ ఉత్సములాకును
20. విషువేణ సంక్రమాణము
21. లాకును అముదు పడిసా
22. తుపళకూను మఱివల్లిని
23. అలాపాల పల్లిని అచ
24. ంద్రాకర్ణముగా నిస్తిమి
25. ఇట్టి క్షేత్రాను సిమంబంఢ్డి
26. ద్రోవతూప్పనను ఇందుం
27. కాలువదీనికి ఇందుల
28. కలువమడుకను ఆగ్నేయా
29. న దక్షిణానను మన్నైఋనై
30. రితిని మఱుల గంగపడు
31. మటను తిరూవళికడువా
32. యావ్యామునను ఱిదొనకొ
33. ండ్డ ఉత్తరానను కనిఋమే
34. ఱు। ఇశాన్యమునను। దే
35. వదొనగట్టు ఇంతవ
36. ట్టను దేవబ్రాంమ్మణక్షే
37. త్ర సీమ ఇక్షేత్రముకొ
38. లచెకొలగోల। పను
39. మూడు బారలకొల। దీ

40. నిర్రిప్పినవారుగంగ క
41. ఱంతను కవిలపొడిచి
42. నారు । పంచ్ఛమహాపాత
43. కులగలిపోఇనారు ॥
44. స్వదత్తము పరదత్తమ్మువా
45. ఓ హరేతివాసుంద్ధరా । ష
46. ష్టిర్వరుష సహస్రాణి
47. విష్టయాం జాయతే క్రిమి ।

KANDUKUR (64). (A.D. 1267–68)

[Pentrála. Telugu. From the fourth side of the same stone. Three separate inscriptions.]

TRANSLATION.

On Thursday, the 10th of the bright fortnight of Áshádha of the year Prabhava, corresponding to the year 1189 of the illustrious and auspicious Ṣaka era, Ṣríman Mahámaṇḍaléṣvara Bijji Ráju Siddaya Déva Chóḍa Mahárájulu gave Davala Kunṭalu (land for religious purposes ?) for offering sandal-wood to Márganáráyaṇa Perumáḷ through the agency of the son of Ṣrímad Márgama Pahiṇḍi Mukkala Víra Tiruvengaḷa, the illustrious establisher of the path of the Védas, to last as long as the sun and moon endure.

1. శ్రీ శుభశకవరుషంబులు
2. ౧౧౮౯ అగు నేటి ప్రభసం
3. వత్సర ఆషాఢ శుద్ధ ౧౦ గురు
4. వారాన శ్రీమన్మహామండ
5. లేశ్వర బిజ్జిరాజు సిద్దయ

6. దేవచోడ మహారాజులు శ్రీ
7. మతు వేదమార్గ ప్రతిష్ఠా
8. చార్యులైన మార్గముప
9. హిండిముక్కల వీర తిరు
10. వెంగళ కొమారుని పురుషా
11. కారానద్దవలకుంటలుమా
12. ర్గనారాయణ పెరుమాళకు శ్రీగం
13. ధము పడికిని ఆచంద్రార్క
14. ముగాని స్తిమి

KANDUKUR (65). (A.D. 1268–69.)

[From the same side of the stone.]

TRANSLATION.

On Thursday, the 15th of the bright fortnight of Chaitra of the year Vibhava, corresponding to the year 1190 of the illustrious and auspicious Ṣaka era, Gaḍi Déva Ráju, son of Ṣríman Mahámaṇḍaléṣvara Sáhattumalla Perumáṇḍi Déva Chóḍa Mahárájulu gave a flower garden in the village and a cow for providing offerings at the sacred festival to Márganáráyaṇa Perumáḷ through the agency of the son of Ṣrímad Márga Pahiṇḍi Mukkala Víra Tiruvengaḍa, the illustrious establisher of the path of the Védas, to last as long as the sun and moon exist.

1. శ్రీశుభస
2. క వరుషంబులు ౧౧౯౦ అ
3. గు నేంటివిభవ సంవత్స
4. ర చైత్రశుద్ధ ౧౫ గురువారా
5. న శ్రీమన్మహామండలేశ్వర
6. స హాత్తు మల్ల పెరుమాండి దే

7. వదోఁడ మహారాజులక్కొడు
8. కుగసిదేవరాజు శ్రీమతు
9. వేదమార్గ ప్రతిష్టాచార్య్య
10. లైన మార్గముపహిండిముక్క
11. ల వీర తిరువెంగడ కొమారు
12. ని పురుషాకారానమార్గనారా
13. యణపెరుమాళ తిరునాళ
14. సేపమునకు ఇచ్చినటూళ్లు
15. పుచ్చుండోంటానుంగలిగొ
16. వూను ఆచంద్రార్కముగా
17. నిస్తిమి

KANDUKUR (66). (A.D. 1269–70.)

[From the same side of the stone.]

TRANSLATION.

On Thursday, the 1st of the bright fortnight of Ṣrávaṇa of the year Ṣukla, corresponding to the year 1191 of the illustrious and auspicious Ṣaka era, Ṣríman Mahámaṇḍaléṣvara Bhíma Rāju Siddaya Déva Mahárájulu gave the village Kúchipúṇḍi for providing offerings . . . to Márga Náráyaṇa Perumáḷ through the agency of the son of Ṣrímad Márgama Pahiṇḍimukkala Víra Tiruvengaḍa, the illustrious establisher of the path of the Védas, to last as long as the sun and moon exist.

NOTE.—In this series of Pentrála inscriptions the donors are in several cases described as descendants of Mukkanṭi Káḍuveṭṭu who is perhaps the Mukkanti who, by tradition, ruled at Nellore as a tributary of the Cholas about the 11th century. In some cases the donors are the ruling Mahárájas while in the rest it is probable that they were connected with the ruling family. The Mahámaṇḍaléṣvara

Mahárájas mentioned are Bhujabala Víra Manma Siddaya Déva Chóḍa (1258–59 and 1261–62), Im'madi Ganḍa Gópála Vijayáditta Déva (1260–61), Bijji Ráju Siddaya Déva Chóḍa (1267–68)[1] Sahattumalla Perumánḍi Déva Chóḍa (1268–69) and Bhíma Ráju Siddaya Déva (1269–70). The appearance of Ganḍa Gópála in the course of Víra Manma Siddaya's reign is not understood.

1. శ్రీశుభ శకవరుష
2. ంబులు ౧౧౯౧ అగు నేంటి
3. శుక్ల స వత్సర శ్రావణ
4. శుద్ధ ౨ గురువారాన శ్రీమ
5. న్మహామండలేశ్వర భీమరా
6. జు సిద్దయదేవమహారాజు
7. లు శ్రీమతు వేదమార్గ ప్రతి
8. ష్టాచార్యులైనమార్గము వ
9. హింఢిమఃకుర్రల తీరతిరువె గ
10. డ కొమారుని పురుషాకారానమా
11. ర్గ నారాయణప్పెరుమాళ్లుశ్రీసే
12. వపడిమాడ్వామక నేపం
13. మునకూచి పూండి ఆ
14. చంద్రార్కముగా నిస్తిమి

KANDUKUR (67).

[Peṭlúru. Telugu of ancient type. From wall of Vírabhadrasvámi temple.]

TRANSLATION.

Hail ! Prosperity ! Konḍivillu, son of Dugiráju, granted land sowable with ten *túms* of seed to Rachchayirru.

---

[1] The correct form of Sahattumalla is Chauhattumalla.

(To face page 606.)

KANDUKUR NO. 67.

The kings of Pedakureṛayu granted. The Raṭoḍi (?) *Kápus* of Inmaḷúru shall protect this.

It is sowable with ten *túms* of seed. Those who injure this (charity) will incur the sin of killing a crore of cows at Bháraṇási (Benares).

(??) Signature of (క్ట్రే) the lord (Prabhu) Rámunḍu.

NOTE.—The transcription was done by Mr. V. Venkayya.

First portion.

1. స్వస్తిశ్రీ [దు]గరాజు [మ]క-
2. స్థు కొండివిల్లు రచ్చయి-
3. [క్షే]కి ఇచ్చినది వస్తు
4. [బు] అల్లిపట్టు పే [పెనుద]·
5. [కు] ఱెఱయురాజు[ల్] [1] దయసే-
6. సిరి [॥*] దీని ఇన్మళూరి ర-
7. [టోడి] కాపు [ఘు] కోచువా [రు][॥*]
8. [వ] దశి వస్తుబు ఆ-
9. ల్లిపటు [॥*] దీని (చె)ఱు -
10. (ఇచ్చి) వారు (గో)ళకోటి (భా)-
11. ర(ణో)సి డఁచినవారు (॥*)
12. (లు)ళ్లి వేఱ

Second portion.

13. ప్రబురా-
14. ముణ్డుక్ట్రేచే [2] (॥*)

---

[1] The symbol which is inserted between *ju* and *da* above the line looks so much like a subscript l that Mr. Venkayya is inclined to take it as the final form of l.

[2] The other two lines on this piece are the last portions of the first and second lines of the first portion of the inscription.

KANDUKUR (68). (A.D. 1406–07).

[Petlúru. Telugu. Opposite Bhímésvara temple.]

TRANSLATION.

Hail! On Monday, the 15th year of the bright fortnight of Vaisákha of the year Vyaya, corresponding to the Srí Saka year 1328, the temple of Bamayadévaru of Peṭlúru being in ruins, Ama Reḍḍi Sigi Reḍḍi of the Kánḍrabóla *gótra*, and who is a Kaṭívari Vritti Sásanandu (?) at the request of all classes of devotees of Petlúru, got the temple constructed and plastered with lime. Káki Máchirázu continued the former gift of a field of two *puṭṭis* for the religious merit of his parents. The *Sthánapati* (the temple servant) is Malla Jiyyaru. The masons of this temple are Máráchári, Sómachári and others.

[Two imprecatory verses.]

Second part.

The field presented by Kómad Raḍḍi on Friday, the 15th of the dark fortnight of Kartika of the year Nandana is one *puṭṭi*.

NOTE.—This second part is a separate inscription.

1. స్వస్తిశ్రీ శకవర్షంబులు ౧౩౨౮ అగు
2. నేంటి వ్యయసంవత్సర వైశాఖ శు ౧౫ సోనా
3. ండు పెట్లూరి బమయదేవరగుడి జీర్ణమైన
4. పెట్లూరి అశంకాడి భక్తులుపంపున
5. ను కాండ్రబోలగోత్ర కటివరి వ్రిత్తిశాసనందు
6. అమరెడ్డి సిగిరెడ్డి గుడిగట్టించి సుంనము
7. పైతముగాను చేయించినాండు కాకిమాచి

8. రాజు తమతల్లి దండ్రులకుం బుణ్యము
9. గాను పూర్వ్వదత్తి యిరుపుట్టిచేను అట్టైసా
10. గించ్చను ఖ౨ యీగుడిస్థానాపతి మల్లజి
11. య్యలు యీగుడిగట్టినవారు. మారాచా
12. రిసోమాచారి సైత మైనరాసిలు.
13. స్వదత్తా ద్విగుణంపుణ్యం పరదత్తానుపాలన
14. నం పరదత్తాపహారేణ స్వదత్తం నిష్ఫలంభవే
15. త్। స్వదత్తంపరదత్తంవా యోహరేర్వ్వసుం
16. ధర షష్టివర్షసహస్రాణాం విష్టాయాం
17. జాయతేక్రిమిః।

Second part.

1. నందనసంవత్సర కార్త్తిక బ ౧
2. ౫ శుక్రోమద్రడి వెట్టినచే
3. పుట్టెండు ఖ ౧

Kandukur (69).

[Peṭlúru. Telugu in Chalukyan character. Opposite Bhímésvarasvámi temple.]

Translation.

Vyengiyarája . . . Dévayanáyu . . . granted . . . mahárájulu. Whoever obstructs this grant will incur the sin of killing at Báraṇási (Benares).

Note.—This was transliterated by Mr. V. Venkayya.

1. . . . (మ)హారా(జు)ల
2. . రికు (వ్వె)ంగియరాజు (ఇలు)రి(ళ్లో)
3. (దే)వయనాయు ఇచ్చిన . . .
4. అస్తు వు . . కు వక్రంబు చే -
5. సినవారు బారణాగి డ-
6. చ్చినవారు (॥ *)

Kandukur (70).

[Polinénipáḷem. Telugu. Near an image of Hanumán. It is mostly illegible.]

1. . స్తు	1. స్వస్తిశ్రీ జయాభ్యుదయ
2. తక మస్తు	2. శకవర్షంబులు . .
	3. . . . . .
3. శకవర్షములు	4. . . . .
4. . తగురెడ్డి	5. . . శుద ౧౧ . .
5. మంరాసంక్రాంతిపుణ్య	కాలమందు . . . .

6. ణ్య . . . .

7. ముగా . . . .

8. . . కోరము శ్రీమన్మహామండలేశ్వర . . .

9. రుహ . . . ఇధర్మాపులు . హారయసిమపూ

10. ర్వత ఇర్వు గం మహాంతర . దక్షిణతతూము . . .

11. స్దాదలవాడు ఉత్తరతగంగ . . . . .

12. స్పారలవాడు . . . . మ . థ . . కవ్రిత్తి

13. కు ౨ వి . . కుంటల ౧ దేవతకు ౧౦ నిరు . కు౧౦ ట.

14. . తివెనల . . . ఖ౧ . . . . స్వద

15. త్తంపరదత్తం వాయోహరేతివసుంధరా షష్టివర్షసహ

16. స్రాణి విష్టాయాంజాయతే।కిమి ॥ విషమహ . .

17. విషమిత్యాహు బ్రహ్మస్వం విషముచ్యతే। విషమేకాకినం హంతి

18. బ్రహస్వంపుత్రపౌత్రుకం॥ . ద్యంధ . . తగారుచినెగరా

19. . . . . స్వ . . . . లం॥

KANDUKUR (71). (A.D. 1517–18 ?)

[Sákavaram. Telugu. To the east in a field.]

TRANSLATION.

This is the charitable edict granted on Wednesday, the 11th of the bright fortnight of Kártika of the year Ísvara by Konda Marasayyagáru after making obeisance to Skandha Somésvaradéva of Kandukúru. I have given 120 *kuntas* of wet land under the tank of Chávatlampúdi, and 2 *gorrus* of dry land for providing *amrita-padi* to the deity as long as the sun and moon endure. Whosoever usurps these lands will incur the sins of cow slaughter and Brahmanicide on the banks of the Ganges. Srí.

1. యీశ్వరసంవత్సర కార్తిక శు ౧౧ బు
2. కందుకూరి స్కంధ శోమేశ్వరదేవునికి
3. కొండ్డ మరసయ్యంగారు దండంపెట్టి
4. యిచ్చిన ధర్మశాసనం చావతంపూ
5. రి చెరువుకిందను వరిమడి గు చ౧౨౦
6. ని వెలిచేను రెండుగొర్లున్ను దేవు
7. ని అమృతపళ్లకు ఆ ంంద్రార్క
8. స్థాయిగాను ఇస్తిని యిక్షేత్రాలు
9. యవరు తప్పినాను గంగకర్త
10. ను గోవున్ను బ్రాహ్మనిన్ని చం
11. పిన పాపానం బో
12. వు వారు ॥ శ్రీ

KAṆDUKUR (72).

[Singaráyakoṇḍa. Telugu. Inscriptions within the temple at Singaráyakoṇḍa.]

TRANSLATION.

(*a*) (On a slab on the floor of the southern gate.)

"The constant and daily service of Kandukúr Sítápati.

(*b*) (On another slab in the same place.)

"The constant and daily service of Kandukúr Séshachári.

(*c*) (On the floor of the eastern gate.)

"The constant service of Kanchiráju Venkatésa.

(*d*) (On the same.)

"The constant service of Chakravarti Sínayya."

(*a*) కందుకూరి శీతాపతి సదా నిత్య శేవ.

(*b*) కందుకూరు శేషాచార్యులు సదా నిత్య శేవ.

(*c*) కంచిరాజు వేంకటేశుండు సదా శేవ శేయుట.

(*d*) చక్రవర్తుల శీనయ్య శేవ శేయుట.

KANDUKUR (73).

[Singaráyakoṇḍa. Telugu. On a stone in the eastern Gópuram. The inscription is in the metre called Sísam.]

TRANSLATION.

(Adoration be to) Ṣrí Ráma ! On the 10th *tithi* (lunar day) of the month Bhádrapada in the year Bháva, the famous Lingá Paṇḍit, resident of Ponnampalli, a village in Koṇḍavíḍu *Mahá Maṇḍala* (kingdom), who is accomplished in doing good to others and who is a man of righteous conduct, joyfully constructed the (pond named) Bhavanási at Singaráyakoṇḍa (Parnasála) for the glory of Ṣrí Narasimha, to last as long as the sun, moon and stars endure, for the religious merit of his son Ganabritpanditárya, so that the work might be praised by the people of the whole world.

శ్రీరామ॥ భావ సంవత్సర భాద్రపద మాసంబు దశమియను తిథి యందుండగవుతాడ । పర్ణశాలంద్దును భవనాశివేయించ శ్రీ నరశింహానికిం కెలువుగాంగ । కొండవీటి మహామండలి యందు పొన్నపల్లి గ్రామపురనివాసు । పరహిత పండితు భవ్యచారిత్ర్యుండు యలమిలింగాపండితు లేఖ మీర తన కుమారుండు గణభృత్పండితార్యునకుం బుణ్యంబుగాంగను బొలుపు మిగుల ఆ చంద్రతారార్కమ వెలయ జేయించె విశ్వమండలి జనులెల్ల వినుతి సేయగా॥

Kandukur (74). (A.D. 1567–68.)

[Singaráyakoṇḍa. Telugu. On the southern pillar in the Mukha maṇḍapam.]

Translation.

Hail! Kanchiráju, son of Vallúr Sarabharáju, who is the karnam of Sómarájapalli, presented (an image of) Garuḍa on Monday, the 12th of the dark half of Vaiṣákha in the year Prabhava, corresponding to the illustrious Ṣaka year 1489.

స్వస్తి శ్రీ శకవర్షంబులు ౧౪౮౯ అగునేటి ప్రభవ సంవత్సర వైశాఖబహుళ ౧౨ సో శ్రీ గరుత్మంతుని సోమరాజుపల్లె కరణం వల్లూరి శరభరాజు కొమారుడు కంచిరాజు సమర్పణం॥

KANDUKUR (75). (A.D. 1449–50 or 1471–72 ?)

[Singaráyakoṇḍa. Telugu. On same pillar.]

TRANSLATION.

Hail! The service of plastering (polishing) dedicated to Ṣrí Narasimha of Parnaṣála, to last as long as the sun and the moon, by Baṇḍári Seṭṭi, son of Baṇḍáni Kámiseṭṭi, and by Kúniseṭṭi, the excellent son of Kommasáni, who are both of the illustrious Góbala *gótra*, on Monday, the 13th of the dark half of Mágha of the year Khara, corresponding to the illustrious Ṣaka year 1371. May it cause great prosperity!

NOTE.—The cyclic year does not correspond to the S.S. year.

స్వస్తి శ్రీ శకవర్షంలుబు ౧౩౭౧ అగునేంటి ఖరసంవత్సర మాఖ బ ౧౩ (సోమవారం) పర్ణశాల శ్రీ నరసింహుని శ్రీముఖభద్రం పునగోబలగోత్రులు బండాని కామిశెట్టి కొడుకు బండారి శెట్టి కొమ్మసానిగారి సుపుత్త్రుండు కూనిశెట్టి ఆ చంద్రార్క-స్తా ఇగాను సమర్పించిన వరుధుంబని మంగళమహా శ్రీ శ్రీ శ్రీం జేయును.

KANDUKUR (76). (A.D. 1528–29.)

[Singaráyakoṇḍa. Telugu. On the northern pillar in the Mukhamaṇḍapa.]

TRANSLATION.

Hail! Dontayya, son of Koṇḍavíḍu Nallambaṭṭi Vissábhadra presented (an image of) Hanumán on the 12th of the dark half of Phálguna of Sarvadhári year corresponding to the illustrious Ṣaka year 1450. May it cause prosperity!

స్వస్తి శ్రీ శకవర్షంబులు ౧౪౫౦ అగునేటి సర్వధారిసంవత్సర ఫాల్గుణ బ ౧౨ లు కు శ్రీ హనుమంతుని కొండవీడు నల్లింజట్టి విస్సాభద్ర కుమారుండు దొంతయ్య సమర్పణము శ్రీ శ్రీం జేయును.

KANDUKUR (77). (A.D. 1527-28.)

[Singaráyakonda. Telugu and Sanskrit in Telugu character. On a stone in front of the temple.]

TRANSLATION.

Telugu.

May there be prosperity! Adoration to Ṣrí Narasimhadéva! On Thursday, the 15th day of the bright half of Ṣrávaṇa of the year Sarvajit, corresponding to the victorious and prosperous Ṣáliváhana Ṣaka year 1449, Ráyasam Ayyapparusu, descendant of the Bháradvája *gótra*, follower of the Ȧsvaláyana *Sútra*, passed master of the Ṛig Veda, who is skilled in ruling the kingdom of the illustrious Rájádhirája, Rájaparaméṣvara, Ṃúruráyaragaṇḍa[1], Ashtadigráyamanóbhayankara[2], Bhásadappuvararáyaragaṇḍa[3], Púrvapaṣchimasamudrádhísvara[4], Karnátarájyalakshmímanóhara[5], Vijayanagarasimhásanádhísvara[6], Ṣrí Víra Pratápa Krishnadévaráya, and who is ruling Udayagiri *durgam* which is the foremost *durgam* in the kingdom of the *ráya* (of Vijayanagar) [issues this edict].

---

[1] This is a Canarese *biruda* and means 'the hero to the three kings, viz., Chera, Chola, and Pándya or else Gajapati (Orissa), Asvapati (Mahomedan ruler) and Narapati (Telugu king).

[2] Sanskrit—one who causes terror to the minds of kings of the eight points of the horizon.

[3] Canarese—the hero who punishes kings who break their word.

[4] Sanskrit—the lord of the eastern and western oceans.

[5] Sanskrit—the beloved of the Fortune of the Karnáṭa kingdom, *i.e.*, ruler of the Karnáṭa kingdom.

[6] Sanskrit—the lord of the throne of Vijayanagar.

Sanskrit.

To one who has seen the temple of Ṣrí Narasimha established by Nárada on the west of the seashore there is no rebirth. The temple was constructed by Rámachandra between the (river) Maniká[1] (Mannéru) and the three hills and is known as Parnasála.[2] This is the edict of Narasimha.

Telugu.

[Ayyapparusu] after making prostrations to Ṣrí Narasimha of Sómarájapalli Parnasála, who is the lord of the whole world and who appeared to Nárada, issues this charitable edict relating to (the gift of) a village.

We have given with a present of gold and libation of water the village named Jillé̤llamúḍi, situated on the southern bank of the Páléru, in the *ṣíma* of Kandukúr, attached to the *rájya* of Udayagiri, as a *Sarvamánya* for (providing) all enjoyments to Ṣrí Narasimhadéva in perpetuity as long as the sun and the moon endure, for the religious merit of Krishnadévamaháráya.

May the deity enjoy the entire lordship of that village with the eight powers and kinds of wealth.

Sanskrit.

The protection of land given by another is twice as meritorious as giving land oneself. By the resumption of land given by another, one's own gift becomes inefficacious.

He who resumes land given by himself or another is reborn a worm in ordure for 60,000 years.

---

1 Maniká is a Sanskritized form of Mannéru.

2 Parnasála—a leafy bower. The Sthalapuráṇa says that Sómarájapalli was formerly a thick forest.

According to the Sthalapurána the temple was founded by Agastya and Nárada.

Telugu.

May it cause great prosperity! Adoration to Krishna! Ṣrí, Ṣrí, Ṣrí!

First side.

(1) శుభమస్తు శ్రీ నరసింహ్వాసామినేనమః । జ
(2) యాభ్యుదయశాలివాహన శకవర్షంబులు
(3) ౧౪౪౯ అగునేంటి సర్వజిత్తు సంవత్సర శ్రావణ శు
(4) ౧౫ గు శ్రీమద్రాజాధిరాజ రాజపరమేశ్వర
(5) మూరరాయరగండ అష్టదిగ్గ్రాయ మనోభ
(6) యంకర భాసదప్పు వరరాయరగండ పూర్వ
(7) పశ్ఛిమ సముద్రాధీశ్వర కర్నాంటరాజ్య లక్ష్మీచు
(8) నోహర విజయనగర సింహ్వాసనాధీశ్వర శ్రీవీర
(9) ప్రతాప శ్రీకృష్ణదేవ మహారాయలరాజ్య
(10) భారధురంధరులైన భారద్వాజగోత్రోద్భవు
(11) ండున్న ఆశ్వలాయన సూత్రపవిత్రులైన రుగ్వే
(12) దపారంగతులైన ఆఖన రాయసం అయ్యప్ప
(13) రుసుంగారు రాయసింహాసనాకు మొదలి
(14) దుర్గమయిన వుదయగిరి దుర్గాధిపతిత్వము సే
(15) యుచున్న సముద్రపశ్చమతటె నారదేనప్ర
(16) తిష్టితం । శ్రీనృసింహ్వాలయం దృష్ట్వా పునర్జన్మ
(17) న విద్యతె॥ మణికా త్రికూటమద్యే రామచంద్రేణ
(18) నిర్మితం॥ పర్ణశాల ఇతిఖ్యాతా నరసింహా
(19) స్య శాసనం॥ శ్రీమత్పకలలోకాధీశ్వరు నార
(20) దప్రసన్నులైన ఆఖనసామరాజుపల్లి పర్ణ
(21) శాల నరసింహ్వులకు సాష్టాంగదండ
(22) ప్రణామంబులు సేసి ఇచ్చిన గ్రామధర్మశాస

Second side.

నం। వుదయగిరి రాజ్యానకుంజల్లి కందుకూరి శీమలోను
పాలేటి దక్షిణతటమందును ఙల్లేళ్లమూండి అనెడి గ్రామము-
సర్వమాన్యముగాను కృష్ణదేవ మహారాయలకు పుణ్యముగాను
సహిరణ్యోదక దానధారాపూర్వకంగాను శ్రీ నరసింహదేవు
నికి
అంగరంగవైభవాలకున్ను ఆ చంద్రార్కస్థాయిగాను ఇస్తిమి
ఆ గ్రామము అష్టభోగ తేజస్వామ్యములున్ను దేవుండు

Third side.

అవధరించ్చుంగాత॥ స్వదత్తాద్విగుణం పుణ్యం పరదత్తాను
పాలనం
పరదత్తాపహారేణ స్వదత్తం నిష్ఫలం భవేత్॥
స్వదత్తాం పరదత్తాం వా। యో హరతి వసుంధరా॥
షష్టివ్వర్ష సహస్రాణి విష్టాయాం జాయతే క్రిమిః॥
మంగళ మహా శ్రీ శ్రీ శ్రీం జేయును శ్రీకృష్ణాయనమః॥ శ్రీ
శ్రీ శ్రీ

KANDUKUR (78). (A.D. 1535–36.)

[Singaráyakoṇḍa. Telugu and Sanskrit in Telugu character. On another slab in front of temple.]

TRANSLATION.

Telugu.

Hail! On Thursday, the 10th of the bright half of Phálguna of the year Manmatha, corresponding to the victorious and prosperous Ṣáliváhana Ṣaka year 1458, while Bhútanátha Rámabhaṭlu, descendant of the Gautama *gótra*, follower of the Âsvaláyana *Sútra*, passed master in the Ṛig Veda, who is skilled in ruling the kingdom of the illustrious Rájádhirája Rájaparaméṣvara, Múruráyaraganda, Ashtadigráyamanóbhayankara, Bhásadappuvaraŕáyaraganda, Púrvapaschimasamudrádhísa,[1] Karnátarájyalakshmímanóhara, Vijayanagarasimhásanádhísvara, Achyutadéva Mahárája, is ruling Udayagiri *durgam*, which is the chief *durgam* in the kingdom of the *ráya* (Vijayanagar), Venkatádri, who has been appointed (by him) to the office of governor of Udayáchala (Udayagiri), who is the moon of the ocean of the family of Yandalúr, who is pure by his descent from the Vishnuvarddhana *gótra*, who has studied the Rig Veda and all other Vedas, who thoroughly knows their meaning and is acquainted with their schools, and who is the excellent son of Timá Jóshya, gives this charitable edict relating to (the gift of) a village, after making adoration with prostrations to Sómarájapalli Parnasála Srí Narasimha, the illustrious lord of the whole world, who appeared to Nárada.

Sanskrit.

To one who has seen the temple of Srí Narasimha established by Nárada on the west of the seashore, there is no rebirth.

Telugu.

We have given with a present of gold and libation of water the village named Chángollu[2] situated on the bank of the river Múshiká[3] (Yelikéru) in the *síma* of Kandukúr, attached to the *rájya* of Udayagiri, as a *sarvamánya*, for the religious merit of Achyutadévaráya and Rámabhatlu,[4] for providing offering (*naivédya*) to Srí Narasimhadéva,

---

[1] The king of the eastern and western seas.

[2] Chángollu is Chágollu in Kandukúr taluk.

[3] Múshika = Rat in Sanskrit and Yelika is the Telugu.

[4] Rámbhatlu was the ruler of Udayagiri and Venkatádri, his deputy.

and for giving food with the remainder (after providing offering to the deity) daily to 24 Brahmans coming from other places to this part of the country.

May the deity enjoy the lordship of that village with the eight powers and kinds of wealth.

(1) స్వస్తిశ్రీ జయాభ్యుదయ శాలివాహన శకవర్షం

(2) బుళు ౧౪౫౭ అగునేంటి మన్మథ సంవత్సర ఫాల్గుణ

(3) శు ౧౦ గు శ్రీమద్రాజాధిరాజ రాజపరమేశ్వర మూ

(4) రురాయరగండ అష్టదిగ్రాయ మనోభయంకర భాస

(5) దప్పువరరా యరగండ పూర్వ పశ్చిమ సముద్రాధీశ కర్నాటరాజ్య

(6) లక్ష్మీమనోహర విజయనగర సింహాసనాధీశ్వర అచ్యుతదేవ

(7) మహారాయల రాజ్యభార దురంధరులైన గౌతమ గోత్రోద్భవు

(8) లైన ఆశ్వలాయన సూత్రపవిత్రులైన రుగ్వేదపారంగతులు

(9) న అయిన భూతనాథని రామాభట్లయ్యవారు రాయసింహా

(10) సనానకుమొదలి దుర్గమైన వుదయగిరి దుర్గాధిప

(11) తిత్వము సేయుచున్న వుదయాచలాధిపత్యమం

(12) దు నిరోగింపంగాను నియుక్తులయిన యందలూ

(13) రి వంశాన్వయాంబుధిచంద్రులైన విష్ణువర్ధనగోత్రపవిత్రులైన

(14) రుగ్వేదాది సకల వేదాధ్యయన అధిత స్వాధ్యాయార్థావబోధ

(15) బుద్ధార్థాచరణచతురులైన తిమాజోస్యవరెయ్య వరతనయున

(16) వెంకటాద్రయ్యవారు సముద్రపశ్చిమతటె నారదేన
ప్రతిష్ఠి

(17) తం శ్రీనృసింహాలయం దృష్ట్వా పునర్జన్మ న్న విద్యతె
శ్రీ మత్సక

(18) లలోకాధీశ్వరులున్ను నారదప్రసన్నులున్ను అయిన సోమ
రాజుప

(19) ల్లిపట్నంశాల శ్రీనరసింహస్వాములకు సాష్టాంగదండప్రమా
ణం బులు

(20) చేసి యిచ్చినగ్రామధర్మశాసనం వుదయగిరి రాజ్యమున
కుం జె

(21) ల్లివచ్చి కందుకూరు సీమలోని మూపకనదీతీరమంద్ద

(22) ను చాంగొల్లు అని యట్టిగ్రామము సర్వమాన్యము

(23) గాను అచ్యుతదేవమహారాయలకున్ను రామాభట్లయ్య

(24) వారికిన్ని పుణ్యముగాను సహిరణ్యోదక దాన ధారా
పూ

(25) ర్వకముగాను శ్రీ నరసింహదేవునికి నైవేద్యము సమ

(26) ర్పించి తశ్శేషము యీమహాదిమార్గమందుం జేరి

(27) యించి పరదేశ బ్రాహ్మణ వర్గానకు ది ౧ కి జ అర కు

(28) అన్నంపెట్టె గట్టడ శేసి యిస్తిమి ఆ గ్రామము అష్టభో
గ తే

(29) జస్వామ్యములున్ను దేవుండు అవధరించ్చుంగా

(30) త

---

[1] Read ప్రణామం.

KANDUKUR (79).

[Sómarázupalli. Telugu. On a big stone in front of the Siva temple. The beginning and the end of the inscription are not to be found. It records the gift of certain lands to a temple and its staff.]

TRANSLATION.

(Some one has given . . .) 100 *kuntas* of land under the Rádimandi bank, 100 *kuntas* under the Malaya tank, 100 *kuntas* under Badiváya, 100 *kuntas* under Marrigunta, and 50 *kuntas* under Muvvalagunta-total, 1,100 *kuntas* of dry land and 1,350 *kuntas* of wet land. The fields were distributed as follows:—To the *pújáris* (priests) for performing worship 600 *kuntas* of dry land and 500 *kuntas* of wet land; pay for worshipping, 100 *kuntas* of dry land and 100 *kuntas* of wet land; pay for *sanku gattu* (blowing the conch ?) 600 *kuntas* of dry land; for flowers, 50 *kuntas*; pay for the dancing girls 440 *kuntas* of dry land, and 500 *kuntas* of wet land.

Let none obstruct this charity. . . . .

[Imprecatory verse.]

90 *kuntas* for pay—*kunta* of wet land (?) . . .

* * * *

First side.

1. రాదిమండిచెఱ్వు
2. కు ౧౦౦ మలయచెఱ్వు
3. కు ౧౦౦ బడివాయ కు ౧౦౦
4. మఱిగుంట కు ౧౦౦ మువ్వల
5. కుంటకు ౫౦। అటువెరషి వెలిసె

6. ను కు ౧౧౦౦ నీరునెలకు ౧౩౫౦।
7. వల్ఘాపూజారులకు అర్చనబోగ
8. ం వెలిసెనుకు ౬౦౦ నీరునెలకు ౫౦౦
9. అల్చనవడి జీతంవెలిసెను కు ౧౦౦
10. నీరునెలకు ౧౦౦ । సంకుగట్టినజీతం
11. వెలిసెను కు ౬౦౦। పూల కు ౫౦। బోగంవారికి
12. జీతంవెలిసెనుకు ౪౪౦ నీరుసెనుకు ౫౦౦
13. చెలు ఇన్ని నిచ్చిరిగారిది। ఎవ్వరు దీనికి అ
14. డ్డంగింపు చేయఉః సమయాలు . .
15. . . స్వదత్తం పరద

Second side.

1. త్తం వా రో హరే
2. తి వసుంధరా
3. షష్ఠివర్ష సహ
4. స్రాణి విష్టాయాం
5. జాయతె క్రి
6. మీ । తోంపది
7. కుజితం నిరు
8. సేల మడికు
9. ంటకు

KANDUKUR (80). (A.D. 1641–42.)

[Sómarázupalli. Telugu. On a stone in front of the Sun temple.]

TRANSLATION.

May there be prosperity! Hail! On the 30th of the dark fortnight of (the month) Áṣvija of the year named Vṛishu, corresponding to 1564 of the illustrious, victorious and prosperous Ṣátiváhana Ṣaka era—Pedanarasaráju, Pina Narsaráju, Krishnamaráju, descendants of the *gótra* of Ṣrí Vasishṭha, grandsons of Venjaḍla Kasvaráju, and sons of Ayyaparáju issued the following charitable edict for the tanks. On this holy occasion of a solar eclipse we have fixed *méras* at the rate of 6 *mánikas* (measures) or every *puṭṭi* of all kinds of grain produced in the fields of Sómarájapalli situated in the territory (*samsthána*) granted to us as *amaram* by Kutub Sháh. Let them give the grain for tank repairs and strengthen the tanks. If any persons, not fulfilling, the conditions of this charity obstruct it in any way, they will incur the sin of killing cows and Brahmans near the Ganges. If Muhammadans rule and do not maintain this charity, they will incur the sin of killing and eating a pig at Mecca. This charitable edict has been executed to-day.

NOTE.—The Kutb Sháh is, no doubt, Abdullah Kutb Sháh of Golkoṇḍa. In KV. the donors' family appears again but Venjaḍla there appears as Vejarlu.

1. శుభమస్తు
2. స్వస్తి శ్రీజయాం
3. భ్యుదయ శాలి
4. వాహాన శత[1] వరు

---

[1] Read శక.

5. పంబులు ౧౫౬౪
6. అగు నేటి క్రిష్ణు
7. నామ సంవత్స
8. ర ఆశ్వీజ బ ౩ం
9. శ్రీవశిష్టగోత్రో
10. ద్భవులయిన వెంజ
11. ర్ల కస్వరాజుంగారి
12. పౌత్రులున్న అయ్య
13. పరాజుంగారి పుత్ర
14. లున్న అన్నా పెద నర్స
15. రాజు పిననర్సరాజు
16. క్రిష్టమరాజుంగా
17. రు చెర్వులకు చేశిన
18. ధర్మశాసన క్రమం
19. మెట్లనను ఖుసు
20. పుశహా గారు షా
21. కు అమరు నడ్పిం
22. చ్చిన సంస్థానము
23. లోను సోమరాజుప
24. ల్లిహొటాన పండిన నానాధాన్యం
25. దోలకం ఖ ౧ కి ఆరుమానికెల
26. లెఖను యీ సూర్య గ్రహణ పు
27. ణ్యకాలమందు యేపాట
28. టు చేస్సి ఖరారు ఖ

29. ండితము చేయించివచ్చినా
30. ము చెర్వుల పనిముఖానకి
31. ఇచ్చి చెర్వులు వూర్జిత
32. ం శేయించంగలవారు ఇ
33. ధర్మానకు లోనై నడ్చక యువ్వ
34. రు కుంతితప్పినాను గంగ
35. కతీర గో।బ్రాంహలను వధియి
36. ంచ్చిన పాపాన బోదురు తురు
37. కలుయేలినా యీ ధర్మం న
38. డపించ్చకుంటేను మక్షా
39. లోను పంది:రి కోసుకొని
40. తిన్న పాపాన పోదురు
41. యీ దినంబ్రాశించిన ధర్మ
42. శాసనము

KANDUKUR (81).

[Sómarázupalli. Telugu. In Narasimhasvámi temple.]

TRANSLATION.

Válicherla Rangamma, a lady of the Vásávári family, caused to be constructed this *mandapa* to please Ṣrí Nṛisimhasvámi.

శ్రీ నృశింహాస్వామివారికి ప్రీతిగా వాసావారి ఆడబిడ్డ వాలి చెర్ల రంగంమ కట్టించిన మంటపము.

KANDUKUR (82). (A.D. 1536-37.)

[Tangeḷḷa. Telugu. On a stone in front of Vénugópálasvámi temple.]

TRASLATION.

May there be prosperity! Adoration be to Krishna! Hail! On the 3rd of the bright fortnight of Chaitra of the current year Durmukhi, corresponding to the illustrious, victorious and prosperous Ṣálivάhana Ṣaka year 1458, Máḷḷúru Chintama Reḍḍi Gangi Reḍḍi . . . gave (this) charitable edict to Janárdana of the village of Tangeḷḷa which is subject to the rule of the illustrious Âḍaya Rudra . . . . To the north . . all kinds (of grain) raised . . . .

NOTE.—It is not clear who this Áḍaya Rudra was.

1. శుభమస్తు ॥ కృష్ణాయనమః ॥ స్వస్తిశ్రీ
2. జయాభ్యుదయ శాలివాహన శ
3. క వర్షంబులు ౧౪౫౮ అగు
4. నేంటి వర్తమాన దుర్ముఖి స
5. ంవత్సర చైత్ర శుద్ధ 3 లు శ్రీమతు ఆడయ రుద్ర ఆధీ
6. నములోనడిచే తంగెళ్ల గ్రామజనార్దనకు
7. మాళ్లూరు చింతమ రెడ్డి గంగి రెడ్డి . . . . బు
8. . . . ధర్మశాసనం.
9. . . . నకు ఉత్తరవు త
10. . . . డోలుంన్ను ఆడు
11. . . . బండిన నానాధా
12. . . . . ,
13. . . . . .

KANDUKUR (83). (A.D. 1526–27.)

[Tangella. Telugu. On stone in front of temple of Janárdanasvámi.]

TRANSLATION.

May there be prosperity! Adoration to Ganésa! Hail! On Thursday, the 10th of the bright half of Chaitra of the current year Vyaya, corresponding to the year 1448 of the illustrious, victorious and prosperous Sáliváhana Saka era . . . who is the excellent son of . . . and the grandson of Júpalli Ráma . . . Náyaningáru, who is illustrious and celebrated, who possesses all the glory of various titles, among others:— Makhámánukúli,[1] Karaválabhairava,[2] Gaṇḍaragaṇḍa,[3] Gaṇḍabhairavagaṇḍa,[4] Uddaṇḍa Puriyamárkkólugaṇḍa,[5] Kaṭakahannibbaragaṇḍa,[6] Hattumuvvaragaṇḍa,[7] Dhíra[8] Sámantabáramaṇḍalikaragaṇḍa[9], Dushtagókulamánamardana,[10] Ranamunambekkandrunáyankulakoṭnattugaṇḍa,[11] Dévichúrakára,[12] . . . . . . gave this edict. To ensure the better cultivation of the wet land under the Tangeḷḷa tank Bráhman inámdars and every one else should contribute to the estate for *amaram* (of the tank) at the rate of one *na*, that is, one *túm* on every *puṭṭi*

---

[1] The meaning is not clear.

[2] A Bhairava armed with a sword.

[3] Canarese = A hero of heroes.

[4] A Bhairava hero to heroes.

[5] Canarese = (?).

[6] Canarese = Conqueror of twelve and ruler of the camp (?).

[7] Canarese = The hero or conqueror of thirteen enemies.

[8] Dhíra = Bravo.

[9] Canarese = The hero who is lord over 12 feudatories.

[10] The destroyer of the pride of the wicked Gókulas (shepherds, *i.e.*, Yádava dynasty).

[11] Canarese = The hero who has vanquished many chiefs in battle.

[12] Meaning unknown.

The donor's name is not legible nor is it clear to what family he belonged.

of the total produce. With this grain the tank bund should be thoroughly repaired every year. Those who obstruct this charity will incur the sin of (committing) the five cardinal sins, viz., killing cows, killing Brahmans, &c. Therefore these conditions should be observed as long as the sun and moon endure . . . .

Turmeric field . . . at this rate . . . .

1. శుభమస్తు ॥ శ్రీగణాధిపతయే నమః ॥ స్వస్తి శ్రీ జయా భ్యుద

2. య శాలివాహన శకవర్షంబులు ౧౪౪౮ అగునేటి వర్తమా

3. న వ్యయ సంవత్సర చైత్ర శు ౧౦ బ్రు శ్రీ మద్విఖ్యాత . . మఖామా

4. నుహూలికరవాల భైరవ గండరగండ గండ భైరవ గండ ఉద్దండప్రరి

5. యమాకొర్తలుగండ కటకహన్నిబ్బరగండ హాత్తు ము వ్వర

6. గండధీరా సామంత బారామండలికరగండ దుష్టగోకు

7. లమాన మర్దన రణమునం బెకర్తంద్య నాయంకుల కొ ట్నత్తుగం

8. డ్డదివిచారకార గసభ్య త్రా . క ప్రశస్తిసహితులైనజా

9. వల్లిరామ . . . . . నాయనింగారి

10. పౌత్రులు . . . . బాగభర పుణ్యో

11. దయులైన . . . . . గెడగ్రామమం

12. దులరితినిప్రజా . . . . శాసనము ! తంగెళ్ల చె

13. రువుకిందను నిర్మాల వ్యవసాయము నడవ ౹ బాంహణ స్థా న మా

14. న్యాయి నగరి కమరు సహితముగాను యెవ్వరైనాను పం
డినధాన్యా

15. నకుసంతరాశిని ఖ ౧ కి న ౧ తూమింట్టి సమస్యను
ద్దిళ్లవెసి అధాన్యా

16. నను యేంటెంటను చెరువుపైకట్ట బహుబాగా వేయించు
వారు

17. యీాధమార్గనకు వేలాహూడినాకు . . . జుంగాసీకం
గాక త

18. ప్పి నడచువారు గోహత్య బ్రంహ్మాత్య మొదలయిన పంచ
మహా

19. పాత కాలాను పొందువారుగాన . . . .

20. కట్టుడ ఆచంద్రార్కస్థాయిగాను . . . .

21. దోంట పసపుందోంట . . . . నతి . . .

22. టలకర్ ! అట్టిగలెఖను . . . . .

23. . . . త్రికి . . . .

KANDUKUR (84). (A.D. 1294–95.)

[Vémpáḍu. Telugu. Near Póléramma temple.]

TRANSLATION.

Hail! On Wednesday, the 15th of Nija Jyéshṭha of the year Jaya, corresponding to the year 1216 of the illustrious auspicious (Ṣaka) era on the occasion of a lunar eclipse, for the prosperity of Hail! Ṣríman Mah-manḍaléṣvara Rudra Déva Maháráya, the gem of the Kákatiya family, and for the prosperity of the kingdom and family of Ṣrímat Muppaḍi Náyani Gáru and for the religious merit of his parents . . Talári Kámúnu (?)

presented with libation of water . . . Bamupáḍu village in Kandukúru *sthala*, having obtained the favour of Ṣrí Tripurántakadéva. Worms will swarm in the mouths of those who obstruct this charity and they will incur the sin of killing a tawny cow and a Brahman on the banks of the Ganges and eating from the skull of their eldest son.

[One imprecatory verse.]

NOTE.—Bampáḍu is presumably Vémpáḍu.

1. స్వస్తి శ్రీ సుభజాతక వ
2. రుషంబులు ౧౨౧౬ వ సేంటి
3. జయ సంవత్సర నిజ జ్యేష్ఠ శుద్ధ
4. ౧౫ బు నాండు సోమ గ్రహణ కాలమ
5. ప్పుడు స్వస్తిశ్రీ మనమహామండ్డలే
6. శ్వరకాక తయ్యకులతిలక రుద్రదేవ మహారా
7. జులకు అభివ్రిద్ధిగాను స్వస్తి శ్రీమతు
8. ముప్పడి నాయనింగారికి రాజ్యాభి వ్రిద్ధియు
9. గులాభివ్రిద్ధియుంగాను శ్రీ త్రిపురాంతకదేవ
10. కృపబొంది (పల్లోము యూరికుంకు) కందుకూరి స్తళం
11. ము బముపాడి అనెయూరి(నల్లంతము)యూరినిమూండు
12. తలారి కామూను తన్మతల్లి దండ్రులకు పుణ్యాము
13. గాను ధారవోసి బిడిచెను ధర్మాన్నకు విఘాత

Second side.

14. ము సేసినాను వారి
15. నోరుతోఁక్రుము
16. లు తోలును గంగక

17. ఱుత బ్రాంహ్మలు గంగికవి

18. ఽలం బోడిచినదోష

19. మునం బోంగలవారు

20. తమ పెద్దకొడుకు మకపాళ్లా

21. నకుడిదిన దోషమునపో

22. యిన వారు॥ స్వదత్తం ప

23. రదత్తం వాయోహరేతి వసు

24. ంధరా షష్టివ్వ౯రుష సహస్రా

25. ణి విష్టాయాం జాయతే క్రిమిః॥

KANDUKUR (85). (A.D. 1516–17 ?)

[Vírapalli. Telugu. To the east, in a field.]

TRANSLATION.

Hail ! On Monday, the 14th of the bright fortnight of Mágha of the year Dháta, corresponding to the illustrious and auspicious Ṣaka year 1411 on the holy occasion of Ṣivarátri, Maradhavi Póṭi Déjatayamgáru has given for the religious merit of his father Pallá Reḍḍi, 100 *kunṭas* of land under the tank of Yírépalli which belongs to us, to the east of the wet fields and by the side of the irrigation channel, for the daily offerings and enjoyments of Nágéṣvara of Yírépalli. I shall bear on my head the feet of those who maintain this charity ; those who fail to continue it will be sinners.

NOTE.—The cyclic and Ṣaka dates do not correspond.

1. స్వస్తిశ్రీ శుభ శకవర్షం
2. బులు ౧౪౭౧ అగునేటి ధా
3. త సంవత్సర మాఘ ౧౪ సో
4. శివరాత్రి పుణ్యకాలమం
5. దును మరధవిపోటి దే
6. జ తయ్యంగారు తమతం
7. డ్రి వల్లారెడ్డింగారికి పుణ్యం
8. గాను యిరేపల్లి నాగేశ్వరు
9. ని నైవేద్య వైభవాలకు
10. మాకుజగ్గివచ్చి యిరే
11. పల్లి చెర్వుక్రిందను వ
12. రిమడి తూర్పుపంట
13. కాలు ఏవంమను ధార
14. చదండాటిన గు ౧౦౦
15. నూరుగుంటలు యిస్తి
16. మి యీధర్మం యెవ
17. రు నడిపినాను (వారి)
18. (పాదాల మాశిరసును
19. ంవ్రిదును) నడపకతప్పి
20. తేనుం వా(రు) దోషులు

KANDUKUR (86). (A.D. 1576–77.)

[Vírépalli. Telugu. In the supply channel of the tank.]

TRANSLATION.

Hail! On Wednesday, the 14th of the dark fortnight of Mágha of the year Dhátṛi corresponding to the Srí Ṣaka year 1498 on the auspicious occasion of Ṣivarátri, Malidévi Donṭi Lingappagáru gave . . . to us also the field irrigated under the Vírépalli tank for the religious merit of his father Pallari Tamvoji.

1. స్వస్తిశ్రీ శకవర్షంబు
2. లు ౧౪౯౮ అగు నేటి ధాతృసంవ
3. త్సర మాఘ బ ౧౪ బు శివరాత్రి పుణ్య
4. (కాలమందు) మలిదేవి దొంటిలింగ్గప్పంగారు ద
5. తండ్రి ఫల్లరి తంవోజికిం పుణ్యం
6. గాను మాకుంన్ను విరేపల్లి చెవుఱ
7. . . కింద పారునట్టి చెను

KANIGIRI (1). (A.D. 1651–52 ?)

[Arivémula. Telugu. From a stone in the temple of Chennakéṣava.]

TRANSLATION.

Hail! (This is) the act of devotion performed to Ṣrí Chennakéṣava by Jangamaráju, who is pure by reason of being of the Átréya *gótra*, and who is the son of Hingi Râmaráju, in planting the *dhvajasthamba* (flag-staff) and celebrating the sacred *kalyânamahôtsava* (the marriage festival) on the 15th of the bright half of (the month) Chaitra of the year Khara, corresponding to 1575 of the illustrious, victorious and prosperous Ṣáliváhana Ṣaka era.

NOTE.—The cyclic and Śáliváhana Śaka years differ by one year.

1. స్వస్తి శ్రీ విజయాభ్యుదయ శాలివాహన శక
2. వర్షంబులు ౧౫౭౫ అగునేంటి ఖర సంవత్సర చైత్ర
3. శు ౧౫ లు శ్రీ చన్నకేశవరాయుడుకు ఆత్రేయ
4. గోత్ర పవిత్రుండైన హింగ్గి రామరాజుకుమా
5. రుండు జంగ్గమరాజు ధ్వజస్తంభ ప్రతిష్టను తిరు
6. కళ్యాణ మహోత్సవము నడిపించిన శేవ శ్రీ

KANIGIRI (2).

[Arivémula. Telugu. In tank to west of village.]

TRANSLATION.

Two *gorrus* of *mányam* of Déva Gurayya in the hamlet of Arivémula in the year Nala . . . . .

1. నళ సంవత్సరం
2. మ్మాన దేవుగుర

3. యమాన్యం గొ తి
4. అరివేముల మజ
5. ర (మనజ)
. . .

Kanigiri (3).

[Chákíréla. Telugu. On pillar of Rámalingasvámi temple. Illegible for the most part.]

1. (వాఖియ .)
2. (. డు వారు దిని)
3. (. ను . .)
4. . . . .

Second side.

(1) ముమ్మడి చెట్టి
(2) మాకు వం . .
3. . . . . ము

Kanigiri (4). (A.D. 1416–17.)

[Dáḍireḍḍipalli. Sanskrit in Telugu character and Telugu. Stone close to tank bund.]

Translation.

May there be no impediment!

(Sanskrit) V. (1) May the primeval Boar protect (you) from the abode of perils — he, the illustrious, whose eternal form is pure like the blue lotus, and who hastens to rescue with his tusk the earth from the copious waters of the unfathomable ocean!

V. (2) In the illustrious Ṣaka year, reckoned by the elephants (8), the worlds (3), the Rámas (3), and the moon (1) [1338], in the year Durmukhi, in the bright fortnight of Śrávana, on the fifth *tithi*, under the Pushya (Nakshatra), on Thursday, the illustrious and honored Kanṭaya Bhávi Nâyaka constructed a tank beneficial to all living beings naming it after his brother Gangaya, to last as long as the moon and stars endure.

(Telugu.) Hail! On Thursday, the 5th of the bright fortnight of Śrávana of the year Durmukhi, corresponding to the year 1338 of the illustrious Śaka era, while Ṣríman Mahárájádhirâja, Rájaparaméṣvara, Chatussamudrádhíśvara, Ṣrí Víra Pratápa, Dévaráya Maháráya, seated on the diamond throne at Vijayanagar, was ruling the kingdom of the earth, while Ṣrí Rámachandra Rája Oḍayalu, son of the aforesaid Dévaráya Mahárája, was ruling with pleasure at Udayagiri—in the fields of Gummaḷḷapádu granted to Bhávináyanigáru, son of Kaṭṭiga Kanṭináyanigáru, in (the village of) Bóyavilla for personal salary, that Bhávináyaningáru constructed a tank named Gangasamudram in the name of that Gangi Náyanimgáru and executed this charitable edict for the spiritual good of his younger brother Gangi Náyanimgáru, and for securing heaven and other pleasures. The sharers who received shares from Bhávi Náyanimgáru for the religious merit of Gangi Náyuḍu at the time of consecration of this tank (are) as follows.

[List of sharers omitted from translation.]

May there be prosperity!

(Sanskrit.) [Imprecatory verses.]

1. अविघ्नमस्तु ॥ श्रीमानगाधजलरा

2. शिपयःप्रपूराद्दष्टांकुरेण

3. धरणीं तरसोद्धरिष्णुः । नीलांबुजा
4. तनिभनिर्मलनित्यमूर्तिः पायाद
5. पायनिलयादयमादिपोत्री ॥ (V. 1)
6. श्रीशाके गजलोकरामहिमगौ
7. संवत्सरे दुर्मुखे शुक्ले श्रावणमा
8. सि पंचमितिथौ पुण्ये गुरोर्वासरे ।
9. श्रीमान् कंटयभाविनायकवरः स्वभ्रा
10. तृगंगाख्ययासर्वप्राणिहितं स
11. मुद्रमकरोदाचंद्रतारावधि ॥ (V. 2)
12. స్వస్తి శ్రీ శకవర్షంబులు ౧౩౩౮ అవునేంటి
13. దుర్ముఖి సంవత్సర శ్రావణ శు ౫ గు॥ శ్రీ
14. మన్మహారాజాధిరాజ రాజపరమేశ్వర చ
15. తుస్సముద్రాధీశ్వర శ్రీ వీరప్రతాపదేవరా
16. య మహారాయరు విజయనగరాన సింహా
17. సనారూఢులై పృథివీరాజ్యము చేయుచు
18. ండంగాను ఆ దేవరాయ మహారాయులకు
19. మారుండు శ్రీ వీరరామచంద్రరాయ ఒ
20. డయలు ఉదయగిరిన సుఖాన రాజ్యము
21. చేయుచుంను కట్టిగ కంటినాయనిగారి కొ
22. డుకు భావినాయనిగారికి అంగ జీతాన
23. కు బోయ వీళ్లలో నిచ్చిన గుంమళ్లపాటి పాల
24. ములోను ఆ బావినాయనింగారు తమ తం
25. ముడు గంగినాయనిగారికి సుకృతము
26. గాను స్వర్గాదిభోగాలు గలుగునట్టుగాను
27. ఆ గంగినాయనిగారి పేరను గంగసముద్ర
28. మని చెరువుగట్టించి చేసిన ధర్మశాసన
29. ము॥ ఈ తటాకప్రతిష్టప్యుడు గంగినాయనిగారికి
30. పుణ్యముగా బావినాయనిగారిచే తనుప్రతిగ్ర

31. హించిన వృత్తిమంతులు॥ ఆచార్యత్వమును
32. న శ్రీవత్సగోత్రం మల్లికార్జున భట్లకు మణుగు
33. ఎన మందుము। కొంకల్ల తిప్పయఓయిలకు ఇ
34. ద్దుము। తంమయజోస్యులకు ఇద్దుము। యిరుగ
35. యజోస్యుల అప్పయజోస్యులకు ముత్తుము।
36. ఆ మంచి భట్లకు ముత్తుము। ఐరాయ ఓఝుల
37. కు నలుతుము। ఆ కొడుకు వీరప్పకు యిద్దుము। క
38. మంపాటి పెదోఝులకు యిద్దుము। మల్లెల అప్పయ
39. ఓఝులకు యిద్దుము। రెనుమడుగు అప్పయభట్ల
40. కు యిద్దుము। వీవులకొలిచెన్లకు యిద్దుము। వడిభా
41. టి మల్లయ ఓఝులకు యిద్దుము। చచిన రామాయఓఝు
42. లకు తూమెడు। సింగపట్నం మాధవవోఝులకు తూమెడు
43. నందవరం నాగాయఓఝులకు తూమెడు మోంత్రవి గం
44. గా ఓఝులకు తూమెడు। వలికుంటమలయగారికి
45. తూమెడు శ్రీకంఠునిగారికి తూమెడు। విష్ణుస్తా
46. నానకు అనంతునికి తూమెడు। యిస్వరస్తానాన
47. కు తూమెడు॥ शुभमस्तु ॥

47. स्वदत्ताद्द्वि गुणं पुण्यं परद
48. त्तानुपालनं परदत्तापहारेण स्व
49. दत्तं निष्पलं भवेत् ॥ सामान्योयं धर्म
50. सेतुर्नृ(पा)णां काले काले पालनिय्यो भवाद्भिः [।]
51. सर्वानेतान् भाविनः पार्थिवेंद्रान्
52. भूयो भूयो याचते रामचंद्रः ॥

KANIGIRI (5). (A.D. 1528–29.)

[Dásalapalli. Telugu. South of Ankálamma temple.]

TRANSLATION.

Salutation be to the illustrious Rámánujá. Hail! On Sunday the 11th of Áshádha of the year Sarvadhári, corresponding to the year 1450 of the illustrious, victorious and prosperous Ṣáliváhana Ṣaka era, Rávúri Rághava Reḍḍi and Timmanáyanigáru son of Veligóṭi Rangánáyaḍu, the servants (devotees) of Ṣrí Tiruvengaḷanátha of Veligonḍa who is the lord of the four worlds and the lord of the crores of universes, presented this charitable edict after making endless salutations. We have presented to the deity with libation of water the village of Dásaḍipalli attached to (the *Ṣíma* of ?) Kanakagiri, Músunúru and Pólacharla, which are in our dominions and belong to the Udayagiri (rájya), and the tax and other fees raised in this village for the enjoyments and sacred food of the deity, for the religious merit of Konḍamarusayyavâru, Rávúri Basuvá Reḍḍi Gáru, and Veligóṭi Rangánáyanimgáru, to last in perpetuity as long as the sun and moon endure. Whoever violates this charity will incur the sin of killing with his own hand his parents, a cow and a Brahman at Benares. Further whoever violates this charity will be regarded as having sucked the yards of a dog and a donkey.

[Two imprecatory verses.]

Ṣrí.

NOTE.—Rághava Reḍḍi, son of Basava Reḍḍi, appears again in K.G. 33 as chief of a *Ṣíma* under the governor of Udayagiri. He may have been connected with the Reḍḍi dynasty.

1. శ్రీమతే రామానుజాయ
2. నమః॥ స్వస్తిశ్రీ జయాభ్యుదయ

3. శాలివాహనశకవరుషంబులు
4. ౧౪౫౦ అగునేట్టి సర్వధారి సంవ్వ
5. త్సర ఆషాఢ శు ౧౧ ఆ॥ చతుర్భువ
6. నాధీశ్వర అఖిలాండ్లకోటిబ్రహ్మాం
7. డనాయకుండైన వెలిగొండ శ్రీతిరువెం
8. గ్గళ్నాతనికి మీదాసులు రావూరిరాగా
9. వ రెడింగారంను వెలిగోటి రంగ్గానా
10. యిని కొమారుండు తిమానాయి
11. నింగారున్ను అనంత్తమైన(దం)డ్లముకు
12. సమర్ప్పించి యిచ్చిన ధర్మ్మశాస
13. నం॥ వుద్దగిరికిం జెల్లిమానాయకా
14. శ్రలోని కనకగిరి మునునూరి పోలచ
15. ర్లకుం జెల్లిదాసడివల్లె గ్రామము
16. కొండ్ల మరుసయ్యవారికిని రావూరి
17. బసువా రెడింగారికిన్ని వెలిగోటి ర
18. ంగానాయినింగారికిన్ని పుణ్యము
19. గాను అంగ్గరంగ్గ వైభవాలకున్ను అమ్మ
20. దపల్లకున్ను ఆచంద్రార్క్క స్థాయిగాను
21. యీగ్రామం సుంకం చూపుటోయ
22. ం మొదలుగాను దేవునికి దారా
23. వోసి సమర్ప్పించ్చి యిస్తిమి యీ
24. పుణ్యానకు యెవ్వరు తప్పినడ
25. చినాను తమమాతృ పితృలా
26. ము సంవారిని గోవును బ్రాంహ్మ
27. ని వారణాసిలో స్వహస్తవద శేసి
28. న దోషానపోదురు మరిని తప్పి
29. నడచిరా కుఖ శేసినమున్ను గాడిదె
30. సిశినమును కుడిచినవారు ॥ శ్రీ
31. దానపాలనయోర్మ్మధ్యే దానా

32. ఛ్రేయోన్యాను పాలునం దానాస్వర్గ
33. మవాప్నోతి పాలునా దచ్చుతం
34. ఫలం॥ స్వదత్తా ద్విగుణంపుణ్యం
35. పరదత్తానుపాలనం పరదత్తాప
36. హారేణ స్వదత్తం నిష్ఫలంభవే
37. తు॥ శ్రీ

KANIGIRI (6).

[Gógulapalli. Telugu. On a stone called Dhanamgunḍu because believed to mark a hidden treasure.]

TRANSLATION.

Hail! In the illustrious and auspicious Ṣaka year Raghusi . . . .

1. స్వస్తి శ్రీ
2. శుభ శకవ
3. రు శంబులు
4. రఘు, శి . .

KANIGIRI (7). (A.D. 1314-15.)

[Gózalavíḍu (*alias* Vágupalli). Telugu. In a garden in the east.]

TRANSLATION.

Adoration be to Ṣrí Sadáṣiva the breaker of the pride of the demon Andhaka, the lion to the elephant which is the demon Táraka, the destroyer of the fifth head of the proud Brahma, the creator of all the pot-shaped (globular) worlds, whose fort is Kailása, whose campis beautiful, whose eyes are the sun, moon and fire, whose form is eight-fold in nature, viz., the sun, the moon, the fire, the earth, the water, the air, the sky and the soul, who grants the eight kinds of wealth, and who is the aggregate of innumerable virtues. Hail! On Thursday the 5th of the bright fortnight of Vaiṣákha of the year Ánanda, corresponding to the Ṣrí Ṣaka year 1236, Iḍumakanṭi Gangi Reḍḍi Gáru, the servant of (Hail!) Bukkaráya Oḍayalu, who is the asylum of the whole world, who is entitled to the five great sounds,[1] Manḍaléṣvara, Múruráyaragaṇḍa,[2] Ariráya vibhála,[3] Báshadappuvaráyaráya (ráyara?) gaṇḍa,[4] the lord of the earth consisting of nine continents, and the worshipper of the divine lotus feet of Virúpáksha Déva, gave in perpetuity to last as long as the sun, moon and stars endure with libation of water for the religious merit of his (Gangi Reḍḍi's) father Peddi Reḍḍi and his mother Chánasáni, one *Singampáṭipuṭṭi*[5] and five *na* (*túms*) of land to the deity Mallikárjuna of Gonuvíḍu and one *Singampáṭipuṭṭi* to the deity Bhíméṣvara and one *puṭṭi* of land for offerings and worship with incense and light.

Second side.

May Brahma Jíyyalu have sons and live long! May he get the seven kinds of progeny! Those who do not maintain this *vritti* will incur the sin of killing their sons and of killing a cow on the banks of the Ganges.

---

[1] 'Panchamahásabda' means literally "five great sounds" and "denotes the sounds of five musical instruments, the use of which was allowed, as a special mark of distinction, to persons of high rank and authority." These persons were heralded in public by these instruments. (*Vide* Vol. V., E.I. footnote 3, page 216.)

[2] The disgracer of three kings (Chéra, Chóḷa and Páṇḍya).

[3] The destroyer of hostile kings.

[4] The destroyer of kings who break their word.

[5] Singampáṭi puṭṭi—a puṭṭi as measured at Singampáḍu (a standard measure presumably).

1. అంధ్దకాసుర మదభంజన తారకా
2. సురగజకంఠీరవ గర్వితవనజాసన
3. పంచమ శిరోహార సకలబ్రంహ్మాండబా
4. ండ్ఞ సంఘటన్యాలాస కటకకమనియ్య
5. స్కంధావార సూరియ్యా సోమాగ్నిలోచన
6. సూరియ్యా సోమాగ్ని మహీజల సమీ
7. ర గగనాత్మ యాష్టమూర్త్తి అష్టైశ్వరియ్యదా
8. యక అపరిమిత గుణకళాప శ్రీసదాసి
9. వ పకాదార్ణత తదాహీ॥ స్వస్తి సమస్త బు
10. వనాశ్రయ పంచమహాశబ్ద మండ్ఞ
11. లేశ్వర మూరురాయరగండ్ఞ అరిరా
12. యవిభాళ బాషదప్పువరాయ రా
13. యగండ్ఞ నవఖండ్ఞ ప్రిత్విస్వర విరూ
14. పాక్షిదేవ ది (వ్య) శ్రీపాద పద్మారా
15. దకులైన శ్రీబుకరాయ ఒడయలబ
16. టు యిడుమకంట్టి గంగిరెడ్డింగారు
17. స్వస్తిశ్రీ శకవర్షంబులు ౧౨౩౬ అ
18. సు నేంటి ఆనందసంవత్సర వైశాఖ
19. ౫ సు। తండ్రి పెద్దిరెడ్డికిని తల్లిచాన
20. సానికింనిం బుంణ్యముగాను గోను
21. వీటి మల్లికార్జునదేవరకు వ్రిత్తిసిం
22. గంపాటి ఖ ౧ న ౫ భీమేస్వర
23. దేవరకు వ్రిత్తి సింగ్గపాటి ఖ ౧
24. దూపేటివ నైవేద్యానకై గా ౧ ఆ
25. చంద్రా తారాకరంబుగా దారవోసి

Second side.

26. రి॥ శ్రీ
27. బ్రంహ జీయ్యలు పు

28. త్రులుంగలిగి బ్రతుకువారు
29. వారు సప్త సంతానంబు
30. బొందినవారు॥ యీవ్రిత్తి చెల్లిం
31. చరు కొడుకుంజంప్పిన పాపాన
32. ంప్పిన దోషానం బోయ్నువారు
33. ద్రోచినారు గంగలో గోవుంజ
34. యీ వ్రిత్తి సాసనము ఎవ్వరు

* * *

KANIGIRI (8).

[Guruvájipéṭa. Sanskrit in old Telugu letters. In a field called Mudám Tóṭa. The transcription was revised by Mr. V. Venkayya.]

TRANSLATION.

This field of 12 *nivartanas* was given by king Kuḍubi Právésa to the temple of Ṣiladévi at Kanḍa Sómésvara. Whoever misappropriates this land is guilty of the five great sins.

NOTE.—There appears to be no reference to this king elsewhere.

1. कण्डसोमेश्वरशिलादे[वी]
2. गृहस्ये तत्[1] द्वादशनिवर्त्तन[ा] वा
3. क्षेत्रं राज्ञाकु[डु]विनाम प्रावेसेन
4. दत्तं एतद्भूमि विलापी पश्च[महा]
5. पातक संयुक्तो भवति ।

---

[1] Read स्येतत्.

KANIGIRI (9). (A.D. 1766–67 ?)

[Guruvájipéṭa. Telugu. From stone near Chenna-késavaswámi temple.]

TRANSLATION.

Ṣrí ! Hail ! On Friday, the 7th day of the bright half of Nija Ṣrávaṇa of the year . . . (Vyaya?) corresponding to the year 1688 of the illustrious, victorious and prosperous Ṣáliváhana Ṣaka era, we Gaja . . . . nemi Náyanimgáru have given as charity to Nágandi Yallayya . . . . to the west of the band as he constructed a tank, and maintained it as a *dasabandha* at Remana in the *síma* of Kanigiri-Pólicherla which was given to us for our chiefdom by Ṣrí Veligóṭi Komára Timma Náyanimgáru. Therefore . . . . they should live happily . . . . (will incur the sin of killing) cows and Brahmans at (Benares). Ṣrí.

		*	
1.	శ్రీ శ్వస్తి శ్రీ జయాభ్యు శా	లి	వాహన శకవరు
2.	సంబ్బుద ౧౬౮౮ అగు శే డు	వ్యయ	సంవత్సర నిజశ్రా
3.	వణశుద్ధసప్తమీ శుక్రవారాన గజ	. .	నేమినాయనింగారు
4.	నాగండి యల్లయ్యకు యిం	. .	ధర్మ్మంగానునుం శ్రీ
5.	వెలిగోటికుమార తిమ్మానా	యనిగా	రు మానాయంకరాన
6.	కుపాలించియిచ్చిన కనిగిరిపోలచె	ర్ల శీమ	లోని రేమానను శ్రీచె
7.	రువు కట్టించినందుకు దసబధం	నడ	పినందుకుపడుమటికట్ట
8.	. . . . . స్తిమిగనుక అందు .	. .	. గానున్న అనభ
9.			వించ్చినాను వారు .
10.			గాన డావు.

1. చ్చలచె . .
2. దించ్చి బ్రతుకు . .

* The letters between these lines are not clear.

3. శిలాంను గోవుబ్రా . .

4. వారు । శ్రీ

KANIGIRI (10). (A.D. 1377–78.)

[Guruvájipéṭa. Telugu. From a stone in front of Chennakéṣavasvámi temple.]

TRANSLATION.

Hail! On Sunday, the 15th day of the bright fortnight of Áshádha in the year Pingaḷa, corresponding to the year 1299 of the illustrious, victorious and prosperous Ṣaliváhaua era, while Ṣríman Mahámanḍaléṣvara, Ṣrí Víra Hari-Hara Maháráyaḍu, Ariráyaganḍa,[1] Basagetappuvaráyaraganḍa,[2] Purva-paschima samudra madhya éka chatrádhipati,[3] Rájádhirája, Rájaparaméṣvara, Kaliyuga Vishnu,[4] the protector of religion, the performer of gifts of food, elephants, girls, land, cows (and other gifts prescribed by Hemádri), the favourite of Lakshmi and the goddess of victory, the worshipper of the divine lotus feet of Ṣrí Virúpákshadéva, the student of the six systems of philosophy, and who is devoted to his spiritual preceptor, [while he] was ruling the kingdom of the earth at Vijayanagar, which is the crest-jewel of virtue, which is an ocean of virtue, which is the southern Benares of the illustrious modern Jambudvîpa . . . .

---

[1] The disgracer of hostile kings.

[2] The disgracer of kings who break their word.

[3] The supreme ruler of the country between the eastern and western oceans (literally having the country between these oceans under his sole umbrella).

[4] Vishnu of the Kaliyuga.

with great pleasure and with delight in holding friendly communications (with his feudatories ?) ; Dérnávúri Koladula Bálináyanimgáru who was ruling over Boyavindlu in Udayagiri *sthala*, bestowed land as follows on Mallikárjunadéva for the religious merit of his parents ; 16 *puṭṭis* of land in Manuvupáḍu. . . . . 5. This endowment of land to the deity should be maintained as long as the sun and moon exist.

[One imprecatory verse.]

May there be great prosperity !

First side.

1. స్వస్తి శ్రీ జయా
2. భ్యుదయ శాలి
3. వాహానశక వర్షంబులు
4. ౧౨౯౯ అగునె
5. టి పింగ్గల సంవత్స
6. ర ఆషాడ శు ౧౫ లు
7. స్వస్తి శ్రీ మన్మహామ
8. ండలేశ్వర అరిరాయ
9. గండ బాసగ త
10. ప్పువరాయరగం
11. డ పూర్వ్వ పశ్చిమ ద
12. క్షిణ సముద్ర మ
13. ధ్య మేకచ్ఛత్రాధి
14. పతి రాజాధిరా
15. జ రాజపరమేశ్వర
16. కలియుగ విష్ణు
17. ణు ధర్మ ప్రతిప్రా
18. లక అన్నదాన
19. గజదాన కన్యా

20. దాన భూ ధాన
21. గోదాన హేమా
(శ్రీ దాన) . . .

Second side.

1. శలు హెూ ౧
2. త్క్ర్యు జయల
3. త్క్ర్మ ప్రసన్న దండ
4. శ్రీ విరూపాక్ష
5. దేవ దివ్య శ్రీ
6. పాదపద్మో
7. రాదక షడు
8. దశకాన సమాన
9. తా గురుభక్త
10. వత్సల శ్రీవీర
11. హరిహర మ
12. హారాయండు
13. శ్రీమదభినవ
14. జంబుద్వీప ద
15. క్షిణవారాణ
16. సినిమాల ధర్మా
17. ంబుధి ధర్మా సిఖా
18. మణిమైన వి
19. జయా నగరమం
20. దు అ . . . ము .
21. ప్రీ తిని సు ఖ సం
22. కథావినోదమునం

Third side.

1. ప్రిథి విరాజ్యంబు
2. (చేయుచు)నుం దాను

3. ఉదయగిరి స్థళ
4. బోయ విండ్లలో దే
5. ణ్ణాం పురు కొలదు
6. లంబాలినాయ్నిం
7. గారు ఏలుచుం
8. డి తమ తల్లికా
9. ద్రులకుం బుణ్యా
10. ముగాను మల్లికా
11. ర్జునదేవరకుం వె
12. ట్టిన ప్రవృత్తిచేను మణు
13. వుపాటి ఖ ౧౬ కామ
14. . . . వరకు
15. . . . . .

Fourth side.

1. . ౫ యా
2. దేవప్రవిత్తు
3. లు ఆచం
4. ద్రాకర్ణ స్థాయి
5. గాను చెల్లి
6. ంచె డి॥ స్వద
7. త్తా ద్విగుణ
8. ం పుణ్యం ప
9. రదత్తాను
10. పాలనం పర
11. దత్తాపహా
12. రేణ స్వదత్తం
13. నిష్ఫలం భవే
14. త్ । మంగళమ
15. హా శ్రీ శ్రీ శ్రీ.

KANIGIRI (11). (A.D. 1254-55.)

[Kambhampáḍu. Telugu. On fallen stone to south of village.]

TRANSLATION.

Hail ! On Wednesday the fifth of the bright fortnight of Chaitra of the year Ánanda, corresponding to the illustrious and auspicious Ṣaka year 1176, hail ! While Ṣríman Mahámanḍaléṣvara Ganḍa . . . . . yadéva Chóḍa Mahárájulu on whose lotus feet the eyes of Trilóchana and all other kings of the earth are set and who is an elephant-goad to (wicked) princes, was reigning over Nellúru . . . . in Pákanáḍu . . . . Ṣríman Mahámanḍaléṣvara Pótayadéva Chóḍa Mahárájulu, on the occasion of Vishuma Sankránti . . . presented . . . Drotapati . . . . for providing decorations, . . . daily offerings . . . . Késavadéva . . . to last as long as the sun and moon endure . . . . Those who violate this charity will incur the sin of killing . . . . near the Ganges.

[Two imprecatory verses.]

Third side.

Ṣrímat Kamabóyiḍu . . . . at Brahmatírtham . . . . caused this temple to be constructed and founded these *vrittis*.

First side.

1. స్వస్తిశ్రీ శుభ శక వరుషంబు
2. ౧౧౭౬ గు నేంటి ఆనంద సంవత్సర చై
3. త్రశుద్ధ ౫ బుధవారమునాండు స్వస్తి

4. చరణసరోరుహ విహిత (విలోచన)
5. త్రిలోచనప్రముఖా (ఖిలప్రిదివీశ్వ)
6. రకుమారాంకుశ (శ్రీమన్మహామ)
7. ండలేశ్వరంగండ (. . . . .)
8. యదేవచోడ మహారాజులు పా
9. కనాంట్టిలోని నెలూరు . రాజ .

Second side.

1. . . . (స్వదత్తా ద్విగుణం పుణ్యం.)
2. (స్వదత్త ద్విగుణంపుణ్యం) పరదత్తాను పాలయతు పర దత్తాపహా
3. రేణస్వదత్తం నిష్ఫలంభవేతు॥ స్వదత్తం పర
4. దత్తం వాయోహరేతి వసుంధరా షష్టివర్ష
5. ష సహస్రాణి విష్టాయాం జాయ
6. తెక్రిమిః॥
7. నిగరాజ్యము సేయుచుండగాం ద
8. త్తాదోవదొషాశ్రుతుండైన శ్రీమ
9. న్మహామండలేశ్వర పొతయ దే
10. వచోడ మహారాజులు విషువ
11. సంక్రాంతి నిమిత్యంబుత్రోమస్మ స
12. . . . బ . న కేశవ దేవరకు వంగ
13. . . . రని వేద్యాంబుఃకు ద్రోతపోట
14. . . . . . . (జబునుం) బట్టి . అ . లు
15. . . . . అచంద్రార్క
16. . . . . వారుగంగ క
17. . . . . జంపినవారు . . వద

Third side.

(1) శ్రీమతు

(2) కమబోఇ

(3) డు దేపరును
(4) వారి పెండవా
(5) బ్రంహ్మ.దీర్ఘం వి
(6) పాళవసులికి
(7) ంతుఖు పెరి
(8) యవిరుదివి
(9) ఇగుడి గట్టి
(10) ంచిఇవ్రి త్తి
(11) వడశినవారు
(12) తు॥

KANIGIRI (12).

[Kánchipuram (*alias* Kámanchipuram). Telugu. To the north in a field. On four sides of stone.]

TRANSLATION.

Hail! On Thursday the 15th of the bright fortnight of . . . . the illustrious year Rákshasa . . . on the auspicious occasion of (Vyatípáta[1]) for the religious merit of Mangiruvaráju (read Mangi Yuvaráju?) Sankidévaráju Gáru . . . field.

Second side.

. . . . on the 15th of the bright fortnight of Áshádha of the year . . . .

Third side.

(Illegible.)

Fourth side.

(Imprecatory verse.)

NOTE.—The king we cannot identify.

---

[1] V yatipáta—a kind of astronomical yoga (or conjunction).

First side.

1. స్వస్తి శ్రీమతు
2. రాతుసంవ్వత్సర . . .
3. . . శు ౧౫ గువారాన
4. (వ్యతీపాత) పున్యకాలమ
5. ందు మంగిరువరాజుం
6. సంకిదేవరాజుం గారికి
7. ధర్మంగాను . . మగ్రస . .
8. . . లి . . . పురి
9. . . . . . చెను . .
10. . . వారము . . .
11. . . . .

Second side.

1. . లు సంత్సర ఆ
2. షాఢ శు ౧౫ . . . .
3. . . . . .
4. . . . .
5. . . త్తినేనింగారు
6. మూంకు . . .
7. . శము నేనిరోగ
8. . . లి గానుమ
9. మ . నింగాలు . .
10. . . . .
12. . . . .

Third side.

1. . . . .
2. . రు . . . . . .
3. . . . .

4. . . . . టి కుం
5. . . . .
6. . . . .
7. . . . . బు . . .
8. . . నా . . . . .
9. . . లిసె . . . .
10. . . ౕ ం . . .
11. . . సుందరాక . . .
12. . . . .
13. . . ణుండు . . .
14. . . సాం . . . .
15. . . . .

Fourth side.

1. స్వదత్తాద్విగుణం పుణ్యం
2. పరదత్తానుపాలనం
3. పరదత్తాప హారేణ
4. స్వదత్తం నిష్ఫలం భవేతు.

KANIGIRI (13).

[Kanigiri. Telugu. On a rock near the pool. Reading and translation doubtful.]

TRANSLATION.

Hari Náráyana! Ṣrí Hanumanta!

Hari-Hari! Ánanḍá Síladáyinénni Reḍḍi son of Dáḍim Reḍḍi made obeisance to Hanumantadéva of Dósapáḍu who took compassion on him and saved him from peril.

1. హరినారాయణ శ్రీ అనుమంతా హరి
2. హరిదాసపాదమతితము హనుమద్దేవ
3. రుం కటాక్షించి కరుణంచేత ఒప్పునట్లు దాడింరె
4. డ్డి పుత్రుండు అనంతా శీల దాయినేంని రెడ్డి
5. దానే అవదకాంచి రక్షించెట్టి పెట్టినట్టి
6. దండములు

Kanigiri (14).

[Kaṭṭakindipalli. From stone in front of Mahálakshmi temple.]

Translation.

On Monday, the 5th day of the bright fortnight of Kártika of the year Yuva, we have given with libation of water to Késavanátha of Polichela 16 *túms* of paddy field near the tank bund (?) of Paidipáḍu, which was formerly in his enjoyment, and dry land, to be enjoyed by sons and grandsons in succession as long as the sun and moon exist. Those who fail to keep up this charity will incur the sin of killing cows and Bráhmans near the Ganges. He should give . . . . 2 *na*(*túms*) on every *puṭṭi*.

1. యువసంవత్సర కా
2. తికశు ౫ సో. పొలిచె
3. ల కేశవనాంతనికి పూర్వాన పె
4. డిన వరిమడి మోడలిక
5. టస్థళం పైడిపాటిఖ ।।। ౧
6. వరి మడిన్ని వెలిచేను
7. ఆచంద్రార్కముగా
8. ను పుత్రపౌత్రకంగాను
9. ధారి దారాపూర్వ

10. కంగాను దారవో
11. సి యిస్తిమి యిందు
12. కుయవ్యళ్లు తప్పి
13. నాను గంగకలుత
14. గోబ్రాంహ్మణి చ.పి
15. న పాపానం పోవు
16. వారు ఖంకి నె ౘ డు
17. పెట్టువాను.

KANIGIRI (15). (A.D. 1579–80.)

[Kuṭṭakindipalli. Telugu. From stone in front Hanumán's temple.]

TRANSLATION.

May there be no impediment!

Ṣrí Róma!

Hail! On the 11th of the dark fortnight of Áshádha of the year Pramádi, corresponding to 1501 of the illustrious, victorious, and prosperous Ṣáliváhana Ṣaka era, while Ṣrímad Rájádhirája, Rájaparaméṣvara, Ṣrí Víra Pratápa Ṣrí Rangaráyadéva Maháráyulu was ruling the kingdom of the earth at the town of Penugonḍa, Chennapa Náyanimgáru, descendant of the Iniyála *gótra*, son of Varadi Náyanimgáru, and grandson of Dámera Dharmá Náyanimgáru, made endless salutations to the illustrious lotus feet of Ṣrímat Akhilánḍakóṭi Brahmánḍa Náyaka,[1] Véda Védánta Védya Purána Purushóttama,[2] Chennaráya (deity) of Pólicherla and granted a charitable edict. On

---

[1] The ruler of all the crores of universes.

[2] The primeval Supreme Soul who is knowable by the Védás and the Védánta.

this holy occasion, on this day we have given with libation of water 3 *puṭṭis* of land in the village of Pólicherla and the hamlets attached to it, in the *ṣíma* of Kanigiri-Pólicherla which was given to us for our chiefdom by Veligóṭi Rangapa Náyanimgáru, for service to the deity and worship on the five *parvas*.[1] Those who obstruct this will incur the sin of killing their parents, cows and Bráhmana on the banks of the Ganges.

[Imprecatory verse.]

The northern flight of steps of the temple of the illustrious Ṣrí Chennaráya.

First side.

1. అవిఘ్నమస్తు॥ శ్రీరామా
2. స్వస్తి శ్రీ జయాభ్యుదయ శా
3. లివాహన శకవర్షంబులు
4. ౧౫౦౧ అగు నేటి ప్రమాది సంవత్స
5. ర ఆషాఢ బ ౧౧ లు¦ శ్రీమదఖి
6. లాండకోటి బ్రంహ్మాండనాయ
7. కులైన వేద వేదాంతవేద్యులైన పు
8. రాణ పురుషోత్తములైన పోలి
9. చెర్ల చన్నరాయని దివ్య శ్రీపాద
10. పద్మాలకు శ్రీమద్రాజాధి

Second side.

11. రాజ రాజపరమేశ్వర వీరప్రతా
12. ప శ్రీ వీర శ్రీరంగ్గరాయదేవ
13. మహారాయలుగారు పెనుగొ
14. ండ పట్ణమందు పృథివిసాంబ్రా

---

1 The full moon day, the new moon day, the first day of the solar month and the 8th and 14th days of the dark fortnight are the five *parvas*.

15. జ్యం చేయుచుండ్డగాను యిణి
16. యాల గోత్రపవిత్రులైన దామె
17. ర ధర్మనాయనింగారి పౌత్రు
18. లున్ను. వరదానాయనింగారి పుత్రు
19. లున్ను అయిన చన్నప్ప నాయనింగా

Third side.

20. రు అనంతములైన దండములు స
21. మర్పించ్చి యిచ్చిన ధర్మశాస
22. నం। వెలిగోటి రంగపనాయనిగా
23. రు మా నాయంకరానకు పా
24. లించియిచ్చిన కనగిరి పో
25. లిచర్ల శీమలోను పోలిచెర్ల
26. గామానన్ను ఆ గ్రామానకు
27. లోనైన పల్లెనున్ను సాగివచ్చేట
28. ట్టు లం ఖ 3 స్వామిధాన్య

Fourth side.

29. ములకున్ను పంచపర్వాలకు
30. న్ను యీ తథాతిథి పుణ్యకాలమం
31. దు ధారవోసి యిస్తిమి యిది
32. యెవ్వరు దప్పినాను దమ తల్లిదండ్రుల
33. ని గోబ్రాంహ్మల గంగానుచరియంద
34. వధియించిన పాపానం బోవువారు। దా
35. నపాలనయోర్మధ్యే దానాచ్ఛేయో
36. నుపాలనం దానాత్స్వర్గమవా
37. ప్నోతి పాలనాదచ్యుతం ప
38. దం। సం శ్రీ శ్రీ చన్నరాయని
39. దెవళానకు వుత్తరపడి కట్టు.

Kanigiri (16). (A.D. 1657–58.)

[Kúṭaguṇḍla. Telugu. Opposite Niruvagopálasvámi temple.]

Translation.

Hail! On the 5th of the bright fortnight of Ashádha of the year Hémaḷambi (Héviḷambi) corresponding to the year 1579 of the illustrious, victorious, and prosperous Ṣálivahana Ṣaka era, Péráreḍḍi, Jangam Reḍḍi, Koṇḍá Reḍḍi, Peda Vengana, Timmá Reḍḍi and China Vengana Gáru, descendants of the Yipparla *gótra*, sons of Lakshmi Reḍḍi, and grandsons of Yérva Koṇḍá Reḍḍi, got the ruined temple of Níruva Gopálasvámi built in stone and dedicated this charity to the deity.

We have given Paṭṭa Paḍamara (?) to Yérva Vengana Gopálasvámi under the orders of Rájaṣrí Viṭhój Pantulu Gáru.

Note.—This official Viṭhoji Pantulu is not mentioned elsewhere in the inscriptions.

1. స్వస్తిశ్రీ జయాభ్యుదయ (యశా)
2. ః వాహన శక (వరుషం)
3. బుఌ ౧౫౭౯ అగు నేంటి
4. హేమళంబి సంవత్సర ఆ
5. షాఢ శు ౫ లు యిప్పర్ల గోత్రో
6. ద్భవులైన యేర్వ కొండా రెడ్డి
7. పవుత్రులును లఛ్మి రెడ్డి పుత్రు
8. లునైన పేరా రెడి । జంగ్గం రెడ్డి । కొండా
9. రెడ్డి పెద వెంగన తింమ్మా రెడ్డి । చిన
10. వెంగనగారు నీరువ గోపాలస్వామికి
11. ఖిలపడ్డ దేవళం శిళా దేవళంగా శేయిం
12. చ్చి యీధర్మం స్వామికి సమ
13. ర్పించిరి.

Second side.

1. రాజశ్రీ విరో౯జి పం
2. తులుగారి ఆనతిని హేఁర్వ
3. వెంకన గో౯పాలస్వామి
4. పట్టపసమగచే
5. ఇంచి సమప్పి౯స్తిమి

KANIGIRI (17). (A.D. 1535-36.)

[Márella. Telugu. In front of Vénugopálasvámi temple.]

TRANSLATION.

Hail! On Sunday the 14th of the dark fortnight of Mágha of the year Manmatha, corresponding to the Ṣrí Ṣaka year 1457, on the holy occasion of Mahá Ṣivarátri, Ṣrímat Venkaṭádri Ayyaváru granted this charitable edict to Jívaraksha Bhaṭṭu Nandi Ráju. We have given you as a Bhaṭa (personal) Agrahára the village of Cheruvupalli which is in the *ṣíma* of Kanagiri which is attached to Udayagiri which is ruled by me and which (village) was formerly enjoyed by you, for the religious merit of Rámabhaṭlayyaváru. May you, your sons, and grandsons in succession enjoy it in peace. Whoever obstructs this charity will incur the sin of killing a cow and a Brahman and his parents at Benares.

[One imprecatory verse.]

Whoever violates this will be regarded as having sucked the yard of a donkey.

1. స్వస్తిశ్రీ శకవర్షంబులు ౧౪౫౭ అగు నేటికి మ
2. న్మథసంవత్సరమాఘ బ ౧౪ (వ) ఆ . . నమహా శివ
రాత్రిపుణ్య
3. కాలమందును శ్రీమతు వెంకటాద్రిఅయ్యవారు జీవరక్ష భ
4. ట్లునంద్దిరాజుకు యిచ్చిన ధర్మశాసనం మేము వేలివుద
యగి
5. రికిం జెలివచ్చి కనగిరికిం జెల్లిపచ్చిన సీమలోను నీకు పూ
ర్వానహ
6. గివచ్చె చెరువుపల్లి అని గ్రామం రామా భట్ల అయ్యవా
రికిపుణ్యాం
7. గానునీకు భటగ్రహారంగాను మేమును యిస్తిమిగాన నీ
8. పుత్రపవుత్ర పారంపరియంగాను అనుభవించి బ్రతుకు
9. వాండవు యీ ధర్మానకు యవ్వరుతప్పినాను నా బహ
10. నితమతల్లిదండ్రిని వారణాసిలోం జంప్పిన పాపానం
బోవువాంహు.
11. స్వదత్తాద్విగుణంపుణ్యాం పరదత్తానుపాలనాం పరదత్తా
12. పహారేణ స్వదత్తానిష్ఫలం భవేతు॥ యిందుకు
13. దప్పినవారు గాడిద శాప్నం కుడిచెనవారు.

KANIGIRI (18.)

[Márelḷa. Telugu. In field to east.]

TRANSLATION.

On the 10th of the bright fortnight of Kártika of the year Ṣukla, Kóḍamagúḷa Peddi Ráju and Chiṭṭe Mandári Guṇḍu . . . .

1. కోడమగూళ పెద్దిరాజు చిట్టెమందారి గుండు
2. శుక్ల సంవత్సర కార్తిక శు ౧౦ .

Kanigiri (19).

[Mârel̤l̤a Telugu. On southern boundary. Illegible for the most part.]

First side.

1. స్వస్తిశ్రీ శకవరుషంబులు
2. . . . . . . సంవత్సర
3. . . . . . . పర . . . . రిజ
4. . . స్వస్తిశ్రీ అనేకదే . .
5. గాజాధి రాజప
6. రపరమ . . ద్ర
7. తిలక నార . జ
8. ష్ట చంద్రఘర ఖట్వా
9. మును . . .
10. తిరు వెంగడన . ది
11. దక కాంచిపుర వరా
12. బికాలబ్బ పర ప్రసా
13. . . . . రక్షు
14. శరణ . . నార .
15. మరకుతీర్థ . . . కవి
16. కులఘటిత చరణకం
17. పుణ్యార ఖర శ్రీ
18. . . కలతక కూతప్రతి
19. కరుద్రకామవైరి
20. . వ్యాగపిప్టీశ్వర
21. . ర్థ శ్రీ త్రిపరాంత

* * * *

Second side.

1. వ ప్ర . .
2. ర . . .
3. రి దే . వన
4. . . వరస .
5. . . .
6. . ర . మాళ్ల
7. . తు . .
8. . ద . . .
9. విక్రయ
10. . . వనము
11. . . . శక
12. . . . .
13. . . . చ
14. . . త్తును
15. . . . .

KANIGIRI (20). (A.D. 1554–55.)

[Márella. Telugu. In front of Vénugópálasvámi temple.]

TRANSLATION.

While Ṣríman Mahárájádhirája Rájaparaméṣvara Ṣrí Sadáṣivaráyadéva Mahárája was ruling the world, on Thursday the 13th of the bright fortnight of Mágha in the year Ánanda corresponding to the year 1476 of the Ṣrí Ṣaka era, Manggaḷa Timmóju Koṇḍójugáru, having done service to Ṣríman Mahámaṇḍaléṣvara Rámaráju Rámayya Déva Mahárájn and having made a request to the king, obtained a royal decree exempting the barbers from the payment of *kaṭṭa méras*,[1] *kóru* tax,[2] *kánike*,[3] *khaḍḍáyam* and *veṭṭi* tax[4] and such taxes throughout the kingdom and set up inscriptions in famous places and set up a stone inscription at Máreḷḷa also. Accordingly the kings who rule over the Kanagiri-Pólacharla *ṣíma* should remit taxes on the barbers. Whoever transgresses this will be considered to have harmed cows and Brahmans on (the banks of the) Ganges.

Ṣrí. Ṣrí. Ṣrí.

Perpetual devotion.

NOTE.—There are several inscriptions of the same sort granting special concessions to barbers.

1. స్వస్తి శ్రీ శకవర్షంబు
2. లు ౧౪౭౬ అగునేంటి ఆ
3. నంద సంవత్సర మాఘ శు
4. ౧౩ గు న శ్రీమన్ మహారాజా
5. ధిరాజ రాజపరమేశ్వర శ్రీ సదా
6. శివరాయదేవ మహారాజులు పృ
7. ధ్వి సామ్రాజ్యం సేయంగాను శ్రీమన్
8. మహా మండలేశ్వర రామరాజు రామ
9. య్య దేవమహారాజులకు వ్రాడికం సే
10. సి మంగళ తింమ్మోజు కొండోజుగా
11. రు రాయలకు మనివి విన్నపం సేసుకొని
12. రామరాజ్యాన నల్లాను మంగళవారికి కట్టమేరలా
13. కోరుపంన్ను కానికె ఖడాయం వెట్టి ఆటిపంన్ను

---

[1] This may mean merely the fixed *méras*.

[2] Perhaps means merely the share of produce usually paid as assessment to the State.

[3] Kánuka according to Brown is a gift to a superior, a sort of 'benevolence'. *Khaḍḍáyam* according to the same authority is compulsory purchase of goods at an exorbitant rate.

[4] A tax for the support of the village *veṭṭi*.

14. శేకుండాను రాయశాసనం పుచ్చుకొని ప్రసి
15. ద్ధిస్థలాలను శాసనాలు వేఇంస్తున్న మా రెళ్ల
16. నున్న సిలాశాసనం వేఇంచ్చిరి గనుక కనగి
17. రి పొలచల్లగ సీమయేలిరాజులున్న యీ
18. క్రమాన్యం మంగ్గళ్ల పంన్న మాని నడుపుకొ
19. నిది యింద్దుకు యపరుదప్పినాను
20. గంగ్గకత్తగ గోబ్రంహ్మల తప్పి
21. నవారు శ్రీ శ్రీ శ్రీ
22. సదాసేవా

Kanigiri (21). (A.D. 1554–55 ?)

[Másáyapéṭa. Telugu. South of village on fallen stone.]

Translation.

Hail! On the 15th of the bright fortnight of Márgaṣira, corresponding to the year 1476 of the illustrious, victorious, and prosperous Ṣáliváhana Ṣaka era, on the holy occasion of a lunar eclipse, the charitable edict setting forth the lands given by Kanṭibóyina Peda Koṇḍama Nenḍu to Nambi Rámanna. We have given one *kucchala* of land in the *sthalam* presented by Íḍiga Náganna to the east of the village in Uppunútu village, which is in our enjoyment, for the religious merit of Veligóṭi Kumára Timmánáyaḍu and Lingamakka Gáru. Therefore may you, your sons, and grandsons enjoy it and live happily. Whoever violates this will incur the sin of killing a cow and a Brahman on the Ganges.

[One imprecatory verse.]

Ṣrí.

1. స్వస్తి శ్రీ జయాభ్యుదయ శా
2. లివాహన శకవర్షంబులు
3. ౧౫౦౮ అగు నేటి ఆనంద సం మార్గశి
4. ర శు ౧౫ సోమగ్రహణ పుణ్యకాల
5. మందు కంటిబోయిని పెదకొండమ నెందు నంబి
6. రామన్నకు ఇచ్చిన భూదాన ధర్మశాసనములు
7. సాగివచ్చి వుప్పునూతుగ్రామమందు వ్రా
8. రికి తూర్పున యీడిగనాగనబెట్టిన స్థలం కుచ్చ
9. లక్షేత్రం వెలిగోటి కుమారతింమ్మనా
10. యునికొన్ని లింగమకర్తగారికిన్ని పుణ్యంగా
11. ను ఇస్తిమి గాన మీపుత్రపారంపర్యం అను
12. భవించి బ్రతుకువాండ్లు యిందుకు య
13. వ్వరుడప్పినాను గంగ్గకతీర గోబ్రా
14. హణ్ని వధించినపాపానంబోదురు.
15. స్వదత్తా ద్విగుణం పుణ్యం పరదత్తా
16. నుపాలనం పరదత్తాప హారేణ
17. స్వదత్తం నిష్ఫలంభవేత్ ॥ శ్రీ ॥

KANIGIRI (22). (A.D. 1586–87.)

[Másáyapéṭa. Telugu. On wall of Ádinárâyaṇa temple.]

TRANSLATION.

Adoration to Ṣiva! Hail! On Monday the 15th of the bright fortnight of Márgaṣira of the year Vyaya, corresponding to the year 1508 of the illustrious, victorious and prosperous Ṣáliváhana Ṣaka era, Lálukhánuningáru (Lál Khán) presented the village of Uppunútula as a tax-free *agrahâram* to be enjoyed in a single share to

Podila Márkanḍa Sómayájulu, Sadáṣiva Sómayájulu, and Yajnéṣvarachayana Panchágni Díkshitulu for the religious merit of Muhammad Kulipátaṣániṅgáru. The act of piety of Séku Issá (Sheikh Isa). May it last as long as the sun and moon endure.

[One imprecatory verse.]

In the illustrious *ṣíma* of Kanigiri . . .

1. శ్రీ శివ॥ స్వస్తి శ్రీజయాభ్యుదయ శాలివాహన శకవర్షం
బులు ౧౫౦౮ అగునేంటి వ్యయసంవ్వ

2. త్సర మార్గశిర శుద్ధ ౧౫ సో॥ మహమందుకులి పాత
శానింగారికి పుణ్యముగాను లాలఃఖానునింగారు పొదిల

3. మార్కండ సోమయాజులు సదాశివ సోమయాజులు
యజ్ఞేశ్వరచయనపంచాగ్ని దీక్షితులుంగారికి ఉప్ప

4. నూతులగ్రామం ఏకభోగ సర్వమాన్య అగ్రహారంగా
నిచ్చెను ఈ। సేకు ఇస్సాపుణ్యం। ఆ చంద్రార్కస్థాయి.

5. ఏషైవభగినిలోకే సర్వేషామేవభూభుజాం నభోగ్యానకర
గ్రాహ్యా విప్రదత్తావసుంధరా ॥ శ్రీ

6. కనిగిరిసీమలోను.

KANIGIRI (23). (A.D. 1393–94?)

[Mogilicherla. Telugu. On north boundary.]

TRANSLATION.

Hail! On Monday the 7th of the dark fortnight of Kártika of the year Ṣrímukha, corresponding to the Ṣrí Ṣaka year 1896, Ṣrí Víra Déva Oḍayalu, who is the son of Ṣríman Mahá Maṇḍaléṣvara Harirâyarahita, Múrurâyaragaṇḍa,[1] Básakutappuvarâyaragaṇḍa,[2] Ahitarâyámvá

---

[1] The disgracer of the hostile kings and the wicked three kings. *Hariráya* is evidently a mistake for *Ariráya*.

[2] The conqueror of kings who break their word.

[1] . . . . Hinduráyasuratráṇa,[2] Ṣrí Víra Harihara Ráya, caused the tank Dévaráyasamudram to be constructed in the holy place of the Lords of the four worlds . . . . Siddhéṣvara and Mandragiri Ṣrí Óbaladévara for the religious merit of his father Hari-Hara Ráya.

May Dévaráya Oḍayulu, who caused this tank to be constructed, rule the four oceans and reign over the earth, protecting religion in perpetuity as long as the sun and moon endure.

May it cause great prosperity.

NOTE.—The Ṣaka date is clear but is of course a mistake. It should apparently be 1316. The construction of the tank is the son of the Vijayanagar king Harabara II who afterwards ascended the throne as Dévaráya I.

1. స్వస్తి శ్రీ సఖవరుషంబులు
2. ౧౮౯౬ అగు నేంటి శ్రీముక సంవత్స
3. ర కార్తిక బ ౭ సో॥ శ్రీమన్మహా మండ
4. లేశ్వర హరిరాయ రహితమూరురాయ
5. రగండ బాసకుతప్పువరాయరగండ అహి
6. తరాయమాంవా . . . హిందూరాయ సుర
7. త్రాణ శ్రీ వీరహరిహరరాయని కొమారుండు
8. శ్రీ వీరదేవరాయఒడయలు తమతండ్రి హరి
9. హరరాయనికిం బుణ్యముగాను చతుర్భువనాధీ
10. శ్వరసకల . . . య్య సిద్ధేశ్వరుండును మంద్రగిరి
11. శ్రీ ఓబళదేవరస్థానమందు కట్టిన చెర్వుదేవ

Second side.

13. రాయసముద్రం యీ చెర్వు వేయిం
14. చిన దేవరాయఒడయులు చతుస
15. ముద్రాలుం నేలిపరివారుడకు అచంద్రా

[1] . . . of wicked kings.   [2] The Sultan among Hindu kings.

16. కఽస్త్రాహిఁగాను ధర్మము ప్రతిపాఁలకంగాంప్రి
17. ద్వి రాఁజ్యాం చెయ్యఁగలవారు మంగళమహాశ్రీ.

Kanigiri (24). (A.D. 1268–69.)

[Nágalavaram. Telugu. Taken from three sides of a standing stone and from 3 fragments in a field.]

Translation.

Salutation be to Ṣrí Lakshmínáráyaṇa!

[One imprecatory verse.]

Hail! On Thursday the 5th of the bright fortnight of Vaiṣákha of the year Vibhava, corresponding to the year 1190 of the illustrious and auspicious Ṣaka era, Ṣrìman Mahámaṇḍaléṣvara Inu(m?)maḍidéva Mahárája, who is the supreme lord of many kings of kingdoms of the earth, who is the supreme ruler, who is descended from an excellent race, who is the ornament of the Pallava dynasty, who is of the Bháradvája *gótra*, who wears the lovely half moon, whose banner is the club (Ṣiva's weapon), who is the protector of others, whose crest is the bull, who is the lord of Kánchi the best of cities and (the residence) of Vengaḍanátha, who has obtained an excellent boon from the goddess Kámakóṭi, who is an Arjuna in valour, who is the ornament of his servants, who is the asylum of his kinsmen, who is the protector of the world, who is a Bhairava characterized by firmness of character, who is a Kandarpa (cupid) among princes, who is an ocean of liberality, who has established seven hundred Agrabáras to the east of Ṣrí Parvata,[1] who is beautiful, having his

---

[1] Ṣríṣailam.

lotus feet touched by the jewelled diadems of numerous hostile kings, who is the maintainer of the duties of the four castes of the earth, and who is a descendant of the race of Mukkanṭi Káḍuveṭṭi,[1] set up the image of Chenna keṣava Perumál, performed the ceremony of infusing life into it for the religious merit of his father Bhímaráju and his mother Siriyádévi, appointed Perumáḍi Nambi, grandson of Ṣrí Rangabhaṭlu, of the blessed Kásyapa *gótra*, resident of the village Ṣrí Suka which is the support of the world, and who is the worshipper of the lotus feet of Tiruvengaḍa nátha, to perform the worship and gave for worship to the deity 13 *túms* of land as measured with a pole of 22 cubits;

For âmṛitapaḍi (sacred food)	14 *túms*.
For all kinds of decorations in Kákanampáḍu, 1 puṭṭi and	10 *túms*.
In Guḍipáḍu	3 *túms*.
In Rávulakola	3 *túms*.

For kariyamadu (food with vegetables) and flowers two gardens.

For the rice (to be distributed) among the travellers of different countries and for sandal to the God—a piece of land given by Masikáṭṭu Toḍuvu Prolé.

For (keeping) the light—a big plate (ఓంటం) given by Námana Appana.

A gong given by Malluka Kámana.

A bell used at time of offering incense and horns (éka sankalu) and for the abhishékam (anointing of the God) with milk—13 cows given by the royal family (racháváru).

---

[1] or Káḍuveṭṭu.

The following are the *vrittis* (shares) to Brahmans :— (Here follows a long list).

[Three imprecatory verses.]

Fifth side.

. . . . whoever causes obstacles to this charity will incur the sin of killing a tawny cow on the Ganges.

First side.

1. శ్రీ లక్ష్మీనారాయణాయన
2. మః సామాన్యోయం ధర్మ
3. సేతుర్నృపాణాం కాలేకాలే
4. పాలనీయోభవద్భి సర్వా
5. నేతాన్భావినః పార్థివేంద్రాన్ భూ
6. యోభూయో యాచతేరా
7. మచంద్ర ॥ స్వస్తి శ్రీ శుభజాతక
8. శకవరుషంబులు ౧౧౯౦ య
9. గు నేంటి విభవసంవత్సర వైశాఖ శు
10. ద్ధ ౫ గురువారము స్వస్తి అనేక మ
11. హీమండల రాజాధిరాజ ప
12. రమేశ్వర పరమవంశోద్భవ పల్లవ
13. కులతిలక భారద్వాజ గోత్ర
14. లలితార్ధచంద్రధర (ఖట్వా)ంగ్గద్వజక
15. డువాయు పలిపోషణ వ్రిషభ

Second side.

1. లాంచ్యన వెంగడనాథ కాంచ్చిపుర
2. వరాధీశ్వర కామకోట్యంబికా
3. లబ్ద వరప్రసాద నోడువడి సాహ
4. సాజున నిజసేవకాభరణ బంధు
5. జనాశ్రయ జగదగోపాల జలదంకరబై

6. రః కుమారకంద్దప్ప త్ర్యాగసముద్ర
7. శ్రీ పర్వ్వత పూర్వ్వాదిగుభాగ సప్తశతా
8. గ్గ్రహార ప్రతిష్ఠిత అనేక రిపునిపతి
9. మణిమకుట ఘటితచరణారవింద
10. సుందర భూల్లోక చాతుర్వ్వర్ణ్యాశ్ర
11. య ధర్మ్మరక్షణ శ్రీమన్మకంటికా
12. దువెటివంశావతారులైన శ్రీ మన్మహా
13. మండలేశ్వర ఇనుమడిదేవ మహారాజులు
14. తమతండ్రి భీమరాజు తమతల్లి శిరియాదే
15. వికి పుణ్యముగాను చెన్న కేశవపెరుమా
16. ళు తిరుప్రతిష్ఠ తిరుమూట్టము కళాం
17. శ నిర్వ్వాహము శేసి ॥ జయంత్రి జగదా
18. ధార శ్రీ శుకగ్రామవాసినాం తిరు
19. వెంగడనాథక్ష్యా పాదపంకజా (దారకం)
20. కాశ్యపగోత్రం శ్రీరంగభట్ల మనుమండు
21. పెరుమాడినంబిని తిరువారాధన శేయం
22. బెట్టిదేవరకు అర్చ్చనభోగమునకు చే
23. ను ఇరువైరెండు మూరలకోలను న ౧౩ అము
21. దుపడికెన ౧౮ అంగరంగభోగానకు కంక
25. సముపాటను ఖ ౧ న ౧౦ గుడిపాటను న ౩ రా
26. వులకోలననున ౩ కరియముచునకూను పూ
27. వుఃకును[1]తోటలు ౨ । జరగు ఉభయనా
28. నాదేశియేవి అముపడిసాతుపడ్లకు మ
29. సికట్టు తోడువుప్రోలె ఇచ్చిన పెంటియ
30. దీపానకు నామనప్పన మాడపల్లిరము
31. మల్లికకామన ఇచ్చినది జేఘంటరాచ
32. వారి ఇవి ధూపఘంట యేకసంకులు
33. దిప్యదారకును గోవులు ౧౩

[1] పు for వు.

Third side.

1. శ్రీ బ్రాహ్మణవ్రిత్తులు ఆపస్తంభయజు
2. సాఖ గౌతమగోత్రం బొల్లెమంచన
3. గారిన ౪ భట్టైనపెద్దిన ౬ బైయ్యేన
4. పెద్దిన ౨ నామన అప్పనన ౭ ప్రోవెమాల
5. చెన ౬ బట్టైన అప్పనన ౩ గంగప్రోలేపు
6. ట్టిసాకునిన ౩ ॥ పిన్నైన ౧ కాశ్యపగో
7. త్రిం మాశెపెద్ది నూహారితగోత్రం గరగన
8. పెద్దిన ౧ కౌండింధగోత్ర మారపెద్దిన ౧ ॥ పై
9. సెన మారపెద్దిన ॥ శ్రీవత్సగోత్రం బయ్యానమం
10. చిన ౧ కౌశికగోత్రం మార్తాండ మంచిగా .
11. . కీశిపెద్దిన ౬ వెంన్నెమంచెన ౮ చెంనిన
12. న ౩ గోవిందపింన్నిన ౩ ప్రోలె అప్పనన ౩
13. ఆంగిరస భారద్వాజగోత్రం విప్రె అ
14. ప్పనన ౬ బైయ్యాన పెద్దిన ౮ కౌశిక
15. గోత్రం మైలార అప్పనన ౪ నందిపెద్ది
16. న ౩ జన్నె అప్పనన ౩ ఆదిత్యమంచేన ౩
17. కౌండిందగోత్రం ప్రోలెపెద్దిన ౪ పోచె పె
18. ద్దిన ౮ ఆదిత్య అప్పనన ౨ శ్రీధర మంచిన ౨
19. గౌతమగోత్రం పోతిపెద్దిన ౩ నారాణ పె

Fourth side.

1. దిన ౩ । భారద్వాజగోత్రం మాధవపెద్ది
2. ౮ అఖిత అప్పనన ౩ శ్రీవత్సగోత్రంపెరు
3. మాడి పెదిన ౪ శౌనకగోత్రం కీశ్చికె
4. చెన ౩ హారితగోత్రంబోయన పెద్దిన ౨ ॥
5. బారద్వాజగోత్ర బ్రమనపెద్దిన ౪ ।
6. కౌశిక పెద్దిన ౨ పెరుమాడి అప్పనన ౩ ॥

7. . . ఎజశాఖ ఆత్రియగోత్ర బాచెనపె
8. దిన ౨ త్రిపురెమాచిన ౫ పాలెకూచిన ౫
9. పినబాచన అప్పన ౪ ॥ కాశ్యపగోత్రం
10. పోచన అప్పనన ౪ పాలెమంచిన ౨ ॥ కొ
11. ణ్డున పెదిన ౨ బారద్వాజగోత్రం సూర
12. అప్పనన ౨ ఆపస్తంబశాఖ కొండింద
13. గోత్ర పఱపోత ఉపాధ్యాలున ౨ శివ
14. అప్పన ౨ మల్లిమంచిన ౨ మాచికూ
15. చిన ౨ భారద్వాజగోత్రం గంగిపెదిన ౩
16. శ్రీవత్సగోత్రం దోనె అప్పనన ౧ ॥ ఆత్రియగో
17. త్రం మారపెదిన ౪ బారద్వాజగోత్రం వేమ
18. నపెదిన ౨ వైజనాథండున ౧ ॥ మారెపం
19. చ్చిన ౩ కొండిందగోత్రం కొంమనమంచెన ౧ ॥
20. దోనపెదిని తంములునున ౩ ॥ డాసికూచ
21. న ౧ ॥ దామిపెదిన ౩ అల్లాడపెదిన ౧ మా
22. ధవగాపాఖండున ౧ ॥ తులసినల్ల మం
23. చన ౧ ॥ కౌశికగోత్రం తూతకిమల్లిన ౩
24. క్రముగున పక ౨ ॥ కొమ్మన అప్పనన ౧౫ ॥ బై
25. యనపెదిన ౨ నాగులవనము జనార్ద
26. న్న దేవరున ౬ శ్రీవత్సగోత్రం వాసుదేవ
27. పినిన ౭ భారద్వాజగోత్ర నాగదేవ పెదిన ౩
28. స్వదత్తాం ద్విగుణం పుణ్యం పూర్వదత్తాను పాల
29. నం పూర్వదత్తాపహారేణ స్వ(ద)త్తంనిష్ఫలంభవేతు
30. దానాత్పాలనాశ్చైవ దానాశ్చె వోపపా
31. లనాతు దానాస్వర్గ మాప్నోతి పాలనాత్పర
32. మంపదం ॥ స్వదత్తం పరదత్తం వా యోహరే
33. తివసుంధరా షష్టిర్వర్ష సహస్రాణి విష్టాయాం
34. జాయతేక్రిమిం॥

Fifth side.

*   *   *   *

*   *   *   *

*   *   *   *

1. ఇధర్మము
2. నకు యొవరువి
3. ఘ్నము చేసినా
4. ను గంగకఱు
5. తను కవిలం
6. బోడిచినవా
7. డు

KANIGIRI (25).

[Nalajanampádu. Sanskrit and Telugu in ancient character. To north-east of village.]

TRANSLATION.

Hail! Ṣrí Bodirájulu who meditated at the feet of the blessed Arhata the great Bhattáraka, who (Bodirája) was a great devotee of Ṣiva, and who was supreme lord. Among them Bá (Bo?) diráju, son of Paḷeyaru, gave land sowable with 3 *puṭṭis* of seed . . . . to me named Paḷayári. Whoever maintains this will obtain the merit of performing several Aṣvamédhas. Whoever obstructs it will incur the sin of killing at Ṣrí Parvata. (This is) written by Pallaváchá(rya), son of Vá . . . dáḷu.

NOTE.—The transcription was done by Mr. V. Venkayya. Who Bodirája was is not apparent.

(To face page 676.)

KANIGIRI NO. 25.

First side.

1. स्वस्ति भ-
2. गघ्वद् हैता[म्प]-
3. रमभट्टारकस्तमा
4. दानुध्यातपरममा
5. हेश्वर परमेश्वर प-
6. ल्लवादित्य श्रीवेडि-
7. राजुल అన్ను పణ్డె-
8. యరికోడుక బాడి [రా]
9. [జె]న్వాస్తి రాజ . .
10. బు మూాస్తి వుట్టు అఱ్ఱి
11. పట్టు క్షేత్రంబును ప . .
12. సి పళ్ళయారి
13. యనబునాకు ఇచ్చి [ని*]
14. దీని రక్షిఞ్చినవాని .
15. అడుగడుగ-
16. శ్వమేధంబున
17. ఫలంబగు
18. దీ [ని] ఉచ్చిన-
19. వానికి చకలు
20. శ్రీ పర్వ్వతంబు
21. ఉచ్చిన పావం-
22. బగు [॥*] వ . .
23. డాళు కొడుకు
24. పల్లవాచా-
25. [జ్య] స్య[1] లిఖి
26. [తం] [॥*]

---

[1] Read య్యాస్యలిఖి

KANIGIRI (26).

[Nallagandla. Telugu. On figure of Vináyaka under tank bund. Illegible.]

KANIGIRI (27).

[Nandanavanam. Telugu. On image in Mallikárjuna temple. Velagonda hills. The last four lines are in a character unknown to us.]

TRANSLATION.

In the place where Rámasvámi released Gautama's wife from her curse while he marched against Lanka, the deities Maléśvara (? or Amaréṣvara) and Umáranga (? or Mahálinga) were set up . . .

1. రామస్వా
2. మి లంకరకు
3. పాయ్యే
4. టప్పుడు
5. గౌతమి
6. మ ఆ [త్యం] సె
7. శినక్తశం (య or) అ
8. మలే (or రే) శ్వర
9. ప్రతిష్ట
10. వుమారం (or లిం) గ
11. ప్రతిష్ట.

12.
13.
14.
15.

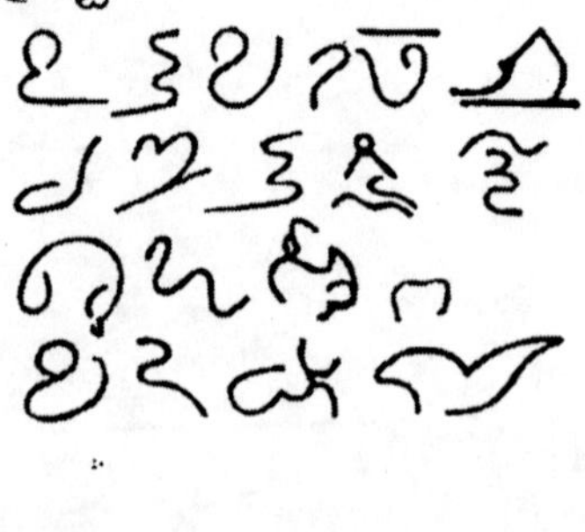

(To face page 678.)

KANIGIRI NO. 27.

(To face page 678.)

KANIGIRI NOS. 27, 29 & 30.

KANIGIRI (28). (A.D. 1785-86.)

[Nandanavanam. Telugu. In village. On doorway of Ánjanéya temple.]

TRANSLATION.

Hail! On the 10th of the bright fortnight of Mágha of the year Viṣvávasu corresponding to the year 1708 of the illustrious, victorious and prosperous Ṣáliváhana Ṣaka era, Sarasi . . Pantulu Váru set up . . in the temple of Hanumantaráyalu. The temple . .

1. స్వస్తి శ్రీ వి
2. జయాభ్యు
3. దయ శాలివా
4. హన శకవర్షం
5. బులు ౧౭౦౮ అగు నేం
6. టి విశ్వావసు
7. నామ సంవ
8. త్సర మాఘ శు
9. ద్ద ౧౦ లు శ్రీహ
10. నుమంత్త రా
11. యులు యుదేవ
12. స్తానం . . సరసి
13. . పంతులవా
14. రు చేయించ్చి
15. న ప్రతిష్ట . . దే
16. వాలయం

KANIGIRI (29).

[Nandanavanam. Telugu. On stone inside Mallikárjunasvámi temple in Velagonda hills. Nothing can be made of the inscription as it contains letters of a peculiar type unknown to us. The only words that can be made out are "Gautama Mahámuni" and "Avadhútasvámi".]

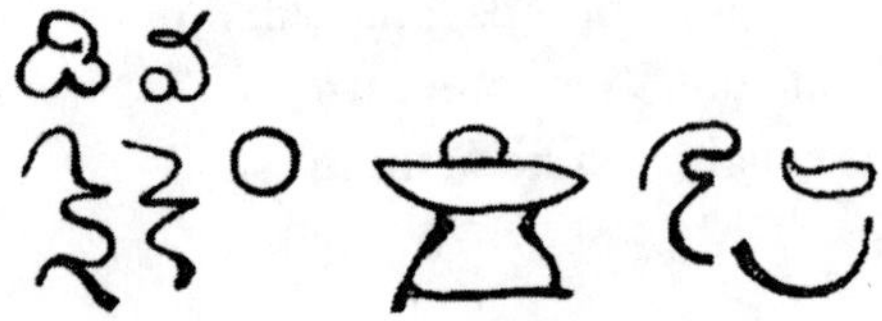

1. గౌతమమహాముని 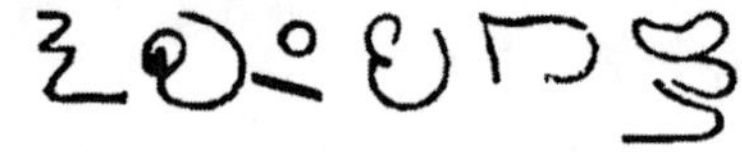

2. రామమహాస్వాముఃవారూ ౪

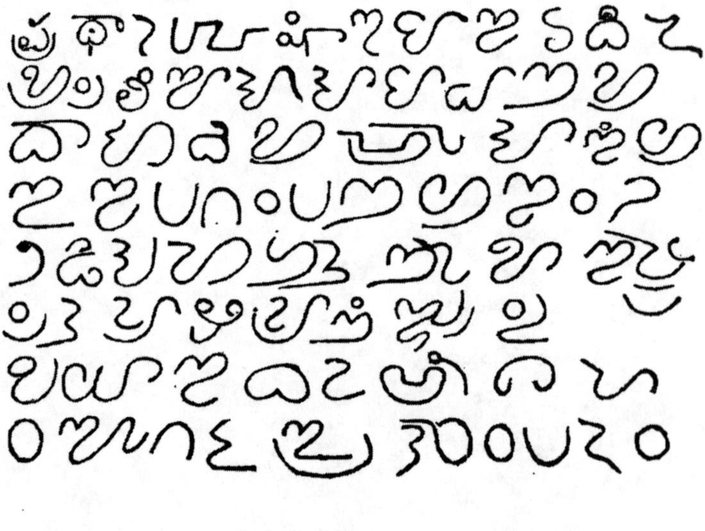

(To face page 680.)

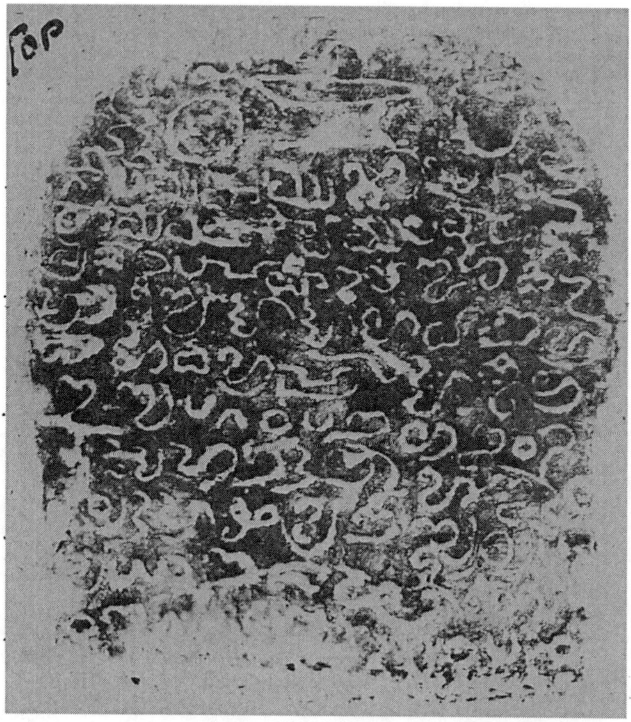

KANIGIRI NO. 29.

(To face page 681.)

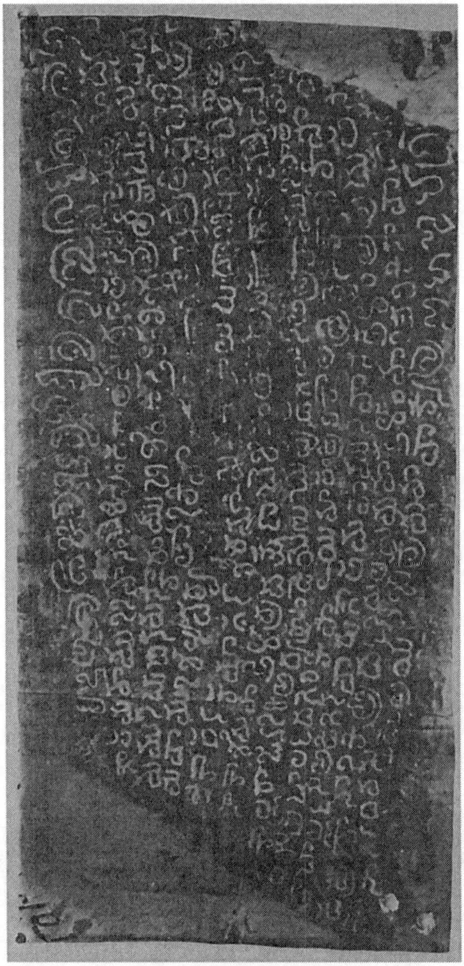

KANIGIRI NO. 30.

KANIGIRI (30).

[Nandanavanam. Telugu. In small tank near Mallikárjunasvámi temple, Velagonḍa hills. The first and last lines contain letters of a type unknown to us. The inscription is incomplete and unintelligible in parts.]

TRANSLATION.

While the great sage Gautama was living (here ?), Avadhútasvámi (came from) Ayódhya, visited and made obeisance to us (and said): "If a *lingam* were established here . . . ." The great sage Gautama went to Ṣalya Parvata (Ṣrí Ṣailam), brought a *linga*, and establishing it there (said that) if Rudrábhishékam were performed in the months of Ṣráváṇa, (Áśvija), Kártika, Márgaṣira and Mágha and (if) a perpetual lamp were maintained, (one would have the merit of) having made a *pradakshanam* (walking round to the right) in the holy place Benares . . . to Lanka. While . . . was superintending and ruling the . . . (?) a kingdom bringing in crores (of rupees) (?), . . . by his father Rámuni having gone to Śukráchárya asked him as follows :—'My father . . . to Benares?' (Thereupon) he said 'This is the abode of the great sage Gautama. Avadhútasvámi (said) that this is a sacred place meet for performing Tirthavidhis (duties at holy places) . . . (He) attained heaven (when this was done). The great word of Śukra.

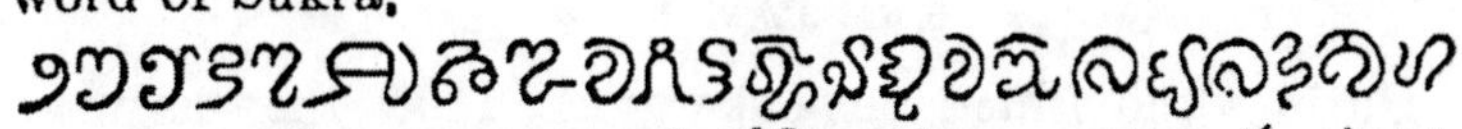

2. గౌతమహామునినివాసంచేశివుండగా అవుదూత స్వామి వారు అయోాద్యను . .

3. మమునిమాచి నమస్కారంముచిశి యీా స్తళం లింగ్గప్రతిష్ట చేస్తె యెమివం . . .

4. మహాముని శల్యపర్వతానికి వారులింగానితెచి ప్రతిష్టచేశి శ్రావ . .

5. జకార్తీక మార్గశిరమాఖమాసాలు రుద్రాభిషేకరం చేశి అఖ (ండ) . .

6. నాకాశిమహాస్తళ ప్రదక్షిణచేశి నంతకులంకకు గౌతమ ముని .

7. కోట్లరాజ్యానికి అద్యక్షుండై యేలుచువుండగ వానితంండ్రి రామునిచాతయేతె

8. ట శుక్రచార్యదగిరికిపోయి మాతంండ్రి లికాలత్రిరెను కాశి కిపోయె (శు)

9. క్రాచార్యను అడిగినవారు గౌతమహాముని వాసస్తళం అవుదూత సా(మివారు) . .

10. దప్రధానానికి త్రిధర్విధులకు మహాస్తళంహాని పలికినా వాడు స . . .

11. మసార్గధివస్తుడు అయను శుక్రమహావాక్య

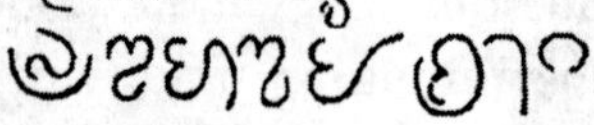

KANIGIRI (31). (A.D. 1184-85 ?)

[Naramárella. Telugu. This stone is now at the Collector's bungalow at Nellore. It bears an armed god or hero and smaller figures, etc. A photograph appears opposite. The inscription is not fully legible.]

TRANSLATION.

During the illustrious Ṣaka year 1106 the master (éliki) of Sankináyaka (gave ?) 50, (?) . . . . (Ba) lakámaḍu the lord of Mannálaváḍu . . . . Sátula

(To face page 682.)

KANIGIRI NO. 31.

Samrōju and Prōlēju (gave) at Gurrālachēnu 2,000 *paṭṭus* of land; Dukirōju (gave) six *maḍis*.

(*Another portion.*)

Balakāmaḍu

Nam Prōlōju field Na (*tūm*) 3.

and at Naḍalōddu one *paṭṭu* of dry land.

Note.—The name of this Balakāmaḍu does not seem to appear elsewhere.

1. శ్రీ శక వర్షంబులు ౧౧౦౬ (అకునేండు)
2. సంకినాయ కుని పలికి ౫౦ యూ(డల . . బ)
3. లకామడు మన్నాలవాడి పతిము (ద్దనల).
4. కర్రసాతు లసంరోజు ప్రోలేజుం (గుఱ్ఱాలచే)
5. లు బట్టుపొలము ౨౦౦౦ దు[కిరో]
6. జానుం యాఱు[మండులాను.]

(*Another portion.*)

1. బలకా
2. మడుసం
3. ప్రోలోజా
4. చేను ౩ న
5. నడలొద్దు
6. నః భూమి
7. ట్ట పట్టు
8. చే ను.
9. ను.

Kanigiri (32).

[Pándavanágalavaram. Telugu. On tank bund.]

Translation.

The perpetual devotion of Koṭiseṭṭi, son of Vákicherla Víriseṭṭi, on Wednesday the 10th of Jyésṭha of the year Sarvadhári.

1. సర్వధారి సంవ్వ
2. త్సర జేష్ట బ ౧౦ భు
3. వాంకిచల్ల వీరిశెట్టి కొమారుడు
4. కోటిశెట్టి నిత్యశేవ.

Kanigiri (33). (A.D. 1526–27 ?)

[Pedda Alavalapád. Telugu. From a rock in the bed of the river.]

Translation.

May there be prosperity ! Hail ! The charitable edict presented by Rápúri Rághava Reḍḍigáru, who has the * *birudas* :—Jaganobba Gaṇḍa,[1] Sangráma Dhannajaya,[2] Hemádridánachintámani,[3] Paṭṭulaláṭaráya,[4] and Basuvasankara,[5] on the holy occasion of a lunar eclipse, on Thursday the 15th of the bright fortnight of Pushya of the illustrious Ṣaka year 1448, for the religious merit of his father Basava Reḍḍi and his mother Amalámbika, after making prostrations and salutations to Lingálakoṇḍa

* *Note.*—These birudas are of the Reḍḍi dynasty with which Rághava Reḍḍi may have been connected.

---

[1] The sole hero of the world.

[2] An Arjuna in battle.

[3] The philosopher's stone of the gifts prescribed by Hémádri (?)

[4] The king whose forehead is adorned with a mark.

[5] Proper name.

Sóméṣvara and Bagádi Ganga. We have presented (the village of) Gangapaṭnam, situated in Kanagiri-Pólacherla-Musumḍúru *ṣíma* which was given for our chiefdom by Konḍa Marusayyangáru for (performing) the sixteen kinds of service to Soméṣvara and Bagádi Ganga. Therefore whoever acts in violation of this charity will incur the sin of killing a cow and a Brahman near the Ganges.

1. శుభమస్తు । స్వస్తి శ్రీ శకవర్షంబులు ౧౪౪౮ అగు

2. నేంటి పుష్యశుద్ధ ౧౫ గురువారమున్ను సోమగ్రహ

3. ణమున్ను అయిన పుణ్యకాలం అందును జగనె[1]

4. బ్బగండ సంగ్రామధనుంజయ । హేమాద్రిదాన

5. చింతామణి పట్టులలాట రాయబసువ శ

6. ంకర బిరుదాంకుండు అయిన రాపురి రాఘవ రెడ్డింగా
రు తమ

7. తండ్రి బస్వరెడ్డింగారికిన్ని తమతల్లిఅమలాంబికకున్ను పు
ణ్యము

8. ఘునట్టుగాను లింగ్గాలకొండ సోమేశ్వరునికిన్ని బగాది
గంగ్గకున్ను

9. సాష్టాంగ్గమున్ను దణ్నముపెట్టి సమర్పించ్చిన ధర్మ
శాసనము

10. కు కొండ మర్సయ్యాంగారు మానాయంకరానకు
ఇచ్చిన కనగిరిపోల

11. చెర్ల ముసుండూసీమలో గంగ్గపట్నం సోమేశ్వరుని
కిన్ని బగాది గ

12. ంగ్గకున్ను సోడసోపచారాలకున్ను సమర్పిస్తిమి గాన
ఇధర్మను ఎ

13. వ్వరు తప్పినాను గంగకత్తర గోవును బ్రాంహ్మణి చం
పిన పాపాన పో

14. వువారు.

---

[1] Read నెబ్బ.

KANIGIRI (34). (A.D. 1409–10.)

[Perugupalli. Telugu. In front of temple on Ranganáyakula hill.]

TRANSLATION.

Hail! On Thursday the 10th of the dark fortnight of Vaiṣákha of the year Viródhi, corresponding to the year 1331 of the illustrious, auspicious and prosperous Ṣaka era, Vammanendu Vennapum Gáru . . . . for the religious merit of Jannapa Náyaḍu . . . . having set up Ṣrí Kaṇṭha Rámésvaradéva of Ṣrí Páléṭikonḍa . . . . presented field . . . . for the deity in perpetuity to last as long as the sun and moon endure . . . Murári Náyani Chennama Náyanimgáru having set up this deity presented him with three *gorrus* of land as a sacred charity. He gave it in perpetuity to last as long as the sun and moon endure. May it cause great prosperity!

1. స్వస్తిశ్రీ శుభకాభ్యుదయ శకవరు
2. షంబులు ౧౩౩౧ అగు నేంటివిరో
3. ధిసంవత్సర వైశాఖ బ ౧౦ గురువా
4. రాన జన్నపనాయనిర్ బుణ్యంగానువమ్మనెం
5. దు వెన్నపుంగారు యీ . . . గెవర్తముదు .
6. పాలేటికొండ శ్రీ కంఠరామేశ్వరదేవర ప్రతిష్ట సేయించి
7. దేవరకుశిప్రు . ౧దుపోల . . . . . జయ .
8. దేవరకుండు చంద్రార్కస్థాయి . . . మురారి
9. నాయిని చెన్నమనాయనింగారు ఇ దేవరను ప్రతిష్ట
10. చెయించి యీ దేవకు తిరుపతిదరుమం కు(మూ)డు గొఱ
11. ల సమర్పించిరి ఆచంద్రార్కసఇతంగాను ఇచ్చిరి
12. మంగళ మహా శ్రీ శ్రీ శ్రీం జేయు.

Kanigiri (35).

[Pólavaram. Telugu. In field to south.]

Translation.

Hail! On Thursday the 15th of the bright fortnight of Mágha of the . . . corresponding to the year . . 6 of the illustrious, victorious, and prosperous Ṣaka era, on the occasion of a lunar eclipse . . .

Second side.

In the field lying to the north of the village *maṇḍapa* for the religious merit of his father Gópináyaningáru he caused a well to be dug, had a water-shed and a temple erected and planted a mango tope, a palmyra tope and a tope of trees yielding all kinds of fruits . . . .

Third side.

. . . . . will incur the sin of killing a cow on the Ganges. May it cause great prosperity!

1. స్వస్తి శ్రీ విజయా
2. భ్యుదయ శకవ
3. రుషంబులు . . . ౬
4. అగు నేంటి సం
5. వత్సరం మాఘ శు
6. ౧౫ గు సోమగ్రహణ
7. కాలమందు . . .
8. . . . . .
9. సము . . .
10. . . . . సా
11. హం . . . . .
12. యకు . . . .

13. జ . . . ససి
14. ణిమా . . .
15. పు . . . క్రిస
16. య . . . . .
17. . రు య . . . .
18. . . . . .
19. ద . . . .
20. ండు . . . యవిళన
21. . త . ను . . .
22. యుం . . .
23. నుచు . . . .

Second side.

1. గ్రామ మంత (ప)
2. పుత్తరపు పో
3. లానను తమ
4. తండ్రి గోపినా
5. థునింగారికిం
6. బుణ్యముగా
7. ను నుయి ద్రవ్వి
8. ంచి చలి మెడీళు
9. నిధర్మ్మణం గుడిం
10. ని పెట్టించి మా
11. మిడి తోపును
12. ను తాటివనము
13. న్ను నానావిధఫల
14. . పాలు పుట్టి . .
15. తులం . . . .
16. . . . . .

17. . . . .
18. . . . .
19. . . . .
20. . . లుకైక్ర
21. . . తలపు
22. . . . .
23 . . . .
24. ను . నుడను
25. డన యొబ్బైయా
26. రు యిచ్చెది.

Third side.

(1) చ్చినాను గంగ్గ కలు
(2) త గోవుంజంపిన పా
(3) పానం బోవు వారు
(4) మంగళ మ
(5) హా శ్రీ శ్రీ శ్రీ
(6) శ్రీ శ్రీ శ్రీ.

KANIGIRI (36). (A.D. ?)

[Punugóḍu. Telugu. From stone in front of Siddhéṣvaraswámi temple.]

TRANSLATION.

Hail! On Friday the 1st of the bright fortnight Ṣrávaṇa of the year Raudri, corresponding to the Ṣrí Ṣaka year 1755834581 [1] Vipaḷam Véja Annapagáru of the family of Malipúṇḍi Aibuḷayyangáru caused to be

[1] The meaning of the date-figures is not understood.

made a thousand *lingas*, consecrated them, and caused to be built a temple. He performed the marriage of Víra-jiyya, son of Tammaḷḷu Mádasivalu; and purchased and presented a field of 10 *Singam*[1] *túms* to the deity. Whoever fails in this will incur the sin of killing a cow near the Ganges. May there be great prosperity!

1. స్వస్తి శ్రీ శకవరు
2. షంబులు ౧౭౫
3. ౫౮౩౪౫౮౧ ఆ
4. గుసేంటి రవుద్రి స
5. ంవత్సర శ్రావణ శు
6. ద్ద ౧ శు । మలిపూం
7. డి ఐబుళయ్యంగా
8. రి విపళంవేజ అంన్న
9. పంగారు వేలింగా
10. ల చేయించ్చి ప్రతిష్ట
11. చేశి గుడిగట్టించి
12. తంమళ్ల మాద శి
13. వులు కొడుకు వీర
14. జయ్యను పెండ్లి చె
15. శను దేవరకు సిం
16. గం పందుము చేను
17. కొని పెటెను యిం
18. దుకు యెవరు తప్పి
19. నాను గంగకరత గో
20. వుం జంపిన పాపా
21. నం బోదురు మంగ
22. ళ మహా శ్రీ శ్రీ శ్రీ

---

[1] Singam is apparently the same as Singampáḍu. The *putti* of that village was probably a standard measure.

Kanigiri (37).

[Rállapalli. Telugu. On a rock to south-east.]

TRANSLATION.

On the full moon day of Mágha of the year Vijaya, Channamanéḍu son of Bíjam Channamanéḍu gave as a *mányam* to Káṣa Koṇḍá Battuḍu a field of one *túm* at the southern extremity of Gollakunṭa in the village of Dúku Nágacheruvupalli for the goddess Gangá.

Whoever violates this (charity) will incur the sin of killing a cow and a Brahman near the Ganges.

1. విజయ సమచ్వర మాఘ శు
2. పవ్రునమీఋ బీజం చన్నమ
3. నేని కుమారుడు చన్నమనేడు
4. దూకు నాగవచెరు ఉపల్లిగ్రామాన
5. గంగాదేవికి గొల్లకుంట దక్షణా
6. కోంస్మన కాశకొండాబత్తి
7. నికి తూమెడు చేను మానెం ఇ
8. చ్చితిమి ఇందుకు యవరు తప్పినా
9. గంగ కతెగ్రో
10. బ్రాంహ్మని చంపిన పా
11. పాన పోదురు.

Kanigiri (38). (A.D. 1517–18?)

[Ṣákhavaram. Telugu. From stone in a field.]

TRANSLATION.

This is the edict issued by Koṇḍamarasayya, after making salutation in favour of the deity Harimskanda-sómésvara[1] of Chunḍḍi, on the 11th day of the dark fort-night of Kártika of the year Īṣvara. We have presented

[1] "Chundi Harimskandasóméṣvara" is probably a misreading for Chundi-puram Skanda Sóméṣvara = Skanda Sóméṣvara of the town of Chunḍi.

to this deity a wet land measuring 120 *gorrus* under the tank of Chávatalampúru [1] and a dry land of . . *gorrus* to last as long as the sun and moon exist. Whoever obstructs this charity will incur the sin of killing a Brahman and a cow on the banks of the Ganges. Ṣri!

1. యీశ్వరసంవత్సర కార్తిక బ౧౧లు చుండ్లి హంశిం సరంద సోమే
2. శ్వరు దెవునికి కొండమరసయ్యంగ్గారు దండం వేటి యిచ్చి
3. న ధర్మశాసనం . . చావతలంపూరు చేరువుకింద్దను వరి
4. మడిగొ ౧౨౦ న్గే(వేలి)చేను యే(. . గొలుసన్నా దేవునికి అ
5. ర్పితము ఆచెందార్కస్తాయిగాను ఇస్తిమి యుత్తే
6. వారిను యెవరు తప్పినా గంగ్గ (కఱుత) బాహ్మణునిగో
7. వును జంప్పిన పాపానపోవువారు శ్రీ.

KANIGIRI (39).

[Tállúru. Telugu. Opposite Channakéṣava temple.]

TRANSLATION.

Salutation be to the illustrious Rámánuja! On Thursday the 1st of the bright fortnight of Chaitra of the year Vikrama, on the auspicious occasion of the consecration of Ṣrí Késavanátha of Táḷúru, the following lands were given by Akáchi Maldéva Rájungáru, 2 *puṭṭis* of dry land, ½ *a chatu paḍi* (?) of wet land, and 3 *kuntas* of garden land. Whosoever transgresses this endowment will incur the sin of killing a cow on the Ganges . . . . will incur the sin of killing a Brahman . . May it cause great prosperity.!

1. శ్రీమతేరామానుజాయనమః విక్ర
2. మ సంవత్సర చైత్ర శు ౧ గు। తాళూ

[1] Chávatalampa is apparently the old name of Sákhavaram.

3. రి శ్రీకేశ్వనాథనికి ప్రతిష్ట పుణ్యా
4. ఘఃమపుడు అకాచి మద్దెవరా
5. జంగారువెట్టిన క్షేత్రం వెలిపాలం
6. ఖ ౨ నీరునేల అర్ధ చతు పడి
7. తోంట మూండు గుంటలు యీాప
8. ధ్ఘతి ఎవండు దో్రసినాను గంగక
9. త్తర గంగి గోవుంజంపిన పాంపా
10. నం బోయినాండు శ్రీ .
11. . . బ్రాహ్మణిం జంపిన బా
12. పానం బోయినాం
13. డు . . . . మంగళం మహా శ్రీ శ్రీ

Kanigiri (40)

[Uppalapáḍu. Canarese. On fallen stone near ruined fort to the south. The transcription was done by Mr. V. Venkayya.]

Translation.

1, 2 and 3. Ṣríman Mahárájádhirája-Rájaparaméṣvara Ṣrí Vírapratápa Dévaráya Maháraya's minister Cháma . . . damanagu . . .

4 and 5. Savaráju . . . . a great devotee of Ṣiva . . . .

6. A man of great fame . . . . in all worlds.

7. believer in Ṣiva . . . .

8. . . . eighteen times . . . .

9. Throne . . . . eighteen times.

14. . . . was given . . . .

15. . . . .

16. in the kingdom of Kamma[nádu ?] . . . . their . . . . look to

17. if not this the rája . . . the (Ṣunkaḍa) fee . . . . .

18. . . . my . . . .

19. . . . for begging purposes . . . . fail to obey

20. Dévaráyamaháráyaru's feet (order ?) . . . . .

21. . . . . five (sins) . . . . . Dévaráya Maháráyaru's order . . . . the edict was executed.

22. May there be prosperity !

1. . . . . శ్రీమన్మ హారా-

2. జాధిరాజరాజ పరమేస్పర శ్రీవీరప్రతాప దేవ [రా యమ]

3. హారాయ . . . . మంత్రి చామ . . . డమ నగు . . . .

4. సపరాజు . . . . వరదాస [ద] వేః [మ] త్రిన సుద్ధ సిహా

5. చారసంపన్నరమప్ప . మ . . . . . తింహాణ

6. సుఖశాల [కీర్తి] సపంన్నరప్పవ . . . . సమస్త లోక

7. సివాకవపారయరు . . . త్రియుగళువారు

8. . నహదినెంటు సమయడస . . . ళ . . బదెపసి-

9. చహసనమ . మానాలుస . . . . హది నెంటు సమయడ

10. . . . .
11. . . . .
12. . . . .
13. . . . .
14. . . త[ళ] వార . . . . ముడియ బిట్టుకొట్ట
నావు . . .
15. నయుగు . యి . . రుషంచాళ[స] . విప్రణమాన
. లవరు
16. ఖండ్ఠపమాన [క] మ్మ రాజ్యదొళగె తఃమ . . .
నోడి కొంబరు
17. యిదు అల్ల వెందు అరుసు [ఆ] డిదరె[సు]ం[ధ]శ్రీళ వా
రగ [వు]
18. ణ్డునాయఃకర వాడిలవనానొ[రణ]ను సం[హా]జ - సం
కకద[చ్చ]మా-
19. డినవను ఆదుద . నతాతం[ష్ట]భిత్తిప్రవిక్తి దేవరా-యమ
20. హాగాయర పాదకుతప్పిడవకు[కా]యఙిచ్చి-యః సంస
21. . . . . వోం అయిదు పాకన్ని దేవ రాయ మహా
రాయరు అను
22. . . . . తి . నసాసనము మంగళ మహా శ్రీ శ్రీ శ్రీ.

Kanigiri (41).

[Válicherla. Telugu. On steps of temple of Íṣvara in the fort. The stone being broken and rough, this is illegible.]

1. .
2. .
3. . మి

4. న్న వద్ద
5. జను
6. శ్వరభు
7. స్వస్తి శ్రీ తి
8. ఫురాంతవ
9. . . అనస్మ
10. సెట్టికి ఆగ .
11. . షం . చి
12. . . . లి అ.
13. . ర . వాము
14. . బరపం
15. ధరు
16. . . . తిము
17. సంతిః
18. . . గ్రామ
19. ం పో . . సి
20. సతః వ
21. . వ్య . . ల్ష
22. వదిస . .
23. స్పషమిము . .
24. స్తిమి . .
25. ము . . .
26 . .

KAVALI (1). (A.D. 1642-43.)

[Ánemaḍugu. Telugu. This inscription was conveyed a few years ago from Ánemaḍugu to the Collector's Cutcherry, Nellore, where it now lies.]

TRANSLATION.

(Adoration to) Ṣrí Ráma! Hail! On Wednesday, the 2nd day of the bright fortnight of Phálguna in the year Chitrabhánu, corresponding to the year 1564 of the illustrious, victorious, and prosperous Ṣáliváhana Ṣaka era, the conditions of the charitable edict issued by Véjarla Narasaráju Gáru, son of Ayyaparáju Gáru and grandson of Kasuva Ráju Gáru, descendant of the *Gótra* of Vasisṭha, follower of the Ápastambha *sútra*, and student of the Yajuṣṣákhá (are as follows):—

We shall continue the grant of *méras* (grain fees) attached to the tank of Ánemaḍugu given us as *amaram* (land held on service tenure) in the *ṣíma* (division) of Kandukúru . . . . For every *puṭṭi*[1] of dry crop, one *kuncham* (8 measures) as *méras* and also an entire *inám* of 40 *gorrus*[2] of wet land under the tank. . . . . (Illegible).

NOTE.—See also under KR. 80.

O ᗜ

1. శ్రీరామా
2. స్వస్తిశ్రీ జయాభ్యుద
3. య శాలివాహన శక

---

[1] 1 puṭṭi = 20 túms or 80 kunchams.
[2] 1 gorru = generally 3·16 acres or 50 kunṭas.

4. వరుషంబులు ౧౫౬౪
5. అగునేంటి చిత్రభాను
6. నామసంవత్సర ఫా
7. ల్గుణ శుద్ధ ౨ బు యజు
8. శ్శాఖాధ్యాయులున్ను
9. అపస్తంభ సూత్రులున్ను
10. వశిష్ట గోత్రోద్భవులు
11. న్ను ఐన కసువరాజు
12. ంగారి పౌత్రులున్ను అయ్యా
13. ప రాజు గారి పుత్రులుం
14. న్ను ఐన వేజర్ల నరసరా
15. జు గారు వేయించిన
16. ధర్మశాసన క్రమమెట్ల
17. ంన్నను కందుకూరు శీమ
18. లోను మాకు అమరం
19. నడిచె ఆ నెమదుగు గ్రా
20. మాన చెర్వుకు నడు
21. చెడివైన మేరస్వాస్త్యం
22. ముసు నడపెడు వారం
23. ము . . .
24. . మెట్టకు పుట్టికి కుం
25. చ్చండి లెఖమేరలు
26. చెర్వుక్రింద మాన్యం
27. గ్రోరు[1] ౪ం సర్వమాన్యం
23. యీమాన్యము . . . .

---

[1] Read గో[illegible]రు.

KAVALI (2).

[Ánemaḍugu. Telugu. In tank bed. Illegible].

KAVALI (3). (A.D., 1124–25 ?)

[Boḍaguḍipáḍu. Telugu. West of village.]

. . . Ṣaka year 1046 . . . . to Mallikárjuna-déva . . . . fields . . . . . Mahéṣvara Máyá Chendraya . . . .

[Three imprecatory verses.]

Second side . . . . . . to Ṣrí Malikárjunadéva . . . .

TRANSLATION.

1. సకవ్వరు సంబుగ ౧౦౪౬ . . .
2. (గట్టియులం౧ . . . అత్రికపె)
3. (ంఙ్లయాలు శ్రీ . . ంవదొక)
4. . . . .
5. (క్రమ . నైచ . య . . . శ్రీ)
6. . . . కామల్లికార్జునదేవర
7. కు శ్రీ . . . .
8. . . డిలగంగకల . .
9. . . . .
10. క్షేత్ర . . . . .
11. ర . . తమహేశ్వర
12. మాయా చేంద్రయ . .
13. . . ॥ సామాన్యోయం ధర్మసేతు
14. ర్నృపాణాం కాలేకాలేపాలనీ
15. యోభవద్భిః । సర్వానేతాన్భావి
16. నః పార్థివేంద్రాన్ భూయోభూ

17. యోయాచతే రామచంద్ర ॥ స్వదత్తాద్వి
18. గుణం పుణ్యం పరదత్తానుపా
19. లనం పరదత్తాపహారేణ స్వదత్తం
20. నిష్ఫలంభవేత్ ॥ స్వదత్తం
21. పరదత్తం వాయోహారేతవసుం
22. ధరా షష్టివర్షసహ
23. స్రాణి విష్టాయాంజాయ
24. తేక్రిమి ॥

Second Side.

1. శ్రీ శ్రీ పచ్చవల్లి . . .
2. శ్రీ మల్లికార్జునదేవరకు
3. వ . . . . . . పత్తి
4. సార్వతర్ష యెకా అతుర అ
5. శుభస్వ . . మార్గ .
6. కర . . జ . సె
7. . ప్నతావేగి . .
8. త్యస్సనాండు
9. మల్లినాంధ . .
10. మ . ంచు మగ్రరాడపి
11. తో . . . .
12. రామాపాయాదవ

Kavali (4).

[Bráhmanakráka. Telugu. On a pillar of a temple. This is an incomplete inscription and is partly illegible. It seems to record a charity to Chenna-késava to last as long as the sun and the moon.]

1. స్వస్తి మనుర్ప్రో .
2. లి ప్రిష్టి కొసాని

3. కడిపాలపాక
4. చంద్రార్కన శేకిన
5. దమ్మోంకై చన్నకై . .

KAVALI (5).

[Bráhmanakráka. Telugu. On a pillar of the same temple. This is also partially illegible.]

TRANSLATION.

We have constructed a temple in Bráhmanakráka attached to Jaladanki *Samatu* in the . . . *ṣíma* to last as long as the sun and the moon.

1. . . సీమకు సంమతుజ
2. లదంకి బ్రాంహాణక్రాకలో
3. కుడిని ఆచంద్రార్కర్ణము
4. గాను కట్టించడము
5. . . .
6. . . . .

KAVALI (6).

[Bráhmanakráka. Telugu. From a pillar in the same temple.]

TRANSLATION.

I believe in Ṣrí Ravi Rámalingasvámi. I believe in the sun and the moon. I always believe (in them).

1. శ్రీరవి శ్రీరామలింగస్వా
2. మిలింసే నంమినాను
3. సూర్య చంద్రాదులు నం
4. మినాను నిత్యం నంమినాను

KAVALI (7).

[Chinna Annalúru. Telugu. From mandapam of Kálabhairavuḍu temple.]

TRANSLATION.

Hail! On the 2nd of . . . . fortnight of Áshádha of the year Sádháraṇa, corresponding to the illustrious, victorious and prosperous Ṣáliváhana Ṣaka year . . . . . Ṣrímad Rájádhirája, Rájaparaméṣvara, Ṣrí Víra Pratápa Ṣrí Víra . . . . Those who fail to do . . . . to this tank will incur the sin of killing cows and Brahmans . . . . .

1. (స్వస్తి శ్రీ జయాభ్యు)
దయ శాలివాహాన శకవర్షంబులు
2. (. . . . . సాధా) రణ సంవత్సర ఆషాడ . ౨
లు శ్రీ
3. (మ(దాజాధిరాజరాజ) పరమేశ్వర శ్రీ వీరప్రతాపశ్రీవీర
. .
4. . . . . మరళ . . .
5. . . . . శాసచెరు
6. . . . .
7. . . . . య
8. . . . . మా
9. . . . .
10. . . . . నిమలో

11. . . . . . నిపఠి
12. . . . . . యచో
13. . . న్నా అ . . . . సీకు యిం
14. . . . . త్త . . . లివి ప్రద్రి . ద్వా
15. . . . . . ను దారఖ . వసరుగాన సర్వ
16. . . . . . మియీూ చెవ్వఁడానకు యెవరు తప్పి
17. . . . . . బ్రాంహాన వధచేసిన పాపానం బో
18. . . . . . తాను వకించినవారు.

KAVALI (8). (A.D. 1188-89.)

[Chinnakráka. Telugu. On a large stone opposite small Ṣiva temple.]

TRANSLATION.

Hail! On the occasion of Uttaráyana Sankránti (winter solstice) in the (cyclic) year Kílaka, corresponding to 1110 of the illustrious Ṣaka era, Pról Désahi, son of Nalagarula Kápa Désahi belonging to the *Désangulu* sect of Vinuradaka (town ?) of Pákinádu, constructed a temple to Páṭi Ṣrí Mallikárjunadéva for the religious merit of Talároru Próli Náyaka and gave one *paṭṭu* of wet land to the east of the village and in rear of the tank, to provide for burnt offerings, (other) offerings, and worship to the deity. None should obstruct the charity of the deity. We have given to this temple a large censer, a small censer, a plate for burning camphor, two perpetual lamps, a bell, and a conch. We have given dry fields in the west (of the village) for the performance of worship at the three *sandhyás* (morning, noon and evening). Tripurántaka Pandit should receive these; he, his sons, and grandsons should maintain the charity.

NOTE.—Náyaks with the prefix Talári or Taláru are mentioned in KV. 10 and R. 47 also, the dates ranging from circ. 1187-88 to circ. 1211-12. R. 72 probably refers to the same family and perhaps KR. 84 of 1294-95 also does so.

1. స్వస్తిశ్రీ సకవర్షంబులు
2. ౧౧౧౦ నెంటి కీలక సంవత్స
3. రంబున ఉత్తరాయణ సంక్రాం
4. త్తిని పాకినాటిలోని వినుకొంధ
5. కిదే సెంగులు నల్గటుల కాపదేస
6. హికొడుకుప్రోల్ దెసహితలాఱి ప్రో
7. లినాయకునికి దమార్త్థముగాంగా
8. పాటి శ్రీమల్లిఖార్జున మహాదేవ
9. రకు గుడి ఎత్తించ్చి ఇదేవరకు హవి
10. బలి అర్చనలకు యారితూర్పున
11. చెఱ్వు వెనక నీరిపాలము పట్టు
12. నేల ఇచితిమి దేవరకు అడ్డే
13. నియుయుంపగీయలమునుం జట్టము
14. నుం ధూపఖండ్డయు ధూపహాతియు [1] దీ
15. పాతియు అఖండదీపములు రెం
16. డునుజయఘంటయు సంఘును ని।
17. చ్చితిమి త్రిసంధ్య పూజచె గలాగము
18. లకు వెలిపాల పడమటి సే
19. నిచ్చితిమి దీనిజేకొని త్రిపురాంత్త
20. క పండితులు పుత్ర పవుత్ర వ్రిద్ధినడప క
21. లవాండు.

---

[1] Read ధూపహారతి.

KAVALI (9).

[Chinnakráka. Telugu. From rough stone gate-posts of temple of Gópálasvámi. Beginning and end wanting.]

TRANSLATION.

In accordance with the charitable deed executed to last as long as the sun and moon exist, one *paṭṭu* of dry land and 100 *paṭṭus* of wet land for lighting a lamp and for daily offering, 100 (*paṭṭus*) of wet paddy fields were given to Ṣrí Gópáladéva by Pótana Bóya and also one *paṭṭu* of dry and wet lands was given by Embanasaddelu Níle Bóyunḍu ; one *paṭṭu* of wet land also——.

. . . ఆచం

1. ద్రా కఁముగానిచ్చి[నధ]
2. మఁశాసనాక్కికిం పట్టి[1]
3. వెస్సేను నూఱుపట్టి[1]
4. వరిచ్చేను దీపముప
5. డిహారము బట్టి[1] వరి
6. ౘెనునీరుపొలమునూఱు
7. శ్రీగోపాలదేవర
8. కు పోతనబోయు
9. ండుపట్టి[1] వెలి
10. ౘెను నీరుపొల
11. ము ఎంబన స
12. డ్డెలునీ (లె) బోయుం
13. డు పట్టనీరిౘెనుంను . . .

[1] May be పట్టు or పట్టి.

KAVALI (10). (A.D. 1187-88 ?)

[Chinnakráka. Telugu. From the same place.]

TRANSLATION.

Hail! On Monday, the 11th of the bright half of Ṣrávaṇa, corresponding to 1109 of the illustrious Ṣaka era, as the idol of Vénugópáladéva was being consecrated, Apápi Reḍḍi (gave) to the Nambi (Vaishnavite priest) one *puṭṭi*[1] of wet land, 14 *paṭṭus* of dry land for providing oblation, offering and worship to Vénugópáladéva so that religious merit might accrue to Dalári Dámi Náyukuḍu.

1. స్వస్తి శ్రీ శకవర్షములు
2. ౧౧౦౯ నెంటి శ్రావణశుద్ధ
3. ఏకాదశియు సోమవార నం
4. దు వేణుగోపాలదేవరను
5. ప్రతిష్టించినందున్న ఆపా
6. పిరెడ్డి దలాఱిదామినా
7. యుకుని దంమ్మర్గాంగవే
8. ణుగోపాలదేవర
9. కు హావిబలి అచర్
10. నలకు నంబారి
11. వసమున నీరుపా
12. లము పుట్టి చె
13. ను వెలిసె ౧౪ నా
14. ల్ఖు పట్టులాను.

* * * *

[1] See note 1 on page 697.

KAVALI (11). (A.D. 1322–23 ?)

[Chinnakráka. Telugu. From the same place.]

TRANSLATION.

Hail! On Thursday, the 11th of the bright half of Áshádha, corresponding to 1244 of the illustrious Saka era, Nallamdérvula Peda Kóti Reddigáru constructed a temple to Srí Gópáladéva for the religious merit of Srí Mahámandalésvara Dasavarma Déva Mahárája, his brothers, and his father Timmadéva Mahárája . . . .

NOTE.—We have not been able to identify this Dasavarma.

1. స్వస్తి శ్రీ శకవర్షంబు
2. లు ౧౨౪౪ అగునేంటి
3 ఆషాఢశుద్ధ ఏకాద
4. శించగురు వాసరో
5. అందు శ్రీమన్మహా మ
6. ండలేశ్వర దశవర్మ
7. దేవమహారాజులు అ
8. న్న తంబులు మరి తండ్రి
9. తిమ్మదేవమహారాజా
10. లకు ధర్మముగా నల్లం
11. డెఱ్వుల పెదకోటిరెడ్డి
12. గారుడి శ్రీగోపాలదే
13. వరగుడి కట్టించ్చిన
14. . . . చేయుము.

KAVALI (12).

[Chinnakráka. Telugu. From the same place. This is an incomplete inscription.]

TRANSLATION.

— Chámaya, son of Dasaráju, gave one *puttu* of paddy field lying due east and cultivated by Dambódanmi

Bhaṭlu as a gift to last as long as the sun and the moon exist so that religious merit might accrue to his grandfather. If any obstruct this ——.

1. మున నా
2. చంద్రార్కము
3. గా దసరా
4. జాకో డుర్కు చా
5. మయ దమ
6. తాతకు ద
7. ముఃపుగా స
8. రి తూప్పుఃన
9. డంబోద న్మిభ
10. ట్లవారి దున్నని
11. వగి చేనుప
12. ట్టి నెలలిచ్చె-
13. దీనికి నెవ్వరు
14. విఫలముదల . .

* * * *

KAVALI (13). (A.D. 1214–15 ?)

[Dúbaguṇṭa. Telugu. To south near the Poliméra stream.]

TRANSLATION.

Hail! On the day of Uttaráyaṇa Sankránti, corresponding to the Ṣaka year 1136, for the religious merit of Ṣríman Mahámaṇḍaleṣvara Manma Siddanadéva Chóḍa

Mahárájulu, son of Rajéndradéva Chóḍa Mahárájulu, on whose lotus feet are set the eyes of Trilóchana and all other kings of the earth, who is the jewelled lamp of the race of Karikála by whom the dam of the Kávéri[1] was built, who is an elephant-goad to wicked princes, who is of the Kásyapa *gótra*, who is sprung from the solar race, who is the lord of the best of cities Orayúr, who is Kírti Náráyaṇa, and who took tribute from Kánchi (?), his younger brother Kaḍanalle Tangadéva Mahárájulu (?) . . . *gópura* and excellent *prákára* (?) . . . .

1. స్వస్తి చరణ సరోరుహ
2. విహాత[2] విలోచన త్రిలో
3. చనప్రముఖాఖిల ప్రిధి
4. వీశ్వర కారితకావేరీ తీర
5. కరికాలకుల రత్నప్రదీపాహి
6. త కుమారాంకుశ శ్రీ మను
7. మహా మండలేశ్వర కాస్య
8. పగోత్ర సూర్యవంశోద్భవ
9. ఒఱయూరి పురవరాధీశ్వ
10. ర కీర్తినారాయణ కాంచింగప్ప
11. ముగొన్నట్టి (జిత) శ్రీ రాజేం
12. ద్రదేవ చోడమహారాజు
13. ల కొడుకు మన్మసిద్ధన దేవచో
14. డ మహారాజులకు ధర్మువు
15. గా వారి తమ్ముండు బసువ
16. (తకలిరి) గోపుర వరప్రాకా
17. ర కడనల్లె తంగదేవమహా
18. రాజులు శకవర్షంములు

---

[1] See note on page 1250.

[2] Read విహిత.

19. ౧౧౩౬ యగునేంటి .

20. యుత్తరాయణ సంక్రాంతి

*   *   *   *

Kavali (14). (A.D. 1441–42?)

[Gaṭṭupalli. Telugu. From stone in bed of tank.]

Translation.

Hail! On Monday, the 1st of the bright fortnight of (Phálguna?) of the year Iva (?), corresponding to, 1363 (?) of the illustrious Ṣaka era, while Rájádhirája Rájaparamésvara, Ṣrí Víra Déva (Uḍeyu?), the son of Ṣrí Hari Hara-Ráya, Mahámaṇḍalésvara, Ariráyaraganda,[1] Bahusamudrádhísvara,[2] Satruráyamanóbhayankara,[3] seated on the diamond throne, was ruling the kingdom of the earth, . . . gave . . . to Rámachandra Óḍeya Perumál, the excellent son of Ánkula Kóṭésvaradévara . . . . to the west of the temple of Múlasthána Mahámudra——of Jaladanki in Pákináḍu——to last as long as the sun and moon, for the increase of life and health of Rámachandra Bhaṭlu. This charity . . . . the seal has been affixed.

May it cause great prosperity!

Note.—The stone is considerably worn and hence illegible in several places. There is apparently some misreading in the case of the year.

1. శ్రీ శకవర్షంబులు ౧౩౬౩ అగు [నే

2. టి] ఇవసం [ఫాల్గుణ] శు ౧ సో [శ్రీ]

3. మనుమహా [మండలేశ్వర] అరిరాయ [ర

---

[1] The conqueror of hostile kings.

[2] Lord of many seas. The usual biruda is chatussamudrádhísvara = the lord of the four seas.

[3] The terror of hostile kings.

4. గండఖ [, . . . మూరురాయ] ర గండభహూ[స]
5. ముద్రాధీశ్వర (. . . శత్రు) రాయమనో భ
6. యంకరండు శ్రీ వీరహరిహరరాయనికుమా[రుండు]
7. శ్రీరాజాధిరాజరాజపరమేశ్వర శ్రీ వీరదేవర [వు
8. డెయులు] వజ్రసింహాసనమందున ప్రిధ్విరాజ్యం
9. చేయుచున్న .
10. కరామచంద్రభటులయ్యలకు అయురాభివ్రిద్ధిగాను [ఆ
11. రోగ్యా] భివ్రిద్ధిగాను అనెనిపాకినాటి జలసంకిలోను
12. ఘటకుమూలస్థాన శ్రీ మన్మహాముద్ర . .
13. దేవరగుడి పక్షుమట దెగ్గరి ఆంకులకోటేశ్వర
14. దేవరగార సుపుత్రరాయవిబ్రదెల . . మ
15. ణ ఆరామచంద్ర ఓడెయపెరు[మాళ్ల]
16. చంద్రార్కముగా . . . .
17. . . . ఇచ్చిన దర్మవు . . .
18. . . వెనని తగిము చెఱవు క్రమన
19. ముద్రవెనిక డంచెను.— మంగళమహా
20. శ్రీ శ్రీ శ్రీ జేయును.

KAVALI (15).

[Gouravaram. Telugu. Two sides of a stone by Chennakéṣvaraṣvámi temple.]

TRANSLATION.

Hail! On the 12th of the bright fortnight of Ṣrávaṇa, corresponding to the illustrious Ṣaka year 1 . . . . the daughter of Ṣrímat Chelvaráju, the lord of . . . . . . konḍa . . . . Rámarámu . . . . gave one *máḍa* for the twilight lamp to Manma Kéṣavadéva to last as long as the sun and moon exist. Perumá Bhaṭṭu should receive this *máḍa* and keep up the lamp. May there be prosperity!

NOTE.—Chelvarázu does not seem to appear elsewhere.

1. స్వస్తి శ్రీ శకవ
2. ర్షంబులు ౧
3. . . . అగు నెంటి
4. శ్రావణ శుద్ధ
5. ద్వాదశి నాండ్డు
6. . కొండప్రబు
7. శ్రీమతు
8. చెలవరాజు
9. (కూంతుఋవం)
10. (ఆ ప్రభుమం)
11. (అచిరా . .)
12. డముబు .)
13. . . .

Second side.

14. నివారితోనాం .
15. మరామగ్రాము .
16. మనుమ కేశవ దే
17. వరకు ఆచంద్రార్క
18. ముగా సంధ్యాదీపము
19. నకు ఇచ్చిన మా (డ) మొ
20. కర్రటి ఈ మాడ పెరుమా
21. భట్టుకై కాని దీపము
22. నడపంగలవాండు
23. స్వస్త్యస్తు

KAVALI (16).

[Gouravaram. Telugu. On pillar to south of Chennakéṣavasvámi temple. Illegible.]

KAVALI (17).

[Gouravaram. Telugu. On pillar to north of Chennakéṣavasvámi temple.]

TRANSLATION.

The pillar of (constructed by) Ṣrí Ádúri Mummaḍi Seṭṭi.

శ్రీ ఆడూరి ము
ంమడి సెట్టిక
ంబ్బము

KAVALI (18.) (A.D., 1422-23.)

[Gouravaram. Telugu. Over door of Párvati temple.]

TRANSLATION.

Hail! On the 15th of the bright fortnight of Chaitra of the year Ṣubhakṛit, corresponding to the illustrious victorious and prosperous Ṣaka year 1344 . . . . .

1. స్వస్తి శ్రీ జయాభ్యుదయ శకాబ్దంబ్బులు ౧౩౪౪ అ
2. శుభకృత్రీ త్స-వత్సర చైత్ర శు ౧౫ క్రాయ . . .

KAVALI (19). (A.D. 1274–75 ?)

[Jaladanki. Telugu. South front pillar of Chennakésavasvámi's temple. The inscription is illegible in various places.]

TRANSLATION.

Hail! On the 30th of the dark fortnight of Kártika of . . . . corresponding to 1196 of the illustrious Ṣaka era . . . . (gave) a lamp to the illustrious Chennakésava of Jaladanki. The wet fields given by him for lighting this perpetual lamp night and day as long as the sun and the moon last . . . . are 6 *gorrus*. Let the charity be maintained as long as the sun and the moon last.

1. స్వస్తి శ్రీ శకవరుషంబులు ౧౧౯౬ వ
2. గు నేంటి . . . . కార్తిక
3. బ ౩౦ లు స్వస్తి। శ్రీ చెన్నకేశవ దేవ
4. రకు బ్ర . . . .
5. దీపం దీని ఆచంద్రార్కముగా
6. ను అఖండదీపము అహోరాత్రిళ్లు
7. ను ముట్టింపుమని ఇచ్చిన నీటిచేలు
8. . . . . ఆరుగొర్రులు
9. . . . . ఆచంద్రార్కముగా
10. నడుపంగలవారు

KAVALI (20). (A.D. 1789–90.)

[Jaladanki. From the same place.]

TRANSLATION.

Hail! On . . . . the 12th (of the dark fortnight of Pushya of the year Sádháraṇa), corresponding to

1712 of the illustrious Ṣaka era, two *guṇṭas*[1] of land were given for the purpose of lighting an evening lamp to Chennakéṣavadéva of Jaladanki as long as the sun and the moon last. Receiving these we shall maintain this charity as long as the sun and the moon last.

1. స్వస్తి శ్రీ శకవరుషంబులు ౧౭౧౨ అగు-
2. నేంటి (సాధారణ సంవత్సరంబున)
3. (. . . . పుష్య బ) ద్వాదశినాడు .
4. జలదంకి చెన్నకేశవదేవరకు స
5. ంధ్యా దీపానకు ఆచంద్రార్కముగ ము
6. ట్టి పమని ఇచ్చిన చేలుగుంట ౨ వీని
7. చేకొని ఆచంద్రార్కము నడపంగలవారము

KAVALI (21). (A.D. 1274–75 ?)

[Jaladanki. Telugu. From the same place.]

TRANSLATION.

Hail! On Saturday the 3rd of the dark fortnight of Vaiṣákha corresponding to the year 1196 of the illustrious Ṣaka era, Purushóttamadévara, son of Perumáreḍḍidéva, gave 66 ewes for the purpose of lighting perpetual lamps every evening to Chennakéṣavadéva, of Jaladanki as long as the sun and the moon last, so that religious merit might accrue to his mother and father. Receiving these 66 ewes, the Nambis should maintain the charity as long as the sun and moon endure. Ṣrí. Ṣrí.

NOTE.—The cycle and S S. years do not agree.

1. స్వస్తి శ్రీ శకవరుషంబులు ౧౧౯౬
2. వగు నేంటి వై । బ । 3 । శనివారము

---

[1] Gunta or kunta = 2,756¼ square feet.

3. నాండు జలదంకి చన్నకేశవదేవరకు పె
4. రుమాంరడి దేవని కొడుకు పురుషోత్త
5. మదేవర తమ తల్లి దండ్రులకు పు
6. ణ్యంముగాను ఆచంద్రార్కముగా అఖండ
7. దీపముల సాయం త్రము ముట్టి పు
8. మని ఇచ్చిన గొఱ్ఱెలు ౬౬ ఈ అ
9.఑వది ఆరుగొఱల జేకొని నం
10. బులు ఆచంద్రార్కముగా నడపంగ
11. లవారు శ్రీ శ్రీ

Kavali (22). (A.D. 1275–76 ?)

[Jaladanki. Telugu. From the same place.]

Translation.

Hail! On Monday the 11th of the bright half of Áṣva (yuja), corresponding to the year 1197 of the illustrious Ṣaka era, Raḍḍi Dámi Raḍḍi, Pandru Próli Raḍḍi, Pinnama Raḍḍi, Kámi Raḍḍi, Prólama Raḍḍi, and Annama Raḍḍi son of Vámmi Raḍḍi gave to the Nambis for Chennakéṣavadéva, with libation of water . . . . and a cow, for the religious merit of Pina Próli Raḍḍi and Pótasáni to last as long as the sun and the moon exist, for a lamp . . . . and to perform ceremony on the Ékádaṣi day and other functions.

1. స్వస్తి శ్రీ శకవరుషంబులు ౧
2. ౧౯౭ వగునేంటి ఆశ్వీ। శు। ౧౧। మ।
3. నాండు రడ్డి దామిరడ్డిన్ని పండ్రుప్రోలి
4. రడ్డిన్ని పిన్నమరడ్డిన్ని కామిరడ్డి ప్రోల
5. మరడ్డిన్ని వమ్మిరడ్డి కొడుకు అన్నమరడ్డి

6. న్ని పినప్రోలి ‘డ్డికిన్ని పోతసానికిన్ని ధర్మః
7. వుగ చెన్నకేశవదేవరకు దీపానికిన్న.
8. . . . ఏకావళి ప్రత్యాపవులందుల
9. . . . . . గోవును ఆచంద్రార్కం
10. గా ధారవోసి ఇచ్చిరి న బులకు

KAVALI (23). (A.D. 1276-77 ?)

[Jaladanki. Telugu. From the same place.]

TRANSLATION.

Hail! On Saturday the 1st of the bright half of Mágha, corresponding to 1193 of the illustrious Ṣaka era, Bamayándli Cheṭṭi, son of Chendimara Kannan gave 18 ewes for the purpose of lighting two evening lamps as long as the sun and the moon last to Chennakéṣavadéva of Jaladanki so that religious merit might accrue to his parents. A *sirasu váká* (the value of this coin is not known) and a cow (have been given) to Chennakéṣavadéva as a charity to last as long as the sun and moon. Those who injure this charity will incur the sin of those who kill their parents on the banks of the Ganges.

1. స్వస్తి శ్రీ శకవరుషంబులు ౧౧౯౩ వగు
2. నెంటి మాఘ శు । ౧ । శ । నాండు జలదం
3. కి చన్నకేశవదేవరకు చెందామ
4. రకన్నని కొడుకు బమయాండ్డి
5. సెట్టి తమ తల్లితండ్రులకు ధర్మము
6. వుగా ఆచంద్రార్కముగా సంధ్యా ప
7. ములు రెండు ముట్టి ప్రమని ఇచ్చి

8. న గోజ్యాలు ౧౮
9. ఆ శిరసు రూకాను గోవ్రాను చెన్న
10. కేశవ దేవరకు నాచంద్రార్కముగాను
11. అని ప్రతిష్ఠ బున్యంబుగ . . . .
12. ఈ ధర్మువు చెఱిచినవారు
13. గంగకటుత తమ తల్లితండ్రు
14. ల వధించిన పాపానం బోవు
15. వారు

Kavali (24). (A.D. 1251–52 ?)

[Jaladanki. Telugu. From north front pillar of the same temple. This is mostly illegible.]

Translation.

Hail ! In 1173 of the illustrious Ṣaka era . . . gave to Chennakéṣavadéva of Jaladanki to last as long as the sun and moon for the religious merit of his father . . . .

1. స్వస్తి శ్రీ శకవర్షంబులు
2. ౧౧౭౩ నెంటి . . .
3. . . . . . .
4. . . . జలదంకి . . చన్న
5. కేశవదేవరకు . . . ఆచంద్రా
6. ర్కముగాను తమ తండ్రికి . .
7. . . ధర్మువుగాను .
8. . . . . . .
9. . . . . . .

KAVALI (25). (1244–45 ?)

[Jaladanki. Telugu. From south back pillar of the same temple.]

TRANSLATION.

Hail! On Thursday the 11th day of the bright fortnight of Kártika under the Uttará Phalguní Nakshatra, corresponding to the year 1166 of the illustrious Ṣaka era, in the reign of Ṣríman Mahámaṇḍaléṣvara Alluntirukaḍgati[1] Déva Chóḍa Maharájulu, the servant of Peddináyaka who is the director of seventy-two offices, for the religious merit of Nágaṇabóyunḍu and for the religious merit of his father and mother, gave a "máḍa"[2] for (the purpose of lighting) evening lamps to the temple of Chennakéṣavadéva of Jaladanki. From the interest derived therefrom the Nambis should maintain the evening lamp. The first "máḍa" should be the principal (or the *máḍa* which is to be the principal should be given to the temple treasury). This charity should be maintained as long as the sun and moon exist.

1. స్వస్తి శ్రీ శకవరుషంబులు ౧౧
2. ౬౬ యగు నేంటి కార్త్తిక శుద్ధ
3. ఏకాదశి గురువారమునం - ఉ -
4. వ - నక్షత్రమునందు స్వస్తి శ్రీమ
5. న్మహా మండలేశ్వర అల్లుంతి
6. రు కడ్గతి దేవచోడ మహారా
7. జుల రాజ్యమున బాహత్తరని యో

---

[1] Dr. Hultzsch reads Allundirukálatidéva (*vide* Ins. No. 208, Epi. Report for 1894–95), but the name seems to be as in the text. Other inscriptions show clearly, however, that Dr. Hultzsch's reading is the correct one.

[2] A máḍa = 2 rupees.

8. గాఢివతిమైనట్టి పెద్దిరాయు
9. కుని బ్రిక్యండు నాగనబో
10. యనికి ధర్మువుగ తల్లితం
11. డ్రులకు ధర్మువుగాను జఃదం
12. కి చెన్న కేశవ దేవరగుడికి సం
13. ధ్యాగిపానకు నిచ్చినది మాడగ ౧
14. దీనివద్ఢికిసంధ్యాదీపము పెల్లు
15. పెట్టి దానపపాగలవారు సంబులు
16. మొదలి మాడబండారులై యు
17. ండంగలవి యీ ధర్మువు ఆచ
18. ంద్రార్కమ్ముగా నడపంగలవా
19. రు

KAVALI (26). (A.D. 1264-65.)

[Jaladanki. Telugu. From north back pillar of the same place.]

TRANSLATION.

Hail! On Wednesday the 7th of the bright fortnight of Áshádha of the year Raktákshi, corresponding to the illustrious Ṣaka year 1186, Pemmáya, son of Kamppanu Boyuḍu gave a "Gadya" (a gold coin) to the Nambi on condition that he should light the evening lamps in a row in half the temple of Chennakéṣavadéva, for the religious merit of his parents, and that he should continue the charity so long as the sun and moon exist.

1. స్వస్తి శ్రీశకవర్షంబులు ౧౧౮౬
2. వగునేంటి రక్తాక్షిసంవత్సర ఆషాఢ
3 శుద్ధసప్తమియు బుధవారము

4. నాండు కంప్పను బోయునికొడుకు పె
5. మ్మాయ తమ తల్లిదండ్రులకు ధ
6. ర్మ్మార్థముగ గుడి సగమువరుసయ
7. ందు సంధ్యాదీపము చెన్నకేశవ
8. దేవరకు ఆచంద్రార్కముగా ధర్మ్మము నడ
9. సంబడినం నంబికి నియామకంచేసి
10. నంబికినిచ్చిన గద్య ౧

Kavali (27). (A.D. 1278–79 ?)

[Jaladanki. Telugu. From the same place.]

Translation.

Hail! On Thursday, the 10th day of the dark fortnight of Mágha, corresponding to the year 1200 of the illustrious Ṣaka era, Orula Siddaya and Perumáṇḍi Nambigáru, Chennakéṣava's son Náraparázu, Singaya, and Pemmaya having bought a fourth part in Jaladanki village and a fourth part within the four boundaries of Jaladanki, gave them, with libation of water, to Késava Nambi and registered (them) in his name. Á!!a Pemmaya and Dhíraba Nambi should maintain (this charity) as long as the sun and the moon exist.

1. స్వస్తి శ్రీశకవర్షంబులు ౧౨౦౦
2. వగు నేంటి మాఘ బ ౧౦ గురువారంనాడు ఒ
3. రులసిద్దయ పెరుమాండినంబిగారు చె
4. న్నకేశవ కొడుకును నారపరాజును శి
5. ంగయాను పెమ్మయను జలదంకిగ్రామ
6. ముద్రమునందలి నాలగంపాలును
7. జలదంకిచతుస్సీమల ప్రావయుడి

8. గల నాలగుపాలును వెలతెగగొని కేశ
9. వనంబికి ధారాపూర్వకము సేసిపేరా
10. యికముపెట్టిరి ఆళ్ల పెమ్మయను
11. ధీరఖనంబి ఆచంద్రార్కముగాను
12. చెల్లించగలవారు

Kavali (28). (A.D. 1276-77 ?)

[Jaladanki. Telugu. From the south back pillar of same temple.]

Translation.

Hail! On Friday, the 3rd of the bright fortnight of Phálguna, corresponding to the year 1198 of the illustrious Ṣaka era, Vallama Prólu Chetti presented 66 ewes for lighting day and night a perpetual lamp to Ṣrí Chennakéṣava of Jaladanki for the religious merit of his parents. The 66 ewes should be accepted and the lamps should be kept up as long as the sun and moon last.

1. స్వస్తి శ్రీశకవర్షంబులు ౧౧
2. ౯౮ వగునేంటి । పా । శు । 3 । శు । నాండు జల
3. దంకి శ్రీచన్నకేశవదేవరకు వల్ల
4. మప్రోలు శెట్టి తమ తల్లితండ్రులకు
5. ధర్మముగ అఖండదీపము అహోరా
6. త్రముముట్టింపు మనిఇచ్చిన గొఱ్ఱు ౬౬
7. ఈ అఱువది ఆఱుగొఱులజకొని
8. దీపాలు అచంద్రార్కముగా నడపం
9. గలవారు

KAVALI (29). (A.D. 1274–75 ?)

[Jaladanki. Telugu. From the north back pillar.]

TRANSLATION.

Hail! On Sunday the 11th day of the bright fortnight of the month of Márgasíra, corresponding to the illustrious Ṣaka year 1196, Búmaya gave 19 ewes as charity on behalf of his parents for lighting two evening lamps in the temple of Chennakéṣava Déva of Jaladanki as long as the sun and moon endure.

1. స్వస్తి శ్రీశకవర్షం
2. బులు ౧౧౯౬ వగు నేంటి మార్గశిర శు ౧౧। ఆ। నాండు
3. జలదంకి చెన్నకేశవ దేవరకు బూమయ దమ తల్లిదం
4. డ్రులకు ధర్మముగా ఆచంద్రార్కము సంధ్యాదీప
5. ములు రెండుమట్టింపుమని యిచ్చిన గొఱ్ఱెలు
6. లు ౧౯

KAVALI (30). (A.D. 1277–78.)

[Jaladanki. Telugu. From the same place.]

TRANSLATION.

On Friday the 3rd of the dark fortnight of Mágha, corresponding to the Ṣaka year 1199, Chendámara Dévanalla Gópála Seṭṭi gave 9 ewes for lighting an evening lamp in the temple of Chennakéṣava of Jaladanki as long as the sun and moon endure so that religious merit might accrue to his father and mother.

1. శకవర్షంబులు ౧౧౯౯ వగు
2. నేంటి మాఘ। బ। 3। శు నాండు జ
3. లదంకి చెన్నకేశవ దేవరకు చెందామ
4. ర దేవనల్లగోపాళసెట్టి తమ తల్లిద

5. ంద్రులకు దమ్మ్రంగా ఆచంద్రార్కము ఏ
6. క సంధ్యాదీపము ముట్టించమ
7. ని ఇచ్చిన గొఱ్ఱులు తొమ్మిది

KAVALI (31.) (A.D. 1217–18?)

[Kaḍanútala. Telugu and Sanskṛit in Telugu character. In enclosure of Mallésvarasvámi temple.]

TRANSLATION.

Hail! On Thursday the 10th of the bright fortnight of Chaitra, on the day under Pushya (the star), corresponding to the illustrious Ṣaka year 1139, (Hail!) Ṣrímat Kámi Reḍḍi, son of Aitama Reḍḍi and his wife Prólasáni, gave a perpetual lamp to Ṣrí Mallikárjunadéva of Kaḍavanúnti situated in Poritináḍu, for the religious merit of Súrapa Reḍḍi and Vennasáni, and presented 50 ewes, to last as long as the sun and moon exist. The *pújári* (worshipper) Prólamaráju should receive this excellent property of the deity and (keep up) 2 lamps.

Second side.

Hail! Ṣrímat Kámasáni, daughter of Srímat Aituma Reḍḍi and Prólasáni, gave a perpetual lamp to Ṣrí Mallikárjunadéva for the religious merit of Mádi Reḍḍi, Márásáni, Próli Reḍḍi, Vémasáni, Próli Reḍḍi, and Gangásáni, and presented 50 ewes. Prólamráju should receive these and keep up the lamp as long as the sun and moon endure.

Sanskrit. Whoever eats (misappropriates) even one-eighth of the size of a sesamum seed of the property of a god, he and all the men of his *gótra* will go to the hell called Raurava.

(To face page 724.)

PART OF KAVALI NO. 31.

1. స్వస్తి శ్రీ శకవర్షములు ౧౧౩౯ అ
2. గు నేంటి చైత్ర శుద్ధ దశమియు బ్రిహ
3. స్పతివారముం బుద్యమునందు పోరిలి
4. నాంటిలోని కడుపనూంతి శ్రీ మల్లికార్జు
5. న దేవరకు శ్రీమతు అయితమ రెడ్డి
6. వెండ్లము ప్రోలాసాని కొడుకు స్వస్తి
7. శ్రీమతు కామిరడ్డి నూరపరడ్డికిని
8. వెన్నసానికిన్ని ధర్మువుఅయ్యెడు
9. మని అఖండదివమొత్తె నాచంద్రా
10. కర్ణమని పంభయిగోటియలిచ్చెను
11. పూజాగి ప్రోలమరాజు దివ్యయీది
12. వ్యాకనముంచెకొని రెండుదీపాలు

Second side.

1. శ్రీమతు అయితమ
2. రడ్డి ప్రోలసాని కూంతుఱు
3. స్వస్తి శ్రీమతు కామసాని మాది
4. రడికి మారాసానికి ప్రోలిరడికి
5. వేమాసానికి ప్రోలిరడికి గంగా
6. సానికిని విరలకును ధర్మువు అ
7. య్యెడమని శ్రీ మల్లిఖార్జున దేవ
8. రకు అఖండ దీపమెత్తె నేంబైగోటి
9. యలిచెను ప్రోలమరాజు సెకొనె నాచ
10. ంద్రార్కం देवद्रव्यातिलार्धार्धं अर्धभ
11. क्षन्तितेनर तेषान्नामानि गोत्रानि रौरव
12. नरकं व्रजेत ॥

KAVALI (32.)

[Kákuṭúru. Telugu. To north of village near Gurrapuráḷḷaguṇṭa.]

TRANSLATION.

. . . . a tank . . . . . . Mára Manchiráju, karnam . . . . . . gave with libation of water. Therefore whoever injures this charity will be considered to have killed a tawny cow and to have taken food in the skull of his eldest son.

[One imprecatory verse.]

1. . . . . . . తిరు
2. లమ . నువుమదిర .
3. భూ॰ ౧౩౦ . . చెరు .
4. ను . . . ము ౧ యువ
5. లు చెరువునున్ను బొవాప
6. డనికి మారమంచ్చిరాజుక
7. రణమును శెవ . . జ
8. . . . . . . నటిరా .
9. దూది . . . . రోన అ
10. పునకు ౧౨ మనమాటి
11. నేండి వది . . . . కద
12. మ్మగ దారాపూర్వకముగ
13. గొంమషానిచ్చినవారుగ
14. నక మావిందుగ విలల బొ
15. డిచినవారు పెద్దకొడుకు క
16. పాలంబున గుడిచినవాం
17. డు॥ స్వదత్తం పరదత్తం వాయో
18. హరేతి వసుంధరా షష్టిర్వ
19. ష సహస్రాణి విష్టాయాం
20. జాయతేక్రిమి॥

KAVALI (33). (A.D. 1382–83 ?)

[Kákaṭúru. Telugu. To the south.]

TRANSLATION.

On Monday the day of Vishama Sankránti, corresponding to the Ṣaka year 1304, Bairapa Náyunḍu, son of Cha . . . . constructed a temple for the increase of wealth to Dánam Guraya, his sons and grandsons, and, for providing daily offerings to Mallikárjunadéva, he constructed a tank and gave . . . . under the tank . . . . for enjoyment of the deity . . . . . to last as along as the moon and stars endure.

[One imprecatory verse.]

1. సకవరుషంబులు
2. ౧౩౦౪ అగునెంటివిషమసంక్రాం
3. తి సోమవారమున చ .
4. . . . నకుకొడుకు బైరపనాయుం
5. డు దానంచెరుగురయకు
6. పుత్రపౌత్రులకు అయిశ్వ
7. ర్యాభివ్రిద్ధిగా గుడిగట్టి మల్లికా
8. ర్జునదేవరకు నిత్యనివేద్యము
9. కుం జెర్వు గట్టించి చెరువు .
10. . భోగమునకు . . కుందా

Second side.

11. . . . . .
12. ది . . పరాభవ . . చంద్ర
13. తారకముగాను ॥ స్వదత్తంపరద
14. త్తంవా యోహరేతివసుంధరా ష
15. ష్టిర్వర్షసహస్రాణి విష్టా
16. యాంజాయతేక్రిమి.

KAVALI (34).

[Kaligiri. Telugu. On tank bund. Illegible.]

KAVALI (35). (A.D. 1309–10).

[Káṭráyapáḍu. Telugu. To west of village, on cattle-stand.]

TRANSLATION.

Hail! On Thursday the 15th of the bright fortnight of Bhádrapada of the year Saumya, corresponding to the illustrious Ṣaka year 1231, on the occasion of a lunar eclipse, under the Púrvabhádra star, Ṣrímat Tiruvéngaḍanátha Mahípála (king) (gave) Tiruvengadanátha Chaturvédimangalam *alias* the *agrahára* Káṭravávi (or Káṭravápi) to Ṣrímat Tyágasamudra Dharma . . máditya Dévaninḍu, Káṭravápi Angáréni Tiruvengaḍa Bhaṭṭu, who is of the Kauṣika *gótra* . . This Káṭravávi *agrahára* is given with libation of water to these who are versed in the Védas, along with the eight kinds of wealth, in perpetuity to last as long as the sun and moon enduro . . . . kings should protect this *vritti* . . . Hail! Those who think of injuring this charity will be considered to have committed Brahmanicide and other sins. They will be considered to have killed a tawny cow on the banks of the Ganges. May there be great prosperity. Ṣrí. Ṣrí.

NOTE.—The donor's name does not seem to occur elsewhere except in No. 37.

1. స్వస్తిశ్రీ శకవర్షం
2. బులు ౧౨౩౧ వగునేటి సౌంమ్య సంవ

3. త్పర బాద్రపదశు ౧౫ పూర్వభద్ర గురు
4. వారమున సోమగ్రహణ కాలమునం
5. ద్దు శ్రీమత్యాగ సముద్ర ధర్మ . . . మా
6. దిత్యదేవ కిందుకు శ్రీమతు తిరువెం
7. గడనాథ మహీపాలుండు యగ్రహా
8. రము కాత్రవావియైన తిరువెంగడ
9. నాథ చతుర్వేదిమంగలము కౌశి
10. క గోత్రజులైన కాత్రవాపి అ
11. ంగారేని తిరువెంగడ భట్లు . . .

Second side.

12. వేద శాస్త్రజ్ఞులు . . . బుజనాథ
13. న . . . . యు
14. ష్ట భోగసామ్యముతో నుదకపు
15. రముగానుం ఆ చంద్రార్కస్థా
16. యిగా నిచ్చిన యికాత్ర వాపి
17. అగ్రహారము యాగము
18. నైన ప . . . వేంద్రులు రక్షింప
19. వలయును యీ ధర్మ ప్రవర్థిన
20. స్వస్తి యీ ధర్మమునకు విరో
21. ధము దలంచ్చిన వాండు
22. బ్రహ్మహత్యాది పాపములు
23. సేసినవాండు గంగక
24. ఱుతం గపిలముంబో
25. డ్చిన పాపానం బడువాండు
26. మంగళ మహా శ్రీ శ్రీ.

KAVALI (36). (A.D. 1312-13?)

[Káṭráyapáḍu. Telugu. From a big stone north of village.]

TRANSLATION.

Hail! On Friday the 11th of the bright fortnight of Phálguṇa of the year Parídhávi, corresponding to the illustrious Ṣaka year 1233, (Sádamabo) Arupálisetti . . . . presented . . . as a *mányam* to Channakéṣa Perumál of *Káṭrávipáḍu* for the religious merit of Hail! Ṣrímat Manḍa . . . Náyankaruváru . . . . while Kákatíya Pratápa Rudradéva Mahárájulu was ruling the earth . . . . . Kákati Rudradéva . . . Siddhárthi year . . . dark fortnight. Monday . . . . with libation of water to last as long as the sun and stars endure.

NOTE.—The cyclic and S.S. years differ by a year.

1. స్వస్తిశ్రీ శకవరుషంబు
2. లు ౧౨౩౩ అగునేంటి పరిధావి
3. సంవత్సర పాలుగుణ శు
4. ద్ధ ౧౧ శుక్రవారం కాట్రావిపా
5. టి చన్నకేశ పెరుమాళ్లు
6. కు స్వస్తి శ్రీమతుమండ
7. . నాయంక్రరువారికి దరుమ
8. ముగాను (సాదమ బో) అరు
9. (పాలిశెట్టి . . . పాలిన)
10. (. . క యొట్ల . వా . ండి)
11. (. . విరారా . . గానం)
12. మాన్యముగాను ద . ము ఇస్తి

Second side.

1. . . . కవ . ంబు .
2. కాక తియప్రతాప రుద్రదేవ
3. మహారాజుగారు దరిశ్రీయెలు
4. (మడా . వారికృత . తానా)
5. (చక్రవాక . . తక)
6. (ంశ క్రాంత . కలాక . .)
7. . . . .
8. . (మ) . . . .
9. (మ . . యం . . . . . మక)
10. (మ . . . . వటి)
11. (న బాదిత్యతి శీ . . . .)
12. (క్రోజయతితి . వసం .
13. . . . . కి చం దునిధాయ)
14. (స్త నిజ . . . . త)
15. (తరకాక తిరుద్ర దెవవేలా)
16. (ని . లం . . . . యెచాత)
17. . . . . ను . . . . విమ
18. (లచికాయ కొస . . . ద్ర)
19. . . . . సిద్ధార్థి
20. సంవత్సరె . . . . .
21. (వ . . తిసవ . కిష్ణ చి)
22. నోవా . . . దా . .)
23. (వమి . . . . . శీపంచ)
24. ద్రాయ శీగయ రంగ్రసా)
25. . . . . . . తారు సమతిమా)
26. . . . . చంద్రయో స్వస్తిశ్రీ.

Third side.

1. పుడినాయచ
2. మాకుం బుణ్యంగాను మా
3. (చానాంవలోన . పిర .)
4. (వకు . . . పరుల . పమ)
5. (గా . రు మంగానున్న)
6. (. . డుశ్వ . . రు . .)
7. (లంగాను . . . గం)
8. జ . . . . . . మగాను)
9. (న్నష్టా . . . . తము)
10. గాను . . తారాకణాము
11. గాను దారా పూర్వకముగాను
12. చెసియియి . . .
13. . . . .
14. . . . . .
15. . . ద్దాత్రితా . . వత్సో
16. . . చ శెసి . సవరా
17. . . . టి ట్లుడు
18. . . . . .
19. . . . . .

Fourth side.

1. . . . శచశ్రీ
2. . . . . వా
3. . శా . . . దేవరకు
4. . . . . . .
5. . . . . . ధారా
6. . ముశ్రీ . య
7. . . దేవరకు . . .

8. న శీ . మతములు
9. ంతుమతు . . .
10. త మ హేశ్వ . . . .
11. . . లకును . కీకశిలు
12. . . . . శ్రీ .
13. . . . . .
14. . . . . సాయ
15. . . . . ల్లినలు నాయ.

KAVALI (37). (A.D. 1309–10.)

[Káṭráyapáḍu. Sanskrit in Telugu character. To the south on the cattle-stand.]

TRANSLATION.

V. 1. May the glorious boar be triumphant—resting on the tip of whose tusk the illustrious earth was resplendent like a *kétaki* tree standing on . . . .

V. 2. In the Ṣaka year reckoned by the Moon (1), the Rámas (3), and the Suns (12), (*i.e.*, 1231), in the year Saumya, ... on (the day of) a holy lunar eclipse, while king Ranganáṭha was ruling the earth . . . the glorious king (of ?) Vengaḍéṣa, who is sinless, presented the *agrahára* Káṭraváya . . . . to Bhímarámésvara.

Ṣrí! Ṣrí!

NOTE.—The donor of this inscription is obviously the same as that of No. 35. The object of the gift is the same. The year is the same. The donor was a feudatory of king Ranganátha, but it is not clear to what dynasty either of them belonged. Ranganátha may be Madurántaka Pottapi Chóḷa Rája Gaṇḍa Gópáladéva.

1. [श्रीव]राहस्स जयतात् यस्य दंष्ट्राग्रसंस्थिस्थ-
2. ता । रेजे . . . श्रीप्रिथिवी[1] कैतकीव . . संश्रि
3. ता । [१*] शाकाब्दे चंद्ररामद्युमणिपरिमि-
4. ते वत्सरे सौम्य . . पुण्ये चंद्रोपरागे म
5. . . [स]ति प्रिथिवीं रंगनाथक्षितीं [द्रे] [।*] प्रादा-
6. त् श्रीवेंगडेशाक्षितिपतिरनघ[:] काट्रवाया-
7. ग्रहारं . . . .
8. . . क्रितां भी[म] रा[मे]-
9. श्वराय [॥*] श्री श्री [॥*]

KAVALI (38). (A.D. 1228–29 ?)

[Kátráyapáḍu. Telugu. On calingulah of tank, north of village.]

TRANSLATION.

On the first Ékádaṣi (11th) day, corresponding to the Ṣaka year 1150, Hail! In the reign of Ṣríman Mahámaṇḍalésvara Gaṇḍagópála Tirukáḷadéva Chóḍa Mahárájulu, Hail! Ṣrímat Patináyakunḍu constructed a temple, for the treasury of (?) Késạvadéva of Kátravavi for the religious merit of his parents and himself and joyfully gave the last field to the east of the tank (Kálukucheruvu) to Perumáḷḷu to last as long as the sun and moon exist.

---

[1] Read श्रीपृथिवी.

1. శక వర్షంబులు ౧౧౨౦
2. అగుయేంటి ప్రథమ ఏకాదశి
3. నాండు స్వస్తి శ్రీమన్మహామం
4. డలేశ్వర గండగోపాల తిరు
5. కాళదేవ చోడమహా రా
6. జుల యేలికిని స్వస్తి శ్రీమతు
7. పాతినాయకుండు తమతల్లి
8. దండ్రులకుం దమకుం దమ్మ
9. వుగా కాట్రవది కేశవదేవరకు
10. భండారువుగా ని గుడియె త్తిం
11. చి . న దేవపెరుమాండ్లను బ్రతి
12. మసమున నాచంద్రార్కముగా ని
13. ల్చెను చేనుకాలుకు చెరువు
14. దూర్పున కొన్నుచెను ౩౦
15. తవ్విః చు.

Kavali (39). (A.D. 1207–08.)

[Kàvali. Mainly Sanskrit in Telugu character. From stone near tank bund. This stone appears to be within the boundaries of Maddurpád village.]

Translation.

Sanskrit.

V. 1. Kaṣyapa was the grandson of Brahma, who was born from the lotus issuing from the navel of (Vishnu) the consort of Ṣrí whose broad chest is tinged with the saffron of the bosom of Ṣrí Kántá (Lakshmí).

His son was the Sun, the lord of the world. His son was the divine Manu. In the race sprung from him, in regular succession from king Ikshváku, was born Ráma, who was united with Ṣrí (Lakshmí, *i.e.*, Síta).

V. 2. In his family was born king Karikála. In his lineage there was king Béta, who was devoted to the worship of the lotus feet of Ṣiva. His son Yerra-siddhíṣvara, endowed with valour characteristic of his race, took the hand of Ṣrí Dévi, which was marked with the lotus, discus and conch.

V. 3. She (Ṣrí Dévi) the virtuous, who resembled the Srí (the goddess of fortune) of his kingdom, who was adorned with the aggregate of celebrated qualities, and who was liberal, brought forth sons, who were endowed with attributes abounding in prowess, and who were equal to Indra.

Of them the eldest, king Nalla Siddha, was anointed; by his favour (his younger brother) Ṣrí Tammu Siddha, lord of men, rules the whole kingdom as supreme lord.

V. 4. Distributing the aggregate of all gifts in company with his mother, protecting the earth, having summoned these venerable Bráhmans, Bandari Tripurárya and others, who are versed in the Veda, who are masters of all the sciences, and who are intent on the six karmas, having worshipped them, he, the wise, gave the village desired (by them) to be enjoyed in a hundred shares by them.

V. 5. In the Ṣaka year, reckoned by the treasures (9), eyes (2), earth (1), and moon (1), (*i.e.*, 1129), in the year Prabhava, on a holy day, at equinox—Ṣrí Tammu Siddhíṣvara presented in perpetuity large gifts and an appropriate *agrahára* called Ṣrípura after his own mother (Ṣrí Dévi), possessed of the triad of human objects of desire (virtue, pleasure and wealth), in the illustrious *Vishaya* (territory) Daddura.

Telugu.

(The boundaries of) the fields of Ṣrípura are :—
on the east, Rácherru (Kávali tank);
on the south, Velpuncherru (a tank);
on the west, the cart-track near the tope of Boḍudévarapâḍu; and
on the north water (a water course ?)

Those who protect this *agrahára* included within these four boundaries will get imperishable reward.

Sanskrit.

V. 6. By many (kings) has the earth been given; by many (kings) has it been protected. Of whomsoever the land is, his is the fruit.

V. 7. He who resumes land, whether given by himself, or by another, is reborn a worm in ordure for 60,000 years.

1. श्रीकांताकुचकुंकुमां
2. कितबृहद्वक्षस्थलश्रीपते
3. र्नाभेरंबुजजन्मसूनुतनयो
4. यःकश्यपस्तत्सुतः । सूर्यो
5. लोकगुरुस्तदंगजानितोदेवोमनुस्त
6. द्भवादिक्ष्वाकोर्नृपते रनुक्रमकुला
7. द्रामोजनिश्रीयुतः ॥ (*v.* 1.) तद्वंशा
8. त्करिकाल मानवपतिर्जातस्तुतस्या
9. न्वयाद्दासीद्बेतमहीपतिर्भवपदा
10. म्भोजानपूजारतः ॥ तत्सूनुः कु
11. लशीलशौर्य्यसहित श्रीयर्रासिद्धोश्व
12. र श्रीदेवीकरमग्रहीत्सरासिजश्री

13. शंखचक्रांकितं ॥ (*v.* 2.) तद्राज्ञश्रीसमा
14. ना प्रथितगुणगणालंकृतिर्द्दानशीला
15. साध्वीसासूत शौर्य्यप्रबलगुणयु
16. तान्नंदनानिंद्रतुल्यान् ॥ तत्रासीन्नक्ष
17. सिद्धिक्षितिपतिरभिषिक्तोग्रजस्तत्कटा
18. क्षादेव श्रीतम्मुसिद्धोनृपतिरखिलसां
19. म्राज्यराज्यं करोति ॥ (*v.* 3.) तन्मात्रा सह स
20. र्व्वदाननिकरं कुर्वन्महीपालयान्वि
21. प्रान्वेदविदस्सुमूलघटिकान्षट्कर्म
22. शीलानिमान् । भंडारित्रिपुरार्य्यमु
23. ख्यसुमुखानाहूय संपूज्य तान् ।
24. भागानाशतसंख्यया परिवृतं ग्रा
25. मं स तेषांसुधीः ॥ (*v.* 4.) शकाब्देनिधिनेत्र
26. भूशशिमिते भूदानमत्राधि
27. कंपुण्येह्नि प्रभवेसमेविषुवति
28. श्रीतम्मु सिद्धीश्वरः ॥ श्रीमद्गुद्दुरु
29. नामधेयविषयेस्वस्यैवमातुश्चिर
30. नामश्रीपुरमग्रहारमुचितंप्रादा
31. त् त्रिवर्गान्वितं ॥ (*v.* 5.)

శ్రీపురమునకుం బొ

32. లము, పూర్వదిక్కున జొచట్లులోను । దక్షిణ
33. దిక్కున వేల్పుంజెఱువు । పశ్చిమదిక్కున (బో?)డ్డ
34. వరపాటితోపుదగ్గటిన బండివసర । ఉత్త
35. రపుదిక్కున నేఱు ॥ ఈ చతుస్సీమముంతోంగూడ
36. నీ యగ్రహారమురక్షించినవారి కక్షయఫలం.
37. बहुभिर्व्वसुधा दत्ता बहुभिश्चानुपालिता । य

38. स्ययस्य यथाभूमिस्तस्यतस्य तथाफलं (v. 6) स्वदत्तां

39. परदत्तांवायोहरेति वसुन्धरां । षष्ठिवर्षस

40. हस्त्राणि विष्टायां जायतेक्रिमि ॥ (v. 7.)

NOTE.—This inscription is in Telugu character and the language is Sanskrit except where the boundaries are given. The Sanskrit portion is all in verse.

It begins with the genealogy of the donor Tammu Siddhi tracing him up to Vishnu.

Vishnu.
|
Brahma.
|
Kasyapa (grandson).
|
Son.
|
Manu.
|
Ikshváku.
|
* * *
* *
|
Rama.
|
* * *
|
Karikála.
* * * *
* *
|
Béta.
|
Yerra Siddhi = Şrí Déví.
|
Nalla Siddhi (crowned). — Tammu Siddhi (regent) Donor. Date S.S. 1129.

Dr. Hultzsch calls the family 'Telugu Choḍas.' The genealogy given in this inscription differs slightly from that of Branch C given on page 18 of Government Epigraphist's Report of the year ending with 30th June 1900, where the succession is given as—

Béta I.

Dáyabbíma. Nalla Siddha. Erra Siddha.

(sons of Nalla Siddha:) Manmasidahi *m.* Sridévi. Béta II. Tammu Siddha.

The donor Tammu Siddha was regent while his elder brother Nalla Siddha was the anointed king.

The object of the grant is an *agrahára* Ṣrípura named after Ṣrí Dévi, the mother of the donor. The inscription states that it was given to Tripurárya and other Bráhmans to be enjoyed in 100 shares which are enumerated on the back of the stone.

KAVALI (40).

[Kávali. Telugu. From gateway of a detached shrine in enclosure of Anjanéṣvara Svámi's temple.]

TRANSLATION.

They have given (the village) Jeldapáḍu to the deity of Jeldapáḍu to last as long as the sun and the moon for the religious merit of Ṣríman Mahámaṇḍaléṣvara Manma Siddhi Déva Chóḍa Mahárája, son of (Ṣrí)man Mahámaṇḍaléṣvara Jagadobba-Ganḍa Kámaya Déva Mahárája.

Those who think of obstructing this will be regarded as having killed cows and children on the Ganges and as having killed their grandsons.

[One imprecatory verse.]

NOTE.—Manma Siddhi is of the family called 'Telugu Choḍas' by Dr. Hultzsch. Jagadobbaganḍa is also a biruda of the kings of the Reḍḍi dynasty and means "the sole hero of the world".

(1) (శ్రీ) మన్మహా మండలేశ్వర జ
(2) గ దొబ్బగండకామయ దే
(3) వ మహారాజుల కొమారులైన
(4) ట్టి శ్రీమన్మహా మండలేశ్వ
(5) ర మన్మసిద్ధి దేవ చోడ
(6) మహారాజులుః ధర్మా త్ర్తమ
(7) గా జెల్లపాటిమదేవరకు
(8) జెల్లపాడ ఆచంద్రార్కము
(9) గ నిచ్చిరి దీనికి యేరుగాని విష్ను
(10) ము తలచేవాండు గంగ కఅత ఆవు
(11) ని పిల్లల చంపినవారు వీండ్ల
(12) కొడుకు కొడుకును వధిం
(13) చినవారు। స్వదత్తం పరద
(14) త్తంవా ఓహారేతి వసుంధరాం
(15) షష్టివరుష సహస్త్రాణి వి
(16) ష్టాయాం జాయతే క్రిమి.

KÁVALI (41).

[Kottapalli. Teluḍu. To north of village.]

TRANSLATION.

55 *kuntas* of paddy field. If any one appropriates this field he will incur the sin of killing Bráhmans, &c.

(1) వరిమడికు ౫౫ ఇమ్మ
(2) డి యెవ్వరు పుచ్చుకొన్న
(3) ను బ్రహ్మహత్యాది పా
(4) త కాలం బొందుదు
(5) రు.

[Maddurpád. See under Kávali.]

KÁVALI (42).

[Mungamúru. Telugu. On south wall of Ganéṣa temple.]

TRANSLATION.

(Adoration be to) the Lord of the Universe (?)

We gave 1,100 *kuntas* of wet land under the tank as a *mányam* to Káṣi Pápá Battuḍu, who constructed these temples. We shall maintain this as long as the sun and moon exist. Every one should maintain this act of piety without fail. Though it yield three crops, whoever wishes to appropriate it or thinks of injuring it, will incur the sin of committing the five cardinal sins.

1. శ్రీ జగబిదా నానుపతి
2. ఈ దేవుళాలుగట్టిన కాశి పాపాభత్తు
3. నికి మావ్యం చెరువుకింద్ద వరిమడి కుంట్ల
4. లుకు ౧౦౦౦ ఆచెంద్రార్కస్థాయిగాను
5. నడపువారు యీ పుణ్యానకు యెవ్వరు
6. న్నా తప్పక నడపువారు ముకాఱుచున్నా పం
7. డినాను యీ మాన్యానకు యెవ్వరు ఆ
8. శించినాను కీడు దలంచినాను పంచమ
9. హాపాతకాలు శేసిన పాపానం బోవు
10. వారు.

KAVALI (43). (A.D. 1263–64 ?)

[Muṅgamúru. Telugu. Stone to east of Nilakanthéṣvara temple.]

TRANSLATION.

On Thursday the 5th of the bright fortnight of Chaitra, of the illustrious Ṣaka year 1185 . . . . of the

Ṣrívatsa *gótrá*, who is the prime minister (Mahápradháni) of Ṣríman Mahámandaléṣvara Manma Siddhi déva Chóḍa Mahárájulu, gave 50 ewes as an act of piety for lighting two twilight lamps to Gauríṣvaradéva of . . . varam in Poritináḍu (a sub-division of) Pákanáḍu. The *Kápus* of the village should receive these ewes (and maintain lights).

The witnesses to this . . . .

శ్రీ శకవర్షంబులు
౧౧౭౫ వటి చైత్ర
శుద్ధ పంచమిన్ని గురు
వారమునాండు పాక
నాంటిలోని పొరితినాంటి
వరము శ్రీ గౌరీశ్వర
దేవరక సంధ్యా దీపము
లు రెంటికి శ్రీమన్మహా
మండలేశ్వర మన్మసి
ద్ధిదేవ చోడమహా
రాజుల మహాప్రదాని శ్రీవ
త్సగోత్రం . . . .
రకొ . . . థ
ర్మంగాను గొఱ్ఱ్యలు ౫౦
గ్రామాన కాంపులు గొన్ని
చెకొని . . . వియ్యపకొ
. నూ జెకె నూం బ్రొ
. . దినికి సాక్ష్యాలు
మదమర్ణము దడినిభ . .
. . . . .

KÁVALI (44). (A.D. 1715-16 ?)

[Mungamúru. Telugu. On south wall of Ganéṣa temple.]

TRANSLATION.

May it be auspicious! Hail! On Thursday the 11th of the bright fortnight of Mágha of the year Manmatha, corresponding to the illustrious, victorious and prosperous Ṣálivṓhana Ṣaka year 1660, as the temple of Gaṇádhipati (Ganéṣa) of Mungamúr which had been constructed as an act of piety was in ruins, Kesima Reḍḍi Lingá Reḍḍi, son of Perumá Reḍḍi who has the *birudas*: Gandaragandá[1] Prajamechchuganḍa,[2] Panḍitapunḍaríkachanḍamártánḍa,[3] constructed a *manḍapa* in front of the temple of Nílakanṭhéṣvara of Mungamúru, a temple to Mátángidévi, a sluice to the tank of Mungamúr, the Máram tank in the village of Kaḍvanútala,[4] and a temple to Vináyakasvámi for the religious merit of his parents, to last as long as the sun and moon endure. May it cause great prosperity. Ṣrí.

[One imprecatory verse.]

NOTE.—The S.S. and cyclic years do not agree. Who this titled Reḍḍi was is not apparent, probably only a big land-holder.

శుభమస్తు

1. స్వస్తి శ్రీ జయాభ్యుదయ శాలివాహన శకవరుషంబులు ౧౬౬౦

2. అగునేంటి మన్మథ సంవత్సర మాఘ శు ౧౧ శు। ముంగ- మూరిగణాధిప

---

[1] Hero of heroes.

[2] Hero who is praised by people.

[3] A powerful sun to the lotuses which are learned men (*i.e.*,) patron of learned men.

[4] Kadanútala.

3. తినగరు క్రితం సేశించిన పుణ్యం ఖిలమఖి పుడ్డంగాను గండరగండ ప్రజమె

4. చ్చగండ పండిత పుండరీక చెండమార్తాండ । బిరుదాంకుండైన పెరుమారెడ్డి కొ

5. మారుండు కేశిమరెడ్డి లింగారెడ్డి ముంగమూరి నీలకంఠేశ్వరుని ముంద్దర మం

6. డపమున్ను మాతాంగ్గిదేవి నగరున్ను ముంగ్గమూరి చెర్వుతూమున్ను కడ్వనూ(*)

7. తులుందు మారంచెర్వున్ను యీ వినాయకస్వామి నగరున్ను తమతల్లి దండ్డ్రాదులకు

8. పుణ్యాంగాను ఆ చెంద్రార్కముంగాను యీ డేచ్చేణము శ్రీ శ్రీ జేయును ॥ శ్రీ ॥ స్వద

9. త్తాద్విగుణం పుణ్యం పరదత్తానుపాలనం పరదత్తా పహారేణస్వద

10. తం నిష్ఫలంభవేత్.

Kavali (45). (A.D. 1230–31 ?)

[Músanúr. Telugu. From tank between Músanúr and Kávali. The inscription is not clearly legible. It is in Telugu verse. The following seems to be the purport] :—

Translation.

Hail! In the illustrious Ṣaka year reckoned by the hands (2), arrows (5), Hara (11), (*i.e.*, 1152), on Monday (the day of Kamalári = the moon) under the Uttará Phalguṇí Nakshatra (asterism) in the reign of Gaṇḍa

Gópála Dípakaltidéva who is possessed of complete glory, and who is the self-chosen lord of the earth.

Karáru Manmarámunḍu, the ruler of Muraṇapura (lit. the beloved of the lady Muraṇapura), the protector of all virtuous people, and who is delightful by reason of his virtues, presented with libation of water, free of encumbrance, two parts under the Táṭicheruvu in this village of Musunḍu (Musunúr) while (his minister) Mantri Kétana presented one part to Ganḍa Gópála.

NOTE.—See under No. 47.

1. స్వస్తిశ్రీ శాకసంవత్స
2. రంబులు కరశరహారసంఖ్యం
3. ఖరగం గోత్తరపు ఫలుగు
4. ణింగమలారి దినమున గం
5. డగోపాలుండఖండ కీర్తి
6. దిపకల్తి దేవ భూవరుని రా
7. జ్యంబున మురణపురాంగనా
8. వరుండు సకల శిష్టరక్షణ
9. గలట్టి కరారు మన్మరాముండు
10. సద్గుణరంజితుండు నేతయీ
11. ముసుండు గ్రామందాటి చెరువు
12. నందుభాగములు రెండు గండ
13. గోపాలునకును మంత్రి కేతనుం
14. డొకపాలు మానుగాంగ నుదకస
15. మర్పణంబుగానిచ్చెను దషయకుండ.

KAVALI (46). (A.D. 1638–39.)

[Músanúr. Telugu. From stone in the garden of Révúr Lakshmayya.]

TRANSLATION.

Hail! Prosperity! (This is) the edict relating to Musanúr tank granted by Velugóṭi Venkaṭapati Náyanivàru,[1] in the victorious and prosperous Ṣáliváhana Ṣaka year 1560, corresponding to the Bahudhánya year, on the 2nd of the dark fortnight of the month of Chaitra. The Sandháta (village official), lessee, amaradar, or ruler of the village should do work to the tank and channel for the *méras* attached thereto. If, not doing it, the ruler of the village, kápu or karnam or any one else, utilizes those *méras* or removes this edict, he will be regarded as having been born to a veṭṭi and the veṭṭi will ravish his wife.

1. స్వస్తిశ్రీ విజయాభ్యుదయ
2. శాలివాహాన శకవర్షంబులు
3. ౧౫౬౦ అగు బహుధా
4. న్యసంవత్సర చైత్ర బ ౨లు
5. వెలుగోటి వెంకటపతి నా
6. యునింగారు ముసునూరి
7. చెర్వు వేఇంచిన ధర్మశాసనం
8. గ్రామం సంధ్ధాతంగుత్త అ
9. మరం యేలిన చెర్వు మేర
10. చెర్వు కాల్వ పని శేఇంచ్చే
11. ది శేఇంచక ఆమేరధా
12. న్యం వూరుయేలే వారు కా

---

[1] A zamindar of Venkaṭagiri.

13. ంపు కరణం యవ్వరు అళి
14. ంచినా శాసనంతీసి వేఞ
15. ంచినా వెట్టివారిక్ పుట్టినవా
16. డు వాడి అల్ని వెట్టి
17. వాండు డెంగును.

Kavali (47). (A.D. 1230-31 ?)

[Músanúr (hamlet Chentsugánipáḷem). Sanskrit in Telugu character. On stone opposite old temple of Vénugópál Svámi.]

Translation.

V. 1. Victorious in the world is king Chóḍa Tikkálati, the jewelled lamp of Jambudvípa (India), whose feet all kings approach with the desire of seeking refuge—whose fame is as white as snow, silver, white grass, the heavenly river, the conch, and crystal.

V. 2. While he, the glorious, whose shout of victory is raised by the kings of the three worlds which have been conquered by his own arm, who is the ornament of the earth, is ruling the kingdom which is pleasing to men,

V. 3. In the Ṣáka year reckoned by the arms (2), arrows (5), the three-eyed (Ṣiva 11) *i.e.*, 1152, on Monday the 12th of the bright half of Kártika, the ruler of Muraṇapura named Kóḍaráma, gave an endowment for lamps to Gópála in Músunúr village which is subject to him to the north-west of the tank . . . .

Note.—This inscription is in Sanskrit verse and in Telugu character.

It records the grant of an endowment for lighting lamps to the deity Gópála.

The donor is Kóḍaráma, the ruler of Muranapura, a feudatory of king Chóḍa Tikkálati.

The stone is defaced in several places and the text is illegible in parts.

The date of this grant is 1152, the same as that of Kávali (45) where the ruler of Muranapura is given as Karáru Manmarámuḍu and said to be subject to Dípakaltidéva, which name is probably a variant of Tikkáltidéva.

Muraṇapuram does not appear in the list of villages in Nellore district.

1. जयति जगति जंबु
2. द्वीपरत्नप्रदीपश्शरण
3. शरणवांच्छायातनाना
4. नरेंद्रः । तुहिनरजतका
5. शाकाशनद्यंबुकंबुस्पाटि
6. कधवलकीर्त्तिश्चोडतिकाल
7. तीशः ॥ (1) ॥ श्रीमति निजभुज
8. विजितात्रिजगज्जनपाल
9. जनितजयशब्दे । तस्मिन्भू
10. तलातिलके राज्यं तन्व
11. ति जनानुरागकरम् ॥ (2) ॥ शा
12. काब्दे बाहुबाणात्रिन
13. यनगणिते कार्त्तिके शु
14. क्लपक्षे द्वादश्यामिंदु
15. वारे मुरणपुरपतिः
16. कोडरामाभिधानः ।
17. प्रादाद्वायोस्तटाके (?) निजा
18. धीश मुमुंरुग्रामके

19. दीपकल्पं गोपालाय

20. श . . . . . ॥ (3)

Kavali (48). (A.D. 1273-74.)

[Peddakondúru. Telugu. To east of hamlet Víráreḍḍi-pálem.]

Translation.

Hail! On Saturday the day of Vishuma Sankránti, in the year Ṣrímukha, in the illustrious Ṣaka year 1195, (Hail!) Ṣríman Mahámaṇḍaléṣvara Nágadévarájulu, who is endowed with all eulogistic titles, gave with libation of water to Mehâyini Tikkináyaḍu of (Prápa) * Konḍúru for the religious merit of Rudradéva Mahárájulu, son of . . . and Nágadévarájulu for providing worship, sacred food, light, and dancing as long as the sun and moon exist. This charity shall be maintained for ever.

[One imprecatory verse.]

* * * *

Those who violate this charity will be considered to have killed 10,000 tawny cows near the Ganges, to have committed the five cardinal sins and to have administered poison in the food given to their parents and to gods and goddesses. Ṣrí, Ṣrí, Ṣrí.

* Note.—Prápakonḍúru is possibly a misreading for Peddakonḍúru.

1. స్వస్తి శ్రీ శకవర్షంబులు ౧౧౯౫ ము విషు

2. మ సంక్రాంతిని శనివారమునాండు

3. స్వస్తి సమస్తప్రశస్తి సహితం శ్రీమన్మ

4. హా మండలేశ్వర నాగదేవరాజుల (పట్టు

5. పర్ణపాశముశిః యాద్ర?) కొడుకు రుద్రదేవ
6. మహారాజులకు నాగదేవరాజులకు
7. ధర్మవుగాను వారియూరి ప్రాపకొండ్డూరు మె
8. హోయిని లికినాయిని సెతికి అచ్బిర్నన
9. భోగానకు అమృత పడికి దీపానకు పాత్ర
10. భోగానకు శ్రీముఖ సంవత్సరమున ధారా పూ
11. ర్వకము సేసి ఆచంద్రతారకముగా నిచ్చె
12. ఈ ధర్మవు ఎల్లకాలము నడపంగలవారు
13. స్వదత్తం పరదత్తంవా యోహరేతివ
14. సుంధరా షష్టివర్ష సహస్రా
15. ణి విష్టాయాం జాయతేక్రిమిః॥
16. జడతుపా . . ఈ ధర్మవునకు
17. దక్షిన గంగ్గకట్ట బదివేల గపిలల
18. బొడ్డినవారు పంచమహాపాతకము
19. సేసినవారు తల్లితండ్రుల దేవిదేవరు
20. కంచ్చాన విషముపెట్టినవారు శ్రీ శ్రీ శ్రీ.

KAVALI (49). (A.D. 1638–39 ?)

[Tállapáḷem. Telugu. From stone in front of old temple.]

TRANSLATION.

Hail! In 1558 of the victorious and prosperous Ṣáliváhana Ṣaka era, corresponding to the cyclic year Bahudhánya on the 5th day of the month Phálguṇa, while the illustrious supreme ruler of kings, Víra Pratápa Ṣrí Víra Venkaṭapatiráya seated on the throne of Penugonda was ruling the kingdom of the earth, we have settled *méras* at one *kuncha* per *puṭṭi* for the tank of Júṭúr village situated in Udayagiri Ṣíma which was given to Veligóṭi Venkaṭapati Náyanivíru (by the Rája) as an *amaram.* If any person covet (the *méras*) and do not give the *kunchas* (*méras*) of that tank to Upparas [diggers] and maintain the tank, he will incur the sin of killing a cow and a Bráhman on the Ganges. His [wife's] honour will be given to a Chanḍála and he will be put on a donkey with a toddy pot tied round the neck and despatched to the town of Yama.

Note.—Bahudhánya corresponds to 1560 S.S. expired and not 1558.

1. స్వస్తిశ్రీ జయాభ్యుదయ శాలివాహన శక
2. వర్షంబులు ౧౫౫౮ వ అగునేడి బహుధాన్య సం
3. వత్సర ఫాల్గుణ ౫ లు శ్రీమద్రాజాధిరాజ పరమేశ్వ
4. ర వీరం ప్రత్తాప శ్రీవీర వెంకటపతిరాయలయ్యవారు పెను
5. ంగొండ శింహాసనాధీశుండై పృథివి సామ్రాజ్యము
6. యేలుచు వెలిగోటి వెంకటపతినాయనివారికి అమ
7. రానకు పాలించినది వుదయగిరి శీమకు చె
8. ల్లివచెడి, జూటూరి గ్రామానను చెర్వుకుంచాలు
9. కట్టిడ శేస్తిమి గనుక ఆ చెర్వుకుంచాలు వుప్పర్లఁవెశా
10. నయిచి చెర్వునీంద వేయించక యెవడు ఆశించినాను
11. గంగ కతఁను గోవు బ్రాంహ్మణి చంపిన పాపానం
12. బోదురు తనమానము చాండాలునికి యిచ్చి గాడిదెను
13. యెక్కి లొట్టిమెడగట్టుకొని యమపురికి యెంగును.

KAVALI (50). (A.D. 1636–37.)

[Tállapáḷem. Telugu. From stone by a pond near the temple.]

TRANSLATION.

Hail! In the victorious and prosperous Ṣáliváhana Ṣaka year 1558 corresponding to the (cyclic) year Dhátu on the 7th day of the dark fortnight of Chaitra, while Víra Venkaṭapati Ráya, seated on the throne of Penugoṇḍa, is ruling the kingdom of the earth, Kunchála Venganna, the agent (mudrakartá) of Venkaṭapati Náyaniváru, under the orders of Venkaṭapati Náyaniváru, commands as follows with regard to the *méras* fixed at one *kuncha*[1] per *puṭṭi* for the tank attached to the village of Kávali in the *ṣíma* of Udayagiri given to Velugóṭi Venkaṭapati Náyaniváru as *amaram* (service tenure) by the Rája (Ṣrí Víra Venkaṭapati).

If any person covet (the *méras*) and do not give the *kunchas* of that tank to Upparas (diggers) and maintain the tank he will incur the sin of killing a cow and a Bráhman on the Ganges. His (wife's) honour will be given to a Chanḍála, and, without respect to the rule of caste, he will be put on a donkey with a toddy pot tied round the neck, eating . . . and despatched to the town of Yama.

1. స్వస్తిశ్రీ జయాభ్యుదయ శాలివా
2. హన శకవర్షంబులు ౧౫౫౮ అగు నేటి
3. ధాతృ సంవత్సరచైత్ర బ ౭ లు శ్రీమద్రాజా
4. ధిరాజపరమేశ్వర శ్రీవీర ప్రతాప శ్రీవీర వేంక
5. టపతిరాయలయ్యవారు పెనుంగొండ సింహా

[1] = 8 measures.

6. సనాసీనుడై పృద్విసామ్రాజ్యమున్ను శేయుచున్న వెలి
7. గోటి వెంకటపతినాయనివారికి అమరానకు పాలి
8. ంచిన వుడయగిరి శీమలోని కావలి గ్రామా
9. న చెల్లెచరువు పుటి[1]కుంచాలు వెంకటపతి నాయనివా
10. రి ముద్రకర్తకుంచాల వెంగ్గన వెంకటపతినాయ
11. నివారి ఆనతి ప్రకారానను చెరువుకె కట్టడ శేశేగనకు ఆచె
12. రువు కుంచాలు వుప్పరవారి వశాన యిచ్చి చెరువుమీం
13. దవేయించక యెవరు ఆశించినాను గంగ్గకర్త గోవు బ్రాం
14. హ్మణచంపినపాపానంబోవును. తనమానిముంచండాలునికి
15. యిచ్చివావివరసలుతప్పి గాడిదెను యెక్కి లొట్టిమెడంగట్టి
16. ంచి . . . బక్షింస్తా[2]ను యమపురికి యెంగును.

Kavali (51). (A.D. 1198–99.)

[Timmasamudram. Telugu. From stone in field bearing Survey Number 170.]

Translation.

Hail! On Sunday, the 11th of the bright half of Vaiṣákha, under the Uttara Nakshatra (asterism), in the year Kálayukta, corresponding to the year 1120 of the illustrious Ṣaka era, Ṣrí Pati Náyuḍu set up the image of Prasannakéṣavadéva at Chintagunṭa for the religious merit of his father, and gave with libation of water four *paṭṭus* of dry land at Kāḷavarmagunta, and 200 *kunṭas* of dry land behind Chintacheruvu, to Kéṣava Bhaṭṭa Nāmbi to provide for burnt offering, other offerings and worship to the deity. Vindla Kéṣami Náyuḍu and Mangala

---

[1] Read పుట్టి.

[2] Read బక్షిస్తాను.

Késami Náyudu gave the Gandávaram póliméra field for providing daily offering, one *pattu* of dry land at Elamanchigunta, 100 *kuntas* of paddy field in rear of Chóda Rámala tank, one *máda* (Rs. 2) for lighting twilight lamps, one *rúka* (probably a silver coin worth 5 as. 8 p.) for the observance of Ekádasi (11th day), and a cow on the day of Uttará Nakshatra. This charity should be maintained as long as the sun and the moon exist.

Those who obstruct this charity will incur the sin of killing their parents and 1,000 cows on the Ganges, and the sin of taking food from the skull of their eldest sons.

1. స్వస్తిశ్రీ శకవర్షంబులు ౧౧౨౦ అ
2. గు నెంటి కాల యుక్తి సంవత్సరాన వైశాఖ
3. శుద్ధ ఏకాదశీని ఆదివారమూను ఉత్తర
4. నక్షత్రమున శ్రీపతినాయుండు తమ
5. తండ్రులకు దర్మ్మువుగాను చింతగుంటన
6. ప్రసన్న కేశవదేవరు ప్రతిష్టచ్చెసి దేవరకు
7. హవిబలి అర్చనలకు కేశవభట్టన
8. ం బిండ్గారికి ధారాపూర్వకము శేసి ఇ
9. చ్చిన వెలిసేను కాళవర్మ గుఁటలోపల
10. ను పట్లు ౪ చిఁతలచెఱువు వెనక
11. వెలిచేని గుంటలు ౨౦౦ బిండ్లకేశ
12. మినాయుండూను మంగళకేశమినా
13. యుండూను గండావరముపోలిమేరచె
14. ల్నినివేద్యమునకు ఎలమంచి గుంటను
15. వెలిసేనుపట్టు ౧ ఇచ్చితిమినని చోడ
16. రామలచెఱువు వెనక ఇచ్చిన వరిచే
17. ని గుంటలు ౧౦౦ సంధ్యాదీపానకు కా
18. సు మ ౧ ఏకాదశి డెళూపనముల శి

19. రసురూకాను ఉత్తరవాసస్వానుగో
20. వ్వాను ఈదర్మంవు ఆచంద్రార్కము
21. చెల్లకలది దీనిం చెఱిచినవారు గం
22. గకటుత తల్లి తంద్రులాను వేయి
23. గోవులానువధియించి పెద్దకొడుకు
24. కపాలమున కసరికూడువండి
25. కుడిచిన పాపానంపోవువారు.

NELLORE (1). (A.D. 1638–39.)

[Allúru. Telugu. On Nandi maṇḍapam opposite Śiva temple.]

TRANSLATION.

Hail! On the 2nd of the bright half of Chaitra of the year Bahudhánya, corresponding to the year 1560 of the illustrious, victorious and prosperous Sáliváhana Śaka era, Śrímat Velugóṭi Venkaṭapati Náyaningáru executed this charitable edict for the tank at Allúru. We have ordered that the tank *méras* of the various villages. collected in the prescribed manner should be spent for the maintenance of the tanks of the respective villages Therefore whether the village be under *sandhátá*, or under an *amaradár*, or lessee, or whoever be the rulers the grain collected as tank *méras* must be spent on the tanks. If, not doing work to the tanks and channel with the grain realized as tank *méras*, any one object, or if any *kápu* or karnam obstruct or if any one remove this inscription, he will be considered to have been born to the *veṭṭi* of this village and to have given his wife to the *veṭṭi* of this village. In these terms has the charitable edict been issued.

1. స్వస్తిశ్రీ జయా
2. భ్యుదయ శాలి
3. వాహాన శకవ
4. ర్షంబులు
5. ౧౫౬౦ అగు
6. నేంటి బహుధా

7. స్య సంవత్సర
8. చైత్ర శు ౨లు.
9. శ్రీమతు వెలు
10. గోటి వెంకటప
11. తినాయనిం
12. గారు అల్లూరు
13. చెర్వుకు వే
14. ఇంచిన ధర్మశా
15. సనం యేయే
16. గ్రామ మూలం
17. చెరువుల మేర
18. లు' యే యే
19. క్రమాన వచ్చె నా
20. మేర అయా
21. గ్రామం చెర్వు
22. మీందవేసి
23. బె ట్టేట్టులు
24. గా నిర్ణయ
25. ం శేశినారం
26. ము గనక ఇ
27. గ్రామం స
28. ంధా తానను
29. ండినా అమ
30. రగానికి ఇ
31. చ్చినాను గు
32. త్తగాంద్రవ
33. శాన నుండ్డి
34. నాను యేదార
35. యేలినాను చెర్వుమే

36. రఙకు నిర్ణయ
37. మైన ధాన్యా
38. లు చెరువు
39. పనిముఖాలు
40. శేఇంచ్చు
41. గలవారు చె
42. రువుమేర
43. ల ధాన్యం చె
44. రువుకాల్వ
45. పనిముఖాలు శే
46. ఇంచ్చుక యవ్వ
47. డు ఆక్షేపిం
48. చ్చినా యే కా
49. ంపు కరణం
50. అడ్డాడినా
51. నున్న నీశాన
52. నం యవ్వరు తీ
53. సివేసినా వాండు
54. ఇవ్వూరి వెట్టివాని
55. కి బుట్టినవాం
56. డే వాండాలిని ఇ
57. యూరి వెట్టివానికి
58. యిచినవాండ్లు
59. అని ఇచ్చిన ధర్మశా
60. సనం

Nellore (2). (A.D. 1533–34.)

[Allúru. Telugu. In Vishnu temple.]

Translation.

May there be prosperity! Hail! On . . . . dark fortnight of Áṣvíja of the year Vijaya, corresponding to the illustrious Śaka year 1455 . . (Manḍa)léṣvara . . . . . . (gave) . . . . to the deity Kéṣavanátha . . . . at Allúr . . . .

1. శుభమస్తు స్వస్తి శ్రీశక
2. వరుషంబులు ౧౪౫౫ అగునే
3. టివిజయ సంవత్సర ఆశ్వీజ బ
4. తడే . . పృథ్వి . .
5. -సేయ . . . . . .
6. వేశ్వర . . లిరుభ . .
7. . . . వైన . . .
8. . . . కేశవనాంధనికిన్నిమా
9. . . . కిమ . . అల్లూరిలోని బోన
10. . . . .

Nellore (3). (A.D. 1756–57.)

[South Ámalúru. Telugu. From stone to east of village.]

Translation.

(May there be prosperity)! Hail! On the 15th of the dark half of Áshádha of the year Dháta, corresponding to the year 1678 of the illustrious, victorious and prosperous Śáliváhana Śaka era . . . . Náyaningáru . . . . . . the *kunchas* of the tank . . . . that *méra* grain . . in the *ṣíma* . . Náyuḍu—they should do work to the tank with the tank *kunchas*. Whoever causes injury to the tank *kunchas* will be considered to have given his (wife's) honour to the *veṭṭi* of the village.

1. . . . . స్తు। స్వస్తి శ్రీ
2. (జ) యాభ్యుద
3. (శా) లివాహ
4. (నశక) వరుషం
5. (బు) లు ౧౬౭౮ అ
6. (గునెటి) ధాతు సంవత్సర
7. (ఆషా) ఢ బ ౧౫ లు పో
8. . నమూరిలోం .
9. . . నాయనింగారు చె
10. (ర్వుకు) ంచాలది ధాన్యం
11. లును ఆమేర
12. ను శ్రీ నెలవె . .
13. ద్రనాయడు . .
14. ఽశీమలో .
15. లూర నడిచె (చెర్వు)
16. కుంచాలు (చెర్వు)
17. మీంద వె (ఇంచగ)
18. లవారు యీకుం
19. చ్చాన్ను యవ్వ(రు)
20. చెరిచినారు (వా)
21. డిమానం వె (ట్టివానికి కిచ్చి)
22. సవాడె.

NELLORE (4). (A.D. 1638–39.)

[Batrakágollu. Telugu. On fallen stone in street the south of village.]

TRANSLATION.

Hail! On the 2nd of the bright half of Chaitra of the year Bahudhánya, corresponding to the year 1560 of the illustrious and victorious Śáliváhana Śaka era, Velugóṭi Venkaṭapati Náyaniváru issued this charitable edict for the *méras* of the tank at Kámgollu. The village *sandhátá*[*gár*], the lessee, the *amara*[*dár*] or the ruler should cause the work to be done to the tank and channel. If, not doing the work, any one covet these *méras*, a *Mádiga* will ravish his wife.

1. స్వస్తి శ్రీవిజయా శాలివాహ
2. నశకవర్షంబులు ౧౫౬౦ బ
3. హుధాన్య సంవత్సర చైత్ర శు ౨ లు వె
4. లుగోటి వేంకటపతి నాయనివారు
5. కాంగొల్లు చెర్వుమేరకు వేయించిన ధ
6. ర్మశాసనం గ్రామం సంధాతం గుత్త అమరం
7. యేలినచ్చెర్వుమేర చెర్వుకాల్వపని చేయి
8. ంచేవి చేయించక నీమేరయవ్వండు అ
9. పించినావాండి ఆండ్ని మాదిగవా
10. ండు దెంగేడి.

NELLORE (5). (A.D. 1653–54.)

[Batrakágollu. Telugu. From same stone.]

TRANSLATION.

Hail! On the 10th day of the bright fortnight of Ásvíja of the year Vijaya, corresponding to the year

1575 of the illustrious, victorious and prosperous Śáli-váhana Śaka era, Boligadacha Vrajagoruvindla . . issued this charitable edict. The residents of the village of Kágollu which has been given as a *mányam* to Páka-nala Kristnappa Náyanivâru are exempted from fees for the marriage of their daughters. If any one collects these fees 'putabitur suxisse pudenda feminæ *Mála.*' If he does not care for it, a *Mádiga* will ravish his wife.

1. స్వస్తిశ్రీ జయాభ్యుదయశాలివాహన శకవర్షం
2. బులు ౧౫౭౫ అగునేటి విజయనామసంవత్సర ఆ(శ్వ
3. జ) శు౧౦ లు । బొలిగడచ వ్రజగోరు విండ్ల . .
4. జగాను పెట్టిన ధర్మశాసనము (పాకనలక్రిష్ణ
5. ప్పనాయనివారి మాన్యలనురాను పాలించ్చి)
6. న కాగొల్లు గ్రామానకు ప్రజలకు ఆండ
7. బిడచుల పెండ్లిసుంఖంమానినారు యీ
8. సుంఖం యవ్వరు తీసుకున్నను మా
9. లదానిపూకు నాకినవాండే
10. అందుకు రోయకుండే వాని ఆలిని
11. మాదిగవాడు దెంగేది.

NELLORE (6). (A.D. 1625–26.)

[Bhujabhujanellúru. Telugu. From stone near the village.]

TRANSLATION.

(Adoration to) Ṣrí Ráma! Hail! On the 3rd of the bright half of Jyéshṭha of the year Kródhana, corresponding to the year 1547 of the illustrious, victorious and prosperous Ṣáliváhana Ṣaka era, the following

*

charitable edict was issued for the tank at the village of Bhujaballi Ráya Nellúru which Velugóṭi Venkaṭapati Náyaniváru gave as an *amaram* to Iṭṭikila Venkaṭagirigáru. Formerly the *méras* were to be collected at the rate of one *kunchaḍu* per *puṭṭi* of all kinds of grain. Therefore we have ordered that hereafter one *kunchaḍu* more should be collected. Therefore they should do considerable work to the tank with the *méras* collected at two *kunchams* per *puṭṭi* of all kinds of grain. Those who fail to keep up this charity will incur the sin of killing cows and Brahmans on the banks of the Ganges. [One imprecatory verse.] Whoever fails to keep this will be considered to have given his wife to the *veṭṭi* of the village. Thus has the charitable edict been issued.

1. శ్రీరామా స్వస్తిశ్రీ
2. జయాభ్యుద (యు) శాలివాహన
3. శకవరుషంబులు ౧౫౪౭
4. అగునట్టి క్రోధన సంవత్సర
5. జ్యేష్ట శు 3 లు వెలిగోటి వె
6. ంకటపతినాయనివా
7. రు॥ యిట్టికిల వెంకటా
8. గిరిగారికి అమరానకు
9. యిచ్చిన భుజబల్లిరా
10. య నెల్లూరి గ్రామానకు చె
11. రువు శాసన క్రమం యె
12. ట్లన్నను పూర్వాననానాథా
13. న్యం ఖ ౧ టికి ౼।[1] లెఖను
14. నడుచు గనుక ఇటు యీా
15. వలమరికుంచడు కట్ట

[1] Symbol for kuncha.

16. డశే స్తి మిగనక
17. పుట్టి ఖంగకి ౼[1] లెఖ
18. ను నానాధాంన్యం పట్ట
19. చెరువు విస్తారంగాను
20. వేయించ్చగలవారు .
21. యీధర్మానకు యె
22. వ్వరు గనుక తప్పినాను గం
23. గకతీ గోబ్రాహ్మనుల
24. చంపిన పాపానపోదు
25. రు॥ స్వదత్తాద్విగుణంపుణ్యం
26. ం పరదత్తాను పాలనం
27. పరదత్తాపహారేణ స్వద
28. త్తం నిష్ఫలం భవేత్ ॥ యి
29. ందుకు యెవ్వరుగనుక త
30. ప్పినాను వాని ఆలిని పూ
31. రివెట్టివానికి ఇచ్చినవాడు
32. అనివేశినధర్మశాసనం

NOTE.—Bhujabhuja Nellúru is apparently a corruption of Bhujabala Ráya Nellúru and the epithet Bhujabala is attached to the Choḍa kings.

NELLORE (7). (A.D. 1638–39.)

[Chennúru. Telugu. In bed of tank.]

TRANSLATION.

Hail! On the 2nd of the bright half of Chaitra of the year Bahudhánya, corresponding to the year 1560 of the illustrious, victorious and prosperous Śáliváhana Śaka era, Velugóṭi Venkaṭapati Náyaningáru issued a

---

[1] = ½ túm = 16 measures.

charitable edict for the tank at Chennúru. The *sandhátá* [*gár*], lessee, *amaradár* or whosoever be ruler of the village should get the work done to the tank and the channel from the different kinds of grain received as *méras*. If any *kápu* or *karnam*, not doing work to the tank or channel. . . the *veṭṭi* will ravish his wife . . . .

. . . . *Kápus* should get work done to the tank. *Karnams* should . . work . . . .

They should collect *méras* at 1 *kuncha* on every *puṭṭi* for the tank . . . . will be considered to have committed the cardinal sins.

1. స్వస్తి శ్రీ జయాభ్యుద
2. యశాలివాహన శకవర్ష
3. ంబులు ౧౫౬౦ అగు నేటి బహుధాన్యసంవ
4. త్సర చైత్ర శు ౧ లు వెలుగోటి వేంకటప
5. తినాయని వారు చెన్నూరు చెర్వుకు వేశ
6. ంచిన ధర్మశాసనం గ్రామసంధాతంగు
7. త్త అమరం యేలినా చెర్వు మేర నానాధాన్యా
8. లు చెర్వుపని కాల్వపని చేశించ్చు
9. వారు (కాంపు కరణం చెర్వుపని కాల్వపని
10. చెశించక . . . . . న్న
11. ట్టివాండిఆలిని వెట్టివాండు . . .
12. . . . .
13. (కాంపులు చెఱువుపని చెయించ్చు)
14. వారు కరణములు పనుల వారు మడు
15. . నాను . . . . . .
16. . దన్ను . . . గామ . .
17. చెరువుల పుట్టికుంచ్చాలు వే
18. యంగలవారు . . . . .

19. ణయ్యలన్నాను . . . . .

20. ండుపున్న . . . . . . పోను

21. . . . . య మహాపా

22. తకాలుచేసినట్టివారు.

NELLORE (8).

[Chennúru. Telugu. From stone in enclosure of Múlasthánésvara temple.]

TRANSLATION.

. . . nugi Peddanamgáru issued this charitable edict after making libation of water in the *Mukha Maṇḍapa* of Múlasthánésvara to . . . Múlasthánésvara of . . . ṭaya panáyani Chennúru, Késavanátha Virésvara, Konapillam Jánakamma of Pallekonḍa and other village deities. He has presented offerings to the deities of these villages with libation of water for the religious merit of his father Basavanáyanimgáru, and his mother Mummammá gáru. Therefore, if any one fails to keep this up, he will incur the sin of killing his parents; he will incur the sin of killing cows and Brahmans on the banks of the Ganges. Whoever rules this village . . he will incur the sin of killing . . . .

[Two imprecatory verses.]

Signature of Peddayya. Srí, Srí, Srí!

1. . . . . టయపనాయని చెన్నూరి మూలస్థా

2. నే శ్వరుండ్డున్ను కేశవనాంథుండున్ను వీరేశ్వరుండ్డు పల్లెకొ

3. ండను కోనపిల్లంజానకమ్మ కున్ను గ్రామదైవాలకు యరవనం

4. . . . . నుగిపెద్దనంగారు మూలస్థానేశ్వరునిముఖ మండ్డ

5\. . . . . మంద ధారవోశియిచ్చిన ధర్మశాసనం
యీ గ్రామదైవాల

6\. వైభవాలు తమతండ్రి బసవనాయనింగారికిని తల్లి ము
మ్మక్క

7\. ంగారికిన్ని పుణ్యంగాను ధారవోశి యిస్తిమి గనక యిందు
కు య

8\. వ్వరు తప్పినాను తమ తల్లిదండ్రాజుల వధియించిన పా
పానపోదు

9\. రు గంగ కతగో బ్రాంహ్మనిచంప్పినపాపాన బోదురు
యీగ్రా

10\. మం యెవ్వరు యేలినాను . . . చంప్పిన పాపానం బో
దురు.

11\. స్వదత్తా ద్విగుణం పుణ్యం (పరదత్తానుపాలనం)

12\. పరదత్తా పహారేణ (స్వదత్తం నిష్ఫలం భవేత్).

13\. యేకైక భగిని లోకే సర్వేషాం (మేవ భూభుజాం)

14\. నబోజ్యా నకర[1] గ్రాహ్యా (విప్రదత్తా)

15\. వసుంధరా॥ . . . . . .

16\. పెద్దయ్యగ్రాలు శ్రీ శ్రీ శ్రీ

Nellore (9). (A.D. 1635-36?)

[Chinna Cherukúru. Telugu. Near the Vináyakudu temple.]

Translation.

On . . . . day of Bhádrapada of the year Yuva, under the orders of Ákula Ranganáthayya, agent (*káryakartá*) of Ṣrímat Velugóṭi Venkaṭapati Náyanimváru, Bóyinapalli Bápanamgáru issued a charitable edict for the *kunchas* of the tank at Cherukúru. If the rulers

---

[1] Read నకర.

of the village, the *kápus*, the *karanams*, the holders of the *mányam* or anybody else, not doing work to the tank with the above said grain, object to it, they will incur the sin of killing cows and Brahmans on the banks of the Ganges. Those who fail to keep it will be considered to have given the honour of their womenfolk to *Málas* and *Mádigas*. Thus has the edict been executed.

NOTE.—This agent is mentioned again in Nos. 110 and 115.

1. యువ సంవత్సర భాద్ర
2. (పద) . . లు శ్రీమతు వె
3. లు గోటి వెంకటపతి నా
4. యని వారి కార్య కర్త
5. లైన ఆకుల రంగ్గనాధ
6. య్య గారి అనుమ తిని
7. బోయినిపల్లి బాపన
8. ంగారు చెరుకూరి చెరు
9. వు కుంట్చాలకు కొల్లుట
10. కు వేయించిన దర్మశా
11. సనం గ్రామం యేలేవా
12. రు కాంపు కరణాలు మా
13. న్యగాండ్లు ఆ ధాన్యం చె
14. ర్వు మీందే ఇంచ్చకయె
15. వ్వరు కీడు ఆడినాను
16. గంగ కతఁను గో బ్రాంహ్మలను
17. వధించిన పాపాన బోయినట్టె
18. అది తప్పి నడిపించ్చిన
19. యాడవాండ్ల మానంమా
20. ల మాదిగలకు ఇ
21. చ్చినవాండ్లు వే ఇంచ్చి
22. న ధర్మ శాసనం.

NELLORE (10). (A.D. 1535–36.)

[Daggadarti. Telugu on boundary between Chennúru and Daggadarti.]

TRANSLATION.

Hail! On Tuesday the 7th of the dark half of Phálguna of the year Manmatha, corresponding to the year 1458 of the illustrious, victorious and prosperous Śáliváhana Śaka era, under the orders of . . . . Governor of Udayagiri *durgam*, the boundary between this village and Chennúru (was settled) in the manner that the people of these four villages:—Jaidanka, Allúru, Gangáram, and Vavvéru acted . . . This inscription has been planted . . .
on the east . . gúlúr, to the south of that . . . . to the west of that . . . . .

1. స్వస్తి శ్రీ జయాభ్యుదయ శాలివాహ
2. న శకవర్షంబులు ౧౪౫౮ అగు నేంటి
3. . కి మంన్మథ సంవత్సర ఫాల్గుణ బ ౭ మ॥ శ్రీమతు
4. వుదయగిరి దుర్గాధిపతిరైయె నెలుకదా . . .
5. య్యవారి ఆనతిని జాఇదంక అలూరు గంగారం
6. వవ్వేరు యీా నాలుగుగ్రామం వాండ్లు నడచిన
7. ట్టి గాను యీాగ్రామ చెంన్నూరి పొలిమెర . .
8. జ . . . . ంచ్చి వేయించ్చిన య్యల్లి
9. . శా సనం పూర్వానకు . . . . నులూరును ఆదక్షి
10. ణం వొడ్డు ఆపడమర . . . . . ల . . . .

NELLORE (11). (A.D. 1638–39).

[Dámavaram. Telugu. South of village.]

TRANSLATION.

On the 2nd day of the bright fortnight of Chaitra of the year Bahudhánya corresponding to the Ṣáliváhana Ṣaka year 1560 this charitable edict was issued for the tank of Dámavaram by Velugóṭi Venkaṭapati Náyuḍu. The village *sandháta*, or the amaradár, or the lessee or the ruler should keep the tank in repair with the *méras*. If, not getting the work done, the *karnam* or *kápu* or any one covet those *méras*, his wife will be ravished by the village *veṭṭi*.

1. శాలివాహన శక
2. వర్షంబులు ౧౫౬౦
3. బహుధాన్య సంవ్స
4. త్సర చైత్ర శు ౨
5. లు వెలుగోటి వెంక
6. ట పతినాయని వా
7. మ (దాం) వరం చెరువు
8. కు వేయించిన ధర్మశా
9. సనం గ్రామం సందా
10. తం కుత్త అమరం యే
11. లిన చెరువు
12. పని చేయించేది చే ఇ
13. ంచక ఆ మేర కరణ
14. ం కాంపు యెవ్వండు ఆ
15. శించినా వాండి
16. ఆలిని వెట్టినాండు
17. దెంగేది

NELLORE (12).

[Duvvúru. Sanskrit in Grantha character and Tamil. From gópuram of Dúrvásula Kóṭéṣvara temple.]

This is a fragment. The beginning is Sanskrit and mentions Rájagaṇḍagópála. In the Tamil portion the cyclic year Vijaya and the village of Pákkam "on the northern bank" are mentioned; it says that some gift was made with libation of water to last as long as the moon and sun endure.

[1] . . . . .

[2] ராஜகண்டகோபால: ஷிக்ஷிதஸிம்ஹ [ஸ்ய] லோகேந்த்ர விக்[ர]ம விக்ரமேண ஸ்ய . . . . .

[3] மமேவிதாய | ஸ்வஸ்திஶ்ரீவக்ஷ . . . . . கமேஷு வகம் ஸகலம் ஸம்ஜி . . . . .

[4] ான்ன வடகரைப்பாக்கத்து . . . . .

[5] தான விஜயஸம்வத்ஸரத்து . . . . .

[6] நமாக உதகம்பண்ணி சந்த்ராதித்தவரை[செல்வ] . .

NELLORE (13). (A.D. 1613–14.)

[Gaṇḍavaram. Telugu. Southern wall of enclosure of Vénugópálasvámi temple.]

TRANSLATION.

Hail! On Sunday, the 7th of the dark half of Jyéshṭha of the year Prámadícha, corresponding to the year 1535 of the illustrious, victorious and prosperous Śáliváhana Śaka era, Vóbánáyaningáru who is pure by reason of descent from the Pácharla *gótra*, who is the moon of the ocean of the Ujaini family, who is the grandson of Chondakunáyaningáru and the son of Pullánáyaningáru, and who is the maintainer of Dharma, caused to be constructed a stone *prákára* (enclosure) to (the temple of) Gópáladéva of Gaṇḍávaram, who is the lord of crores of worlds of the whole universe to last as long as the sun and moon last, for the religious merit of his preceptor Tirumala Tátáchárlu Ayyaváru, Veligóṭi Venkaṭapati Náyaningáru, who is the ruler of the *ṣíma*, his father Pullánáyaningáru, and his mother Dharmáyammagáru. May it cause great prosperity!

(1) స్వస్తిశ్రీ జయాభ్యుదయ శాలి వా
(2) హన శకవర్షంబ్బులు ౧౫౩౫ అగు నేటి
(3) ప్రమాదీచ సంవ్వత్సర జేష్ట బ ౭ ఆదివా
(4) రాన పశ్చర్లగోత్ర పవిత్రులున్ను వుజైని
(5) వంశపారావారసుధాంశులున్న చో
(6) ండకునాయనింగారి పవిత్రుండును పుల్లా
(7) నాయనింగారి పుత్రుండును ధర్మ. . .
(8) ప్రతి పాలకులున్ను అయిన వోబా
(9) నాయనింగారు అఖిలాండ్డ కోటిబ్ర
(10) హ్మాండనాయకులయిన గండ్డావరం గో
(11) పాలదేవునికి ఆచంద్రార్కస్థాయిగా మా
(12) ంకు గురువులు తిరుమల తాతాచార్యుల
(13) అయ్యవారికిన్ని శీమయేలే వెలిగో
(14) టి వెంకటపతి నాయనింగారికిన్ని తమ
(15) తండ్రి పుల్లానాయనింగారికిన్ని త
(16) మతల్లి ధర్మాయమ్మంగారికిన్ని పు
(17) ణ్యంగాను శిలాప్రాకారం గట్టించె
(18) ను శ్రీ శ్రీ శ్రీ జేయును

Nellore (14).

[Gaṇḍavaram. Telugu. Eastern wall of enclosure of Vénugópálasvámi temple.]

Translation.

Ṣrí Ráma!

Timmana, son of Janná Jéjam Śeṭṭi caused (this) well to be constructed and presented it to Gópálasvámi of Gaṇḍavaram. Śrí!

1. శ్రీ రామ గం
2. డ వరం గోపాల
3. స్వామికి జన్నా జే
4. జం సెట్టి కొమారుం
5. డు తింమన నుయ్యి
6. గట్టించి సమర్పిం
7. చెను శ్రీ.

Nellore (15).

[Gaṇḍavaram. Telugu. From a stone bearing also a Tamil inscription to north of gate of Udayakáléṣvara temple.]

Translation.

That successful man (danyuḍu) who obtained the village of Bonḍaváḍa by the grace of Allun Dirukálti, the ornament of kings, who is a Vishnu (Murári) to the Dánavas who are his proud enemies, and who is the crest jewel of the Pallava family, got a tank excavated in that village, constructed a village which he named after his father Dámávaram, to the knowledge of the world, and, out of love, gave that village to Udayakalavatí-ṣvaradéva in perpetuity as long as the moon, water, sun and stars exist and also constructed a *mandapa* in the name of his mother Kaṭṭaḍi Prólama and published this as a charitable edict.

. . . స

4. మదశాత్రవదాన
5. వమురారి పల్లవ
6. వంశ శేఖరుండు నవ
7. అత నల్లుందిరుకాల్తి
8. వసుమ తీశ్వర తిలక
9. ంబుచేం బ్రాభవశక్తి
10. యెప్పఁడంగ బొండవా
11. డనా గ్రామంబు వడ
12. సి యందొనరందటాకం
13. బు గట్టించి లోక మెఱ
14. ంగ్గం దమతండ్రి పేరి
15. ంట్ట దామావరం బు
16. ను పేరిడి యాయూ
17. రు ప్రీతి నుదయక
18. లవతీశ్వర దేవునకు
19. చంద్ర జలార్క తారక
20. ంబుగా నిచ్చిన ధన్య

On the north side.

21. ం గన్నతల్లి పెర.
22. మండపమునుం .
23. ం . యోం దమ్మఁం
24. గ్గాను ననంగ్గ కట్ట
25. డి ప్రోలమ విసుతి సే
26. యం

NELLORE (16). (A.D. 1182–83.)

[Gaṇḍavaram. Sanskṛit in Grantha. From the same stone as No. 15.]

TRANSLATION.

Próli Reḍḍi of Prabhugaṇḍavára the best of villages (obtained) from the illustrious king Alluntikka who is the crest-jewel of kings, who is a blossom among blossoms (or Pallavas), who is blessed with courage . . . to the god Vallíśvara whose forehead is adorned by the moon, ... the village . . Bontapáḍu in the *vishaya* (country) called after Báta in the month when the sun was adorning the *nakra* (crocodile) (Márgaḷi) in the Śaka year 1104 expressed by bána (5), arkka (0), vichandra (11) corresponding to the cyclic year Śóbhakrit.

[Imprecatory verse.]

[1] ஶ்ரீ(ஃ) ஶக ர·[ஜ]
[2] ஶிரொர[ர*]ந்ராத்
[3] பல்லவாங்கிவ
[4] பல்லவாத் [|*] ஸ-
[5] ஹஸாங்கஶ்ரீ ப-
[6] ராக்ஷாத் ஸ்வயம் ஷி-
[7] ரபதெ ஶ்ரியஃ [||*]
[8] ஶ்ருத்ராஶவரா-
[9] த் தஸ்யாத் வர [ஹ]-
[10] ஹணாபாரஸ்யவ [|*]
[11] ஷெராமிரொஸ்தி
[12] ஊகி வ்யாதொகா வர-
[13] ஸாயக க . .
[14] வக உதை . .

[15] [வஜ்ஜி] ஸ்ரிதெவா-

[16] ஜ தெவாயி . .

[17] விக . . .

[18] மாரஉ . . . ல-

[19] வாய வநுரா-

[20] ககெஉளவெய

[21] ஷாண[ா]ககு-ஷ ஷி-

[22] வநுமணிகெ ம-

[23] கவகஷெர மெ-

[24] ாஹகுஜ வகஷெ-

[25] ர நகுஉவுஂக-லு-

[26] தி ஷாலுதி ெப-

[27] ாகநாஉலுஉா-

[28] வெ்வு விஷயெ ெ-

[29] . ெபாஜபாட

[30] . ட-லு-ாவுஉதி

[31] . . . ட-ரஷ தஷ ரு-

[32] . . . . .

[33] . . . . . . ஞ-

[34] . . . . . . லுதி-

[35] ககுஷ [டாதிககுஷ வ]ா ெ-

[36] யா [ஹூெரக] வல-ட-

[37] நு [ராஂ ஷஜுவ] ஷ-

[38] லஹூஸுாணி

[39] விஷூாயாஜு[ாய]-

[40] கெ குதிஃ-||

NELLORE (17).

[Gaṇḍavaram. Telugu. By the Ṣiva temple.]

TRANSLATION.

Hail! (He whose feet are adorned by the coronets of kings and form a shelter to those who prostrate themselves humbly before him . . . . . .) Ṣrímanmahámaṇḍaléṣvara Kulóttuṅga Chóḍa, Chitrakhaṇva, Tribhuvana Chakravarti Kulóttunga Chóḍadévara . . . Ṣrí Tribhuvana Chakravarti Kullóttungadéva Chóḍa executed an edict and gave to the deity Mahádéva and his wife Udaya Kalavati 20 *paṭṭis* of wet land at Bódemaram. This was given to Nambi Vasamuradévalenḍu with libation of water. He should receive and enjoy it in peace. This is the stone inscription. Those who maintain this charity will be considered to have given a charity five and twelve times greater than this. One *kuncham* of grain should be given for every *puṭṭi* of produce. Nine cows were given. The tope should last for ever.

Signatures. BIDDANA VÍRACHÓḌA.
(Signed) KARNAM NÁRANAYA.
(Signed) SÓMANAVAPA PEGGADA GÓVINDANA.

1. స్వస్తి శ్రీ . . . . . విన
2. యు వినమిత నిస్త్రింద్రిడ . . .
3. మకుటతర . . . తస్తగిత
4. . . . ణో త్తి . . . చరణ సర
5. స . . . విమలచిత్తమైనయనేక
6. స్వస్తి శ్రీమన్మహామండలేశ్వర కులో
7. త్తుంగచోడ చిత్ర ఖణ్వ . త్రిభువన

8. చక్రవర్త్తికులోత్తుంగ చోడదేవర
9. . . . . నార
10. . . . పౌనమైన . . . బోడమార
11. మున ఉదయకలపతి సమేతమైన మహాదే
12. వరకు శ్రీత్రిభువన చక్రవర్త్తి శ్రీకులోత్తు
13. ంగ చోడదేవరు విరువది పట్టికిరు నీరు నేలసాస
14. న బద్ధముగాన . . . తానసంబి పసము
15. రదేవలెండు ధర్ముపుగానున్న పీరికి ధారవోశితి
16. చేకొని సుఖమనుభవించి శెప్పడ శిలాశాసన
17. ముగా నప్పకముంచి కొన్నది దీనికి పూను
18. వారు సేనుంబండ్రెండుద్దుల సాసనము
19. సిచ్చితి బుట్టికి ఒక మోదలు తొంప్రండ
20. నిరంతము . . బిడ్డని పీరచోడ కణ్ణానారన
21. యప్రాలు సోమనవప పెగ్గడ గోవిందనప్రాలు

NELLORE (18).

[Gaṇḍavaram. Telugu. To south of Udayakálésvara temple. From a stone bearing also a Tamil inscription. Illegible.]

NELLORE (19).

[Gaṇḍavaram. Tamil. From the same stone as No. 18. Beginning lost.]

TRANSLATION.

The five vélis of demarcated dry land in that village which we left when we visited that *Maṇḍalam* to the *pújári* (dévarkaṇmi) and to the overseers of the Sri Máhésvaras of the temple of the god Vallésvara at Kaṇṭhanáráyanapuram *alias* Kulóttuṅgachóḻapuram situated in Muṇḍai-náḍu in . . . Kulamáṇṇikkavalanáḍu (a sub-division of) . . . Chóḷamaṇḍala for three rice offerings and the five vélis . . . of land in the village of Tunamasiṛídúr, which, in accordance with the request contained in a letter received by us, we gave on the same day for celebrating the festival to that god, for feeding the ascetics at the *math*, for paying those who attended to the sacred flower garden . . . . (mutilated portion) This is the signature of Kulóttuṅgachóḻappallavaraiyan. Year 41, day 125.

[1] ஸ்வ . . . . .
[2] . . . .
[3] . . . . . . சொழம-
[4] . . . . . . குலமாணிக்கவளநா-
[5] [ட்டு] முண்டைநாட்டு கண்டநாரா[யணபுர]-
[6] மாக குலொத்துங்க சொழபுரத்து உடையார்
[7] வல்லிஸ்ராமுடைய ஊஹாதெவர்கன்மிகளுக்கும்
[8] ஸ்ரீ ஊரொஹஸ்ராக்கண்காணிசெய்வார்களுக்கும் அத்-
தெவ-
[9] ர்க்கு முன்பு நாம் அம்மண்டலத்துக்கு வந்தபொழுது
மு[வ]-
[10] முதுபடிக்கு அவ்வூரில் புஞ்சை நிலத்தில்த்[திரு]த்தி
க்கொ-
[11] ள்கைக்கு விட்ட அஞ்சுவெலிநிலமும் அந்நிக்கெ அத்
தெ-
[12] தவர்க்கு திருவுத்ஸவத்துக்கும் மடத்திலுண்ணுதவஸி-
[13] களுக்கும் திருநந்தவானஞ்செய்வார்க்கும் இந்நமசிறி
தூ[ரி]ல்
[14] நாம் பெறவெண்டுமென்று நமக்கு ஓலைவந்த .
[15] . எட்டி நா . . . . . . அமுதுபடிக்கு வி-
[16] ட்ட நிலம் அஞ்சுவெலியெ இ . . . யான இநாற்பா
[17] . . . . . . டக்கு நடத்தி . .

[18] ஃ னு . . . . . .

[19] . வெளி நிலம் . . . . . விட்ட சொக்கொ-ட்டு ஆக

[20] . . . . . . நிலமும் கைக்கொ-

[21] காண்டு . . . . வெப்ப . . ண்ணி . . ருட்டி-

[22] [மூந்று] வாரம் செய்யப்பண்ணுக இவை கு-

[23] லோத்துங்கசோழப்பல்லவரை[ரய ன்] எழுத்து உ

[24] யாண்டு சம[க] நாள் ௱உ௰௫.

NELLORE (20).

[Guḍipallipáḍu. Telugu. Stone opposite Śiva temple.]

TRANSLATION.

On the 10th day of the bright half of Bhádrapada of the year Yuva, Ṣrímat Velugóṭi (Timmánáyanigáru) . . . . whoever fails to keep it up . . . . will be considered to have given his honour to *Málas* and *Mádigas*. Thus has this charitable inscription been issued.

1. యువ సంవత్సర భాద్ర
2. పద శు ౧౦ లు శ్రీమ
3. తు వెలుగోటి తి . . . . .

* * * * * * *

* * * * * * *

1. ఆది తప్పినడి
2. పిచ్చి (రాయని ?)
3. వాండ్ల మానం
4. మాల మాదిగె
5. లకు ఇచ్చినట్టు

6. వా ర్గు శిటని
7. కేయించ్చిన
8. ట్టి ధర్మ శా
9. సనం . .

NELLORE (21). (A.D. 1272–73 ?)

[Ídúru. Sanskrit in Grantha and Tamil. West wall of Chokkanáthaswámi temple.]

This inscription which is only a fragment begins with a Sanskrit introduction giving the birudas of a king named Nágadévamahárája. The Tamil portion which follows states that in the expired Śaka year 1193 corresponding to the cyclic year *Ángirasa*, on the date corresponding to Monday, with the *nakshatra* Púśa, being the tenth day of the month of Mágha, one Nágadevan of Nellúr *alias* Vikramasingapura gave (with libation of water) to the lord Bhímanádéva *alias* the god of Veṭṭuván Paṭṭaiviḍu, for offerings, some lands in Angapaḻandanáḍu free of tax to last as long as the moon and sun endure.

NOTE.—Angiras corresponds with 1194 expired, not 1193.

[1] ஸ்வஸ்தி ஸ்ரீ ஸதுஸமுத்ர ஸ்வர்ணமெஸ்வர [ஷெ] நாமாஜ-ட-னை விலவஜித நாமெஸ்வர ஸக்ர [மெமமெ] ய நாமமெதவ ஸஹா-ரா[ஜ] . . . . .

[2] [ன்] சகரையாண்டு ௲௱௯௰௩ சென்ற ஆங்கிர ஸம்-வத்ஸரத்து மாஸமாஸத்து தஸமியும் ஸோமவாரமும் பெற்ற பூசத்துநாள் . . . . .

[3] ல்லூர் ஆன விக்ரமஸிம்ஹ புரத்து வெட்டுவான் பட்டைவிட்டு உடையார் பீமநாதெவருக்கு அங்கபழந்த நாட்-டில் சாந்தனம் பக் . . . . .

[4] சையும் அமுதுபடியும் சந்திராதித்தவரை நடத்துவ தாக வல்லபோதநமாக இக்கொயிற் . . . . உடி . . .

[5] பண்ணிக்குடுத்தென் நாமதெவனென் இத்தன்மத்தை குலைக்குமவன் கங்கைக்கரையிற் குரால்பசுவை வ த்தான் பாவங்கொள்வான.

NELLORE (22).

[Indukúrpéṭa. Tamil. From gópuram of Narasimhaswámi temple. Beginning lost.]

TRANSLATION.

. . . . kávanúrkiḻavan Malaikiḻiyaninṟán Pichchaṉ Uḍaiyár of Máḻigaikávanúr (situated) in Póḻigainádu in Maṇaviṟkóṭṭam (a sub-division) of Jayaṅkoṇḍachóḻa-maṇḍala gave, to last as long as the moon and sun last, 750 (*kuḻi*) consisting of sacred flower garden and mango tope.

If anybody should cause obstacles to this charity, he will incur the sin of one who kills a cow on the banks of the Ganges.

[1] த்திச்செய்த கழுநடி குழு . . . . மவல க்கறதி-
[2] ருநந்தவானமாத்தொட்ட நில எழுநூற்றை-
[3] ம்பது சந்திராதித்தவரை செல்வதாக விடுவி-
[4] த்தாந் செயங்கொண்டசொழமண்டலத்-
[5] து மணவிற்கொட்டத்துப்பொளிகைநாட்டு
[6] மாளிகைக்காவனூர் காவனூர்கிழவன் மலை-
[7] கிளியநின்றான் பிச்சன் உடையார் இத்தன்-
[8] மத்துக்கு விக்கம் பண்ணிநூனாகில் கெ-
[9] ங்கைக்கரையில் தொவதை பண்ணினன்
[10] செய்த பாவத்திலெ பொவாந்.

Nellore (23).

[Indukúrpet. Telugu. On threshold of gópuram of Vírabhadrasvámi temple.]

Translation.

The grain realized from the *kunchas* of the tank should be spent by these in repairing the channel and the tank. If there should be any balance, it should be given for the repairs of these temples. Whoever fails to keep this will be considered to have given his (wife's) honour to the menial servant of the village. If the *mányagáḍu* hides (the grain) and says anything, the same censure will apply to him.

1. యీా చెర్వు కుంచా
2. లవల్ల వచ్చిన ధాన్యం కాల్వ
3. లం నూరి చెర్వుల మీ
4. ందను వీరు వేయించ్చాగ
5. లవారు మీగులు గలిగినా
6. యీా దేవళ్ళాలపని ముఖా
7. లకు యియ్యగలవారు యి
8. ంద్దుకు యవ్వరు గనక త
9. ప్పినాను వాని మానం గు
10. లాపువానికి ఇచ్చిన వా
11. డె మాన్యగాడు దాంచి
12. చెప్పినాను యిదే వట్టు

NELLORE (24).

[Kákaṭúru. (Hamlet Pátachennuḍu gunṭa.) Telugu. In bed of tank.]

TRANSLATION.

(Adoration to) Ṣrí Ráma !

On the 15th of the bright half of Kártika, corresponding to the Śaka year 156 . on the holy occasion of a lunar eclipse, ... granted (the village) as an *amaram*. Therefore the different kinds of grain received from this village as *méras* should be spent on doing earth work to the tank. Therefore we have given this with libation of water on the holy occasion of a lunar eclipse on this abovesaid *tithi*. They should therefore do the tank work as long as the sun and moon exist. Those who fail to do so will incur the sin of killing cows and Brahmans on the river Ganges. They will be considered to have given their (wives') honour to the *toṭi*; they will be considered to have sucked the yard of a horse. If they fail to keep this they will be considered to have given their (wives') honour to the *veṭṭi*. Thus (has) the charitable edict (been issued).

1. శ్రీ రామ
2. శక సంవత్సర
3. ంబులు ౧౫౬ .
4. ం అగు కా ర్తిక
5. శు ౧౫ లు సోమగ్రహణ
6. . . . . కామర
7. . . . ఎనాన
8. . . . . . తిని
9. ఖని . . . తుచుంన

10. య . . . . డపా
11. . . . . రికి
12. . . . . మం
13. టచును అమరా
14. నకు పాలించినారు గనక
15. యీ గ్రామన వచ్చిన
16. మెఱలు నా
17. నాధాన్యాలున్ను చెర్వు
18. మీంద మట్టివేసే
19. వారు
20. యిందుకు
21. ఇతథాతి
22. థి శోమగ్ర
23. హణపుణ్యా
24. కాలమంద్దు
25. ధారవోసి ఇ
26. స్తిమి గనక ఆచ
27. ంద్రాకస్థాఇ
28. గాను చెర్వుపనిచే
29. యంగలవారు
30. ఇ(యికపుచ్చు ండు)
31. నను గంగలోను
32. గోవును బ్రాంహ్మని
33. చంపిన పాపా
34. నం బొందురు గు
35. లాపువానికి మా
36. నం ఇచ్చి పోదు
37. రు గుఱపు బొ
38. డ్డ గుడిచిన వాం

39. ఢి యింద కు

40. తప్పినా వెట్టివాని

41. కిం మానంబిచ్చిన వా

42. ండె ఇట్టవెంటిధ

43. ర్మశాసనము

Nellore (25).

[Kandamúru. Telugu. To north in Survey No. 61.]

Translation.

On the 30th day of the dark fortnight of Áshaḍah of the year Sarvadhári, on the holy occasion of a solar eclipse, Bairapa Reḍḍi Annayya of Pánḍéru gave with libation of water 200 *kunṭas* of dry land to Channa Késavanátha of Kandamúru for the religious merit of Basuvarusayya Ayyávaru. Whoever causes obstruction to this land will incur the sin of killing a cow and a Brahman on the banks of the Ganges. May it cause great prosperity!

1. సర్వ్వధారి సంవత్సర ఆషాఢ బ ౩౦ లు సూ
2. ర్యగ్రహణ పుణ్యకాలమందు కందమూరి చ
3. ంన కేశవ నాథనికి బసువరుసయ్య అయ్యవా
4. రికిపుణ్యముగాను పాండేటి బైరపరెడి అన్నయ్య
5. వెలిచేను ఇన్నా (రు) ౨౦౦ కుంటలు దారవోస్తిమి
6. ఇక్షేత్రానకు యవ్వరుగనక తప్పినాను గం
7. గకతట గోంబ్రాంహ్మని చంప్పిన పాపా
8. నంబోవరు ॥ మంగళమహా శ్రీ శ్రీ
9. శ్రీ చేయునూ॥

NELLORE (26). (A.D. 1638-39.)

[Kanupartipádu. Telugu. In field No. 30 to north of village.]

TRANSLATION.

On the 2nd of the bright half of Chaitra of the year Bahudhánya, corresponding to the year 1560 of the Śáliváhana Śaka era, Velugóṭi Venkaṭapati Náyanivárn issued a charitable edict for the *méras* of the tank of Kanuparti. The village *Sandháta*, lessee, *amaradár*, or ruler should cause the work to be done to the tank and channel. If, not doing the work, the *amaradár*, *kápu*, *karnam* or any one else covet the tank *méras*, the *vetti* will ravish his wife.

1. శాలివాహన శకవ
2. ర్షంబులు ౧౫౬౦ అగునేం
3. టి బహుధాన్య సంవత్సర
4. చైత్ర శు ౨ లు వెలుగోటి వెంక
5. టపతినాయని వారు కనుపర్తి
6. చెర్వు మేరకు వేయించ్చిన ధర్మశాస
7. నం గ్రామం సంధాతం గుత్త అమరు
8. యేలినిని న్యాయమైన మేర చెర్వు కా
9. ల్వ పని చేయించ్చేది చేయించక చెర్వుల
10. మేర అమరగాండు కాపుకర
11. ణం యవ్వరు ఆశించినవాండి
12. ఆల్ని వెట్టివాడు దెంగును.

(To face page 789.)

NELLORE NO. 27.

NELLORE (27).

[Kanupartipáḍu. Tamil. From field No. 383 to east of village.]

TRANSLATION.

Hail! Prosperity! In the 37th year of the reign of the emperor of the three worlds, the glorious Rájarájadéva, I, Pramaladévi, had the steps leading to the shrine (paḷḷichchandam) of the Jain temple (called after) Karikálachoḷa, built on behalf of Matiságaradéva.

[1] ஸ்வஸ்திஸ்ரீ திரிபுவந-
[2] சக்ரவத்திகள் ஸ்ரீராஜ-
[3] ராஜதெவற்(க்)கு ஆண்டு
[4] ௩௰௭ வது மதிசாகரத்-
[5] [தெ]வற்காக கரிகாலசொ-
[6] ழஜிநாலயத்துப்பள்-
[7] ளிச்சந்தம் இறங்க-
[8] ல் யிட்டுக்குடுத்தெ-
[9] ன் பிரமலதெவி[ய்]-
[10] யென்.

NELLORE (28). (A.D. 1346–47.)

[Koḍavalúru. Telugu. Near western gate of Nágéṣvara temple. The last few lines perhaps form a separate inscription.]

TRANSLATION.

May there be freedom from impediment! Hail! On Sunday the 7th of the bright half of Kártika of the year Vyaya, corresponding to the year 1268 of the illustrious Śaka era, Mudra Chiddi Sáyanna Oḍayalu who is the prime minister (Mahápradháni) of Kampaṇati Oḍayar, who is the lord of the eastern and western seas (presented) . . for a perpetual lamp to Ṣrídhara Pẹrumál who dwells at Koḍavalúr for the expiation of all sins of his parents· Prólé Bainṭi and Prólelu Víralivi, the sons of Rámiseṭṭi Pólisetṭi, presented a *sarva mányam*, half each (?), for the perpetual lamp to the temples of Ṣrí Dhara Perumál and Nágéṣvara, though these deities have many ewes (?), to last in perpetuity as long as the sun and moon last.

1. అవిఘ్నమస్తు
2. స్వస్తి శ్రీ శకవ
3. ర్షంబులు ౧౨౬౮
4. అగు నేటివ్యయ
5. సంవత్సర కార్తిక
6. శుద్ధ । ౭ । భాను
7. వారాన కొడువ
8. లూరి ప్రసంన్నుండు అఖి
9. నా శ్రీధర పెరుమా
10. ళ్లకు అఖండ దీపా
11. నకును పూర్వాప
12. శ్చిమ సముద్రా
13. ధి పత్యకంపణలి
14. ఒడయర మహా
15. ప్రతాని ముద్రచి
16. డ్డి సాయన్న ఒడ్డ
17. యలు తమతల్లి
18. దండ్రులకు సకల
19. ప్రాయశ్చితము
20. గాను ।శిధర పెరుమా
21. ళ్లకును నాగేశ్వర దే
22. వకును అఖండ దీ

23. పాలకు రామిసెట్టి
24. పోలిసెట్టి కొడుకు
25. లు ప్రాలేబైంటిని
26. ప్రోలెఱు పీరలిని
27. జీవధనము య
28. (నే) కలిగినాను శా
29. (శ్వత) మాన్యము ఆ
30. చంద్రస్తాయిగాను
31. ఈ రెండు స్తానాల
32. కను చెఱిసగం
33. యిచ్చెను.

NELLORE (29).

[Koḍavalúru. Telugu. From gateway on southern side of Ṣrídharasvámi temple.]

TRANSLATION.

Whoever causes any injury to this permanent charity will fall into 21 hells. The fruit of this charity is unlimited.

[One imprecatory verse.]

This charitable inscription was engraved by Poḍḍarasu under the orders of Sáyánna Oḍayalu. This should last as long as the sun and moon last.

1. యి శాశ్వత
2. దమ్మఃవుకు
3. యవ్వరు యే
4. మి యుప
5. హాః పుట్టి

6. ంచ్చినాను వాకు
7. యేకవింశతి న
8. రకాలోను పడు
9. వారు ౧ యిద
10. ర్మవునకు ఫ
11. లము । అపరి
12. మితము॥
13. సామాన్యో
14. యం ధర్మసే
15. తుర్నృపాణాం
16. కాలే కాలే పా
17. లనియ్యో భవ
18. ద్భిః । సర్వ్వానేతా
19. న భావినః పా
20. ర్థివేంద్రాన్ భూ
21. యో భూయో
22. యాచతే ॥ రామ
23. చంద్రః ॥ యీ
24. దర్మ్మశాసన
25. ము సాయాన్న
26. ఒడయల ఆన
27. తిని పొడ్డరసు
28. వ్రాయించ్చిన
29. శాసనము ఆ
30. చంద్రసూర్య్య
31. ల కలంత్తాను చె
32. ల్లం కలది॥

NELLORE (30). (A.D. 1268–69.)

[Koḍavalúru. Telugu. From eastern gateway of Ṣrídharasvámi temple.]

TRANSLATION.

Hail! On . . corresponding to the Śaka year 1190, the children of Náraparáju and Appalaráju have made a partition of the *vrittis* between themselves into two shares in Rámapuram; the sons of Náraparáju of Guḍlúr (have divided) their property into 7 parts; Tikkana, &c., sons of Gutto Appaḷaráju (have divided) their property into 7. The witnesses for this are the elders of the village Mahájanulu), the sun and moon . . .

1. స్వస్తి శకవ
2. రుషంబులు
3. ౧౧౯౦ నే
4. ంటి నారప
5. రాజుబిడ్డ
6. లూను అప్ప
7. ళరాజు బిడ్డ
8. లూందమలో
9. వ్రిత్తులు పం
10. చిన భంగ్గి
11. రామాపుర
12. ము రేండు
13. గుడ్లూరి నార
14. పరాజు కొ
15. డుకులు భాంగం
16. టి వేండు, గు
17. త్తో అప్పల్లా

18. జా గౌడుకు

19. లు తికర–నమా

20. లోం బంప్వ

21. వేండు దీనికి

22. సాక్షిమ

23. వాజను

24. లుం చెంద్ర సూ

25. యాాణలూను

26. . . . .

Nellore (31). (A.D. 1284–85.)

[Koḍavalúru. Sanskrit in Grantha character and Tamil. From a fallen stone in the tank bed.]

Translation.

The beginning which is in Sanskrit is not very clear. It seems to state that in the Ṣaka year (expressed by rasa 6, *na* 0, drik 2 and bhú 1) or 1206, in the month Mágha, a certain image of a god was set up.

Tamil portion.

Hail! Prosperity! In the 3rd year of the reign of Manumagaṇḍagópáladéva, corresponding to the cyclic year Târaṇa, on the date of Saṅkránti, on Monday the first day of the bright half of the month of Pushya, the sons of the ryots Kámireḍḍi and Chóḷappireḍḍi, gave as a charity on behalf of their parents for the deity, the lord Tirunágéśvara, at Koḍavalúr (situated) in Muṇḍainádu, and to Aṇṇappiḷḷai Náyakkar in order that he may reside in the building constructed on the banks of the sacred pond attached to the temple of this god, to the temple treasury, the money (collected) at the rate of half a *chinnam* per month on every loom.

If there be anybody who hinders this (charity) (he will incur the sin) of killing a cow on the banks of the Ganges.

First part.

[1] ஸ்வஸ்தி ஸ்ரீ
[2] ஶகவர்ஷ ஸ-
[3] ஹ ஸ்ரஸதஷ்ரு-
[4] க்ஷ ஹ-ஞஸவ்ரு-
[5] யாஸ யுதெ-
[6] க ஷெண [ஷ]-
[7] [த்ரு] ரோஷி [ஷ]
[8] [ஸ்ஹ]ாயநாஶம [illegible]
[9] . ஹஷெ காரீ-
[10] வ்ரு ஷொஸா-
[11] வ்ருஷெய ஷெஜ-
[12] ந்ருாயாய [illegible]
[13] . கவிஷ வாடு
[14] ஸஹஸித ஷ்தா-
[15] வ்ஜீரூதரம் ஸ-
[16] காஃ வ்ஜஸ்தீகீ-
[17] க்தீ-வெஷ நய-
[18] ாவஷவதி

Second and third parts.

[1] ஸ்வஸ்தி ஸ்ரீ மனுமக-
[2] ண்ட கொபாலதெ-
[3] தவற்கு யாண்டு ௩
[4] ஆவது தாரண ஸ-
[5] [illegible]

[6] ஊ வ்யயமையுந்தி-
[7] ங்கள் கிழமையும் ெ-
[8] பற்ற ஸங்க்ராந்திநா-
[9] ள் முண்டைகாட்-
[10] டில் கொடுவெலூரி-
[11] ல் உடையார் திருநா-
[12] கிஸ்வரமுடையநா-
[13] யநார்க்கு தெவதா-
[14] னமாக மாஸமொ-
[15] ன்றுக்குத்தறி ஒன்று-
[16] க்கு அரைச்சின்னம்
[17] இன்னுயனுர் சிப-
[18] ண்டாரத்துக்கு
[19] இட்டு இன்னு-
[20] யநார் திருக்கொ-
[21] யிலில் திருப்ப[திக்]-
[22] குட்டையிலெ மடை-
[23] விளாகமாகக்கட்டி
[24] இருப்பபரா-
[25] க [அ]ண்ண-
[26] ப்பிள்ளைநா-
[27] யக்கருக்கு-
[28] ம் காமிரட்டிக்-
[29] குடியார் குடி-
[30] சொழப்பிர-
[31] ட்டி குடியா-
[32] ர்க்கு தந்மம்-
[33] மாக இவர்-
[34] கள் பிள்ளை-
[35] கள் எற்றிவி-
[36] த்தார்கள் இ-
[37] துக்கு விலங்-

[38] குச்செய்தாரு-
[39] ண்டாகில்க-
[40] ங்கைக்க-
[41] ரையில் பசு-
[42] வை வதித்த.

NELLORE (32). (A.D. 1314–15 or 1354–55 ?)

[Kóḍúr. Telugu. At Chennakéṣava temple on stone bearing figure of Anjanéṣvara.]

TRANSLATION.

Hail! On Sunday, the 15th of the bright half of Ásviyuja of the year Jaya, corresponding to the year 1236 of the illustrious Śaka era, on the holy occasion of Tulá Sankramaṇa, the offerings presented to Kóṭéṣvaradéva and Kéṣavaperumál of Kóḍúr (are these): The fields which were formerly in the enjoyment (of the deities)—A field of 200 *kunṭas* in "the Rájá's fields" by the side of Nallapagunṭa under the tank, 300 *kunṭas* below the above said tank, and 500 *kunṭas* in the Gundani Muluva land. They formerly gave in total 1,000 *kunṭas*. Those who fail in this charity will incur the sin of killing a Brahman and a cow.

NOTE.—The Saka and cyclic year do not agree.

1. స్వస్తి శ్రీ శకవరుషంబు
2. లు ౧౨౩౬ అగు నేంటి జయ సంవ
3. త్సర ఆశ్వియుజ శు ౧౫ ఆ తు
4. లాసం క్రమణపుణ్యకాలమందు కో
5. డూరకోటేస్వర దేవర కేశవ పెరుమా
6. ళ్ల భోగాలువారికి ప్రూర్వానం జెల్లి త్తే

7. త్రంము చెఱువుక్రింద నల్లవగుంట
8. (వాముపడి) ని రాజుల చెల్లోనుచేను
9. కుంటలు ౨౦౦ ఆ చెఱు దిగువను కుం
10. టలు ౩౦౦ గుండ నిములువునం
11. గుంటలు ౫౦౦ వుభమును గుంటలు
12. ౧౦౦౦ పూర్వాన ఇచ్చిరి మరి యీ ద
13. ర్మానకు యవ్వరు దప్పినను బ్రహ్మ హత్య
14. గోవాత్య . . శేసిన పాతకాన
15. ం బోవువారు.

NELLORE (33). (A.D. 1645–46.)

[Kodúr. Telugu. In a street of the village.]

TRANSLATION.

Hail! On the 2nd of the bright half of Chaitra of the year Párthiva, corresponding to the year 1567 of the illustrious, victorious and prosperous Śáliváhana Śaka era while Śrímat Rájádhi Rája Rája Paraméṣvara (Śrí Vírapratápa Venkaṭádri Ayya)váru, seated on the diamond throne at the city of Penugonḍa, was ruling the kingdom of the earth, Krishnappa Náyaningáru gave as an *amaram* to Rávula Venkaṭádrigáru the village of Kóḍúru attached to the *ṣíma* of Sarvémpalli which was granted as an *amaram* to Rávéla Muddu Krishnappa Náyaniváru by Venkatádri Ayyaváru. Therefore this is the charitable edict relating to the *méras* of the tank issued by Venkaṭádrigáru. It is ordered that one *kuncha* should be given (as *méra*) on all sorts of grain raised in and all income of this village. Therefore this grain should be spent on the tank. Whoever desire to appropriate it will incur the sin of killing cows and Brahmans on the banks of the Ganges. If the *sandhála*, revenue inspector (Parupatagáḍu), lessee, *amáragánḍlu*, *Kápus*, *karanams* or whoever they may be, desire to appropriate it, they will incur the sin of . . . . . . will be regarded as having killed . . . . . Whoever covets the *méras* or removes this stone inscription, elephants, horses, donkeys, pigs, and dogs. . will have intercourse with his wife.

(1) స్వస్తి శ్రీజయా
(2) భ్యుదయ శాలి
(3) వాహాన శకవర్ష
(4) బులు ౧౫౬౭ అ
(5) గు నేడి పార్థివ
(6) సంవత్స చైత్రశుద్ధ ౨
(7) శ్రీమద్రాజాధిరాజ
(8) రాజపరమేశ్వర [శ్రీ వీరప్ర
(9) తాప వెంకటాద్రి అయ్య]
(10) వారు పెనుగొండ పట్న
(11) ణమందు వజ్ర శింహాస
(12) నారూఢులై పృథివి
(13) సామ్రాజ్యమును పాలి
(14) ంపుచున్న రావేల ము
(15) ద్దు క్రిష్ణప్పనాయని
(16) గారికి ఇచి అమరానకు
(17) వెంకటాద్రి అయ్యవారు అ
(18) వధరించిన సర్వేంపల్లి
(19) శీమకుచెల్లె కొండూరు
(20) గ్రామాను క్రిష్ణప్పనాయుని

Second side.

(21) గారును
(22) రావుల వెంక
(23) టాద్రిం గా
(24) రికి అమరా
(25) నకు యిచ్చిరి
(26) గనక వెంక
(27) టాద్రింగారు
(28) వేయించ్చినట్టి
(29) చెర్వు మేర
(30) ధర్మశాసనం
(31) యీ గ్రామానను
(32) నానాధాన్యాన
(33) కున్ను సకలాయం
(34) ఖ ౧ కి ౧ లెఖ
(35) ఏప్పాటు గనక
(36) ఆ ధాన్యం చెర్వు
(37) మీంద వేయి
(38) ంచ్చగలవార
(39) ంయిందుకు
(40) యవండు ఆ
(41) శించ్చినాను
(42) గంగకర్త
(43) గోబ్రాంహాలా
(44) నుచ ంపిన పాపా
(45) నం బోవువారు
(46) యీ కోడూరిం
(47) యీాండూరి గ్రా

Third side.

(48) మాలను చ
(49) నే సంధాత వ
(50) రుపతగాం
(51) డు గిత్తకాం
(52) డు అమరగా
(53) ండ్లు కాం
(54) ఫుంకరణాలు
(55) యెవ్వరు ఆశిం
(56) చ్చినాను (యేల
(57) తిసి వేస్ని) పా
(58) తకంబున బొ
(59) యినవాండ్లు
(60) వధించినవాం
(61) డు యెవం
(62) డు ఆశించ్చినా
(63) ను యీ శాసన
(64) ంరాయిని యెవం
(65) డు తీశివేసినా
(66) ను వాండి ఆలిని
(67) యేనుగలు గు
(68) ఱ్రాలు గాడిదె
(69) లు పందులు
(62) న్ను కుకరాలును
(71) . . . .
(72) డెంగును
(73) . . . . . .

NELLORE (34).

[Koḍúr. Telugu. In Koṭéṣvarasvámi temple. On ceiling near the door.]

TRANSLATION.

Rájayya, son of Ṣrímat Sítayya (constructed) a temple to the excellent goddess Ṣrí Naṭarájésvarí of Ṣikralapáḍu . . . .

1. శ్రీమ సీతయ్యయొక్క
2. కుమార్డు రాజయ్య
3. . మనివల్ల వొబ
4. శిక్రలపాటినందు చే
5. వివర శ్రీనటరా
6. జేశ్వరికి గుడి . . .
7. రి (వారిదా) . . . . .

NELLORE (34A). (A.D. 1525–26.)

[Kommarapúḍi. Telugu. On a step in the temple on Narasimhakoṇḍa.]

TRANSLATION.

Hail! On Wednesday the 15th day of the bright half (of Phálguṇa of the year Párthiva), corresponding to the year 1448 of the illustrious, victorious and prosperous Śáliváhana Śaka era, while Ṣríman Mahámaṇḍaléṣvara . . . Achyutadéva Mahárájulu, seated on the diamond throne at Vijayanagar, was ruling, Timmaráju Nandayyagáru, the agent in the city of Udayagiri of Ṣríman Mahámaṇḍaléṣvara (Ṣrí) Ráju China Tirumala Ráju Mahárájulu, after making prostrations to the divine lotus feet of

Védádri Ṣrí Narasimhadéva, issued a charitable edict as follows :—On the holy occasion of Utthána (the day of the awaking of Vishnu) the 12th he presented the village, otherwise named Komarapúḍi, situated to the south of the hill Védádri and to the west of . . in the *ṣíma* of Prabhákarapaṭnam, in Pánka *náḍu*, in Udayagiri *Rájya*, which is attached to the chiefdom of Ṣrí Ráju China Tirumalayyadéva Mahárájulu, to Ṣrí Narasimhadéva for sacred food (*amritapadi*), to secure long life, health and increase of wealth to Achyutadévaráyalu. May the deity enjoy it ! Thus runs the charitable edict.

1. స్వస్తి శ్రీ జయాభ్యు
2. దయశాలివాహ
3. న శ ౧౪౪౮ అగు నేటి
4. (పార్థివ సంవత్సర పాల్గు
5. ణ) శు ౧౨ బు। మున
6. (శ్రీమన్మహామండలేశ్వ
7. ర . . . . . .) అచ్యుతదే
8. వమహారాయలువారు విజయన
9. గరమందు వజ్రసింహాసనా
10. రూఢులై పలుచుండ
11. వుదయగిరి పట్నంబున
12. శ్రీమన్మహామండలేశ్వర (శ్రీ)
13. రాజు చిన తిరుమలరాజు
14. మహారాజులవారి కార్యక
15. ర్తలైన తిమ్మరాజు నందయ్య
16. గారు వేదాద్రి శ్రీ నరసింహ
17. దేవుని దివ్య శ్రీపాదపద్మంము
19. లకు సాష్టాంగదండప్రణామ
20. ం బులు సమర్పించి యిచ్చి

21. న ధర్మశాసన క్రమమెట్లన్నను.
22. (స్వా)మిని శ్రీరాజాచినతిరమ
23. లయ్య దేవమహారాజులకుం
24. నాయంకరానకుం జెల్లె
25. వుదయగిరి రాజ్యంపాంక
26. నాండు ప్రభాకరపట్నం శీమలో
27. వేదాద్రికి దక్షిణం న . . .
28. పడ్మర కొామరపూడి అనెడు
29. పరనామముగల అచ్యుతదేవ
30. రాయులకు ఆయురారోగ్య అ
31. ఇశ్వర్యాభివృద్ధి అవునట్లగాను వు
32. ద్దానద్వాదశి పుణ్యకాలమందు
33. శ్రీ నరసింహ్మ దేవునికి అమృ
34. తపడ్లకు సమర్పించె దెవుండు
35. అవధరించెడి ధర్మశాసనం.

NELLORE (35).

[Kommarapúḍi. Telugu. On outside wall of temple on Narasimhakonḍa.]

TRANSLATION.

On the 15th of the bright half of Kártika of the year Pingaḷa, Ṣríman Mahámanḍalésvara Cháḷikya Náráyaṇa Chauhattamalla[1] Ranavijaya[2] Velamapáṭi Tirumala

---

[1] Chauhattamalla—(1) A hero having the strength of four elephants—Chaṭurhastimalla. (2) Vishnu—Chaturhastamalla.

[2] Ranavijaya—A conqueror (Arjuna) in war.

Rájayadéva Mahárájulaváru performed service to Védádri Ṣrí Narasimhadéva and the shrine (of that deity).

NOTE.—Compare Nellore No. (112) where the name of a different man of perhaps the same family is given as Chálukya Náráyana Chauhattamalla Ranavijaya Vengaḷayya.

1. పింగళ సంవత్సర కార్తీక శు ౧౫లు శ్రీమన్మహామండ
లేశ్వర చాళిక్యనారాయణ చౌహత్తమల్ల
2. రణ విజయ వెలమపాటి తిరుమలరాజయదేవ మహారా
జుల వారు వేదాద్రి శ్రీ నరసింహ
3. దేవునకి తీర్థానకుగల వుభయం.

NELLORE (36).

[Koruṭúru. Telugu. East wall of Puttanáthéṣvara temple.]

TRANSLATION.

On the 9th day of the dark fortnight of Phálguṇa of the year Hévalambi, Changappa, son of Barhari Kónari Seṭṭi of the . . . Paṭinḍala *gótra* founded an endowment for providing a daily offering of 3 measures of rice daily to Puṭṭanátha (god) and Párvatidévi (goddess) of Kóraṭúru for the religious merit of his father Kónéri Seṭṭi and his mother and put it in the possession of the temple servants. The temple servants should maintain this in perpetuity as long as the sun and moon last.

1. హేవళంబి సంవ్వత్సర పాల్గుణబ౯లు . . . . .
2. పటిండల గోత్రం బర్హారి కోనరి సెట్టి కొడుకు
3. చంగప్పతమ తండ్రి కోనెరి సెట్టికిన్ని తమ తల్లికిని పుణ్యం
4. గాను కొరటూరి పుట్టానాధునికిన్ని పార్వతి అమ్మవారలకు
నిత్య

5. నైవేద్యానకు దినముదినము మూండుపళ్లుబియ్యము స్వా
మి ఆ

6. రాధనకున్ను కట్టడసెసి స్తానికులవశాన యిచ్చెను యీ

7. పుణ్యం స్తానికులు ఆచంద్రార్కస్తాయిగా న

8. డుపువారు.

NELLORE (37).

[Koruṭúru. Telugu. From west wall of Puṭṭanáthé-ṣvara temple.]

TRANSLATION.

Basudévu gave golden ornaments to Ṣrí Putanádha (deity). These jewels will last as long as the sun and moon exist. Such being the case, those who misappropriate them will incur the sin of killing cows and Brahmans near the Ganges.

శ్రీ పుటనాంధునికి ప్పింప్పంబసు
దేవు సమర్పించిన బంగారంపట్టలు
యీ పట్టం ఆచంద్రార్కస్తాయిగా
ను వుండును యిది గనక య
వ్వారు అపహరించ్చదలచెవారు
గంగకతర్గోవు బ్రాహ్మణుని
వధించిన పాపానుం బోవువారు.

NELLORE (38).

[Koruṭúru. Tamil. From wall of enclosure of temple.]

TRANSLATION.

. . . . . . for sacred food, and flowers . . . . these lands . . . . (free of tax) to last as long as the moon and sun endure . . . . . . this charity.

[1] . . . . . க்கு அமுதுபடி சாத்துப்படி தி-
[2] . . . . . பொம் இந்நிலங்களுக்கு . ரொ-
[3] . . . . . வலு-ஷமாநருமாகச் சந்திராதித்தவ-
[4] . . . . . ள்வதே கொ . . . . இத்தன்
மத்து.

NELLORE (39).

[Koruṭúru. Tamil. East wall of temple. Unintelligible.]

NELLORE (40). (A.D. 1190-91 ?)

[Kóvúru. Tamil and Sanskrit in Grantha character. Opposite Vishnu temple.]

TRANSLATION.

Hail! Prosperity! This is the edict of the glorious (god) Gópálanátha, the lord of the world, who is worshipped by crores of gods and kings.

In the Śaka year expressed by *pra*(2), *khya*(1), *yó*(1), *gyo*(1), (or 1112), the king Siddhi gave to the god Góvinda (some portion here is not clear) the village of Kóvúr.

In the Śaka year one thousand one hundred and twelve corresponding to the 14th year of the reign of the emperor of the three worlds who was pleased to take Madurai and the crowned head of the Páṇḍya, the glorious Kulóttuṅgachóḷadéva, Madurántakapottapichóḷa (*alias*) . . . . raiyan . . . . . at Tiruváyppáḍi in Nellore *alias* Vikramasiṅgapura, (situated) in Piḍánáḍu in Chédikulamáṇikkavaḷanáḍu (a sub-division) of Jayaṅkoṇḍachóḷamaṇḍala . . . .

Note.—This stone bears two Telugu inscriptions also. Of these one seems to be a portion of a Telugu copy of the above while the second is a fragment, dated S.S. 1468. The regnal year was originally read as the 32nd but has been changed on local inspection to 14th. As a fact it should be the 12th apparently.

[1] ஸ்வஸ்திஶ்ரீ ஶாகே ஶில்லா-
[2] ண கோடி ர[ஸ கோடி] ஸ-
[3] ங்க்யே [1*] ஶ்ரீமத் ராஜ-
[4] ராஜநாய [ஸ்ய] ஸோம
[5] நாயஸ்ய [ஸ]ரஸ்வத் [11*]
[6] ஶ்ரீபரம ராஜநாத [வாய]
[7] ஸ்வஸ்ரியா [தேவ] ஸ [ஜரா]-
[8] ஜாதி விர்யாத்ர் ஜா-
[9] விடாயா தயக் வதி-
[10] [ஹு] த: கோஷ்ஸ்வர் வ்ர-
[11] த்யெர்மெத்ர ஸகாலெ
[12] சகவருஷம் ஆயிரத்தொ-
[13] ருநூற்றொருபத்திரண்டா-
[14] வதில் திரிபுவனச்சக்கர-
[15] வத்திகள் மதுரையும்
[16] பாண்டியன் முடித்த-
[17] லையுங்கொண்டருளின
[18] ஸ்ரீகுலோத்துங்கசோ-
[19] ழ தேவற்கு யாண்டு [௩] வதுவ-
[20] து ஜயங்கொண்ட சோ-
[21] ழ மண்டலத்துச் செதிகு-
[22] ல [மாணிக்கவ] ளநாட்டுப்பி-
[23] டா[நா]ட் [டு] நெல்லூரான வி-
[24] க்கிர[மசி]ங்கபுரத்துத்தி[ரு]-
[25] வாய்ப்பாடியில் . . .

[26] . க்கு மதுராந்தக[ப்பொ]-
[27] [த்*] தப்பிச்செ . . . . .
[28] யரையன் . . . . . ட .
[29] ட்டிற்குள் . . . . ந்தி
[30] ரந்த்தவ . . . . . தாக
[31] திருவிள . . . . . க்க
[32] குடுத்த . . . . .

Nellore (41).

[Lébúru. Persian. On pillars of gópuram of Chenna-késava temple.]

Translation.

This building was constructed by Muhammad Husain Beg Khán. If, in the present building, the descendants of Husain Beg Khán live, they must look after the condition of the fakirs. Should they hesitate, his younger brother Hamza Husain Khán will be invested with full powers . . .

این حویلي ساخت محمد حسین بیگ خان اگر در این
حویلي حال والاد حسین بیگ خان باشند آگاه از حال
درویش باشد و اگر فکرے مي کنند برادر خرد ایشان حمزه
حسین خان را حاکم نموده *

Nellore (42).

[Lébúru. Persian. From pillar of *gópuram* of Chenna-késava temple.]

Translation.

Prayers and benediction. This building has been presented to Imám Husain for the purpose of an Áshúr

Khána (temporary house erected in the Muharram for the purpose of prayer). Ghulám Muhammad Husain Beg Khán.

صلاة و درود *

[illegible]

[illegible]

Nellore (43).

[Lébúru. Telugu. In the Válésvara temple.]

Translation.

They should utilize on the tank the *kunchams* of grain (set apart) for the tank in the village of Vémúru. They should give the balance to the temple. Those who speak evil of this, or desire to appropriate that grain, will incur the sin of killing cows and Brahmans on the banks of the Ganges.

1. వేమూరిగ్రామాన చె
2. రువు కుంచ్చాల ధాన్యం
3. చెరువుమీందనే వేశిం
4. చ్చంగలవారు మిగిలిదె
5. వుళాలుగుండినిచ్చువారు
6. ఇందుకు యెవ్వరు కీడా
7. డినాను అధాన్యం ఆశిం
8. చినాను గంగకత
9. గోబ్రాం హ్మాణుల వధి
10. ంచిన పాపానం బోవు
11. వారు.

NELLORE (44).

[Lébúru. Telugu. In the Válésvara temple.]

TRANSLATION.

I have given a field in the swampy land for providing enjoyments in this temple. I have made the gift so that it may be maintained as a *Sarvamánya* (tax free).

1. యీా దేవళంలోను
2. దానుంబోంగాను
3. . . . వాంకనుచే
4. నునిచ్చినాను సర్వమా
5. ంన్యంగాను నడుపువా
6. ంక్షని యిచ్చినవాం
7. డ్లను. . . .

NELLORE (45).

[Lébúru. Tamil. From interior of Kunkálamma temple. Illegible.]

NELLORE (46). (A.D. 1591–92?)

[Marripádu. Telugu. On a stone near the choultry.]

TRANSLATION.

Hail! In the year 1513 of the illustrious, victorious and prosperous Śáliváhana Śaka era, ... Venkaṭádri Náyaningáru, the servant (?) of Vengappa Náyaningáru, who is the grandson of Póli Náyaningáru, and the son of Vengappa Náyaningáru, granted with libation of water the village of Marripáḍu situated in Rápur *ṣíma* and in Udayagiri *rájya* which was granted to Venkaṭapati

Náyanivárn, who is the grandson of Peda Koṇḍama Náyaningáru and the son of Ammánáyanigáru, in ratification of the former gift to last as long as the sun and moon endure . . . . .

Whoever whether among you or any one else covets this charity will incur the sin of killing a cow and a Brahman near the Ganges, and will incur the sin of killing his parents and his *gurus*.

Thus has this charitable edict been issued. Ṣrí ! Ṣrí ! Ṣrí !

1. స్వస్తిశ్రీజయాం
2. భ్యుదయ శాలి
3. వాహన శకవర్షంబులు
4. ౧౫౧౩ ది పెదకొం
5. డ్డమనాయని
6. ంగారి పౌత్రు
7. లైన అంమ్మనా
8. యనిగారింపు .

Second side.

9. త్రులైన వెం
10. కర్ణటపతినా
11. యనివారిక
12. ఋయ్యా నవ
13 ధరించిన వు
14. దయగిరి రా
15. జ్యములోని
16. రాంపూరి శి
17. మలోను నడిచె
18. మరిపాశ్రిగ్రా

19. మం ధారవోసి
20. . . .
21. . . పోషి
22. నాఇనింగారి
23. పౌత్రులును
24. వెంగప్పనాఇ
25. నింగారి పుత్రు

மதக்ககா } These Tamil
க்கதம்மக } letters appear.

Third side.

26. దు వెంగ్గప్పనా
27. ఇనింగారి పా
28. లించిన వెంక
29. ట్రాద్రి నాఇనిం
30. గారు పునః ప్ర
31. తిష్టగాను ఆ
32. చంద్రాకర్కాంగా
33. ను నడిచెట్టుగాను
34. . . కశ
35. . డ
36. . .
37. . లఇ
38. లముఖ
39. చ్చిర యీధర్మాపు
40. మీలోనుగాకయ
41. వ్వారు ఆశించ్చినా
42. ను గంగ్గకర్తాంగో

Fourth side.

43. బ్రాంహ్మ ని
44. వధియించ్చిన
45. పాపానను
46. తల్లిదండ్రా
47. జాలు గురు
48. వులయుం వ
49. ధియించి
50. న పాపానం
51. పోదురు ఇ
52. ట్టనిబ్రాఇం
53. చ్చిన ధర్మ
54. శాసనం శ్రీ
55. శ్రీ శ్రీ .

NELLORE (47). (A.D. 1638–39.)

[Móḍeguntạ. Telugu. Near choultry to west.]

TRANSLATION.

(Adoration to) Ṣrí Ráma! Hail! on the 2nd of the bright half of Chaitra of the year Bahudhánya, corresponding to the year 1560 of the illustrious, victorious and prosperous Śáliváhana Śaka era, Velugóṭi Venkaṭapati Náyanivάru . . issued this charitable edict for the tank . . . . vetti . . . .

* * * *

1. శ్రీరామా
2. స్వస్తి యాభ్యు
3. దయ శాలివాహాన

4. శకవర్షంబులు
5. ౧౫౬౦ అగు నేటి
6. బహుధాన్య సంవత్స
7. ర చైత్రశు ౧ లు వెలు
8. గోటి వెంకటపతి
9. నాయనింవారు .

Second side.

10. . . . . . . గారు చెర్వుకు
11. వెళ్ళించిన ధర్మశాసనం
12. . . . .
13. . . . .
14. . . . .
15. . . . .
16. . . . .
17. . . . .
18. . . . .
19. . . . .
20. . . . వెట్టివాడు

NELLORE (48).

[Náyuḍupāḷem. Telugu. Fallen stone in field to north of village.]

TRANSLATION.

* * * *

. They will enjoy. The field given to Prakóḷa Dévata is to be maintained by Biḍḍalakú Mallináthunḍu.

He who obstructs this will incur the sin of eating food from the skull of his eldest son. He who maintains it . . . . May it cause great prosperity !

* * * *

1\. . . . .

2\. . . . .

3\. అనుభవించువారుగాను

4\. సెసి ప్రకాళ దేవతకూను

5\. ఇచ్చిన చేనుకు బిడ్డల

6\. కూ మల్లినాథుండు

7\. సెల్లించెదీనికి విఘాత

8\. ముసేసినవాండు తన

9\. పెద్దకొడుకు కపాలము

10\. న వన్నము పెట్టికొని కుడి

11\. చిన పాపానంబొందు

12\. వారు దినిపాలించినవానికి

13\. . . అనై తలనుండు

14\. . . . .

15\. న మంగళమహా శ్రీ శ్రీ

16\. (సిద్ధము వానలిండు

17\. నట్టిన వాడికి . రిలాప)

* * * *

NELLORE (49).

[Nellore. Telugu. From a Muhammadan tomb at Dargamiṭṭa.[1] Evidently the stone was taken from an older building. An unintelligible fragment.]

1. రా మేశ్వర శ్రీకాళకాటవికర్ప రేశ్వరదేవ
2. శ్రీపాదపద్మారాధకులైన తిరుపతిబు
3. ద్గాతివ్యాభావతత్స్ఫధలాలన్సు నెలూరు
4. ను మాధుగర, దేయఃభూంతలికివనాయ
5. గధద్రోహులకు లోనుగాకతమలోందాము
6. స్తున్న పుచ్చుకొన్నం వోరిమపాత్రం తిరుపతికులా
7. రువచ్చిన దాంకాను తర్లివచ్చినవారు.

---

[1] Of Dargamiṭṭa it is said in the District Manual that tradition declares it to have once been the site of a large town surrounded by a forest known as Dandakáranyam. Tradition has it, further, that the ghosts of the lions which once inhabited that forest still wander roaring about the locality. These ghostly noises so terrify sleeping elephants that they die of fright (cause and effect; there are no elephants in the neighbourhood). Dargamiṭṭa is now the European quarter of Nellore and takes its names from a group of tombs of Muhammadan saints. Of the chief of these it is related that he lost his head in battle and, carrying it with him, wandered about the world looking for a place for his grave. When he got to Nellore he was so pleased with it that he decided to settle there, which he did and over his remains was raised one of the tombs now standing. The tombs are said to have been discovered two centuries ago by Muhammad Rahimtulla ancestor of the present inamdar along with an iron plate bearing an inscription that twelve martyrs were buried on the spot. This plate is said to have been presented by the finder to the ruler Nek Nám Khán (obviously a fancy name) who established the existing inam. While on the subject of Nellore we may mention that there is in one of the temples of that town a seated figure, about life-size, which now bears the Vaishnavite mark, but which is clearly a Buddha or a Jain saint, probably the latter. It is called the Kónéṭi Ráyi, having been dug up when a pond, or kóneru, was constructed, half a century or so ago, in front of the Collector's cutcherry. Scattered here and there about the town and, indeed, about the District generally, are numerous small images of a Jain type but we know of no other approaching the Kóṇéṭi Ráyi in size.

NELLORE (50).

[Nellore. Tamil. Built into the big Muhammadan tomb at Dargamiṭṭa.]

TRANSLATION.

We shall maintain (the charity) as long as the moon, and the sun endure. With this promise, Kitti Álvaṇ, goldsmith of Kúvam and son of Mávedụttán, presented one evening lamp and Perụmáḷ the goldsmith, son of Tondáravén, the son of Oṟṟikoṇḍár of Palantaṇḍala, presented one evening lamp. (For these lamps they give a *máḍai*). This *máḍai* to be lent out on interest . . . . Madurántaka Potta . . . . . whoever injures this will incur sin. (The second side is of the reign of Kulóttunga Chóḷadéva and seems to record the grant of some land to the god Akkasálíṣvara).

[1] இத்தவரை செலுத்தக்கடவொ-
[2] ம[ாக] கூவத்தில் விஸ்வகர்ம்மா-
[3] வாண மாவெடுத்தான் மகந்
[4] கி[த்]தி ஆழ்வாந் வைச்ச சந்-
[5] தி விளக்கு க பழந்தண்ட-
[6] வத்து விஸ்வகர்ம்மா ஒற்றிகொ-
[7] ண்டார் மகன் தொண்டாரவெ-
[8] வன் மகந் பெருமாள் இட்ட
[9] சந்திவிளக்கு க இம்மாடை
[10] எறை இழிச்சி இறை இ . . . . .
[11] மதுராந்தகப்பொத்த . . . . .
[12] னென் இதுக்கு அகி . . . . .
[13] யில் ஜொவவெயெ பண் . . . . .

Second side.

[1] ஸ்வஸ்தி ஸ்ரீ குலொத்துங் . . . . .
[2] வது அக்கஸாலிஸ்வரமு . . . . .

[3] ரவனென் பெரி ளரிகிழ் . . . . .
[4] உதருமா சம புஞ்சை ந . . . . .
[5] பறச்செரிக்கு தெற்கு . . . . .

NELLORE (51).

[Nellore. Tamil. Built into the big Muhammadan tomb at Dargamiṭṭa.]

This inscription is made up of two fragments. One of these records the gift of gardens by Pottapichóḷa *alias* Gaṇḍagópála with libation of water to the deity Akkasáli, and prays that it may be kept under the protection of the Máhéṣvaras. It gives boundaries but they are not complete.

The second appears to be a gift to the god Tirunágéṣvara. It was received by Dévapiḷḷai, son of . . . and Káḷatti Uḍayár and they bind themselves to maintain the charity as long as the moon and sun endure.

[1] . . . . . . சை இந்த க்ஷேத்ரத்து யாராவ-ஒல்லுத்து வண்ணணி.
[2] . . . . . வனெனக் . பண்டாரிக்கொயில் மட விளாக
[3] . . . . . ழிதியும் வழிக்கு வடக்கும் தொட்டம் குழி ௫
[4] . . . . . ளிக்கு மெற்குத்தொட்டம் செங்கழனி குழி
[5] . . . . . ழி சாஉய இத்தொட்டங்கள் அக்க-ஸாலி-
[6] . . . . . ற்கு பொத்தப்பிச்சொழன் கண்ட-கோபா-
[7] . . . . ஜ-த்து வண்ணணினெக் ஸ்ரீமாஹெஸ்வர.

Second side.

[1] . . . . . டும் திருஞகிசாமு-
[2] . . . . . மகக் தெவப்பிள்ளை . .
[3] . . . . . காளத்தி உடையார் . . .
[4] . . . . . ப்பிள்ளை உள்ளிட்டார் . .
[5] . . . . . கைக்கொண்டோம் . . .
[6] . . . . . து வரை செலுத்த
[7] . . . . . ம.

NELLORE (52). (A.D. 1635–36.)

[Nellore. Telugu. From the bund of the big Nellore tank.]

TRANSLATION.

Hail! On the 15th day of the bright half of Śrávaṇa of the year named Yuva, corresponding to 1557 of the illustrious, victorious and prosperous Ṣáliváhana Ṣaka era, Arula Rághayamgáru issued a charitable edict as follows for the *mérás* of the tank of Nellore under the orders of Ṣrímat Velugóṭi Venkaṭapati Náyanáyyamváru. We have granted with libation of water the *mérás* collected from all the fields under this tank within the four boundaries and ordered that they should be spent on the tank by the residents of the town (?). Therefore those who walk by those places, the cultivators, the *kápus*, and the *karnams*, should give the grain derived from the *mérás* of this tank to Upparas and get the tank put in order by them. If any fail to carry this out they will be considered to have[1] given their honour to Málas and Mádigas. In such terms has the charitable edict been executed.

---

[1] The phrase apparently means "prostituted their wives."

1. స్వస్తిశ్రీ విజయాభ్యుదయ శాలి
2. వాహన శకవరుషంబ్బు
3. లు ౧౫౫౭ అగునేంటి యువ
4. నామ సంవత్సర శ్రావణ శు
5. ౧౫ లు శ్రీమతు వెలుగో
6. టి వెంకటపతినాయనయ్యం
7. వారి ఆనతిని అరులరాఘు
8. యంగారు నెల్లూరు చెర్వుమేరా
9. కుగాను యిచ్చిన ధర్మశాసనపద్ధ
10. తి యీచెర్వ్య కింద్దపొలఁయల్లచ
11. తుకీమాను వారలు సహితంగా
12. ను నడిచె చెర్వు మెరనగరం బడసిద్ధారా
13. పూరంచెసిచెర్వుమీందనె వేయించేట
14. ట్టుగాకట్టడశెస్తిమి గనక అకఁడ స్తళ్ళాం
15. త్తరాల నడ్చెవారు సేత్యగాండ్లుకా
16. ంపు కరుణాలు ఆచెర్వ మేరవల్ల వ
17. చ్చిన ధాన్యం ఉప్పల్లఁకిచ్చి చెర్వుమీ
18. ద వేయించ్చంగలవారు యింద్దు తప్పి
19. నట్టిదాయినా వాండ్లాలిం మాలుమాదిగ
20. కుఃములు వాండ్లకు యిచ్చినవాండు
21. గానిచ్చిన ధర్మశాసనపద్దతి

NELLORE (53).

[Nellore. Telugu. Alongside the Madras road.]

TRANSLATION.

The charitable *maṭham* of the illustrious Dattátrêya Svámi, who presides over the whole universe, who is a *paramahamsa*, the excellent *guru*.

NOTE.—There was doubtless a maṭham of a guru near this stone.

Paramahamsa is the title assumed by a Hindu sannyási after a certain stage in his spiritual progress.

1. శ్రీమద్వి
2. శ్వాధిష్ఠాపన
3. పరమహంస
4. సద్గురు దత్తా
5. త్రేయ స్వాము
6. లవారి ధర్మ
7. మఠం॥

Nellore (54). (A.D. 1573–74.)

[Nellore. Telugu. From northern wall of Ranganáyakulasvámi temple.]

Translation.

Hail! On the 15th of the bright half of Vaiṣákha of the year Ṣrímukha, corresponding to 1495 of the illustrious, victorious and prosperous Ṣáliváhana Ṣaka era, Venkaṭapa Naiḍu, the secretary (mudrakartá) of Veligóṭi Timmapa Náyaningáru the agent (káryakartá) of Ṣrímad Rájádhirája, Rája Paraméṣvara, Śrí Víra Pratápa Śrí Víra Ṣrí Rangaráyadéva Maháráya, for the religious merit of the Ráyalu (Rangaráya) and Timmapanáyani-(ngáru), made the following arrangements, for showing respect to Panchahánas[1] during the festival days of Paḷikonḍanátha of Nellore. We shall show respect to all the Panchahánas who come in the car as at Tirupati (?)

---

[1] The five classes of artizans.

The *Sthala Karanams, Kápus, Seṭṭis* and *Páka Reḍḍis*[1] having been made to agree to the observance of this etiquette, if any obstruct this etiquette, they will incur the sin of killing cows, Brahmans and newly-born infants near the Ganges.

Ṣrí

This edict has been written by Karanam Muttaráju Venkaṭádri.

1. స్వస్తి శ్రీ జయాభ్యుదయ శాలివాహన శకవరుషంబులు ౧౪౯౫ అగునేంట్టి శ్రీముఖసంవత్సర వయిశాఖ శు ౧౫ లు శ్రీమద్రాజాధిరాజ రాజపరమేశ్వర శ్రీ వీరప్రతాప శ్రీవీరశ్రీరంగరాయ

2. దేవమహారాయులు అయ్యవారి కార్యకర్తలయిన వెలిగోటి తిమ్మపనాయనింగారి ముద్రకర్త వెంకటప్ప నాయండు రాయలవారికిన్ని తిమ్మపనాయనికిన్ని పుణ్యముగాను । నెల్లూరి

3. పలికొండనాథునికి తిరుగ నిప్పించి తిరుతిరునాళ్లకు।పంచ్చహాణం వారికినడపి మర్యాదకు కట్టండ చేసిన వివరము॥ తేరుయెక్కి-వచ్చియందుకు తిరుపతిమర్యాదను పంచ్చహాణం వారికి నడపాగలవారము

4. యీ మర్యాదకు స్థలకరణాలనున్ను కాంపులనున్ను శెట్టి పాకరడ్లనున్ను వొప్పించి యా యామర్యాదకు యప్వరుదప్పినాను గంగకర్తను గోబ్రాంహల పుట్టిన శిశువులనున్ను వధించిన పాపాన బోవువారము। శ్రీ। కరణంముత్తరాజు వెంకటాద్రి వ్రాశిన శాసనము

---

[1] This seems to mean "Reḍḍis of Pákonáḍu."

Nellore (55). (A.D. 1197–98.)

[Nellore. Tamil. North wall of Ranganáyakala-swámi temple.]

Translation.

Hail! Prosperity! The following is engraved from verbal orders received:—

This is the edict of Chitraméḷa who is the son of the illustrious Bhúdéví, and who was sprung from the fourth class (Śúdra), (promulgated) for the benefit of all the world . . . . . .

In the Śaka year one thousand one hundred and nineteen, the inbabitants of (a number of) *náḍus* (Pédainádu, Péráttinádu, Muṅgaláṟattainádu, Kaḍaiyaśinganáḍu, Pûṅgainádu, Tongaipúnuḷnáḍu, Chakalanáḍu, Pottappináḍu) of Jayaṅkondachóḻamaṇḍala having all assembled at Chittiraméḻimaṇḍapa in Tiruppáṟkaḍaṟchittiraméḻivinnagar, gave to the god at Chittiraméḻivinnagar, free of tax, lands to the extent of 2,200 *kuḻi*. We shall give this (extent of land). He who hinders this will incur the sin of stabbing a tawny cow on the banks of the Ganges.

Thus agreeing we have made the gift.

(Then follows a list of signatures of those who consented to this grant).

[1] ஸ்வஸ்திஸ்ரீ திருவாய்க்[கெ]ழ்வி முன்னுடைத்தாக ஸ்ரீ-
பூதேவீபுத்ரஸ்ய சதுர்த்தகுலஜாதஸ்ய ஸகலலோக-
ஹிதார்த்தாய சித்ரமேளஸ்ய ஶாஸநம் அரம்வளர்க . .
. ப்புகழ்பெருக . . . . . நியாய நடாத்துகின்ற ஜயங்
கொண்டசொழமண்டலத்துப் பெடைநாட்டு இவிலைய .
. . . . இவிலையத்தொழும் பொரத்திநாட்டு வ-

[2] யி[ர]விஜையத்தொழுங்கொ[ர]றத்தைநாட்டு விஜை-யத்தொழுங்கடையச்சிங்கநாட்டு விஜையத்தொழு[ம்] பூங்-கைநாட்டு விஷையத்தொழுந்தொங்கைப்பூநு[ள்]நாட்டு வி-ஜையத்தொழுஞ்சகலநாட்டு விஷையததொழும்பொ,த்தப்பிநா-ட்டு விஜைய,த்தொ[ம்'] உட்பட்ட பெரியநாட்டு விஜையத்-தொம் சகாயாண்டு ஆயிரத்தொருநூற்றெருபத்தொன்பதாவ-

[3] (த்)துத்திருப்பாற்கடற் சித்திரமெழிவிண்ணகரிற்சித்-திரமெழிமண்டபத்துக்குறைவறக்கூடி நிறைவற நிறைந்திருந்து இச்சித்திரமெழிவிண்ணகரெம்பெருமானுக்கு எங்கள் திரு-விடையாட்டமாக வைத்துக்குடுத்த பரிசாவது பெருநாள் வை ஆயிரங்குழியும் நடுவுதாத்தாள்கள் எழுநூற்றைம்பது-குழ்யுஞ்சிற்சாள்வை ஐந்நூறுகுழியும் டள்ளிபட-

[4] இப்படி விடி[த்தார்]பெரிய நாயநார்க்குப்பழைத்தார்-பட இது விடக்கடவர்களாகவும் இது விலக்கினூர் கெங்கைக்-கரைக்குராற்பசுக்குத்தினுன் பாவத்தெப்படவாராகவும் இப்படி சம்மதித்து வைத்துக்குடுத்தொம் பெரியநாட்டு விஷையத்-தொம் பணியாள் சித்திரமெழிவெளான் எழுத்து இப்படிக்கு இவைகடுவெலிவிஜைய செறுபதி எழுத்து இப்படிக்கு

[5] இவை முதிபுறத்துக்கங்கைகொண்டானெழுக்து இப்-படிக்கு இவை கண்டநாராயணபுரத்துத்தாமிரட்டகுடி எழு-த்து இப் டிக்கு இவைகொள உருப்பிரட்டகுடி எழுக்து இப்-படிக்கு இவை வெங்கூர் சொமிரட்டகுடி எழுத்து இப்படிக்கு இவை அல்லூர் முப்பிட்டகுடி எழுத்து இப்படிக்கு இவை அல்லூர் அயித்தமி-

[6] ப்படிக்கு இவை விரியூர்ச்சியபயநாயக்கனெழுத்து இப்படிக்கு இவை . . . ப . . . .

NELLORE (56).

[Nellore. Tamil. From northern wall of Ranganáyakulaswámi temple.]

This inscription refers to the grant of land in various villages.

[1] ஸ்வஸ்திஸ்ரீ சிறுகப்பைநாடு மன்[று]பொழில் குழி ஐநூறும் அப்[பூ]ர் குழி . . நூறுக்குழூர்குழி ஐஞ்ஞூறுகறுப்பூர்குழி ஆயிரம் குடிச்செறுகுழி முன்னூறு சிறுக்கனப்பூண்டி குழி இருநூறும் இவலூர்குழி முன்னூறு ஒட்டப்பூண்டி குழி ஐஞ்[ஞூறு]

[2] மிறுத்தியூத்தக்கா குழி முன்னூறு குருத்தஊர் குழி ஐஞ்ஞூறு ஊட்டக்கூர் குழி மூன்னூற்றைம்பது கொம்மலப்பூண்டி குழி இருநூறு விங்தூர் குழி நானூறு பென்னிலக்கூர் குழி இருநூறு பிடியூமுன்னூறு

[3] சாதெயன்கொண்டுர் குழி இருநூறு விருகங்கபொ[ல்]லி குழி முன்னூறு சொமெயன்பூண்டி குழி இருநூறு பாழிசெல்மை குழி நூற்ரம்பது முங்கொடுகுழி நூறு வெமூர் குழி. முன்னூறு முஊக்கலதாணை பூண்டி குழி

NELLORE (57).

[Nellore. Tamil. North wall of Ranganáyakulaswámi temple.]

This inscription is not complete. It is dated in the cyclic year Pingaḷa corresponding to the second year of the glorious Kólóttungachóḻadéva who was pleased to take Madurai, Íḻam (Ceylon) and the crowned head of the Páṇḍya king, and the fifteenth year of the reign of the glorious Kulóttungachóḻadéva who was pleased to take the crowned head of Vírapándya, on the date corresponding to Friday with the *nakshatra* Révati, the fourteenth day of the month of Vriśchika. It records grant of 250 *kuḻis* of land and closes with a number of signatures.

The year of the former Kulóttunga was read first as second but on check *in situ* as twentieth.

[1] ஷையத்தொழும் . . . . . விஷயத்தொழும்
காட்டுவிஷையத்தொழுங்கெ . . ட்டத்பாடு நாட்டுவி-
ஷயத்தொழுங்கடைப நாட்டுவிஷயத்தொ-
ழுங் . . ; . . நாட்டு விஷயத்தொழுங்கடை . .
. . .

[2] பிங்குல ல[வொ]லவரத்து மதுரையும் ஈழமுழுங்கொ-
ண்டு பாண்டியன் முடித்தலை கொண்டருளின ஸ்ரீகுலத்துங்க-
சொழதெவர்க்கு யாண்டிரண்டு(?)பாண்டியன் முடித்தலைகொ
ண்டருளின ஸ்ரீகுலோத்துங்க சொழதெவர்க்கு யாண்டு பதி-
னை[ந்தா]வது வ்ரு ஸ்சிகநாயற்றுப்பதி[காலாந்தி]யதியான வெ-
ள்ளிக்கிழமையும் ரெவதியுமான நாள் இம்மண்டலத்து நெல்
லூரான விக்கிரமசிங்கபுர . . . . .

[3] இக்கண்ணவை இருநூற்றைம்பது குழியும் நிர்நிலத்-
திலெ விட்டு காலு மூலையிலுந்[த்]திருவாழிமஞ்சித்திரமெழியும்
இட்ட கல் நட்டுச்சந்திராதித்தவரை செல்லக்கடவதாக விடக-
டவொமாகவும் இப்படி மிவ-ரணபுரசெவகம் விற்றுள்ளனு-
தெமெழியிடத்து மக்கடவர் எல்லாமும் விடக்கடவ . . .
. . ாகவும் . . . . .

[4] இவை நெல்லூர் உடையான் எழுத்து இப்படிக்கு
இவை குறட்டப்பூண்டிப்பிரட்டகுடி எழுத்து இப்படிக்கு இ-
வை கொடுவரூர் வெளான் எழுத்து இப் . . . ண்டிப்
பிரட்டகுடி எழுத்து இப்படிக்கு இவை கொடுவரூர் வெளர்
எழுத்து இப்படிக்கு இவை உருலூர் உலகுய்யாகொண்ட சொ-
யத்தாட்டி எழுத்து இப்படிக்கு இவை பூத்தக்கூர் இராயிட்ட-
குடி எழுத்து இப்படிக்கு . . . . .

[5] டிகுடி எழுத்து இப்படிக்[கு*] இவை மூங்கமூர்ப்-
பொ . . . . . சிரட்டகுடி எழுத்து இப்படிக்கு இவை
குமிழூர் இராசெந்திரசொழவெந்த . . . . திரட்டகுடி
எழுத்து இப்படிக்கு இவை குமிழூர் இராசெந்திரசொளமூ-
வெந்வெளனெழுத்து இப்படிச்கு இவை செறுவனூர்த்திருக்-
காளத்திதெசிரட்டி எழுத்து இப்படிக்கு இவை சறுமவனகா-
ட்டி நாயக்கனெழுத்து இ . . . . .

NELLORE (58).

[Nellore. Tamil. On the northern wall of the Ranganáyakulaswámi temple appear lists of lands granted to the temple. It has not been thought necessary to print them.]

NELLORE (59).

[Nellore. Telugu. Western wall of Ranganáyakulasvámi temple.]

TRANSLATION.

Up to (on) the 5th of the dark fortnight of Chaitra in the year Ṣrímukha, the dancing girl of Ṣrí Talpagiri Ranganátha Svámi gave a *paṭṭi* of dry land in Páta Chintapalli for providing services with sandal and basil (*Ocymum sanctum*). . . . . of Venkaṭá Chári . . . . .

శ్రీముఖనామ సంవత్సర చై
త్ర బ ౫ లు వరకు శ్రీతల్పగిరి
రంగనాథస్వామివారి సానిది

చందనం తులసి కైంకర్యములకు
పాతచింతపల్లి వెలిచేనూపట్టి
ని యీా వెంకటచారిదిండ్ని చేటాం . .

NELLORE (60). (A.D. 1301–02.)

[Nellore. Tamil. Western wall of Ranganáyakulaswámi temple.]

TRANSLATION.

Hail! Prosperity! In the Śaka year 1224 Plavanga (Plava?) corresponding to the 12th year of the reign of the emperor of the three worlds, the glorious Rájagaṇḍagópáladéva, on the date corresponding to Monday with the *nakshatra* Róhiṇi, the tenth day of the bright half of the month of Makara, I, Madurántakapóttapichóḷa *alias* Ránganáthan *alias* Rájagaṇḍagópáladéva, gave to last as long as the moon and sun to (the god of) Chitraméḷivinnagar namely Paḷḷikoṇḍaperumáḷ at Tiruppáṟkaḍal in Nellúr *aliàs* Vikramaśiṅgapura (situated) in Paḍainádu in Chédikulamánikkavaḷanáḍu (a sub-division) of Jayaṅkoṇḍachóḷamaṇḍala, for ceremonies including sacred food, ornaments, daily offerings and temple repairs, free of tax and as exclusive property, the dry and wet lands included within the four boundaries of the village of . . . in Paḍainádu.

If there is anybody who obstructs this charity, he will incur the sin of killing of a tawny cow on the banks of the Ganges.

NOTE.—The date was first read as 1228 but on check *in situ* appears as 1224. The cyclic year is given as Plavanga, but we should doubtless read Plava which is S S. 1224 current. To agree with other inscriptions, however, we ought to have the *expired* Ṣaka year 1224.

[1] ஸ்வஸ்தி ஸ்ரீ சகரையாண்டு ௲௨௱௨௰௪ [பிலவங்க-
ஸம்வத்ஸரி திரிபுவனச்சக்கரவத்திகள் ஸ்ரீ இராசகண்டகொ-
பாலதெவற் (க்)கு யாண்டு

[2] பன்னிரண்டாவது மகரநாயற்று பூர்வபக்ஷத்து தச-
மியும் திங்கட்கிழமையும் பெற்ற உரொசணிநாள் மதுராந்-
தக—

[3] ப்பொத்தப்பிச்சொழன் ரெங்கநாதன் ஆன இராசகண்-
டகொபாலதெவனென் செயங்கொண்டசொழ-

[4] மண்டலத்துச்செதிருலமாணிக்கவளநாட்டுப்படைநா-
ட்டு நெல்லூரான விக்கிரமசிங்கபுரத்து

[5] திருப்பாற்கடல் சித்திரமெழிவிண்ணகரான பள்ளி-
கொண்ட பெருமாளுக்கு அமுதுபடி சாத்துப்படி உள்ளிட்ட
நிமந்த-

[6] ங்களுக்கும் திருப்பணிக்கும் உடலாக படைநாட்டுத்-
தண்டி . ப்பூறு நாற்பாற்கெல்லைக்கு உட்பட்ட நன்சை-
புன்சை நிலம் திருவி-

[7] [டையாட்டம்] ஸர்வமானியமாக சந்திராதித்தவரை
செல்வதாக விட்டென் இதுவிலக்கிருண்டாகில் கெங்கை-

[8] [க்கரையில் குரா]ற்பசுக்கொன்றான் பாவத்திலெ|படு
வான்.

NELLORE (61).

[Nellore. Tamil. From western wall of Ranganayakulaswámi temple.]

TRANSLATION. (*Abstract*).

Hail! Prosperity! In the . . . of the reign of the emperor of the three worlds, the unequalled among kings, Sundara Páṇḍyadéva, we (the king) gave at the recommendation of Kálingaráyar the village of Mávaḍikuṇḍai in Muṇḍanáḍu, all the lands in the village, wet, dry, house sites, gardens and other lands, taxes and rights of ryots, ínevari (?), sittáya (toll ?) and all kinds of taxes accruing from the village, from the month of Ávani of the same year, for offerings in the hall constructed in our name (and) called Sudarapáṇḍyaśandi and at festivals and for daily offerings to the god Chittiraméḻivinṇagar namely Paḷḷikoṇḍaperumál at Nellúr *alias* Vikramásiṅgapuram situated in Paḍaináḍu in Chédikulamáṇikkavaḷanâḍu.

[1] ஸ்வஸ்தி ஸ்ரீ திருபுவனச்சக்கரவத்திகள் கொனெரின்மை-
கொண்டான் சுந்தரபாண்டியதெவற்கு யாண்டு . . . .

[2] வணிமாதமுதல் செதிகுலமாணிக்கவளநாட்டுப்பெ-
டைநாட்டு நெல்லூரான விக்கிரமசிங்கபுரத்துத்திரு . . .
. .

[3] சித்திரமெழிநண்ணகரா[வி]பள்ளிகொண்டாழ்வாற்கு நம்-
பெரால் கட்டின சுந்திரபாண்டியன் சந்திக்கும் திருநா . .
. . .

[4] அமுதுபடி சாத்துப்படி உள்ளிட்டு வெண்டும் நித்த
நிமன்தங்களுக்கு முண்டநாட்டு மாவடிகுண்டை . . . .

[5] ல்லைக்கு உட்பட்ட நிர்நிலமும் கறுஞ்செய் .
புன்செயும் நத்தமும் தொட்டமும் குழுமகுள ப்பரிவ்வும் மற்று.
. . . . .

[6] ட்டவையிற்றுக்குடி இருக்கும் கடமை[யி]னெவரி சித்-
.தாயமும் மற்றும் எப்பெறப்பட்ட வரிகளும் உட்பட ஸ .
. . .

[7] மாகத்திருவிடையாட்டமாக இடப்பெற வெணுமென்-
று காலிங்கராயர் சொன்னமையில் இவ்வாழ்வார்க்கு . . .
. .

[8] ணை செல்வதாக இவ்வூர் குடுத்தோம் இதுவிலக்[ங்]கு-
ருண்டாகில் கெங்கைக்கரையிற் குரால் பசுவைக் . . . . .

Nellore (62). (A.D. 1299-1300.)

[Nellore. Tamil. Western wall of Ranganáyakula-swámi temple.]

Translation.

In the expired Śaka year 1221 corresponding to the 9th year of the reign of the emperor of the three worlds, the glorious . . . [Gaṇḍa] Gópáladéva, on the date corresponding to Monday with the *nakshatra* Anusha . . . . . of the bright half of the month of Makara, [Madurántakapo] ttapichóḻa, the glorious Raṅganátha *alias* Rájagaṇḍagópáladévan gave to the god of Chitraméḻiviṇṇagar namely Paḻḻikoṇḍaperumáḷ at [Tiru]ppárkaḍal in Nellúr *alias* Vikrama[śiṅgapura] (situated) in Paḍainâḍu in [Chédi]kulamáṇikkavaḷanáḍu (a sub-division) of Jayaṅkoṇḍachóḻa[maṇḍala] for daily offerings and temple repairs, as long as the moon and sun last, free of tax with libation of water, the dry and wet lands included within the four boundaries of the village of . . . ṅgalakkoṇḍai.

He who obstructs [this] charity will incur the sin of killing a tawny cow on the banks of the Ganges.

[1] க . . . . . [ண்டு] கதுஉாஉ௰க செல்லாநின்ற திரிபுவனச்சக்கரவத்திகள் ஸ்ரீ-

[2] . . . . . . பாலதெவற்கு யாண்டு ௯-வது மகர-நாயற்று வலுபக்ஷத்து

[3] . . . . . ட்கிழமையும் பெற்ற அனுழத்திநாள் ஜயங்கொண்டசோழ-

[4] . . . . . . குலமாணிக்கவளநாட்டுப்படைநாட்டு நெல்லூரான வி[கூ]-ம|

[5] . . . . . . ப்பாற்கடற்சித்திரமெழிவிண்ணகரா-ன பள்ளிகொண்டபெருமாளுக்கு

[6] . . . . . . படி உள்ளிட்ட நித்தநிமந்தங்களுக்குந்-திருப்பணிக்கும் உடலாக-

[7] . . . . . . ாத்தப்பிச்சொழன் ஸ்ரீரங்கநாதரான இராஜகண்டகொபாலதெவன் நந்தா-

[8] . . . . . . ங்கலக்கொண்டை நாற்பாற்கெல்லை உட்பட்ட நன்சையும் புன்சை-

[9] . . . . . . யுந்திருவிடையாட்டமாகச்சந்திராதி-த்தவரை செல்ல உதகவ-[illegible]-மாக

[10] . . . . . . [illegible]ம் விலக்கினார் கெங்கைக்கரையில் குராப்பசுக்கொன்றான் பாப-

[11] . . . . . . டவன் க

NELLORE (63).

[Nellore. Tamil. Southern wall of Ranganáyakula-svámi temple.]

TRANSLATION.

Hail! Prosperity! In the reign of the emperor of the three worlds, who was pleased to take Madurai and the crowned head of the Pándya, the glorious Kulóttunga-chóladéva, . . . gave to Chittiraméḷivinnagar *alias* Paḷḷikoṇḍaperumáḷ . . Seṭṭi of Tiruppáṛkaḍal in Nellur *alias* Vikramasingapura (situated) in Piḍanáḍu in Chédi-kulamáṇikkavaḷanáḍu, (certain villages, names not clear) free of tax. We the authorities of this temple agreed to provide, as long as the moon and sun endure, rice, food, food with vegetables, ghee and curds.

[1] ஸ்வஸ்தி ஸ்ரீ திரிபுவனச்சக்கர[வர்]த்திகள் மதுரையும் பாண்டியன் மு[டி]த்தலையுங்கொண்டருளின ஸ்ரீ கு[லொத்-துங்]க சொ[ள]தே- . . . . .

[2] செதிகுலமாணிக்க வளநாட்டுப் பிடநாட்டு[ெ]நல்லூ-ரான விக்கிரமசிங்கபுரத்து திருப்பா[ம்]கடற் சித்திரமெழிவிண்ணகரான பள்ளிகொண்டபெருமாள் கொ . . . . .

[3] மசெட்டியாற்குச் சிவிதமான முண்டைநாட்டு பெரும் பள்ளி நி[ம்]ம[ல்] யின்ஞயஞர் திருவிடையாட்டமான தாமணம் வெற்கலந்த . . . . .

[4] முதுபடிகாயமு[து*]நெய்யமுது தயிரமுதுடனேங் ச-திராதித்தவரை செல்வதாகச் சமித்தொம் இக்கொயற்தானத்-தொம் .

Nellore (64).

[Nellore. Tamil. Southern wall of Ranganáyakula-svámi temple.]

This is a fragment dated evidently in the reign of Kulóttuṅgachóḻadéva who was pleased to take Madurai and the crowned head of the Páṇḍya and it appears to grant the village of Peṭṭiḍakuṇḍai . . . . . at Nellúr *alias* Vikramaśiṅgapura (situated) in Paṭṭainéḍu.

[1] . . . . தாகமதுரை[யு] . . . . .

[2] ணிக்கவளநாட்டு பட்டைநாட்டு நெல்லூரான விக்கி-ரமசிங்க[புரத்து] . . .

[3] [ம]ஹாதெவியர் சிறுகட மை நாட்டுப்பெட்[டி]லகொண்டைத் . . . . .

[4] . . ஊரான பெட்[டி]டகுண்டையில் உடலானது இந்நாயஞர்க்கு

[5] . . . . . . வையவலவர்க்கும் வ[வாஸிகளுக்கும்] செல்வதாகச் சிவாபூதன் வான-

NELLORE (65).

[Nellore. Tamil. Southern wall of Ranganáyakulasvámi temple.]

TRANSLATION.

Hail! Prosperity! The following is the list of evening lamps given up to the month of Chittirai of the 35th year of the reign of the emperor of the three worlds, the glorious Kulóttuṅgachóḻadéva who was pleased to take Madurai and the crowned head of Páṇḍya, it being promised that the lamps will be kept lighted by means of the interest accruing on one *máḍai* for each lamp for the god of Chittiraméḻivinṇagar namely Paḻḻikoṇḍaperumáḻ.

[Then follows a list of the donors of lamps.]

[1] ஸ்வஸ்தி ஸ்ரீ மதுரை[யு]ம் பாண்டி[யன்மு]டி[த்தலை]யுங்-கொண்டருளின திருபுவனச்சக்கரவர்த்திகள் ஸ்ரீ குலொத்துங்-கசொழதெவர்க்கு யாண்டு ௩௰௫

[2] ஆவது சித்திரமெ[ழிவி]ண்ண[கர]ான பள்[ளி]கொ-ண்டபெருமாள் கொயிலுக்கு இவ்வாண்டை சித்திரை மாஸ-வரை செ[லு]த்த சந்திவிளக்கு பொலி-

[3] யூட்டாக மாடை ஒன்று[க்கொ]ரு விளக்கு-[எற்றுவ]-தாக மாடை இட்ட சந்திவிளக்குக்கு முதல் சிவபூதன் வானவ-நாயகன் விளக்கு நா[ற்]பதும் இளங்கிழவன் திருக்க[ா]

[4] ளத்தியுடையான் விளக்கு மூன்றும் நளம்பியங் வ . ை . . . மதெவன் விளக்கொன்றும் மெற்படிகூத்தர் விளக்கொன்றும் சிவ[ா]தன் சொக்கர் மானவர் [பிடிய]பி]ள்-ளை]விள-

[5] . . . .

Nellore (66).

[Nellore. Tamil. South wall of Ranganáyakulasvámi temple.]

Translation.

Hail! Prosperity! In the 28th year of the reign of the emperor of the three worlds, the glorious Rája-rájadéva, in the month of Áni, one *máḍai* was presented for an evening lamp (to be burnt) before Tirukkéḷi Uḍaiya Viyaláḻvár by Vaitumban Pitusuramuḍaiyán.

[1] ஸ்வஸ்தி ஸ்ரீ திரிபுவனச்சக்கரவத்திகள் ஸ்ரீ[ரா]-
[2] ஜராஜதெவர்க்கு யாண்டு இருபத்தெ-
[3] ட்டாவது ஆனிமாசத்தில் வைதும்பன் [பி]து-
[4] சுரமுடையான் திருக்கெளி உடைய [ய] விய[லா]-
[5] ழ்வார்மின் இட்ட மாடை ஒ[ன்று]க்கு சந்திவி-
[6] ளக்கு ஒன்று.

Nellore (67).

[Nellore. Tamil. South wall of Ranganáyakalasvámi temple.]

Translation.

Hail! Prosperity! Under orders verbally received (the following is engraved). In the 31st year of the reign of the emperor of the three worlds who was pleased to take Madurai and the crowned head of the Páṇḍya king, the glorious Kulóttuṅgachóḷadéva, in the month of Mésha, (the undermentioned) was left (free of tax) by Periyasiddappanáyakka a follower of Madurán-takapottapichóḷa *alias* Nallasiddharaśa, to the god Chittaraméḻivinnagar *alias* Paḷḷikoṇḍaperumáḷ at Tirup-páṟkaḍal in Nellúr *alias* Vikramaśiṅgapura (situated) in

Pédainádu in Chédikulamáṇikkavaḷanádu (a sub division) of Jayankoṇḍachóḷamaṇḍala.

He gave with libation of water the village of Viṟkáḍu free of tax to Paḷḷikoṇḍaperumáḷ, the village being included within the four following boundaries viz., on the east the boundary of Kóḷúr, on the south the boundary of Méṟappayúr, on the west the boundary of Yámalúr and on the north the boundary of Kuṟaṭṭúr, after setting up in (that village) Viṟkáḍu (situated) in the same náḍu (Péḍainádu) (the image of) Viddharasa-siddharasa.

Those who violate this (charity) will incur the sin of those killing a cow on the banks of the Ganges, and the sin of those who kill their parents.

[1] ஸ்வஸ்திஸ்ரீ திருவாய்கெழ்விமுன்னுடைத்தாக மதுரை யும்பாண்டியன் முடித்தலையுங்கொண்டருளிந திரிபுவநச்சக்ர-[வ]த்திகள் ஸ்ரீகுலொத்துங்கசொழதெவற்கு யாண்டு ௩௰கா-வது ௦-

[2] [மஷ]நாயற்று ஜயங்கொண்[டெ]சாழமண்டலத்துச்-செதிகுலமாணிக்கவளநாட்டுப்பெடைநாட்டு நெல்லூரான வி-க்ரமஸிங்கபுரத்துத்திருப்பாற் [கடற்சித்]தரமெழி விண்ணகரா-ன பள்-

[3] [ளி]கொண்டபெருமாளுக்கு மதுராந்தகப்பொத்தப் பிச்சொழநான நல்லஸிஂரவர் கன்மிகளில் பெரிய ஸித்தப்ப-நாயக்கன் திருவிடையாட்டமாக விட்ட பரிசாவது [யிந்நா]-

[4] ட்டுவிற்காடு ஸிஂாவஸிஂாவூ)ரையிடுவித்து நிர்வார்-பித்து குடுத்[த]னிதற்கு கிழ்பாற்கெல்லை கொ[ளூரெ]ல்லைக்கு மெற்கும் தென்பாற்கெல்லை மெறப்பயூரெ[ல்லை]க்[கு வட]-

[5] க்கும் மெல்பாற்கெல்லை யாமலூரெல்லைக்கு கிழக்கும் வடபாற்கெல்லை குறட்டுரெல்லைக்கு மிந்நாற்பாலெல்லைக்குட்ப-ட்ட விற்காடு திருவிடையாட்டமாகப்பள்ளிகொ[ண்டபெரு-மாளு]-

[6] க்துக்குடுத்தான் இது வில[க்கு]வார் கெங்கைக்கரை குராற்பசு கொன்றார் பாவ[த்]தைப்படுவான் தன்-மாதாபிதாக்களைக்கொன்றார் பாவத்தெ பொவார்

NELLORE (68).

[Nellore. Tamil. Southern wall of Ranganáyakulasvámi temple]

TRANSLATION.

Dévándai, son of Ṣivapútan Senda Piḷḷai, presented one *mádai*, for one evening lamp.

Mérvaigunda Piḷḷai presented one evening lamp to Tirumavár (?). Méradiyáḷaṇḍai presented one evening lamp.

[1] சிவபூதன் செந்தபிள்ளை
[2] மகன் தெவாண்டை இட்ட
[3] மாடை ஒன்றுக்கு சந்தி-
[4] விளக்கு ஒன்று மெ[ற்]
[5] வைகுந்த[பிள்ளை] திரு-
[6] மவாற்கு வைத்த ச[ந்தி].
[7] விளக்கு ஒன்று மெற-
[8] டியாளண்டை வைத்[த]
[9] சந்திவிளக்கு ஒன்று

NELLORE (69).

[Nellore. Tamil. Eastern wall of Ranganáyakulasvámi temple.]

TRANSLATION.

Hail ! Prosperity ! In the tenth year of the reign of the emperor of the three worlds, who was pleased to take the crowned head of the Páṇḍya and Madurai, the glorious Kulóttuṅgachóḷadéva, we, the Mudalis belonging to the army and the citizens of the three streets of Nellúr *alias* Vikramaśiṅgapuram (situated) in Péḍainádu in Chedikulamáṇikkavaḷanáḍu (a sub-division) of Jayaṅkondachóḷamaṇḍala gave the money, 10 *chinnams*, accruing from certain dues (the details are not clear owing to the mutilated state of this portion) to Tiruppáṛkaḍal Paḷḷikoṇḍaperumáḷ of this city (Nellúr).

We the villagers . . . gave . . . so that it may be maintained in other *maṇḍalams* also.

He who obstructs this charity will incur the sin of killing a tawny cow on the banks of the Ganges.

[1] ஸ்வஸ்தி ஸ்ரீ திரிபுவனச்சக்கரவர்த்திகள் பாண்டியன் மு-
டித்தலையு[ம]துரையுங்கொண்டருளின ஸ்ரீகுலொத்துங்கசோ.
[2] ழதெவர்க்கு யாண்டு ய வது செயங்கொண்டசொழ-
மண்டலத்துச்செ[சதிகுல]மாணி[க்க]வளநாட்டுப்பெடை-
[3] நாட்டு நெல்லூரான விக்[கி]ரமசிங்கபுரத்துப்படை-
முதலிகளும் மூன்றுதெருவில் நகரத்தொமும் இவு-
[4] [ர்]த்திருப்பாற்கடல் பள்ளிகொண்டபெருமாளுக்கு
நாங்கள் ஆயம் வைத்து குடுத்த . . . . . ப்பளிகி-
[5] று[ம்]பன் உட்பட்டாருக்கு . [செ]னல்லாத்திலும்
பிள்ளையார்குத்திரந்த தங்கத்தில் . . . . ங்கொ-
[6] ள்ளக்கடவர்களாகவும் மணலங்களிற்கொண்டப[த்து]-
ச்சின்னமுங்குடுத்த [வன்தார் சின்ன]மும் இ[ட]க்-
[7] கடவர்களாகவும் இப்படி பரமண்டலங்களிலும் செல்-
வதாகவும் வைத்துக்கு[டுத்தெ]தாம் சடைம . . . . ணத்தன்
[8] . . . உளொம் இதுவிலக்குவான் கெங்கைக்கரை
குராற் பசுக்குத்தினை [பாவத்தெ படுவான்]

NELLORE (70).

[NELLORE. Tamil. Eastern wall of Ranganáyakula-svámi temple.]

TRANSLATION.

Hail! Prosperity! In the 31st year of the reign of the emperor of three worlds, who was pleased to take the glorious Madurai and the crowned head of the Páṇḍya, the glorious Kulóttuṅgachóḻadéva, I, Vémayáḻván the son of Véṭṭandandainambiyáṇḍi of the city of Púndamali (situated) in Puliyúrkóṭṭa *alias* Kulóttuṅgachóḻavaḷanáḍu, a sub-division of Jayaṅkoṇḍachóḻamaṇḍala, gave to Śrivaráha Emberumáṉ whose image was set up by my father Nambiyáṇḍi in the inner sacred enclosure of the temple of Chittiraméḻiviṉṉagar (*alias*) Paḷḷikoṇḍaperumáḷ at Tiruppaṟkaḍal in Nellúr (*alias*) Vikramaśiṅgapuram (situated) in Péḍainádu in Chédikulamáṇikkavaḷanáḍu, (a sub-division of) this maṇḍala (Jayaṅkoṇḍachóḻa-maṇḍala), free of tax, two shares in this Tiruppaṟkaḍal city made up of the shares bought from my father Uṟaṅgávillidásár (otherwise called Nambiyáṇḍi) and Mádhavabhaṭṭaṉ of this city.

I, Vémiyáḻváṉ (the son of) Veṭṭandai, gave (these two shares) to last as long as the moon and sun.

[1] ஸ்வஸ்தி ஸ்ரீ திரிபுவநச்சக்கரவத்திகள் ஸ்ரீ மது[ரையும்] பாண்[டிய]ன் முடித்தலையுங்கொ-

[2]ண்டருளின ஸ்ரீகுலொத்துங்கசொழதேவர்க்கு யாண்டு ௩௰௧ வது ஜயங்கொண்ட-

[3] சொ[ழ]மண்டலத்து புலியூர்க்கொட்டமான குலொத்-துங்கசொழவளநாட்டு நகரம்

[4] பூந்தமலி வெட்டந்தைநம்பி[யா]ண்டி மகன் வெமயாழ்-வானென் இம்மண்டலத்·

[5] து செதிகுலமாணிக்கவளநாட்டுப்பெடைநாட்டு நெல்
லூரான விக்கிரமசிங்கபு[ர]-

[6] த்து திருப்பாற்கடல் சித்திரமெழிவிண்ணகரான பள்-
ளிகொண்டபெருமாள் கொயி-

[7] ல் உட்திருச்சுற்றில் [எ]ன்தவப்[ப]நம்பியாண்டி
உகந்தருளுவித்த சிவராகளம்பெருமானு-

[8] க்கு திருவிடையாட்டமாக இத்திருப்பாற்கடல் அகரத்-
து முன்று[ளி]ல் என்தவப்பன்

[9] உறங்காவில்லிதாஸர் பாடுகொண்டு விட்ட பாகம்
ஒன்றும் இவ்வாண்டுரான இவ்வக-

[10] ரத்து மாதவபட்டன் பாடுகொண்டு விட்ட பாகம் ஒன்-
றும் இவ்விரண்டுபாகமு-

[11] ம் சந்திராதித்தவரை செல்வதாக கொண்டு விட்டேன்
வெட்டந்தை வெமயா-

[12] ழ்வானென்

NELLORE (71). (A.D. 1296–97.)

[Nellore. Tamil. From shrine of Ranganáyakulasvámi temple.]

TRANSLATION.

Hail! Prosperity! In the expired Śaka year 1218 which corresponds with the 6th year of the reign of the emperor of the three worlds, the glorious Vijayagaṇḍa-gópáladéva, on the date which fell on Wednesday with the Nakshatra Uttiráḍa and Saṇkrama, the first day of the bright half of the month of Makara, we, Madurántaka-pottapichóḷan *alias* Raṅganáthan *alias* Rájagaṇḍagópála-dévan gave for the daily offerings including rice, ornaments, etc., and for sacred building purposes, to the god

Chittiraméḻivinnagar *alias* Paḻḻikoṇḍaperumáḷ at Tiruppáṟ-kaḍal in Nellúr *alias* Vikramasiṅgapura (situated) in Piḍainádu in Chédikulamáṇikkavaḷanáḍu (a sub-division) of Jayaṅkoṇḍachóḻamaṇḍala, with libations of water, free of tax, the dry and wet lands situated within the four boundaries of (the village of) Alaṅgáḍu in Muṇḍainádu.

Those who obstruct this charity will incur the sin of killing a tawny cow on the banks of the Ganges.

[1] ஸ்வஸ்தி ஸ்ரீ சகரையாண்டு ரு[உா]மஅ—செல்லாநி-
ன்றதிரிபுவனச்சக்கரவத்திகள் ஸ்ரீவிஜ[யகண்டகொ]பால--

[2] தெவற்கு யாண்டு சூவது மகரநாயற்று வ—ஒவு—ல்பக்ஷ-
த்து வுரகமையும் புதன்கிழமையு[ம்] பெற்ற

[3] உத்திராடமும் சங்கிரமுமான நாள் ஜயங்கொண்ட-
சொழமண்டலத்துச்செதிகுலமாணிக்க-

[4] வளநாட்டுப்பிடைநாட்டு நெல்லூரான வி[க்*]கி[ர*]
மசிங்கபுரத்துத்திருப்பாற்கடர்சித்திரமெழிவிண்ண-

[5] கரான பள்ளிகொண்டபெருமாளுக்கு அமுதுபடி சா-
த்துப்படி உள்ளிட்ட நித்தநிமந்தங்களுக்கும் திருப்பணிக்கும்

[6] உடலாக மதுராந்தகபொத்த[ப்பி]சொழன் ஸ்ரீரங்க-
நாதரான இராஜ[கண்] டகொபா[ல]தெவன் முண்டைநாட்டு
அலங்காடு

[7] நாற்பாற்கெல்லைக்கு உட்பட்ட நன்[சை]புன்[சை]யும்
உள்ளடங்கலுந் திருவிடையாட்டமாக[ச்ச]ந்திராதித்தவரை-
செல்ல உதக-

[8] வ—ஒவு—மாக குடுத்தோம் இதழிம்[வி]லக்கினர் கங்கை-
க்கரையிற்குராற்பசு[க்கொ]கான்றான் பாவத்திலே படக்கடவன்

NELLORE (72).

[Nellore. Tamil. From Ranganáyakulasvámi temple.]

TRANSLATION.

Hail! Prosperity! Under orders verbally received (the following is engraved).

In the 26th year of the reign of the emperor of the three worlds, who was pleased to take Madurai and the crowned head of the Páṇḍya, the glorious Kulóttuṅgachóḻadéva, we, Madurántakapottapichóḻa *alias* Tammusiddharaśa gave to Paḷḷikoṇḍaperumáḷ at Tiruppáṟkaḍal *alias* Chittiraméḻiviṇṇagar at Nellúr *alias* Vikramasiṅgapura (situated) in Péḍainádu in Chédikulamáṇikkavaḷanáḍu (a sub-division) of Jayaṅkoṇḍachóḻamaṇḍala, as long as the moon and sun last, (the village of) Támaraimaḍuvu (the lotus tank) *alias* Chitraméḻinallúr in Muṇḍainádu free of tax.

[Then follows the imprecatory portion which is incomplete.]

[1] ஸ்வஸ்தி ஸ்ரீ திருவாய்க்கெழ்விமுன்னுடைத்தாகத்திரிபு-
வனச்சக்கரவர்த்திகள் மதுரையும் பாண்டிய-

[2] ன்முடித்தலையுங்கொண்டருளின ஸ்ரீகுலோத்துங்க
சொழதெவர்க்கு யாண்டு உய[கூ]வது செயங்கொண்ட-

[3] சொழமண்டலத்துச்செதிகுலமாணிக்கவளநாட்டுப்-
பெடைநாட்டு நெல்லூரான விக்கிரமசிங்கபுரத்துத்-

[4] [தி]ருப்பாற்கடற்சித்திரமெழிவிண்ணகரிர்ப்பள்ளி-
கொண்டபெருமாளுக்கு திருவிடையாட்டமாக மதுராந்தகப்-
பொ-

[5] த்தப்பிச்சொழனான த[ம்மு]ஸிஜியரைசனென் மு-
[ண்டை]நாட்டுத்தாமரைமடுவான சித்திரமெழிநல்லூர் சந்-
திராதித்-

[6] தவ்ரை செல்வதாகக்கொடு [த்தோம்] இது விலக்கு-
வான் கங்கைக்கரைக்குராற்பசுவை அன்னியாய . வதைதா-

Nellore (73). (A.D. 1280–81 ?)

[Nellore. Tamil. From shrine of Ranganáyakulasvámi temple.]

Translation.

In the Ṣaka year 1202 Vaitumápperumáppiḷamá and Pámaṇḍai (gave) the interest on . . . for an evening lamp to Paḻḻikoṇḍaperumáḷ.

[1] சகரையாண்டு க[௲]உ௱உவது
[2] வைய்துமாபெருமாப்பி-
[3] ளமாயும் பாமண்டையும்
[4] பள்ளிகொண்டபெருமாளுக்கு
[5] பொலியிட்டு யிட்ட சன்திவிளக்கு

Nellore (74). (A.D. 1315–16).

[Nellore. Tamil. From shrine of Ranganáyakulasvámi temple.]

Translation.

Hail! Prosperity! In the Ṣaka year 1237 expired which corresponds to the 25th year of the reign of the emperor of the three worlds, the glorious Rájagaṇḍa-gópáladéva on the date which corresponded to Wednesday with the *nakshatra* Punarpúṣa, the tenth day of the bright half of the month of *Mína*, Madurántakapottapichóḻa *alias* . . . . Rájagaṇḍagópáladévan . . . . gave . . . . for the sacred lamp and ghee to the god at Chitramélivinnagar, Pallikondaperumál at Nellúr *alias* Vikramasingapuram (situated) in Pidainádu in Chédikulamánikkavalanádu (a sub-division) of Jayankondacholamandala.

[Imprecatory lines.]

NOTE.—The regnal year was first read as 25th but on check *in situ* as 15th. A further reference to the estampage confirms the reading 25th. The Ṣaka year too is doubtful and we may read either 1227 and 15th or 1237 and 25th. The Ṣaka year was first read as current but on check as expired.

[1] ஸ்வஸ்தி ஸ்ரீ சகரையாண்டு ௲உ௱[௨]௰௭ செல்லா[நி]ன்ற [திரிபுவனச்ச]க்கரவத்திகள் ஸ்ரீஇராஜகண்டகொபா . . . .

[2] யாண்டு உ௰௫வது மினநாயற்று வ-இஷ்-பக்ஷத்து [தெசமியும் புதந்]கிழமையும் பெற்ற புணர்பூசத்திந . . . . . . ,

[3] கொண்டசொழமண்டலத்துச்செதிகுலமாணிக்க[வள-நாட்டு]ப்பிடைநாட்டு நெல்லூ[ரான] . . . . .

[4] கபுரத்துத்திருப்பாற்கடற் சித்திரமெழி[விண்ணக]ரா-ன பள்ளிகொண் . . . . .

[5] திருவிளக்குக்கும் நெய்பமுதுக்கும் உட[லா]க மது[ரா ந்த]கப்பெ[பா]த்தப்பிச்சொழன் ஸ்ரீ . . . . .

[6] இராஜகண்டகொபாலதெவன் .நிலன.மவ . . . . . ணவிடொம் இது விலகினொர்

NELLORE (75).

[Nellore. Tamil. From Dwajasthambam of Ranganáyakulasvámi temple.]

This is a Grantha fragment which mentions Tammusiddhi and his ancestors Kalikála and Bédabhanátha. (Beta ?)

[1] ஶ்ரீஶாகே: ஶகேந்த்ரவஸுதக்ஷித்ர-
[2] வெயகாத்ய: ஶஶிகாஞ்செவ ! வெ-
[3] ஶமெபாவத்ய ஶக்லம்ஶுக்ஷிழ-
[4] ஶஹ டெநா பெட்ஹந யு ஷ்க ஜ்ஜ
[5] ஶ்ரீஶத்ரு-ரவிஸிஹஶ: ஸ்வஸ்தஶ்ரீ
[6] [ராஶ] ஶிஹ்ரஸத்ரிகெத்ரு ஶத்ரு-ரவிஸி

Nellore (76). (A.D. 1400–01 ?)

[Nellore. Tamil. Ranganáyakulasvámi temple; outer wall, facing river.]

Translation.

Hail! Prosperity! In the Ṣaka year 1322 which corresponded to the twenty-fifth year of the reign of Rájaparaméśvara Harihararáya, on the date corresponding to Sunday bearing the *Nakshatra* Púśa, during the bright half, the 15th of Vaigáśi, the big *maṇḍapa* in the temple of Śayyanáráyaṇaperumáḷ at Vikramasiṅgapuram *alias* Nellúr was the charity of Puḷavadalvar *alias* Chamayattár.

[The remaining portion of the inscription is mutilated, mentions the emperor Sundarapáṇḍya and appears to record the gift of five sacred lamps.]

[1] ஸ்வஸ்தி சகரை ஆண்டு ௲௩௱௨௰௨வது ராசபரமெசுர
[2] ஆன அரிஅரராயனுக்கு ஆண்டு ௨௰௫வது வைய்கா-
சிம-
[3] ாதம் ௰௫க்கு பூர்வபக்ஷத்தில் நாயற்றுக்கிழமையும் பூ-
[4] சமுபெற்ற நாள் விக்கிரமசிங்கபுரமான நெல்லூரில்
சய்-
[5] யநாராயணப்பெருமாள் கொயில் பெரியமண்ட-
[6] பம் புலவதல்வரான சமயத்தார் கட்டுவிச்ச தர்மம்

[7] புலவதல்வரில் சுந்தரபாண்டியச் சக்ரவதிகள் இந்தா
ண்டு . . . . .

[8] . . . . . ட்டத்திருவிளக்கு || ருப்ப .

NELLORE (77).

[Nellore. Telugu. From threshold of Ánjanéya temple in Santhapet.]

TRANSLATION.

(*a*) The perpetual devotion of Gádam Seṭṭi Séshayya.
(*b*) The perpetual devotion of Gadde Rangáyya.
(*c*) The perpetual devotion of Kommá Chenchu Vóbuḷu

(a) 1. గాదం శెట్టి శేషయ్య
2. నిత్య శేవా॥
(b) 1. గద్దె రంగాయ్య నిత్య శేవా
(c) 1. కొంమ్మా చెంచువోబు
2. ళు నిత్య శేవా.

NELLORE (78). (A.D. 1364–65.)

[Nellore. Telugu. From gate jambs of Irukalamma Temple.]

TRANSLATION..

Hail! On Friday the 5th of the dark fortnight of Márgaṣira of the year Kródhi corresponding to the year 1286 of the illustrious Ṣaka era, while Sríman Mahámandaléṣvara Víra Ṣrí Sávaṇṇa[1] Oḍayalu was ruling the earth, the people of all countries came to agreement in connection with the Friday market established by

---

[1] It may be Sáyaṇṇa.

Kánchaṇṇamgáru in Nellore. They arranged to devote (the fees raised in the market) to providing all sorts of enjoyment for Irukalá Paraméśvari for the religious merit of Kánchaṇṇamgáru the best of officials (adhikáru). They have settled that this charity of this village should be maintained as long as the sun and moon last. Whoever causes obstacles to these conditions will incur the sin of committing the five cardinal sins. This charity has been founded with the consent of the people of different countries. May it cause great prosperity!

1. స్వస్తి శ్రీ శక
2. వరుషంబు
3. లు ౧౨౭౬ అగు
4. నెంటి క్రోధిసం
5. వ్వత్సర మార్గశి
6. ర బ ౧౨ శు శ్రీమ
7. మహామండలేశ్వ
8. ర వీర శ్రీసావం
9. ణ ఓడయలు ప్రి
10. థివిరాజ్యము సే
11. యంగాను నెల్లూర
12. ను కాంచంణ్ణంగారు
13. చెయించిన శుక్రవా
14. రము సంత్తను నానా
15. దేశి పెకరండ్రాను ఒడం
16. బడిరి అధకారి సె
17. కరు కాంచణ్ణంగా
18. రికి ధర్మముంగాన
19. యిరుకలాపర
20. మేశ్వరి కేలుబగ

21. పినసట్టి కట్టడనుం
22. గట్టవెట్టి నడచెడులా
23. గు అంగరంగ బో గాలకు
24. కాను ఆ చెంద్రా
25. ర్కముగా యా గ్రామ
26. మాన ధర్మువు

Second side.

27. చెల్లం శెతిడిరి
28. యామేరకు ఎ
29. వ్వరు విఘ్నము
30. చేసినాను వంశ
31. మహాపాతకా
32. లు చేసిన పాపా
33. నం బోవువాండు
34. నానా దేశాల పెకరం
35. డ్ర పంపునాంను
36. (ముల) ధర్మువు
37. చెసినట్టి। మంగ
38. ళ మహా శ్రీ శ్రీ
39. శ్రీం జేయును.

NELLORE (79).

[Nellore. In Dévanágari character. From pillar of shrine of Irukalamma temple.]

TRANSLATION.

The stone of Irukalá Paraméṣvari.

इरुकलापरमेश्वरिचीला

NELLORE (80). (A.D. 1314–15 ?)

[Nellore. Telugu. From shrine of Irukalamma temple.]

TRANSLATION.

Hail ! On Monday the 15th of the dark fortnight of Bhádrapada of the year Ánanda corresponding to the Sṛí Śaka year 1239, while Ṣríman Mahámaṇḍaléṣvara Kákatiya Pratáparudradéva Mahárájulu was ruling the earth in pleasant communication (with his feudatories), Nágayánulóka Bóyuḍu and Brammana Bóyuḍu, the sons of Hari Déva, the servant of Nágaṇagaṇa, caused to be constructed behind . . . Ṣrí Ranganátha for the merit of the agent and viceroy of that Pratáparudradéva Mahárajalu, (namely) Ṣrí Muppaḍi Náyani Gáru and of Pedda Rudra Dévani Gáru for the prosperity of the kingdom, for the falling of rain thrice a month at Nellúr and for the increase of wealth. . . Pina Bóyunḍu and Siddaya Bóyuḍu . . . Irukalá Paraméṣvari in Nellúr . . . . we have granted. He who does harm to this charity will incur the sin of killing a tawny cow on the Ganges and the Bhágírathi. This charity should last as long as the sun and moon exist. Thus have we granted . . . . . . May it cause great prosperity.

NOTE.—Ananda is S.S. 1237 current but perhaps we should read Anala (A.D. 1316–17).

1. స్వస్తి శ్రీ శకవర్షంబు ౧౨౩౯ అగు నేంటి ఆనంద సం
వత్సర భాద్రపద శుద్ధ ౧౫
సో॥ శ్రీ మన్మహా మండలేశ్వర కాకతియ్య ప్రతాప రుద్రదేవ
మహారాజులు సుఖసంకథావి

2. నోదంబున పృథివీరాజ్యము చేయుచుండగాను ఆ ప్రతా
ప రుద్రదేవ మహారాజుల

వారి కార్యకర్త శ్రీతిరుధిగారు స్వస్తి శ్రీ ముప్పడి నాయనిం
గారికిం పెద రుద్రదేవరంగారికి రాజ్యాభి

3. వృద్ధిగాను నెల్లూరి భూమికి నెలమూండువర్షములు కు
వర్ష ధనకనక సమృద్ధిగానున్న నాగణ
గణభృత్యుండు వారిదేవని కొడుక్లు నాగయానులోకబోయుం
డూను బ్రంమనబోయుండూను శ్రీ రంగనాధుండుని
వెనుక

4. (గట్టించిరి) పినబోయండూను సిద్దయబోయుడూను . . .
యబోయుండూను . . . . రహరహభ . .
లూను .
క . . తం ఇ . : . . నెల్లూరిలోంన ఇరుకలా పరమే
శ్వరికి నెలమి అఱుస . . డ జఱ వముగాను చెనదా

5. . . ను . . నెలమండడకులక . . లమేర . డి నపు
వాండు ఇ కాంపును . . . . .

6. రి కిస్తిమి ఇ ధరమ్మమునకు నెవ్వండు విఘలము తలంచి
నాను భాగీరధి గంగకఱుత కపిలలను వధి

7. ఇంచినదోషం వారు ఇదరమ్మము చంద్రసూర్యులు క
లంతకాలము నుండునటుల ఇచ్చినవారు . . .

8. శ్రీ య్యఖిల . . . .
మంగళమహా శ్రీశ్రీశ్రీంజేయును

NELLORE (81).

[Nellore. Tamil. Irukalamma temple.]

This is the pillar presented by Ammaṇadévanátha to the god Salísvara.

[1] [உட]யார்ச[வி]சுரமு(டெ)-
[2] டைார்கு அம்ம-
[3] ணதெவநாதென்
[4] இட்ட தூண்

Nellore (82).

[Nellore. Tamil. From a house in Kápu street.]

This is a fragment and appears to record the grant of lands in Eṟṟampaḷḷi in Púṅgainádu as temple land to the god Nágaríśvara in Nellúr *alias* Vikramaśiṅgapuram in Chedikulavaḷanáḍu by Madurántakapottapichóḷa *alias* Manumasiddarasa.

[1] ணிச்கவளநாட்டு பள . . . . .
[2] ல் நெல்லூரான விகரம . . . . .
[3] புரத்து ஸ்ரீ[ந]மரிஸ்வரமு . . . . .
[4] யிநாயனுற்கு பூங்கை . . . . .
[5] ட்டில் எற்ற[ம்]பள்ளியா . . . . .
[6] ர்நாற்பாலெல்லைக் . . . . .
[7] . . . . தெ[வ]தா[ன] . . . . .
[8] . . . ந்தகப்பொத்த[ப்] . . . . .
[9] . . முநான மனும[சித்] . . . . .
[10] [ற்]கும் [செ]சல்ல கொ . . . . .

Nellore (83).

[Nellore. Tamil. In a house in the Chinna bazaar.]

Translation.

Hail! Prosperity! (In the reign of) the emperor of the three worlds, the glorious Kulóttuṅga (chóḷadéva), who was pleased to take Madura and the crowned head (of the Páṇḍya king), Irá . . . . pallá . . . of Murónóttamaṅgala in (Va)luvanáḍu presented a sacred lamp to Manuma(késavaperumál ?) of Nellúr *alias* Vikkiramasiṅgapuram (situated) in . . . . (a sub-division) of Jayankoṇḍachóḻamaṇḍala.

[1] ஸ்வஸ்தி ஸ்ரீ திரிபுவநச்சக்கரவத்திகள் மது . . . . .
[2] தலை கொண்டருளிக ஸ்ரீகுலொத்துங்க . . . . .
[3] ஜயங்கொண்ட சொழமண்டலத்து . . . . . .
[4] வநெல்லூர் விக்கிரமசிங்கபுரத்து மநும . . . .
[5] ளுவநாட்டில் முரொநொத்தமங்கலத்து இரா . . .
[6] பல்லாச் . கயெந் வைத்த திருநந்தாவி . . . .

NELLORE (84).

[Nellore. Tamil. From coping of well by Dharmarájá temple. Illegible.]

NELLORE (85).

[Nellore. Tamil. Over a drain in Big Mosque street.]

This inscription which is dated in the [ninth ?] year of [Kulóttuṇgachóḻadéva] who was pleased to take Madurai, Ceylon and the crowned head of the Páṇḍya, appears to record some gift to the god Manumaśidíśvara at Nellúr *alias* Vikramaśiṇgapura by Madurántakapottapichóḻa *alias* Nallasiddharaśa.

[1] ஸ்வஸ்திஸ்ரீ மதுரையும் ஈழமும் பாண்டியன்மு . .
[2] பதாவது மகரநாயற்று பூர்வபக்ஷத்து ஸ . . .
[3] டலத்து நெல்லூரான விக்கிரமசிங்கபுரத் . . .
[4] த்தப்பிச்சொழந் நல்லசித்தியரசன் தேவ . . .

[5] டையார் மநுமசித்திஸ்வரமுடையருய . . . .

[6] . . . வெகுடியிருந்து ஞபஞர் கொயிலுக்கு

. . . .

NELLORE (86).

[Nellore. Tamil. Built into the Collector's cutcherry.]

This is the end of an inscription being the imprecatory portion thereof.

[1] . . . . . . ம் வெட்டிக்கொள்வது

[2] . . . . . ஜ பண்ணுவார் ஊரங்கை-

[3] ய்தார் செய்த பாவத்

NELLORE (87).

[Nellore. Tamil. Built into the Collector's cutcherry.]

TRANSLATION.

Hail! Prosperity! In the 36th year of the reign of the emperor of the three worlds the glorious Kulóttunga-déva, amongst . . . . the Śivabrahmanas of the temple—Śrímádévabhaṭṭa, (of the) Bháradvája (gótra), Madanugrahacharaṇabhaṭṭa, Aṭkoṇḍapiḷḷai and Sittáṇḍár agreed to light one evening lamp without failure, beginning from the month of Tai of the 36th year, as long as the moon and sun last, in a niche in the temple of the lord Áḷuḍaiyár Manumamasiddhíśvara at Nellúr *alias* Vikkiramasiṅgapuram in the Jayaṅkoṇḍachóḷamaṇḍalam.

(To face page 854.)

NELLORE NO. 87.

[1] ஸ்வ[ஸ்தி] ஸ்ரீ திரிபுவனச்சக்கரவர்த்திகள் ஸ்ரீ குலொத்-துங்கதெவர்க்கு யாண்டு ௩௰[௬வது]

[2] ஜயங்கொண்டசொழமண்டலத்து நெல்லூரான விக்-கிரமசிங்கபுரத்து அளுதை-

[3] டயார் மனுமசித்தீசு [ர*]முடையனாயனார்க்கு ௩௰௬வது தைய்மாஸமுதல் மாடைக்கு

[4] னித்தமொரு சந்திவிளக்கு முட்டாமைச்சந்திராதித்த-வரை யெரிப்பார்களாக இசை[சந்]-

[5] து இக்கொயிலில் சிவப்பிராமணரில் பாரத்துவாசனா-ன ஸ்ரீமாதெவபட்டனுமாத-

[6] னு[க்கிரகச்சர]ணபட்டனும் ஆட்கொண்டபிள்ளையும் சித்தாண்டாரும் இன்னாயி-

---

NELLORE (88).

[Nellore. Tamil. Built into the Collector's cutcherry.]

This is a fragment mentioning the name of a god Manumasittíśvara.

[1] . . . . . . ார் கொயிலில் தான[த்*]தார் கண்டு-விடைமனும-

[2] . . . . . . யான மனுமசித்திசுரமுடைய நாயனா-ர்கெ கட்

NELLORE (89).

[Nellore. Tamil. Built into the Collector's cutcherry.]

This inscription is a fragment dated in the 25th year of the reign of the glorious Víraréjéndracholadéva.

[1] . . . . . . ள் ஸ்ரீவிராஜெந்திரசொழதெவற்க்ரு-
குயாண்டு உ௰[ரு] ஆவது மதுராந்தகப்பொ-

[2] . . . . . . ள தெவதானபற்றிலும் சாலியகு[ட]-
மனைகுமாற்றுமிடத்து நமக்கு இறுகற்ப-

[3] . . . . . . சொன்னொம் இப்படிக்கு க[ல்*]விலு
ம்செம்பிலும் வெட்டிகொள்வாத

Nellore (90).

[Nellore. Tamil. Built into the Collector's cutcherry.]

This is a fragment which mentions Nellúr.

[1] . . . . . தெவர்க்கு யாண்டு முப்-
[2] . . . . . காண்டசொழமண்-
[3] . . . . . மதுராந்தக்ப்பொ-
[4] . . . . . ரெலை நெல்லூர் ஆளு-
[5] . . . . . ரயஞர் திருமடைவிளா-
[6] . . . . . குடி அறுபதும் . .

Nellore (91).

[Nellore. Tamil. Built into the Collector's cutcherry.]

This inscription, the beginning of which is lost, records the grant of one *máḍai* for an evening lamp to Manumasiddhiśvara by one Vaḷuváṇḍán, the son of Kumárandaiperumâḷ. The money was received from the month of Tai of the 36th year of some king's reign by Áṭkoṇḍapillai, Siddáṇḍár and Bharadvája Mahádéva. It ends with stating that they made the gift so that the lamp might be burned as long as the moon and sun last.

[1] . . . . . . ருபுதிரவாணிகன குமாரக்கைபெரு மாள் மகன் வறுவாண்டாங் க-

[2] . . . . . [மனு]மசித்திசுரமுடை[ய]நாயகா[ர்]-க்கு வைத்த சந்திவிளக்கு ஒன்று விட்-

[3] . . . . . . கொன்றுக்கு ஆட்கொண்டபிள்ளையு-ம் சித்தாண்டாரும் பரத்துவாசிமாதெவ-

[4] . . . . . . ப்பரும்மாதிராசனுக்காக சரணபட்-டனுமன் முப்பத்தாறுவது தைய்ம-

[5] . . . . . . மமுதல் கைய்க்கொண்ட மாடை க இ-ம்மாடை ஒன்றுக்கும் பலிசை-

[6] . . . . . . ல் உள்ளது கொண்டு சந்திராதித்தவ-ரை எரிக்கடவளாக இவ்விளக்கு வைத்தான்

NELLORE (92).

[Nellore. Tamil. Built into the Collector's cutcherry.]

This inscription is dated during the reign of Kulóttuṅgachóḻadéva. The object of the grant is not ascertainable.

[1] ஸ்வஸ்தி ஸ்ரீ குலொத்துங்கசொழ . . . . .
[2] ம் பெற்ற சொதினுள் ஜயங்ெ . . . . .
[3] திஸ்லரமுடையநாயகார்க்கு . . . . .
[4] தகப் பொத்தப்பிசொழன் . . . . .
[5] டு மனுமசித்திஸ்லரமுடையந . . . . .
[6] ம் இருப்பார்களாக வாணிய . . . . .

NELLORE (93).

[Nellore. Tamil. Built into the Collector's cutcherry.]

This inscription is dated in the thirtieth year of the reign of the emperor of three worlds, who was pleased to take Madurai and the crowned head of Páṇḍya, the glorious Kulóttuṅgachóḻadéva, at the time of the equinox during the month of Aippasi.

[1] [ஸ்வ]ஸ்தி ஸ்ரீ திரிபுவனச்சக்கரவத்திகள் மதுரை . . . . .

[2] யுங்கொண்டருளிய ஸ்ரீ குலொத்துங் . . . . . .

[3] ப்பதாவது ஐப்பசி விஷுவ்நா . . . . .

NELLORE (94).

[Nellore. Tamil. Built into the Collector's cutcherry.]

TRANSLATION.

Kaḍambáṇḍi . . . . son of . . . . rutu (ru) ḻán Pariyáṇḍi placed (presented) one evening lamp to . . . the god Nágéśvara . . . (Jayan?)koṇḍa Piḷḷai and Sittáṇḍár . . . . received one *máḍai* (for keeping it). In order that with this *máḍai* they may burn (the lamp) as long as the moon and the sun endure (I have presented) this lamp.

[1] . . . . . ருது[ரு]ழான் பறியாண்டி மகன் கடம்-பாண்டி வ-

[2] . . . . . ஞகிசுரமுடை[ய*]நாயந[ா*]ர்க்குவைத்த சந்திவிளக்கு ஒன்று

[3] . . . . . ங்கொண்டபிள்ளையும் சித்தாண்டாரு-ம் பாத்துவாசமாதெ-

[1] . . . . . ங்க . . சாண்பட்டனும[ன்பு யட்டு]-
தாருவது ஹை த . .

[5] . . . . . கொண்ட மாடை க இம்மாடை ஒன்றுக்-
கும் பலனை-

[6] . . . . . ண்டு சந்திராதித்தவரை எரிக்[க*]கட-
வ[ர்க*]ளாக இவ்விளக்குவை-

NELLORE (95).

[Nellore. Tamil. From stone lying by the gate of the Collector's cutcherry.]

This is a fragment and no meaning can be made out of it.

[1] . . . . . ளன் . . . . .
[2] . த த[ரவ]னும் செசவபெருமாளுக்கு சந்தி-
[3] . . . ணியார் . காம்மாசாணியார் வி
[4] . . . தி . . சாத அப்பசாணியார்விட்ட ச-
[5] . . மகன் ப[ரச]க்கனப்பெற்தமமாா

NELLORE (96). (A.D. 1706–07?)

[Nellore. Telugu. Nílakanṭhéṣvara temple.]

TRANSLATION.

Hail! On the 14th of the dark fortnight of Mágha of the year Vyaya corresponding to the year 1628 of the illustrious, victorious and prosperous Śáliváhana Śaka era this vritti (was given) after salutation to the Omnipotent Nílakanṭha Svámi associated with Párvatí residing at Ṣrí Víravikramasimhapura who is the lord of all the crores of universes. The following are the details of the charitable stone-edicts planted in the villages:

Vírasimhapuram, Nellúru, Allúru, Várijákadi Véru, Saidápuram, Kámpúr, Chennúru, Gúḍúru, Kaluváy, Duttalúru, Mahimalúru, Bráhmalakáka Jaladanki, Kávali, Allúrpelleru, Pulugulapáḍu, Pallelapáḍu, etc. In the temple of Nílakanṭhanáthasvámi . . . . . Nellúru . . . they shall maintain . . . .

1. స్వస్తి శ్రీ జయాభ్యుదయ శాలివాహన శకవరుషంబులు
2. ౧౬౭౫ అగు నేంటి వ్యయసంవత్సర మాఘ బ ౧౪ లు

. . . .

3. ద్ధ కాలి బ్రంహ్మాండనాయకుండైన శ్రీ వీరవిక్రమ సింహ పురిని వు . . .
4. దె శ్రీ పార్వతీసమేతుండుగ నీలకంఠేశ్వర స్వామివారి శా వాచె
5. సి ద్రిష్టియకు అందుల వీరసింహపురం నెల్లూరు అల్లూ రువా రిజా
6. కడివేరు సైదాపురం కాంపూరు చెంన్నూరు గూండూరు కలువాయి

Second side.

7. దుత్తలూరు మహిమలూరు బ్రాంహ్మలకాక జలదంకి కావ లి అల్లూరు పెల్లెరు
8. న్ను పులుగులపాడు పల్లెలపాడు మొదంయిన శీమలోనిం గ్రామాలం వే
9. ఇంచ్చిన ధర్మ, శిలాశాసన క్రమ మెట్లన్నను నెల్లూరు . . . .
10. నీలకంఠ నాథస్వామి దేవాలయ . . . . . లానుం
11. . . . . . . నడపంగలవాడు

NELLORE (97). (A.D. 1267–68?)

[Párlapalli. Tamil. From stone in front of Alaganáthasvámi temple.]

This inscription which is mutilated records the gift of a perpetual sacred lamp to Aḷagaperumáḷ by somebody (name not clear) in the month of Áḍi of the *Ṣaka* year 1189 corresponding to the cyclic year Bhava which should probably be Prabhava.

* * * *

* * * *

[1] ஶகவஷ-௰ ௲[௱]௮-
[2] ௰௯ [சென்ற] ஸவ-
[3] ஸம்வத்ஸரத்து
[4] ஆடிமாஸம் வெ-
[5] ங்[கநா . ததமத்]-
[6] தடியென் நாயனு-
[7] ர் அழகப்பெரு[ம]-
[8] ாளுக்கு திருநந்தா-
[9] விளக்குக்கு இன்று

* * * *

* * * *

NELLORE (98).

[Párlapalli. Tamil. From stone bearing another inscription in front of Alaganáthasvámi temple.]

TRANSLATION.

Hail! Prosperity! In the . . . year of the reign of Vijayagaṇḍagópáḷadéva corresponding to the cyclic year. . . . on the date corresponding to Monday, *nakshatra* rósani, the thirteenth day of the bright half of the month of Dhanu, the father Véṅgaḍamuḍaiyán (*alias*) Éṛan and his sons gave with libation of water before the god 85 ewes for a sacred lamp to (the god) Aḻagaperumáḷ at Vikramachóḻachaturvédimaṅgala.

Let there be prosperity !

[1] ஸ்வஸ்தி [ஸ்ரீ விசைய-
[2] கண்டகொ . பா[ல]
[3] தெவற்கு யாண்டு .
[4] வது . . . ஸம்வஸ்-
[5] ஸரத்து [தநு]நாயற்று பூ-
[6] ர்வபக்ஷத்து த்ரயெ[ா*]தசியு-
[7] ந்திங்கட்கிழமையும்பெ-
[8] பற்[ற] ரொஹணி . . . . .
[9] நாள் விக்கிரமசொழ-
[10] ச்சதுர்வெதிமங்கலத்து
[11] [அ]ழகப்பெருமாளுக்குத்-
[i2] திருநந்தாவிளக்குக்கு வெங்க-
[13] முடுடையான் எறன் தந்தை-
[14] யனும் பிள்ளைகளும் திரு-
[15] முன்னெ தாரவார்த்துக்குடு-
[16] த்த ஆடு சயடு [ஸ்ரீமஹேஸ்வர].

NELLORE (99). (A.D. 1638–39.)

[Párlapalli. Telugu. To east of village.]

TRANSLATION.

Hail ! On the 2nd of the bright half of Chaitra of the year Bahudhánya, corresponding to the year 1560 of the illustrious, victorious, and prosperous Śálivâhana Śaka era, Ṣrímat Velugóṭi Venkaṭapati Náyaningáru . . . . . . situated in Nellore *ṣíma* . . Nellore . . .

Whether the *méra* grain is with the village *Sandháta* . . . . . . whoever be the ruler . . . . . . they should get work done to the tank . . . . If, without doing the work to the tank, (any one appropriates) the *méra* grain or removes (this inscription), (the *veṭṭi*) of the village (will ravish) his wife.

1. స్వస్తి శ్రీ జయాభ్యుదయ శాలివాహన శకవ
2. ర్షంబులు ౧౪౬౦ అగు నేంటి బహుధాన్యసం
3. వత్సర చైత్ర శు ౨ లు శ్రీమతు వెలుగోటి వెంకట
4. పతి నాయనింవారు నెల్లూరి శీమలోం చెల్లె
5. . . . న . . శ్రీ . చె . . .
6. . నెల్లూరి . . . . చెరిసవి గనక
7. మేర ధాన్యం సంధాతానవున్నా . . . ండా వేయిం
చినాను
8. . . . . . . రలుగానినాను యెవ్వరైనా
9. . . . . . . పని . . . చేపట్టినారు చెర్వు మేరలు
10. . . . . చెర్వు . . . . . యవ్వరు
11. . . . . చెర్వు (పని) చేయిం . . . .
12. . . . . వేయించినాను యెవ్వరు తీసినా . . .
13. . . . . . . ర్చినవాండ్లు వాండ్ల ఆలిని ఆవూరి . . . .
14. . . . . నాండు.

NELLORE (100.)

[Rámatírtham. Telugu. Above door of the temple.]

TRANSLATION.

(For the merit of) Bhujabala[1] Malla Siddi Chóḍa Mahárája . . . son of Chóḍéṣvara . . . . at Rámatírdham . . . . .

---

[1] The inscription is mutilated. It may be Nalla Siddhi.

1. చోడేశ్వరకు
2. మాణుఁడు
3. భుజబలము
4. ల్లిసిద్ధిచోడ
5. మహారాజుకు . .
6. ణర . . రామ
7. తీర్థమందు
8. దానూటి కూ
9. . దొవమ ఆ
10. . . . నీయు
11. . . . .

Nellore (101).

[Rámatírtham. Tamil. Over shrine of temple.]

Translation.

Hail! Prosperity! In the 31st year of the reign of the emperor of the three worlds, the glorious Kulóttuṅgachóḷadéva who was pleased to take Madura and the crowned head of the Páṇḍya (king), Madurántakapottapichóḷa *alias* Tirukkáḷattidéva gave to Manumákéśava Perumáḷ of Manumakéśavapura (a suburb) of Nellúr *alias* Vikramasiṅgapura (situated) in Pérúrnáḍu in Chédikulamáṇikkavaḷanáḍu (a sub-division) of Jayaṅgoṇḍachóḷamaṇḍala, free of tax, the village of Iḍappúr situated in Maṇḍainádu (a sub-division) of this náḍu (Chédikulamáṇikkavaḷanáḍu).

The boundaries of this village are: on the west the boundary of *Śâṇi*; on the south the boundary of *Váriḳai*;

(To face page 864.)

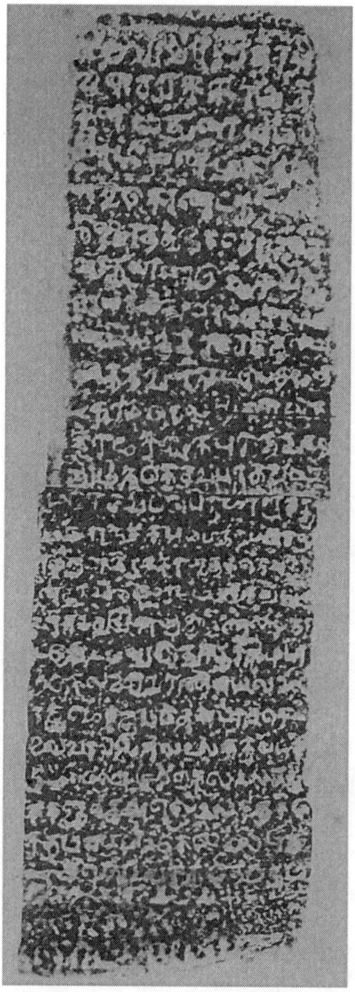

NELLORE NO. 101.

on the west the boundary of *Tirukkâñjéru*; and on the north the boundary of *Puruṇḍil*.

*　　*　　*　　*

*　　*　　*　　*

*　　*　　*　　*

[1] ஸ்வஸ்தி ஸ்ரீ திரிபு-
[2] வனச்சக்கரவர்த்தி-
[3] கள் மதுரையும் ப[ா]-
[4] ண்டியன் முடிதலை-
[5] யுங்கொண்டருளின [ஸ்ரீ]
[6] குலொத்துங்கசொழதெ-
[7] வற்கு யாண்டு ௩௰௧ வது
[8] ஜயங்கொண்டசொழம-
[9] ண்டலத்துச்செதிகுலமா-
[10] ணிக்கவளநாட்டுப்பெரு-
[11] ர்நாட்டு நெல்லூரான விக்-
[12] கிரமசிங்கபுரத்து ம-
[13] னுமக்கெசவபுரத்து [மனு]-
[14] மகெசவப்பெருமாளுக்கு
[15] மதுராந்தகப்பொத்தப்பிச்செ-
[16] ாழனை திருக்காணத்திதெவநெ-
[17] ன் திருவிடையாட்டமாக இட்ட [ப]
[18] ரிசாவது இன்று[ட்டு] மண்டைகா-
[19] ட்டு இடப்பூர் இதுக்கு கிழ்பா-
[20] ற்கெல்லை சாணியெல்லை-
[21] க்கு மெற்கும் தென்பாற்கெல்-
[22] லை வாவிகெல்லைக்கு வடக்-
[23] கும் மெல்பாற்கெல்லை திரு-
[24] க்கஞ்செறு எல்லைக்கு கிழ-
[25] க்கும் வடபாற்கெல்லை புரு-
[26] ண்டிலெல்லைக்கு தெற்கும்

NELLORE (102). (A.D. 1227–28.)

[Sangam. Telugu. From northern wall of temple.]

TRANSLATION.

Hail! On Thursday the 7th of the bright half of Chaitra corresponding to the illustrious Śaka year 1149, on the day of Vishu Sankránti, Kandamúri Baichana Api Reḍḍi Prólisáni (presented) an evening lamp to Sangamésvara for the religious merit of her husband. . . .

1. స్వస్తిశ్రీ శకవర్షములు ౧౧౪౯ నేట్టి చైత్రంబు
2. నందు శుద్ధసప్తమియు గురువారము విషుసంక్రా
3. ంతినాండు కందమూర బైచ్న అపిరెడ్డి ప్రోలిసాని తన
4. పెన్మిటికి ధర్మ్మువుగా సంధ్యాదీపము సంగమేశ్వరునికి. .

NELLORE (103). (A.D. 1218–19.)

[Sangam. Telugu. On the northern wall of the temple.]

TRANSLATION.

Hail! On Tuesday the 3rd of the dark fortnight of Phálguna, corresponding to 1140 of the illustrious and auspicious Śaka era, Páti Reḍḍi, Surapa Reḍḍi, and Brahmanayu gave three slaves to Sangaméṣvara Mahádéva, so that religious merit might accrue to their parents. May there be great prosperity! Ṣrí! Ṣrí!

1. స్వస్తి శ్రీ శుభసకవర్షంబులు
2. ౧౧౪౦ నేంటి భాల్గుణక్రిష్ణ
3. త్రితియయు మంగ్గడవార
4. మునదు పాతిరడసురవ

5. రడి బ్రహ్మనయు దకుతల్లిద
6. ంద్రికి దమ్మఱంగా సంగమేస్వ
7. రమహాదేవరకు దాసులు
8. ముప్ప్వర నిచ్చిరి మంగ్గళ
9. మహా శ్రీ శ్రీ శ్రీ.

NELLORE (104). (A.D. 1551–52.)

[[1] Sangam. Telugu. On the western wall of the temple.]

TRANSLATION.

Hail! On Sunday the 7th of Chaitra of the year Viródhikṛit, corresponding to 1473 of the illustrious, victorious and prosperous Ṣáliváhana Ṣaka era, while Ṣrímad Rájádhirája Rájaparaméṣvara Víra Prátápa Ṣrí Sadáṣivadéva Maháráya, seated on the diamond throne at Vijayanagar, was ruling the earth, Rámi Reḍḍi, son of Duvvúri Konḍávara Nandi Reḍḍi, granted a charitable edict as follows after making obeisance to Sangaméṣvaradéva, for the religious merit of Chivvakalúri Bayacha Rájayya, who is the governor (ádhipati) of Udayagiri *rájya* which belongs to the chiefdom of Ṣríman Manḍaléṣvara Rámarájayya Ṣrí Tirumalayya déva Mahárájulayya. We have presented with libation of water the proceeds realized from the sale of the produce of the tope planted by us in the *sthala* of Sangam in Udayagiri *rájyam* for providing worship with light to Sangaméṣvara. We have done this under the orders of Ṣrí Mahá Manḍaléṣvara

---

[1] At Sangam is a fine monolithic Sthambam, the top of which is unfortunately broken off. The obelisk bears a graceful scroll-pattern.

apratihata (invincible) Paricheja Mummayadéva Chóḍa Mahárája. Duvvúri Rámi Reḍḍi.

1. స్వస్తిశ్రీ జయాభ్యుదయ శాలివాహన శకవర్షంబు ౧౪౭౩ అగునేంటి విరోధి కృతు సంవ

2. త్సర చైత్ర బ ౭ ఆ। శ్రీ మద్రాజాధి రాజ రాజపరమే శ్వర శ్రీ వీరప్రతాప శ్రీ సదాశివదేవ

3. మహారాయులు విజయనగరమందు వజ్రసింహాసనా రూఢులై ।పిధివి సామ్రాజ్యాం

4. ముసేయుచుండంగాను శ్రీ మన్మహామండలేశ్వర రామ రాజయ శ్రీ దిరుమలయ్య దే

5. వ మహారాజులయ్యవారి నాయంకరానకు చెల్లి వుదయగిరి రాజ్యానకు అధిపతిఅయిన (అ

6. ఉ) చింవ్వకలూరి బయచరాజయ్య వారికి పుణ్యముగాను దువ్వూరికొండా వరనంది రెడ్డి

7. ంగారి కొమారుండు రామిరెడ్డి సంగమేశ్వరదేవునికి దం డంపెట్టి సమర్పించి యిచ్చినధర్మశా

8. సన క్రమమెట్లన్నను వుదయగిరి రాజ్యంలోని సంగాము స్తళమందును తాము వేయించిన తోంపును మావల్ల ఫలపరుపు

9. టకు రొఖం సంగమేశ్వరు దిపారాధనము సాగెయస్లు గాను ధారవోసి సమర్పింస్తిమి శ్రీ మహామండలేశ్వర అప్రతి

10. హతపరిచెజముమ్మయ దేవచోడ మహారాజులంగారికి నాయంకరానకు చెల్లిపడశేస్తిమి, దువ్వూరి రామిరెడ్డి

NELLORE (105). (A.D. 1570–71.)

[Sangam. Telugu. From stone in front of temple. Translation conjectural in parts.]

TRANSLATION.

Hail! On Monday the 7th of the dark fortnight of Chaitra of the year Pramódúta corresponding to the victorious and prosperous Śálivâhana Śaka year 1492 when Śrímád Rájádhi Rája, Rája Paraméṣvara, Ṣrí Víra Pratápa Sadáṣiva Maháráya, seated on the diamond throne was ruling the earth, we Veligoṭi Timmappa Náyanimgáru, the agent (káryakarta) of Śríman Mahá Maṇḍaléṣvara Rámarája Ṣrí Ranga Rájayyadéva Mahárájulayya, after making obeisance to Sangaméṣvaradéva, have given this charitable edict. On the holy occasion of Mésha-Sankránti, with a libation of water, for providing all enjoyments and worship to Sangaméṣvara, we have remitted the taxes on cattle and sundry articles of merchandise and the service for the river channel and the *veṭṭi* fees for the religious merit of Rangarájayya. Therefore, if any person obstructs this charity, he will incur the sin of killing his parents at Kási. This charitable deed has been granted in perpetuity to last as long as the sun and the moon exist. Ṣrí ! Ṣrí !

1. స్వస్తిశ్రీ జయాంభ్యుద
2. య శాలివాహన శకవ
3. ర్షంబులు ౧౪౯౨ అగు
4. నేటి ప్రమోదూత సంవ్వ
5. త్సర చైత్ర బ ౭ సో శ్రీమ
6. ద్రాజాధిరాజ రాజపర
7. మేశ్వర శ్రీ వీరప్రతాపశ్రీ
8. సదాసివదేవ మహారాయ
9. లు వజ్ర సింహాసనారూఢు
10. లై పృథివి సామ్రాజ్యమున్ సే
11. యుచుండంగాను శ్రీమన్
12. మహామండలేశ్వర రామరాజ
13. శ్రీరంగరాజయ్య దేవమహా
14. రాజులయ్యవారి కార్యకర్

15. ర్త్తలైన వెలిగోటి తింమ్మప్పనా
16. యనింగారు సంగమేశ్వర
17. దేవునికిం దండం సమర్పించి

Second side.

18. యిచ్చిన ధర్మశాసనం
19. యీ సంగాననగరికి ఔ ట్టెబేడి
20. గొఖడాయం సంగమేశ్వరునితీ
21. ధర్ం కానికదానః శ్రిరంగ్గరాజయ్య
22. వారికి బుణ్యంగాను మేషసం
23. క్రాంతి పుణ్యకాలమందు అం
24. గరంగవై భవ ఆరగింపులుకు
25. న్ను ధారాపూర్వంగాను సంగమేశ్వ
26. రునికి ధారపోసి యిచ్చిపట్టువ
27. సులు చిల్లర పరకస్తులు యేటి
28. కాల్వ వెట్టిసహా మానితిమిగన
29. క యీ ధర్మానకు యవ్వరు అయిన
30. విరోధం శేశి తప్పినాను గంగ్గ
31. కర్త గోబ్రాహ్మలను వధియి
32. ంచిన పాపానం బోవువారు
33. తమ తల్లిదండ్రులను కాశి
34. లోను వధియించినపాపా
35. నంబోవువారు । ఆ చంద్రా
36. ర్క స్థాయిగాను ఇచ్చిన ధ
37. ర్మశాసనము ॥ శ్రీ శ్రీ.

NELLORE (106). (A.D. 1183–84.)

[Sangam. Telugu and Tamil. In survey number 253 to east of village.]

TRANSLATION.

Hail! On Thursday the 5th of the bright fortnight of Chaitra, corresponding to the Ṣrí Śaka year 1105, Kóllapúḍi Nílama Náyakuḍu, Kétam Náyakuḍu and Mámiḍi Nílama Náyakuḍu presented the tank of Koṇḍakarrikili lying to the east of the temple of Sangaméṣvaradéva situated on the northern bank of the river Penna (Pennér) in perpetuity to last as long as the sun and moon exist for providing incense, worship with light, offerings and gifts to Sangaméṣvaradéva.

Those who cause delay (obstruction) to this charity will incur the sin of killing a thousand tawny cows on the banks of the Ganges.

[One imprecatory verse in Telugu characters.]

[The same in Grantha characters.]

1. స్వస్తి శ్రీ శకవర్షం
2. బులు ౧౧౦౫ సెం
3. టి చైత్ర సుద్ధ పం
4. చ్చమి యు గురువా
5. రామునాడు . పెన్న
6. తీరము నుత్తరము
7. న సంగమిశ్వర దేవ
8. రగుడి తూర్వ్వన
9. కొండకఱికిలిచె
10. ఱువు బిలియూరి
11. కోల్లపూడి నీలమ
12. నాయకుండు కేత

13. మ న్నాయకుండు మా
14. మడినీలమనాయ
15. కుడును సంగమీశ్వ
16. ర దేవరకు దూపదీప
17. నైవేద్యములకు దాన
18. మానములకు ఆచం
19. ద్రాకర్కస్థాయిగానిచ్చిన
20. చెఱు ఇధమ్ము వున
21. కు నెవ్వ రేని విలంబ
22. ము సేసినవారు గంగ

Second side.

23. కఱుతవేయి
24. క విలల జంపిన
25. పాపమునబోయి
26. నవారు ॥ స్వదత్తం
27. పరదత్తంవాయో
28. హారేతి వసుంధరా
29. షష్టిర్వ్వరుష సహ
30. స్రాణి విష్టా యాంజాయ
31. తే క్రిమి.
32.
33.
34. The above slóka is re-written in Grantha character—Tamil.
35.
36.
37.

NELLORE (107).

[Sangam. Tamil. From northern wall of temple.]

This inscription records the gift of some money (?) as long as the moon and sun last for a sacred lamp by one Náyakkayakka.

[1] த்தநாயக்கயக்கனென் திருநுந்த[ா]-
[2] விளக்கு தரணி வாவியிலெப்பயிர் ப[யி]-
[3] தறைகுடுத்தெக் சந்திராதித்-
[4] தவரை

NELLORE (108).

[Sangam. Tamil. From two sides of a stone which also bears two Telugu inscriptions.]

TRANSLATION.

Hail! Prosperity! In the fifth year of the reign of Rájáyirájadéva, we, Nílamanáyakkar, Kéttamanáyakkar and Mummaḍi Nílamanáyakkar who govern Viriyúr (and) Kollappúṇḍi, gave for incense, lights, sacred food, and other expenses, to Márideva known as Kadikkili (whose image is) situated at the north-east corner of the temple of Sangaméśvara (situated) on the north bank of the Peṇṇár at Viriyúr in Pákkainádu (situated) within Jayaṇkoṇḍachóḻamaṇḍala.

He who injures this charity will incur the sin of killing thousand tawny cows on the banks of the Ganges.

[1] ஸ்வஸ்தி ஸ்ரீ
[2] ராஜாயிராஜ-
[3] தெவற்கு யா-

[4] ண்டு அஞ்சா-
[5] வது செயக்-
[6] கொண்டெ-
[7] சாழமண்ட-
[8] லத்துள் பா-
[9] க்கைநாட்டி-
[10] ல் விரியூரில்
[11] பெண்ணாற்-
[12] றில் வடக்கை-
[13] [ரயி]ல் ஸ்ரீசங்-
[14] [க]மிச்சரமு[ட]
[15] [ய]ாற்கு விரி[யூ]-
[16] [ர்க்] [ெ]கால்ல-
[17] பமூண்டிநா-
[18] யக்கஞ்செய்-
[19] வர்கள் நிலம-
[20] நாயக்கரும் கெ-
[21] த்தமநாயக்க-
[22] ரும் மும்மடி
[23] நிலமநாயக்-
[24] கரும் சங்கமீ-
[25] சுரமுடையார்
[26] கொயிலுக்கு வ-
[27] டகிழக்கு கொ-
[28] ண்ட க[தி]க்கிலி-
[29] யெங்றுமாரி-
[30] தெவற்கு தூபதீ-
[31] பங்களுக்கும்
[32] அமுதுபடிக்கு-
[33] ம [ற்று].ள்ளதாகம-
[34] ாக அழிவுகளுக்-
[35] கும் குடுத்தொம்

[36] இத்தந்மத்தை
[37] யாவர் சிலாழி-
[38] பார் கங்கைக்கர-
[39] யில் ஆயிரங்குரா-
[40] ற்பசுவை கொந்று-
[41] ந் பட்ட நரகத்தில்
[42] படுவாந்.

NELLORE (109). (A.D. 1221–22 ?)

[Talamanchi. Tamil. On gate of Rámalingasvámi temple.]

TRANSLATION.

Hail! Prosperity! In the Śaka year one thousand one hundred and forty-three . . . . the interest on the gold deposited in previous years by various persons for the gods Sénapatipiḻḻaiyár (Subrahmaṇya) and Uḍutómuḍaiyár in the temple of the lord of Áḍúr (situated) in Rájéndrachóḻamaṇḍala . . . . for oil . . . .

[1] ஸ்வஸ்தி ஸ்ரீ சக-
[2] வருடம் ஆயி-
[3] ரத்தொருநூ-
[4] ற்றுநாற்பத்தி-
[5] மூன்றில ராஜெ-
[6] ந்த்ரசொழமண்-
[7] டலத்து முண்[டை]-
[8] நாட்டு ஆ[டு]ர்-
[9] த்தெவ[ர்]கள் செ-
[10] னாபதிப்பிள்-
[11] ளையார்க்கும் உ-
[12] டு தொமுடையா-

[13] ர்க்கு மூன்றுனில்
[14] [ப]ல[ரும்] வைத்-
[15] த பொன் கொண்-
[16] டு பெ[ரவி]யூட்ட-
[17] த்துக்கும் பிடவா-
[18] ரி எண்ணைக்கு[ம்]-

NELLORE (110).

[Tóṭapalligúḍúru. Telugu. In street to the east.]

TRANSLATION.

* * * *

under the orders of Ákula Ranganáthayyagáru, agent of Rája Ṣrí . . . . . Venkaṭapati Náyanigáru, Bóyanipálli Bápannagáru issued this charitable edict for the grain to be collected at 1 *kunchuḍu* for the tank of the village. If the rulers of the village, the *kápus*, *karnams* or *Mányagáḍus* or any one else fail to spend that grain on the tank and object to it, they will incur the sin of killing a cow and a Brahman on the banks of the Ganges. They will be considered to have been born of a donkey.

1\. . . . . .
2\. . వ . . . .
3\. జే శ్రీ . . . .
4\. వెంకటపతి నాయనింగారి కా
5\. ర్యక ర్త్తలైన ఆకుల రంగ్గనా
6\. ధయ్యగారి అనుమతినిబో
7\. యిని పాల్లి బాంపనంగారు
8\. ను యూరి చెరువుకుంచాల ధా
9\. న్యాలకు వేశించ్చిన ధర్మశాస

10. నం గ్రామం యేలువారు కాపు
11. కరణాలు మాన్యగాండ్లు ఆ
12. ధాన్యం చెర్వు మీంద వేశించ్చక
13. యెవ్వరు అపేక్షించ్చినా గంగ్గ
14. కత్తీరను గోబ్రాంహణి చం
15. పిన పాపానం బోదురు
16. గాడిద కడుపున పుట్టిన
17. వాండు.

Nellore (111). (A.D. 1204–05?)

[Tóṭapalligúḍúru. Tamil. Opposite Vináyaka temple.]

Translation.

Hail! Prosperity! In the Śaka year (one) thousand one hundred and twenty-six, on the date corresponding to Wednesday . . . . with the *nakshatra* Róhini, the fourth day of the bright half of the month of Tulá, Malaikiḷiyaninṛán Pichchan Uḍaiyán, the headman of Kávanúr forming part (?) of the village of Máligaikkávanúr (situated) in Pónagaináḍu in Maṇaviṛkóṭṭa gave to last as long as the moon and sun, with libations of water, to (the temple of) the lord Siddappa at Póyinḍanpaḷḷi (situated) in Piḍaináḍu in Chédikulamáṇikkavaḷanáḍu (a sub-division) of Jayáṇkoṇḍachóḷamaṇḍala, after having set up in the temple (an image of) Madurántakapottapichóḷa *alias* Peddaraśa, as temple land, one thousand five hundred *kuḷi* of areca-nut plantation situated to the south of the temple.

If there be anybody who cause disregard of this charity, he will incur the sin of one who kills a tawny cow on the banks of the Ganges.

[Then follows what is evidently a separate inscription dated in the month of Aippasi of the thirty-fifth year of the emperor of the three worlds.]

[1] ஸ்வஸ்தி ஸ்ரீ ஸக[வருஷ]-
[2] மாயிரத்தொருநூ-
[3] ற்றுயி[ருபத்]தா[று]-
[4] வது து[லா]நா-
[5] [ய] ற்று [பூர்வ்வபக்ஷ]-
[6] த்து [சதுர்த்]தி ெ-
[7] பற்ற புதன்கி-
[8] ழமையுங்க-
[9] . வி . . . தி[ரு]-
[10] [ம]யும் [உ ெ]ரகி-
[11] ணியுமான நாள்
[12] [ெ]ஜயங்கொண்-
[13] டசோழமண்ட[ல]-
[14] த்துச்செதி-
[15] குலமாணிக்க-
[16] வளநாட்டுப்பி-
[17] டைநாட்டுப்-
[18] பொயிண்டன்
[19] பள்ளியில் சித்த-
[20] ப்பமுடையக[ர]-
[21] யனார்க்குத்தே-
[22] வதானமாக ம-
[23] துராந்தகப்ெ-
[24] பாத்தப்பிச்ெ-
[25] சாழனை பெ-
[26] த்தராசரை இடு-

[27] வித்து இக்கொ-
[28] யிலுக்கு தெ-
[29] ற்கடைந்த க-
[30] முகங்தொட்ட-
[31] மான நிலம் ஆ-
[32] யிரத்தைந்நூ-
[33] று குழியும் ஊரா-
[34] . . . . .
[35] . . . . . . சங்
[36] கி[ராதி]த்தவரை செல்-
[37] வதாக விட்டான் ம[ண]-
[38] விற்கொட்டத்துப்பெ-
[39] பா[ண]கைநாட்டு மாளி-
[40] கைக்கா[வ]லூர்க்காவ-
[41] நார்[தலை]வன் மலைகிளிய-
[42] நின்றான்[பி]சசன் உடை-
[43] [யான்] இத்தன்மத்துக்-
[44] கு [அவமானம்] பண்ணி-
[45] ஞ[று]ண்டாகில் ஙஂகை-
[46] ககரையில் குரால்-
[47] பசுவை வதித்தார் ப-
[48] ண்ணின பாவத்திலெ
[49] பொவார் திரிபுவன-
[50] ச்சக்கரவத்திகளுக்கு
[51] ய[ாண்]டு முப்பத்தை-
[52] ஞ்[சா]வதில் ஐய்-
[53] ப்[ப] சிமாசத்தில உ-
[54] . . . . டிந . . க . .

NELLORE (112). (A.D. 1558–59.)

[Vangallu. Telugu. From tank bund.]

TRANSLATION.

Hail! On the 8th of the bright half of Mágha of the year Kálayukti corresponding to the year 1480 of the illustrious, victorious and prosperous Śáliváhana Śaka era, this is the lease of the tank in Duvvúru *sthalam* in the *síma* of Udayagiri granted by Sríman Mahámaṇḍaléṣvara Rámarájuyara Timmaya Dévara Mahárájulugáru to Ṣríman Mahámaṇḍaléṣvara Cháḷukya Náráyaṇa Chauhaṭṭamalla[1], Raṇa Vijaya[2] Velmapáṭi Veragaḷayya (Vengaḷayya?) Déva Mahárájulu Ayyaváru.

This charitable edict was issued for the tank at Yókámbram Vávélúru . . . . for the religious merit of Máḷu Vengaḷarájayyaváru. Whoever obstructs this charity will incur the sin of killing cows and Bráhmans on the banks of the river Ganges.

(a)

1. స్వస్తి శ్రీ జయాభ్యుద
2. య శాలివాహన శకవర్ష
3. ంబులు ౧౪౮౦ అగు నేంటి కా
4. ళయుక్తి సంవత్సర మాఘశు ౮
5. లు శ్రీమన్మహా మండలేశ్వ
6. ర రామరాజయ్యర తింమ్మయ
7. దేవర (మ)హారాజులుంగారు శ్రీ
8. మన్మహా మండలేశ్వర చాళుక్య

---

[1] Chauhattamalla=(1) Vishnu—Chaturhastamalla.
(2) a hero having the strength of four elephants—chaturhastamalla.

[2] Rana Vijaya—an Arjuna in war.

9. నారాయణ చౌహాత్త మల్ల ర
10. ణ విజయ వెల్మపాటి వెరగళ
11. య్యు దేవ మహారాజులు అ
12. య్యవార్కి పాలించ్చిన పుద
13. యగిరి శీమలోను దున్నూ
14. రి త్తళాన చర్వుమీలగుత్త

Second side.

15. మాళు వెంగళరాజు
16. య్యవారికి పుంణ్యం
17. గా యోకాంబ్రం పా
18. వేలూరి చెర్వుకట్ట యి
19. దమంటి
20. కట్టడశేశి ఇచ్చిన
21. ధర్మశాసనం ఇ
22. పుంణ్యాసక యె
23. వ్వరు గాదంనా
24. ను గంగ్గకత్తే గో
25. బ్రాంహ్మని వధి
26. యుంచిన పాపా
27. నం బోదురు.

NELLORE (113).

[Varakavipúḍi. Telugu. To south of village.]

TRANSLATION.

The village Varakalapánḍu which was received as a gift by Tirumala Sómayájulu. . . . has also got the name Tiruveṅkaṭa(námagrámam).

* * * *

Venkaṭa Ayyarpaṭnam (in Tamil characters). . .

1. తిరుమల సోమ
2. యాజులు ప్ర
3. తిగ్రహించిన
4. పరకల పాండు
5. గ్రామానికి ప్ర
6. తి నామమైన
7. తిరు వెంకటనామ
8. గ్రామము . . .
9. . . . . .
10. . . . . .
11. வெகட அயரபட்ண

Nellore (114). (A.D. 1638–39.)

[Varigonḍa. Telugu. From stone by path to east of village.]

Translation.

Hail! On the 3rd of the bright half of Chaitra of the year Bahudhánya, corresponding to the year 1560 of the illustrious, victorious and prosperous Ṣáliváhana Śaka era, Velugóṭi Veṇkaṭapati Náyaningáru issued this charitable edict for the tank at Varigoṇḍa. The village being dealt with under *Sandhátá* lease, or *amaram*, the *méra* grain settled for it should be used on the tank. If, not doing the work, any *kápu* or *karnam* or any one else covets the grain, the *veṭṭi* will ravish his wife.

1. స్వస్తి శ్రీ విజయాభ్యుదయ
2. శాలివాహన శకవర్షంబు
3. లు ౧౫౬౦ అగు నేటి బహు .

4. ధాన్య సంవత్సర చైత్రశు 3
5. లు వెలుగోటి వెంకటప
6. తినాయుడు వరిగొండ చె
7. ర్వుకు ఇచ్చిన ధర్మశాసనం
8. గ్రామం సంధాతం గుత్త అ
9. మరంచేసి నిర్ణయమైన
10. చెర్వు మేరధాన్యం చెర్వు
11. పని చేయించేది శేయించక
12. కాపు కరణం యవరు అశి
13. ంచిన వాండి అల్ని వెట్టి
14. వాడు దొంగేది॥

NELLORE (115). (A.D. 1635–36 ?)

[Vávilétipáḍ. Telugu. Now at Collector's bungalow.]

TRANSLATION.

On the 8th day of the bright fortnight of Bhádrapada of the year Yuva, under the orders of Ákula Ranganáthayya the agent of Ṣrímat Velugóṭi Veṇkaṭapatináyanivâru, Bóyanapalli Bápanayagáru issued a charitable edict for the *kuncha* grain of the tank. If the ruler of the village Vávilétipáḍu or the *kápus* and *karanams* or the *mányadárs* fail to get the tank repaired with the *kuncha* grain or if any speak ill of the charity and decline to give (the grain) they will incur the sin of killing a cow near the Ganges. They will incur the sin of killing their parents. Those who do not maintain this (charity) will be considered to have given their honour to Málas and Mádigas. In these terms has this charitable edict been issued. Ṣrí! Ṣrí! Ṣrí!

1. యువసంవత్సర భాద్రపదశుద్ధ ౧ లు శ్రీమతు వెల గో
2. టి వెంకటపతి నాయునివారి కార్యకర్తలయిన ఆకులరంగ
3. నాధయ్యంగారి అనుమతిని బోయిని పల్లిబాంపనయగారు
4. చెరువు కుంచ్చాల దాన్యాలకు వేయించిన ధర్మ శాసనం
వాని
5. లేటిపాటి వూరుయే లేవారు కాంపు కరణాలు మన్యగాండ్లు
6. కుంచాలధాన్యం చెర్వుమీద వేయించ్చక యవ్వరు ఇయ్యక
కీడు
7. ఆడినాను గంగ కరుతను గోవును చంపిన పాపానపోదురు.
8. వారి తలితండ్ర్యుల వధించిన పాపాన పోదురు అ
9. ది తప్పి నడిపించ్చిరా వాండ్ల మానం మాలమాదిగెలకు
10. ఇచ్చ్చివాండ్లై ఇటని వేయించిన దమ్మశాసనము శ్రీ
11. శ్రీ శ్రీ.

Nellore (116). (A.D. 1638–39.)

[Vávilḷa. Telugu. Opposite the Vishnu temple.]

Translation.

On the 2nd of the bright fortnight of Chaitra of the year Bahudhánya, corresponding to the Ṣáliváhana Ṣaka year 1560, Velugóṭi Kumára Timmánáyanivåru gave grain to the tank of Vávilḷa; the village . . . Sandhátá . . . . should get the work done to the tank. If any Kápu or karnam, etc., fail to get the work done to the tank and utilizes the *méra* grain it will be considered that his wife has been given to the *veṭṭi* of this village.

1. షాలివాహాన శకవర్షంబు
2. లు ౧౫౬౦ అగునేంటి బహు
3. ధాన్య సంవత్సర చైత్ర శు ౨ లు
4. వెలుగోటి కుమా(రతిమ్మ) నాయుని
5. వారు వావిళ్ల చెర్వుకిచ్చినధాన్య

6. నను . . గ్రామ . . . . స
7. ంధాతా . . . . .
8. . . . . చెరువువని సేయించ్చేది
9. సేయించక యీ మెరధాన్యం ఎ
10. కాంపుకరణం యవరు అయిన్నావా
11. రించినవాడి ఆలిని ఇవ్వూరి
12. వెట్టివానికి ఇచ్చినవాండు

NELLORE (117). (A.D. 1572–73.)

[Vavvéru. Telugu. In a garden to the east of village.]

TRANSLATION.

Hail! On the 11th of the bright half of Śrávana of the year Angírasa, corresponding to the year 1494 of the illustrious, victorious and prosperous Śáliváhana Śaka era, this "Ranga" fountain was caused to be constructed by Mámandu (Muhammad) Miyá for the religious merit of the illustrious Rájádhi Rája Rája Mahárája Rájaśrí Kóvaṭi (Kónéṭi ?) Ranga Raogáru. May it cause prosperity!

1. స్వస్తి శ్రీమతు
2. జయాభ్యుదయ
3. శాలివాహన శకవర్షం
4. బులు ౧౪౯౪ అగు నేంటి
5. అంగీరస సంవత్సర శ్రావణ
6. శు ౧౧ లు శ్రీరాజాధిరాజ
7. రాజమహారాజ రాజశ్రీ కో
8. వటి రంగారావుంగారికి పుణ్య
9. ంగాను మామందు మియ్యాగట్టి
10. ంచ్చిన రంగ్గచలము॥ శ్రీ శ్రీ
11. ంజేను.

NELLORE (11?). (A.D. 1193–94.)

[Vavvéru. Telugu. In purohit's *mányam* to south of village.]

TRANSLATION.

In the year 1115 of the illustrious Śaka era. . .

* * * *

శ్రీశక వర్షం
బు ౧౧౧౫ దగు
జు నేటి (నాసగమేశదా)
ము . సే . జుకదోజలుకు
ప్రా లేటి విడినికి ఇచ్చినాను
. . శకమ సదాచెను ప .
. దేవగా నివ్వినచేసు
న్న జా గుంటలో
జెను . అం . జా
. టలు శ్రీ . . .
. ని . నాలుగు . .
* * * *
* * * *

NELLORE (119).

[Vavvéru. Telugu. In Chennakéśava temple.]

TRANSLATION.

The service to the goddess. The perpetual devotion of Gummaráju Guravayya.

అంమ్మవారి వుభయం గుమ్మ
రాజు గురవయ్య సదాశేవ.

NELLORE (120).

[Végúru. Tamil. From enclosure of Kailásanátha temple.]

TRANSLATION.

Hail! Prosperity! In the 21st year of the reign of the emperor of the three worlds, the glorious Kulóttunga-chóḻadéva, I, Śevvan Póyinḍan gave to the God of Śríkailása at Veṅgúr for Ámavásipaḍi[1] 330 *kuḻi* of land measured with the twenty *śáṇ*[2] rod settled by Tantipóyinḍan.

If anybody would injure this land, he will incur the sin of killing a cow on the banks of the Ganges.

This charity (is placed under) the protection of all the *Mâheśvaras*.

[1] ஸ்வஸ்தி ஸ்ரீ திரிபுவநச[க்]-
[2] கரவத்திகள் ஸ்ரீ குலொ[த்]-
[3] த்துங்[க*]சொழதெவ-
[4] ற்கு யாண்டு உ௰க ஆவ-
[5] தில வெங்கூரில் ஸ்ரீ
[6] கைலாயமுடையாற்-
[7] கு ஆமவாசிப்படிக்கு செ-
[8] சவ்வங்பொயிண்டன்-
[9] நென் வெங்கூரார் கை-
[10] கய்யிலெ கொண்டுவி-
[11] ட்டநிலம் தன்திபொயி-
[12] ண்டன் தூரவரந்து இரு-
[13] பதின்சாண்கொலால்
[14] அளன்து விட்ட நிலம்

---

[1] Endowment to the temple in memory of a certain disease having been cured [ஆமம் = disease; வாசி = cure (Winslow)]. Donations of this kind to temples are very common.

[2] Sáṇ = 9 inches.

[15] கடாகடம்குழி இந்த நில-
[16] ம் இறக்குவான் கஂகெ-
[17] ங்கரையில் பசு-
[18] வைக்கொன்றான் பா-
[19] வத்திலெ படுவான்
[20] ஸ்ரீசோமெஹஸ்வரரமெகெக்ஷ

Nellore (121). (A.D. 1243–44?)

[Végúru. Tamil. From enclosure of Kailásanátha temple.]

Translation.

Hail! Prosperity! In the Śaka year one thousand one hundred and sixty-five during the Chittirai equinox, the ryot Púśali Reḍḍi, the son of the ryot Piḍammi Reḍḍi of Kaṭṭappúṇḍi gave for a sacred lamp to the god of Śrí Kaiḷása at Vélúr (situated) in Muṇḍainádu in Nellúr-náḍu in Paiyyuriḷaṅkóṭṭa (a sub-division) of Jayaṅkoṇḍa-chóḷamaṇḍala 50 full-grown undying and unaging sheep.

(The gift of) these sheep should last as long as the moon and sun endure.

If anybody obstructs this charity, he will incur the sin of killing a tawny cow on the banks of the Ganges.

(*Slóka*) He who misappropriates land given by himself or by others will be born a worm in ordure for sixty thousand years.

[1] ஸ்வஸ்திஸ்ரீ ஸகவருஷம் ஆயிரத்து ஒரு[நூற்று *]-
[2] அறுபத்துஅஞ்சாவது சித்திரை வி[ஷுவில்]
[3] ஜயங்கொண்டசொழமண்டலத்து

[4] பையூரிளங்கொட்டத்து நெல்லூர்நா[ட]-
[5] டு முண்டைநாட்டில் வெ[லூர்] ஸ்ரீ க[யிலா]-
[6] சமுடையநாயநாற்கு கட்டப்பூண்[டி]
[7] [யி]டம்பிரட்டகுடியார் மகன் பூ-
[8] [ச]விரட்டகுடியென் வைத்த திரு-
[9] நந்தாவிளக்குக்கு வைத்த சாவா-
[10] மூவாப்பெராடு ரூ௰ இந்த
[11] ஆடு சந்த்ராதித்தவரை செல்-
[12] வக்கடவதாவதென்ய-
[13] ஜ-ல இறக்குவார் கங்கைக்க[ரை]ர-
[14] [யி]ல் குராற்பசுவை வதித்தான் பாவ-
[15] த்திலெ படுவான் - ஸ்வத த-
[16] த்தாம் பரதத்தாம் வா யோஹரெ-
[17] த வஸுந்தராம் [|*] ஷஷ்டிர்வர்ஷ-
[18] ஸஹஸ்ராணி விஷ்டாயாம்-
[19] ஜாயதெ க்ருமி: [||] ஸ்ரீ || ஸ்ரீ-

NELLORE (122). (A.D. 1524–25.)

[Vellanṭi. Telugu. Opposite to Ánjanéya temple.]

TRANSLATION.

Hail! On Sunday, the 10th of the bright half of Kártika of the year Tárana, corresponding to the year 1447 of the illustrious Śaka era, Śríman Mahámaṇḍaléśvara Dantalúr Chágaṇṭi Déva Mahárájulu (gave for the religious merit) of his father Vóbularáju . . . . . . (for providing) offerings to the deity Hanumán. We gave to Mahádéva . . . . under (the tank) . . . and dry field to the south of the field . . . . .

to the east of the field . . . .
We gave one hundred *kunṭas* of dry field to Késavadéva for offerings. Whoever fails in this will incur the sin of killing cows and Brahmans on the banks of the Ganges. May it cause great prosperity!

NOTE.—We have not identified the donor.

1. స్వస్తిశ్రీ శకవరషంబులు (పయి
2. ని) ౧౮౮౭ అగునేంటి తారణస
3. ంవత్సర కార్తిక శు ౧౦ ఆ। శ్రీ
4. మహామహా మండలేశ్వర దంత లూ
5. రి చాగంటి దేవమహారాజులుత
6. మతండ్రి వోజులరాజుంగారి

Second side.

7. చేతం ఇచ్చి . . . . . .
8. హానుమంతునికి నివేద్యానకు
9. . . . .
10. . . . . క్రింద మహాదేవునికి . .
11. ర చేనికి దక్షిణం వరిమడి . . .
12. నచారియ చెనితూర్పున . . .
13. నను ఇచ్చితిమి వెలిసెను కు ౧౦౦
14. కేశవదేవనికి నైవేద్యానకు ఇ
15. స్తిమి ఇపుణ్యంకు యవ్వారు త
16. ప్పినాను గంగకర్తెను గోవును
17. బ్రాంహానిం జంపిన పాపానం
17. బోవువారు ॥ మంగళమహా శ్రీ.

NELLORE (123).

[Vellanṭi. Telugu. In street to the south.]

TRANSLATION.

On the 2nd of the bright half of Áshádha of the year . . . . the *méra* given to (by ?) Velugóṭi Venkaṭapati Náyanimgáru . . . . . . We gave . . . . on the east. They should enjoy its produce as long as the sun and moon exist. Those who fail to keep this charity will incur the sin of killing cows and Brahmans on the banks of the Ganges. [One imprecatory verse.]

1. . . . . . సంవత్సర
2. ఆషాఢ శు ౨ లు వెలిగోటి వెంకటప
3. తినాయనింగారికి యిచ్చిన మేర
4. . . . . . శెకంగంబు మొదలయినవి క
5. . . . . గానేను . . . ను తూర్పుగా . . .
6. స్తిమి గనక అందుల ఫలం ఆ చం
7. (ద్రార్కముఅనుభవించువారు)గనక తప్పినాను గంగకతీ
నుగో
8. (బ్రాహ్మల వధించినపాపానఁబోయినవారు)॥ స్వదత్తం పర
దత్తం
9. (వాయోహరేతివసుంధరా షష్టివర్ష) సహస్రాణి విష్ఠా
యాం జాయతే క్రిమి॥

NELLORE (124). (A.D. 1582–83.)

[Viḍavalúru. Telugu. From rock on Póléramma-mitṭa.]

TRANSLATION.

Hail! On the 5th of the bright half of Chaitra of the year Chitrabhánu, corresponding to the year 1504 of the illustrious, victorious and prosperous Śáliváhana Śaka era, while Śrímad Rájádhirája, Rája Paramésvara Śrí Víra Pratápa Śrí Víra Rangaráyadéva Mahárájulugáru, seated on the diamond throne at the city of Penugonḍa, was ruling the earth, Kónéṭi China Timma Náyanimgáru of the Vellaṭla *gótra*, grandson of Rávéla Kanṭi Náyanimgáru, and son of Tirumalayyagáru, issued a charitable edict for the tank. The old grant of *méras* at 1 *kuncha* per *puṭṭi* for the tank at the village of Viḍavalúru, situated in Udayagiri *śíma*, which was granted for our chiefdom by the king has been discontinued. Therefore we have again granted *méras* at 1 *kuncha* per *puṭṭi* on all kinds of grain raised in the village, including fields leased by the estate, garden lands, and *bhaṭa vritti mányams* (personal inams), for the religious merit of the above said China Kónéṭi Timmanáyanímgáru and to last as long as the sun and moon exist. We have also given 100 *kunṭas* under the tank to the south of the *báḍava* (marshy land) as a *mányam*. This is the charitable edict issued for doing work to the tank every year, with the yearly income derived from the *mányam* and the *méras* at 1 *kuncha* per *puṭṭi*. Those who fail in this will incur the sin of killing cows and Brahmans on the banks of the Ganges, and will incur the sin of killing their parents at Benares.

If any one speaks ill of this, the Upparas will ravish his wife; also Angírula Súraḍu will ravish his wife. Ṣrí! Ṣrí! Ṣrí! [One imprecatory verse.]

1. స్వస్తిశ్రీ జయాభ్యుదయ శాలివా

2. హాన శకవర్షంబులు ౧౫౦౮ అగు నేటి చిత్రభా

3. ను సంవత్సర చైత్ర శు ౫ లు శ్రీమద్రాజాధిరాజ రా

4. జ పరమేశ్వర శ్రీ వీరప్రతాప శ్రీ వీర రంగరాయ దే

5. వ మహారాయలుంగారు పెనుగొండనగరమందు వజ్రశిం

6. హాసనారూఢులై పృథ్వి సామ్రాజ్యముచేయుచును

7. వెల్లట్ల గోత్రులైన రావేల (కం) టి నాయనింగారి పౌత్రు లైన తి

8. రుమలయ్యంగారి పుత్రులైన కోనేటి చిన తిమ్మానాయనిం

9. గారు ఇచ్చిన చెరువు ధర్మశాసనం రాయలవారు మా నాయం

10. కరానకు పాలించిఇచ్చిన పుదయగిరిశీమలోని విడవలూ రి గ్రా

11. మానను చెర్వు ప్రట్టికుంచాలు పూర్వాన సాగింది ఖిలపడి వుండు

12. గనక అచినకోనేటి తిమ్మనంగారికి పుణ్యంగాను అచంద్రా ర్కంగా

13. ను గ్రామానను పండిన నానాధాన్యానకు నగరి కమతా లనుములు

14. వులను భటవ్రిత్తిమాన్యాలును సహా వి త్తినపుటికల ప్రట్టికి కుం

15. చడు మేరసాగింస్తిమి మాన్యం చెరువుకింద్దను బాడవ లోన

16. దక్షిణం నూరుకుంటలు ఇస్తిమి మాన్యంవల్లను పుట్టికుంచా

17. లవలను యాటవచ్చినవి యాంట చెరువుమీాండ పనిశే యుటకు

18. ఇట్టని ఇచ్చిన ధర్మశాసనం ఇందుకుతప్పినవాండుగంగ కర్త్త

19. గోవు బ్రాంహని చంపిన పాపానపోదురు వారణాసిలోను తమ

20. తల్లితండ్రుల వధించిన పాపానపోదురు ఇందుకు యవ్వ

21. ండు కీడాడిన వానిఆలిని పడందిసియ యెటివుపరవారు

22. దెంగుదురు మరి వానిఆలిని అంగీరుల నూరడు

23. దెంగును శ్రీ శ్రీ శ్రీ స్వదత్తా ద్విగుణంపుణ్యం పర

24. దత్తానుపాలనం పరదత్తాపహారేణ స్వధత్తం నిష్ఫలం

25 భవేత్ ॥

ONGOLE (1).

[Addanki. Telugu. From roof of Náncháramma temple.]

TRANSLATION.

The servant of Báṇa Sindhúru . . . . the dark fortnight of Chaitra . . . . Ṣrí Pina Kampi Mallani . . . . the excellent charity of Víráṛya at Vémanúru

NOTE.—There are 8 short inscriptions on the pillars of the Nágéṣwara temple at Addaṅki. They are not worth printing.

1. బాణ సింధూరి బృత్యుండువు . . . .
2. చైత్రవలతు పతువిలశిత్ శ్రీ . . . .
3. రువారు శ్రీబిన కంపిమల్లని . . .
4. ణ తవీరార్య బువివెమ నూర ధర్మము . . .

ONGOLE (2). (A.D. 1404–05 ?)

[Addanki. Telugu. From eastern wall of Rámaswámi temple.]

TRANSLATION.

Hail! On the 12th of the bright fortnight of Kártika . . . . . corresponding to the illustrious Ṣaka year 1326, Chinni Dontama Seṭṭi plastered the wall of the temple for the religious merit of his father and of his mother Bayya Sáni and of himself.

May it cause great prosperity!

NOTE.—Two small inscriptions on the maṇḍapam are not worth printing.

1. స్వస్తిశ్రీ శకవర్షంబులు ౧౩౭౬ అగు నేం (టి . . .) . . .

2. కార్తిక శు ౧౨బు చిన్నిదొంతుమ శెట్టి త (. . .) . . . .)

3. తమ తల్లి బయ్యసానికిన్ని తనకున్నను (. . . . .) . . . .

4. నగరికి గోడతాలు వడెను వరుంబని (. . . .) (మంగళంమ)

5. హా శ్రీ శ్రీ శ్రీ.

Ongole (3).

[Addanki. Telugu in Chálukyan character. In a backyard.]

Translation.

. . . . In the first year after the coronation of the king . . . . , having gone to war, the lord Bantaragu (Pánḍurangu?) having been appointed to the command of the army . . . .

Tribhuvanánkuṣa of Véginánḍu . . . . having planted a pillar (?), having captured the fortress Kiṭṭepudurgam,[1] (?)

Pánḍurangu Parama Mahéṣvara granted land sowable with 8 *puṭṭis* of seed in Dhammapuram (Dharmapuram) as charity to Ádhitya Bhaṭṭára. Whoever protects this will acquire the merit of a horse sacrifice.

1. . . . . . . భూపాలకుడ్డు

2. పట్టబుం గట్టి[న] ప్రథమబుం నేణ్డు బలావర్వ[ం]బో

---

[1] For Kiṭṭepudurgam we should perhaps read Kíranapuram.

(To face page 896.)

ONGOLE NO. 3.

3. ప్పగ బై లేచి శేన పట్టబుం గట్టిఞ్చి ప్రభు
4. బణ్ణరగు బణ్డాన సెమక్త పమ[వశో]బోయ
5. కోట్టబుం ల్పణ్డై్డు . . వేగింనాణ్టి గొండల్లము
6. శ్రీభువనాంకుశ [బాణ] నిల్పా కిశ్టైపుదుర్గ్గణబుం గ[డు]
7. బయల్సేసి కణ్డుకబ్బ జవహామిఞ్చి వచ్చి
8. పాణ్డురంగు పరమమాహేశ్వరణ్డు ఆదిత్యభటారని
9. కి ఇచ్చిన భూమి ఎనుబోది పుశ్లె అఘ్లు పట్టు నేల ద
10. న్మపురబున దమ్ములు [విని] రక్షిఞ్చినవారికి అశ్వ
11. మేదబుంన పలబుం అగు [॥*]

—

ONGOLE (4). (A.D. 1578–79.)

[Allúru. Telugu. Opposite Vírabhadra temple.]

TRANSLATION.

On Monday, the 12th of the dark fortnight of Márgasira of the year Bahudhánya, corresponding to the Śáliváhana Saka year 1500.

The leading people of Párvatipuram and the residents of the fifty-six countries with a joyful heart founded (méras) as *Múlavisam*[1] in the village of Ayyapalli which is the abode of the best of Brahmans for providing worship to Śrí Vírabhadra.

Those who do not pay (these méras) will incur the sin of killing a cow and a Brahman.

Pepper, gingelly-oil and frankincense are intended for lighting and fragrance.

Fees to be collected on head loads of grain and oil *per putti* . . . .

(The text is not thoroughly understood.)

[1] This phrase is not understood.

1. శాలివాహనశెఖవరు
2. షంబులు ౧౫౦౦ అనేటి బా
3. వు ధాన్య సంవత్సరు మాగశ
4. శిర బైశ ౧౨ సో శ్రీ పీరభద్ర
5. నికి నిలయింగిపులకు ఆయ్యే
6. పల్లి విప్రముఖ్యమైన చాయు
7. ముల సహృదయన పార్వతి
8. పురజన ముఖులన పలువురు
9. జనలును యిడంవారు యాం
10. బై ఆరుదేశాలవారు పొగించిన
11. మాలపీసాలు ఇయ్యనివారు
12. గోబ్రాంహ్మణ చంప్పిన పాతకంన
13. పోదురు మిర్యాలు నూనే గుగ్గిలం ఘూ
14. ప డీపాలకుం ముం
15. దాన్యాదులకు రసవగాణకు రు
16. తల మూటకు క ఖ ౧

Ongole (5).

[Allúru. Telugu. On stone in front of Aḍivi Rámálinga-swámi temple.]

Translation.

Malleṣwara Swámi, the self-existent, consecrated by Ṣrí Paraṣuráma, graciously protected Immánéni Kóṭi-lingam, the son of Bápayya.

For offerings and worship with the lamp eight *kucha-las* of dry land and one *gorru* of wet land where ¾ *puṭṭi* of seed can be sown were given in the fields of Allúru. Besides this mányam, the ryots who cultivate the sandy fields according to the deed of gift executed by them should give at the rate of one anna for every *kunṭa* of land of high assessment and at 4 pies for every *kunṭa* of land of low assessment. It is the duty of the Karnams to collect and give this amount. They must utilize it for the deity.

This is the truth.

1. శ్రీ పరశురామ ప్రతిష్ట
2. శ్రీ వుఝ్ఝలుడు మల్లేశ్వరస్వామి
3. వారు యిమ్మానేని బాప
4. య్యా కొమారుడు కోటి
5. లింగం హృధిస్థితులై రచ్చించెను
6. యీ స్వామి వారి నయివేద్యం దీ
7. పారాధనలకు అల్లూరు పొ
8. లంలో మెట్ట యెన్మది కుచ్చ
9. ళ్లు మాగాణి ఖం ౪ు విత్తులగొ
10. ట్రు మాన్యాగాక యినాంపాలం
11. సాగుబడి చేసేవారు వ్రాయించి యి
12. చ్చినదాన పత్రం ప్రకారం హెచ్చు
13. శిస్తుగల పయిర్ల భూమికి
14. కుంటకు అణాన్ను తగ్గు శిస్తు ప
15. యిర్లకు కుంటకు డబ్బున్ను
16. యీవలసినది కరణాలు జరిగిం
17. చి యిచ్చే నిర్ణయం యిందు స్వామి
18. కి జరిగించుదురు. సత్యము.

Ongole (6). (A.D. 1268–69 ?)

[Allúru. Telugu. In Amarésvara temple.]

Translation.

Hail! On the occasion of Uttaráyaṇa Sankránti corresponding to the Srí Ṣaka year 1190 for the religious merit of (Hail!) Ṣríman Mahámaṇḍalésvara Kaḷáráyanánṭa Singaḍadéva Mahárájulu, 240 *guṇṭas* of dry field were given to Kondavíḍu Kumára Svámidévaru of Ongole for providing worship, enjoyment and *nivédya* and 40 *guṇṭas* of wet land situated in the tank bed to Sámidévaru . . . to Nágésvaradévara . . . .

1. స్వస్తిశ్రీ శక
2. వర్షంబులు ౧౧౯౦
3. అగునేంటి ఉత్తరాయ
4. ణ సంక్రాంతి నిమిత్యంబున
5. స్వస్తి శ్రీ మన్మహామండలే
6. శ్వరుడు కళారాయనాంట
7. సింగడదేవ మహారాజు
8. లకు దమార్త్తముగాను
9. ఒంగోలని కొండవీడుని
10. కొమాఱస్వామి దేవరకు
11. అర్చ్చన భోగనివేద్యము
12. లకు నిచ్చిన వెలిపొలము
13. గుంటలు ౨౪౦ చెర్వు
14. సాకిపట్టు మడి గుంట
15. లు ౪౦ సామిదేవరకున్ను
16. నాగేశ్వర దేవరకున్ను
17. . . . .
18. . . . .

ONGOLE (7). (A.D. 1314–15.)

[Allúru. Telugu. On a big stone in the temple of Ishṭa Káméṣvara.]

TRANSLATION.

[One imprecatory verse.]

Hail! On Wednesday, the 10th of the bright fortnight of Chaitra of the year Ánanda, corresponding to 1236 of the illustrious and prosperous Ṣaka era, on the day of Vishvu Sankránti, Rudranáyakulu made a charitable gift to Ishṭa Káméṣvaramahádévara of Aṛalúru, consisting of kóru land wherein 15 *marttu* can be sown, to last as long as the sun and moon exist. This *vritti* is given as a *sarvamánya*. Whatever ryots cultivate these fields they will not have to pay tax. This is given for the religious merit of Pratáparudra Mahárája. Those who protect this (charity) will get religious merit. On the contrary, any one who thinks of injuring it, will be considered to have committed incest with his sister and to have allowed his wife to be covered by a donkey.

NOTE—See also O. 99.

స్వదత్తం । పరదత్తంవా । యోహరేతి । వసుంధరా
షష్టిర్వర్ష సహస్రాణి విష్టాయాం జాయతే క్రిమిః
స్వస్తిశ్రీ శుభ శకవర్షంబులు ౧౨౩౬ అగునేంటి ఆనం
దసంవత్సర చైత్రశుద్ధ ౧౦ బుధవారమునాండు
విషువు సంక్రాంతి దినమునప్పుడు అఱలూరి
శ్రీ ఇష్టకామేశ్వర శ్రీ మహాదేవరకు రుద్ర
నాయనింగారు చేసిన దమ్మర్దానం కొరునేలపెట్టిన మ
త్తూర్లువేసి ౧౫ ఆచంద్రతారార్కము ఈ వ్రిత్తి సర్వ
మాన్యము ఈచేలు ఏకాంపులు దున్నా

ను పుణ్యములేను ఈ ధర్మువు ప్రతాప
రుద్రదేవ మహారాజులకుం బుణ్యము
గానిచ్చినది ప్రతిపాలించినవారికిం బుణ్య
ము అస్లుగాక చెఱ్పందలంచినవాడు దమ
చెలియలిం తాంబోయిన వాండు పన
ఆడిది గాడిదలం దెంగ్గించినవాండు

Ongole (8). (A.D. 1317–18.)

[Allúru. Telugu. Inside the Ishṭa Kámésvara temple.]

Translation.

Hail! On Wednesday, the 10th of the dark fortnight of Srávaṇa of the year Pingaḷa, corresponding to 1239 of the illustrious and prosperous Saka era Gála Muddana Bóyuḍu and Dana Mádhava, in the presence of Pinnaya Venkangáru, the Reḍḍis of Aralúr, the karnams and all people, gave as charity 50 *kunṭas* and 1 *kunchaḍu* of ghee per month for lighting the lamp to Ishṭa Kámésvara of Aralúru, for the religious merit of Sríman Mahámaṇḍa-lésvara Pratápa Rudradéva Mahárájuluváru and will acquire merit. Those who protect this charity will acquire religious merit.

Note.—The modern village of Allúr according to this inscription was formerly called Aralúr.

స్వస్తిశ్రీ శుభ
శకవర్షంబులు
౧౨౩౯ అగునేం
టి పింగళ సంవత్సర
శ్రావణ బహుళ ౧౦.

బు స్వస్తిశ్రీ మన్మహా మ
ండలేశ్వర ప్రతాపరుద్ర
దేవమహారాజులకు
ంబుణ్యమ్ముగాను పిన్న
య వెంకంగారుఁను అఱ
లూరి రెడ్లున్ను కరణాలున్ను
సమస్త ప్రజానె అంగ్గను గా
లముద్దన బోయుండు డన
మాడవ్రులు పంబదికు
౫౦ కల్నును అఱలూరి ఇ
ష్ట కామేశ్వర దేవర
రికిని అఖండ్డ దీపమున
కు నెలకుం గుంచండు నె ఇ
వోసి పుణ్యము అనుభ
వించువాండు ఈ ధర్మ
వు ప్రతిపాలించ్చి పుణ్య
మునం బొంద్దువారు
పలికలు—

ONGOLE (9). (A.D. 1320–21.)

[Allúru. Telugu. On stone by the Ishṭa Kámésvara temple.]

TRANSLATION.

Hail! In the month of Áshádha of the year Rávudri corresponding to 1242 of the illustrious and prosperous Ṣálivahana Ṣaka era, Ṣríman Bamma Náyaningáru gave as *vritti* 400 *kunṭas* of dry land to the deity Ṣrí Ishṭa Kámésvara Mahádéva of Aṛalúr, and 100 *kunṭas* for worshipping, to last as long as the sun and moon exist to secure religious merit for (Hail !) Śrímau Mahámaṇḍaléśvara Pratápa Rudra Déva Mahárájulu. Let these two charities be maintained (?). We have given 100 *kuntas* of dry land as a *sarvamánya*.

NOTE.—The donor re-appears in the following inscription.

స్వస్తి శ్రీ
శుభ శాలివాహన
శకవర్షంబు
లు ౧౨౪౨ అగు
నేంటి రౌద్రి సంవ
త్సర ఆషాఢన
స్వస్తిశ్రీ మన్మహా
మండలేశ్వర ప్రతా
ప రుద్రదేవ మహా
రాజులకుం బుణ్యం
బుగాను శ్రీమత్
బమ్మయినాయ్నింగారు
ఆఱిలూరి శ్రీ ఇష్ట కా
మేశ్వర మహా దేవరకు
వ్రిత్తి ౪౦౦ గుంట
లు వెలిసెను అక్షన వ్రిత్తి
౧౦౦ గుంటలు ఆ చంద్రా
ర్కముగా నిచ్చిరి దమ్ము
వుంజంట . సెసెడివారు
రిపలిసెను ౧౦౦ గుంటలు
. . . సర్వమా
న్యములుంగ మాన్యము
ఇస్తిమి

ONGOLE (10). (A.D. 1320-21.)

[Allúru. Telugu. On the same stone by the temple of Ishṭa Káméṣvaradéva.]

TRANSLATION.

Hail! On the 11th of the bright fortnight of Ashádha of the year Ravudri, corresponding to the year 1242 of the illustrious and prosperous Ṣáliváhana Ṣaka era, Ṣrímat Bamaya Naiḍu Gáru gave to Ishṭa Káméṣvaradéva of Araḷúru 400 *kunṭas* as *vritti* and 100 *kunṭas* of dry land as *archana vritti*[1] for the religious merit of (Hail!) Ṣríman Mahámanḍaléṣvara Pratápa Rudradéva Mahárájulu to last as long as the sun and moon exist. He has given for (lighting) a lamp to the deity 50 *kunṭas* of dry land at Nannalapáḍu as a *sarvamánya* free from tax. To those who make this great gift will accrue the merit of performing many gifts, and the gift of cows; to those who injure (the charity) there will be hell and all kinds of misery.

[One imprecatory verse.]

First side.

స్వస్తిశ్రీ
శుభ శాలివహాన
శకవర్షంబు
లు ౧౨౪౨ అగు
నేటి రౌద్రి సంవం
త్సర ఆషాఢ శు
ద్ధ ౧౧
స్వస్తిశ్రీ మన్మహా

---

[1] Land granted for the purpose of conducting worship.

మండలేశ్వర ప్రతా
ప రుద్రదేవ మహా
రాజులకుం బుణ్యా
ముగాను శ్రీమతు
బమయ నాయ్నింగారు
అఱులూరి శ్రీ ఇష్టకా
మేశ్వర దేవరకు
. . వ్రిత్తి ౪౦౦ గుంట
లు వెలిసెను అర్చనవ్రిత్తి
౧౦౦ గుంటలు ఆ చంద్రా
ర్కముగా నిచ్చిరి దేవరకు
వుండెంటి సేసి దివానకు
కి వెలిసెను ౩౦ గుంటలు
నన్నలపాటందు సర్వమా
న్యము పంగమాన్యము

Second side.

ను నిచ్చిరి
ఈ మహాదానం
చెల్లించ్చిన దానా
లనేకం ఇట్ల గోవు
ల దానమును సేసిన
ఫలమును పొ
ందువారు ఉప
ద్రమ్ము సేసినవారి
కి నరకము సకలా
దిగ ద్రోహాలు
స్వదత్తాం పరదత్తాం
వా యోహరేతి

వసుంధరాం ష
ష్టి వరుష సహ
స్రాణి విష్ఠాయాం
o జాయతే క్రిమి

ONGOLE (11).

[Allúru. Telugu. On east side of enclosure of Ishṭa Kámésvara temple.]

TRANSLATION.

Hail! Ṣrímat Rudrama Náyaningáru presented . . . . for the cattle of Araḷúru . . . . and for the cattle of all people. Whoever upholds this charity will get unlimited merit. On Sunday, the 9th of the bright fortnight of Ásháḍha of the year Ánanda, Hail! Ṣríman Rudradéva Náyaningáru . . . . we have given . . . as a *sarvamánya* for (providing) offerings to Ishṭa Kámésvara.

Those who uphold this charity will acquire the merit of giving . . . . cows.

స్వస్తి శ్రీమతు రుద్రమ
నాయనంగారు అఱలూరి పసు
లకు . రిఁరి విడిచిం . . కాలా
సకును సర్వమైనవారి పసులకు
ఈ ధర్మం పాలించినవారికి అనంత పుణ్య
ము ఆనంద సంవత్సర ఆషాఢ శుద్ధ ౯
ఆదివారాం స్వస్తి శ్రీమతు రుద్రయనా ఇ
నింగారి . . . ర బెరము . . .
ఇష్ట కామేశ్వర దేవరకు నైవేద్యానకు సర్వమా

న్యముగ నిస్తిమి . . . సాలందున . డు . దిపా
నకుం చాయువారు ఈ ధర్మము పాలించినవారు
ననేక గోవుల . ఫలములు.

Ongole (12).

[Ammanabrólu. Telugu. From eastern pillar of mandapam of Chenna Késava temple. Not quite clear in parts.]

Translation.

On the 10th of the dark fortnight of Jyéshṭha of the year Yuva, Tiruvírunendu, Gudhani Nírigáru, and the *Kápus* of Ammanabrólu, Yádattiḍiráya, Dammála Pápandu, Yaranalúri Mallayya, Nallapáṭi Póllayya, the *motarfa*[1] *Kápus*, the karnams, the *sthalakarnams*, and Mélúri Anantayya, after making obeisance, issued this charitable edict to the deïties and barbers of Ammanabrólu.

Formerly *méras* used to be in the possession of Késava-déva in Ammanabrólu.

In addition to the following items granted by us the Kápus, namely, 10 *puṭṭis of sáluva* (?), 4 *túms* of dry, 4 (?) of land under the tank, the *Panta Reḍḍis*,[2] karnams and cultivators should give (méras) at 3 *túms* on every *puṭṭi* of produce, and 3 *puṭṭis* . . . . (?)

The ten *puṭṭis* of land that have been given should not be taxed. [What follows is not clear; the general

---

[1] This phrase is not understood. Does it mean the headmen charged with the collection of the motarfa tax?

[2] A sub-division of the Reḍḍi caste.

meaning is that, if objections are taken to the grant, Náráya Konḍóji is to see that it is carried out. The inscription ends with certain signatures.]

First side.

1. యువసంవత్సర జేష్ట
2. బ ౧౦ లు అమ్మనబ్రో
3. లు గ్రామకే పళ్లకు మం
4. గళకు తిరుపీరు నెండుః గు
5. ధనినీరిగారును అం
6. మ్మ నంబ్రోలిం
7. కొంఫ్రలు
8. యాదత్తిడి
9. రాయ, డం
10. మ్మాలపా
11. పండు, య
12. రనలూరి మల్లయ్య
13. నల్లబాటి పోల్లయ్య
14. మోతర్పా కొంపులు
15. కరణాలు స్థలకర
16. ణాలు మేలూరి అనం
17. త్తయ్యను దండంసమ
18. పించి ఇచ్చిన ధర్మ
19. శాసనము
20. అంమ్మనం
21. బ్రోలిగ్రామా
22. నను కేశవ
23. దేవమేర పూ
24. ప్వంసాగివ

25. ఛ్చేదికాం
26. ఫుణమయ్ను
27. మావల్లసా
28. భువ ఖ ౧౦ పూర్వనవెలిస్సే
29. ను ఖం ౦౪ న్ను తథాతిథిపె
30. ద్యైన చెర్వుణను |౪| లమంద్దు
31. నున్న యీ అధికారంసాగిం
32. చ్చినది నుంన్నూ కూడాను పం
33. డ్డై పుట్లపంటకు ఖం ౦ ౩
34. పంటరెడ్లున్న కరణా
35. లు వ్యవసాయాన్ను పూ
36. ర్వాణన సాగివచ్చేటట్టు ౩ స్తాను
37. నున్న తథాతిథినపూర్వం
38. సాగించినదినిగాన్ను పం
39. ధారంపది పుట్లపంప్పు
40. కూడుదుమున్న

Second side.

41. యిది పది పుట్లపంప్పు
42. ను పంగమును లేవు ఇతరులు
43. ఎవరు కీడాడి ఓనికి
44. లెకర్ సేసిమే
45. ర పెట్టివా
46. రము అ
47. ట మీదా
48. చక కరణాల వ్యవసాయం
49. వల్ల పదిపుట్లపంటకు తూ
50. మెండ లెఖను పూర్వంసడచి
51. న పీంన్ని హరిస్టిమి అవి

52. న్ని. పుట్టిపుట్లుపెచ్చునవుర్వ
53. తకుకానను కీడాడి జనికిని
54. వారుకేరమాడినా పు
55. త్రకంగాను కాంపులు
56. కరణాలు అందరిగా
57. లాను పూర్వం సాకు
53. మాట్లాడెడివారు అడ్డం
59. కిపెట్టెట్టు నడుపు
60. వారు యేమికీడాడిన
61. ను నారయకొంచో'జు న
62. డుపువారు
నడుమసాగించ్చి యిస్తిమిగా
న ఆచంద్రతారార్కంగాను నైవేద్యాలుకా
అవధరించెది యప్పుడానాం
యప్వరుగాన్యాను గంగకత
నుగోవుబ్రాహ్మణిని వధశేసి
న పాపానబోవువావారు త
మ తండ్రులను వారణా
శిలో చంపిన పా
పానం బోవువారు
తిమ్మయ గంగయ్య
వ్రాలు సర్వయవ్రాలు
అయ్యగాని

Third side.

వ్రాలు చెన్నయ్య వ్రా
లు పెద్దయ్యవ్రా
లు

ONGOLE (13).

[Ammanabrólu. Telugu. Opposite Ṣiva temple.]

TRANSLATION.

Salutation be to the glorious Raghunáyaka (Ráma)!

V. 1. Salutation be to Ṣambhu (Ṣiva) who is charming, as with a *chámara*, with the moon which kisses his lofty head, and who is the main pillar of the creation of the city of the three worlds.

V. 2. May the staff-like tusk of Hari, who assumed in sport the form of a Boar—resting on which the earth with Mount Méru as its apex resembled an umbrella—protect you.

Vs. 3 and 4. May that descendant of Yadu, who though without support is of immense size,—in regard to whom the moon is the growing nail, the celestial tree is the line of the fingers of the hand, the cow of plenty is this nectar-like speech, the desire-fulfilling stone is the eye, the line of clouds is the incomparable hue of the body, and the ocean of nectar is the mercy—protect you always.

V. 4. Náráyana, in a palace of gems, resembling the Ṣvétadvípa where celestial trees abode, in the milk ocean, is adored by Sanaka and other sages, Garuda and the lord of serpents. His glory is eternal bliss and knowledge and is supreme (without a second). Being the soul of all, and the origin of truth, he is eternally resplendent; and his form is characterized by the lotus which is the face of Ráma.

V. 5. From his navel-lotus was formerly born the creator (Brahma) from whom the world was created. His mind-born son was Vasishṭha, the best of sages

His son was Ṣakti, the store-house of good precepts, the ocean of compassion. His son was the sage Paráṣara of pure intellect, devotee of Vishnu, thereby excelling all.

In his exalted *gótra* were born Vyása, the gem of preceptors, the Brahmans, Ṣuka and others, granters of the merit of the scriptures which deserve to be praised.

V. 6. . . . . . Then shines king Singa who was like a lion . . . . to the elephants . . . . ., who was possessed of might resembling that of . . . .

[V. 7. The verse as it stands makes no sense. Its purport seems to be that Singárya was esteemed by the Carnatic kings.]

V. 8. His son was Bhava, the prince of ministers, who acquired victory by polity; who made king Apa a dependant on his feet by means of the profusion of the splendour of his fame which shines like the milk ocean and the autumnal cloud, who made all the elephants of the cardinal points shine like Indra's elephant, able to read the thoughts of others, of illuminating speech. His son was the glorious king Rámachandra, who was as handsome as Indra's son (Jayanta), who by the fierce sword resembling Ráhu destroyed the moon and the sun of the fame and valour respectively of his enemies, who was eminent in might, who in valour resembled lighted fire, who in great fortitude resembled the mountain of gems (Méru), who was always a *Kámadhénu* (cow of plenty) to his relations.

Ṣrí Ráma—

Devoted to Dharma, who had destroyed the heap of his enemies' arrows . . . . . . army, whose . . .

was possessed of Ganesa's strength, who resembled the son of the daughter of ocean (Káma) devotee of Rághava —Mádhava.

He, king Ráma, married a wife named Telingama who resembled Anasúyá in virtue, of radiant speech, the earth (abode) of fame, sprung from the Lohita race, of great splendour, daughter of the Gangárya race, famed in the three worlds for chastity.

The ocean which was Ráma bore on the Ganges which was Talingama five sons who resembled the celestial trees (5), liberal to the gods (scholars).

Timma Malla Suréndra

Bháskara Chamúpati . . . . .

Bha . . nárya

The worshipper of the feet of Srí Raghuráma, the benefactor of intelligent men, serene, whose speech resembled nectar towards sages, calm.

Srí Timma . . famed as Kártavírya.

Srí China Timma Mantritilaka was peerless.

The brothers China Timma and Bháskara Chamúnátha possessing the splendour of Ráma and Lakshmana, praiseworthy like Ráma and Krishna, possessed of glory, flourish as if they were the sole fortresses to the garden which is the excellent town of Kondavídu.

Like the párijáta among celestial trees, like Gándíva (Arjuna) among the five Pándavas, he among them . . . .

(Incomplete.)

NOTE.—We have not been able to identify these chiefs.

1. श्रीर[घु]नायक[।।*]

2. नमस्तुंग सिरश्चुं[बि]-

3. चंद्रचामर चारवे ।
4. त्रैलोक्य नगरारंभ-
5. मूलस्तंभाय शंभ-
6. वे । [१*] हरेर्लीलावरा-
7. हस्य दंष्ट्रादं तस्स-
8. पातुवः । हेमाद्रिक-
9. लशा यत्र धात्री छत्र-
10. श्रीयं ददौ ॥ [२*] शुभ्रांशु
11. :[शि]खरोत्कररसुरतरुः श्री
12. पंचशारवांगुळिः [श्रेणी]
13. [कामग] नी सुधा[सु]म-
14. . . चिंत्तामणी द[श्यतां]
15. श्रीकादंबिन्यतुलां-
16. गकांतिरमृतां भो-
17. धिः कृपायस्यत्रः शश्व-
18. त्पातु स यादव
19. [श्चि]रम[ना] धारोप्युदा-
20. राकृतिः । [३*] क्षीरा[ब्धौनतक]-
21. ल्पपादप सित द्वीपेनु-
22. रूपे मणिप्रासादे सन-
23. कादि योगि खगराट्
24. नानाधिपाराधितः । सो
25. व्या[न्यं]थ चिर[द्यु] तिर्य
26. [दु*] भवः(।) सर्व्वात्मकः . .
27. नित्यं भाति रमात्र-

28. घृ [जयप] ताकारोहि-
29. नारायणः । २ । तंना
30. भीनलिनाभिजात . . . .
31. रातिकर्ता जग[ज्जा]ते मा
32. नसनंदनो सयमिरा
33. द श्रेष्ठो वसिष्ठोभवत् ।
34. शक्तिः सूक्तिनिधिः कृपां[बु]
35. धिरभूत्तस्यात्मज [स्रासु]
36. धीरासीद्विष्णुपरः पराश
37. रमुनिः सर्पातिशायी
38. ततः । गोत्रे तस्य महो
39. न्नते गुरुमणिर्व्या
40. से शुकादिद्विजः स्तो . .
41. . . . म सत्फल प्र-

Second side.

Some lines lost.

1. लागा . . . . . .
2. र्व्वारण गा[ढ]
3. ताप . नय
4. . . . पंचाननं
5. दि . द्यशा जातो
6. भाति नृसिंह
7. साम्य विभ[वो]
8. संग्गेन शिग्गाधि
9. पः । ९ कर्णाट

10. भूपतिलकै क
11. थि तात्मवंशो
12. पूर्वाक्षितीश
13. हितमंत्रि
14. वसिष्ट चर्ये । शिं
15. गार्य[मौ]नि
16. सुधियस्थिरनी
17. तिकार्य धुर्या
18. विचार्य कविता
19. : किलमंत्रि व
20. र्याः । . । तस्या
21. सीत्तनयो न[यो*]
22. र्जित जयः [पा]
23. दाश्रितापोधि
24. पः क्षीरांभो
25. निधि शारदां
26. बुधलसत्कीर्त्ति
27. प्रभापूर्त्ति
28. पः । दिद्रं
29. त्ति प्रवरान्[स]
30. दाश्रमु[ख]
31. रानेवाखिलान्
32. भासयन् भा
33. व[ज्ञ]: प्रति
34. भाति भासुर

35. वचा श्रीभो .

36. मंत्रीश्वरः ।

37. सूनुरतस्य

38. सुरेंद्रसू

39. नु सुषमः स्वा .

Some lines damaged.

Third side.

1. . . . .

2. नारातियशः प्रता-

3. पसितरुग्भानु प्रभा-

4. वोंन्नतः । तेजोदीप्त कृ-

5. शानुरुंन घृति श्री

6. रत्न सानुर्ग्ग . वं

7. दी वांधव कामधेनु-

8. रनिशं श्रीर[ां]मदं

9. डाधिपः [२] सधौत्रा

10. . . . . . .

11. . . . .

12. राढया शतधर्मगो

13. चरपरो लूनारि बा

14. णोत्करः (।) सेना , हि-

15. कड्गणाथिप बलोपा-

16. थोधि भूनंदनः श्री

17. राम प्र . . .

18. नुभजि[त] श्रीराघ

19. वोमाधवौ । ८ । भा
20. ष्पौ . . . . . .
21. . . . . . . गुणशा
22. [खा]नसूयां स्फु
23. रद्धार्णां लोहि
24. तगोत्र संभवय
25. शः क्षोणिमुदार
26. श्रियं गंगाया
27. न्वयवर्द्धिनीं त्रि
28. वनप्रख्यात साध्वी
29. पदां पत्नीपुर्य . .
30. यमदा[त्ते]लंगम
31. नाम्नीं स[रा] [मा*] धिपः । [९*] ।
32. रामाध्विरा . तिलं
33. गमांब्बर निम्नगा
34. यां पंच्चामरद्ट
35. मसमान् सुमनोव
36. दान्यान् पुत्रान

Fourth side.

1. सूत . . . .
2. यति मम[ल्ल]
3. सूरेंद्र भास्क[र]
4. चमूपति भ .
5. नार्यान् । १० । . .
6. श्रीरघुराम पा

7. दभ्रजनः [क्षेमा]
8. करो धीमतां
9. शांतः शांत[सु]
10. छानुकारिन .
11. चाःदांत . .
12. रांतरः । श्री[तिं]
13. मोघ्यणच . .
14. . वतयु . .
15. गतो कार्थवी . .
16. ति श्रीचिनतिंम
17. मंत्रितिलक .
18. त्राद्वीतीय्यो
19. सः । ११ । कि वे
20. रभावसोदरी प्र
21. तिभा तापु . .
22. . तले सौभ्रा . .
23. तराम लक्ष्मण
24. विभूतिं रामकृ
25. ष्णाविति । संस्तु त्यौ
26. चिनतिंम्म भास्कर
27. चमूनाथौ स ना
28. थौश्रिया वर्धते
29. वरकोंडवीडु नग
30. रोद्यानैक दुर्ग्गवि
31. वा ॥ १२ ॥ तेषु द्यु

32. वृक्षेष्विव पारिजा

33. तः सगांडिवः [पं]

34. [च]सु पांडवेषु ।

35. . . . .

Incomplete.

ONGOLE (14).

[Bollapalli. Telugu. On a boundary stone.]

TRANSLATION.

The pillar planted after walking round the boundaries of the village of Yasali otherwise called Bollápalli and Konḍa Munjalúru.

1. యసలిగ్రా
2. రిప్రతినా
3. మ బోల్లా ప
4. ల్లి కొండము
5. ంజలూరి పొ
6. లిమేర నడచి వె
7. ట్టిన కంభం

ONGOLE (15). (A.D. 1545–46.)

[Bollapalli. Telugu. In front of Ánjanéya temple.]

TRANSLATION.

Salutations be to the illustrious Rámánuja.

Hail! On Thursday, the 12th day of the dark fortnight of Áshádha of the year Viṣvávasu, corresponding to the year 1467 of the illustrious, victorious and prosperous Ṣálivábana Ṣaka era, while Ṣrímat Rájádhi Rája

Rája Paraméṣvara, Ṣrí Víra Pratápa, Ṣrí Sadáṣivadeva Maháráyulu, seated on the diamond throne at Vijayanagar, was ruling the kingdom of the earth, he granted with libation of water and gift of gold the village named Bollapalli in Addanki *ṣíma* attached to Kondavídu *rájyam* as an *agraháro*, to last in perpetuity as long as the sun and moon endure, ... to Kóṭi Tiruvengaḷanáthayya, the son of Ṣrímat Táḷapáka Tirumalayyagáru, who is the establisher of the two schools of the Vedánta.

[One imprecatory verse.]

May it cause prosperity!

Note.—See also Nos. 21 and 141. Kóṭi stands for Kónéṭi apparently.

1. శ్రీమతే రామానుజాయనమః। స్వస్తిశ్రీ
2. జయాభ్యుదయ శాలివాహన శకవర్షంబులు
3. ౧౪౬౭ అగు నేటి విశ్వావసు సంవత్సర ఆషా
4. ఢ బ ౧౨ గు। శ్రీమదుభయవేదాంత ప్రతిష్ఠాపనా
5. చార్యులైన తాళ్పాక తిరుమలయ్యంగారి కొ
6. మారుండు కోటితిరువెంగళనాథయ్యంగారికి
7. శ్రీమద్రాజాధిరాజరాజపరమేశ్వర శ్రీవీర ప్ర
8. తాప శ్రీ వీరసదాశివదేవమహారాయలు విజ
9. యనగరమందు వజ్రసింహాసనాశీనుండై పృధ్వీ
10. సామ్రాజ్యముచేయుచు కొండవీటి రాజ్యా
11. నకు చెల్లివచ్చె అద్దంకిశీమలోని బొల్లాపల్లి అనే
12. గ్రామమును హిరణ్యోదక దానధారాపూర్వ
13. కముగాను ఆచంద్రార్కస్థాయిగాను ధార
14. పోసిఇచ్చిన అగ్రహారము॥ దానపాలన యో
15. ర్మధ్యే దానాచ్ఛ్రేయోను పాలనం దానాత్స్వ
16. ర్గమవాప్నోతి పాలనాదచ్యుతంపదం॥
17. శ్రీ శ్రీ శ్రీ ం జేయను॥

ONGOLE (16). (A.D. 1271–72?)

[Bollapalli. Telugu. Fallen stone opposite Agasthéṣvara temple.]

TRANSLATION.

Hail! On Saturday, the full moon day, under the Krittiká *nakshatra* in the month of Kártika, corresponding to the Ṣaka year 1193, Ṣrímat Svayapa Náyaka dedicated (this) to Agastéṣvara Mahádevara.

[One imprecatory verse.]

1. మల్లికార్జు   న ఫలము
2. స్వస్తి సకవరుషంబులు ౧
3. ౧౯౩ గునేంటి కార్తికమా
4. సంబున పున్నమ క్రిత్తికా
5. నక్షత్రము సనేశ్వరవా
6. రమున శ్రీమతు శ్వ
7. య్యపనాయకుండు
8. అగస్తేశ్వర మహాదే
9. వరకర్పించిన వారము
10. స్వదత్తం పరదత్తం
11. వా ఒ హ రేపివసుంధ
12. రా షష్టివర్ష సహస్రాణి
13. విష్ఠాయాం జాయతే క్రిమిః

ONGOLE (17). (A.D. 1218–19?)

[Bollavárapáḍu (hamlet Daiválarávúru). In front of Chenna Késava temple. From line 22, a second inscription begins. The meaning is doubtful in parts.]

TRANSLATION.

(1) Hail! During the illustrious Śaka year 1140 Ṣríman Mahámaṇḍalésvara Kákatiyya Gaṇapatidéva Mahárájulu, having seen the old inscription and having learnt that the agraháram had been given to Brahmans, gave Dayyálarévúru (Káḍiveṭṭi Chitri Káṇḍa?) situated in Kammanáḍu.

Boundaries are—

On the east—Renkulakunṭa (pond). On the south-east—Bammanipáḍu and Mrontavikunṭa (pond).

On the south— . . . . river bed.

On the south-west—Mandikalakunṭa (pond).

On the west—Baireḍḍikunṭa (pond) and north of it Bulumaḍikunṭa (pond).

On the north-west—Machavárikunṭa (pond).

On the north—Durgamúlakunṭa (pond).

On the north-east—Two ponds.

Those who obstruct this will be regarded as having killed 1,000 cows on the Ganges, as having committed murder at Benares and having eaten . . . . from the skull of their eldest sons.

(A.D. 1227–28?)

(2) Hail! On the year 1149 of the illustrious Śaka era Hail! Ṣríman Mahámaṇḍalésvara Mallidéva Chóḍa Mahárajulu, whose lotus feet are adorned (by the prostrations

of) all illustrious rulers of the earth, to wit, the Vilóchana, Trilóchana and others, and who shines like a gem in the family of Karikála who built the dam[1] across the Kávéri, knowing (?) . . . . gave Takkellapáḍu and old Dayyálarévúru situated in Kammanáḍu.

[One imprecatory verse.]

1. స్వస్తిశ్రీ శకవర్షంబులు ౧౧౮౦
2. శ్రాహిశ్రీమన్మహా మండలేశ్వర
3. కాకతియ్య గణపతిదేవమహా
4. రాజులు అనాదిశాసనము సూ
5. చి కమ్మనాంటిలోని దయ్యాల
6. రెవ్రూరు కాడివెట్టి చిత్రికాండ
7. విప్రాగ్రహారంబు అనాదిగా నెటి
8. ంగిచ్చితిమి త . . తూర్పు-
9. న రెంకులకుంటయు ఆగ్నేయ
10. మునఁ బమ్మనిపాడును ప్రోంత్త
11. (వ) కుంటయు దక్షిణంబున
12. . . కుల్య నైరిత్యమునమండిక
13. లకుంట పడుమటం బైతెడ్డికుం
14. ట దానియుత్తరమునం బులుసు
15. డి కుంట వాయవ్యమున మచ్చ
16. వారి కుంట ఉత్తరమున దుర్గమూ
17. లకుంట ఈశాన్యమున రెండికుంటలు
18. ఈ ధర్మమునకు యవ్వరుదప్పినాను
19. గంగకటుత వేయిగవిలలంబొడ్చి
20. నవారు వారణాసివచ్చినవారు పె
21. ద్దకొడుకు కపాలమునం గుడిచినవా

---

1 See note on p. 1250 about this.

22. రు స్వస్తిశ్రీ శకవర్షంబులు ౧౧౭౭ శ్రా
23. హి స్వస్తిచరణసరోరుహా విహిత వి
24. లోచన త్రిలోచన ప్రముఖాఖిల పృద్వీశ్వ
25. రకారిత కావేరీ తీరకరికాల
26. కులరత్నప్రదీపాహిత శ్రీ
27. మన్మహా మండలేశ్వర మల్లి
28. దేవచోడ మహారాజులుకమ్మ
29. నాంటిలోని తకెఱ్లపాడు అనా
30. ది దయ్యాలరేవూరి ప్రవిష్ట
31. ముగా నెఱింగి ఇచ్చితిమి ॥
32. స్వదత్తం పరదత్తం వాయో
33. హరేతివ సుంధ్ధరాష్ఠి
34. వర్ష సహస్రాణి ః ష్టా
35. యాం జాయతే క్రిమి॥

Ongole (18). (A.D. 1155–56?)

[Bollavárapáḍu (hamlet Daiválarávúru). Telugu. Under tank bund to west of village.]

Translation.

Hail! In the Śaka year 1077 on (the occasion of) Vishama Sankránti, all the elders (*mahájanas*) of the illustrious Dayyálareyúru gave ten *puṭṭis* of land in the fields of the deity Rámésvara to Mádajiyya who is the *sthánapati* (temple servant) of the temple of Śiva for (providing) worship, offering, lighting, enjoyments and decorations for Rámésvaradéva, to last as long as the moon and sun endure. Those who uphold this will acquire the merit of making a gift of a crore of cows;

those who do not maintain it will be regarded as having killed one thousand tawny cows on the banks of the Ganges and as having eaten from the skull of their eldest son.

1. స్వస్తి శకవర్షమ్ములు ౧౦౭౫
2. శ్రాహి శ్రీమద్దయాల
3. రెయూరి అశేషమహాజెన
4. మ్ము విషువసంక్రాన్తిని రామేశ్వర
5. దేవరకుం బూజనివేద్య దీపభోగ
6. రాగము లకు శివాల్యముస్థాన ప
7. తిమైన మాడజియ్యకు దేవరకునాచం
8. ద్రాకర్ణముగానిచ్చిన భూమి రామేశ్వర . . .దేవరహా
9. లమ్ము పకర ఖ౧౦ దీని నడపినవా
10. రు గోకోటిదానమ్ము సెసిన ఫలంమ్మునుబొందు
11. దురు నడపనివారు గంగకత్త వేయు కవిల
12. లంబొడ్చినవారె వారణాసినిప్రచ్చినవారు
13. పెద్దకొడుకు కపాలమున కుడ్చినవారు

ONGOLE (19). (A.D. 1153–54?)

[Bollavárapáḍu (hamlet Daiválaravúru). Telugu. Under the tank bund.]

TRANSLATION.

Hail! On Vishama Sankránti, corresponding to the Ṣaka year 1075, in the reign of Hail! Ṣríman Mahá-máṇḍaléṣvara Tribhuvanadéva Chóḍa Mahárája, on whose lotus feet the eyes of Vilóchana, Trilóchana and all other kings of the earth are set, who is the jewelled lamp of the race of Karikála by whom the dam[1] of the Kávéri was built, and who is a goad to wicked princes, all the mahájanas of Dayyálaréyúru which is the abode of men who have practised yama, niyama, svádhyáya, dhyána, samádhi, and are endowed with good qualities, and which is situated in Kammanáḍu issued this edict, and presented the land formerly given to Madhácharya to this Ráméṣvaradéva . . . .

We shall maintain this as long as the moon and sun endure . . . .

(Those who do not uphold this charity) will be regarded as having killed a tawny cow near the Ganges and as having killed at Benares.

[One imprecatory verse.]

1. స్వస్తిశ్రీశకవర్షంబులు ౧౧౭౫ గు శ్రా . . . . . .
2. విషువ సంక్రాన్తిని స్వస్తిచరణ సరోరుహ లిహిత
3. విలోచన త్రిలోచన ప్రముఖాఖిల ప్రిథ్వీశ్వరకారిత
4. కావేరితీర కరికాలకులరత్న ప్రదీపాహిత (కుమా)
5. రాంకుశ శ్రీమన్మహా మండలేశ్వర త్రిభువన
6. దేవచోడ మహారాజుల ఎంలికంగమ్మనాటిలోని (య)
7. మనియమస్వాధ్యాయధ్యాన పారీణమేనాను
8. పసమాధిహ్యోమాదిశీలగుణ సంపన్నులైన .
9. దయ్యాలరేయూరిశాసనము అశేషమహా (జన)
10. ము ఈ రామేశ్వదేవరకు సమర్పణం
11. సెసిన ముదాచార్యుర్గాన . . . .
12. పూర్వ్వనను సేసిఇచ్చిన భూమి . . .
13. నాచంద్రార్కర్కముసడపంగలవారు . .
14. గంగకటు (త).

---

[1] See note on p. 1250.

15. గవిలం (బొ)
16. డిచినవారు .
17. వారణాసిం
18. చంప్పినవారు .
19. స్వదత్తాం పర
20. దత్తాం వాయో
21. హరేతి వసుం
22. ధ్ధరాం షష్టివర్షస
23. సహస్రాణి విష్టాయాం
24. జాయతేక్రిమి

ONGOLE (20).

[Bollavárapáḍu (hamlet Daiválarávúru). Telugu.
Opposite Chintalamma temple.]

TRANSLATION.

Hail! All the elders (*mahájanas*) of the illustrious Dayyálaréyúru, which is endowed with all eulogistic titles, gave a field of one *puṭṭi* to Pattél Káṭana for conducting the worship and offerings of this goddess. Whoever does not continue this as long as the moon and sun endure will be regarded as having killed one thousand tawny cows on the banks of the Ganges.

Hail! For the merit of Ṣrímat Yéravaráti Muduvéṇayya, Néyikánu Bóyunḍu granted a field of one *puṭṭi* for the offerings of this goddess.

Whoever . . . . this . . . .

1. స్వస్తి సమస్త
2. ప్రశస్తి సహిత
3. శ్రీ మదయ్యాలరే

4. యూరి అశేషమహా
5. జనమును ఈదేవిపూ
6. జనివేద్యములు నడపు
7. మని పట్టెలు కొటనకిచ్చి
8. నచెను ఖ ౧ దీని నైవ్యం
9. రైనా నా చంద్రార్క౯ంమునడపరేని
10. గంగకట్ట వేయిగవిలలంబొడిచినవారు.

Second side.

1. స్వస్తి శ్రీమతు పరపతా
2. తిముదువేణయకు
3. ధమ్మ౯వుంగా నేయికొంను
4. బొయుండుదెవతకు
5. నివేద్యమునంకిచ్చినచె
6. ను ఖ ౧. దినినైవ్వతెని . . .
7. ముష్థాయిగా నడపునది

ONGOLE (21). (A.D. 1545–46.)

[Búdaváḍa. Telugu. In front of Gópálaswámi temple.]

TRANSLATION.

Salutation be to the illustrious Rámánuja!

Hail! On Thursday, the 12th of the bright fortnight of Áshádha of the year Viṣvávasu, corresponding to 1467 of the illustrious, victorious and prosperous Śáliváhana Ṣaka era, while Ṣrímat Rájádhirájá, Rájaparaméṣvara, Ṣrí Vírapratápa, Ṣrí Sadáṣivadéva MáhAráyulu was seated on the jewelled throne at Vijayanagar and was ruling the kingdom of the earth, he granted the village of Mallavaram situated in Addanki *síma*, attached to Koṇḍavíḍu *síma*, in perpetuity to last as long as the sun and moon, with gift of gold and libation of water, as an *agrahára* to Chinanna Tiruvengaḷanátha, the son of Ṣrímat Táḷapáka Tirumalayangáru, who is the establisher of the path of the vedas.

[One imprecatory verse.]

May it cause great prosperity!

NOTE.—The donees of this and of No. (15) are apparently brothers. In No. (15) the phrase Kondaviḍu *rájyam* appears, whereas here *síma* is used probably by mistake.

1. శ్రీమతే రామానుజాయనమః॥ స్వ
2. స్తి శ్రీ జయాభ్యుదయ శాలివాహన శకవర్షం
3. బులు ౧౪౮౭ అగు నేంటి విశ్వావసు
4. సంవత్సర ఆషాఢ శు ౧౨ రు॥ శ్రీమతు వే
5. ద మార్గ ప్రతిష్ఠాచార్యులైన తాళపాక
6. తిరుమలయ్యంగారి కుమారుండు
7. చినంన తిరువెంగళనాథునికి శ్రీమతురా
8. జాధిరాజ రాజపరమేశ్వర వీరప్రతాప
9. వీరసదాశివదేవ మహారాజులు విజ
10. యనగరమందు రత్నశింహాసనా శీనుం
11. డై పృథివిసాంమ్రాజ్యము శే
12. యుచున్న కొండవీటిశీమకు
13. చెల్లివచ్చె అద్దంకిశీమలోని ప
14. ల్లవరంఅనే గ్రామము సహిర
15. ం ణ్యోదక దానధారాపూర్వక
16. ముగాను ఆచంద్రార్కంము
17. గాను దారపోశి సమర్పించిన
18. అగ్రహారము॥ దానపాల నం
19. నోర్మధ్యే దానశ్రేయో
20. ను పాలనం

21. దానాత్స్వర్గమ
22. వాప్నోతిపా
23. లనా దచ్యుత
24. ం పదం । మ
25. ంగళమహా
26. శ్రీ శ్రీ శ్రీం జే
27. యనూ॥

ONGOLE (22).

[Búdaváḍa. Telugu. From fallen stone in an inám land.]

TRANSLATION.

The field given as *vritti* to Ṣrí Pangalúri Bhíméṣvara. Whosoever says "no" to this *vritti*, will incur the sin of killing a cow and a Brahman on the banks of the Ganges.

Ṣrí! Ṣrí! Ṣrí!

1. శ్రీ పంగులూరి బీమేశ్వరు
2. నికి ఇచ్చిన వ్రిత్తిచేను ఇవ్రి
3. త్తిచేనికియవ్వరు లేదు అన్నా
4. ను గంగ్గకతట గోవుబ్రాంహ్మనిం
5. జంపిన పాపానంబోవు
6. వారూ శ్రీ శ్రీ శ్రీ

Ongole (23). (A.D. 1533–34.)

[Chandalúru. Telugu. From stone against wall of Chennakéṣava temple.]

Translation.

May there be prosperity!

Hail! On Thursday, the 11th of the bright fortnight of Kártika of the year Vijaya, corresponding to the year 1456 of the illustrious, auspicious and prosperous Ṣáli-váhana Ṣaka era, while Ṣríman Mahámaṇḍaléṣvara, Rájádhirája, Rájaparaméṣvara, Ṣrí Vírapratápa Achchuta-déva Maháráyulu, seated on the diamond throne at Vijayanagar was ruling the earth, Mallarusayyaváru, the son of Chennékanṭi Viṣvanáthayya, of the Ṣrívatsa *gótra*, of the Ápastambha *sútra* and of the Yajus *sákha*, having performed the consecration and marriage of Kéṣavanátha of Chandalúru village which is in Konḍavíḍu *durgam* which he (Achchutadéva) was pleased to grant to the prime minister (*mahápradháni*) Bácharusayyaváru and which is in Addanki *ṣíma* which Bácharusayyaváru was pleased to grant to us, for providing decorations and sacred food for the deity,

granted with libation of water and *aksha* (consecrated rice) lands to the south of the village Chandalúru, to the east of Rávinútalapáḍu tank, to the east of the village . . . . and also one *puṭṭi* . . . . . of lands . . . . in Késaripáḍu.

Therefore let the deity be pleased to enjoy the produce thereof in perpetuity as long as the sun and moon last.

[One imprecatory verse.]

Ṣrí!

We have granted a field of one *kuchchela* as a *sarva-mányam* to Káṣivírabhaktu, who performed the above ceremonies.

Who have granted a field of 2 *kuchchalas* to Tirumalu Sarva Sánindási, the dancing girls of the Tiruvíthi sacred street, who do service to this deity. Let them therefore enjoy it in perpetuity as long as the sun and moon endure and live happily. Those who violate this charity will be regarded as having killed cows and Brahmans.

Ṣrí !

1. శుభమస్తు ॥ స్వస్తి శ్రీ శుభశాసనాభ్యుదయ శాలివా
2. హన శకవర్షంబులు ౧౪౫౬ అగు నేంటి విజయ
3. సంవత్సర కార్తీక బ౧౧ గు శ్రీమన్మహా మండలే
4. శ్వర రాజాధిరాజ రాజ పరమేశ్వర శ్రీవీర ప్ర
5. తాప అచ్చుతదేవ మహారాయలుంగారు విజయ
6. నగరమందు వజ్రసింహాసనా రూఢులై స్వ
7. స్థి రాజ్యం శేయుచుండ శ్రీమహాప్రధానులైన
8. బాచరుసయ్యవారికి। పాలించ్చుయీ నవధరించ్చి
9. న కొండవీటి దుర్గంలోని। బాచరుసయ్యవారు
10. మాకు యీ నవధరించిన అందంకి శీమలోని
11. చందలూరిగ్రామం కేశవనాధని వివాహ ప్రతిష్టచే
12. శి దేవునికి అంగ్గరంగ్గ వైభవాలకున్ను అమృతపళ్ల
13. కున్ను శ్రీవత్సగోత్రం ఆపస్తంభసూత్రం యజుశా
14. ఖాద్యాయులైన బెన్నేకంటి విశ్వనాధయ్య కొమాళ్లు
15. మల్లరుసయ్యవారు చందలూరిపాలాన ఇచ్చిన క్షేత్రం
16. గ్రామం దక్షిణపుదిక్కున రావినూంతులచెరువుకు తూ

ర్పున

17. నాను పూరితూర్పునాను కూడాను కేసరిపాటిని క్షే

త్రం ౪౧ అక్షరా

18. దక ధారాపూర్వకముగాను ఇస్తిమిగాన అందుఫలః ఆచ

19. ంద్రాకర్ణస్థాయిగాను అనుభవించి ఆపధరించుడి॥ దాన
పాలన

20. యోర్మధ్యే దానాచ్ఛ్రేయోనుపాలన । దానాస్వర్గ
మవాప్నోతి పా

21. లనా దచ్యుతంపదం॥ శ్రీ॥ వుభయపనులను [illegible]శిన కాశీ పీ

22. రాభక్తునికి వొకకుచ్చెలచేను సర్వమాన్యంగాను ఇస్తిమి॥

23. యీదేవుని శావశేశే తిరువీధిసాంస్లు తిరుమలు సర్వ

24. సానిందాశికి ఒ రెండుకుచ్చళ్ల చేనుయిస్తిమిగాన ఆచం
ద్రా

25. కర్ణస్థాయిగాను అనుభవించి బ్రతుకేది । యీధర్మానకుం
డప్పి

26. నవారు గో బ్రాహ్మనికించంప్పినవారు॥ శ్రీ ॥

ONGOLE (24).

[Chandalúru. Telugu. From garbha wall of Chenna-késava temple.]

TRANSLATION.

. . . . for providing worship and enjoyments to the deity. 400 *kuṇṭas* measured with a pole of 12 bárlu (fathoms); 600 *kuṇṭas* to Tirupani Dási; for *Sáni*[1] *mányam* 2,000 *kuṇṭas* of which 200 *kuṇṭas* are for Dontamma, 200 *kuṇṭas* for Mélunán Koni Nára, 200 *kuṇṭas* for Ventuchu Pátrabayya, for lights one field (?) . . . .

1. . . . . (దే)
2. వక్లకం అచ్చన
3. ...గమునకు
4. క్షేత్రము పండ్రె

---

1 Sáni=dancing girl.

5. ండు బారలు ఘ
6. డను కుంటనా
7. ౮౦౦ లు ॥ తిరు
8. పణిదాసికికుం ౧౦
9. ౦రు। సామాన్య
10. లకు కుంటలు రే
11. ండువే ౨౦౦౦ లు
12. ఏనిలోనవొంత
13. మకు (కాచినూ ?)
14. కుంటలు ౨౦౦
15. యి। మేలునాంకో
16. ని నారకుం ౨౦౦
17. క వెంతుచు పాత్రబ
18. య్యకుకుం ౨౦౦
19. యి। దీపములకు
20. గానుమ ౧డి ఘ
21. పాడిప ౧టి

* * * *

ONGOLE (25).

[Chandalúru. Telugu. From wall of garbha of Chenna-késava temple.]

TRANSLATION.

Hail! . . . . who is the worshipper of the illustrious lotus feet of (Hail!) Ṣrí Sáyaṇamdévarulu, who is entitled to the five great (musical) sounds, Mancha Mallésvara, who is an excellent Máhésvara, who is of upright character, whose ornament is modesty, who is the excellent lord of the town of Anumakonḍa . . . .

NOTE.—Anumakonḍa is said to have been the original seat of the Kákatíya dynasty but Sáyaṇam Dévara is probably the officer referred to in No. 28. Mancha Mallēṣvara may be a misreading.

స్వస్తిసమధిగ
తపంచమహా
శబ్దమంచమల్లేశ్వ
ర పరమమా
హేశ్వరపరిది
వచరిత వినయ
విభూషణ అ
నుమకొండ
పురవధీ
శ్వర శ్రీసాయం
ణం దేవరుల
శ్రీపాదపద్మా
(రాధ)కుడైన

* * * *

ONGOLE (26).

[Chandalúru. Telugu. In front of Chennakéṣava temple.]

TRANSLATION.

The devotion of Péraḍláḷa Jiyyamgáru! Ṣrí! Ṣrí! Ṣrí! The dedication to the deity. On Thursday, the 15th of the bright fortnight of Kártika of the year Vikriti.

1. పేరడ్లాళ జియ్యంగారి
2. సేవ శ్రీ శ్రీ శ్రీ

3. వికృతిసంవ్వత్సర కా
4. ర్తిక శు ౧౫ గు । స్వా
5. మికి సమర్పణ ॥ శ్రీ.

ONGOLE (27). (A.D. 1253–54 ?)

[Chandalúru. Telugu. From two sides of the stone before Rámalingéṣvara temple from which No. (28) is taken.]

TRANSLATION.

Hail! On the 7th day of Vaiṣákha of the Ṣaka year reckoned by the senses (5), the mountains (7), the moon (1), and Dhátri (1) (*i.e.*, 1175) Máyidéva Peggaḍa who is the beloved of Videya (learning) who belongs to the fourth caste, who worships the learned, who is possessed of all praiseworthy attributes, who is the illustrious prime minister (*mahápradháni*) and who is the principal authority (sarvádhikári), presented a *vritti* to Chenámallináthadévara of Chandalúru for the prosperity of Addanki Singaḷadéva who was his liege lord and of himself. Of this *vritti*, Máyídéva Preggaḍa presented 50 *kunṭas* to Viṣvanátha, and 50 *kunṭas* to the same deity and 50 *kunṭas* in these *vrittis* are for Divyakóla Brahmayya.

NOTE.—This minister's name does not appear elsewhere in the collection. Apparently he succeeded Sómarázu as Mahápradháni.

శ్రీ శాకా
బ్దములింద్రి
యాద్రిశశి
ధాత్రిసంఖ్య

గావిస్ఫు
రద్వైశాఖం
బునసప్త
మినిదివస
క్రీద్వారంబు
నం వడ్విజగీ
శుంబ్రీతింబ్ర
తిష్టసేసెవ
రభోగేంద్రు
ండుసేపైక వి
ద్యావరుం
డు చతుర్త
పంశుండు బు
ధాధారుం
డు మారం
డి లగా॥
స్వస్తి సమ
స్త ప్రశస్తి
సహితం
శ్రీమన్మ
హాప్రధా
ని సర్వా
ధి కారి
మాయిదే
వ పెగ్గడ
తం నేలిన
అద్దంకి సిం
గళ దేవని
కి తనకూ

అభివ్రిద్ధి
గా చెందలూ
రి చెంనామ
ల్లి నాథదే
వర . .

Second side.

ఇవ్రిత్తై
న విశ్వనా
ధునకు
కు ౫౦
ఇతనికె మా
యీదేవపె
గడపెట్టిన
వ్రిత్తి కు ౫౦
ఇవ్రిత్తిలో
నె దివ్యకో
ల బ్రమ్మయకు
కు ౫౦॥

ONGOLE (28). (A.D. 1253–54?)

[Chanḍalúru. Telugu. From two sides of a stone opposite Rámálinga temple.]

TRANSLATION.

Hail! On Sunday, the 7th of the bright fortnight of Vaiṣákha, corresponding to the Ṣaka year 1175, while Ṣríman Mahámanḍaléṣvara Kákatiya Gaṇapatidéva Mahá-rázulu, who is entitled to the five great (musical) sounds, who is Mahámaṇḍaléṣvara, who is a great devotee of Ṣiva, who is filled with good will towards others, who is adorned with humility, who is the excellent lord of the city of Anumakoṇḍa, who is the worshipper of the illustrious lotus feet of Ṣrí Svayambhudéva, and who is the vanquisher of hostile armies, was ruling the earth, his feudatory (Hail !) Ṣrí Maṇḍaléṣvara Chakra Náráyaṇa Ṣrí Singadéva Mahárájulu, who is possessed of all eulogistic titles, who is a Révanta amongst those who ride very unruly horses, who is death to hostile armies, who is a fortress of adamant to his refugees, who is the protector of life, and who is a hero without fear, makes a gift of the following, for securing prosperity.

Vritti for the *pújári* measured with a pole of 12 fathoms. For Padmajiyya and Dévajiyya 250 *kuṇṭas*. For decorations and enjoyments to the deity a field of 2,000 *kuṇṭas*. May it cause great prosperity!

Out of that land, 60 *kuṇṭas* are for Ekásedámója, 100 *kuṇṭas* for Mélunáyaninúnkayya and one *ma* for the lamp of the deity. The sun and moon, wind, heaven, earth, water . . . . . Yama, day and night, the two Sandhyas and Dharma, know the mind of man.

[One imprecatory verse.]

స్వస్తి సమధిగత
పంచమహాశ
బ్ద మహామండ
లేశ్వర పరమ
మహేశ్వర ప
రహిత చరిత వి
నయ విభూష అ
నుమకొండ పు

ర వరాధీశ్వర శ్రీ
శ్వయంబు దేవ
దివ్య శ్రీపాద
పద్మారాధక పర
బలసాధక శ్రీమ
న్మహా మండలేశ్వ
ర కాకతియ్యా గ
ణపతి దేవ మ
హారాజులు ప్రి
థివీ రాజ్యంబు
సేయుచుండంగా
॥ వారిసామంత్తు
ండు స్వస్తి సమ
స్త ప్రశస్తి సహి
తం శ్రీఅండలే
శ్వరం అతివిష
మ హయారూ
ఢ ప్రవుఢ రేఖా
రేవంత పరబ
ళ్క్రితాంత శరణా
గత వజ్రపంజ
ర మండలీకరవ
ండోళ్ళి జీవరక్షి (తు)
విశ్ఫంకటమల్ల చ
క్ర నారాయణ శ్రీ
సింగదేవ మహా
రాజులుకభ్యు
ధయంబుగా॥
శకవర్షంబు

లు వేయినూట
డెభ్భదేనగు సేంటి
వైశాఖ శుద్ధ
సప్తమీ నాదివా
రమున ॥
౧౧౭౫ గు
నెండు ॥
పూజారిబ్రి
త్తి పండ్రెండు
బారల కోలను
పద్మజియ్య
జీవజియ్య
లకు కు ౨౫౦
అంగ్గరంగ్గబో
గానకు క్షేత్ర
ముకు ౨౦౦౦
లు ఇచ్చిరి మ
ంగళ మహా
శ్రీ శ్రీ శ్రీ ॥
ఆక్షేత్రము
లోన నేకాసెదా
మోజానకు
కు ౬౦ యి ॥
మేలునాయి
వి నూంకయ
కు కు౧౦౦
లు ॥ చేవర దీ
పానకు గాను
ను ౧ ॥ అది

త్య చంద్రా అని
లో నలశ్చద్యో
భ్యూమి రాపో
హ్రిదయం యె
మశ్చ । అహశ్చ
రాత్రిశ్చ ఉభే
చ సంధ్యా ధర్మ్మ
శ్చజానాతి
నరశ్యవి త్తం[1]
॥ స్వదత్తం ద్వి
గుణం పుణ్యం
పర దత్తాను
పాలనం పర
దత్తాపహారే
ణ స్వదత్తం నిష
ఫలం భవేత్ ॥

ONGOLE (23-A). (A.D. 1166–67.)

[Chandrapáḍu. Telugu. In front of Ṣiva temple.]

TRANSLATION.

Hail! On Tuesday the 15th of dark half of Márgaṣira of the year Vyaya, corresponding to the illustrious Ṣaka year 1089, on account of a solar eclipse, Konḍapa Náyakunḍu owner of (?) Chandrúru on the bank of the Gunḍḍi river, who is the dutiful son of Eṛṛamanáyaka, who is like the moon (Sudhákara) to the ocean of the

---

[1] Read వృత్తం

Manumapála family, who declares the good properties of Mahéṣvara, and who bends his head to the lotus feet of his own guru (priest), gave 55 she-goats to Ṣrí Nágéṣvaramahádéva of Chanḍrúru for a perpetual light. Rabbena Ṣeṭṭi, son of Nangaréku Naḍvi Ṣeṭṭi, should receive these and maintain the grant. He, his sons and grandsons should give for the lamp every day one mánika of ghee as long as the sun and moon exist. This charity will continue as long as the earth exists. Thanks to Gaṇéṣa. Three *puṭṭis* of land were given to Srí Nágéṣvara Mahádéva.

1. స్వస్తిశ్రీ శకవరుషంబులు ౧౦౮౯ అ
2. వునేంటి వ్యయసంవత్సర మార్గ్గశిర
3. బహుళపంచదశియు మంగ్గళవారము
4. సూర్య్యగ్రహణ నిమిత్తమున గుండ్డి
5. కత్తిలోని చంద్రూరును లకునిపూరతీ
6. యుంగల యజ్ఞమనాయకునకి సు
7. పుత్త్రుండు మనుమపాల వార్ద్ధిమ
8. దాన సుధాకరుండును మహేశ్వర
9. గుణాధికరుండును నిజగు
10. రు పాదాబ్జ శిరశేఖరుండును
11. నైన కొండపనాయకుండు
12. చంద్రూరి శ్రీనాగేశ్వర

Second side.

13. మహాదేవరకు నఖండదీపమునకు
14. బెట్టినమేంకలు ౫౫ వీనినంగ్గరేకు నడ్వి
15. సెట్టికొడుకు రబ్బెనశెట్టి సేకొనిరక్షించేది
16. పుత్త్రాసుపౌత్రము ఆచంద్రార్కము నిత్యము
17. మానెండు నెయ్యిదీపమునకు నడపం

18. గ్గలవాండు యీధర్మము బ్రిథ్వికలంత్త

19. కాలము వర్ధింపంగలది. గణేశ్వరా

20. యనమ

21. శ్రీ నాగేశ్వరమహాదేవరకు బెట్టిన

22. ది ఖ 3.

ONGOLE (29). (A.D. 1565–66.)

[Chedalaváḍa. Telugu. On Kalyánamandapam.]

TRANSLATION.

Salutations be to Rámachandra.

Hail! On Thursday, the 11th of the bright fortnight of Áshádha of the year Kródhana, corresponding to the year 1488 of the illustrious, victorious and prosperous Śáliváhana Śaka era, while Ṣríman Mahárájádhirája Rája-paraméṣvara Ṣrí Víraprátápa Sadáśivadéva Maháráyalu was ruling the kingdom of the earth, in the kingdom (*rájya*) of Koṇḍavíḍu which he granted to Ṣríman Mahá-maṇḍaléśvara Ráma Rájayaṛan Tirumala Rájayya Déva Mahárájulungáru, in Koṇḍavíḍu *rájya* which he was pleased to grant to Ṣríman Mahámaṇḍaléśvara Siddhiráju Rangaparájayyadéva Mahárájulungáru, in Addanki Ammanabrólu *ṣíma*, to Ṣrí Raghunáyakulu of Chadalu-váḍa;

Rangapa Rájayyadéva Mahárájulungáru, the great grandson of Siddhirájungáru, the grandson of Vóbuḷará-jungáru, the son of Timmaráju, presented on the holy occasion of the first *ekádasi* (eleventh day of the lunar fortnight) with libation of water and gift of gold to Ṣrí Raghunáyakulu of Chadaluváḍa the income derived from the *aḍḍagaḍa sunkam* [1] and *kaṭnálu* (presents) (?) in Chadaluváḍa, Mallavaram, Alavaiapáḍu, and other villages, the *sunkam* from the *bharitas* (residents ?) of the *sthala*, and the *múlavisálubodi* [2] and other taxes. Therefore Rangapárájayyagáru, the grandson of (as before) with a devout heart presented this charity to Ṣrí Raghunáyakulu of Chadaluváḍa. Therefore it should be maintained in perpetuity as long as the sun and moon endure.

[Three imprecatory verses.]

Ṣrí ! Ṣrí !

1. శ్రీరామచంద్రాయ
2. నమః ॥ స్వస్తి శ్రీజయా
3. భ్యుదయ శా జ .శ్వర లివాహ
4. న శకవర్షంబులు ౧౪౭
5. ౭ది అగు నేంటి క్రోధన స
6. ంవత్సర ఆషాఢ శు ౧౧ గు
7. శ్రీమన్మహా రాజాధిరా
8. జరాజపరమేశ్రీవీర
9. ప్రతాప సదాశివదేవమహా
10. రాయలు పృథ్విసా మ్రా
11. జ్యం చేయుచున్న శ్రీమ
12. న్మహామండలేశ్వర రామ
13. రాజయఅందిరు
14. మలరాజయ్యదేవ మ
15. హారాజులుంగారికి

---

[1] Aḍḍa sunkam means a tax levied on the sellers of sheep. Gaḍa sunkam might perhaps mean tax payable at fixed periods. But possibly "gaḍa" is merely a jingle and in that case we should translate "tax levied on the sellers of sheep and similar things".

[2] See glossary.

16. ం బాలించిన కొండపీటి
17. రాజ్యకాందును। శ్రీమ
18. న్మహామండలేశ్వర సిద్ధిరా
19. జురంగపరాజయ్యదేవమహా
20. రాజులుంగారికిం బాలించం
21. నవధరించిన కొండవీటిరా
22. జ్యములోని అద్దంకి అమ్మనం
23. బ్రోలి శీమలోన చదలువా
24. డ శ్రీరఘునాయకులకు సి
25. ద్దిరాజుంగారి ప్రపౌత్రులున్న
26. వోబుళరాజుంగారి పౌత్రు

Second side.

27. లున్న తిమ్మరాజుంగారి
28. పుత్రులునైన రంగపరా
29. జయ్యదేవమహారాజు
30. లుంగారు చదలువాడ
31. శ్రీరఘునాయకుల
32. కు చదలువాడ మల్లవర
33. ము అలవలపాడు మో
34. దలైన గ్రామాల అడ్డగడ
35. సుంకం ని(వి ?)హిత కట్నాలు
36. స్థలభరితాలు సుంకం
37. మూలవీసాలు బడి
38. మొదలైన సుంక ఆదా
39. యము సిద్ధిరాజుం
40. గారి ప్రపౌత్రులున్న వో
41. బుళ రాజుంగారి పౌత్రు
42. లున్న తిమ్మరాజుంగారి

43. పుత్రులునైన రంగపరాజ
44. య్య దేవమహారాజులు
45. ంగారు చదలువాడ శ్రీ
46. రఘునాయకులకు ప్ర
47. థమైకాదశి పుణ్యకాల
48. మందును స హిరణ్యో
49. దక దానధారాపూర్వ
50. కముగాను ధారవోశి
51. సమర్పించిరి గనక ఈ
52. ధర్మము సిద్ధిరాజుం

Third side.

53. గారి ప్రపౌత్రులున్ను వోబ
54. శ రాజుంగారి పౌత్రులున్ను
55. తిమ్మరాజుంగారి పౌత్రులు
56. నైనన రంగపరాజయ్య దేవ
57. మహారాజులుంగారు చె
58. దలువాడ శ్రీరఘునాయ
59. కులకు త్రికరణంగాను సమ
60. ర్పించిరి గనక ఆచంద్రార్క
61. స్థాయిగాను నడచునది ॥
62. స్వదత్తాం పరదత్తాంవాయో
63. హరేత వసుంధరాం షష్టి
64. వర్ష సహస్రాణి విష్టాయా
65. ంజాయతేక్రిమిః । స్వదత్తాం
66. ద్విగుణం పుణ్యం పరద
67. త్తానుపాలనం పరదత్తా
63. పహారేణ స్వదత్తం నిష్ఫ
69. లం భవేత్ । మద్వంశజాః

70. పరమహీపతి వంశజా
71. వయద్వంశజా సతత ము
72. జ్వల ధర్మచిత్తాః మద్ధర్మ
73. మేవమనఘాః పరిపా
74. లయంత్వి తత్పాదుక
75. ద్వయమహం శిరసా
76, పహామి ॥ శ్రీ శ్రీ

NOTE.—There is a lot of repetition in this inscription. The reference to the two grantees of the Kondaviḍu rájyam is not understood.

ONGOLE (30). (A.D. 1482–83.)

[Chedalaváḍa. Telugu. In front of Ṣrí Raghunátha temple.]

TRANSLATION.

Hail to Rámachandráya! After reading the copper-plate grants formerly caused to be granted, for providing all enjoyments, through Prauḍha Déva Ráya Mahárayalu by Panṭa Maila Reḍḍi as an *agrahára* to Raghunátha of Chadaluváḍa, on the 11th day on the bright fortnight of Mágha of the year Ṣubhakrit corresponding to the Ṣrí Ṣaka year 1404, Timmareḍḍi, the son of Hinduráyu Suradháṇi Sariyapati Timmáreḍḍi likewise granted (the agraháram) to the deity as a *sarvamánya*. Therefore those who obstruct this charity so that it does not go to the deity of Chadalaváḍa will incur the sin of cow slaughter and Brahmanicide on the banks of the Ganges.

The women of those who abuse the ruler of the village or the king of the *síma* or endeavour to obtain the sovereignty will be given to Dommara villagers.

NOTE.—The allusion is to Dévaráya II. The date S.S. 1404 relates to the later grant.

1. శ్రీరామచంద్రాయనమః
2. స్వస్తి శ్రీ శకవరుషంబులు
3. ౧౪౦౪ అగు సేంటిశుభ
4. కృత్తు సంపత్సరమాఘు
5. శు ౧౧ ఆచెదలువాడ ర
6. ఘునాంతనికి అగ్రహారము
7. గాను అంగ్గరంగ్గవైభవాల
8. కు పూర్వానను ప్రౌడదేవరా
9. యమహారాయల చేతను ప
10. ంట మైలారెడ్డింగారు యిప్పిం
11. చిన తామ్రశాసనాలు చదివిం
12. చుకొని అటువలెనె హిందూ
13. రావు సురధాణి సరియపతి
14. తిమ్మారెడ్డింగారి కుమారుండు
15. తిమారెడ్డింగారు సర్వమాన్యము
16. గాను దేవరకు యిచ్చిరిగాన యీ
17. చెదలువాడదేవరకుం జెల్లనీక
18. యెవ్వరు అంకిలి శేశివాను గంగ్గ
19. కర్తను గోవున్ను బ్రాంహ్మనిన్ని
20. ం జంపినపాపానం బోవువారు
21. యీగ్రామము యీశీమకర్తను
22. రాజును ఆడినవారి ఆడిగించ్చి
23. నవారి యేలేనని అపేక్షించిన
24. వారి ఆండ్లను దొంమ్మరి పిళ్ల
25. వారికి యిచ్చిన వారు.

ONGOLE (31). (A.D. 1558–59.)

[Chedalaváḍa. Telugu. In front of Raghunáyaka temple.]

TRANSLATION.

Salutations be to Ṣrí Rámachandra.

Hail! The following are the particulars of an inscribed pillar planted in Chadalaváḍa *sthala* in Ammanabrólu *síma* for the religious merit of Ṣiddhiráju Timmarájayya by Mandapáṭi Appaḷa Ráju on the 15th of the bright fortnight of Phálguṇa of the year Kálayukti, corresponding to the Ṣrí Ṣaka year 1481, while Ṣrímat Rájadéva Rája Rájaparamésvara Ṣrí Vírapratápa Ṣrí Sadásivadéva Ráyulu, seated on the jewelled throne at Vijayanagar, was ruling the kingdom of the earth, while Ṣrímán Mahámaṇḍaléṣvara Ṣiddhi Ráju Timmarájayyadéva Mahárájulu was ruling over Konḍavíḍu. We have presented to Ṣrí Raghunáyakulu the taxes levied on articles sold in Chadalaváḍa village, the *sthala* of Raghunáyakulu, and on grain, the *aḍagaḍa sunkham*, the *múlavisálu* collected in Addanki and Ammanabrólu *símas*, and the *sunkham* and the old *kaṭnam* collected in Ṣrí Raghunáyakulu *sthala*. Therefore the temple people themselves should credit the taxes to the estate of Ṣrí Raghunáyakulu and grant receipts to the merchants who buy there and receipts for the taxes raised in the two *ṣímas*. For the daily offerings to Raghunáyakulu we have remitted the taxes levied on paddy and other articles bought in Konḍavíḍu *ṣíma*, on paddy and other articles purchased and brought during festivals, on articles brought for sale by merchants during festivals, on articles purchased and taken away by merchants during festivals, and the fees collected in Addanki and Ammanabrólu *ṣímas*. We have remitted the *Randinulappulári*(?) from the time of hoisting of the flag during festivals and big festivals up to the 30th of Phálguṇa.

Those who henceforth do not maintain this but violate it, will incur the sin of killing a cow and a Brahman near the Ganges.

[One imprecatory verse.]

NOTE.—See notes under No. 29.

1. శ్రీరామచంద్రాయ
2. నమః । స్వస్తి శ్రీశకవరుషంబు
3. లు ౧౪౮౧ అగు నెంటికాల
4. యుక్తిసంవత్సర ఫాల్గుణ
5. శు ౧౫ లు శ్రీమద్రాజాధి
6. రాజరాజ పరమేశ్వర శ్రీవీ
7. రప్రతాప శ్రీ సదాశివదేవ
8. మహారాయలుంగారు వి
9. జ్యనగరమందు రత్నసింహా
10. సనారూఢుండై పృథివి సామ్రా
11. జ్యం శేయుచుండంగాను శ్రీ
12. మన్మహామండలేశ్వర శిద్ధిరా
13. జు తింమ్మరాజయ్యదేవ మ
14. హారాజులుంగారు కొండ్ర
15. వీడు పాలించుచున్న వుం
16. డ్డంగాను మంగపాటి అప్పళ
17. రాజుంగారు సిద్దిరాజు తిమ్మ
18. రాజయ్యవారికి పుణ్యము
19. గాను అమ్మనంబోలి శీమలో
20. ని చదలువాడ స్థలమందు
21. నిలిపిన శాసన స్తంభ క్రమ మె

22. ట్లన్నను శ్రీరఘునాయకులస్థ
23. లం చదలువాడ గ్రామానను
24. అంమ్మికొనే పదార్థాలకున్ను
25. ధాన్యాలకున్ను వచ్చే అద్దంకి
26. అమ్మనబ్రోలిశీమల అడ
27. గడ సుంఖము మూలపీసా
28. ల్ను శ్రీరఘునాయకుల స్థ
29. లము సుంఖ్యన్ని బాతకట్నము
30. న్ను శ్రీరఘునాయకులకు స
31. సమర్పింస్తిమి గనక స్థానము
32. వారేసుంఖము రఘునాయకు
33. ల నగరికి ఆయము శేశి కొనుకా
34. పోయీ వర్తకులకు రెండు
35. శీమలసుంఖాల్యకున్ను చెల్లుం
36. జెల్లువెట్టు వారు రఘునా
37. యకుల నిత్యనైవేద్యాలకు కొండ
38. వీడు శీమలోను కొనితెచ్చేవడ్లు

Second side.

39. మొదలైనపదా
40. ర్థాలకున్ను తిరు
41. ణాల్లకు కొనితెచ్చె
42. వడ్లు మొదలైన ప
43. దార్థాలకున్ను
44. తిరునాళ్లలో వత
45. ర్తకులు అమ్ముకోను
46. తెచ్చేపదార్థాల
47. కున్ను తిరుణాళ్లలో
48. వర్తకుఃబుకొను

49. ర్తిపోయే పదార్థా
50. ణాలకున్ను అర్ధంకిర
51. అమ్మనంబోలి శీసు
52. ల సుంఖ్యంపూల
53. వీసాలు మానితిమి
54. తిరుణాళ్లు మహోత్స
55. వంద్వజారోహ
56. ణం మొదలు పా
57. ల్గుణ బ ౩౦ యీప
58. ర్యంతం చదలువా
59. డస్థలమందు (రండి
60. ండస్థలాతిమిః)
61. మానితిమి యీ వెం
62. బడిని యవ్వరుగన
63. కనడపక తప్పినా
64. ంగంగ్గ కర్తను గో
65. వుబ్రాహ్మనిం జం
66. ప్పిన పాపానం బో
67. వువారు । స్వదత్తా
68. ద్విగుణం పుణ్యం
69. పరదత్తాను పాలనం
70. పర దత్తాప హా
71. రేణ సదత్తం నిష్ఫ
72. లం భవేత్ ।

ONGOLE (32). (A.D. 1633–34?)

[Chedalaváḍa. Telugu. Opposite Raghunáyaka temple. The meaning is not clear in parts.]

TRANSLATION.

Salutations be to Rámachandra.

Hail! On Thursday, the 7th of the dark fortnight of Jyeshṭa of the year Ṣrímukha, corresponding to the year 1565 of the illustrious, victorious and prosperous Ṣáliváhana Ṣaka era, while Ṣrímat Rájádhirája Rájáparamé-ṣvara Vírapratápa Ṣrí Víra Ṣrí Rangadéva Maháráyalu, seated on the jewelled throne, was ruling the kingdom of the earth, according to the copper-plate granted to Dávan-ḍakúri Agnyammakunḍa (?) Immaḍi Ṣítájuhiva Voḍayalu, Polayareḍḍi of Cheḍaluváḍa village in Ammanabrólu *ṣíma* gave . . . for the religious merit of his ancestor Khásuningáru and his mothers Krishṇamma, Gangamma and Singamma and planted boundary pillars at the junction of Chadaluváḍa, Chiraváṇa and Uppalapáḍu, naming the gift three times, for providing all enjoyments to Ṣrí Raghunáyakulu of Chedalaváḍa.

Those who do not uphold this shall incur the sin of cow slaughter and Brahmanicide on the banks of the Ganges.

[Two imprecatory verses.]

NOTE.—The cyclic and S.S. years differ. This Immaḍi Ṣítájuhiva Oḍaya has not been identified.

1. శ్రీరామచ
2. ంద్రాయనమః
3. స్వస్తిశ్రీ జయా
4. భ్యుదయ శాలి

5. వాహన శక
6. వరుషంబులు
7. ౧౪౯౫ అగు నే
8. టి శ్రీముఖ సం
9. వ్వత్సర జేష్ఠ
10. బ ౨ గు శ్రీమ
11. ద్రాజాధిరాజ
12. రాజపరమే
13. శ్వర శ్రీ వీరప్రతాప
14. శ్రీ వీర శ్రీరంగ్గ దే
15. వ మహారాయలు
16. ంగారు రత్నసింహాస
17. నారూఢుండై పృ
18. ధ్వీ సామ్రాజ్యాం
19. జేయుచు నుండగా
20. దావండకూరి ఆ
21. జ్ఞం మాకుండ్ల ఇమ్మ
22. డి శీతాజుహివ వో
23. డయులుంగారికి వ్రా
24. యించ్చి ఇయ్యా నవ
25. ధరించ్చిన అస్మ్మన
26. ంబ్రోలు శీమలోన
27. చెదలువాడ స్థలం
28. పోలయరెడ్డి దేవ
29. రాయలు సమప్పిం-
30. చ్చిన తామ్రశాసన
31. నాల పద్ధతిని చద
32. లువాడ చిరవాన ఉ
33. వ్వలపాటి సంద్బుకా

34. డ నాటిపద్దతిని (?) పొ
35. లిమేర కంభాలుం
36. తమపెద్ద ఖాను
37. నింగారికిన్ని తమత
38. ల్లులు క్రిష్ణమ గంగ్గ
39. మ సింగ్గమంగారికి
40. పుణ్యంగాను చదల
41. వాడ శ్రీరఘునాయ
42. కుల అంగరంగ వైభో
43. గాలకును త్రివాచి
44. కంగాను సమర్పిస్తిమి
45. యీధర్మానకు ఎవ్వరు
46. గనా తప్పినాను గంగ్గక
47. తర్గో బ్రాంహ్మని వధం
48. చిన పాపానం బోవుదురు.
49. స్వదత్తా ద్విగు
50. ణంపుణ్యం పర
51. దత్తానుపాలనం
52. పరదత్తాపహా
53. రేణ స్వదత్తం ని
54. ష్ఫలం భవేత్॥ స్వ
55. దత్తాం పరదత్తా
56. ం వ్వయో హరేతి
57. వసుంధరా షష్టి
58. వ..ష సహస్రా
59. ణి విష్టాయాం
60. జాయతే క్రిమి॥

ONGOLE (33).

[Chezerla. Telugu. To south of Chennakéșava temple.]

TRANSLATION.

Hail! On the 10th of the bright fortnight of Áshádha in the year Paridhávi, corresponding to the illustrious, victorious and prosperous Șáliváhana Șaka year . . . . the (following) charitable edict was granted by Rámanáyaningáru after making innumerable salutations to the lotus feet of Șrí Chéjarla Kéșavadéva (and) to Rávi Parákéșamáryara. In the south-western quarter of Pina Chéjarla in Ammanabrólu *síma* granted to us by Dévarájayyavåru, I have presented land under the tank for the daily offerings, lights, and all enjoyments of the deity. I have also given two *puțțis* of land under the tank as a *sarvamánya* . . . . The grazing fee levied on this field . . . . for the daily offerings . . . . and all enjoyments . . . .

1. స్వస్తిశ్రీ జయాభ్యుదయ శాలివాహన శకవరు
2. షంబులు (. . . .) అగునెంటి పరిధావి సం
3. వత్సర ఆషాఢ శు ౧౦ లు శ్రీచెజర్ల కేశవ
4. దేవరకు . . పదంబులకు రావి పరా
5. . కేశమార్యరకు రామానాయనిం
6. గారు అనంతములయిన దండములు
7. సమర్పించియిచ్చిన ధర్మశాసనం ॥ యీ
8. . యరం దేవరాజయ్యవారు మా
9. కు అంమనంబోలి సీమలో
10. నం బిన చేంజర్లను నైరుతిభాగం
11. లోను స్వామినిత్యనైవేద్యక దీపా

12. లకు అంగ్గరంగ్గ వైభవాలకున్ను చెర్వు
13. క్రిందపాటి నిచ్చిరి . . పుణ్యక్షే

Second side.

14. త్రముంను చెరు
15. వు క్రింద్దను రెండ్డు పు
16. ట్లు క్షేత్రమున్ను
17. సర్వమాన్యంగాను
18. సమర్పించ్చిని.
19. యీ క్షేత్రంవల్ల వ
20. చ్చిన పుల్లరి . . .
21. . నిత్య నైవేద్య . .
22. దకు. . . . . .
23. అంగ్గరంగ్గ భోగానికిన్ని
24. లు సో . . . . .
25. . . . . దాయ
26.. . యివ్వ . . ్పి
27. లుం కోరు శేంద కి
28. కీర్తి . . .
29. . . . . .
30. . . . . .
31. . . . . .

ONGOLE (34). (A.D. 1248–49 ?)

[Chezerla. Telugu. To north of Chennakéṣava temple.]

TRANSLATION.

Hail! In the illustrious Ṣaka year 1570, on the occasion of Uttaráyana Sankránti, Ṣríman Sómaráju, the prime minister (*mahápradháni*) gave 200 *kuntas* of land to the Múlasthánadéva . . . . for the religious merit of his master Chakra Náráyaṇa Singaḷadéva Mahárája; 30 *kuntas* of land to . . . . déva . . . . for *vritti*.

The *sthánapati* (temple servant) is Kapóta . . . . son of Prammira . . . .

NOTE.—A reference to Nos. 6, 103 and 151 shows that the Ṣaka year should be 1170.

1. స్వస్తిశ్రీ శకవరుషంబులు
2. ౧౫౭౦ నెంటి ఉత్తరాయ
3. న సంక్రాంతి నిమిత్తంబు
4. న శ్రీమన్మహా ప్రధానిసోమ
5. రాజు తన్నేలిన చక్రనారాయ
6. ణ సింగళదేవ మహారాజుల
7. కు ధర్మముగను యా
8. . . మూలస్తాన దేవరకిచ్చిన
9. చేనుగుంటలు ౨౦౦ .
10. . టిమి దేవరకు వ . .
11. . . గుంటలు ౩౦ యి .
12. . . . . నుకు

Second side.

13. ఏక వ్రి త్తి కి
14. స్తానాపతి వ్ర
15. మ్మిర కొడుకు
16. కపోత . టి

ONGOLE (35). (A.D. 1338–39.)

[Dénuvakoṇḍa. Telugu. Opposite Vénugópáḷaswámi temple.]

TRANSLATION.

Hail! On Thursday, the 11th of the bright fortnight of Áshádha of the year Bahudhánya, corresponding to the illustrious Śaka year 1260, this charitable edict was granted to Dhénuvukoṇḍa Gópálakṛishna by Poddilapalli Śingamanáyanimgáru after making obeisance. We have given the land known as . . . . in the western fields of Dhénuvukoṇḍa which belongs to our chiefdom for (providing) offerings to the deity.

Whoever violates this charity will incur the sin of killing a cow on the banks of the Ganges.

[One imprecatory verse.]

NOTE.—This Singama does not appear elsewhere in our collection. He was probably of no importance.

1. స్వస్తిశ్రీ శకవర్షంబులు ౧౨౬౦
2. ౦ బహుధాన్య సంవత్సర ఆషాఢ శు
3. ౧౧ గు। ధేనువుకొండ గోపాలక్రిష్ణని
4. కి పొద్దిలపల్లి శింగ్గమనాయనింగారు దం
5. డం పెట్టి ఇచ్చిన ధర్మశాసనం। మానాయం
6. కరానకుం జెల్లే ధేనువకొండ్డ పడమటిపొ

7. లానను [ఫుకె సంవిం అ] నరక్షేత్రం
8. దేవుని నవిద్యానకు ఆ చంద్రార్క స్థాయిగా నిస్తిమి
9. యీా ధర్మానకు యెవ్వండు దప్పినాను గంగకరత
10. గోవును వధియించ్చిన పాపానం బోవువారు.
11. స్వదత్తం ద్విగుణం పుణ్యం పరదత్తా
12. ను పాలనం పరదత్తాప హారేణ స్వదత్తం ని
13. ష్ఫలం భవే.

Ongole (36).

[Dharmavaram. Telugu. From threshold of Sítarámaswámi temple.]

Translation.

[Two imprecatory verses.]

The famous Épirán (or Pírán), commander of the elephants, with the permission of the emperor Ékalásakhán, who always protects his subjects with the valour of his arm, founded that Punnúru.

Note.—The emperor's name is not recognizable in the form it bears here. Probably one of the Golkonda dynasty is referred to.

1. దానపాలనయోర్మధ్యే దా
2. నాచ్ఛ్రేయోను పాలనం
3. దానాత్స్వర్గ మవాప్నో
4. తి పాలనా దచ్యుతంపదం॥ (1)
5. సామాన్యోయం ధర్మసేతు
6. నృపాణాం కాలేకాలేపాల
7. నియ్యోభవద్భిః। సర్వానేతా
8. న్భావినః పార్థివేంద్రా
9. భూయో భూయో యాచ
10. తే రామచంద్రః॥ (2) భజబ

11. లమునం బాలించ్చుం బ్రి
12. జనెపుడే కలాసఖానపా
13. ధిఙ వుండాభూరి బుజా శ
14. లవునం గావించ్చెఙ । గజ
15. రాయుండు తత్పున్నూరి
16. ఘనుండే పిరాను ॥

ONGOLE (37).

[Dharmavaram. Telugu. Stone in enclosure of Sítarámaswámi temple.]

TRANSLATION.

On Thursday, the 12th of the bright fortnight of Áṣvíja of the year Promódíta, the cavalry of the Hiválá (area subordinate to a havâldár ?) and the infantry having come, (?) the following charitable endowments were made for the religious merit of Khán Ajyam Khája Abul Saheb by all the people of the suburbs Yékalásá-puram and Bálupuram. On every bag of vegetables and grain raised on land, at the rate of 1 dha (?); on every *ráṭam* (spinning-wheel) at 2 dha; on *sellá* (muslin) at 1 vam (?); on sundries at 1 (va)? (This portion is not understood.)

In this manner we have made an arrangement. Therefore if any one fails to continue this charity, if a Telugu, he will incur the sin of killing a cow and a Brahman on the banks of the Ganges, if a Mussalman, he will incur the sin of killing a pig in Mecca . . . . he is the son of a donkey.

NOTE.—Khán Ajyam may stand for Khán-i-Azam. The same form appears in KR. 41. The references are, no doubt, to some official of no great importance.

1. ప్రమోదూతసంవత్సర ఆశ్వీజశు ౧౨ గురువారా
2. న ఖానే ఆజ్యం ఖాజ్జే అపులుసాహేబులుగారికి పు
3. ణ్యంగాను, హివాలాశిలేదారును, కాయినదండుస్న్
4. పెట్టి యేకలాసాపురం చాలుపురాల సమస్తపెకండ్రు
5. న్ను సాగించ్చిన ధర్మకార్యాలువివరం భూమినింగాసిన
6. కాయధాన్యం గోనే ౧ కి ధ। లెఖానురాటం ౧ కి ధ॥ లె
7. ఖ్ఖాను శెల్లా ౧ కి వం। లెఖ్ఖాను చిల్లరలో ౧ కి ప।
8. లెఖ్ఖాను యీ ప్రకారం నిర్ణయంబడిచేసినడిపివు
9. న్నామగనక యీధర్మాను యవ్వరుదప్పినాను తెలగా
10. లూ దప్పిరాయనా గంగ్గకతటంగోవుబ్రెంహ్మ
11. న్నివధించ్చిన పాపానపోవువారు తురుకలుదప్పి
12. రాయనా మఖాకలాను పంద్దిచంప్పినపాపా
13. న పోవువారు శ్రీ శ్రీ శ్రీ గాడి
14. ద కడుపున పుట్టినవారు.

ONGOLE (38).

[Dharmavaram. Telugu. On a rock in Ūrubōḍu hill.]

TRANSLATION.

The pond constructed by Nágaravutu, son of Kóṭivuṣáravutu.

1. కోటివుశా
2. రవుతు కొమా
3. రుండు నాగరవు
4. తువేయించ్చిన
5. దోన.

ONGOLE (39).

[Dharmavaram. Telugu. East of village in Survey No. 381.]

[The first part is unintelligible. It mentions Guṇakenalla whose name is immediately preceded by the words Ayyapa Ráju tammuṇḍu (younger brother) Bejeyaṇḍu. There appears also a reference to Baṇḍarangapura and Páṇḍuranga and the burning of Kíranapuram which last identifies Guṇakenalla with Vijayáditya III].

TRANSLATION OF END.

In the . . . . year of the glorious reign of (Vijayáditya) whose fame illuminated all the countries of the earth, the hero (?) of Páṇḍuranga, . . . at Dharmapuram, who is adorned with all the virtues, on the occasion of Uttaráyana Sankránti . . hail! . . the asylum of the whole world, ...

NOTE.—The transcription into modern letters was furnished to us by Mr. V. Venkayya.

1. [కొట్టు] రపురమునీ శానంబుః[నుం]డి నిల్పిన దీఱః[కొ] డుకున్న సమ . . .

2. ౦ . . ఠియమఱెవొనాన్ని నల్లాతడ్డ[య్య] అయ్యపరాజు తమ్ముణ్డు బెజెయ

3. ణ్డు గుణకెనల్లుణ్డు క[చ్చి]నబణ్డరంగపూ[ర]పాణ్డరంగుస . . . .

4. . . . . రుతంబు [పలె] నాడునచేఃపుర [ముః] . ట్టిన చలముణ్డువల్ల . .

5. రిచొ[టి]ని జేకొని కాది భూలోకంబెఱఃగ కిరనపురము దహ[ణ్డ]ం

(To face page 967.)

ONGOLE NO. 40.

6. . . పనజి [లాజ్యావి] సకీఅడ్డను . . . . .
ముడిచోట్లణ్డు . . . . .

7. . . . . [చిన] వల్లబు కొల్వు
ననెల్లి నెలుంగకన్నరగూ . .

8. . లు[క]ల . . నీబుతె [అ] నెడటి . .
[మ] లనడవిసో . . ళాన

9. [మ]స్త మహీమణ్డలప్రకాశిత కీర్తి శ్రీమత్పాణ్డ రంగుక
[ఢుఅ దుర్గ]

10. . స్తితిక్షమ్మ్ర్వురమ్మ్ఙన . . . . . ణ్యాసే
కగుణ గణాలంక్రిత . [శ్రీ]

11. [విజ] యరాజ్య సంవత్సరంబు . . . . .
గునేడ్డి ఉత్తరాయనసం

12. . . నస్వస్తి సర్వలోకాశ్రయ . . . . . .
భీమమ . . . . .
.

ONGOLE (40).

[Dharmavaram. Telugu. South wall of Malla-karjuna temple.]

TRANSLATION.

Maya Bajeyarâju (Vijayarâju?) having attained increasing glory, being godfearing, devoted to gods, Brahmans and spiritual preceptors; who is a great statesman well versed in the politics of all the neighbouring kingdoms . . . who constructed . . . . . niches for lamps, the prâkâra (enclosure wall) and the portico . . . . Preggaḍa Pâṇḍarangu, who is equal to Brihaspati among men, who is the minister of Vijayarâju . . . made grants . . . .

in the village of Páṇḍurangapuram . . . . Ayyapayya and Ṣakaraṣá . . . . as Kártikéya to Íṣvara . . on the full moon day of Pushya of (Pra ?)bhava. The illustrious Véy(Vijay ?)aráju who is adorned with the aggregate of virtues . . . .

NOTE.—This transcription also was done by Mr. V. Venkayya.

1. బుస్సేని దీపగుడ్లు ప్రాకారబుకటంబునునమ . .

2. సపన్నుణ్ణమయ బజెయరాజు [వృ]ద్ధి యేశ్వరంబుగలసి నివ్వి

3. . . . శ్వరపత్తపాతి దేవబ్రాహ్మనగురు [భ]క్తి పరుణ్డు సక్తాతిస

4. సు . బమసంసరా [జ్యాన్త] రనిరూపిత మహా మన్త్రాక్షిపతి . .

5. ధారి . . . [బ] జె యరాజు సమత్తుర్గ . . . మన్మత[బు]న బ . న ప్ర

6. న్మ . . . దోగ్యగమ్ముసర బృహస్పతిసమ్మానుల య్య పెగ్గడ . .

7. [పా]ణ్డరం[గు]బ అల్లుమ పెద్ద . ము . రనమ్ముఖ పణ్డరంగునూ[పు ?]రం . .

8. న్ను అయ్యపయ్యయు సకఅశా . . . . యు అయ్యన . .

9. . . . . కేస్వరునకు దా[?]త్తికేయుణ్డు బోశె పౌషపూలవినార .

10. . . భవ . . . శ్రీమతువేయ రాజు గుణ గణా రనుణ్డు దన

ONGOLE (41). (A.D. 1528–29.)

[Doḍḍavaram. Telugu. By a path to the east.]

TRANSLATION.

Hail! On Thursday, the 30th of the dark fortnight of Kártika of the year Sarvadhári, corresponding to the illustrious and prosperous Ṣaka year 1450, on the holy occasion of a solar eclipse, in the lands which Pángula Chumpiri presented with prostrations to Mallikárjunadéva of Vúrudoḍḍáram (Doḍḍavaram village) in Ammanabrólu *ṣíma*, he has given two *túms* of land in Késaripáḍu, viz., the field Gánḍakaṭṭachénu, lying in the north, near Gaḍeyana street for the sacred food (*amritapaḍi*) of the deity.

[Imprecatory verses.]

1. స్వస్తిశ్రీ శకవర్షాబ్యుదయంబులు
2. ౧౪౫౦ అగునేంటి సర్వధారిసంవ్వతర కార్తి
3. క బ ౩౦ గు సూర్య్యగ్రహణ పుణ్యకాలమం
4. ద్దులను అమ్మనంబ్రోలి శీమలోని ఊరుదొడ్డా
5. రంబున మల్లికార్జునదేవునికి పాంగుల చుంపిరి
6. సాష్టాంగదండ్డంబెట్టియిచ్చిననేలలో(సనద్దం)యీపూరు
7. చేనిని అమృతపడ్లకు వుత్తరపుపాలాన గడెయన
8. తెరువున గాండకట్టచేను కేసరిపాటిం ఇద్దుము ఇచ్చిరి
9. స్వదత్తా ద్విగుణంపుణ్యం పరదత్తానుపాలనం పర
10. దత్తాపహారేణ స్వదత్తం నిష్ఫలంభవేతు॥ స్వదత్తాం

పర

11. దత్తాం వాయోహరేతి వసుంధరా షష్టివర్షసహ

స్రాణి విష్టాయాం

12. జాయతేక్రిమి । యేకైవభగినీలోకే సర్వేషామేవభూ

బుజాం

13. నభోజ్యానకరగ్రాహ్యా విప్రదత్తా వసుంధరా.

ONGOLE (42).

[Doḍḍavaram. Telugu. To the east in a tope; from three sides of a stone.]

TRANSLATION.

On Monday, the 3rd of the bright fortnight of Bhádrapada of the year Sarvadhári, this charitable edict was granted by Pongula Mítinénigáru after making obeisance to Vináyaka (Ganésa) of Doḍḍavaram. The *mányam* bought from Mádani Venkusáni (is given) for worship with a light (?) We gave formerly (?) the eastern field to Venkaṭayya. Therefore he should enjoy it as long as the moon and sun endure.

[Four imprecatory verses.]

1. సర్వదారి సంవత్సర భాద్ర
2. పద శు 3 సో। దొడ్డవరం
3. వినాయ
4. కునికి పొంగులమితినేనింగారు దం
5. డ్డంపెట్టి యిచ్చిన ధర్మశాసనం
6. ము। మా
7. దనివెంకుసాని వచ్చి దొడ్డటికొన్నమాన్యం దీ
8. పారాధ్యాలకు తూర్పుపొలం వెంకట
9. య్యాను పూర్వకం చెల్లించె స్తిమిగాన ఆచంద్రా
10. రకంగాను అనుభవించువాండ్రు। స్వదత్తా ద్విగుణం
11. పుణ్యం పరదత్తానుపాలనం పరదత్తాపహారేణ స్వ
12. దత్త నిష్ఫలంభవేతు। ఏకైవ భగినిలోకే సర్వేషా

మేవభూబుజాం

13. నభోజ్యా నకరగ్రాంహ్యా విప్రదత్తా వసుంధరా। స్వద

త్తాం

14. పరదత్తాం వాయోహరేతివసుంధరాం షష్టివర్షసహ
స్రాణి

15. విష్టాయాం జాయతే క్రిమిః । మద్వంశజాః పరమహీపతి

16. వంశజావాయే భూమిపాః సతత ముజ్వలధర్మచిత్తా । మద్ధ
ర్మమేవ

17. సతతంపరిపాలయంతు త్వత్పాదుకాద్వయమహం శిర
సావహే

18. మి॥

ONGOLE (43).

[Doddavaram. Telugu. To the east in a field. One portion is the end of some inscription with two imprecatory verses. The other is a fragment recording a gift to a deity for offerings.]

1. విమలా । యేకైవభగినిలోకే సర్వేషా
2. మేవభూభుజాం నభోగ్యా
3. నకరగ్రాహ్యా విప్రదత్తా వసు
4. వుంధరా॥ శ్రీ. స్వదత్తా ద్వి
5. గుణం పుణ్యం పరదత్తాను
6. పాలనం పరదత్తాపహారేణ స్వ
7. దత్త నిష్ఫలం భవేత్ ॥

1. (. ం కలమ అ) స
2. మర్పించ్చితి
3. అమ్మనం .
4. పాలించ్చి ఇయ్య
6. త . . . (విధు)
7. నే . యము .
8. నైవేద్యానకు

9. గంగ్గాన
10. వినయు.

ONGOLE (44).

[Gonasapúḍi. Telugu. From Dhvajasthambam of Vishnu temple. Unintelligible.]

1. స్వస్తి రావిపూడి
2. . . . వ . హా . డ
3. . . . ర . . .
4. రయస్మ జీజ గట్టి
5. నధమ్మాణముజ కొ
6. డవా వికుల కరు
7. . శహంరుచే ధమ్మాణ
8. రాజేసి వాండు . .
9. కి వారిరివి.

ONGOLE (45). (A.D. 1218-19.)

[Gonasapúḍi. Telugu. To west of Káṣiviṣvéṣvara temple.]

TRANSLATION.

Hail! On Wednesday, the 11th of the bright fortnight of Kártika of the year Bahudhánya, corresponding to the year 1140 of the illustrious Śaka era, Ṣrímat Súryagiri Danḍanáyaka Chandra set up the image of Ṣrí Chandréṣvara Mahádéva naming it after himself in Mánópalli otherwise called Baṭṭirrapaṭṭam, which is on the coast of the eastern sea in Kammanáḍu for the religious merit of Ṣrímat Gaṇapatidéva Mahárája. He constructed a temple along with an illustrious *maṇḍapa* and granted in perpetuity, to last as the sun and moon endure, Erra Cheṛugonasapúndi for providing all enjoyments to Ṣrí Chanḍéṣvara Ṣrí Mahádéva, for the religious merit of Ganapatidéva Mahárája.

[One imprecatory verse.]

1. స్వస్తిశ్రీ శకవరుషంబులు
2. ౧౧౮౦ యగు నేంటిబహు
3. ధాన్య సంవత్సర కార్త్తిక శు
4. ద్ధపక్ష ౧౧ యుర బుధవాం
5. బునం గంమనాంటిలోనం
6. బూర్వ్వ సముద్రతీరంబున (బట్టి
7. (ర) పట్టణంబైన మానోపల్లియ
8. ందు నిజనామాంకితంబుగా
9. శ్రీచంద్రేశ్వర శ్రీమహాదేవుని శ్రీ
10. మతు గణపతి దేవమహారా
11. జులకు ధర్మ్మవుగా బ్రతిష్టిం
12. చెను శ్రీమండప సమన్వితం
13. బుగాగుడి ఎత్తించి శ్రీమశ్శూబయ్యర్
14. గిరి దండనాయక చంద్రనం
15. ధు శ్రీచంద్రేశ్వర శ్రీమహాదేవు
16. నికి అంగరంగ భోగంబుల
17. కు ఎఱ్ఱచెఱుగోన సపూండి
18. ని చంద్రార్కస్తాయిగా గణపతిదే
19. వ మహారాజులకు ధర్మ్మవుగాని
20. నిస్తిమి దీనికి స్వదత్తాం పరదత్తాం
21. వాయో హరేతి వసుంధరా
22. షష్టిర్వ్వర్ష సహస్రాణి విష్టా
23. యాం జాయతేక్రిమి॥

ONGOLE (46). (A.D. 1510-11.)

[Gonugunṭa. Telugu. In front of Vírabhadraswámi temple.]

TRANSLATION.

Hail! On the holy occasion on Tuesday, the 11th of the bright half of Kártika of the year Pramódúta, corresponding to the year 1433 of the illustrious, victorious and prosperous Ṣaliváhana Ṣaka era, while Ṣríman Mahámaṇḍaléṣvara Rájádhi Rája Rájaparaméṣvara Rája Téjónidhi (treasury of splendour) Ṣrí Kṛishnadéva Mahaáráyulu was ruling the kingdom of the earth, Súrnáyani Abbánáyanivárú was pleased to give Gónugunṭa, attached to Kocharlakoṭa *Kaṭaka* in Ammanabrolu *ṣíma* which Sáḷuva Timmarasayya was pleased to give to Súrnáyani Abbánáyanivárú and which is situated in Konḍavíḍu *rájya* which was given to him (Timmarusayya) by the Rája, for the religious merit of Timmarusuváru for providing *amritapaḍi* to Amaréṣvara of Gonugunṭa which is subject to him (Abbanáyanivárú).

. . . . on the west, Gonugunṭa, the western extremity . . . . on the east of . . . . the *méra* grain realized from the *amaram*, on the north of the village . . . . on the west of the tank, on the east of Yélumnáḍu, on the south of Ṣévúru, near Chellikúru . . . . to . . . Vórungirammakúr . . . . at the junction of that field and Gonugunṭa . . . . the field granted *puṭṭi*, per *puṭṭi* . . . to the village . . . to the west of mádigalachénu to the south of the village, the *mányam* to the east . . . torikump . . . . shall belong to Amarasvara . . . Those who violate this will incur the sin of killing cows and Brahmans near the Ganges. If any one obstruct and do not give (méras) he will incur in perpetuity as long as the sun and moon endure the sin of eating from the skull of his eldest son, and of killing cows, and his parents.

[One imprecatory verse.]

Note.—(1) Note the use of Kaṭaka in this inscription. It seems to mean nothing more than a fort and its *entourage*.

(2) On the gópuram of the temple of Rámalingéṣvara at Gonuguṇṭa there is a long inscription describing a grant made by a zamindar of Venkaṭagiri to the temple. It is probably modern and is of no interest.

1. స్వస్తిశ్రీ జయాభ్యుదయ శాలివాహన శకవర్షంబులు ౧౪౩౩ అగు నేంటి ప్రమోదూ

2. త సంవత్సర కార్త్తీక శుద్ధ ౧౧ మంవార పుణ్యకాల మందున శ్రీ మన్మహా మండలేశ్వర రాజా

3. ధి రాజ రాజ పరమేశ్వర రాజతేజోనిధి శ్రీకృష్ణదేవ మహారాయులు పృథివీరాజ్యము చే

4. యుచును సాళువతింమరసయ్యరువారికి దయచేసి యి య్యంగా నంగరంగ వైభవాలతో

5. ను రాజ్యముచేయుచును తిమరసయ్యవారు తమకుచెల్లి వచ్చె కొండవీడురాజ్యం

6. లోను సూనార్యని అబ్బానాయనివారికి డయచేసి యిచ్చిన అమ్మనబ్రోలు సీమలోను కొచ్చర్ల

7. కోటకటక సాలుంగపట్టునగోనుగుంటన సూనార్యని అబ్బానాయనివారు డయచేసి

8. తిమ్మరుసువారికి పుణ్యముగాను తమర్తచేసె దమకు జెల్లివచ్చెడి గోనుగుంటను అమరేశ్వర

9. దేవునకు అమృతపళ్లములకు . . . . పడ మటను గోనుగుంట పడమటి కొమ్మున . . .

10. . యఽరి వూరికి తూప్పూనను అమరానకువచ్చె మేర పంటను వూరికి వుత్తరమునను . .

11. చెరువు వడమటను యెలుంనాటికి పూర్వానాం [శేవూరికి దక్షిణము తట్టునను చెల్లి కూరివద్ద]

12. . . . . వోరుంగి ఉామకు వూరికి . . . . వూ . ం బో అ చేనుగోనుగుంట సందున వుట్టి [పతు]

13. . . . . పెట్టిన క్షేత్రం ఖ ౧ వుట్టికి . . . వూరికి . . . లోన్యాలానను మాదిగల చేనుకుపడుమటను . . .

14. అమరేశ్వరునికి వూరికి ధక్షిణమున . . . . వోరి కుంటకు తూప్పూనుంచివచ్చి మాన్యా . . . . చెల్లంగలది

15. . . . . చ్చవ అ . . . . యింమకు యశ్వరు తప్పివాను గంగ కఱుత గోవుబ్రాంహ్మలను

16. వధించిన పాపానం పొందుదురు . . . . యవ్వరియ్యాక సరిగా

17. . విరోధించినయకల పెద్దకొడుకు కపాలమున గోవుల తమ తల్లితండ్రుల . . . . కుడిచిన . . . .

18. అచంద్రార్కాము అనుభవించువారు స్వదత్త ద్విగుణం పుణ్యాం . . . .

19. . . . .

ONGOLE (47). (A.D. 1519–20.)

[Gundḷapalli. Telugu. Near Polameramma temple.]

TRANSLATION.

Hail! On Sunday, the 15th of the bright fortnight of Kártíka of the year Pramádi, corresponding to the illustrious and auspicious Ṣaka year 1441, on the holy occasion of a solar eclipse, we, Jíyaràju, have given 200 kunṭas of dry land in the fields of Vírachirudapalli which belongs to our chiefdom, on the boundary line of Kottakóṭa and Nettipáḍu as a *sarvamánya* for the Gópáḷa tank.

Note.—This chief's name does not recur in our collection.

1. స్వస్తి శ్రీ శుభ శకవరుష
2. ంబులు ౧౪౪౧ అగు నేటి ప్ర
3. మాది సంవత్సర కార్తిక శు ౧౫ ఆ
4. సోమ గ్రహణపుణ్య కాలమందు
5. ను (వెట్టినచెంను) జీయంరాజుమా
6. నాయంకరానకు జెంల్లె వీర చిరుదప
7. ల్లి పొలంలోను కొత్తకోట(నె)త్తి
8. పాటి పొలిమేరం వెంటచెను
9. గోపాళుని చెరువుకు సర్వం
10. మాన్యంగాను యిస్తిమి ౨౦౦ కు.

Ongole (48).

[Gunḍlapalli. Telugu. Opposite Ṣiva temple.]

Translation.

First part.

* * * *

Those who obstruct this resemble those who kill at Benares and will be regarded as having disobeyed Tribhuvanánkuṣa (the Chálukyan king Vijayáditya III). Seal.

Second part.

Hail ! . . . . the terror of all foes . . .

* * * *

Note.—The transcription was done by Mr. V. Venkayya.

1. [ని]చ్చినట్టి కఌది . బు దేవు
2. లయ్యకవ్వారి జా . ను ఇల్లు
3. లనుద్దాగిన [వారు] ల . ద్రి
4. . ద్దలు ప ణ్డలు రి . . . .
5. పాలు ఆ . స్థ . బలుపుష్టి
6. పాలలు దీనికిన్ప్రక్రంబు వచ్చిన
7. వారు బారనాశి న్డచ్చినవారు
8. త్రిభువనకుశంబు వ [క్రి] శినవారు
9. [ముద్ర ?]

(*b*)

1. స్వస్తి సకల రిపుదర్ప మ

* * * *

ONGOLE (49). (A.D. 1298-99.)

[Íḍamúḍi Telugu. Inside shrine of Ṣiva temple.]

TRANSLATION.

Hail! On Sunday, the 2nd of the bright fortnight of Ṣrávaṇa of the year Viḷambi, corresponding to the Ṣaka year 1221, Putávari Káma Boppaningáru, the minister (*pradháni*) of Ṣríman Mahámaṇḍaléṣvara Kákatíya Pratápa Rudradéva Mahárájulu presented . . . . to Kandamúḍi Rámájósyulu for the religious merit of his ather (Dévaya) and his mother (Punnavalakshmi) . . . .

1. స్వస్తి శకవర్షంబులు ౧౨౨౧ అ
2. గునేటి విళంబి సంవత్సర శ్రావణ
3. సు ౨ ఆ। నాండు శ్రీమన్మహా
4. మండలేశ్వర కాకతీయ ప్రతా

5. ప రుద్రదేవ మహారాజుల ప్రధా
6. ని పుత్రాహరి కామబొప్ప
7. నింగారు తమతండ్రి (దేవయ) గారికి
8. న్ని దమగల్లి (పున్నవలక్ష్మికిన్ని) పు
9. ణ్యముగాను కందమూండి రామాజో
10. స్యులకు . . . . ఇచ్చెను . .
12. . . . . .
13. . . . . .

ONGOLE (50). (A.D. 1154–55.)

[Janakavaram (hamlet Pongulúru). Stone in enclosure of Bhíméṣvara temple.]

TRANSLATION.

Hail! In the year Bháva, corresponding to the Ṣrí Saka year 1076 on the occasion of a solar eclipse, we, Ṣríman Mahásámanta (provincial chief) Viyavélaru have given with libation of water ten *matlu* of land in our village Pangalúru, situated in Kammanáḍu for providing oblation, a sacrifice and worship to the great deity Tiruvengaḷabha.

[Two imprecatory verses.]

Whoever obstructs this will be regarded as having killed 1,500 tawny cows on the banks of the Ganges, as having eaten from the skull of his eldest son, and as having killed at Benares.

NOTE.—Perhaps Vijavélaru of 50 is the same as Jiyyaru of 51. There is probably some mistake about the name which does not seem to appear elsewhere. Perhaps we should read Vijaya instead of Vija and Jiyyaru.

1. స్వస్తి శ్రీమతు సకవరుషములు ౧౦౭౬ అ
2. వునెండు భావపట్టున తిరువేగళభ మహా

3. దేవరకు శ్రీమనుమహాసామంత జియ
4. వేలారు కమ్మనాంటిలో నదముయూర్రై నపం
5. గులూరు హవిబలి అర్చ్చనంకు సూర్య్య గ్ర
6. హణ నిమిత్తమునం వ ౧౦ మట్లు భూమి
7. దారా పూర్వ్వకముసేసి ఇచ్చితిమి । బహుభి
8. ర్వ్వ సుధాదత్తా బహుభిర్వ్వాను పాలితం యస్యయ
స్యయ
9. దా భూమితస్యత స్యదదాఫలం । స్వదత్తాం పర
10. దత్తాం వాయోహరేతి వసుంధరా షష్టివర్షస
11. సహస్రాణి విష్టాయాం జాయతే క్రిమి । దీని
12. నెక్కరేని విలమముసేసినవారు గంగ క
13. ఱుత ౧౫౦౦ కవిలల వధించినవారు
14. జేష్ట పుత్రుని కపాంణమున కుడిచి
15. నవారు ॥ బాణరాణి వ్రచ్చినవారు॥

Ongole (51). (A.D. 1155-56.)

[Janakavaram (hamlet Pangalúru). Telugu. In enclosure of Bhímésvara temple.]

Translation.

Hail! In the 10th year of the victorious reign of Srímad Rájarájadéva, on Sunday, the 1st of the dark fortnight of Ásviyuja of the year Yuva, corresponding to the Saka year 1077, Mahá Sámanta Jiyyaru, the servant of the divine feet of Srímad Rájarájadéva and the protector from fear, gave on Vétiparva day from the fields of Guḍimaṇiyam one kucheḷa of land to Múlasthána Bhímésvaradéva of Pangulúru for the temple. This should last as long as the moon, sun and stars endure. Those who think of doing evil to this will be regarded as having killed at Benares.

Setajiyya, son of Vírajiyya, the temple servant of the *múlasthána* (chief deity) should build the temple and *mandapam* and perform daily offerings, and worship with lights. Those who prevent the trustee of this edict from keeping up the charity will incur the sin of killing a tawny cow on the banks of the Ganges.

[One imprecatory verse.]

1. స్వస్తి శ్రీ మద్రాజ రాజ దేవర విజ
2. య రాజ్య సంవత్సరములు ౧౦ శ్రాహి శక వ
3. ర్షములు ౧౦౭౭ నేంటి యువ సంవత్సర ఆ
4. శ్వియుజ బహుల బాద్యమి నాదివారము వేణి
5. వర్షముణాణ్ణు శ్రీమద్రాజ రాజ దేవర దివ్యశ్రీ
6. పాద శేవకా భయదాయమాన మహాసామంత
7. జియ్యరువారు వంగులూరి మూలస్థాన శ్రీభీమేశ్వర దే

వరకుం

8. గుడిమణియమునగు చ్చెలమాన్యం ఇచ్చితిమిదియాచంద్రా

ర్కతా

9. రకము దీనికహితము దలచినవారు బాణరాసింవ్రచ్చిన
10. వారు మూలస్థానపతి వీరజియ్యల కొడుకు సేతజియ్య
11. లు ఈ గుడియుని మండపమును గట్టించి నిత్య నివేద్యము
12. దీపము నడపంగలవాండు ఇస్థానాపతిని దత్తినెవ్వరేని జె

ర్చి

13. నవారు గంగకత్తం గవింంవధించినవారు బహుభిర్వ సు

ధాద

14. త్త బహు ఖచ్చానుపాలితా యెస్యయెస్య యదాభూమి

తస్య తస్యయదా

15. ఫలం ॥ స్వదత్తం పరదత్తం వాయోహారేతి వసుంధరా

షష్టి వర్షసహ

16. స్రాణి విష్టాయాం జాయతే క్రిమి॥

ONGOLE (52). (A.D. 1632–33.)

[Janakavaram (hamlet Pangalúru). Telugu.
Stone to east of Bhíméṣvara temple.]

TRANSLATION.

Hail! On Monday, the 14th of the dark fortnight of Mágha of the year Ángírasa, corresponding to the illustrious, victorious and prosperous Ṣáliváhana Ṣaka year 1554, this charitable edict of land was caused to be granted by Muḍupali Tirumalayya, the agent (kárya-karta) of Ṣrí Veligóṭi Komára Timmánáyanivâru, after making endless salutations to the great god Bhíméṣvara of the illustrious Pangulúru. On this holy occasion of Ṣivarátri we have given with libation of water for the religious merit of Kumára Timmánáyanigáru, the Linga-gunṭa field of two *gorrus* as an entire *inám* in the Nesari-páṭi Kuchela field having on the n rth the path to Chandalúru and the boundary line of Chandalúru on the east and Góparázuváru waste land on the south and Góparájuváru field on the west. Therefore . . . . . these two *gorrus* of land with the eight kinds of ownership and powers . . . .

NOTE.—This agent is not mentioned elsewhere.

1. స్వస్తి శ్రీ జయాభ్యుదయ శాలివాహనశక వ
2. ర్షంబ్బులు ॥ ౧౫౫౪ ॥ అగు నెంటి ఆంగ్గీర (స) సం
3. వ్వత్సర మాఘ బ ౧౪ సో శ్రీమతు పంగ్గులూరి భీ
4. మేశ్వర శ్రీమహాదేవునికి శ్రీవెలిగోటి కొమా
5. రతిమ్మానాయినివారి కార్యకర్త్తలైన ముదుపలి తిరు
6. మలయ్య అనంతములైన దండ్డములు సమర్పించ్చి యి
7. ప్పించిన భూదాన ధర్మశాసనం శివరాత్రి పుణ్యకాల

మంద్దు స్వా

8. మి అంగ్గ రంగబోగములకుంగ్గాను నె సరిపాటికుచ్చిలక్షే
త్రము రెండు

9. గోర్లచేను లింగ్గికుంటచేను వుత్తారాన్ను చందలూరి
దోవాను తూర్పు

10. న చెంద్గలూరి పొలిమేరానున్ను దక్షిణాను గోపరాజు
వారి బీడును

11. పడుమట గోపరాజువారి చేనునున్ను . ఇలోనను
. . సర్వమాన్యం

12. గాను . . కుమారతిమ్మానాయినింగారికి పుణ్యంగాను
ధారాపోసి ఇస్తిమిగానయిా

13. రెండుగోర్ల . . . చెను అందుగల అష్టభోగ తేజ
స్వామ్యము ఆ

ONGOLE (53). (A.D. 1293–94.)

[Kanḍlagunta. Telugu. From four sides of a stone opposite Gokanéṣvara temple.]

TRANSLATION.

Hail! On Monday, the 1st of the bright fortnight of Chaitra of the year Vijaya, corresponding to the illustrious Śaka year 1215, Hail! while Ṣríman Mahámaṇḍaléṣvara Kákatíya Pratápa Rudradéva Mahárája was ruling and holding pleasant intercourse (with his feudatories), *mányams* were given to Polamara stbána constructed for Brahma (?), *vrittis* to god and Brahmans and a field up to its four boundaries(?) . . . Báhata Dévarája caused the village . . . . to be given as charity to Bhíméṣvara Ṣrí Mahádévara (whose image is) set up at Rávinútula for his enjoyment as long as sun and moon exist for the religious merit of his ruler Rudradéva Maháràja. May it cause great prosperity!

[Two imprecatory verses.]

NOTE.—In O. 129 we have the same donor mentioned. His name there appears as Báhaḍa. He seems to have been a petty chief who is not mentioned elsewhere.

1. స్వస్తిశ్రీ శక
2. వర్షంబులు
3. ౧౧౧౫ అగు
4. నేంటి విజ
5. య సంవత్స
6. ర చైత్ర శుద్ధ
7. ౧ సో । స్వస్తి
8. శ్రీ మన్మ
9. హా మండ్లే
10. శ్వర కాక
11. తియ్య ప్ర
12. తాప రుద్ర
13. దేవ మహా
14. రాజులు సు
15. ఖ సంక (తావినోద ?)

Second side.

16. ంబుల రాజ్యము
17. సేయుచుండంగా
18. ను కమ్మనాంటిలో
19. విరావి నూంతుల
20. స్థలమున బ్రమ్మ
21. నికింనిం గట్టిన
22. బోలామర

23. వనస్థాన మాన్యం
24. ములును దో
25. వ బ్రాహ్మణ
26. ప్రిత్తులూహూ
27. ఫుచ్చి చతుస్సీ
28. మ సహిత
29. మైన క్షేత్రమా
30. ంత్ర బెట్టెను
31. గ్రామా య
32. . . ము

Third side.

33. గాను బాహ
34. తదే వరా
35. జులు ద
36. న్నైలిన రుద్ర
37. దేవ మహా
38. రాజులకు
39. ధర్మణాపుగ
40. ను రావినూ
41. ం తులంబ్ర
42. తిష్ట సేసిన
43. భీంబేశ్వ
44. ర శ్రీమహా
45. దేవరకును
46. అంగరంగ్గ
47. భోగముల
48. కును ఆచ
49. ం ద్రాకకాము

50. సెల్లు నట్లు
51. గాను ధర్మ
52. ము సేయిం

Fourth side.

53. చ్చెను మంగళ
54. మహా శ్రీ శ్రీ
55. శ్రీ ॥ శ్లోకం ॥
56. దానపాల నయో
57. ర్మధ్యే దానాత్శ్రేయో
58. నుపాలనం । దానా
59. త్స్వర్గ మవాప్నో
60. తి పాలనా ద
61. చ్యుతం పదం ॥ స్వ
62. త్తా ద్విగుణం పు
63. ణ్యం పరదత్తాను
64. పాలనం పర
65. దత్తాప హా
66. రేణ స్వద
67. త్తం నిష్ఫ
68. లం భవే
69. త్ శ్రీ

ONGOLE (54). (A.D. 1306–07 ?)

[1] [Kanuparti. Telugu and Sanskrit in Telugu character. On a small stone by the Vishnu temple. Lines 1 to 4 form a Sanskrit verse which as it stands makes no sense, but appears to be a Jain invocation of Dharma.]

TRANSLATION.

On Friday, the day of Ṣatabhisha, the first day of Kártika of the year Rappava (Bhava or Parábhava ?), corresponding to the illustrious Ṣaka year 12 . . with the consent of the Rája, Ṣrimat Kámaya Boyyanḍu of Alinanánḍu gave to Malamandala (Alamanḍala ?) Perumálu of Moṭṭupalle 200 *maḍis* of wet land in Chadalaváḍa *sthala* under the Kámasamudram (a tank ?) of Kanuparti for providing worship, *amritapaḍi*, vessels and *tirupaḍiyáram*. This *paḍisesham* to Rámuḍu (Ráma) should be maintained as long as the sun and moon exist. May the kingdom and Dharma prosper!

NOTE.—The inscription has been made out with difficulty from the original stone.

1. स्वस्ति श्री लोकेधर्मा
2. ध्यंते लोकांस्तां प्रण
3. म्यहं । पालयें तस्तु
4. मां भवंतु पृथिवीश्वर

---

1 Mr. Boswell in the District Manual talks of "an immense stone ṣásanam" at Kanuparti, but we have been unable to find it; possibly sand has drifted over it. Kanuparti was evidently a place of some importance once and much larger than it is at present. Carved stones are to be found scattered about but the most conspicuous feature is the number of *lingams*. In the next inscriptions it is spoken of as possessing a thousand *lingams*.

5. శ్రీ శకవరుషములు ౧౩ . . .
6. రప్పవ సంవత్సర కార్తిక క. శు
7. ౧ శుక్రవారమాను శత భిశం
8. మును అలినినాండు । శ్రీమతు
9. కామయబోయ్యుండు రాజానుగ్ర
10. హముతోడ మోట్టుపల్లెమల
11. మండ్డల పెరుమాళ్లకు సమా
12. రాధనకు అమ్రుతపడి బాత్రము
13. లకు చెదలవాడస్తలమున, కసు
14. పలితి కామసముద్రం క్రిం
15. దను తిరుపడియారముకు
16. గాను నిచ్చిన వరిచెని మడు
17. లు ౨౦౦ మడులుండును
18. ఆచంద్రార్కము రా
19. ముడు పడిశేషముగా
20. నునడపంగలది రాజ్యమూ
21. ను దర్మమూను వర్ధించ
22. డము.

Ongole (55). (A.D. 1426–27.)

[Kanuparti. Sanskrit verse in Telugu character. From stone removed from above the gate of the Vishnu temple.]

Translation.

V. 1. In the illustrious Ṣaka year, reckoned by the elephant (8), the oceans (4), the fires (3), and the moon (1), *i.e.*, 1348, on the 11th *tithi* of the bright fortnight of Mágha in the year Bhava preceded by Para (Parábhava), there was a holy city called Kóśámbika, which is situated at the junction of the Brahmakunḍi (Gundlakamma) with the sea, at a distance of *yójanas* reckoned by the eyes (2) and the moon (1), *i.e.*, 12, to the east of Ṣrísáila, and which was the abode of 1,000 lingas.

V. 2. King Víra Amala (Abala), of great valour, scion of the solar race, son of king Núnka, being entreated by kings who were his equals " Be our refuge " gave to the pious Brahmans, whose conduct was pure and approved by the védas, and who were enjoying lands given by him in that town, wealth consisting of the eight species of property and the eight species of enjoyment to last as long as the sun and moon endure.

Kósambika = gold.

Kósambikapuri = city of gold, Kanakapuri a Sanskritized form of Kanuparti.

Inscriptions (55) and (56) are of the same date and the donors' fathers seem to be the same. But the stone is rough and the inscriptions had to be read *in situ* and there may be some mistakes. Kanuparti contains a large number of *lingams* even now.

1. श्रीमच्छके गजाब्धि
2. ज्वलनशाशिमिते श्रीप
3. रादौ भवाब्दे माघे
4. मास सितैकादशातिथिस
5. मये ब्रह्मकुंड्यब्धि
6. गयो श्रीशैलस्यैन्द्र
7. भागे नयनशाशिमिते
8. योजने संस्तिताया
9. पुण्या कोशांबिका पु
10. र्यपि च दशाशतस्याणु
11. लिंगाकरोभूत् ॥ (1)

12. भूपालैरात्मतुल्यैर्भ

13. वशरणमिति प्रार्थितो

14. ग्रप्रतापःश्रीमद्वीरो

15. भलक्ष्मापतिरिनकुलजो

16. नूंकभूपालसूनुः ।

17. तस्यांभुक्तक्षितिभ्यःशृ

18. तिमतविमलाचारस

19. द्ब्राह्मणेभ्यश्चाष्टैश्च

20. र्याष्टभोगान्वितसुख

21. मकरोद्यावद्दादित्य

22 चंद्रौ ॥

ONGOLE (56). (A.D. 1426–27.)

[Kanuparti. Sanskrit in Telugu character and Telugu. From the stone by the Vishnu temple referred to in the preceding inscription.]

TRANSLATION.

[One imprecatory verse in Sanskrit.]

(Telugu) Hail! On Thursday, the 11th of the bright fortnight of Mágha in the year Parábhava, corresponding to the illustrious Ṣaka year 1348, Víra Ávu Bhúdéva Chóḍa Maháréja, the son of Ṣríman Mahámaṇḍaléṣvara Vennu Samberạ Álamandala Núkayadéva Chóḍa Mahárája, who has the *biruda* Tribhuvana, (gave) Kanupaṛti which is situated to the south-east of Ṣríparvata (Ṣríṣaila) which is the place of 1,000 lingas and which is the holy place of the junction of the Brahmakuṇḍi (Gundlakumma) with the sea to the holders of *vrittis* of deities and the Brahmans of that town, as a *sarvamánya* with all its income and free from all burdens and made them happy, for the religious merit of Vijaya Bukka Ráya Mahárája, son of Ṣríman Mahámaṇḍaléṣvara Rajádhirája Rájaparaméṣvara Ṣrí Víra Dévaráya Maháráya and his queen Demá Ammá.

A royal charter in stone was issued (in these terms).

To the kings who protect the charity set out in this charter which has been set up to last as long as the sun and moon exist and which has also been engraved on stone in a spirit of righteousness, there will be prosperity to the kingdom, to the ministers increase of life, health and wealth, to the officials abundance of wealth, gold, property and vehicles, and to the subjects increase of progeny.

[One imprecatory verse.]

Adoration be to Ṣrí Ráma !

Those who cause obstacles to this charity will be regarded as having committed the five cardinal sins, *Brahmahatyá* and the rest.

[One imprecatory verse.]

NOTE.—The mother of Víra Vijaya or Vijaya Bukka is commonly called Hemámbiká. Probably Dema Ammá is a misreading for Héma Ammá. It seems pretty clear that for Víra Ávu we should read Víra Abala. The titles should apparently precede the name of Vijaya Bukka instead of that of Víra Dévaráya.

1. सामान्योयं धर्मसेतु
2. र्नृपाणां कालेकाले पालनी
3. य्यो भवर्द्भि । सर्वानेतान् भाविन
4. पार्थिवेन्द्रान् भूयोभूयो
5. याचते रामचंद्रः ॥

6. శకవర్షంబులు ౧౩౭౮ అగునేంటి
7. పగా భవసంవత్సర మాఘ శు ౧౧ గు
8. శ్రీమన్మహా మండలేశ్వర రాజాధిరా
9. జ రాజ పరమేశ్వర శ్రీ వీర దేవరాయ
10. మహారాయులకుంను ఆదేవులు దే
11. మా అమ్మంగారికిన్ని ఆపద్దం కుమా
12. రుండు విజయ బుక్కరాయ మహా
13. రాయలుకుంన్ను పుణ్యముగాను శ్రీ
14. మన్మహా మండలేశ్వర త్రిభువనాభి
15. రుద్రుల వెన్ను సంబెట ఆలమండలనా
16. కయదేవచోడ మహారాజుల కు
17. మారుండు విర అవు భూదేవ చోడ మ
18. హారాజులు కనుపర్తి శ్రీపర్వత పూర్వ
19. దక్షిణమున్ను సహస్రలింగస్థాన బ్రంహ
20. కుండి సాగర సంగమ పుణ్యక్షేత్ర
21. మన్ని అందుంగల దేవబ్రాం
22. హ్మణవిశ్వల వారికి క్రితానకష్టం
23. ఆయాలు సహితం ప అవాంతరా
24. లుంబుట్టకుండాను సర్వమాన్యం
25. గాను రాయలు ఇచ్చిన రాయిసప
26. త్రశాశనము సిలాశాసనముగాను
27. ధర్మసహాయుండై ఆచంద్రార్కస్థా
28. ఇగాను ప్రతిష్టించి వుద్దరించిన ధ
29. ర్మశాసనములోని ధర్మముంబాలి
30. ంచిన రాజులుకు రాజ్యాభివృద్ధిన్ని ప్ర
31. దానులకు ఆయురారోగ్యైశ్వర్యాభివృద్ధి
32. న్ని అధికారులకు ధనకనక వస్తువా
33. హానసమృద్ధిన్ని ప్రజలకు పుత్రపౌ
34. త్రాభివృద్ధిన్ని అవును दानपालनयो

35. मध्ये दानाच्छ्रेयोनुपालनं दाना

36. त्स्वर्गमवाप्नोति पालनादच्युतं

37 पदं ॥ श्रीरामचंद्रायनमः

38. ఇదమార్గనకు విరోధించినవారు బ్రహ్మ

39. హత్యాది పంచమహాపాతకము

40. లు చేసినవారు॥ स्वदत्तां परदत्त

41. वा यो हरेति वसुंधरां षष्टि

42. वर्षसहस्राणि विष्टायां

43. जायते कृमिः ॥

ONGOLE (57).

[Kanuparti. Telugu. From threshold of gate of Ṣiva temple.]

TRANSLATION.

Hail ! Prosperity ! . . . . Vijayáditya Mahárája, supreme lord . . . . Paramabhaṭṭáraka (very devout) . . . . will realize the desires . . . . whoever destroys this will incur guilt such as that of one who distroys 1,000 good Brahmans, 1,000 cows, 1,000 temples and 1,000 tanks in Benares . . .

1. [స్వస్తిశ్రీ] . . . .
2. విజయాదిత్య మహారాజాధి రాజ . .
3. . . . .
4. . . . .
5. . . . .
6. . . . .
7. వర్యస్య వరద . . . .
8. ఔప నిధి . . . . . .

9. యాధిపతే [విజ్ఞా] జ . . . . . రాజాదర [ప]
10. రంభట్టారకప్రసా . . . . . దయాను . .
11. శ్చాంతనమీశా . . . . థయ . మనవా
12. చితఫలమ్ప్రాప్తి . . . ద [యే]న వినాశ చి . .
13. యిత్వాతేన [వారాణశీ] మహాబ్రాహ్మన సహస్రఘ్న
14. సహస్రకపిలాఘ్న సహస్రదేవాలయఘ్న సహ
15. స్రతటాకఘ్న మహాపాతకో భవతి విజయదిత్య
16. స్తు జన్మనాభ . . . . . నాశమ . . సతిత
. యమ .
17. . . . పెదయ దాన . . . . . .
18. . . . .

NOTE.—The transcription was done by Mr. V. Venkayya.

ONGOLE (58). (A.D. 1310–11.)

[Karavadi. Telugu. From a boulder in enclosure of Rámalingaswámi temple. Second side unintelligible in parts.]

TRANSLATION.

Hail! On Thursday, the 10th of the dark fortnight of Srávaṇa of the year Sádháraṇa, corresponding to the year 1232 of the illustrious and prosperous Ṣaka era, while Pratápa Rudradéva Mahárája was ruling the earth, this charity was presented to the deity Rámanátha of Karuvadi, which is situated on the southern bank of the Gunḍéru (Gunḍlakamma river) by Kámaya Boppanḍu Dévaya Reḍḍigáru, the Reddis, the Kápus, and the Seṭṭies, and the 18 castes. We have given the field to the deity free from taxes and miscellaneous fees . . . . Vendors and purchasers should give half a kásu on all their goods and grain (?) The Behris (hawkers) who sell goods for thousands (on a large scale) should also pay (?) Those who obstruct the charity by not giving these *méras* will incur the sin of killing a tawny cow near the Ganges. They will be considered to have drunk toddy from the skull of their eldest son. They will incur the guilt of the five great sins.

* * * *

స్వస్తిశ్రీ శుభశకవరుష
ంబులు ౧౨౩౨ అగునేంటి
సాధారణ సంవత్సర
శ్రావణ బహుల ౧౦ గు
ప్రతాప రుద్రదేవ మహారాజు
లు ప్రిధ్వీరాజ్యము సేయం
గాను గుండ్డేటి దక్షిణాన కలు
వది రామనాథ దేవరకు కా
మయ బొప్పండూను, దేవ య
రెడ్డింగారూను, రఝ్జూను, కాంపు
లూను, సెట్లూను, పదునెనిమిది జా
తులవారూం గూడం జేసిన దమ్మ
ము దేవక్షేత్రము ఎంత్తగలవారు

Second side.

నువట్టి . . . పంగ్గము సిల్లఱ సుంకరాము
బేయును . . . వ్య లేకుండా నిస్తిమి, తమ స
ర కమ్మి . . ధమ్మము సురముభండ్డి వరు
పుడు . . చీర, సకలధాన్యాలూను పసరక
మ్మినాను . . . విసామూను పణమున నరకా
నూని ర్కుయించి సరకుగొన్నవారు వెళ్టేడిది

వెలు . . . అమ్మైడి బెహారి పెట్టెడిది ఇ
మెర . . తూను పెట్ట నీకవిఘ్నము సేసిన
వారు . . గంగ కతీరంగవిలం బొడిచిన
వారు . పెద్ద కొడుకు కపాలానం గల్లు ద్రా
వినవారు - పంచమహాపాతకాలుబడువారు
కు భక్తుని పెరనడ్డు సెస్తిమి(?).

ONGOLE (59). (A.D. 1167–68 ?)

[Koṇḍamunjalúru. Telugu. One side of Nága stone to west of village.]

TRANSLATION.

Hail ! On Tuesday, the second of the dark fortnight of Kártika, corresponding to the year 1089 of the illustrious Ṣaka era, in the 21st year of the victorious reign of Ṣrímat Rája Rájadévara, Yerrama Náyakuḍu, son of Nimbrólu Sabbanáyaka the superintendent of the treasury (koṭṭari presumably corresponds with koshtádhikári in No. 60) of Ṣríman Mahámaṇḍaléṣvara Kulóttunga Rájéndra Chóḍa Rája, having set up a *linga* in the name of his father in Koṇḍamunjalúru in Kammanáḍu, erected a temple and presented eight *kunchams* for offerings at the three *sandhyás* to Sabbéṣvara Mahádéva.

Seven *maruts* of wet land in rear of the Ṣilácheruvu to the south of the village along the tank bund for rice . . . and two *puṭṭis* of dry land; two *túms* of jonna field to Mallajiya, a gingelly field of one *puṭṭi* west of the village for the perpetual lamp, five cows and four she-buffaloes for the five kinds of sacred food, for ghee, for curds, for festivals and for offerings. Mallajíyalu the son of Vémajiyalu, should receive these and he, his sons and grandsons should maintain (the worship) as long as the sun and moon endure. Those who, not maintaining this charity, cause obstruction to it will be regarded as having killed their parents and will incur the sin of killing tawny cows on the Ganges.

. . . . of Rájéndra Chóḍa . . . . presented, ... two *puṭṭis* of land to Sabbéṣvara for the great offerings; he presented a gingelly field of . . . . *puṭṭis* for the perpetual lamps to last as long as the moon and sun endure to the west of the village of Konḍamunjalúr . . . . no trouble by force should be caused to this (charity) by any one on earth. If any one seizes what has been given by others he becomes guilty of the five cardinal sins. So has it been declared by Vyása.

[Two imprecatory verses.]

NOTE.—Mr. V. Venkayya supplied the transcript of the Sanskrit portion.

1. స్వస్తి శకవర్షంబులు ౧౦౮[౯]
2. గు నేంటి కార్త్తిక బ ౧ మంగ్గల వా
3. రమున శ్రీమద్రాజరాజ దే
4. వర విజయరాజ్యం సంవత్స
5. రంబులు ౯౧ శ్రాహి శ్రీమన్మహా
6. మణ్డలేశ్వర కులోత్తుంగ్గ రాజేం
7. ద్రచోడ రాజుల కొట్టరి, నింబ్రో
8. లి సబ్బినాయకుకొడుకు ఎఱ్ఱి
9. మనాయకుండు కమ్మనాంటిలో
10. ని కొండముంజలూరం దమ తం
11. డ్రి పేర లింగ్గ ప్రతిష్టసేసి గు

12. డి గట్టించ్చిం ఆసబ్బేస్వర మహాదే
13. వరకుంద్రి సంధ్యల నివేద్యము
14. నకుంగా ఎన్మిది కుంభములు
15. . . బీయమునకు నూ
16. రి దక్షిణదిక్కునం జెఱ్వగట్లోన
17. శిలా చెఱ్వ వెనుకం బుట్టిన్ని వరి
18. పొలము పనుమఱుతులును
19. రెండు పుట్లునేల వెలిపొలము
20. ను మల్లజీయలకు జొన్నపొ
21. లముఖ ౨ అఖణ్డవర్తి దీప
22. మునకునూరి పడుమటంబు
23. ట్టి జెనుక్వం జేనును పంచ్చాద్రి
24. తాలకును స్థానమునకు నేతికింబెర్గువు
25. త్సవానకు నివేద్యమునకుంగాంబెట్టినట్టిమొ
26. దాలు ౫ సద్దలు ౪ వీనింజేకొనివేమ
27. జియ్యలుకొడుకుమల్లజీయల పు
28. త్రాను పవుత్రకముగానా చంద్రార్కతా
29. రంగా నడుపంగలవాణ్డుంయి ధ
30. మ్మర్వు[1] నడపక విఫలనము[2]సేసి
31. నవారు దమతల్లిదండ్రుల వధించ్చి
32. నవారు గంగకవిలల వదించ్చిన పోవ
33. మున బోయన[3]వారు ॥ . . . .
34. . . . .
35. . . . . त्र महानैवेद्यार्त्थं द्वि-
36. खण्डप्रमितमपि परं तत्र सब्वे-
37. श्वराय प्रादद्राजेंद्रचोड-
38. . तिवल्यपतिस्सोयामित्या-

1 Read ధర్మ్మార్వు. 2 Read విఘటనరు.

3 Read బోయినవారు.

39. . . . क्षेत्रं खण्कि . .
40. तत्र तिला . . मखण्डदीपाय प्रादा-
41. दाचंद्रार्कं ॥ पश्चिमतः कोण्डमु-
42. जरुग्रा . . . . स्योपरि न बलाद्वा .
43. . . . . . केन चिद्धात्र्यां । यदि ह-
44. रति परैर्द्दत्तं पञ्चमहापातका-
45. न्वितस्स भवेत् ॥ तथा [च] व्यासेना-
46. प्युक्तं[1] [॥*] స్వదత్తాం పరదత్తాంవాయో హ
47. రేత వసుంధరా షష్టిర్వర్షసహస్రా
48. ణి విష్టాయాంజాయతేక్రిమిః ॥ బ
49. భిర్ వసుధాదత్తా బహుభిశ్చానుపా
50. లిత యస్యయస్య యధాభూమి
51. తస్య తస్య తధాఫలం ॥ శ్రీ ॥

Ongole (60). (A.D. 1167–68 ?)

[Koṇḍamunjalúru. Sanskrit in Telugu character. From Nága stone to west of village.]

Translation.

V. 1. Hail! The son of king Chóḍa of the illustrious Velnáḍu, who had destroyed hostile kings, was Gonka, whose mind was pure on account of following truth and righteousness, famous for great valour, whose mind was resplendent with meditation on the pair of lotuses which is the feet of Ṣankara (Ṣiva); his wife was the illustrious Subbamámbá, chaste and endowed with virtues.

---

[1] The rest of the inscription consists of two imprecatory verses beginning with స్వదత్తాం and బహుభిః.

V. 2. His son, named Rájéndra Chóḍa, renowned, who had acquired polity, whose eternal prosperity was famous, who was praised by good men, who was the constant worshipper of the pair of lotuses which is the feet of Him whose crest is the young moon (Ṣiva), who vanquished with joy the crowd of hostile kings, and who was a second Arjuna in valour, brought under his control, the sea-girt (earth).

V. 3. His Superintendent of the treasury was Errama Náyaka (residing) in the village named Ṣrí Nidumbrólu—situated in the middle of the well-known district named Velanáḍu—wealthy, famous, blessed, excellent, grandson of the blessed Ṣrí Muduva of pure lineage, intelligent, of great fame, son of the illustrious Sabbana.

V. 4. Liberal, resembling Indra in enjoyment, a very Ṣiva, who is saluted by his devotees, who is a *Mandara* in fortitude, a very Káma to beautiful women who is well known, who is the abode of Ṣrí (fortune), handsome, a Harichandan to relations, excellent poets, Brahmans, good men, and . . ., whose fame is white, the son of Kommámbiká.

V. 5. "Let my father obtain union with Ṣiva" with this wish, having named a famous *linga* Sabbéṣvara, after him (his father), and having caused it to be set up, he, the illustrious Eṟṟama Náyaka reverently caused to be constructed for it a temple in the village named Ṣrí Munjalúr well known as being preceded by the word *parvata* (*hill*, *konḍa* in Telugu, *i.e.*, Konḍa Munjalúr).

V. 6. In the Ṣaka year reckoned by 9, by the serpents (8), the sky (0) and the moon (1) (*i.e.*, 1089), on the second *tithi* of the dark fortnight of the month named Kártika, on an excellent day (of the week), when the *nakshatra* was Kumbha (lit. at the rise of Kumbha)—he, the illustrious, the very wise, who is of good disposition, respectfully dedicated a *kalaṣa* (dome) (to be placed) on the top of the temple of Sabbéṣvara which had been constructed.

V. 7. In this village, in the country known as Kammaráshṭra (Kammanáḍu) . . . .

NOTE.—The transcription of Mr. V. Venkayya has been adopted.

First side.

1. स्वस्ति श्रीवेल-
2. नांटिचोडत्रि[1]
3. पतेर्ध्वस्तारिधा-
4. श्रीपतेस्सूनु-
5. रसूनृतधर्म्मनि-
6. र्म्मलमतिः प्रख्यात-
7. शार्योन्नतिः । गोक्क-
8. श्शंकरपादपंकज-
9. युगध्यानस्फुरन्मा-
10. नसः पतिनी[2] तस्य प-
11. तिव्रता गुणयु-
12. ता श्रीसब्बमांबा-
13. भवत् । [१*] ख्यातस्तत्तन-
14. य . . जितनयः[3]
15. प्रस्तुत्यनीत्योदयः[4] ।

---

[1] Read °चोडनृ.°

[2] Read पत्नी instead of पतिनी.

[3] The reading appears to be सचोर्जितनयः which is correct. समार्जितनयः suits the context better.

[4] Read नित्योदयः.

16. सद्वंद्यस्तरुणेंदु-
17. मौलिचरणद्वंद्वाभिवं-
18. द्वी सदा । लीलालोडित-
19. वैरिराजनिचयो रा-
20. जेन्द्रचोडाह्वयः ।
21. स्वाधीनामकरोत्पयो-
22. धिरशनां शौर्य्याद्विती-
23. यार्ज्जुनः ॥ [२*] तस्याभू-
24. द्वेलनांडुनाम्नि विष-
25. ये मध्ये प्रसिद्धे घनी ।
26. ग्रामे श्रीनिडुंब्रोलिना-
27. म्नि विदितः कोष्ठाधिकारी
28. कृती । श्रेष्ठ[:*] श्रीमुदु-

Third side.

29. वाह्वयस्य कृ-
30. तिन! [पौ]त्रः पवि-
31. त्रान्वयो । धी-
32. मानेङ्गमना-
33. यकस्तुतय-
34. [शा][:*] श्रीसब्बना-
35. ख्यात्मजः ॥ [३*] त्या-
30. गी भोगपुरंद-
37. र[:*] श्रितनुतश्रीक-
38. न्धरस्सुंदरी (।) कं-
39 दर्प्पो [1]भ्रितिमंद-
40. रस्सुविदितश्री-
41. मंदिरस्सुदं[रः*]
42. बन्धूनां सुक-

---

1 Read धृति.°

43. वींद्रसूरिवसु-
44. धाब्रिंदारका-[1]
45. णां सतां ब्रि-
46. नां[2] हरिचंद्दन-
47. स्सितयशाः को-
48. म्मांबिकानंदनः
49. ॥ [४*] सायुज्यं स्वचि
50. ता शिवस्य ल[भ*]ताम्ना-
51. मेति सब्बेश्वरं त-
52. न्नामोपपदं विधा-
53. य विदितं लिग्गं
54. प्रतिष्ठाप्य सः । ग्रा-
55. मे पर्व्वतनामपू-
56. र्व्वविदिते श्रीसु-
57. जलूराह्वये । श्री-
58. मानेङ्कमनाय-
59. को ऽपरचयत्प्रा-
60. सादमस्यादरात्
61. ॥ [५*] शाकाब्दे नवनागरवें-
62. द्दगाणिते कृष्णद्वितीय-
63. यातिथौ । मासे का-
64. र्त्तिकनाम्नि वास[र*]वरे
65. कुंभोदये सुस्थिते ।
66. प्रासादस्य विनिर्मितस्य शि-
67. खरे सब्बेश्वरस्यादरात्
68. सत्स . कलशार्प्पणं[3]

---

[1] Read बृंदारकाणां. In the translation I make सुविदितः a separate word.

[2] त्रिनां is unintelligible.

[3] The anusvara stands at the beginning of the next line.

In line 68 after सत्स a letter is lost. The reading may be सद्वृत्तः as in the translation.

69. समकृत श्रीमानु-[1]
70. सुधीमानसौ ॥ [१*] ग्रामे-
71. स्मिनु[2] कम्मराष्ट्राक्षि-
72. तितळविदिते दक्षि-

(Incomplete.)

ONGOLE (61).

[Konijédu. Telugu. On stone in Janárdanaswámi temple.]

TRANSLATION.

To propitiate Ṣrí Gópinátha of Koḍinjéḍu, Naraṣingi Śeṭṭi, son of Balasáyani Singama Śeṭṭi, of the Vinḍila *gótra*, of the Kómaṭi sect of Kandukúru, caused the enclosure wall of the eastern side of the temple to be polished by Santanútalapáḍu Punnayya for the religious merit of his mother Yalasáni and father Śingama Śeṭṭi.

1. శ్రీ కొడింజేటి శ్రీ గోపినా
2. ధునికి ప్రీతిగాను కందు
3. కూరి కోమటివారు విండి
4. లగోత్రుఁడు బలసాయని
5. సింగమ శెట్టి కొడుకు నర
6. శింగి శెట్టి తమతల్లి యలసాని
7. కిని తమతండ్రి శింగమ శెట్టి
8. కిని పుణ్యముగాను నగరికి

---

[1] Read श्रीमान्.   [2] Read ° स्मिन्.

9. తూర్వ్పదిక్కునను ఒక గుడివప్రన (ప్రాకార)
10. సంతనూతుల పాకుపుణ్ణయ
11. వరుంబని చెయిం చెను
12. ఈధర్మము శ్రీ శ్రీ శ్రీ

ONGOLE (62). (A.D. 1533-34?)

[Konijéḍu. Telugu. On a stone near the well of Chakradhara.]

TRANSLATION.

The well caused to be constructed on the 15th day of the bright fortnight of Áshádha of the . . . . year, corresponding to 1455 (S.S.) by Ṣríchakradhara as a work of charity for the religious merit of his father and mother.

1. ౧౪౫౫ అగునేంటి
2. సంవత్సర ఆషాఢశు ౧౫
3. నాడు శ్రీ చక్రధరు
4. డు తమ తల్లితండ్రికి ధర్మము
5. గాను సుకృతంగాను
6. కట్టించినట్టి భావి

ONGOLE (63).

[Koṇiki. Telugu. From fallen stone by Bhíméṣvara temple.]

TRANSLATION.

Hail! The *vritti* given by Ṣríman Mahámaṇḍaléṣvara Pratápa Rudradéva Maháráyulu . . . . He gave 4 *puṭṭis* in perpetuity . . . . Whoever obstructs this, of whatever family he may be, will incur the sin of killing a tawny cow on the banks of the Ganges . . . .

1. స్వస్తి శ్రీమన్మహా మండ
2. లేశ్వర ప్రతాప
3. రుద్రదేవ మహారాజులవారు
4. యిచ్చినవ్రిత్తి। . .. ము హా
5. ఐబలిమున పు . . .
6. వేకంబ నిత్యముగాను పట్టి ర
7. ట్టి కూడు తరుజావిచ్చెను దీ
8. నికి వీరివంశమునందు యె
9. వ్వరు విఘ్నముసేసితె గంగకరు
10. త గపిల గోవును . . . .
11. లేక

Ongole (64).

[Koṇiki. Telugu. From the same stone.]

Translation.

The *vritti* given by Kódinka Laḍḍa Varma of Kammánáḍu for the religious merit of Sankáma Mahárája Siddhana. Whoever obstructs this *vritti* will be regarded as having eaten from the skull of his eldest son . . . . and as having killed at Benares . . . . .

Note.—It is not clear what Siddhana is alluded to.

1. కంమనాంటికోని కో
2. డింకలడ్డవర్మ సంకామ
3. మహారాయ సిద్ధనకుం బు
4. ణ్యముగాను వ్రిత్తివెట్టెను యె

5. ష్వరు విఘ్నుంసేసినాను దమాపె
6. ద్ద కోడురుకపాలమున కుడిచి
7. నవారు బారణాసి వ్రచ్చిన
8. వారు (ముకసకరమును)
9. (శుటికం శుక్ర . .) శ్రీను
10. . . వామశ్రీ చందలూరి
11. . . . . . వడిరాదుదె

ONGOLE (65).

[Koṇiki. Telugu. Three inscriptions from Garuḍa stone opposite Raghunáyakula temple.]

TRANSLATION.

The perpetual devotion of Addépalli Singaráju to Ṣrí Raghunáyakulu of Koṇiki.

The service of Góparáju Pérayya.

Commencing from the 5th of the bright fortnight of Mágha of the year Kródhi to the bright fortnight of Kártika of the year Raktákshi . . . .

1. కొణికి శ్రీ రఘు
2. నాయకులకు అద్దేప
3. ల్లి శింగ్గరాజు నిత్యశేవా
1. గోపరాజు పేర
2. యశేవా ॥
1. క్రోధినామ సంవత్సర
2. మాఖ శుద్ధపంచమిల ఆ
3. రంభ్భు మొదలు కొని ర
4. క్తాక్షినామసంవత్స

5. రకా ౖత్తిక శు . . .
6. . . . .
7. . . . .

ONGOLE (66).

[Kopparapáḍu. Telugu. Opposite Mallésvaraswámi temple.]

TRANSLATION.

Hail! This is a gift to the deity made by Betrumanáyakuḍu, prime minister of Mahámaṇḍalésvara Mallidéva Chóḍa Mahárájulu, for the religious merit of his parents. Whoever desires this will be regarded as having killed his parents.

NOTE.—This official is not mentioned elsewhere in this collection.

1. స్వస్తి శ్రీ మన్మహా మ
2. ండలేశ్వర మల్లిదేవ చో
3. డమహారాజులు మహా ప్రధా
4. ని బెట్రుమున్నాయంకు
5. ండు తమతల్లితండ్రు
6. లకు ధర్మార్థముగా
7. ం బెట్టినదేవదత్తి నిది
8. నివారించ్చినవాండు
9. తమతల్లిదండ్రుల
10. వధించ్చినవాండు

A COLLECTION
OF THE
INSCRIPTIONS ON COPPER-PLATES AND STONES
IN THE
NELLORE DISTRICT

A COLLECTION
OF THE
INSCRIPTIONS ON COPPER-PLATES AND STONES
IN THE
NELLORE DISTRICT

MADE BY

ALAN BUTTERWORTH,

OF THE INDIAN CIVIL SERVICE (MADRAS)

AND

V. VENUGOPAUL CHETTY,

OF THE INDIAN CIVIL SERVICE (MADRAS)

IN THREE PARTS

PART III

GYAN

Published by

Gyan Publishing House
5, Ansari Road
Daryaganj, New Delhi-110002
Phone: 011-47034999, 9811692060
E-mail: books@gyanbooks.com

Distribution Network
gyanbooks.com
India, USA, Canada, UK, Australia, France

ISBN : 978-81-212-3814-4 (Set)
ISBN : 978-81-212-9722-6 (HB)
First Published, 1905

2nd Impression 2020

Printed at: Gyan Press, Delhi.

A Collection of the Inscriptions on Copper-Plates and Stones in the Nellore District, Part-III
Author: Alan Butterworth, V. Venugopaul Chetty

A COLLECTION

OF THE

INSCRIPTIONS ON COPPER-PLATES AND STONES

IN THE

NELLORE DISTRICT

MADE BY

ALAN BUTTERWORTH,

OF THE INDIAN CIVIL SERVICE (MADRAS)

AND

V. VENUGOPAUL CHETTY,

OF THE INDIAN CIVIL SERVICE (MADRAS).

IN THREE PARTS.

PART III.

MADRAS:

PRINTED BY THE SUPERINTENDENT, GOVERNMENT PRESS.

1905.

CONTENTS

PART III.

APPENDICES.

ABBREVIATIONS USED IN THIS WORK.

Prefixed to a Number	A.	stands for	Átmakúr Taluk.	
„ „	C.	„	Copper-Plate.	
„ „	D.	„	Darsi Division.	
„ „	G.	„	Gúḍúr	Taluk.
„ „	KG.	„	Kanigiri	„
„ „	KR.	„	Kundukúr	„
„ „	KV.	„	Kávali	„
„ „	N.	„	Nellore	„
„ „	O.	„	Ongole	„
„ „	P.	„	Podili Division.	
„ „	R.	„	Rápúr Taluk.	
„ „	S.	„	Súlúrpet (or Pólúr) Division.	
„ „	U.	„	Udayagiri Taluk.	
„ „	V.	„	Venkatagiri Division.	

B.	stands for	Brown's Telugu Dictionary.
Epig. Carn.	„	Epigraphia Carnataca.
E.I.	„	Epigraphia Indica.
I.A.	„	Indian Antiquary.
M.P.C.	„	Madhurántaka Pottapi Chóḷa.
M.K.	„	Mukkanṭi Káḍuveṭṭu.
M.M.	„	Mahá Maṇḍalésvara.
S.M.	„	Srímanmahámaṇḍalésvara.
W.	„	Wilson's Glossary of Revenue terms.

ERRATA.

(1) *Page* 1430, *sixth line from bottom.—For* "therefore" *read* "therefrom".

(2) *Page* 1431, *first line.—For* "Mauma" *read* "Manma".

(3) *Page* 1436, *eighth line.—For* "not" *read* "given".

(4) *Page* 1441, *tenth line from bottom.—For* "Peddami" *read* "Peddanu".

A COLLECTION

OF THE

COPPER-PLATE AND STONE INSCRIPTIONS

IN THE

NELLORE DISTRICT.

PART III.

ONGOLE (67). (A.D. 1254-55 ?)

[Koppólu. Ṭelugu. Opposite Bhíméṣvara temple.]

TRANSLATION.

Hail! On the occasion of Uttaráyaṇa Sankránti, corresponding to the illustrious Saka year 1176, Hail! Ṣrí . . . . who is a Révanta in riding most unruly horses, who is the protector of the lives of his feudatories, who bears the *biruda* Chakra Náráyaṇa . . . . . . (for the religious merit of) his father Maḍa . . . . and his mother Mádamma, gave dry land as *vritti* to Bhíméṣvaradéva of Kroppólu for worship . . . . in Bhanṭikolanu, 300 *kunṭas* of paddy field, to Gunḍima Kaṭṭi Mallináthadéva as *vritti* . . . . . *kunṭas*; this is given to the sons and grandsons of Prólajiyyalu the *sthánikuḍu* (temple servant), to last as long as the moon and sun endure to . . . one *kunṭa*; to the goddess ¾ of a *kunṭa*. The following are the *vrittis* of Bráhmans: (Here follows a list which is not quite clear.)

Second side.

His gift was made in the presence of the *mahá-pradháni* (prime minister) and the feudatories. This *vritti* to Srí Mallináthadéva should be protected . . .

Kámi Reḍḍi.

Reḍḍi Sannapa Reḍḍi . . . . .

NOTE.—The inscription is partially illegible. No doubt we have here to do with the same dynasty as in O. 89.

1. స్వస్తి శ్రీ శుభ శకవరుషంబులు ౧౧౭౬ ఆగు
2. నేంటి ఉత్తరాయణ సంక్రాంతిని మిత్తంబున స్వస్తి ఆతి
3. విషమహాయాకూథ ప్రౌఢ రేఖా రేవంత
4. క మండలీకరవందోళిజీవరకు . . . .
5. . . . . చక్రనారాయణశ్రీ
6. తమతండ్రి మడ . . . తమతల్లిమాదంమ (ఇ)
7. చ్చినవిత్తి క్రొప్పాలునందు భీమేశ్వరదేవరకు
8. . . . రాచ్చూనలకు ఇచ్చిన వెలిపొలము
9. భంటికొలను[?]కు ౩౦౦ పట్టివరిచేను గుండి
10. మకట్టి మల్లినాథదేవరకు ప్రిత్తికు . . దేవర
11. దీనిస్థానికుండు ప్రోల జియ్యల పుత్రపౌత్రులకు ఆచంద్రా ర్కముగా నిచ్చెను
12. కుంచెగు ౧I . దేవతకు గు-ఖ్యా ఇందుల బ్రాహ్మణవిత్తుబు తగ్చి పెద్దికగు ౧౦౦
13. . పెద్దిగుణం అక్షరాల గు ౨౦౦ ఆనం . . . గు ౫౦
14. గుగం దేవరకు దీనికగు ౨౦౦ తులసి అగ్నే పెదిగు ౧౦ సూరపెద్ది గు ౫౦
15. రికని గు౫౦ విజ్యపరాజునకు మంచిరాజునకు గు ౨౦౦
16. రాజు గు ౫౦ యరపరాజు గు ౨౩ తాడయ భక్తికి గు ౫౦ జో
17. శ్రీమన్ మహాదేవర్శ వరిపంట

Second side.

శ్రీమత్ మహాప్రతాప సామంత . . .
జనమున దీని దత్తించె శ్రీ మల్లి
నాధదేవరకు ఇచ్చి ప్రవిత్తిపాలింబడిన
పనులు . ఫం యెత్తిడి కామిరెడ్డి
రెడ్డి సన్నపరెడ్డి సోమరలి

ONGOLE (68). (A.D. 1534–35.)

[Koppólu. Telugu. To the north in the shroff *mânyam.*]

TRANSLATION.

Hail! On Thursday, the 15th of the bright fortnight of Vaiṣakha of the year Jaya, corresponding to the Ṣrí Ṣaka year 1456, on the holy occasion of the sacred marriage festival of . . . Vému Mádharu, this charitable edict was granted by Pólavíra . . . Nágini Náyuḍu of the Ravóli *gôtrá* . . . . . belonging to our chiefdom . . . grandsons maintained. They gave 5 *túms* of land for (providing) oil for anointing and offerings to the deity.

NOTE.—This chief is not mentioned elsewhere in the collection.

1. స్వస్తి శ్రీ శకవర్షంబులు
2. ౧౪౫౬ అగు నేటి జయసం
3. వత్సర వైశాఖ శు ౧౫ గు శ్రీద .
4. . . . . . . వేము మాధరు తిరు
5. కల్యాణోత్సవ పుణ్యకాలమం
6. దును . . రవోలి గోత్రుండైన
7. పోలవీర . . . నాగినినాయుండి
8. చ్చిన ధర్మశాసనం ఈమాన్యం .
9. కి . . . వ . . నుదాచలు . య్యా

10. వారు మాకి . . యంగరాం స్త్రైకుడు
11. . . . . తిరుణాలు
12. . . . . లు పౌత్రులూను
13. నున్ను పరిపాలించిరి యెందు
14. ము క్షేత్రం స్వామివి దేవన
15. నైవేద్యమునకు సమర్పించం
16. చెను

ONGOLE (69).

[Korisapáḍu. Telugu. On wall of Venugópálaswámi temple.]

TRANSLATION.

We have given with libation of water with a pure heart on the holy occasion of *tithi* . . . . With the Rája's share of the crop raised on that field they should repair the bund of the tank. Whoever fails to maintain this charity in that tank . . . .

1. తిథిపుణ్యకా
2. లమంద్ద త్రిక
3. రణ శుద్ధిగాను
4. ధారవోసి ఇస్తిమి
5. ఆ క్షేత్రానం బండ్డి
6. న ధాన్యాదులను
7. రాచభాగంవల్ల
8. చెరువుకట్ట వేశిం
9. చ్చంగలవారు ఇ
10. పుణ్యానకు యెవ్వ
11. రు తప్పినాను ఆచె
12. రువులో న .

ONGOLE (70). (A.D. 1275-76.)

[Maddipáḍu. Telugu. From stone by Narasimha temple.]

TRANSLATION.

Hail! On Thursday, the 10th of the dark fortnight of Mágha of the year Yuva, corresponding to the Ṣrí Śaka year 1197, Manchiráju Ganapáya and Kámáya-preggaḍa, the younger brother of Póchiráju, presented to Ṣrí Rámanáthadéva of Móṭupalli (the village of) Maddipáḍu lying on the Gunḍikarri (Gundlakamma) for providing oblation, offering and worship and all enjoyments, as long as the sun and the moon last, for the religious merit of Ṣríman Mahámanḍalésvara Kákatiya Rudramadéva Mahárája and of their own parents. Those who obstruct this charity will incur the sin of killing a tawny cow on the Ganges and at Benares. They will be considered to have taken food from the skull of their eldest son.

[Imprecatory verse.]

స్వస్తి శ్రీ శకవ
ర్షంబులు ౧౧౯౭
అగునేంటి యువ
సంవత్సర మాఘ
బ ౧౦ గు మో
టుపల్లి శ్రీరామ
నాథదేవరకు మ
ంచిరాజు గణప
యానుపోచిరా
జు తమ్ముండు
కామాయప్రెగ్గడ

సు స్వస్తి శ్రీమన్మ
హామండలేశ్వ
రకాకతియ్యరు
ద్రము దేవమ
హారాజులకు
తెమతల్లితండ్రు
లకు ధర్మ్మముగాను . . . .
గుండ్లకుర్తిలో
న మద్దిపాడు
అహోబలి అర్చ
నలకు అంగరం
గ్గభోగాలకు ఆ
చంద్రార్కముగా
నిచ్చితిమి తలా
రి ము కానీక . .
అన్నవారు గంగ
కత్తె (క) పిలం జ
ంప్పిన పాపానం బో
యినవారు శ్రీ
వారణాసి(వచ్చి
నవారు తనపెద్ద
కొడుకు కపాలము
లో కుడిచినవారు
స్వదత్తాం పరదత్తాం
వాయో హరేతివ
సుంధరా షష్టిర్వ
రుష సహస్రాణి విష్టా
యాం జాయతే క్రిమి

ONGOLE (71). (A.D. 1517-18?)

[Maḍanúru or Mannúru. Telugu and Sanskrit in Telugu character. On a stone in the temple of Rámalingéṣwara.]

TRANSLATION.

(Invocation in Sanskrit and Telugu.)

May Rámésvara Mahádéva who resides on the sea-shore and who is the lord of the town of Maḍanúru protect the worlds for ever!

Hail! On Thursday, the 15th of the bright half of Mágha of the year Íṣvara, corresponding to the year 1421 of the Ṣrí Śaka era, on the holy occasion of a lunar eclipse, under the orders of Ṣríman Mahámaṇḍaléṣvara, Rájádhirája Rájáparaméṣvara, Múruráyágaṇḍa, Ashta Digráyamanóbhayankara, Básadappuvaráyaragaṇḍa, lord of the eastern, southern and westerns seas, Yavanarájya-stbápanácbárya, Ṣrí Vírapratápa Krishṇadéva Maháráya, the illustrious Sáḷuva Timmarasu, the protector (*pratipálaka*) of the whole kingdom of Ṣrí Krishṇadéva Mahárája and who is able to protect gods and Brahmans, gave the village of Maḍanúru which was formerly in the enjoyment of Rámésvaradéva, having dismantled the (old) *arddha manḍapa* and *garbhagṛiha* (sanctuary), having caused to be erected a pinnacle, and having built a new *bhóga manḍapa* and an enclosure wall for the temples of the attendant deities, Sáḷuva Timmarasu (gave Maḍanúru) to Kaṭṭa Malaya for this purpose, for providing *amritapaḍi* (sacred food) and all enjoyments to the deity, for the religious merit of Ṣrí Krishṇadéva Maháráya. He presented the village of Maḍanúru with libation of water to Rámésvaradéva with the eight enjoyments and with the eight powers, so that this charity may be maintained.

(One of the usual imprecatory verses.)

The description of the fields on the four boundaries of Maḍanúru :—On the east of the fields is the sea, on the south Pokádhénunḍḍi, on the west Inangaléru, on the south-west Inangaléru Modugaluvampu, from that vampu (a bend, as of a river) to the north-west as far as the pond named Padártaguntạ, extending further north up to junction of Ítamukkala and Maḍanúru which is bounded on the east and west by Pótugaṭṭa, proceeding further to the east as far as a well with a Kapila,[1] further to the east as far as Veligunṭa, the line then goes west, east, south, then to the south-east, then east up to Jógidinna and east beyond that. To the east of that is the sea. These are the fields given and these are the boundaries.

NOTE.—For the other inscriptions of this place see under Mannúru. The year Íṣvara is S.S. 1440 current, not 1421.

The S.S. year has been assumed to be incorrect. Note the biruda "Yavanarájyasthápanácharya" applied to Krishnadéva. To what incident this relates is not clear to us.

1. सिंधुतीरनिवासोयं मड
2. नूरिपुरीश्वरः रामेश्वरमहादे
3. वो लोकान् रक्षतु शाश्वतं ॥
4. శకవరుషంబులు ౧౪.౨౧ అగునేంటి యీ
5. శ్వర సంవత్సర మాఘ శు ౧౫ గు । సోమగ్ర
6. హణపుణ్య కాలమున శ్రీమన్మహా
7. మండలేశ్వర రాజాధిరాజ రాజప
8. రమేశ్వర మూరురాయరగండ అష్ట

[1] Kapila = picottah or water-lift.

9. డికుడురాయ మనోభయంకర బాస
10. దప్పురరాయరగండ పూర్వదక్షి
11. ణ పశ్చిమ సముద్రాధీశ్వర యవన
12. రాజ్యస్థాపనాచార్య । శ్రీ వీరప్ర
13. తాప క్రష్ణదేవ మహారాయుల అ
14. నతిని శ్రీ క్రిష్ణదేవ మహారాయుల సమ
15. స్తరాజ్యానకున్ను ప్రతిపాలకుండును
16. దేవబ్రాంహ్మణ ప్రతిపాలకము
17. చెయ్యగల శ్రీ సాళువ తింమరసు
18. లుంగారు పూర్వాన రామేశ్వర దే
19. వునికిసాగి వచ్చే మడనూరు
20. అర్ధమండ్డప గర్భగృహము
21. లు విచ్చిసిఖరంగట్టియ్యాడం
22. కున్ను భోగమంటపము పరివా
23. ర దేవరగుళ్ల ప్రాకారంగకట్టిం
24. చ్చియ్యాండంకున్ను దేవుని అమ్రు
25. త పళ్లకున్ను అంగ్గరంగ్గ వైభోవా
26. లకున్ను శ్రీ కృష్ణదేవమహారాయ
27. లకుం బుణ్యంగాను సాళువ తిమ్మ
28. రుసయ్యంగారు కట్టమలయ్యకు
29. యిప్పించి యీధర్మము సెల్లించ్చె
30. మామడనూరు అష్టభోగ. అష్ట
31. స్వామ్యంగాను రామేశ్వరదేవు
32. నికి ధారా పూర్వకముగాను సమ
33. ర్పణసేసెను । స్వదత్తా ద్విగు
34. ణంపుణ్యం పరదత్తానుపాలనం
35. పరదత్తాపహారేణ స్వదత్తం ని
36. ష్ఫలంభవేత్ । మదనూరిశచె
37. తుస్సీమపొలం వివరము తూ

38. ర్పు పొలానకు సముద్రము
39. ను దక్షిణానకు పొకాధేనుండ్లి
40. పశ్చమానకుయినంగ లేరు
41. పశ్చమానకు నైరుతియినుంగ లేరు
42. విధిములు మోందుగలువంప్పు
43. వంప్పగనుండి వాయువ్యానకు
44. పదార్ణంగుంట అంతకు పు
45. త్తరంన యీాంతముకుక్కలమడ
46. నూరిసంద్దు తూర్పుణంజడముర
47. లకు పోతుగట్టు అందుకుతూర్పు
48. కపులబావి దానికి తూర్పునం
49. వెలిగుంటవ
50. డ్మ(వ)రచ్చి తూర్పు
51. నచ్చి దక్షిణపుతట్టు
52. తూర్పుకొమ్ముననచ్చి
53. తూర్పురాంగాజో
54. గిదింన్న అమానతూ
55. ర్పు॥
56. అందు తూర్పు స
57. ముద్ర దటమందు లి
58. ప్పించిన ఇవిపొలము
59. ఈ హద్దులశ్రీ

Ongole (72). (A.D. 1441–42.)

[Mainampáḍu. Sanskrit except the last line which is Telugu. From stone on tank-bund.]

Translation.

V. 1. May the illustrious Tirupurántaka, who is the gem of Śríṣaila hill, protect his devotees, devotion in whom like a tree of paradise yields to Brahma and others the fruit consisting of the four objects of human desires.

V. 2. There is a celebrated king of the earth, the illustrious Dévaráya, the son of Vijaya. While he, of pure fame, was ruling the earth as Indra (was ruling heaven) which is filled with divine glory,

V. 3. There was, in the beautiful town named Údayagiri, which is in the middle of the kingdom of the Carnatic, a righteous-souled Bráhman named Narahari, of the Bháradvája *gótra*.

V. 4. His son was named Timmayamantri; his son was Mallanárya, renowned on earth, endowed with the disposition to worship Sadáṣiva, devoted to the worship of excellent Bráhmans, and intelligent.

V. 5. Having approached the head of the Śaiva church, and having requested him (to tell him) the means of emancipation, he, by his command,

V. 6. With his mind intent on the daily performance of worship and offering to Tirupurántakadéva the crest-gem of Álaṣaila (Śríṣaila ?),

V. 7. Having strongly built a tank to the east of the temple of Tirupurántakadéva in the village of Maindanapáḍu (Mainampáḍu), and having secured the field to the north of it,

V. 8. In the Śaka year reckoned by the guṇas (3), tarkaṣ (6), Ramas (3), and the moon (1), (*i.e.*, 1363), in the year Durmati, on Monday, on the *parva* of Kártika, the lord, Ṣrí Mallanárya, presented to Puráráti (Śiva) land in the town named Maindanapáḍ, and a flower garden for the perpetual performance of daily worship.

V. 9. The lord also presented a village (a field ?) of great prosperity for a perpetual lamp and sacred food, and a spotless bronze vessel for daily offering.

V. 10. May the lord of Arunagiri, whose crest-jewel is the moon, taste daily the offering presented by Mallayya-mantri ; may he grant him the fulfilment of his desires ! May it cause great prosperity !

NOTE.—There is an exact copy of this inscription in the big temple at Tirupurántaka in Márkapúr taluk, Kurnool district.

The language is Sanskrit (in Telugu characters).

Álaṣaila may be another name of Śríṣaila.

1. श्रीशैलशिखररत्नं श्रीमान्[1] त्रिपुरान्तकोवताद्र

2. क्तान् यद्भक्तिकल्पवल्ली फलति चतुर्वर्गफलमजादीनां ॥ (*v.*1) अस्ति प्र

3. शस्तः पृथिवीतलेन्द्रः श्रीदेवरायो विजयात्मज

4. न्मा तस्मिन्महीं शासति पुण्यकीर्तौ । दिवं मरुत्वानिव दिव्य

5. लक्ष्मीं ॥ (*v.*2) वुदयगिरि नाख्य[2] नगरी[3] कान्ते कर्नाटकटक-मध्यस्थे । भार

6. द्वाजसगोत्रो नरहरिनामा द्विजोस्ति धर्मात्मा ॥ (*v.* 3,तदा

7. त्मजस्तिम्मय मंत्रिसंज्ञस्तत्सूनुरासीत् भुवि म

---

[1] Read श्रीमतिन in the text. [2] Read उदयगिर्याख्य or उदयगिरिनाम्नि.

[3] Read नगरे.

8. छनार्यः । सदासिवा[1] श्यर्चनदशीलयुक्तो द्विजेन्द्रपूजा निरतोम

9. नीषी ॥ (*v.* 4) सोभ्येत्य शैवसाराज्यकर्तारं मुक्तिसाधनं भिक्षावृत्त्या य

10. तिश्रीरतं[2] । प्रार्थयित्वा[3] तदाज्ञया ॥ (*v.* 5) त्रिपुरान्तकदेवस्य आल शैल

11. शिरोमणिः[4] । नित्यं पूजाञ्च नैवेद्यं कर्तुमुद्युक्तमानसः ॥ (*v.* 6)

12. मैन्दनपाटिग्रामे त्रिपुरान्तकदेवशीम्नि[5] पूर्वस्मिन् । ब

13. ध्वा दृढं तटाकं । लब्ध्वा क्षेत्रं च तदुत्तरक्षेत्रं ॥ (*v.* 7) शाका

14. ब्दे गुणतर्करामशशिभिर्युक्ते तद्दा[6] दुर्मतौ प्राप्ते कार्तिकपर्व

15. णीन्दुदिवस श्रीमल्लनार्यविभुः । प्रादान्मैन्द

16. नपाटि नामनि पुरे क्षेत्रं पुरारातये । पुष्पाराममम

17. जस्रमप्यनुदिनं नित्यार्चनासिद्धये ॥ (*v.* 8) ग्रामं च सुखसंदो

18. हं नित्यदीपाभृताय च । विमलं कांस्यपात्रं च नैवेद्याय

19. ददौ प्रभुः ॥ (*v.* 9) मल्लयसमर्पितमनुदिनमामोद्यता[7]

20. रुणगिरिनाथः । नैवेद्यमिन्दुमौलिः तस्य दद्यात्तथा फलसि.द्धिम्[8] ॥ (*v.* 10)

21. श्री श्री श्री जेयनु

---

[1] Read सदाशिव.

[2] Read यतिश्रेष्ठं ।

[3] प्रार्थयित्वा is grammatically wrong अर्थयायित्व अनुप्राथ्र्य.

[4] Read शिरोमणेः ।

[5] Read सीम्न.

[6] Read तथा.

[7] Perhaps the reading is अनुदिनमास्वाद्यदरुणागिरिनाथः

[8] Perhaps the reading is तस्य विदध्यात् यथष्टफलासाद्ध ।

ONGOLE (73). (A.D. 1355–56?)

[Mallavaram. Sanskrit in Telugu character. To north in Survey No. 247.]

TRANSLATION.

V. 1. May the glorious sportive Boar who is as brilliant as a tender blue lotus, and whose tusk resembles a young lotus root and a plantain flower, protect you long. Carried by him (the boar), the earth whose blue garment of the ocean was gradually slipping off and whose body was wet appeared beautiful as though (hot with) love.

V. 2. From the foot of the god, the consort of Lakshmi (Vishnu), whose body is adorned with the Kaustubha gem, and who resembles the lotus in brilliance, arose in turn the race of the fourth caste like the holy Gangá (Ganges), the source of holiness, lasting as long as a *kalpa*, diligent in protecting the three worlds, prolific in magnanimity and bravery.

[The epithets refer to both the Ganges and the fourth caste which both arose from the foot of Vishnu.]

V. 3. In the ocean of that family there was born Vémaya who was the fullmoon to the eyes of all mankind, the abode of the gods on earth (Brahmans), founder of the dynasty; since his fierce valour always shines like the sun, there was not on the necks of the women of his enemies the lustre of the rows of stars which were their necklaces of pearls.

(The meaning is that in the glare of the sun of his valour the lustre of the stars, viz., the pearls of the women of his enemies, was dispelled, *i.e.*, they did not wear necklaces as their husbands had been killed by him.)

V. 4. By him was begotten Kómaṭi Próla, the incarnation of good to the collection of Brahmans, excelling men in virtues as Indra excels the *Maruts*, the foremost of heroes, who was a very garuḍa to the serpents which are hostile kings.

V. 5. The chaste Annayambá was Kómati Próla's wife just as the daughter of the mountain (Párvati) was of Ṣiva, as the goddess Sarasvati was of the lotus-born (Brahma), as the daughter of the ocean (Lakshmi) was of Vishnu, as the Ganges was of the ocean, as Suvarcchala was of Súrya (sun), and as the holy Rohini was of the moon.

V. 6. To Kómaṭi Próla she the virtuous bore in succession five sons just as the milky ocean (gave birth) to the (five) celestial trees of the gods—first, Máchaya Peddaya of great valour, next the glorious king Véma, next Doḍḍaya, next Annaya, and next the glorious commander of the army Malla.

V. 7. Men truly thought them who were resplendent with truthfulness, strength, valour, beauty and intellect to be the sons of Pándu again descended on earth for the protection (of the earth).

V. 8. Then king Véma, the asylum of all the wise, rules the whole earth, resembling the god Krishna incarnated on earth for protection, vanquishing proud and wicked kings of the Kali age,

V. 9. The proud Ándhras . . . . like the river washing away trees . . . . who was the rise of the full moon to the white lotuses which were the confederate kings . . . . other kings . . . .

Second side.

1. Malla, who was a very wind to the cotton which is other kings, (ruled) for a long time. How can this hero the glorious king Kómaṭi Véma be described?

2. He who was dear to the learned, having given excellent villages (which had been) won by valour on the banks of the Krishna, on the banks of the Kundija (Guṇḍlakamma), and on the sides of the Gódávari to Brahmans, caused his fame to be proclaimed to the world of Brahma by the vedic recitations of Brahmans. By whom is this king Véma, the purifier of the world, not worthy of being praised?

3. The tree of paradise which gives land was made to sprout by Bali, the son of Viróchana; it was made to blossom by Ráma and now it is made to yield fruit by the glorious king Véma.

4. There is a country named the glorious Púngi extending from the vicinity of the eastern fort of Ṣrígiri (Ṣrí Ṣailam) up to the eastern sea, on both sides of the river Kunḍi (Gunḍlakamma).

5. In that (country) greatly shines the city named Addanki,[1] having beautiful mansions and *gópuras*, always adorned by *apsaras* (celestial nymphs) and having happy citizens. This glorious king Véma, by the valour of whose club-like arms which were very staves of death to the circle of fierce feudatory chiefs the multitude of foes was conquered, who is heroic like the king of the mountains, and who is 'Jagannobbaganḍa' (the sole hero in the world), rules this town.

[Thus the eulogistic description of the donor. Next the eulogy of the donee.]

6. May the glorious and famous lords Ráma and Lakshmana who were set up by the glorious lord Rája

---

[1] The exaggeration of Sanskrit verse was never more ridiculously misapplied. Addanki is a collection of poor huts.

Malla, in the beautiful . . . . at the town of Chedalaváḍa—Lakshmi—the foot of whose mansions are kissed by the waters of the river Kuṇḍi—be triumphant.

7. [Rághava (Ráma) was] the destroyer of Táṭaká, the protector of the sacrifice of the head of the Kuṣika family, valiant . . . . of Subáhu, the breaker of the bow of Ṣiva—the ocean . . . . the well-established powerful Haihaya . . . . lahari. Is it possible to describe king Rághava, the destroyer of Rávana, his sons and grandsons?

8. In the Ṣáka year reckoned by the mountains (7), the oceans (7), the suns (12), *i.e.*, 1277, on the day at the setting of Aṣvin, on the lunar eclipse day, on Thursday, on the sands of the holy river . . . . king Véma very joyfully gave the city . . . .

9. . . . . naming it Ṣrí Doddimalla . . . . the gift.

10. The boundaries of this village: on the east . . . . .

[Three imprecatory verses.]

Note.—In verse 7 there seems to be an allusion to some historical person as well as to the god Ráma (Rághava), but the inscription is not clearly legible at this point.

1. श्रीमत्कोमलनीलनीरजरु[चि]र्लीलाव-
2. राहश्चिरं नातिप्रौढमृणालकंदल-
3. लसद्दंष्ट्रांकुरः पातु वः । यस्मिन्न-
4. द्वहति क्रमेण विगळ[त्पा]थोधिनीलां-
5. शुका रागाद्रार्द्रतनूरिव क्षणम-
6. भूदामोदिनी मेदिनी । [१*] असीत्कौस्तुभरत्न-
7. मंडिततनोर्देवस्य लक्ष्मीपतेः पा-

8. दात्पद्मनिभत्विषो भगवती गंगेव पुं-[1]
9. ण्योदया । आकल्पस्थिरजीव[ना]
10. त्रिजगतीसंतारणोद्योगिनी पर्य्या-
11. येण चतुर्थवर्णविततिर्गांभी-
12. र्य्यधैर्य्यप्रसूः । [२*] तद्वंशाब्धौ सकल-
13. जनतानेत्रसंपूर्णचंद्रो जातः [क्षो]-
14. [णी]विबुधसदनं वेमयो वंशक-
15. र्त्ता । यस्योदग्रे स्फुरति सततं भा-
16. स्वती[व] प्रतापे नासीत्किंठेप्वरिमृग-
17. दृशां हारतारावलिश्रीः । [३*] तेनाज-
18. नि द्विजनिकायहितावतारः श्रेया-
19. न्गुणैस्तनुभृतां मरुतामिवें-[1]
20. द्रः । शूराग्रणीर्जगति कोमटिप्रोल-
21. नामा प्रत्यर्थिभूपतिभुजंगविहं-[1]
22. गराजः ॥ [४*] शंभोरद्रिसुतेव पंकज-
23. भुवो देवी यथा भारती विष्णोस्सागरसं-[1]
24. भवेव सरितांपत्युर्य्यथा जाह्न-
25. वी । सूर्य्यस्येव सुवर्च्चला शशभृतः
26. [पु]ण्या य[था] रोहिणी रू[ढा] कोमटि-
27. प्रोलयस्य सदृशी भार्य्यान्यमां[बा]
28. [स]ती ॥ [५*] . . . त्रिदिवौकसां सुरत[रू]-
29. न् क्षीरा . . . यथा पुत्रा[न्] कोम-
30. टिप्रोलयाद्गुणवती सासूत पंच क्र-
31. मात् । अग्रे माचयपेद्दयोजित[म]-

[1] The anusvára stands at the beginning of the next line.

32. [थ] श्रीवेमपृथ्वीपतिं पश्चादाङ्कयमं-
33. नयं च तदनु श्रीमल्लसेनापतिं ॥ [६*]
34. सत्येन [1]सत्वेन पराक्रमेण रूपेण बुध्या[2]
35. च विराजतस्तान् । त्राणाय भूयोपि ध-
36. रावतार्णानूनं जनोमन्यत पांडुदु-
37. त्रान्॥[७*] अथ सकलबुधानामाश्रयः पा-
38. लनाय क्षितितलमवतीर्णः[3] कंसम-
39. र्दीव देवः । कलिसमयविदृप्यद्[ष्ट]-
40. भूपान्निरस्यन् वहति सकलपृथ्वीं वे-
41. मयक्ष्मानुपालः । [८*] दृप्तानंध्र . .
42. जम्भूरुहमहास्रोतोवहा . . .
43. . . . संगतराजकैरववनीसंपू-
44. र्णचंद्रोदयः । . . . . न्यनृपा-
45. ल . . . .

Second side.

1. [4]लनूलपवनो गङ्ग . . . [श्रिरं] । श्री-
2. मत्कोमटिवेमभूपतिरसौ वीरः कथं व-
3. र्ण्यते ॥ [१*] कृष्णारोधासि कुंडिजापरिसरे
4. गोदावरीपार्श्वतः कृत्वा ग्रामवरान्
5. पराक्रमाजितान् विद्वत्प्रियो विप्र-
6. सात् । स्वाध्यायैरुदघोषयद्वि[ज]-

---

[1] Read सत्त्वेन. [2] Read बुद्ध्या.

[3] Read °तीर्णः

[4] There seem to be traces of some lines of writing at the top of this side. Hence both the lines and the verses have been numbered separately and not in continuation of the first part.

7. नुषामाब्रह्मलोकं निजां कीर्त्तिं

8. यस्स न कस्य वेमनृपति[:*] स्तुत्यो जगत्पा-

9. वनः ॥ [२*] वैरोचनेन बलिना पल्लवितो भू-

10. मिदानकल्पतरुः । रामेण पुष्पितो-

11. सौ श्रीवेमनृपेण सांप्रतं फलितं ॥ [३*]

12. अस्ति श्रीगिरिपूर्व्वपादनिकटादा पू-

13. र्व्वपाथोनिधेर्देशः कुंडितरंगिणीमु-

14. भयतः श्रीपूंगिनामांकितः । तस्मिन्

15. भासुरसौधगोपुरवती नित्याप्सरोलं-[1]

16. कृता नंदत्पौरजना विभाति नितरा-

17. मद्दंकिनामा[2] पुरी ॥ [४*] उद्दंडमंडलिक-]

18. मंडलकालदंडदोर्दंडविक्रमावि-

19. निर्जितवैरिलोकः । सोयं बिभर्त्ति नग-

20. रीं नगराजधीरः श्रीवेमभूपतिर[मुं]

21. जगनोब्बगंड्डः ॥ [५*] इति दातृप्रशस्तिः [॥*]

22. अथ प्रतिगृहीतृप्रशस्तिः ॥ कुंडीनदी-

23. सलिलचुंबितसौधमूले लक्ष्मी . .

24. वेदलुवाडपुरा . रम्ये । श्री[रा]-

25. [ज]मल्लविभुना रचितप्रतिष्ठौ । श्रीरा-

26. मलक्ष्मणविभू जयतां प्रसि-

27. द्धौ ॥ [६*] संहर्त्ता ताटकायाः कुशिक-

28. कुलपतेः पालिन(:)स्सप्रतंतोः प्रौढो

29. . . . सुबाहुस्सदसि पुरजितो . .

---

[1] The anusvára stands at the beginning of the next line.

[2] Read नाम्नी.

30. . . . नः कार्म्मुकस्य । [श]क्रा[न्] हैहय . .

31. . . . लहरीसुंस्तभितां[1] मोघिरा[ड्]-

32. किं वर्ण्यः पुत्रपौत्रान्वितदशवदनध्वं-

33. सनो घवेंद्रः ॥ [७*]शाकाब्दे शैल[वार्द्धि]-

34. द्युमणिपरिमिताहोश्विनस्यावसा-

35. ने राहुग्रस्ते [हिमांशौ] सुरगुरु-

36. दिवसे सैकते पुण्यनद्याः ।

37. . . . .

38. . . . .

39. . पुरमधिकमुदा द[त्त]वान् वे-

40. मभूपः ॥ [८*] श्रीरेड्डिमल्लनामा . .

41. येन दा[नो] . . . . .

42. . . . .

43. . . . . . . ॥ [९*] अस्य ग्रामस्य सीमानः [पू]-

44. र्व्वतः . . . .

45. . . . .

46. . . . .

47. . . . .

48. . . . .

49. . . ॥ स्वदत्तां परदत्तां वा[2]

---

[1] Read °संस्तभि°. instead of सुस्तभि°.

[2] The rest of the inscription consists of the continuation of this verse, of two other imprecatory verses beginning with स्वदत्तात् and सामान्योयं and of the syllables श्री श्री श्रीं.

ONGOLE (74).

[Maṇikéṣvaram. Telugu. Opposite Páṇḍukéṣvara temple. The stone bears inscriptions on four sides.]

TRANSLATION.

Hail! In the illustrious sixth year of the reign of Ṣríman Mahámaṇḍaléṣvara Chóḍamadéva Maháraja, who is the asylum of the whole world, who is the beloved (lord) of the illustrious earth, who is a great devotee of Mahéṣvara, who is the ornament of the solar race, who is the best of the Chóḍa family, who is the destroyer of the Páṇḍya family, who is Víra Chóḍa Rája Késari Varma (Dharma in the text), the emperor of the three worlds, we have given with libation of water to Máṇḍukéṣvara Ṣrí Mahádéva of Buddapúṇḍi on the banks of the river Gaṇḍi, in Kammanáḍu in our territory, that village of Buddapúṇḍi for providing all enjoyments, we have given this to last as long as the moon and sun endure. The *sthánapatis* (temple authorities) Komma Ráju, Chóḍama Ráju, and Kuṇḍama Ráju should perform this for the deity and live in happiness. Those who maintain this (charity) will be blessed with increase of desired objects, sons, prosperity and long life. Those who are against it are like those who have administered poison to their parents, like those who have eaten in the skull of their eldest son, like those who have killed at Benares.

First side.

1. స్వస్తి సమస్తభువ
2. నాశ్రయ శ్రీప్రి
3. థ్వీ వల్లభ మహారాజా

4. ధి రాజపరమ మహే
5. శ్వర పరమ భట్టార
4. క రవికుల తిలకచో
7. డకులశేఖర పాండె
8. కులాన్తక వీరచోడ
9. రాజకేసరి దమ్మణనా
10. దిగళు త్రిభువన చ
11. క్రవర్త్రిణ శ్రీ మన్మ
12. హా మండలేశ్వర చో
13. డ మదేవ మహారాజుల
14. దివ్య సంవత్సరాలు ౬ (౪౦)
15. శ్రాహిమాభూమిక
16. మ్మనాటిలోనిగుం
17. డి నదీతీరమునం

Second side.

18. దు బుద్ధపూం
19. డి మాండుకేశ్వర
20. శ్రీ మహాదేవర
21. కు ఆబుద్ధపూండి ధా
22. రా పూర్వముగాను
23. ఆంగ్గరంగ్గ వైభ
24. వాలకున్ను ఇ
25. స్త్రిమి ఆచంద్రా
26. కర్ణముగా ని స్తిమి దీని
27. కి స్థానాపతులు కొ
28. మ్మరాజును చోడ
29. మరాజునుకుండ
30. మ రాజూను దేవరకు

31. నడిపి సుఖమనుభ
32. వింప్పంగలవారు ఈ
33. క్షేత్రము చెల్లించినవారికి
34. ని అభిమతార్థప్రసిద్ధియు
35. పుత్రసమృద్ధియూను ఆయు
36. వృవర్ధన మూనున్ను ఈధ
37. ర్మ్మువునకు నెవ్వరు కంట
38. డ పరచిరి వారు తమతల్లి
39. దండ్రికంచాన విషము
40. పెట్టినవారు పెద్దకొడుకు క
41. పాలానంగుడ్చినవారు
42. వారణాశింవ్రచ్చినవారు

Ongole (75). (A.D. 1280–81.)

[Maṇikéṣvaram. Telugu. From stone inscribed on four sides. Opposite Páṇḍukéśvara temple.]

Translation.

[One imprecatory verse.]

Hail! On Monday, the 1st of the bright fortnight on Márgaṣira of the year Vikrama, corresponding to the illustrious Ṣaka year 1202, on the holy occasion of Makara Sankránti, I, Ṣríman Mahámaṇḍaléṣvara Nágadéva Mahárája, gave a mango tope, a flower garden, and a field of 9 *puṭṭis* in Buddepúndi (a portion not understood) to Máṇḍukéśvaradéva of Buddepúṇḍi as *vritti* for providing worship for the religious merit of Rudradéva Mahárája, to last as long as the sun and moon endure. Those who keep up (the charity) of the garden and this field will have increase of life, health and wealth. Those who think of causing obstruction to this charity will be regarded as having committed the five cardinal sins.

[At the beginning and end of the inscription the same imprecatory verse is quoted.]

1. స్వదత్తం పరదత్తం వా
2. యో హరేతి వసుంధరా
3. షష్టిర్వర్ష సహస్రాణి వి
4. ష్ఠాయాం జాయతేక్రిమిః।
5. స్వస్తిశ్రీ శకవర్షంబులు
4. ౧౨౦౨ అగునేంటి విక్ర
7. మ సంవత్సర మార్గశిరశు
8. ౧ సోమవారాన మకరస
9. ంక్రాతి పుణ్యకాలమప్పుడు
10. స్వస్తి శ్రీమన్మహా మండలే
11. శ్వర నాగదేవ మహారాజులు
12. బుద్ధెపూండి మాండుకేశ్వర
13. దేవరకు బుద్దెపూండి డేంకొండ
14. లెరవు రూప్పన డేంకొండల
15. అనసుంది కంమ్మ దొడ్డిమడు
16. లోపలను అర్పన భోగాన
17. కు ప్రతి త్రిరుద్ర దేవమహారాజు
18. లకు ధర్మార్తముగా నాంచంద్రాంకర్క
19. ముగాఖర్ క్షేత్రమూలన కొల్లవి
20. రేచ్చెసిపుళ్ళ్వందొంటాను మామి
21. డ్లూను ఇస్తిమి ఈచేనూందో
22. టాదుం జెల్లించినవారికి ఆ
23. యురారోగ్యైశ్వర్యాభివ్రి
24. ద్ది యగు ఈ ధమ్మంబునకు
25. విఘ్నముదలంచ్చినవారు

26. పంచమహా పాతకమూ చేసిన
27. వారు । సదత్తం పరదత్తం వాయో
28. హారేతి వసుంధరా షష్టివర్షస
29. సహస్రాణి విష్టాయాం జా
30. యతే క్రిమిః॥

ONGOLE (76). (A.D. 1208–09.)

[Maṇikéṣvaram. Telugu. From a stone inscribed on four sides opposite Páṇḍukéṣvara temple.]

TRANSLATION.

Hail! On Monday, the 10th of the bright fortnight of Bhádrapada of the year Vibhava, corresponding to the illustrious Ṣaka year 1130, Hail! Ṣríman Mahámaṇḍalóṣvara Ṣrí Mádhava Mahá Rája, who is endowed with all eulogistic titles, who is a Révanta in controlling most unruly horses, who is death to hostile forces, who is a fortress of adamant to refugees, who is the protector of life, who is Chakra Náráyaṇa . . . . on the occasion of Sankránti, gave a field of 40 *puṭṭis* in the land of Koṭikalapúṇḍi to the west of the Gunḍḍakamma and . . . . to Máṇḍukéṣvara Ṣrí Mahádéva. Those who protect this will have increase of sons and grandsons; those who violate this will be regarded as having eaten from the skull of their eldest son.

[One imprecatory verse.]

1. స్వస్తి సమస్తప్రశస్తి
2. సహితంబున శ్రీ
3. మన్మహా మండలే
4. శ్వర అతివిషమమ

5. హా యారూఢప్రౌఢరే
6. ఖారేవంత పరబళక్రి
7. కాంత్త శరణాగత వజ్ర
8. పంజర మండలీకరవం
9. దోళి జీవరక్ష చక్రనారా
10. యణ శ్రీమాధవమహా
11. రాజులు స్వస్తిశ్రీ శకవర్ష
12. ంబులు ౧౧౩౦ అగునేం
13. టి విభవ సంవత్సర భాద్ర
14. పద శు ౧ం సోమవారామున
15. అయనసంక్రాంతి నిమిత్యం
16. బున మాండుకేశ్వర శ్రీమ
17. హాదేవరకు గుండ్లకంమ
18. పడుమటి కొటికల పూండిపొ
19. లమున ఖ ౮ం చేనును గుత్తి
20. . . . మ్మని బోయునికొడు
21. కు . . . రగంనులూను . ం
22. . . వానకొను ఆచంద్రా
23. కణంముగా ఇస్తిమి దీని క్రతివా
24. వించనవారికిం బుత్రపౌత్రాభి వృద్ధి
25. యగు దోంసం దలంచ్చినవారు
26. దమ పెద్దకొడుకు కపాలమునం గూ
27. ండు గుడిచినవారు
28. స్వదత్తం పరదత్తంవాయోహరేతి
29. వసుంధరా షష్టివర్షసహస్రాని
30. విష్టాంయాం జాయతేక్రిమిః।
31. గొల్లడు . ధియ . . .
32. . . కదలపునేకనివిత్యతి
33. ండు దిపాకుంబోయి వా .

ONGOLE (77). (A.D. 1534-35?)

[Maṇikéṣvaram. Telugu. In a street to the west.]

TRANSLATION.

May it be well! Hail! On the 15th of the bright fortnight of Phálguṇa of the year Jaya, corresponding to the illustrious, victorious and prosperous Ṣáliváhana Ṣaka year 1455, Bába Káṣayyaváru who was skilled in bearing the burden of the kingdom of Ṣrí Achyutadéva Mahárâyalu and who was ruling Koṇḍavíḍu presented a field to Mallinátha, son of Vennalakanṭivi . . Kántayya . . . . to Késavadéva . . . a *puṭṭi* to the east of . . . to Koṇḍa Ṣrí Narasimha . . ; caused to be made . . . .

NOTE.—The cyclic and S.S. years differ by a year. The name of this governor of Koṇḍavíḍu does not seem to appear elsewhere, but perhaps we should read Bácharusayyá and then compare O. 23.

1. శుభమస్తు ॥ స్వస్తిశ్రీ జయా
2. భ్యుదయ శాలివాహన శకవ
3. ర్షంబులు ౧౪౫౫ అగునేంటి జ
4. య సంవత్సర ఫాల్గుణ శుద్ధ ౧౫
5. లు శ్రీ అచ్యుత దేవమహారాయ
6. ల సాంమ్రాజ్య ధురంధరుండైన
7. బాబకాశయ్యవారు కొండవీ
8. డు యేలుచుండి వెన్నెలకంటివి .
9. కాంత్తయ్య కుమారుండు మల్లినా
10. థుండు . మ ఇసెను . . .
11. ండు కేశవ దేవుని . . . .
12. . ఇచ్చిన ఖ శానపండియ . .
13. తి తూర్పుద్వాహరావి . .
14. కొండ శ్రీ నరసింహుని . . .

15. రిశే ఇంచ్చి మ . . వెట్ట . .
16. పు కట్టించి ఆవెనకను . విశో
17. . కపెద్ద మనేలుచుండి ఆ . .

. . .

ONGOLE (78). (A.D. 1353–54.)

[Maṇikéṣvaram. Sanskrit in Telugu character and Telugu. In enclosure of Máṇḍukéṣvara temple.]

Prosperity!

V. 1. The glorious sage Marichi was the mind-born son of the primeval Brahma. By him by reason of his penances was begotten a son Kaṣyapa who was capable of being influenced by mercy. In course of time in his family was born the glorious Rámarája of good deeds, blessed, a Káma to women. His son was the lord Manchana.

V. 2. To the glorious Manchirája was born a son Rámarája, the store-house of virtues. Then by him (Rámarája) the faultless, the glorious Mallamámbá had a son Mallinátha the receptacle of glory (fortune), who, though young, was of great valour and of clever mind and accomplished in all (branches of) knowledge, and who obtained the great glory of sovereignty from the glorious king Véma.

V. 3. Thereafter she, the virtuous wife of Rámaya, again bore four sons like the elephants of the quarters; the glorious Manchirája, then the excellent Vamaya-mantri; then the glorious Erranárya, and Késayamantri.

V. 4. When Mallinátha, who was honoured by the glorious king Annavóta, died, afterwards, his younger brother Manchirája the blessed, the intelligent, having performed his funeral obsequies according to rules, caused to be brought from Lingaṣailam (Ṣríṣailam) two beautiful *lingas* (which were) in the Patálagangapattu in Ṣrígiri (Ṣríṣailam).

V. 5. In the Ṣaka year reckoned by the arrows (5), the mountains (7), and the suns (12) [*i.e.*, 1275] on the bright fortnight of Jyéshṭha, on the day of Ṣiva, the glorious Manchirája, intelligent, blessed, performed the consecration of Siddhalinga to the south of the famous temple of Máṇḍukéṣa Ṣambhu in the place which resembled Váranáṣi (Benares) in order that his brother Mallinátha might obtain the abode of Ṣiva.

V. 6. Ṣiva, viz., the lord Mallinátha (the above linga) the ruler of the city of the glorious Rávinúntala, who was set up by his younger brother the glorious lord Manchirája, being the friend of Máṇḍukéṣa Ṣambhu, will long enjoy pleasures on earth.

V. 7. On that same day, and in that beautiful and excellent temple the glorious lord Manchirája, of meritorious conduct, caused to be set up there the other linga Sóma Ṣrígiri Siddhalinga, representing his own linga (?) He there set up a golden vessel resembling Kubera's car and brilliant as the reflection of the shining sun.

V. 8. He caused to be constructed steps to the Kuṇḍika (Gundlakamma), a new *manṭapa* at the gate and a new *prákára* (enclosure), made also with plaster a circular hall to represent (the moon) Sóma (?); and he gave . . . The glorious lord Manchirája, the blessed, constructed a beautiful kitchen room for the glorious lord Máṇḍukéṣa.

V. 8. And around the temple of Máṇḍukéṣa Ṣambhu, he caused to be planted cocoanut trees. Rámaya Mantri Manchirája gave a golden lotus containing the nine kinds of gems.

Telugu.

Manchiráju, who was the son of Ṣrí Rámarája, son of Manchiráju, son of Ṣrí Rámaprégaḍa minister of Ṣrí Véma, and Mallamámbá, in order to please Máṇḍukéṣvaradévara, constructed at the northern gate . . . . in the east manda(ta) . . . . a kitchen room, planted 200 cocoanut trees and presented a lotus containing the nine gems, a mosquito curtain, sajjavettam (?), mid-day food, árati-pallalu (plates ?) and other services to the deity. Subsequently when his brother Anna Paruvata Mallinátha died, his younger brother Manchiráju brought (two) lingas from Ṣríparvata and set one of them up in the temple of Máṇḍukéṣvara linga (?) designating it Ravinúntala Parvata Mallináthalinga on Saturday, the 14th of the bright fortnight of Jyéshṭha of the year Vijaya, corresponding to the Ṣaka year 1275. At the same moment in the manḍapa in front of it, he caused to be set up the other linga designating it Ṣrígiri linga and representing his own *linga*. For the service of these two lingas he presented a khanḍriga as *vritti* in his agrahára Méḍúr which was in his ownership.

. . . . gave . . . . (to) Máṇḍukéṣvaradévara

. . . . May it be auspicious !

NOTE.—The genealogy given by this inscription is—

Brahma.
|
Marichi.
|
Kaṣyapa.
|
* * *
|
Rámarája Preggaḍa (minister to king Véma).
|
Manchana.
|
Rámarája—Mallamámbá.
|

Mallinátha (minister of Anna Véta.)	Manchiráju (Donor).	Vámaya-mantri.	Erranárya.	Keṣaya-mantri.

1. श्री [॥ *] आसीदादिविरिंचि-
2. मानससुत [: *] श्रीमा
3. न्मरीचिर्म्मुनिस्तेनायं[1]
4. तपसोदपादि करु-
5. णावश्यस्सुतः कश्यपः।
6. तद्वंशे क्रमतोजनिष्ट
7. सुकृती श्रीरामराजः कृ-
8. ती रामापंचशरस्स मं-
9. चनाविभुः तस्याभवं नं-
10. दनः ॥ [१ *] पुत्र[: *] श्रीमंचिरा-
11. जादजनि गुणानिधी रा-
12. मराजस्ततोस्माल्लेभे श्री-
13. मल्लमांबा सुतमन-
14. घगुणात् श्रीनिधिं म-
15. ल्लिनाथं। बालोपि प्रौढ-
16. तेजाः चतुरतरमतिः स-
17. र्वविद्याप्रवीणः श्रीवेम-
18. क्षोणिपालादलभत मह-
19. तीमाधिराज्याश्रियं यः। [२ *]
20. श्रीमंचिराजमनु [व]ाम-
21. यमंत्रिवर्य्यं श्रीए-
22. ल्लुनार्य्यमनु केसय-
23. मंत्रिणं च। प्रासूत
24. सा तदनु रामयधर्म्म-

---

[1] The anusvára stands at the beginning of the next line.

25. पत्नो दिग्वारणानिव पुनश्चत-
26. रस्तनूजान् ॥ [३ *] तस्मिन् श्री-
27. वंनवोतक्षिति-

Second side.

28. तलपतिना लालि-
29. ते देवभूयं सं-[1]
30. प्राप्ते मल्लिनाथे
31. तदनु तदनुजो
32. मंचिराजः कृता-
33. त्मा। कृत्वा तस्योष्ठि[मं]-
34. त्यां विधिवदथ
35. सुधी[ः *] श्रीगिरौ द्वे म-
36. मोझे लिंगे पाता-
37. लगं [गा *] पथिसाकिलसमे
38. मायल्लिंग्गशैला-
39. त ॥ [४ *] शाकाब्दे बाणशी-
40. लद्युमणिपरिमि-
41. ते ज्येष्ठशुक्ले शिवा-
42. हे भ्रातु[ः *] श्रीमं-
43. चिराजः शिवप-
44. दगतये मल्लिना-
45. थस्य धीमान्। प्रख्या-
46. ताद्वारणासीसम-
47. इति भुवने मां-
48. डुकेशस्य श-

---

[1] The anusvára stands at the beginning of the next line.

49. मोरावासाद्दक्षि-
50. णस्यामकृत दिशि
51. कृती सिद्धलिंग-
52. प्रतिष्ठां ॥ [२*] श्रीरा-
53. विनूत्लपुर [वल्ल]-
54. भमाल्लिनाथ नाथ-[1]
55. ः शिवरतदनुजेन कृ-
56. तप्रतिष्ठः । श्रीमं-
57. चिराजाविभुना
58. भुवि मांडुके-
59. शशंभोस्सरखानुभ-
60. विता चिरम . भोगान् ॥ [६*]

Third side.

61. [त] स्मिन्नेव दिने सुरालयवरे
62. तस्मि [न्न] वारथापयत्सोमश्रीगि-
63. रिसिद्धलिंगमपरं स्वप्राणलिं-
64. गात्मकं । रम्ये पुष्पकवत्सु-
65. [2]वर्नकलशं दीप्रार्कबिंब[प्र]-
66. भं तत्र स्थापयति स्म पुण्य-
67. चरित[:*] श्रीमंचिराजप्रभुः । [७*]
68. सोपानान्यभिकुंडिकं व्य-
69. रचय[द्*]द्वारे नव[3] मंटमं
70. प्राकारं च नवं व्यधत्त सुध-

---

[1] The anusvára stands at the beginning of the next line.

[2] Read °वर्ण°

[3] Read नवे.

71. या सोमात्मकम्मंडलं ।
72. प्रादाच्चारु . . . . यां
73. श्रीमांडुकेशप्रभो रम्यन्निर्म्मित-
74. वान्महानसगृहं श्रीमंचिराजः कृ-
75. ती ॥ [८*] परितोस्य च मांडु-
76. केशशंभोस्सदनं रोप-
77. यति स्म नारिकेलान् । नव-
78. रत्न[1] सुवर्न्नपद्ममस्मै [व्य]-
79. तरद्रामयमंत्रि-
80. मंचिराजः ॥ [९*] శ్రీవేమ
81. మంత్రి శ్రీగామ ప్రెగడ పు
82. [త్రు] లైన మంచిరాజు కొడుకు-
83. శ్రీరామ రాజుంగారికి
84. మల్లమాంబికంను సు
85. [ఖుండు] మంచి రాజుంగారు
86. మాండుకేశ్వర దేవరకు ప్రీ-
87. [తిగా] ను ఉత్తరపు వా
88. కిటాన . . . లనూ . టు
89. ప్పు మండ . . . . . మ
90. ల్లం గట్టించి రెండు కోట
91. లు . . చుట్టుం నారికేళా

Fourth side.

92. లుం బెట్టించి నవరత్న [స]
93. మలము దోమతెర గ

---

[1] Read °सुवर्ण° instead of सुवर्न्न.

94. జ్జ వట్టుంను మధ్యాహ్న
95. [పు] అవసరము ఉప
96. హారముంను ఆరతి
97. పల్యాలు మోదలైన జే
98. వోపచారాలు సేఇం
99. చెను । ఆ వెనకను త
100. మ తోంబుట్టిన అన్న
101. పరుత కమ్మల్లినాథ [నిం]
102. గోరు శివునంద్రై తేని
103. ఆ తమ్ముండు మం [చి]
104. రాచుంగారు శ్రీపర్వ్వ
105. తలింగాలం దెప్పిం [చి]
106. మాండుకేశ్వర లింగో
107. [లూ] ర చక్రచ్చాయను శ
108. [క] వర్షాలు ౧౨౭౫ అగు వి
109. [జ] య సంవత్సర శ్రేత్ర
110. శు ౧౮ వ రావినూంట్ల పర్వ్వ
111. తమల్లి నాథలింగమని
112. ప్రతిష్ఠ సేసె [॥*] ఆ ముహూ
113. ర్త్తానసే ఆ ముందటి మ
114. ంటపానం దన ప్రాణలిం
115. గ [పు] శ్రీగిరి లింగం పేర
116. ప్రతిష్ఠసేసెను [॥*] ఇరెం
117. డు లింగాల అంగరంగభో
118. గార్థ్థంగాం దమ అగ్రహా
119. [రం] మేడూరను తమ స్వా
120. మ్యానసే ఖండిక ప్రతిపట్టు [పో]
121. ల . ను ఇచిరి (ను) ॥ వంచ
122. . . కగిరేషా . . . . .

123. . रवोपेतान् । अयुता-

124. ष्मांडुकेशस्य [ददौ] श्री-

125. मल्लेनप्रभुः ।

126. నాథనింగారు . . .

127. . . . మాణ్డు కేశ్వర దే ·

128. వర . గా ఇచెను ॥[శు*]భమ[స్తు]॥

ONGOLE (79). (A.D. 1111–12 ?)

[Mannúru or Maḍanúru. Sanskrit in Telugu character and Telugu. By dhwajasthambam in Rámalinga temple.]

TRANSLATION.

Hail! On Sunday, the 2nd of the dark fortnight of the month of Phálguṇa, corresponding to the illustrious Ṣaka year 1033, when the *nakshatra* was *Hasta*, Gósanayya, the son of Víreḍḍi, presented with a full and joyful heart five *gadyánas* for the perpetual lamp in the temple of Rámé-ṣvaradéva of Ítamukkala. Ṣímábhaṭṭa, the *stánádhipati* (temple servant) of this (temple) . . . . he and his descendants in succession should burn the perpetual lamp as long as the moon and sun endure. Thus has this stone edict been put up.

Sanskrit.

In the Ṣrí Ṣaka year, reckoned by the *tridaṣas* (33), the sky (o) and (l) (*i.e.*, 1033) on Sunday, the 2nd of the dark fortnight of Phálguṇa, under the *nakshatra* arkabha, Kósanayya, of the fourth caste, revered by good men, gave a lamp and five *yadyánas* for interest for the pleasure of Ráméṣvara, to last as long as the brilliance of the moon and the stars exists.

[The translation of the last two lines is conjectural, the text being doubtful.]

1. స్వస్తి శ్రీ శకవర్షంబులు ౧౦౩౩ అ
2. వునేణ్డి ఫాల్గుణమాస క్రిష్ణపాడిమి
3. నాదిత్యహస్తమున నింతముకుర్ల రామేశ
4. ర దేవరకు నిమ్మనంబెడరుంజోకొట్టుగట్టి
5. న వీరడ్డి కొడుర్గొసనయ యఖండ దీప
6. ం బునకుంబెట్టిన యేను గద్యానములువ
7. ణ్డియుంజేకొని యిందుల స్థానాధిపతి సీమా
8. భట్టాంచంద్రార్కర్కము సంతానక్రమమ్మున దేవరకుం
9. నఖండవిర్తి మెత్తంగలవాణ్డు గాంబెట్టిన
10. శిలా శాసనము ॥ शाकाब्दे दशनांबरैक
11. गणिते दीपं ददौ फाल्गुन कृष्णेसूर्यदिनेर्क
12. मे विधितिथावांचंद्रतारोज्वलन् । सत्सेव्यः को
13. (सनय्यतो) यधिपथस्तोरेचतुर्थान्वयोगद्या
14. (णान् सकुसीदकान् शरमितान्) रामेश्वर प्रीतये ॥

ONGOLE (80).

[Mannúru or Madanúru. Telugu. On boundary to the south.]

TRANSLATION.

In the fields of Ṣrí Maḍanúru half the *khanḍrika* is the land of Ráméṣvara (?)

1. శ్రీ మడనూరిపొలం
2. లోను సగంఖండికెవు
3. రబుగం రామేశ్వరంని
4. పొలం

Ongole (81).

[Muktinútalapáḍu. Telugu. By the steps of the Ṣiva temple.]

Translation.

* * * *

We have constructed the temple for charity on the occasion of Vishuma Sankránti. Those who obstruct the charity will be considered to have killed 1,000 cows near the Ganges.

* * * *

1. విషుమస్న
2. క్రాంతి నిమిత్తం.
3. ఋన ధర్మ
4. వుగాను గుడిని
5. ని గట్టినాము
6. వి త్తి క్రిప్పిన
7. వారు గంగ క
8. ఱుత వేయి ఆ
9. వులల పోడ్చి
10. నవారు

Ongole (82). (A.D. 1275–76.)

[Muktinútalapáḍu. Telugu. On the Nandi stone in front of the Ṣiva temple.]

Translation.

East side.

Ṣrí! Hail! 770 kunṭas of (vritti) land are from time immemorial in the enjoyment of the deity Ṣrí

Mallináthadéva of Ṣrímat Muṛikinúnttipáḍu. There is no tax on this *vritti.*

West side.

* * * *

For the religious merit of Keḷachapiḷa Choṭṭi. The *sthánapati* (temple servant) of this (temple) is Bayyarázu, son of Vásirázu. We have given to him, to be enjoyed by his sons and grandsons as long as the sun and moon last.

Hail! On Tuesday, the 2nd of the dark fortnight of Áṣvayuja of the year Yuva, corresponding to the year 1197 of the illustrious Ṣaka era on the occasion of Vishuma Sankránti 10,000 *kunṭas* of dry land are given to the deity Mallináthadéva of Muṛkinútipáḍu by Keḷachapiḷa for the religious merit of his sons and grandsons, etc. There is no tax on this *vritti.* 100 *kunṭas* of land are given to Bhairavadéva.

South side.

Any one who says before the throne (*gadyá*) that the deity has not a sixteenth portion will incur the sin of eating from the skull of his eldest son.

1. శ్రీ స్వస్తి శ్రీ
2. మతు ము
3. రికి నూంత్తి
4. పాటి శ్రీ మ
5. ల్లినాథ దేవర
6. కు ననాది సంపి
7. ద్ధమునం జెల్లు
8. చు నున్న వ్రిత్తి కుంటలు

9. ౭౭౦ ఆ దెవదత్తికి
10. పంగాయములు లేవు

West side.

1. కెళచపి
2. ళసెట్టికి ధ
3. ర్మ్మవుగాను
4. దీనికి స్థానాపతి వ్రాసిరా
5. జుకొండుర్తి బయ్యరాజు వీ
6. రి పుత్ర పౌత్రులకు ఆ
7. చంద్రార్కముగాను ఇచ్చి
8. తిమి
9. స్వస్తి శ్రీ శకవర్షంములు
10. ౧౧౯౭ అగు నెంటి యువసం
11. వత్సర ఆస్వయుజ చ బహుళ ౨ మంగ
12. లవారమున విషువ సంక్రాంతి
13. నిమిత్యముగాను ముత్కూనూ
14. తిపాటి మల్లినాధ దేవరకును
15. ంకెళచపిళ తనపుత్ర పౌత్రా
16. జవర్గంబునకును పుణ్యముగాను
17. వ్రిత్తిని మెట్టను పెట్టిన వ్రిత్తి
18. వెలికు ౧౦౦౦౦ వ్రిత్తికి వ
19. ంగము లేవు భైరవదేవ
20. రకు వ్రిత్తికు ౧౦౦

South side.

1. దేవరకు ౪
2. ద్యానావి
3. సాము దీ
4. ని వెవ్వరేని లే

5. దన్నవారు
6. తన పెద్దకొ
7. డుర్కు కపాళ
8. మును గూడ్చిన
9. దోషమును బొందు
10. దురు

Ongole (83). (A.D. 1415–16 ?)

[Muktinútalapáḍu. Telugu. On stone in front of Ṣiva temple.]

Translation.

Hail! On Monday, the 15th day of the bright fortnight of Chaitra of the year Manmadha,* corresponding to the year 1327 of the illustrious, victorious and prosperous Ṣáliváhana Ṣaka era, the Náyak of Addanki, Báṇála Lingana, the son of Akkana and the grandson of Vírappa, who is of the Viṣvakarma (goldsmith) caste, who is a follower of the Ápastamba sútra and who is descended from the Suparva *gótra*, executed the following charitable deed of land to the deity Muktinútalapati Chenna Mallikhárjunadéva, who is the lord of all the croresof worlds. He caused the temple to be constructed and at the time of consecrating the deity gave one *tuchchala* of land of Késaripáḍu on the east side of the way to Ongole in the fields of Muktinútalapáḍu.
(Ṣlokam.)

Note.—The cyclic year corresponds with S.S. 1337 expired.

First side.

1. స్వస్తి శ్రీ జయాభ్యుదయ
2. శాలివాహన శకవర్షంబు
3. లుగ ౧౩౫౭ అగునేంటి మన్మధ
4. నామసంవత్సర చైత్ర శు ౧౨ సో
5. అఖిలాండకోటి బ్రంహాండ
6. నాయకులైన ముక్తి నూతలు
7. పాటి చెన్న మల్లిఖార్జున దే
8. వునకు విశ్వకర్మవర్గోద్భులైన
9. సువర్ణస్యా గోత్రోద్భవ ఆపస్త
10. ంభ సూత్రులైన అద్దంకినాయకుం
11. డు వీరప్ప పౌత్రులైన ఆకర్ణనపుత్రుండు
12. ను ఖాణాలలింగన యిచ్చిన భూ
13. దాన ధర్మశాసనపత్రికె
14. యేమన్నను ముక్తి నూతలపాటి

Second side.

15. ల పొలానను వొంగోలు దోవ
16. లు దోవ తూర్పునకే
17. సరిపాటి కుచ్చలక్షే
18. త్రం దేవళం కట్టించ్చి దేవుని ప్ర
19. తిష్టకాలమందు సమర్పిణం
20. చెను స్వదత్త ద్విగుణం పుణ్యం
21. పరదత్తాను పాలనం పర
22. దత్తాపహారేణ స్వదత్తు ని
23. ష్ఫలంభవేతు.

Ongole (84).

[Muktinútalapáḍu. Telugu. On floor of Ṣiva temple.]

Translation.

. . . . We have given . . . . for the religious merit of . . . . Vidyaráju. Those who obstruct this will be regarded as having killed a thousand cows on the banks of the Ganges . . . .

1. . . . .
2. పీ . ర
3. . . .
4. . . వరు
5. . . . .
6. . . . .
7. . . . .
8. . . న . .
9. . . . . .
10. వసలుమ
11. నిను . .
12. వకాకయ చి
13. మమమర .
14. . . ధవిద్య
15. రాజునకు ధర్మ
16. ముగను సమ
17. పీంచినాము .
18. వారి త్రిప్పిన .
19. వారు గంగ క
20. ఉుత వెయిక
21. విలల విద్యా
22. నవారు .
23. . . . .

ONGOLE (85). (A.D. 1428-29.)

[Nágaluppalapáḍu. Telugu. By west wall of Ṣiva temple.]

TRANSLATION.

Hail! On Tuesday, the illustrious 11th day of the dark fortnight of Jyéshṭa in the year Kílaka, corresponding to the year 1350 of the illustrious and auspicious Śaka era the following charitable edict granting *vrittis* to the deity, Brahmans and the Jangam sect and Bamalas (?) of Náguluppalapáḍu was issued by Gangayadéva Chóḍa Mahárájulu, son of Ṣríman Mahámanḍaléśvara Tribhuvana (lit. whose *biruda* is Tirubhuvana) Vennu Sambeṭa Álamandala Anavótaya Dévachóḍa Mahárájulu. I have granted (remitted) with libation of water the pannu (tax), kaṭnam (present) and kánika (present) due by you formerly on your *writti*, with the eight kinds of enjoyment and with the eight kinds of ownership, for the religious merit of my grandfather Tirumala Rájugáru, my grandmother, Peddamadévalammagáru, my father Anavótayya, and my mother, Chennamadévalammagáru to last as long as the sun and moon exist. They, their sons, and grandsons should keep up the ceremony prescribed by this edict. Thus has this stone edict been planted.

(Those who obstruct this charity) will incur the sin of killing cows and Brahmans near the Ganges, the sin of killing their eldest son and eating his cooked flesh, and also the sin of those who commit the five great sins. Those who keep up this charity will obtain all kinds of merit and those who do not keep it up will go to many hells.

[One imprecatory verse.]

May there be prosperity! May it cause great prosperity!

Note.—Compare this with Kanuparti Vishnu temple inscription No. (56).

1. స్వస్తిశ్రీ శుభ శకవరుషంబులు
2. ౧౩౫౦ అగు నేంటి కీలక సంవత్స
3. ర జేష్ట బ౹శ్రి ౧౧ మ శ్రీమన్మహా
4. మండలేశ్వర త్రిభువనాభిరుద్రుల
5. వెంన్న సంబెట ఆలమందల అనవో
6. త యదేవచోడ మహారాజుల కుమా
7. రుండు గంగయ దేవచోడ మహారాజులు
8. నాగులుప్పలపాటి దేవబ్రాంహ్మన జంగా
9. లవ్రి త్తి బమల వారికి ఇచ్చిన దర్మశాసనం
10. మీరు పూర్వానంబెట్టి వ్రిత్తిపంన్న కట్నం కానిక స
11. ర్వమ్మసలటువెంటి ఇంకా మాతాత తిరుమలరా
12. జుంగారికింన్ని మాముత్తా పెద్దమ్మదేవులంమంగా
13. రికిన్ని మాతండ్రి అనవోతరాజుంగారికింన్ని మాతల్లి
14. చెంనమదేవులంమంగారికింన్ని పుణ్యాంముగాను ధార
15. వోసి అష్టభోగ తేజస్వాంమ్యముగాను అష్టై
16. శ్వర్య ఆచంద్రార్కముగాను నిస్తిమి పుత్రపౌత్రము
17. యీ శాసనము మరియాదను
18. నడపువారును యిట్లని వేయించిన శిలా
19. శాసనము
20. గంగకఱుత గోబ్రాంహ్మలం జంపి
21. న పాపానం బోవువారు తమ పెద్దకొడుకుంజంపి
22. వండిన కూటింకుడ్చిన పాపానం బోవు
23. వారు పంచమహాపాతకాలు సేసిన పా
24. పానం బోవువారు యీధర్మం నడపిన వారికి

25. సకలధర్మములును చెందును యిందుకు త
26. ప్పినవాండు అతినరకమున పడుదురు స్వదత్తా
27. ద్విగుణం పుణ్యం పరదత్తానుపాలనం పరదత్తా
28. పహారేణ స్వదత్తం నిష్ఫలంభవేత్ శుభమస్తు।
29. మంగళమహా శ్రీ శ్రీ శ్రీం జేయును

Ongole (86). (A.D. 1239–40.)

[Nágaluppalapáḍu. Telugu. From stone lying to east of Ṣiva temple.]

Translation.

Hail! In the year Vikári, corresponding to the year 1161 of the illustrious and auspicious Śaka era on the occasion of Vishu Sankránti, Mádéva Náyakuḍu set up the image of Malléśvara at Návuluppalapáḍu and presented land for providing oblation, offering and worship to that deity for the religious merit of Ṣríman Mahámaṇḍaléśvara Gaṇapatidéva Mahárájulu who is possessed of all praiseworthy attributes and for the religious merit of his father and mother—land measured with a pole of 12 fathoms in length as follows :—

* * * *

The temple servants are Tara Pandit the younger brother of Má . . . . Túnuváru and his sons and grandsons as long as the moon, stars and sun endure.

The Brahman *vrittis* are :—(Here comes a list of the shares).

[One imprecatory verse.]

1. స్వస్తి శ్రీశుభ శకవర్షంబు
2. లు ౧౧౬౧ గు వికారిసంవ
3. త్సర విషుసంక్రాంతి నిమిత్తం
4. బు స్వస్తి సమస్త ప్రశస్తి సహిత
5. తంబున శ్రీమన్మహామండలేశ్వ
6. ర గణపతిదేవ మహారాజు
7. లకు దమార్త్థముగా మా
8. దేవనాయకుండు తమతల్లిద
9. ండ్రులకు దమ్మార్త్థముగా నా
10. వుల ఉప్పలపాడను మల్లేశ్వ
11. ర మహాదేవరం ప్రతిష్టించ్చి
12. ఆ దేవునికి హావి బలిఅర్చ్చన
13. లకు నిచ్చిన క్షేత్రము పంండ్రెం
14. డు బారలుం డెవుండుఘు

* * * *

Second side.

1. స్తానపతులు మా
2. తూనువారి తమ్ములు
3. తరపండితులు వీరి
4. పుత్రాను పౌత్రిక మాచం
5. ద్రతారార్కము । వ్రిత్తులు
6. బ్రహ్మలుదంబిరాజు చేసు
7. గుంటలు ౨౦౦ గోపాల పె
8. ద్దిగుంటలు ౨౦౦ నల్లపరా
9. జు గుంటలు ౧౦౦ కామరా
10. జు గుంటలు ౧౦౦ అన్ని
11. పెద్దిగుంటలు ౧౦౦ మల్ల
12. మరాజు గుంటలు ౧౦౦

13. దవపెమఃఘూదిగుంటలు

14. ౧౦౦ పెద్దల కొమఃరాజు

15. గుంట్లలు ౧౦౦ నిమిష

16. కవిసూరపరాజు గుం

17. ట్లలు ౫౦౦ దవతచెను

18. గుంటలు ౧౦౦ స్వదత్త

19. ంపరదత్తంవా ఓ హా రే

20. తివసుంధరా షష్టివషః

21. . . .

22. . . .

ONGOLE (87). (A.D. 1297–98.)

[Nágaluppalapáḍu. Telugu. From a stone near Ṣiva temple.]

TRANSLATION.

Hail! On Thursday, the 1st day of the bright fortnight of Jeshṭa of the year Hévaḷambi, corresponding to the year 1219 of the illustrious and auspicious Ṣaka era, for the religious merit of Ṣríman Mahámaṇḍaléśvara Kákatiyya Pratáparudradéva Mahárájulu, Ṣrímat Muppaḍiniyaningáru gave 500 *kuntas* of land and 1,500 *kuntas* of land . . . and 300 *kuntas* of land in all 2,300 *kuntas* of land to Múlasthána Mallinátha of Náguluppalapáḍu. This charity should be enjoyed in succession by the sons and grandsons of the grantee as long as the sun and moon last. If any one should obstruct this he will be considered to have eaten from the skull of his eldest son and to have killed [cows and Brahmans near the Ganges.

[One imprecatory verse.]

1. స్వస్తిశ్రీ శుభసకవర్షం
2. బులు ౧౧౬౧గ్ అగు నేంటి
3. హేవళంబి సంవత్సర జేష్ట సు ౧ గు
4. రువారము స్వస్తి శ్రీమన్మహామండలే
5. శ్వర కాకతియ్య ప్రతాప రుద్రదేవ మ
6. హారాజులకు ధర్మముగాను
7. శ్రీమతు ముప్పడినాయునింగారు
8. నాగులు ఉప్పలపాటి మూలస్థాన
9. మల్లినాథునికి ఇచ్చిన వ్రిత్తుకు ౫౦౦
10. న్ను వ్రిత్తికు ౧౫౦౦ . . . వ్రిత్తి ౩౦౦
11. వెరశిను ౨౩౦౦ యీధర్మము ఆచం
12. ద్రార్కముగాను పుత్రపౌత్రికము దీనికి యెవరు
13. ద్రిప్పినాను తన పెద్దకొడుకు కపాలమున కూడు
14. కుడిచినవారు గంగకటత గోవుబ్రాహ్మలను
15. జంపినవారు । స్వదత్తం పరదత్తంవ్వా యో
16. హరేతివసుంధరా షష్టివర్షసహస్రాణి
17. విష్టాయాం జాయతేక్రిమి

ONGOLE (88). (A.D. 1239-40.)

[Nágaluppalapáḍu. Telugu. From a stone opposite Ṣiva temple.]

TRANSLATION.

(*c.*) Hail! In the year Vikári, corresponding to the year 1161 of the illustrious and auspicious Śaka era, on the occasion of Vishuma Sankránti (equinox)—Hail! Mádhava Náyaka consecrated the temple of Mallésvara of Nágaluppalapádu and gave fields as follows for providing oblation, offering and worship to that deity, for the religious merit of Sríman Mahámandalésvara Ganapatidéva Mahárája who is endowed with all praiseworthy attributes and of his own parents:—1,000 kuntas measured with a pole of 12 'bárlu' (fathoms) in length, 200 *kuntas* measured with the same pole are given for the cows, and 200 kuntas for Ganésvara.

The *sthánapantulu* (temple servants) of this (endowment) are Márajiyyalu and his younger brother, Bhairajiyyalu, their sons and grandsons and as long as the sun and moon last.

The shares (*vrittis*) of the Brahmans are:—(Here follows a list).

* * * *

These gifts are given in the year Kródhana to last as long as the sun and moon exist.

100 *kuntas* of land in rear of the tank of Pedalúru and 100 *kuntas* of wet fields in Ghrasulúru are given to karnam Dásiráju who wrote this (inscription).

200 *kuntas* of land are given to the dancing girls of the deity, drummers, servants, *palláyamulu* (?)

[Four imprecatory verses.]

One additional (same as in 91, Ongole)

Médusvadugáru's son Yinisvalangáru's vritti 300 *kuntas* of land.

First side.

1. స్వస్తి శ్రీ శుభశ
2. కవరుషంబు

3. లు ౧౧౬౧
4. అగునేంటి
5. వికారిసంవ
6. త్సర విషువ
7. స్సకాంతి నిమి
8. త్తంబు స్వస్తి స
9. మస్త ప్రసిస్తి
10. సహితంబున
11. శ్రీమన్మహా మ
12. ండలేశ్వర గ
13. ణపతిదేవ మ
14. హారాజులకు ధ
15. ర్మార్థముగా
16. మాధవనాయకు
17. ండు తమతల్లిద
18. ండ్రులకు దమ్మార్థం
19. గా నాగుల ఉప్పల
20. పాటి మల్లేశ్వర
21. మహాదేవరకు
22. ప్రతిష్టించి ఆదేవు
23. ని హావి బలి అ
24. ర్చనలకు నిచ్చిన
25. క్షేత్రము పండ్రెం

Second side.

26. ౧డు భారలుండె
27. వ్వెండు ఘడను ఇ
28. చ్చిన చేను గుంట్ల

29. లు ౧౦౦౦ అఘ
30. డను నావులకిచ్చి
31. న చేను ౨౦౦ గణే
32. శ్వరుని కిచ్చిన
33. చేను గు ౨౦౦ దీ
34. నికి స్థానాపంతు
35. లు మారజియ్యు
36. లు పీరితమ్ములు
37. భైరజీయ్యులు పీ
38. రలపుత్రానుషా
39. త్రిక మాచంద్ర
40. తారకము బ్రా
41. హ్మణ బ్రిష్తలు
42. క్షేత్రము తంబి
43. రాజు గు ౨౦౦ గో
44. పాల పెద్ది గు ౨౦౦ నల్ల
45. పరాజు గు ౧౦౦ కామ
46. రాజు గు ౧౦౦ అన్న పెద్ది
47. గు ౧౦౦ మల్లమ రాజు
48. గు ౧౦౦ దేవ పెరుమం
49. డి గు ౧౦౦ పెద్దిల కామం
50. రాజు గు ౧౦౦ నిమిష క
51. వి సూరపరాజు గు ౨౦౦ దె
52. మంచన గు ౧౦౦ పాపరా
53. డ్వి గు ౧౦౦ దిట్టిలి వాసరాజు
54. గు ౧౦౦ దేవర దివ్యకునాచ
55. గో పాళపటేల
56. ల్లుండు మారపెద్ది
57. చేని గు ౧౦౦ దా

Third side.

58. చదివి లష్మన
59. పెద్ది లింగ యల
69. వ్రిత్తి గు ౧౫౦
61. చేరా మనిర గా
62. సు మ ౧ గణే
63. స్వరుని గాను మ
64. ౧
65. దన్నాడ అమరేశ్వ
66. ర దెవునిర గు ౧౦౦
67. భైరవునికి క్షే-
68. త్రము గు ౫౦
69. గుండు లిసందు
70. చరవిష్ణునాంక
71. దాలింగదేవనికి
72. దమ్మువుగాను తి
72. రుమన బోభ
74. ట్టిచ్చినట్టి వెలికు
75. (౨౦) సాంకినార్రి
76. ణకిచ్చిన క్షేత్ర
77. ము గు ౪౦
78. క్రోధన సంవ
79. త్సర ఆయం
80. దానాంమ బా
81. పియగు ౧౦౦
82. వెన్నహిత పెద్ది వ్రిత్తి
83. క్షేత్ర గు ౨౦౦
84. చీతమ రాజు
85. వ్రిత్తి క్షేత్రము

86. గు ౧౦౦
87. వామాధరహిమ వ్రిత్తి గు ౨౦౦
88. కాస్స కొమ్మాజు వ్రిత్తి గు ౫౦౦
89. పోచెద పెద్ది వ్రిత్తి
90. క్షేత్రముకు ౨౦౦

Fourth side.

చంద్ర తారకముగా నిచ్చి
న దానములుం దీని
వ్రాసిన కరణము
దాసి రాజు పెడ
లూర చెఱువెనక
గు ౧౦౦ ఘుర్సులూ
ర వరిచెని గు ౧౦౦
దెవుని సానివారికి
మద్దెల కానికి అమ
జకానికి పుల్లాయ
ముల వారికి క్షేత్రం
ము గు ౨౦౦౦॥ స్వద
త్తం పరదత్తంవా ఓ
హరేతి వసుంధరా
షష్టివరుష సహ
స్రాణి విష్టాయాం
జాయతిఃకిమిః ॥
స్వదత్త ద్విగుణం పు
ణ్యం పరదత్తానపా
లినం పరదత్తాప
హారేణ స్వదత్తం నిష్ప
లంభవెత్ । 3 అకర

స్సకరరికారి గోసహ
స్ర పధస్మి్రితె । కరస్ర
వి త్తివిచ్ఛేదో గోకో
టి పాలమశ్నుతె॥
బహుభి ర్వసుధా
ద త్తరాజభి సగరా
జభియస్యయస్య
యధాభూమితస్య
తస్య తధా ఫలం॥
మొమశ్వదుగారి కొ
డుకు యునిశ్చవ
లంగారి వ్రిత్తి
క్షేతము గు ౩౦౦

Ongole (89). (A.D. 1254–55 ?)

[Nágaluppalapáḍu. Telugu. From four sides of a stone opposite Gópálaswámi temple.]

Translation.

Hail! In the year Ánanda, corresponding to the year 1175 of the illustrious and auspicious Śaka era, on the occasion of Vishuma Sankránti (passage of the sun to the next sign at the equinox)—Hail! Ṣrímat Sárangapáṇi Dévarasu consecrated Ṣrígópáladéva naming him Chakranáráyaṇa Mádhava Gópinátha of Návuluppalapáḍu, and gave land to the Nambi (priest) for providing oblation, offering and worship to that deity, for the religious merit of Ṣríman Mahámandaléśvara Gaṇapatidéva Mahárája who is possessed of all praiseworthy attributes and of his father Mádhava Náyakaḍu and his mother Chúḍubávi. He measured with a pole 12 'bárlu' long 500 *kuṇṭas*.

Second side.

1,500 *kuṇṭas* of land given as a *bhaṇḍáram* for the performance of all enjoyments to the deity, daily worship and occasional festivities . . . . 10 cows.

The vritti-holder of this sthána (temple) are Nambyári Ṣrí Krishṇa Pedda, his sons and grandsons and as long as the sun and moon last.

Third side.

The shares of the Brahmans are :—(Here follows the list).

* * * *

[Two imprecatory verses in Sanskrit.]

Fourth side.

The writer of this inscription is karṇam Jákaráju.

The managers of this charity are—

Basaya Náyaku.

Víraya Náyaku and his son Patumana Boyunḍu.

May there be great prosperity!

Dharma (religion) is victorious.

[One usual imprecatory verse in Sanskrit. Another not common]—

He who imposes taxes on lands free from tax incurs the sin of killing 1,000 cows, but he who removes taxes obtains the merit of protecting crores of cows.

NOTE.—At the top of the first side there is one line apparently meant to have been inscribed at the end of the second side, viz.:—"Ku Peddi's share 100 k (kuṇṭas)."

The S.S. and cyclic years differ by a year.

1. కు పెద్దివృత్తి కు ౧౦౦
2. స్వస్తి శ్రీ శుభశ
3. ఖ వర్షంబులు
4. ౧౧౭౫ గు నేం
5. టి ఆనంద సంవ
6. త్సర విషుమ సం
7. క్రాంతి నిమిత్తం
8. బున స్వస్తి సమస్త
9. ప్రశస్తి సహితం
10. బున శ్రీమన్మహా మ
11. ండలేశ్వర గణప
12. తి దేవమహారా
13. జులకు దర్మము
14. గా శ్రీమతు శ్రీ సా
15. రంగపాణి దేవ
16. రసరు తమతల్లి
17. తంద్రులు మాధవ
18. నాయకునికి చూడుమానికి
19. ధర్మార్థముగా
20. నావులుప్పల పాటి
21. ను చక్రనారాయణ

Second side.

22. మాధవ గోపినా
23. తుండని శ్రీ గోపా
24. లదేవర బ్రదిష్టిం
25. చ్చి ఆ దేవునికి హా
26. నిబలి అర్చనల
27. కుం సంఖ్యారిచె ద

28. ర్తము సేసి ఇచ్చి
29. న క్షేత్రము పంద్ర
30. ండు బారలుండె వ్వె
31. ండు ఘడను గుంట్టలు ౨౦౦
32. అంగ్గరంగ్గ భోహ
33. పరివారక పల్లా
34. యన్నైమిత్తికముల
35. కు వినియోగము
36. లకు భండారము
37. గా నిచ్చిన చేను
38. గుంటలు ౧౨౦౦
39. గోవులు ౧౦ ఇస్తా
40. నమునకు ప్రవిత్తిమ
41. ంతుండైన నంబ్యా
42. రిశ్రీ క్రిష్ణ పె
43. ద్ద వీరల పుత్ర
44. పౌత్రిక మాచం
45. ద్ర తారకము

Third side.

46. బ్రాహ్మణ ప్రవిత్తిలు
47. పెద్దిరాజు గు ౩౦౦
48. మంచిరాజు గు ౩౦౦
49. మాధవుని గు ౧౦౧
50. కొమ్మన పెడ్డి గు ౧౦౦
51. నల్ల రాజు పెద్ది గు ౧౦౦
52. మైలార పెద్ది గు ౭౬౦
53. సూదనభట్టు గు ౭౭౦
54. బిద్యమ గోపాల్ని ౧౦౦

55. మంగణ గు ౨౨౦
56. జోగయ గు ౧౦౦
57. లక్కపెద్ది గు ౪౦౦
58. ప్రోలిపెద్ది గు ౪౦౦
59. కుఅలాడిపెద్ది గు ౧౦౦
60. పదుమయ గు ౫౦
61. వామహావళ్లు గు ౫౦
62. కూచింగారి గు ౫౦
63. కాహాకోవగడు గు ౪౫
64. సజ్జిక సమందు గు ౩౦
65. అద్దంకి మాధవ పె
66. రుమాళ్లు గు ౫౦
67. పెరుమద్రాజు గు ౧౦౦
68. స్వదత్తాం పరదత్తాంవా
69. యోహరేతివసుం
70. ధరా షష్టివరుష స
71. హస్రాణిం విష్టా
72. యాజాయతెక్రిమి॥
73. స్వదత్తం ద్విగుణంపు
74. ణ్యం పరదత్తాను పా
75. లనం పరదత్తాపహారే
76. ణ స్వదత్తం నిష్ఫలం
77. భవేత
78. భాగొమ్మవల్ల
79. భ పెద్ది గు ౧౦౦

Fourth side.

80. దీని వ్రాసిన కరణ
81. ము జాకరాజు ఇ

82. దమ్ము౯వు ప్రతిపా
83. లించిన వారు భూస
84. యనాయకు వీర
85. యనాయకు వీర
86. నపుత్రుండు పతు
87. మన బోయుండు
88. మంగళ మహా శ్రీ
89. శ్రీ దమో౯జయతి
90. బహుభిర్వసుధాద
91. త్తంరాజభిస్సగరాధి
భిః యెస్యయెస్యయె
92. ధాభూమి తస్యత
93. స్య తథాపలం ॥ అ
94. కరస్స కరరికారిగో
95. సహస్రవధ స్త్రీత
96. కరప్రప్రవి త్తి విశ్చే దో
97. గోకోటి పాలమశ్ను
89. తె॥
99.
100.

ONGOLE (90). (A.D. 1187-88 ?)

[Nannúru. Telugu. From stone bearing inscriptions on four sides opposite the Amma temple.]

TRANSLATION.

Hail! In the Śaka year 1109, on the occasion of Vishuva Sankránti, Hail! Ṣríman Mahámaṇḍaléśvara Kámana Chóḍa Mahárája, on whose lotus feet the eyes of Trilóchana and all other kings of the earth are set, who is the jewelled lamp of the race of Karikála by whom the dam[1] of the Kávéri was built, and who is a goad to wicked princes, gave Nannúru exempt from all taxes to Hónkáradévi (goddess) of Nannúru in perpetuity to last as long as the sun and moon endure.

The men of my lineage or those of the lineage of others should protect this (charity).

[Two imprecatory verses.]

NOTE.—Revised by Mr. V. Venkayya.

1. స్వస్తి సకవర్షంబులు ౧౧౦౯
2. శ్రాహివిషువు సంక్రాంతినిమిత్తంబు
3. న స్వస్తి చరణసరోరుహ
4. విహితవిలోచనత్రిలో
5. చన ప్రముఖాఖిల ప్రి
6. థ పీశ్వర కారిత కావేరీ
7. తీర కరికాలకుల రత్న
8. ప్రదీపాహిత కుమారాం
9. కుశ శ్రీ మన్మహామణ్డ
10. లేశ్వర కామనవోడ మ
11. హారాజులు ననూరి హొంకా
12. రదేవికి నన్నూరు సర్వకార (కర)
13. పరిహారము ఆ చంద్రార్క
14. మునకు నిచ్చితిమి దీని మా
15. వంసమున వారైన నొణ్డు
14. వంసమున వారైన నీదమ్ము
17. వు రక్షించునట్టిది ॥ స్వ
18. దతపంరటత్తం వాంయోహ

[1] See note on p. 1250.

19. రేతివన్నూరా షష్టివర్షసహ
20. హస్రాణి విష్ఠాయాంజా
21. యతే క్రిమీ । మద్వంశజః
22. జః పరమహీపతివంశజావా
23. (పాపాదపేత్త మనసాభువిభా)
23. రి రూపయ పాలియంతి మమద
25. స్మర్ణమిదా సమస్తంతె సమ్మయా
26. క్రితమిదంజలిరె వసుపః

Ongole (91).

[Nannúru. Telugu. From the same stone opposite the Amma temple.]

Ttanslation.

Hail! Ṣrímat Ujvala Chóḍa Balaya Chóḍa Mahárájulu, who is Kírtináráyaṇa and Jagadobbagaṇḍa . . . . gave with libation of water . . . . on this side of Nannúru . . . . to Hónkáradévi (goddess) of the very sacred Nannúru. This is endowed for the religious merit of the solar race?

Note.—Revised by Mr. V. Venkayya.

1. స్వస్తి శ్రీమతు
2. కీర్తి నారాయణ
3. జగదొబ్బగణ్డ
4. ఉజ్వల చోడ బల
5. యచోడ మహా
6. రాజులు మాకడుకు
7. రాయసెవా తిత్తి
8. రు నన్నూరి హొబాంకా

9. రదేవికి నన్నూరి
10. కేవలంను చూపె
11. సర్వ నమస్సవ్య
12. ను పేర ధారాపూ
13. ర్వ కము సేసిరి
14. సూర్య్యవంశు
15. లకుం ధర్మ్మము
16. గాంబాకనాం
17. టి ప్రతిష్ట
18. గా ంనిర్పినది

ONGOLE (92). (A.D. 1088-89 ?)

[Nannúru. Telugu. From the same stone.]

TRANSLATION.

Hail! Balleráju (was) the son of Chági Venkana of the illustrious solar race, his son (was) Kanṭruvankyaráju, his son (was) Nanni Chóḍa, his son (was) Súraparáju, and his son Ṛájamahéndra Po[te]pi Chóḍa gave land exempt fro mall taxes to Hónkáradévi at Nannúru. The date of his gift is the first day of the month of Mésha, corresponding to the Śaka year 1010.

He gave it . . . . for *amṛitapaḍi* (sacred food) to Chóḍéṣvara linga . . . .

NOTE.—Revised by Mr. V. Venkayya.

1. స్వస్తి శ్రీ సూర్య్యవ
2. ంశజు నేంటి చాగి వెంకన
3. కొడుకు బల్లెరాజు వీరి
4. పుత్రుండు కంట్రువంక్యరా

5. జా ీరికొండుర్ల నన్నిచోడ
6. వీరి పుత్రుండు సూరపరా
7. జా ీరి పుత్రుండు రాజను
8. హేంద్ర పా [తె] పిచోడు నమ్నారి
9. బొబ్బాంకారదేవికి సర్వ కర
10. పరిహారముగా నిచ్చిరి వీ
11. రయిచిన కాలసంఖ్య
12. లు శకవర్షంబులు ౧౦౧౦
13. యగునేంటి మేషమా
14. సమున పుతమదివ
15. నమునాండు యిచిరి
16. చోడేశ్వర లింగానకుం
17. అమృత పడిగండ (ది)
18. వెంపడి ముం . .
19. పగ వారిశుపు . పు
20. . , యిచ్చిరి బోలము

ONGOLE (93).

[Nannúru. Telugu. From the same stone opposite the Amma temple. The reading and translation are conjectural in parts.]

TRANSLATION.

The king (Ṛéndu) of the important village Nannúru, situated on the bank of the Gundi (Gundlakamma river),

* * * *

who is elder brother of king (Ṛéḍu) Kima (Timma ?), became king (Vibhunḍu). This member of the Vallava (or Pallava) *gótra* had the lord of the monkey tribe

(Hanumán) as the emblem on the royal flag, extended his family and reigned there.

NOTE.—It is not clear what dynasty is alluded to.

1. ఱొలమి గుండి
2. కఱుతు ఒప్ప
3. గం బరగుచున్న
4. నెరద నన్నూరి తె
5. ండుగా నా (నో ?) సగాత్రు
6. ండు గనునజే (ఘనచ?) కి
7. ఘ్రుడణ గంనత (బర?)
8. గుచున్న కిమ (తిమ్మ?) తె
9. ని యగ్రజుండు
10. శ్రీ విభుండ
11. య్యోనని వ (వ ?) ల్లవ
12. గోత్రుంవ (డ?) న్నగ
13. జెఱకు లేశ్వ
14. లాసు (రుండు వాని ?) బెచిన్న
15. ములు వడసె
16. వంగ వర్ధనుణ్డు
17. వ్రేలి యచట

ONGOLE (94).

[Niḍamanúru. Telugu. Opposite temple of Bhímésvaraswámi.]

TRANSLATION.

Núrinimanḍapanírungáru should perform the services at the six times in the temple for the *amritapaḍi* of Bhairava who attends upon Ṣrí Bhímésvara Dévara in three places in that temple (?).

[Two imprecatory verses.]

Pedda Pinna gave with libation of water Gaṇapápuram with its four boundaries and the boundary of Jaḍevágu to the east of the village . . . . to the west . . . . formerly gave *mányas* . . . .

* * * *

Paddy field . . . . this village.

* * * *

Pina Pina Ganapapuram.

శ్రీ భీమే
శ్వర దే
వర మూ
ండుచోట్ల
మూండు
కీ పీరగు
డి పరివా
రము భై
రవునికి అ
మురు (త) వ
డికిని ఈ గు
డికి నూరి
ని మండప
సీరుంగారు
ఆరకాలా
లు నడపం గ
లవాడు ॥

1\. స్వదత్తం ప
రదత్తం వా
యో హరే
త వసుం

దర షష్టి
ర్వ్షర్షా సి
హస్రాణి
విష్ఠాయా
ం జాయతే
క్రిమి॥ (స్వ
దత్తా ద్వి
గుణం
పుణ్యాం పర)
దత్తాను పా
లనం పర
దత్తాప
హారేణ స్వ
దత్తము
నిష్ఫలం
భవేతు॥
పెదపిన్న
గణపా
పురము
చతుస్సీమ
మమును
ఊరి తూ
ర్పున క
జడె వా
ంగు సీమ
మును న్ను
. . . .
. . . .
. .

. . .

సుపడు

మటికి

(విత్తీణాపా

టి నడవ

. . .

వ్రూను ధా

రా పూర్వక

ముగాను

మాన్యాలు

యిచ్చెను

. . . .

. . . .

వరిచెను

ఇగ్రామా

న . . .

. . .

పిన పిన

గణప

పురము

ONGOLE (95).

[Niḍamanúru. Telugu. In front of Bhíméśvara temple.]

TRANSLATION.

They have given this village with all its income with libation of water—(the village) having for its boundaries the boundaries of Daiyyálárâyúru, on the north the boundary of the path leading from Niḍa Mrána to Daiyyáláráyúru—two-thirds to Śṛí Paramésa and one-third to Śṛí Vaiśva Vaṇéśvara Dévara, to provide for decorations and enjoyments for these deities in perpuitety to last as long as the sun and moon endure.

1. పవిత్ర పావనము
2. దైయ్యాలా యూర
3. బోల మెరలు
4. సీమగానున్న ఉ
5. త్తరానకు నిడ
6. మ్రానునుండి దై
7. య్యాలా యూ
8. రికి బొయ్యే
9. న్న డొంక సీమాను
10. యీ గామ.
11. ము సకలాయ
12. సహితముగా
13. ను శ్రీ పరమే
14. శునకు మూ(డు)
15. కు పాలును
16. శ్రీ వైశ్వ
17. వణేశ్వర దే
18. వరకు నొక
19. పాలుంగాను
20. ఈ దేవర అంగ
21. రంగ్గ భోగా
22. లకు న్రా చంద్రా
23. కణము సెల్లునట్లు
24. గా ధారా
25. పూర్వకము సెసిరి

ONGOLE (96). (A.D. 1315-16?)

[Niḍamanúru. Telugu. In front of Bhímésvara temple.]

TRANSLATION.

Hail! While Ṣríman Mahá Maṇḍaléṣvara, Múrúráyalagaṇḍa, Kákatiyya Pratápa Rudradéva Maháraja was ruling the kingdom of the earth hail! On . . . . corresponding to the illustrious Śaka year 1237. . . .

1. స్వస్తి శ్రీమన్మ
2. హా మండ
3. లేశ్వర మూ
4. రురాయల
5. గండ కాక
6. తియ్య ప్రతాప
7. రుద్రదేవ మహా
8. రాజులు పృ
9. థ్వి సాంమా
10. జ్యంబు సేయుచు
11. నుండంగాను
12. స్వస్తిశ్రీ శకవ
13. ర్షంబులు ౧౨౩౭
14. అగు నేంటి

. . . . .

. . . . .

ONGOLE (97). (A.D. 1446–47 ?)

[Niḍamanúru. Telugu. In front of Bhíméśvaraswámi temple.]

TRANSLATION.

Hail! On Thursday the 15th of the bright half of Vaiśákha of the year Vyaya (Kshaya ?), corresponding to the year 1368 of the illustrious Śaka era . . . . . Biródi Gaṇḍa [1], Bhairava Náyankaragaṇḍa [2], Śrímat Paṭalampula . . . . Náyanimgáru issued this charitable edict to the people who live in the *síma* of (Daivarúrirúru ? Daiyálaráyúru) . . . . to Álatu Bóyi. . . . Náyaḍu . . . .

NOTE.—The cyclic and S.S. years do not correspond.

1. స్వస్తి శ్రీ (శక వరుషం)
2. బులు ౧౩౬౮ అగు నేటి
3. వ్యయ సంవత్సర వైశాఖ
4. శు ౧౫ గురువారాన (బి
5. . తురుడ) బిరోది గండ భైర
6. వనాయంకరగండ శ్రీ
7. మతు పటలంపుల వా . .
8. (నా) ఇనింగారు (గనకారిపు)
9. (దై వలూరిరూర) సీమల
10. వారికి ఇచ్చిన ధర్మము శా
11. స ము ఆలతుబోయి . .
12. నాయనికి . . . . .
13. . నూ . . పలుదేవలం
14. . . . .

---

[1] and [2] are birudas.

15. .
16: .
17. .
18. .
19. పుణ్యం
20.

ONGOLE (98). (A.D. 1310–11.)

[Niḍamanúru. Telugu. In front of Bhíméśvara temple.]

TRANSLATION.

Hail! On this holy occasion, on Monday the 30th of the dark fortnight of Pushya of the year Sádháraṇa corresponding to the year 1232 of the illustrious, auspicious (victorious and prosperous) Śaka era, Vipapáṭi Mallayyamgáru presented for the religious merit of his father Bairinénigáru . . . . and settled that (*méras* should be given) at one *kuncha* per *puṭṭi*. If the rulers hinder the construction of this tank, they will incur the sin of killing cows and Brahmans near the Ganges.

1. స్వస్తిశ్రీ శుభా . .
2. రక బ్యుదయ శకవ
3. ర్షంబులు ౧౨౩౨ అగు
4. నేంటి సాధారణ సంవ
5. త్సర పుష్య బ ౩౦ సో ।
6. పు॥ కాలాన విప పా
7. టి మల్లయ్యంగారు త
8. మతండ్రి బయిరినేనింగా
9. రికి పుణ్యంగాను . . .

10. నిమ్ప్ర . . . .
11. పులా . . నాయు
12. . . . .
13. దానయంకరన
14. న్నవోడం బరచి
15. యిచ్చిన పుట్టికుం
16. చ్చాలు యిచ్చేరువు
17. కు కట్టడ నా
18. ను రాజ్యంవారు
19. నడ్పక విఘాతం జే
20. సినాను గంగక
21. తః గోవుబ్రాంహ్మ
22. నిం చంప్పిన
23. పాపాన పోవువారు

Ongole (99). (A.D. 1290–91.)

[Ongole. Telugu. In the Ṣiva temple.]

Translation.

Hail! On the occasion of Uttaráyana Sankránti corresponding to the illustrious Śaka year 1212, Hail! Rudraya Náyakulu (*Gaja Sáhini*) the commander of (the force of) elephants of Ṣríman Mahárája gave 100 *kunṭas* of dry land to Chóḍa Gópinátha of Ongole and one *kunṭa* for the lamp as a charity on behalf of his parents. The temple servant (*sthánikuḍu*) is Sáranguḍu and the trustees of this are Déśi Reḍḍi, Brammi Reḍḍi, Máchama Náyuḍu, Pinnama Reḍḍi (and) Perumánḍi Reḍḍi.

Note.—This is probably the Rudra Náyaka of O. 7 and, if so, the king referred to is Pratápa Rudra.

స్వస్తిశ్రీ శకవర్షంబులు ౧౨౧౨ యగునేంటి ఉత్తరాయణ నిమిత్యంబ్బున స్వస్తిశ్రీ కాస్మహారాయ గజాసాహిణి రుద్రయనాయంకులు తమ తలితండ్రులకు ధర్మార్థముగాను వంగోలిని చోడ గోపినాథునికిచ్చిన వెలిపొలముకు ౧౦౦ నూరు దీపనకుగాను౧ త్తని (స్థాని ?) కుడు సారంగుడు దీనికి నరసోసనము దేశిరెడ్డి బ్రమ్మిరెడ్డి మాచము నాయుడు పిన్నమరెడ్డి పెరుమాండిరెడ్డి.

ONGOLE (100).

[Ongole. Telugu. On a stone by the side of the Great Northern Road to the east of M.R.Ry. D. Márkandayya Ṣástri's garden.]

TRANSLATION.

. . . .[1] On the occasion of Makara Sankránti, the illustrious Karnam Baicharáju Nágaráju gave 100 *kunṭas* of dry land for providing daily offerings, worship and enjoyments . . . . to Vaijéśvara Dévara of Ongole for the religious merit of his liege lord Ṣríman Mahámanḍaléśvara Chakra Náráyaṇa Ṣrí Vaijéga Déva Mahárája.

The temple servants of this charity are the sons of Pandit Víréśvara, viz., Bayyana, Appana, Manchena and their sons and grandsons. These are the temple servants. The trustees of this charity are Pápa Nárapa Reḍḍi, Dési Reḍḍi, Koṭi Reḍḍi, Machana and Pinnama Reḍḍi. This charity was given with the consent of these two sets of persons. This charity was given by Dévi Ṣeṭṭi's sons.

NOTE.—This king does not seem to be mentioned elsewhere. See under "certain chiefs subordinate to the Kákatíya kings" in Appendix I.

---

[1] The stone is broken at the top left-hand corner.

నాంటి మకర సంక్రాంతి నిమిత్యమున స్వస్తి శ్రీ కరణము బైచరాజు నాగరాజు తన్నెలిన స్వస్తిశ్రీ మన్మహా మండలేశ్వర చక్రనారాయణ శ్రీ వైజేగదేవమహారాజులకు ధర్మార్థముగాను ఒంగోలని త్రైజేశ్వర దేవరకు నిత్యనివేద్య అర్చన భాగానకిచ్చిన వెలిచేను కుంటలు ౧౦౦ దీనికి స్థానపతి వీరేశ్వర పండితుల కొడుకులు ఐయ్యన, అప్పన, మంచ్చెన వీరి పుత్ర పౌవిత్రలు స్థానికులు దీనికి నరసాసనము పాపనా రవరెడ్డి దేశిరెడ్డి కొటిరెడ్డి మాచన పిన్నమరెడ్డి వీరి ముఖ యున్మతమున కిచ్చిన దత్తి ॥ యీ ధర్మం సేసినవారు దెవిశెట్టి కొడుకులు.

Ongole (101). (A.D. 1273–74?)

[Ongole. Telugu. On stone now removed to Sub-Collector's bungalow.]

Translation.

Hail! On the occasion of Uttaráyaṇa Sankránti in the year Ṣrímukha corresponding to 1194 of the illustrious and auspicious Ṣaka era, Hail! while Ṣrí Mádhava Déva Maharáyalu, who is Ṣríman Mahá Maṇḍaléśvara, who is a Révanta in riding very rough horses, who is Kṛitánta (Yama) to the enemy's army, who is a fortress of adamant to refugees, who is a protector of the life of his feudatories (?), who is strong-armed, who is a hero without fear, and who is Chakra Náráyaṇa, was ruling, the persons who walked along the boundary line of Ongole and Murikinúntipáḍu are Dammuka Dévanáyuḍu, Gangaráju, Chandári Bairapa Náyuḍu and the Reḍḍis of the eight families of Áṛuluru and Pellúru *sthalas*. With the consent of both these parties Boṭṭuvíḍu Próli Reḍḍi walked over the boundary line of Ongole.

Mádhava Mahárájulu presented a *vritti* of 200 *kunṭas* (to them) to be enjoyed by their sons and grandsons in perpetuity as long as the sun and moon endure.

The trustees (*Narasásana*) of this are Pápana Reḍḍi, Déśi Reḍḍi, Boṭṭivívaṭi Reḍḍi, Pinnama Reḍḍi, Máchinayuḍu.

Twelve *kunṭas* are granted as *vritti* to Bairava (deity) on the hill.

Whoever obstructs this will be regarded as having killed a thousand tawny cows near the Ganges and as having eaten from the skull of his eldest son.

[One imprecatory verse.]

NOTE.—The cyclic and S.S. years differ by one year.

1. స్వస్తిశ్రీ శుభ శకవరుషంబులు ౧౧౯౪
2. అగునేంటి శ్రీముఖ సంవత్సర యుత్తరాయ
3. ణ సంక్రాంతి నిమిత్యమున స్వస్తి । శ్రీమన్మహా
4. మండలేశ్వర అతివిషమ హయారూఢ ప్రౌఢరేఖా
5. రేవంత పరబళ కృతాంత, శరణాగత వజ్రపంజర, మండ
6. లీకర వండోలి జీవరక్ష బుజబల భయుని శంకరమల్ల
7. చక్రనారాయణ శ్రీమాధవదేవమహారాజుల రాజ్యం
8. మున ఒంగోలని మురికినూంతిపాటి పా
9. లి మేర నడబంప్పుమ వచ్చినవారు దంమక
10. దేవనాయుండును గంగరాజును చందారి బై
11. రప నాయుండును ; అటులూరి పెల్లూరి స్త
12. లము యొమ్మదియుళ రెడ్డును వీరియు
13. భయాన్మ తమ్ము న వంగోలిని బొట్టువీటి
14. ప్రోలిరడ్డికిం బొలి మేరనడచినను మాధ
15. వదేవమహారాజులు యిచ్చిన వ్రిత్తి కు
16. ంటలు యిన్నూలు ౨౦౦ వీరి పుత్ర

17. షావృత్తులకు ఆ చంద్రార్కముగా
18. నిచ్చిరి దీనికి నరసాసనము పా పన
19. రెడ్డి, దేశిరెడ్డిని, బొట్టు వీవటి డ్రెడి పి
20. న్నమ రెడ్డి మాదినాయుడు వీరు.

Second side.

21. వ్యాకె కుంటలు ౧౨
22. కొండమీంది వైరేనికి పెట్టిన బ్రిత్తి
23. దీని నెవ్వరు దప్పి వాడు గంగ క
24. టుత వెయిగవిలం బొడిచినవారు పెద్ద కొడు
25. కు కపాళమున గుచ్చినవారు స్వదత్తాం
26. ద్విగుణం పుణ్యం పరదత్తానుపాలనం పరదత్తా ప
27. హారేణ స్వదత్తం నిష్ఫలం భవేతు.

ONGOLE (102). (A.D. 1762–63.)

[Ongole. Telugu. A paper grant in the possession of M.R.Ry. D. Márkandayya Şástri Gáru.]

TRANSLATION.

(Adoration be to) Şrí Ráma.

Hail! This is the charitable grant of a gift of lands written and given by Mandapáṭi Kumára Rámabhadrarája, student of the Yajuș śákha, follower of the Ápastamba sútra, descendant of the Kásyapa *gótra*, grandson of Rámabhadraráju, and son of Rámachandraraja to Dhárá Mṛityunjaya Şástri, student of the Yajus Şákha, follower, of the Ápastamba sútra, descendant of the Kaundinya *gótra* grandson of Peddi Bhoṭla, and son of Venkaṭávadhánulu in the victorious and prosperous Sáliváhana Saka year 1684 corresponding to the (cyclic) year Chitrabhánu, on the 15th of the bright fortnight of Srávaṇa. The conditions of the grant are—We have given you, exempt from all taxes, cultivable land measuring two (2) kuchela [1] in the fields of Koppólu, which we enjoy as mirási lands for doing service as 'Kávali déśamukh' and as 'ijárá' lands; situated in the taluk of Chímakurti, according to the prescribed rules, on a holy occasion, with a gift of gold and libation of water. Therefore having taken possession of this land, let you, your sons and grandsons in succession enjoy the various grains raised on it every year as long as the sun and the moon last and be happy.

Verse. The ratification of another's gift is superior to one's own gift. By gift one obtains heaven; but by protection of another's gift one reaches absolute bliss. The protection of land given by another is twice as meritorious as one's own gift; by resuming another's gift one's own gift becomes inefficacious.

[Signature] RÁMABHADRA RÁJA,

Rája of Yenḍlúru, Ongole Taluk.

స్వస్తిశ్రీ విజయాభ్యుదయ శాలివాహన శక
వర్షంబులు ౧౬౮౪ అగునేటి చిత్రభాను సం
వత్సర శ్రావణ శు ౧౫ లు యజు శ్శాఖాధ్యాయు
లుంన్ను ఆపస్తంబ్బ సూత్రులుంన్ను కౌండిన్య స
గోత్రులున్ను పెద్దిభొట్లగారి పౌత్రులుంన్ను వెంక
టావధానులవారి పుత్రులయ్ని ధారా మృత్యుం
జయశాస్త్రులవారికి యజుశ్శాఖాధ్యాయు
లున్ను ఆపస్తంబ్బ సూత్రులుంన్ను కాశ్యపస

[1] Kuchela = 8 'gorrus' of land.

గోత్రోద్భవులున్న రామభద్రరాజుగారి పౌ
త్రులైన్ను రామచంద్రరాజుగారి పుత్రులు
న్న అయ్యిన మంద్దపాటి కుమార రామభద్ర
రాజుగారు వ్రాయించ్చియిచ్చిన భూదాన ధర్మ
శాసన పత్రికె క్రమమెట్లను మాకుమన్నె కావ
లి సరిదేశముఖ మిరాసీలుౠన్ను యిజారాకున్ను
నకుపత్తావున్న చీమకుర్తి సముతులో
కొప్పోలు పొలానీ మీకు కయిలుపాటునకు ౨
రెండ్డు కుచ్చళ్లపొలిం సర్వమాన్యం యీ తథా
తిథి పుణ్యకాలమంద్దు సహిరణ్యోదక దాన
ధారాపూర్వకంగ్గా శ్రీ అర్పితంగ్గా యి
స్తిమి గనుక యీ క్షేత్రం ఫలవరుచుకుని యం
దుకల ప్రతి సంవత్సరం ఫలించ్చిన నానా ధాన్యము
లు మీ పుత్ర పౌత్ర పారంపర్యము ఆచంద్రా
కర్కస్థాయిగా అనుభవిస్తూ సుఖానవుండ్డు
నది ॥ శ్లోకం ॥ దానపాలనయోర్మధ్యే దా నా
చ్ఛ్రేయోనుపాలనం దానాత్స్వర్గ మవాప్నో
తి పాలనా దచ్యుతం పదం ॥ స్వదత్తా ద్విగుణం
పుణ్యం పరదత్తాను పాలనం పరదత్తాపహా
రేణ స్వదత్తం నిష్ఫలం భవేత్ ॥

ONGOLE (103). (A.D. 1250–51 ?)

[Ongole. Telugu. From stone in supply channel of a tank. Now at Sub-Collector's bungalow, Ongole.]

TRANSLATION.

Hail! This is the gift made by Ṣrí Sómarája, the prime minister, on the occasion of Uttaráyaṇa Sankránti, corresponding to the illustrious Ṣaka year 1172, for the religious merit of his liege lord Chakra Náráyaṇa Singaḷa Déva Mahárája, to the deity of Ongole.

స్వస్తిశ్రీ శకవరుషంబులు ౧౧౬౨
అంగుసెంటి యుత్తరాయణ సంక్రాంతిని నిత్యంబు
శ్రీ మన్మహా ప్రదానియైన సోమరాజు తన్నేలిన చక్ర
నారాయణ సింగళదేవ మహారాజులకు ధర్మార్థ
ముగాను ఒంగోలుని . . . .
దేవరకు యిచ్చినది.

ONGOLE (104). (A.D. 1424-25.)

[Paidipáḍu. Telugu. From Mallésvara temple.]

TRANSLATION.

Hail! On Saturday, the 10th of the bright fortnight of Śrávaṇa of the year Kródhi, corresponding to the Śaka year 1346, Śríman Mahámanḍaléśvara Birudóráya, Chauhattamalla, Ghanṭánádaka, Ghanṭadhvaniparichitavobbanḍalómandalíśaktivíra, Cháṇúrámallapraharaṇa (Baturómáḍam Nulpa) . . . . . Karibháti Śrípari-pandhita, Prabhuvaratanaya, Śrínidhi, Mummiḍi Reḍḍi gave this endowment while Mailára Reḍḍi, son of Panṭa Mummaḍi Reḍḍi was ruling Pahinḍipáḍu. Near the fields belonging to the gods and Brahmans of this village in the time of Vémayya Reḍḍi seven *kunchams* of land were given as a *sarvamányam* (?) At that time Manta Reḍḍi, the person having authority, settled the *vrittis* of that village. Having enquired into the former settlement in the time of Mummaḍi Vémayya Reḍḍigáru, Mayilára Reḍḍigáru gave for the gods and Brahmans of Payinḍipáḍu *vrittis* free from presents (kaṭnálu) to last long as the sun and moon.

Those who protect this charity will be regarded as having performed all religious acts; those who do not protect it will be regarded as having committed the five cardinal sins, as having killed a tawny cow on the banks of the Ganges, as having murdered their parents and as having eaten from the skull of their eldest son.

[One imprecatory verse.]

May it cause great prosperity!

1. స్వస్తిశ్రీ మన్మహా మం
2. డలీకరబిరుదో రా
3. య, చౌహత్తమల్ల, ఘ
4. ంటా నాదకక ఘంట
5. ధ్వని పరిచిత బబ్బం
6. డలో మండలీ శక్తి వి
7. రశ్ప్రాణూరా మల్ల ప్ర
8. హారణను(బతురో
9. మాడంనుల్ప) . క
10. రి భా. శీపరివంధి
11. త ప్రభువర తనయ
12. శ్రీ నిధి ముమ్మిడి రెడ్రు
13. పెట్టిన శకవర్షం
14. బులు ౧౩౮౬ అగునే
15. టి క్రోది సంవత్సర
16. శ్రావణ శు ౧౦ శ వం
17. ట ముమ్మడి రెడింగారి
18. కుమారుండు మైలార
19. రెడ్డింగారు పహిండి
20. పాడు పలుచున్న యీ
21. యూరి దేవ బ్రాంహ్మణ

22 క్షేత్రాలకాడ వే
23. మాయరెడ్డింగారి కా
24. లమందు సర్వమాన్య
25. ంపండుకుంచాలన కుం
26. మంతరడి అదికారు
27. లు ఆ వూరానుంసేసిన
28. వ్రిత్తి కట్టులు ముంమ్మ
29. డివె మాయురెడ్డింగా
30. రి కాలమందుల పూర్వ
31. మర్యాద విచారించి
32. మయిలార రెడ్డిం
33. గారు వయిండిపా
34. టి దేవ బ్రాంహ్మణ
35. క్షేత్రాలకు ఆ చంద్రా
36. కస్థాయిగాను వ్రిత్తి
37. కట్నాలు మానిగా ఇ
1. చ్చిరి ఈ దమ్మనాము ప్రతి
2. పాలించినవారు సక
3. ల ధమార్ణలును చేసినవా
4. రు ఈ ధమ్మర్ణం ప్రతిపాలి
5. ంపనివారు పంచమ
6. హా పాతకములున్ను
7. చేసినవారు గంగ కలు
8. త కపిలగోవుం జంప్పి
9. నవారు తమతల్లితం
10. డ్రులం జంప్పినవా
11. రు తమ పెద్దకొడుకు క
12. పాలనం కాటికపట్టి
13. నా వారు॥ స్వదత్తా ద్విగు

14. ణం పుణ్యం పరద
15. త్తాను పాలనం పర
16. త్తాపహారేణ స్వద
17. త్తం నిష్ఫలం భవేతు.
18. మంగళ మహా శ్రీ

Ongole (105). (A.D. 1366–67 ?)

[Pallamalli. Telugu. Opposite Ṣiva temple.]

Translation.

Hail! . . . . of the year Plavanga, corresponding to the illustrious and prosperous Ṣaka year 1289, Pallámalli Kanṭamamantapamadya Náyinenḍu of Kammanáḍu . . . . presented . . . . to last as long as the moon and sun endure . . . .

స్వస్తిశ్రీ శుభ శకవ
ర్షంబులు ౧౨౮౯ అ
గు నెంటి ప్లవంగ సం
వత్సర క
మ్మనాండు పల్లామ
ల్లి కంటమ మంటప
మద్య నాయి నెండు
(మసనిత) . . . రుడు
రమ . . . . . .
పెట్టినవ . . .
. . టిరె . బు .
ఇ . . . నెలిటి . ను
దాంభ . ఆ చం
కాము . త్న . .

సో . పోతల్లి ఆవ .

. . . .

ను . . .

లం గొండామన .

సెంపెది.

ONGOLE (106). (A.D. 1739–40 ?)

[Pallamalli. Telugu. South of village under tank bund.]

TRANSLATION.

Hail! On the 10th of the bright fortnight of Ṣrávaṇa of the year Siddhárthi, corresponding to the illustrious, victorious and prosperous Ṣáliváhana Ṣaka year 1660, Rámasvámi Gurvupadyi Ayyannagáru, descendant of the Tállúr *gótra*, grandson of N(G ?)ánginéḍigáru and son of Polneḍigáru caused this tank to be constructed for dedication to the god, ... wells, channel . .

NOTE.—The cyclic and S.S. years do not agree.

1. స్వస్తిశ్రీ జయాభ్యు
2. దయ శాలివాహన
3. శకవర్షంబులు ౧౬౬౦
4. ఆగు నేటి శిద్ధార్థి
5. సంవత్సర శ్రావణ
6. శుద్ధ ౧౦ లు
7. తాల్లూరి గోత్రో
8. ద్భవులున్న
9. నాంగినేడి
10. గారి పౌత్రు

11. లుంన్ను పొత్నే
12. డి గారి పుత్రు
13. లుంన్ను అయిన
14. రామస్వామి గురువ్వ
15. పడ్య అయ్యన్నగా
16. రు యీశ్వరాపణ
17. ణంగాను కట్టిం
18. చ్ని చెరువు . . .
19. బావులు కాలు
20. వ.

ONGOLE (107).

[Pallamalli. Telugu. Below a hill to the west.]

TRANSLATION.

Hail! On the 10th of the bright fortnight of Márgaśira of the year Raktákshi, corresponding to the illustrious victorious and prosperous Ṣáliváhána Ṣaka year . . . Rámasámi and Guruvappa, descendants of the Táḷúr *gótra*, grandsons of Ganginénigáru, and sons of Pólinaváru, caused this pond to be constructed for dedication to Paraméśvara.

1. స్వస్తిశ్రీ జయా
2. భ్యుదయ శాలి
3. వాహన శకవరుషం
4. . . . . . .
5. అగు నేటి రక్తాక్షినామస
6. ంవత్సర మార్గశిర
7. శు ౧౦ లు తాళూరిగోత్రో

8. ద్భవులున్ను గంగ్గినేనిగా

9. రి పౌత్రులున్ను పోలిని

10. వారి పుత్ర్రులున్ను

11. రామసామి గురువప్ప వ

12. రమేశ్వరాపీఠతంగ్గాను త

13. ప్పించిన కోనేరూ.

ONGOLE (108).

[Pallamalli. Telugu. West of Gangamma temple.]

TRANSLATION.

. . . . Those who violate this (charity will be regarded as) having killed a Brahman at Benares.

[One imprecatory verse.]

1\. . . . . .

(2) మరుమీ . .

(3) దాలివ . తోన ౨౦

4\. . . తప్పిన వారణాసిలో

5\. బ్రాంహాని వధియించ్చిన బ (హు)

6\. భిర్వసుధాదత్తా బహుభి

7\. చ్చాను పాలితః యస్యయస్య యదాభూ

8\. మి తస్యతస్య తథాఫలం.

9\. . . . . . .

10\. . . . . .

11\. . . . . . .

12\. . . . . . య

13\. . ను . . . . . . కొంత

14\. వ . . యె . . . . .

15\. . దాచంద్ర్రమునుం

16\. . . . . డుపు . .

ONGOLE (109). (A.D. 1337–38.)

[Pérayapáḷem (hamlet Módépalli). Telugu. On a hill opposite Ánjanéya temple.]

TRANSLATION.

Hail! On the 13th of the dark fortnight of Kártika of the year Íśvara, corresponding to the illustrious, victorious and prosperous Ṣaka year 1259, the following charitable edict was granted to Lakshminarasimhadévara of Virunapáḍu and to Chépe Ásinta Dásari by Ṣrímat-Kasakurti Bávináyaningáru, Ivipáṭináyaningáru . . is given as a village mányam and as a *sarvamányam* to Lakshminarasimhadévara of Virunapáḍu . . . . On the southern side is the *brindávanam* (garden) of the deity.

1. స్వస్తిశ్రీ జయాభ్యుదయ శకవ
2. ర్షంబులు ౧౨౫౯ అగు నేటి
3. యీశ్వర సంవత్సర కార్తిక బహుళ
4. ౧౩ లు శ్రీమతు కస
5. కుర్తి బావినాయునింగారు
6. యీవిపాటి నాయునింగారు
7. విరునపాటి లక్ష్మి నరసిం
6. హ దేవరకు చేపె ఆసిం
9. త దాసరికి యిచ్చిన ధర్మ
10. శాసనము వీరునపాటి ల
11. క్ష్మి నరసింహ దేవరకు వూరి
12. మాన్యముగా నను సర్వమా
13. . . . . దక్షిణపు దరిని
14. దేవర బ్రిందావనము.

ONGOLE (110). (A.D. 1221–22.)

[Pernamiṭṭa. Telugu. From stone by Rámálingaswámi temple.]

TRANSLATION.

Hail! In the year Vṛishu corresponding to the year 1143 of the illustrious Ṣaka era Mainápalli Ma . . . granted 400 *kuṇṭas* to Bhúnáthadéva of Pernamiṭṭa for the religious merit of his parents. If any one obstructs the charity (by collecting cess) he will be considered to have killed a black cow near the Ganges, and to have taken food in the skull of his eldest son. Kunkaṭi Márajíya Bhaṭṭalu's son Dévapánu Víralunḍu Prolajiyula should conduct the deity's service for this *vritti*.

[One imprecatory verse.]

1. స్వస్తిశ్రీ శకవరుష[ంబులు
2. ౧౧౪౩ గు నేంటి విశువ . . .
3. త్సరున మైనాపల్లి మా . . .
4. తమతల్లి తండ్ర్లకు [పుణ్యము]
5. కు పెఱినమిట్ట గ్రామంబున
6. భూనాథ దేవర వ్రిత్తి ౪౦౦ కు
7. ను యవ్వరయినాను పంగము కు [ధ]
8. ర్మువునకు నెవరు విఘలము సేస్నివారు గం [గకరు]
9. తం గవిలంజంపినవారు తమపెద్దకొడు
10. కపాలమున గుడిచినవారు ఇవ్రిత్తికి
11. నొడయులు కుంకటిమారజీయ భట్టలు కొనా
12. రుండును డేవపానువీరలుండు ప్రొలజియ్యల దేవభో

గము

13. నడపంగలవారు । స్వదత్తం పరదత్తంవా
14. యోహరేతి వసుంధరా షష్టిర్వర్ష సహస్రా
15. ణి విష్టాయాం జాయతే క్రిమి

ONGOLE (111). (A.D. 1627–28.)

[Pernamiṭṭa. Telugu. On a pillar in Vishnu temple.]

TRANSLATION.

Hail! On the 15th of the bright fortnight of Phálguṇa of the year Prabhava, corresponding to the year 1548 of the illustrious, victorious and prosperous Ṣáliváhana Ṣaka era, Parnaśála, Timmana, Vengaḍa, Rámanna, Súrapa and Rangana, these six who are the grandsons of Rámachandruni Timmaráju and (his wife) Rangamma and who are sons of Bhávaráju and (his wife) Tirumalamma, who are of the Kauṇḍinya *gótra*, of the Ápastamba *sútra*, who are students of the *yajuṣṣákhá* and who are the *sthala karanams* of Konḍavíḍu and village karanams of the 5 villages, viz., Péraṇamiṭṭa, Mangamúru, Tangaṭúru, Vávilēṭipáḍu and Pachuva . . . . .

NOTE.—The cyclic and S.S. years differ by one year.

1. స్వస్తిశ్రీ విజయాభ్యుదయ
2. శాలివాహన శకవరుషం
3. బులు ౧౫౪౮ అగు నేంటి
4. ప్రభవసంవ్వత్సర ఫాల్గుణ
5. శుద్ధ ౧౫ లు యజుశ్శాఖాధ్యా
6. యులు ఆపస్తంభసూత్రు
7. లు కౌండిన్యగోత్రులునున్న కొం
8. డవీటికి స్థలకరణాలు
9. న్న పేరనమిట్ట మంగ్గ
10. మూరు తంగటూరు
11. వావిలేటిపాడ

(To face page 1099.)

ONGOLE NO. 112.

12. పచువ । యాగ్రామా
13. లు ౫ కి గ్రామకరణా
14. లు అయిన రామచం
15. ద్రుని తిమ్మరాజు
16. రంగమ్మ । పౌత్రులు
17. భావరాజు । తిరుమలంమ । పు
18. త్రులు । పనజాశాల । తిమ్మన । వెంగ
19. డ। రామన్న।సూరప। రంగన। జ ౬
20. కి ॥

ONGOLE (112).

[Pernamiṭṭa. Telugu in Chálukyan character. From a rock known as Goḍugubanḍa, on the hill.]

TRANSLATION.

Hail ! . . . . . . who was a mountain to the Ganga dynasty (?) lord of the city of Máhishmati, descendant of the Áyihaya race . . . .

NOTE.—The transcription into Telugu character was done by Mr. V. Venkiah. On p. 66 E.I. vol. IV reference is made to Chóḍa Vikrama Rudra, son of Rájapareṇḍu of the Haihaya *vamsa*, lord of the Kóṇa country and ornament of the city of Máhishmati which has been identified with Mandla. Ayihaya clearly stands for Haihaya (*i.e.*, Kalachuri).

1. స్వస్తి గంగాపారియాత్ర[1] మాహిష్మతీ పురేశ్వర
2. అయిహయ [వం*] శోద్భవ శివ . . .

---

[1] Páriyátra means the western Vindhya mountain.

ONGOLE (113).

[Pondúru. Telugu.]

TRANSLATION.

On Thursday the 15th of the bright fortnight of Kártika of the year Kródhi, Kondama Náyaningáru, son of Rávipervata Náyanimgáru, and Ráminávanimgáru gave the village of Pondúru to Tállapáka Tirumalayyan Gáru in the presence of Tiruvengadanátha for the religious merit of Sadáśivaráya. Therefore he is entitled to enjoy the eight kinds of enjoyment of that village as long as the sun and moon exist.

Those who obstruct this charity will incur the sin of killing cows and Brahmans near the Ganges. They will be debarred from the worship of Hari and Hara, will be born in the womb of a donkey and will go to the city of Yama.

The protection of another's gift is twice as meritorious as one's own gift. By resuming another's gift one's own gift becomes inefficacious.

1. క్రోధిసంవత్సర కార్తిక శు
2. ద్ధ ౧౫ గు తిరువెంగడనాథుని స
3. న్నిధిని సదాశివరాయుల
4. కుం బుణ్యంబుగాను తాళ్ల
5. పాక తిరుమలయ్యం
6. గారికి రావి పర్వతనా
7. యనింగారి కొమారుడు
8. కొండమ నాయనింగా
9. రున్ను రామి నాయనిం
10. గారును పొందూరు గ్రామ
11. ము సమర్పించిరిగాన ఆగ్రామా

12. నః గల అష్టభోగఫలప్రాప్తి ఆచం
13. ద్రార్క స్థాయిగాను అనుభవించు వా
14. రు యీ ధర్మానకు యవ్వరుగా
15. ని తప్పినాను గంగకతీర గోవుబ్రాహ్మల
16. వధించినపాపానం బోదురు
17. హరిహరాదులశాపకు వెలిఅగా
18. ధర్మభజన్మానజనించి యమపురికిం
19. బోవువారు । స్వదత్తాద్విగుణంపుణ్యం
20. పరదత్తానుపాలనం పరదత్తాపహారేణ
21. స్వదత్తం నిష్ఫలంభవేత్ ॥

ONGOLE (114).

[Pótavaram. Telugu. In a street.]

TRANSLATION.

When it was represented to Timmárasayya that the tank in Pótavaram village towards Nágula Vuppalapáḍu caused to be dug by Póledayya, for the religious merit of his parents, on the 14th day of the bright fortnight of Pushya of the year Bahudhánya, had no water, Malliyarayya made a gift of a field of 2 *gorrus* to the east of the village.

Whoever maintains this field without failure will acquire merit. If any one fails to maintain this field and destroys the tank, the donkey of the Dommara will cover his wife. Therefore the tank is given to the public . . . .

1. బహుధాన్యసంవత్సర పుష్యశుద్ధ ౧౪ లు
2. చెల్లివచ్చిన పోతవరంగ్రామానమూ తమత ల్లిదండ్రులకు-

3. ణ్యముగాను పోలెదయ్య వేయించిన నాఉఃవుప్పల

4. పాడతెరువు చెరువు యీ గ్రామానకు నీళ్లు లేకుండంగాను తిమ్మ

5. రసయ్యకు చెప్పితేను మల్లియరయ్య యిచ్చిన ధర్మదానం

6. వూరికి తూరుపు పాలాన రెంఉః గొలుః

7. చేను యీ చేను యవ్వరు తప్పక నడిపిరి వారికి యీ పుణ్యం చెందును

Second side.

8. యెవ్వరు తప్పి యీ చెరు

9. వు తెను (కోరుపట్టేలి) వా

10. ని ఆలిని దొశ్మరవా

11. నిగాడిదె విషయించు

12. గనుక అష్టలోక ధర్మసా

13. చి ప్రజలకు చేనువు

14. న్న కుంటను అది ప్రొద్దు

Ongole (115). (A.D. 1134–35.)

[Ráchapúḍi. Telugu. In a field to south of village.]

Translation.

Hail! On Thursday the 11th of the bright fortnight of Áshāḍha of the year Ánanda, corresponding to the illustrious Ṣaka year 1356 . . . . May this be maintained as long as the sun and moon endure. I have just begun it. Whoever maintains or protects this charity will acquire merit. Those who injure this will incur the sin of caressing the dugs of a donkey.

స్వస్తిశ్రీ శకవరుషం
బులు ౧౩౫౬ అవునేటి

ఆనంద్ద సంవత్సర ఆషా

డ శు ౧౧ గురువారము

తంచి . . . . .

చితకీగి . . . . .

ల్బ్బ సాగించి .

ద్రాకర్ణముగాను చెల్లగలది మొదటయుపుకు సా

గించినాను యీాధర్మవుం అను

పాలించి

స. వారికి

ధర్మవు

గలుగును

చెసిచిన యీ గ్రామంవారు గాడి

దె స్తనము కవుగలించిన

పాపానం పోదురు

Ongole (116).

[Rámakúru. Telugu. On rock opposite Rámalingéśvara temple.]

Translation.

O Ráma! May Gaṇapéśvarasvámi resplendent with greatness and splendour on the east . . . Prólámba, the ornament of gods who receive worship from learned men (   ) on the south . . . Rámappa who resides with Párvati on the summits of a mountain on the west . . . Hanumantamúrti the peaceful who protects the north . . . May these lords of the universe shower prosperity and happiness in all directions . . . protect the residents of Amarapura and increase the virtue of people! Ráma! (?)

Note.—This is a verse called Sísam.

1. గణపేశ్వరస్వామి ఘనతతోం దూర్వాన వైభవంబులతోడ వున్న (మీరు . . . .)

2. దక్షిణభాగాన దైవాలతిలకమై ప్రాలాంబ విభుదుల పూజ వసి . . . .

3. పడమట రామప్ప పార్వతిసహితుండై పర్వతాగ్రంబునం బరిగ నిలచె . . .

4. వుత్తరభూమిన వొనరంగశాంతుండు హనుమంత మూర్తి దాను (మరియూరి . . .)

5. యిట్టి లోకైకనాధులు యెల్లదిక్కుల అఖిల మంగళ సౌ ఖ్యాంబులమరు . . .

6. అమరపుర దాసులను (చు . . యుండు) ప్రజలు ధర్మం బు మీర గ నొప్పారామా॥

Ongole (117).

[Rámakúru. Telugu. On rock opposite Rámalingéśvara temple.]

Translation.

To Ráméṣvara Dévara we Ṣríman Mahá Maṇḍaléṣvara . . . . nannichóḍa 'Mahárâyulu . . . . have given . . . . as *vritti* $3\frac{1}{8}$ *puṭṭis* of field . . . . Those who obstruct . . . . near the Ganges.

1. శ్రీరామేశ్వర దేవరకు కోమరుశ్వ
2. శ్రీన్మహా మండలేశ్వర . . .
3. ంనన్ని చోడమహారాజులు . . . .
4. ఋలమానుకుం . . . . .
5. ఇద్దణాను జనసూ . . . .
6. స్థివరుప్పుగుడో . . . . . .

7. చ్చితిమి వీరికి శ్రీ . . . . . .
8. ప్రతిష్ఠ (౩౽) ఇల్యునక .
9. . . లసున చక్రకవాటినిన .
10. . . తప్పినవారు గంగ్గకతః . . .
11. . . . . . .
12. . తకవి . . . . . .
13. . . అచిరు . . .

Ongole (118).

[Rámakúru. Telugu. On rock opposite Rámalingéśvara temple.]

Translation.

Mallavarapu Timmayya by the grace of Srí Rámésvara.

1. శ్రీ రామే
2. శ్వర వరప్రసా
3. దేన మల్లవర
4. పు తిమ్మయ

Ongole (119).

[Rámakúru. Telugu. On rock opposite Rámalingeṣvara temple.]

Translation.

On the 2nd of the bright fortnight of Mágha of the year Paridhávi, Chévula Dattayaváru planted this flower garden for the worship of Rámésvara.

1. పరిధావి సంవ్వత్సర మాఘ శు
2. ౨ లు రామేశ్వరని పూజకు పుష్ప

3. లతోంట చెవుల దత్తయ్యవారు బుణ్యం
4. గాను శేశెను శ్రీంజేయును

ONGOLE (120). (A.D. 1217–18.)

[Rámakúru. Telugu. From rock near Dhvajasthambham of Rámalingéśvara temple.]

TRANSLATION.

* * * *

Chóḍa Déva Chóḍa Mahấráyalu who is the son of Mahá Maṇḍaléśvara Kámaya . . . . who is possessed of all praiseworthy attributes, who bears names such as Jagad (obba)gaṇḍa, Kírti Náráyaṇa, Páráyaṇa and Chandraśékhara, who is of the Káṣyapa *gótra* . . . . who is the excellent ruler of Vorayúripura, who is a goad to hostile kings, hail! On Friday, the 15th day of the dark fortnight of Ṣrávaṇa of the year Íṣvara, corresponding to the illustrious Ṣaka era 1134, on the occasion of the solar eclipse, for the religious merit of his parents and the prosperity of his kingdom . . . .

1\. . . . . . .
2\. . ర శ్రీ . . . .
3\. . కరితూ . . . .
4\. . తబు . . ధగా . . . .
5\. బలా . . మా . . మా . డును .
6\. యడు . శ్వర . .
7\. జంబుత . . . దనచరణపద్మ
8\. . . . . వీరడు . .
9\. వేరితిచో . . . . వరనృపతి వరకుమారాంకుశబర

10. ధయూరి పురవరాధీశ్వర . . . కాశ్యపగోత్ర జగ . . .
11. . . గండ . . . . కీర్తినారాయణ పరాయణ
12. చంద్రశేఖరనామాది సమస్త ప్రశస్తి సహిత శ్రీమన్మ
హామండ
13. లేశ్వర కామయ . . . యాపుత్రుడు చోడదేవ చో
డమహా
14. రాజులు స్వస్తి శ్రీ శకవర్షంబులు ౧౧౩౯ అగునేంటి
ఈశ్వరసంవ్వత్సర
15. శ్రావణ బహుళ ౧౨ యు శుక్రవారమునాండు . . . .
16. సూర్యగ్రహణ నిమిత్తంబున దమతల్లిదండ్రులకు ధర్మాను
17. గాను మాకు రాజ్యాభివ్రిద్ధి అగునట్లుగాను . .

* * * *

ONGOLE (121).

[Rámakúru. Telugu. On rock opposite Rámalingéśvara temple.]

TRANSLATION.

Ṣrí Rághavéṣvarunḍu set up the image of Ráma, and presented . . . . paddy field as a charity for the daily (service) of the deity.

[One imprecatory verse.]

1. శ్రీ రాఘువేశ్వరుండు . .
2. రామయ్యను ప్రతి
3. ష్టసేసెను దేవరప్రతినిత్యం
4. కు యవకాయ . . చెను
5. ధర్మముగా నిచ్చిన వరిచేను
6. దేవరకి అర్పదాని సేనివె క్షై

7. స్వదత్తా ద్విగుణం పుణ్యం
8. పరదత్తాను పాలనం
9. (పరదత్తాపహారేణ)
10. . . . .

Ongole (122).

[Rámakúru. Telugu. On rock opposite Vishnu temple.]

Translation.

The plastering work done for Lakshmaṇadéva. The field given as *vritti* to Lakshmipati 4 *kuntas*.

1. లక్ష్మణదేవునికి
2. వరుపుంబని లక్ష్మీపతి
3. దేవర వచ్చృత్తినూ ఖ ౪ ॥

Ongole (123). (A.D. 1281–82.)

[Rámakúru. Telugu. On same stone as preceding inscription to east of Ánjanéya temple.]

Translation.

Hail! On the occasion of Vishuma Sankránti in the year Vrishu, corresponding to the illustrious Ṣaka year 1203, for the religious merit of (Hail!) Ṣríman Mahá Mandalésvara [Manumádripati] Rájulu and [Dévabágiya] Mahárajulu, *vrittis* were presented to Gaṇapéśvara and Bhímésvara of Rámakúru in Pávativárikunṭa . . . .

Note.—The names, unfortunately, are uncertain.

1. స్వస్తి శ్రీశకవర్షంబులు ౧౨౦౩ అగు
2. నేంటి విషు సంవత్సర విషుమసం
3. క్రాంత్తి కాలము స్వస్తి శ్రీ మన్మహా
4. మండలేశ్వర [మనుమాదిపతి] రా
5. జులుకు [దేవబాగీయు] మహారా
6. జులకుం బుణ్యముగాను రామకూ
7. రను గణపేశ్వర భీమేశ్వరదేవర
8. కుంబెట్టి నవృత్తి పావతివరికుంట
9. ను .
10. ప్రయ్యా . వ . . . వృత్తిన
11. కివాపురజే

ONGOLE (124).

[Rámakúru. Telugu. On stone to east of Ánjanéya temple. The inscription merely gives a list of the property in land and the méras possessed by the temple.]

1. శ్రీరామేశ్వర దేవరకిచ్చిన వృత్తి ఖ ౧ పుట్టి
2. శ్రీగణపేశ్వరు దేవరకిచ్చిన వృత్తి ఖ ౨ వరకుంటయ
3. ంశ చెఱువు వెనకన ౧౨ పాగనూరచేనిలోన ౧౦ ద
4. ఱుడి వెనకన ౩ ఉ తూర్పునసున ౫ దూవెనకు ౫ కు

వ్రుతి

5. వల్లిని నరకప్పల వెల్లినెన ౫ చంద్రాలకుంట ధఋణాను
6. కు ౧౨ పాకనాటి చెరువు తూర్పునన ౩ అడ్డ తెరువు
7. ఉత్తరానన ౧౦ ఎంముచేటి వాంగుపడమటన పాగెనా
8. కేమరువు పడుమటన ౨ అని చెరువు పడుమట చెవ్వ్రకొ
9. ననుప ౧౦ ట్టి పొలము సందునిసేనూ ఖ ౧ న ౭ రేడ

చెఱువు

10. లోన 3 మఱ్ఱిలకుంట దక్షిణాన ౧౨ తం గేలికుంట దక్షిణా
11. నన ౫ చుద్రాటకుంట దక్షిణాన ౫ పాంకనాంటి అయో
12. దడుమెట్టన ౫ గారగుండి వెనకన ౫ ను ఇఱ్వి త్తిమా
13. . . . . దెవర్విత్తులు ॥

ONGOLE (125). (A.D. 1277–73 or. 1337–38 ?)

[Rámakúru. Telugu. From stone east of Ánjanéya temple.]

TRANSLATION.

First side.

Hail! Ṣríman Mahá Maṇḍaléṣvara . . . . (Níla ?) Kaṇṭha Chóḍa Déva Mahárázulu in the year Íṣvara, corresponding to the Ṣaka year 12 . . . . for his own religious merit.

Second side—illegible.

Third side.

The field (given) to the god, one *puṭṭi* (rest illegible).

Fourth side.

Illegible except imprecatory verse at the end.

First side.

1. స్వస్తి శ్రీమ
2. న్మహా మ
3. ండలేశ్వర
4. (. . కంఅ) కంఠ .
5. చోడదేవ
6. రాజులు తమ

7. కు ధర్మాతారం
8. సునా శకవ
9. ర్షంబులు ౧౨. .
10. అగునేండా
11. ఈశ్వర సం
12. వత్సర

Second side.

1. . . .
2. బుగి .
3. . . .
4. . . .
5. . లో . .
6. . పణమా
7. . . . .
8. . . . .
9. . . .
10. . . .
11. . . .
12. . . .
13. . . .
14. . . .
15. . . .
16. . . .

Third side.

1. వరకుంబెట్టి
2. నక్షేత్రము
3. ఖ ం | చెను

4. బుట్టిరి తంగణ
5. కు . పక్షము
6. . . . .
7. ముల . . బ . న
8. క్ష . . ౧౨
9. . . .
10. . . .
11. . . .

Fourth side.

1. . రుక ౧ త .
2. తమతల్లి
3. . . .
4. పల్లి . .
5. శ్రీ మహావర
6. . ప్పభశరి
7. మడుదేవరకు
8. . . . . కి
9. అంగరంగనికి
10. . . . వినది
11. . సమప్పించి
12. . . ఇచ్చితిమి
13. స్వదత్తా ద్విగుణం
14. పుణ్యం పరదత్తా
15. ను పాలనం పర
16. దత్తాపహారేణ
17. స్వదత్తం నిష్ఫలం
18. భవేత్తు

Ongole (126).

[Rámakúru. Telugu. On boundary stone east of village.]

Translation.

Pillars showing the three boundaries north-east and east of Rámakúru (?)

1. యూాస్వ
2. ర దూారుపు
3. రామకూా
4. రులో క త్తరా
5. ము మూాండు
6. దిశలం దెల సీ
7. కంభములు.

Ongole (127).

[Rámakúru. Telugu. On rock opposite Rámalinga temple. Not forthcoming; this has probably been printed above and entered separately by mistake.]

Ongole (128). (A.D. 1118–19?)

[Ráparla. Telugu. On fallen stone by Vishnu temple.]

Translation.

Hail! On the eleventh of the bright fortnight of Jyéshṭha on the occasion of Uttaráyana Sankránti, corresponding to the Ṣaka year 1040, while Ṣríman Maha Chóḍa Déva Maháráyalu, who is endowed with all good attributes, who is the lord of Vilóchana, Trilóchana and all other kings of the earth, who is the jewelled lamp of the race of Karikála by whom the dam [1] of the Kávéri was built, and who is of unlimited valour, (was ruling) the kingdom in Kammanáḍu . . . .

Will be regarded as having killed a Brahman and as having killed 100 brown cows and as having eaten from the skull of his eldest son.

[One imprecatory verse.]

* * * *

1. స్వస్తి సమస్త సహిత
2. విహిత విలోచ
3. న త్రిలోచన ప్రముఖా
4. ఖిల ప్రిధ్వీశ్వరకారి
5. త కావేరితీర కరికాల
6. కులరత్న ప్రదీపాం అ
7. పరిమిత ప్రతాప శ్రీ మ
8. న్మహా మణి . న్యంకలి
9. . . చుడ దెవుల రాజ్య
10. శకవర్షంబులు ౧౦౪౦
11. నేంటి జేష్ట శు ౧౧
12. ఉత్తరాయణ సంక్రాంతి
13. నిమిత్తమున కమ్మినాం
14. ంటిలోని . . .
15. . . . . .
16. తమ . . .
17. . . లశుద్ధ .

---

[1] See note on p. 1250.

18. . . . . .
19. . . . .
20. . . . .
21. . . . . . .
22. . . . . . .
23. బ్రాంహ్మని వధిం
24. చ్చిన పాపానం పో
25. ఇనట్టి వాండె కవిల
26. వధించ్చిన వా
27. రు తన పెద్ద కొడుకుం
28. లముల గూడుకుడ్చిన
29. వారు స్వదత్తం పర
30. దత్తం వాయో హరె
31. తి వసుంధరా షష్టి
32. వర్ష సహస్రాణి
33. విష్టాయాం
34. జాయతే క్రిమి
35. . . .
36. . . . .
37. . . . .

ONGOLE (129). (A.D. 1293–94.)

[Rávinútala. Telugu. Opposite Mallésvara temple.]

TRANSLATION.

Hail! On Monday the 1st of the bright fortnight of Chaitra of the year Vijaya, corresponding to the illustrious Ṣaka year 1215, while (Hail!) Ṣríman Mahámaṇḍaléśvara Ḳákatiya Pratápa Rudra Déva Mahárájuʼu was ruling the kingdom in pleasant communication (with his feudatories ?) . . Pólamma . . in Brammánipáḍu of Rávinútala *sthala* and Brammánipáḍu in Kammanáḍu, Báhaḍa Déva Rájulu gave in perpetuity with libation of water lands to Bhiméṣvara Ṣrí Mahá Dévara whose image he had set up at Rávinútula for the religious merit of Rudra Déva Mahárája who was his liege lord for providing all enjoyments as *mányams* for the temple and *vrittis* for Brahmans.

[Imprecatory verses.]

1. స్వస్తిశ్రీ శకవ
2. ర్షంబులు ౧౨౧౫
3. అగునేంటి విజయ
4. సంవత్సర చైత్ర
5. శు ౧ సో స్వస్తిశ్రీ
6. మన్మహా మండలే
7. శ్వర కాకతియ్య
8. ప్రతాప రుద్ర దేవ
9. మహారాజులు సు
10. ఖ సంకథా వినోద
11. ంబుల రాజ్యము సే
12. యుచుండుగాను క
13. మ్మనాంటిలోని
14. వినూంతుల స్థల
15. మున బ్రహ్మని పా
16. టం గట్టిన బోలామ్మ

Second side.

17. బాహడ దేవరాజు
18. లు దన్నెలిన రుద్రదేవ

19. మహారాజులకు ధర్మ
20. వుగాను రావినూంతు
21. లం బ్రతిష్ట సేసిన భీ
22. మేశ్వర శ్రీమహా
23. దేవరకును అంగరంగా
24. ది భోగములకునున్న
25. . . . . క్షే
26. త్రము దేవస్థాన మాన్య
27. ములును దేవ
28. బ్రాహ్మణ వ్రిత్తు
29. లును పంచ్చ చతు
30. స్సీమ సహితమైన
31. క్షేత్ర మంత పట్టు
32. ను చెల్లె గ్రామం స
33. హితముగాను

Third side.

34. ఆచంద్రార్క
35. ము సెల్లున
36. ట్లుగాను దారా
37. వోసి యిచ్చెను
38. మంగళ మ
39. హా శ్రీ శ్రీ॥
40. దానపాల నయో
41. ర్మధ్యే దానాశ్చే)
42. యోనుపాలనం
43. దానాత్స్వర్గమ
44. వాప్నోతి పాలి
45. నా దచ్యుతం

46. పదం ॥ (2) స్వద
47. త్తా ద్విగుణం పు
48. ణ్యం పరదత్తా
49. నుపాలనం పర
50. దత్తా పహారేణ స్వ
51. దత్తం నిష్ఫలం భ
52. వేతు॥

Fourth side.

53. స్వదత్తం పరద
54. త్తంవాయోహారే
55. త వసుంధరా ష
56. ష్టివర్ష సహస్రా
57. ణి విష్ఠాయాం
58. జాయతె క్రిమిః ॥

Ongole (130). (A.D. 1283–84?)

[Rávinútala. Sanskrit in Telugu character. Opposite Vishnu temple.]

Translation.

In the Ṣaka year reckoned by the senses (5), the sky (0) and the suns (12) (*i.e.*, 1205), on the 1st of Chaitra, Ṣrí Padmaya the Brahman who is the ornament of the ministers of king Ṣrímat Kṛishṇadhara firmly planted a pillar bearing a garuda, conferring prosperity and being the edict of his good fame, for Ṣrí Késava, at the town of Rávinútala in Ṣrí Kammanáḍu.

Note.—We cannot identify this king.

1. श्री कंसक्ष्मात
2. ल रावेनूत

3. ल पुरे श्रीकेशवा
4. याकरोत्स्तंभं
5. गारुडमिंद्रि
6. या भ्रमिंद्दिरे
7. शाकेसमासंमि
8. ते श्रीमनुक्-णध
9. रेशमंत्रितिलक
10. श्रीपद्मयक्ष्मासु
11. रश्रैत्रादौस्वसुकी
12. त्तिशासममि
13. ति श्रेयःप्र
14. दं सुस्थिरम् ॥

Ongole (131).

[Santanútalapáḍu. Telugu. From stone in Chenna-késava temple.]

[The stone is broken at the top and what is visible of the first two lines is therefore not intelligible. The broken portion seems to give the name of the donor of the charity.]

Translation.

We have given the fields belonging to us in Ammana-brólu *ṣíma*, commencing from the northern extremity of the tank of Nútulapáḍu, bounded on the east by the boundary line of Yenḍlúru, on the west by the boundary line of Piṇundula Guḍipáḍu on the north and south by the boundary line of Mainampáḍu, after fixing the boundaries, for the performance of daily worship, lighting and all enjoyments to the deity, on the holy occasion of a lunar eclipse, with libation of water and gift of gold.

Therefore this service should be continued always as long as the sun and the moon last.

Those who obstruct this charity will incur the sin of killing Brahmans and cows on the banks of the Ganges.

V. The protection of another's gift is twice as meritorious as one's own gift; by resuming another's gift, one's own gift becomes inefficacious.

V. Whoever resumes land given by himself or by another will be reborn a worm in ordure for 60,000 years.

1. న్వొంవెట్టి సమపి౯ంచి

2. య్యవారు వ్యమ్యసానిచిన తిమ్మప్పకు పాలించ్చి ఇయ్యన వ౯గించి

3. అమ్మనబ్రోలి శీమలోను మా నాయంకరానకు సాగివచ్చి

4. నూతులపాటినం చెరువు వుత్తరపు కొమ్మునుండి పూర్వాటికి యండ్లాగి

5. పాలిమెరాను పశ్చిమానికి పిణుందుల గుడిపాటి పాలిమెరాను అంద్వక్షిణో

6. త్తరానకు మైనంపాటి పాలిమేరాను మితంచేశి పాంం ఖండ్డిత్తంగాను దేవునికి నిత్యనై

7. వెద్య దీపారాధన పర్వతిథులు- అంగరంగ వైభవాలు న్ను సాగివచ్చి అట్టుగాను

8. యీ తథాతిథి సోమగ్రహణ పుణ్యకాలమందును సహిరణ్యోదక దానధారా పూ

9. ర్వకంగాంను సమపి౯ంస్తిమి గనక ఆచంద్రాక౯స్థాయిగాను యీకైంకర్య అ

10. వర్తరించ్చునది॥ యీ పుణ్యానమయవరూ అచ్చినానుడిం గంగక

11. తెఃను గో బ్రాహ్మనిని వధిఇంచిన పాపాన బోవువారు॥ం స్వదత్తా ద్విగుణంపుణ్యం

12. పరదత్తానుపాలనం పరదత్తాపహారేణ స్వదత్తంనిష్ఫలం భవేత్ । స్వదత్తాం పరదత్తాం వాయోహా

13. రేతివసుంధరా షష్టివఃషః సహస్రాణి విష్టాయాంజాయతే క్రిమి॥

ONGOLE (132). (A.D. 1443–44.)

[Singarikoṇḍa. Telugu. From fallen stone below the hill.]

TRANSLATION.

May there be prosperity!

Hail! On Thursday the 10th of the bright half of Phálguna of the year Rudhiródgári, corresponding to the year 1365 of the illustrious Ṣaka era, on the auspicious occasion of a solar eclipse, Manúri Devala under the orders of Daḷaváyi (commander-in-chief) Devarájaya Vaḍayulaváru (? ?) granted the following charity for the religious merit of Ṣrímad Rájádhi Rája, Rájaparaméśvara, Ṣrí Víra Pratápa Déva Ráya Maháráya.

During Koṇḍa Ṣrí Narasimhadéva's great festival which falls on Punnama (the 15th day of the bright half) in spring, while the 18 sects of people of all the countries and all the devotees (bhaktas) of the 56 countries are serving the deity, we have remitted the taxes on articles of merchandize carried for sale on the road leading to (Tirupati) this holy place during the 7 days from the 10th day of the bright half of Phálguna to the end of

1st day of that dark fortnight and the tax on marriages on carts, slaves, horses, bullocks, cows, buffaloes, and other live stock, on all kinds of grain, oils, women's cloths and other beautiful articles, also the tax due to temples, watcher's fees, (the meaning not very clear) palace (or government) tax, and granted the privilege of this exemption, with libation of water, so that it may last as long as the sun and moon exist. Therefore all the officials of the 18 sects of all the countries and all persons who reside in the 56 countries have granted this for performing divine service to Narasimhadéva. Those who do not maintain the charity are like Arabs and will incur the sin of committing the five great sins; they will incur the sin of killing the sacred cow near the Ganges; they will incur the sin of killing their eldest son and eating from his skull (at the burial ground).

[Imprecatory verse in Sanskrit!]
The charity should be maintained.
May it cause great happiness!

1. శుభమస్తు స్వస్తిశ్రీ శకవర్షంబు
2. లు ౧౩౬౫ అగునేంటి రుదోద్గారి స
3. ంవత్సర పాల్గుణ శు ౧౦ శ్రీమద్రాజా
4. ధిరాజ రాజపరమేశ్వర శ్రీవీరప్రతాప
5. దేవరాయ మహారాయలుకుం బు
6. ణ్యముగాను సూర్యగ్రహాణ పు
7. ణ్యకాలమునందును దళవాయి దేవరా
8. జయ వడయుల వరస్యానతిం మనూరి దె
9. వలులకు సేసిన దమ్మ్ణము (.) కొండ శ్రీన
10. రసిహ్మదేవుని వసంత పున్నమ తిరు
11. నాళ్ల మహోత్సవం అఖిలదేశాల పదినె
12. న్మిదివండి శ్రీవష్ణవులున్ను యెంబైఆ

13. రు దేశాల చాలుమూల సమస్తభక్తులు
14. న్ను వేంచేసి కొలువంగాను తిరుపతి
15. మార్గహోను అంమికొని సరకులకు
16. ఫాల్గుణ శు ౧౦ మొదలు ఆ బ ౧ తుద
17. గాను ది ౭ లోనున్న పెండ్లికి రూకలూను
18. న్ను బండి ఛానిసలు గుజాలు యెద్దు
19. లుం ఖసులు యెనుపశులు మొద
20. లయిన జీవధనాలున్ను నానాధాన్యా
21. లున్ను రసవర్గాలు చీర సరుకులు
22. మొదలయినటువంటి రమ్యమయి
23. న సరకులకున్ను సుంఖపుతలారి
24. దేవలం తీరువలేక సుంఖకమతలా
25. రికట్నం నగరికట్నం నుచితముగాను
26. మాని ధారాపూర్వముసేసి ఆ చం
27. ద్రార్క స్థాయిగాను సర్వమాన్యం సే
28. సిరిగాన అఖిల దేశాల పదినెనిమి
29. ంది శ్రీవ్యవస్థాపులున్ను యంబై ఆరు దే
30. శాల చాలుమూల సమస్త పెకం
31. ధృన్ను శ్రీనరసింహదేవుని తిరుప
32. డి కొత్తిమి యిద్దమర్ణాము యిచ్చినది
33. యిది యీ ధమర్ణాము యిదిపాలిం
34. ప్పక యెవ్వరు తప్పినాను ఆరబ్బు
35. నటువంటివారు పంచమాది మహా
36. పాతకాలు సేసిన పాపానం బోవువా
37. రు గంగకఅత గంగగోవుం జంపి
38. న పాపానం బోవువారు పెద్దకొడు
39. కుం జంపి కాపాళ్లాన కాటిక కుడ్చి
40. న పాపానం బోవువారు॥
41. స్వదత్తా ద్విగుణంపుణ్యాం పర

42. దత్తాను పాలనం పరదత్తా ప
43. హారేణ స్వదత్తం నిష్ఫలం భ
44. వేతు ॥ అన్నారుగాన యీాదర్మ
45. ము పాలించ్చేది మంగళమహా
46. శ్రీ శ్రీ శ్రీ జేయును.

ONGOLE (133).

[Ṭangaṭúru. Telugu. In a street to the east—a fragment.]

TRANSLATION.

. . . . should be maintained. (Whoever obstructs) this will be regarded as having killed a tawny cow on the banks of the Ganges, and as having eaten from the skull of his eldest son.

1. . . . . .
2. సు . . . . .
3. చెల్లంగల దీనికి కి .
4. గంగ్గకరుతు కబిలపా . .
5. వారు పెద్దకొడుకు . . .
6. ఊచిన . . . . య . . .
7. నాగరా . . . మ
8. నులా . . . వాని శు
9. సంగాని . . ఖ న
10. మ సంగయ గోల.

ONGOLE (134).

[Tangaṭuru. Telugu. Threshold of Keśavaswámi temple. Illegible.]

ONGOLE (135).

[Trovagunṭa. Telugu. On a stone in the Ṣiva temple.]

TRANSLATION.

Ṣríman Mahámandaléśvara Bayyanadéva Mahárája and China Bayyanadéva Máhárája gave 1,000 *kunṭas* of land to the illustrious Mahádéva of the temple (múlasthána) of Tógunṭa—10 *kunṭas* to Kannéśvara Mahádéva, 10 to Ṣrí Mahádéva of Yeṟṟaguḍipáḍu, 10 to Veṭṭipali (?) Gaṇeju-peṣvaṟa (?) Ṣrí Mahádéva, 5 to Víréśvara Ṣrí Mahádéva of Paḍúru and 10 to Ṣrí Konḍúrudéva.

NOTE.—The inscription consists of 19 lines, of which the last 12 are engraved on the right of the first 7. The village Trovagunṭa appears as Tógunṭa in this inscription. We cannot identify the rulers mentioned.

1. శ్రీమన్మహా మండలేశ్వర
2. బయ్యనదేవ మహారాజులు
3. చిన బయ్యనదేవ మహారాజు
4. లుతో గుంట మూలస్థాన శ్రీమన్మ
5. హా దేవరకుం ఇటిన క్షేత్రం
6. కు ౧౦౦౦ కన్నేశ్వర శ్రీమన
7. మహాదేవరకు న౧౦ పది
8. ఎఱ్ఱగుడి
9. పాటి శ్రీ మహా
10. దేవరకున ౧౦ ప
11. ది వెట్టి పలిగణె
12. జుపెశ్వర శ్రీమ
13. హా దేవరకు న ౧౦
14. పది పడూరి వి రేశ్వర

15. శ్రీ మహాదేవర

16. కు న ౫౪ కొండూ

17. రి దేవరకు

18. న ౧౦ పది

19. ఇచ్చెను.

Ongole (136). (A.D. 1300–01?)

[Trovaguṇṭa. Telugu. On stone in temple of Chinnakéṣava.]

Translation.

Hail! Tóguṇṭa Náráyaṇappa of the *gótra* of Gautama caused to be constructed a temple, and maṇḍapams to Chennakéśavasvámi in the month of Chaitra in the year Ṣárvari corresponding to the Ṣrí Ṣaka year 1224 and caused the image to be set up. He gave land to the temple. He (also) established worship with lamps.

Note.—The year Ṣárvari corresponds to Ṣ.S. 1223 current.

1. స్వస్తిశ్రీ శకవరుషం

2. బులు ౧౨౨౪ నెంటి

3. శార్వరి సంవత్సర

4. చైత్రమా సంవరకు

5. గౌతమ గోత్రోద్భవు

6. లైన తోగుంట నా

7. రాయణప్ప శ్రీచెం

8. న్నకేశవస్వామికి ఆ

9. లయ మంటపాను

10. లు కట్టించి ప్రతిష్ట చె

11. యింది ఆలయా
12. నకు క్షేత్రం ఇచ్చెను
13. దీపారాధనను
14. నిన్నూ౯ఇంచెను.

ONGOLE (137). (A.D. 1778–79.)

[Trovagunṭa. Telugu. On a stone in the Kóḍanda Rámaswámi temple.]

TRANSLATION.

Hail! As the temple which was formerly constructed by Tóvagunṭa Sítarámuḍu got out of repair, Rámanna son of Tóvagunṭa Venkaṭappa, rebuilt the temple and consecrated Ṣrí Ráma (the idol) in it on the 15th day of the bright fortnight of Jyeshṭa of Viḷambi year corresponding to 1700 of the victorious Ṣáliváhana Ṣáka era. Those who did this belong to the *gótra* of Gautama and are *mirásidars* of the village.

1. స్వస్తిశ్రీ విజయ
2. శాలివాహన శ
3. కవర్షంబులు
4. ౧౭౦౦ అగు
5. నేటి విళంబినం
6. వత్సర జేష్ట శు
7. ద్ధ ౧౫ లు పూర్వం
8. తోవగుంట సీ
9. తారాముఃడు ప్ర
10. తిష్టచేశిన ఆలయ
11. ంశీలం అయితే తి

12. ర్గి తోవగుంట కేం
13. కటప్ప కొమారుడు
14. రామన్న ఆలయం
15. కట్టించి శ్రీరాము
16. లవారిని ప్రతిష్ట
17. చెశెను॥ యి ప్రతి
18. ష్ట చెశినవారు
19. గౌతమ గోత్రు
20. లు॥ గ్రామా
21. ను మిరాశి
22. దాలుగా

ONGOLE (138). (A.D. 1247-48.)

[Uppugundúru. Telugu. From stone near gate of Gouréśvara temple.]

TRANSLATION.

Hail! On Sunday the 15th of the bright fortnight of Adhika Jyéshṭa of the year Kílaka in 1170 (Ṣaka) a gift was made for the religious merit of Ṣrímat Gaga (Gaja ?) Sáhiṇi Jámulunáyaka consisting of 50 *kunṭas* of wet land in rear of the tank constructed by Uppugonḍúru Próliređḍi, to the north of Pinnagaṭṭu, and 50 *kunṭas* of dry land. To the deity (were given) 20 *kunṭas*. The following are *vrittis* to Brahmans.

(Here follows a list of shares.)

NOTE.—Jámulu Náyaka was probably the commander of the force of elephants to one of the Kákatiya kings. Compare No. 99.

1. ౧౧౭౦
2. కీలక సంవత్సర అధిక జేష్ట

3. శుద్ధ ౧౫ ఆదివారం శ్రీమతుగ
4. జసాహిణి జామూలు నాయకుని
5. కి ధర్మువుగా ఉప్పుగొండూరి
6. ప్రోలిరెడ్డి పిన్నకట్టి ఉత్తరా
7. నం వెట్టించిన చెఱ్వు వెనక
8. నిరునేల దేవరకు గు ౫౦ వె
9. లిపాలము గు ౫౦ దేవుడికి గు ౨౦

Second side.

10. బ్రాహ్మన క్షిత్తులు పొంక్ష్ము
11. ండి పెద్దికి కు ౧౫ కొమ్మనపెద్ది
12. కి కు ౨౫ నరసింహపెద్దికి కు ౩౫
13. నరసింహ్మంవారికి కు ౭౫ రామపెద్ది
14. కి కు ౨౫ అపా అప్పనకు ౨౫ నారా
15. యణునకు కు ౨౫ అనంతునికు
16. ౨౫ అకొండయ ౨౫ యరపె
17. ద్ది కు ౨౫ పెరుమాది కు ౫

ONGOLE (139). (A.D. 1218-19?)

[Uppugundúru. Telugu. Near Gouréśvara temple.]

TRANSLATION.

Hail! (Vai)tama Seṭṭi who is the son of Śrímat Minda Guddali Chendi Seṭṭi, who is possessed of all praiseworthy attributes, who is the worshipper of the illustrious divine lotus feet of Śrí Gouríśvaradévara, who is the chief ruler of Nellore *sthala* (in) Pákanáḍu . . . . twenty . . . . thousand (?), having constructed the big tank of this Uppugonḍúrupalli, having put up *achchukaṭṭus* (bunds) to the paddy fields all round the village for the religious merit of his lord Gaṇapatidéva Mahárája and of his parents and of himself, on Sunday the fifteenth . . . . of the bright fortnight of Kártika under the star Krittika, corresponding to the Ṣaka year 1140 to Gouríśvara Mahádéva of Uppugonḍúru presented 200 *kunṭas* of wet land under the Taḍa tank and 3 *puṭṭis* of dry land. Nellore Minda Guddali Vaitama Seṭṭi did this. Whoever upholds this charity will get merit and those who obstruct this will be regarded as having killed tawny cows near the Ganges and will be infested with worms in hell for sixty thousand years.

NOTE.—The donor's father was apparently governor or headman of Nellore town. He is not mentioned again in this collection.

1. స్వస్తి సమస్త ప్రశస్తి సహి
2. తంబున శ్రీగౌరీశ్వర దేవర
3. దివ్య శ్రీపాదారాధకులైన పాకనాంటి ఇ
4. రువైదీశ వేయింటికి నెల్లూరి స్తళమునకు ప్ర
5. బు ముఖ్యుడును శ్రీమతు మిందగుద్దలి చె
6. ండిసెట్టి కొడుకు తమసెట్టి ఇయ్యు
7. ప్పుం గొండూరు పలి ఊరిపెద్ద చెఱువు
8. కట్టించి ఊరిచుట్టును వరి మడ్లకు
9. అచ్చుకట్టు సేసి తన్నేలిన గణపతిదేవ మ
10. హారాజునకు తమ తల్లితండ్రులకు .తనకు పుణ్యం

Second side.

11. గాను శకవరుషంబులు
12. ౧౧౪౦ అగునేంటి కార్తిక శు
13. ప వనమియుం క్రిత్తికలు నాది
14. వారమునాండు ఉప్పు గొండూరి
15. శ్రీ గౌరీశ్వర మహాదేవరకు నెల్లూరి మిండగు

16. ద్దలిపై తమసెట్టి తడచెఱ్వు సెఱుకట్టనీరు నే
17. లగు ౨౦౦ వెలి పాలముఖ ౩ ఆధమ్మఁవు
18. ఎవ్వరైనను నడపి ఫుణ్యా నడపెంది
19. దీని త్రిప్పినవారు గంగకఱుత కపిల పా
20. డిచినవారు అర్వది వేలెండ్లు తొంకత్రు
21. మఖ తొలువంగానఱకానమండంగలవారు.

ONGOLE (140).

[Valaparla. Telugu. From rock near the Yerragunṭa.]

TRANSLATION.

The tank of Kárempúḍi Peddanayamgáru.

1. కారెంపూండి
2. పెద్దనయంగారి
3. చెఱ్వు

ONGOLE. (141). (A.D. 1544-45.)

[Valaparla. Telugu. Stone near Aravapalli Vírabramham's yard wall.]

TRANSLATION.

Adoration be to the illustrious Rámanúja.

Hail! On Thursday the 12th of the bright fortnight of Ásvíja of the year Kródhi, corresponding to the year 1466 of the illustrious, victorious and prosperous Ṣáliváhana Ṣaka era, Ṣrímad Rájádhirája Rája Paraméṣvara, Srí Víra Pratápa, Ṣrí Víra Sadáṣivadéva Maháráyulu, being seated on the jewelled throne at Vijayanagar and ruling the kingdom of the earth, granted the village of Volaparli in

Addanki *șíma* attached to Kondavídu *Durgam* as an *agraháта* with libation of water and gift of gold to Kónéṭi Tiruvengaḷanáthayyagáru, son of Șrímad Táḷḷapáka Tirumalayyan Gáru, who is the founder of the path of the vedas.

[One imprecatory verse.]

May it cause prosperity!

1. శ్రీమతే రామానుజాయనమః।
2. స్వస్తిశ్రీ జయాభ్యుదయ శాలివాహన శకవ
3. ర్షంబులు ౧౪౬౭ అగునేంటి క్రోధి సంవ్వ
4. త్సర ఆశ్వీజ శు ౧౨ గు శ్రీమద్వేదమార్గ ప్రతి
5. ష్టాచార్యులైన తాళ్లపాక తిరుమలయ్యంగారి కు
6. మారుండు కోనేటి తిరువెంగళనాథయ్యంగారికి
7. శ్రీమద్రాజాధిరాజ రాజపరమేశ్వర శ్రీవీరప్రతా
8. ప శ్రీవీర సదాశివదేవ మహారాయలు విజయన
9. గరమందు రత్నసింహాసనాసీనుండై పృథ్వీ సా
10. మ్రాజ్యము సేయుచున్న కొండవీటి దుర్గానకు
11. ం జెల్లివచ్చె అద్దంకి శీమలోని వొలపల్లె అనేగ్రామ
12. ము సహిరణ్యోదక దానధారాపూర్వకముగా
13. ను ధారపోశి యిచ్చిన అగ్రహారము। దానపాలన
14. యోర్మధ్యే దానాచ్ఛ్రేయోనుపాలనాత్ । దానాత్స్వ

ర్గమ

15. వాప్నోతి పాలనాదచ్యుతం పదం శ్రీ శ్రీ శ్రీం జే
16. యు

ONGOLE (142). (A.D. 1148-49?)

[Valaparla. Telugu and Sanskrit in Telugu character. In front of Vénugópálaswámi temple.]

TRANSLATION.

Hail ! In the 16th year of the victorious reign of Ṣrímat Tribhuvana Chakravarti Ṣrí Kulóttunga Chóḍadévara, corresponding to the Ṣaka year 1070, on the occasion of Vishama Ṣankránti, we, Ṣríman Mahámanḍaléṣvara Tribhuvana Malladéva Chóḍa Maháráyulu, have given with libation of water the (village) Volupaṛa in Kammanánḍu, which is under our rule, to Ṣrí Késavadévara of Kontṛidona for oblations, offerings, worship, dancing girls and furniture (?), and for the maintenance of the worshippers, to last as long as the moon, sun and stars endure. Those who, not doing good to this charity, think of injuring it will be regarded as having killed 1,500 cows on the banks of the Ganges and as having killed at Benares.

[Three imprecatory verses.]

1. స్వస్తి శ్రీమత్త్రి
2. భువన చక్రవర్త్తిᵒ శ్రీ
3. కులోత్తుంగ చోడదే
4. వర విజయరాజ్య
5. సంవత్సరములు
6. ౧౬ గు సా౹హిం సకవ
7. రుషంబులు ౧౦౭౦ య
8. గు నేణ్టి విషుమ సం
9. క్రాన్తి నిమిత్తమున
10. శ్రీమన్మహా మణ్డ

11. శేశ్వర త్రిభువనమ
12. ల్ల దేవచోడ మహా
13. రాజులు కొంట్ఱుదొన
14. శ్రీ కేశవదేవరకు మా
15. జీవితమ్మున కమ్మనా
16. ట్టిలోని ఒలుపఱిహా
17. వి బలిఅచ్చర్ణనలకు సా
18. నులకు మానులకు
19. దేవాశ్రితులకు జీవి
20. తా త్తర్ణముగా ధారా
21. పూర్వకముసేసి ఆచ
22. ంద్రార్క తారకముగా ని
23. చ్చితిమి యీకృత్తికి హి
24. తమ తలంచి కావి అహి

Second side.

25. తము దలచిన
26. వారు గంగకఱత
27. వేయి నేనూఱు గవి
28. లల వధియించ్చినవా
29. రు వారణాసి వ్రచ్చిన
30. వారు॥ స్వదత్తం పరద
31. త్తం వాయో హరేతి
32. వసుంధర షష్టిర్వర్షస
33. హస్రాణి విష్టాయాం
34. జాయతే క్రిమి॥ బహు
35. భిర్వసుధా దత్తా బహు
36. భిశ్చానుపాలిత యెస్య
37. యెస్య యదా భూమి స్త

38. స్య తస్య తదాఫలం॥
39. అకరస్యా కరి కరణే గో
40. సహస్ర వధ సితః కరణే
41. ప్రవిత్తి విచ్ఛేద గో కో
42. టి ఫల మశ్నుతే॥

ONGOLE (143). (A.D. 1267–68 ?)

[Valaparla. Telugu. On stone bearing a garuḍa opposite Vénugópála temple.]

TRANSLATION.

Hail! On the occasion of Arddhódaya, corresponding to the illustrious Ṣaka year 1189, Ṣríman Mahá Maṇḍaléṣvara Kákatiya Rudradéva Maháráyalu, being given to understand that Ṣrímat Kovvidona (?) Tribhuvana Mallapraháṛi Ḳéṣava Dévara was in possession of an ancient edict for (the grant of) the village named Volupaṛa in Kammanáḍu, presented it (to him) for the religious merit of Gaṇapadéva Mahárája.

[One imprecatory verse.]

1. స్వ స్తిశ్రీ శక
2. వరుషంబు
3. లు ౧౧౮౯ అ
4. గునేంటి అర్థో
5. దయ నిమి
6. త్తమున శ్రీ
7. మన్మహా మం
8. డలేశ్వర కా
9. కతీయ్య రు

10. ద్రదేవమ
11. హారాజులు
12. శ్రీమతు శా
13. వ్యి దోన త్రిభు
14. వన మ్లవ్ర
15. హారి కేశవ
16. దేవరకు కం
17. ష్మనాంటిలో

Second side.

18. ని ఒలుపటి అనే
19. డి ఊరు పూర్వ శా
20. సనమును గల
21. గుట ఎరింగి గణ
22. పద్దేవ మహారా
23. జునకుం బుణ్యము
24. గాను ఇచ్చితి
25. స్వదత్తం పరదత్త వా
26. యో హరేతి వసుం
27. ధరా షష్టి వరుష స
28. హస్రాణి విష్టాయాం
29. జాయతే క్రిమి

ONGOLE (144).

[Vallúru. Telugu. South of Vénugópálaswámi temple. Illegible.]

ONGOLE (145).

[Vallúru. Telugu. Opposite Vénugópalaswámi temple.]

TRANSLATION.

The wet and dry fields given as a *vritti* by Kámaya Boppaṇḍu to the descendants of Mattugáru . . . .(?) of Mattugáru . . .

1. కామయ బొప్పండు
2. పెట్టిన వ్రిత్తికిరు వెలిమ
3. త్తుగారి మాకమరదికి
4. బిడ్డబిడ్డ తరము కుడు
5. చువారు వ్రాసినవా
6. రు . డమా . మి
7. . . . .

ONGOLE (146).

[Vallúru. Telugu. North of Sóméṣvara temple.]

TRANSLATION.

Hail! On Thursday the fullmoon day of the bright fortnight of Ṣrávaṇa of the year Vibhava, corresponding to the illustrious Ṣaka year 1 . . 0 (gave) to . . . . . . belonging to his chiefdom. Those who fail in this will be regarded as . . . . in the river Ganges and as having eaten in the skull of their eldest son . . .

1. స్వస్తిశ్రీ శకవరు
2. షంబులు ౧ . . . ౦ అగునేంటి
3. విభవ సంవత్సర శ్రావణ శుద్ధ పౌర్ణ
4. మి గురువారాన య . నాయంకుని వా

5\. . రం . ప్రోరమవా . . . . . . వాొకి శ్రీశ
6\. కైహా నెవరకుమనం నెనిబితి . . . .
7\. దినా దీనిం చెంత మర . . . .
8\. మాళవి సావి . . . .
9\. జ నిచ్చిని దీనికిం తప్పినవారు గంగానది . . . .
10\. ప్పినవారు పెదకొడుకు కపాలానం గుడిచినవారు
11\. . . . . . . నెంజు . . నికి . . . . . .
12\. ఇప్పనిం . . . .
13\. డే . . . .
14\. . . . .
15\. . . . .
16\. . . . శేసినవారు
17\. కిని దుటాని . తల

Ongole (147).

[Vulichi. Telugu. On steps of Vénugópáḷaswámi temple.]

Translation.

The charitable edict granted by Rudrápaningáru, son of Hinḍirá Bhúnárí Sobhamgáru of Hiragalúru belonging to Ṣrí Paschahadana Gópáḷa on Thursday the 30th of the dark fortnight of Mágha of the year Íṣvara . . . . If aný one obstructs this charity . . . . he will incur the sin of killing a cow and a Brahman on the banks of the Ganges.

1\. యీశ్వర సంవత్సర మాఘు
2\. బ ౩ం గు శ్రీపశ్చహాద
3\. న గోపాళుని హిరగలూ

4. రి హింండిగా భూనారీ శో
5. భంగారి కుమారుండు రుద్రా
6. పనింగారు సెయించ్చి ధర్మశాసనం
7. . . . . . . న్ని వచ్చి మా
8. . . . పాలాన చింగ్గన నానా
9. (దా) న్యాన రాంన్నం జేడ్డిమానిరి
10. . . . యీ పున్యానకు యి
11. . స్వబం పుచ్చుకొంన్నాను గం
12. . . గోవుబ్రాహ్మనిం జంపిన పా
13. పానం బోదురు గనక . . . .
14. . . . . . .

ONGOLE (148). (A.D. .)

[Vulichi. Sanskrit in Telugu character and Telugu. East of village.]

A. (*Sanskrit.*)

Hail! . . . . the worshipper of the divine and glorious lotus-feet of Ṣrí Tirupurántakadéva which are illuminated by the gems of the diadems of all the gods and demons, the abode of the goddess of universal sovereignty obtained by the excellent favour of the glorious king Karikála Chóḍa, who has the ensigns—the clouds, the umbrella, white wing (vehicle), chámara, álaveṭṭa (fan) and an ornament containing pearls and other gems, who has the greatness of being heralded by a conch, Iruvettuganḍa (conqueror of twenty), Ráyaganḍagópáḷa, the supreme lord of the Nallambhaṭṭu country, the paramour of the prostitutes who are titled chiefs, Singára . . . . hostile army . . . . a hero on the battle field, the destroyer of hostile armies, Mádaya Narasimhaya, who is great in valour, (a lion) destroying the rut on the temples of the elephants which are hostile rulers, a fierce king, the lion to the elephants which are enemies, Áruvattuganḍa (conqueror of sixty), Ráyaganḍagópáḷa, Ráyanáyanka vítí . . . .

B. (*Telugu.*) (A.D. 1416–17 ?)

Hail! On Wednesday the 7th of the bright fortnight of Kártika of the year Durmukhi, corresponding to the Srí Ṣaka year 1340, Ṣrí Rámanangáru granted to Chandréṣvara and Soméṣvara the field *Bevanachénu* . . . the southern field, and others in all 4 *puṭṭis* and 10 *túms* . . . .

NOTE.—B is evidently a separate inscription. There is a difference of a year in the S.S. and cyclic years. In A, for Nallambhaṭṭu, we should perhaps read Noḷamba.

A.

1. स्वस्ति [1]समस्तसुधासुरमौळिमणिगणरंजितश्री-
2. त्रिपुरांतकदेवदिव्यश्रीपादपद्माराधक श्रीक-
3. रिकालचोडनराधिपवरप्रसादसाधितसकल-
4. साम्राज्यलक्ष्मीनिवास [2]लाच्छनमेघ[।]डंब्ब-
5. रयातपत्र[3]धवलपत्रचामरयाल्वङ्गसमौ-
6. क्तिकमणिगणालंकार [4]येकशंक्कादिमहाम-
7. हिमान्वित यिरुवत्तुगंड्ड रायगंड्डगोपाल न-
8. ळुंब्बहुतलाधिराय राहुत्तवेस्या [5] भुजं-

---

[1] Read 'सुरासुर॰ instead of सुधासुर.

[2] Read लांछन॰.

[3] Read धवलछत्त.

[4] Read एकशंखा॰

[5] Read 'वश्या॰ instead of वेस्या.

9. ग पिंगार . . . परबल . . समरतल[वी]-

10. र परदहिविभाळ मादयनरसिंह्य साहसोत्तुं

11. ग [1]वैरिनायंककुंब्बिकुंबस्थल[2]मदाविदाराणिह

12. मंडुनपार्तव[3] तोडरगजकेसरी यरुवेत्तुगंड रा-

13. यगंडगोपाल रायनायंकवीटि . . पां-

14. चाल

B.

14. స్వస్తిశ్రీ శకవరుషంబులు [4]వెయిన్ని తొంమనూ

15. ంట నలుపయగు నేంటి . . . దుర్మ్ముఖి సంవత్సర కార్త్తిక శు

16. 2 బు సిరోమనంగారు చాంద్రేస్వర సోమేస్వర దేవ

17. రకు సి . . . . . . చుండ్డి పూజము వి[చా]రించి బె

18. [వ] నసేను . దక్షణపు పేను మోదలుగనం నాలుగు పుట్టులు

19. ను వంద్దము సేనున్ని స్త్రిమి బీడు గాసి సు . . . .

20. . . . . పిన దోశాన బోవంద్దు [॥*]

---

[1] The anusvára stands at the beginning of the next line.

[2] Read °कुंभिकुंभस्थल°.

[3] Read °पार्थिव instead of पार्तव

[4] Apparently వెయిత్తోం మున్నూంటుకలుపై is meant.

ONGOLE (149). (A.D. 1310–11.)

[Yendlúru. Telugu. Opposite Ṣiva temple.]

TRANSLATION.

Hail! On . . . . , in the month of Mágha of the year Sádhárana, corresponding to the illustrious Ṣaka year 1232, on the holy occasion of a lunar eclipse, for the religious merit of Ṣríman Mahámanḍaléṣvara Ṣrí Víra Pratápa Rudradéva Mahárájulu . . . . formerly . . . . to Mallináthadévara . . . . to Mahadéva.

100.
100 *kunṭas* in Mangamúru.
100 *kunṭas* in Gónugunṭa.
100 *kunṭas* in Kákuṭúru.
100 *kunṭas* in Búdaváḍa.
50 *kunṭas* in Pulikonḍa.
100 *kunṭas* in Chanimpáḍu.
100 *kunṭas* in Maindanipáḍu.
100 *kunṭas* in——múnḍi.
100 *kunṭas* in Manchikalapáḍu.

* * * *

1. స్వస్తిశ్రీ జాతక
2. శకవరుషంబులు ౧౨౩౨ అగునేంటి సా .
3. ధారణ సంవత్సర మాఘమా . . . సోమగ్ర
4. హణ పుణ్యకాలమందు శ్రీమన్మహా మండలేశ్వర
5. శ్రీవీరప్రతావ రుద్రదేవ మహారాజులు౽ పుణ్యంగాను
6. . . . . . . మల్లినాథ దేవరకు పూర్వము
7. . . . . . సమంగాను
8. . . . . మహాదేవరకు
9. . . . . . య
10. . . . . . . వారుషూం

Second side.

1. రకు ౧౦౦ మంగ మూరకు ౧౨౦ గోనుగుంటను
2. కు ౧౦౦ కాకుటూరకు ౧౦౦ బూదవాడకు ౧౦౦
3. పులికొండకు ౫౦ . . . . . . చంనిం
4. పాతుకు ౧౨౦ మైందనిపాడి కు ౧౦౦
5. మూండికు ౧౦౦ మంచి కలపాడకు ౧౨౦
6. . . . .
7. . . . . . .

ONGOLE (150). (A.D. 1256–57 ?)

[Yeṇḍlúru. Telugu. From 3 sides of a stone in enclosure of Mádhavaswámi temple.]

TRANSLATION.

Hail! Ṣríman Mahámaṇḍaléṣvara Chakravaráyaṇa Ṣrí Sárangapáṇidévarája who is possessed of all praiseworthy attributes, who is skilful as Révanta in subduing unruly horses, who is Kṛittánta (Yama) to the enemy's army; who is a fortress of adamant to those who seek refuge; who is praised by his feudatories; who is the protector of life; for the increase of his life, health, and wealth, for the increase of his possessions and *váhanams* (vehicles), for the prosperity of his kingdom, for the increase of wealth and gold; while Ṣríman Mahá Maṇḍaléṣvara Kákatíya Gaṇapatidéva Mahárája was ruling the earth and holding pleasant intercourse (with his feudatories); (Hail!) on Wednesday the 5th of the bright fortnight of Vaiṣákha of the year Nala, corresponding to 1174 of the Ṣrí Ṣaka era, in order that his

(Govinda Náyakulu's) father Mádhavadévarája might obtain Vaikunṭa (heaven); his (*i.e.*, Sárangapáṇi's) servant (Hail!) Ṣríman Mahápradháni (prime minister) Govinda Náyakulu founded this endowment. The charity given to Ṣrí Mádhava Perumál for providing all enjoyments, consisting of daily offering, lighting and all other pleasures!

We have given Éndalúru, 12,500 *kunṭas* (in extent), as a sarvamánya.

On the east Pernamiṭṭa.

On the south Nútulapáṇḍu.

On the west Mayandanapáḍu.

On the north Yaḍlúru.

In this way they have given it as a sarvamányam to Ṣrí Mádhava Perumál.

The enjoyers of this *vritti* are Chennaya Nambigáru, son of Mádhava Nambigáru, and his sons and grandsons as long as the sun and moon last.

[Two imprecatory verses and afterwards comes a list of shares in the grant.]

Note.—The year "Nala" corresponds with S.S. 1179 current.

1. స్వస్తి సమస్త ప్రశస్తి
2. సహితం శ్రీమన్మ
3. హా మండ్డలేశ్వర అ
4. రి విషమ హయా
5. రూఢ ప్రౌఢ రేఖా రే
6. వంత్త వరబళ క్రితా
7. ంత్త శరణాగత వ్రజప
8. ంజర మండలీకర వందోళి
9. జీవరక్ష చక్రనారాయణ
10. శ్రీ సారంగ్గపాణి దేవరాజు

11. లు తమకు ఆయురా రో
12. గ్యైశ్వర్యాభివృద్ధియు
13. వస్తు వాహన సంమృద్ధియు రా
14. జ్యాభివృద్ధియు ధనకనక సమృ
15. ద్ధియుంగాను శ్రీమన్మ
16. హామణ్డలేశ్వర కాకతి
17. య్య గణపతి దేవమహారా
18. జులు సుఖసత్కథా వినో
19. దంబున ప్రిథ్వీరాజ్యము
20. సేయుచుండంగాను స్వస్తి
21. శ్రీ శక వరుషంబులు ౧౧
22. ౭౮ అగునేంటి నల సంవ
23. త్సర వైశాఖ శు ౫ బు తమ
24. తండ్రి మాధవ దేవ రాజునకు
25. శ్రీ వైకుంఠలోక ప్రాప్త్య
26. ర్థమై పెట్టి నిజభృత్యు
27. లైన (న?) । స్వస్తి శ్రీ మన్మహా
28. ప్రధాని గోవింద నాయ

Second side.

29. ంకులు నిల్పిన ప్రతిష్ట । శ్రీ
30. మాధవ పెరుమాళ్లకు
31. ను అంగరంగ భోగనైవేద్య
32. దీప ముఖ్యమయిన సర్వ
33. వస్తు భోగమునకు ఇ
34. చ్చిన దంమ్మూర్వు । పండ
35. లూరు సర్వ భోగ సాంప్ర
36. తగాను ఇచ్చిరి కుంట
37. లు ౧౨౫౦౦ । పూర్వతః పె

38. రన మిట్ట దక్షిణతః నూం
39. తులపాడు పశ్చిమతః
40. మఱిందనపాడు ఉత్తర
41. తఃయర్ల్లురు ఇట్లు సర్వ
42. మాన్యముగాను శ్రీమా
43. దవ పెరుమాళ్లకు ఇ
44. చ్చిరి యీ వ్రిత్తి కొడయలుమా
45. దవనంబింగారి కొడుకు చె
46. ంన్న యనంబింగారు విరిపు
47. త పౌత్రులకు ఆచం
48. ద్రార్కము । స్వదత్తం పరద
49. త్తం వాయోహరేతి వసు
50. ంధరా షష్టివర్షసహ స
51. హస్రాణి విష్టాయాం జా
52. తే క్రిమి । స్వదత్త ద్విగుణం
53. పుణ్యం పరదత్తాను పా
54. లనం పరత్తా పహారం
55. ౘ్ఛ స్వదత్తండనిష్ఫలం భ
56. వేతు ॥ మల్లినాధ దేవర
57. కు ౧౨౦ గొవింద పెరుమాళ్ల
58. కు ౧౦౦ అవనం కకు
59. ౧౦౦ దేవత కు ౩౦ విరుల కు
60. ౨౫ కోనిట్ల ఘుండవసం కు
61. కు ౨౫.

Third side.

1. గోవింద నాయనికు ౮౦౦
2. బపరాజుకు ౩౦౦ చురి పె

3. ద్దికు ౧౨౦ అని పెద్దికు ౧౨౦
4. పెరుమాండ్రాజు కు ౧౦౦
5. చమిరాజు కు ౧౦౦
6. శు చెకు ౨౫ పదుమనాభికు
7. ౨౫ చందయ కు ౧౦౦ నరస
8. భట్టుకు ౧౦౦ తిపురారి దే
9. వని కు ౨౦౦ మయిలారు
10. భట్టుకు ౧౦౦ వల్ల భయి
11. దేవన కు ౧౦౦ మయిదే
12. వన కు ౧౦౦ లకుం భాయికు
13. ౧౦౮ నరన దేవన కు ౧౦౦
14. తిడుపబాయికు ౧౦౦ గడ
15. యాకు ౫౦ బాందు దేవభ
16. ట్టుకు ౧౦౦ పొలిమెరకు
17. ౧౦౦ మరెమంచి ౬౦
18. అత్తిరాజ కు ౫౦ . .
19. బట్టనప్పన కు ౬౦ మం
20. చ కు ౨౦ కూచిరాజకు ౨౦
21. శ్రీ దామ అప్పనకు ౨౦౦ శ్రీ
22. బయితెడికు ౧౦౦౦ శ్రీ
23. పొలప్పన కు ౫౦

Ongole (151). (A.D. 1248–49 ?)

[Yendlúru. Telugu. From three sides of stone near Mádhavaswámi temple.]

A.

Translation.

Hail! Prosperity!

During the year 1170 of the illustrious Ṣaka era, on the occasion of Uttaráyaṇa Sankránti, Hail! Ṣríman Mahámanḍaléṣvara Chakra Náráyaṇa Singaladéva Mahárájulu's minister . . . . Hail! who is resplendent in the post of Mahámátya (prime minister) to which he has been appointed for ruling the whole kingdom, who is great in honor, who is endowed with the triad of royal attributes, namely, lordship, counsel and courage, who is the conqueror of the seven external enemies, who is the possessor of wealth, who is the commander-in-chief of the whole army and who is well skilled in managing the affairs of the king, has given to Ṣrímallináthadéva of Ongole for worship, enjoyment, and daily offering,

Second side.

three hundred *kuntas* of dry land on the west of the village. The trustees for this are Kondapareḍḍi, Mallireḍḍi, Pápa Próreḍḍi, Nárapareḍḍi, Káṭavareḍḍi, and Sómireḍḍi. The temple servant for this is Víraya Pandit, son of Sakaléṣvara Pandit.

(Those who obstruct this charity) will be considered to drink from the skull of their eldest son.

[Usual imprecatory verse.]

B.

Náganabóyundu, son of Dévanabóya, ordered the grant to the deity Mallinátha of ewes and cows (to supply) one half *munta* (అవ్వతు) of ghee for the lighting of a lamp for the religious merit of Jagadéva Mahárájn. (This is apparently a separate inscription.)

1. శ్రీ స్వస్తిశ్రీ శకవరుషంబులు
2. ౧౧౭౦ నెంటి యుత్తరాయణ
3. సంక్రాంతి నిమిత్తమున స్వస్తిశ్రీ
4. మన్మహా మండలేశ్వర చక్రనారాయ
5. ణ సింగళదేవ మహారాజుల ప్రధాని
6. స్వస్తి సమస్త రాజ్యభరణ నిరూపి
7. త మహామాత్య పదవి రాజమాన
8. మానోన్నత ప్రభుమంత్రోత్సాహ శక్తి
9. త్రయగుణ సంపన్నులును బావా
10. సప్తారిని యోగాధి పతియు
11. ను సకల లక్ష్మిమి పతియును స
12. మస్త సేనాధిపతియునుం బ
13. ది కార్య్య దురంధరుండును

Second side.

14. ను ఒంగోలని
15. శ్రీ మల్లినాథ
16. దేవరకు అర్చ
17. నాభోగ నిత్య నివే
18. ద్యముల కిచ్చిన వెలి
19. పొలము ఊరిప
20. శ్చిమ భాగమున
21. గుంటలు ౩౦౦ డీనికి
22. నరసాసనము కొండపరె

23. డ్డి మల్లిరెడ్డిని పావఠ్రోరె

24. డ్డి నారవరెడ్డిని కాటవ

25. రెడ్డిని సోమిరెడ్డిని దీనికి

26. స్థానికులు సకలేశ్వర పండి

27. తులు కొడుకు వీరయపండి

28. తులు

Third side.

29. పెద్దకొడుకు కపాళము

30. సం గుడిచిన వారు

31. స్వదత్తం పరదత్తం వా

32. యోహరేతి వసుంధర

33. షష్టిర్వ్వ౯రుష సహస్రాణి

34. ం విష్టాయాం జాయతే క్రి

35. మి । శ్రీ జెగదేవ మహా

36. రాజులకు దమ్ము౯వు గాను దె

37. వన బోయిని కొడుకు

38. నాగన బోయుండు తన నా

39. గొత్తెంగదువు (మల్లినకుని

40. దేవరకు దీపా ం

41. తవ్వండు నెధచెయి)

42. వాండు౹నది పెప

PODILI (1).

[Budamanaráyalapáḍu. Telugu. Near Gangamma temple. This inscription—deciphered by Mr. V. Venkayya—is written from the bottom upwards; a rare occurrence. The translation is more or less conjectural.]

TRANSLATION.

Hail! In the 12th year of the prosperous and victorious reign of the glorious Vishṇuvardhana Mahárája, ... granted in the northern part of Bállam Bhanṭáraḷa which is in the domain of . . . Veḷḷakiváḍu his father-in-law, a field requiring four *puṭṭis* of seed, in the northern quarter. (He) gave to Ishṭa Sómu . . . . Whoever obstructs this field of Sómu will incur (the sin of) . . . . Whoever protects this will . . . .

* * * *

1. స్వస్తి శ్రీ [విష్ణువ] ర్ధన మహారా-
2. [జు *] [ల] కు ప్రవర్ధమాన విజయరా-
3. [జ్య *] [సం] వత్సరంబు [లు] ద్వాదశవ [ర్షం] బున
4. . దు . ప్రి [థి *] విరాజ్యంబు . యవారిమామ
5. . . య్యవెళ్ళకివాడి పళువు
6. బాల్లమ్ భంటారళ [ఉ] త్తరంబున దేశమునా-
7. లుగుపుట్టు ఆట్లపటు సే . చ్చి [రి] ష్ట సోము
8. కు ఇచ్చిరి దీనికి ప్రతిరవలు వచ్చువారు
9. [ఈ] సో [మి] చేనుకు పా . . . . . లిదుఅ
10. [వా] రగళు [1] దీని గాచినవారు . రట్టాన . . .

11. [ర] . . . లరు . . క ఇ [చ్చిన] వారు . . .
12. వంబురాక . . నడచినవారు కీరిమా [స్థ] . . .
13. . బడితిమ . . . . . . లిము . .
14. . ట్టుకో . . . బున . ఆనిఇచినా
15. . . ను । శ్రీ

PODILI (2).

[Buḍumanaráyalapáḍu. Telugu. Near Gangamma temple. In old character.]

TRANSLATION.

Hail! In the first year of the reign of the prosperous and victorious Vishṇuvardhana Mahárája, Ṣivápparájul made a grant to Ubilíṣvara Bhaṭṭár. May the kingdom of the Gangas[1] resemble Paradise(?)

* * *

Second side.

. . . . . is the deed of gift.

This should be continued as long as the sun and moon endure. The grant made by Maṇḍavi Kamma, born in (the kingdom of) Chóḷa, to Ubilíṣvara Bhaṭṭáraka. The gift made by Sivápparáju should be continued as long as the sun and moon endure.

Third side.

A well and a temple in Ṣrí Niṭṭasómuḷa erected by Ṣrí Komorapólu Koṇḍayya, best of Kings(?) A temple built

---

[1] Or 'the dominion of the goddess Ganga.'

by Vallúri Áṭaṟla Márayya. The Reḍḍis (గొరవఙ్ల) being pleased gave land.

Whoever obstructs this grant will incur guilt.

NOTE.—Who this king was is not known.

Fourth side.

Whoever injures this (grant) will incur the sin of destroying 1,000 temples, 1,000 tanks, 1,000 cows, five Brahmans (?) and five maidens in Benares.

1. స్వస్తిశ్రీ వి[ష్ణు]-
2 వర్ధన మహా[రా]-
3. జు లోకు ప్రవ-
4. ర్ధమాన వి[జ ?]
5. రా[జు] ప్రథమరా[జ్యం]
6. బున శివాప్పరా-
7. జుల్ ఉ[బిలీ]
8 శ్వర భటారళా-
9. కు ఇచ్చిన దత్తి
10. గంగరాజ్యం బునాక
11. ఉద్యోగం బ[య్యె]ద

Mutilated at the bottom.

Second side.

Lines 1 to 5 are much damaged.

6. ఇచ్చిన పన్నా[స]
7. చన్ద్రాయిత్తకాలం
8. బు చరిగిన్చువారు [॥*]
9. మణ్డ[వి]చోళ[జక]
10. మ్మ ఉబిలీశ్వర
11. భట్టారక పన్నాస

12. శివాప్ప గాజు ఇచ్చి-
13. [న] దత్తి చన్ద్రార్కయి-
14. త్తకాలంబు చరి .
15. గిన్పువారు .

Third side.

1. శ్రీనిట్ట
2. సోముళ
3. . వసిన
4. వావియు
5. దేగులాబును
6. శ్రీ కొమొరపా
7. లు కొణ్డయ్య
8. ఘనరాచ[మ]
9. ణి లిఖితస్య
10. వల్లురి ఆట
11. ల్లి మారయ్య
12. పణికొసి-
13. న గుడియు
14. గొరవల్మిచ్చి
15. చే నిచ్చిరి వ-
16. [కర్కి]బు వచ్చిన
17. ఇ పన్నాస [వి]
18. [స్థ ?] అయ్యెద [॥ *]

Fourth side.

1. దీనికి అ
2. హితన్చి[పి]
3. న్చిన వాణ్డు
4. భారణాసి [ని]

5. వెయు గుళ్ళవు
6. వెయు చెలఃవు
7. ళు వెయు గవి
8. లాళు వేవురు
9. పాఅను వేవు
10. కన్న్యళనుము
11. టిచ్చిన[వి]
12. [ప్య?] అమ్యె [దు] [॥ *].

NOTE.—The transcript into modern character was supplied by Mr. V. Venkayya.

PODILI (3).

[Buḍamanaráyalapáḍu. Telugu. Near Gangamma temple. A small inscription on a stone close to No. (2), unintelligible.]

PODILI (4). (A.D. 1514-15.)

[Chilamakúru. Telugu. To south of village.]

TRANSLATION.

Prosperity! Hail! On Thursday, the 30th of the dark fortnight of Srávaṇa of the year Bháva, corresponding to the illustrious, victorious and prosperous Ṣáliváhana Ṣaka year 1437, on the holy occasion of a solar eclipse, for the religious merit of Ṣríman Mahárájádhirája, Rájáparamésvara, Ṣrí Víra Pratápa Kṛishṇadéva Maháráya, the lord of Ṣríkarnáṭa Vijayanagar, Ráyasam Koṇḍa Marusayyangáru granted this edict to Bhíméṣvara Mahádéva and Kailásanátha Mahádéva of Podela. We formerly granted the village of Chilumakúru situated in the east in Podila *síma*, on the western bank of the Musi, which was formerly in the enjoyment of these two deities, as a rent-free *Inám* to these two deities for providing all means of enjoyment to them, in the proportion of four shares to Bhímésvara and two shares to Kailásnátha. Those who render help to this charity will acquire the merit accruing from the sixteen great gifts beginning with *Tula purusha*.

Whoever violates this charity will incur the sin of killing a cow and a Brahman near the Ganges. Ṣrí.

1. శ్రీ స్వస్తిశ్రీ జయాభ్యుదయ శాలివాహన శకవర్షం
2. బులు ౧౪౩౭ । అగునేటి భావసంవ్వత్సర శ్రావణ
3. బహుళ ౩౦ గు । అందు సూర్య్యగ్రహణ పుణ్యకా
4. లమంద్దు శ్రీమన్ మహారాజాధి రాజ రాజపర
5. మేశ్వర శ్రీ కన్నాటవిజయ నగరాధీశ్వర శ్రీవీరప్ర
6. తాప శ్రీకృష్ణదేవ మహారాయలకు పుణ్యగాను రాయసం

కొండ్డ

7. మస్సయ్యంగారు పొడెల భీమేశ్వరమహాదేవునికిన్ని కై
8. లాసనాథ మహాదేవునికిన్ని ఇచ్చిన ధర్మశాసనము
9. పూర్వాన దేవళ్లకు ఇద్దరికిన్ని చెల్లేటిగ్రామ పొదిలశీమ
10. లోని తూర్పు ముశికిపడమటిగడ్డ చిలుమకూరి
11. గ్రామంము సర్వ్వక్రాంత్రిముగాను దేవళ్లకు యి
12. ద్దరికిన్ని అంగ్గరంగ్గవైభవాలకున్ను భీమేశ్వరదే
13. వునిక్ని ౪ నాలుగుపాళ్లున్ను అరాన్ను కైలాసనాథునికి
14. ౨ రెండ్డుపాళ్లున్ను అరాను నడచితిమిగాను పూ
15. ర్వ సాగించ్చి ఇస్తిమి యీధర్మానకుస హాయులై
16. నడచినవాళ్లకు తులాపురుషం మోదలైన షోడశమహాదా
17. నాలున్ను చేశిన పుణ్యంకలుగును । ఇధర్మానకు యెవ్వరు

తప్పిన

18. డచిరి గంగ్గకర్తగోవు బ్రహ్మనిత్సంపిన పాపానపోదురుశ్రీ

PODILI (5). (A.D. 1518–19.)

[Chilamakúru. Telugu. On the same stone.]

TRANSLATION.

Hail! On Thursday, the 15th of the bright fortnight of Mágha of the year Bahudhánya, corresponding to the illustrious, victorious and prosperous Ṣáliváhana Ṣaka year 1440, the temple trustees (Samsthánakuḷu) of Kailásanátha and Bhíma granted one *kucchala* of dry land on the boundary and 10 *kunṭas* of wet lands as a *sarvamánya* to Médarameṭṭa Singirináyaḍu, who walked over the boundary line of Chilamakúru (settled the boundary dispute). They have granted (the lands) so that they may be enjoyed by the sons, and grandsons (of the grantee) as long as the sun and the moon endure. Therefore he should enjoy it.

1. స్వస్తిశ్రీ జయాభ్యుదయ
2. శాలివాహన శకవర్షం
3. బులు ౧౪౪౦ అగునేంటిబహు
4. ధాంన్య సంవత్సర మాఘ శు ౧౫ గురు
5. వారాన్ను చిలమకూరిసందు పొ
6. లిమేరనడచిన మేదరమెట్ట శింగి
7. రినాయనికి కైలాసనాధండు భీ
8. మనిధం సంస్థానికులు ఇచ్చిన వెలిచే
9. ను పొలమేరనుకుచ్చిలచేనున్ను వ
10. రి మడి గు ౧౦ పది గుంటలున్ను సర్వ
11. మాన్యంగానిచ్చిరి కాన పుత్రపౌత్రపా
12. రంపర్యం ఆచంద్రార్కర్ణమై ఇచ్చిరి గను
13. భవించి బ్రదుకువారు॥

PODILI (6). (A.D. 1312–13.)

[Chimaṭa. Telugu. Opposite Bhíméṣvara temple. In great part illegible.]

TRANSLATION.

Hail! On the day of Sankránti, on Tuesday the 13th of the dark fortnight of Pushya of the year Paridhávi, corresponding to 1234 (also in letters) of the illustrious Ṣaka era . . . Náyaningáru issued this charitable edict, pouring water in the presence of Bhímanáthadéva, for the enjoyments of the temple of Bhímanáthadéva of Chimaṭa and for the services in connection with *bhóga*, to last in perpetuity as long as the sun and moon endure, for the religious merit of Ṣrímat Ahivi Moḷayanáyanikulu the Superintendent of the palace of (Hail!) Ṣríman Mahámaṇḍalésvara Kákaṭiya Pratápa Rudradéva Mahárája . . . . the sons, karanams and *kápus* granted 12 . . .

NOTE.—This is Pratápa Rudradéva II. The palace official is not mentioned elsewhere in this collection.

1. స్వస్తిశ్రీ శకవరుషంబులు వెయిన్ని ఇన్నూ
2. ంటముప్పైనాల్గు ౧౨౩౪ అగునేంటి పరీధావిసం
3. వ్వత్సర పుష్య బ ౧౩ మంగ్గళవారాన సంక్రాంతినాండు
4. స్వస్తిశ్రీమన్మహా మండలేశ్వర కాకతియ్య ప్రతా
5. పరుద్రదేవ మాహారాజుల నగగినాయంకులు శ్రీ
6. మతు అహివి మోళయనాయంకుంలకుం బుణ్యముగా
7. న చిమట భీమనాథదేవర గుడిభోగానకు భోగవను(లకు)
8. గాను యన్నాకాలమూన్ను సురియ చంద్రులు గలంతకాల

ము

9. ను వుండునట్టుగాను భీమనాథదేవరసన్నిధిని ధారవోసిన

వారు

10. . . . . నాయినింగారి దాసినాఇనింగారు ఇచ్చివుండిన ధర్మం

11. . . . . వకొాడుకులూను కరణాలూను కాంపులూను

12. . . . . ను ఇచ్చిన పన్నునిళు చిమట దన . . . . . పిసన

13. . . . . . మంకాచింత్తలువ . . రుకు . . . . విలివా

14. . . . . . ఇరుసన్నంనూర . . . .

15. . . . . . నాఖాం . . .

16. . . శాగం . . . . . పూ ఆర . . . . .

17. . లవ క ంలకూ . . . ికు . . . .

18. . . . పూ . . మర . . . ంపెర . . .

19. . . . . కక . . . న . . .

20. . . . . . వారి . . . స్మాక్త్న . . .

21. . . . . లవాప . కజని .

22. పాతు . . వార . . ప .

23. . . . .

24. . . . .

25. . . . కు . . . నవ్రిత్తి ఖ ౭ న ౧ం బోగవ్రిత్తి ఖ౭ . . . . వ్రిత్తి

26. . . . నియ దాసినాండ పెద్దివ్రిత్తిన రుద్రదేవరకు . . . . ను స్రా

27. . . . జు భోగానుకు బ్రాంహణవ్రిత్తి దేవరకుఇచ్చికవి . . మడ్డిండు

28. . . వే . . వవ్రిత్తి ఖ ౧౧ డుపుట్ల . . వ్రిత్తిని . . ఐగవను . . నవాస్సవ 3

29. . . శ్రీ వారిపుణ్యానపోదురు పెట్టనివారికి పరియ్యనివారు ప్రభువ్వలు

30. . . . . . . శ్రీ శ్రీ శ్రీ

PODILI (7). (A.D. 1260-61 ?)

[Dondaléru. Telugu. East of Mádiga hamlet.]

TRANSLATION.

Hail! On Thursday, the 15th of the dark fortnight of Bhádrapada of the year Raudri, corresponding to . . . of the illustrious, victorious, and prosperous Saka era, in the reign of Sríman Mahámandalésvara Kákati Ganapatidéva Mahárája, in the reign of Sríman Mahámandalésvara Bhímarája Peddanu(Siddana?)déva Mahárája, descendant of the lineage of Sríman Mahámandalésvara Vimaláditya, who (Bhímarája) is Chálukya Náráyana and who is versed in polity, in Kammanádu . . . . the illustrious, who is the abode of all kinds of prosperity, who is the supporter of his relations, who is devoted to doing good to others, Gourísvara . . . Dévundu, Chennagúri . . . svarundu . . . presented as charity for the religious merit of Siddhiráya . . . for perpetual lamp . . . Therefore . . . (to last as long as the sun and moon (endure) . . .

NOTE.—For date compare Podili (No 10).

1. స్వస్తిశ్రీ విజయాభ్యుదయ . . . . . .
2. . . అగు నేంటి రౌద్రి సంవత్సర భాద్రపద బ ౧౫
3. లు గురువారము నాండు
4. శ్రీమను మహామండలేశ్వర కాకతి గ
5. ణపతిదేవమహారాజు రాజ్యంబున
6. శ్రీమనుమహా మండలేశ్వర చాళుక్య నా
7. రాయణ నీతిపారణ విమలాదిత్య వంసావతా
8. ర శ్రీమనుమహా మండలేస్వర భీమరాజు పెద్ద
9. ను దేవమహారాజు రాజ్యంబున సిద్ధి

10. రాయనికిం బుణ్యంబుగ్గాను
11. కంమనాంటిలోని శ్రీమతు
12. సకలలక్షి నివాసుండు బం
13. ధుజనాశ్రితుండును బ
14. రహితాంబరనుం(డ్స)గాత్ర
15. . . .
16. . . .
17. సంబర గౌరిస్వర . .
18. దేవుండును చెంన్నగూరి . .
19. . . . స్వరుండునుం లనేటి
20. . . . . న వెట్టించి మెటి
21. . . . . . ధర్మ్మవుగా
22. . . . టి శె. . . . అఖండదీపానకు .
23. . . . . గనకస . . .
24. . . . . . . మారమకు . .
25. . . చంద్రా
26. . . . .
27. . . . .

PODILI (8).

[Dondaléru. Telugu. Near a well.]

TRANSLATION.

. . . of Phálguna of the year Durmu(khi) corresponding to . . . 83 of the (Ṣa)ka era . . . .

1. . . . . . .
2. . . . . . .
3. . నిచిన ననుభవిం . .

4. . . ండ్డి యాతండు . .
5. . . కవహణాంబులు . .
6. ర౩ గు నేంటి దుమ్మణ . .
7. . ం వత్సరము న పొల్లు
8. . . దాచవశ . .

Podili (9). (A.D. 1257–58.)

[Dondaléru. Telugu. Opposite ruined Malléṣvara temple.]

Translation.

Hail! On Thursday, the 7th of the bright fortnight of Márgasira of the year Piṅgala, corresponding to the Ṣrí Saka year 1179, Ṣrímat Madádidévunḍu, who is possessed of all the glory of various titles, such as Ṣríman Mahámaṇḍaléṣvara, the lion to the mountain which is the race of Vijaya (victory), who is a Harischandra in truthfulness, whose locks of hair are sprinkled with the pollen of the lotus of the illustrious and divine feet of Kulóttunga Chóḍadéva, who is a skilful Paraṣuráma in the battle field, ... a Rádhéya in truth, the king who is as pure as the Sobhánjana (a tree), (Soubhánjaninga Malaráya[1]?), ... Vikrama Simhádri, ... a Vasanta (spring season) to the host of good men, a Jayanta to lovely women, the lord of the town of Vivarangadási (?) . . . . whose conduct is characterized by mercy, who is a Révanta[2] in horsemanship, who can fight with two heroes, who can fight with the whole world, ...

---

[1] Malaráya = Hill chieftain(?).

[2] Révanta, a son of the Sun.

Konḍuganḍa, Chalamartiganḍa, the destroyer of the pride of Gajapati, Pekandrunu Kétuganḍa (the hero who has vanquished many men), Ganḍáraganḍa (hero of heroes), Bhimaḷamanda (?), who is death to the hosts of the enemies of the holy kingdom of the Chóḍas, who is a hero to those having *birudas* . . . . who is Bhojéndra, who is a Kshatriya of the Hárita *gótra* (?) . . . . who is Brahma in destruction, whose seat is Garuḍa, whose glory is praised in the three worlds, whose fame is sung by soldiers and ministrels, who is . . . . Sankéṣvara, who is a son to other men's wives, and whose consort is the goddess of victory: for the religious merit of his lord (Bhíma?) ráju Siddayunnu Rudra Mahádéva and of . . . . . Mahárája, presented for providing worship and all kinds of enjoyment to Dontaléṭi Mallináthadéva.

The *Sthána Pantulu* (temple servants) of this temple Mallajiya, Menṭa . . . . pólajiya, should enjoy this in peace.

[Two imprecatory verses.]

Whoever fails in this charity will be considered as having eaten from the skull of his eldest son.

NOTE.—This Madádi Devunḍu does not seem to appear elsewhere. He seems to have been a subordinate of the king Bhímarája Siddanadéva who is mentioned in P. 7 and who seems to have been a vassal of the Kákatíya Gaṇapati. It is not apparent in what position Kulóttunga Chóḍadéva stood to these various personages nor what Chóḷa king is alluded to under that name. Possibly Kulóttunga III is referred to and it is meant that Madádi Devunḍu was a descendant of that king.

1. స్వస్తిశ్రీశకవర్షంబులు ౧౧౭౯ అగు నేంటిపింగళసంవ
త్సరమా

2. గాసిరసుద్ధ ౭ గురువారమునాండు శ్రీమన్మహామండ

3. ేశ్వరవిజయకులాచలమ్రిగేంద్ర సత్యహరిశ్చంద్ర కులో
త్తుం

4. గ చోడదేవదివ్యశ్రీపదపంకజరజః కలితకుంతల సిర స
మర

5. ముఖప్రాజ్ఞాపరుసరామ . . . . . సత్యరాధేయసా

6. భాంజనింగమలరాయ। విక్రమసింహాద్రి . . . సిహా సు
జనవన

7. వసంతకామినీజయంత వివరంగదాసినగరిపతి వనజా

8. (సనకస్తూరి . . నోరథతమధుసూద స్తరాజ మనోజ)
ఆహావ

9. (వహోగ్ధ . ర . . హా ర్తికకోనవతలికలన మావంగాసు .
ధాత)

10. (లాదిరాజు) దయచారచారిత్ర తురగరేవంత . . .

11. (మనాకు) సంతయుభయ మాకోఱలు జగధియ మా
కోఱలు (వకి)

12. (లని)బైకొండుగండ చలమర్తిగండ గజపతి మదనాపహా

13. (ర ఇనివాలినం . .)మ నైనపెకంద్ర నూకేతుగండగండ
రగం

14. డ . చోడభీమలమండల శత్రుకులయాంతకబిరుదర

15. గండ . సచోడ(గ హాకిసాలతో)బోజేంద్రన హరితక్షత్రజ

16. (. నివ . . . సంహార) చతుర్ముఖ గరుడాసన సంజా

17. యమాన త్రిజగన్నుతమాన (. . మడివాదేవర) భటనట

18. జననాథ కీర్తి (యాంక నాధిక్య త్రమాకేంశరలం) సం
కేశ్వర

19. పరాంగనాపుత్ర విజయలక్ష్మీకలత్రయ నామాదిస

20. మస్తప్రశస్తిసహితం శ్రీమతుమదాది దేవుండుగంతన్నెలి

21. న . . . మరాజు సిద్ధయున్న రుద్రమహాదేవుల
కుం

22. న . . . మహారాజులకుం బుణ్యముగాను దొంతలటిమలి గా

23. థదేవతాపూజలకుం అంగరంగ బోగానకుం ఇప్పిం

24. (చ్చిరి) ఇగుడిష్ఠానావంతులు మల్లజియ్యాను వెంట

25. . . పోలజియ్యాను (ది . .) సుఖము యనుభవించువారు

26. బహుభిర్వసుధాదత్తా బహు భిశ్చానుపాలిత ఎస్యఎస్య యదా భూమి

27. తస్యతస్యతధావలం । స్వదత్తంపరదత్తం వా యోహ రేతి వసుంధరా ॥

28. ష్టిర్వషసహస్రాణి విష్టాయాంజాయతే క్రిమిః॥ దీని దొ

29. వ్వరుదప్పినా వారిని పెద్దకొడుకు కపాలాన కుడిచినవాం డు.

PODILI (10). (A.D. 1260–61.)

[Dondaléru. Telugu. From fallen stone near ruined Mallésvara temple.]

TRANSLATION.

Hail! On Thursday, the 1st of the bright fortnight of Chaitra of the year Raudri, corresponding to 1182 of the Srí Saka era, Srímat . . . . . . Preggada . . . . . . who is the worshipper of the illustrious feet of Sríman Mahámandalésvara Kákatiya Ganapatidéva Mahárája, who is (agent) for all (his) affairs . . . . . . for the religious merit of . . . . .

1. స్వస్తిశ్రీ స

2. కవర్షంబులు ౧౧౮౨

3. అగునేంటి రౌద్రి సంవ

4. త్సరంబున చైత్ర సుద్ధ॥

5. ౧॥ గురువారమున శ్రీ
6. మన్మహామండలేశ్వర
7. కాకతియ్య గణపతిదేవ
8. మహారాజులు దివ్యశ్రీ పాదపద్మా
9. రాధకులయిన శ్రీమతు సర్వ
10. కార్యా . . . . . .
11. సంప్రెగ్గడ . . . జ . .
12. ం జగాను

PODILI (11).

[Dondaléru. Telugu. From fallen stone near Mallésvara temple.]

TRANSLATION.

Hail! In Kammanádu, which is attached to the chiefdom of Visva-bhujya, Víra . . . . . . tumarája . . . . . . of Srímán Mahámandalésvara Kákatiya Ganapatidéva Mahárája, who is possessed of all the glory of titles . . . . . .

NOTE.—Visvabhujya does not seem to be mentioned elsewhere in this collection.

1. స్వస్తి సమస్త ప్రశస్తిస
2. హితం శ్రీమన్మహా మండలే
3. శ్వర కాక తియ్యగణపతి
4. దేవమహారాజుల
5. . విశ్వభుజ్య . . విర
6. . [తుమ మ రాజ] . . .
7. . యింకరి అముగా
8. (చెన్నస) కమ్మనాంటిలో . . .

PODILI (12). (A.D. 1447–48.)

[Gárladinne. Telugu. On stone in Hanumanta temple situated in the temple of Veligoṇḍaráyasvámi.]

TRANSLATION.

Hail! On Saturday, the 5th day of the dark half of Kártika of the year Prabhava, corresponding to 1369 of the illustrious Ṣaka era, Nimmáju Hétimgáru consecrated Hanumanta Perumáḷ, for the religious merit of the illustrious Náradarájungáru. May there be prosperity! May it cause great prosperity!

1. స్వస్తిశ్రీ
2. శకవరుషంబు
3. లు ౧౩౬౯ అగు
4. నెంటి ప్రభవసంవత్స
5. ర కార్తిక బ ౫ వ । శ్రీ
6. నారద రాజుం
7. గారికిం బుణ్యం
8. గాను నింమ్మాజు హేంతి
9. ంగారు హానుమంత
10. పెరుమాళ్ళ ప్రతి
11. ష్ట సేయించిరి
12. శోభనమస్తు
13. శ్రీ శ్రీ శ్రీ జేయును.

PODILI (13). (A.D. 1642–43.)

[Gárladinne. Telugu and Sanskrit in Telugu character. In Veligoṇḍa temple.]

TRANSLATION.

Hail! On Thursday, the 11th of the dark fortnight of Jyéshṭa, on the holy occasion of (the aforesaid) tithi of the year Chitrabhánu, corresponding to 1564 of the illustrious, victorious and prosperous Ṣáliváhana Ṣaka era, Bárugugáru, descendant of the *gótra* of Pallela, grandson of Námu Obanáyanigáru, and son of Lingappa-náyanigáru, after making daily at the three twilights innumerable prostrations to Tiruvengaḷanáthasvámi of Veligoṇḍa performed the following acts of devotion.

He caused to be put up an image of Chakra Perumáḷ on the steps, graciously caused to be performed *utsavas* and *Kaḷyáṇa Mahótsava* (the carrying out and wedding of idols) sent for all the Ṣrí Vaishnava people by the four main gates, converted the temple servants to Ṣrí Vaishnavism, brought the shrine to its former glory, made it like another Tirupati, instituted the distribution of holy food and water, and willingly made an agreement with these people. Thus he established this religious service permanently to last as long as the sun and moon endure. Those who object to this are not of the Ṣrí Vaishnava religion (Sanskrit verse):—Those kings, whether born in my lineage, or in the lineage of other kings, who with minds always intent on righteousness always protect (this) good charity, I bear the pair of their sandals on my head (as obeisance).

May it cause prosperity!

NOTE.—The Sanskrit verse at the end does not, of course, imply that the donor was of royal descent.

1. శ్రీ స్వస్తిశ్రీ జయా
2. భ్యుదయశాలి వాహ
3. నశకవర్షంబులు ౧౫౬౪ అ
4. గు నేటిచిత్రభాను సంవత్సర జే
5. ష్ట బ ౧౧ గురువారమ్మునతథా తిథి

6. పుణ్యకాలమందు పల్లెలగోత్రోద్భవులైన
7. నాముఓబా నాయనిగారి పౌత్రుండును
8. లింగప్పనాయనిగారి పుత్రుడున్ను ఆ
9. యినట్టి బారుగుగారు వెలిగొం
10. డతిరువెంగళనాథస్వామికి నిత్యం
11. త్రిసంధ్యమున్ను అనంతములైన
12. సాష్టాంగములు సమర్పించ్చి శే
13. యించిన కైంకర్యవిధము పడకట్టు
14. నచక్రపిరుమాళ్లను శేయించి వుత్సవ విధు
15. లునాప్రతిగాతిరుగా కళ్యాణమహోత్సవము
16. శేయించి నాల్గుసింహాసనాలదారిని సకల
17. శ్రీవైష్ణవజాతమును రప్పించి స్తానికుల
18. కుశ్రీవైష్ణవము యిప్పించి స్థలంపూర్వ
19. రీతిని దివ్యతిరుపతి శేయించి తీర్థ
20. ప్రసాదాలు పెట్టించ్చి దృప్తితో విండ్ల
21. కరారు శేయించ్చి గనుకయీ కైంకర్య
22. ము ఆచంద్రార్కస్థాయిగాను క
23. ట్టించ్చెను యిందుకు యవ్వరు ఆక్షేప
24. ణ శేశురో వారు శ్రీవైష్ణవద్రోహం
25. లో వారుగారు । मद्वंशजाः
26. परमहीपतिवंशजा वा
27. ये भूमिपास्सततमुज्व
28. ल धर्मचित्ताः सद्धर्म
29. मेवसततं परिपालय
30. न्ति तत्पादुकाद्वयम
31. ह शिरसावहामि श्री
32. శ్రీయుం జేయును.

Poḍili (14). (A.D. 1517–18 ?)

[Gárladinne. Telugu and Sanskrit in Telugu character. In Velagoṇḍa temple.]

Translation.

Prosperity! Hail! On Thursday, the 15th of the bright half of Vaiṣákha in the year Isvara, corresponding to 1443 of the illustrious, victorious and prosperous Ṣálivâhana Ṣaka (era), on the holy occasion of a lunar eclipse, while Ṣrí Mahámanḍaléṣvara, Rájádhirája, Rája-paraméṣvara, Víra Pratápa Krishṇadéva Mahárája, was ruling the earth at Vijayanagar, Ráyasam Koṇḍa Maru-sayya, who was skilled in bearing the burden of his kingdom, having made obeisance to Tiruvengaḍa (Tiruven-kaṭa)nátha of Veligoṇḍa, issued the (following) charitable edict under the orders of Śrí Krishnadévaráya. We have given the villages Gárladinne and Kattiráḷḷagumpu, situated in Podali *síma* (district) in Udayagiri which are in our jurisdiction and which were given before our grandfather's time to the deity. Koṇḍamarusayya has given (them) to the deity in perpetuity to last as long as the sun and the moon exist for the religious merit of Krish-ṇadevaráya with the eight sorts of ownership and with the eight sorts of enjoyment of this village, namely, hidden treasure, deposit, *akshini* (imperishables), *ágámi* (future produce ?), water, stone, actuals and outstandings, for (providing) all kinds of enjoyments and sacrifices to the deity.

Those who maintain this charity without interruption will enjoy the pleasure of sovereignty in this world and heaven in the next world. Those who obstruct this charity will incur the sin of those who commit the following sins :—Murder of parents, slaughter of cows and Brahmans at Kási and Benares.

V. 1. The protection of another's gift is twice as meritorious as one's own gift. By resuming another's gift, one's own gift becomes inefficacious.

V. 2. He who resumes land which has been given by himself or by another is born as a worm in ordure for 60,000 years.

V. 3. In the world there is only one sister of all kings, namely, land given to a deity; she must not be enjoyed, nor married (also, taxed). Ṣrí, Ṣrí, Ṣrí!

NOTE.—The cyclic year Iṣvara = S.S. 1440 current.

1. శ్రీ స్వస్తిశ్రీ జయాభ్యుదయ
2. శాలివాహన శకవర్షంబులు
3. ౧౪౪౩ అగునేంటి ఈశ్వరసంవ్వత్స
4. ర వైశాఖ శు ౧౫ గు సోమగ్రహణ పు
5. ణ్యకాలమందును శ్రీమన్ మహా
6. మండలేశ్వర రాజాధిరాజ రాజపర
7. మేశ్వర శ్రీవీరప్రతాప శ్రీక్రిష్ణదేవ మ
8. హారాయలుంగారు విజయనగా
9. రంమందు పృధివీసామ్రాజ్యం శేయు
10. చుండంగాను వారిరాజ్యభారాధుర
11. ంధరుండైన రాయసంకొండ మరుస
12. య్యంగారు శ్రీక్రిష్ణదేవరాయలంగారి
13. ఆనతిక్రమాన శ్రీవెలిగొండ తిరువెంగ్గ
14. డనాధునికి దండంసమర్పించ్చి ఇచ్చినధర్మ
15. శాసనం మాకు జల్లెడి వుదయగిరి పొదిలసీమ
16. లోనిగాల్లదిన్న గ్రామమున్ను కర్త్రరాళ్లగుంపున్ను తా
17. తపూర్వాన సాగివడేటిది నేమున్ను సాగించిశ్రీస్వామి దేవుని
18. కి అంగరంగ్గవైభవాలకున్ను అమృతపడికున్ను అష్ట
స్వామ్యగాను

19. ఈ గ్రామలంగల నిధినిక్షేప అక్షీణ్య ఆగామి జలపా
20. షాణసిద్ధిసాధ్యాలు అనెడి అష్టభోగలు స్వామ్యేంగా
21. ను కొండ్డ మరుసయ్యంగారు క్రిష్టదేవరాయలుకు
22. ం బుణ్యంగాను సాగించి ఆచంద్రార్క స్థాయిగాను
23. దెముకు సమర్పింస్తిమి ఈధర్మము యెవ్వరు త
24. ప్పక నడిపిడివారు ఇహమందుల రాజ్యభోగ
25. మున్ను పరమందున వైకుంటమున్ను అనుభవింత్తురు
26. ఇధర్మం యవ్వరుతప్పిన. కాశిలో వారణాసిలోను మాతృ
27. పితృవధ గోహత్య బ్రంహాత్యాది పాతకాలుచేసిన
28. పాపానంబోపువారు॥

28. स्व दत्ताद्दिगुणं पुण्यं
29. परदत्तानुपालनं परदत्तापहारेण स्वदत्तं
30. निष्फलं भवेत् । स्वदत्तां परदत्तां व्वा यो ह
31. रेति वसुंधरा । षष्ठिर्वषसहस्राणि विष्टायां
32. जायतेक्रिमिः । येकैव भगिनी लोके सर्वेषा
33. मेवभूभुजां । न भोग्या न करग्राह्या दैव
34. दत्ता वसुंधरा । శ్రీ శ్రీ శ్రీ

PODILI (15). (A.D. 1517-18.)

[Gárladinne. Telugu and Sanskrit in Telugu character. On a stone in the village. This seems to be an exact copy of the one in Veligonda temple (No. 14), but it is illegible in part.]

NOTE.—The S.S. year appears to be 1440 current.

PODILI (16).

[Góruguṇṭapáḍu. On Venugópalásvami temple. A few letters only.]

PODILI (17).

[Gotlagaṭṭu. Telugu. Opposite Siva temple.]

TRANSLATION.

Hail! The paramount lord of many *mahá maṇḍalas* of the earth, the king of kings, who is of the Paramavamṣa, who is the ornament of the Pallava dynasty, who is of the Bháradvája *gótra*, who wears the lovely half-moon, whose banner is the Kaṭvánga (club), ... the lord of the city of Kánchi, who has obtained an excellent boon from the goddess Kámakóṭi, whose crest is the Bull, (worshipper of ?) Véyangaḍanátha . . . . .

NOTE.--The Véyangaḍanátha means, apparently, lord of Tirupati, *i.e.*, Vishnu. In U. 6 the usual form of Véngaḍanátha appears.

1. స్వస్తి అనేకమహా మం
2. డల రాజాధిరాజరాజ
3. పరమేశ్వర పరమవంశో
4. ద్భవ పల్లవ కులతిలక భా
5. రద్వాజగోత్ర లలితార్ధచం
6. ద్రధర కట్వాంగధ్వజ కడు
7. గో . పురీవణ కాంచిపు
8. ర రాధీశ్వర కామకోటియం
9. బి కా లబ్ధ వీరప్ర సాదవృ
10. శభలాంచనవేయంగ డనా
11. త . . . . . .

Second side.

1. జ . . .
2. బగ
3. తగోగశ్చతిక్షతా
4. భగణ గా
5. తీడిగాంధా
6. శప్తం . .
7. . లజ

PODILI (18). (A.D. 1369–70.)

[Gurrálamaḍugu. Telugu. Opposite Ánjanéya temple.]

TRANSLATION.

Prosperity! Hail! On Thursday, the 30th of the dark fortnight of Jyéshṭha of the year Saumya, corresponding to 1291 of the illustrious, victorious and prosperous Ṣáliváhana Ṣaka era, this charitable edict of gift of land was granted for maintenance to Kórumámaḷḷa Raghupatíṣvara Sástrulu for the religious merit of Sáyapanéni Venkaṭádri Náyanivâru. They have given us Gurálamaḍugu village as an *amaram*. Therefore you supported Nílávaru Venkaṭasámi and the temple of Sanjívaráyuḍu. Therefore I have given a field to the north-east of those two ways(?)

[One imprecatory verse.]

Ṣrí Ṣrí Ṣrí!

1. శ్రీ స్వస్తి శ్రీ జయాభ్యుదయ శాలివాహ
2. న శకవర్షంబులు ౧౨౯౧ అగునేంటి సౌ
3. మ్యనామ సంవత్సర జేష్ట బ ౩౦ గు
4. సాయపనేని వెంకటాద్రినాయని

5. వాంకి పుణ్యంగాను భూదానము
6. న శోరుమామిళ్ల రఘుపతీశ్వర శాస్త్రు
7. గ్లకు బత్తానికి ఇచ్చిన భూదానశాసనము
8. మాకు గురాలమడ్డు గ్రామం అమరంకు
9. యిచ్చిరిగనుక నీలావరు వెంకటస్వామి
10. నిన్ని సంజీవరాయుల దేవుళాను యుద్ధరి
11. స్తితి గనుకను నా రెండు దోవ ఉత్తరం
12. తూర్పు భాగాన కైఅ[1] ఇచ్చినారతండు
13. స్వదత్తా ద్విగుణం పుణ్యం పరదత్తానుపా
14. లనం పరదత్తా పహారేణ స్వదత్తం నిష్ఫలం
15. భవేత్ ॥ శ్రీ శ్రీ శ్రీ

PODILI (19). (A.D. 1563-64 or 1575-76?)

[Ígalapáḍu. Telugu. Near Sangaméṣvarasvámi temple.]

TRANSLATION.

May there be prosperity! Hail! On the 15th of the bright fortnight of Áshádha of the year Rudhiródgári, corresponding to the year 1497 of the illustrious, victorious and prosperous Ṣálivábana Ṣaka era, while Śrímad Rájádhi Rája, Rájaparaméṣvara Śrí Víra Pratápa, Śrí Sadáṣivadéva Mahaáráyulu, seated on the jewelled throne at Vijayanagar, was ruling the kingdom of the earth, Tirumalanáyaningáru, the grandson of Rávela Tippánáyaningáru and son of . . . ppánáyaningáru, after making endless salutations, granted the following charitable edict of gift of land to the deity Sangaméṣvara. Land at Podila-Tummalúru lying on the north-east corner of the fields of Íngalapáḍu, which is attached

---

1 కైఅ = కయ్య.

to our chiefdom, which is in Podila *ṣíma*, and which is attached to Udayagiri *durgam*, was granted for the charitable Edict for maintaining worship at the temple of Sangaméṣvara Déva (?)

Its boundaries are:—East—Pámulachénu; South—Márgasavári field and Ballamguṇḍu to the west of that boulder. We have presented a *puṭṭi* of field in Tirumangám (?) with libation of water, as a *sarva mánya* as an absolute gift on the holy occasion of a lunar eclipse. Therefore this charitable edict has been given on the condition that the income derived from this field be spent for providing *amṛitapadi* (sacred food) and all enjoyments to the deity.

(Sanskrit verses.)

V. 1. He who resumes land whether given by himself or by another is born as a worm in ordure for 60,000 years.

V. 2. Of kings born in whatever lineage, whether born in my lineage, or in the lineage of other kings, who, with minds always intent on righteousness, ever protect my act of charity, I bear the sandals on my head (as a mark of respect).

NOTE.—The cyclic and S.S. years do not agree.

1. శుభమస్తు । స్వస్తి శ్రీ జయాభ్యుదయ
2. శాలివాహన శకవర్షంబులు ౧౪.
3. ౯౭ అగునేంటి రుధిరోద్గారి సంవ
4. త్సర ఆషాఢ శు ౧౫ లు శ్రీ మద్రాజాధి
5. రాజ రాజపరమేశ్వర శ్రీ వీరప్రతాప శ్రీ స
6. దాశివదేవ మహారాయలుంగారు విజయనగ
7. రమందు రత్నసింహాసనాసీనులై పృదివి సామ్రాజ్యం
8. చేయుచుండంగాను రావెల తిప్పారాయనింగారి పవుత్ర

9\. . . . ప్పానాయనింగారి పుత్రులైన తిరుమలనా
యనిం

10\. గారు సంగమేశ్వర దేవుడికి అనంతములైన దండము
లు స

11\. మర్పించి ఇచ్చిన భూదాన దర్మశాస్త్రి క్రమమేట్లం
స్నను

12\. దయగిరి దుర్గానకు సాగివచ్చి పొదిల సీ

13\. మలోను పొదిలతుమ్మలూరా నను

14\. మానాయంకరానకు నడచివచ్చిన

15\. యింగలపాటి పొలం యీశా

16\. న్యపుమూలగాను సంగమేశ్వ

17\. రదేవునికి నగర్కి కడ్డంక్ష

18\. తానకు జరప దర్మశాసన

19\. మునకు తనకు ధర్మాలు

Second side.

1\. నతూపుర్నకు పాములచెను . . . .

2\. ఖర దక్షిణానకు మోర్గసవారి బొలము

3\. బల్లంగుండ్లు ఆ పశమటి దిక్కుగుండు తిరిముం

4\. గామలోనైన పుట్టెడు క్షేత్రమును సో

5\. మగ్రహణ పుణ్యకాలమందు సర్వాగ్రాంతు

6\. సర్వ మాన్యంగాను ధారపోసి సమర్పిస్తిమి గనక అ

7\. క్షేత్రానవచ్చిన ఫలము స్వామి అమృతపడ్లకు అం

8\. గ్గరంగ్గవైభవాలకు నడచునటులదిట్టం చేసి యిచ్చిన ద_ర్మ

9\. శాసనము v (1) स्वदत्तां परदत्तां वा

10\. योहरेति वसुंधरां षष्टि वर्षसह

11\. स्राणि विष्ठायां जायते क्रिमि ॥ मद्वं

12\. शजाः परम महीपतिवंशजा वा यद्वंश

13\. जा स्सततमुज्वल धर्मचित्ताः मद्धर्ममेव

14. परिपालनमाचरंति त
15. त्पादुकद्वयमहं शिरसां व्व
16. हामि ।

PODILI (20).

[Kákarla. Telugu. On image opposite Vishnu temple.]

TRANSLATION.

The 10,000 salutations made daily by Ṣílam Timmá-reḍḍi to Venkaṭéṣvaradéva.

1. శీలం తిమ్మారెడి వెం
2. కటేశ్వరునికి నిత్య
3. పదివేల దండాము
4. లు.

PODILI (21). (A.D. 1426–27 ?)

[Kalujuvvalapáḍu. Telugu.]

TRANSLATION.

May there be prosperity ! Hail !

On . . . of the dark fortnight of Chaitra of the year Parábhava, corresponding to the year 1347 of the illustrious, victorious and prosperous Ṣaka era, Ṣríman Mahámanḍaléṣvara Manma Anta Rájulu . . . Murári-gáru . . . Víradéva Pra . . .

NOTE.—The cyclic and S.S. years differ by a year. Who the Mahámanḍaléṣvara is does not appear.

1. శ్రీ శుభమస్తు స్వస్తి శ్రీ జ(యాభ్యుదయ)
2. శకవర్షంబులు ౧౩౪౭ (అగునేంటి)

3. (ప) రాభవ సంవత్సర చైత్ర బ . . .
4. మహా మండలేశ్వరమన్న అంతరా
5. జాలు మురారిగారు వుప్పర . . .
6. . . . . నాకుపీరదేప్రప .

Podili (22).

[Kalujavvalapáḍu. Telugu. In the temple.]

Translation.

Hail! The illustrious Tóṇḍayyarázu, who is the ornament of the race sprung from the Solar dynasty, who is of the *gótra* of Kásyapa and who is of the lineage of Karikhala, has graciously given this land named Chanpa Kunṭhi situated south of Tammalúru (village) for the enjoyment of the deity of the temple constructed by Tammalúru Vankiya Ráddóḍiya. Chhévatala Chárjunḍiruvúddi and Yáḍlu Paddayya have obtained the field free of tax and *kóru*. The original founders of this are Múyánpuna Kolliya, Ráḍḍoḍya, Khalinganvi Chamunḍa Ráddóḍlu, karnam Ṣamudrayya, Vémana Peggéḍa, Sunkarí Múliyya. This is the charter granted by Tamma Dhanḍani in the presence of these as witnesses. Those who obstruct this (charity) will be regarded as having killed at Benares and as having comitted the five great sins and as having killed cows. May there be prosperity to the engraver of this inscription Danḍya Mólgajílára Sarvadéva, to (his) mother and to (the builder of the temple) Tammalúri Vankiyaraddóḍi.

Note.—This stone inscription is beautifully engraved. It is in Telugu characters of the Chalukyan type. The language is Telugu, but some words are not intelligible. The sense rather than a literal rendering has been given.

The inscription states that Tondayyaráju the ornament of the solar race, of the Kásyapa gótra and of the lineage of Karikála, gave a bit of land named Chanpakunṭa to a temple. The builder of the temple was one Tammalúri Vankiyaraddóḍi. From the donor's name and lineage one may infer that he was a Chóḍa. The royal officer who issued the edict was Tamma Dhanḍani and the engraver was Daṇḍya Mógajílára Ṣarvadéva (?)

The date is not given, but from the characters we may place the inscription at about the 10th century.

Some of the names of the individuals mentioned are peculiar.

1. స్వస్తి శూర్జ్య వంశోద్భవకులతి(ల) క
2. కాస్యపగ్గోత్ర కరిఖలాన్వయశ్రీ
3. మాత్తోణ్డ యరాజు త్తమ్మలూరి వంకి
4. యరద్దోడియెత్తిచ్చినగుడిదేవ
5. భోగమునకు దివ్యచిత్తమ్మున ని
6. చ్చిన భూమి త్తమ్మలూరి దక్షిన
7. సారిస్వంబున చన్పకుణ్ట ఛేవతల చాఱ్ఱణ్డిరు
8. వూద్దియాడ్ల పద్దుయ్యేవ్వరు అఁని
9. యును బేడకోరు లేకుండంబడసి
10. న స్తితి దీనికి బూర్వ్వస్తాపనంబున
11. వారు మూయాప్పర్వన కొల్లియ రాద్దోడియు
12. ఖలిగణ్వి చాముణ్డరాదోడ్లు ఖరనమున శముద్ర
13. య్యరు వేమనపెగ్గడబు సుంకరీమూలి
14. య్యయు ఈ యేవురుశాక్షి మన్తుల్గగానూ
15. త్తమ ధణ్డనియ్యిచ్చిన సాసనబద్ధము
16. దీనిం చెఱిచ్చినవారు ఛారనాసిప్రచ్చి
17. వారు పఞ్చ మహాపాతకంబు సేసినవారు
18. వసులబుఅనుంచ్చిప్రమినవారు *
19. ఇప్పని సేసిన య్యాచార్ఱణ్డు దణ్డ్య మోగజిలా
20. రశవ్వదేవనికి తల్లికి తమ్ తమ్మలూరి వంకి
21. యరద్దోడికిన్మాస్వస్తి శిశిలవాణ్డుణ్డు

PODILI (23). (A.D. 1519-20.)

[Kalujuvvalapádu. Telugu and Sanskrit in Telugu characters. In a field. This is a copy of No. 14, but the year is Pramádi corresponding to S.S. 1442 current.]

PODILI (24). (A.D. 1551-52.)

[Kásipuram. Telugu. On a stone by Venugopálasvámi temple.]

TRANSLATION.

Hail! On Thursday, the 10th of the bright fortnight of Áshádha of the year Viródhakrit, corresponding to the illustrious, victorious and prosperous Sáliváhana Saka year 1473, while Srímad Rájádhirája Rájaparamésvara, Srí Víra Pratápa, Sadásivadéva Maháráya, seated on the diamond throne at Vidyánagar, was ruling the kingdom of the earth, in Podila *síma* which he was pleased to grant to Sríman Mahámandalésvara Jillella Rangapatidéva Maháráya, in the village of Pámulapádu granted for *vunjali* (?) to Rájayyadéva Mahárája, grandson of Sríman Mahámandalésvara Mólakárájayyadéva Mahárája and son of Vallavarája.

Ráchirájadéva Mahárája of the lunar race, of the Átréya *gótra*, grandson of Malaká ráchi Rája, and son of Vallabha Rája, caused to be made an image of Srí Madanagopála, caused a temple to be constructed for it and performed the ceremony of infusing life into the image. On that holy occasion, this charitable edict was issued granting gift of land with libation of water and gift of gold for providing *amritapadi* (sacred food) and all means of enjoyments to Srí Madanagópál.

To the south of the village . . . in the street . . . 1 *kucchala* in Úrikondaya *sthala* (place), to the south, 1 *kucchala* in Ponpúripólaya *sthala* to the south of the extremity . . . . both aggregating 2 *kucchalas*, a garden containing a well in rear of the *kunta* (*pond*) to the north of the village.

This is the charitable edict setting forth the gift of land and presenting the above lands with libation of water for the religious merit of his father Vallabharáju, and of his mother Kónamamma.

Note.—This ruler of Podili *Síma* is mentioned again in P. 35. (In D. 35, Note, we find Jillalla Mangaparázu holding the office of governor in this neighbourhood in 1682 or thereabouts.) The genealogy of the other donee is given as—

Mahámandalésvara Mólaká Rájayyadéva Mahárája or Malaká Ráchi Rája.

|

Vallava (or Vallabha) Rája m. Kónamamma

|

Rájayyadéva Mahárája or Ráchirájadéva.

He does not seem to appear elsewhere. He claims to be of the lunar race.

1. స్వస్తి శ్రీ జయాభ్యుదయశాలివా
2. హనశకవరుషంబ్బులు ౧౪౭౩ అగునేంటి
3. విరోధకృత్తు సంవత్సర ఆషాఢ శు ౧౦ గు
4. శ్రీమద్రాజాధిరాజరాజ పరమేశ్వర శ్రీ వీ
5. రప్రతాప సదాశివరాయదేవ మహారాయలు
6. విద్యానగరమందు వజ్రసింహాసనారూఢులై
7. బృథివీసామ్రాజ్యమున్ను చేయుచుండంగాను
8. శ్రీమన్మహామండలేశ్వర జిల్లెళ్లరంగపతి దేవమహారా
9. జులుంగారికి పాలించి యియ్యనవధరించిన పొదిల
10. సీమలోను శ్రీమన్మహామండలేశ్వర మోలకారాజయ్య
11. దేవమహారాజులుంవారి పౌత్రులయ్యున వల్లవరాజుగారి

పుత్ర

12. లయిన రాజయ్యదేవమహారాజులుంగారికి వుంజిళ్లికి
13. పాలించ్చియిచ్చిన పాములపాటిగ్రామానను సోమకులో
ద్భవు
14. లయిన ఆత్రేయగోత్రులయిన మలకారాచిరాజుపవుత్రుల
యిన వ
15. ల్లభరాజుపుత్రులయిన రాచిరాజుదేవ-మహారాజులుంగా
రు శ్రీ
16. మదనగోపాల విగ్రహమునుం జేయించి దేవళముగట్టిం
17. చి ప్రాణప్రతిష్టచేశిన పుణ్యకాలమందు శ్రీమదనగో
18. పాలుని అమృతపళ్లకుంను అంగరంగవయిభవాల
19. కుంసహిరంణ్యోదక దానధారాపూర్వకముగాను
20. ధారవోసియిచ్చిన భూదాన ధంర్మశాసనం గ్రామా
21. నకు దక్షిణము . . . .

Second side.

1. . . . న కుంటకు బోయిన తెరువులూ.
2. . లూరికొండ యస్థళంకుచ్చల గన్ని దక్షిణంతు
3. . . . టికొంము దక్షిణాన పొంపూరిపోలయస్థళంకు చె
4. . ల గన్ని వుభయంకు చ్చెల్లు-అన్న వూరికివుత్తరం
కుంట
5. వెనక నూంతితోంటను తమతండ్రివల్లభరాజు
6. కుంన్ను తమతల్లికోనమంమంగారికింన్ని పుంణ్య
7. ంగాను ధారవోశి యిచ్చినభూధాన ధంర్మశా

PODILI (25). (A.D. 1546–47 ?)

[Kátragunṭa. Telugu. Near gate of Veligonḍasvámi temple.]

TRANSLATION.

Prosperity ! Hail. On . . . corresponding to 1468 of the illustrious, victorious and prosperous

Ṣáliváhana Ṣaka era, while Ṣríman Mahámaṇḍaléṣvara Ṣrí Víra Pratápa Venkaṭarangapatidéva Mahárája, seated on the diamond throne in Vidyánagar, was ruling the earth (Punigani) Gaṇaparapura Ṣríman Náginénigáru planted this charitable edict regarding a *pullari mányam.*

For the religious merit of Ṣríman Mahámaṇḍaléṣvara Venkaṭarangapatidéva Mahárája . . . .

1. శ్రీస్వస్తి శ్రీ జయాభ్యుదయ
2. శాలివాహనశకవరుషంబు
3. లు ౧౫౭౯ అగునేంటి . . . .
4. శ్రీమన్మహామండలేశ్వర
5. శ్రీవీరప్రతాప వేంకటరంగ
6. పతిదేవమహారాజులవారు
7. విద్యానగరమందు వజ్రసింహా
8. సనారూఢులై పృథ్వీరా
9. జ్యము చేయుచునుండగా(పు
10. ని గని)గణపరపుర శ్రీమాను
11. నాగినేనిగారు వెట్టిన పుల్లరిమా
12. న్యం ధర్మశాసనం శ్రీ
13. మన్మహామండలేశ్వర వెం
14. కటరంగపతి దేవమహా
15. రాజులగారికి పుణ్యంగాను

Podili (26). (A.D. 1426-27.)

[Kúchapúḍi. Telugu. Opposite Ándhrarámalinga-svámi temple.]

Translation.

Hail! On Sunday, the 1st of the bright fortnight of Chaitra of the year Parábhava, corresponding to the Ṣrí

Ṣaka year 1348, Hail! Ṣríman Mahámaṇḍaléṣvara, Médiní-mísaragaṇḍa[1], Kaṭhári[2], Sáḷuva[3] Samburáyadéva Mahá-rájulu caused to be constructed (a temple) to Áṇḍhra . . . dévara for the religious merit of his father Ráya Vibháḷadéva Mahárája. May it cause great prosperity!

1. స్వస్తిశ్రీ శకవ
2. ర్షంబులు ౧౩౪౮
3. అగునెంటి పరాభ
4. వ సంవత్సర చైత్ర
5. శు ౧ ఆస్వస్తి శ్రీమ
6. న్మహామండలేశ్వర మేదినీ
7. మీసరగండ్డ కఠారి సా
8. ళు వ సంబ్బురాయదేవ
9. మహారాజుతమతండ్రి
10. రాయవిభాళదేవ మ
11. హా రాజుకుంబుణ్యము
12. గాను ఆంధ్ర . . . దేవ
13. రులకు గట్టించ్చెను మంగళ
14. మహా శ్రీశ్రీశ్రీం జేయును

Podili (27). (A.D. 1483–84 or 1515–16 or 1575–76 ?)

[Kunchepalli. Telugu. In front of Ánjanéya temple.]

TRANSLATION.

On the 15th of the bright half of Jyéshṭa in the year Yuva, corresponding to 1407 of the illustrious, victorious and prosperous Ṣáliváhana Ṣaka era, while Ṣrímad Rájá-

[1] Médinímísarágaṇḍa = Champion over the moustache-wearing heroes of the world.

[2] Kaṭhári = axe.

[3] Sáḷuva = hawk; compare this inscription with No. 39.

dhirája, Rájaparamésvara, Ṣrí Vírapratápa Ṣrí Rangadéva Maháráyalayyaváru Rájádhirája, was ruling the kingdom of the earth at Vidyánagar, he granted the village of Kunchepalli, situated in Podilá *ṣíma* which was ruled by Velugóṭi Kumára Timmánáyaningáru, to Brityári Timmamúṇḍuḷa Atnógá Cháryulayyaváru as charity. Therefore those who obstruct (the enjoyment of) that village will incur the sin of killing cows and Brahmans near the Ganges.

[One imprecatory verse in Sanskrit.]

Ṣrí, Ṣrí, Ṣrí.

Note.—The cyclic and S.S. years do not correspond. The last figure of the date is not clear.

1. శ్రీజయాభ్యుదయ
2. శాలివాహన శకవర్షంబులు
3. ౧౪౦౭ అగునేంటి యువ సంవత్సర
4. జెష్ట శు ౧౫ లు శ్రీమద్రాజాధిరాజరాజపర
5. మేశ్వర శ్రీ వీరప్రతాప శ్రీరంగదేవమ
6. హారాయలయ్యవారు పిద్యానగరమం
7. దుప్రిథివిసామ్రాజ్యమును చేయుచున్న వెలుగో
8. టి కుమారతిమ్మనాయినింగారికి ఫాలించ్చిన
9. పొదిలశీమలోని కుంచ్చేపల్లిగ్రామంలో బ్రిత్యా
10. రి తిమ్మమూండుళ అత్నోగాచార్యులయ్యవారికి
11. దీని ధర్మంయిచ్చినాండుగనుక ఆగ్రామానుకాయ
12. వ్వారు డప్పినానుగంగకర్తణ గోవుబ్రాహ్మాలను వ
13. ధియించిన పాపాన్నిబోయ్నువారు । ఏకైవభ
14. గినీలోకే సర్వేషామేవ భూభుజాం
15. న భోజ్యాన కరగ్రాహ్యో విప్రద
16. త్తా వసుంధరా శ్రీ శ్రీ శ్రీ

PODILI (28).

[Marripúḍi. Telugu. Below Dvajasthambam of Venugópálasvámi temple.]

TRANSLATION.

The dedication of a Gárada pillar by Punnam Seṭṭi to Gópinátha on Wednesday the 2nd of the bright fortnight of Mágha of the year Pramódúta.

1. ప్రమోదూతస్వత్సర
2. మాఘ శు ౨ బు గోపి
3. నాథునకి గారడకంబము
4. పున్నమసెటి సమర్పణం
5. శ్రీ

PODILI (29). (A.D. 1515–16.)

[Pámulapáḍu. Telugu. In a garden.]

TRANSLATION.

Hail! On Monday, the 15th of the bright half of Mágha of the year Yuva, corresponding to 1437 of the Ṣrí Ṣaka era, on the holy occasion of a lunar eclipse, the (following) charitable deed was granted to Dúḍala Mallikhárjuna (deity) of Podila by Ṣríman Mahárája, Rájádhirája, Rájaparaméṣvara, Ṣrí Víra Pratápa Ṣrí Krishṇadéva Mahárája, King of Vijayanagar of the Carnatic (and) Ráyasam Konḍamarusayyamgáru. We formerly granted the village of Kiraḷḷapalli which is situated on the south of the (river) Musi in Podila *ṣíma* and which formerly belonged to the deity as an absolute gift for providing all kinds of enjoyments to the deity. Those who help this charity will acquire the religious merit derived from performing the sixteen great gifts (*Mahádánas*) such as the *tulá purusha*[1]. . . . Those sinners who obstruct this charity will go to the hells Kumbhipáka, Roura, &c. (Sanskrit verse). The giver of land abides in heaven for 60,000 years, but he who resumes it or he who permits (resumption) goes to hell for the same number of years.

If those who resume this grant are Muhammadans they will incur the sin of eating pork. Those who cause this charity to fail will incur the sin of killing cows and Brahmans near the Ganges. His (wife's) honour will be given to tawny cattle (?). May it produce great prosperity!

Note.—Another inscription here is illegible and a third, referred to by Mr. Sewell, could not be found; a fourth resembles the one here printed.

1. స్వస్తిశ్రీ శకవర్షంబులు ౧౪
2. ౩౭ అగునేంటి యువ సంవత్స
3. ర మాఘ శు ౧౫ సో సోమ
4. గ్రహణ పుణ్య కాలమందు
5. శ్రీమన్మహా రాజాధిరాజ రా
6. జ పరమేశ్వర శ్రీకన్నాంట విజ
7. య నగరాధీశ్వర శ్రీవీరప్రతాప శ్రీ
8. క్రిష్ణదేవ మహారాయలు రాయసం
9. కొండ మరుసయ్యంగారు పొదిల
10. దూడల మల్లిఖార్జునికిచ్చిన ధర్మశాస
11. నం పూర్వాన దేవునికిం జెల్లి గ్రామము
12. పొదిల సీమలో ముసికి దక్షిణపు గ
13. డ్డ కిరణ్ణపల్లి గ్రామము సర్వాగ్రాంతు
14. గాను దేవునికి అంగరంగ వైభవాలకు

---

[1] Tulá purusha is the weighing a man against gold.

15. ను నడచియ్యాట్లు గాను పూర్వం సాగిం
16. చ్చి యిస్తిమి యీ దమ్మానకు సహాయు
17. లై నడచినవారలకు తులాపురుషం
18. మొదలైన సోడశ మంహా దానాలు
19. న్ను సెసిన పుణ్యం గలుగును యిందు
20. కు ప్రతిహారులై చెరిచిన పాతకమ్ములకు
21. కుంభ్బి పాకము మొదలైన రౌరవాదిన
22. రకాలం బడుదురు . . . षष्टि र्वर्ष सहस्रा
23. णिस्स्वर्गे तिष्ठति भूमिदः । अपहर्ता चा
24. नुमंता च ताण्येव नरकं व्रजेत् ।
25. కవారైరా కందిం దిన్న పాపానం బో
26. దురు యీధర్మం తప్పించినవారు
27. గంగకత్తీరను గోవు బ్రా
28. హ్మనింజంపిన దోషా
29. నం బోవును వానిమానం
30. గపిల గోవులకిచ్చును
31. శ్రీ శ్రీ శ్రీం జేయు
32. ను

PODILI (30). (A.D. 1547–48.)

[Pátagárlapéṭa. Telugu. To the south in the puróhit's field.]

TRANSLATION.

Hail! This is the charitable edict setting forth the gift of land made to Kondúri Obayéṣvara by Chintagumpalli Pedda Náyaningáru, on Monday, the 15th of the bright fortnight of Kártika of the year Plavanga, corresponding to 1469 of the illustrious Ṣaka era. In

Gárlapáṭa (village) in Podila *ṣíma* on the holy occasion of a lunar eclipse we have granted . . . with libation of water as a sarvamánya. You, your sons and your grandsons, in succession should enjoy this and live (happily).

[One imprecatory verse.]

May it cause prosperity!

1. స్వస్తిశ్రీ శకవరుషంబులు ౧౪౬౯ నే
2. టి ప్లవంగ సంవత్సర కార్తిక శు ౧౫
3. సో॥ చింతగుంపల్లి పెద్దానాయనిం
4. గారు కొండూరి ఓబయేశ్వరుకిచ్చి
5. న భూదాన ధర్మశాసనం పొదిలసీమ
6. లోను గార్లపాటను . . . .
7. . . . . . . సోమగ్ర
8. హణ పుణ్యకాలమందును సర్వమాన్యంగా
9. ధారా పూర్వకంగాను ఇస్తిమి మీపుత్ర పౌ
10. త్ర పారంపర్యం అనుభవించి బ్రతుకువారు
11. స్వదత్తాద్విగుణం పుణ్యం పరదత్తానుపాల
12. నం పరదత్తాపహారేణ స్వదత్తం నిష్ఫలం
13. భవేత్॥ శ్రీ శ్రీ శ్రీం జేయును

Podili (31).

[Pedárikaṭla. Telugu. In front of Chennakéṣavasvám, temple.]

Translation.

Hail! On Thursday, the 11th of the bright fortnight of Ṣrávana of the year (Sarvadhári) corresponding to . . . of the illustrious Ṣaka era, Hail, Ṣríman

Mahámaṇḍaléṣvara . . . who is endowed with all the glory of titles . . . Vibhavámaréṣvara.

* * * *

1. స్వస్తిశ్రీ శకవర్షంబులు . . . .
2. గునెంటి (సర్వదారి) సంవత్సర శ్రావ
3. ణ శు ౧౧ గు సమస్త ప్రస
4. స్తి సహిత శ్రీమన్మహామం . .
5. కు
6. విభవామరేశ్వర . .
7. . . .
8. . . .
9. శ్రీమ . . .
10. వ . .
11. వితా . . . . స

PODILI (32). (A.D. 1289–90?)

[Podili. Telugu. Stone outside Vírabhadra temple. The stone is broken.]

TRANSLATION.

On Thursday, the 1st of the bright fortnight of Phálguṇa, corresponding to the illustrious Ṣaka year (1211) Hail! Ṣríman Mahámaṇḍaléṣvara ráyajaná . . sisvará, Chakravartulára Mána mardda . . . . . Samudrala Sura . . . maṇa Dharma Vijayádityadéva Mahárája (?), who is possessed of all praiseworthy attributes, gave 100 puṭṭis (?) free from taxes to Tirupurántaka Kommanappa (?) of the Vangípura Gótra, for the religious merits of (Hail!) Ṣríman Mahámaṇḍaléṣvara,

Mahámaṇḍalika dánava murári Hari (ari?) ráyagaṇḍa-góp̣áḷa, ráhutta . . . Maṇumagaṇḍagópáḷa Déva Mahárája, who is endowed with all praiseworthy attributes.

NOTE.—The identity of this Vijayáditya is not clear.

(స్వస్తి) శ్రీ శకవరుషంబు—
(లు ౧) ౭౧౧ అగునేంటి పాలు
(గుణ) శు ౧ గు। స్వస్తి సమస్త
(ప్రసస్తి) సహితంబున శ్రీ
(మన్మ) హామండలేశ్వర
(మహా) మండలిక దానవ
(మురా)—రిహరి రాయగ
(ండ) పాళ, రాహుత్త
(—) మనుమగండ్గ
(పా) ళ దేవ మ
(హా) రాజులకుం బు
(ణ్యంబు) గాను స్వస్తి స
(మస్త)—ప్రశస్తి సహితం
(బుగ) శ్రీమన్మహా మం
(డలేశ్వ) ర రాయజనా
(—)సిశ్వర చక్రవ
ర్తులార మానమర్ద్ద
(. .) సముద్రలసుర
( ) మణ దర్మ విజ
(యాది)త్య దేవ మహారా
—(యు)డకునూరు శివ 100
(ఎరి)—హారముగాను
—గో త్రివంగిపు
(ర)నున్నైన త్రిపురా

(.)కి కొమ్మనవ్వనకూ
ంబికి అన్నికూంచయు.

PODILI (33). (A.D. 1515-16.)

[Podili. Telugu. On a stone in the mosque. The inscription is practically identical with No. 29.].

PODILI (34). (A.D. 1583-84?)

[Podili. Telugu. Stone near Muhammadan Darga.]

TRANSLATION.

Hail! On the 11th day of the bright fortnight of Ṣrávaṇa in the year Svabhánu corresponding to the victorious and prosperous Ṣáliváhana year 1501, Komára China Timmánáyaningáru, son of Komára Timmánáyaningáru, grandson of Ṣríman Veligóṭi Peda Timmanáyaningáru of the Récherla family, issues this charitable edict to pious Brahmans and *agrahárams* in Podile sthalam, also to Bhaṭavirti mányams belonging to pious Bráhmans of villages in Podile *ṣíma* for carrying on work connected with learning. For the religious merit of Timmánáyaningáru and Lingammakka we have exempted your mányams from payment of taxes for ever. You may cultivate your mányams and enjoy them as long as the sun and the moon last. Those who obstruct in any manner this gift will incur the sin resulting from killing cows and Bráhmans near the Ganges.

V. 1. Of giving one self and protecting (another's gift) protecting is more meritorious. By giving (one self) one attains heaven, (but) by protecting (another's gift) one attains the abode of Vishnu.

May it cause prosperity.

NOTE.—Subhánu is S.S. 1506 current.

1. స్వస్తిశ్రీ జయాభ్యుదయ శా
2. లివాహన శకవరషంబులు
3. 1505 అగు నేటి స్వభాను సంవ్వ
4. త్సర శ్రావణ శు ౧౧ లు శ్రీమతు
5. రేచర్ల గోత్రోద్భవులైన వెలిగోటి పె
6. ద తింమ్మానాయునిగారి పౌత్రులైన కొ
7. మార తింమ్మానాయినింగారి పుత్రు
8. లైన కొమారచ్చి తింమ్మానాయనింగారు
9. పొదిలె స్థలం దేవబ్రాంహణులకు అగ్రహా
10. రాలకు పొదిలె శీమలోని గ్రామాల
11. దేవబ్రాంహణ భటవిర్తి మాన్యాల
12. కు విద్యావసులకు సవరిగాను యిచ్చి
13. న ధర్మశాసనం—తిమ్మానాయినిం
14. గారికిని లింగంమ్మకరుంగారికిన్ని పుణ్యా
15. ంగాను మీమాన్యాల జేడిగె యెల
16. కాలానకుం మన్నించ్చిమి మీ మాన్యా
17. లు మీరు యెప్పటివలెనే వ్యవసా
18. యాలు సెసుక అచంద్రార్కస్థాయి
19. గాను అనుభవించ్చి బ్రతికిడి యీ
20. పుంణ్యానకు యంవ్వర దప్పినాను
21. గంగ్గకర్త్ర గోవుబ్రాంహణి
22. వధియి
23. ంచ్చినా పాపానం బోవువారు
24. దానపాలన యోర్మధ్యే-దానాశ్చే)
25. యోనుపాలన దానాస్వర్గమ

26. వాంప్నోతి పాలనాత్ అచ్యుతం
27. పదం శ్రీ శ్రీ శ్రీం చేయును॥

Podili (35) (A.D. 1547–48.)

[Podili. Telugu. In Ánjanéya temple.]

TRANSLATION.

May there be prosperity! On Sunday, the 15th of the bright half of Kártika of the year Plavanga, corresponding to the victorious and prosperous S.S. 1469, while Ṣríman Máhárája Rájádhi Rája Rájaparáméṣvara, Ṣrí Víra Pratápa Ṣrí Sadáṣivadéva Maháráyalungáru was ruling the earth, seated on the jewelled throne at Vijayanagar, under the orders of Ṣríman Mahámaṇḍaléṣvara Aliyagáma (ráma?) Rájayyadéva Mahárájalungáru who bears the burden of the kingdom, Jilleḷḷa Rangapatidéva Mahárájulungáru issues this charitable edict to the barbers of the villages of Podili *ṣíma* which is attached to his chiefdom. Chippagiri Mangaḷa Timmóju Koṇḍóju Bhadrójú having pleased by his (or their) service the king Rámarájayyaváru, the barber caste in the kingdom of the king was exempted from taxes. Therefore we also exempt the barbers of Podila *ṣíma* and of the *Sthalam* from taxes including veṭṭi's fees. This gift is made under the orders of the king to the barbers of Podile *ṣíma*. Therefore we have exempted you from all taxes including veṭṭi's fees. You may take possession of the fields and enjoy them in full, you, your children and grandchildren in regular succession as long as the sun and moon last.

May Nimmanátha and Gópinátha, the gods of Podile, (two deities for each of whom there is a separate temple in Podili) (protect). This is the stone inscription written by Yellamrâju, the Sthalakarnam of Podila.

Those who obstruct the continuance of this gift will incur the sin of killing cows and Brahmans near the Ganges and also the sin of killing one's parents at Benares and will be regarded as having been born of donkeys.

Note.—In line 15 Mangala pójulaku looks as if it might mean "to the armies of barber."! It is not quite clear whether one person or three persons are referred to. In another inscription we find Mangaḷa Konḍóji and in a third Mangaḷa Timmóju Konḍóju.

1. శుభమస్తు స్వస్తిశ్రీ జయాభ్యుదయ శాలివాహన
2. శకవర్షంబులు ౧౪౬౯ అగు నేంటి ప్లవంగ్గసంవత్సర
3. కార్తిక శు ౧౫ భా॥ శ్రీ మన్మహారాజరాజాధిరాజరాజ
4. పరమేశ్వరశ్రీ వీరప్రతాప శ్రీసదాశివదేవమహారాయ
5. లుంగారు విజయనగరమందుల రత్నశింహ్వాసనాసీ
6. నులై బ్రదివిరాజ్యంచేయుచుండంగాను వారిరాజ్యభా
7. ర ధురంధరులైన శ్రీమన్మహామండలేశ్వర అళియ గా
8. మరాజయ్యదేవ మహారాజులుంగారి ఆనతిని జిల్లెల్లరంగ
9. పతిదేవ మహారాజులుంగారు మానాయంకరానకు
10. ం జెల్లె పొదిలశీమగ్రామాలం మంగ్గళ్లకిచ్చిన ధంమశా
11. సనం రాయలు రామరాజయ్యవారి శావచేసి చిప్పగిరి
12. మంగళ తిమ్మోజు కొండోజు భద్రోజులంగా
13. రు మెప్పింస్తైను రాయరాజ్యాన తమకులంమంగళ
14. వారికి పంనువరాయాలుమానినారు గనక పొదిలశీమ
15. మంగ్గళ్లకున్ను స్తళంమంగ్గళపొజులకు పంన్నువరాయాలు
16. వెట్టివెములు సర్వమాన్యంగాను మానితిమి (.) యీధర్మ

శాస

17. నం రాయుల ఆనతిక్రమానను పొదిలెశీమమంగ్గళవారిప
18. న్నువరాయులువెట్టి వేములుమానితిమి (.) గాన మీపుత్ర

పౌ

19. త్ర పారంపర్యంగాను ఆచంద్రార్కస్థాయిగాను మీస్వ
20. యికంచేసుకొని పరిణామాన వుండువారు (.) యి
21. పొదిలె నిమ్మనాథుండున్ను గోపినాథుండున్ను
22. పొదిల శీమ స్థలకరణం యెల్లరాజు వ్రాసిన శిలాశాసన
23. నము॥ యీ ధర్మానకు యెవ్వరు దప్పినాను గంగకట్టను

గో

24. బ్రాంహ్మలంజంపిన పాపానఁబోవువారు తమ తల్లితండ్రు
25. ల వారణాశిలోఁజంపిన పాపానఁబోవువారు
26. గాడిదె కడుపునం బుట్టినవారు.

Podili (36). (A.D. 1514–15.)

[Podili. Telugu. In front of Nirumaléṣvara temple.]

Translation.

Hail! On Thursday, the 30th of the dark half (*i.e.*, new moon day) of Ṣrávaṇa in the year Bháva, corresponding to the victorious and prosperous S.S. 1437, on the auspicious occasion of a solar eclipse, Ráyasam Koṇḍappamasayya (Koṇḍamarusayya ?) gáru for the religious merit of Ṣrí Víra Pratápa Krishṇadéva Mahárája, who is the king of Vijayanagar of the Carnatic, and who is Ṣríman Mahá Rájádhirája Rájaparaméṣvara, granted this charitable edict to the deities Bhíméṣvaradéva and Kailásaráya of Podila. We have granted with pleasure the village of Chirramakúru which lies on the western bank of the river Músi which is to the east of Podila *ṣíma* and which was formerly enjoyed by both these deities, as an absolute gift for providing all kinds of enjoyments to these deities in the proportion of four parts to Bhíméṣvara, and two to Ráma Kailásanátha. Those who help this charity will derive the religious merit of performing the 16 *mahádánas* (great gifts), viz., *tulá-purusha* (weighing a man against gold and giving it to him) and others.

1. స్వస్తిశ్రీ జ
2. యాభ్యుదయ
3. శాలివాహ
4. న శకవరుషం
5. బులు ౧౪౩౭
6. అగు నేటి
7. భావ సంవత్స
8. ర శ్రావణ బ
9. ౩౦ గు॥ సూ
10. ర్య గ్రహ
11. ణ పుణ్య
12. కాలమందు
13. శ్రీమాన్ మహారా
14. జాధి రాజరాజ
15. పరమేశ్వర

Second side.

1. శ్రీ కర్నాంట
2. విజయనగరా
3. ధీశ్వర శ్రీ వీర
4. ప్రతాప శ్రీకృష్ణ
5. దేవమహారా
6. యలకు పుణ్య
7. ముగాను రా
8. యసము కొం

9. డప్పమసయ్య
10. గారు పొదిల
11. భీమేశ్వర దేవు
12. నికిని కైలాస
13. రాయనికిని
14. యిచ్చిన ధర్మ
15. శాసనము—పూ
16. ర్వాన దేవళ్లకు
17. యిద్దరికిన్ని చెల్లే గ్రా
18. మం పొదిల శీమ

Third side.

1. లోని తూర్పు ముసి
2. కి పడమటిగట్టు చిలి
3. మకూరి గ్రామం
4. ము సర్వాక్రాంతము
5. గాను దేవళ్లకు అం
6. గ రంగవైభవాలకు
7. న్ను భీమేశ్వర దేవునికి
8. ౮॥ నాల్లుగు పాల్లున్ను అ
9. రామకైలాస నాథున
10. కు ౨॥ రెండుపాళ్లు
11. న్ను ఆరానుసడచి అ
12. ట్లను పూర్వం
13. సాగించ్చి ఇస్తిమి

14. యాత్రమార్నకు
15. సహాయములై నడచి
16. నవాలర్కు తులాపు
17. షర్ం మొదలైన షో
18. డశ మహాదానాలు
19. చేసిన పుణ్యం కలుగు
20. ను

PODILI (37).

[Podili. Telugu. On Pillar in Nirmalésvara temple. Last part unintelligible and inscription rough.]

TRANSLATION.

Under the orders of (Hail!) Śrímat Pótaya Sáhiṇin Gáru, son of Víraya Sáhiṇi, the excellent son of Dádi Pótaya Sáhiṇingáru (subordinate) of Śrímaḍ Vírayadéva-chakravartulu and of the Lakumámba, the illustrious Jákamma Venkamgáru gave to the *Kámpus* of Podiyala *sthalam*. . . . .

NOTE.—Sáhiṇi = commander-in-chief. The identity of the emperor is not obvious. From D. 12 it appears that a Kákatíya may be referred to.

1. శ్రీమ
2. ద్వీరయ
3. దేవచక్ర
4. వర్తులదా
5. దిపోతయ
6. సాహిణింగా

(To face page 1201.)

PODILI NO. 36.

7. రికిని లకుమాంబకూ

8. ను సుపుత్రుడైన పీరయసాహి

9. ణికొండుకు స్వస్తి శ్రీమతు పోతయసాహిణింగారి ఆనతి

10. నిస్వస్తిమతుజాకంమం యీ వెంకంగారుపాది యలస్థల
ము కాంపులకు యి

11. చ్చినసత్ । క్రతానంజలిసుత్

12. షుత్రానుకే నిస్తిమి

13. దుంనా విద్వానుం గలదమ

14. చెతం బత్రాలుగొని చేహొవులుగడెం

15. చినవారి లోపలి వెలుపలి పదలవరము

16. యెలుకా

PODILI (38). (A.D. 968–69 ?)

[Sannamúru, Sanskrit in Telugu character and Telugu. Opposite Rámaliṅgéṣvara temple.]

TRANSLATION.

Hail! On Friday, the full moon day of Vaiṣákha of the year corresponding to (Ṣaka) 890, the illustrious Aggaparáju, who was born in the family of *Mahábali* the members of which were made the gatekeepers of Paraméṣvara who is the lord of gods and demons and worshiped by all the three worlds; whose (Aggaparázu's) banner was a black-buck (?), who was heralded in public by the *Paiṣácha pataha* (a drum given by a piṣácha or demon); whose signet was the bull, who was the lord of Nandigiri (Nandidrug ?) and the supreme lord of Parigipura, who was Báṇa . . . . lgaṇḍa, who was the Arjuna of the family of Bali, ... granted with his own hand to Annagúri Agastîṣvara Bhaṭṭára twenty-four . . . of land in . . . . . the big kingdom and in the small kingdom. The progeny of the kings of . . . . . (big) kingdom and the small kingdom shall continue the enjoyment (of the same). Witness to this: Jésa Raṭṭaya, Márupúri Tikkana, and . . . . . Kalleka. With the consent of all these (this was) written by Tippama.

[One imprecatory verse.]

NOTE.—This was transcribed by Mr. V. Venkayya. The (symbol on the ?) banner was a black-buck according to Dr. Fleet, see p. 162, Vol. V, E.I. Parigipura appears elsewhere as Parivipurí. The "G" here may be a misreading for "V". The king, whose name does not seem to appear elsewhere, was evidently a Báṇa.

1. स्वस्ति सकलजगत्रया-[1]
2. भिवन्दितसुरासुराधीशप-
3. रमेश्वरप्रातिहारीक्रित[2] म-
4. हाबलिकुलोद्भव कृष्णध्वज-
5. विराजित पैशाचिकपटहघो-
6. षण वृषभलाञ्छन नन्दि-
7. गिरिनाथ पारिगिपुरपरमे-
8. श्वर बाण . लगण्ड बलिकु-
9. लार्ज्जुन गडुसण्डिय . व-
10. . . . . . श्रीमत्
11. [అ]గ్గ పరాజు సవత్స[3] [౮౯౦]
12. యగునే ॥ జ్యే వైశాఖ పుణ్ణమి శు-
13. క్రవారంబు నాణ్డు [అ]న్నగూరి [అగ]

---

[1] Read जगत्त्रया.

[2] Read कृत

[3] Read సంవత్సర

14. [శ్రీ] శ్వరభటారనికి పెద్దరాజ్యాన
15. . . . యు కొణ్డుకరాజ్యానం చేతంగోని ఇ-
16. చ్చిన భూమి ఇరువోదినాలుగు . .
17. . . . . . . రాజ్యానయు కొణ్డు
18. కరాజ్యానయు స్వస్తిభోగము నడ-
19. పేవారు [॥*] దీనికి సాక్షి జేసరట్టయ
20. యు మాలుపూరి తికరనయు . . .
21. కల్లెకయు పిరి ఉభయసమ్మథ[1]బు
22. న వ్రాసినవారు తిప్పమయ్యం [॥*][2][స్వ*] దత్తాం
23. (వా) . . . . .

PODILI (39). (A.D. 1438–39.)

[Tippaldévipalli. Telugu. To the west by a ruined tank.]

TRANSLATION.

May there be prosperity! Hail! This charitable edict relates to the consecration of the tank (caused to be constructed) near Ankepalli village on the holy occasion of Sunday, the third of the bright fortnight of Vaiṣákha of the year Kálayukti, corresponding to the Ṣrí Ṣaka year 1360 by Tippaladévi, the daughter of king Pedaráya Vibháḷa who is the younger brother of the king Ṣríman Mahámaṇḍaléṣvara, Médínimísaragaṇḍá[3], Kaṭhári[4], Sáḷuva[5], Dharaní Varáha[6], Telunguráyáḷésuṇḍa Bhúpa

---

[1] Read సమ్మతంబున

[2] The rest of the inscription consists of the continuation of the imprecatory verse beginning with these words.

[3] Médinimísaragaṇḍa = champion over the moustaches (heroes) of the world.

[4] Kaṭhári = the axe.

[5] Sáḷuva = the hawk.

[6] Dharaní Varáha = the boar on earth.

Góvinda, who is the son of the king Ṣríman Mahámaṅḍaléṣvara, Médinímísaragaṇḍa, Kaṭhári, Sáḷuva, Dharaní Varáha, Peda Samburáya, of the lunar race and of the Átréya *gótra*, for the religious merit of her husband king Jagatábasinga[1] of the solar race and of the Káṣyapa *gótra*, her son king Timma and (for the religious merit of the members) of the families of her mother and father. She made it in order to last so long as the sun and moon endure. Ṣrí, Ṣrí, Ṣrí. She granted with libation of water the village Tippaladévi to Tinta Tammanárya of the Bháradvája *gótra* . . . . as an agrahâram to be enjoyed as a single share.

NOTE.

King Rája Vibhála (from No. 26, Podili).

King Peda Samburáya (from No. 39, Podili).

King Telunguráyalésunḍa Bhúpa Góvinda. King Pedaráya Vibhála

King Jagatába Singa. = Tippala dévi.

King Timma.

[In volume VII, E.I., it is stated that in the temple at Simháchalam in Vizagapatam district there is an inscription, dated S.S. 1350 of Telunguráya, son of Samburáya of Kannaḍadéṣa and that there is another of Telunguráya dated Ṣ.Ṣ. 1350 at Santarávúru in Bápatla taluk in Kistna district in which the kings described as Mahámandaléṣvara Mísaragaṅḍa, Kaṭhári, Sáḷuva, Telunguráya. Samburáya and Telunguráya of Podili, No. 39, are evidently the same as these kings.

[1] Jagatábasinga is possibly the same as Jagadobbasinga = the sole lion of the world.

In an inscription at Tekal in Mysore Góparája is called the "Setter-up of Ganga Hale Sambáráya"—(*Epig. Carn. vol.* I, p. 208.)

In No. 26, Podili, the same Samburáya is given. His father was Ráya Vibhála.]

1. శుభమస్తు స్వస్తిశ్రీ శకవరు
2. షఀంబులు ౧౩౬౦ యగునేం
3. ౬౩. కాలయుక్తి సంవత్సర ఖ
4. ం దుల*వైశాఖ సుద్ధ తది
5. యాం భానువార పుణ్య
6. కాల భంద్దు సోమవంసో
7. ద్భవుండు అత్రియగోత్ర
8. ంను శ్రీమన్మహామండ
9. లేశ్వర మేదిని మీసరగం
10. డ్డ కంఠారి సాళువ ధరణి
11. వరాహుండైన పెదసం
12. బురాయతన్మా పాల తన
13. యుండు శ్రీ మన్మహా
14. మండలేశ్వర మేదిని మీస
15. ర గండ్డ కఠారి సాళువధర
16. ణి వరాహులైన తెలుంగ్గురాయా
17. ళైసండ్డ భూపగోవిందత్మా పా
18. లాను జుండైన పెదరాయ విభా
19. ళత్మా పాలసుత తిప్పలిదేవిసూ
20. ర్య వంశోద్భవుండు కాశ్యప
21. గోత్రుండైన తనపతి జగ

22. తాబ సింగత్మపాలుకు

23. ను తన తనయుండు తిన్మ

24. త్మాపాలుకును తనమా

25. తృ పితృవంశము వాటాణ

26. కున్ను పుణ్యంగాను అంకే

27. పల్లిగ్రామ సమీప బంకు త

28. టాక ప్రతిష్టా ధర్మశాసనం

29. - బాచంద్రార్కణ స్థాయిగానో

30. నరించెన్ను శ్రీ శ్రీ శ్రీ

31. భారద్వాజగోత్రం తింత్త

32. తమ్మ నార్యులకు ఏకబో

33. x అగ్రహారంగాను

34. ధారబోశి ఇచ్చును తి

35. ప్పలి దేవిగ్రామం

PODILI (40).

[Tuvvapáḍu. Telugu. By the Vaḍlaváḍi pond.]

TRANSLATION.

On Monday, the 10th of the dark fortnight of Ṣrávaṇa of the year Bahudhánya, Ṣrímat Ṣrí Velugóṭi Komára China Timma Náyaningáru issued this edict to the Jangála (priest) who worships Kúḍali Sangaméṣvara. We have granted this charity . . . for the religious merit of Timma Náyaningáru and Yáchema Náyaningáru. Whoever obstructs the (Jangála) priest will incur the sin of killing a cow on the Ganges.

1. భహుధాన్యే సంవ
2. త్సర శ్రావణ బ ౧౦ సో। శ్రీమత్
3. శ్రీ వెలుగోటి కొమారచిన తిమ్మ
4. నాయనింగారు కూడలిసంగమే
5. శ్వరుని పూజించె జంగాలకు
6. యిచ్చిన ధర్మశాసనం (న
7. డుం త్రాన పటిస అం
8. హిటంగాను) తిమ్మనా ఇని
9. ం గారికిన్ని యాచెమనా
10. యినికి పుణ్యంగాను
11. నిస్తిమి దంమ్మర్ణం య
12. (శ్వరు) జంగాలను విరోధించి
13. న్నం గంగ్క త్తర్ణగోవును
14. వధియించినవారు

PODILI (41).

[Uppalapáḍu. Sanskṛit in Chalukyan character. On floor of Rámalingasvámi temple. It makes no sense.]

కీర్త్ణ శ్రీ { సర్వ్ణ లోక / కాన్తి విజ }

(యా) ళ్ళబాజ్ణ నా కాగ్రో॥

PODILI (42). (A.D. 1376-77.)

[Vágimaḍugu. Telugu. Opposite Vírabhadrasvámi temple.]

TRANSLATION.

Hail! On the 15th of the bright fortnight of Márgaṣira of the year Nala, corresponding to 1297 of the illustrious Ṣaka era. . .

NOTE.—Nala or Anala corresponds with S.S. 1298, expired.

1. స్వస్తిశ్రీ శకవ
2. రుషంబులు
3. ౧౨౯౮ అగు నేంటి
4. నల సంవత్సర మా
5. ర్గశిర శు ౧౫
6.
7.
8.
9. నశు .
10. . . బనేకలు
11. వంబున . . .
12. . . . స్థ
13. . . . . .
14. . . . . .

RAPUR (1).

[Ákilavaisa. There is a defaced inscription on the tank bund.]

RAPUR (2).

[Áltúrti. Tamil. Opposite Chennakéṣvara Swámi temple. Illegible.]

RAPUR (3). (A.D. 1638-39.)

[Ákupalli. Telugu. Near tank to west of village.]

TRANSLATION.

Hail! On the 2nd of the bright half of Chaitra of the year Bahudhánya, corresponding to the year 1560 of the illustrious, victorious and prosperous Ṣáliváhana Ṣaka era, Ṣrímat Velugóṭi Venkaṭapati Náyanimgáru issued this charitable edict for the tank at Ákupalli. He has ordered that the tank work should be done with the *méra* grain in the same manner in which it was formerly collected and utilized. Therefore they should get the work done to the tank with the *méra* grain settled for it, whether the village be under *sandhátá*, or under an *amaradár*, or a lessee, or whoever be the ruler. If the rulers do not get the work done to the tank, if any one misappropriate it (the *méra*), or if any one covet it or if any kápu or karnam object to it or if any one remove this inscription, he will be considered to have been born to the *veṭṭi* of this village and to have given his wife to the *veṭṭi* of this village.[1] Thus has this charitable edict been issued.

1. స్వస్తిశ్రీ జయాభ్యుద
2. య శాలివాహన శకవ
3. ర్షంబ్బులు ౧౫౬౦
4. అగునెటి బహుధాన్య సం
5. వత్సర చైత్రశు ౨ లు శ్రీ
6. మతు వెలుగోటి వెం
7. కటపతి నాయనింగారు
8. ఆకుపల్లె చెరువువేయించి
9. న ధర్మశాసనం యిగ్రా
10. మాన చెరువుమేరలు పూ
11. ర్వాన యేదారిగాను నడి
12. చినవో ఆమేరధాన్యంచె
13. రువు పనిమోఖం శాయం
14. గట్టడ శేయించ్చినారు గ
15. నక యిగ్రామం సంధాతా
16. న వున్నాను అమరగాని
17. వశాన యేదొర యేలినాను
18. గుత్తగాని వశాన వున్నాను
19. ఛెరువుకు నిర్న్ణయమైన
20. మేరధాన్యం చెరువు వ
21. నిముఖం శేయించ్వా గ
22. లవారు చెరువుపని

Second side.

23. ముఖం
24. గాను పలి

[1] This excellent old tank-builder (would there were more zamindars of his kidney) generally concludes his edicts with some such expression.

(To face page 1211.)

RAPUR NO. 4.

25. నవారు చే
26. యించ్చుక యవ్వ
27. రు అనుభవిం
28. చ్చినాను యవ్వ
29. రు ఆసిం
30. చ్చినాను మేకాం
31. పు కరణం ఆత్రే
32. పించ్చినాను యీ
33. శాసనం యివ్వ
34. రు తీసివేసినా
35. ను వాండు యీ
36. వూరి వెట్టివా
37. నికి బుట్టినవా
38. ండు వాని ఆలిని
39. యీవూరి వెట్టివానికి
40. యిచ్చుకున్న ట్టై అ
41. ట్లని యిచ్చిన ధ
42. ర్మశాసనం

RAPUR (4).

[Chágaṇam (hamlet Rázupáḷem). Tamil. On a rock below the hill to north of village.]

[1] திருபுவநச்சக்கரவத்திகள் ஸ்ரீகு-
[2] லொத்துங்கசொழதெவற்கு ஆ-
[3] ண்டு இருபத்துமுன்றுவது விக்கி-
[4] ரமசிங்கபுரமான நெல்லுரிற்க-
[5] ழை இட்ட காடெச்ச[ரு]தெவற்கு சிலைக-
[6] [ளும்] காட்டில் ஊட்டுக்கூக[ண்]ம-
[7] லை மலையடியில்ப்[பி]ச்சண்டிகாய-

[8] க்கர் கட்டுவித்த எரி நல்லசித்தசாரரும்
[9] உள் உடுக்கூரில் வெள்ளாளரும் கூடி
[10] சிமுப்பிலிசிங்கமச்சரும்
[11] இவ்வெரி இட்ட காமிச்சுரமுடைய-
[12] நாயநாற்கும் பிராமணற்கும் குடு-
[13] த்தொம் இந்த தம்மம் சந்திராகதித்தவ-
[14] ரை செல்வதாகவும் குடுத்தொம் இந்த தம்ம இ-
[15] டக்[கி]நாருண்டாகில் கெங்கைகரையிற்கு-
[16] ராப்பசுக்கொன்றான் பாவங்கொள்வான்.

Translation.

In the twenty-third year of the reign of the emperor of the three worlds, the glorious Kulóttungachóḻadéva, Pichchaṇḍi Náyaka gave images to the temple of the lord Kaḻai Iṭṭa Káḍuchcharudéva at Nellúr *alius* Vikkiramasingapuram and caused to be dug a tank at the foot of Úṭṭukkúkaṉ hill of the country.

We, Nallasittaśárar(?), the *Vélálás* of Úḍukkúr and Śímuppili Singa Amachcha gave this tank to the god.

Iṭṭakaramáśvara (Isṭhakáméśvara ?) and Brahmans.

We gave it so that this charity might be maintained as long as the moon and sun endure. If there is anybody who obstructs this charity, he will incur the sin of killing a tawny cow on the banks of the Ganges.

Rapur (5). (A.D. 1636–37.)

[Cháganam. Telugu. From stone in middle of village.]

Translation.

Hail ! On the 30th day of the dark fortnight of Pushya of the year Dháta(ri), corresponding to the year

1558 of the illustrious, victorious and prosperous Ṣáliváhana Ṣaka era, while the illustrious Rájádhirája, Rájaparaméṣvara, Ṣrí Vírapratápa, Ṣrí Víra Venkaṭapatidéva Mahárájulu, seated on the diamond throne at the town of Penugonḍa, is ruling the kingdom of the earth, Velugóṭi Venkaṭapati Náyanimgáru has given Dágdama *agrahára* in Nellore *ṣíma* which is ruled and presided over by himself to Púsala Venganna Kaḍappa as an *amaram*. Therefore Venganna Kaḍappamgáru granted this charitable edict for the tank *kunchas* (*i.e.*, at 1 *kuncha* per *puṭṭi*). Its terms are as follows. He settled this for (the upkeep of) the tanks. They should spend the *méras* on tanks and not remit them to the palace (zamindar). Having thus ordained, we have given a stone inscription on this holy occasion of a solar eclipse for the tanks with libation of water so that religious merit may accrue to Venkaṭapati Náyanimgáru.

Therefore any one who fails in this will be considered to have given his honour to the veṭṭi (*gulápuváḍu*). In these terms has the charitable stone edict been granted for work (to the tank.)

1. స్వస్తి శ్రీ విజయాభ్యుదయ శాలివాహాన శ

2. కవర్షంబులు ౧౫౫౮ అగు నేంటి ధాత (తు) సంవత్సర

పుష్య

3. బ ౩౦ లు శ్రీమద్రాజాధిరాజరాజపరమేశ్వర శ్రీవీ

4. రప్రతాప శ్రీవీర వెంకటపతి దేవ మహారాయల అయ్యవా

5. రు పెనుంగొండ నగరమందు వజ్రసింహాసనారూఢుం

6. డై పృథివిసామ్రాజ్యం జేయుచుండి వెలుగోటి వెంకట

7. పతి నాయనింవారు పాలించి నవహరించ్చిన నెల్లూరి శీమ

8. లోను దాగడమనే అగ్రహారం వెంకటపతి నాయనివారు

ఫ్రా

9. సాల వెంగ్గన అకడప్పం గారికి అమరానకు బాలిచ్చినా
10. రు గనుక వెంగన కడపం గారు చెరువు కుంచ్ఛాలకు యి

11. నధర్మశాసన క్రమమెట్లన్నను దీని చెరువులకుంగాను
12. నిర్ణయించెనునమేర ధాన్యాలు నగరంబెట్టక చెరువుల
13. మీందను పనిముఖం శేయించంగలవారు అని నిర్నయం
14. చేశి యీా సూర్యగ్రహణ పుణ్యకాలమందున వెంకట
15. పతినాయనివారికి దర్మంచేసూ రేటట్లుగాను చె
16. రువులకు దారవోశి సిలాశాసనం వేయుంస్తిమి గనుక ఇ
17. ందుకు తప్పినవాండు కులావువానికి మానమిచ్చి
18. న వాండే యీపనిర్వేయించిన శిలాధర్మశాసనము

RAPUR (6). (A.D. 1636-37.)

[Cháganam. Telugu. North of village on Tirragatrála Bóḍu.]

TRANSLATION.

Hail! On the 30th day of the dark fortnight of Pushya of the year Dhátri, corresponding to the year 1558 of the illustrious, victorious and prosperous Ṣáliváhana Ṣaka era, while Ṣrímad Rájádhirája, Rája-paraméṣvara, Ṣrí Víra Pratápa Ṣri Víra Venkaṭapatidéva Mahárájulu, seated on the diamond throne at the city of Penugoṇḍa, was ruling as universal sovereign . .

1. స్వస్తి శ్రీ విజయాభ్యుదయ శాలి
2. వాహన శకవర్షంబులు ౧౫౫౮
3. అగునేటి ధాతృసంవ్సర పుష్యబ
4. ౩౦ లు శ్రీమద్రాజాధిరాజ రా

5. జపర మేశ్వర శ్రీవీరప్రతాప
6. శ్రీవీర వేంకటపతి దేవమహా
7. రాయులయ్యవారు పెన
8. గొండ నగరమందు వజ్రసింహా
9. సనారూఢులై సకలసామ్రాజ్యం

* * * *

Rapur (7). (A.D. 1638-39.)

[Chíkavólu. Telugu. On tank bund.]

Translation.

Hail! On the 2nd day of the bright half of Chaitra of the year Bahudhánya, corresponding to the year 1560 of the illustrious, victorious and properous Ṣáliváhana Ṣaka era, Ṣrímat Velugóṭi Venkaṭapati Náyaningáru issued this charitable edict for the tank at Chikkavólu. He has ordered that the *méras* collected for the tank of this village at one *kuncha* for every *puṭṭi* should be spent on the tank. Therefore whether the village be under the *sandhátá*, or an *amaradar*, or lessee, or whoever be the ruler, the *méra* at one *kuncha per puṭṭi* (must be expended and) if, not doing work to the tank, any one misappropriate the *méras* collected at one *kuncha per putti*.

1. స్వస్తి శ్రీ జయాభ్యుదయ శాలివాహనశకవర్షం
2. ంబులు ౧౫౬౦ అగునేంట్టి బహుధాన్యసంవ్వ
3. త్సర చైత్రశు ౨ లు శ్రీమతు వెలుగోటి వెంకట
4. పతినాయనింగారు చికకావోలుగ్రామ చెర్వుకు వేయించిన
ధర్మ
5. శాసనము యీగ్రామాన చెర్వు మేరలు
6. . . . పుట్టి కుంచాలవల్ల వచ్చిన ఆమేర

7. ధాన్యం చెర్వు పనిముఖంశాయ కట్టడ శేసేరి

8. గనుక మేరపుట్టింటికి ఖ ౧ కి కుంచెడు

9. తెఖను మేరధాన్యం ఇగ్రామసంధాతాను

10. వశానను అమరగానివశాను పవారయేలినా

11. నున్న్న గుత్తగానివశాన పున్నాను చెర్వ్వకు

12. పనిముఖంచేయించక మేరధాన్యంచెర్వ పు

13. ట్టి కుంచాలు . . . . . .

Rapur (8). (A.D. 1213–4.)

[Chíkavólu (hamlet Yerraguntapalem). Sanskrit in Grantha and Tamil. To the north in Survey No. 510. The first portion, written in very incorrect Sanskrit, expresses the same meaning as the Tamil portion with the addition of the Saka year expressed by *rasa* (6), *guṇa* (3), *ṣaṣi* (1), *bhú* (1) or 1136. The translation of the Tamil portion is given below :—]

Translation.

In the 36th year of the reign of the emperor of the three worlds, the glorious Kulóttunga Chóladéva, I, Tukki Náyaka, the younger brother of Vayirappa Náyaka, who is the younger brother of Piḍiyári Kósani Náyaka, the son of Kaṭṭaśádi who was the son of Vayirappa Náyaka, who was one of the followers (Paḍiyár) of Chóḷa Tirukká-ḷattidéva, the son of Piḷḷaiyár Manumasiddarasa, gave on behalf of Piḷḷaiyár Tirukkáḷattidéva, to last as long as the moon and sun endure to Késava Perumál (whose image) I set up in the month of Chittirai at Takkuḷam in Mándainádu, with libation of water, the village (evidently of Takkuḷam) including all taxes leviable within its four boundaries.

He who obstructs this charity will incur the sin of stabbing a cow on the banks of the Ganges.

NOTE.—Some years ago this stone is said to have fallen on and killed several people who were digging under it for hidden treasure. For another inscription from this hamlet see No. (79).

Sanskrit.

[1] ஸ்வஸ்தி ஸவஸ்து-..
[2] ஸபுவநாக்ஸஶ்ரீ-
[3] ஊரஸ-ப ஸ்ரீ ஒவர-
[4] ஊதிக்க [நு] வதிவ-
[5] ஷ்ரு-ரிரா கூ்லவஶிகு-
[6] தகெஸவாடா-
[7] நஶக் ஞாகேஷ-
[8] க்ஷாஷிஂ யாவஜ-
[9] ஜயஶிஸ்ரீதேத்ரு-
[10] ஜெ ஶகா-
[11] நாஂ ஈஸகஜெ
[12] ஸ-பணஶஶி-
[13] ஷ-ஞஸசீ ஜெ
[14] ஒவெதுரோ-
[15] (ஒ) ஸ ஞாஉ-
[16] ஒ[ஜ]வாயஜுஸ-
[17] ஷகுதிஉதி வு-
[18] ஜாதீ கு-
[19] தகெஶவ-
[20] ாய யஸு
[21] ஞாகாவி-
[22] தாவஷுபஶி-
[23] தஶ-பணஷ-
[24] ஒரள ஒஹொர-
[25] வெள் ஜா-
[26] ஷுஉ-பவெ்ள
[27] ஒஸாஜய-்ா-
[28] ஒஸாவி ஷி-

[29] ரொஜவதி
[30] க்ரவஸநய-
[31] ஶ்வொஊதி-
[32] க்ஷ்வநா
[33] யஃ |

Tamil.

[1] த்ரிஹுவநச்ச-
[2] க்ரவர்த்திகள்
[3] ஸ்ரீ குலொ-
[4] ாத்துங்கெ-
[5] சாழதெவ-
[6] ற்கு யாண்டு
[7] ௩௰௪வது
[8] பிள்ளையார்
[9] மநுமசித்தர-
[10] சர் மகநார் செ-
[11] ளத்திருக்கா-
[12] ளத்திதெவர்ப்-
[13] டியார்களில்
[14] படியாள் வயிர-
[15] ப்பநாயக்கன்-
[16] மகன் கட்டசா-
[17] தி மகந் பிடியா-
[18] ரி கொசநிநாய-
[19] க்கந் தம்பி வயி-
[20] ரப்பநாயக்-
[21] கந் தம்பி துக்-
[22] கிநாயகநெ-
[23] ந் மாந்தைந[ா*]
[24] ட்டுத் தக்குள-
[25] த்தை நாந் சி-
[26] த்திரைஊவ-
[27] த்தில் நாந் வர-
[28] திஷை பண்ணி-

[29] ந கெசவப்ெ-
[30] பருமாளுக்குப்-
[31] பிள்ளையார் தி-
[32] ருக்காளத்திெ-
[33] தவர் பக்கெ-
[34] லப்பெற்பட்-
[35] ட வரியுட்பட
[36] நாற்பாலெ-
[37] ல்லைக்குள்-
[38] ளு சந்திராதித்-
[39] த்தவரை செல்-
[40] வதாக கிரட்டு-
[41] வித்துக்கொடு-
[42] த்தெந் படி-
[43] யாரி துக்கிந-.
[44] ாயக்கநெந்-
[45] இது துக்கி ந-
[46] ாயக்கந் தம்-
[47] மம் இத்தந்ம-
[48] ம்மிழப்பா-
[49] ந் கெ-
[50] ங்கைக் க-
[51] ரையிற் குராசற்-
[52] பசுவை குத்தி-
[53] நாந் பாவத்-
[54] தைப் படுவான்.

Rapur (9).

[Chintalátmakúru. Ṭelugu. Opposite Áñjanéya temple.]

Translation.

On the 3rd day of the dark fortnight of Ṣrávaṇa of the illustrious year Kílaka, Anumantu, son of Chiru Mámiḷḷa Gópanna caused to be made an image of Sanjíva

Ráya in Chintalátukúru and consecrated it. He caused to be planted five lamp posts. The sun and moon are witnesses of this. Śrí.

1. శ్రీకీలక సం
2. వత్సర శ్రా
3. వణ బ ౩ లు
4. చిరుమా
5. మిళ్ల గోపం
6. న్న కొమా
7. రుండు అ
8. నుమంతు
9. చింత లా
10. తు కూరి
11. ం లోన స
12. ంజీవరా
13. యంణ్ని చే
14. యించ్చి ప్ర
15. తిష్ట శే శేను
16. అయిదుం
17. టి గారుడ
18. కంభములు
19. యత్నించి
20. వాండు సూ
21. ర్యచంద్రు
22. ల సాక్షిగా
23. నుందురు
24. శ్రీ

Rapur (10).

[Chípinápi. Telugu. Near the Oṭaguṇṭa to south of village.]

Translation.

Hail! On the 3rd of the bright fortnight of Ásvija of the year Manmatha, Ga—raju Timma Rájugáru, the agent (*káryakarta*) of Ṣríman mahámaṇḍaléṣvara Táḍigoṭla Timmarájuváru gave . . . . to the goddess Ammagáru of Vávilla. Therefore this gift should be utilized for providing food (*amritapaḍi*) and worship with light to the Ammagáru of Kamma Váivalle.

Note.—This Timmarájn is not apparently mentioned elsewhere in this collection.

1. స్వస్తి మన్మ
2. త సంవ్వర ఆ
3. శ్వీజ శు ౩ లు శ్రీమను
4. మహామండలే
5. స్వర. తాడిగోట్ల తిమ
6. రాజువారి కార్యకర్తలైన గ.
7. రాజు తిమ్మరాజుగారు వావి
8. ల్లన అమ్మంగారికి ఇచ్చిరి .
9. గనుక యిచ్చిన కంమ్మవాఇవల్లె
10. అంమ్మంగారికి అమృత
11. పడ్లకుంన్న
12. దీపారాధ
13. నకున్న
14. . . . రి
15. . . . ..
16. . . . .

Rapur (11). (A.D. 1570–71 ?)

[Chittalúru (hamlet Ádúrupalli). Telugu. In the tank bed. Mostly illegible.]

Translation.

Hail! . . . . corresponding to 1492 of the Śrí Śaka era . . . (issued) this charitable edict.

* * * *

If any persons obstruct this charity, they will incur the sin of killing a cow and a Brahman on the Ganges, and will incur the sin of killing their parents and children at Kási . . . .

(1) స్వస్తి శ్రీశవర్షంబు ౧౪౯౨ .అగు నేంటి
(2) . . . . . నాడు
(3) . . . . . శంన
(4) . . . . . .
(5) . . . . . .
(6) దూరి . . . .
(7) ధర్మశాసనం . . . .
(8) . . . . . .
(9) గాను పూర్వాలం . . .
(10) దు . . . . దు । ద
(11) . . ల పెద . .
(12) . . . ద . .
(13) . . . .
(14) . . . . .
(15) . . . న అవల . .
(16) . . . ప . . .
(17) ప్పినం గంగకతర గోబ్రాంహ్మల జంపి
(18) పాపాన బోదురు తల్లి తండ్రిని
(19) పిల్లవాండ్ల కాశిలో వధించిన పాపనంబోవువా

(20) రు . చె . . నాను చెర .
(21) . . . న ప . . రు .
(22) . . నా . కు . . . న మర్యనవె
(23) . . . . . ధర్మశాం

Rapur (12).

[Chittalúru. Telugu. On the tank bund. Incomplete.]

Translation.

On the 10th of the bright fortnight of Ṣrávaṇa of the year Ṣrímukha Dummarapu Venkátâdri Náyanigáru set up this charitable edict for the tanks of the villages of Chittalúṛu and Ádúrupale. For the tanks of the villages of Chittalúru and Ádúrupale, granted to us as an *amaram* by Velugóṭi Venkaṭapati Nayanivâru . . .

1. శ్రీము
2. ఖ సంవ్వత్సర శ్రా
3. వణ శు ౧౦ లు దు
4. మ్మరపు వెంకటా
5. ద్రి నాయనిగారు
6. చిత్తలూరు ఆదూ
7. రుపలె గ్రామాల చె
8. రువులకు వేశిన దమా
9. శాసనం వెలుగోటి వెంకట
10. పతినాయనివారు మాకు అమరా
11. నకు యిచ్చిన చిత్తలూరు ఆదూ
12. రుపలె గ్రామాల చెరువులకు ని . .
13. . . న వెలిపఇర్ల . .
14. గ్రాను . . .

RAPUR (13).

[Chittalúru. Telugu. Near a well to east of village.]

TRANSLATION.

This is the great *linga* carved by Náyiṇḍu for the flower garden to the west of the Nágináyini well . .

(1) నాగినాయిని .
(2) భావికి పడుమ
(3) టి పుష్పాల తోం
(4) టం లోకి నాయి
(5) ండు చెక్కిం ఇంచి
(6) మహాలింగం . . .

* * * *

RAPUR (14).

[Chittalúru. Telugu. Near the same well.
Incomplete.]

TRANSLATION.

* * * *

Whoever fails in this charity, will incur the sin of killing a cow on the Ganges.

(1) స్వ . .
(2) వారిను యీధర్మా
(3) నకు యెవ్వరు తప్పి
(4) నారుం గంగ కర్త గో
(5) వు చంపిన పాపానం బో
(6) ద్యురు

Rapur (15). (A.D. 1684–85.)

[Dátsúru. Telugu. One side of a tall stone bearing inscriptions on three sides, to east of village. Incomplete.]

Translation.

Hail! In Adhika Áshádha of the year Raktákshi, corresponding to the year 1607 of the illustrious, victorious and prosperous Sáliváhana Saka era . . . .

1. స్వస్తి శ్రీ
2. . . [వి] జ
3. యాభ్యుద
4. య శా
5. లివాహ
6. న శకవర్షం
7. బులు ౧౬౦౭ అగు
8. నే టి రక్తాక్షి
9. సంవత్సర అ
10. ధిక అషాఢ
11. . . . .
12. . . .

Rapur (16).

[Dátsúru. Telugu. From the same stone.]

Translation.

Prayer to (Tva)ḍári Ganga who resides in the boundary (between the villages) . . . (unintelligible). By the feet of Raghunátha, by Bhúdévi (goddess of earth) and Ánjanidévi, Piṭalammá, Váravári, Om, hrám, Ṣrím, hrím, paṭṭu phaṭṭu sváhá, bálá, paṭṭu phaṭṭu sváhá. To the lord (deity) of cattle.

Having dug a pit at the entrance of the cattle shed cook food in it, milk a cow that gives plenty of milk offer incense, worship with light and offering, put three marks of blood (on the face) put three marks of—, and divide the red food (red with blood) (among the people present). Prepare medicine with márédu (Ægle marmelos), dondakúra (Coccinea indica), gingelly, budu-ma (cucumis), mustard, salt, pepper, garlic, urine, jaggery, and sour butter milk.

You must make obeisance.

Administer one tube of this medicine to the sick cattle.

NOTE.—This seems to be a mantra and prescription for cattle diseases. Some parts are unintelligible.

1. పొలిమేరయందలి
2. (త్వ) డారి గంగ్గ
3. జపం (జరు ఫ్రా
4. డి నెంద్దు గోం
5. డ్డు పటు పేరు పె
6. ట్టే) రఘునాధుని
7. పాదమాన భూదే
8. వి అంజనీదేవి ఆ
9. న పిటలంమ్మా వా
10. ర వారి వోం హ్రాం
11. శ్రీం హ్రీం పట్టు
12. ఫట్టు స్వాహా బాలా
13. పట్టు ఫట్టు స్వాహా

14. పసులనాథున
15. కు॥ పసుల దొ
16.డ్డి వాకిట గాడిగా
17. దొవ్వి బత్యము
18. లం . పాండి అల
19. మీంద ఖారి జే
20. పు కొంమ్మ పితి
21. కి ధూప దీపనా
22. వేద్యమిచ్చి మూం
23. డు నెత్తురు బొట్లు
24. బెట్టి మూండు . రి
25. లవు బొట్లు పెట్టి
26. యెఱ్ఱగూడునూం
27. బంచ్చి వేశ్యేది॥ మా రే
28. డు దొండకూర తిల
29. లు బుడుమ అవా
30. లు పుప్పు మిరియా
31. లు పెల్లుల్లి కాలు
32. మడి బెల్లం పులిమ
33. జ్జిగతో మందుచేసి
34. మీరు మొకుగ్గాలు పెట్టే
35. ది గొట్టండు లోవ లి
36. కి పెట్టేది

Rapur (17).

[Dátsúru. Telugu. From the same stone.]

Translation.

Hanumán of five faces, who is like Páta̤la (the nether world) in devouring the sun, who is valiant in fiercely driving away foes with his bow, who is unconquerable by gods and demons, having arms like columns to do the will of Ráma, who has a tail like a pillar, who has an eye in the middle of his forehead, who is the son of Anjani, who is a fierce Yama (destroyer) to wicked people, who is the leader of monkeys, who is a swift mover, the nectar of the semen of Ṣiva, a giant to stormy seas (?), . . . who captures the cardinal points, hero, *sura*, *paṭṭu*, fierce Hanumanta, Sánumanta (mountain dweller).

Note.—This seems to be a mantra or spell, in the name of Hanumán. Some of the epithets are unintelligible.

1. . . డిబం .
2. . ణపంము
3. ఖహానుమం
4. త సూర్యభక్ష
5. చపా తాళకోద
6. ండవు।గహా పుచ్ఛా
7. టనవీరవిక సూరసు
8. రనిరాఘాటన । దాశా
9. రథపతి౯ని బాహుద
10. ండ్డ బాలదండ్డ భా
11. లనేత్ర అంజనీతన
12. య ఘోర ఘోరకా
13. లాంత్తక కపినాయః
14. క శీఘ్రుహారం శివు
15. నివీర్యసుధా శీఘ్రుర
16. ద్భిదానవ బాకోటి
17. దిగ్బంధ్ధన వీరసుర
18. పట్టి పుగ్రహానుమ
19. ంత సానుమంత

Rapur (18). (A.D. 1622-23.)

[Dátsúru. Telugu. From two sides of a stone near the police station.]

May there be no impediment!

Hail! On the 11th day of the bright fortnight of Phálguna of the year Dundubhi, corresponding to the year 1544 of the illustrious, victorious and prosperous Ṣáliváhana Ṣaka era, Venkaṭapati Náyanigáru, descendant of the Récharla *gótra*, grandson of Veligóṭi Koṇḍama Náyaningáru and son of Venkaṭappa Náyaningáru, issued this charitable edict for the repairs of Dátsúru tank as follows. Its terms are: we have ordered that one *kuncha* should be given for every *puṭṭi* for the upkeep of the tank. Therefore we shall spend, as long as the sun and moon endure, on the tank (the grain thus collected on) all the crops raised under the tank. If any persons, not maintaining (the charity), injure, or cause obstacles to, this charity or if any fail to keep it up, they will incur the sin of killing cows and Brahmans at Kási and that of killing their fathers.

[Two imprecatory verses.]

May it cause prosperity!

1. అవిఘ్నమస్తు
2. స్వస్తి శ్రీ విజయాభ్యు
3. దయ శాలివాహన శక
4. వర్షంబులు ౧౫౪౪ అగునేటి దు
5. ందుభి సంవత్సర ఫాల్గుణ శు ౧౧ లు
6. శ్రీమతు రేచర్ల గోత్రోద్భవులున్న వె
7. లిగోటి కొండమ నాయనింగారు పౌ
8. త్రుండు వెంకటప్ప నాయనిం

9. గారి పుత్రుండు వెంకటపతి నాయ
10. నిగారు దా ఛూరుని చెరువుకు సా
11. గించిన ధర్మశాశన క్రమము ఎ
12. ట్లన్నను చెరువు పూర్తితు కావ
13. లెనని పుట్టితి కుంచాలు కట్టడశే ఇ
14. ంచినవారం గనక చెరువుల కింద పం
15. డె పొలాన కారుగిండలు మోడ
16. లైన సకల ఫలాదులున్ను ఆచం
17. ద్రార్క స్థాఇగా చెరువు మీందనే
18. వేయించగలవారము చెరు [వు] నడి
19. పించక యీపుణ్యముకు యవ్వరు
20. తలంగినాను విఘాతంగా చేశినా
21. నడిపించక పోయినవారు కాశి
22. లోపల గోబ్రాంహ్మాల వధించిన
23. పాపానను పోవువారు [వా]లఽదండ్సృలి
24. వధియించ్చిన పాపానం
25. పోగలవారు॥ స్వదత్తా ద్విగు
26. ణం పుణ్యం పరదత్తానుపా
27. లనం పరదత్తాపహారేణ స్వ
28. దత్తం నిష్ఫలం భవేత్॥
29. స్వదత్తఖా పరదత్తం వా
30. యో హారేతి వసుంధరా
31. షష్టివర్ష సహస్రాణి వి
32. ష్టాయాం జాయతే క్రిమి॥
33. శ్రీశ్రీశ్రీం జేయును.

RAPUR (19). (A.D. 1541–42 ?)

[Dátsúru. Telugu. From the same stone. Mostly illegible.]

TRANSLATION.

Hail! In 1463 of the illustrious Ṣáliváhana Ṣaka era . . .

1. స్వస్తి శ్రీ శాలి
2. వాహాన శ
3. క వర్షం
4. బులు
5. ౧౪౬౩ అగునే
6. టు (దరిటి).
7. (లమర తిథి)
8. (పను దాకూ)
9. (మ ల. ణ.)
10. (. . .)
11. నాయిండు
12. . . . . .
13. జనాలు. . . .
14. . . . . .
15. . . . . .

RAPUR (20). (A.D. 1247–48.)

[Dévaravémúru. Telugu. East of village in survey No. 350.]

TRANSLATION.

Hail! On Thursday, the 8th of the bright half of the month of Mágha of the year Plavanga, corresponding to the year 1169 of the illustrious Ṣaka era, while Ṣrímat Alu Tirukáladéva Chóḍa Mahárája was ruling the kingdom, Ṣrímat Chivapani Seṭṭi, son of Lakshmi Seṭṭi descendant of the Brahma *sákha gótra* and the favourite servant of Vijayádityadéva Chóḍa Mahárájá the younger brother of the abovesaid king, gave land for providing offering to the deity for the religious merit of . . and of Vijayáditya Rája.

1. స్వస్తి శ్రీ సకవరుశంబులు
2. ౧౧౬౯ అగునేంటి ప్లవంగసం
3. వత్సరము మాఘమాసమునం
4. దుల ౮ శుద్ధపక్షమున బ్రిహస్ప
5. తివారమునాండు శ్రీమతు అలు
6. తిరుకాలదేవ చోడమహారాజుల రాజ్యం
7. మున శ్రీమతు ఆ రాజుతమ్మండు విజ
8. యాదిత్య దేవచోడ మహారాజులకు
9. ఇష్టబ్రిత్యుండైన లక్ష్మిం సెట్టికొడుకు బ్రమ్మశా
10. క (గోత్రుండు) శ్రీమతు చివపని సెట్టి
11. . మూను . . బుణ్యంగాను . . . .
12. దును . . . దేవరకు నైవాద్యా
13. . . . . దేవరబ్రిత్తి . . విజయాది
14. త్యరాజునకు ధర్మంగాముర క ౧ మీ దేవరకు
15. . . . యకు . . దారము . . .
16. క్రొ . . . . . .
17. పి . . . . . .

RAPUR (21).

[Dévaravémúru. Telugu. Near Vénugópálasvámi temple. Incomplete.]

TRANSLATION.

. . . The charity for the tank at one *kuncha*. He has ordered that the *méra* grain settled at one *kuncha* for every *puṭṭi* for the tank should be spent for the maintenance of the tank. Therefore whether the village is under *sandhátá* or in the possession of an *amaradár*. . . .

1. చెరువుకుంచెండు ధర్మ . . . .
2. యీగ్రామచెరువులకు పుట్టికుంచాలూ
3. . . . గాను కట్టడ శేసిచ్చినట్టి ఇమేర
4. ధాన్యం చెరువుపనిముఖం శాయంగ
5. ట్టడ శేఇంచినారు గనుక ఇగ్రామాన సం
6. ధాతానవున్నాను అమరగాని వశానను . . .

RAPUR (22). (A.D. 1623–24.)

[Duggunṭa (hamlet Konagallúru). Telugu. On tank bund to south.]

TRANSLATION.

On the 5th of the bright half of Jéshṭa (Jyeshṭha) of the year Rudhiródgári, Ṣrímat Velugóṭi Venkaṭapati Náyanigáru . . . the paddy field under the tank Dugunṭa called Koṇangu and measuring 4 *gorrus*. This inscribed pillar was planted to last as long as the sun and moon exist.

1. రుధిరోద్గారిస
2. ంవత్సర జేష్ట శు
3. ౫ లు శ్రీమతు వె
4. లుగోటి వెంక
5. టపతినాయనిం
6. గారు దుగుంట
7. చెరువుకింది క
8. రిమడికి కొణంగ
9. లసిరిపాలంనాలు
10. గోల . . . . .
11. నక ఆ చంద్రార్కం
12. ముగానుండంగలందుకు
13. వేయించిన శాసనం
14. న స్తంభము

Rapur (23).

[Gilakapáḍu (hamlet Vébinábi). Tamil. On Boyela tank bund.]

[1] ஸ்வஸ்தி ஸ்ரீ திருபுவனச்சக்கரவத்திகள்
[2] ஸ்ரீகுலொத்துங்கசொழதெவற்கு
[3] ஆண்டு முப்பத்தெட்டாவதிலா-
[4] ந யூவை சம்வச்சரத்திலாக மா-
[5] சிமாசத்தில் வெமிநாப்பி மாசவிச்சவி-
[6] ண்டிநாயக்கர் மகன் மாசவிபெத்திநாய-
[7] க்கனென் ஸ்ரீவல்லீடத்தில் உக்ஷிணஸ்வாரஸோ-
[8] ந விஜுவ[டெ]ஸ்வரதெவற்கு பெத்தசமு-
[9] த்திரமாக [எரியும் கு]டுத்து என்னுடைய
[10] மகனையும் விஜுவடெஸ்வரதெவர் ஸிவ-
[11] காமஞ்சாத்திநென் மாசிவிபெத்திநா-
[12] யக்கநென் பெத்தசமுத்திரமாக எ-

[13] ரி கட்டின வெள்ளாளர் செலநாட்-
[14] டில் கிரச்சமாலையும் பொத்தப்பிநாட்-
[15] டில் மன்னூர்காணியு (உ)டைய வாகநதி-
[16] தி பொயிண்டர் மல்லிரட்டிய[ர*]ர் மகன்
[17] . . . .
[18] குதன்மரட்டிய[ர*]ர் மகந் தச்ச-
[19] மரட்டியும் தாடிவேலை காணியுடை-
[20] யவன் கொந்தறு பொயிண்டர் தே-
[21] ரப்பரெட்டியார் மகன் நாகிரட்டி-
[22] யாருமான இந்த யிம்மூவரும் பெத்-
[23] தசமுத்திரமான எரிகட்டின குடிமக்கள்
[24] மூவ்வற்கும் எரிகிழ் நிங்கின நஞ்சை முக்க-
[25] ால் நிலமும் மூன்றுமாவும் சாச(ந)ம-
[26] ாக குடுத்தோம் மாசிவிபெத்திநாய-
[27] கநேன் எரியிங்கிழ் நிலம் ஓடவ[ர]-
[28] ய் அனுபவித்தும் [ஸ்ரீ]பண்டாரத்தில் ஸி-
[29] த்தவடேஸ்வரதேவர்[க்கு]ஸ்ரீமாநதுவும் ஊவ்-
[30] வெரி கட்டின குடிமகன் மு(வ்)வற்கு குடுத்த
[31] நிலமாநதுவும் ஆரொருமொருவர் விழ்ழ் வ-
[32] ண்ணினாருண்டாகில் ஆயிரங்குராற்பசுவை-
[33] வ கொன்ற பாபத்திலெ படுவார்கள்
[34] ஸாமாந்யோயந்தர்ம்மஸெ[து-]ந்ருபாணாம் காலெ-
[35] லெ காலெ பாலநியொ ஭வத்பி:[|*]ஸர்வ்வாநெ-
[36] தாந் ஭ாவிந: பார்த்திவெந்த்ராந் ஭ூயொ஭ூ-
[37] யொ யாசதெ ராமசந்த்ர:[||*] . . . . .

TRANSLATION.

Hail! Prosperity! In the month of Mási of the cyclic year Yuva which corresponded to the 38th year of the reign of the emperor of the three worlds, the glorious Kulóttungachóladéva, I, Másavipetti Náyaka the son of Véminappi Másivichchavindi Náyaka gave the tank named Peddasamudram to Sitthavaṭésvara (who resides) to the south of Ṣríparvata and also gave the sacred name of Sitthavaṭéṣvara to my son.

I, Másivipettináyaka, also gave to the three Veḷḷálas who dug the tank Peddasamudram, viz., . . . the son of Vágantiti Boyinḍar Maḷḷi Reḍḍiyár, possessing rights at Kirachchamálai in Sélanáḍu and Mannúr in Pottapináḍu, Tachchama Reḍḍi the son of . . . Reḍḍiyár Paṇma Reḍḍi and Návi Reḍḍi the son of Kondaru Boyinḍar Tórappa Reḍḍi possessing rights at Táḍivelai; to these three ryots who dug the tank Peddasamudram land measuring three-fourths of a 'ground' (nilam = véli) and three *má* in the wet lands remaining under the tank as a grant. I, Másivipetti Náyakkan (repeated in the text).

If there are any persons who cause obstacles to the grant of the proceeds of the lands under the tank being paid into the sacred treasury to be used as charity for the god Sittavatéṣvara, and to the enjoyment of the land given to the three ryots who dug the tank, they shall incur the sin of killing a thousand tawny cows.

[One imprecatory verse in Sanskrit.]

NOTE.—For another inscription of this hamlet see No. (76).

RAPUR (24). (A.D. 1538–39.)

[Griḍḍalúru. Telugu. Stone in middle of village. Incomplete.]

TRANSLATION.

May there be prosperity! Hail! While Ṣríman-Mahámaṇḍaléṣvara, Rája, Rája Paraméṣvara, Ṣrí Achyutadéva Mahárája was ruling the kingdom of the earth as conqueror of the cardinal points, on Sunday the 30th of the dark half of Pushya of the year Vilambi, corresponding to 1460 of the Ṣálivâhana Ṣaka era. . . . .

1. శుభమస్తు
2. స్వస్విశ్రీమన్మహా
3. మండలేశ్వరరాజ
4. రాజపరమేశ్వర శ్రీ
5. అచ్యుతదేవ మహారా
6. జులు ప్రిథివిరాజ్యం
7. దిగ్విజయంగానే ప
8. లేకాలమందు। శాలి
9. వాహన శకవర్షంబు
10. లు ౧౪౬౦ అగునేం
11. టి విళంబి సంవత్సర
12. పుష్య బ ౩౦ ఆ
13. ం దివారాము

* * * *

RAPUR (25). (A.D. 1638–39.)

[Griḍḍalûru. Telugu. From the same locality. Mostly illegible.]

TRANSLATION.

Hail! On the 5th of the bright fortnight of Márgaṣira of the year Bahudhánya, corresponding to 1560 of the illustrious, victorious and prosperous Ṣáliváhana Ṣaka era.

* * * *

1. స్వస్తిశ్రీజయాభ్యు
2. దయ శాలివాహ

3. న శకవర్షంబులు
4. ౧౫౬౦ ఆగునేటి బ
5. బహుధాన్య సంవత్సర
6. మార్గశిర శు ౫ లు
7. నాండు. . .
8. . . . .
9. . . . .
10. . . . .
11. . . . .

Rapur (26).

[Gundavólu. Telugu. Below tank bund to south of village. Beginning missing.]

Translation.

[Yangappa was pleased to present ?]

Therefore whether the *méra* grain of the tank is in the possession of the village *sandhátá*, or of the *amaradárs* (or the *amaradárs* [1]) or of the lessee, or whoever be the ruler, they should spend this *méra* grain on the tank work. If, not doing the work, any one enjoys the *méra* grain or if any one obstructs or removes this inscription, he will be considered to have given his honour to the *veṭṭi* of the village, or if the grain thus fixed is utilized by a *Voḍḍa*, he will be regarded as having given his wife to the *veṭṭi* of the village.

1. (యంగప్ప దశెయిచ్చునరం ?) [దయచేసి]
2. గనుక ఆగ్రామం సంధాతా

---

[1] Repeated in the text.

3. నవున్నా అమరగా నివశాన
4. వున్నా అమరగాని వశాన వు
5. న్నా యెఘోరయేలిన సుత్తశాని
6. వశానవున్నా చెర్వు మేరధాన్యం
7. చెర్వుకు పనిముఖం శేయించ్చ
8. గలవారు శేయించ్చక ఆదాన్యంయె (వ)
9. రు అనుభవించినాను యవరు ఆతే
10. పించ్చినాను యీా శాసనం యవ్వరుతీ
11. శి వేయించ్చినావాండు యీావూరివెట్టిరి-మా
12. నంయిచ్చివున్నటె యని నియిణంచ్చినధాన్యం
13. పట్టినవడ్డెవాడి ఆలిని యీా
14. వూరి యెట్టివానికి యిచ్చు
15. కున్నట్టే—

Rapur (27). (A.D. 1392–93.)

[Gundavólu. Telugu. From two stones near the calingula of the tank. Incomplete and partly unintelligible.]

Translation.

Hail! . . . of the year Ángírasa, corresponding to the year 1314 of the illustrious (Saka era).

* * * *

This edict was given to Gundapróli Bairu.

* * * *

(a) 1. స్వస్తి శ్రీ శ . . . .
2. షంబులు ౧౩౧౪ . .
3. ఆంగీరసంవత్సర .
4. . . .

(b) 5. గుండ గ్రోలిబై ఇ
6. రుకునిచ్చిన శాసనం
7. త్రోలంజెల్లి రెడ్డిపాలు
8. నేనవ పాలుమీ
9. ఇ పాలితేజ ము
10. ందలాను లంమ
11. రియాం దంనుస
12. హింగానువుం
13. డిబ్రముక .

* * * *

RAPUR (28). (A.D. 1638-39.)

[Guruváyapálem. Telugu. Near calingula of tank.]

TRANSLATION.

Hail! On the 2nd of the bright half of Chaitra of the year Bahudhánya, corresponding to the year 1560 of the illustrious, victorious and prosperous Sáliváhana Saka era Srímat Velugóti Venkatapati Náyaningáru issued this charitable edict for the tank at Guruváyapalli. The *méras* should be given at one *kuncha* for every *putti* of produce on all lands under the tank, on dry lands including *Dévadáya* and *Bráhmanádáya* lands. They should get the work done to the tank from the *méra* grain settled for the tank whether it is with the *sandhátá*, *amaragádu*, or the lessee of this village, whoever be the ruler. If, not doing the work, any one misappropriate the (*méra*) or if any one object to it, or if any *kápu* or *karnam* object to it, or if any one remove this inscription, he will be considered to have been born to the *vetti* of this village and to have given his wife to the *veṭṭi* of this village. Thus has the charitable edict been issued.

1. స్వస్తి శ్రీజయాభ్యుదయశాలివాహ
2. న శకవర్షంబులు ౧౫౬౦ అగునేటి బహు
3. ధాన్యసంవ్వత్సర చైత్ర శు ౨ లు శ్రీమతు
4. వెలుగోటి వెంకటపతి నాయనిం గారుగు
5. రువాయపల్లిం చెర్వుకు యిచ్చిన దరవ్మ
6. శాసనము చెర్వుక్రిందు వెలిధాన్యం దేవా
7. దాయబ్రాంహ్మణాదాయాలు నహా పుట్టి
8. ౧ కి ఖం ౦। లెఖను మేము యియ్యగలరు
9. యీ గ్రామం సంధాతానవుంన్నాను అ
10. మరగావశాన యేధార యేలిన గుత్తగాని
11. వశాన వుంన్నాను చెర్వుకు నిర్ణయమై
12. న మేరధాన్యం చెర్వుపనిముఖం శేయుంచే
13. ది పనిముఖాలు శేయించ్చక యవ్వరు అనుభ
14. వించినాను యవ్వరు ఆక్షేపించ్చినాను యే
15. కాంవుకరణం ఆక్షేపించ్చినాను యీ శాస
16. నం యవరు తీశివేశినాను వాండు యీవూరి
17. వెట్టివానిగ్రాంబుట్టినవాండే వాని ఆలిని యీవూరి
18. వెట్టివానికి యిచ్చినట్టె యిట్లని యిచ్చిన ధర్మ
19. శాసనం ॥

RAPUR (29).

[Inukurti. Telugu. On west bank of a ruined tank. Incomplete.]

TRANSLATION.

* * * *

They should do work to the tank. Whether the *méras* are with the *sandhátá* of this village, or with the *amaragáḍu*, or with the rulers, or with the lessee; if, not doing work to the tank and the channel, any one creates obstacles to (this charity), whatever *kápu* or *karnam* objects, or whoever removes this inscription, he will be considered (to have given his honour) to the *veṭṭi* of this village.

* * * *

1. చెర్వుపని ముఖంశేయించు
2. వారు యీగ్రామం సెందాతాన
3. వున్నాను అమరగాని వశాన వున్నా
4. యేధొరయేలినాను గుత్తగాని (వ) శాను
5. న్నాను చెర్వుపని ముఘంకాలువ వ
6. ని ముఘాలూ శేయించ్చక యెవ్వరు
7. ను వేపించ్చినాను యెవ్వరు ఆశిం
8. చ్చినాను యేకాంపుంగరణాం (ఆ
9. క్షే) పించ్చినాను యీశాసనం యె
10. వ్వరుతీసివేయించ్చినాను వాండు
11. యీపూరివెట్టివాని . .

* * * *

RAPUR (30). (A.D. 1638–39.)

TRANSLATION.

[Kalichéḍu. Telugu. On eastern tank bund.]

(Adoration be to), Ṣrí Sámbhaṣiva! Hail! On the 2nd of the bright fortnight of Chaitra of the year Bahudhánya, corresponding to 1560 of the illustrious, victorious and prosperous Ṣáliváhana Ṣaka era, Ṣrímat Veligóṭi Venkaṭapati Náyaningáru caused to be planted this charitable edict for the tank of Kalichéḍu. If the tank work be not done with the *méra* grain collected in the manner in which the *méras* of the various tanks were formerly collected, if any one obstruct, if the *sandháta* (village official), the *amarajádu*, the *kápu*, or the *karnam* receive this *méra* grain of the tank and do not get work done to this tank and thus misappropriate it, he will be considered to have given his (wife's) honour to the *vetti* Boddivádu.

1. శ్రీ సాంబ్బశివా స్వస్తిశ్రీ జయాబ్ధియు శాలివా
2. హన శకవర్షంబులు ౧౫౬౦ అగు నేంటి బహుధా
3. న్య సంవత్సర చైత్ర శు ౨ లు శ్రీమతు వెలిగోటివెంకట
4. పతినాయ్యంగారు కలిఛెట చెర్వ్వకు వెళించ్చిన ధర్మశాస
5. నం యి యేగ్రామాల చెర్వ్వమేర పూర్వ్వాన ఎదారిగా న
6. డ్చినదో ఆమేర ధాన్యం చెర్వ్వవనిముఖం శేయించ్చక
7. కీడు ఆచరించ్చినా సంద్దాతానవుంన్నా యే అమరగాడు
8. గాని కాంపుగాని కరణంగాని చెరువుమ్యేరకునియీచె
9. ర్వ్వమేరధాన్యం యీచెరువువని సేయించ్చక ఆత్మేపించి

అను

10. భవించిన యీవ్వారి వెట్టిబొడ్డువానికి మానంయిచ్చి.

[న]

Rapur (31).

[Kalichédu. Telugu. On north bund of tank. Incomplete.]

Translation.

* * * *

We have endowed. May you, your sons and grandsons enjoy this as long as the sun and moon endure.

[One imprecatory verse.]

If any one obstructs this charity, he will incur the sin of killing a cow and a Brahman near the Ganges.

* * * *

1. రాపూ గరిగా న . . . .
2. స్య పెట్టితిమి మీపుత్ర పౌత్రా
3. ఖి వృద్ధిగాను ఆచంద్రార్కముగాను
4. అనుభవించి బ్రతుకువారు। స్వదత్తా
5. ద్విగుణం పుణ్యం పరదత్తానుపాలనం పర
6. దత్తాపహారేణ స్వదత్త నిష్ఫలం భవేత్।
7. యీపుణ్యం యెవ్వరు తప్పినాను గంగకర్త
8. గో బ్రాంహ్మనిం జంపిన పాపానం బోదురు.

Rapur (32).

[Kanuparti. Telugu. North of village near Ṣiva temple.]

Translation.

On the 15th of the full moon day of the bright half of the month of Áshádha of the year Khara, corresponding to . . . . The southern sluice was constructed . . . Fields measuring 100 *kunṭas* . . . .

1. . . . .
2. నేడు ఖ
3. రసంవర
4. ముసు ఆ
5. శాడమాస
6. ముసు సు ౧౫
7. రిపౌన్నానాడు
8. కతువానా
9. . . . .
10. . . . .

1. . . . .
2. . . . .
3. . మా .
4. . బో .
5. . ప .
6. . ను మాడు
7. . హం అ(శ్రీ
8. మతు దక్షను
9. చినతూము .
10. తూముకట్టినది . .
11. రుపాజానకు హం?.).
12. రచెను ౧౦౦ ఖం
13. టబు (విజరావు
14. . . . .

RAPUR (33). (A.D. 1629–30 ?)

[Kanuparti. Telugu. East of village in survey No. 129.]

TRANSLATION.

Hail! On the 3rd day of the bright fortnight of Kártika in the year Ṣuklá, corresponding to the year 1558 [1] of the illustrious and prosperous Ṣáliváhana Ṣaka era, the edict issued by Ákula Peda Veṇgana, the minister (*Mudrakarta*) of Ṣrí Velugóṭi Venkaṭapati Náyanivâru in respect of the *méra* due for the tank of Kanuparti (is as follows):—If the graiu payable at a *kuncha* per *puṭṭi* on the produce from the dry and wet lands of this village be not utilized for the improvement of the tank bund but be appropriated by the village officers, they will incur the sin

---

[1] The years do not correspond.

of killing their parents in Benares. They will incur the sin of killing cows and Brahmans near the Ganges. (They will incur the sin of one) who kills his teacher . . . . Whoever fails (in this) . . . . will be regarded as having sucked the yard of a donkey.

Note.—This *mudrakarta* was perhaps the father of the *kiryakarta* mentioned in N. 9, 110 and 115.

1. స్వస్తి శ్రీ విజయా
2. భ్యుదయ శాలివా
3. హన శకవర్షంబులు ౧౫౫౧ అ
4. గు నేటి శుక్ల సంవత్సర కార్తీక
5. శుద్ధ 3 లు శ్రీమతు వెలుగోటి వెంకట
6. పతినాయని ముద్రకర్త ఆ
7. కుల పెదవెంగనకానుపర్తి చెరువు మే
8. రకు వేయించ్చిన ధర్మశాసనం యీా
9. వూరి వెలి పాలం వరమళ్లను వచ్చిన
10. పుట్టి కుంచాల ధాన్యం చెరువుకు
11. కట్ట మీందను వేయించక గ్రామ
12. ం పాలివారు యవ్వరు అనుభవిం
13. చ్చినాను వారణాశిలోను తల్లి
14. దండ్రాజుల వధియించిన పాపా
15. న బోదురు.
16. గంగకర్తగో బ్రాంహ్మల
17. చంపిన పాపానం బో
18. దురు గురువును చ
19. ంప్పినవాండు . .
20. ప్ప . . . . దప్పిన
21. వాండు గాడిద శిశ్నం
22. కుడిచినవాండె.

Rapur (34). (A.D. 1638-39 ?)

[Kompéḍu or Kommipáḍu. Telugu. From bund of tank to west of village.]

Translation.

Hail ! . . . , . corresponding to the year 1560 of the illustrious, victorious and prosperous Ṣáliváhana Ṣaka era Velugóṭi Venkaṭapati Náyaningáru granted this charitable edict for the village Kommi. The *méras* of the tank of this village should be collected on all the tank-fed lands, on *mányas*, on *Dévádáya* [1] and *Brahmádáya* [2] *mányas* and on fields under the pond of Dárabandapáḍu at one *kuncha* on every *puṭṭi*, and on dry lands and *mányas* at one *kuncha* on every *puṭṭi*. With the grain thus realized, they should do work to the tank. Whether the *méras* of the village are with the village *sandhátá* or *amaradár* or whoever be the ruler or whether they are with the lessee, the grain should be spent by the *kápu* or *karnam* on doing work to the tank and the irrigation channel.

1. స్వస్తిశ్రీ జయాభ్యుదయ (శాలివాహన)
2. శకవర్షంబులు ౧౫౬౦ అగునేటి . .
3. . . . . . .
4. వెలుగోటి వెంకటపతి నాయనింగారు కొ
5. మ్మిగ్రామానికి యిచ్చిన ధర్మశాసనం యీగ్రా
6. మాన చెర్వుమేర చెర్వుక్రింద్ధు (స్థాళాయ)
7. భూములునున్న మాన్యాలకు దేవాదాయ బ్రం
8. హ్మాదాయ మాన్యానకు ధారబంద్ధపుపాడి నుం
9. ట చెలు ఖ ౬౦। లెఖ వెలిపొలానకు మాన్యాల

[1] Dévadáya land = land given to a temple.

[2] Bráhmadáya land = land given to Brahmans.

10. మీది ధాన్యం ఖ ౧ కి ౯ ౦ । లెఖను యీవచ్చిన దా
11. న్యాలు చెర్వుపని ముఖాలు చేయించువారు
12. యీ గ్రామ సంధాతాన అమరగానివశాన యేదొర
13. యేలినా గుత్తగానివశాన వున్నా యేకాంపు కర
14. ణమైన మేరధాన్యం చెర్వు పనిముఖాలు
15. కాలువ పనిముఖాలు చే
16. (యించువారు). . . .

Rapur (35). (A.D. 1634—35 ?)

[Kompéḍu. Telugu. To the south of the village. Illegible in parts.]

Translation.

Hail! On the 15th of the bright half of Mágha of the year Tárana,[1] corresponding to the year [1] 1556 of the illustrious, victorious and prosperous Ṣáliváhana Ṣaka era, while Ṣrímat Rájádhirája, Paraméṣvara, Ṣrí Víra Pratápa, Ṣrí Venkaṭapati Ráya Déva Maháráyalu, seated on the diamond throne in the city of Penugoṇḍa of the Karnáṭa kingdom, was ruling the kingdom of the earth, Lakshmappa Náyanimgáru, son of Sári Lakshmi Ṣrí Náyanimgáru of Udayagiri, the *karnam*, *kápus* and *vuḍḍas* . .

* * * *

(Illegible.)

1. స్వస్తి శ్రీ జయాభ్యుదయ
2. శాలివాహన శకవరుషంబులు

---

[1] The dates do not correspond. If Tárana is right, the date will be A.D. 1644-45. If not, it is probably A.D. 1634-35.

3. ౧౫౫౬ అగునేంటి తారణసంవత్సర మా
4. ఘ శు ౧౫ శ్రీమద్రాజాధిరాజ పరమే
5. శ్వర శ్రీవీరప్రతాప శ్రీవెంకటపతిరాయ
6. దేవమహారాయులవారు కర్ణాటక మ
7. ందు పెనుకొండ పట్ణమందు వజ్రశింహ్మా
8. సనారూడులై పృథివి సాంబ్రాజ్యం చే
9. యుచునుం పుండగాను సారి లక్ష్మప్ప నా
10. యనింగారి పుత్రులైన లక్ష్మప్ప నా
11. యనింగారు కరణం కాంపులు వొడ్డ
12. . . . దికా సతశివాజ
13. . . . . . పాపిరెడ్డి కలు
14. . . . . . వరిమడి పొల
15. . . . . ను నన వకటిహా
16. . . . . లిర మానా
17. . . . అమ . . ఐన పుద
18. . . . . జ్యానం లోకా
19. . . . . డు నరకం ఇ
20. పుడుగా.

RAPUR (36). (A.D. 1217-18 ?)

[Kompédu. Telugu. From a high stone near a ruined temple.]

TRANSLATION.

Hail! On Monday the 5th of the bright half of Pushya corresponding to the Ṣaka year 1139, Kónangi Siddapa Ṇáyaka, the brother-in-law of Bairava Náyaḍu, who was the feudatory and door-keeper of Víra Nalla Siddanadéva Chóḍa Mahárája, on whose lotus feet the eyes of all kings of the earth, Trilóchana and others, are set, who is the jewelled lamp of the race of Karikála by whom the dam [1] of the Kávéri was built, who is Kumárá *Sámanta* [2] (?); who is Ṣríman Mahámandaléṣvara . . Goppara, (?), who is strong of arm, and Siddapa Náyaka, son of Kámi Náyaka, on the occasion of Uttaráyana Sankránti, set up the images of Ishṭa Káméṣvaradéva, Nágéṣvaradéva and Mallikárjunadéva at Bommini in Ṣrí Pákinádu, constructed temples for them so as to resemble a hill of three peaks, and *maṇḍapas*, and to the north near the temples (constructed a temple) to Chennakéṣava, for the religious merit of their parents and Bairava Náyaka.

1. స్వస్తి శకవ
2. ర్షంబులు
3. ౧౧౩౯ వ నే
4. ంటి పోష్య శుక్ల
5. పంచమియు
6. సోమవారము
7. ను స్వస్తి చరణసరో
8. రుహా విహాత వి
9. లోచన త్రిలోచ
10. న ప్రముఖాఖిల
11. కారిత కావేరీతీర
12. కరికాలకులరత్న
13. ప్రదీపకుమారా

---

[1] The allusion is perhaps to the "Grand Anikat" of the Kávéri. This ancient work, the largest surviving example of native engineering, is ascribed by tradition to the second century A.D., but is probably later. Enlarged and strengthened by Sir Arthur Cotton, it is still doing its duty.

[2] Sámanta = feudatory.

14. సామంత శ్రీమన్మహా
15. మండలేశ్వర
16. . . గొప్పరో
17. . . భుజ
18. బల వీరసల్ల
19. సిద్ధన దేవచోడ
20. మహారాజులకు
21. ప్రీతిహార సా
22. మంత పదాత్తం
23. బు వడసిన
24. భైరవనాయ
25. కుని బావకో
26. సంగి సిద్ధన నా
27. యుడు కాఱి
28. నాయకు కొడుకు
29. సిద్ధప నాయకు
30. డు యుత్తరాయణ
31. సంక్రాంతినిమి
32. త్తమున తమ
33. తల్లి దండ్రుల
34. కు భైరవ నా
35. యకునికిని ధ
36. ర్మువుగా శ్రీ
37. పాంక నాంటిలో
38. ని బొమ్మి ని యిష్ట
39. కామేదేశ్వర దేవరా
40. ను నాగేశ్వరదే
41. వరాను మల్లి
42. కాఱాన దేవ

43. రాను ప్రతిష్ఠిం
44. చి త్రికూట
45. ంబుగా గుడ్లె
46. త్తించి మండ
47. పంబు గట్టిం
48. చ్చి యీ గుడ్ల
49. సమీపంబు
50. న ను త్తరమున
51. చెన్న కేశవ.

RAPUR (37).

[Kóṭúrupalli shrotriem. Telugu. From a stone two miles to the east of the village. Incomplete.]

TRANSLATION.

Hail! Nárapa Ṣáhiṇi Bhímanáyakunḍu, who is the worshipper of the lotus feet of Hail! Ṣríman Mahámandaléṣvara Erra Siddhi Chóḍa Maháraja, on whose (Erra Siddhi's) lotus feet are set the eyes of Trilóchana and all other kings of the earth, who (Erra Siddhi) is the jewelled lamp of the race of Karikála by whom (Karikála) the dam of the Kávéri was built, who (Erra Siddhi) is of unlimited valour, who is a constant worshipper of the consort of Lakshmi, who is the lord of the excellent town of Orayúr, who is a Jayanta to very charming ladies, who is the beloved of the goddess of victory, who is the lord of Kánchi the best of cities, who is styled Trinétra, who is of the Kásyapa *gótra*, and who is possessed of all praiseworthy attributes consisting of various titles, such as *Ayyana Singa*,[1] and *Sáhasóttunga*,[2]—who (Bhíma Náyaka) is adorned with numerous virtues, a hero in vanquishing enemies, who is a Vikramáditya in liberality, who is Prasta áditya (?), who is like Indra in prosperity, who is the lord of the excellent town of Alatúr . . . (?), who is the worshipper of the lotus feet of Ṣríkarakanṭhadéva, presented . . . . to his preceptor Ṣríkarakanṭha Késayyangáru, who (Késayyangáru) is the servant and worshipper of the lotus feet of Karakanṭhadéva, who (Karakanṭhadéva) is the cause of the origin, preservation and destruction of the whole universe, whose splendour is that of innumerable crores of suns, who transcends the Véda, who is able to punish and to protect the host of all the gods, whose ornament is the digit of the moon, and who is the lord of the three worlds, who (Késayyangáru) is the worshipper of the Creator of the world who (the Creator) is revered by Bhuvarlóka, the hosts of gods and all the worlds (?), hail! who (Kesayyangáru) is endowed with all praiseworthy attributes, who is devoted to *yóga* consisting of the group of the eight[3] spiritual powers *yama*, *niyama*, *ásana*, *dhyána*, *dhárana*, *pránáyáma*, *pratyáhára* and *samádhi* and who practises the vow of fasting and who is the chief of *yógis* (sages) . . . .

---

[1] Ayyana Singa = lion of his father.

[2] Sáhasóttunga = eminent in valour.

[3] Yóga = ecstatic union with the Divine Being.
Yama = paramount duty; obligatory morality.
Niyama = occasional or minor duty.
Ásana =
Dhyána = deep meditation.
Dhárana = mental concentration.
Pránáyáma = holding of the breath.
Pratyáhára = Abstention from the objects of the senses.
Samádhi = final stage of yoga practice—profound ecstatic meditation.

1. స్వస్తి సమస్త భువనఉ
2. త్పత్తిస్థితిలయకారణ
3. స్వరూపుండునుం అన
4. ంతకోటిసూర్యప్ర
5. భావేదయతీతస్వరూ
6. పుండును సకలదేవ
7. నికురుంబవిగ్రహా
8. నుగ్రహసమర్థుం
9. డునుం చంద్రకళా
10. వతారు[1]ం డును త్రిలో
11. కనాథుండునైన కలి
12. కంఠదేవ భ్రిత్యులు
13. (జగత్కర్త్తలాడిన భూ
14. వర్లోకముదేవగ
15. ణంబుల సర్వలోక
16. ము) మహాసనాంబు
17. జపాదారాధకుండు
18. స్వస్తి సమస్త ప్రశస్తిసహి
19. తం యమనియమా
20. సనధ్యానదారణప్రా
21. ణాయామప్రత్యాహా
22. రసమాధియాష్టవ
23. గయోగనిరతుండు
24. ను నిరాహారనియ
25. మాన్వితుండును వ
26. రమయోగీంద్రుండు
27. నుంనైన శ్రీకర
28. కంటకేనయ్యగారికి

[1] తంను.

29. స్వస్తి చరణసరోరు
30. హావిహాత[1]విలోచన
31. త్రిలోచనప్రముఖా
32. ఖిలశ్రీప్రిథ్వీశ్వరకా
33. రితకావేరితీరకరికా
34. లకులరత్నప్రదీప అప
35. రిమితప్రతాపసతత
36. సమభ్యర్చిత లక్ష్మీశ్వ
37. రయోరాఅయూరిష్వకవా
38. రాక్షీశ్వర అతిచతురకా
39. మినీజనజయంత విజ
40. యలక్ష్మీకాంత కాంచీపుర
41. వరాధీశ్వర త్రిణేత్రకాస్యప
42. గోత్ర అయ్యనసింగ సాహ
43. సోత్తుంగ నామాది సమ
44. స్తప్రసస్తిసహితం శ్రీమ
45. న్మహామండలేశ్వర ఎఱ్ఱ
46. సిద్ధిచోడమహారాజు
47. లపాదపద్మారాధకులై
48. న స్వస్తి సమస్తప్రశస్తిస
49. హితం అనేకగుణవిభూ
50. షణరిపువిదారణ వీ
51. ర. వితరణ విక్రమాది
52. త్యప్రస్త అదిత్యవిభ
53. వామరేశ్వర అలతూ
54. రిపురవరాధీశ్వర (అ
55. తివెంటి అడుదు) శ్రీ

---

[1] Read విహిత.

56. కఱకంటదేవరపత్రా
57. రాఘకుంఢైన నారవ
58. సాహిణి భీమినాయ
59. కుండు తమ గురు
60. వు కఱకంటకేస
61. య్యంగారికి రాజ్యం

* * * *

Rapur (38).

[Linganapálem. Tamil. To the south.]

[1] திரிபுவனச்சக்கரவ-
[2] த்திகள் ஸ்ரீராஜ-
[3] ராஜதெவர்க்-
[4] கு யாண்டு எட்டா-
[5] வது ஜயங்கெ-
[6] ாண்டசொழம-
[7] ண்டலத்துப்ப-
[8] ாக்கைநாட்டு
[9] நெல்லூரான விக்கி-
[10] ரமசிங்புரத்து ம-
[11] துராந்தகப்பொத்த-
[12] ப்பிச்சொழ எறசித்த-
[13] ரசர் மக்திரி படியாரி பயி-
[14] ரப்ப நாயக்கரும் திக்கந-
[15] ாயக்கனும் இவர்கள் த-
[16] மையனூர் குசனி நாயக்-
[17] கனும் துக்கிநாயக்க-
[18] னல் எடுத்து பொவிசை
[19] [பூ]ட்டில் பூசல் துக்கி பட-
[20] க்கனுக்கும் துக்கி நாயக்க

[21] எரிகாகி நாயக்கர் மக-
[22] பநாயகனென் எது-
[23] மார் மூவற்குந்தனி இத்-
[24] தெவற்கு இட்ட திருநன்-
[25] [ஒன்றுக்கு] . . .
[26] [இக்கொயில்] . . .

* * * *

TRANSLATION.

In the eighth year of the reign of the emperor of the three worlds the glorious Rájarájadéva, the servants (paḍiyári) of the minister of Madurántaka Pottapi Chóḻa *alias* Erra Sittarasan of Vikkiramaṣiṅgapura *alias* Nellúr in Pákainádu (a sub-division of) Jayankonḍachóḻa Manḍala, Bayirappa Náyakka and Tikka Náyakka and their elder brother Kusaṇi Náyakka, these three, with the sum of money deposited for interest by Tukki Náyakka (portion not clear) . . . . presented a sacred lamp to this deity . . . .

RAPUR (39). (A.D. 1243–44?)

[Marupur. Tamil. By the little tank.]

[1] ஸ்வஸ்தி ஸ்ரீ ஸ-ஹம் ச
[2] க(ல)வஷ-ம் ஆயிர-
[3] த்தொரு [நூற்று]-
[4] அறுபத்தைஞ்-
[5] சாம் வருஷத்தி-
[6] ல் உத்திராயண-
[7] த்திலெ வைஸா-
[8] வவ-ஸ்லவக்ஷத்தி-
[9] லெ ஸ்ரீமன்மஹா-

[10] மண்டலெஸ்வரன் ம-
[11] துராந்தகப்பொத்-
[12] தப்பிசொழ[நார]
[13] திலகநாராயணன் [ம]னு-
[14] மசித்தரசு ம[ஹா]-
[15] ராஜ்யத்திலெ ஸ்ரீக-
[16] ண்டசெட்டி கு-

TRANSLATION.

Hail! Prosperity! In the auspicious Ṣaka year one thousand one hundred and sixty-five, in the bright half of the month of Vaisákha while the sun was in its northern course, Ṣríkaṇṭha Cheṭṭi (residing) in the great kingdom of Ṣríman Mahámanḍaléṣvara Madurántaka Pottapi Chóḻa *alias* Tilakanáráyana *alias* Manumasidharaṣa . . . .

RAPUR (40). (A.D. 1638–39.)

[Marupur. Telugu. On the big tank bund.]

TRANSLATION.

Hail! On the 2nd of the bright fortnight of Chaitra of the year Bahudhánya, corresponding to 1560 of the illustrious, victorious and prosperous Ṣáliváhana Ṣaka era, Velugóṭi Venkaṭapati Náyanivάru issued this charitable edict for the tank of Marupúr. The *sandhátá*, lessee, *amaradár*, or the ruler of the village should get the tank and channel work done with the *méras* settled on the tank. If, not doing the work, the *kápu* and *karnam* obstruct the charity, or if any one misappropriate this *méra* grain, or remove this inscription, the *veṭṭi* will ravish his wife.

1. స్వస్తి శ్రీ విజయాభ్యుద
2. యశాలివాహాన శకవర్ష
3. ంబులు ౧౪౯౭ అగునేటి బ
4. హుధాన్య సంవత్సర చైత్ర
5. శు ౨ లు వెలుగోటి వెంక
6. టపతినాయనింవారు మరు
7. పూరిచెర్వుకు ఇచ్చిన ధర్మశాస
8. నం గ్రామసంధాతం గుత్త అ
9. మరంయేలిన నిర్ణయమై
10. నచెర్వు మేరచెర్వు కాల్వ
11. నివశేషం బేది శేషంచక
12. కాంపుకరణంలు భేదంచేశినా
13. ఈ మేరదాన్యం యవ్వరైనను
14. [1]అరించిన శాసనం తిశివేశినా
15. వాండి ఆల్ని వెట్టివాండు
16. (దెంగుదురు)

RAPUR (41). (A.D. 1575-76.)

[Mogallúru. Telugu. In the middle of the village.]

TRANSLATION.

Adoration to Srí Ráma!

Hail! On Thursday the 10th of the dark fortnight of Vaisákha of the year Yuva, corresponding to 1497 of the illustrious, victorious and prosperous Ṣáliváhana Ṣaka era, while Ṣrímad Rájádhirája, Rájaparaméṣvara, Ṣrí Vírapratápa, Ṣrí Víra Ṣrí Rangaráyadéva Maháráya, seated on the jewelled throne of Penugoṇḍa, was ruling, we have set up the image of Chennakésavaráya in the village of Mogaḷúru granted as an *amaram* by Prattikonda

---

[1] హరించిన.

Timmarája in the *síma* of Udayagiri, and presented to this deity for providing food to the deity a paddy field of 10 *túms* under the big *anikat*, two *túms* of dry land in the field of Bellamkoṇḍa Vengalayya, and two *gorrus* of saline land belonging to Póla Gangayya. Therefore, if any one, not maintaining (the charity) obstruct this *mányam*, he will incur the sin of killing a cow and a Brahman on the Ganges. For this purpose has this charitable edict been granted.

May it cause prosperity !

(1) శ్రీమతే రామా
(2) స్వస్తిశ్రీ జాయాభ్యు
(3) దయ శాలివాహన శక
(4) వర్షంబ్బు ౧౪౯౭ అగునే
(5) ంటి యువ సంవత్సర వైశాఖ బ
(6) ౧౦ గురు వారాన అగునట్టి శ్రీ
(7) మద్రాజాధిరాజరాజ పరమేశ్వర
(8) శ్రీ వీరప్రతాప శ్రీ వీరశ్రీరంగ్గరా
(9) యదేవ మహారాయలయ్యవారు పె
(10) నుంగొండను రత్నసింహ్వాసనా రూఢులై
(11) రాజ్యం సేయుచుండ్డి ప్రత్తికొండ్డ తిమ్మరాజయ్యవారు
(12) వుదయగిరి సీమను అమరంపాలించ్చిన మొగళ్ళూరి గ్రా
(13) మానచంన్న కేశ్వర రాయన్ని ప్రతిష్ట సేఇంచ్చి దేవుని పళ్ళి
గలు
(14) వరిచేనిడి పెద్ధ అనకిందను చోడెవంద్దుము వరి
(15) మడిన్ని వెలిపొలం బెల్లంకొండ్డ వెంగ్గళయ్య చే
(16) నిస్త్రళం రెండ్డుగొర్లున్ను చవనేల పోలగంగ్గయ
(17) చేను రెండ్డుగొర్లున్ను యిస్తిమి గనక యీ
(18) మాన్యము నడుపక ఎవ్వరుతప్పినాను గ

(19) ంగ కర్తాం గోబ్రాహ్మణ్ని జంపిచ్చిన పాపానం
(20) బోవువారు యుందుకని నిల్పిన ధర్మశాసనం
(21) శ్రీ శ్రీం జేయును.

Rapur (42).

[Mogallúru. Telugu. From the same locality.]

Translation.

If any one, not doing work to the tank, enjoys the *méra* grain attached to the tank, he will incur the sin of killing a cow and a Brahman on the Ganges. Ṣrí!

(1) చెర్వు మేర ధాన్యం యవరు
(2) చెర్వుమీద వేయక అను
(3) భవించినాను గంగ్గ క
(4) త్తర గోబ్రాంహ్మణ్ని వ
(5) ధించ్చిన పాపాన
(6) బోదురు శ్రీ

Rapur (43). (A.D. 1638-39.)

[Mogallúru. Telugu. On tank bund to east of village.]

Translation.

Hail! On the 2nd day of the bright half of Vaisagha of the year Bahudhánya, corresponding to the year 1560 of the illustrious, victorious and prosperous Ṣáliváhana Ṣaka era, Ṣrímat Velugóṭi Venkaṭapati Náyanimgáru issued this charitable edict for the tank of Mógallúru. The tank work should be done with the *méra* grain collected at one *kuncha* for every *puṭṭi* on all lands including *Dévadáya* and *Brahmadáya* lands. Whether the village be under *Sandhátá* or in the hands of an koṇḍa

Amaragáḍu or of a lessee or whoever be the ruler, the tank work should be done with the *méra* grain settled for the tank. If, not doing the work, any one misappropriate it or object to it, or if any *kápu* or *karnam* object to it, or if any one remove this inscription, he will be considered to have been born to the *veṭṭi* of this village, and to have given his wife to the *veṭṭi* of this village. Thus has this charitable edict been issued.

1. స్వస్తి శ్రీ జయాభ్యుదయ శాలివాహన శకవ
2. ర్షంబ్బులు ౧౫౬౦ అగు నేటి బహుధాన్య సంవత్సర వైశా
3. ఖ శు ౨ లు శ్రీమతు వెలుగోటి వెంకటపతి నాయనింగారు
4. మోగల్లూరి చెరువుకు యిచ్చిన దామర్శాసనం చె
5. రువు మేరదాన్యం వు ఖ ౧ కి ౦౦। లెఖను దేవాదాయ
6. బ్రాహ్మోదాయాలు మోదలుంగాను వచ్చిన ధా
7. న్యం చెరువుపని ముఖం శేయించ్చగలవారు యిగ్రా
8. మం సంధాతాన వున్నాను అమరగాని వశాన యే
9. ధొర యేలినాను గుత్తగానివశానవున్నాను చెరువుకు
10. నిర్ణయమైన మేరధాన్యం చెరువుపని ముఖం శే
11. తురీపని ముఖంలు శేయించ్చక యవ్వరు అనుభవించినాను
యె
12. వ్వరు ఆత్షేపించ్చినాను యే కాంపు కరణం ఆక్షేపించ్చి
నాను
13. యీ శాసనం యవరు తీసివేశినాను వాండు యీ వూరి
వెట్టి
14. వానికిం బుట్టినవాండ్లు వాని ఆలిని యీ వూరి వెట్టి
15. వానికిం యిచ్చుకున్నవాడి యిటని యిచ్చిన ధ
16. మశాసనం॥

RAPUR (44).

[Muḍigóḍu. Telugu. Opposite the temple of the village goddess.]

TRANSLATION.

If any one removes this inscription, he will be considered to have been born to the *veṭṭi* of this village and to have given his wife to the *veṭṭi* of this village. In these terms has this charitable edict been issued.

1. యీ శాసనం యెవరు తీ
2. శివేశినాను వాండు యీ
3. వూరి వెట్టివానికి బుట్టిన వాం
4. డి అని ఆలిని ఇవూరి వెట్టి
5. వానికి ఇచ్చు కుంన వాండ
6. ని వేయించ్చిన ధర్మ
7. శాసనం.

RAPUR (45).

[Nandiváya. There is said to be an inscription here which is entirely defaced.]

RAPUR (46).

[Nernúru. Telugu. Opposite to the Désamma temple, three miles from the village.]

TRANSLATION.

This is the charitable edict issued by Ku. . palli Naragayya to Ṣrímat . . Vurti Késa(va) déva. For providing offerings and worship with light to the deity (he presented) a *mánya* in Nirayaniḍi in Rápúr *Ṣíma* in Udayagiri which is ruled by [1] M. R. Koṇḍamarasa(yya) váru.

(1) [శ్రీ వణరి]
(2) శ్రీమతు . .
(3) వుత్ర్రి కేశ (వ)
(4) దేవునికి కు . '
(5) వల్లినరగయ
(6) గారు యిచ్చి (న)
(7) ధర్మ్మశాసనము (సా)
(8) మి నైవేద్య దీపా
(9) రాధనలకు మ.రా.
(10) కొండమరుస (య్య)
(11) వారు వుదయగిరి
(12) ంబాలించ్చిన రా
(13) పూరి శీమలో
(14) ని అయనిడిలో
(15) మానపాలము.

Rapur (47). (A.D. 1211–12?)

[Pálicherlapáḍu. Telugu. From four sides of a stone on the tank bund in front of the Siva temple.]

Translation.

Hail! On Monday the day of Dhanishta nakshatra, the 7th of the dark fortnight of Márgaṣira, corresponding to the Ṣaka year 1133.

Dámi Náyakuḍu, son of Taláṛa Denimija Náyakuḍu, and the righteous wife of this Dámi Náyakuḍu Ṣrímati

---

[1] M.R. = Mahárája.

Pótasáni built a temple to Srímat Bhujabala Mallikárjuna Mahádéva in Pálachélam situated in Chedupúlinádu (?) . . . . for the religious merit of Víra Tikkakálatidéva Chóḍa Mahárája, on whose lotus feet the eyes of all the kings of the earth, Trilóchana and others, are set, who is the jewelled lamp of the race of Karikála by whom the dam of the Kávéri was made, who is of unlimited valour, who is always revered by his feudatories, who is the lord of the best of cities Orayúr, who is of the Káṣyapa *gótra*, who is a Jayanta to very charming ladies, who is a Revanta[1] with horses, who is a Vikramáditya in the pastime of liberality, who is a powerful sun to the enemy Ténjanáditya,[2] who is Jagadobbagaṇḍa, who is an Indra to the mountains, to wit, the host of proud and hostile kings, who is a fortress of adamant to his refugees, who is the lord of Kánchi the best of cities, the scatterer in all directions of rival feudatories, who is Kírti Náráyaṇa, and who is strong-armed . . . . and presented for (providing) oblation, offering and worship to this deity 50 *kuṇṭas* of wet land in the southern quarter of our village, 20 *paṭṭus* under our tank, dry land 25 for the enjoyment of the deity, for dancers 5, for the drummer 1, for the *lávadondu* (musician ?) 1, for the *pátra* (dancing girl) 1, for the blower of the conch 1, for the gardener 1, and for *piccha kavva* (?) 1 . . . . and 14 *vrittis* for Brahmans near Pandévati Erracheruvu of that village. We have given to these for enjoyment dry lands as follows :—

[Here comes a list of the shares.]

---

[1] Révanta—son of the sun (an expert rider).

[2] The reference to "Tenjanáditya" is not understood.

[One imprecatory verse.]

1. స్వస్తి (చ) రణ స
2. రోరుహ విహిత
3. విలోచనత్రిలో
4. చన ప్రముఖాఖి
5. ల ప్రిథ్వీశ్వరకారి
6. త కావేరితీరక
7. రి కాలకుల రత్న ప్ర
8. దీప అపరిమిత
9. ప్రతాప సతత సా
10. మంత్తార్పిత ఒటి
11. యూరి పురవరా
12. దీశ్వర కాశ్యపగోత్ర
13. అతిచతుర కామినీ
14. జనజయంత తుర
15. గ రేవంత వితరణ
16. వినోద విక్రమాది
17. త్య తేంజనాదిత్యరిపు
18. విపులమార్తాండజ
19. గదొర్బగండ గర్వతా
20. రాతి కుమారకుల కు
21. ధరకులిశధర శరణా
22. గత వజ్రపంజర కాం
23. చీపుర వరాధీశ్వరదా
24. యాదిమండలీకదిశా
25. స్పష్టి కీర్తినారాయణ
26. భుజబల వీరతికర్కా
27. లతిదేవ చోడమహా
28. రాజులకు ధర్మవు

29. గాను తలాఱిదేనిమి
30. జనాయకుని కొడుకు దామి
31. నాయకుండును యీ దామి
32. నాయకునికి ధర్మపత్ని
33. యైన శ్రీమతు పోతసాని
34. యును చెదుపులినాంటిలోని
35. పొలచేలమలందు శ్రీమతు
36. భుజబల మల్లికార్జున మ
37. హాదేవరకు గుడి యెత్తించ్చె
38. శకవర్షంబులు ౧౧౩౩
49. యగునేంటి మార్గశిర బ
30. హుల సప్తమిన్ని సోమవార
41. మున్ను ధనిష్ట నక్షత్రము నా
42. ండు యీ దేవరకు హావి బ
43. ల్యార్పనాదులకు మాయూం
44. రి దక్షిణదిగ్భాగంబునం
45. మ నీరిపొలమునకు వేభ
46. మూలన చెఱ్ఱువను ఇరువది
47. పట్టు ౨౦ వెలిచెను దేవభో
48. గమునకు పాఱిమోకరి అం
49. డువారు ౫ మద్యలిండు ౧
50. లావదొండు ౧ పాత్రె ౧ సం
51. కు వాండు ౧ తోంటవాండు ౧
52. పిచ్చకవ్వ ౧
53. ఆయూరి పండేవ
54. టి యజ్ఞం జెఱ్ఱువ బె
55. నిపట్టిం నారులోనుగాను
56. బదు నాల్వు ౧౪ బ్రా
57. హ్మణ క్షిత్తులు పిరి

58. కి వెలిచెను బొల్లపె
59. ద్దింగారికి చేను రెండు
60. పట్ల ౨ యార అప్పన
61. ంగారికి చేను రెండు
62. పట్టి ౨ మల్లి మలి
63. ంగారికి చేను రెండు
64. పట్టి ౨ అజాంనార
65. పెద్దికి చేనువట్టి ౧
66. కామయ దేవ భట్లకు చే
67. నుపట్టి౧ విస్తనూ చెంగా
68. రికి చేనువట్టి ౧ పిన్నపి
69. న్నకు చేనువట్టి ౧ నాగచే
70. వపెద్దింగారికి చేనవ
71. ట్టి ౧ మారమం జెంగారి
72. కి చేనువట్టి ౧ అర్ధి పె
73. ద్దింగారికి చేనుపట్టి ౧ వె
74. ని పెద్దింగారికి చేనుపట్టి ౧
75. కామదేవ మంచెంగారికి
76. నువట్టి ౧ కామంగారికి
77. చేనుపట్టి ౧
78. మడె అప్పనంగారికి
79. పద్దచెఱ్వు వెనక నీటి
80. నేల గు ౨౦౦ వెలి చేను మూ
81. ండుపట్లు ౩ బుద్దిమద్దు
82. నికి వెలిచేనువట్టి ౧ కేశ
83. భట్టనకు నీరినేలగు ౧౦౮
84. వేవి అప్పనంగారికి నీరినేలగు ౧౮౧
85. వెలిచేనుపట్లి ౩ నీరదరఌం వీరం
86. గారికినీరి వేలగు ౧౦౦ చెనుపట్లి

87. కొమ్మన పిన మద్దులకు వెలిచే
88. సుపట్టి ౧ గోవిందుని అనంకు వె
89. లిచేనుపట్టి ౧ కొడ్డు వ్రెపలయలకు
90. కన్నుమూరిద్దా . . కుంద్ర
91. కు వెలిచెనుపట్టి ౧ నిరిసేల గు ౬౦
92. సూరపగాజును దేవ గు ౨౦ అర
93. బండారి బ్రిత్తులకు వెలిచె
94. సు పట్టి ౧ దేవర
95. కు చేను . . .
96. నం . . . .
97. మ . . . అనుభవిం
98. చేట్ల ఇచ్చితిమి
99. స్వదత్తాం పరదత్తాం వా యో
100. హారేతి వసుంధరా షష్టి
101. వర్ష సహస్రాణి విష్టాయాం
102. జాయతే క్రిమి

RAPUR (48).

[Pallakoṇḍa. Telugu. Near Ankamma temple.]

TRANSLATION.

The charity given by (Hechu Savunaṭi) of Rápúr.

Hail! On . . . . of Chaitra . . . . . of the illustrious, victorious, and prosperous Ṣáliváhana Ṣaka era.

1. రాపూరి హె
2. చ్చు శౌన టి
3. . చ్చిన ధ

4. . ం . . . .
5. స్వస్తి శ్రీ జయాభ్యు
6. . య శాలివాహన .
7. . వర్షంబులు . .
8. . . నెంటి . .
9. . . చైత్ర . .
10. . . లు కాలము
11. . . . .
12. . మ . .
13. . . . .
14. . . . .

RAPUR (49). (A.D. 1638-39 ?)

[Penubarti. Telugu. Opposite the Ṣiva temple.]

TRANSLATION.

Hail! On this auspicious occasion, on Monday the 3rd of the dark fortnight of Adhika Śrávana of the year Bahudhánya[1], corresponding to the year [1]1559 of the illustrious, victorious and prosperous Ṣálivâhana Ṣaka era, there is an endowment to Udumésvara Svámi in the *sarvamánya agrahára* called Koḍḍavásili Banḍáru Penubarte, otherwise named Krishnaráya Samudra, in Udayagiri *Rájya*, in Nellore *vaṇita* (country ?), and in Rápur *ṣīma*. A quit-rent (béḍiga) of five [2]*máḍas* (?) is collected from the endowment of Uḍuméṣvara Svámi. Venkaṭáchalam, who is of the fourth caste, grandson of Voḍḍe Arjinéni, and son of Kónéṭayya, has remitted that (quit-rent of) five *máḍas* (?), saying it three times, with

---

[1] The dates do not correspond.

[2] Repeated in the text.

a pure mind [saying it, three times][1] for the religious merit of Arjanéni and Kónéṭayya. Therefore if any one think of obstructing this endowment and speak ill of it, he will incur the sin of killing cows and Brahmans near the Ganges. If any think of obstructing this, they will incur the sin of killing cows and Brahmans and that of causing abortion at Kási, Gaya, or Prayág.

[Three imprecatory verses.]

NOTE.—It is presumed that máḷu in the text is the plural of máḍa (=R. 2). The text is very involved and the meaning obscure. The term *vanita* does not seem to occur in any other inscription.

1. స్వస్తి శ్రీ విజయాభ్యుదయశాలి
2. వాహన శకవర్షంబులు ౧౫౫౯ అగు
3. నేంటి బహుధాన్య సంవత్సర అధిక। శ్రావ
4. ణ బ ౩ సోవారాన యీా పుణ్యకాలమం
5. ద్దు ఉదయగిరిరాజ్యం నెల్లూరి వణితంలోను రాపూరి
6. సీమలోను కొడ్డవాసిలిబండారు పెనుబరితి
7. ప్రతినామమ నేటి క్రిష్ణరాయసముద్ర
8. మనే అ సర్వమాన్య అగ్రహారమంద్దు వుడు
9. మేశ్వరస్వామికి నడిచె స్వాస్థ్యనఁచటు
10. ర్ధగోత్రులైన వొడ్డె అర్జునేనికి పౌత్రు
11. లైన కోనేటయ్యకు పుత్రులైన వెంకటాచ
12. లంగారు వుడుమీశ్వరస్వామి స్వాంస్థ్యా
13. ను బేడ్డి అయిడుమళు నడుస్తావుఁడ్డె గను
14. క ఆ అయిదుమాళున్ను అర్జునేండుకో
15. నేటయ్యగారికి పుణ్యంగాను త్రివాచి
16. కంగాను త్రిక[రు]ణసిద్ధిగాను త్రివాచికంగా
17. బేడిగ అయిదుమాళున్ను మానితిమిగన
18. క యీాస్వాస్థ్యానుకు యెవ్వడు అవరోధం దల

[1] Repeated in the text.

19. చి కీడోడి నాగానివాండ్లు గంగ్గకర్త గో
20. బ్రాహ్మని వధించిన పాపాన బోవువాండు ఖుం
21. దుకు యివ్వడు అవరోధం దలంచి నాశౌశిగయ
22. ప్రయాగమందు గోహత్య బ్రంహ్మ అత్య బ్రూణహ
23. త్య చేశిన పాపానబోవువాండు। స్వదత్తాం ప
24. రదత్తాం వా యో హరేతి వసుంధరా షష్టివర్ష
25. రుష సహస్రా (స్రా)ణి విష్టాయాం జాయతే క్రిమిః
26. దానపాలనయోర్మధ్యే దానాచ్ఛ్రేయోనుపాలనం దా
27. నాస్స్వర్గ మవాప్నోతి పాలనా దచ్యుత పదం॥ స్వ
28. దత్తాద్విగుణం పుణ్యం పరదత్తానుపాలనం ప
29. గదత్తాపహారేణ స్వదత్తం నిష్పలం భవేతు

Rapur (50). (A.D. 1638-39.)

[Penubarti. Telugu. From the tank bund.]

Translation.

Hail! On the 8th day of the bright fortnight of Chaitra of the year Bahudhánya, corresponding to the year 1560 of the illustrious, victorious and prosperous Ṣáliváhana Ṣaka era, Ṣrímat Velugóṭi Venkaṭapati Náyanigáru issued this charitable edict for the maintenance of tanks of the villages situated in the Rápur *ṣíma* (district). He has ordered that in the manner in which the *méras* of the tanks of the respective villages were formerly utilized, the said *méras* should be spent in repairing those tanks. Therefore, whether the village be under direct management (*sandhátá*), or be in the hands of an *amaradár* or a lessee, or whoever be the ruler, they should get the tanks repaired, with the *méras* settled for the tanks. From the *méras* settled for the tanks, the tank work should be maintained. If any person think of not utilizing these *méras* for the tank or if any object to do so or if any *kápu* or *karnam* object to do so or if any one remove this inscription, he will be considered to have been born of the *veṭṭi* of this village and he will be considered to have given his wife to the *veṭṭi* of this village. In these terms has the charitable edict been granted.

1. స్వస్తి శ్రీజయాభ్యుదయ శాలివాహన శకవర్షంబులు ౧౫౬౦ బ

2. హుదాన్య సంవత్సర చైత్రశు ౧ లు శ్రీమతు వెలుగోటి వెంకటపతినా

3. యనింగారు రాపూరిశీమలోని గ్రామాల చెర్వులకు యిచ్చి నధ

4. ర్మశాసనము యేయే గ్రామం చెర్వు మేరలు పూర్వాన యేదారిగా

5. ను నడ్చినవో ఆ మేర ధాన్యం చెర్వు బనిచేయంగట్ట

6. డ శెయించ్చినారుగనుక ఆ గ్రామానఁ ధాతానను అమర గాని వ

7. శాన వున్నాను యెథోర యెలినాను గుత్తగానివశాన వున్నాను

8. చెరువునకు నిర్ణయమైన మేరధాన్యంవల్ల పనిముఖం శెయించం

9. గలవారు చెరువుమేరలు ధాన్యంచెరువు పనిముఖంకిచ్చె వి ముఖాలు శేయిం

10. చ్చక యెవ్వరు అనుభవించినాను యెవ్వరు ఆక్షేపించినాను యే కాం

11. పుకరణం ఆక్షేపించినాను యీా శాసనం తీసివేయి

12. ంచినాను వాండు యీా వూరి వెట్టివానికిఁ బుట్టినవాం

13. డి వాని ఆలిని యీ వ్వూరి వెట్టివానికి యిచ్చికున్నట్టె
14. యిట[ట్లు]ని యిచ్చిన ధరుసంనం[ధర్మశాసనం]

RAPUR (51). (A.D. 1638-39.)

[Perumállapáḍu. Telugu. On four sides of a stone on tank bund.]

TRANSLATION.

Hail! On the 2nd day of the bright half of the year Bahudhánya, corresponding to the year 1560 of the illustrious, victorious and prosperous Ṣáliváhana Ṣaka era, Ṣrímat Velugóṭi Venkaṭapati Náyanimgáru issued this charitable edict for the tank at Perumállapáḍu. He has ordered that the *méra* grain levied on dry and wet fields including *Dévadáya* and *Brahmadáya* lands should be utilized for the tank of this village. Therefore, whether the village be under *sandhátá* or in the hands of an *amaragáḍu* . . . . If any one, not doing work to the tank, misappropriate it or if any object or if any *kápu* or *karnam* object, or if any one remove this stone inscription, he will be considered to have been born to the *veṭṭi* of this village, and to have given his wife to the *veṭṭi* of this village. Thus has this charitable edict been issued.

1. స్వస్తి శ్రీ జయాభ్యుదయ శాలివాహన
2. శకవర్షంబ్బులు ౧౫౬౦ అగునేటి బహుధాన్య స
3. ంవ్వత్సర చైత్ర శు ౨ లు శ్రీమతు వెలిగోటి వెంకట
4. పతి నాయనింగారు పెరుమాలపటి గ్రామానికి
5. చ్చిన ధర్మశాసనం యీ గ్రామాన చెర్వు మేరలు
6. మొదలయ్ను వెలిపాలాన్ని వారిమడి దేవ (బ్రాహ్మ)

7. మ్యనాలకు సహాను వచ్చిన ధాన్యం .
8. యీగ్రామం చెర్వుకు ఇయకట్టడశే (ఇచ్చినాము)
9. గనుక గ్రామం సంధాతాను వున్నాను
10. అమరగానివశాన వున్నాను . .
11. . . . . .
12. శాయ్య పనిముఖం శేఇం(చ)క యవరు అను
13. భవించినాను యవ్వరు అక్షేపించ్చినాము
14. యే కాంపుకరణం అక్షేపించ్చినాను
15. ఈ శాసనం యవ్వరు తీసివేసినాను వాండు
16. యీవూరి వెట్టివానికి బుట్టినవాండె
17. వాండి ఆలిని యీవూరి వెట్టివానికి
18. ఇచ్చుకున్నట్టె ఇల్లని ఇచ్చిన ద
19. ర్మ శాసనం

Rapur (52).

[Perumállapáḍu. Telugu. In a tope.]

Translation.

The village of Penumbálapáḍu is presented to the deity Múlasthánéṣvara of Udayagiri with libation of water. This edict giving this charity is issued by Koṇḍa Marusayya for the religious merit of Krishnaráya. Whoever causes obstruction to this will incur the sin of killing cows and Brahmans on the bank of the Ganges and the sin of having killed one's eldest son. Ṣrí, Ṣrí, Ṣrí!

1. వుదయగిరి మూలస్థానేశ్వరునికి
2. ధారపోసినగ్రామం పెనుం బా
3. లపాడు యీధమ్మర్ణం క్రిష్ణరా
4. యనికి పుణ్యముగాను కొండమ

5. రుసయ్య ఇచ్చిన ధర్మశాసనం
6. ఇందుకు తప్పినవారు గంగకతీరాం
7. గోవు బ్రాహ్మణి చంపిన ప
8. పాన పోదురు తన పెద్ద కో
9. డుకు చంపిన పాపానం బో
10. దురు శ్రీ శ్రీ శ్రీ

NOTE.—Penumbálapáḍu is evidently Perumállapáḍu.

RAPUR (53). (A.D. 1638-39.)

[Podalakúru. Telugu. Near a well by the Vináyaka-svámi temple. On two stones.]

TRANSLATION.

Hail! On the 2nd of the bright fortnight of Chaitra of the year Bahudhánya, corresponding to 1560 of the illustrious, victorious and prosperous Ṣáliváhana Ṣaka era, Ṣrímat Veligóṭi Venkaṭapati Náyaningáru granted this charitable edict for the tank of Poddalakúr. He has ordered that the *méra* grain should be utilized for the tank work in the manner in which the tank *méras* were formerly being collected. Therefore, whether the village be under *sandhátá*, or in the hands of an *amaradár* or of a lessee, whoever be the ruler, they should get the tank work done with the *méra* grain settled on the tank. If, not doing the tank work or the channel work, any one enjoy (the *méras*) or if any one obstruct, or if any *kápu* or *karnam* obstruct, or if any one remove this inscription, he will be considered to have been born to the *veṭṭi* of this village. He will be regarded as having given his wife to the *veṭṭi* of this village. In these terms has the charitable edict been issued.

1. స్వస్తి శ్రీ జయాభ్యుదయ శాలివా
2. హన శకవర్షంబులు ౧౫౬౦ అగు
3. నేటి బహుధాన్య సంవత్సర చైత్ర శు ౨లు
4. శ్రీమతు వెలిగోటి వేంకటపతినాయ
5. నింవారు పొద్దాలకూరి చెర్వుక ఇచ్చిన
6. ధర్మశాసనం
7. ఇ తీర్మానాన చేర్వు మేరలు పూర్వాన యేదా
8. రిగా వచ్చునట్టి ఆ మేర ధాన్యం చెర్వుపని
9. ముఖం శాయకట్టత పేఇంచ్చినారు
10. గనక ఇ గ్రామం సంధాతాన వున్నాను
11. ఆమరగాని వశాన యే ధోర యేలి
12. నాను గుత్తకానివశన వుంనాను చె
13. ర్వుకు నిర్ణయమైన మేరధాన్యం
14. ను చెర్వు పనిముఖం శేఇంచ్చ
15. గలవారు
16. చెర్వు పని మా(ము)ఖం కాల్వ పని శే
17. యించ్చక యవ్వరు అనుభవించ్చి
18. నాను యవ్వరు ఆక్షేపించ్చినాను
19. యేకాంపు కరుణం ఆక్షేపించ్చి
20. నాను ఇశాసనం యవరు తీశివే
21. శినాను వాండు యివూరి వెట్టివా
22. నికి పుట్టినవాడె వాని ఆలి
23. ని ఇవూరి వెట్టివానికి ఇచ్చి
24. నవాడె ఇటని ఇ(చ్చి)నధర్మ
25. శాసనం

NOTE.—The vowel ఇ represents the long vowel ఈ in lines 7, 20 and 23.

Rapur (54). (A.D. 1638-39.)

[Pótegunṭa or Pátagunṭa. Telugu. From bund of tank to east of village.]

Translation.

Hail! In the year Bahudhánya, corresponding to the year 1560 of the illustrious, victorious and prosperous Sáliváhana Saka era, Śrímat Veligóṭi Venkaṭapati Náyanimgáru caused this charitable inscription to be set up for the tank at Pótegunṭa. The *méras* of the tank of this village, viz., 1 *kuncha* on every *puṭṭi* of dry land, 1 *túm* on every *puṭṭi* under the tank, and the *méra* grain on the produce raised under Tana tank and Nellúru Dvára tank should be utilized for the repairs of the tank. Whether the village is under *sandhátá* or an *amaragáḍu* or lessees, or whoever be the ruler, they should do work to the tank. If any one, not doing the work, enjoys the *méras*, . . this village.

1. స్వస్తి శ్రీ జయాభ్యుదయ శాలి
2. వాహన శకవర్షంబులు ౧౫౬
3. ౦ బహుధాన్యం సంవత్సరంన
4. శ్రీమతు వెలిగోటి వెంకటపతినా
5. యనింగారు పోతే గుంటచెర్వుకువె
6. యించిన ధర్మ శాసనం యీగ్రా (మ)
7. చెర్వు మేరలు పుట్టి ౧కి వె (లిన)
8. కుచ్చెండు చెర్వు క్రిందు ను
9. తూమెడు లెఖన్నూ (లుటి)
10. (తర్మ) తమ చెరువుక్రింద
11. పండె నెల్లూరి దార చెర్వు
12. మేరాలు ధాన్యాలునుం
13. న్నుం చెర్వు పనిముఖం చే

14. యించ్చు వారు గ్రామా సంథా
15. త అనురుగాని వశౌనను యేదో
16. ర యేలినాను గుత్తగాని వశౌనవున్నా
17. ను చెరువు పనిముఖం చే
18. ఇంచువారు చేయించక
19. యెవ్వరు అనుభవించినాను యీవూరి

* * * *

RAPUR (55).

[Pulikollu. Telugu. To east of village near Polimera stream. Incomplete.]

TRANSLATION.

* * * *

We, Rivamati Anantam, Sílaparvalamu Tippaṇḍu, Bóya Krishnayya, Krishnamma, and the sons of Kantha Baviri, Vírakshâṭaya, Gangayya, Bhánu Manchinaya, Gópaya, Góvindaya, Venkaṭádri, ... Perlá Appana, Sáyahiri, Gánugabandlaggóla, Kothnam, Eri Ádi Rangarájularu, Rághavamma have done. . . . . Therefore we have given . . . . to last as long as the sun exists. Accepting it they should worship. . .

1. . . . . . .
2. రివమాతి అనంతం శీలపర్వాల
3. ము తిప్పండు భోయక్రిష్ణయ్య క్రి
4. ష్ణమ్మా కంతా బవిరి బిడ్డలు వీరక్షా
5. టయ గంగయ్య భాను మంచిన యె
6. గోపయ గోవిందయ వేంకటాద్రి . .
7. కి పెర్లా అప్పన శాయహిరి గానుగబ

8. ంక్ష గ్గోలకాత్మం ఎరిఆది రంగరాజుల
9. రు రాఘువమ్మాను క్రిత జలానను
10. . . . ంగన వయునులు నెరపిరి అ
11. . . . . ధలఖడిరి గనక ఇ జల్మాన హా
12. . . . ని అయ్యావ అక్రూ-రాముగాను
13. . . . పాలవెలసి నంతాకం ఇస్తిమి
14. . . . తీసుకొని పూజగొన వెంకటనిర
15. . . . .

RAPUR (56).

[Rápúru. Telugu. In front of Rápúramma's temple. Legible only in parts.]

TRANSLATION.

Ṣrímın Mıhám . . . . we all . . . . have caused to be constructed a *mukha mıṇḍıpa* for Ammagáru of Rápúru . . . . Nárânayya . . . . in the villages of the *síma* of Rápúru—they should give grain . . . . gave. Therefore those who maintain this charity as long as the sun and moon endure will acquire merit. May it cause great prosperity !

1. శ్రీశ్రీమన్ మహానా
2. . . . యావన్మంది
3. . . . వరదేవనిభామ
4. టు అయిన రాంపూరి అమ్మ
5. గారికి ముఖమండపంనం గట్టించి
6. వాము . . . . . చాలామ స్తవలంధ్ధ
7. . . . . . . ను అయ్యా వ
8. . . . యం నారణ రయ్యాను

9. . . . . మనులు డయిాలు
10. . . . . . లరు యిచ్చిన శాసనము
11. . . . . . రాపూరిశీమం గ్రామమందుల
12. . . . . . కునన్నుల విమారు రుమి
13. . . . . . య్యెల తీవం రతురలూడమకో
14. . . . . . ధాన్యంగాను యిచ్చేవాండ్లు
15. . . . . . ఇచ్చెను అందుకు
16. ఆచంద్రార్కం యిా పుణ్యా అ
17. పుణ్యం బొందుదురు మంగళ మహా
18. శ్రీ శ్రీ శ్రీం జేయును।

RAPUR (57).

[Saidápuram (hamlet Molakalapúṇḍla). Telugu. On a rock on Dévará Tippa.]

TRANSLATION.

May there be prosperity!

On Wednesday, the 7th of the bright half of Pushya of the year Svabhánu, Vaddu Airináya Bhánuṅḍu of Gummaḍúru caused to be constructed *manḍapas* and consecrated (Vináyaka) by the grace of the deity Vináyaka.

శుభమస్తు

1. స్వభాన సంవత్స
2. ర పుష్య శు ౭ బుధవారం
3. గుమ్ముడురి వద్దు ఐరినాయ
4. భానుండు వినాయకపు
5. స్వామి కృపను మండపాలివి క
6. ట్టించి ప్రతిష్టించెను

Rapur (58).

[Tánamcherla. Telugu. From a stone on the tank bund. Mostly illegible.]

Translation.

Hail! On . . . . the . . . . . *tithi* (lunar day) corresponding to the illustrious Ṣaka year . . . gáru issued this charitable edict.

1. స్వస్తి శ్రీ శాలివాహన శ
2. క వరుషంబులు . . . . అగు నేటి
3. . . . థితివాడు . . . . .
4. . . ర్బములు శ్రీ . . . . .
5. . . హరింగారు . . . .
6. . . ధర్మశాసనం . . .
7. కింది నెంతి . . . . మరి . . .
8. ట్టినం నిట్లు . . . . . .
9. . . . .
10. నిధ . . . ంసూర్యచం . . .
11. . . . . . లుసేయించి
12. నట్టి ధర్మము మవురు:

Rapur (59).

[Tánamcherla. Telugu. From the same stone. Incomplete.] . . . .

Translation.

They shall attend to the weir work, tank work and bund work, ... whether the *kuncha* grain be with the village *sandhátá* or . . . . . , if any object to this charity or if any appropriate it, or if any remove this inscription, he will be considered to have been born to the *veṭṭi* of this village and to have allowed his wife to be outraged by the *veṭṭi* of this village. In these terms has the charitable edict been granted.

. : .

. . .

1. అ
2. లుగు
3. పనిచె
4. వృ౯కు
5. పని
6. కట్టల
7. కుం పని
8. (ము) ఖం చెసె
9. డివా
10. రు . .
11. . . .
12. . . .
13. . . .
14. (రవ
15. రాం
16. దెవె)
17. చెరువు (కుం) . . .
18. చెడి గ్రా . . .
19. సంర (ధా?) . . .
20. తానె . . .
21. నినాను . . .
22. ధమ౯ని
23. కి యవ్వ (రు)

24. ఆశ్లేం
25. పించినాను ఆశ్రయిం
26. చ్చినాను యీ శాసనం యెవరు
27. తిసివేశినాను వాండు యీ
28. పూరి వెట్టివానికి బుట్టిన
29. వాండు వాడాలిని యీపూ
30. రి వెట్టివాడు చెరచికొన్నట్టె
31. యిట నిచిన ధర్మశాసనం.[1]

RAPUR (60) (A.D. 1612–13.)

[Tegacherla. Telugu. To the south on tank bund.]

TRANSLATION.

Hail! On the 15th day of the bright fortnight of the month of Srávana of the year Paridhávi, corresponding to the year 1534 of the illustrious and prosperous Ṣáliváhana Ṣaka era, while Ṣrimad Rájádhirája, Rájaparaméṣvara, Ṣri Víra Pratápa Ṣrí Víra Venkaṭapatiráya Déva Maháráyulu was ruling the kingdom of the earth at the town of Penugoṇḍa, Kumára Timmánáyanivâru, grandson of Veligóṭi Kumára Timmanáyanivâru, and son of Koṇḍamanénivâru, descendant of the Récharla *gótra*, and Rudrappanáyanivâru, grandson of Chintapaṭla Singamanéni and son of Chanchamanéni, descendant of the Peṣáli *gótra* caused a low-level sluice to be built for this tank. As the former high level sluice fell out of order they got this sluice built. Let this charity be maintained as long as the sun and moon remain so that his

---

[1] Read ఇష్టని యిచ్చిన ధర్మశాసనం

(Rudrappanáyaniváru's) parents Chanchamanéni and Kanchamma may acquire religious merit.

1. స్వస్తి శ్రీ విజయాభ్యుదయ
2. శాలివాహన శకవరుషం
3. బులు ౧౫౩౮ అగు నేటి పరి
4. ధాది సంవత్సర శ్రావణ శు
5. ౧౫లు । శ్రీమద్రాజా
6. ధిరాజ రాజపరమే
7. శ్వర శ్రీ రప్రాతాప శ్రీ
8. వీరవేంకటపతిరాయ దే
9. వ మహా రాయలయ్యవా
10. రు పెనుగొండ పట్నమం
11. దు పృథివీ సాంమ్రాజ్యము
12. సేయుచుండంగాను రేచ
13. ర్ల గోత్ర పవిత్రుండునను
14. వెలిగోటి కుమారతిమ్మ
15. నాయని పౌత్రులైన కొండమనే
16. ని పుత్రులైన కొమారతింమా
17. నాయనివారు
18. పెశాలి గోత్రుండు
19. చింతపట్ల శింగమనేని
20. పౌత్రుండైను చంచమనేని
21. పుత్రులైన రుద్రప్పనాయ
22. నింగారు ఈచెర్వుకు వాం
23. ఖతూము కట్టించినా
24. రు పూర్వాన నడపించి
25. న మిట్ట తూముకిల
26. పడిందినింగాన ఆ తూ
27. ము కటించినారు

28. గనక తమతండ్రి చ
29. ంచను నేనికి తమతెల్లి
30. కాంచమం గారిత్ని పు
31. ణ్యంగా ఆ చంద్ర
32. సహితం ఇ పుణ్యం
33. ఇడేచుఃకో గాత

Rapur (61).

[Tegacherla. Telugu. On the boundary towards Gónupalli.]

Translation.

Adoration to Srí Ráma!

On Sunday, the 5th of the bright half of Pushya of the illustrious year Naḷa, Narasimham of Tegacherla,—bha suru, Sundhu Malli Ve . . . ., Tokkalu mai vunnam gáru, ... Ku . . . . . . ri, *Kárukún* (Revenue Inspector) of the estate, the *Sthaḷa Karanams*, Kullúru Viracháru, and also the young and old of Yerrapalli Nágalavelli Doru Mámudúru and other villages have constructed the street as follows: Ráti Kaṭṭa (stone bund), Kuchanṭa baṭa, Vadamakunṭa, Yarapápukunṭa, Mára Sánikunṭa, stone of Chintala Pápayakunṭa and onward towards the east. This is the boundary.

శ్రీరామా

1. శ్రీనళ సంవత్సరపుష్యశు ౫ లు ఆదివారం
2. తెగచలః నరశిమ్హు . . .
3. బ్బ శూరు సంధూమల్లివె . .
4. తొకలు మైవున్నంగారుకు . .

5. రిదివాణం కారుకూనలుస్త
6. ళ కరణాలు కూలూరుల వీరా
7. చారు యఱ్రపల్లి నాగలవెల్లి దో
8. రు మాముడూరు మొదలైన గ్రమా
9. ల పిన్న పెద్దలు తెవ్పుగా వేఇం
10. చిన వివరం రాతికట్టకు
11. చంటబటవడమకుంట
12. యర పాపుకుంట మారసా
13. నికుంట చింతలపావ
14. యు కుంటరాయియికాను
15. తూర్పుగాణదుచానినో
16. యందాలి మేర.

RAPUR (62).

[Tummalatalapúr. Telugu. On tank bund to north of village.]

TRANSLATION.

The *méra* grain settled for the tank of Tummala ṭalapúru is at 2 *kunchas* per *puṭṭi*. If any one misappropriate (the *méra*) or if any one object or if any *kápu* or *karnam* object or if any one remove this inscription, he will be considered to have been born to the *veṭṭi* of this village, and to have given his wife to the *veṭṭi* of this village. The *mérás* of the tank should be spent on the upkeep of the tank. Thus has the charitable edict been issued.

1. తుమ్మల తలుపూరు చెర్వుకు వేయించిన
2. చెర్వు మేర ఖ ౧ కి ఖం ౦౪ ౦౨

3. ఖను . . . యవ్వరు అ.ను భవిం
4. చినాను యవ్వరు ఆక్షేపించినాను
5. యే కాంపుకరణం ఆక్షేపించినాను యీశా
6. సనం యవ్వరు తీసివేశించ్చినాను గ్రామ
7. వెట్టివానికి బుట్టినవాండౌ వాండి
8. ఆలిని యీవూరి వెట్టివానికి యిచ్చుకున్నక్లొ
9. . . చెర్వుక్రింది వూళ్లపాలెపుమె
10. చెరువుమీద వెయించగలవారు యి
11. ట్లని యిచ్చిన ధర్మశాసనం

RAPUR (63). (A.D. 1638-39.)

[Turimerla. Telugu. On south bank of tank.]

TRANSLATION.

Prosperity! Hail! On the 6th of the bright half of Chaitra of the year Bahudhánya, corresponding to 1560 of the illustrious, victorious and prosperous Ṣálivâhana Ṣaka era, Ṣrímat Velugóṭi Venkaṭapati Náyaningáru granted this charitable edict for the tank of Tullimerla. He has ordered that the *méra* grain collected in the manner in which it was collected formerly for the tank of this village should be utilized for the tank work. Therefore, whether the village be under *sandhátá* or with an *amaragáḍu* or lessee, or whatever rulers rule, they should get the tank and channel work executed with the *méras* settled on the tank. If, not getting the work done, any one should obstruct or enjoy the *méras* or remove this (inscription) he will be regarded as having been born to the *veṭṭi* of this village and as having given his wife to the *veṭṭi* of this village.

1. శ్రీ స్వస్తి శ్రీ జయాభ్యుద
2. య శాలివాహన శక వర్షం
3. బులు ౧౫౬౦ అగు నేటి బహు
4. ధాన్య సంవత్సర చైత్ర శు ౬ లు శ్రీమతు
5. వెలుగోటి వెంకటపతినాయనింగారు
6. వారు తుర్లి మెలచెర్వుకు ఇచ్చిన ధ
7. ర్మశాసనం యీగ్రామాన చెర్వుమే
8. రలు పూర్వాన గ్రాం వారిగా నావచ్చినట్టివిన్ని
9. ఆమేర ధాన్యం చెర్వుపనిముఖం శాయ
10. ంగట్టడ శేయించ్చినారం గనక యీ గ్రామం
11. సంధాతాన వున్నాను అమరగాడు యే దొ
12. రలు యేలినాను గుత్తగాని వశాన వున్నా
13. ను చెర్వుకు నిర్ణయమైన మేరధాన్యం
14. చెఱ్వు పనిముఖం కాలువ పనిముఖా
15. లు చెయ్యగలవారు శేయించక యవ్వ
16. రు భేదించినాను యవ్వరు
17. అనుభవించినాను యవ్వరు తీశివే
18. యించినాను వాండు యీవూరి వె
19. ట్టివానికిం బుట్టినవాడె వాని
20. ఆలిని యీవూరి వెట్టివా
21. డు దెంగును

Rapur (64).

[Tsuṭṭupāḷem. Telugu. Near Komiṭi gunṭa.]

Translation.

Yanamadam Suddama of Mátlapúndi for the worship of . . . . .

1. మాళ్లపూండి
2. యన మదం
3. సుద్ధ మ శం .
4. పూజ్యాలకు .
5. టిపు . మిరు
6. రూపు (తోంను) .
7. న్న చానుమే .
8. . రా . య

RAPUR (65). (A.D. 1231-32 ?)

[Úṭukúru. Tamil. In the middle of the village.]

[1] சகரை ஆ[ண்டு]
[2] ஆயிரத்தொ-
[3] ருநூற்றைம்பத்-
[4] துமூன்று [ஸவுர]
[5] வத்தி ஸ்ரீகு-
[6] லொத்துங்-
[7] கசொழதெ-
[8] வற்கு யாண்டு
[9] ௰௬ வது மது
[10] ராந்தகப்பெ[ர]-
[11] த்தப்பிச்சொ-
[12] ழன் கண்டகெ-
[13] ாபா[ல]ன் திருக்க-
[14] [ாளத்]தி தெவன்

TRANSLATION.

In the 16th year of the reign of the Emperor, the glorious Kulótuṅgachóḻadéva, corresponding to the Ṣaka year one thousand one hundred and fifty-three, Madurántaka Pottapichóḷa (*alias*) Gaṇḍagópála (*alias*) Tirukkálattidéva. . . . .

Rapur (66).

[Úṭukúru. Tamil. From stones dug up on the site of an old temple near the chávidi.]

[1] . . . . . . [கு]லொத்து[ங்க சொ]ழதெவ[ற்கு யா]-

[2] ண்டு ௩௰௭ வது மதுராந்தகப்பொத்தப்பிச்சொழன் திருக்கா-

[3] ளத்திதெவன் இராச்சியத்தில் வெள்ளைசெரியில் மெ ல்லைப்பா-

[4] கத்தில் காணியாளன் செங்கனப்பொயன் முப்பிடிஇர-ட்டி மகன்

[5] கல்லப்பஇரட்டியென் சிங்கட்டைநாட்டில் ஊட்டக்-கூரில்

[6] நல்லிகர்பென்று சிவாலையமெடுப்பித்து இதுக்கு நாச்-சான் வாவியின்கி[ழ்]

[7] குழி ஐம்பதும் பெரிஎரிகிழ் குழி ஐம்பதும் நஞ்சை-நிலம் பட்டியும் உ

[8] பொன் ஆனூர் விமரசன்பொ[ய]ன் திக்கரசனும்-தெவன் பொயிண்டனும்

[9] நல்லப்பஇரட்டியும் புடொலம்இரட்டியுமுப்பிடி-இர ட்டியும் ஊற்கு

[10] வடக்கெ எரிகட்டி இதின் கிழ் நீர் பாய்ந்து விளைகிற நிலமும்புஞ்சை

[11] நிலம் பட்டியும் நல்லிகாதெவற்கு அமுதுபடி சந்திரா-தித்தவரை

[12] செல்வதாக இவ்வனைவொவும் தாரைவார்த்து தெவ-தானமாக

[13] விட்டோம் இதுவில்லையெனவெங் கெங்கைகரையில்-குராற்பசு-

[14] வை கொங்ற பாவத்திற்பொவாங் தஙமத்த மகாகால-த்தில் பிச்சை

[15] பண்ணிஙர் பாவத்திற்பொவான் கொமொசனுக்கு கு

TRANSLATION.

In the 37th year of the reign of . . . . . . Kulóttuṅgachóḻadéva, Kallappa Reḍḍi the son of Seṅganppóyan Muppiḍi Reḍḍi possessing rights in Melálaippákam (a suburb) of Veḻḻaiṣéri situated in the kingdom of Madurántaka Pottapichóḻa (*alias*) Tirukkáḻattidéva built a *Ṣiva* Temple named after Nallikádéva at Úṭṭakkúr (a village) in Siṅgaṭṭai Náḍu and gave to this (temple) fifty *kuḻi* of land under the Náchchán well and fifty *kuḻi* of land under the big tank (constituting) one *paṭṭi* of wet land and 2 *pon.* (In addition to the above lands), Vímaraśanpóyaṉ Tikkaraśan of Ándúr, Déva Póyinḍan, Nallapa Reḍḍi, Puḍolam Reḍḍi and Muppiḍi Reḍḍi dug a tank in the north of the village (Úttukkúr) and gave the land irrigated by the water of this tank and one *paṭṭi* of dry land.

All of us (the abovementioned) donors gave the lands as temple lands with libation of water for providing sacred food (amudupadi) to Nallikádéva to last as long as the moon and sun endure.

If there is anybody who says the contrary he will incur the sin of killing a tawny cow on the banks of the Ganges and of begging at a time when there is no money at all. . . . . . .

RAPUR (67).

[Úṭukúru. Telugu. This is a defaced inscription in the middle of the village.]

RAPUR (68). (A.D. 1682–83.)

[Úṭukúru. Telugu. To the east of the drinking water well. Mostly illegible.]

TRANSLATION.

Hail! . . . . of the year Dundubhi, corresponding to 1605 of the illustrious, victorious and prosperous Ṣáliváhana Ṣaka era, under the orders of Ṣrímat . . . .

(1) స్వస్తి శ్రీ జయాభ్యుదయ శాలివాహన
(2) శక వరుషంబులు ౧౬౦౫ అగునేంటి దు
(3) ందుభి సంవత్సర . . . .
(4) లు శ్రీమతు. . . . గా
(5) రి అనతిని . . . . .
(6) . మెర . . . . .
(7) నయ శ్రీ . . . . .
(8) . . . .
(9) . . . .
(10) . ధ . . . . . న్య
(11) లకు . . . . . .
(12) . ఖ . . . . . .
(13) . . . .
(14) గలవారు ఋ . . . .

RAPUR (69).

[Útukúru. Telugu. On three sides of a stone in the middle of the village. This inscription is unintelligible. The first four lines are printed at right angles to the rest.]

First side.

1. తంకళ వెంకట్రటన
2. రుసు। వూటుకూ
3. రి కరణం పామరా
4. జూ ఆరలార
5. మరి బఁలవి
6. మవారూను
7. నంటిమివా
8. రారి అంగ్గు
9. సంటిరివె
10. దురువేరి
11. పింల్లివాలి
12. పంచ్చలు
13. కునహింపు
14. టీలలు। రంకృ
15. పావంబుంలు
16. రాజగోపవా
17. జలు। వూట
18. కూరి గ్రామం
19. శెలివాంచ్చిన
20. వరి చెలు
21. ను నంజెల్లిరా
22. యుని మంద్ద
23. శ్రీ . లు

Second side.

1. యిమా
2. జె శ్రీ దా
3. వ్రాటి
4. . వెలు
5. శకులి
6. డరిని
7. జోమా
8. జోనుగ
9. కులము
10. ల్రదినద
11. నలంటగ
12. ణాపుల
13 నిగుగా
14. శెంకుర్ల ౧
15. డమలుల
16. ఖాదాలి
17. వారా
18. రావిరడి
19. సవిలో
20. రల్లుపు
21. కుదం స
22. లసదుపు
23. తి గ్రాడు
24. ల వెంగ్లర
25. ణ రలు కూ
26. గ్రదతు
27. శెగలుర
28. లజా

29. తుగు

30. లు

Third side.

1. యూఆ

2. తవాంగి

3. తంముద

4. పూరు

5. రు ముల్ల

6. ములుమా

7. రు . రుమా

8. ట మాటి

9. ట వారు

10. ద పెటినవా

11. రేలునవు

12. డు వూటకూ

13. రి అప్పతి

14. రామరాయ

15. రు వరగలి

16. ం వాను .

17. శ్రీ రంగ . ర

18. ం రొా .

19. రాడి కింమ

RAPUR (70). (A D. 1236–37 ?)

[Uṭukúru. Tamil. From site of old temple opposite the chávidi.]

[1] ஸ்வஸ்தி ஸ்ரீ ஸகர-
[2] யாண்டு[1] ஆயிரத்தொரு-
[3] நூற்றம்பத்தெட்டா[வது*]

[1] Expressed by an abbreviation.

[4] மாஶிமாஸத்தில் சி-
[5] வராத்ரி அம[ா]வாஸையு-
[6] ன்று ஊட்டுக்கூரில் ரா-
[7] மெஸ்வரமுடையாற்கு
[8] ராஜராஜதெவற்கு யா-

TRANSLATION.

Hail! Prosperity! In the Ṣaka year one thousand one hundred and fifty-eight on the date corresponding to the new moon day after Ṣivarátri in the month of Máṣi, in the reign of Rájarájadéva. . . . to Rámêṣvaram Uḍaiyár at Úṭṭukkúr.

RAPUR (71).

[Vaḍlapúḍi. Telugu. Opposite Ponnúramma temple. The impression of this rough inscription appears to have been lost.]

RAPUR (72).

[Vaḍlapúḍi. Telugu. Half a mile south of the village.]

TRANSLATION.

On the 11th of the bright fortnight of Mágha of the year Párthiva, I, Dámi Náyuṇḍu, son of Páḍumu . . di Náyuḍu, have presented to Ṣrí Kálahastíṣvara, with libation of water, a wet field in Pina Voḍlamúṇḍi which is attached to my chiefdom, and 100 *kuṇṭas* of land in Dárabandampáḍu village of Nellúru, and to the south of Perumáḷḷuchénu, in perpetuity to last as long as the moon endures. He who enjoys this land will present a large fan (álavaṭṭam) to the deity . . . .

1. పార్థివ సంవత్సర మాఘ శు
2. ద్ధ ౧౧ లు శ్రీకాళహస్తీశ్వరునకు పాదుము .

3. డి నాయని కొమారుండు దామినాయనింగారు తమ
4. నాయంకరంలోని పినవొడ్లమూండిని దారవో
5. సిన వరివుడి పెరుమాళ్లు చేనికి దక్షిణం నె
6. ల్లూరిదార బందం పాటి కు ౧౦౦ నూరుగుంట
7. లు ఆచంద్రస్థాయిగాను ఇస్తిమి ఇటుల భోగప్రా
8. పి దేవునికి ఆలవట్టం (నయినాథ?)
9. సమర్పించువాండు

Rapur (73).

[Vaḍlapúḍi. Telugu. From stone in front of temple of Ponnúramma. Incomplete and partially illegible. The translation is conjectural in places.]

Translation.

* * * *

Any one obstructing this charity will incur the sin of one who commits cow slaughter, Brahmanicide and murder of one's spiritual preceptor at Káṣi and will incur the sin of killing his mother. In these terms the Mahá Rája Ṣrí has granted this charitable edict . . . . the charitable edict now set up by Tanapusala Venkaṭa Reḍḍi of Vaḍlapúḍi . . . . cows (were given) for the perpetual lamp. In addition to Timmá Reḍḍi's *mányam* Venkaṭádri's *mulum* (garden land) was given.

We Timmá Reḍḍi, Venkaṭa Reḍḍi and others, *kápus* . . . have given cows . . . .

(1) . . . . . చె
(2) ద్చినవాడు కాశిలో గోహత్య బ్రహ్మహత్య
(3) గురువుహత్య అతడిపాపాన పోదురు తల్లిని చం (పిం)
(4) చిన పాపాన పోదురు యిట్లు మ-రాజ-శ్రీవారు యి

(5) చ్చిన ధర్మశాసనం యిప్పుడు . . వ

(6) డ్లపూడి తనవుసల వెంకటెద్దుం వేశిన ధర్మశాసనం

(7) . . గణసరిగోవులు అఖండం తిం

(8) మ్మారెడ్డిమాన్యగాక వెంకటాద్రిములుము

* * * *

(10) మె . . . . .

(11) .ణసరిగో . . . (తి)

(12) మ్మారెడ్డి మ . . (వె)

(13) కటరెడ్డి వగైరా మ . .

(14) . . కాంపువాండ్ల . .

(15) నుమెము యించ్చిడు . .

* * * *

RAPUR (74). (A.D. 1638–39.)

[Vaḍlapúḍi. Telugu. Near sluice of tank to the west.]

TRANSLATION.

Hail! On the 2nd of the bright half of Chaitra of the year Bahudhánya, corresponding to the year 1560 of the illustrious, victorious and prosperous Ṣáliváhana Ṣaka era, Ṣrímat Veligóṭi Venkaṭapati Náyanimgáru executed this charitable edict for the tank at Voḍlapúnḍi. This charity settles the manner in which he has presented the *méras* for the tank of this village. For the charity they should be collected at one *kuncha* on dry fields and at . . on wet fields . . The *méra* grain . . . . .

1. స్వస్తి శ్రీ జయాభ్యుదయ శాలి
2. వాహన శకవరుషంబు
3. లు ౧౫౬౦ అగునేటి బహుధా
4. న్యం సంవత్సర చైత్ర శు ౨ లు

5. శ్రీ మతు వెలిగోటి వెంక
6. టపతి నాయనింగారు దో
7. డ్లపూండి చెర్వ్యకుగానిచ్చిన ధ
8. ర్మ్మశాసనం యీ గ్రామాను చె
9. రువుమేరటు విధాంనిచ్చిరో ఇ
10. ధర్మ్మ ధర్మ్మాలకు వెలిపాలా
11. న కుంచడుగాను. నీటిపాలాన
12. . . . . . మేరధాన్యం

RAPUR (75).

[Vaḍlapúḍi. Tamil. From the Baineṭi hill near the village. Illegible.]

RAPUR (76).

[Vébinábi. Telugu. From a stone in a street to the west. These are two spells to avert epidemics among men and cattle. They were translated by M.R.Ry. Védam Venkatráya Sástri Gáru, Sanskrit Pandit at the Christian College, Madras. Some words in these spells are mystical, and a few, being perhaps incorrectly transcribed, yield no sense.]

TRANSLATION.

A.

Óm Hrím. (By) oath on the feet of the Sanyási. (This is) a barrier, a barrier, a great barrier, the (village) boundary. (These are) the barriers constructed by the sages, the great sages and the sanyásis. Phat Swáhá. Taking the food and the animal sacrifices (offered to you)

. . . oath on the feet of the venerable Inda, the great sage. Go away, taking away with you the bowl of blood, the sharp knife and the noose. This is the binding spell with which was bound the great destructive goddess Murámáriya (probably the name of the goddess of epidemics).

B.

Great . . . sacrifices. A binding made by the great and venerable sage Inda and other sages. Binding of the upper canine teeth. Bindings made by the priest. Binding of the canine teeth. The priest's bindings save these and form the safeguard of the cattle. Therefore (?) milk, tails and pasturage (are) bound. It is said that the great sage bound these. The priest's tie . . . . The tie of Virayya, the priest. (This is) Máriya's tie (*i.e.* Máriya is bound by this). This safeguard has been made after ascending to and descending from the foot of our sage Inda. The great and venerable Óm. [a] Priest's favour, the priest [a]. Do this ten lakhs of times.

A.

1. ఓం హ్రీం సన్న్యాశిపాంచ
2. మూన కట్టకట్ట మ
3. హోకట్ట పొలిమేర
4. మునులు మహోము
5. నులు సంన్యాసులు
6. కట్టినకట్టులు పట్టు
7. స్వాహాః పటలు ఆహాః

---

a—a Perhaps "గురుప్రసాద గురు" stands for "కురు ప్రసాదం కురు" which means "do favour, do."

8. రము తీసుకొని (వ్రి
9. ధము) శ్రీయుంద మహా॰
10. ముని పాదమాన పా
11. విరక్తముకొట్ట వా
12. లు కత్తి పాశము
13. తీసుకొని పోవే
14. మహాశక్తినీ క
15. ట్టిన కట్టు మం
16. త్రము ॥
17. (మురామురియ॥)

B.

1. మహా॰ . . (బ)
2. లుఖు॥ శ్రీ యుంద (మ).
3. హా॰ముని మునులు కట్టిన కట్టు
4. మీందికోరలు । కటు గురువు
5. కట్టులు కోరలు బిందకటు
6. వీరికాపాడి పసువులకు గురి
7. గురుకటులు (కాలఖట్టి పా
8. లుశోకలు) బైలుకటు
9. మహా॰ముని కట్టినారట
10. గురుకటు (లఖిచిరకట్టె
11. ట్టు) గురు । వీరయకట్టు
12. దిగి । మాయకట్టు మాయం
13. దు గురుపాద యొక్క దిగి స్వా
14. ట్టినారిగురి । మహా॰ శ్రీ
15. ఓం గురుప్రసాదగురు

పదిలక్ష

లు గురు

Rapur (77).

[Yépúru. Telugu. From stone on tank bund.]

Translation.

The tank of Channamgáru, daughter of Veligóṭi Timmánáyuḍu (constructed) on Wednesday the 10th of the dark fortnight of Phálguna of the year Vijaya.

1. విజయసంవ్వత్స
2. ర ఫాల్గున బహుళ
3. ౧౦ బుధవారం
4. వెలిగోటి తింమ్మా
5. నాయుడి కుమా
6. ర్తె చంనంగారి
7. సముద్రము

Rapur (78). (A.D. 1401–42.)

[Yépúru. Telugu. West of village in survey No. 78. Inscription on three sides of a stone. The fourth side is illegible.]

Translation.

Hail ! On Tuesday, the 4th of the bright half of Kártika of the year Vṛishu, corresponding to the year 1323 of the illustrious Ṣaka era Vánḍadéva (?) . . ttaṣanka . . . ganḍa, Ganḍaraganḍa, Manyabhúmi Náyanimgáru, son of Manujávaḷi Náyuḍu, for the forgiveness of his sins, gave with submission a wet paddy field under the Pulicheruvu . . . . to Ṣrígirinátha, who is the conqueror of foes and the deliverer from Asuras . . . . 100 *kunṭas* of dry land . . . . This should last as long as the sun and moon exist. Those who fail to maintain the charity will incur the sin of killing on the banks of the Ganges.

1. స్వస్తి శ్రీ
2. సకవరు
3. షంబులు
4. ౧౩౨౩ అ
5. ను నేటి వృ
6. ష సంవ
7. త్సర కా.ర్తిక
8. క శు ర మ
9. వాండ దేవ .
10. త్ర శంక .
11. బ . . . గ
12. ండగండర
13. గండ మను
14. జావళినాయ
15. ని కొడుకు మ
16. స్య భూమినా
17. యనింగా
18. రు తనకు
19. తప్పు యా
20. రయనయ
21. పూర్వకం
22. ఆరిపీరా
23. సురత్రా
24. ణి శ్రీ గి
25. రినాంధు
26. నికి పులి
27. చెరువు

28. క్రింద నీ

29. రు నేలవ

30. చెరి నూను

31. . . . మ

32. . . .

33. పాలము మ

34. డి కు ౧౦౦

35. అక్షరా

36. లాను నూఱు

37. లూనూరుగు

38. ంటలును

39. (మెట్టని) ఆ

40. చంద్రాక

41. ముగాం జె

42. ల్లంగలబ

43. యూ ధర్మాంకు

44. . . య

45. వ్వరు దప్పి

46. నాను గంగ

47. కటుత వ

48. ధించిన పా

49. పానం బో

50. దురు

* * * *

(ఆరయ)

(మీరల)

(నీ చేనుజ)

(డ మాల)

(నీతిమ)

RAPUR (79). (A.D. 1638–39.)

[Yerraguntapáḷem (hamlet of Chíkavólu). Telugu. On the tank bund. Incomplete.]

TRANSLATION.

Hail! On the 5th of the bright fortnight of Chaitra of the year Bahudhánya, corresponding to 1560 of the illustrious, victorious and prosperous Ṣálivàhana Ṣaka era, Ṣrímat Velugóṭi Venkaṭapati Náyaningáru issued this charitable edict for the tank Yarraguntapálem. He has ordered that *méra* grain for the tank should be levied at 1 *kuncha* per *puṭṭi*, even on *inám* lands. Therefore whether the village be under *sandhátá* or under an *amaradár*, or whoever be the rulers . . . .

(1) స్వస్తి శ్రీ జయాభ్యుదయ శా
(2) లివాహన శకవర్షంబు
(3) లు ౧౫౬౦ అగు నేటి బహు
(4) ధాన్యసంవత్సర చైత్ర శు ౫
(5) శ్రీమతు వెలుగోటి వెంకటా
(6) పతినాయనింగారు యరగుం
(7) ట పాలెం చెరువుకు యిచ్చినధ
(8) ర్మశాసనం పుట్టి వకటికి కుంచ్చ
(9) లక్షైను మాన్యలకు సహాగాను
(10) వచ్చిన చెరువుమేర దాన్యాంశా
(11) యం గట్టడ శేయించ్చినారం గనక యీ
(12) గ్రామ సంధాతాన వున్నాను అమ
(13) రగాని వశాని యె ధొర . .
(14) లగాని వున్నా . . .

SULURPET (1).

[Mannár Pólúru. Tamil. From threshold of gópuram of Alagumaláru Krishṇasvámi temple.]

TRANSLATION.

. . . (Alluṇ)tikka Mahárájan presented the land included within these four boundaries, viz., North . . . . South . . . . East, the street . . . . West . . . . for providing sacred food (*amudupaḍi*) during festivals to (deity) . . . .

If any one obstructs this charity, he will be regarded as having killed a tawny cow on the banks of the Ganges and will incur the sin of killing a Bráhman. May this charity be maintained as long as the moon and sun endure.

[1] . . . . . . ல்லுன்திக்கமஹாராஜன்
[2] . . . . . . சித்தவல் . . . யக்-
[3] . . . . . . யாற்கு த்திருமலைய . .
[4] . . . . . . விட்ட வடபாற்கெல்லை
[5] . . . . . . ளிரண்டு ஜய . . .
[6] . . . . . . த்தெற்கும் தென்பாற்கெல்-
[7] . . . . . . க்குன்றுன் . . .
[8] . . . . . . லவுலகுயிக்ததெருவுக்கு
[9] மெற்கும் மெல்பாற்கெல்லை
[10] . . . க்கு கிழக்கும் இந்நாற்பாலெ-
[11] ல்லை உள்பட்ட விலத்து-
[12] க்கு திருவிளா[தொரும்] அமுதுபடி
[13] . . டயெங் இத்தந்மம் இறக்கிநாரு-
[14] ண்டாகில் கெங்கைக்கரை-
[15] யில் குராப்பசுக்கொந்றுந் ஹுஹூ-
[16] [,ஹதி] கொள்வாந் இத்தந்(ம)ம் சந்-
[17] [திராதித்தவரை] செல்லக்கடவது.

SULURPET (2).

[Mannemuttéri. Tamil. In street to west.]

TRANSLATION.

The charity of Nalla Sittarasan (Nalla Siddha) of the Pallava race . . . . . lottu . . . . . rent free to the deity . . . . . Whoever obstructs this charity will incur the sin of killing a tawny cow on the banks of the Ganges. May it be auspicious.

[1] . . . . . து-
[2] . . . . . லொத்து-
[3] . . . . . ருவிடையாட்-
[4] . . . . . ானயமர்க்கு தெ[வ]-
[5] . . . . . பல்லவவங்ஶத்தில் நல்-
[6] லசித்தரசன் தன்மம் இத்-
[7] தன்மம் விலக்கினாருண்டா[னா]-
[8] ல் கெங்கைக்கரையில் கு-
[9] ரால்[ப]சு கொன்ற பாவத்தி-
[10] லெ பொவான் ஶுபமஸ்து.

SULURPET (3).

[Súlúrpéṭa. Tamil. From pillar in Nágéśvara temple.]

TRANSLATION.

Hail! Prosperity! In the 24th year of the reign of the emperor of the three worlds, the glorious Vijayagaṇḍagópáladéva . . . . endowed the following charity to the god Tirunágíśvara at Śingaḷántapuram *alias* Śúralúr (a village) in Mélnáḍu to carry the god in procession on the new moon day.

[The details of the grant are not decipherable, but it appears to be of land as a *Sarvamánya* and the proceeds of certain tolls.] We bind ourselves to maintain this charity as long as the moon and sun endure. He who lessens this charity will incur the sin of all those who kill cows between the Ganges and Cape Comorin.

This charity is (placed) under the protection of all the glorious *Máhésvaras.*

[1] ஸ்வஸ்தி ஸ்ரீ திரிபு-
[2] வனச்சக்கரவ-
[3] த்திகள் ஸ்ரீ விஜ-
[4] யகண்டகொபா-
[5] லதெவற்கு யாண்-
[6] டு ௨௰௪ வது [மெல்]-
[7] [காட்டு]ச்சிங்களா-
[8] ந்தபுரமான சுர-
[9] ஊர் உடையார்த்தி-
[10] ருஞெசுரமுடை-
[11] யநாயனுர்கு க-
[12] மாவாவை௱ப்படி
[13] எழுந்தருளும்படிக்-
[14] கு . . . . .
[15] வெண்டு . .
[16] ள்ளுக்குமாக . ஓன்
[17] றுக்கு அரைமாை-
[18] டக்குச்சூரஊர்
[19] . . . . .
[20] . . . . . .
[21] . . . . .
[22] . . . . .
[23] கம்ம கண்ண . .
[24] ளும் ஸர்வமானிய-

[25] மாக நூடு பெத்து விட்-
[26] டென் சுங்கம் தவி-
[27] த்தருளும் நாண்மைமு-
[28] தல்களும் இத்தன்ம[ம்]
[29] சந்திராதித்தவரை-
[30] ர செலுத்தக்கடவோ-
[31] ம் இத்தன்ம இறக்குவா-
[32] ன் கெங்கை இடை-
[33] க்குமரி இடை குரா-
[34] ற்பசுக்கொன்றான் ப-
[35] ாபத்தெப்படுவான்
[36] இது ஸ்ரீமாஹேஸ்வர-
[37] [ர் ர]க்ஷை.

SULURPET (4).

[Súlúrpéṭa. Tamil. Southern wall of Nágéśvara temple.]

TRANSLATION.

Hail! Prosperity! (In the reign of) the emperor of the three worlds, the glorious Vijaiyá . . . . [déva] . . . Tanikkúttukkaṇḍáḷ, the consort of Taimmáḍidévan . . . . presented one sacred perpetual lamp (in the temple of) the lord Tirunágíśvara of Śúralúr[1] *alias* Śiṅgaḷántapura in Veṅgánáḍu (a sub-division) of Paiyyúrilaṅkóṭṭam.

For this lamp and for . . . . Tirumárgaḷi festival (I gave land) free from all kinds of taxes . . . . 100 *kuḷis* measured with a pole of 22 spans

---

[1] Śúralúr is evidently Súlúrpet.

of the standard land measure of Maraiyúr in the field . . . . to the east of Iraṭṭaikkuḻi—total 600 *kuḻis.* I, Tanikkúttuk. . . . have given this land so that these two charities may be maintained as long as the moon and the sun endure . . . . will incur the sin of killing . . . . . (this charity is placed under) the protection of all the *Máhéśvaras.*

[1] ஸ்வஸ்திஸ்ரீ திரிபுவனச்சக்கரவத்திகள் ஸ்ரீவிஜைய . . . . . ண்ட ஜொழமண்டலத்து பைய்யூரிளங்கொட்டத்து வெ-

[2] ங்காநாட்டுச்சூர[ஓர]ான; சிங்க[ள]ாந்தபுரத்து உடையார் திருநாகிசுர . . . . . ஜன் தைம்மாடிதெவன் தெவி தனிக்கூத்துக்கண்டாளெ-

[3] ன் வைத்த திருநந்தாவிளக்கு ஒன்றுக்கும்திருமார்கழி த்திரு . . . . . ழ் கழனியில் இரட்டைக்குழிக்கு கிழக்கு எப்பெர்ப்பட்ட இறை-க-

[4] ளும் இழிச்சிக்கொண்டு மறையூர் நிலவளவு இருபத்தி-ருசாண் கொலால் திருநு . . . . . . குழிநூறும் ஆக இக்குழி அறுநூறும் இத்தன்மம் இரண்டும் சந்ரா-

[5] ாதித்தவரை செல்லக்கடவதாக இந்நிலங்கொண்டு வி-ட்டென் தனிக்கூத்துக் . . . . கொன்றான் பாவத்தை படுவான் ஸ்ரீமாஹெஸ்வரரக்ஷை.

SULURPET (5).

[Súlúrpéṭa. Tamil. South wall of Nágéśvara temple.]

TRANSLATION.

Hail! Prosperity! In the 5th year of the reign of the glorious Kulóttungachóladéva, Muraiyúrudaiyán

(Uṛaiyúruḍaiyáṇ ?) *alias* Nediyan *alias* Tiruppálaivanam-uḍaiyán *alias* Duraiaraśavéḷán presented one evening lamp (in the temple) of the lord Tirunágéśvara of Śúralúr. The money which we, the Bráhmaṇs who have rights (káṇi) in this temple, received to burn this lamp as long as the moon and sun last, is four "old" *káśus*. We have received the four *káśus*. (The charity is placed under) the protection of all the *Máhéśvaras*.

[1] ஸ்வஸ்தி ஸ்ரீ குலொத்துங்கசொழதெவற்குயாண்டு [௫] ஆவது சுரலூர் திருநா[கி]சுரமுடையநாயனா[ர்]க்கு

[2] முனை[ற]யூருடையான் நெடியன் திருப்பாலைவன[மு]-டையானான துரைஅரைசவெளான் வைத்த

[3] சந்திவிளக்கு ஒன்றும் சந்திராதித்தவரை எரிக்ககடவ-தாக இக்கொயிலின் காணியுடை-

[4] யுடைபகல்ப்பிராமணரொம் கைக்கொண்டக பழங்கா-சு நாலு நாலுங்கைக்கொண்டொம்

[5] பன்மாகெசுரரக்ஷை.

SULURPET (6).

[Súlúrpéṭa. Tamil. Western wall of Nágéṣvara temple.]

TRANSLATION.

Hail! Prosperity! In the twelfth year of the reign of Rájarájadéva, Oḷukaraiyán (*alias*) Kulóttuṅgachóḷattali-varáya (*alias*) Púṅgunṛamuḍaiyár (*alias*) Ráviḷḷanáyakan (*alias*) Kúndatennavataraiyan presented one evening lamp to last as long as the moon and sun endure to the god Tirunágíśvara of Śúralúr.

We, the Siva Brahmans of this temple, received for every day three good, old *káśu* as interest on his (donor's)

behalf (binding ourselves) to maintain (the lamp) in this manner.

[1] ஸ்வஸ்தி ஸ்ரீ ராஜராஜதேவர்க்கு யா-
[2] ண்டு பன்னிரண்டாவது சூரலூர் திருநா-
[3] கேசுரமுடையநாயனார்க்கு ஒழுகறையான் கு-
[4] லோத்துங்கசோழத்த[லிவராய]பூங்குன்ற-
[5] முடையார் [ராவிள்ளாக]யகன் கூந்த-
[6] தென்னவதரையனென் சந்திராதித்தவரை
[7] செல்வதாக வைத்த சந்திவிளக்கு ஒன்றும் இ-
[8] ப்படி செலுத்துவதாக இக்கோயில் காணியு-
[9] டைய சிவபிராமணரோம் பொலிஊட்டாக
[10] இவர் பக்கல் கைக்கொண்ட அன்றாடு
[11] நற்பழங்காசு மூன்றும் கைக்கொ-
[12] ண்டோம் சிவபிராமணரோம்.

SULURPET (7).

[Súlúrpéṭa. Tamil. Western wall of Nágéśvarasvámi temple.]

TRANSLATION.

Haríḥ! Hail! Prosperity! In the thirteenth year of the reign of Rájarájadéva, . . ngóḍan Śómadévan, *alias* Áṇḍapiḷḷai *alias* Koṅgaráya *alias* . . . . of Áyalúr (situated) in Kákkalúrnáḍu in . . . káṭṭúkóṭṭa . . . . Śúralúr *alias* . . . . (situated) in Vélúr-náḍu in Paiyúriḷaṅkóṭṭa . . . .

[1] ஹரிஃ ஸ்வஸ்திஶ்ரீ ராஜராஜதேவற்கு யாண்டு பதின்-மூன்றாவது . . . .

[2] க்காட்டுக்கோட்டத்துக்காக்கலூர்நாட்டு ஆயலூர்க்கெ . . . .

[3] ரங்கொடடன் சொமதெவன் ஆண்டபிள்ளை ஆன கொ-
ங்கராய . . . .

[4] னென் பையூரிளங்கொட்டத்து வெலூர்நாட்டு குர-
லூரான . . . .

SULURPET (8).

[Súlúrpéṭa. Tamil. Western wall of Nágésvarasvámi temple.]

TRANSLATION.

In the second year of the reign of [Vijayagaṇḍa]-gópáladéva, Rájéndrachóḷa Mummuḍi Vaidumba Máhárájan presented 500 *kuḻis* of land for one lamp in Eṇṇáyiraparaiyúr Putteri . . . . and (for the performance of a festival) during Tiruvádirai (in the month of) the sacred Márgaḻi to . . . . Náyanár (deity) . . . . in Jayankoṇḍa . . . . Whoever obstructs this charity (will incur the sin of killing) a tawny cow on the banks of the Ganges.

NOTE.—A Mummaḍi Vaitumba Mahárája appears in G. 88 also. *See* also No. 66.

[1] . . . . . ண்டகொபாலதெவற்கு இரண்டாவது
ஜயங்கொண்-

[2] . . . . . டைய நாயனார்க்கு இராஜெந்திரசொ-
ழமும்முடி வைதும்பமஹாரா-

[3] . . . . . திரைச்சிறப்புக்கும் எண்ணாயிரபறை-
யூர்ப்புத்தெரியில் க-

[4] . . . . . ாவிளக்கு ஒன்றுக்கு விட்ட குழி ஐஞ்
ஞூறும் திருமார்கழி திருவாதிரைக்கு விட்ட

[5] . . . . . னென் இத்தன்மம் இறக்குவான் கெங்-
கையிடை குமரியிடை குராற்பசுக்-

SULURPET (9).

[Súlúrpéṭa. Tamil. South wall of Nágéśvarasvámi temple.]

TRANSLATION.

Hail! Prosperity! In the thirty-eighth year of the reign of the emperor of the three worlds, the glorious Kulóttuṅgachóḻadéva, the things given to last as long as the moon and sun endure to the deity Tirunágéśvara at Śúralúr *alias* Śiṅgalántagapura (situated) in Vélúrnáḍu in Paiyurilaṅkóṭṭa (a sub-division) of Jayaṅkoṇḍachóḻamaṇḍalam . . . .

[End mutilated.]

[1] ஸ்வ[ஸ்தி ஸ்ரீ திரிபுவந]ச்சக்கரவத்[தி]-
[2] கள் சிரிகுலொத்துங்கசொழதெ[த]-
[3] வற்கு யாண்டு முப்பத்தெட்டாவ-
[4] து ஜெயங்கொண்டசொழமண்-
[5] [டல]த்துப்பையூரிளங்கொட்ட-
[6] த்து வெலூர்நாடு சூரலூரான சிங்க-
[7] [ளாந்த]கபுரத்து திரு[நாகீசுர]-
[8] முடைய[நாய]நாற்குச்சந்திராதித்தவ[ரை]
[9] [செல்]வதாகக்குடுத்தமைக்கு காவ்வார் ஆ-
[10] . . . . . ண்டி சிங்க-
[11] . . . . . க்கன் ஒன்று . . . நாரசிங்க.

SULURPET (10).

[Tummúru. Telugu. From roof of Nílakanthasvámi temple. Illegible.]

1. . . . .
2. . . . . . . వనా . . . . . .

3. శావం . . . . తక్షిండి . . .
4. . . . . రంమ . . . వా . . . .
5. . . . ధనంవా . మ . . . .
6. . . . . . అ . . నదాసం ఓభ . . . . .

Sulurpet (11). (A.D. 1513-14.)

[Tummúru. Tamil. From pillar of western porch of Kariyamánikasvámi temple.]

Translation.

Hail! Prosperity! In the victorious and prosperous expired Sálivábana Saka year 1435, corresponding to the year *Srímukha*, on Monday, the 11th day of the bright half of the month of Mithuna (the following) is the grant agreed to by the glorious Krishnaráya Mábáráya the glorious Máhárájádhirája Rájaparaméśvara Víra-pratápa (and made) to the temple treasury of the God Tirukkálahastísvara.

The following are the villages granted with libations of water as charity on behalf of Narasánáyaka, Immuru Mátákkal and Narasimha . . . on this sacred day of *prathama ékádasi* for the daily worship of the God *Vináyaka* with bathing perquisites, scents for anointing the body, including camphor, saffron, *tastákattai* (sandal-wood paste?), and flower garlands made of *pannír* and Champak flowers, a sacred lamp as well as rice and cakes, camphor balls and other daily offerings, for arranging a sacrificial bath for the god (Kálahastíśvara) on the date of our (the king's) birthday under the *Nakshatra* Jyéshtá in the month of Vaikáśi, and for celebrating in the month of Ádi (the festivals including) the hoisting of the flag, the car festival, *Tiruchchándu*, sacred marriage, &c., and in the month of Vaikási the great festival, after first dedicating to the god Tirukkáḷa-hastíśvara a crown inlaid with the nine precious stones.

The villages are: Puliyúr in Pónagainádu; Tonpák-kam in Kamalainádu; one share belonging to the temple treasury in the village Chennáḷi in the same *náḍu*; the village of Nitti; the village of Karumbéḍu attached to the city of Tagalaṇipaṇi; plantations in the village of Śattambaiyúr (portion not clear here); the village of Tummúru in Mádainallúrsíma in this *náḍu*. All the dues from these villages, including the dues appertaining to water, land, &c., were given by us with libations of water, to the temple treasury of the god Tirukkáḷahastíśvara free of tax.

With the produce of these villages all the donations to the god Tirukkáḷahastíśvara, including food, referred to in this stone grant, as well as the sacred flower garden, shall be maintained as long as the moon and sun last. This charitable grant was made on this understanding.

If any one fails to keep this charity, he will incur the sin of killing his parents in the Ganges, of killing a cow of . . . . of killing a Brahman, and other sins.

[Three imprecatory verses.]

[1] ஸ்வஸ்திஸ்ரீ விஜயாப்யுதய ஸாலிவாஹந ஸகவருஷம்
[2] த்து சாங்கடுருன்மெல் செல்லாநின்ற ஸ்ரீபவஸம்வத்ஸரா-
[3] த்து ரியாத நாயற்று வடுஷ்டேவகஷத்து வாயு[தூ]-
தெஸமியும்
[4] ஸொமவாரமும் பெற்றநாள் நாயனார் திருக்காளஹஸ்தி-
[5] ஸ்வரநாயனார் ஸ்ரீபண்டாரத்துக்கு ஸ்ரீவீரமஹாராஜாதி-
ராஜ ராஜ-

[6] வாஜேய ஸ்ரீவீரவரதாவ ஸ்ரீவீரகுருஹாராயஹேமா-
ராயர் ஸ்வஸ்தி-

[7] த்த ஸாவஸரதீ . . . . . ஷாக்கள் நரஸாதயக்க-
உடையர்க்கும் ஷம்மு-

[8] [று]ஜாகாக்கள் நாஸ[ஹ] . . . . . . ச்கும்
யஜுர்ஜாக நாயனார் திருக்காளஹஸ்தீஸ்ராகாய-

[9] ார்க்கு நகரதவவித்ஜாக ஸாமணவ்ரஹாஷியும் ஸஜ-
லீத்து நாளது முதலாக நித்த-

[10] ப்படி விநாயகபூஜையபிஷேகத்ர [வ்ய] மிதக்மெறப்-
பூசுக்கற்பூரம் குங்குமம் கஸ்தூரிகட்டெ

[11] மொழுகு பன்னீர்ச்செம்பதிருமாலை திருநக்ஷாவிள-
க்கு அமுது செய்து அருள நைவேத்யத் வஞ்ச-

[12] [ந]வகைப்பண்ணியாரம் திருக்கணுமெண்ணெ ஆடைக்-
காயமுது கற்பூரஉருண்ணை முதலா-

[13] ன நித்தப்படித்தாம் நடத்தத்தக்கதாகவும் வைகாஸிஜோ-
ஷஸ்பிலெ நம்முடைய ஜநந-

[14] க்ஷத்ர ஜெஷ்டாநக்ஷ[த்ர]த்திலே சுவஸ்தகஸ்நானம்
பண்ணித்தக்கதாக ஞுஷிஜாவஸ கஸகஷாராற்ப-

[15] ணஜ்ஜாரொஹண ஈயோத்ஸ [வ]த் திருச்சாந்து தி-
ருக்கல்யாணம் முதலான வைகாஸிஜோஷஸ

[16] யில் உத்ஸாதஸவத் நடக்கத்தக்கதாகவும் மிந்த வ்ரயஜ
எகாஜெஸிவஷணுகாலத்திலே தாரா-

[17] வஷுர்ஜாக ஸவேத்தி[த்த ஹுரா]மங்கள் பொனகை-
காட்டுப்புலியூர் ஹுராமம் உட[டை]யநாட்டில்

[18] செ[த]ன்பாக்கம் கிராமம் இன்நாட்டுச் சன்றுனி ஸ்ரீஹ-
ணாரப்பங்கு ஆக நடக்கிற பங்கு ஒ-

[19] ன்று கித்திரஹுராமம் [தகல]ணிபணிபுரத்து[ஸ்தல]த்தி-
ல் கரும்பெட்டு ஹுராமஸத்தம்பையூறத்-

[20] தொட்டத்தில் . . . . . ஆக பங்கு ஷத்த ஹுராம
மூன்றெமுக்காலுமாக இங்-

[21] நாட்டுக்குள் [மாடைகல்லூர்]சிர்மையில் தும்மூர்
[க்]ராமமு[ம்] இந்த ஹுராம ஒன்றுக்-

[22] குடுக்கிற ஊத்த ஆதாயம் [ஸுவர்ண]யாயம் ஆய-ம் மகமை தலையாரிக்கம்பட்டடை [ப]ா-

[23] லய [வஸ்து]க்களையும் [ஜல படி]த்துறை முதலாக ஸ-ர்வ ஆதாயமும் ஸர்வமாந்யமா-

[24] க யாநயாஸர்வ்வமாக நாயனார் திருக்காளஹஸ்தி-ஸ்வரநாயனார் ஸ்ரீபண்டாரத்துக்கு

[25] ஸம்வத்ஸரதொம் இக் கிராமத்தில் [உ]ண்டான முதல் கொண்டு நாயனார் திருக்காளஹ-

[26] ஸ்திஸ்வரநாயனார்க்கு ஸாஸனப்ரகாரத்தில் நித்தப்படி-யும் [ப்ர]சாதித்தருளு சிலாவெளை-

[27] க முதலானவை பொகங்களும் நம்முடை திருநந்தவ-னமும் ஆசந்த்ரார்க்க-

[28] க நடத்திவரக்கடவார்கள் ஆகவும் என்று குடுத்தயஜ்ஞ-ஸர்வமாந்யம் இந்த யஜ்ஞத்துக்கு

[29] யாதொருவன் தப்பினாலும் தங்கள் மாதாபிதாக்களையும் [கங்கை]யிலெ வதைத்த

[30] பாவத்திலெ பொகக்கடவனாகவும் கொஹத்தி ப்ரஹ்ம-[சிசுஹத்தி] ஸ்ரீஹத்தி ப்ராஹ்மணஹத்தி

[31] முதலான பாவங்களிலெ பொகக்கடவன் ஆகவும் ஸ்வ-தத்தாத்த்விகுணம் புண்யம் பர-

[32] த்தாநுபாலநம் | பரதத்தாபஹாரெண ஸ்வதத்தம் நிஷ்-பலம் பவெத் || ஸ்வதத்தாம் பரத[த்தா]ம் வா-

[33] யொ ஹரெத வஸுந்தராம் || ஷஷ்டிவர்ஷஸஹஸ்ராணி விஷ்டாயாம் ஜாயதெ க்ருமி: || தாந-

[34] பாலநயொர்மத்யெ தாநாச்ச்ரெயொநுபாலநம் | [1*] தாநாத் ஸ்வர்க்கமவாப்நொதி பால-

[35] நாதச்யுதம் பதம்

SILURPET (12).

[Tummúru. Tamil. East wall of Kariyamánikyaráya temple.]

TRANSLATION.

Hail! Prosperity! In the thirteenth year of the reign of the emperor of the three worlds Rájarájadéva, the temple and the sacred place for Karumáṇikkaperumáḷ of Tumbaiyúr *alias* Jayaṅkoṇḍachóḻachaturvédimaṅgalam (situated) in Mélaipaṭṭayanáḍu in Paiyyúriḷaṅgóṭṭa (a sub-division) of Jayaṅkoṇḍachóḻamaṇḍala, were the charity performed by Tyágasamudrapaṭṭai Vímaraśan the lord of the best of cities Ayódhyá situated in the kingdom of Madurántakapottapichóḻa *alias* Gaṇḍagópála *alias* Tirukkáḷattidéva.

NOTE.—What Ayódhyá is referred to is not known. Possibly the donor claimed descent from the Chalukyas and the words "in the kingdom" refer to the locality where the charity was performed and not to the situation of Ayódhyá.

[1] ஸ்வஸ்தி ஸ்ரீ திரிபுவனச்சக்கரவர்த்திகள் ராஜராஜதெவ-ற்கு யாண்டு ௰௩ ஜயங்கொண்டசொழமண்டலத்து பையூரிளங்கொட்டத்-

[2] து மெலைப்பட்டயனாட்டுத்தும்பையூரான ஜயங்கொ-ண்ட சொழச்சதுர்வெதிமங்கலத்துக்கருமாணிக்கப்-பெருமான் கொயி-

[3] லும் திருமாளிகையும் மதுராந்தகப்பொத்தப்பிச்சொ-ழனை கண்டகொபாலன் திரு[க்]காளத்திதெவயிராச்சியத்தில் அயொத்யாபுரவரா-

[4] வராதிஸ்வரரான தியாகசமுத்திரப்பட்டை விமரசன் செய்வித்த தன்மம்.

SULURPET (13).

[Tummúru. Tamil. East wall of Kariyamánikyaráya temple. Illegible.]

SULURPET (14).

[Tummúru. Tamil. South wall of Kariyamánikyasvámi temple. A fragment recording the gift of a lamp.]

[1] தப்பநாக காயப்பநாயக்கநெக் இ-
[2] . . . . க்குச்வநூராதித்ருவரை ஒருசந்திவிளக்கு
[3] . . . . . க்க இதுக்கு . . . .
[4] . . . .

SULURPET (15).

[Tummúru. Tamil. From gate of Kariyamánikyaráya temple.]

TRANSLATION.

Hail! Prosperity! In the 16th year of the reign of the emperor of three worlds, the glorious Rájarájadéva . . . . laikáṇiyáḷa Iruṅkaṟṟipóyan *alias* Siddamanáyakka . . . . in the Chitra . . viṇṇagar *alias* Kanamáṇikkaperiya . . . . . at Tumbaiyúr (*alias*) Jayáṅkoṇḍachóḻachaturvédimaṅgalam (situated) in Paṭṭaiyanáḍu in Paiyyúriḷaṅkóṭṭa.

[1] ஸ்வஸ்தி ஸ்ரீ திரிபுவனச்சக்கரவத்திகள் ஸ்ரீராஜராஜதே-வற்கு யாண்டு ய[சா] ஆ[வ]-

[2] து பையூரிளங்கொட்டத்துப்பட்டையநாட்டுத்தும்-பையூ-

[3] [ர்] ஜயங்கொண்டசொழச்சது[ர்வே]திமங்கலத்துச்-சித்திரமெ-

[4] . . [வி]ண்ணகராக கணமாணிக்கப்பெரிய . . . யில குவரை

[5] . . . . ஊல காணியாளர் இருங்கற்றிபொயளுண சித்தமநாயக்கர் த

SULURPET (16). (A.D. 1593–94.)

[Tummúru. Telugu. From gate of Kariya-mánikyaráya temple.]

TRANSLATION.

Hail! On Sunday the 12th of the bright fortnight of Márgaṣira of the year Vijaya, corresponding to the year 1516 of the illustrious, victorious and prosperous Ṣáliváhana Ṣaka era, Velugóṭi Ráya Channáyani Lingam Gáru caused a *Mukhamaṇḍapa* (a hall) to be constructed to Káli Máṇikya Náyanar (deity) of Tummúru for his own religious merit. Salutation be to Ṣrí Venkaṭéṣvara. May it cause prosperity!

1. స్వస్తిశ్రీ విజయాభ్యుదయ శాలివాహన శకవర్షంబులు ౧౫౧౬ అగునేని విజయసంవత్సర

2. మార్గశిరశుద్ధ ౧౨ ఆ- వెలుగోటి రాయచన్నాయని లింగం గారు తమకు పుణ్యముగాను తుమ్మూరి కలి

3. మాణిక్యపు నాయనిర్ ముఖమండపం కట్టించినారు శ్రీ శ్రీ వేంకటేశ్వరా(య)నమః. శ్రీ శ్రీ శ్రీం జేయును.

SULURPET (17).

[Tummúru. Tamil. From shrine of Kariyamáṇikyaráya temple.]

TRANSLATION.

Hail! Prosperity! In the 23rd year of the reign of emperor of the three worlds, the glorious Rájarájadéva, Eramireḍḍi, the son of Viḷakkandaikkávisimuppareḍḍi *alias* Rájéndrachólamúvéndaveḷáḷan who possessed rights in Tiruvánbúr (a village) of Kíḻaippaṭṭaiyanáḍu, gave one *máḍai* to the Karumáṇikkaperumáḷ of Tumbaiyúr (a Mélaippaṭṭaiyanáḍu).

We, the three priests of this temple, agreed to light without failure one evening lamp as long as the sun and moon endure with the interest accruing from this *máḍai* at the rate[1] of half a *chinnam* per month and received it.

[1] ஸ்வஸ்தி ஸ்ரீ திரிபுவநச்சக்கரவத்திகள் ஸ்ரீராஜராஜதெவ-
ற்கு யாண்டு

[2] உ௰௩ வது மெலைப்பட்டையநாட்டு தும்பையூர்க்கரு-
மாணிக்க-

[3] ப்பெருமாளுக்குக் கிழைப்பட்டையநாட்டுத்திருவா-
ன்பூர்க்காணி-

[4] யாளன் இராஜெந்த்ரசொழமூவெந்தவெள்ளானான வி-
ளக்கந்தை-

[5] தக்காவிசிமுப்பரட்டி மகன் எறமிரட்டியென் இட்ட
மாடை

[6] ஒன்று இம்மாடை ஒன்றும் திங்கள் அரைச்சின்னம-

[7] ாக வந்த பலிசைக்குச்சந்திராதித்தவரை ஒரு சந்தி-
விளக்கு ஒன்-

[8] று முட்டாமல் செல்லுவதாக இக்கொயில் நம்பிமார்
மூவரும்

[9] கைக்கொண்டொம் ப௦

---

[1] The rate is 150 *per cent. per annum*, the *chinnam* being one-fourth of the *méḍai*.

SULURPET (18). (A.D. 1794-95.)

[Tummúru. Telugu. From tank bund.]

TRANSLATION.

Hail! On the 11th of the dark fortnight of Áshádha of the year Ánanda corresponding to the year 1716 of the illustrious and victorious and prosperous Ṣáliváhana Ṣaka era, Mahárája Rajá Ṣrí Velugóṭi Kumára Yáchama Náyanivíáru presented a *khandriga* on which ten *túms* can be sown in the fields of Tumbúr to Nílakanṭhésvara-svámi. Máram Reḍḍi Krishṇa Reḍḍi and our Revenue officer should utilize this for the offerings of the deity and perform festivals.

1. స్వస్తిశ్రీ విజ
2. యాభ్యుదయ
3. శాలివాహన శకవ
4. షరాంబులు ౧౭౧౬
5. అగునేటి ఆనందసంవత్స
6. ర ఆషాఢ బ ౧౧లు శ్రీనీలక
7. ంఠేశ్వర స్వామివారికి మ
8. హారాజరాజశ్రీ వెలు
9. గోటి కుమార యాచ
10. మనాయనివారు తుం
11. బూరు పొలంలో ప్ర
12. ల పొధుం వి త్తనాల
13. పట్టు ఖండ్రిగె మారం
14. రెడ్డి కృష్ణారెడ్డిని మాఅ
15. మీలును నయివేద్యం ము
16. లకు తిరువాళ్ల యు
17. న్ను చేయించువారు.

SULURPET (19).

[Utsúru. Tamil. From door of Chennakéṣava temple.]

TRANSLATION.

Hail! Prosperity! In the 23rd year of the reign of Vijayagaṇḍagópálaḍéva . . . . for the erection of the sacred door-way for the sacred *maṇḍapam* of Chennakéśavaperumáḷ of Uchchiyúr. . . . . This is a great charity.

[1] ஸ்வஸ்தி ஸ்ரீ
[2] விஜயகண்
[3] டகோபால-
[4] [தே]வற்கு யாண்[டு]
[5] [இ]ருப[த்]து[மூன்று]-
[6] [வ]து உச்சியூர்செ-
[7] ன்னகேசவப்-
[8] பெருமாளை
[9] திருமண்டப[த்.]-
[10] து திருக்லை ஒ-
[11] வஸி . . சமுச்-
[12] . . . ட்படை
[13] . . . டி திக்கு
[14] ெெரச செய்க்-
[15] குமடிப்பெரு-
[16] ன் தன்ம இது.

SULURPET (20).

[Utsúru. Telugu. Opposite Bhíméṣvarasvámi temple.]

TRANSLATION.

On Tuesday the 13th of the dark fortnight of Mágha of the year Vikrama, on the holy occasion of Ṣiva Rátri

Pina Kúpi Náyuḍu, son of Rávúri Pápí Náyuḍu, presented with libation of water to Bhímésvaradéva Dáravonta (the name of a field?) (situated) in the fort and under the Ponnéri *gunṭa.* Whoever thinks of injuring (this charity) will incur the sin of killing a cow and a Brahman on the banks of the Ganges. If any one puts obstacles in the way, his honour will be given to Málas.

1. విక్రమసంవత్సర మాఘబహుళ ౧౩ మ సివరాత్రి పు
2. ణ్యకాలమందు రావూరి పాపినాయిని కోమారుండు
3. పినకూపినాయిండు దారవోసిన బీమేశ్వరదేవునికి కోటలో
4. ను పొన్నేరి గుంటకిందును దారవొంత ఎవరునంతు తల
5. ంచినాను గంగకరలగోవు బ్రాంహ్మణింజంపినపాపానబోవు
6. వారు. ఇందుకుయవరుఆటంక(వ?)రిస్తేసువానిమానముమా
7. లలకు ఇత్తురు.

SULURPET (21).

[Utsúru. Telugu. By tank bund.]

TRANSLATION.

On the 12th of the dark fortnight of Vaiṣákha of the year Vikṛiti . . . .

1. వికృతిసంవత్సర వైశాఖ బ ౧౨ లు
2. . . . . . కుజా మీరుండ్లు
3. . ర చెవ్రు . . . . . చెరు
4. వు చెరు . . . . . .
5. . . . .
6. . . . . . . పాబోవు

Udayagiri (1). (A.D. 1568–69?)

[Alimélumangapuram. Telugu. From stone near Ánjanéya's figure.]

Translation.

May there be prosperity! Hail! On Thursday, the 13th day of the bright half of Srávaṇa of the year Vibhava,[1] corresponding to the year 1444 of the illustrious, victorious and prosperous Sálivâhana Saka era, Singála Akkalayya, having caused an image of Hanumanta Perumal to be made and having consecrated it, caused to be built a temple, so that it may last in perpetuity as long as the moon exists, at Bóyamaḍugu, for the religious merit of his father Koṇḍamanéni and his mother Rangamma. The constant worship of Akkalayya.

May it cause great prosperity!

1. శుభమస్తు॥ స్వస్తిశ్రీ జయాభ్యుదయశా
2. లివాహన శక వర్షంబులు ౧౪౪౪ అగునేంటి వి
3. భవసంవత్సర శ్రావణ శుద్ధ ౧౩ గు। శింగాల అక్కలయ్య
4. తమతండ్రి కొండమనేనిక్కిన్ని తమతల్లి రంగ్గమ్మంగారిక్కి
5. న్ని పుణ్యమానట్టుగాను ఆచంద్రార్కస్థాయిగాను బోయిమడు
6. గున హనుమంత్త పెరుమాళ్లను శేయించ్చి ప్రతిష్ట శేయించ్చి గు
7. డి గట్టించెను అక్కలయ్య సదా శేవ॥ శ్రీ శ్రీ శ్రీం జేయును।

---

[1] S.S. 1444 corresponds to Vrisha and 1431 and 1491 to Vibhava.

UDAYAGIRI (2). (A.D. 1568–69 ?)

[Alimélumangapuram. Telugu. From another stone near the image of Ánjanéya.]

TRANSLATION.

May there be prosperity! Hail! On the 13th day of the bright fortnight of Srávana of the year Vibhava,[1] corresponding to the year 1444 of the illustrious, victorious and prosperous Śálivâhana Śaka era, while S.ímat Rájádhirája, Rájaparaméṣvara, Śrí Víra Pratápa, Śrí Víra, Bhujabala,[2] Tirumaladéva Mahárájulu Ayyaváru, seated on the diamond throne, was ruling the kingdom of Vidyánagara, he was pleased to grant an *amaram* to Kammarajangam Vaḍla Prasannamgáru of Udayagiri for (doing) his Amara service . . . . . We have given two *gorrus* in Bindala Vasili Naḍimi field and three *gorrus* in Chimbam Vunnavaḍi field, in all 5 *gorrus* excluding the land given for providing *amṛitapadi* (food) with libation of water to Hanumán by Jangam Prasannam, who is the ruler of the village named Bóyamaḍugu, for the religious merit of his father and mother. Therefore, if any one fails to keep up this charity, he will incur the sin of killing cows and Brahmans near the Ganges. He will incur the sin of carnally knowing his mother.

[One imprecatory verse.]

NOTE.—This Jangam Prasannam is not mentioned elsewhere in this collection.

1. శుభమస్తు । స్వస్తిశ్రీ జయా
2. భ్యుదయ శాలివాహాన శక వర్ష

[1] S.S. 1444 corresponds to Vrisha and 1431 and 1491 to Vibhava.

[2] Bhujabala = Strong-armed.

3. ంబులు ౧౪౭౪ అగు నేంటి
4. విభవ సంవత్సర శ్రావణ శు ౧౩
5. లు॥ శ్రీమ ద్రాజాధి రాజ రాజ పర
6. మేశ్వర శ్రీవీర ప్రతాప శ్రీవీర భు
7. జ భల తిరుమలదేవ మహారాయ
8. లయ్యవారు వజ్రసింహాసనాసీనుండై వి
9. ద్యానగరం మేలుచుండి వుదయగిరి క
10. మ్మర జంగ్గం వజ్లప్రసన్నంగారికి అమరమ
11. డంగివనులకుగాను అమరం పాలిం
12. చ్చి ఇయ్య నవధరించ్చినాలు . . .
13. . . . . బోయమద్దు గ్రామం
14. యేలుచుండె జంగ్గం ప్రసన్నంగారు
15. తమతల్లి దండ్రాదుల పుణ్యంగా
16. ను హనుమంతుని అమృత ప
17. ళ్లకు దారవోసి ఇచ్చిన క్షేత్రంబోను
18. బిదళవాసిల నడిమిచేను ౨ గోలుఁన్ను
19. చింబంవున్నవాడిచేను ౩ గోలుఁన్ను కూ
20. డా ౫ గోలుఁచేను ఇస్తిమి గనుక యీ
21. పుణ్యాన్ను యవ్వరు తప్పినాను గంగ
22. కతఁను గోబ్రెంహ్మన్ని వధిఇంచినం పాపానం
23. పోవువారు కన్నతల్లిని కాంగిలించ్చిన పాపాన బోయి
24. నవారు॥ స్వదత్తం ద్విగుణం పుణ్యం పర
25. దత్తానుపాలనం పరదత్తాపహారేణ స్వదత్తం నిష్ఫలంభ
వేత్ ॥

UDAYAGIRI (3). (A.D. 1244–45.)

[Ayyavváripalli. Telugu. From four sides of an upright stone. Above the inscription are figures of the Linga, bull, sun and moon.]

TRANSLATION.

Hail! [To Siddhanátha déva,] (same as paragraph 1 of No. 11 below); this charity has been given for the religious merit of Ṣríman Mahámaṇḍaléṣvara Bhujabala Chóḍa Tirukáḷti (kálati) Déva Mahárája, &c. (as in paragraph 2 of No. (14)) and for the religious merit of Alu Tika (Tikka) ráju Tirukála déva.

This is the gift of Tende tank made to Siddhanátha-déva.

On Thursday, the 10th of the bright half of Chaitra of the year Kródha, corresponding to 1167 of the Ṣaka era, they have given (it) after pouring water in the hand of Kédavarma.

If the three persons Átukúr Rámireḍḍi, Gaṇḍavaram Vammireḍḍi and Káḍuváluti Chóḍapareḍḍi fail to keep up this charity, or if any one obstruct it, he will incur the sin of killing a tawny cow on the Ganges.

East side.

1. స్వస్తి సమస్త భువనా
2. ధీశ్వర శ్రీ శ్రీ శైల
3. శిఖర సింహాసనకే
4. ళిలోల విష్ణో నేత్రాం
5. బుజ ప్రసవగ
6. న్థ కుసూమాలా మం
7. గళ మణి దీపికా
8. యమూన మానసేక

9. మాణిక్య శిలాతల ప్ర
10. భా పటల ఘటిలిత
11. పురందర లోకపాల
12. క అర్చిత సనకస
13. నంద సనత్కుమార
14. నారదాది ముని నికాయ

South side.

15. సకల సురాసు
16. రోరగేంద్ర సిద్ధ
17. విద్యాధరాద్య
18. నేక పరివార
19. పరివ్రితాస్థానా
20. రస రసాయన
21. పదాంజన ఖ
22. డ్గయాగ
23. ఘుటికా- కంన్య
24. శావాద మంత్ర
25. వాద దూమ్రం
26. గరుడవాద
27. రాస వాదదే
28. తిగళని సిద్ధ
29. వ్యాళినాగజు
30. ని నగబుద్ధకో
31. రంటిక గధన [1]
32. రత్నఘోష
33. విష్ణుగుప్త చం
34. ద్రగుప్త బాణా

---

[1] In No. 11 instead of గదన we have శదంబక and శాదంబ.

35. శ్యాదిం నిఖిల
36. సిద్ధ జనామనో
37. భిలశిత ప్రదా
38. యక భక్తజన

West side.

39. భుక్తిముక్తి ప్రదాయక శ్రీ
40. పర్వత ప్రియ నివాస [స్వస్తి వి]
41. ళ్లోచన [1]త్ర్యిళ్లోచన కారిత
42. కావేరి తీర కరికాలకు
43. లకడు ప్రదీప అపరి
44. మిత ప్రతాప సతత
45. [సి]మంత[2] లక్ష్మీశ్వర ఒలయా
46. రిపురావారావాధీశ్వరాకాం
47. చ్చీపుర వరాధీశా శ్రీమ
48. నుమహా మండలేశ్వ
49. ర భుజబళ చోడంతి
50. రుకల్తి దేవా మహా
51. రాజానకు పుణ్యం
52. ముగాను అలుతికరా
53. ంజు తిరుకాల దేవుడికి
54. పున్యముగాను ఇచ్చి
55. న ధర్మువు తెండె చెలు
56. వు సిద్ధనాతం దేవరకు
57. నిచ్చినదత్తిం । శాకా
58. వరుశ్యంబులు.
59. ౧౧౬౭

[1] త్రిలోచన. [2] సముత్ప్యచిత in No 11.

North side.

60. క్రోధి సంవత్స
61. రమున చైత
62. త్ర సుద్ధ ౧౦ ద
63. శమి గురువార
64. మున కేదవ
65. రుమ చేతదా
66. రవోసి ఇచ్చిరి
67. ఆతుకూరిగామి
68. రెడ్డిని గడంవర
69. వమ్మి రెడ్డిని
70. కాడువాలుతి
71. చోడవ రెడ్డి
72. ముప్వురును ఈ
73. ధర్మవుంత
74. ప్పిన వారా ఎవ్వడే
75. ను విఫలము సే
76. సిన వాడు గం
77. గ కలుతందా
78. ఇ కవిలం పొడి
79. చిన పాపానం
80. పోయినవాడు.

UDAYAGIRI (4). (A.D. 1514–15.)

[Dásarapalli. Telugu. From steps in a cave.]

TRANSLATION.

Hail! On the 3rd day of the dark fortnight of Jeshta (jyéshṭha) of the year Bháva, corresponding to the year 1436 of the illustrious, victorious and prosperous Sáliváhana Saka era, under the orders of Srí Krishnadéva Mahárâya, Ráyasam Konda [marusayya Gáru] . . . .

Note.—Ráyasam Konda Marusayya is referred to in other inscriptions as the governor of Udayagiri. His name is not Konda Narasayya as given by Mr. Sewell.

There are two other inscriptions in this cave, but they contain only a few words and are not worth recording.

1. స్వస్తిశ్రీ జయాభ్యుదయ శాలివాహన శకవర్షంబులు ౧౪౩౬ అగు నేంటి

2. భావ సంవత్సర జేష్ట బ ౩ లు శ్రీ కృష్ణదేవ మహారాయు లు ఆనతిన రాయసం కొండ [మరుసయ్యగారు]

* * * *

Udayagiri (5).

[Guvvádi. Telugu. Incomplete.]

Translation.

* * * *

The *Vritti* (share, land) given with libation of water to last as long as the sun and moon exist. Those who obstruct this charity are sinners. They will incur the sin of killing (kine) near the Ganges.

[Two imprecatory verses.]

* * * *

1. ఆ చంద్రార్కము
2. గాను ధారాపూ
3. ర్వ వ్రిత్తి దీనికి
4. నెవ్వరు ద్రోచినాను పా
5. పము సేసినవారు గంగ కఱుల
6. వధియించిన పాపంబునం పోయినవారు

7. స్వదత్తం పరదత్తం వా యో హరేతి
8. వసుంధరా షష్టిర్వర్షసహస్రాణి విష్టా
9. యాం జాయతే క్రిమి॥ స్వదత్తాద్విగుణం
10. పుణ్యం పరదత్తానుపాలనా పరదత్తాపహారేణ
11. స్వదత్తం నిష్ఫలం భవేత్ ॥

Uḍayagiri (6).

[Jaḍadévi. Telugu. On bank of Pilappéru, south of village. From two sides of a stone.]

Translation.

Prosperity! Hail! Ṣríman Mahámanḍaléṣvara Dórapa Ráju, the over-lord of many countries of the earth, the supreme king of kings, the ornament of the Pallava family, of the Bháradvája *gôtra*, whose banner was the club of the wearer of the beautiful crescent moon (Ṣiva), who is Révanta in riding troublesome horses, the lord of Kánchi the best of cities, the possessor of a boon from Kámakóṭi, whose ensign was the bull, the worshipper of Véngaḍanátha, who was an Arjuna in valour, who was venerated by his subordinates and who was beloved by his kinsmen, fierce in war, the incarnation of Náráyaṇa Rudra, the lotuses of whose feet were touched by the jewelled diadems of many hostile kings, who resembled Káma (in beauty), who was desirous of the conquest of the cardinal points (the world), and who was a descendant of Konḍavíṭṭi (Káḍuveṭṭi?), had five sons, Iruga Ráju, Samarta Ráju, Yamma Ráju, Bhíma Ráju, and Bandu Ráju. Of these Yamma Ráju, *alias* Ṣríman Mahámanḍaléṣvara Nandivarma Maháraja, was crowned at Chóḍapuram in the month of Rishabha of the year Chitrabhánu, corresponding to the illustrious Saka year 1024. While he was ruling Ponugóḍu and Máḍurévi (?), enjoying pleasant correspondence (with his feudatories), on the occasion of a lunar eclipse in the month of Kanyá, he presented (the villages) Mridikallu, Guḍimiṭṭa, Baddimaḍuva, Jókúru, Uppalapura, Rávipáḍu, Iddukalapáḍu, Jadrupaḍiya, Sangam, Gónuguṇṭa, and Guḍipáḍu, (situated) in Pungináḍu, as *agrahàras* to Brahmans, constructed two temples, *manḍapas*, *gópuras*, and *prákáras* to Dá[o?]résvara and Irugésvara of Páḍaṭúru, his favourite village (?), constructed a temple named Vindhyavási, dug a tank named Podarasamudram . . . . . excavated a channel named . . . . after himself, built a sluice for the tank, planted a flower garden (?) and gave lands (?) to the deities Rishabhakésvara and Baddidórísvara. He erected a . . . . and *manḍapa* in the name of Durgidévi . . . . tank to the north of Vindhyavási temple, and erected a *prákára* and *gópura* in the name of Samarthaṭi Ráju.

Second side.

. . . . Irugésvaradéva . . . . Vi[?]dhyavási Brahmaṇa . . . . ráyaṇa Bhaṭṭa 400 *puṭṭis* (?) . . . . under the tank . . . . the perpetual lamp to . . . . . ra dévara, to Irugésvara dévan and for 12 dancing girls, and 12 Brahmans, gave Manumúru (?) with libation of water . . . and presented lands under . . . samudram (tank) to . . . . . We have granted 50 ewes for the perpetual lamp of Ghaṭikésvaradéva, 50 ewes for the perpetual lamp of . . . . in Doyúru, 50 ewes for the perpetual lamp of (Iru)gésvaradéva, and 50 ewes for the perpetual lamp of Vindhyavási. We have given these 200 (ewes) into the charge of Mahayadúmanḍéṭi (?) dévana, to last as long as the moon and sun endure.

[Two imprecatory verses.]

Those who injure these charities will incur the sin of killing 1,000 tawny cows near the Ganges. Those who maintain the service in this temple (?) will get the fame . . . . . Benares . . . . . edict . . . . .

May it cause great prosperity.

(The signature of) Murya, son of Dévaya, and servant of Nadivamma.

NOTE.—Compare P. 17 which relates to the same dynasty. We cannot trace any other references to the rulers mentioned here. Véngaḍam is Tirupati. For Konḍaviḍu we should doubtless read Káḍuveṭṭu.

1. శ్రీ స్వస్తి అనేక మహీమణ్డల రాజాధిరాజ రాజప

2. రమేస్వర పల్లవకులతిలక భారద్వాజగోత్ర లలితార్థ
చంద్రధరకట్వాం

3. గధ్వజ కడుహయారూఢ రేఖా రేవంత కాంచీపురవరాధీ
శ్వర కామకోటిలబ్ధవరప్ర

4. సాద రిషభలాంచ్ఛన వెంగడనాధకోడువడి, సాహసార్జు
న నిజసేవకాభావ బన్ధుజనా

5. శ్రయ సమరప్రచణ్డ హోరిదగోపాల చలదంభోరవ భు
వని నారాయణ రుద్రావతార

6. అనేక రిపునివలిమణిమకుట ఘట్టిత చరణారవిన్ద కుమార
కందర్ప దిగ్విజయా

7. ర్థ కొండువీటి వంశావతారులైన శ్రీ మనుమహామణ్డ
లేశ్వర దోరపరాజునకు దృగ్గి

8. దాంవిరి మనోహరాజ్యాగాను డీయించి నంసు ప్రత్రులైన
యిరుగరాజును సమర్తరాజును యమ్మరా

9. జును భీమరాజును బస్వరాజును నాసేగతినమెవురులోన
శ్రీ మన్మహామణ్డలేశ్వర నంది

10. వర్మణమహారాజులైన యమ్మరాజులు శ్రీ మత్సకవరుషం బులు వేయింనిరువాదవనాలవు నేం

11. టి చిత్రభానుసంవత్సరంబున రిషభమాసంబున చోడుపు రం బట్టముగట్టి పొనుంగోటిమాడురె

12. స్నీసుకసంకతావినోదంబుల రాజ్యంబుసేయుచు గన్న మాసమున సోమగ్రహణంమునన్దు జన్నత్రి

13. . . న పూంగినాంట్టిలోన త్రిదికల్లును గుడిమిట్టయుం బద్దిమడువునూ జోమూరుంను ప్పలవు

14. రును రావిపాడుంన్నిద్దు కలపాడును ఐద్రుపడియయు సంగాముంగోను గుంటయు గుడిపాడును

15. బ్రాహ్మనుల కగ్రహారంబులుగానిచ్చి తమరంజపల్లిరైన పాదటూరదా(దొ)రేస్వర మున్నిరుగేస్వ

16. ర నుంనారెండుటి ఆలయములు మణ్డపప్రాకారగోపురం బులెత్తించి వింద్యవాసిగుడి ౫

17. త్తింపోడరసముద్రంబని చెరువుగోప్పి బచలార్ద కతీర వుదనితన పేరంగాల్వదీప్పించి

18. చెఱువునకు దూముగట్టించిన . నవనమువెట్టి రృపటీభ కేశ్వర దేవరకుంబద్దికోరిస్వరదేవ

19. తకు బెట్టియిచ్చినది వింధ్యవాసిగుడిం నుత్తరాన్నచెఱు వు . . . హహె . . నెత్తించి మండపము దు

20. గిఱ దేవిపేరనెత్తించి ప్రాకారువునుం గోపురంమ్మునుం సమర్థఱటి రాజుపేరనెత్తించి.

Second side.

1. . . కు బెట్టియున్నరగేశ్వరదేవరకుంబెట్టియుం వింద్యవా సికిం బెట్టియుబ్రహ్మ

2. ణ . . . రాయణభట్టులకున నూఱురు(పు?)టిలుగా జె ఱుపు క్రింద్ద పాడెబేర

3. . . . రదేవరకుం నిరుగేస్వరదేవరకుం (నఖండకొఱకు) ఋన్నిద్దఱుసానుల

4. వన్నుండిచ్చు బ్రాంహ్మనులకుమర్థిం మనునా(మూ ?)రు దేవ భోగముగాదారాయెత్తి పు(ఘ ?)టికె

5. శ్వరదేవరకుమయ్యా రజ . వ్నాంబిమలూరబెట్టిరి . . వునిగాలువట్టిదేవ . . .

6. (గాన) . మరమునజు . . . రి భోజ్యకొడుకులునై (పాజ్య జెల్లెవరి)

7. . త్యఖాడితం . . సిముద్రముకింన్దబండె నేలయిచ్చిఘటి కేశ్వరదేవరకు నఖణ్డ

8. వత్తికి నేజైగొటియలు దోయూర నఖణ్డవత్తికి నేభైగొటి యలా.

9. . నేశ్వర దేవరకు నఖణ్డవత్తినైభైగొటియలు వింద్యవాసి కిం నఖణ్డవత్తికినైభై

10. గొటియలు నిస్తిమి యిన్నాటుని (మ) హాయదూమన్డేటి దేవన వసమున నాచంద్రార్కమూ

11. . . . నముగం న్నిచ్చితిమి॥ స్వదత్తం మనన్తపుణ్యం పర దత్తానుపాలయతు పరదత్తా పహ

12. రేణ స్వదత్తం నిష్ఫలంభవేతు॥ బహుభిర్వ్యా సుధాద త్తరాజుభిసగరాదిభి యస్య

13. యస్యయదాభూమి తస్య తస్య తధాఫలం॥ స్వదత్తం పాయోహరేతి వసున్ధరా

14. షష్టి వర్షసహస్రాణి విష్టాయాం జాయితేక్రిమి॥ యీ ధర్మవులుచె

15. అచినవారు గంగకటుత వేయిగ విలలబోడిచిన పాపమున బడుదురు యీ (గు)డిపని

16. సెసినకాసిలోకీర్తి (జు జీ . .) హాదిత్య పీరిదియిసాన నము హారియుంజ . కకు వణ్డ . . . .

17. ప్రము మంగలమహా శ్రీ శ్రీ శ్రీ దేవయకొడుకు నవివమ్మ డిహరిమూర్త్య.

UDAYAGIRI (7).

[Nallagoṇḍa. Telugu. From Narasiṃha temple on the hill.]

TRANSLATION.

The stone temple and sacred tank dedicated to Ṣrí Ṛangarāju (God) of Nallagoṇḍa by Abbá Pandit, younger brother of Narasimha Pandit, son of Gangádhara Pandit and his wife Appasáni Ammá, who belongs to the *gótra* of Kauṣika, who is a studenṭ of the Yajus Ṣákhá, on Friday the 10th of the bright half of Mágha of the illustrious year Kródhana.

శ్రీ క్రోధన సంవత్సర మాఘ శుద్ధ దశమీ సుక్రవారం కౌశిక గోత్రం యజుశ్శాఖాధ్యాయులయిన గంగాధరపండితుల అర్ధాంగ లక్ష్మీలయిన అప్పసాని అమ్మ కొమాళ్లు నరశింహ్వా పండితుల తమ్ముండు అబ్బాపండితులు నల్లంగొండ శ్రీ రంగరాజులకు సమర్పించిన కలుగుడి తిరువళ్లము.

UDAYAGIRI (8). (1536 A.D. Circ ?)

[Nallagoṇḍa. Telugu. From same place.]

TRANSLATION.

Hail! (This is) the charity given by Venkaṭádri Ayya, son of Rámajósulu, after making salutations, for providing food (amṛitapaḏi) to the god of Dúbagunḍála village in the *Néla* (territory) of Udayagiri . . . Protection of a gift is better (than giving one self);

By giving one attains heaven, but by protecting (another's gift) (one attains) the state of eternal bliss.

* * * *

NOTE.—Venkatádri here referred to is probably the deputy governor of Udayagiri of that name whose date was about 1536 A.D.

1. స్వస్తిరామాజోశుల పుత్రుండు వెంకటాద్రి అయ్యవారు దండంవెట్టి ఇచ్చిన ధర్మంవు

2. దయగిరి సేలం దూబగుండాలనే గ్రామం దేవుని అమృతవల్లకు తథా . . . .

3. పాలనం । దానాత్సగ్గ మవాప్నోతి పాలనా దచ్యుతంపదం । [దృశత్యాది గ్రామం].

Udayagiri (9).

[Nallagoṇḍa. Telugu. From same place.]

Translation.

Adoration to Ṣrí Rámánuja (the Vaishnavite reformer)! Hail! In the victorious and prosperous year—

Ṣrí Vírapati . . . . Rájádhirája Rájaparaméṣvara caused to be given on the holy occasion of—*tithi* (lunar day) . . . the village . . . .

. . . Vara Bhúpálaká Vírapratápágraníh. Hail!

Note.—1. Vara Bhúpálaká—excellent king.

2. Vírapratápágraníḥ—the first of heroes.

1 and 2 are evidently birudas or titles of the king.

1. శ్రీమతే రామానుజాయ్నమః స్వస్తి శ్రీజయాభ్యు . . .

2. లుసవర। శ్రీమద్రాజాధిరాజ రాజ పరమేశ్వర శ్రీవీరపతి . .

3. తిథి పుణ్యకాలమందు । సమర్పించి ఇప్పించిన శ్రీ గ్రా . .

4. . . . రు వర భూపాలక వీరప్రతాపాగ్రణి స్వస్తి . .

UDAYAGIRI (10).

[Nallagoṇḍa. Telugu. From same place.]

TRANSLATION.

(This is) the grove planted by Ṣrí Rangarája Chámarája Voḍayar.

NOTE.—We do not identify this Voḍayar.

1. శ్రీరంగరాజుల
2. చామరాజువొడర్
3. విధించిన వనము

UDAYAGIRI (11).

[Nallagoṇḍa. Telugu. From the Vináyaka Mandapam.]

TRANSLATION.

May there be prosperity! On the 13th of the dark half of Mágha in the illustrious year Prabhava, Lingâreḍḍi, son of Lingáreḍḍi Timmáreḍḍi, caused to be constructed at his own expense a temple to Vighnéṣvara of Nallagoṇḍa. May it cause prosperity!

1. శుభమస్తు శ్రీమతు ప్రభవ సంవత్సర మాఘ బ ౧౩ లు లింగారెడ్డి తిమ్మారెడ్డి కొమారుండు లింగారెడ్డి నల్లంగొండ్న విఘ్నెశ్వరు
2. నికి దేవస్తానం తనవుభయంగాను కట్టించెను శ్రీ. శ్రీ. శ్రీం జేయును

UDAYAGIRI (12).

[Nandavaram. Telugu. Opposite Chennakeṣava temple.]

TRANSLATION.

* * * *

for the increase of sons and grandsons . . . náyakunḍu, son of Bramminàyakunḍu . . .

[One imprecatory verse.]

* * * *

* * * *

* * * *

* * * *

* * * *

* * * *

. . . . పుత్ర

ప పుత్రా వర్ధిగాను

* * * *

న శ్రీ . . . . . బ . . . బైన

. . బ్రమ్మినాయకుండు

ను కొడుకు . . . నాయకుండు

ను నం . నామకుండ్లన . .

* * * *

* * * *

* * * *

* * * *

* * * *

నరస . . .

* * * *

* * * *

*   *   *   *

*   *   *   *

*   *   *   *

.   . శ్ర .   .   .   .

స్వదత్తం పదత్తం వాయోవా
రేతి వసు దరా షష్టిర్వర్ష సహాని శ్రీణివిష్ణా
యాంజాయతెక్రిమ

Udayagiri (13).

[Nandavaram (hamlet Rámanaiḍupalli). Telugu. On sluice of tank.]

Translation.

The details of the endowment made for the tank Kottacheruvu constructed in the village of Nandavaram by Sauryanáyani Raghupati Náthaya on the 2nd of the bright fortnight of Mágha . . . are:—

The rulers of the village should collect *méras* at 1 *kuncha* per *kirái* (?) *puṭṭi* of all grain raised under that tank, give it to the *méradar* of the tank and see that the repairs are done to the tank and the channel. Whoever misappropriates this will be regarded as having disobeyed his parents, as having transgressed his customs and as having killed a cow at Benares. In these terms has this charitable edict been engraved on this sluice.

To Śingázavupura Gópayya a land which can be sown with 10 *túms* . Komaṭi . .. to . Káśiruvibattanéningáru a land which can be sown with 10 *túms*.

1. .   .   .   .   .

2. .   మా ఖ శు ౨ లు సౌ
య్యణనాయని రగుప

3. తినాథయ నంద్దవరం

4. గ్రామాన్ను తాము

5. గట్టిచ్చిన క్రొత్త నర్వ (కు)

6. కాను దృడంగ సేసినవివరం

7. ఆ చెర్వుక్రిందను పండిన

8. నానా ధాన్యానకుంన్ను

9. కిరాయి పుట్టి ఖ ౧ కి కుం

10. చ్చాల లెక్కను చెర్వు [పుతి ?]

11. చెర్వుకాలవమీందనుం

12. వేయించి దాన్యాగ అయా

13. ంటనే చెర్వుమేర వారివశా

14. న్ను యిప్పించ్చి చెర్వు కాల్వ

15. పరిగ్రామం యెలేటివారు

16. వేయించ్చంగలవారు

17. యిందుకు యవరు అ

18. శించ్చినాను వారి త

19. ల్లి తంండ్రజాలకు తప్పి

20. నవారు వారి ఆచారా

21. దులకు తప్పినవా

22. రు గంగకతఁను గో

23. వును వధించినవారె

24. యీనాదిని తూముకో శ

25. లును కాడను వేశినధ

26. ర్మ శాసనము

27. శింగాజ

28. వుపుర గో

29. పయకు వం

30. డ్డుము వి త్తనా

31. ని . . కోమటి

32. . . . న్యం శాశీరు
33. వి బత్తనేనింగారికి
34. పఁడుము విత్తనా
35. లు.

Udayagiri (14). (A.D. 1245–46.)

[Nandipád. Telugu. From a four-sided stone surmounted by a Nandi in a field about half a mile from the store-shed.]

Translation.

Hail! To the deity Ṣrí Mudriká Ṣrí Siddhanáthadéva, who is the supreme ruler of the whole universe, who disports himself on the throne of *Ṣólaṣikhara* (Sholinghar?); who is fond of the fragrance of the flower of the lotus-like eye of Vishnu [1] (*i.e.*, of the *arka* flower); who is worshipped by Purandara (Indra, king of the gods) and other regents of the world who are resplendent with the lustre of the pavement of big rubies which resemble jewelled lamps; whose court is surrounded by the host of sages—Sanaka, Sanandana, Sanatkumára, Nárada and others, and by all the gods, demons, lords of serpents, *siddhas*, *vidyádharas*, and other numerous attendants; who grants the desires of all the *siddhas* (sages)—Vádigala, Siddha Vyáḷi, Nágárjuna, Nága Buddha, Kóranṭika, Kadambaka, Kádamba, Ratnaghósha, Vishnugupta, Chandragupta, Báṇa, and others, who are versed in the science of mercury, the elixir of life, in the art of painting the feet (probably a species of magic for

---

[1] The eye of Vishnu is the sun. Siva is said to be fond of the sunflower (Sanskrit *arka*).

making oneself invisible), in the art of fencing, in *ghutika* (a species of magic), in the science of maidens (love ?), in the science of spells, in metallurgy, in the science of smoke (the art of producing optical illusions in smoke), in the science of birds (omens ?), in alchemy and other sciences,[1] who confers prosperity and salvation on his devotees, who grants the spiritual powers consisting of the 505 *ghutikas* (different kinds of skill in magic) (described by the sage) Ṣrí Vámarási (Vámakési ?), and whose favourite abode is Ṣríparvata (Srísaila).

2. Hail ! for the religious merit of Ṣríman Mahámaṇḍaléṣvara Chóḍadéva Tirukálti (Kálati) déva Mahárája, on whose lotus feet the eyes of all the kings of the earth, Trilóchana (Pallava) and others are set, who is the jewelled lamp of the race of Karikála by whom the dam of the Káveri was built, whose valour is unlimited, who is a constant worshipper of the consort of Lakshmí (Vishnu), who is the lord of Orúripura the best of cities (Orayúr the capital of the Choḷa kingdom), who is the lord of the excellent town of Kánchi, who is strong-armed, (this edict has been issued) for providing rest-houses for travellers visiting the holy place of Siddhanátha.

3. On Tuesday, the 15th of the bright half of Chaitra of the year Viṣvávasu, corresponding to 1168 of the Ṣaka era ;—Aludiḍlayyadéva Maháráyá, Ganḍávaram Próli Reḍḍi, Átukúr Désáhi, and Duvvúri Súramareḍḍi, having agreed among themselves and having obtained the consent of the king, gave with libation of water (the village) Nagulavanam in the names of Kêdáradéva and

[1] Eleven sciences are mentioned and 11 experts in these are given—one for each.

Dandapáṭi déva (two deities) for providing rest houses to travellers, to last as long as the sun and moon endure.

4. Whoever obstructs this (charity) will incur the sin of killing a tawny cow on (the banks of) the Ganges, will incur the sin of killing a hind (?), will be considered to have committed the five cardinal sins and will be regarded as having eaten dog's flesh and as having drunk toddy from the skull of his eldest son.

[One imprecatory verse.]

May the king be victorious! May there be prosperity to cows and Brahmans!

1. స్వస్తి సమస్త భువ
2. నాధీశ్వర శ్రీ శ్రీ
3. శ్రీశైళ శిఖర సింహాస
4. సనా కేలి లోల విష్ణో
5. నేత్రాంబుజ ప్రసవ
6. గంధ కుతూహల
7. మంగళ మణి దీపికా
8. యమాన మానసేక
9. మాణిక్య శిలాతల ప్ర
10. భా పటల ఘుటితిత
11. పురందర లోకపాలక
12. అర్చిత సనక సనంద
13. న సనత్కుమార నారదాది
14. ముని నికాయ సకల సు
15. రాసురోరగేంద్ర సిద్ధ వి
16. ద్యాధరాద్యనేక పరివా
17. ర పరి వ్రితా స్థాన ర
18. స రసాయినా ప
19. దాం జన ఖడ్గ

20. యోగ ఘుటిక
21. కంస్యకావాద
22. మంత్రవాద ధా
23. ·త్రువాద ధూ
24. మ్రవాద గారు
25. డవాద రస
26. వాద వాదిగళ్
27. నీ సిద్ధ వ్యాళీ
28. నాగార్జుని న
29. గ బుద్ధ కోరం
30. టిక కదంబక
31. కాదంబ రత్న
32. ఘోష విష్ణుగు
33. ప్త చంద్రగుప్త
34. బాణాక్యాది
35. నిఖిల సిద్ధ జ
36. న మనోభిల
37. షిత ప్రదాయ
38. క భక్త జన
39. భుక్తిముక్తి ప్రదాయ
40. క శ్రీవామరాసి ప చో
41. త్తరపంచశతఘుటికా
42. సిద్ధిప్రదాయక శ్రీవ
43. ర్వత ప్రియ నివాస శ్రీమ
44. ద్వి)కా శ్రీసిద్ధనాధదేవరకు
45. స్వస్తి చరణసరోరుహావిహా[1].
46. తవిల్లోచన [2] త్రిల్లోచన ప్రముఖా

---

[1] విహిత in a Rápur Inscription.   [2] Read త్రిలోచన.

47. ఖిల ప్రిథ్వీశ్వర కారితకావే

48. రతీరకరికాలకులకడుప్రదీ[1]

49. వ ఆపరిమితప్రతాప సతత

50. మభ్యర్చితలక్ష్మీశ్వర ఒఱియూ

51. రిపురవరాధీశ్వర కాంచీపు

52 రవరాధీశ శ్రీమనుమహా

53. మండలేశ్వర భుజబళచోడతి

54. రుకాత్తిదేవ మహారాజున

55. కు పుణ్యముగాను పి

56. ఘనాధ క్షేత్రానకు వ

57. చ్చినదేశాంత్రులకు ఛత్రం

58. బుబెట్టుమని । శకవరు

59. షంబులు ౧౧౬౮ నేంటి

60. విశ్వావసు సంవత్సరము

61. న చైత్ర శుద్ధ ౧౫ మ

62. వారముచంమ అలు ది

63. క్ష య్యాదేవమహారాయ

64. గండావ్వరము ప్రోలిరెడ్డి

65. ని అకుకూరి దేశాటిని దూ

66. వూరి సూరమరెడ్డిని లంవోల్స్య ప్ర

67. భువ్నల సంధాన

68. కేదార దేవరిం

69. దండపాటి దే

70. వనిబేర దేశాం

71. త్రుల ఛత్తానకుజు

72. నాగులవనము

73. ఆ చంద్రార్కము

---

[1] Line 48. In an inscription of Rápur रत्नप्रदीपक is used for कट्टप्रदीप and seems to be the proper reading.

74. గా ధారాపూ
75. ర్వకము సేసి
76. ఇచ్చి దత్తి దీనికి
77. నెవ్వడే నొకడు వి
78. ఘలముచేసిన వా
79. డు గంగకఱుత
80. గవిలం వధించినపా
81. పంబునం బోయిన
82. వాడు యిరులవధి
83. యించి న పాపంబు
84. నం బోయినవాడు
85. పంచ మహాపాత
86. కము సేసినవా
87. డు పెద్దకొడుకు
88. కపాళమున కు
89. కర్మమాంసము కంలు
90. వేసికొని తిన్నవా
91. డు॥ స్వదత్తాం పర
92. దత్తాం వా యో హ
93. రేతి వసుంధరామ్
94. షష్టివర్షరుశ సహ
95. స్రాణాం వ్రిష్టాయాం జా
96. యతే క్రిమి। రాజా విజ్య
97. భవతు। గోబ్రాహ్మణ
98. సుభమస్తు॥

UDAYAGIRI (15).

[Nandipád. Telugu in ancient characters. From a stone bearing a Nága Kanyaká near the above stone. There are two other inscriptions about a mile from the rest-house, but they are defaced; one records a gift of land.]

TRANSLATION.

Hail! The service of fanning was done to Padâksha Lakshmayanátha (deity) of Srí Murudupuri.

1. స్వస్తి శ్రీ మురు
2. దు పురి పదాక్ష
3. లక్ష్మయనాథ్ను
4. కు వీవ్న ఫల
5. ప్రణీత
6. ము.

UDAYAGIRI (16).

[Pallavolu. Telugu. From two sides of a stone near Avulamma temple.]

TRANSLATION.

Adoration be to Sambhu. }
(Adoration be to) Ráma! } Nandi.

On the 10th of the bright fortnight of Bhádrapada of the year Dundubhi, Saiyid Abdulla Sáhib gave 10 *gorrus* in Raudulachénu as karnam *mányam*, and 1 *gorru* as Avulamma *mányam* (grant for the goddess Avulamma). This is the edict written by Kávali Ráju Venkatapati, Sákamúri Anantappa, and Sítárásidana (?). If any Muhammadans object to this, they will be regarded as having killed a pig at Mecca. If the ryots of this *péṭa* (village) object (to this), they will be regarded as having killed a cow at Káṣí.

1. శ్రీ శం } నంది
2. భోనమోస్తు }
3. శ్రీరామా దుందు
4. భినామ సంవత్సగ బా
5. ద్రపద శుద్ధ ౧౦ లు
6. సైదు అబ్దుల్లా సాహే
7. బులవారు రౌదుల
8. చేని కరణవారి మూం
9. న్యానకు గోలుర్ ౧౦ ఆవు
10. లమాలెకు మాంస్య
11. ం గోరుర్ చేనుయి
12. చ్చినాం కావలిరా
13. జు వెంకటపతి శా
14. కమూరి అనం
15. త్తప్ప శితాగా
16. శిదన శాసెనము
17. యుందుకు
18. తులుకలు
19. ఆక్షేపణసేస్తే మా
20. కాలో పందిని
21. చంపినట్టు
22. ఈ పేట కాపువారు
23. ఆపెదాని చేస్తె కా
24. శిలో గోవును
25. చంపినట్లు

UDAYAGIRI (17). (A.D. 1447-48.)

[Périsettipalli. Telugu. On a rock on a hill known as Sásanálabódu. The inscription is much defaced.]

TRANSLATION.

Hail! On . . . day the 15th . . . fortnight of Chaitra of the year Prabhava corresponding to the illustrious Ṣaka year 1369 . . . . (Venugopála) déva.

Hail! For the benefit of the kingdom to Ṣrímanmahámandaléṣvara . . . vibhála, Básatappuvaráyaraganḍa, Múruráyaraganḍa, Ashṭádigráya Manóbhayankara, ... Ṣrí Víra Dévaráya, Maháráya, son of Víra Harihararáya . . . . . gave . . . . . for various enjoyments of the deity . . . .

This will last as long as moon and sun endure. . . . .

1. స్వస్తి శుభశకవరు షంబులు ౧౩౬౯ అగునేటి ప్రభవ సంవత్సర చైత్ర . . . ॥ ౧౫ ॥ . . వారము . . . . . (వేణుగోపాల) దేవ . . . . .

2. . . . దేవరకు స్వస్తిశ్రీ మన్మహా మండలేశ్వర . . దవిభాళ, బాసతప్పువరాయరగండ మూరురాయరగండ అష్ట దిగ్రాయమనోభయంకర . . . . .

3. డీశ్వరుండైన శ్రీవీరహరిహరరాయుని కుమారుండు శ్రీ వీర దేవరాయ మహారాయనికిని ప్రిథివిరాజ్యాభివ్రిద్ధిగాను దేవుని అం గ్గరంగ్గ వైభవాలకును . . . .

4. ఆ చంద్రార్కస్థాయిగాను చెల్లది . . . . దేవతకు పు . ల . . . .

5. పు . . ఒమ . . . . . . డి డి . . .

UDAYAGIRI (18*a*).

[Rávimánidinne. Sanskrit in Telugu character. From fragments of a stone in Siddhéṣvara Kóna. Only a few lines are legible as indicated below.]

1. . . . .
2. . . . .
3. . . . .
4. . ఠి . . . బా బాబూసం
5. . . .
6. .. . . రస
7. . . . రా .
8. వప్పు . . . . బుల శ్రీయం
9. . . . . పా . ద్వరుహ చెరవిః
10. . రా మౌక్తిక మణిదేవ సమా
11. . . వమదావరె బోక్తుం రాజాసు
12. . . . జరితస్సృ . ముభూ దక్షి . ణ

NOTE.—This is illegible.

UDAYAGIRI (18*b*).

1. . న . . టం . . శు . .
2. . వక్రీతియామా . . . .
3. కిస తిఃణంశి . . . . .
4. . ప్రసంసతా . . . చనా .
5. . . నోగ్రలగ్నా . . .
6. . లా భూరి . ప్ర . . . . స
7. . స్ఫు భగవాన్సచ సేవి . . . చతు
8. బాద శావరి నూడిన్విబిహా . . . సకల
9. శురిచిరం కలియుగ . . . యిస్సనిపు
10. (నిడిద) బుకరారా జాత్మనా ॥ . . . య

11. సరతిస హరిశ్చంద్ర . . . . . నిడిభు
12. భి బాళముదినా . . . . . ర మేర్పర
13. . రతాగోమమె . . . ణయ . . . తి
14. . శోయంతిమూరు రాయరగండా .
15. రు రాయర గండ చండప్రతీకాహిత
16. . . . యొస్తా . . . . . . యరిశ్వ
17. . . . . . . క్షు . . .
18. . . . . . నుకడ
19. . . . . హార
20. . . . . . .
21. . . . . . .
22. . . . . . .

Note.—This refers to the Vijayanagar dynasty. Bukkarája's son is mentioned with usual birudas.

Udayagiri (18*c*). (A.D. 1386–87?)

1. . . . . . . क्षितिपातिर्निखिलानि देवस्थाना . . .
2. . . . . सिद्धवटयोर्मध्ये बहु . . . . .
3. . . . कण्ठघुटिकासिद्धेश्वरं तीर्थं । . .
4. . . . मूर्त्तित्रयैकात्मनो निर्य्यातं . .
5. . . सूरयः । तस्मिन् पुण्यजनावगाह . .
6. . . . कल्पयातिस्म मानससरःकल्पं . .
7. . . . सरंतस्तत्र मारुताः । दू . . .
8. . . . ज्जुतां ॥ [1]शरजन्मशार्ङदुर्गाभिर . . .
9. . . . कल्पा राज्ञा तेनैव मंटपा र[चि]ताः . . .
10. . . . देश्वरस्यांगणप्रासादाः पव . . .
11. . . . क्रीडंत्यामिव देवरायनृपते . . .

---

[1] Read शार्ङ्ग instead of शार्ङ.

12. . . . तनक्षितिम जां कीर्तिर्वियद्व्यापिनी . . . .
13. . . . पतिं राजराजे च . . . .
14. . . . द्येंदुभैरवा क्षिते . . . . . .
15. . . . देस्तस्तद्राजाधिराजे हरिहरनर . . .
16. . . [कुं]जराभ्रज्वलनशशिमिते १३०८
17. . . . स्फुटरुचिघुटि . . . . . .

(Mutilated.)

NOTE.—The left half of the inscription being defaced it is impossible to give a complete translation of it. The transcription was done by Mr. V. Venkayya. It mentions that a certain king built a temple for Siddhéșvara. He also built a tank there for holy men to bathe in which resembled the *Mánasa* lake. The same king built maṇḍapas for certain deities, Durgá and others. He also constructed front halls for the temple. There then comes a reference to king Dévaráya and it goes on " when Rájadhirája Harihara . . . . . (was ruling) . " . . . . in the Şaka year reckoned by the elephants (8), the "sky (0), the fires (3), and the moon (1), in 1308 (in Telugu figures)." The end is missing.

UDAYAGIRI (18*d*).

1. రాజాధిరాజ యరిరాయ
2. (గ్రవీ) య్యాఞరాయం హిందురాయ
3. . విప్నయం కృపా . . . . . ష
4. . . . వేదండక . . . . ప్హ
5. . . . . బలికృత్యాస . . దః కృతా
6. . జంగతా । త్స . . . . .
7. . . . వోహారి . . . .
8. . . . వణిజాన్వై . . . .
9. . . . నిజం . . . . .
10. రాతం . . . . ల . . . .
11. . . . .

12. . . . .

13. . . . .

14. . . . .

Note.—This is illegible. The following words appear :—
Rájádhirája, Ariráyagravíryarája, Hinduráya.

Udayagiri (18*e*).

1. వసమంటవ గొప్ప రాద్యతిధి
2. ని నిత్య విభవానికి నిత్యజి సం
3. మన్యతెస రాజేంద్ర । ఉదయగిరి
4. మూలా స్త్రత్ర సపివృల స్యమోహాంతి
5. క్రదయంతి నిర్ఝరనదింయన్నిఝుౝర
6. నక్ర తెరం మ్య శిలా (కు) ట్టి మైః కుం (ద)
7. మహీకర్బిషః (తరుశాఖాచలద్వి .
8. , రానిషా , యంతివషు రితానినిధి
9. . . . . జరాద్రిసు.

Udayagiri (18*f*).

1. రిపవస
2. . . . .
3. . . . .
4. ధిపతిః భం
5. విభూషణం .
6. నాఁవరిణ్యాశ్శ్య .
7. హూ మపెతదేక,

Note.—This is illegible.

Udayagiri (18*g*).

1. . . యస్యఘుట . .
2. . . . . (వశోంకారవ)

3\. . . . . . రవరతి వప్ప

4\. . . . .

5\. . . . .

NOTE.—This is illegible.

UDAYAGIRI (19). (A.D. 1615-16?)

[Tóṭacheruvupalli. Telugu.]

TRANSLATION.

In the year corresponding to 1537 of the Ṣáliváhana era, Ṣrímat Rájádhirája, Rájaparaméṣvara, Venkaṭapati Ráyadéva Mahiráyalu gave the village Kumáraka Koṭi situated in Kampináḍu to Kámarti Mánikédári. The village Ráva otherwise named . . . situated in the *Ṣthiti* (district) of Arivélam attached to the *Amaram* (land on service tenure) granted to us while Timmayadéva Mahárájulu Ayyaváru, seated on the diamond throne, was ruling, is given for doing service to Raghunáyakulu (deity). The land, with its treasures, hidden deposits, imperishable and future produce, actuals, outstandings and all other produce, should be utilized to provide enjoyments (to the deity) as long as the sun and moon endure.

1\. శాలివాహన వర్ష

2\. ంబులు ౧౫౩౭ అగునేంటి

3\. శ్రీమద్రాజాధిరాజ రాజ పర(మేశ్వర వేంక)

4\. టపతిరాయ దేవ మహారా (య)

5\. ర కంప్పినాడు లో కుమారక కో టి

6\. నికామర్తి మాణికేదారికి యిచ్చిరి (శ్రీమ)

7\. ద్రాజాధిరాజ పరమేశ్వర తింమ

8\. య దేవమహారాయలు అయ్య(వారు)

9. వ్రజసింహా సనా రూఢులై యేలు
10. చునుండి మాంకు అమరానకుం
11. జెల్లె అరివేలము స్త్రితిలోని [రా
12. వ] అనేగ్రామానకు ప్రతినామ
13. [* వు] గ్రామము రాంఘునాయ
14. ంకులసేవసేసుకొని వుండేది
15. అంగరంగ బోగాలకు నిధి నిక్షేప అక్షీ
16. ణ్యా ఆగామి సిద్ధి సాధ్యాలు గ
17. లిగిన సకలఫలాలున్న భూమి ఆచం
18. ద్రార్కముగా అనుభవించి
19. సుఖాన వుండునది.

Uḍayagiri (20).

[Udayagiri Village. Telugu. From Ranganáyaka-svámi's temple.]

Translation.

"Ḍambádu Kamma" (these letters in the first line are unintelligible).

Timmarájú, son of Ṣrímanmahámaṇḍaléṣvara Ráma Ṛája Konéṭayya Déva Mahárája, caused to be made a tower (Góp̣ura), a hall (Maṇḍapa), a compound wall, and a reservoir and other pious services to Raghu-náyakulu (deity). [He] performed the car festival and planted a stone inscription prescribing the ceremonials to be observed in future festivals. According to this, when the deity in the car passes through the holy streets, when the Naṭṭuvas (dancing girls) and servants are inside the car, a member of the *Panchaháṇas*,[1] wearing a head

---

[1] The five classes of artizans.

cloth, wrapping a cloth loosely round the waist, and having only a sandal mark between the eyebrows, and not chewing betel, should go round, in front of the car, with a chisel, a mallet, a nail, and a sickle in his hands. This formality should be observed without failure.

1. డంబాదుకమ్మ శ్రీమన్మహామండలేశ్వర రామరాజుకొనే

2. టయ్యదేవ మహారాజు కొమారుండు తిమ్మరాజుగారు

3. రఘునాయకులకు గోపురమండప ప్రాకారాలు కోనేరు మొదల

4. యిన సకలకైంకర్యాలున్నుం జేయించి తేరు తిరుణాళ్లు సాగించ్చి

5. పుత్రరోత్తరాలకు నడచు మర్యాదకు శిలా శాసనం వేయించినప్ర

6. కారానసనడవుండు తేరుమీందను తిరువీధుల వేంచేసి యిప్పు

7. డు తేరుమీందను నట్టువముట్టువకాండు పరిచారకులువుండిరు

8. ంతరువునను పంచాహాణంవారు వొకరంతలపాగచుట్టుక మోలను

9. పచ్చడం పిరిచుట్టు చుట్టుకం నొసలగంధం బొట్టుమాత్రం వె

10. ట్టుకొని విడెంశాయక పులిన్ని గూంటమున్ను చేతంబట్టుక చిలకొడ

11. వలంతీచ్చుకకవచ్చువారుయీమర్యాదకుతప్పకనడచువారు

Udayagiri (21).

[Udayagiri Village. Telugu. From the same place. Incomplete.]

Translation.

On the 12th day of the bright fortnight of Áshádh (Nija) of the year Parábhava to the treasury of Srí Raghunáyakulu of Udayagiri, the *Panchahánas* of Udayagiri, Nellore, Koratúr, Gandavaram, Duvúr, Átukúr, Jaladanki, Kodavalúr, Allúr, Kóvúr, Vovvéru, Prabhákarapatnam, Krishnaráyapatnam, Sariyapalli, Rápúr, Kandukúr, Podile, Kenagiri, and Kegipa, and other villages in the kingdom of Udayagiri and the Ahanas (*i.e.*, Panchahánas) of the fifty-four countries of the earth and other *Panchahánas* made obeisance and gave . . . .

1. ం పరాభవ సంవత్సర నిజ ఆషాడ శు౧౨లు వుదయగిరి
2. శ్రీరఘునాయకుల భండారానకు।వుదయగిరి । నెల్లూరు
3. కొరటూరు । గండ్డవరం । దువూరు । అతుకూరు। జలదంకి
4. కొడవలూరు । అల్లూరు । కోవూరు।వవ్వేరు ప్రభాకరప

ట్నం । క్రిష్ణ

5. రాయపట్నం । సరియపల్లె।రాపూరు । కందుకూరు । పొ

దిలె ।

6. కెణగిరి । కెగిప। మొదలయినం వుదయాగిరి రాజ్యానంగల
7. పంచహాణం వారును పృథివి డేబై నాలుగు అహాణాలు
8. మొదలయిన పంచహాణంవారున్ను దండం వెట్టియిచ్చినవో.

Udayagiri (22). (A.D. 1552-53.)

[Udayagiri Village. Telugu. From same place.]

Translation.

Hail! Prosperity! On Friday, the 30th of the dark fortnight of Pushya of the year Paridhávi, corresponding to the year 1474 of the illustrious, victorious and prosperous Sáliváhana Saka era, Timmayadéva Mahárájulu, son of Sríman Mahámandalésvara Rámaráju Konétayyadéva Mahárájulu, gave a charitable edict in the following terms to Víragangayya, son of Chapparti Pina Kávidha Srí Bhatluváru, who is of the Háritasagotra, who is a follower of the Ápastambha *sútra*, and a student of the Yajussákha.

While Sríman Mahárájádhirája, Rájaparamésvara, Srí Víra Pratápa Srí Sadasivadéva Maháráyalu, seated on the diamond throne at Vijayanagar, was ruling the kingdom of the earth (Timmayyadéva issued the following edict). The income which is derived from sundry articles in the villages situated in Udayagiri *durgam* which belong to us and were formerly attached to (the temple of) Srí Raghunáyakulu should be utilized for always providing daily offerings, worship with lights and miscellaneous offerings in the temple. While speaking these pleasant words, we have presented on the auspicious occasion of a solar eclipse, with libation of water and gift of gold, this endowment to the accountant in the temple of the deity, to last as long as the sun and moon endure. These Karnams and *Mirási kápus* should contribute at the rate of one *Chakra Varahá* (Rupees four) per month, 12 *Chàkra Varahás* per year, and 4 measures (of rice) per day for sacred food (prasáda).

Receiving these contributions and writing the accounts of the temple of Raghunáyakulu, you, your sons and grandsons in succession should enjoy the charity which has been given to last as long as the sun and moon exist and live at ease. In these terms has this charitable edict been granted.

[Two imprecatory verses.]

May it cause prosperity!

1. శుభం స్వస్తి శ్రీ జయాభ్యుదయ శాలివాహన శకవరుషం బులు ౧౪౭౪ అగు నేంటి పరిధావి సంవత్సర పుష్య శ్రీ ౩౦ లు శు శ్రీమర్త మహామండలేశ్వర రామరాజు కోనె

2. టయ్యదేవ మహారాజుల కుమారుండు తింమయదేవ మహారాజులుంగారు హారితసగోత్రులు ఆపస్తంభసూత్రంయజుశ్శాఖాధ్యాయులైన చప్పర్తి పినకావిధ శ్రీభట్లు

3. వారు కుమారుడు వీరగంగయ్యకు ఇచ్చిన ధర్మశాసః పత్రిక క్రమం - శ్రీమర్త మహారాజాధిరాజ రాజపరమేశ్వర శ్రీ వీరప్రతాప శ్రీ సదాసివదేవ మహారాయులు విజయనగా

4. రమందు వజ్రసింహాసనారూఢులయి సకలసామ్రాజ్యము చేయుచుండంగాను మానాయం కరానకు జెల్లివచ్చె వుదయగిరిదుర్గమందును శ్రీ రగునాయకు

5. లకుపూర్వానకు నడచివచ్చె గ్రామాలు చిల్లర సరుకులవల్లనువచ్చె ఆదాయమున్ను నిత్యమున్ను కోవిలకు నిత్యనైవేద్యాదులు దీపారాధన జరిగించెడి ఉపహార్థా

6. లునుయిప్రియాలుమాటలాడుతాను దేవునిగుడిలో లేఖ సంప్రతినకు తథాతిథిసూర్యగ్రహణ పుణ్యకాలమందు సహిరణ్యోదక దానాధారాపూర్వకముగాను

7. ఆచంద్రార్కముగాను ధారవోసి ఇస్తిమి ఈ కరణీక శాణయాచికావులను కట్టడినెల ౧ కి చక్ర ౫౧ వరహా లెఖను వేంశు ౧ కి చక్ర ౯౧॥ పండ్రెండువరహా

8. లున్న దినం ౧ కి ప్రసాదం వర నాలుగు పండ్లున్ను యీా కట్టడిన పుచ్చుకరఘునాయకుల కోవిల లెఖ ప్రాసుక మీపుత్ర పౌత్ర పారంపర్యం త్తం ఆ చంద్రార్కస్థాయిగాను

9. యిచ్చినధర్మమును అనుభవించి బ్రతుకువారు అనియిచ్చి న ధర్మశాసనము దానపాలన యోర్మధ్యే దానాత్ శ్రేయోను పాలనం దానా స్వర్గమ వాప్నోతి పాలనాద

10. చ్యుతంపదం।సామాన్యోయంధర్మసేతుర్నృపాణాం కాలే కాలే పాలనీయో భవద్భిః సర్వానేతాన్ భావినః పార్థివేం ద్రాన్భూయో భూయో యాచతే రామచంద్రః ॥

11. శ్రీ శ్రీ శ్రీం జేయును

Udayagiri (23). (A.D. 1586–87.)

[Udayagiri Village. Telugu. From same place.]

Translation.

(Obeisance to) Ṣrí Ráma! Hail! On the 12th of the bright fortnight of Áshádha of the year Vyaya, corresponding to the year 1508 of the illustrious, victorious, and prosperous Ṣálivábana Ṣaka era, this charitable edict was issued, after making many salutations, under the orders of Kúchináyaningáru, who belongs to the fourth caste (Sudra), who is the grandson of Kamppináyanimgáru and the son of Chalamayya and who is the agent (Káryakartá) of Ṣrímad Rájádhirája Rájaparaméṣvara Ṣrí Víra Pratápa Ṣrí Víra Venkaṭapati Ráyadéva Mahárájulu Ayyaváru, to the deity Ṣrí Raghunáyakulu of Udayagiri who is the lord of the universe of all the worlds.

Hail! Prosperity! While Ṣrímad Rájádhirája Rájaparaméṣvara, Ṣrí Víra Pratápa, Ṣrí Víra Venkatapati Ráyadéva Mahárájulu Ayyaváru, seated on the diamond throne at the city of Penugoṇḍa, was ruling the kingdom of the earth, (Kúchi Náyaningáru) gave, after making obeisance, the village of Appanimádara in Udayagiri *Sthala* for performing *Vasanta Mahótsava* (spring festival) to the deity for the religious merit of Venkaṭapati Ráyulu Ayyaváru and for the religious merit of his father, mother and others. This is the charitable deed issued for performing *Vasantótsava* and providing all enjoyments to the deity from the income derived from this village.

[One imprecatory verse.]

*Note.—This inscription was copied as two inscriptions, but they appear to be only parts of one inscription. This agent's name does not appear elsewhere in the collection. In the next inscription of the same year a different Káryakarta is mentioned. See also A. 1.

1. శ్రీ రామ స్వస్తి. శ్రీ జయాభ్యుదయ శాలివాహన శకవ ర్షంబులు

2. ౧౫౦౮ అగు నెంటి వ్యయ సంవత్సర ఆషాఢశుద్ధ౧౦లు శ్రీ

3. మదఖిలాండకోటి బ్రంహాండనాయకులైన ఉదయగిరి

4. శ్రీరఘునాయకులకు శ్రీమద్రాజాధిరాజ రాజపరమే

5. శ్వర శ్రీవీరప్రతాప శ్రీ వీర వేంకటపతిరాయదేవమహారా

6. యుల అయ్యవారి కార్యకర్తలైన చతుర్థ జాతులున్ను కంప్పినాయ

7. ని పౌత్రులున్ను చలమయని పుత్రులున్ను ఆయినకూచి నా

8. యనింగారి ఆనతిని అనేక దండములుపెట్టి ధర్మార్థ నిచ్చినధర్మశాసనము.

9. స్వస్తి శ్రీ శ్రీమద్రాజాధిరాజ రాజ పరమేశ్వర శ్రీ వీర ప్రతాప శ్రీ వీరవేం

10. కటపతి రాయదేవమహారాయుల అయ్యవారు పెను కొండపట్టణ

11. మందు వజ్ర సింహాసనాసీనులై పృథివి సాంబ్రాజ్యము జేయుచును

12. ండంగాను ఉదయగిరి స్థళము తాను ఆ [ప్పనిమాద]ర గ్రామానదముర్

13. వుగానిచ్చి ఆ గ్రామము స్వామి వసంతమహోత్స వానకు వేంకటపతి

14. రాయులయ్యవారికి పుణ్యముగాను తమతల్లి తండ్రాదు లకు పుణ్యంగా

15. ను దండంసమర్పించియిచ్చిరి ఆ గ్రామంనవచ్చు విత్తము లో స్వామివసంతవుత్సవము

16. లకును అంగరంగవైభవాలకున్ను అవధరించెటట్టు సమ ర్పించిన

17. ధర్మశాసనం దానపాలనయోర్మధ్యే దానాచ్ఛ్రేయోను పాలనం

18. దానాస్వర్గమవాప్నోతి పాలనా దచ్యుతంపదం. శ్రీ శ్రీ శ్రీ జేయును.

UDAYAGIRI (24). (A.D. 1586–87.)

[Udayagiri Village. Telugu. From same place.]

TRANSLATION.

[Obeisance to] Ṣrí Ráma—Hail! On the 12th of the bright fortnight of Áshádha of the year Vyaya, corresponding to the year 1508 of the illustrious, victorious, and prosperous Ṣáliváhana Ṣaka era—Venkaṭa Pinnaya Náyaningáru, who is of the fourth caste, who is the grandson of . . . Náyaḍu, and the son of Pinnama Náyaḍu, and who is the agent of Ṣrímad Rájádhi Rája Rájaparaméṣvara Ṣrí Víra Pratápa Ṣrí Víra Venkaṭapati Ráyadéva Maháráyulu, after making infinite salutations, presented this charitable edict to Raghunáyakulu of Udayagiri, who is the lord of the universe of all the worlds. While Ṣrímad Rájádhi Rája Rájaparaméṣvara

Ṣrí Víra Pratápa Ṣrí Víra Venkaṭapati Ráyadéva Mahá Ráyulu Ayyaváru, seated on the diamond throne at the town of Peṇukoṇḍa, was ruling the kingdom of the earth, a tank was constructed in the village of Pranava Viṣikhara (?) situated in Udayagiri *rájya*. At the time of consecration of the deity we presented that village for performing the great garden festivals of the deity for the religious merit of Ṣrí Rangaráyulu Ayyaváru. Therefore the income of that village should be enjoyed as long as the sun and moon endure for providing offerings, enjoyments, and festivals.

NOTE.—Perhaps this means that the village was granted for the merit of Ranga II and that the tank was constructed immediately after in the time of his brother Venkata I in whose first year this inscription was set up.

1. శ్రీ రామ స్వస్తి శ్రీ జయాభ్యుదయ శాలివాహన శక వర్షంబులు

2. ౧౫౦౮ అగు నేంటి వ్యయసంవత్సర ఆషాడశుద్ధ ౧౦లు శ్రీ మదఖి

3. లాండకోటి బ్రాంహ్మాండ నాయకుండు ఉదయగిరి శ్రీ రఘునాయ

4. కులకు శ్రీ మద్రాజాధిరాజ రాజపరమేశ్వర శ్రీ వీరప్ర తాప శ్రీ వీర వేంకటప

5. తిరాయదేవ మహారాయుల అయ్యవారి కార్యకర్త యున్న చతుర్థ వంశోద్భవులున్న

6. . . . నాయని పౌత్రులున్న పిన్నమనాయని పుత్రులున్న అయ్యా వెంకటపిన్నయ

7. నాయనింగారు అనంతములయిన దండములు పెట్టి సమర్పించిన ధర్మశాసనము

8. శ్రీ మద్రాజాధిరాజ రాజపరమేశ్వర శ్రీ వీరప్రతాప శ్రీ వీరవేంకటపతిరాయ

9. దేవమహారాయులు అయ్యవారు పెనుగొండపట్టణమందు వజ్రసింహాస్న

10. నారూఢులై పృథివి సాంమ్రాజ్యమును చేయుచును ఉం డంగాను ఉదయగి

11. రి రాజ్యములోను ప్రనవవిశికర గ్రామాన చెరువుకట్టిరి ఆ గ్రామమున

12. . . . స్వామి తోపుతిరుణాళ్ల మహొత్సవానికి శ్రీ రంగ్గరాయుల అయ్య

13. వారికి పుణ్యముగాను స్వామి ప్రతిష్ఠకాలమందు సమ ర్పించి

14. నాముగనుక ఆగ్రామఫలమును ఆరగింపులకును భోగ ములకు పు

15. త్రవం ఆ చంద్రార్కముగాను అనుభవించువారు.

Udayagiri (25).

[Udayagiri Village. Telugu. Incomplete. From Ahóbala Narasimhasvámi's temple.]

Translation.

Gingelly, black gram, rice, oil-seeds, and other grains and produce at 8 for every *góna* (bag) of jonna, horse gram, and all grains at . . . . for every *góna* of horse gram . . . . This charity has been given in perpetuity to last as long as the sun and moon exist . . . .

1. డు ములు నూలూను మినులు బియ్యం ఆముదాలుంన్ను యీ మొదలైన కాయధాన్యాలు . . . .

2. లుగోన ౧ కి ౮ టి లెఖజొన్నలు వులవాలు అన్నిధాన్యా లకు లోగోన ౧ కి . . లెఖ

3. వులవస . . బిసట సనికాయుశఃదన శాసయకరవ

. . . . .

4. హోవరు . . . . గాను ఆచంద్రస్థాయిగాను

. తు. అవి

5. దమఁ . . . .

6. యూ యూ య . . . .

Udayagiri (26). (A.D. 1661–62.)

[Udayagiri Hill.[1] Persian. From stone near Forest Bungalow inscribed in Persian and Telugu (see No. 22).]

Translation.

1. In the days of the king of kings, Kutb Sháh Abdulláh, a king who is the crown of the kings of the Dakhan.

2. One of his trusted courtiers is Saiyid Muzaffar ;— and Shaikh (Hasan)

(May the lamp of the house of the [abovesaid] exalted Saiyid, become as resplendent as the moon,)

3. secured eternal blessings through God's favour, since he laid out a beautiful garden of his own device :

4. In an auspicious place in the fort of Udayagiri, such that the angel was so delighted by his wanderings therein that he exclaimed "how beautiful."[2]

5. To its generous fruits the whole world is indebted. Shall I not call it a paradise? Nay, I can call it the highest paradise.

---

[1] Udayagiri Hill rises to a height of over 3,000 feet. The top is a rugged plateau borne a loft upon immense red cliffs and thickly strewn with remains of buildings and fortifications. Except at one or two points it must have been unassailable.

[2] Ahsan—A play upon the name of the founder Hasan.

6. A thousand and sixty and ten and two from the prophet's hijrat (1661-62 A.D.).

Through the work of God it became a garden of paradise.

(1) در عهد شاه شهان قطب شاه عبدالله *

شهي كه افسرشا نهانست پائي تخت دكهن *

(2) ايك از ملازم سيد مظفر است و شيخ *

چراغ سيد عالي چومه بود روشن *

(3) سعادت ازلي يافته زلطف كريم *

چه طرح باغ فكندش بطبع شيخ حسن *

(4) كه درمقام مبارك و قلعه ادگير *

زمير خرمي او ملك بگفت احسن *

(5) كه فيض اوست رسيده بعالم ازثمرش *

چه خلد گويم و خلد برين توان گفتن *

(6) هزار وشصت وده ودوز هجرت نبوي *

زصنع قدرت حق شد رياض او گلشن *

UDAYAGIRI (27). (A.D. 1661-62.)

[Udayagiri Hill. Telugu. From the same stone.]

TRANSLATION.

In the illustrious lunar Plava year, Sultan Abdulláh Pádsháh (reigning), Saiyid Muzaffar Zill ul láh u taála (may God's shadow rest on him) gave to Shaikh Hasan's garden the name of Pársmisál (Persia-like, Persia being noted for its gardens) and erected an inscribed pillar. Those who deface or remove it, shall incur the sin of killing cows, Brahmans and children in Kási (Benares). Knowing this act charitably. Hail.

NOTE.—The above is the rendering of Saiyid Mustafa Sahib. The phrase Zill ūl láh u taála is incorrectly transcribed in the Telugu.

1. శ్రీ చాంద్రమాన ప్ల
2. వ నామ సంవత్సరంలో
3. ను సులుతాను అబ్దుల్లా
4. పాదుశాహా సయిదు
5. ముజాఫరు సరిఖెలు
6. శాహి ముతాలీకు శే
7. కు హాసను తోంటకు
8. పౌర్ణమి సాల్ పేరుపె
9. ట్టివ్రాసి కంభం నిలిపినాడు
10. యిది యెవ్వరు చెరిచినా
11. తీసిసినా కాసిలో గోహ
12. త్య బ్రంహ్మ హత్య శిశు హత్య
13. చేసిన పాపాన పొందుదు
14. రు యిది యెరిగి ధర్మాన న
15. డిచేది శ్రీ

UDAYAGIRI (28). (A.D. 1470–71 ?)

[Udayagiri Hill. Telugu. From stone near Baptist Mission Bungalow. The stone bears the sun, moon, lingam and bull.]

TRANSLATION.

May there be prosperity! Hail! On Sunday, the 11th of the bright fortnight of Srávana of the year Vikriti,[1] corresponding to the year 1382 of the illustrious, victorious and prosperous Ṣáliváhana Ṣaka era, Tamaráyaningáru, son of Kanṭamaráju Valabhala,[2] having built a temple to the deity Káṣi Viṣvéṣvara on the hill of

---

[1] Vikriti was S.S. 1393 and not 1382. Perhaps Vikrama is meant.

[2] Valabhayya in No. 29.

Udayagiri and consecrated the deity, gave for (providing) daily offering and worship with lights to the deity $1\frac{1}{4}$ *chódana* of rice for each day, green gram న[1] (*túm*) $\frac{1}{8}$ and ghee న (*túm*) $\frac{1}{16} + \frac{1}{32}$. For providing all enjoyments to this deity (he gave) 1,000 (*kunṭas*) of land in rear of the *amara* tank under the middle sluice. We have given this wet field so that it may be enjoyed free from all burdens. May the rulers of this *Durgam* (fort) maintain this charity without fail and prosper!

May it cause great prosperity!

NOTE.—Symbols used in the text for fractions are—

⌒| = $1\frac{1}{4}$.

= = $\frac{1}{8}$.

—|| = $\frac{1}{16} + \frac{1}{32}$.

Chódana is now a liquid measure of Malabar containing 96 ollucks, or $341\frac{1}{4}$ cubic inches. It does not appear to be now used in this district.

1. శుభమస్తు॥ స్వస్తి శ్రీ జ
2. యాభ్యుదయ శాలివా
3. హన శకవరుషం
4. బులు ౧౩౪౨ అగునే
5. టి వికృతి సంవత్స
6. ర శ్రావణ సు ౧౧ ఆ -
7. కంటమరాజు వలభల
8. కుమారుండు తమ (తమ్మ)
9. రాయనింగారు వుదయ
10. గిరిమీంది మన్యానం
11. కాసి విశ్వేస్వర దేవరకు
12. నగరు గట్టించి ప్రతిష్ట
13. సేయించి యీ దేవునికి నైవే

[1] న denotes the *túm*

14. ద్యానకును దీపారాద్నకు
15. ను దినానకు బియ్యం చో
16. దెన ౧। పెసలు స= వెఇని—॥
17. యీ మరియాదను సేను న
18. సిఽంచ్చిరి యీ దేవునికి అం
19. గరంగ వయిభవాలకును
20. అమర చెరువు వెనకను న
21. డిమితూముంకించను వరి
22. చేను ౧౦౦౦ యీ వరిమడి ని
23. రోహాని లేక చెల్లి అట్లుగాను
24. పెటితిమి యీ ధర్మ
25. శాసనానకు తప్పక
26. యీ దుర్గం యేలినవా
27. రు పాలించి బ్రతుకు
28. వారు మంగళ మహా
29. శ్రీ శ్రీ శ్రీం జేయును

Udayagiri (29). (A.D. 1470–71 ?)

[Udayagiri Hill. Telugu. From a stone near the Baptist Mission Bungalow.]

Translation.

May there be prosperity! Hail! On Sunday, the 11th day of the bright fortnight of Srávaṇa of the year Vikriti[1] corresponding to the year 1382 of the illustrious, victorious, and prosperous Ṣáliváhana Ṣaka era, Tammaráyaningáru (probably Náyaningáru), king (Rája) of the race of Raghu, the grandson of Mádhavavarma who caused

---

[1] Vikriti was S.S. 1393 and not 1382. Perhaps we should read Vikrama.

the city of Bezwáḍa to be built, and the son of Kanṭamarája Vallabhayya who had the *birudas*: Raṇaranga Bhairava,[1] Mallikávallabha,[2] Sahakára Bándhava vása,[3] Birudaragaṇḍa[4] and Danambaragina,[5] constructed a temple (*Nagaru*) and consecrated Gópálakrishna on the hill of Udayagiri. $1\frac{1}{4}$ *chódana* of rice, $\frac{1}{8}$ *túm* of green gram, $\frac{1}{16}+\frac{1}{32}$ *túm* of ghee (should be given) every day for offerings and lighting lamps to this deity. He has presented this endowment. He has presented free from all burdens with libation of water 1,000 *kunṭas* of land in rear of the *amalu* (amara) tank under the middle sluice for providing all enjoyments to this deity. May the rulers of the *durgam* whoever they are maintain this charity and prosper!

V. The protection of another's gift is twice as meritorious as one's own gift. By resuming another's gift, one's own gift becomes inefficacious.

May it cause great prosperity!

NOTE.—It is not known to what dynasty (if it was a dynasty) this Tammaráya belonged—See No. 28 also. Some of the birudas seem merely fancy titles, such as occasionally occur. Note that Mádhavavarma is said to have built Bezwáḍa. At Tirumala there is a similar inscription (see page 17 E.R. for 1903–04).

1. శుభమస్తు ॥ స్వస్తి శ్రీ జ
2. యాభ్యుదయ శాలివా
3. హన శకవరుషంబులు
4. ౧౩౮౨ అగునేంటి వికృతి
5. సంవత్సర శ్రావణ శు. ౧౧ ఆ
6. రఘువంశంరాజు బెజవాడ పా

---

[1] A Bhairava on the battle field.

[2] The beloved of the jasmine?

[3] The kinsman and friend of the mango?

[4] A hero to those who claim birudas.

[5] Not clear.

7. డిగడించిన మాధవవర్మ మనుమ
8. ండు రణరంగ భైరవ మల్లికా వల్ల
9. భ సహకార బాంధవవాస బిరు
10. ధర గండండనంబరగిన కంటమరా
11. జు వలభయ్య కుమారుండు తంమ్మ
12. రాయనింగారు వుదయగిరిమీంది మ
13. న్యానను గోపాలక్రిష్ణునికి నగరు క
14. ట్టించ్చి ప్రతిష్ట సేయించిరి యీ
15. దేవునికి నైవేద్యానకున్ను దీపారా
16. దనకున్ను దినానకు బియ్యం చో
17. డెన ౧। పెసలు న= నెయ్యి న— ॥ యీ
18. మరియాదను సమర్పించిరి
19. యీ దేవునికి అంగరంగ వైభ
20. వాలకున్ అమలు చెరువు వెనక
21. ను నడిమి తూముకిందను
22. కు ౧౦౦౦ యీపట్టి వరిమడ్ని
23. నిరోహరి లేక చెల్లి అష్టుగాను
24. ధారవోసి సమర్పించిరి । యీ
25. మరియాదను దుర్గంయె
26. వ్వరు పాలించినాను యీకట్టు
27. ను సమర్పించి బ్రతుకువారు
28. స్వదత్తాద్విగుణం పుణ్యం ప
29. గదత్తాను పాలనం పర
30. దత్తాపహారేణ స్వదత్తం
31. నిష్ఫలంభవేత్
32. మంగళం మహాశ్రీ
33. శ్రీం జేయును.

*   *   *   *

UDAYAGIRI (30). (A.D. 1542–43.)

[Udayagiri Hill. Telugu. On a big rock near the Madáru gate. Imperfect and the meaning obscure.]

TRANSLATION.

May there be prosperity! Hail! On Wednesday, the 11th day of the bright fortnight of Kártika of the year Ṣóbhakṛit, corresponding to the year 1465 of the illustrious, victorious, and prosperous Ṣáliváhana Ṣaka era, while Ṣríman Mahárájádhirája Rájaparaméṣvara Ṣrí Víra Pratápa, Múruráyaragaṇḍa,[1] . . . ráya . . . kára,[2] Ṣrí Sadáṣivadéva Mahárájulu, seated on the diamond throne in Vijayanagar, was ruling the earth, against (or, on) Udayagiri Durgam, which was governed by Aḷiya Rámayadéva Mahárájulu Gáru (and?) Rámaráju Timmayyadéva Mahárájulu Gáru. . . .

1. శుభమస్తు ॥ స్వస్తి శ్రీ విజయాభ్యుదయ శాలివాహన శక వర్షంబులు ౧౪౬౫ అగునేం

2. టి శోభకృతు సంవత్సర కార్తిక శుద్ధ ౧౧ బు శ్రీమన్ మహారాజాధి రాజపర మేశ్వర శ్రీ వీరప్రతాప

3. మూరురాయర గండ (అరి) . . రాయాకార శ్రీ సదాశివదేవ మహారాయులు విజయనగరమందు వజ్రసింహా

4. సనారూఢులై పృథివి రాజ్యంబు చేయుచున్ ఉండి అళియ రామయదేవ మహారాజులుగారు రాము

5. రాజు తిమ్మయ్యదేవ మహారాజులంగారు పాలించిన వుదయ గిరి దుర్గంమీద . .

* * * *

[1] The conqueror of the three kings (Chéra, Chóla, and Páṇdya).

[2] This is probably Ariráyamanóbhayankára — the terror of the minds of hostile kings.

Udayagiri (31).

[Udayagiri Hill. Telugu. Beginning not found. From same place.]

Translation.

Line 1.—For *Amritapadi* (food) to the deities :—Narasimha, Gópinátha, Késava Nátha, Késava Mádhava, and Hanumán.

2. Gutti Ráju Tirumala Ráju, Teruva Kondlu, Bóyalarantla Narasingaya, Bágu Rámaya, Délinéni Bayappa, Nandu Návuri Busaya (?)

3. Túli Seja Machurlu, Kollúri Náginendu, Bandi Kondamanendu, Vetakurchi, Chevayya, Guni Ráminendu, Malinéni Srí Rangayya and Rácha Pátrundu.

* * * *

4. They will incur the sin of killing . . . .

5. Of giving and protecting (another's gift), protecting is better. By giving one attains heaven; but by protecting (one attains) the state of imperishable bliss.

1. (? ద్వంసుం ?) నారసింహుండు గోపినాథుండు కేశవనాథుండు కేశవమాధవుండు యీ హనుమంతుండు యీ దేవళ్లకు అమ్రుతపళ్లకు

2. గుత్తిరాజు తిరుమలరాజుగారున్ను తెరువకొండ్లు బోయలరంట్ల నరిసింగ్గయ బాగురామయ దెలినేని బయప్ప నందునావూరిబుసయ

3. తూళిసెజమచ్చుర్లు కొల్లూరినాగినెండు బండికొండమన్నెండు వెతకుర్చి చెవయ్య గునిరామినెండు మలినేని శ్రీరంగయ్య రాచాపాత్రుండు

* * * *

4. వధించిన పాపానబోవువారు . దానా .

5. పాలనయో ర్మధ్యే దానాచ్ఛ్రేయోను.

6. పాలనం దానాస్వర్గమవాప్నోతి పాలనాదచ్యుతంపదం

NOTE.—Lines 4–6 are inscribed so as to run on with 1–3.

UDAYAGIRI (32).

[Udayagiri Hill. Telugu. From same place.]

TRANSLATION.

Yatahi Vengaya . . . Satavan Prítigamayya, Ninagam Lingaya, Bachalaya, Nirmita Mabbaya, La . . ḍa, their father Garamalayya . . . after making obeisance to Narasimhadéva have agreed and granted this charitable edict. We shall give . . . without fail one *irasam* (a measure). If any one does not maintain this charity, he will (incur the sin of killing) cows and Brahmans near the Ganges.

1. శ్రీ యతహి వెంగయ . . . నుసతవన్ ప్రీతిగమ
య్యనినగం లింగ్గయ బచల . . . .

2. య నిర్మిత మబ్బయల . . డవింఙ్ల తండ్రి గరమల
య్య (అలోరాండు పెరూన?)

3. నారసింహాదేవునికి దండంవెట్టి వొడబడియిచ్చిన దర్మశాస
నం [నెలగనబట్టుకుట్టి?] రసం లెఖ

4. ను తప్పక యిచ్చువారం యీ పుణ్యానకు యవ్వరులోను గా
కుంనాను గంగకతర గోబ్రాంహ్మ

* * * *

UDAYAGIRI (33).

[Udayagiri Hill. Telugu. From same place.]

TRANSLATION.

China Vallabhayya, son of Chinnanna made endless obeisance to Narasimhadéva (deity) who is on the (Udayagiri) *Durgam.*

(1) (వుదయగి
(2) రి) దుగ౯ంమీదినరసింహుని
(3) కి చిన్నన్న కొమారుడు చినవ
(4) ల్లభయ్య అనంతాలుగా
(5) ను శేవించుకొన్నాడు

UDAYAGIRI (34).

[Udayagiri Hill. Telugu. From same place.]

TRANSLATION.

. . . ni Ammana, Saragóvu Dásari, Archipa Náyulayya, Kommaṭi Sarama, Tiruvengaḍa Nadhuni Havi Cheṭṭi, Timmaya, Bhógam Singaya, Bachana Dammayya, Tipudátam Yallaya, Chaṭukubondi Vidiyalayya, Páṭi Timmaya and others of Yaralúr, Yanimitta Mabbayya . . . lakaviradla Táṭi Garamalayya and Alavadonḍu Phirangi. These persons after making salutations agree and execute this charitable edict to Narasimhadéva. They have given grain (?) . . . If any one obstructs this charity (he will incur the sin of killing) cows and Brahmans on the Ganges.

1. ని అంమ్మన శరగోవుదాసరి అచ్చి౯పనాయులయ్య కొ
మ్మటిశరమ తిరువెంగడనాథునిహావిశెట్టి తింమయ భోగంశింగయ
బచన

2. దంమ్మయ్య్య తిపుదాతం యల్లయ చతుకు బొందివిడి

3. యలయ్య్యపోటి తిమ్మయ్య్య యఅలూారు మొదలైనవారు

4. యు నిమిత్తే మబ్బయ్య్య . . . లకవిరఢ్ల తాటి కరమలయ్య్య ఆలవదొాండు ఫిరంగి

5. వ నరసింహ్వా దేవునికి దండం పెట్టి వొాడబడియిచ్చిన దమ్మ శాాసనం। నె అ ౧౩ బర్జుంకంవిసం లెఖ

6. ను తప్పక యిచ్చినవారు యీాశ్ర్ణాన్యనకు యవ్వరులోానం గాాకుంన్నాను గంగకరుతం గోబ్రాహ్మ

* * * *

UDAYAGIRI (35).

[Udayagiri Hill. Telugu. On a rock near the western postern above the Forest Bungalow.]

TRANSLATION.

(Obeisance be to) Ráma. The day of the fight on the Durgam was Monday the third of the bright half of Pushya in the year Vikári.

NOTE.—It is not known to which fight this refers. In the 16th century Vikári corresponded to 1539–40. So the reference cannot be to the capture of the Fort by Krishnadéva Ráya.

శ్రీరామ వికారినామ సంమ్మచ్చర పుష్యశుద్ధ తదియ సోమవా రంనాడు దుగ౯ం పొట్ల రినాధినిమూా

UDAYAGIRI (36). (A.D. 1660–61.)

[Udayagiri Hill. Persian. From the little mosque.]

TRANSLATION.

(1) During the days of Abdulláh Kutb Sháh, the pride of kings.

Husain Khán secured the blessings of God.

(2) In that he constructed a new mosque and embellished it.

May God accept it for the purpose of prayers.

(3) A thousand and sixty and ten and one elapsed from Hijra (A.D. 1660–61).

(He) Destroyed a temple and constructed the House of God.

(1) بدور فخر شهان قطب شاه عبدالله *
بيانت حسن معادت حسين خان زاله *
(2) بنائي مسجد نورا بداد زينت و زيب *
خدا كناد قبولش زبهر طاعت جاه *
(3) هزار شصت وده و يك گذشته از هجرة *
شكست خانه بت را ببست بيت الله *

Udayagiri (37).

[Udayagiri Hill. Canarese.[1] From the rock known as Vráta gundu. It is written with an unusual slope.]

Translation.

Mahárájádhirája, Rájaparamésvara, Srí Víra Pratápa Srí Krishnadéva Maháráya having attacked Udayagiri Durgam and pursued Pratápa Rudra Gajapati up to Kondavídu, besieged Udayagiri and captured Tirumala[2] Rághava Ráya, the uncle of Pratápa Rudra Gajapati. On his return to Vijayanagar, he presented to Rámachandradéva (deity) of Udayagiri, the village named Kanuparé (Kanuparti ?) in the *síma* of Prabhákarapattana (Prabhagiripatnam ?); to Kónevallabha Rája (deity)

---

[1] The old names 'Canara' and 'Canarese' are mere anglicized versions of the native word Kannada, and we retain the initial C which is sanctioned by old usage.

[2] In Nos. 38, 40 and 41 this name appears as Tirumala Kánta Ráya.

(To face page 1385.)

UDAYAGIRI NO. 39.

UDAYAGIRI (39). (A.D. 1642–43.)

[Udayagiri Hill. Persian. From the big mosque.]

TRANSLATION.

(1) Gházi Ali, lord of the age, victor in war;

Such a man that from him originated speech (or versification);

(2) With the help and support of the virtuous king, pivot (*Kutb*) of the world, king (Sháh) of the throne of the Dakhan;

(3) From one end to the other he (Gházi Ali) burnt away the sweepings of idolatry;

His justice cleansed the garden of its impurities;

(4) With the fire of his sword (he) burnt in one moment the idol of idol worshippers;

(He) killed all, that breaker through (annihilator) of the army;

(5) When he captured the fort of Udayagiri, the world became full of jessamine;

(6) (He) began to construct the mosque and the date was,

"Founder of the mosque—(Gházi) Ali, the iconoclast."

[Hijra 1052 or 1642–43 A.D.]

NOTE.—The Gházi Ali alluded to was presumably a general of Abdullah Kutb Sháh. A photograph of part of this inscription is appended.

(۱) غازي علي خان زمان فتح جنگ *
آنکه سخندان شده از وے سخن *
(۲) از مدد و ياوريِ شاه سعيد *
قطب زمان شاه سرير دکهن *
(۳) سر بسر او سوخت خس و خاشاک کفر *
گشت عدلش باب شکار چمن *

(۴) زآتش شمشیر بت بتپرست *
سوخت بیکدم همه زوصف شکن *
(۵) قلعه اُدگیر چو تسخیر کرد *
گشت جهان پرز گل یا سمن *
(٦) کرد بنا مسجد و تاریخ شد *
بانئ مسجد علي بت شکن *
۱۰۵۲

Udayagiri (40). (A.D. 1514–15.)

[Udayagiri Hill. Telugu. From rock by the Lakshmamma temple.]

Translation.

Hail! On the 2nd day of the dark fortnight of Jyeshṭha of the year Bhava, which was current after the expired year 1436 of the illustrious, victorious and prosperous Ṣáliváhana Ṣaka era, Ṣríman Mahárájádhirája, Rájaparaméṣvara Ṣrí Víra Pratápa, Ṣrí Víra Krishna Ráya Maháráyulu Gáru encamped on Udayagiri hill, pursued Pratápa Rudra Gajapati up to Koṇḍavíḍu, captured Udayagiri Durgam after besieging it and seized [1] Tirumala Kánta Ráya, the paternal uncle (younger) of Pratápa Rudra Gajapati and returned. He has now presented one village namely Ṣikallu (Ṣríkallu of No. 37) situated in Nellore *síma* to the deity Kónavallabha Ráya of Udayagiri. From the revenue and grain derived from the village we shall perform worship and (provide) daily offering and all enjoyments to the deity for ever as long

---

[1] Note.—In the Canarese inscription No. 37 the name is given as Tirumala Raghava Ráya.

as the sun and moon last. In these terms this charitable edict has been issued.

[Imprecatory verse.]

1. స్వస్తిశ్రీ జయాభ్యుదయ శాలివాహన శకవర్షంబులు ౧౪౩౬

2. చెల్లంగానామీంద నడచే భావ సంవత్సర జ్యేష్ట బ ౨ లు శ్రీమన్మహా రాజా

3. ధిరాజ రాజపరమేశ్వర శ్రీవీర ప్రతాప శ్రీవీరక్రిష్ణరాయ మ హారాయలు వుద

4. యగిరి దుర్గంమీద విడిశి ప్రతాప రుద్రగజపతిని కొండ వీడుపర్యంతం విరుగంబొడిచి వుదయగిరి

5. దుర్గానకు మేణతవేయించి దుర్గంపుచ్చుకొని ప్రతాప రుద్రగజపతి వారి పిన్న తండ్రి తిరుమలకాంతరా

6. యనివి పట్టుకొని తిరిగివిచ్చేశి యిప్పుడు వుదయగిరి కోన వల్లభరాయనికి సమర్పించిన నెల్లూరి శీమలోని

7. శికల్లు గ్రా ౧ యీ గ్రామంవల్లం బుట్టిన రొఖధాన్యంల వల్ల దేవునికి పూజ పునస్కార నైవేద్య సర్వభోగాలున్ను.

8. ఆచంద్రార్కస్థాయిగాను నడపంగలవారము అని యిచ్చి న ధర్మశాసనము దానపాలన యోర్మ

9. ధ్యే దానాచ్ఛ్రేయోను పాలనం దానాత్స్వర్గ మవాప్నో తి పాలనా దచ్యుతం పదం శ్రీ శ్రీ జేయును.

UDAYAGIRI (41).

[Udayagiri Hill. Canarese.[1] From same place. This is a mere copy of No. 40 except as regards the name of the uncle of Pratápa Rudra Gajapati.]

---

[1] The Canarese inscriptions are in Telugu character.

1. శుభమస్తు స్వస్తిశ్రీ జయాభ్యుదయ శాలివాహన శకవ
ర్షంగళు ౧౪౩౮ సందు మేలె నడవ భావసం

2. వత్సరద జ్యేష్ఠ బ ౨ లు శ్రీమన్ మహారాజాధిరాజ రాజ
పరమేశ్వర శ్రీవీరప్రతాప శ్రీవీరకృష్ణరాయ మహా

3. రాయరు ఉదయగిరియ దుర్గదమేలె బిట్టు ప్రతాపరుద్ర
గజపతియనుకొండ వీడుపరియంతరలూ ముఱియ

4. లిఱిదు ఉదయగిరియ దుర్గకెర్ల విడియవనూ హొక్కి దుర్గ
వనూ తెకొండు ప్రతాపరుద్రగజపతియవర చికప్ప తిరుమల

5. కాంతరాయననూ హిడిదుకొండు తిరిగి బిజయమాడు
వాగకోనవల్లభరాయనిగె సమర్పిసి నెల్లూరు సీమెయొళగణ

6. శ్రీ కల్రగ్రామగె యాగ్రామదల్లి హుట్టిద రొఖదాంశ్యగ
ళింద దేవరిగె పూజపునస్కార నైవేద్య స

7. వర్ణ భోగగళనూ ఆ చంద్రార్కస్థాయి ఆగి నడసలుళ్ళ
వరుయెందుకొట్ట ధర్మశాసన॥ దానపా

8. లన యోర్మధ్యే దానాచ్ఛ్రేయోనుపాలనం దానా స్వ
ర్గమవాప్నోతి పాలనాదచ్యుతం పదం॥

Udayagiri (42). (A.D. 1533–34.)

[Udayagiri Hill. Telugu. From same place.]

Translation.

Hail! On Thursday, the 14th of the dark fortnight of Mágha of the year Vijaya, corresponding to the year 1455 of the illustrious, victorious and prosperous Ṣáli-váhana Ṣaka era, Mádinendu, son of Golavóbanéḍu, the door-keeper of Ṣrímanmahámaṇḍaléṣvarat Salarája Pina Tirumalayyadéva Mahárájulu, consecrated 12 Áḷvárs (Vaishnava saints) on the east of the temple of Kónavallabharáya of Udayagiri, constructed a *kónéru* (reservoir) for bathing for the removal of all sins for the devotees of Hari and for Vaishnava disciples and constructed *Maṇḍapas* on both sides of it. Having made ten thousand salutations daily to the divine and illustrious feet of Kónavallabharáya, Mádinéni Gáru presented to Kónavallabharáya, the *kónéru* and a garden on the holy occasion of Mahásivarátri.

NOTE.—This is the Salaka Rája Chinna Tirumalayyadéva of Sewell, a great officer under the Vijayanagar dynasty. Udayagiri appears to have been within his jurisdiction.

1. స్వస్తిశ్రీ జయాభ్యుదయ శాలివాహ
2. న శకవర్షంబులు ౧౪౫౫ అగునేటి వి
3. జయ సంవత్సర మాఘ బ ౧౪ గు
4. శ్రీమన్ మహామండలేశ్వర సలరాజు పి
5. న తిరుమలయ్య దేవ మహారాజులుంగారివా
6. కిలికాచే గొలవోబనేని కొమారుండు మా
7. దినేండు వుదయగిరి కోనవల్లభరాయని నిధిమీందవ(దే ?) వునితూర్పు
8. భాగమందు పన్నిద్దరు అళ్వారను శ్రీహరిదాసులు వైష్ణవ శిస్యులకు సర్వపాప
9. పరిహారంగాను సానంసేయను కొనేరు కట్టించి వుభయ పారిశ్యాలును మండపగ
10. ట్టించి మాదినేనుంగారు వల్లభరాయని దివ్య శ్రీపాదాలకు నిత్యమున్ను పద్వేలు దండాలు
11. పడి మహా శివరాత్రి పుణ్యకాలమందును కొనేరును వన మును కోనవల్లభరాయనికి సమర్పణ సేశను.

Udayagiri (43).

Translation.

[Udayagiri Hill. Telugu. From the same place.]

On Thursday, the 11th of the dark fortnight of Phálguna of the year Bahudhánya, Tirumalayya of the Vallabharáya family caused a *Bhóga Maṇḍapa* (a pleasure-hall or cooking-room for the deity) and a flight of steps to be constructed.

1. బహుధాన్య సంవ్వత్స
2. ర ఫాల్గుణ బ౧౧
3. వల్లభరాయని తిరు
4. మలయ్య భోగమం
5. డపం కట్టించ్చి సోపా
6. నాలు కట్టించినారు.

Udayagiri (44).

[Udayagiri Hill. Telugu. From within the Lakshmamma temple.]

Translation.

All the acts of devotion projected by Timmarájn, son of Konéṭaya, have been successfully brought to a close.

1. కోనేటయ కొమారుండు తిం
2. మరాజు సేయించిన సకలకైంక
3. ర్యము యీడేరెను.

UDAYAGIRI (45).

[Udayagiri Hill. Telugu. From a rock below the Madáru gate.]

TRANSLATION.

The son of the chief (Rázu) of the bearers of Udayagiri Durgam has suffered [*or* the son of Boyarázulu of Udayagiri Durgam has suffered].

ఉదగిరి దుర్గం బోయరాజుల బాలిసుడు కష్టపడినాడు

UDAYAGIRI (46). (A.D. 1426-27.)

[Venkatapuram. Telugu. From stone on tank bund.]

TRANSLATION.

Hail! On Thursday, the 15th of the bright half of Srávana of the year Parábhava, corresponding to the illustrious Saka year 1348—Hail! while Srímanmahamandalésvara Srí Víra Pratápa Déva Ráya Maháráyulu was ruling at Vijayanagar, Bayichana Bóyudu, the grandson of Mutta Ráju Singanaráju and Tudirula Dharmasáni gave this sale-deed. We have sold you the Dasabandam tank constructed by us at Bóyavídu and Kudichalapádu in Udayagiri *Rájya*. You may enjoy all the income derived from this tank in perpetuity as long as the sun and moon exist.

[One imprecatory verse.]

1. స్వస్తి శ్రీ శకవర్షంబులు
2. ౧౩౪౮ అగు నేటి పరాభవసం
3. వత్సర శ్రావణ శు ౧౫ గు స్వస్తి శ్రీ
4. మన్మహామండలేశ్వర శ్రీవీర
5. ప్రతాప దేవరాయ మహారాయలు

6. విజయనగరమంద్దు సాంమ్రా
7. జ్యము శేయుచుండగాను
8. ముత్తరాజు సింగ్నరాజుగారికి తు
9. దికుల దర్మసాని మనుమడు
10. బయిచనబోయుడు యిచ్చినక్రయ శాస
11. నం ఉదయగిరి రాజ్యమందు
12. బోయవిడిలోవలను కుడి
13. చలపాటనుం నేము ధనపందాన
14. కు కట్టించ్చిన చెరువు మీక క్రయ
15. ముగాను యిత్సిమి యీచెరువందు
16. ల సకలలాభాలు ఆచంద్రార్క
17. స్తాఇగా అనుభవించితిరి సా
18. మాన్యోయం ధర్మశేతుర్ నృపాణా
19. ంకాలేకాలేపాలనియ్యోభవెద్భిః
20. సర్వాంనేతాన్ భావినాపార్థివేంద్రాన్
21. భూయోభూయోయాచతేరామచంద్రః

Udayagiri (47).

[Vírúru. Telugu. East of village on the south bank of Upputéru.]

Translation.

On the 3rd of the bright fortnight of Phálguṇa of the year Pramádi, the paid servant of the ruler of Vírúru granted this charitable ediot of gift of land to Bommaláṭa Vírappa. We have granted to you with libation of water the villages Aṣavémula, Viḷátilangam & Rarlapalli (?) as *sarva agrahára* for the religious merit of Voḍa Komára Venkaṭádrináyanivàru. Therefore you should take possession of these three villages and you, your sons and grandsons should enjoy them.

Whoever, coveting this charity, speaks ill of it will be considered to have eaten the excrement of his son and to have sucked the yard of a donkey . . . (?)

1. ప్రమాది సంవత్సర ఫాల్గుణ శుద్ధ
2. 3 లు వీరు రిథోంన్కై జీతపువారు బొమ్మలా
3. ట వీరప్పకు ఇచ్చిన భూధాన ధర్మశాసనం అశ
4. వేముల విశ్వాతి లంగంఅర్లపల్లె వొడకొమార
5. వెంకటాద్రినాయని వారికి పుణ్యంగా సర్వ గ్రహారంగా
6. దారదత్తంచెసి మీకి స్తింగనక ముమ్మూరు చేసుక పు
7. త్రపుత్ర పారంపర్యం అనుభవించి బ్రతికేది యీపుణ్యా
8. లకు యెవండు అసించి కీడాడిన కూడు
9. కి పియ్యి తిన్నవాండెగాడిదె శిస్నం
10. దీంకినవాండే యీ కొలంతిగోని
11. పింగుగుడిచినవాండే,

Udayagiri (48). (A.D. 1252–53.)

[Yépilagunṭa (hamlet of Chilakapád). Telugu. On three sides of a stone. The three sides seem to make up one inscription though they do not run on very well.]

Translation.

Hail! While Ṣríman Mahámaṇḍaléṣvara Pasáhita (?) Tikkayadéva Mahárájulu, who is possessed of all praiseworthy attributes, was pleasantly passing his time at Vadólagaṭṭu, listening to pleasant converse in company with his chief minister Ṣríman Siddana Pregaḍa, who is possessed of all praiseworthy attributes, his minister (Pregaḍa) Tikkayanátha, his father, his younger brother, and a party of men venerable with age and famous, his (Tikkayadéva's) father, having considered what is *dharma* (virtue) and what is *adharma* (vice), (provided) for decorations and other enjoyments for Tirukalésvara Srí Máhadéva.

On Vaddavâram (Friday) the 15th of the dark fortnight of Phálguna in the year Paridhávi corresponding to the illustrious Śaka year 1174, in the 9th year of (the reign of) Srí Víra Rájéndra Chódachakravarti, on the occasion of an eclipse of the sun, he (Tikkayadéva) who is the worshipper of the illustrious lotus feet of Tirukálesvara (presented) to Tirupurántaka déva; (and) his younger brother (gave) to Kédáradéva.

There is (a village) Bódapádu in Chilakapáti Kampanagalam. They presented (Bódapádu ?) with libation of water to last as long as the sun and moon exist. Any one who denies the existence of this charity will have worms in his mouth (?). Those who obstruct it will incur the sin of killing a cow near the Ganges. They will be considered to have eaten the flesh of a dog from the skull of their eldest son.

[One imprecatory verse.]

NOTE.—This chief minister does not seem to be mentioned elsewhere in the collection.

1. స్వస్తి సమ
2. స్త ప్రశస్తి స
3. హిత శ్రీమ
4. న్మహా మండ
5. లేశ్వర [పసా
6. హిత ?]తికరయ
7. దేవ మహారా
8. జులు సమ
9. స్త ప్రశస్తి సహి
10. త శ్రీమన్మహా

11. ప్రధానులైన
12. సిద్ధనపెగడ
13. తికర్రయ నాథ
14. రిపెగడయు
15. ం దమతిాం
16. డినం తోడు
17. నింతమవట్ల
18. నుంగూడి
19. యు వయోా
20. న్స్యతప్రము
21. ఖులై య
22 శవగణంబుతో వదొాల
23. గట్టునం దిష్ట కథ వి
24 నోదంయులం నున్నయ
25. వసరంబునధర్మాధర్మం
26. విచారించి తమతండ్రి
27. తిరుకాళేశ్వర శ్రీమహా
28. దేవరకునంగభోగరం
29. గ భోగంబులకు. । స్వస్తి శ్రీ
30. సకవరుషంబులు
31. ౧౧౭౪ నేండు శ్రీ వీ
32. ర రాజేంద్ర చోడచక్ర
33. వతిా .౯. శ్రాహి. బరిధా .
34. వి సంవత్సర ఫాల్గుణ
35. బహుళ॥ ౧౫ వడవా
36. రమునాంటి సూర్య
37. గ్రహణమునాండు తి
38. రుకాళేశ్వర దేవర దివ్య
39. శ్రీపాదపద్మా రాధకులై

40. త త్రిపురాంతక దేవునికిన్ని
41. అతనితమ్ముండు గేదా
42. ర దేవనికిం చిలుక
43. పాటి కంపన
44. లములో బోగ
45. డ పాడ నుం
46. న్నది ఆచం
47. ద్రార్కముగా
48. ధారాపూర్వ
49. ముసేసి ఇ
50. చ్చినవాండు
51. దీనిం నెవ్వ
52. డు లేదన్నవా
53. ని నోర తోం
54. కప్రుప్పులు
55. ద్రొలుదీనికి వి
56. క్రితంచేస్తే వా
57. రు గంగ్గ కటు
58. తం గపిలం పొ
59. డిచినవారు
60. తమ పెడకొడుకు
61. కపాలానంస్వ
62. నరమాంస భ
63. క్షణంబుసేసి
64. నవారు స్వదత్తాం
65. పరదత్తాంవ్వాయోహ
66. రేతివసుంధరా షష్టి
67. వర్షసహస్రాణి
68. విష్టాయాం జాయతే క్రిమి.

VENKATAGIRI (1). (A.D. 1230–31.)

[Chápalapalli. Tamil. From Vishnu Temple. The inscriptions on this temple are very long and in order to save space we have omitted those portions which merely describe the mode of sharing the endowments.]

TRANSLATION.

Hail! Prosperity! In the expired Ṣaka year one thousand one hundred and fifty-two corresponding to the 15th year of the reign of the emperor of the three worlds, the glorious Rájarájadéva, on a date in the month of Ṭai, Bejjádévi the consort of Yádavaráya Bhujabalasiddharasa, . . . to give as . . . . in Pákkainádu (a sub-division of) Jayaṅkoṇḍa-Choḻamaṇḍalam.

[The inscription then goes on to describe the lands and the shares, 46 in number, given to Brahmans.]

According to the cadjan document signed by . . . pillayár to these persons I, Kamala Mahádévi *alias* Bejjádévi, consort of Rájámalladéva *alias* Bhujabalasiddharasa *alias* Yádavaráya caused this to be inscribed on stone.

If there should be any who injures this charity, he will incur the sin of one who kills a tawny cow on the banks of the Ganges. I shall place on my head the illustrious feet of those who protect this charity.

Having engraved this stone . . . 40 *kuḻis* of the mango tope, the jack fruit tope . . . .

[1] ஸ்வஸ்திஸ்ரீ சகரை ஆண்டு ஆயிரத்து ஒருநூற்றை[ம்ப-த்திர]ண்டு சென்ற திரிபுவனச்சக்கர[வ]த்திகள் ஸ்ரீராஜ[ரா]-ஜதெ[வ]ர்க்கு யாண்டு ௰௫வது தைமாஸதொருநா[ள்] யாத-

வராயஹ ஜவசூவஸிஸாவஸாதெவிபெச்சாதெவியென் ஜயங்கொ-ண்டசொழமண்டலத்துப்பாக்கைநாட்டுப்பநாட் . . . .

[2] மாநக்குடிப்பெ[பநா]நக்கொவிப்பின் . . . . . .

[11] . . . . வகள் பக்கல் பெற்ற இப்பபெருக்கு பிள்-ளையார் திருவெழுத்து இட்டுக்குடுத்தகை பொலைப்படியெ பெ-ற்ற பெறைப்பெர்வஸம் கல்வெட்டுவித்தொர் யாதவராப-ரீஹ-

[12] ஜவசூவஸிஸாவஸரான ராஜமல்லதெவருடைய தெவி கமசூஹாதெவியார் வெஜ்ஜதெவியென் இஸ்ஜ்ஞு[நூா] ஜிதஸ்-வரை செல்வதாக மதுராந்தகப்பொத்தப்பிச்சொழன் எறவி . . . . .

[13] . . . . . பத்திலெ இப்படி கல்வெட்டுவிதென் இஸ்ஜத்துக்கு அழிவு நினைத்தாருண்டாகில் கெங்கைக்கரை-யில் குரால் பசுக்கொன்றான் பாபதலெபுகுவார் இஸ-

[14] ஜெனை ரக்ஷிதாந் ஸ்ரீ வாதயஜி எந்தலைமெனை ஸஜூஜா இக்கல்வெட்டு . . . . . திலங்கள் பெத்-திற இடத்து மாவெணாப்பும் பிலாதொப்புங்குழி காற்பதும் . . . . பொவி .

VENKATAGIRI (2).

[Chápalapalli. Tamil. North wall of Vishnu temple.]

TRANSLATION.

Hail! Prosperity! In the twenty-first year of the reign of the emperor of the three worlds, the glorious Rájarajadéva, in the month of Ádi, I, Savaṇar Áḷuḍaippiḷḷai gave recently one *máḍai* as interest for three evening lamps presented by me to (the god) Yádavanáráyaṇaperumáḷ in the city of Nágapuḍól *alias* the glorious Rájamallachaturvédimangala.

This one *máḍai* . . . .

NOTE.—There is a village called Nágavólu in Venkatag'ri Division. Possibly Nágapuḍól is the old name of the same place.

[1] ஸ்வஸ்திஸ்ரீ திரிபுவனச்சக்கரவத்திகள் ஸ்ரீ ராஜராஜ தெ-வற்கு யாண்டு இருபத்தொன்றாவது ஆ(ட்)டி ஜோலஷ்காரஷ நா-கபுடோலான ஸ்ரீராஜஸ்யேச்சதுர்வேதிமங்கலத்து

[2] யாதவநாராயணப்பெருமாளுக்கு லவணர் ஆளுடை-யபிள்ளையெங் கைவத்த சந்திவிளக்கு [மூந்]றுக்கும் பெ விழு-ட்டி இன்னாளில் குடுத்த மாடை ஒன்று இம்மாடை ஒன்று[ம்]

VENKATAGIRI (3).

[Chápalapalli. Tamil. Inscription going round the Vishnu temple.]

TRANSLATION.

Hail! Prosperity! In the 15th year of the reign of the emperor of three worlds, the glorious Rájarájadéva, on a date in the month of Tai, Bejjádévi, the consort of Yádavaráya *alias* Bujabalasiddarasar gave to the god Emperumán Yádavanárayaṇa in the city which we established at Nágapuḍól, for the maintenance of a sacred perpetual lamp as long as the moon and sun last, land (measuring) two hundred and twenty *kuḻi* out of the two thousand *kuḻi* granted free of tax under this tank made up of (1) one hundred *kuḻi* situated to the east of the land belonging to the Brahmans of Mókkaḍai, to the south of Kunḍili the *dévadáyam* of the lord . . lanisvara and to the north of the supply channel and

(2) one hundred and twenty *kuḷi* of land under the tank called Déviyáréri *alias* Kamalamahádévićrí which I caused to be dug.

The priest Tiruvénkadabhattan having received this two hundred and twenty *kuḷi* before the sacred door way of Yádavanáráyaṇaperumáḷ is bound to maintain this sacred perpetual lamp as long as the moon and sun last.

I, Bejjádévi, the consort of Yádavaráyar *alias* Bujabalasiddharasar left in the hands of this priest Tiruvenkadabhattan this land (measuring) two hundred and twenty *kuḷi* so that he may also, without hindrance from any man, raise a hot weather crop therein . . . . Let there be prosperity.

[1] ஸ்வஸ்தி ஸ்ரீ திரிபுவநச்சக்கரவர்த்திகள் ஸ்ரீராஜராஜதேவர்க்கு யாண்டு ௰௩ வது தைம்மாஸத்தொருநாள் யாதவராயர் ஹுஜபலஸித்தரஸர் தேவி பெஜ்ஜாதேவியென் இஷாழபு-டொவில் நாங்களெற்றின அகரத்தில் எம்பெருமான் யாதவநாராயணப்பெருமாளுக்கு ஒரு திருநந்தாவிளக்குச்சந்திராதித்தவரை செல்லக்கடவதாக இவ்வெரிகீழ் திருவிடையாட்டநிலம் குழியிரண்டாயிரத்தில் மொக்கடைய ஸுரஹணருடைய நிலத்துக்கு கிழக்கு

[2] . . . லகிஷ்ராமுடையநாயநார் தேவதாநமான குண்டிவிக்குத்தெற்கு நிர்கட்டிவாக்காலுக்கு வடக்கு இவடத்திலெ நூறு குழியும் நாங் கல்லிவித்த தேவியாரெரியென்கிற கமலமஹாதெவிப்பெரிகீழ் கிலாரிபுலத்தொடு தடிசொக்குழி நூற்றிருபதுமாகக்குழி இருநூற்றிருபதும் யாதவநாராயணப்பெருமான்திருவடிபிடிக்குநம்பியார் திருவெங்கடபட்டன் கைக்கொண்டு இத்திருநந்தாவிளக்கு ஒன்றும் சந்திராதித்தவரை செலுத்தக்கடவநாகவும் இப்படி இத்திருநந்தாவிளக்கு ஒன்றுக்கு விட்ட நிலம் ஊரமிக்குங்கொடைப்பயிர் செய்யுமிடத்து நலொரபாதியென்று சொ-

[3] லலக்கடவதன்றாக இந்நிலமிருநூற்றிருபதுமினம்பியார் திருவெங்கடபட்டன் வசம் விட்டேன் யாதவராயர் ஸ்ரீராஜவ- ஙவிஉபஸருடைய தேவியார் வெஜஜாதேவியேன் ஸ்வஸ்தி ஸ்ரீ

VENKATAGIRI (4).

[Chápalapalli. Tamil. From the Vishnu temple.]

TRANSLATION.

In the 19th year of the reign of the emperor of the three worlds, the glorious Rájarájadéva, in the month Aippaśi, Kaśáṇmai the son of Yádavaráyar, gave to Emberumán Yádavanáráyaṇaperumál, at Rájamallachaturvédimaṅgalam (situated) in Pákkainádu one *máḍai* for the maintenance as long as the moon and sun last of one evening lamp endowed by him.

I, Tiruvéṅgaḍabhaṭṭai, bind myself to maintain the evening lamp with this *máḍai* as long as the moon and sun last.

[1] திரிபுவனச்சக்கரவத்திகள் ஸ்ரீராஜராஜதேவற்கு யா- ண்டு ௰௯வது ஐப்பசி மாஸம் பாக்கைநாட்டு

[2] ஸ்ரீராஜமல்ல ச்சதுர்வேதிமங்கலத்து எம்பெருமான் யா- தவநாராயணப்பெருமாளுக்கு யாதவராயர்

[3] மகன் கசாண்மையென் வைத்த சந்திவிளக்கு ஒன்று- ஞ்சந்திராதித்தவரை செலுத்தக்கடவ[ரா]க இக்கோயிலின்

. . . . .

[4] டை ஒன்று இம்மாடை ஒன்றுக்கும் சந்திராதித்த[வ- ரை]ச்சந்திவிளக்கு செலுத்தக்கடவேன் திருவெங்கடபட்டனே . .

VENKATAGIRI (5).

[Chápalapalli. Tamil. From Vishnu temple.]

TRANSLATION.

Hail! Prosperity! In the 13th year of the reign of the emperor of the three worlds, the glorious Rájarájadéva on the date of Chittirai equinox, Attiyammai the daughter of Iraṭṭáḍi Bhímabhaṭṭan of Tumbaiyúr (situated) in Paṭṭaiyúrnáḍu . . . . town of Nágarpuḍól (situated) in Paḍikámanáḍu in Pákkainádu . . .

[1] ஸ்வஸ்தி ஸ்ரீ த்ரிபுவனச்சக்கரவத்திகள் ஸ்ரீராஜராஜதே-வற்கு யாண்டு ௰௩வதில் சித்திரை விஷுவத்தி நாள் பட்டை-யூர்நாட்டு தும்பையூரகரத்து இரட்டாடி பீமபட்டன் பெண்-பிள்ளை அத்தி

[2] யம்மையென் பாக்கைநாட்டு ப[டிக]ாம நாட்டு அகர-ம் நாகர்புடோலான ஸ்ரீ . . . .

VENKATAGIRI (6).

[Chápalapalli. Tamil. From Vishnu temple.]

TRANSLATION.

Hail! Prosperity! In the 11th year of the reign of the emperor of the three worlds, the glorious Rájarája déva, on the date of the Uttaráyaṇasaṅkránti, I Toṇḍaimán Áṟṟúr Kántaráyan, the prime minister of Yáḍavaráyan (*alias*) Kaṭṭidévarasan gave to Emberumán Yáḍavanáráyaṇaperumáḷ at the town of Nágapuḍól *alias* the glorious Rájamallachaturvédimaṅgalam, four cows for the maintenance as long as the moon and sun last of four evening lamps.

For these four cows were given (four) *máḍai* in the hands of Koṇḍuperumáḷ of Náyaṟunáḍu.

[Then follows one line which forms part of another inscription.]

Emberumán Yádavaráyan of Śrí Rájamallachaturvédimangalam.

[1] ஸ்வஸ்தி ஸ்ரீதிரிபுவனச்சக்கரவத்திகள் ஸ்ரீராஜராஜதெ-
வற்கு யாண்டு யக வது ரிஷப[ய]ணஸம்க்ரம[த்து] நாள் அக-
ரஉ ஸாகபுடொலான ஸ்ரீராஜமல்லச்சது வெதிமங்கலத்து
எம்பெருமான் யாதவராயணப்பெருமாளுக்கு யாதவராயன்
கட்டிதெவராசன் வரயா-

[2] கி தொண்டைமாநாற்றூர் காஸராயதெவன் நாலுச-
ஸிவிளக்குச்சந்திரா[தித்த*]வரை செல்லக்கடவதாக நான் வி-
ட்ட பசு நாலு இப்பசு நாலுக்குமாக நாயறுநாட்டுக்கொண்-
பெருமாள் வசங்குடுத்த மாடெ[ந] . . .

[3] க்ககம ஸ்ரீராஜமல்லச்(ச்)சதுர்வெதிமங்கலத்து எம்-
பெருமான் யாதவராயன் நா-

VENKATAGIRI (7).

[Chápalapalli. Tamil. From Vishnu temple.]

TRANSLATION.

I, Yádavarájan, who bear the birudas :—the glorifier of the *Yádava* race, the one entitled to the five great musical sounds (instruments), Mahámaṇḍaléṣvara, (great provincial chief), the lord of the best of cities Kanuchára . . . . the worshipper of the lotus feet . . . . . the destroyer of hostile forces, who bear the name "Samastarájásráya" (*i.e.*, the asylum of all kings), the king of the race of Ṣaṣikula Chálukki which is endowed with all eulogistic titles; gave lands (as follows) as exclusive property of the deity . . . . city which formed part of Nágapudol in Pagámanádu in Pákkainádu in Chólamandala :—2,000 *kuli* of wet land under the tank of this city . . . . . 13,000 *kuli* of dry land marked off as exclusive property of the deity (Emperumán) . . . . Kamalamahádéviputtéri (a tank) caused to be constructed by . . . (Kamala Mahá ?) dévi ; I caused to be granted with libation of water on behalf of the Vellálas of Kanumili by (Madurántaka) Pottapichóla Erasiddharasa whom I brought (for this purpose), ten *mádais* to this deity (Emperumán) . . . Tiruvenkatabhattan who possesses rights in this temple, and who worships the sacred feet . . . . as long as the moon and the sun endure . . . .

[1] யாதவகுலதிலகனாஸயிமதவஜுஹொஸஜுஹொணேயெ-
ஸ்வரன் கடவராவபுரவராயிவ . . . . ராஜேந்த்ரசொ-
ளாது வரவதுஸாயகன் ஸஹஸ்ரராஜா நாயகாஹயெயது ஸஜ-
ஸ்த்வஸ்ஸ்தி ஸமிகந்தசொளுக்கிவம்ஸா ரிசு ஞன யாதவராஜந்-
. . . . .

[2] முமண்டலத்துப்பாக்கைநாட்டுள் பகாமநாட்டில் நாக
புடொலிற்பிறிவான அகரம் . . . . . கு நான் விட்ட
திருவிடையாட்டங்களாவன இவ்வகரத்து எரிகீழ் நஞ்சைநி-
லங்குழி ௨௲மும் இவ்வெம்பெருமான் திருப்புற . . . . .

[3] தெவி கல்லிவித்த கமலமஹாதெவிப்புத்தெரியும் இவ்-
வெரிக்கு கீர்ப்பாய் இவள் கண்ட . . . . . ம்பெருமானு-
க்குத்திருவிடையாட்டமாக பிறிந்த புஞ்செய் குழி ௰௩௲மும்
கனுமிலி வெள்ளாளர் பக்கல் ஞன் பொன்னறமிட்டு மண்ண-
றக்கொண் . . .

[4] தகப்பொத்தப்பிச்சொழன் எ்றஸிதரஸரை இடுவித்-
து கீர்வார்ப்பித்துக்குடுத்து இவ்வெம்பெரு . . . . .
மாடை பத்து இம்மாடை பத்தும் இக்கொயிலில் காணியாளன்
திருவடிப்பிடிப்பான் திருவெங்கடபட்டன் சந்திராதித்தவரை-

VENKATAGIRI (8 & 9).

[Chápalapalli. Tamil. From Vishnu temple.

These are two fragments, the first recording the grant of one *máḍai* to Aṅgaḍabhaṭṭar by Yádavaráyar of the town of Nágarpuḍól *alias* the glorious Rájamalla-chaturvédimaṅgalam (situated) in Pákkainádu; the second mentioning Témáṇḍi Ammai the wife of Bhuja-balasiddarasar.]

(8).

[1] மண்டலத்துப்பாக்கைநாட்டு அகரம் நாகர்புடோலான ஸ்ரீராஜ[8]ல்லச்சதுர்வெதிமங்கலத்து யாதவராசர்

[2] அங்கடபட்டர் வசம் குடுத்த மா[டை] ஒன்றும் கொண்டு சந்திராதித்தவரைக்கடவார்

(9).

[1] தவராயர் புசபலசித்தளாசர் மூப்பியார் தெமாண்டி அம்மையென் பாக்கநாட்டுப்பகாமநாட்டு அகரம் நாகபுடோலான

VENKATAGIRI (10).

[Chápalapalli. Tamil. From Vishnu temple. Translation doubtful.]

TRANSLATION.

In accordance with the village inscription engraved by us on stone for the town founded by us in Nágapuḍól in . . . Náḍu, Piḷḷaiyár Bhujabalasiddharasar having declared his intention of founding this town in Nágapudól in the 39th year of the reign of Kulóttuṅga-chóḻadéva, Nárumidan Piṟṟaiyáṇḍán (gave) in the second year of (the reign of) this Rájarájadéva . . . .

including the tank of . . . . . . dévi, demarcated it with stones on the four sides, set up the image of (?) Madurántakapottapichóḷa *alias* Siddharasa, dedicating the village with libations of water, and granted the lands included within these four boundaries, *i.e.*, all the wet and dry lands excluding the tax-free lands—all the temple lands . . . . of Nágéṣvara Uḍayár in this town, the garden lands forming the boundary of this town and lying to the east of Tondaimán *kuḻi*, and 800 *kuḻi* of garden land near the temple of Piḍári,—Piḷḷaiyár's share 32, my share 14—total 46 shares—as follows, (here follow the shares of various Brahmans).

[1] நாட்டு நாகபுடோவில் நாங்களேற்றின அகரத்துக்கு நான் ஸ்ரீராஜஸராவஸகம் கல்வெட்டுவித்தபடி குலொத்துங்கசோழதேவர்க்கு ௩௰௯ வது நாளிலெ பிள்ளையார் ஹஜவஷஸிஙா-வர் இநாகபுடோவிலெ அகரமெற்றுவாராகக் கொவிச்செல்லாகிற்க நாறுமிகன் பிற்றைபாண்டான் இவ்விராசராசதேவருக்கு இரண்டாவது நாளிலெ எ[று]டயாரியை அழகா-

. . . . .

[2] ம் தெவியார் எரியுமுள்ப்பட இநாமபுடோவிலெ கிழக்கடய ஊர்ப்பிறிவாகப்பிறித்து நாற்பாலெல்லையுங்கல்லு நடுவித்து மதுராந்தகப்பொதப்பிச்சொழனென ஸித்தரஸனைபிடுவித்து அகரமாக நிர்வாரிப்பித்துக்கொண்டு இந்நாற்பாலெல்லைக்குள்ப்பட்ட நிலத்தில் இவ்வகரத்தில் நாயனார் திருநாகீஸ்வரமுடையார்க்கு இ . . . . .

[3] ள்ளகொத்தமத்தனையும் தொண்டைமான் குழிக்கிழ் இவ்வகரத்தெல்லையாக நஞ்சைநிலமான கொத்தமும் பிடாரிகொயிலருகில் கொல்லைகுழி எண்ணூறும் இவை திருவிடையாட்டமாக விட்டு நீக்கி நின்ற நிலம் புஞ்சை நஞ்சைய்யுள்ள நிலமத்தனையும் பிள்ளையார் அகரப்பங்கு முப்பத்திரண்டும் எங்ககரம் பங்கு பதினாலும் ஆகப்பங்கு நாற்பத்தாறாக நி [புது]

[4] பெர்வசம் தம்முடய திருவெழுத்திட்ட திருமுகங்குடுத்த பொக்குமுதல் வங்கிப்புறத்து லக்ஷ்மணஹட்டன் பங்கு ஒன்று இவன் பிள்ளை திருவெங்கடஹட்டன் பங்கு ஒன்று குஞ்சப்பூர் லக்ஷ்மணஹட்டன் பங்கு ஒன்று பிருந்தூர் மலைகின்றான்ஹட்டன் பங்கு ஒன்று குஞ்சப்பூர் ஆவுடையான்ஹட்டன் பங்கு ஒன்று.

VENKATAGIRI (11).

[Chápalapalli. Tamil. From Vishnu temple.]

TRANSLATION.

Hail! Prosperity! In the . . year of the reign of Kulóttuṅgachóḷadéva, I, Rájamalladévan *alias* Bhujabalasiddharasa the son of . . . . . Kaṭṭidévarasan (who bears the birudas), the best of the Yádava dynasty, the light of the Yádava race, he who possesses the five Mahásabdas, Mahámaṇḍaléśvara (the great provincial chief), the lord of the best of cities Kañchavárapura, the lord of Veṅgi, the receiver of gifts from the goddess Piṭaradévi, the worshipper of the lotus feet of the glorious Veṅkatanátha, he who bears the name samastharájáśrayan (the refuge of all kings), the head of the famous race of Śaśikulachálukki, created, through Madurántakapottapichóḷa *alias* Eṛasiddharasa, the town of Nágapuḍól (situated) in Pagámanáḍu in Pákkainádu (a sub-division) of Jayaṅkoṇḍachōḷamaṇḍala as a separate city demarcated on the four sides with stones, (and granted it) with libation of water and divided the lands therein into forty-six shares.

[The inscription also says that, in dividing the land into shares, certain tax-free land belonging to the god Tirunagésvara and to the god Yádavanáráyaṇa Emberumán, a flower garden, etc., were excluded.]

[1] ஸ்வஸ்திஸ்ரீ குலோத்துங்கசோழதேவற்கு யா[ண்டு]
. . . . . வது [ய]தூவம்ஸகுலோத்தமன் யாதவகுலதீ-
வகு ஸமயிம [தவ] ஞஸோரஸு ஜேஸ[ர] ஜேஜுவெஷுரகு [க]
ம்வாரபுரவராயி[ஸ]ரகு வெங்கிவல்லஹகு வி[ம]ரதேவிவர-
ஹஸாதக]ன் ஸ்ரீகாளஹஸ்தி, உராகருன்யமதீயார ஸ்ரீமற்-
வெங்கடநாயஸ்ரீவாதாரவிதஸேவா[ன்] வாரவஷவாயகன்
ஸஹேஸ்ராஜாஸ்யஙஜேயயன்.

[2] ஸஹேஷ பரஸஹஸிஸஸிகுலசாளுக்கி வம்ஸாயிவ நா . .
. ன் கட்டிதேவரசன் மகன் ராஜமல்லதேவனுஹன ஹூஜ-
வஷஸஙரஸநென் ஜயங்கொண்டசோழமண்டலத்துப் பாக்கை-
கநாட்டுப்பகாமநாட்டு நாகபுடோல அகரம் [மதுராந்தக]ப்-
பொத்தப்பிச்சோழன் எறஸிஙரஸமெரயிடுவித்து அகரமாக
கிர்வார்ப்பித்து நால்பாலெல்லையும் பிறித்துக்கல்நடுவித்து-
இந்நால்-

[3] பாலெல்லைக்குமுட்பட்ட நிலத் திலிவ்வூரில் நாதவரதி-
வெஷயாயிருந்துள்ள ஹோதேவர் திருந[ா *]மஸமுடையார்
தேவதாந [ந]ஞ்சை நிலம் இரண்டாயிரத்தை[ந்நூ]றும் நஞ்சை
திருவிடையாட்டத்தில் நிலம் ஐனூற்றெட்டும் பூளிவாதமெட்-
டில் நிலம் எழுபத்தெட்டும் மணபதியார்குண்டில் குழி இருப-
தும் ந[ான் எழுந்த]ருளுவித்த எம்பெருமான் யாதவநாராய-
ணப்பெருமாளுக்கு இவ்வகரத்திலெரிகிழ் திருவிடையாட்டமாக
விட்ட நஞ்சை நிலம் குழி இரண்டாயிரமும் திரு-

[4] ப்புறக்குடைத்திருநந்தவனம் குழி நூற்றொருபதும்
மாந்தோப்புக்குழி இருபதும் பிலாந்தோப்புக்குழி இருபதும் எ-
ளுகமுடையாள் கமலமாதேவி யார்கல்லுவித்த கமலமாதேவிப்-

புத்தெரியுந்திருவிடையாட்டமாக விட்டு நிக்கி நின்ற கொத்தமெ-ல்லாம் நாற்பத்தாறுஹாஸமாக நிவேயித்து இதில் நான் குடுத்த-ஹாஸம் முபத்திரண்ணடும் கம்லமாசெடிவிதநூ 8 மாகக்குடுத்த ஹாஸ வெடி . . . . . .

VENKATAGIRI (12).

[Chápalapalli. Tamil. West wall of Vishnu temple. Illegible.]

VENKATAGIRI (13).

[Chápalapalli. Tamil. An inscription going round the Vishnu temple.]

TRANSLATION.

In the 39th year of the reign of Kulóttuṅgachóḷadéva, Rájamalladévan *alias* Bhujabalasiddharasan, the son of Kaṭṭidévarasan (who has the birudas) . . . . (the best of the *Yadu* race), (gave) a flower garden called after Rájamallan (donor) measuring 100 *kuḻi*, a mango tope measuring 20 *kuḻi*, and a jack fruit tope measuring 20 *kuḻi*, ... including Puruvalakkál *alias* Vishayasamudra (evidently a reservoir) which was granted as temple property . . . . in . . . . Jayankoṇḍachoḷamaṇḍala. All this . . . .

[1] ஸ்வஸ்தி ஸ்ரீ குலொத்துங்க[சொழ]தெவற்கு யாண்டு கூயிகூ ஆவது யதுவம்ஸகுலொத்தமன் . . . . .

[2] கட்டிதெவரசன் மகன் ராஜமல்லதெவனான ஹுஜப-லஸித்தரஸனென் ஜயங்கொண்டசொ . . . . .

[3] க்குடையில் ராஜமல்லந் திருநந்தவனங்குழி ௱ம் மாந்-
தொப்புக்குழி உ௰ பிலாந்தொப்புக்குழி உ௰ சமைய-ஜனா
. . . . .

[4] தெருவிடையாட்டமாக விட்ட புறவலக்காலான வி
வைஷயவஸ்ருஜமும் உட்பட இத்தனையுமதுராந்-

VENKATAGIRI (14).

[Chápalapalli. Tamil. East wall of Vishnu temple.]

TRANSLATION.

Hail! Prosperity! In the 25th year of the reign of the emperor of the three worlds, the glorious Kulóttuṅgachóḻadéva, in the month of Ádi, I, Nilamareḍḍi Kaṭṭaiyaṇ, (gave) . . . . . for one evening lamp to (Yádavanárá)yaṇaperumáḷ and for reading the Bhárata on the sacred temple doorway . . . . (a sub-division) of Jayankonḍachóḻamanḍala.

[1] ஸ்வஸ்திஸ்ரீ திரிபுவனசக்ரவத்திகள் ஸ்ரீகுலொத்துங்கசொ-
ழதெவற்கு யாண்டு உ௰௫ வது ஆ(ட்)டிமாசம் ஜயங்கொண்ட-
சொழ . . . . .

[2] யணப்பெருமாளுக்கு நிலமரட்டி கட்டையனெந் சந்தி-
விளக்கு ஒந்றுக்கு இக்கொயிற் திருவடிப்பிடிபாரதஞ்செ-

VENKATAGIRI (15).

[Chápalapalli. Tamil. East wall of Vishnu temple.]

TRANSLATION.

In the 12th year of the reign of the emperor of the three worlds, the glorious Rájadéva, on the date of

Chittirai equinox, the *mádai* which I gave for one evening lamp to last as long as the moon endure to (the god) Yádavanáráyaṇaperumáḷ . . . . .

[1] திரிபுவனச்சக்கரவர்த்திகள் ஸ்ரீராஜதெவற்கு யாண்டு ௰௨ ஆவது சித்திரைவிஷுவிறுள் [ஸி]ள்ளையார்ய[ாதவநா]-

[2] ராயணப்பெருமாளுக்கு (ஸி)வந்திராதித்தவரை செல்வதாக ஒரு சந்திவிளக்குச்செல்வதாக நான்குடுத்தமாடை.

VENKATAGIRI (16).

[Chápalapalli. Tamil. East wall of Vishnu temple.]

TRANSLATION.

I, (who bear the *birudas*) Véṅgívallabhan (the lord of the Veṅgi country), Piṭaradévivaraprasádhan (the receiver of boons from the goddess Piṭaradévi), the worshipper of the illustrious feet of the lord of Śríkáḷahasti, . . . Veṅkaṭa granted the big channel named after Kamalamahádéví, the Toṇḍaimáṇ tank and certain . . . . lands under this tank, and also 33 cows for one perpetual lamp and also the interest on . . . . for ten evening lamps, to our lord Yádavanáráyaṇaperumáḷ set up by me in Śrí Rájamallichaturvédimaṅgala.

NOTE.—The ruler referred to is probably the Yádavarájan of preceding inscriptions. Kamala Mahádéví is mentioned in No. 1.

[1] . . . . . ண வெங்கிவல்லுஹ[ந] பிடாரதெவிவரப்ரஸாதக[ந] ஸ்ரீகாளஹஸ்திநாயஸ்ரீபாதாராதக[ந] ஸ்ரீவெங்கடநாம உ-

[2] . . . . . ஸ்ரீராஜமல்லிச்சதுர்ப்பெதிமங்கலத்து நானுகந்தருளுவித்த எம்பெருமான் யாதவநாராயணப்பெருமாளுக்கு.

[3] . . . . . . கமலசேகராதெவிப்பெருவாய்க்காலும் தொண்டைமானெரியும் இவ்வெரியைச்செ[ர]ப்பலகெ எட்டு கிலம் இவ்வெ-

[4] . . . . . மானுக்கு திருநந்தாவிளக்கு ஒன்றுக்கு பசு நடுநடம் சந்திவிளக்கு பத்துக்கு பெவிபூட்டாககுடுத்-

---

Venkatagiri (17).

[Mópúru. Tamil. From south wall of Chennakéśava temple.]

Translation.

This is a fragment dated in the 18th year of the emperor of the three worlds, the glorious Rájarájadéva and mentions Kéśavaperumáḷ of Muṇoyúr.

Note.—Muṇoyúr, Muṇoppúr and Periyamuṇoppúr seem to be the place now called Mópúru.

[1] திருபுவனசக்கரவத்தி
[2] ஸ்ரீராசராசதெவர்க்கு ய-
[3] ாண்டு பதிநெட்டா-
[4] வது முதல் முனெ-
[5] யூர் கெசவப்பெருமாள்.

Venkatagiri (18).

[Mópúru. Tamil. From south wall of Chennakéśava temple.]

Translation.

This is a fragment and records the gift of 2½ *máḍai* by a relation of Tikkamaraḍḍi for an evening lamp.

[1] சந்திராதித்தவரை-
[2] செல்லக்கடவத[ா*]க
[3] இக்கமரட்டியு-
[4] ரற் பெரிதயநும் சங்-
[5] திவிளக்குக்கு குடுத்த-
[6] [மாடை ஊரு இ]க்கொயி-
[7] வ காணியாளன் ஆ-
[8] ன்தபிள்ளையும் ந[ாரகி]-
[9] யணி-
[10] . ம்-
[11] . . .
[12] கைெ-
[13] காண்ட-
[14] ரங்கன்-
[15] . . . .

VENKATAGIRI (19).

[Mópúru. Tamil. South wall of Chennakéśava temple.]

TRANSLATION.

Hail! Prosperity! In the eighteenth year of the reign of the emperor of the three worlds, Rájarájadéva Choḻadévar, Chóḍappiraḍḍi (*alias*) Dásamanáyakkan gave as charity in the name of Chalukkinaráyaṇa *alias* Manumasittiyarasar of Periyamuṇoppúr (situated) in Pagámainádu, for interest, one *máḍai* for an evening lamp to the temple of Késavaperumáḷ.

Having received this *máḍai* to maintain this lamp, I, Anantamúrtibhaṭṭan, the possessor of rights in this temple . . . . as long as the moon and sun last.

[1] ஸ்வஸ்தி ஸ்ரீ திரிபுவநச்சக்கரவத்திகள் ராஜராஜசோழ-
தேவர்க்கு யாண்டு எட்டாவது [ப]காலை[ம]ருட்டுப்பெரியமு
னைப்பூர்ச்சளுக்கிநாராயண மருமசித்தி[யரசர்] யஜ்ஞமாந
கேசவப்பெருமாள் கோயில் சோட-

[2] ப்பிரட்டித்தாசநாயக்கனென் பொலியூட்டா[க*] சந்-
திவிளக்குக்கிட்ட மாடை ஒன்று இம்மாடை[க்கு]ச்சந்திவிள-
க்கு க செலுத்துவதாகக்கைக்கொண்[டு] இக்கோயிலில்கா-
ணியாளனான அநந்தமூற்திபட்டனென் சந்திராதித்தவரை

VENKATAGIRI (20).

[Mópúru. Tamil. On stone to north of Śiva temple.]

TRANSLATION.

Hail! Prosperity! In the 22nd year of the reign of the emperor of the three worlds, the glorious Rájarájadéva, Viṭṭami Reḍḍi, the son of Vayirappa Reḍḍi, a Reḍḍi resident in Muṇoppúr, gave one evening lamp to the god of Tiruvéṅgaḍam; Nárappa Reḍḍi, the son of Paṇḍári Kéttama Reḍḍi, gave one evening lamp; and Payatitappa Reḍḍi (the son of) Dharma Reḍḍi gave one evening lamp; and Tiraiyappa Reḍḍi gave one evening lamp. These together came up to four. One perpetual lamp . . . . Thus five lamps (have been presented). (Let them be maintained) as long as the moon and sun endure.

[1] ஸ்வஸ்தி ஸ்ரீ திரிபுவனச்சக்கரவத்திகள்
[2] ஸ்ரீ ராஜராஜதேவற்கு யாண்டு
[3] உ௰உண்டாவது முனை[ர]ப்பூர் ரெ-
[4] ட்டிகுடி வயிரப்பரெட்டியார் ம-

[5] கங் விட்டமிரெட்டியார் ஸ்ரீதி[ருவெங்]-
[6] க[ட*]முடையநாயநாருக்கு யிட்ட சந்திவிள-
[7] க்குவொன்றும் பண்டாரிக்கெத்தமரெ-
[8] ட்டியார் மகநாரப்பரொட்டியா[ர்*] யிட்ட
[9] சந்தி வி[ளக் *]கு ஒன்று பயதிதப்பரெட்டி தர்ம-
[10] ரெட்டி யிட்ட சந்திவிளக்கு ஒன்று தி-
[11] ரையப்பரெட்டியார் யிட்ட சந்திவி-
[12] ளக்கு ஒன்றுமாக சந்திரா[தித்தவரை]
[13] நாலுயகண்டவி[ள*]க்கு ஒ . .
[14] ய[ெ]டவிக்குயஞ்சும் வைத் . .
[15] ந்திராதித்தவரை தெ[வி]ல்க . .
[16] கடவது

VENKATAGIRI (21).

[Páḷemkóṭa. Telugu. On Venkatagiri drug near the spring.]

TRANSLATION.

On the 10th day of the dark fortnight of Bhádrapada of the year Táraṇa, Bhujabaḷa Boppayya Déva Mahárájulu constructed a cistern on the Kalimili Durgam.

NOTE.—It is not clear who is referred to in this and the following inscription. The epithet Bhujabaḷa suggests a Chóḍa descent. The present Rája of Venkaṭagiri has informed us that he does not think the inscriptions 21 and 22 can refer to any of his ancestors.

1 తారణ భాద్రపద
2 బ ౧౦ లు భుజబళ బొ
3 ప్పయ్య దేవమహారా
4 జులు కలిమిలి దుర్గ
5 మీంద చెలమ గట్టిం
6 చెను.

VENKATAGIRI (22).

[Páḷemkóṭa. Telugu. On Venkatagiri drug near the spring.]

TRANSLATION.

On the 5th day of the dark fortnight of Mágha of the year Prabhava Mádirázu, son of Kalimili Bopparáju, repaired the fortress (Durgam).

1. ప్రభవసంవత్సర మా
2. ఘ బ ౫ లు కలిమిలిబొప్ప
3. రాజుకొమారుడు మా
4. దిరాజు దుర్గాంసవరణ
5. శేయిచ్చును

SUBRAMANYAM.

NOTE.—Subramanyam. In the temple here are several inscriptions in Telugu, Tamil, Sanskrit and Hindústání descriptive of the founding of the suburb of Subramanyam and the endowment of the temple by the zamindars. The date from the close of the eighteenth century and it has not been thought necessary to print them.

VENKATAGIRI (23). (A.D. 1659–60 ?)

[Vazzavári páḷem. Telugu. In a field north of the Village.]

TRANSLATION.

Hail! On the 12th day of the dark fortnight of Jéshta of the year Vikári corresponding to the year 1580 of the illustrious, victorious and prosperous Śáliváhana Śaka era, while Házarat Álam Ennasá, seated on the diamond throne, was ruling the earth, Rangapparázugáru, grandson of Buchirázu Veṅgaḷarázu and son of

Kámarázu of the Átri *gótra* of the Ápastambha sútra and of the Yajuśśákha, and . . Bhaṭlaváru, grandson of . . . and son of . . . . of the Átri *gótra* of the Áśvaláyana *sútra*, and of the Rukśákhá, issued a charitable edict bestowing a grant of lands . . . in Udayagiri *sīma* . . .

Note.—The cyclic and Śaka years do not exactly agree. The Sultán referred to is perhaps Aurungzib under the name of Álamgír, though what 'Enna' stands for is not, in that case, apparent. The authority of the Golkoṇḍa dynasty must have been much shaken for the Delhi Emperor to be named, yet we find Sultán Abdullah Kutb Sháh mentioned in later grants, viz., U. 26, 27 and 36 which suggests that he is referred to in this inscription. In the next inscription two or three years later the ruling sovereign mentioned is the Penugoṇḍa Vijayanagar king. The territory round Udayagiri seems to have been torn from the Vijayanagar kingdom before that to which V. 24 relates.

1. స్వస్తిశ్రీ విజయాభ్యుదయ శాలి
2. వాహన శకవరుషంబులు ౧౫౮౦ అగు నే
3. టి వికారినామసంవత్సర జేష్ట బ ౧౨ లు
4. హజరతు ఆలం ఎన్నసావారు బ్రి . .
5. . . . . . రత్న సింహాసనానంద . .
6. సాంమ్రాంజ్యం చేయుచునుండంగాను ఆ
7. త్రిగోత్ర అపస్తంభసూత్ర ఎజుశ్శాఖా .
8. ను బుచ్చిరాజు వెంగళరాజు పౌత్రులైన కామ
9. రాజుగారి పుత్రులైన రంగప్పరాజుగారు ఆత్రి
10. గోత్ర ఆశ్వలాయనశూత్ర రుక్శాఖా . .
11. . . . . . . టవారి పౌత్రులు . .
12. . . . . లవారిపుత్రులు య . శాభట్లవారు
13. యిచ్చినట్టి భూదాన ధర్మశాసనము
14. . . వుదయగిరి శీమలోను . . . . .
15. . . . . నాయనివారు . . . . .

16. . . . . నామము . . . .
17. . . . అగ్రహారము . . .
18. . . . . తూర్పుకు . . .
19. . . . . కావు . . . . .
20. . . . .
21. . . . .
22. . . . .

VENKATAGIRI (24). (A.D. 1662-63.)

[Vazzaváripáḷem. Telugu. In a street.]

TRANSLATION.

On the 14th of the bright fortnight of Jyeshṭa of the year Śubha(kṛit), corresponding to the illustrious, victorious and prosperous Śáliváhana Śaka year 1584, while Śrímad Rájádhirája, Rájaparaméśvara, Śrí Vírapratápa Śrí Víra Bhujabala Víra Veṅkaṭapatiráyadéva Maháráyalayya Váru, seated on the diamond throne in the city of Penugonḍa, was ruling the earth, Śríman Mahámanḍaléśvara Kochúri Jaggarájayyadéva Mahárájalayyaváru issued a charitable edict in the following terms for the tank of Inugunṭa. Oju Rájayya Tirumalammagaru . . . having caused the tank with sluices (?) to be constructed, granted in perpetuity (?) *kunchams* per *puṭṭi* (on the produce?) of dry lands to the tank (?).

Whoever refuses to grant this, or misappropriates it, will incur the sin of killing cows, Brahmans and his parents near the Ganges.

NOTE.—To what family the Mahámanḍaléṣvara belonged is not apparent.

1. స్వస్తిశ్రీ విజయాభ్యుదయ శాలివాహనశకవరుషంబులు
౧౫౨౪

2. అగు నేటి శుభశ్వత్సర జేష్టశుద్ధ ౧౪ లు శ్రీమద్రాజాధి

3. రాజ రాజపరమేశ్వర శ్రీవీరప్రతాప శ్రీవీరభుజబలవీర
వేంక

4. టపతిరాయదేవమహారాయలయ్యవారు పెనుగొండనగర
మం

5. దు వజ్రసింహాసనారూఢుండై పృధ్విసామ్రాజ్యం సేయు
చుండ

6. గాను శ్రీమన్ మహామండలేశ్వర కోమారిజగ్గరాజయ్య

7. దేవమహారాజలయ్యవారు యినుగుంటచెరువుకు ఇచ్చిన
ధ

8. రమశాసనక్రమమెట్లన్నను ఒజరాజయ్య తిరుమలం

9. మగాకూ . . . . . . ను చెరువుకట్టించి కుండతూ
ములు

10. వెలిచేలపుట్టికుంచాలు యలపడిచెరువుకు ఇచ్చిరి

11. ఇయ్యమని యవ్వరు కీడాడినాను యవ్వరు ఆశిం

12. చినాను గంగ్గకతర్ గోవుబ్రాంహ్మలను వధి ఇ

13. ంచిన పాపానబోదురు తమతల్లితండ్రుల వధిఇం

14. చిన పాపానబోదురు.

VENKATAGIRI (25).

[Vazzavároipálem. On the north wall of Vénugópála-svámi temple. Quite illigible. Apparently, Telugu.]

VENKATAGIRI (26).

[Vazzavároipálem. (Hamlet Inuguṇṭa.) Tamil. North wall of Bhíméśvara temple.]

TRANSLATION.

Hail! Prosperity! In the 39th year of the reign of the glorious Kulóttuṅgachóḻadéva, Uṇḍiyappaḍavaḷavan, the son of Vaḍugappaḍavaḷavan of Perumpúṇḍi, placed an evening lamp (in the temple) of Késavaperumáḷ of Iluṅguṇḍai in Pákkainádu . . . .

[1] ஸ்வஸ்தி ஸ்ரீ கு-
[2] லொத்துங்க-
[3] சொழதெவற்-
[4] கு யாண்டு ௩௰௯
[5] ஆவது பெரும்பூ-
[6] ண்டி வடுகப்ப [ட]
[7] வளவன் மகன் உ-
[8] ண்டியப்படவள
[9] வனென் பாக்கை-
[10] நாட்டு இலுங்கு-
[11] ண்டைக்கெஶ-
[12] வப்பெருமாளு-
[13] க்குச்சந்திவிளக்கு
[14] ஒன்றுக்குப்பணர்-
[15] க்கழஞ்சியில் யிடை
[16] . . . . . . குய

VENKATAGIRI (27).

[Vazzavárípálem. (Inuguṇṭa hamlet.) Tamil. South wall of Bhíméśvara temple.]

[This is a fragmentary inscription of the reign of the emperor of the three worlds, the glorious Rájarájadéva and mentions the temple of Víméśvara at Iruṅguṇḍai.]

[1] திரிபுவனச் சக்கரவத்திகள் ஸ்ரீராஜராஜதெவற்கு . . . . .

[2] டன் இருங்குண்டை விமெசுரமுடையருயரு . . . . .

VENKATAGIRI.

NOTE.—Venkatagiri. In the Śiva and Vishnu temples of Venkatagiri town there are numerous inscriptions in Telugu, Tamil, Sanskrit, Mahráthi and Hindústáni. They all belong to the close of the eighteenth century and describe the endowments granted to the temples by various zamíndárs. It has not been thought worth while to print them.

POSTSCRIPT.

No. 1.

Victory has been achieved by the Holy one! Hail! From (his) residence, the victorious camp Mêtmâtura,—Dharmamahârâja Srî-Simhavarman of the Pallavas,—who are the receptacles of the royal glory of other kings that have been overcome by their valour and who have performed many sacrifices of horses procured according to established rules,—who is of enviable prowess, who wishes to surpass sage-like princes by (his) multitude of good qualities, who wishes to surpass virtue (itself), who (always) meditates on the feet of the Blessed one (Bhagavat), who is the disciple of the feet of the venerable Bappa, who is an excellent worshipper of the Holy one, who belongs to the Bhâradvâja-gôtra,—the great-grandson of the *Mahârâja*, the glorious Vîravarman, who was the most pious one, who acquired by the strength of his arm a great abundance of the penances (peculiar) to the powerful Kshatriyas, who conformed to all (such) injunctions as are prescribed, who was firm ins teadiness (of conduct), who was broadminded and who was the unsurpassed hero on the face of the earth,—the grandson of the high-minded *Mahârâja*, the glorious Skandavarman, who was endowed with great power and success, who subjugated by his prowess the assemblage of kings, who possessed all prosperity produced by devotion to the Holy one and by (his) goodness, who had increased store of religious merit by making many gifts of cows, gold, land, etc., who had skill in ruling people, who was the fifth Lôkapâla of the Lôkapâlas,—the son of the true-hearted *Yuva Mahârâja*, the glorious Vishṇugôpa, who honored the gods, the twice-born, spiritual preceptors and old men, who was very modest, who possessed brilliant fame (on account of) victories gained in many battles (accompanied by) violence and destruction and who was always ready to uplift virtue (Dharma) from the sin of the Kali age in which it is sunk,—issues the (following) order to the villagers and those in authority at this (village) (*viz.*) all supervisors, favourites and those who carry out orders, at the village of Pîkiri in Muṇḍarâshṭra :—" On the third day of the bright half of the month Âśvayuja of the fifth year of (our) increasing and victorious reign, for the increase of our lifetime, strength and victory, this village, which has been made into a *Brahmadêya*, has been given by us to Vilâsaśarman of the Taittirîya (-śâkhâ), who belongs to the Kâśyapa-*gôtra*, with all immunities, excluding the cultivated lands enjoyed by temples. Accordingly, this village has to be exempted with all immunities (by you); (and you) have to cause it to be exempted (by others also). The wretch who transgresses this, our order is liable to corporal punishment." And here are verses composed by the Ṛishis. [Three imprecatory verses.]

No. 2.

Hail! Victory has been achieved by the Holy one! Hail!

From the victorious (city of) Kâñchîpura,—Dharma-mahârâja Śrî-Kumâra-Vishṇu of the Pallavas,—who are the receptacles of the royal glory of other kings that have been overcome by their valour and who have performed many sacrifices of horses procured according to established rules,—who is devoted to the occupation of pleasing and ruling people and to the vow of truth always; who possesses brilliant fame (on account of) victories gained in many battles (accompanied by) violence and destruction; who is always ready to uplift virtue (*dharma*) from the sin of the Kali age in which it is sunk; who wishes to surpass sage-like princes by (his) multitude of good qualities; who wishes to surpass virtue (itself); who (always) meditates on the feet of the Blessed one (Bhagavat); who is an excellent worshipper of the Holy one; who belongs to the Bhâradvâja (*gôtra*); who is the disciple of the feet of the venerable Bappa;—the great-grandson of the *Mahârâja*, the glorious Skandavarman, who was endowed with great power and success, who subjugated by his prowess the assemblage of kings, who was the unsurpassed hero on the face of the earth; the grandson of the *Mahârâja*, the glorious Kumâra-Vishṇu, who honored the gods, the twice-born, spiritual preceptors and old men, who was very modest, who had increased store of religious merit by making many gifts of cows, gold, land, etc., who had skill in ruling people, who was the fifth Lôkapâla of the Lôkapâlas, who was true-hearted; the son of the *Mahârâja*, the glorious

Buddhavarman, who possessed all prosperity produced by devotion to the Holy one, whose many virtues vied with (those of) the primeval kings (and) who was broad-minded,—issues the following order to the villagers, all officials in authority and the (king's) favourites in the village of Chandalûru in Karmâka-râshṭra:—"On the fifth day of the bright half of the month Kârttika in the second year of the prosperous and victorious reign, for the increase of our lifetime, strength, victory and wealth, 800 paṭṭikâ of royal land (within) the four boundaries and 432 paṭṭikâ of communal land,—all this land in this village of Chendalûra in the district of Kavachakâra-bhôga (a subdivision) of Kammâka-râshṭra, has been given by us to the learned Brahman Bhavaskandatrâta, a resident of Puṭṭukâkâ, who belongs to the Kauṇḍinya-*gôtra* and followed the Chhandôga-*sûtra*, as a *Brahmadêya*, excluding the cultivated lands enjoyed by temples, with all exemptions. Knowing this, exempt this *Brahmadêya* land with all immunities, and have it exempted (by others also). The wretch who transgresses this, our order is liable to corporal punishment." And here are verses from the Brahmagîtâ [Four imprecatory verses]. Let cows and Brahmans rejoice at this order! May all subjects be happy!

No. 3.

The style and wording of this grant which belongs to the Eastern Châlukya dynasty is very similar to that of ancient Pallava grants. The titles *Mahârâja* and *Sarvalôkâśraya* of the king are mentioned, but his actual name is omitted. The compound after which the name of the king may be expected ends with the word *vijaya-siddhi.* On the seal of the grant the legend is *Srî-Vijayasiddhi.* From these two facts it may be concluded that the name of the king was Vijayasiddhi, which has evidently been omitted by mistake by the writer or engraver. The king was the great-grandson of the glorious Vishṇuvardhana-mahârâja, the grandson of the illustrious *Mahârâja* Indrabhaṭṭârakavarman surnamed Siṁhavikrama and the son of the illustrious Vishṇu-vardhana-mahârâja surnamed Makaradhvaja. His ancestry shows that the king must be identical with Mangi-Yuvarâja of other Eastern Châlukya grants, who is known to have reigned for 25 years (*Cir.* Śaka 586–87 to *Cir.* 611–12). It is also possible that the donor of the present grant is a hitherto unknown brother of Mangi-Yuvarâja.

The grant portion records the gift of the village of Chendalûru in Kammarâshṭra to several Brahmans of the Kauṇḍinya gôtra and the Chhandôga-śâkhâ.

The names of the donees are peculiar as they end in the word *bôya.* The *Âjñapti* (messenger) of the grant was the glorious Aṇaghavarman, who belonged to the Ayyaṇa family. Then follow two imprecatory verses.

The grant was made on the day of a lunar eclipse in the month Vaiśâkha of the second year of the increasing and victorious reign of the king. The inscription closes with the name of the person who wrote the grant.

INDEX TO APPENDIX I.

APPENDIX I.

NOTES ON VARIOUS DYNASTIES.

BÁṆA DYNASTY.

An indication of the dominion of the Báṇa dynasty is found in P. 38 under date 967-8 or 968-9. The Báṇa King is Aggaparázu whose name does not seem to occur elsewhere.

CHÁLUKYA DYNASTIES.

Inscriptions of the Eastern and Western Chálukyans occur but not frequently and they are rarely dated in a Ṣaka year. Those of the Eastern branch seem to be confined to the northern part of the district and it is probable that the south remained outside the limits of its dominion prior to amalgamation with the Chóḷa line.

CP. 19 is of Amma II and gives the usual genealogy. In addition it gives Parachakrarárma as a name for Vijayáditya III and describes how, after the death of Vikramáditya, the crown became an object of contest between Yuddhamalla, Rája Mártanda, Kanṭhika Vijayáditya and others until it was assumed by Rájabhíma. It also mentions that Amma II ascended the throne in his twelfth year in Ṣaka 867 (A.D. 945-46).

P. 1 is of the twelfth year of a certain Vishnuvardhana Maháraja but which one is not apparent.

A similar remark applies to P. 2.

C.P. 24 is of the Western Chálukyan Vikramáditya I and is granted in his sixth year, *i.e.*, about 663-64. It is probably the oldest inscription in the collection. It was found in the Nellore taluk but the villages which formed the subject of the grant do not appear in the survey list for that taluk. If it relates to this district, it may be taken as an indication of the dispossession of the Pallavas by the Western Chálukyans.

D. 2 also refers to one of the Chálukyan Vikramádityas.

KG. 12 is a grant for the religious benefit of Mangiruvárázu Sankidévarázu. This looks as if it should be Mangi Yuvarázu Sankidévarázu, but there is nothing to connect him with the Mangi Yuvarája of the Eastern Chálukyan line as our notes do not show that the inscription is in an ancient character.

In O. 57 we find reference to Vijayáditya Mahárája Paramabhaṭṭáraka. It is possible that this is Vijayáditya Bhaṭṭáraka the Eastern Chálukyan.

The name Vijayáditya appears in O. 39, O. 40 and P. 32 also. In the last case the identity of the chief is not apparent; he was a subordinate of Manma Gaṇḍagópáladéva and his date is 1289–90 apparently.

In the case of O. 39 and O. 40 we have clear reference of the Eastern Chálukyan King Vijayáditya III or Gunakenalla. The date of O. 40 seems to be 847–48 and we get a reference to the minister Páṇḍuranga for whom see also pages 123 and 130, volume V, E.I., but both these Ongole inscriptions are partially illegible. We must attribute to the same reign O. 3 which mentions Tribhuvanánkuṣa of Vénginánḍu and, apparently, Páṇḍuranga, the commander of the army. The capture of Kiṭṭepudurgam is also alluded to and this may be a misreading for Kíraṇadurgam or Kíranapuram. O. 48 also mentions Tribhuvanánkuṣa.

G. 54 mention a Pallava king Nandipóttarasar and a grant made under the orders of Chalukkiarasar. It is not unlikely that we have here a reference to the Western Chalukyan King Vikramáditya II. who reigned in the eighth century. It appears also that S. M. Bhímarázu Peddanu (Siddana ?) déva Mahárája of P. 7 was a chief of Eastern Chálukyan origin. He is called "descendant of the lineage of S. M. Vímaláditya" and "Chalukya Naráyaṇa" and seems to have been a vassal of the Kakatíya Ganapati. The inscription is apparently of 1260–61. The same person probably is referred to in P. 9 where we find (Bhíma ?) rázu Siddayunnu Rudra Mahádéva.

Kings of the combined Eastern Chalukyan and Chóḷa line appear under the Chóḷas.

CHÓḶA DYNASTY.

Though numerous, the inscriptions of this dynasty are of little interest. Most of them are in Tamil and the title Tribhuvana

Chakravarti is commonly prefixed to the name. As will be seen later on, the same title is used also by certain Chóḻas not generally recognized as belonging to the main dynasty with which we are at present concerned.

We will now deal in order with the rulers concerned, premising that nothing anterior to Kulottunga I seems to have been found. The three kings first mentioned appertain to the Eastern Chálukyan line as well as to that of the Chóḻas.

(1) *Kulóttunga I.*—G. 87 is of the 32nd year of this monarch whose *alias* Rájendra Chóḻa is also mentioned. It is probable that N. 19 refers to the same. It is dated "year 41 day 125" and the king calls himself "Kulóttunga Chóḻa Pallavaraiyan", referring, presumably, to the overthrow of the Pallavas by his son Ádoṇḍai. There seem to be no other inscriptions which can be identified as belonging to this reign except, perhaps, O. 74, but this is of the sixth regnal year and calls the king Tribhuvana Chakravarti a title which, it would appear (page 131, Vol. III, part II, 'South Indian Inscriptions'), had not been assumed by him so early in his reign.

(2) *Vikrama Chóḻa.*—This king seems to be represented only in G. 94 of the eighth year.

(3) *Kulóttunga II.*—According to page 181 of Vol. III, part II, of 'South Indian Inscriptions,' Vikrama Chóḻa's date has been brought down to 1135 and it appears that the initial date 1123 for Kulóttunga II entered on page 21 E.R. for 1898–99 has been discarded. In the present collection O. 142 which must refer to this king makes the date of accession 1132–33 or 1133–34.

This is the only inscription which can be definitely assigned to Kulóttunga II, though out of the 48 inscriptions which contain the name of Kulóttunga it is likely that more than one appertain to the second sovereign of that name.

(4) *Rájarája II.*—Our collection seems to fix the initial date of Rájaraja II which must, as O. 51 and O. 59 show, have been 1146–47. This agrees with the date recently settled by Professor Kielhorn (see page 12 E.R. for 1903–04).

As Kulóttunga III ascended the throne in 1178–79, the last year of Rájarája II (assuming that he reigned up to the accession of Kulóttunga III) must be the 33rd and it will be seen from the remarks below under Rájéndra III that Rájarája III cannot have reigned more than 28 years. But we find here an inscription of the 30th year and another of the 36th year. The last may be a mistake in transcription but the former, if correctly referred to Rájarája II, brings his date to 1175-76. He certainly reigned at least 20 years as shown by O. 59, and seems to be the last of the main line whose inscriptions are found in the northern part of the district. When Rájádhirájadéva comes in is not apparent, if these dates be accepted.

It seems probable to us that Kulóttunga Chóḻa is a mere title borne by a succession of princes and that the Rájarája who reigned for 30 and 36 years is Kulóttunga III.

(5) *Kulóttunga III.*—There are numerous inscriptions of this king who in three inscriptions appears under the name Tribhuvana Víradéva.

His initial date being known, we find an error of one year in the Ṣaka date of G. 50, if that inscription appertains to this king, and in N. 40 there must be a misreading in the case of the regnal year which should be the twelfth.

N. 57 contains a reference to two regnal years which is not intelligible to us. It is of the cyclic year Pingala "corresponding to the twentieth" (first read as second) "year of Kulóttunga "Chóḻadéva who was pleased to take Madura, Ceylon and the "crowned head of the Páṇḍya king and the fifteenth year of "Kulóttunga Chóḻadéva who was pleased to take the crowned "head of Víra Páṇḍya."

G. 96 gives to some Kulóttunga Chóḻa the *alias* Chokka Náyanár.

The last regnal year given in these inscriptions is the 39th, which brings the reign up to 1216-17.

(6) *Rájarája III.*—The recognized date of accession, viz., 1216-17 is confirmed by V. 1. R. 70 must belong to this reign and the completion of the grant referred to in V. 10 took place in the second year of this king. From R. 65 it seems clear that Rájarája III was also called Kulóttunga Chóḻadéva.

(7) *Rájéndra III.*—If P. 9 of 1257-58 refers to this king, then he too bore the *alias* Kulóttunga Chóḻadéva which, in that case, must have been a mere title assumed as a matter of form on ascending the throne. But it is possible that the reference is to Kulóttunga III and that nothing more is implied than that the

donor was one of his descendants. From P. 7 it appears that the sovereign ruling at the time in the north of the district was the Kákatiya king Gaṇapati.

The year of accession of Rájendra Chóḷa III is fixed as 1244–45 by G. 39, G. 85 and U. 48. Also N. 89 shows that he reigned for at least 24 years, *i.e.*, until 1268–69.

The distribution of the inscriptions of the recognized main line of Chóḷa emperors is shown below :—

Name.	Talnk or division.									
	Átmakúr.	Darsi.	Gúdúr.	Nellore.	Ongole.	Podili.	Rápúr.	Súlúrpet.	Udayagiri.	Venkatagiri.
Kulóttunga ...	3	1	12	18	1	1	5	2	...	5
Rájarája	...	...	27	3	2	...	2	5	...	12
Rájendra	...	...	4	1	...	...	...	...	1	...

It will be observed that none of the inscriptions comes from Kandukúr, Kanigiri or Kávali.

We now pass to the consideration of certain other Chóḷa kings who assume the style Tribhuvana Chakravarti and may be regarded as carrying on the line of Chóḷa emperors.

(1) The first of these rulers is Irumaḍi Tirukálattidéva who is said to have ascended the throne in 1278–79 (see G. 45).

(2) The second is Vijaya (or Rája) Ganḍa Gópáladéva.

According to G. 115, N. 62, N. 71 and N. 74 his initial date was 1291–92, but N. 60 seems to make it 1290–91.

He certainly ruled till 1304–05 and, if KV. 37 relates to the same man, he was ruling in 1309–10. He bore the *alias* Ranganáthan.

A peculiar feature of his inscriptions is that the donor in every case is Madurántaka Pottapi Chóḷa Ranganáthan *alias* Rája Ganḍa Gópála. This fact suggests that the Madurántaka Pottapi Chóḷa also bore the imperial title though, of course, they may be distinct persons.

OTHER RULERS OF CHÓḶA LINEAGE.

We have dealt above with those Chóḷas who bore the imperial title Tribbuvana Chakravarti. We now proceed to a series of rulers who claim to be of Chóḷa lineage but do not arrogate supreme authority. Affairs are complicated by the simultaneous existence of chiefs of Pallava descent. In no case in this collection are distinctive Pallava titles attached to any ruler bearing the name Chóḷa or Chóḍa, for, though the title "lord of Kánchi" is occasionally borne by the latter, it need not be taken to mean more than the alternative title "levier of tribute from Kánchi" which refers to the overthrow of the Pallavas by the Chóḷas. Therefore we have excluded from the lists of Chóḷa chiefs all those who claim Pallava descent but the result is that we have a Pallava Allun Tirukálti and a Chóḍa Allun Tirukáḷattidéva, a Pallava Nallasittarasan and a Chóḍa Nallasittarasan. This co-incidence is sufficiently remarkable to raise some doubt whether the same individual may not have claimed descent from both families, but in the absence of clear proof of this we have thought it safer to assume the contrary.

(1) The first of the subordinate Chóḷa families which we will deal with is that of the chiefs of *Velanáḍu*. A genealogical table of these chiefs appears on page 35, Vol. IV, E.I. Number 16 of that table is Kulóttnuga Rájendra Chóḍa and we meet with him in D. 45, O. 59 and O. 60. The first is dated 1169–70 or 1170–71. The second is three years earlier and from it we gather that he was a vassal of the Chóḷa emperor Rájarája II. The third is of 1166-67 or 1167-68 and gives us the accepted pedigree.

Chóḍa of Velnáḍu
|
Gonka *m.* Subbamámbá.
|
Rájendra Chóḍa,

If KV. 13 refers to the same king, as is possible, we learn therefore that he had two sons called Manma Siddanadéva and Kaḍanalletangadéva (the latter name is probably a misreading) and the former was apparently ruling in 1213-14 or 1214-15. Whether R. 8 refers to the same Manma Siddanadéva under the name Manma Siddarasa Piḷḷaiyár is not clear. If the inscription is of 1213–14, it may well do so but there is some error about the date. It is likely enough that the Mauma Siddanadéva of KV. 13 is Gonka III who was also called Manma Gonka.

There seem to be no other inscriptions of this dynasty.

(2) The next group to engage attention may for convenience be called the *Madurántaka Pottapi Cholas*, because under this head we have placed all those Chóḍas who bear this title. The manner in which they were connected with each other, with other Chóḍas and with the imperial Chóḷa family is obscure and much time has been vainly spent by us on the attempt to make a consistent classification of the family.

(*a*) *Manmasiddha*.—According to KV. 13 which is dated 1213-14 or 1214-15 Manma Siddanadéva was the son of Rájendradéva Chóḍa who might be the Velnáḍu chief of that name but KV. 40 which bears no date makes Manma Siddhi Déva Chóḍa the son of Jagadobba Gaṇḍa Kámayadéva. Apparently, then, two Chóḍas bore the name Manmasiddharasa but we cannot place them for want of a date to KV. 40. R. 39 gives 1242–43 or 1243–44 and the additional name Tilaka Náráyaṇa. The date of G. 39, so far as it relates to Manma Siddharasa, may be taken as 1258–59. KV. 43 is of 1262–63 or 1263–64. The Bhujabala Víra Manma Siddayadéva of KR. 60, 61 and 63 is probably the same and the dates are 1257–58 or 1258–59, 1258–59 or 1259–60 and 1261–62. V. 19 seems to give 1233–34 for Chálukki Náráyaṇa Manmasittiyarasar of Periyamunoppúr which is the modern Mópúru in Venkatagiri division. This last inscription may belong to a different family but the dates 1242–43 or 1243–44, 1257–58 or 1258–59, 1258–59, 1258–59 or 1259–60 and 1261–62 probably refer to the same individual. There remains G. 86 which must be of 1213-14. This states that M. P. C. Manmasittarasan married Páchchaldévi, daughter of Rájarájapaṭṭai Pettarasan, lord of the middle country. It is probable that KV. 13 and G. 86 relate to the same man.

It seems then that we have—

(1) M. P. C. Manmasiddharasa son of Rájendradéva Chóḍa 1213–14.

(2) Chálukki Náráyaṇa Manmasittiyarasar of Periyamuṇoppúr (a different family?) 1233–34.

(3) M. P. C. Manmasiddharasa called also Tilaka Náráyaṇa and Bhujabala Víra (the son of Kámayadéva ?) about 1243–44 to about 1261–62.

(*b*) *Tirukkáḷattidéva.*—Of princes of this name there seem to be several. The first appears to be the one referred to in R. 8 where he is called Piḷḷaiyár and described as the son of Manumasiddarasa. The date is probably 1213-14. The same person may be referred to in N. 101 of 1208-09 where he is called Madurántaka Pottapi Chóḷa; in R. 47 of 1210-11 or 1211-12 where he is called "lord of Orayúr, Jagadobbagaṇḍa, Bhujabala," etc.; in KR. 29 of 1209-10; in R. 66 which is of 1215-16.

A second prince perhaps is referred to in the following group:—

KV. 38 dated 1227-28 or 1228-29 where we have Gaṇḍa Gópála Tiruká̆ḷadéva Chóḍa; S. 12 which must be of 1228-29; KV. 45 dated 1229-30 or 1230-31 where the same person appears under the misreading Gaṇḍa Gópála Dípakaltidéva; KV. 47 of the same date; R. 65 which is probably of 1231-32 and where, as in S. 12, he receives the title Madurántaka Pottapi Chóḷa; G. 60 of 1228-29 alludes to the same prince. As to G. 77 it has the peculiarity of being dated in the regnal year of the Madurántaka Pottapi Chóḷa instead of that of the Chóḷa emperor. If it refers to this Tiruká-lattidéva, then he had the prefix Allun. If it refers to the Allun Tirukkálatti who follows, then that prince also had the *alias* Gaṇḍa Gópála. Possibly a single individual ruled from 1228-29 to 1252-53 or thereabouts. It is perhaps a distinct prince who appears in the following inscriptions where he is distinguished by the prefix Allun:—

KV. 25 of 1243-44 or 1244-45 where Allun Tirukálati appears as Allun Tirakadgati in the transcription; U. 3 of 1244-45 which is a grant for the benefit of two persons, one, Bhujabala Chóḍa Tirukaltidéva who is given the usual Chóḍa birudas, and the other, Alu Tikarázu Tirukáladéva; U. 14 of 1245-46 mentions Chóḍadéva Tirukáltidéva with the usual birudas and also one Aludidlayyadéva (*read* Alu Tikkayyadéva?); A. 7 of 1246-47 tells us that Allu Tirukáḷatidéva ruled at Kánchi and that his father-in-law was Tirukáḷa Mahárája; R. 20 of 1247-48 gives Alu Tirukáladéva Chóḍa as ruling sovereign and mentions his younger brother Vijayádityadéva; U. 48 of 1252-53 is a grant by Tikkayadéva who is called Pasáhita. It is not unlikely that the S. M. Gaṇḍa . . . yadéva Chóḍa Mahárája who, according to KG. 11, was ruling at Nellore in 1254-55 was Gaṇḍa Gópála *alias* Allun Tirukáḷattidéva. The connection between the different parties mentioned in this last group of inscriptions is not clear. The ruling prince from 1243-44 or 1244-45 to 1252-53 (or 1247-48 at all events) seems to have been Allun Tirukáḷattidéva, but there were in existence at the same time his father-in-law also called Tirukáḷa and a second person called Alu Tikkarázu Tirukáḷadéva or Alu Tikkayadéva. It has already been mentioned that there is a Pallava-descended chief called Allun Tirukkálti or Allun Tikka. He is mentioned in N. 16, dated 1182-83 and also in N. 15.

(c) *Nallasiddha.*—KV. 39 and R. 36 bear Ṣaka dates. The latter is of 1216-17 or 1217-18 and gives the common Chóḍa titles. The former is of 1207-08 and gives us the information that Nalla Siddha was the son of Yerra Siddhiṣvara and Ṣrí Déví and the grandson of Béta and further that, although Nalla Siddha was the anointed king, his younger brother Tammu Siddha was the actual ruler of the country.

The dates of G. 1 and N. 85 are uncertain. The dates of other inscriptions which contain the name, coupled sometimes with the title Madurántaka Pottapi Chóḷa, are R. 4, 1200-01; G. 34 and G. 76, 1204-05 (the latter names his descendant Mayilamadévi Pattarasa); N. 67, 1208-09; and A. 18, 1212-13 (in this he is spoken of as being "of Nelloré").

The dates of Nallasiddharasa thus range from 1200-01 to 1216-17 or 1217-18.

It is possible that N. 100 refers to this king but his father's name there appears as Chóḍéṣvara. This disagrees with KV. 39 and we must conclude either that there were two Nalla Siddhis or that Chóḍéṣvara in N. 100 is merely used loosely in the sense or "Chóḍa Chief." It is rendered probable by KR. 26 that there were two kings called Nalla Siddhi. According to that inscription one Vallu Rája and other petty Yádava chiefs of the northern part of the district agreed to take Pákináḍu on a grazing lease from king Nalla Siddhi of Nellore. They failed to pay the sum due and Nalla Siddhi attacked and defeated them. The date of the battle is given as S.S. 1170 Káḷayukti. If we read S.S. 1180 Káḷayukti we get 1258-59. As already mentioned S. 2 calls Nallasittarasan a Pallava and we have therefore treated that person separately. No date is given in this inscription.

(d) *Errasiddha.*—As already stated, KV. 39 of 1207-08 relates to Nalla Siddha, son of Errasiddha. This person is clearly distinct from the Errasiddha of A. 38 which is of 1216–17 or 1217–18 and which gives the prince the titles Ṣríman Mahámaṇḍaléṣvarâ, lord of Orayúr, Ayyana Singha, Bhujabala Víra, levier of tribute from Kánchi and so on. It adds that the protector of his kingdom (Pratipálaka) was one Gollapayiṇḍi Biyyapa Náyaka.

The other inscriptions of Errasiddha do not bear Ṣaka dates but the regnal years show that they are of 1223–24, 1225–26 and 1226–27 (see R. 38, G. 59 and G. 58). R. 38 calls him Madurántaka Pottapi Chóḷa and implies that he ruled at Nellore. G. 58 mentions his brother-in-law Siddarasa V. 7 and V. 11 seem to imply that Errasiddha was subordinate to a certain Yádavaráyan or Rája Malladévan of Eastern Chálukyan lineage who is dealt with elsewhere. V. 11 bears as date some year of Kulóttunga Chóḷa. This must be Kulóttunga III and the year is doubtless his last because, otherwise, we should have the reigns of Errasiddha and Nallasiddha overlapping. This is made clear by V. 10 which relates to Errasiddha under the name Bhujabalasiddharasa and is of the 39th year of Kulóttunga III.

A. 45 may relate to this ruler.

(e) *Peddarasa.*—We find in N. 111 which bears date 1203–04 or 1204–05 a reference to Madurántaka Pottapi Chóḷa Peddarasa and it is possible that he is the Pattarasa who, according to G. 76, was the son of Nallasiddha.

(f) *Tammusiddha.*—We find from KV. 39 that this chief was the younger brother of Nallasiddha and acted as regent for him. The date of that inscription is 1207–08, but Tammusiddha is mentioned earlier, viz., in N. 72 of 1203–04, where he is styled Madurántaka Pottapi Chóḷa. N. 75 also relates to him and his ancestor Béta is there called Bédabhanátha (*read* Bédabhúnátha ?).

(g) *Gaṇḍa Gópála.*—It has already been stated that between 1290–91 or 1291–92 and 1304–05 or 1309–10 there was ruling a certain Tribhuvana Chakravarti Gaṇḍa Gópála *alias* Ranganáthan and that along with him there existed a person of the same name styled Madurántaka Pottapi Chóḷa and it has been suggested that they were identical.

There was also a certain chief of Pallava origin who bore the name Vijaya Gaṇḍa Gópála as indicated by A. 25, dated 1284–85 or 1285–86. He is dealt with separately under the Pallavas.

It has further been mentioned that Gaṇḍa Gópála was an *alias* of the M. P. C. Tirukkálattidéva who was ruling in 1227–28 or 1228–29 and two or three years later and that it was also an *alias* of Allun Tirukálattidéva who may have been the same chief or his successor.

We find also in KR. 62 S. M. Immaḍi Gaṇḍa Gópála Vijayádittadéva Mahárája who may be the S. M. Immaḍidéva Mahárája of KG. 24 (1268–69) and, if so, was of Pallava origin.

Further, we have in N. 31 mention of Manuma Gaṇḍa Gópaladéva. The Ṣaka date is given as *rasanadrikbhu* equivalent to 1206. The cyclic year is Táraṇa which agrees with S.S. 1206, expired or A.D. 1284–85. The regnal year is the third; so we learn that Manma Gaṇḍa Gópáladéva ascended the throne 1282–83. In the list of Chóḍas on p. 18 of E.R. for 1899–1900 the last name is Manma Gaṇḍa Gópála with date S.S. 1219. It will however be observed that, according to A. 25, a Vijaya Gaṇḍa Gópála of Pallava origin was ruling in 1284–85 or 1285–86, and so far as the wording of N. 31 is concerned, it might relate to this chief. P. 32, which seems to be of S.S. 1211, may refer to the same person.

Finally G. 50 gives another Madurántaka Pottapi Chóḷa Rája Gaṇḍa Gópálan *alias* Ranganáthan ruling in 1192-93 or 1193–94 under the emperor Kulóttunga III.

The identity of the Víra Gaṇda Gópáladéva of G. 67 is not certain and a similar remark applies to the [Vijaya Gaṇḍa] Gópáladéva of S. 8.

(3) *Certain miscellaneous Chóḷa chiefs.*—Under this head we group various persons who claim Chóḷa descent but who do not bear the title Madurántaka Pottapi Chóḷa although it is likely enough that they belong to the family of the Madurántaka Pottapi Chóḷas.

(*a*) A. 29 of 1275–76 probably refers to a Chóḍa when it says that S.M. (Náne?) déva Mahárája was ruling as universal sovereign at Nellore.

(*b*) P. 22 is undated, but the character appears to belong to the 10th century or thereabouts. It is a grant by Tóndayya Rázu "the ornament of the race sprung from the solar dynasty, belonging to the Káṣyapa gótra and sprung from the lineage of Karikhala."

(c) O. 125, which may be of 1277-78 or 1337-38, mentions S. M. (Níla ?) Kaṇṭha Chódadéva Mahárája.

(d) D. 38 of 1166-67 or 1167-68 mentions S. M. Pantadéva Chóḷa Mahárája.

(e) N. 40 of 1189-90 or 1190-91 refers to king Siddhi who evidently bore the title Madurántaka Pottapi Chóla but which Siddharasa is referred to is not clear as the inscription has been defaced. The Ṣaka date is not clearly as 1112. The regnal year was first read as 32nd of Tribuvana Chakravarti Kulóttunga Chóḷadéva who took Madura and the head of the Pandya: on further inspection *in situ* the year is reported to be the 14th. Probably we should read 12th and refer the inscriptiou to the time of Kulóttunga III.

(*f*) O. 55 of date 1426-27 gives us a king of the solar race called Víra Amala (*read* Ábala or Obala ?) the son of king Núnka, and O. 56 of the same date is a grant for the merit of the Vijayanagar king Viḷaya Bukka by Víra Âm Bhúdeva *read* Víra Abaladéva ?) Chóḍa son of S. M. Vennu Sambeṛa Álamanḍala Núkayadéva Chóḍa Tribhuvana.

O. 85 relates to same family for, under date 1428-29, it gives—

Tirumala Rázu *m.* Peddamadévalamma.

S. M. Tribhuvana Vennu Sambáṭa Álamanḍala Anavótayadéva Chóḍa. *m.* Chennamadévalamma.

Gangayadéva Chóḍa (donor).

It does not seem possible to identify the Núnka and Obala of the above inscriptions with the persons of the same name in D. 13.

(g) *Singayadéva Gaḍidéva.*—In D. 24 of 1267-68 we find mention made of " S. M. Singayadéva Gaḍidéva who is the sovereign of the earth, on whose feet the eyes of Trilóchana and other kings are set, the jewelled lamp of the race of Karikála, lord of Orriyúr, the Tripura Trinétra of Kánchi, of the Káṣyapa gótra." Reference is at the same time made to " Rudramahárája, the ruler of Konḍaviḍu in the kingdom."

This Singayadéva is clearly a Chóḍa and presumably he was a vassal of the Rudra Mahárája who is so casually mentioned.

Contemporaneous with this Singayadéva was another ruler of the same name who has been referred to under the sub-head " The

Chakra Náráyaṇa line" under the head "Certain chiefs subordinate to the Kákaṭiya kings." There is apparently nothing to suggest that the Chakra Náráyaṇa chiefs were Chóḍas beyond the fact that one of them bears the *biruda* "Bhujabala." We assume, then, that the two Singa (or Singaya) dévas are distinct.

(*h*) *Vijayáḍityadéva.*—A. 55 mentions that Malidéva Mahárája (date 1290–91) was the son of S. M. Vijayádityadéva Mahárája. R. 20 of 1247–48 mentions that Vijayádityadéva Chóḍa Mahárája was the younger brother of the ruling chief Ṣrímat Alu Tirukáladéva Chóḍa Mahárája.

P. 32 is of doubtful date but seems to be of 1288–89 or 1289–90. It mentions a Vijayádityadéva Mahárája on whom are conferred certain partially defaced titles and who made a grant for the religious benefit of Manma Gaṇḍa Gópáladéva Mahárája.

D. 43 (date uncertain but may be of 1150–51) mentions S. M. Vijayádityadéva Mahárája, a descendant of Mukkanṭi Káḍuveṭṭu. This person is dealt with under the Pallavas.

The first three inscriptions seem to give—

...

Alu Tirukáladéva Chóḍa (1247–48). | Vijayádityadéva Chóḍa.

Malidéva (1290-91).

(*i*) *Malidéva or Malladéva.*—O. 142 is of Ṣaka 1070 (1147–48 or 1148–49) and the 16th of Tribhuvana Chakravarti Kulóttunga Chóḍadéva. It records the grant of a village in Kammanáḍu which was under the rule of S.M. Tribhuvana Malladéva Chóḍa Mahárája. D. 69 under date 1217–18 or 1218–19 gives the following titles to S. M. Abhidéva Malidéva Mahárája—Paraméṣvara, ornament of the Pallava family, of the Bháradvája gótra, whose flag is a club, lord of Kánchi, whose crest is the bull, who is descended from Mukkanṭi Káḍveṭṭu (dealt with under the Pallavas). O. 17 (2) of 1226–27 or 1227–28 mentions S. M. Mallidéva Chóḍa Mahárája, whose lotus feet are adorned by the prostrations of Vilóchana, Trilóchana, etc., who shines like a gem in the family of Karikála. K.R. 22, dated 1236–37 or 1237–38, mentions one Mallidévarája along with Chikkirája and Chóḍadéva Chóḍa Mahárája. A. 55, dated 1290–91, is a grant by one Pinnama Náyaka who is described as grandson of Badhya Madrarázu, the lord of Orayúru. The grant is of a village called Bayindipáḍu in the kingdom of S. M. Malidéva Mahárája, the son of S. M. Vijayáḍityaḍéva Mahárája.

D. 6 of 1290–91 or 1291–92 mentions a grant by . . . . Chóḍa Malidéva Mahárája for the merit of Pratápa Rudra Mahárája.

O. 66 mentions Betruma Náyaka the prime minister of Mahámanḍalésvara Mallidéva Chóḍa Mahárája.

D. 13 mentions a certain Vémula Maliḍéva, who is referreḍ to elsewhere.

In G. 67 (Tamil) we have a reference to one Mallidévarasan *alias* Tyágasamudrapaṭṭai, the date being 9th of Víra Ganḍa Gópáladéva.

O. 19 of 1152–53 or 1153–54 mentions S. M. Tribhuvanadéva Chóḍa Mahárája of the race of Karikála and this may be Tribhuvana Malladéva.

Our present inscriptions give us—

(1) Tribhuvana Malladéva Chóḍa ruling Kammanáḍu in 1147–48 or 1148–49 and 1152–53 or 1153–54.

(2) Abhidéva Malidéva ruling in 1217–18 or 1218–19 and claiming descent from the Pallavas and *Mukkanṭi* Káḍuveṭṭu.

(3) A Mallidéva Chóḍa claiming descent from Karikála and dated 1226–27 or 1227–28.

(4) A Mallidéva of 1236–37 or 1237–38 who seems to have had a relative called Chóḍadéva Chóḍa on the throne.

(5) Malidéva, the son of Vijayádityadéva, ruling in 1290–91 and (if D. 6 refers to the same man) a subordinate of the Kákaṭíya king Pratápa Rudra.

(*j*) *Mummayadéva Choḍa.*—N. 104 of 1551–52 says that certain grant was made under the orders of the invincible Ṣrí Mahámanḍalésvara Paricheja Mummayadéva Chóḍa Mahárája. It is not, however, clear what position this person occupied, for the sovereign was Sadáṣivadéva and the grant was made in Udayagiri *rájyam* which formed a part of the territories under Rámarájayya Tirumalayyadéva and which was ruled by a governor called Bayacha Rájayya. Apparently the Chóḍa occupied some position subordinate to the great Vijayanagar officer Tirumalayyadéva.

(*k*) *S. M. Haridéva Chóḍa Mahárája* of the race of Karikála appears in D. 28 under date 1254–55. If, as is probable, the donor of D. 25 also was Haridéva Chóḍa, then he was a vassal of the Kákaṭíya king Gaṇapati.

(*l*) *Manuma Gaṇḍa Gópáḷadéva.*—The Tamil and Sanskrit inscription N. 31 bears an uncertain date and it is possible that the inscription consists of two separate parts. If, however, the Ṣaka date is correct and applies to both parts, then the year 1183–84 or 1184–85 was the third year of one Manuma Gaṇḍa Gópáḷadéva. There is, however, a wide discrepancy between the Ṣaka and cyclic years and probably the Ṣaka date should be 1206 and the date of our era 1284–85.

The name re-appears in P. 32 which is apparently of 1288–89 or 1289–90. Therein S. M. Vijayádityadéva Mahárája, to whom various titles are attached, makes a grant for the religious benefit of S. M. Mahámanḍalika Dánava Murári Ariráya Gaṇḍa Gópáḷa rahutta . . . . Manuma Gaṇḍa Gópáḷadéva Mahárája.

It is possible that this is the son of Nallasiddha who appears with the Ṣaka date 1219 on p. 15 of E.R. for 1899–1900.

(*m*) *Pottapi Nanni Chóḍa.*—According to D. 48 (1145–46) and D. 49 (1166–67) Pottapi Nanni Chóḍa appears in the following pedigree :—

Pottapi Nanni Chóḍa.
|
Venka.
|
Káma.
|
Balli of the race of the Sun and Karikála.

The undated inscription O. 117 seems to be one of the same Nanni Chóḍa. A Manni Choḍa appears in the genealogy in O. 92.

(*n*) *Venka.*—This person, the son of Pottapi Nanni Chóḍa, seems to be referred to only in D. 48 and D. 49.

(*o*) *Káma.*—A grandson of Pottapi Nanni Chóḍa of this name appears in D. 48 and D. 49. The name appears in the following inscriptions also :—

O. 90, dated 1186–87 or 1187–88, is a grant of two villages by S. M. Kámana Chóḍa Mahárája "on whose feet the eyes of Trilóchana and other kings are set; the jewelled lamp of the race of Karikála; the goad to wicked princes."

O. 120 of 1217–18 is a grant by Chóḍadéva Chóḍa Mahárája, son of Mahámaṇḍalésvara Kámaya (Mahárája ?); who has the titles "Jagadobba Gaṇḍa, Kírti Náráyaṇa, Páráyaṇa, Chandrasékhara, of the Káṣyapa gótra, ruler of Vorayúripura, the goad to hostile kings."

KV. 40 (undated) gives us S. M. Manma Siddhi Déva Chóḍa Mahárája, the son of S. M. Jagadobba Gaṇḍa Kámayadéva Mahárája.

(p) *Balli Chóḍa*.—Appears under date 1145–46 and 1166–67 in D. 48 and D. 49 as the great grandson of Pottapi Nanni.

He appears also with the usual titles in D. 68 which is apparently of 1147–48.

O. 91 (undated) mentions Ṣrímat Ujvala Chóḍa Balaya Chóḍa Mahárája with the titles Kírti Náráyaṇa and Jagatkarta.

An earlier Balle Rázu, also of the Chóḍa family, appears in O. 92 of 1087–88 or 1088–89 in the following pedigree:—

Chági Venkana.
|
Balle Rázu.
|
Kastruvankya Rázu.
|
Nanni Chóḍa.
|
Rájamáhéndra Po[te]pi Chóḍa.

(q) *Chóḍadéva*.—He appears in O. 120 of 1217–18 with the usual titles as son of Kámaya.

KR. 22, dated 1236–37 or 1237–38, relates to Chóḍadéva Chóḍa Mahárája in conjunction with Mallidévarája and Chikkirája.

(r) *Pótayadéva*.—We get S. M. Pótayadéva Chóḍa Mahárája under date 1254–55 in KG. 11. Apparently Gaṇḍa Gópáladéva Chóḍa was his overlord.

(s) A group of inscriptions from Penṭrála in Kandukúr taluk next claims attention.

These are summarized below:—

KR. 60, dated 1257–58 or 1258–59, is a grant to a priest by S.M. Bhujabala Víra Manma Siddayadéva Mahárája.

KR. 61 is a similar grant of 1258–59 or 1259–60 made for the prosperity of the kingdom of S. M. Bhujabala Víra Manma Siddayadéva Chóḍa by S. M. Alláḍu Suddhadéva Mahárája grandson of Podakanúri Siddi Rázu a descendant of Mukkanṭi Káḍuveṭṭu.

KR. 62 of 1259–60 or 1260–61 is a similar grant for the prosperity of the kingdom of S. M. Immaḍi Gaṇḍa Gópála Vijayádittadéva by Madusúdhanadéva Mahárája grandson of S. M. Andalúri Vijayaditta Déchini of the race of Mukkanṭi Káḍuveṭṭu.

KR. 63 of 1261–62 is a similar grant for the prosperity of the kingdom of S. M. Bhujabala Víra Manma Siddayadéva Chóḍa by Siddama Dévulu Vijaya Dévanḍu, son of S. M. Ka . . . . ráya Bhímadéva Mahárája of the race of Mukkanṭi Káḍuveṭṭu.

KR. 64 of 1267–68 is a grant by S. M. Bijji Rázu Siddayadéva Chóḍa Mahárája.

KR. 65 of 1268–69 is a grant by Gaḍidéva Rázu, son of S. M. Sáhattumalla Perumánḍidéva Chóḍa Mahárája.

KR. 66 of 1269–70 is a grant by S. M. Bhíma Rázu Siddayadéva Mahárája.

The above inscriptions seem to give us a Chóḍa ruler called Víra Manma Siddayadéva *alias* Immaḍi Gaṇḍa Gópála Vijayádityadéva reigning in 1257–58 or 1258–59 to 1261–62. He may have been followed by Bijji (or Bhíma ?) Rázu Siddayadéva with dates 1267–68 and 1269–70.

Where Perumánḍidéva Chóḍa would come in is not clear. His son Gaḍidéva is not, apparently, the Singayadéva Gaḍidéva of D. 24.

The connection between the various descendants of Mukkanṭi Káḍuveṭṭu who are mentioned in these inscriptions is not apparent.

The Siddana Dévulu Vijaya Dévanḍu, son of Bhímadéva Mahárája, and descendant of Mukkanṭi Káḍuveṭṭu who appears in KR. 63 under date 1261–62 is apparently not the S. M. Bhímarája Peddami (*read* Siddana ?) déva Mahárája of P. 7 dated apparently, 1260–61. This latter person is described as a descendant of S. M. Vimaláditya and as "Chálukya Náráyaṇa" and he dates his grant in the reign of Kákaṭíya Gaṇapatidéva whose vassal he evidently was.

(*t*) O. 148 relates to some Chóḷa chief whose name may have been Mádaya Narasimhayya. He is called the possessor of universal sovereignty obtained by king Karikála Chóḍa, possessor of the symbols of the cloud, the umbrella, the white wing (?), the chámara, the álaveṭṭa etc., heralded by a conch, Iruvettugaṇḍa,

Ráya Ganḍa Gopála, supreme lord of the Nallambhaṭṭu (Noḷamba ?) country, Aruvattu Ganḍa, Ráyanáyankavítí, etc.

(4) We may now sum up the facts set out in the preceding sub-heads (2) and (3) regarding the Chóḷas or Chóḍas in Nellore district excluding the main line and the Velnáḍu family. The inscriptions come from all parts of the district but are rare from the northern parts. There the Chóḍas seem to have been at one time in subordination to the Kákaṭíya kings but in the south they seem to have generally acted as viceroys to the Chóḷa emperors. The later members were doubtless subject to the Vijayanagar dynasty. The title borne by the principal members of the group shows that they derive descent from a person connected with Pottapi who had acquired renown in war against the Páṇḍyans. Pottapi has not hitherto been identified and we have found nothing to settle the site of that town but one of these inscriptions mentions that the Pottapi náḍu was in Jayankoṇḍamaṇḍalam which included the southern part of the district. Some of the Chóḍas seem to have made Nellore town their capital: others apparently ruled at Kánchi. We do not find anything to support the view that they had any special connection with Kandukúr (see p. 19 E.R. for 1889–90). Below is a list of the various Chóḍas mentioned in sub-heads (2) and (3) *supra* with their dates where ascertainable; doubtless some of those who appear in the list did not themselves occupy positions of authority :—

Mádaya Narasimhayya (?)	....
Tóṇḍayya Rázu	perhaps 10th century.
Chagi Venkana	....
Ballerázu	....
Kantru Vankya Rázu	....
Nanni Chóḍa	....
Rájamáhéndra Po[te]pi	circ. 1088–89.
Pottapi Nanni	....
Venka	....
Káma	....
Balli	1145–46, 1147–48 (?).
Tribhuvanamalladéva	circ. 1148–49 and circ. 1153–54.
Panṭadéva	circ. 1167–68.
Kámaya	1166–67 and circ. 1187–88.
Siddhi	circ. 1190–91 (doubtful).

M. P. C. Ganda Gópála *alias* Ranganáthan	circ. 1193-94.
Béta	....
M. P. C. Errásiddha	....
M. P. C. Nallásiddha, son of Errasiddha and grandson of Béta ..	1200-01 to circ. 1217-18.
M. P. C. Tammusiddha, brother of and regent for Nallasiddha ..	1203-04 and 1207-08.
M. P. C. Peddarasa	circ. 1204-05.
M. P. C. Tirukkálattidéva, son of Manmasiddharasa	1208-09 to 1215-16.
M. P. C. Manmasiddharasa, son of Rájéndradéva Chóḍa	1213-14.
Chódadéva Chóḍa, son of Kámaya..	1217-18.
Manmasiḍḍhidéva, son of Kámaya	....
M. P. C. Errasiddha..	circ. 1217-18 to 1226-27.
Mallidéva	circ. 1227-28.
M. P. C. Tirrukkálattidéva *alias* Gandagópála	circ. 1228-29 to 1231-32
Mallidéva with Chóḍadéva Chóḍa ruling	circ. 1237-38.
M. P. C. Manmasiddharasa ..	1234-44 to circ. 1261-62.
M. P. C. Allun Tirukkálattidéva *alias* Gandagopála	circ. 1244-45 to 1247-48 or 1252-53 or 1254-55.
Vijayádityadéva, brother of the above	....
Alu Tikkayadéva	....
Pótayadéva	1254-55.
Haridéva	1254-55.
M. P. C. Nalla Siddhi, son of Chóḍéśvara(?)	circ. 1258-59.
Vira Mana Siddayadéva	circ. 1259-60 and 1261-62.
Immadi Ganda Gópála Viyayádittadéva (?)	circ. 1260-61.
Singayadéva Gadidéva	1267-68.
Bijji (Bhīma?) Rázu Siddayadvéva	1267-68.
Chauhattamalla Perumánḍidéva ..	....
Gaḍidéva Rázu, son of Perumánḍidéva	1268-69.
Bhīma Rázu. Siddayadéva ..	1262-70.
(Náne?) déva	1275-76.

Manuma Ganḍa Gópáladéva ..	ascended 1282-83. (doubtful) and circ. 1289-90. circ. 1289-90 (?).
Malidéva, son of Viyayádityadéva.	1289-90 (?) and 1290-91.
M. P. C. Ganḍagópála *alias* Ranganáthan	circ. 1291-92 to 1303-05 or 1302-10.
(Nila ?) Kantha Chóḍadéva ..	1337-38 or 1277-78.
Vennu Sambáta Alamandala Nukayadeva	....
Vira Amala (Obala ?)	1426-27.
Tirumala Rázu	....
Tribhuvana Vennu Sambeta Alamanḍala Anavotayadéva Gangayyadéva	1428-29.
Paricheju Mummayadéva	1551-52.

Some of the names in the above list are to be found in the table on p. 18 of E.R. for 1899-1900, but the construction of a genealogical tree out of the materials available seems impossible.

(5) *Other Chiefs Subordinate to the Chóḷas.*—P. 9 of 1257-58 mensions S. M. Mádádidévundu, a subordinate of Kulóttunga Chóḍadéva. The latter may, possibly, be Rájéndra Chóḷa III. The former receives various titles, but it is not clear to us how he should be classified.

(6) Further information regarding the complicated lines of chiefs referred to in paragraph 4 above appears below. The chiefs herein referred to prefix to their names the name of a Chóḷa emperor followed by the word "Paṭṭai." Mr. V. Venkayya has explained to us that this word must be taken to indicate subordination to the emperor whose name is used in conjunction with it. Several of the chiefs concerned may be identified with rulers mentioned in the list appearing in paragraph (4) *supra*. The word 'Paṭṭai' is preceded by the name Kulóttunga Chóḷa in one case, by the name Rájarája in other cases and in G. 67 and S. 12 by the name Tyágasamudra. The former, G. 67, is of the 9th year of Vira Ganḍa Gópáladéva who was no doubt of Chóḷa lineage though his identity is not certain. In this we have Tyágasamudra Paṭṭai Mallidévarasan. S. 12 is of the 13th of Tribhuvana Chakravarti Rájarájadéva who is probably Rájarája III., in which case the date is 1228-29. It gives us Tyágasamudra

Paṭṭai Vímarasan and it seems to say that he was lord of Ayódhyá and that he made a grant in the kingdom of Madurántaka Pottapi Chóḷa Gaṇḍagópála *alias* Tirukkáḷattidéva.

As regards the inscriptions which relate to chiefs bearing the prefix Rájarája Paṭṭai, they are as follows :—

G. 53 is of the 26th of Kulóttunga Chóḷadéva who took Madura and the crowned head of the Páṇḍyan, so the date may be put at 1203–04. This is a grant by Peddarasar, the son of Rájarájapaṭṭai Vattiyarasar, and the birudas given are "lord of the Paṇámaṇḍalam, lord of Ahischatra, Ṣivapádṣékhara, of the Átriya gótra."

G. 86 is of the 36th year of Tribhuvana Chakravarti Tribhuvana Víradéva who is, no doubt, Kulóttunga III. The date is thus 1213–14. It is a grant by Rájarája Paṭṭai Sittarasan, the son of the provincial chief of the Mattimadésam Rájarájapaṭṭai Pettarasan, and mentions his older sister Páchchaldévi the wife of Madurántaka Pottapi Chóḷa Manuma Sittarasar. It is not clear whether Peddarasa was still alive at the time. Thus we get :—

Rájarájapaṭṭai Vattiyárasar.

Rájarájapaṭṭai Peddarasa (1203–04).

Páchchaldévi *m.* Madurántaka Pottapi Chóḷa Manma Siddharasa.

Rájarájapaṭṭai Siddharasa (1213–14).

From G. 92, which is of the same date as G. 86, we find that the aforesaid Siddharasa married Irumaḍi Ṣríyá Dévi, the daughter of a Chóḷa of Uraiyúr called Ṣúraḷvár Kaṭṭidévar.

In the following case we have the prefix Kulóttunga Chóḷa Paṭṭai :—

G. 78 is of the 18th year of Rájarájadéva "who took Madura and the head of the Páṇḍyan." It is a grant by Siddharasa, son of Kulóttunga Chóḷa Paṭṭai Ṣékharadéva, lord of Ahischatrapura and the middle country and Paṇamaṇḍalam, of the Átriya gótra and bearing the biruda Ṣivapádṣékhara.

If the Rájarája herein referred to is Rájarája III., then the date is 1233–34. It is not clear whether the Kulóttunga Chóḷa Paṭṭai Sékharadéva herein mentioned as the father of Siddharasa is the same as the Pattarasa of G. 86.

On p. 210, Vol. IV, E.I., it is stated that Ahichchhatra is Rámnagar and on p. 230, Vol. III, E.I., it is stated that Sinda, the eponymous ancestor of the Sinda dynasty, a descendant of the Serpent-king, was born at that place. That family bore the Phaṇipatáká or Nágadvaja which seems to be recalled by the statement in our inscriptions that the chiefs referred to therein were lords of the Phanamaṇḍalam.

Regarding the term "the middle country" see p. 169 *et seq*, Vol. XXII, I.A, from which it appears that it lay north of the Vindhyas.

A DARŚI DYNASTY.

D. 13 is an inscription of Rákshasa and S.S. 1317. If we should read S.S. 1357, the date will be 1435–36. It relates to the construction of a tank by S. M. Ásnadéva Mahárája in the name of his mother Áryamadévi and traces his pedigree from Gonkarázu who receives the following *birudas* amongst others :—

" Supreme lord of kings ; Parama Bhaṭṭáraka ; descendant of the race of Panéndra ; having as emblems the elephant, crocodile, serpent and boar ; having as emblem the moon adorned with a serpent ; belonging to the lunar race ; of the Vishnu family ; of the Hárita gótra ; he who planted pillars of victory in the mountains to the east and west of the Mahánadi river ; lord of the three worlds ; descendant of the race of Nága ; vanquisher of three kings ; Britti Manivvara Gaṇḍa ".

The line of descent is—

Gonkarázu *m.* Sandhyádévi.
|
Manabaḷidéva.
|
Nága.
|
Póta.
|
Vémula Malidéva
|
Núnka.
|
Ásnadéva (donor —1435-36 ?).
|
Núnka.
|
Obalayya.

The grantor seems to be the antepenultimate chief, because he assigns a village for the religious benefit of his son Núnka.

In the last part of the inscription the donor's mother is called Lakshyamadévi. As she is previously called Áryamadévi, it is probable that there is some error in transcription. The donor is said to be "of Darsi."

We do not know to what dynasty this line of chiefs should be assigned. O. 55 and O. 56 do not apparently relate to any of these persons, though the former gives us Víra Amala (Obala ?) son of Núnka under date 1426-27; for the Ongole people are Chóḍas.

It is just possible, though hardly likely, that the Nága of the Darsi list is the Nágadéva of A. 51, KV. 48, N. 21 and O. 75. This person was a vassal of the Kákatíya king and his inscriptions bear date circ. 1272-73 to 1280-81.

The Potarázu of the Darsi inscription is clearly not the Póta Rája of C.P. 18 or the Pótayadéva Chóḍa of KG. 11.

LATE GAJAPATI RULERS.

In C.P. 16, dated 1515-16, a reference is made to Krishṇadévaráya having captured at Konḍavíḍu Vírabhadra Mahárâya the son of king Rudra and having made him his servant.

U. 37, U. 40, and U. 41, which are of 1514-15 or thereabouts, describe how Krishṇadéva Ráya drove Pratápa Rudra Gajapati to Konḍavíḍu and, in capturing Udayagiri, captured also Tirumala Rághava (or Kánta) Ráya, the younger brother of the father of Pratápa Rudra Gajapati.

If the records quoted from Dr. Hunter on p. 204 *et seq* of Vol. II of Sewell's 'Antiquities' are to be trusted, Purushottama Déva, the predecessor of Pratab Rudradéva on the throne of Orissa, invaded the Southern country and defeated the Conjeevaram king. It seems probable that in this expedition Konḍavíḍu and Udayagiri were seized and they fell into the hands of Krishṇadéva Ráya in the reign of the next king Pratab Rudradéva. It is pretty clear that Pratab Rudradéva was still ruling in 1514-15 and the traditional dates on p. 188 of Vol. II of Mr. Sewell's 'Antiquities' are, in that case, inaccurate. Vírabhadra was, no doubt, merely the governor of Konḍavíḍu and perhaps Pratab Rudradéva's uncle Tirumala Rághava Ráya was in command at Udayagiri.

GOLKONḌA SULTANS.

All the inscriptions of the Muhammadan sovereigns seem to relate to Abdullah Kutb Sháh. V. 23, indeed, mentions Házarat Alam Emasá. There seems some mistake about this name. If

Alamgír is meant, the reference may be to Aurangzíb, or, perhaps, Alamgír was another name of Abdulla Kutb Sháh, in which case the Alamgír of the Kocherlakóṭa *Sthalapurána* (D. 35, note) may be the same person.

The other inscriptions all come from Udayagiri and Kandukúr and range from 1640–41 to 1661–62 ; see U. 26, U. 27, U. 36, U. 39, KR. 20, KR. 44, KR. 47, KR. 48 and KR. 80.

KÁKATÍYA DYNASTY.

The first inscription of this dynasty seems to be O. 139 of 1217–18 or 1218–19, which mentions Gaṇapatidéva Mahárája but does not identify him as a Kákaṭiya. He is, however, so identified in O. 17 of the same date and, no doubt, the same person is referred to in O. 45 of 1218–19.

There is thus evidence of the existence of a Kákaṭiya king called Gaṇapatidéva in 1218–19.

Twenty-one years later the name re-appears under date 1239–40 and thirteen years afterwards we come upon it again as shown below :—

O. 86 and O. 88 are both of 1239–40 and though Gaṇapati is not described therein as a Kákatíya, there is no reason to doubt that the reference is to the predecessor of Rudramma.

O. 28, dated 1252–43 or 1253–54, speaks of a Kákatíya Gaṇapatidéva who was lord of Anumakoṇḍa and O. 150, which may be of 1252–53 or 1256–57, mentions the same ruler. Further references appear in D. 25 (1254–55), D. 27, O. 89 (probably 1254–55), P. 7 and P. 10 (both of 1260–61) and P. 11. C.P. 17 (1254–55) is of the same reign and shows that Gaṇapati was the son of Mahádéva and the grandson of Prólaya. Finally, in O. 143, dated 1266–67 or 1267–68, we find Rudradéva making a re-grant for the merit of Gaṇapaṭidéva. This is, no doubt, an inscription of the successor (male or female) of Gaṇapati. The aforesaid inscriptions seem to render necessary some slight alteration in the dates commonly accepted, for they show one or more Gaṇapatis extending from 1218–19 to 1260–61.

It is noteworthy that the inscriptions of Gaṇapati appear only in Ongole, Podili and Darsi and from this we may gather that the southern boundary of his dominions took in only the extreme north of the Nellore district.

Under the name of Pratápa Rudradéva appear a large number of inscriptions which belong to Atmakúr, Darsi, Kandukúr, Kávali, Nellore, Ongole, Podili and Udayagiri. The absence of inscriptions from the extreme south suggests that the authority of the Kákaṭiyas did not extend over that portion of the country for, at all events, any appreciable time. The southward extension since the time of Gaṇapati will be noted. The first date is given by KR. 26, which declares that in the Kaliyuga year 3965 the Oraganṭi Pratápa was ruling. This date is, however, clearly erroneous and the utmost we can deduce from this inscription is that a king of Orugallu who was called Pratápa may have been ruling on a date which is probably 1248-49.

Another date which may be dismissed from consideration is the Ṣaka year 1033 which appears in the *Sthalapurána* of Kocherlakóṭa (D. 35, note). If that *purána* could be trusted, it would give us the following pedigree :—

Ṣiva Deváke Oḍaya.
|
Kákati Ṛudra.
|
Pratápá Ṛudra of
Orugallu (reigned for 24 years).
|
Haripálaka (reigned 8 years and
was ousted, apparently, by
the Gajapati family about 1142-43).

But it is not safe to place any reliance on this *purána*.

Leaving these out of consideration, our first date is perhaps given by P. 9 of 1257-58, but the reference there is not clear enough to allow of certainty. Thenceforward we get dates as follows :—

1266-67 or 1267-68	1280-81	1305-06	1317-18
1267-68	1291-92	1310-11	1320-21
1268-69	1293-94	1312-13	1322-23
1272-73	1294-95	1313-14	1329-30
1273-74	1297-98	1314-15	
1275-76	1298-99	1315-16	

There is no hint in these inscriptions that the throne was ever occupied by a queen Rudramma but this can be explained as shown on p. 199 of Vol. XXI of Ind. Ant.

The first lot of inscriptions may, therefore, refer to the queen Rudramma and, presumably, it terminates with 1293–94.

Of this group we may notice especially D. 24 of 1267–68 which is a grant on behalf of Singayadéva Gadidéva, the sovereign of the earth, and for the religious merit of "Rudra Mahárája, the ruler of Kondavídu in the kingdom." The position assigned to Rudra by this inscription suggests that of a mere governor. D. 57 may refer to this ruler but there is some error about the date which makes the point uncertain. With KR. 84 of 1294–95 we seem to begin the reign of Pratápa Rudradéva II, because the minister (Muppadi Náyudu) mentioned therein re-appears in subsequent, but not in anterior, inscriptions.

The inscriptions of this monarch run certainly to 1322–23, but they appear to go further, for KR. 28 of 1329-30 seems to refer to the same king under the name of Víra Pratápa Rudradévapatirája, lord of the Carnatic country.

Apparently C.P. 21 and C.P. 22 relate to this dynasty. In the former we find one Vírabhadraráya called "Mahánubháva, Paramabhattáraka, lord of the Drávila mandalam and lord of Kalubarga and the nine crores of the Carnatic." Similar titles, as well as "lord of Ganda" are attached in C.P. 22 to Víra Srí Gajapati Káketa Rudra Venkataráya Srí Partápadéva Mahárája.

CERTAIN CHIEFS SUBORDINATE TO THE KÁKATÍYA KINGS.

It seems as well to group together certain rulers, some evidently of very inferior rank, who acknowledged the supremacy of the Kákatíyas. These appear below. It will be noticed that we have excluded all persons bearing the title "Chóda." They are dealt with separately.

(1) *Nágadéva.*—KV. 48 of 1273–74 is a grant by Sríman Mahámandalésvara Nágadévarájulu, "who is endowed with all eulogistic titles," for the merit of Rudradéva Mahárája.

O. 75 of 1280–81 is similar.

A. 51 of 1273–74 or 1274–75 is a grant by a subordinate of Nágadéva Mahárája.

N. 21 is of 1271–72 or 1272–73. It is a Tamil grant to a temple and mentions a king Nágadéva Mahárája as ruling.

It is not clear whether the same person is referred to in these four inscriptions. If so, it is more probable, perhaps, that he was a mere officer of the Kákaṭíyas than that he was a local chief, having in view the wide distribution of his inscriptions.

(2) *Dévari Náyaningáru.*—D. 35 of 1310–11 describes a grant made in the time of Pratápa Rudra by Ṣrímat Dévari Náyaningáru and gives him various titles, such as, Chalamartiganḍa, master of polity, hero of the world, destroyer of kings in battle, Vírabhadra of the Kaliyuga. His father's name was Máchaya Náyaka.

(3) *Báhaḍadéva.*—O. 129, dated 1293–94, mentions Báhaḍadéva Rájulu as a vassal of Pratápa Rudra. There may be some error in the reading. The name seems an unlikely one.

(4) *The Chakra Náráyana line.*—We now come to a dynasty which, for convenience, we call "Chakra Náráyaṇa" from the title borne by its members. This dynasty is referred to in the inscriptions summarized below:—

C.P. 17 states that Kákaṭíya Gaṇapati had a vassal called king Mádhavadéva who was the son of Sauri Suravara. This Mádhavadéva is called the ruler of the city of Addanki. To him was born a son called Ṣárngadhara who is described as being "a good son, a ruler of men, of the Ṣálankáyana gótra, destroyer of enemies, of excellent fame." He is also called "the illustrious Chakra Náráyaṇa, the ruler of the earth." This king bestowed a village in the Ongole taluk upon Brahmans in the year 1254–55.

D. 72 of 1272–73 is a grant by Mallaṇadévilamma the daughter of Gópáladéva the uncle of S. M. Chakra Náráyaṇa Ṣrí Mádhavadéva Rája the governor of Addanki *sthala.*

O. 28, dated 1252–53 or 1253–54, states that S. M. Chakra Náráyaṇa Ṣrí Singadéva Mahárája, having titles similar to those in O. 76, was the feudatory of Kákaṭíya Gaṇapatidéva.

O. 6, dated 1267–68 or 1268–69, mentions S. M. Kaḷáráyanánṭa Singadéva Mahárája.

O. 27 of 1252–53 or 1253–54 is a grant by Máyidéva Preggaḍa, the prime minister and Sarvadhikári of Addanki Singaḷadéva.

O. 34, which is apparently of 1248–49, refers to a prime minister of Chakra Náráyana Sigaḷadéva Mahárája.

O. 76, dated 1208–09, is a grant by S. M. Ṣrí Mádhava Mahárája who is spoken of as "endowed with all eulogistic titles, a Revanta in controlling unruly horses, death to hostile forces, an adamantine stronghold to refugees, the protector of life, Chakra Náráyaṇa."

O. 86 and O. 88 of 1239–40 are grants by one Mádhava Náyaka in honour of Kákaṭiya Ganapatidéva. The connection of this Náyaka with the family in question is established by O. 89 of 1253–54 or 1254–55, wherein Ṣrímat Sárangapáṇi Dévarasu consecrates Ṣrí Gópáladéva, naming him Chakra Náráyaṇa Mádhava Gópinátha, for the merit of Gaṇapatidéva, his own father Mádhava Náyaka and his mother Chúḍubávi. Probably O. 67 of 1253–54 or 1254–55 refers to the same dynasty.

O. 100, which is undated, is a grant by a karnam for the merit of his lord S. M. Chakra Náráyaṇa Ṣrí Vaijégadéva Mahárája.

O. 101 is of 1273–74 and of the time of S. M. Ṣrí Mádhavadéva Mahárája who is given titles similar to those in O. 76 and is called in addition "Bhujabala" and "Bhayani Ṣankkamalla."

O. 103 of 1249–50 or 1250–51 states that Ṣrí Sómarája was the prime minister of Chakra Náráyaṇa Singaḷa Déva Mahárája.

O. 150 may be of 1252–53 or 1256–57 and is a grant by Govinda Náyaka, the prime minister of S. M. Chakra Náráyaṇa Ṣrí Sárangapáṇidéva Rája who is given attributes as in O. 76. It is stated that Kákaṭiya Gaṇapatidéva was ruling the earth at that time.

O. 151 of 1247–48 or 1248–49 is a grant by a prime minister and commander-in-chief of S. M. Chakra Náráyaṇa Singaḷadéva Mahárája.

The head-quarters of this petty dynasty was apparently Addanki and, although it claims somewhat magniloquent titles, its authority seems to have been confined to the neighbourhood of that town. The genealogy is not clear and the following table is based on surmise :—

Sauri Suravara.

|

Mádhavadéva or Mádhava Náyaka (1208–09 and 1239–40) m. Chúḍubávi.

Singaḷadéva or Singadéva (1247–48 or 1248–49, 1249–50 or 1250–51, 1252–53 or 1253–54).	Sárngadhara or Sárangapáṇidéva (1252–53 or 1256–57, 1253–54 or 1254–55 and 1254–55).	Gópáladéva.
Kalaráyanánta Singadéva (1267–68 or 1268–69.	Mádhavadéva (1273–74).	Mallanadévilamma (1272–73).

Where Vaijégadéva comes in cannot be guessed as O. 100 is undated.

We find no reference to this dynasty in any inscription heretofore published but on p. 37 of the introduction to Vol. VII, Epig. Carn., there appears a pedigree of the Sévuṇas which agrees in some particulars with our inscriptions.

We have there —

(1) Jayatugi.
(2) Bhillama, son of (1).
(3) Singhaṇa (1215).
(4) Sárangapáṇi or Krishṇa Kandhára.
(5) Mahádéva, brother of (4).
(6) Rámachandra or Rámadéva (1295).

Mr. Sewell's list (p. 254, Vol. II, 'Antiquities') differs from the above. He gives dates 1209 to 1247 for Singhaṇa, 1247 to 1260 for Krishṇa Kandhára and 1260 to 1271 for Mahádéva. Probably we have here a mere coincidence, but it is singular that our Singaḷadéva should have a prime minister and factotum called Máyidéva Preggaḍa, while the Sévuṇa Singhaṇadéva has, as his chief minister, Máyidéva Paṇḍita.

In this connection reference may be made to O. 13. This is unfortunately defaced and incomplete and the date is missing. It mentions kings called Singa, Bhava and Rámachandra the last-named of whom married Telingama and had five sons. These so-called kings were apparently, however, only ministers and there is nothing to clearly connect them with the Sévuṇa line.

In this connection see the remarks against D. 24 under the Chóḍa Singayadéva Gaḍidéva.

CERTAIN OFFICIALS UNDER THE KÁKAṬÍYA KINGS.

(1) *Muppaḍendra or Muppaḍi Náyuḍu.*—A. 56 (date wanting) mentions that Kákaṭi Rudradéva had placed the burden of the kingdom on Ṣrí Muppaḍendra.

KR. 84, dated 1294-95, is a grant for the prosperity of Rudradéva Mahárâya and for the prosperity of the kingdom and family of Ṣrímat Muppaḍi Náyanigáru.

In KR. 1 of 1315-16 we find Ṣríman Muppaḍi Náyanka Puraharu, the Mahá Pradháni and servant of Pratápa Rudra.

N. 80 of 1314–15 or thereabouts calls Muppaḍi Náyanigáru the agent (*káryakarta*) and viceroy (*pratinidhi*) of Pratápa Rudradéva.

O. 87, dated 1297–98, is a grant by Muppaḍi Náyaningáru for the merit of Pratápa Rudra.

KR. 23 mentions Muppuṛi (*read* Muppaḍi) Náyakuḍu, the Mahá Pradháni of Pratápa Rudra, and names his father Nági Náyaḍu and his mother Gangasánamma.

The dates of this minister of Pratápa Rudradéva II. thus runs from 1294–95 to 1315–16 at least.

It was this officer who captured Kánchi in S.S. 1238 (*vide* p. 5, E.R., for 1892–93).

(2) *Tripurári Déva.*—In D. 1 of 1272–73 this person is styled Mahámanḍaléṣvara, Mahárája, worshipper of the lotus feet of Rudradéva, Chalamarttuganḍa, Múrurâyajagadaḷa, Manḍalíka Bramha Rákshasa, Ganḍapenḍáru and director of 72 offices.

D. 57 is wrongly dated. It refers presumably to the same person under the name of Tripurántaka Mahárája, says that he acquired the lordship of the whole kingdom and gives him titles similar to those in D. 1.

D. 59, which is not dated, is similar to D. 1.

This person was evidently a great officer under Rudradéva *alias* Rudramadéví.

It is probable that in D. 12 (1313–14) a deity is referred to under the name of Tripurántaka Mahádéva.

(3) *Pótaya Sáhini.*—In D. 12 of 1313–14 Pótaya is called the servant of Pratápa Rudradéva.

He seems to re-appear in P. 37 where his descent is shown as follows:—

Dádi Pótaya Sáhiṇi *m.* Lakumámbá.
|
Víraya Sáhiṇi.
|
Pótaya Sáhiṇi.

The grandfather is described as the subordinate of Ṣrímad Vírayadéva Chakravartulu.

The title suggests that the family held high military office.

(4) *Rudra Pregaḍa.*—KR. 50 of 1268–69 calls Rudra Pregaḍa the prime minister (mahápradháni) of Rudradéva.

(5) *Rudra Náyadu.*—In O. 7 of 1314–15 Rudra Náyakulu makes a grant for the merit of Pratápa Rudra.

O. 11 is of Ananda which may be 1314–15. It refers to a grant by Śrímat Rudramá Náyaningáru.

O. 99, under date 1290–91, probably refers to the same man under the name "Rudrayá Náyakulu, commander of the elephants of Śríman Mahárája." Perhaps the Rudra Pregaḍa above is the same person.

(6) *Káma Boppa.*—O. 49 of 1298–99 says that Putávari Káma Boppaṇingáru, son of Dévaya, was the minister (*pradháni*) of Pratápa Rudra.

It is probably the same man who appears in O. 40, O. 54, O. 18 and O. 145. These give dates from 1306–07 (probable) to 5321–22 or 1322–23. In one case he is spoken of as belonging to Aliṇanáṇḍu, in another as ruling at Kandukúr.

The Kámaya Pregaḍa of O. 70 (1275–76) is, presumably, a different person.

(7) *Ahivi Moḷaya Náyanikulu.*—P. 6 under date 1312–13 mentions that this person was superintendent of the palace (*Nagari Náyak*) to Pratápa Rudradéva.

(8) *Kommi Náyaḍu.*—D. 24 of 1267–68 is a grant by Śrímat Kommi Náyuḍu, the governor (Rakshádhíśvara) of Táḍlúru. He was, apparently, a subordinate of Pratápa Rudra, though, perhaps, more directly connected with a ruler Singayadéva whose connection with the Kákaṭíyas is referred to elsewhere.

THE KOCHERLAKÓṬA STHALA-PURÁṆA.

An abstract of this is given in the note to D. 35 and from Mr. Sewell's remarks on p. 136, Vol. I, 'Antiquities,' it seems that it had been brought to his notice too. The *purána* is by no means trustworthy. It gives dates which are certainly, in some cases, widely inaccurate, but it preserves a certain vague adherence to historical sequence. Certain of the events alluded to in the *purána* have not been confirmed from other sources but they may be correct and it has therefore been thought well to include a summary of the document in this collection.

It starts with one Mallikharjuna Gaṇapati whose son Gajapati founded Kocherlakóṭa in 995–96 and afterwards retired to Telingána. His son Mukkanṭi followed as ruler of Kalinga.

Pratápa Rudra then drove out this family and we read of an edict issued by a king of that name in 1110–11. Pratápa Rudra's father is called Şivadévaka Oḍaya and his grandfather Kákata Rudra. He had a son Haripálaka who succeeded him and reigned for 8 years.

The Kákaṭíyas were driven out again by the Gajapati kings about 1142–43 and they held the country for 38 years when they in turn seem to have been ousted by the Reḍḍi chief Véma who is said to have belonged to the Gona (Kona ?) family. Véma's date is given as 1179–80 which is much too early. If, as Mr. Sewell says, we take his date as 1328, we work back to 1258 as the beginning of Pratápa Rudra's reign and this agrees nearly enough with accepted facts. In that case Haripálaka (not known from other sources) dates from 1282 and the Gajapati restoration from 1290. Mukkanṭi, it may be mentioned here, is commonly regarded as a Pallava, but the *purána* suggests that he was a Gajapati. The list of Reḍḍi kings as given in the *purána* differs from the accepted list as shown below :—

Purána list.	Years ruled.	*Accepted list.*	Years ruled.
Pólaya Véma	12	Pólaya or Próla Véma	11
Anapota Bhúpati	30	Ana Véma	30
Ana Véma	15	Aliya Véma	12
Komára Véma	25	Komáragiri Véma	14
Kori Véma	4	Kómaṭi Venka	28
Komáragiri	14	Rácha Venka	4

There is enough resemblance between the lists to make it appear probable that the *purána* list is an incorrect version of the real list and not a genuine list of a separate branch of the family ruling locally. It is, however, possible that we have here a line of local rulers descending from Prólayya's son Anna Bhúpa.

The *purána* then proceeds to the Vijayanagar dynasty which it dates from S.S. 1222, wrongly said to correspond with Pramáthin. The line is given as—

Achyutadéva.
|
Pravududéva.
|
Narasimhadéva.
|
Achchitadéva.

This is, of course, altogether wrong and the inaccuracy shows how little reliance can be placed on the *purána*. It is curious that it should speak of Krishṇadéva Ráya as if he were a mere assistant to Achyutadéva. If the statement that the litigation about the *Sthala karnamship* was settled before the Rája in person at Vijayanagar is true, it is an interesting indication of the reality of the sovereignty exercised by the Vijayanagar kings in this distant part of their dominions.

After a reference to Ráma II. of the third dynasty, the *purána* then proceeds to the Mussalmán rulers and their subordinates. It preserves its inaccuracy to the end, for it starts with Alamgir Pádisháh ascending the throne in 1479–80. This is probably a vague reminiscence of Aurungzib or, perhaps, Abdulla Kutb Sháh of Golkoṇḍa had the names Alamgir as an *alias* (see note under Golkonda sovereigns).

CHIEFS OF KÓNA MAṆḌALAM.

In O. 112 we have a reference to a ruler who was "a mountain to the Ganga dynasty (?), lord of the city of Mahishmati, descendant of the Áyihaya race." This is probably a Kóna chief (see p. 86, Vol. IV, E.I.). A memory of this dynasty seems to survive in the Kocherlakóṭa *sthalapurána* where the Reḍḍi chief Véma is said to have belonged to the Gona family.

PALLAVA DYNASTY AND ITS DESCENDANTS.

Inscriptions of the main Pallava dynasty are almost non-existent in this collection, but G. 54 which is of the 15th year of Nandipóttarasar may be assigned thereto. The inscription is in Tamil which is described by Mr. T. P. Krishṇasámi Sástri as being of Pallava type and, while dated in the reign of Nandipóttarasar, the grant is said to have been made under the orders of Chaḷukkiarasar. If the references are to Nandivarman or Nandipótarája and Vikramáditya II., this inscription must be assigned to the 8th century and it is, then, one of the oldest, if not the oldest, stone inscription found in Nellore.

G. 63 which is of the 20th year of Vikrama Varmadéva and from the same temple may belong to the same dynasty but it probably refers to a Páṇḍyan. There appears to be nothing else of this line but the Pallavas have left a clear trace of their dominion in the form of families which long after the main line ceased to exist, laid claim to a Pallava origin. Of these the principal group consists of the descendants of Mukkanṭi Káḍuveṭṭu, whose inscriptions are set out below.

It may be mentioned that the Reḍḍi dynasty called itself "Pallaváditya" and "Pallava Trinétra."

(1) *Descendants of Mukkanṭi Káḍuveṭṭu.*—By tradition a chief called Mukkanṭi reigned at Nellore about the 11th century and the Mukkanṭi Káduveṭṭu who appears so frequently in this collection as the ancestor of ruling chiefs is, no doubt, the same person. Whether he ever existed is uncertain. Probably he is a mere personification of the Pallava dynasty. In the *sthalapurána* of Kocherlakóṭa (D. 35, note) we are told that Mukkanṭi was the son of Gajapati and grandson of Mallikhárjuna Gaṇapati and that he ruled over Kalinga in the 11th century. No reliance can, however, be placed on these statements.

The following is an abstract of the inscriptions of the rulers who describe themselves as descendants of Mukkanṭi Káḍuveṭṭu (or Káḍuveṭṭi, either form being possible) :—

D. 43 of 1150–51 or thereabouts refers to S. M. Vijayádityadéva Máharája descended from M. K.

D. 69 of 1217–18 or 1218–19 is a grant by S. M. Paraméṣvara Abhidéva Malidéva Máharája who is called a descendant of M. K. and a member of the Pallava dynasty and receives the title of lord of Kánchi and various other Pallava birudas.

KR. 61 of 1258–59 or 1259–60 is a grant by S. M. Alláḍu Suddhadéva Máharája, grandson of Podakanúri Siddi Rázu a descendant of M. K., for the prosperity of the kingdom of S. M. Bhujabala Víra Manma Siddayadéva Chóḍa.

KR. 62 of 1259–60 or 1260–61 is a grant made by Madusúdhanadéva Mahárája, grandson of S. M. Andulúri Vijayáditta Déchini a descendant of M. K., during the reign of S. M. Immaḍi Gaṇḍa Gópála Vijayáditta.

KR. 63 of 1261–62 is a grant by Siddanadévulu Vijayadévanḍu, son of S. M. Ka . . ráya Bhímadéva Mahárája a descendant of M. K., for the prosperity of the kingdom of S. M. Bhujabala Víra Manma Siddayadéva Chóḍa.

KG. 24, dated 1268–69 gives—

Bhímarázu *m.* Siriyádévi.

|

S. M. Immaḍidéva Mahárája.

The last named is given various titles, *e.g.*, lord of Kánchi, ornament of the Pallavas, descendant of M. K.

U. 6 gives the usual Pallava titles to S. M. Dórapa Rázu who is called the supreme king of kings and a descendant of Kondavitti, which is clearly a misreading for Káduvetti. His sons were Iruga Rázu, Samarta Rázu, Yamma Rázu, Bhíma Rázu and Bandu Rázu. Yamma Rázu was also called S. M. Nandivarma Mahárája and was crowned at Chódapuram in S.S. 1024 (A.D. 1101-02 or 1102-03). He is said to have made a grant of twelve villages of Punginádu to Brahmans while ruling Ponugódu and Mádurévi. One of these twelve villages was Sangam in the Nellore taluk. The king's favourite village is said to have been Pádatúru. There is a Punugódu village in Atmakur taluk and there are villages called Chódavaram in Kandukúr, Kanigiri and Kávali, but the Chódapuram of the inscription may refer to a Chódavaram outside the district.

We get, then, the following table :—

(1) Dórapa Rázu.

(2) His sons Iruga, Samarta, Yamma crowned at Chódapuram in 1101-02 or 1102-03 under the name of Nandivarma Mahárája, Bhíma and Bandu.

(3) Vijayádityadéva, about 1150-51.

(4) Abhidéva Malidéva, 1217-18 or 1218-19.

(5) Alládu Suddhadéva, 1258-59 or 1259-60, grandson of Podakanúri Siddi Rázu and a vassal of the Chóda Víra Manma Siddayadéva.

(6) Madusúdhanadéva, 1259-60 or 1260-61, grandson of Andulúri Vijayáditta Déchini and subordinate to Immadi Ganda Gópála Vijayáditta.

(7) Siddanadéva Vijaya Dévandu, 1261-62, son of Ka . . ráya Bhímadéva and vassal of the Chóda Víra Manma Siddayadéva.

(8) Immadidéva, 1268-69, son of Bhímarázu and Siriyádévi.

The connection between these persons is not apparent and it is not probable that all of them were ruling chiefs. Their inscriptions which range from 1101-02 to 1268-69 belong to Darsi, Kandukúr, Kanigiri and Udayagiri. It appears probable that the S. M. Immadi Ganda Gópála Vijayádittadéva Mahárája of KR. 62 is the S. M. Immadidéva Mahárája of KG. 21.

Others claiming Pallava descent.—In the following cases, though the claim to Pallava descent is obvious, there is no distinct reference to Mukkanṭi Káḍuveṭṭu. A. 25 of 1284–85 or 1285–86 gives us S. M. Vijaya Gaṇḍa Gópála Mahárája, the lord of Kánchi, and assigns to him Pallava titles During his reign a grant was made by Káma and Dévi, sons of Ṣríman Golapundi Késima Náyaka who is called the lord of Orriyúru, the beheader of Burágaṇḍa, and by various other titles (see also p. 1434 of Appendix I).

N. 16, dated 1182–83, mentions Allun Tikka the crest-jewel of kings, a blossom (or sprout) among the Pallavas."

N. 15 mentions Allun Dirukálti "the crest-jewel of the Pallava family."

S. 2 (Tamil) speaks of one Nalla Sittarasan of the Pallava race. These give us the following:—

(1) Allun Tikka *alias* (probably) Allun Tirukálti, 1182–83.

(2) Vijaya Gaṇḍa Gópála, 1284–85 or 1285–86, with a vassal chief at Uraiyúr.

(3) Nallasittarasan.

The inscriptions are of Atmakúr, Nellore and Súlúrpet.

In KR. 26 we are told that in or about 1258–59 one Nalla Siddhi was ruling at Nellore and this is in conformity with tradition which tells of Siddi Rája who ruled at Nellore about the 12th century but whether he was of Pallava descent cannot be ascertained from the inscriptions. Whoever he was, he had Pákináḍu under his authority. We have seen that, a century and a-half before, Punginádu was ruled by Nandivarma, *alias* Yamma Rázu, a descendant of the Pallavas.

PÁṆḌYAN DYNASTY.

N. 61 states that Tribhuvana Chakravarti Sundara Páṇḍyadéva gave, on the recommendation of Kálingaráyar, the village of Mávaḍi Kuṇḍai in Munḍanáḍu for the benefit of the temple at Nellore. The Páṇḍyan king is very likely Sundara Páṇḍya I who, as we find from Inscription No. 904, p. 145 (App.), Vol. VII, E.I., "performed the anointing of heroes at Nellúrapura." The Kálingaráya, at whose request the grant was made, may well be the Kákaṭiya Ganapati I who seems to have suffered defeat at the hands of the Páṇḍyans. It is possible that the Vikrama Varmadéva of G. 63 is the Páṇḍyan King Vikrama mentioned on p. 7, E.R. for 1899-1900.

A very late Sundara Páṇḍya Chakravarti is mentioned in N. 76 under date 1399-1400, or 1400-01. The name of the Vijayanagar King Harihara II appears in the same inscription but in what relation the two kings stood is not apparent.

Probably there are other Páṇḍyan inscriptions in our collection but we have not noticed any and it is likely that the Páṇḍyan dominion never extended to the north of the district. See note under A. 37.

RÁVÉLA, RAVULA OR RAVILLA FAMILY.

Persons bearing the name Rávéla, Rávula or Rávilla are mentioned in G. 52, G. 84, N. 33, P. 19, N. 124, S. 6, D. 35 note and G. 112.

The earliest date seems to be the 12th of Rájarájadéva in S. 6, where we find a Rávilla Náyakkan.

D. 35 note says that Alamgír Pádisháh (Aurangzib?) appointed Rávilla Timma Náyaka to rule over the Kocherlakóṭa *síma*, that he was succeeded by his son Venkaṭádri and that finally it was divided up among six members of the family.

P. 19 of 1563-64 or 1575-76 states that Tirumala Náyaka, grandson of Rávéla Tippa, made a grant of land in Podili *síma* which was under his control. N. 124 of 1582-83 gives Rávéla Kanṭi Náyaka, his son Tirumalayya and his grandson Kónéṭi Timma of whom the last held Udayagiri *síma*.

G. 112 of 1616-17 or 1617-18 gives—

Vengalappa.
|
Rávula Venkaṭappa or Venkaṭapati.
|
Rávula Vengalappa.

The second received Víranna Kanupur as an *amaram* from king Venkaṭapati.

N. 33 of 1645-46 says that Rávula Venkaṭádri received Kódúr as an *amaram* from (Rávéla Muddu) Krishnappa Náyaḍu and that the latter received Sarvapalli *síma* from king Venkaṭádri.

G. 84 of 1688-89 and G. 52 of 1712-13 both refer to Rávéla Muddukrishnappa Náyaḍu.

REḌḌI DYNASTY.

Genealogies of the Reḍḍi dynasty appear in C.P. 5, KR. 15, KR. 16, KR. 18, KR. 19, KR. 21, KR. 34, KR. 35, KR. 43 and O. 73. They are not, however, consistent, the difficulty arising over C.P. 5 and KR. 21, which give Véma as the grandfather of Ṣrígiri and, in the former case, as the father of Pina Komaṭi. On the other hand the table on p. 24, E.R. for 1899–1900, shows Malla as grandfather of Ṣrígiri and this is supported by other inscriptions in the present collection. We assume, therefore, that Véma occupies the place of Malla in C.P. 5 and KR. 21 either because he was a person of more importance than his younger brother or by reason of a mere error. This being granted, the genealogy seems to work out as shown below :—

- Vémaya.
  - Kómati Próla or Pró'aya *m.* Annayambá.
    - Mácha Satri or Máchaya Peddaya.
    - Kómaṭi Véma (1354–55 or 1355–56).
      - Anavóta (1353–54).
    - Doḍḍayya.
    - Annaya or Annabhúpa.
      - Véma.
        - Malla Bhúpa.
        - Ten other sons.
    - Malla (called commander-in-chief).
      - Pina Kómaṭi *m.* Gaurámbiká.
        - Ṣríṣa Ṣrígiri *m.* Gangámbiká (1397–98 or 1398–99 and 1400-01 (?)).
          - Kómaṭi (1430-31).
            - Tippaya Reḍḍi.
            - Tippaya Ṣrígiri.
            - Rámayya.
            - Dévaráyuṇḍu.
            - Náráyaṇadévara.
          - Mallaya or Ṣrígiri Malla. (1406-07, 1408-09).
          - Ana Véma.
          - Náráyaṇa.
        - Rácha Véma (1397–98 or 1398–99).
        - Mácha.
        - Anna Déva.
        - Peddi.

This table supplements that on p. 24 of E.R. for 1899–1900 by giving the father of Kómaṭi Próla and the descendants of Ṣrísa Ṣrígiri.

In C.P. 5 Véma, son of Kómaṭi Próla receives the following titles :—Jagannobbagaṇḍa, Jita Gópála, Pallava Trinétra, Vairivíra and Basava Ṣankara and he is said to have built the steps at Ṣríṣaila. The grant is by his alleged great-grandson and relates to villages attached to Chuṇḍi in Kandukúr. The donor is called Mahárája.

KR. 15, which is of Raktákshi year, mentions the fact that the dynasty belonged to the Panṭa division of the Reḍḍi caste speaks of Véma, the son of Anna Bhúpati, as having ruled the earth and names the Treasurer of Véma's son Malla Bhúpa. It relates to Chunḍi.

KR. 16 gives the genealogy of Kommana Sómayájulu, the prime minister of Kómaṭi, the son of Ṣrígiri. It relates to Chunḍi.

KR. 18 gives Véma, the son of Kómaṭi Próla, *birudas* similar to those in C.P. 5 and records a grant in Chunḍi by Mallaya, son of Ṣrígiri.

KR. 19 calls Véma "the lord of the eastern country" and Malla, his brother, "Emperor of the Earth." His successor Kómaṭi and Ṣrígiri are called king (Bhúmipála) : and the same, or a corresponding, title is bestowed on the latter's sons by one of whom a grant is made in the town of Chunḍi.

KR. 21 relates to the Mallayya who is incorrectly (?) called great-grandson of Vémáya and describes certain works carried out by him in Chunḍi.

KR. 34 calls Prólaya the crest-jewel of kings and talks of both him and his son Véma as conquerors of their enemies. The latter's brother Malla is termed *kshitiṣah*, or king, and he, too, is represented as a conqueror. The inscription is incomplete.

KR. 35 recites Véma's meritorious deeds ; alludes to his getting the Rámáyana translated into Telugu ; mentions that Malla's son Kómaṭi ruled the earth as did *his* son Ṣríṣa Ṣrígiri who constructed thousands of tanks ; calls Rácha Véma the destroyer of other kings and describes how he constructed a tank in Kandukúr taluk in the time of his brother Ṣrígiri.

KR. 43 is wrongly dated as transcribed. Probably we should read S.S. 1322, *i.e.*, A.D. 1400-01. It gives either Ṣrígiri or his father Kómaṭi the following birudas:—Jaganobbaganḍa, Víra-náráyaṇa, Bhujabala, Chóḷa Páṇḍyagaja Késari, Vairivíra and Basuva Ṣaṅkara, and says that Ṣrígiri was ruling while his son Kómaṭi Rája governed the town of Kandukúr. The grant is of the last-named.

O. 73 calls Véma the founder of the dynasty, calls his son Kómaṭi Próla the foremost of heroes, says that, after Próla, his son Véma ruled the earth and that assisted by his brother Malla who commanded the army, this ruler, who bears the title Jaganobba-ganḍa, subdued his enemies on all sides. The inscription mentions conquests on the banks of the Kistna, Gódávari and Gunḍla-kamma and states that Véma made a grant of Addanki in the Púnginádu which extended from the eastern fort of Ṣríṣailam to the eastern sea. The inscription relates to the putting up of *lingams* by Manchirája a descendant of one Rámarája a minister to king Véma, and Manchirája's brother Mallinátha was, apparently, granted by king Annavóta the village of Rávinútala. The date is 1353–54.

It will be observed that the inscriptions discovered in Nellore do not throw so much light on the Reḍḍi dynasty as might have been expected. They range in date only from 1353–54 to 1430–31 and mainly relate to the town of Chunḍi where members of the branch descended from Malla, son of Próla, appear to have settled. Whether these Chunḍi people claimed independence is not clear, but it is probable that they were in subordination to the Reḍḍi ruler at Konḍavíḍu. There is nothing suggestive of independent sovereignty in the titles bestowed except in the case of Próla Véma son of Próla, Véma son of Annaya, Malla son of Próla, Pina Kómaṭí and Ṣrísa Ṣrígiri and, even in respect of them, the inscriptions usually contain only a bare statement that they ruled the earth. There is nothing in these inscriptions to confirm the statement that the Reḍḍi capital was originally Addanki (see p. 23, E.R. for 1899–1900). The relics of the rule of the Reḍḍis at Chunḍi consist of a few small ruined temples and a fine monolithic column.

A descendant of the Reḍḍi dynasty is, perhaps, the Ganga Reḍḍi of C.P. 16, who seems to have helped Krishnadévaráya in driving out the Gajapati ruler from Konḍavíḍu.

VAITUMBA CHIEFS.

This line is mentioned in Vol. VII, E.I., see pp. 142, 143, 144. We find several references to them in our collection, as follows :—

G. 88 of the 8th of Rájarájadéva records a gift by Mummuḍi Vaitumba Mahárája *alias* Vishnudévan *alias* Durai Arasan.

G. 61 of the 9th of Rájarájadéva records a gift by Aṭṭamasiddi Bhuvané Kaní Kadhéran *alias* Páṇḍyagaja Késari *alias* Rája Brahma Chóḷa Vaitumbana *alias* Vanan Mahárájan *alias* Madanudévan *alias* Dasaiyarasan.

N. 66 of the 28th of Rájarájadéva records a gift by Vaitumba Pitusuramuḍaiyán.

S. 8 of the 2nd of (Vijayagaṇḍa) Gópáladéva records a gift of land by Rájéndra Chóḷa Mummuḍi Vaitumba Mahárája.

These chiefs, therefore, seem to have had authority in the southern part of Nellore in the 13th century. S. 8 may be of the time of Tirukáḷattidéva Chóḍa who was also called Gaṇḍa Gópála.

FAMILY OF THE VENKAṬAGIRI ZAMINDARS.

The Venkaṭagiri family has long occupied a position of importance in Nellore but the inscriptions of this family though numerous are confined to recording grants to temples and tanks and such domestic matters. The family name is Velugóṭi and the first of this name met with is Kastúri Rangapati in C.P. 12. The Ṣaka date of that grant is 1360, but it does not agree with the cyclic year and is, therefore, doubtful. On p. 242, Vol. II of Sewell's "Antiquities" Kastúri Rangappa appears under date 1579.

KG. 5, dated 1528–29, mentions Timma and his father Ranga and G. 82, dated 1533–34, possibly refers to the same Timma.

KG. 21, dated 1553–34 or 1554–55, mentions Kumára Timma.

N. 105, dated 1570–71, refers to Timmappa as does N. 54, dated 1573–74.

P. 27, which is perhaps of 1575–76, mentions Kumára Timma.

P. 34, dated 1579–80 or 1583–84, gives us Kumára Chinna Timma son of Kumára Timma and grandson of Pedda Timma.

N. 46 is dated 1590–91 or 1591–92 and seems to be of the time of the Venkaṭapati referred to below but the date is too early and it has probably been incorrectly transcribed.

A. 40, dated 1610–11, is of Timma.

P. 60, dated 1612–13, probably relates to the same Timma who is there described as Kumára Timma, son of Kondamma, and grandson of Kumára Timma.

Of Venkatapati, the son of Kumára Timma (or Venkatappa according to R. 18) and grandson of Peda Kondama, there is a large number of inscriptions ranging from 1612–13 to 1638–39. This was, apparently, the most distinguished member of the family but, curiously, does not appear in the family pedigrees given by Messrs. Boswell and Sewell. He deserves to be remembered on account of his efforts to encourage irrigation. In the single year 1638–39 we find twenty-five grants to irrigation works. He appears to have acquired some renown as a soldier too, as indicated by A. 35.

The pedigree of Venkatapati and his immediate predecessors seems to have been—

Ranga
(1528-29).
|
Pedda Timma
(1533-34).
|
Kumára Timma
(1553-54 and 1575-76).
|
Kumára Chinna Timma
(1579-80 or 1583-84).
|
Pedda Kondama.
|
Kumára Timma
(1610-11 and 1612-13).
|
Venkatapati
(1612-13 to 1638-39).

G. 110 which speaks of Venkatapati Rázu son of Veligoti Rájayyapátúru falls within the period of Venkatapati son of Kumára Timma and doubtless relates to him. The meaning of the suffix Pátúri is not apparent.

O. 53, though dated 1632–33, refers to Kumára Timma as though he were still living. This is unintelligible and there seems to be no mistake in the date, the cyclic and Saka years agreeing.

N. 116, dated 1638–39, declares that Kumára Timma made a grant in that year. This is possible as Venkatapati's inscriptions end with this year. He must, then, have been succeeded by another Kumára Timma.

After a long interval we come to KG. 9 which is apparently of 1766–67 and refers to yet another Kumára Timma though it does not distinctly say that he was contemporaneous with the inscription.

S. 18 of 1794–95 and Kumára Yáchama closes the list.

It will be observed that several members of this house held the office of *Káryakarta*, or agent, to great officers of the Vijayanagar dynasty.

By tradition the family owes its elevation to the patronage of the Orangal Kákaṭíya dynasty. Pedigrees of this family appear on p. 713 of the District Manual and p. 240 of Vol. II of Mr. Sewell's 'Antiquities.' They differ widely from the short pedigree suggested by the inscriptions but, as the name Velugóṭi is found in at least one case (in P. 40) in connection with the name Yáchama which also is borne by the Venkaṭagiri zamindars, there seems no reason to doubt that these Velugóṭi people belonged to the family of the present zamindars.

VIJAYANAGAR DYNASTIES.

First Dynasty.

There are numerous inscriptions of the Vijayanagar dynasties but they add little to our knowledge on the subject.

C.P. 15 professes to be a grant by Harihara I. It declares that his original capital was Kunjarakóna (Anegunḍa) and that he founded Vijayanagar city. It says further that Sangama I was the son of one Bukka by Mágámbiká. The father of Sangama I is not apparently known from other sources and the statement on the subject in C.P. 15 cannot be trusted as the grant appears to be a forgery.

Nevertheless we find in KG. 7 allusion to a certain Bukkaráya Oḍayalu with titles as follows :—Asylum of the world, entitled to the five great sounds, Manḍaléṣvara, Múruráyaraganḍa, Ariráya Vibhála, Báshadeppuvaráyara (ya ?) ganḍa, lord of the earth with its nine continents. This inscription is dated 1314–15 which seems too early for Bukka I of Vijayanagar and it appears not impossible that the chief referred to was the father of Sangama.

It is known that the Nellore district was very early connected with the Vijayanagar crown, for the Bitragunṭa grant (our C.P.

20, printed at p. 21, Vol. III, E.I.) shows that the son of Kampa, the brother of Bukka I, was governing part of Nellore and implies that Kampa himself held sway there.

It is pretty clear, then, that part of Nellore was included in the dominions which were governed by the family which afterwards became the first Vijayanagar dynasty at the time when they were mere vassals of the Hoysalas or some other paramount dynasty. In other words part of Nellore formed a portion of the original Vijayanagar kingdom.

Of Kampa I only one inscription seems to exist, viz., N. 28 which mentions a grant made by Mudra Chiḍdi Sáyanna Oḍayalu; the prime minister of Kampaṇati Oḍayar the lord of the Eastern and Western seas. The date is 1346–47.

Of Sangama II we have only the Biṭragunṭa grant.

We now come to Harihara II. KG. 10, dated 1377–78, was inscribed during the reign of this king and shows that the country round Udayagiri was then attached to the Vijayanagar kingdom. KG. 23 is wrongly dated but is apparently of 1393–94. It is a grant by the son of Harihara II, Víra Déva Oḍayalu, presumably the prince who afterwards became Dévaráya I and who, at the time, was apparently holding the post of governor in Nellore district. N. 76 is a Tamil inscription and is important in giving the regnal year of Harihara II. It declares that S.S. 1322 was the 25th year of the reign; so Harihara II apparently came to the throne in 1376–77. U. 18 (*b*) and (*c*), the latter being of S.S. 1308, are other inscriptions of the same king.

It has been noted above that Harihara II was ruling in 1393–94 and from page 36, Vol. III, E.I., it appears that later inscriptions of this monarch have been found, but C.P. 1, dated 1390–91, is issued in the name of Dévaráya I. The explanation seems to be that in that year Dévaráya visited Nellore district in command of his father's army, that he then granted the land referred to and that the grant was confirmed by Dévaráyá's son, the governor of Udayagiri, after Dévaráya's accession to the throne. In other words C.P. 1 bears the date of the original grant and not that of the formal confirmation of the same.

Other inscriptions of Dévaráya I are D. 46 and KG. 4, the former of which shows that Dévaráya was ruling in 1415–16 while the latter advances his date to 1416–77 which dates are later than those generally accepted. There are a few other inscriptions of this king which need not be noticed.

In this connection reference must be made to KV. 14 and U. 17. The former bears date Iva (?) and S.S. 1363 and states that Víradéva, son of Harihara, was then on the throne. The latter is dated Prabhava and S.S. 1369 and it, too, refers to Víra Dévaráya, son of Harihara, as ruling. In the case of U. 17 the cyclic and Ṣaka dates agree and this fact suggests that the Ṣaka date 1363 in KV. 14 is correct. If so, the reference must be to Dévaráya II and we can only conclude that his father Víra Vijaya must have been also called Harihara.

Before leaving Dévaráya we must mention certain descendants of his who do not appear in the line of sovereigns. C.P. 1 shows that Dévaráya I had a son called Rámachandra who is spoken of as Yuvarája and was governor of Udayagiri. He is said to have completely vanquished the Mussalmán king who may be Firóz Sháh the Bahmani Sultán.

C.P. 2 is a grant by one Dévaráya Voḍaya, the ruler of Udayagiri kingdom, and it gives his lineage thus:—

Rámachandra Ráya *m.* Lakshmí Déví.
|
Parvataráya *m.* Párvatí Déví.
|
Dévaráya Odaya.

The cyclic and Ṣaka dates of this grant differ. If the latter is correct, it is of 1435–36.

D. 19 and KG. 4 both seem to refer to Rámachandra, the former being dated 1406–07 and the latter 1416–17. O. 132 mentions the Commander-in-Chief (Daḷavâyi) Dévarájaya Odaya under date 1443–44 and it is probable that this is the grandson of Rámachandra Ráya whose dates are therefore 1406–07 and 1416–17, while his grandson's are 1435–36 and 1443–44.

We now come to Víra Vijaya *alias* Vijaya Bukka. O. 56 refers to this prince under date 1426–27, a date which seems to encroach on the reign of his successor as recorded on p. 36 of Vol. III, E.I.

To the time of Dévaráya II belong several inscriptions ranging in date from 1426–27 to 1447–48 if we include the two inscriptions KV. 14 and U. 17 referred to above. The ruling monarch is spoken of as Dévaráya Praudha Dévaráya or Pratápa

Dévaráya. The Satyamangalam plates (p. 35 of Vol. III, E.I.) call Pratápa Dévaráya a younger brother of Dévaráya, but there is nothing in the Nellore inscriptions to show that Dévaráya II had a brother.

As to the rest of the first dynasty, the only trace of them seems to be in A. 31 which refers to Ṣrí Víra Pratápa Ṣrí Virupáksha Ráya Maháràja and his minister Viḍayanchami Jangamayya. The inscription is dated Chitrabhánu and the reference probably is to Virupáksha the son of Dévaráya II. To sum up, we have in Nellore inscriptions of the reigns of the following members of the first dynasty :—

Bukka Oḍaya.
Kampa.
Sangama II
Harihara II.
Dévaráya I and his son Rámachendra Ráya and other descendants in that line.
Víra Vijaya.
Dévaráya II.
Vírupáksha (son of Dévaráya II ?).

Second Dynasty.

After an interval of half a century or so we come to inscriptions of the second dynasty, beginning with those of Krishnadéva Ráya. These range from 1510–11 to 1529–30, that is, within the accepted period of his reign.

U. 37, 40 and 41, which are probably all of 1514–15, describe the pursuit of Pratápa Rudra Gajapati to Konḍaviḍu and the capture of Udayagiri fort and of Tirumala Rághava (or Kánta) Ráya the uncle of Pratápa Rudra Gajapati. C.P. 16 declares that in 1515–16 Krishnadéva made a grant after he had captured Vírabhadra Máharája, the son of King Rudra, in the city of Konḍaviḍu and made him his servant. All these matters are well known from other sources except, perhaps, the name of the uncle.

It is clear from the inscriptions that Udayagiri was in the hands of the first Vijayanagar dynasty. When that dynasty became decrepit the fortress must have been seized by the

Gajapatis and the recapture of it was one of Krishnadéva's first acts.

Most of the taluks supply inscriptions of Krishnadéva and it appears that the district appertained mainly to the Udayagiri *rájyam*, the extreme north falling within the limits of the Kondavídu *rájyam*, while the south belonged to the Chandragiri *rájyam*.

Of Achyuta we have three copper-plate grants, namely, Nos. 10, 13 and 23, dated, respectively, 1536–37, 1541–42 and 1347–48; of these the last is evidently a forgery. The stone inscriptions number seven and call for no special remark except N. 31 A which declares that Achyuta was ruling in 1525–26. The cyclic year in this inscription is not clear, but seems to be Párthiva which would agree with the recorded Ṣaka date. There must, however, be some mistake as Krishnadéva was certainly ruling in 1525–26.

The inscriptions of Sadáṣiva range from 1542–43 to 1570–71. It appears from p. 27 (Introd.) of Vol. III of Epig. Carn. that Sadáṣiva's reign extended to 1576.

The Nellore inscriptions of the second dynasty thus refer to the times of—

Krishnadéva.
Achyuta.
Sadáṣiva.

Third Dynasty.

In the case of this dynasty there are certain inscriptions which clearly relate to the ruling sovereigns, but also a number as to which it is difficult to say whether the rulers mentioned therein are members of the royal family or not. We have grouped all of these under the head of the third dynasty on the supposition that they appertain to the Áravídu family.

Ranga.—Under this name come the following:—

P. 25, dated 1545–46 or 1546–47, states that Ṣríman Mahámaṇḍaléṣvara Víra Pratápa Venkaṭa Rangapati Mahárája was then reigning at Vijayanagar.

N. 105, dated 1570–71, mentions Rámarája Ranga Rájayya-déva as holding office under Sadáṣiva.

N. 54, dated 1573-74, mentions Vira Rangaráyadéva Mahárája.

R. 41, dated 1575-76, says that Víra Pratápa Víra Rangaráyadéva was reigning at Penugonḍa and gives him royal titles.

P. 27 is wrongly dated. If we read S.S. 1497 for 1407, we got Víra Pratápa Rangadéva with royal titles ruling at Vijayanagar in 1575-76.

KG. 15, dated 1579-80, and N. 124, dated 1582-83, correspond with R. 41.

O. 32 is wrongly dated. If S.S. 1556 be substituted for S.S. 1565, we get Víra Pratápa Víra Rangadéva as reigning in 1633-34.

C.P. 7, dated 1647-48, is a grant by Ranga, the adopted son of Gópála.

As Sadáṣiva was reigning in 1545-47, the date of P. 25 must be presumed to be wrong. Some of the other inscriptions probably relate to Ranga II, the son of Tirumala I, and it would appear that he first assumed royal dignity in 1575-76. Having regard, too, to R. 41 and P. 27, it would appear that the seat of Government was transferred to Penukonḍa in that year, but Mr. Sewell (p. 250, Vol. II, 'Antiquities') gives an earlier date.

C.P. 7 relates to Ranga VI.

Which Ranga O. 32 relates to is not clear to us.

U. 24 under date 1586-87 makes an allusion to a Ṣrí Rangaráyulu Ayyaváru who may not, however, have any connection with the family in question.

Timma or Tirumala.—C.P. 14 bears date 1549-50 and refers to Tirumala I. The sovereign Sadáṣiva is herein disposed of with the remark that he is an excellent man while his subject is loaded with titles of honour.

A. 15 mentions Konéru Timmarasu.

A. 16, dated 1549-50 or 1556-57, says that *Kónéṭi* Timmarájayya built the Átmakúr tank.

U. 20 speaks of Timmarázu son of the Mahámandaḷéṣvara Rámarája Konéṭayyadéva Mahárája.

U. 22, dated 1552-53, mentions Timmayadéva the son of the same person.

U. 44 speaks of Timma Rázu son of Kónéṭayya.

N. 104, dated 1551–52, mentions that Udayagiri *rájyam* formed a part of the dominion ruled by Mahámandalésvara Rámárájayya Tirumalayyadéva Mahárája.

A. 17, dated 1548–49, refers to a grant made under the orders of Sadáṣiva by Mahá Manḍaḷéṣvara Rámarázu Timmayadéva Mahárája to certain barbers in the Udayagiri *rájyam*.

G. 46, dated 1548–49, makes a reference to the same man and so does N. 112, dated 1558–59.

U. 19, dated 1615–16 or 1614–15, mentions a grant made by Timmayadéva Mahárája Ayyaváru but implies that he was no longer living. In this inscription he is referred to as having sat on the diamond throne.

U. 30, dated 1542–43, is not very clear but apparently means that Rámarázu Timmayadéva Mahárája and Aḷiya Rámayadéva Mahárája were in joint command of Udayagiri fort.

G. 113 and G. 114 of 1559–60 (?) and 1555–56 (?) refer to Mahámanḍaléṣvara Ráma Rázu Tirumala Rájayya.

O. 29, dated 1565–66, says that Sadáṣiva granted Konḍavíḍu *rájyam* to M. M. Ráma Rájayaran Tirumala Rájayyadéva Mahárája along with (apparently) Siddhirázu Rangaparájayyadéva.

V. 2 which bears an incorrect date gives Víra Pratápa Víra Tirumaladéva royal titles as well as the *biruda* Bhujabala.

The above inscriptions seem to refer to two persons. One of these is Kónéṭi Timma son of Rámarázu Kónéṭayya who plainly belonged to the branch of the Áravíḍu family headed by Pedda Konḍarája (see p. 4, Vol. IV, E.I.). His date is about the middle of the 16th century and he evidently held some important office in connection with Udayagiri.

The other person referred may be Tirumala I the grandson of Ráma I. If U. 30 refers to him, then, in 1542–43, he was governor of Udayagiri fort. Later he rose to a higher position, for he governed territories which included the Udayagiri *rájyam* and also apparently, Konḍavíḍu *rájyam*. Ranga II, the son of Tirumala I, seems to have assumed royal titles only about 1575–76, and it is not clear how Tirumala I can have ever formally occupied the throne, because Sadáṣivá's authority was nominally recognised up to that date. It is possible, therefore, that U. 2 and U. 19 refer to Tirumala II.

Venkaṭapati or *Venkaṭaráya.*—The inscriptions containing this name are as follows:—

U. 23 and U. 24; 1586–87 (ruling at Penukoṇḍa).
C. P. 6: 1602–03.
A. 53; 1602–03 (ruling at Vijayanagar).
A. 35; 1612–13.
R. 60; 1612–13 (ruling at Penukoṇḍa).
U. 19; 1614–15 or 1615–16.
A. 1; 1616–17.
G. 112; 1616–17 or 1617–17.
A. 48; 1621–22 (not quite clear as to whether Venkaṭapati was still ruling at the time).
R. 35; 1634–35 or 1644–45 (ruling at Penukoṇḍa).
R. 5; 1636–37 (ruling at Penukoṇḍa).
R. 6; 1636–37 (ruling at Penukoṇḍa).
KV. 10; 1636–37 (ruling at Penukoṇḍa).
KV. 49; 1636–37 or 1638–39 (ruling at Penukoṇḍa).
N. 33; 1645-46, says that Víra Pratápa Venkaṭádri Ayyaváru was ruling at Penukoṇḍa.
V. 24; 1662–63 (ruling at Penukoṇḍa).

Of the above inscriptions the first nine clearly relate to Venkaṭa I and they bring his latest date a little beyond that generally fixed.

Leaving out of consideration A. 48, the next five inscriptions appear to relate to Peda Venkaṭa II. The next, N. 33, may perhaps be of Chinna Venkaṭa III. The last inscription relates to a king whom we do not identify. He may have been ruling at Penukoṇḍa while Ranga VI was ruling at Chandragiri. It seems clear, at all events, that Penukoṇḍa remained a seat of government during part of the seventeenth century and that a century after Tálikóṭa the Vijayanagar dynasty had not lost its hold on the southern part of Nellore district. Mr. V. Venkayya, however, on page 15 E.R. for 1903–04 calls the reference to Penukoṇḍa in inscriptions of Venkaṭa I a mere boast. It will be noted that the capital is said in 1602–03 to be Vijayanagar whereas in 1586–87 and 1612–13 Penukoṇḍa is mentioned instead.

Ráma.—Ráma II seems to be referred to in the following inscriptions where he is styled Aḷiya, *i.e.*, son-in-law, on account of his marriage to the princess Tirumalámbá.

U. 30 of 1542-43, where he is mentioned as being in authority at Udayagiri, apparently along with Rámarázu Timmayadéva.

P. 35 of 1547-48, where we should doubtless read 'Ráma' for 'Gáma' and which describes him as bearing the burden of Sadáṣivá's kingdom.

G. 48 where we should read 'Rámayya' for 'Rávulaya'.

KG. 20 of 1554-55 is one of several grants to barbers. This is by Rámarájn Rámayyadéva which the others are by Aḷiya Rámayyadéva and Ráma Rázu Timmayyadéva. In KG. 20 also Ráma II seems to be referred to.

A. 3, dated 1628-29, shows Vira Pratápa Víra Rámadéva as ruling with royal titles. On page 26 of Vol. III of Epig. Carn. (introduction) we find it stated that Ranga II (son of Tirumala I) was succeeded on the throne by his son Venkaṭa whose grandson was Rámadéva whose date appears as 1620-25. The Rámadéva of A. 3 may be this man but the table opposite page 238 of Vol. III, E.I. does not agree with that given by Mr. Rice.

GOVERNORS OF UDAYAGIRI UNDER THE VIJAYANAGAR KINGS.

Under the Vijayanagar dynasty we have referred to several of the governors of Udayagiri because the fortress was considered of such great importance that the charge of it was frequently entrusted to some prince of the blood, even to the heir apparent. Udayagiri was, in fact, at one time the capital of, to speak roughly, the Nellore district and in KR. 27, it is called the chief fortress in the kingdom of Krishnadéva Ráya. A few other governors of Udayagiri fort and *rájyam* remain to be noticed. It seems from KR. 78 that the ruler of the *rájyam* occasionally employed a deputy to discharge his duties.

One of the most conspicuous of the governors of Udayagiri was Ráyasam (sc. secretary) Koṇḍa Marusayya who is mentioned in eighteen inscriptions of Udayagiri, Atmakúr, Kandukúr, Kanigiri, Podili and Rápúr all of which, no doubt, fell within the territories administered from Udayagiri, though it may be mentioned that the term *rájyam* is not employed in any of these inscriptions which range from 1514-15 to 1528-29. He was the son of one Timmarusayya and is called the *Káryakarta* for Krishnadéva Ráya. He is said to have built the large tanks at Anantaságaram and Kaluváya. He was evidently the first governor of

Udayagiri under the second Vijayanagar dynasty and Mr. Sewell's remark that Rámabhaṭlu was the first is erroneous.

Koṇḍamarusayya must have retired from office before 1528–29 (his last certain date is 1520–21 for KR. 77 shows that in 1527–28 the governor of Udayagiri was Ráyasam Ayyapparusu. Apparently he was transferred from Udayagiri, for in D. 33 of 1529–30 we find him governing the Koṇḍaviḍu *rájyam* as deputy, apparently, of Ráyasam Timmarusayya. His father's name is given as Vémarusayya.

There is no other clear reference to Ráyasam Timmarusayya.

N. 34 A of 1525–26 gives M. M. Rázu China Tirumala Rázu as being the ruler of Udayagiri with a local agent called Timmarázu Nandayya.

G. 108, dated 1530–31, gives Salakarázu Tirumalayyadéva various titles and says that the Chandragiri *rájyam* was in his dominions.

G. 82 of 1533–34 mentions Timma Nayuḍu the agent of M.M. Salaká . . . Tirumala Déva.

U. 42, dated 1533–34, mentions M.M. Salaṛázu Pina Tirumalayyadéva.

It is not quite clear whether these last four inscriptions relate to the same man. If they do, he would appear to have followed Koṇḍamarusayya as governor of Udayagiri and to have also governed the Chandragiri *rájyam*. Salakaráju Chinna Tirumalayyadéva is mentioned in the list of great officers of the Vijayanagar kings appearing on page 249, Vol. II of Mr. Sewell's 'Antiquities.'

Under date 1535–36, in KR. 78, we find Bhútanátha Rámabhaṭlu ruling Udayagiri *durgam* with Venkaṭádri as deputy. The latter is mentioned again in V. 8 and is no doubt the donor in KG. 17. Another subordinate governor (ádhipati) was Chivvakalúru Bayacha Rájaya whose date was 1551–52 (see N. 104). The name suggests the Bácharusayya of O. 23, but they are probably not the same.

In addition to the above, the Konéṭi family seems to have had some official connection with Udayagiri. That family is referred to under the third Vijayanagar dynasty.

From A. 53, of 1602-03, it seems that one M.M. Satti Rája Srí Muddayyadéva Mahárája bestowed the *rájyam* of Udayagiri on M.M. Muddayyadéva Mahárája Venkata I being then on the throne.

These persons are the last governors of Udayagiri mentioned in this collection and there do not seem to be any references to them elsewhere.

GOVERNORS OF KONDAVÍDU UNDER THE VIJAYANAGAR KINGS.

(1) It seems to be now established that Sáluva Narasimha, the principal minister of the last king of the first Vijayanagar dynasty, usurped the throne before the advent of the second or Tuluva dynasty and that he had a son Immadi Narasimha and an elder brother Timma.

One Maparusayya appears in A. 27 as the son of Srímat Sáluva Narusappaya and the following two Ongole inscriptions show that the family held important office under the second dynasty:—

O. 46, dated 1510–11, mentions that Saluva Timmarusayya received Kondavídu *rájyam* from the king (Krishnadéva).

O. 71 (date doubtful but perhaps 1517–18), calls Sáluva Timmarasu the protector (Pratipálaka) of the whole kingdom of Krishnadéva.

It will be observed from O. 46 that the *rájyam* of Kondavídu was bestowed on Sáluva Timma before the stronghold of Kondavídu was captured from the Orissa king and Timma made a grantof land in the *rájyam* in 1510–11. From this it is to be gathered that the Gajapati king was not in effective occupation of the northern parts of Nellore though he held the forts of Udayagiri and Kondavídu. For Sáluva Timma see also p. 86 (Appendix) of Vol. VII, E.I. and p. 249, Vol. II of Sewell's 'Antiquities.'

(2) O. 23, dated 1533–34, gives Bácharusayya as prime minister of Achyutadéva and ruler of Kondavídu *durgam*. Doubtless we get the same officer in O. 77 of 1534–35 (?) where he appears as "Bába Kásayyavárn who is skilled in bearing the burden of the kingdom of Achyutadéva." The name has been transcribed wrongly in one or the other.

(3) O. 31, dated 1558–89, mentions M.M. Siddhi Ráju Timmarájayyadéva as ruler of Kondavídu in subordination to Sadásiva.

D. 14 probably relates to the same person.

(4) O. 29 of 1565–66 gives the following pedigree :—

Siddhirázu
|
Obuḷarázu
|
Timmarázu
|
Rangappa Rázu.

Apparently the last-named was ruling the Konḍavíḍu *rájyam* along with Rámaráju Tirumala Rájayadéva for whom see under the Vijayanagar third dynasty. He is plainly the son of the Timmarájayya of O. 31.

CERTAIN OTHER SUBORDINATES OF THE VIJAYANAGAR KINGS.

There remain to be mentioned certain other persons who held positions of some importance under the Vijayanagar kings either as vassal chiefs or officials.

(1) P. 26, dated 1426–27, mentions Şríman Mahámanḍaléşvara Médiní Mísaraganḍa Kaṭhári Sáḷuva Samburáyadéva Mahárája the son of Ráya Vibháḷadéva Mahárája.

P. 39, of 1438–39, refers to the same family and gives the following pedigree :—

S.M.M. Médiní Mísaraganḍa Kaṭhári
Sáḷuva Dharaní Varáha Peda Samburáya
of the Lunar race.
|
(Titles as above) Telungaráyaḷésunḍa Bhúpa Góvinda — King (Kshmápála) Pedaráya Vibhála.
|
King (Kshmápála) Jagatába Singa of the Solar race married Tippaladéví (1438–39).
|
King (Kshmápála) Timma.

We have unfortunately no other references to this line of chiefs. The question of its connection with the second Vijayanagar dynasty is discussed by Mr. J. Rámayya at p. 74 *et seq.* of Vol. VII, E.I.

It is not apparent who is referred to under the name Jagatába (Jagadobba?) Singa of the Solar race.

(2) N. 28, under date 1346–47, records a grant by Mudra Chiddi Sáyanna Oḍaya the prime minister (Mahápradháni) of Kampaṇáṭi Oḍayar, the lord of the Eastern and Western seas.

From the same place comes the undated inscription N. 29 which mentions Sáyánna Oḍaya.

N. 78, dated 1364–65, declares that S.M. Víra Ṣrí Sávaṇṇa Oḍaya was ruling the Earth O. 25 mentions Ṣrí Sayaṇam Dévara and calls him "entitled to the Panchamaháṣabda, Mancha Malléṣvara, Parama Mahéṣvara, lord of the town of Anumakoṇḍa."

Probably all these inscriptions refer to the same person who seems to have held high office under Kampa I and his son Ṣangama II.

Mr. Sewell, on p. 125, Vol. II, 'Antiquities,' gives an inscription of Sáyaṇa Uḍaiyár from Conjeeveram.

(3) N. 35, of the year Pingaḷa, mentions S.M.M. Cháḷikya Náráyaṇa Chauhattamalla Raṇa Vijaya Velamapáṭi Tirumala Rájayadéva Mahárája.

N. 112, of 1558–59, states that the *ṣíma* of Udayagiri was granted by S.M.M. Rámárájuyara Timmaya Dévara Mahárája to S.S.M. Vera (Ven?) galayya Déva Mahárája, bearing titles as in N. 35. This person seems to have claimed Chálukyan ancestry but we cannot identify him.

(4) O. 31, dated 1558–59, mentions one Mandapáṭi Appala Ráju as governing the *ṣímas* of Ammanabrólu and Addanki in subordination to the governor of Koṇḍaviḍu

Possibly the Rája of Yenḍlúru, Mandapáṭi Kumára Rámabhadra Rája, referred to in O. 102 of 1762–63, was a member of the same family of which an account is given on p. 735 of the District Manual.

(5) C.P. 18 is a grant of Dévaráya II, dated 1428–29. It gives the genealogy of a certain Panṭa Mailára as follows :—

Súra
|
Póta
|
Mummaḍíndra (married) Mumbámbá
|
Panṭa Mailárá or Panṭa Malla.

Mailára had the *birudas Dharanivaráha* and *Chauhatta Malla*. He was also *Ghanṭanáḍa*. It appears that he had helped Dévaráya in war and at his request the king granted a village in Ongole Taluk to certain Brahmans. We find the same chief referred to in O. 30 and O. 104. The former is of 1482–83 and alludes to a grant formerly made by Panṭa Maila Reḍḍi through Prauḍha Dévaráya

Maháraya. The latter, of 1424–25, refers to a grant made by one Mummiḍi Reḍḍi called Ṣríman Mahámanḍalêṣvara, Chauhatta-malla, Ghanṭanáḍaka, etc., while Mailára Reḍḍi, son of Panṭa Mummaḍi Reḍḍi, was ruling Palinḍipáḍu. Whether the donor Mummaḍi Reḍḍi made the grant previously and was the father of Mailára Reḍḍi who confirmed it is not, however, quite clear.

YÁDAVARÁYA CHIEFS OF EASTERN CHÁLUKYAN DESCENT.

On page 208, 'South Indian Inscriptions,' Vol. III, part II, Vol. XXIX of the new series of the Archæological Survey of India, Dr. Hultzsch mentions—

(1) Yádavaráya Tirukkáḷattidéva of the 16th and 17th of Kulóttunga III and

(2) his son Yádavaráya Víra Narasimhadéva of the 36th and 37th of Kulóttunga III and the 8th of Rájarája III.

Dr. Hultzsch adds that they bore the *birudas* Véngivallabha and Ṣaṣikula-Cháḷukki, thus claiming descent from the Eastern Chálukyas. He mentions also "Simha *alias* Víraráksbasa Yádavarája son of Yádavárája *alias* Tirukkáḷattidéva" of the 15th of Kulóttunga III; and inscriptions of the 34th and 40th years of Tribhuvanachakravarti Víra Narasimhadéva Yádaváraya and of the [8]th of Tribhuvanachakravarti Tiruvéngaḍanátha Yádaváraya.

We find in our collection the following references to these rulers:—

V. 1 of 1230–31 and the 15th of Rájarájadéva (III) gives us Kamala Mahádéví *alias* Bejjadéví, the wife of Rájamalladéva *alias* Bhujabalasiddharasa *alias* Yádaváraya.

V. 3 of the 15th of Rájarájadéva (*i.e.*, 1230–31) is a grant by the same lady and states that the town of Nágapuḍól was founded by her (probably meaning her husband).

V. 4 of the 19th of Rájarájadéva (*i.e.*, 1234–35) is a grant by Kásáṇmai the son of Yádaváraya.

V. 6 of the 11th of Rájarájadéva (*i.e.*, 1226–27) mentions Toṇḍaimán Arrúr Kántaráyan, the prime minister of Yádaváráyan *alias* Kaṭṭidévarasan.

V. 7 calls Yádavarája "the glorifier of the Yádava race, Mahá Maṇḍalésvara, lord of Kanuchára (Kanchi ?), of the race of Ṣaṣikula Chálukki." It also states that he caused a grant to be made by Madurántaka Pottapi Chóḷa Errasiddharasa whom he "brought (for the purpose)." This seems to imply that Errasiddharasa was ruling in subordination to him.

Vs. 8 and 9 mention Yádaváraya of Nágapuḍól and Témáṇḍi Ammai the wife of Bhujabala Siddharasa.

V. 10 says that Piḷḷaiyár Bhujabala Siddharasa declared in the 39th of Kulóttunga Chóḷadéva (1216–17) his intention to found the town of Nágopuḍól and that in the second of Rájarájadéva (1217–18) the image of (?) Madurántaka Pottapi Chóḷa [Erra] Siddharasan was set up.

V. 11 says that Rájamalladévan *alias* Bhujabala Siddharasa was the son of . . . . Kaṭṭidévarasan who was "the best of the Yádavas, possessor of the five Maháṣabdas, Mahámaṇḍalésvara, lord of Kanchavárapura (Kanchi ?) and Vengi, samastharájaṣráyan, head of the Ṣaṣikula Chálukki race." It adds that he created through Madurántaka Pottapi Chóḷa Errasiddharasa the town of Nágapuḍól in Pákkaiṇáḍu.

V. 13 refers to the same chief and is of the 39th of Kulóttunga Chóḷadéva.

V. 16 is a grant by Véngivallabhan who is one of the same line no doubt.

All these inscriptions are of Chápalapalli village. How these rulers stand relatively to each other and to those named by Dr. Hultzsch is by no means clear.

The same line may be represented in V. 19 which mentions (probable date 1233–34) a chief of Mópúru or Periyamunoppúr called Chalukki Náráyaṇa Manumasittiyarasar.

APPENDIX II.

INDEX OF INSCRIPTIONS IN ACCORDANCE WITH DATES.

(This index excludes those inscriptions which do not bear a Ṣaka date.)

10th Century.

945–46, C.P. 19,
968–69, P. 38.

11th Century.

1088–9, O. 92,

12th Century.

1111–12, O. 79 (?),
1118–19, O. 128,
1124–25, KV. 3,
1134–35, D. 41,
1141–42, D. 39,
1144–45, D. 40,
1145–46, D. 48,
1147–48, D. 68,
1148–49, O. 142,
1153–54, O. 19,
1154–55, D. 43, O. 50,
1155–56, O. (18), O. 51,
1166–67, D. 49, O. 28 A,
1167–68, D. 38, O. 59, O. 60,
1170–71, D. 45,
1182–83, N. 16,
1183–84, N. 106,
1184–85, KG. 31,
1187–88, KV. 10, A. 24, O. 90,
1188–89, KV. 8,
1190–91, N. 40,
1192–93 (?) G. 50,
1193–94, N. 118,
1197–98, N. 55,
1198–99, KV. 51.

13th Century.

1204–05, N. 111,
1207–08, KV. 39,
1208–09, O. 76,
1209–00, KR. 29,
1211–12, R. 47,
1213–14, R. 8,
1214–15, KV. 13,
1217–18, R. 36, KV. 31, A. 38, O. 120,
1218–19, D. 69, N. 103, O. 17 (1), O. 45, O. 139,
1219–20, D. 57, D. 60,
1221–22, N. 109, O. 110,
1223–24, V. 19,

1226–27, V. 6,
1227–28, N. 102, O. 17 (2), V. 15, V. 20,
1228–29, KV. 38, V. 5,
1230–31, V. 1, KV. 45, KV. 47, V. 3,
1231–32, R. 65,
1233–34, V. 17,
1234–35, V. 4,
1236–37 R. 70, V. 2,
1237–38, KR. 22,
1239–40, O. 86, O. 88,
1242–43, G. 8,
1243–44, R. 39, N. 121,
1244–45, U. 3, KV. 25,
1245–46, U. 14,
1246–47, A. 7,
1247–48, G. 27, R. 20, O. 138,
1248–49, O. 34, O. 151,
1249–50, G. 17,
1250–51, O. 103,
1251–52, KV. 24,
1252–53, U. 48,
1253–54, O. 27, O. 28,
1254–55, KG. 11, D. 25, D. 28, P. 17, O. 67, O. 89,
1256–57, G. 39, O. 150,
1257–58, P. 9,
1258–59, KR. 26, KR. 60,
1259–60, KR. 61,
1260–61, P. 7, P. 10, KR. 62,
1261–62, KR. 63,
1263–64, G. 85, G. 90, KV. 43,
1264–65, KV. 26,
1267–68, KR. 64, D. 24, N. 97, O 143,
1268–69, KG. 24, G. 11, KR. 50, KR. 65, N. 30, O. 6,
1269–70, G. 9, KR. 66,
1271–72, O. 16,
1272–73, KR. 57, D. 1, D. 72, N. 21,
1273–74, KV. 48, KR. 53, O. 101,
1274–75, KV. 19, KV. 21, KV. 29, A. 14, A. 51,
1275–76, KV. 22, A. 29, O. 70, O. 82,
1276–77, KV. 23, KV. 28, G. 29,
1277–78, KV. 30, KR. 58, A. 13,
1278–79, KV. 27,
1279–80, G. 45, A. 11,
1280–81, KR. 43, N. 73, O. 75,
1281–82, O. 123,
1283–84, A. 25, O. 130,
1284–85, N. 31,
1286–87, A. 57,
1289–90, P. 32, G. 66,
1290–91, A. 55, O. 99,
1291–92, D. 6,
1293–94, O. 54, O. 129,
1294–95, KR. 84,
1296–97, N. 31,
1297–98, O. 87,
1298–99, O. 49,
1299–00, G. 115, N. 62,
1300–01, O. 136.

14th Century.

1301–02, N. 60,
1302–03, KR. 52,
1305–06, D. 70,
1306–07, O. 54,
1309–10, KV. 35, KV. 37,
1310–11, D. 35, O. 58, O. 98, O. 149,
1312–13, KV. 36,

15*th Century.*

16*th Century.*

17th Century.

1636–37, R. 5, R. 6, KV. 49, KV. 50,
1637–38, R. 49, R. 50, R. 53,
1638–39, R. 3, R. 7, R. 25, R. 28, R. 30, R. 34, R. 40, R. 43, R. 51, R. 54, R. 63, R. 74, R. 79, KV. 46, N. 1, N. 4, N. 7, N. 11, N. 26, N. 47, N. 99, N. 114, N. 116,
1640–41, KR. 20,
1641–42, KR. 80,
1642–43, U. 39, P. 13, KV. 1,
1643–44, KR. 12,
1644–45, KR. 4,
1645–46, N. 83,
1647–48, C.P. 7,
1650–51, KR. 44, KR. 47, KR. 48,
1651–52, KG. 1,
1652–53, C.P. 81,
1653–54, N. 5,
1657–58, KG. 16,
1659–60, V. 23,
1660–61, U. 36,
1661–62, U. 26, U. 27,
1662–63, V. 24,
1672–73, D. 31,
1675–76, D. 62,
1682–83, R. 68, KR. 46,
1683–84, KR. 41,
1684–85, R. 15,
1687–88, C.P. 9,
1688–89, G. 84,
1697–98, A. 23,
1698–99, G. 19.

18th Century.

1706–07, N. 96,
1709–00, D. 3,
1712–13, G. 52,
1715–16, KV. 44,
1718–19, D. 61,
1726–27, D. 3,
1739–40, O. 106,
1746–47, C.P. 4,
1756–57, N. 3,
1762–63, A. 9, O. 102,
1766–67, KG. 9,
1771–72, A. 50,
1778–79, O. 137,
1781–82, A. 10,
1785–86, KG. 28,
1789–90, KV. 20,
1791–92, G. 83 (?),
1794–95, S. 18.

19th Century.

1802–03, KR. 42.

APPENDIX III.

WEIGHTS AND MEASURES.

The following particulars are gathered from Macleane's "Manual of Administration" under the heads Nellore and Chingleput :—

Weights.

1 pagoda weight = 52½ grains troy.
1 tola = 180 grains troy.
10 kurruck pagodas or 3 tolas = 1 pollam.
8 pollams or 24 tolas = 1 pucka seer.
5 seers or 120 tolas = 1 viss.
8 viss or 960 tolas = 1 maund (100 pounds troy).
20 maunds = 1 candy or puṭṭi.

Land measures.

1 cubit = 19·68 inches.
32 cubits = 1 rod.
1 rod square = 2,756¼ square feet = 1 gunṭa = ·0633 acre.
50 guntas = 1 gurtu or gorru = 3·1637 acres.

For garden lands a rod of 21 cubits or 34⅔⅔ English feet was employed. The gunṭa was then ·02725 acre and 116 went to the gurtu or gorru.

Grain measures.

4 chittis = 1 sola = 70 tolas of rice heaped.
4 solas = 1 munta = 280 tolas or 3½ pucka seers.
4 muntas = 1 kuncham = 1,120 tolas or 14 pucka seers.
4 kunchams = 1 túm, about a hundred-weight.
20 túms = 1 candy or puṭṭi, about a ton.

The túm corresponds with the markál which was subdivided into 8 measures.

The following relate to the Chingleput District, but may be found applicable in the case of some of the inscriptions from the south of Nellore :—

Weights.

3 tolas = 1 pollam.
8 pollams = 1 cutcha seer.
40 pollams = 1 viss or 3·0857 lbs. avoir.
50 pollams = 1 túk.
5 viss = 1 túlám.
8 viss = 1 maund of 24·6857 lbs. avoir.
20 maunds = 1 candy or bárum.

There is also a pucka seer of 72 tolas.

Land measures.

28 aḍis = 1 kol (24 Eng. feet).
1 square kol = 1 kuzhi = 576 square feet.
100 kuzhis = 1 káni = 57,600 square feet = 1·3 acres.

There were, however, several kánis in existence.

Grain measures.

124 tolas' weight of rice = 1 paḍi (measure).
8 paḍis = 1 markál.
12 markáls = 1 kallam.
33⅓ kallams = 1 garce.

There were, however, local variations from these measures.

APPENDIX IV.

THE MONTHS.

(FROM THE INDIAN CALENDAR BY R. SEWELL AND S. BALAKRISHNA DIKSHIT.)

Serial No.	Zodiacal sign.	Tamil name.	Sanskrit name.	
			Old.	New.
1	Mesha	Chittirai ...	Mádhava ...	Vaiśákha.
2	Vṛishabha ...	Vaigási or Vaiyási.	Śukra	Jyéshtha.
3	Mithuna ...	Áni	Śuchi	Áshádha.
4	Karka	Áḍi	Nabhas ...	Śrávaṇa.
5	Simha	Ávaṇi	Nabhasya ...	Bhádrapada.
6	Kanyá	Puraṭṭási or Puraṭṭádi.	Isha	Áśvina.
7	Tulá	Aippaśi or Arppiśi.	Úrja	Kárttika.
8	Vṛiśchika ...	Kárttigai ...	Sahas	Márgaśírsha.
9	Dhanus ...	Márgaḷi ...	Sahasya ...	Pausha.
10	Makara ...	Tai	Tapas	Mágha.
11	Kumbha ...	Mási	Tapasya ...	Phálguna.
12	Mína	Panguni ...	Madhu	Chaitra.

APPENDIX V.

TERRITORIAL DIVISIONS.

The inscriptions mention various territorial divisions but it is not possible to give the modern equivalents with any approach to accuracy. Not all the divisions mentioned were in existence simultaneously and such Sanskrit terms as *déśa* and *vishaya* are probably intended generally as mere translations of local vernacular terms, though in later times the former word represented a definite area.

The unit is, of course, the village or *úru* and the first grouping of villages is perhaps the *sthaḷa*, though that term is also used in the general sense of "locality" and apparently in the sense of "chief town" too. The *sthiti* and the *daṇḍampáḍ* are rarely used except when the former has the general sense of "place." Whether these two terms denoted fixed territorial divisions is doubtful. The *sammatu* is another rare term.

The most common division in the Telugu inscriptions is the *śíma* which clearly formed a part of the *náḍu*. Perhaps the *śíma* corresponded as nearly as anything else to the modern *firka*. In one inscription the Rápúr *śíma* appears as a sub-division of the Nellore *vanita* a word which does not recur in this collection. The term *kampana* appears also once or twice, perhaps as equivalent to *śíma*.

The *náḍu* is a very common term in both Telugu and Tamil inscriptions and the Sanskrit *vishaya* is sometimes used as equivalent thereto as we find from V. 19 of C.P. 20 where reference is made to the *vishaya* of Páka, *i.e.*, Pákináḍu. It was a large area in some cases as shown by O. 73 where Púnginádu is described as extending on both sides of the Gunḍlakamma river from the vicinity of the eastern fort of Ṣrígiri (Ṣríśailam in Kurnool) to the eastern sea. Roughly the Telugu *nádu* may correspond with the modern taluk.

In the Telugu inscriptions nothing seems to be recognized between the *nádu* and the *rájyam* which latter was an area ruled by an important governor in the days of the Vijayanagar empire when the bulk of the district fell within the Udayagiri *rájyam*, though the extreme north appertained to Kondavíḍu *rájyam* and the south to the Chandragiri *rájyam*.

In the Tamil inscriptions the *koṭṭam* comes in between the *náḍu* and the *maṇḍalam* which latter term may be taken to correspond with the Telugu *rájyam*.

The Tamil inscriptions also refer to places as being within such-and-such a *náḍu* forming a portion of such-and-such another *náḍu*. These sub-*náḍus* appear to take the place of the *śímas* of the Telugu inscriptions.

In fact it may be doubted whether the Tamil *náḍu* itself amounted to much more than the Telugu *śíma* having in view the large number of *náḍus* into which the southern half of the district is divided in the Tamil inscriptions.

We give below, separately for the Telugu and the Tamil inscriptions, the various divisions of the Nellore district as they appear in this collection :—

TELUGU.

Rájyams.

Udayagiri.
Konḍavíḍu.
Chandragiri.

Náḍus.

Páka or Pánka or Páki.
Tonkakúḍúru (?).
Angaḍamanta.
Púngi.
Kamma.
Vela.
Cheḍupúli (?).
Paḍa.
Kandukúru (?).

(It is doubtful whether any part of this district fell within the Velanáḍu.)

Símas.

Udayagiri.
Rápúr.
Nellúru.
Pórúru (*alias* Nidugantakóṭa and Piḍainádu).
Konḍamapáḍu.
Venkatagiri.
Korṭúru.
Kullúru.
Prabhákarapaṭnam.
Eastern Paḍanáḍu (?).
Sarvapalli.
Kanigiri.
Kanigiri-Pólicherla.
Musumḍúru.
Podili.
Addanki.
Ammanabrólu.
Daiyálaráyúru.
Kandukúru.
Chúnḍi.
Jaladanki.
Duddura (?)
Puritináḍu (?)

TAMIL.

Maṇḍalams.

Jayankonḍachóḻa *alias* Rájendrachóḻa.
Malai.

Koṭṭams.

Paiyúrilam.
Maṇaviṟ.
Puliyúr.
Pavvattiri or Kaḍalkonḍa Pavvattiri.

Náḍus.

Mándai.
Séla.
Pottappi.
Singaṭṭai or Singapai (?)
Pákkai.
Mél.
Paṭṭaiyúr.
Nellúr.
Angaḍipátta.
Mélaipaṭṭaiya.
Kíḻapaṭṭaiya.
Chedikulamánikkavala (with a sub-division Paḍai or Maḍai).
Valluva.
Pérúr.
Péraṭti.
Mungaláṟattai.
Kaḍaiyasinga.
Púngai.
Poḷigai (or Pónagai ?).
Tongaipúnul.
Chakala.
Kulóttungachóḻavaḷa.
Venga.
Kákkalúr.
Vélúr.
Kamalai.
Jayakulamánikkavala.

Sub-Náḍus.

Madainallúr.
Munḍainádu.
Rápúr.
Paḍainádu (also called Péḍai, Piḍai and Paṭṭai).
Paḍikámanáḍu (also Pagámanáḍu).
Okkáṭṭunáḍu.
Maḍainádu (perhaps Paḍainádu).

It will be noticed that the Tamil *náḍus* Pákkai and Púngai and sub-*náḍu* Paḍai bear the same names as three of the Telugu *náḍus* while the Tamil *náḍu* Nellúr and sub-*náḍu* Rápúr bear the same names as two of the Telugu *śímas*.

The *náḍus* and *śímas* can sometimes be roughly located by the mention of villages situated therein, but the preparation of any sort of map showing the old divisions of the district is impossible.

In Muhammadan times we get such territorial terms as the *Sarkár* (Udayagiri S., Sarvapalli S., Kambham S.), the *Zilla* and the *Pargana*. For the last two we find modern equivalents in the terms "District" and "Division" respectively. The Sarkár is mentioned in C.P. 4 where it is used to denote an area which may best be translated by "Division."

GLOSSARY OF REVENUE AND OTHER TERMS.

A

Aḍḍa, a measure equal to 2 *mánikas* or one-eighth of a túm.

Ágámi, future profits, a term used in grants and leases.

Agrahâram, a grant of land to Brahmans.

Akshini "imperishables", a term used in grants and leases.

Amaradár or amaragáḍu, the holder of an *amaram*.

Amaram, a grant of the revenue of a tract of land on condition of military or police service.

Amji, labour customarily exacted without payment in regard to certain works, *e.g.*, the repair of tanks and channels.

Amritapaḍi, the food of a god, ambrosia.

Anikat, a dam across a river.

Archaka, chief priest in a temple.

B

Báṛa, a fathom, 6 feet.

Bhanḍáram, W says this means a village managed directly by the proprietor, but in O. 89 the word clearly means a grant of land on favourable rent. This agrees with B's explanation of the phrase *banḍáraváḍa grámam*.

Bhóga, enjoyment, the food offered to an idol.

Bhóga manḍapam, the part of a temple where food is prepared for the idol.

Biruda, a title.

Bráhmanáḍáyam or Brahmáḍáyam, a grant to a Brahman.

C

Chakra Varahá, perhaps the same as B.'s *Karuku Varahá* which is Rs. 4. The ordinary *chakram* according to B is $\frac{1}{16}$th of the pagoda.

Chinnam, a weight and also a coin worth $\frac{1}{2}$th of the pagoda or 7 annas.

Chódana, a liquid measure. In Malabar it is 341$\frac{1}{4}$ cubic inches. In Nellore the measure seems to be no longer used.

Chunam, lime, mortar.

D

Danḍam, a measure of 10 *hasta* or cubits.

Daśabandham, an assignment of revenue for the upkeep, usually if not always, of a tank. According to B the grantee pays one-tenth of the usual assessment; according to W nine-tenths. According to other authorities the grantee appropriates ten-sixteenths and pays six-sixteenths to the grantor.

Déṣai, the administration of a *pargaṇa*; the principal revenue officer of a district according to W, but in KR. 41 the word must refer to a less important class of officer; we may translate as "Divisional officer."

Déṣamukh, the chief revenue and police officer over the group of villages constituting the *déṣa*.

Désastha, apparently merely a title of Mahrátha Brahmans.

Dévadáyam, a grant to a temple.

Dharmakarta, the trustee of a charitable grant or temple.

Dommara, the juggler and acrobat caste.

Duggáṇi, ten *kásu*, about half an anna.

Durgam, a fort, fastness.

E

Ekabhógam, land held by a single individual or family.

G

Gadya, a coin, value not known.

Gadyánam, perhaps the same as *gadya*.

Gócharma, 10 *nivartanas*, apparently a square of 4,500 feet.

Gópuram, the pyramidal gateway of a Dravidian temple.

Gorru, a variable measure of land, commonly equal to 3·1637 acres.

Gótra, the family stock within which marriage is prohibited.

Gunṭa, a pond, also a land measure equal according to B, to $\frac{1}{50}$th or $\frac{1}{125}$th of a *gorru* which is generally about $3\frac{1}{8}$ acres. In these Nellore inscriptions the *gunṭa* may be taken as equal to $2,756\frac{1}{4}$ square feet or ·0633 acre, being $\frac{1}{50}$th of a *gorru*. In the case of garden lands, however, the *gunṭa* is only ·02725 acre or $\frac{1}{116}$th of a *gorru* (see Macleane's 'Manual of Administration').

Gurtu, the same as *gorru*.

Guru, a spiritual teacher.

H

Havildar for the various meanings see W. In these inscriptions it probably means a subordinate revenue officer.

I

Ijára, a lease or farm of land or revenue or taxes.

Inám, a grant of land or assignment of revenue.

Irasan, a measure. B. says half a *túm* which would be 28 pucka seers, but W. says 24 seers.

J

Jangam, a sect worshipping Basava and obnoxious to Brahmans as denying their claims to sanctity.

Jonna, the great millet, known also as chólam and jowári.

K

Kalanju, the weight of $1\frac{1}{3}$ pagoda coins.

Kampana, a territorial division.

Kánuka, a gift to a superior, a compulsory "benevolence."

Kápu or *Kámpu*, a cultivator. The word is also used in the sense of *Peddakápu* or principal ryot or village headman.

Kárkún, a subordinate revenue officer, a revenue inspector.

Karnam, the village accountant.

Káru, preceding the name of a crop indicates that it is sown in the wet season.

Káryakarta, an agent.

Kasba, the chief town of any given area.

Kasba Kápu, the headman of a *kasba* town.

Kásu, a coin of gold, silver or copper; the copper *kásu* was worth about $\frac{1}{20}$th of a penny.

Katnam, a present to a superior, a compulsory "benevolence."

Kávali, watch and ward.

Kétaki, a plant which B terms *Pandanus odoratissimus* (*i.e.* the screw-pine).

Khandrika, a portion of a village granted free or at a favourable rent.

Kómati, the shopkeeper caste.

Kóru, land the produce of which is shared by Government. Commonly used in opposition to the terms zamíndárí and inám.

Kuchchala, a land measure equal to 8 *gorrus*; it may be taken at 25 acres in Nellore, though B gives the equivalent in Kistna as 29 acres.

Kuli, a square measure varying, according to W from 1 square foot to 25,600 square feet. In these inscriptions it is probably used to denote 576 square feet.

Kuncham or *kunchadu*, 4 *mánikas* or *muntas* or $\frac{1}{4}$ of the *túm* which is, roughly, a hundred weight.

Kunta, same as *gunta*.

L

Lagna, the rising of a sign of the zodiac, the moment of the sun's entry into a sign.

Lingam, the representation of Siva in the form of the male organ.

M

Má, a land measure equal to $\frac{1}{20}$th of a *véli*.

Máda or *mádai*, half a pagoda, *i.e.*, Rs. 2 or Rs. 1—12—0.

Madi, a wet field but it seems to have been also a definite measure of land—*vide* O. 54.

Mádiga, the cobbler caste.

Mahájanam, the principal people of the village.

Mála, a Pariah.

Mandalam, a division of territory; perhaps we may translate it "province."

Mandali Kápu, headman of a village according to W, but perhaps of rank superior to the ordinary headman.

Maṇḍapam or *manṭapam*, a porch, portico or pavilion supported on pillars.

Mandya, some measure of land.

Mánika, one-fourth of the *kuncham* or 280 *tólas*.

Mányam, a grant of land or revenue in return for services to be rendered to the community.

Marutu, an unknown measure of grain and land.

Maṭha, an establishment of religious persons, monastery, college.

Maṭlu, plural probably of *maṭṭu* and used to denote some measure of land.

Méra, a fee in grain or money paid by villagers for the upkeep of certain offices, services or institutions.

Mirásidár, one having a hereditary title to property or office.

Mótarfa, the tax upon the profits of those exercising manual arts or professions.

Mudám, a village police-officer.

Mukhása, land assigned in return for service to be discharged. For other meanings see W.

Mulumu, according to B, a stubble field; according to W, land cultivated with millet; translated as garden land in the text. The word does not seem to be in common use in Nellore.

Múlavisálabaḍi perhaps means "the original tax levied proportionately upon the profits of traders." See W. under *Visabaḍi*.

Munta, one-fourth of the *kuncham*; apparently in Nellore the same measure as *mánika*.

N

Náḍu, a division of the *manḍalam* or *rájyam* or province.

Nakshatra, a star, one of the 27 constellations through which the moon passes.

Nambi, a priest performing ordinary rites in a Vaishṇava temple.

Nayaka, a military chief, poligar, assistant to a revenue officer—often assumed as a title of honour.

Nishka, a gold coin said by B. to be equivalent in value to the máḍa.

P

Pádisháh, king, sultán.

Panḍit, a learned Brahman, especially one who studies Sanskrit.

Pannu, tax, tribute, customs.

Pargana, a sub-division of the zilla or district.

Párupatagáḍu, W gives Canarese Párupatyagára as meaning a manager or superintendent. This is, doubtless, the same word. We have translated it "revenue inspector."

Parva, a sacred period such as full-moon day, the 8th, 11th and 14th day of the lunar half-month, the solstices, equinoxes and so on (W).

Paṭṭi, apparently the same as *paṭṭu*.

Paṭṭu, evidently a definite measure of land but B and W do not give the word in this sense.

Pon, a gold coin of variable value. Under the Company it was the star pagoda worth about Rs. 3½. It is probably the same as the *hún*. *Pon* and *honnu* are etymologically the same word and *hún* seems to be derived from the latter.

Prākāra, the enclosure in which a temple stands.

Pullari, a tax on pasture lands.

Puṭṭi, a measure of 20 *túms* or, roughly, a ton. As a land measure, according to W, it equals about 8 acres being, presumably, the area which can be sown with a *puṭṭi* of grain.

Pújári, a temple priest.

R

Rájyam, territory ruled by an independent king or by a dependent ruler or governor.

Rishi, an ascetic, inspired teacher.

Rūka, a silver or gold coin of variable value.

S

Śákha, a sub-division of the Vedas.

Samatu, apparently a division of the *Śíma*.

Sán, a measure of, it is said, 9 inches.

Sanad, a grant, charter, patent.

Sandhátá, apparently the Canarese *Sandáyita*, which W. describes as meaning land, not let, but managed by the proprietor or an officer of government direct. The same word seems to be used to denote the manager of such land.

Sandhyá, sunrise, noon and sunset.

Sankránti, the point of time at which the sun enters a fresh zodiacal sign. There are 12 of these *Sankrántis* and four correspond with the equinoxes and solstices.

Sarvá-mányam, a grant made free of all charges so far as regards the grantor.

Śásanam, an edict, inscription.

Seṭṭi, a merchant.

Síma, a division of the *náḍu*.

Sthala, a 'place', but also seems to denote some definite sub division of territory, probably a small group of villages; also, apparently, used in much the same sense as *kasba*.

Sthala Karnam, the accountant for the tract known as a *sthala*.

Sthiti, some territorial division apparently, also used generally in the sense of locality.

Sunkam, toll or tax.

Sútra, creed, precepts, institutes, sect.

T

Tavvaḍu, half a *munta* or 140 tólas.

Tithi, a lunar day; one-thirtieth of the time taken by the moon to move through a synodical revolution.

Tóṭi, an inferior village servant or *veṭṭi*; a scavenger.

Túm, roughly represents a hundred weight; it is 4,480 tolas. As a land measure, according to B, the *túm* is $\frac{1}{1}\frac{2}{5}$ths of an acre, but this seems improbable if the *puṭṭi* is only 8 acres.

U

Uppara, the tank-digging caste.

Utsava, the ceremony of carrying the idol out of the temple ; a festival.

V

Vaḍḍa or *Voḍḍa* appertaining to the Woḍḍar or tank-digger caste.

Vanita, some sort of territorial division.

Varahá, the coin known as the pagoda ; generally worth Rs. 3½, but sometimes Rs. 3 and sometimes Rs. 4.

Véli, a land measure consisting of 5 *kánis* or $6\frac{3}{10}$ acres.

Veṭṭi, the lowest village servant paid, as usual, by grant of land or grain-fees or, now-a-days, in money.

Visabaḍi, the tax upon the profits of trade.

Vishaya, a territorial division, probably the same as the *ṇáḍu*.

Vritti, (maintenance), a grant of revenue to a Brahman ; usually denotes the share held by each Brahman in an *agrahâram* granted to several.

Y

Yajussákha, commonly appears in the sense of the sect of Brahmans who especially study the Yajur Veda.

Yójana, a measure of 12 miles 1,280 yards according to B, but in C.P. 20 Biṭraguṇṭa is described as being 3 *yójanas* north of Nellore and this would make the *yójana* just about 8 miles.

INDEX OF PRINCIPAL PERSONAL NAMES OCCURRING IN THE INSCRIPTIONS.

[A. Stands for Átmakúr Taluk.
C.P. do. for Copper plates.
D. do. for Darsi Division.
G. do. for Gúdúr Taluk.
KR. do. for Kandukúr do.
KG. do. for Kanigiri do.
KV. do. for Kávali do.
N. do. for Nellore do.
O. Stands for Ongole Taluk.
P. do. for Podili Division.
R. do. for Rápúr Taluk.
S. do. for Súlúrpet (Pólúr) Division.
U. do. for Udayagiri Taluk.
V. do. for Venkaṭagiri Division.]

A

B

C

D

N

R

S

T